D0882441

The World Almanac of Islamism
2021 Edition

Contents

1 World Overview

Welcome to the 2021 edition of the American Foreign Policy Council's *World Almanac of Islamism.*

The *Almanac* represents a unique scholarly compilation designed to examine the current state of the political phenomenon of Islamism worldwide. It is intended to provide a snapshot of contemporary Islamism, as well as of the movements and trends it inspires and the governments it impacts. For the purposes of this collection, the term Islamist is used to describe movements, groups, and individuals that harness religious values and ideals in the service of a political agenda aimed at spreading or imposing Islamic law locally, regionally, or internationally. However, while it showcases a broad spectrum of Islamist ideology, the *Almanac* does not—and is not meant to—provide a comprehensive chronicle of the full range of political thought prevalent in the Muslim World.

The past year has witnessed significant shifts in Islamist political currents worldwide. A major driver of these changes was the collapse, in the Spring of 2019, of the territorial *caliphate* in Iraq and Syria of the Islamic State (ISIS) at the hands of the United States and the Global Coalition. That seminal event precipitated a significant shift in the tactics, operations and activities of the group and its ideological fellow travelers—as well as a change in their respective areas of operation, as both ISIS and its assorted affiliates shift to new and more hospitable global locales.

In the Middle East, the collapse of ISIS territorial control has had a number of concrete effects. It has significantly strengthened the hand of Syrian dictator Bashar al-Assad, who is now once again definitively in control of that country. Nevertheless, the Assad regime remains beset by insurgent forces, including Islamist ones, and is deeply dependent on both Russian and Iranian military support for internal stability. Notably, the retraction of ISIS has also created a power vacuum in Syria that external forces—including Russia and Iran, as well as neighboring Turkey—are attempting to fill, laying the groundwork for potential future geopolitical and sectarian conflict.

Significant, too, has been the impact of the Trump administration's policy of "maximum pressure" against the world's leading state sponsor of terrorism: Iran. This approach—entailing a U.S. withdrawal from the 2015 Joint Comprehensive Plan of Action and the imposition of sweeping economic penalties on the Iranian regime—was formally enacted in May of 2018. Since that time, Iran's economic fortunes have deteriorated significantly, as has its ability to project power regionally. The corollary effects can be seen in a reduction of Iranian sponsorship of (though not of Iranian control over) organizations such as Lebanon's Hezbollah militia. Notwithstanding the effects of "maximum pressure," however, the Iranian regime remains deeply involved in attempting to influence the internal affairs of regional states such as Iraq, Syria and Yemen through its support of Islamist proxy forces in those places.

Finally, official policy toward Islamist currents on the part of regional governments appears to be hardening. This is not only the case in Egypt, where the government of President Abdel Fatah al-Sisi has pursued a broad campaign to isolate and marginalize the Muslim Brotherhood since taking power in 2013. It is also evident in places like Jordan, whose top court formally outlawed the Brotherhood in July 2020, and in the Persian Gulf, where regional governments are taking an increasingly assertive tack against the Brotherhood (as well as its regional patron, Qatar).

But if Islamist movements appear increasingly on the back foot in the Middle East, a very different situation prevails in Africa. The collapse of the ISIS *caliphate* in Iraq and Syria has driven a surge of Islamist activity and religiously-motivated violence throughout the continent. Organizations such as Nigeria's Boko Haram and Somalia's al-Shabaab remain active and potent threats to regional stability, while Mali and the Lake Chad region continued to be plagued by religiously-driven violence. Additionally, new hotspots of extremist activity—such as Mozambique and Ethiopia—signal an alarming expansion of Islamist activism, one with which local governments and, increasingly, the United States will be forced to contend in the years ahead.

In Europe, the subject of Middle Eastern and African migration remains a topic of considerable controversy, as well as an animating factor in the politics of a number of nations. At the same time, occasional attacks by ISIS-inspired elements throughout the continent demonstrate the continued appeal of the group's radical ideology, in spite of the destruction of its physical *caliphate*. They also highlight the ongoing vulnerability of the Eurozone to terrorist penetration, as well as its ongoing attractiveness as a target for such actors.

In years past, the countries of Eurasia served as a major source of Islamist mobilization. This trend, however, appears to have become more muted in tandem with increasing political interaction among, and cooperation within, with the five nations of Central Asia. For these nations, however, the question of nearby Afghanistan remains an overriding one—and the Trump administration's plans to withdraw forces from the country pursuant to its February 2020 truce with the Taliban has fostered worries over a potential resurgence of Islamist influence there and in the broader region. Islamism also appears on the wane in the Russian Federation, thanks to assertive (and repressive) counterterrorism measures taken by the government of Vladimir Putin in recent years. However, Islamist currents remain prevalent in the country's restive Caucasus republics, as well as—to a lesser extent—in its Volga region.

Islamism continues to impact Asia as well. Indonesia remains a notable example of Islamic tolerance, thanks in large part to the extensive political and societal influence exerted by the country's mass Muslim movements. However, other parts of the region, including Malaysia and the Philippines, have a more fraught relationship with Islamism. Islamism also finds expression in the long-simmering political and territorial conflict between regional rivals India and Pakistan, which has grown more acute over the past year. And in China, the PRC's broad-based campaign of repression against the country's Uyghur Muslim minority continues apace, as yet without a meaningful response from the international community.

Finally, the advent of the global coronavirus crisis has added a further layer of complexity to the evolving Islamist phenomenon in the Muslim World. In the early months of the pandemic, government responses (including national lockdowns, business closures and widespread social distancing measures) helped diminish the mobility of local populations, and made it more difficult for Islamist actors to organize and mobilize. Over the longer term, however, the impact of the virus on social cohesion and economic stability in a number of vulnerable nations has the very real potential to provide Islamist ideology with added appeal, and to give Islamist actors new avenues for recruitment and action.

By its nature, the *Almanac* represents a massive intellectual endeavor and a formidable administrative challenge. Its completion was made possible through the diligent work of a team of dedicated researchers, including Margot Van Loon, Cody Retherford, Ritika Bhat, Doug Dubrowski, Rachel Schaer, Ella Gagne, Isaac Schlager, Rebecca Van Burken, Delaney Amonino, Tilly Moross, Ethan Pann, Brendan Burtker, Lauren Szwarc, Jessie Kaplan, and Noah Garber. Each of them deserves our heartfelt thanks.

Ilan Berman, Executive Editor
Jacob McCarty, Managing Editor

Washington, DC
December 2020

The Americas

2 Argentina

Quick Facts

Population: 45,479,118 (July 2020 est.)
Area: 2,780,400 sq km
Ethnic Groups: European (mostly Spanish and Italian descent) and mestizo (mixed European and Amerindian ancestry) 97.2%, Amerindian 2.4%, African 0.4% (2010 est.)
Religions: Nominally Roman Catholic 92% (less than 20% practicing), Protestant 2%, Jewish 2%, other 4%
Government Type: Presidential republic
GDP (official exchange rate): $637.6 billion (2017 est.)

Source: CIA World FactBook (Last Updated July 2020)

Introduction

Argentina is home to one of the largest Muslim populations in Latin America.[1] *A growing percentage of this community is made up of Argentine converts to Islam, a significant number of whom have been recruited and radicalized by Islamist operatives working throughout the country.*

The Argentine Muslim community has gone largely unnoticed since the 19th century. However, significant financial investments in the 1990s, such as those from Saudi Arabia, brought it into the national spotlight. Since then, the community has been stigmatized in particular for its connection to radical Islamist networks tied to Iran and its proxy, Hezbollah. Via these networks, Iran has used intelligence operatives to infiltrate Muslim society and recruit members from a community that shows signs of increasing radicalization who can operate independent of one another.

These networks can pose a danger to Argentina, whose policy toward Iran and other Arab states has often been ambivalent and inconsistent. Moreover, Argentina's failing economy and its strained relationships with Western allies during the presidency of Cristina Fernández de Kirchner made it even more vulnerable to

Iranian advances and activities in the region. Successive Argentine governments since then, however, have taken progressively more drastic domestic counterterror measures to respond to modern threats.

ENDNOTES

1. The Argentine national census does not record religious data, so statistics vary by source, with some reports citing Argentina as home to the largest Muslim population in Latin America (1,000,000 members) and others citing Brazil (35,000 to 1.5 million members). For more information, see the U.S. Department of State, International Religious Freedom Report for 2015, 2016, http://www.state.gov/j/drl/rls/irf/religiousfreedom/index.htm#wrapper.

Due to publishing constraints, this chapter is provided here only in summary form. To view the full study, please visit the online edition of the Almanac at almanac.afpc.org.

3 Bolivia

Quick Facts

Population: 11,639,909 (July 2020 est.)
Area: 1,098,581 sq km
Ethnic Groups: mestizo (mixed white and Amerindian ancestry) 68%, indigenous 20%, white 5%, cholo/chola 2%, black 1%, other 1%, unspecified 3% ; 44% of respondents indicated feeling part of some indigenous group, predominantly Quechua or Aymara (2009 est.)
GDP (official exchange rate): $37.78 billion (2017 est.)

Source: CIA World FactBook (Last Updated July 2020)

Introduction

Bolivia, a country of more than 11.6 million people, has a Muslim population of approximately 3,000. But while the practice of the religion in Bolivia remains small and dispersed, the election of President Evo Morales in 2005 brought about a more amiable relationship with Islamic countries in the Middle East, and significantly opened official domestic policy towards Islam in the years since.[1]

Bolivia's Muslim population counts among its members' descendants from Bangladesh, Pakistan, Egypt, the Palestinian territories, Iran, Syria, and Lebanon. These communities are generally spread out between the major cities of La Paz and Santa Cruz, with a smaller presence in Sucre, Cochabamba, and Oruro and other remote cities throughout the country. There are at least twenty different Islamic organizations, both Shi'a and Sunni, operating within Bolivia, funded primarily by either Saudi Arabia or the Islamic Republic of Iran.

Since opening an embassy in La Paz in 2008, Iran has been a driving force in increasing the Islamic presence in Bolivia, within both society and the state. Iran has proposed several bilateral agreements with Bolivia, ranging from economic development projects to military-to-military exchanges. Iran has also reportedly funded state-owned media networks in the country. In return, Bolivia has lifted visa restrictions for Iranian citizens, supported its efforts in the UN, and facilitated the increased presence of Iranian officials in this Andean nation. However, the November 2019 resignation of Evo Morales and transition to the interim government of President Jeanine Añez has shifted the official posture of Bolivia on Iran, including closing its embassy in the Islamic Republic in June 2020 because of a lack of resources.

Endnotes

1. Pew Research Center, "Global Muslim Population: A Report on the Size and Distribution of the World's Muslim Population," October 2009.

Due to publishing constraints, this chapter is provided here only in summary form. To view the full study, please visit the online edition of the Almanac at almanac.afpc.org.

4 Brazil

Quick Facts

Population: 211,715,973 (July 2020 est.)
Area: 8,515,770 sq km
Ethnic Groups: White 47.7%, mulatto (mixed white and black) 43.1%, black 7.6%, Asian 1.1%, indigenous 0.4% (2010 est.)
Religions: Roman Catholic 64.6%, other Catholic 0.4%, Protestant 22.2% (includes Adventist 6.5%, Assembly of God 2.0%, Christian Congregation of Brazil 1.2%, Universal Kingdom of God 1.0%, other Protestant 11.5%), other Christian 0.7%, Spiritist 2.2%, other 1.4%, none 8%, unspecified 0.4% (2010 est.)
Government Type: Federal presidential republic
GDP (official exchange rate): $2.055 trillion (2017 est.)

Source: *CIA World Factbook (Last Updated November 2020)*

Introduction

The Federative Republic of Brazil is Latin America's largest and most populous country. It has the largest Islamic community in the region, which numbers around one million.[1] *A growing portion of this population is made up of converts, as dawa (Islamic proselytization activities) is in full effect in most major cities.*

With antecedents going back some 500 years to Brazil's founding, Islam is accepted within society, and many successful Muslim entrepreneurs have assimilated into Brazilian culture. Unfortunately, however, a radical element is forming within the country's larger Muslim population, fueled by ties to Middle Eastern Islamist terror networks. Iran and Hezbollah have historically propagated these networks in Brazil. Recently, however, there has been a rise in Islamic State (IS) followers and sympathizers within the country.

Considered an important logistical center and recognized "safe haven" by extremist groups, Brazil enacted its first piece of national anti-terrorism legislation in March 2016. The law gave the government legal authority to surveil, apprehend, and arrest members of Islamist terrorist organizations. Just four months after the anti-terror law was passed, the Brazilian Federal Police foiled a major terrorist plot by IS affiliate Ansar al-Khilafah. The attack targeted the 2016 Summer Olympic Games in Rio de Janeiro in what would have been the worst Islamic terrorist attack in Latin America in the last twenty years.[2] *In May of 2017, the Brazilian Federal Court convicted eight Brazilians of terrorist activity in the country's first legal sentence of its kind.*[3] *On March 8, 2019, newly-elected president Jair Bolsonaro formally approved law 13.810, which makes Brazil compliant with sanctions against people who are investigated or accused of terrorism, as required by the United Nations Security Council. The new bill updates and tightens rules to combat criminals and companies involved in money laundering and terrorist financing, including a provision to block assets of those who are investigated or accused of terrorism. Such an action previously required a judicial order, but it remains dependent on the approval of the Executive.*[4]

Endnotes

1. The Brazilian Census of 2010 puts the number of Muslims in Brazil at 35,207, while religious authorities speak of far higher numbers: between one and two million. Based on the scope of Islamic activities in Brazil, the number of one million seems a more plausible estimate.
2. Zorthian, Julia. "Brazilian Police Arrest 10 Suspected of Plotting Olympics Terror Attack." TIME, July 21, 2016. Accessed May 30, 2019. http://time.com/4417762/rio-olympics-brazil-terror-plot/.
3. Reda. "Juiz Usa Lei Antiterror Pela 1ª Vez Para Condenar Réus Da Hashtag." Fausto Macedo. May 06, 2017. Accessed June 03, 2019. https://politica.estadao.com.br/blogs/fausto-macedo/juiz-usa-lei-anti-terror-pela-1a-vez-para-condenar-reus-da-hashtag/.
4. "LEI No 13.810, DE 8 DE MARÇO DE 2019 - Imprensa Nacional." Ir Para Imprensa Nacional. Accessed June 03, 2019. http://www.in.gov.br/materia/-/asset_publisher/Kujrw0TZC2Mb/content/id/66191195.

Due to publishing constraints, this chapter is provided here only in summary form. To view the full study, please visit the online edition of the Almanac at almanac.afpc.org.

5 Canada

Quick Facts

Population: 37,694,085 (July 2020 est.)
Area: 9,984,670 sq km
Ethnic Groups: Canadian 32.3%, English 18.3%, Scottish 13.9%, French 13.6%, Irish 13.4%, German 9.6%, Chinese 5.1%, Italian 4.6%, North American Indian 4.4%, East Indian 4%, other 51.6% (2016 est.)
GDP (official exchange rate): $1.653 trillion (2017 est.)

Source: CIA World FactBook (Last Updated September 2020)

Introduction

Canada is a free and peaceful society with a large and generally successful immigration program. Newcomers to Canada tend to learn the local language (English or French), integrate into the economy, adopt Canadian values, and develop a positive Canadian identity. Muslims are no exception, and most Muslim communities in Canada are better integrated than their European counterparts. That said, Canada has also earned an unsavory reputation as a terrorist haven. Terrorist groups flocked to Canada in the decades prior to the September 11, 2001 attacks on the United States, prompting the Canadian government to belatedly enact stricter anti-terrorism laws. In the past two decades, however, Islamist and terrorist groups have hidden amid Canada's immigrant communities – including its Muslim population. Stubborn and subversive Islamist groups have penetrated the community and established terrorist cells, fundraising operations, communal organizations, mosques, and schools.

Following two attacks on members of the Canadian military in 2014, the Canadian government once again strengthened its counterterrorism response through legislation (including the 2015 Anti-Terrorism Act, known as Bill C51). However, Canada's approach to combating Islamism has shifted once more under current Prime Minister Justin Trudeau, whose government has taken an active role in assisting the repatriation of Islamic State fighters.[1]

Endnotes

1. Alison Crawford, "Deradicalization must be tailored to Canadian cities, says expert," CBC News, October 7, 2017, https://www.cbc.ca/news/politics/deradicalization-terrorism-extremism-1.4343689; Amanda Connolly, "Conservatives accuse Trudeau of smug approach to returning foreign fighters," *Global News*, December 4, 2017, https://globalnews.ca/news/3895418/conservatives-accuse-trudeau-of-smug-approach-to-returning-foreign-fighters/.

Due to publishing constraints, this chapter is provided here only in summary form. To view the full study, please visit the online edition of the Almanac at almanac.afpc.org.

6 Nicaragua

Quick Facts

Population: 6,203,441 (July 2020 est.)
Area:130,370 sq km
Ethnic Groups: Mestizo (mixed Amerindian and white) 69%, white 17%, black 9%, Amerindian 5%
Government Type: Presidential republic
GDP (official exchange rate): $13.81 billion (2017 est.)

Source: CIA World FactBook (Last Updated July 2020)

Introduction

Islam's presence in Nicaragua dates back to the late 19th century, when Muslims from what was then known as Palestine migrated to Central America. According to one estimate, as many as 40 families from Palestine settled in Nicaragua during this period.[1] However, both this first wave of immigration and a subsequent one in the 1960s did little to establish Islam in Nicaragua. The most recent group of Middle Eastern immigrants, however, arrived in the early 1990s and helped establish a small but thriving Islamic community.

Nicaragua's Islamic community consists of Muslim descendants of Arab emigrants from the territories of Palestine and Lebanon. A relatively small number of Nicaraguan nationals have also converted to the Muslim faith.[2] There are also Shi'a Muslims in Nicaragua, mainly of Iranian origin.[3]

The first mosque built in Nicaragua was constructed in 1999 with local funding, as well as the assistance of Panamanian Muslims. Construction on a second mosque was subsequently completed in 2009. In keeping with his political leanings, President Daniel Ortega's re-assumption of power in 2006 represented a stark, positive a positive change in the relationship between Nicaragua's government and the country's Muslim community.

Endnotes

1. Roberto Marín Guzmán, *A Century of Palestinian Immigration into Central America: A Study of Their Economic and Cultural Contributions,* (San Jose: Editorial de la Universidad de Costa Rica, 2000), p. 49–59.
2. U.S. Department of State, "International Religious Freedom Report," September 13, 2011, https://www.state.gov/j/drl/rls/irf/2010_5/168223.htm.
3. Roberto Tottoli, ed., *Routledge Handbook of Islam in the West*, (Routledge, 2015), p. 166.

Due to publishing constraints, this chapter is provided here only in summary form. To view the full study, please visit the online edition of the Almanac at almanac.afpc.org.

7 United States

Quick Facts

Population: 332,639,102 (July 2020 est.)
Area: 9,833,517 sq km
Ethnic Groups: white 72.4%, black 12.6%, Asian 4.8%, Amerindian and Alaska native 0.9%, native Hawaiian and other Pacific islander 0.2%, other 6.2%, two or more races 2.9% (2010 est.)
GDP (official exchange rate): $19.49 trillion (2017 est.)

Source: CIA World FactBook (Last Updated July 2020)

Introduction

The United States remains committed to countering Islamist terrorism abroad and thwarting violent acts by Islamic extremists at home. The Trump administration's counter-terrorism strategy, issued in 2018, arguably broadened the scope of U.S. counterterror efforts by enshrining a need to counter Islamist ideology – although such an approach is not yet in evidence.

In the meantime, non-violent political Islam in the country continues to grow. While commentary and investigations by media, academia and political organizations have focused overwhelmingly on jihadist networks and extremist activities, other movements and manifestation of Islamism have flourished quietly. The most active Sunni non-violent Islamist forces in America today include the Muslim Brotherhood, Jamaat-e-Islami, Salafis, and Deobandis, along with growing networks representing Qatari and Turkish state Islamism. Shi'a Islamists, aligned with the Iranian regime and the Lebanese terror group Hezbollah, also operate across North America.

Islamist Activity

While American Islam is extraordinarily varied, the dozens of religious sects and movements that constitute American Sunni Islam have distinctly little say in how their own views are represented; the lack of a hierarchical clergy within Sunni Islam and the sheer diversity of Islam – its competing schools of theology, schools of jurisprudence, sects, ethnicities, cultures and mysticisms - produce a natural political vacuum. Islamist groups that fill the political gap are non-violent, with most embracing the idea of introducing an Islamic state through gradual political transition.[1]

Muslim Brotherhood

Of all the nonviolent Islamist movements across the globe, the Muslim Brotherhood is perhaps the best known. It was certainly the one best prepared to assume the leadership of American Islam.

In the United States, Muslim Brotherhood activists who studied in America during the 1960s founded the Muslim Student Association (MSA). The MSA functioned as the organizational beachhead of Muslim Brotherhood activism in the U.S. Through conferences and events, publications, websites, and other activities, the MSA promoted Islamism on university campuses throughout North America. It was the predecessor to American's most prominent Muslim organizations, including the Muslim American Society (MAS), Council on American-Islamic Relations (CAIR), Muslim Public Affairs Council, North American Islamic Trust, and the Islamic Society of North America.[2]

In 2007, federal prosecutors named many of thesc Islamist groups or their officials as "unindicted co-conspirators" in the Holy Land Foundation terrorism financing trial. America's (self-proclaimed) Muslim leadership groups, the government discovered, were part of a network working to fund terrorism abroad and advance extremism at home.[3] These activist organizations are among the most prominent Islamic groups in American civil society; they are influential in politics at all levels and have established relationships with media outlets, academics, charities, and other faith groups throughout the country.

Publicly, these groups are professionally-led activist organizations concerned with civil rights, religious education, political awareness, grassroots organization, and other benign activities.[4] However, internal Brotherhood documents revealed that these groups promote "the main goal of Islamic activism," which is "establishing the nation of Islam, the rule of God in the lives of humans, making people worship their Creator and cleansing the earth from the tyrants who assault God's sovereignty, the abominators in His earth and the suppressors of His creation."[5]

A new set of Muslim Brotherhood-linked organizations have gained prominence since the 2008 Holy Land Foundation trial. The most prominent of these is Islamic Relief, one of the largest Islamic aid charities in the world. Since 2008, Islamic Relief's American branch, Islamic Relief USA, has become the largest Muslim charity in the United States. Islamic Relief maintains branches and offices in over 20 countries and reports hundreds of millions of dollars per year in income, which include sizeable grants from Western governments. The charity was founded in 1984 by Brotherhood activists Hani El Banna and Essam El Haddad (who also served as Egyptian President Morsi's foreign policy advisor). In recent years, Islamic Relief has openly partnered with and funded several Hamas fronts.[6]

Islamic Relief USA is chaired by Khaled Lamada, who is also the founder of Egyptian Americans for Democracy and Human Rights, one of the Egyptian Muslim Brotherhood's American lobbying groups. Lamada has praised the "jihad" of the "Mujahidin of Egypt" for "causing the Jews many defeats". He has shared social media posts that praise Hamas for inflicting a "huge defeat" against the "Zionist entity."[7]

Jamaat-e-Islami (JI)

Founded in British India in 1941 by the prominent Islamist theorist Abul Ala Maududi, Jamaat-e-Islami (JI) today is active across the Indian subcontinent and within the South Asia diaspora in the West.[8] Maududi popularized the idea of Islamic revolution, writing that "the objective of the Islamic 'Jihad' is to eliminate the rule of an un-Islamic system and establish in its stead an Islamic system of state rule."[9]

In the United States, the Islamic Circle of North America (ICNA) has long operated as the chief U.S. representative body of JI. Originally named Halaqa Ahbab-e Islami, its self-described mission was "to strengthen the Jamaat-e-Islami Pakistan."[10] In 1977, Halaqa Ahbabe Islami formally changed its name to ICNA.[11]

The organization's charter calls for the "establishment of the Islamic system of life" in the world, "whether it pertains to beliefs, rituals and morals or to economic, social or political spheres."[12] ICNA's curriculum promotes the teachings of Islamist scholar and JI founder Maududi.[13] The organization's 2010 *Member's Handbook* lists five stages that involve going through the individual, family, societal, state, and global levels "to establish (a) true Islamic society" that "will lead to the unity of the *Ummah* (global Muslim community) and towards the establishment of the *Khilafah* (Caliphate)."[14]

Twice a year, ICNA hosts conferences in Chicago and Baltimore, in collaboration with the Muslim American Society (MAS). These conventions – which are known to host Salafi clerics with histories of inciting hatred against Jews, women and homosexuals – also include Jamaat representatives from South Asia.[15]

JI has long operated in partnership with the Muslim Brotherhood. Qazi Ahmad Hussain, a former head of Jamaat in Pakistan, has declared: "We consider ourselves as an integral part of the Brotherhood and the Islamic movement in Egypt.... Our nation is one."[16] In the West, JI and the Brotherhood often work in tandem – an alliance sometimes referred to as the Ikhwan-Jamaat duopoly.[17]

ICNA has established two prominent aid charities: ICNA Relief, which works within the United States, and Helping Hand for Relief and Development (HHRD), which operates overseas. HHRD funds and partners with Jamaat-e-Islami's welfare arm in South Asia, Al Khidmat Foundation, whose president is closely involved with the designated Kashmiri *jihadist* group Hizbul Mujahideen.[18] JI's own website reports that Al-Khidmat has also funded Hamas.[19] In 2017, HHRD openly partnered with an arm of Lashkar-e-Taiba (LeT), the Pakistani terrorist organization responsible for the 2008 Mumbai attacks.[20]

Salafism

Salafism in America takes four forms: quietists, activists, modernists and *jihadists*.

Quietists and Activists

Most of the quietists have long been strongly supportive of the Saudi regime, and have opposed political participation and involvement in *jihadist* causes. Consequently, the quietists have been staunchly opposed to many other Islamist movements.[21]

Activist Salafis, meanwhile, primarily operated through the Islamic Assembly of North America (IANA) in the 1990s. Salafi commentator Umar Lee notes in his memoir of Salafism in America that IANA was opposed to the Saudi regime but "in favor of a global Islamic movement to bring about an Islamic state."[22] Prominent Islamic figures involved with IANA included the notorious American Islamic leader Ali Al-Tamimi, who would later be convicted for supporting and encouraging *jihad*.[23]

Separate from IANA, a new generation of Salafi clerics and activists grew out of the Nation of Islam and Warith Deen Muhammad organizations. Some – including prominent clerics such as Siraj Wahhaj – were enticed to study in Saudi Arabia; others were entranced by new charismatic leaders such as Jamil Abdullah Al-Amin (formerly known as H. Rap Brown), along with movements such as Darul Islam.[24] Some of these new clerics and movements fused activist Salafi ideas with various elements of black nationalism and consciousness.

While activist Salafis shared goals with political Islamist movements such as the Muslim Brotherhood, the alliance was not fruitful because of religious dogma and competition among adherents. Different Islamist ideas competed for relevance in prominent East Coast institutions such as Dar ul Hijrah in Virginia (whose *imams* later included Anwar Al-Awlaki, who went on to lead Al Qaeda in Yemen).[25] Umar Lee recounts that "the 'Ikhwanis' [Muslim Brotherhood] and Salafis fought in the area like the Bloods and Crips."[26]

Quietists Salafis now have little influence and few supporters.[27] A new modernist Salafi network was subsequently born, leading to an enormous collection of different clerical and activist organizations. The most prominent Salafi groups in America today are either the original activist Salafis, who continue to mostly reject collaboration with political Islamist movements; and a new generation of modernist Salafis, who support an "intersectional" political Islam that has produced alliances with other movements.

Modernists

Modernist Salafis, best known by organizations such as the Al-Maghrib Institute, no longer fight the influence of the Muslim Brotherhood or JI. Modernists have partly embraced the Muslim Brotherhood with modish mainstream political trends, cementing alliances with leading Brotherhood community organizations. Clerics such as Yasir Qadhi and Omar Suleiman regularly partner with leading Muslim organizations such as CAIR, MAS and Islamic Relief. They have also embraced the idea of mixing old world Salafism with some elements of new world progressivism, mingling sermons about the ostensible evils of homosexuality and feminism with praise of the Black Lives Matter movement and protests against the Trump administration's immigration policies.[28] MAS-ICNA and ICNA-MAS, two annual conferences organized by American Muslim Brotherhood and JI activists, rely heavily on modernist Salafi clerics to fill its speaker rosters.[29]

Quietists and activists share concerns over the purported dilution of Salafism – and of Islam – by the modernists. Some clerics preach that "Islam in the West is a resistance movement against totalitarian liberal ideology," and have looked at the activities of modernist Salafis with alarm.[30] Activist and quietist Salafis accuse the modernists of trying to "westernise Islam" by appealing to progressive impressions of Islam.[31]

Modernist Salafis have been remarkably successful, earning the trust of other politically-savvy Islamist movements. They have established seminaries, schools, mosques, lobby groups, and even think tanks to feed their growing presence.[32] Previously subservient to the agendas of Muslim Brotherhood and JI community organizations, modernists now represent a distinct, media-savvy, politically-astute movement.

Jihadists

There are a number of small U.S.-based formal and informal Salafi groups and networks that support violent *jihad*, but do not necessarily engage in violence themselves. Most of their activities consist of provocative public statements and demonstrations.

Following the June 2017 London Bridge terror attack, Western media briefly turned their attention to an American cleric. The BBC reported that one attacker was radicalized by Ahmed Musa Jibril, a prominent Salafi preacher in Michigan.[33] Jibril has reportedly been a source of inspiration for a number of other Western terrorist operatives. But since his exclusion from several mosques in Michigan, Jibril and his network of supporters have primarily operated online. His YouTube videos and social media accounts attract tens of thousands of supporters from around the world.[34] One study found that 60 percent of foreign fighters in Syria at that time followed Jibril on Twitter.[35]

There have been other attempts to form Salafi-*jihadist* networks that skirt the line between ideological support for *jihad* and direct incitement to violence. Revolution Muslim [RM] was a New York-based *jihadist*-activist group that grew out of al-Muhajiroun, a prominent British Salafi *jihadist* movement.[36] Founded in 2007 "to invite people to proper Islam... and command the good... while forbidding the falsehood," RM's mission "is to one day see the Muslims united under one Khalifah [caliph] and under the commands of Allah."[37] RM maintained an active blog and website, which served as a forum for a dissemination of its views and support for violence. In April 2014, Revolution Muslim co-founder Yousef al-Khattab was sentenced to two-and-a-half years in prison for advocating violence against the Chabad Jewish organization's headquarters in Brooklyn.[38]

Deobandis

Adherents of Deobandi Islam follow the Hanafi *maddhab* [school of jurisprudence], and most are of South Asian ethnicity. In a similar vein to Salafi networks in America, Deobandi Muslims in America are split over whether followers should embrace civil society or isolate oneself from it. Broadly, most American Deobandis can be found in three camps: conservatives, modernists and Tablighi Jamaat (TJ).

Conservatives

Conservative Deobandis primarily operate through mosques and seminaries. Darul Uloom Al-Madania in Buffalo and the Institute of Islamic Education in Chicago operate the two longest running and largest Deobandi madrassas in the United States, wherein "strict gender segregation is a norm ... as is a general pattern of social isolation from the broader American society."[39]

While some conservative Deobandis eschew political participation, condemn music and dancing, and avoid proselytization efforts outside their own communities, not all isolate themselves from American society.[40] An increasing number of conservative Deobandis can be found involved with interfaith activities, establishing television channels, participate in political Islamist organizations linked to the Muslim Brotherhood and JI.[41]

Even forward-facing Deobandi institutions, however, maintain ties with hardline Pakistani *madrassahs* and clerics, and have had a number of congregants turn to terrorism. Adnan Shukrijumah, a former prayer leader at the Darul Uloom Institute in Florida, for instance, became one of Al Qaeda's highest-ranking officials.[42] Other congregants of the Darul Uloom Institute have included: Jose Padilla, who plotted to detonate a radioactive bomb in the continental United States, as well as Imran Mandhai and Shueyb Mossa Jokhan, who used the Darul Uloom Institute to plot a bombing campaign.[43] While the *imam* of the Institute, Shafayat Mohamed, has been praised by the media as a moderate – citing his interfaith dialogue efforts – in 2005 he wrote an article attacking Jews and claiming the 2004 Indian Ocean Tsunami was punishment for homosexuality.[44] Other institutions with terrorist congregants and students have included Dar Al Uloom Al Islamiyah, where the San Bernardino shooters prayed and married; and the Flagler Mosque in Miami, whose *imam*, Hafiz Khan, was convicted in 2013 of funding the Taliban.[45]

A number of conservative Deobandis in the United States are involved with Khatme Nubuwwat (Finality of the Prophecy), an international movement headquartered in Pakistan that encourages violence against Ahmadiyyah Muslims, whom many Islamic movements consider heretical. *Khatme Nubuwwat* refers to the tenet held by most Islamic sects that there can be no prophet after Muhammad. Most Ahmadi Muslims, however, believe there was in fact another prophet. This belief, Canadian *imam* Usman Ahsan claims, is "enough to wage war" against them.[46] *Khatme Nubuwwat* offers a rare example of collaboration between Barelvi and Deobandi Muslims. In the United States, the *Khatme Nubuwwat* movement is run predominantly by Deobandi clerics. In 2017, conservative Deobandi clerics from across America gathered in Virginia for a *Khatme Nubuwwat* conference, which was sponsored by several American Deobandi mosques.[47]

Missionaries

Conservative Deobandis have a lot in common with Tablighi Jamaat, a missionary movement linked to dozens of terror plots. TJ is active along the East Coast of the U.S., as well as in Houston, Los Angeles and San Francisco.[48] Its most prominent hub is the Al Falah Mosque in Corona, NY, which openly acknowledges its affiliation with TJ.[49] A 2009 document seemingly authored by the New York Police Department states that dozens of the mosque's congregants and visitors have been linked to jihadist operatives and terror plots, and claims that several congregants are members of Sipah-e-Sahaba, a designated Pakistani Deobandi terrorist organization.[50]

Modernists

Modernist Deobandis work closely with Muslim Brotherhood and JI, and partner closely with modernist Salafis. The most prominent example of a modernist Deobandi institution is the Qalam Institute. Founded in 2009, the Qalam Institute established a full-time seminary in 2013. Its two leading officials, Hussain Kamani and Abdul Nasir Jangda, were both trained at traditional Deobandi seminaries: Kamani studied at Darul Uloom Bury, a U.K. seminary which British newspapers have reported "preaches contempt for non-Muslims and warns of the 'repulsive qualities' of Christian and Jewish women"; while Jangda studied at Jamia Binoria in Karachi, which Pakistani officials have linked to terror groups.[51]

Both Jangda and Kamani are regular speakers at conferences organized by ICNA, the MAS and prominent mosques such as the Islamic Society of Boston.[52] Qalam Institute officials rely heavily on social media platforms and have amassed hundreds of thousands of followers. Clerics like Jangda take a more liberal approach to the question of watching movies or listening to music, which conservative Deobandi clerics generally teach is forbidden.[53] Despite these flashes of liberalism, Qalam officials have expressed support for female sex slavery, encouraged the killing of adulterers, expressed virulent anti-Semitism, and excused violent misogyny.[54]

Shi'a Islamism

Iranian Regime Network

An important component of the Iranian regime network in the United States is the Alavi Foundation. Established as the Pahlavi Foundation in 1958, it was seized by the new Islamic regime following the 1979 revolution and renamed the Alavi Foundation in 1992. Since the early 1980s, the Alavi Foundation has built and funded a number of prominent Shi'a centers, including the Islamic Education Center in Houston, the Islamic Education Center in New York, the Islamic Education Center in Maryland and the Qoba Foundation in California. All four institutions openly advocate for the Iranian regime and commemorate Ayatollah Khomeini.[55] The Alavi Foundation has also given financial donations to other Khomeinist Shiite institutions across North America.[56] In 2017, a federal jury found the Alavi Foundation guilty of funding the Iranian regime's activities.[57]

There have also been several attempts by American Shi'a to establish counterpart organizations to national Sunni groups like CAIR, ISNA and ICNA. In 2005, the Islamic Education Center of Houston founded the Muslim Congress, a hardline alternative to the Sistani-leaning Universal Muslim Association of America, which, as reported by the Associated Press, openly promotes a virulent anti-Semitic and pro-Tehran narrative.[58] The Muslim Congress does not hide its Islamist links: the group organizes marches for Al Quds Day, its annual events feature hardline pro-regime Shiite clerics, and its website distributes the writings of Ayatollah Khamenei.[59]

Several organizations active in the U.S. lobby and campaign in support of the Iranian regime and against sanctions and U.S. military action. These groups include:

- The National Iranian American Council (NIAC), which partners closely with the Iranian regime, and is referred as the U.S. "Iranian lobby" by regime media.[60]

- The Campaign Against Sanctions & Military Intervention in Iran (CASMII), whose members and board comprise leading regime supporters and officials.[61]
- The American Iranian Council, whose officials have reportedly referred to the organization as an Iranian regime lobbying group. Its staffers have included NIAC founder Trita Parsi.[62]

With the exception of the institutions listed above, however, most of the Iranian regime's network operates through local religious organizations. This contrasts with Sunni Islamism in America, which initially sought to establish far-reaching national organizations and umbrella groups. The Islamic Institute of New York, for example, reportedly serves as Ayatollah Khamenei's liaison office in the United States, and regularly hosts events with Iranian regime officials.[63] Moreover, Khomeinism is preached openly in a number of mosques in Dearborn, Michigan. The Islamic House of Wisdom, for example, was founded in 1995 by prominent Iranian regime supporter Ali Elahi.[64] According to a report published by the U.S. Institute of Peace, Elahi first came to the United States to "inspect American branches of [Hezbollah] and to reinforce Tehran's influence on Shi'ite communities."[65] Elahi is also a member of the Ahlulbayt World Assembly (a globally important institution for the regime), speaking at its general assembly in Tehran in 2015.[66]

Hezbollah

The violent enmities of Lebanese politics have also long affected Lebanese American Twelver communities. In Dearborn, Michigan, for example, "it is commonly said that the [Islamic Center of America] is more sympathetic to the Harakaat Amal of Lebanon; [while] the institute generally is seen as being closely aligned with the [Hezbollah] movement."[67] The Islamic Institute's founder and *imam*, Abdul Latif Berry, studied under Ayatollah Fadlallah – Lebanon's late leading Shiite cleric, frequently referred to as Hezbollah's "spiritual advisor."[68] In 1995, the Treasury Department designated Fadlallah as a terrorist, referring to him as a "leading ideological figure" of Hezbollah.[69] Mosques and other institutions that support Hezbollah in America tend to be aligned with two *maraji*: Iran's Supreme Leader and Ayatollah Fadlallah.

While there have a few examples of violent Shiite Islamist plots in North America, including a 2011 effort to assassinate the Saudi ambassador, Hezbollah's activities on the continent are mostly relegated to propaganda and fundraising.[70] Dozens of American Shiites have been indicted or convicted on charges relating to Hezbollah activity, and numerous Hezbollah cells have been involved with money laundering enterprises.[71] The DEA reportedly believed that Hezbollah was amassing $1 billion a year through drug and weapons trafficking, bank fraud, and other criminal pursuits.[72]

Islam and Society

In 2017, the Pew Research Center, in one of the more extensive polls of the topic conducted, estimated that 3.45 million people who identify as Muslim live in the United States.[73] Sixty-five percent of these people identify as Sunnis, 11 percent as Shi'a, and 24 percent as having no specific affiliation (describing themselves as "just a Muslim").[74] 58 percent of Muslims in the U.S. are first generation immigrants while 42 percent are native-born. Ethnically, 41 percent of American Muslims identify as White (which includes Arab and other Middle Eastern origins), 28 percent as Asian (mostly South Asian), 20 percent as black, and 8 percent as Hispanic.[75]

Surveys of American Muslim opinion remain relatively shallow because they often do not consider movements, sects, or schools of thought. Rather, they focus on broader groups like ethnicity and denomination. Unsurprisingly, then, surveys on Muslim attitudes towards society and extremism are typically inconsistent. Notwithstanding, the 2017 Pew survey found that 76 percent of American Muslims believe that political or religious violence can never be justified. Previous surveys found that 21 percent of Muslim Americans believe there is either a great deal or a fair amount of support for extremism within their community, with 48 percent saying that Muslim community leaders are not doing enough to challenge extremists.[76]

There is no good estimate for the number of Islamists within American Muslim communities; however, some analysts argue that, because leading Islamist organizations do not publish membership numbers, they have little popular support.

Islamist networks have recently established their own research bodies that poll American Muslims. The Yaqeen Institute, for example, is part of the modernist Salafi network, and mixes polls of American Muslims, studies of anti-Muslim sentiment, and the efficacy of counter-extremism initiatives with analyses of Islamic theology.[77] Another group, the Institute for Social Policy and Understanding (ISPU) was founded in 2002 to "[empower] American Muslims to develop their community and fully contribute to democracy and pluralism in the United States."[78] As part of its annually published "American Muslim Poll", ISPU concluded that, in 2018, 80 percent of Muslims believed individual attacks on civilians is never justified and 84 percent opposed a ban on visas to Muslims wishing to enter the United States. Muslim respondents stated that they believe 12 percent of other American Muslims are hostile to the United States and another 18 percent believe that they are prone to violence.[79] A 2019 "American Muslim Poll" conducted by IPSU focused on the attitudes of different religious and ethnic groups toward the American Muslim community.[80]

Another ISPU report states that someone perceived to be Muslim and accused of a terror plot will receive seven and half times the media coverage as someone not perceived to be Muslim.[81] However, over the last decade, perhaps as a response to claims of Islamophobia, investigative reporting of trends within American Islam has mostly disappeared. Peter Skerry notes that "Boston's media, academic, and political elites have refused to acknowledge any concerns about, much less the existence of, ties between the [Islamic Society of Boston (ISBCC)] and the Brotherhood." Skerry adds that despite the implication of numerous American Islamists in the 2008 Holy Land Foundation trial, groups like the Council on American-Islamic Relations (CAIR) and their spokespersons continued to be treated as representatives of American Muslims: "The FBI's rebuke of CAIR has gone largely unnoted. In fact, most major media outlets continue to seek out CAIR spokespeople for comments…without ever mentioning CAIR's history and provenance."[82] However, Skerry makes it clear that while Islamist elements like the Muslim Brotherhood do exists, they ultimately do not pose an existential threat to the United States.

Islamism and the State

The U.S. government has moved aggressively to disrupt homegrown terror plots; since March 2014, 177 individuals have been charged in the U.S. with offenses relating to the Islamic State.[83] A report released in January 2018 by the Departments of Justice and Homeland Security found that a majority of terrorists convicted of "international terrorism-related charges" in the U.S. since 2001 were foreign-born. Out of 549 convictions for international terrorism-related charges in U.S. federal courts between September 11, 2001 and December 31, 2016, approximately 402 were foreign-born.[84]

The Trump administration's *National Strategy for Counter-Terrorism* (NSCT) is closely in line with other the counterterrorism strategies of other Western governments. Alongside the usual promises to defeat terrorism using the military, law enforcement, and security services, the administration pledged to "prevent and intervene in terrorist recruitment, minimize the appeal of terrorist propaganda online, and build societal resilience to terrorism. This includes leveraging the skills and resources of civil society and non-traditional partners to diminish terrorists' efforts to radicalize and recruit people in the United States."[85] The NSCT explicitly names Islamist ideology as the underlying cause of Islamist violence: "To defeat radical Islamist terrorism, we must also speak out forcefully against a hateful ideology that provides the breeding ground for violence and terrorism." Strategy architects do not elaborate further, however, and avoid mentioning lawful Islamist movements active in the United States. Nonetheless, this is a marked change from previous administrations, under which government documents deliberately avoided mentioning Islam or Islamism.

Soon after assuming office, President Trump signed an executive order which immediately barred entry of individuals into the U.S. from seven Muslim-majority nations—Iran, Iraq, Libya, Somalia, Sudan, Syria, and Yemen. Dubbed "Protecting the Nation from

Foreign Terrorist Entry into the United States," the order also put a hold on the U.S. refugee program for 120 days and indefinitely barred Syrian refugees from entering the country.[86] The travel ban generated widespread controversy among the American public, resulting in President Trump issuing Executive Order 13780, which considered certain legal objections and removed Iraq from the list of targeted countries.[87] On September 24, 2017, Presidential Proclamation 9645 superseded Executive Order 13780, adding North Korea and Venezuela to the list of designated countries.[88] The Supreme Court upheld President Trump's controversial travel ban on June 26, 2018.[89] The "Muslim Ban," as it is popularly known, remains controversial among both secular and Islamist organizations.[90]

Under the Obama administration, the Department of Homeland Security (DHS) had set up the Terrorism Prevention Partnerships (TPP) "to address the root causes of violent extremism by providing resources to communities to build and sustain local prevention efforts and promote the use of counter-narratives to confront violent extremist messaging online."[91] Part of TPP included a Countering Violent Extremism (CVE) program to "build prevention programs that address the root causes of violent extremism and deter individuals who may already be radicalizing to violence."[92] Despite widespread criticism of CVE pilot programs, Congress approved $10 million for CVE grants to "community partners" in 2016. Since then, however, these grants have been either cancelled or returned under the Trump administration.[93]

Meanwhile, in Congress in 2018, the House Committee on Oversight and Government Reform opened an investigation into the 2014 decision of Obama administration to give $115,000 to the Islamic Relief Agency, which the U.S. government had designated as a terrorist organization in 2004.[94] Also in 2018, members of Congress wrote to federal agencies demanding more information on an alleged investigation by the FBI, IRS and Office for Personnel Management into Islamic Relief's activities.[95]

The federal government continues to give millions to Islamic organizations controlled, or linked, to radical Islamist movements. ICNA, for instance, received over $10 million for disaster relief work in 2016 and 2018. Among many other examples, branches of

CAIR and the MAS collectively received over $310,000; $31,000 was handed to the Islamic Center of Passaic County, whose *imam*, Mohammad Qatanani, is accused by federal agencies of coordinating with Hamas.[96]

The distribution of federal funds continued in October 2019 when President Trump granted an additional $100,000 to CAIR as "the product of the DHS's Nonprofit Security Grant Program." MAS also received $57,000 in federally allocated funds. In 2019, it was discovered that these funds contribute to the grand total of "over $41 million of federal grants… since 2007."[97]

Endnotes

1. That is not to say that adherents of groups such as the Muslim Brotherhood never commit violent acts, and, internationally, it has certainly produced violent offshoots, such as the designated terrorist organization Hamas. Non-violent Islamism is also referred to in the West as lawful Islamism.
2. "Muslim Student Association," Investigative Project on Terrorism, n.d., http://www.investigativeproject.org/documents/misc/84.pdf
3. "Attachment A," *United States of America vs. Holy Land Foundation for Relief and Development et al.*, No. 3:04-CR-240-. G, United States District Court for the Northern Division of Texas, Dallas Division.
4. See, for example: Esam Omeish, "MAS President Letter to the Washington Post," Muslim American Society Website, September 16, 2004, http://www.unitedstatesaction.com/documents/omeish/www-masnet-org_pressroom_release-asp_nycmexs4.pdf
5. "Exhibit 0003918-0003919," (Letter from "The Political Office" re: the founding of the Islamic Association for Palestine by "the Group"), *U.S. v. Holy Land Foundation et al.*, 5.
6. Zeid al-Noman, as quoted in "Elbarasse Search 2," *U.S. v. Holy Land Foundation et al.*
7. *Islamic Relief: Charity, Extremism & Terror*, Middle East Forum, July 2018.
8. Ibid.
9. Nadeem F. Paracha, "Abdul Ala Maududi: An existentialist history," *Dawn*, January 1, 2015, https://www.dawn.com/news/1154419.
10. Paulo Casaca, "Maududi: The founder of modern Jihadism," *New*

Delhi Times, March 3, 2017, http://www.newdelhitimes.com/maududi-the-founder-of-modern-jihadism123/,

11. Zaheer Uddin, "ICNA: A Successful Journey and a Promising Road Ahead." *The Message International* 23, no. 8 (1999), 24.
12. "The Charter And By-Laws," Islamic Circle of North America, n.d., https://web.archive.org/web/20101227052638/http:/www.icnasisterswing.com/charterbylawfiles/ICNA_CBL.pdf.
13. Ibid.
14. "Promoting Radical Ideas—What ICNA Demands of its Members," *IPT News*, August 10, 2010, https://www.investigativeproject.org/2098/promoting-radical-ideas-what-icna-demands-of-its; "ICNA Still Promotes Radical Texts," *IPT News*, September 9, 2011, https://www.investigativeproject.org/3155/icna-still-promotes-radical-texts; "ICNA's Radical Reading List," *IPT News*, April 27, 2010, https://www.investigativeproject.org/1919/icnas-radical-reading-list.
15. "Member's Hand Book," *Islamic Circle of North America*, n.d., 9-10, https://www.investigativeproject.org/documents/misc/475.pdf.
16. "Sh. Yusuf Islahi," ICNA Convention Website, December 24, 2017, https://icnaconvention.org/sh-yusuf-islahi/; "MAS-ICNA/ICNA-MAS Background," *Middle East Forum*, January 4, 2019, https://www.scribd.com/document/396807493/MAS-ICNA-MAS-LA-conference-speakers-2018
17. Lorenzo Vidino, *The New Muslim Brotherhood in the West* (New York: Columbia University Press, 2010), 34; This term was coined in Kalim Siddiqui, *Stages of Islamic Revolution* (London: The Open Press, 1996). It refers to groups tied to the Muslim Brotherhood (*Al-Ikhwan al-Muslimeen*) and the Pakistani Islamist party, *Jama'at al-Islami*.
18. "US-based charity announces establishment of rehab center," ICNA Website, March 10, 2017, https://www.icna.org/us-based-charity-announces-establishment-of-rehab-center/; "Welfare in Sindh: 'Al Khidmat spent Rs140m last year,'" *The Express Tribune*, June 28, 2016, https://tribune.com.pk/story/1132200/welfare-sindh-al-khidmat-spent-rs140m-last-year/; Abha Shankar, "IPT Investigation Reveals ICNA Partner's Close Ties to Kashmiri Jihadists," *IPT News*, December 5, 2017, https://www.investigativeproject.org/7011/ipt-investigation-reveals-icna-partner-close-ties; Sheikh Abdulmayed, "S Syed Salehuddin, Martyrdom Brings a New Spirit to the Freedom Struggle," *Jasarat* [Urdu], August 7, 2016, https://www.jasarat.com/2016/08/07/karachi-sayed-salahuddin-and-hafiz-naeem-ur-rehman-press-conference.

19. "JI donates Rs. 6 m to Palestinians," Jamaat-e-Islami Pakistan," Jamaat Islami, August 17, 2006, https://web.archive.org/web/20071003065109/http:/www.jamaat.org/news/2006/aug/17/1001.html
20. Sam Westrop, "Pakistani Islamism Flourishes in America," *National Review*, January 24, 2018, https://www.nationalreview.com/2018/01/pakistani-terror-groups-charitable-guises-us-funds/
21. Alexander Meleagrou-Hitchens, "Salafism in America: History, Evolution, Radicalization," George Washington University Program on Extremism, October 2018.
22. Umar Lee, *The Rise and Fall of the Salafi Dawah in America: a Memoir by Umar Lee* (E-book: St. Louis Stranger, 2014)
23. Jerry Markon, "Muslim Lecturer Sentenced to Life," *Washington Post,* July 14, 2005, http://www.washingtonpost.com/wp-dyn/content/article/2005/07/13/AR2005071302169.html
24. There are numerous accounts and studies of this complicated period of Salafi upheaval in America. For more information about the intra-Salafi politics and the effect of Black Consciousness, see, inter alia: Shadee Elmasry, "The Salafis in America: The Rise, Decline and Prospects for a Sunni Muslim Movement among African-Americans," *Journal of Muslim Minority Affairs* 30, no. 2, June 2010; Abin Chande, "Islam in thc African American Community: Negotiating between Black Nationalism and Historical Islam," *Islamic Studies* 47, no. 2 (Summer 2008), pp. 221-241; Lee, *The Rise and Fall of the Salafi Dawah in America: a Memoir by Umar Lee.*
25. J.M. Berger, "Anwar Al-Awlaki's Links to the September 11 Hijackers," *The Atlantic*, September 9, 2011, https://www.theatlantic.com/international/archive/2011/09/anwar-al-awlakis-links-to-the-september-11-hijackers/244796/
26. Lee, *The Rise and Fall of the Salafi Dawah in America: a Memoir by Umar Lee.*
27. Hitchens, "Salafism in America: History, Evolution, Radicalization."
28. Tim Stelloh and Rima Abdelkader, "Imam reveals story behind haunting image at border processing facility," *NBC News*, June 24, 2018, https://www.nbcnews.com/storyline/immigration-border-crisis/imam-reveals-story-behind-haunting-image-border-processing-facility-n886201; "Worst of the ICNA-MAS Conference 2017," *Islamist Watch*, April 18, 2017, https://www.meforum.org/islamist-watch/52341/worst-of-the-icna-mas-conference-2017
29. "MAS-ICNA/ ICNA-MAS Background," *Middle East Forum*, Jan. 4, 2019, https://www.scribd.com/document/396807493/MAS-ICNA-

MAS-LA-conference-speakers-2018

30. Shadee Elmasry, Facebook Post, August 24, 2015, https://www.facebook.com/DrShadeeElmasry/posts/1030454433641121?__tn__=-R
31. Abu Ibraheem Hussnayn, Facebook Post, September 2, 2015, https://www.facebook.com/abuibraheemhh/posts/1036452506388485
32. Hitchens, "Salafism in America: History, Evolution, Radicalization."
33. Martin Evans, Nicola Harley and Harry Yorke, "London terrorist had twice been referred to police over his extremist views," *Telegraph* (London), June 4, 2017, https://www.telegraph.co.uk/news/2017/06/04/london-terrorist-had-twice-referred-police-extremist-views/
34. Hitchens, "Salafism in America: History, Evolution, Radicalization."
35. Joseph A. Carter, Shiraz Maher, and Peter Neumann, "#Greenbirds: Measuring Importance and Influence in Syrian Foreign Fighter Networks," International Centre for the Study of Radicalisation, April 2014, 19.
36. Jesse Morton and Mitchell Silber, "The Origin of Revolution Muslim," in *From Revolution Muslim to Islamic State*, New America, June 4, 2018, https://www.newamerica.org/international-security/reports/revolution-muslim-islamic-state/the-origin-of-revolution-muslim/
37. "Mission Statement," Revolution Muslim Website, n.d., http://www.revolutionmuslim.com/index.php?option=com_content&view=article&id=3&Itemid=17
38. Matt Zapotosky, "New Jersey man sentenced to prison for extremist Islamic Web posts," *Washington Post,* April 25, 2014, https://www.washingtonpost.com/local/crime/new-jersey-man-to-be-sentenced-for-extremist-islamic-web-posts/2014/04/24/406e65a8-cbc4-11e3-93eb-6c0037dde2ad_story.html?utm_term=.95898084ffe5.
39. "Zareena Grewal and R. David Coolidge, "Islamic Education in the United States: Debates, Practices, and Institutions," in Juliane Hammer and Omid Safi (eds.), *The Cambridge Companion to American Islam* (New York: Cambridge University Press 2013), 254.
40. Sulaiman Abdur-Rahman, *Friday Inspires Muslim Success* (United States: Sulaiman Abdur-Rahman's Publishing House, 2018), 194
41. Darul Uloom Institute in Florida and Darul Uloom New York regularly runs events with the Council on American-Islamic Relations and the Islamic Circle of North America. See Facebook Post, CAIR Florida, July 19, 2018, https://www.facebook.com/CAIRFlorida/photos/a.200962816585241/2190705467610956/?type=3&theater; Facebook Post, ICNA Relief, August 21, 2017, https://www.

facebook.com/ICNARelief/posts/10155592062667770?__tn__=-R; Founder Biography, Darul Uloom Institute, n.d., http://www.alhikmat.com/shaikhshafayatfounder/founderbio.html; Al-Hikmat TV is a project of the Darul Uloom Institute in Florida: "About Us," Al-Hikmat Website, n.d., http://www.alhikmatlive.com

42. Dina Temple-Raston, "Al-Qaida Mastermind Rose Using American Hustle," *NPR*, October 11, 2010, https://www.npr.org/templates/story/story.php?storyId=130434651
43. Bob Norman, "A Tale of Two Mosques," *Miami New Times*, August 8, 2002, https://www.miaminewtimes.com/news/a-tale-of-two-mosques-6349890
44. Shafayat Mohamed, "Tsunami," *Al-Hikmat*, 2005, http://web.archive.org/web/20050305194351/http://alhikmat.com/tsunami.htm (Due to a quirk in the archive service, the text in this source is white on a white background – select the text to read)
45. Jay Weaver, "Miami imam convicted of Taliban-related terrorism charges in federal court," *Miami Herald*, March 4, 2013, https://www.miamiherald.com/latest-news/article1947872.html; "Dar Al Uloom Al Islamiyah-Amer mosque," *CBS News*, n.d., https://www.cbsnews.com/pictures/san-bernardino-california-shooters/11/
46. Sam Westrop, "Deobandis Meet in Virginia to Incite Violence against Persecuted Islamic Minority," *Daily Caller*, November 22, 2017, https://www.meforum.org/7036/deobandis-meet-in-va-to-incite-violence-against-minority
47. Ibid.
48. Fariba Nawa, "Internal struggles at US mosques seep into secular courts," *Reveal*, August 31, 2015. https://www.revealnews.org/article/internal-struggles-at-us-mosques-seep-into-secular-courts/; Also see a TJ blog listing TJ institutions: "Worldwide Tablighi Markaz Address," All About Tablighi Jamaat, May 13, 2008, https://tablighijamaat.wordpress.com/2008/05/13/worldwide-tablighi-markaz-address/
49. *Paracha v. Adulaleem*, Supreme Court of New York, Queens County, July 14, 2011
50. "Amended Investigative Statement," Policy Department, City of New York, May 27, 2009, http://web.archive.org/web/20150919003935/http://enemieswithinbook.com/documents/TEI_Tablighi%20Jamaat.pdf
51. Sam Westrop, "Training Tomorrow's Extremists," *Daily Caller*, November 22, 2016, https://www.meforum.org/islamist-watch/51075/training-tomorrow-extremists

52. "MAS-ICNA/ ICNA-MAS Background," *Middle East Forum*, Jan. 4, 2019, https://www.scribd.com/document/396807493/MAS-ICNA-MAS-LA-conference-speakers-2018; "Islamic Society Of Boston (Once Again) Shows Fondness For Sex Slavery Advocates," Americans for Peace and Tolerance, August 5, 2016, https://www.peaceandtolerance.org/2016/08/05/islamic-society-boston-once-again-shows-fondness-for-sex-slavery-advocates/;
53. Abdul Nasir Jangda and Ustadh Abdul Rahman Murphy, "The Hangout – Part 2 – On recreation and entertainment – sports, movies, and music," Podcast, Qalam Institute, March 11, 2016, http://www.qalaminstitute.org/2016/11/the-hangout-part-2-on-recreation-and-entertainment-sports-movies-and-music/#.XJUrNShKhaQ
54. Westrop, "Training Tomorrow's Extremists."
55. Hassan Dai, "Pro-Iranian regime network of Islamic Centers in the US," Iranian American Forum, October 17, 2016, http://iranian-americans.com/pro-iranian-regime-network-of-islamic-centers-in-the-us/
56. "Alavi Foundation in Focus," Alavi Foundation, July 2016, http://alavifoundation.org/wp-content/uploads/2016/07/History-of-Alavi-Foundation-2016.pdf; Ryan Mauro and Justen Charters, "Iranian Front Group Funds Institutions Across US," Clarion Project, October 16, 2018, https://clarionproject.org/iranian-front-group-funds-us-institutions/
57. "Acting Manhattan U.S. Attorney Announces Historic Jury Verdict Finding Forfeiture Of Midtown Office Building And Other Properties," U.S. Attorney's Office, Southern District of New York, Department of Justice, June 29, 2017, https://www.justice.gov/usao-sdny/pr/acting-manhattan-us-attorney-announces-historic-jury-verdict-finding-forfeiture-midtown
58. "As the Muslim Congress gathered in Dearborn, American Shias struggle with their future," Associated Press, June 20, 2009, https://www.mlive.com/news/us-world/2009/07/as_the_muslim_congress_gathere.html
59. Dai, "Iran sponsored "Muslim Congress" in Dallas, August 18-20"; "The Letter of Ayatollah Khamenei to Youth in the West," Muslim Congress, January 28, 2015, http://muslimcongress.org/wp/the-letter-of-ayatollah-khamenei-to-youth-in-the-west/; "Boston's Al Quds Day," Americans for Peace and Tolerance, July 11, 2016, https://www.peaceandtolerance.org/2016/07/11/bostons-al-quds-day/
60. "Parsi's collaboration with Iranian ambassador to UN," Iranian American Forum, n.d., http://iraniansforum.com/index.php/fact-

book/384-parsi-and-zarif; "Trita Parsi and NIAC in the Iranian regime newspapers inside the country," Iranian American Forum, n.d., http://iraniansforum.com/index.php/factbook/458-niac-governmentpress

61. "Agents of the Ayatollahs: CASMII's Links to the Iranian Regime," Stand for Peace, January 2013, http://standforpeace.org.uk/wp-content/uploads/2013/01/Agents-of-the-Ayatollahs-CASMII%E2%80%99s-Links-to-the-Iranian-Regime.pdf
62. "American Iranian Council," Iranian American Forum, n.d., http://www.iraniansforum.com/lobby/index.php/other-orgs/86-american-iranian-council
63. Liyakat Nathani Takim, *Shi'ism in America* (New York: New York University Press, 2009), 148; Dai, "Pro-Iranian regime network of Islamic Centers in the US."
64. "Bio of Imam Elahi," Islamic House of Wisdom, n.d., http://www.islamichouseofwisdom.com/bio-of-imam-elahi
65. Daniel Pipes and Khalid Durán, "Muslims in the West: Can Conflict Be Averted?" United States Institute of Peace, August 1993, http://www.danielpipes.org/232/muslims-in-the-west-can-conflict-be-averted
66. Dai, "Pro-Iranian regime network of Islamic Centers in the US."
67. Linda S. Walbridge, "Thc Shi'a Mosques and Their Congregations in Dearborn," in Yvonne Haddad and Jane Smith, eds., *Muslim Communities in North America* (Albany: State University of New York Press, 1994), 347-348.
68. David Kenner, "The Sheikh Who Got Away," *Foreign Policy*, July 6, 2010, https://foreignpolicy.com/2010/07/06/the-sheikh-who-got-away-2/
69. "List of Specially Designated Terrorists Who Threaten To Disrupt the Middle East Peace Process," Office of Foreign Assets Control, Department of the Treasury, *Federal Register* 60, no. 16, January 25, 1995.
70. John Mueller, *Terrorism Since 9/11: The American Cases* (Washington D.C: The Educational Publisher, 2017).
71. Levitt, *Hezbollah: The Global Footprint of Lebanon's Party of God*; "Hezbollah," Anti-Defamation League, Feb. 6, 2013, https://www.adl.org/sites/default/files/documents/assets/pdf/combating-hate/Hezbollah-backgrounder-2013-1-10-v1.pdf
72. Josh Meyer, "The secret backstory of how Obama let Hezbollah off the hook," *Politico*, December 2017, https://www.politico.com/interactives/2017/obama-hezbollah-drug-trafficking-investigation/

73. Besheer Mohamed, "A new estimate of the U.S. Muslim population," Pew Research Center, January 6, 2016, http://www.pewresearch.org/fact-tank/2016/01/06/a-new-estimate-of-the-u-s-muslim-population/.
74. Michael Lipka, "Muslims and Islam: Key findings in the U.S. and around the world," Pew Research Center, February 27, 2017, http://www.pewresearch.org/fact-tank/2017/02/27/muslims-and-islam-key-findings-in-the-u-s-and-around-the-world/.
75. "U.S. Muslims Concerned About Their Place in Society, but Continue to Believe in the American Dream," Pew Research Center, July 26, 2017, https://www.pewforum.org/wp-content/uploads/sites/7/2017/07/U.S.-MUSLIMS-FULL-REPORT-with-population-update-v2.pdf.
76. "Muslim Americans: No Signs of Growth in Alienation or Support for Extremism". Pew Research Center, Washington, DC (August 30, 2011). https://www.pewresearch.org/politics/2011/08/30/muslim-americans-no-signs-of-growth-in-alienation-or-support-for-extremism/
77. "Publications and Articles," Yaqeen Institute, n.d., https://yaqeeninstitute.org/research/.
78. "About Us," Institute for Social Policy and Understanding, n.d., https://www.ispu.org/who-we-are/.
79. Youssef Chouhoud and Dalia Mogahed, "American Muslim Poll 2018," Institute for Social Policy and Understanding, April 30, 2018, https://www.ispu.org/american-muslim-poll-2018-full-report/
80. D. Mogahed and A. Mahmood, "American Muslim Poll 2019: Predicting and Preventing Islamophobia," *Institute for Social Policy and Understanding,* February 24, 2020, https://www.ispu.org/american-muslim-poll-2019-predicting-and-preventing-islamophobia/
81. Kumar Rao and Carey Shenkman, "Equal Treatment?: Measuring the Legal and Media Responses to Ideologically Motivated Violence in the United States," Institute for Social Policy and Understanding, 2018, https://www.imv-report.org.
82. Peter Skerry, "American Brotherhood," *Foreign Affairs*, April 8, 2017, https://www.foreignaffairs.com/articles/united-states/2017-04-08/american-brotherhood.
83. "Terrorism in the United States," *GW Extremism Tracker*, February 2019, https://extremism.gwu.edu/sites/g/files/zaxdzs2191/f/Feb19%20Update.pdf
84. Department of Homeland Security and Department of Justice, "Executive Order 13780: *Protecting the Nation from Foreign Terrorist Entry Into the United States*," January 2018, 2, https://www.dhs.gov/

sites/default/files/publications/Executive%20Order%2013780%20 Section%2011%20Report%20-%20Final.pdf.

85. White House, "National Strategy for Counterterrorism of the United States of America," October 2018, 2, https://www.whitehouse.gov/wp-content/uploads/2018/10/NSCT.pdf
86. White House, "Executive Order Protecting the Nation from Foreign Terrorist Entry into the United States," January 27, 2017, https://www.whitehouse.gov/presidential-actions/executive-order-protecting-nation-foreign-terrorist-entry-united-states/.
87. White House, "Executive Order Protecting The Nation From Foreign Terrorist Entry Into The United States," March 6, 2017, https://www.whitehouse.gov/presidential-actions/executive-order-protecting-nation-foreign-terrorist-entry-united-states-2/
88. White House, "Presidential Proclamation Enhancing Vetting Capabilities and Processes for Detecting Attempted Entry Into the United States by Terrorists or Other Public-Safety Threats," September 24, 2017, https://www.whitehouse.gov/presidential-actions/presidential-proclamation-enhancing-vetting-capabilities-processes-detecting-attempted-entry-united-states-terrorists-public-safety-threats/
89. Brent Kendall and Jess Bravin, "Supreme Court Upholds Trump Travel Ban," *Wall Street Journal*, June 26, 2018, https://www.wsj.com/articles/supreme-court-upholds-trump-travel-ban-1530022794
90. "CAIR Action Alert: Repeal the Muslim Ban," Council on American-Islamic Relations, Jan. 31, 2019, https://www.cair.com/update_cair_action_alert_repeal_the_muslim_ban
91. Department of Homeland Security, "Terrorism Prevention Partnerships," n.d., https://www.dhs.gov/terrorism-prevention-partnerships.
92. Ibid.
93. Peter Beinart, "Trump Shut Programs to Counter Violent Extremism," *The Atlantic*, October 29, 2018, https://www.theatlantic.com/ideas/archive/2018/10/trump-shut-countering-violent-extremism-program/574237/
94. "Report: Congress investigates $200,000 given to terrorist-designated group by US," *JNS*, October 16, 2018, https://www.jns.org/report-congress-investigates-200000-given-to-terrorist-designated-group-by-us/
95. "MEF Reveals Islamic Relief under Investigation; Congress Demands Answers," Middle East Forum, October 18, 2018, https://www.meforum.org/7281/mef-reveals-islamic-relief-under-investigation
96. All data available at usaspending.gov; For information on Qatanani,

see John Rossomando, "DHS: Hamas-Tied NJ Imam Must Prove Why He Shouldn't Be Deported," Investigative Project on Terrorism, December 7, 2016, https://www.investigativeproject.org/5723/dhs-hamas-tied-nj-imam-must-prove-why-he-shouldnt

97. Sam Westrop, "DHS Approves $100k Grant of Taxpayers' Money to CAIR," Middle East Forum, January 17, 2020, https://www.meforum.org/60302/dhs-approves-100k-grant-to-cair

8 Venezuela

Quick Facts

Population: 28,644,603 (July 2020 est.)
Area: 912,050 sq km
Ethnic Groups: Spanish, Italian, Portuguese, Arab, German, African, indigenous people
GDP (official exchange rate): $210.1 billion (2017 est.)

Source: CIA World FactBook (Last Updated August 2020)

Introduction

Nicolas Maduro has continued his predecessor Hugo Chavez's welcoming stance toward the propaganda, recruitment, and fundraising of Islamist groups that fit into the anti-American and anti-Semitic worldview inherent in the anti-imperialist ideology of the Bolivarian revolution and the Venezuelan regime. Maduro continues to provide various Islamist elements with assistance and safe havens for a range of financial and extra-territorial activities in Venezuela and beyond.

The roots of this affinity stretch back to Chavez's years as a militant in the 4-F movement, during which time the future Venezuelan president fell under the sway of individuals with a sympathetic view of a variety of "non-aligned" Middle Eastern rogues. Members of that group included now-embattled Syrian despot Bashar al-Assad, the late Libyan dictator Muammar Qadhafi, former Iraqi strongman Saddam Hussein, and the leaders of the Iranian Revolution.[1] *These early lessons provided the basis for the foreign policy that Chavez pursued from the start of his presidency in 1999—a foreign policy that has, since 2013, been perpetuated by Maduro, and which has made Venezuela a close ally of the Islamic Republic of Iran and an array of radical Islamist groups, chief among them Hezbollah.*

Aside from its traditional terrorist activity, Hezbollah has increasingly become involved in the world of transnational organized crime. Years of state support to various criminal groups and the ever-worsening economic and humanitarian crisis in Venezuela, have transformed Venezuela into a global hub of crime-terror convergence in the Western Hemisphere, further entrenching Islamist presence in the country.

ISLAMIST ACTIVITY

Venezuela is an attractive way station for Islamist groups, which have a quiet but longstanding and profitable presence there. That includes fundraising, smuggling, money laundering, and training. The U.S. Southern Command (SOUTHCOM) estimates that "Islamist terrorist groups raise between three hundred million and five hundred million dollars per year through illicit and licit activity in various free trade zones throughout Latin America, including in Maicao, Colombia, and Margarita Island, Venezuela."[2] Among the most prominent is Hezbollah, Iran's main terror proxy.

One of the most notable Hezbollah financiers in South America is Assad Ahmad Barakat, who was sanctioned by the Treasury Department in 2004 and served a stint in a Paraguayan prison for tax evasion from 2002-2009.[3] More recently, Barakat was arrested again in Brazil in 2018 for immigration fraud, and was extradited to Paraguay in July 2020.[4] Barakat comes from a large Lebanese clan in the Tri-Border Area (TBA) where Paraguay, Argentina, and Brazil intersect – a hotbed infamous for its role in the 1994 AMIA terrorist attack in Argentina. In Argentina, Assad Ahmad Barakat has been implicated by authorities in the AMIA attack for his role in facilitating communications between the TBA and Lebanon. He did this through an array of front companies, some stretching as far north as the Andes.

One such company, Saleh Trading LTDA, was established in 2001 in the duty-free zone of Iquique, Chile, and later on the Caribbean coast in Margarita Island, Venezuela.[5] According to research by Venezuelan legislator Carlos Papparoni, in 2001, Saleh Trading LTDA signed preferential business deals with the Venezuelan Ministry of Education, which was controlled by Hugo Chávez.[6] This contract provided a precedent for the special relationship between the Venezuelan government and Iran's chief terrorist proxy, Hezbollah.

Venezuela provides political, diplomatic, material and logistical support to Hezbollah. In turn, the group uses Venezuela for fundraising and various forms of money-laundering, smuggling, and illicit finance. The basic model is a simple "pay to play" system, in which local Lebanese merchants are persuaded by Hezbollah fixers, facilitators, and financiers, through varying degrees of coercion, to "tithe" to Hezbollah.[7]

There have been several reports of the Venezuelan regime providing identification documents to suspected members of Hezbollah and other Islamist terrorist organizations from the Middle East. One former director of Venezuela's immigration agency has suggested that the number of documents provided to Islamist militants number in the tens of thousands.[8] Another official, a former legal attaché to the Bolivarian Republic's embassy in Iraq named Misael Lopez-Soto, provided an eyewitness account and documentary evidence that the Venezuelan embassy in Baghdad was selling passports and other identification documents to suspected members of Hezbollah.[9] In one case, Lopez-Soto identified an acquaintance of one of the 9/11 hijackers who fled to Venezuela after the attack on the World Trade Center and Pentagon.[10]

A 2017 CNN documentary pointed to the country's former Vice President (and current Minister of Petroleum) Tareck El Aissami as the most prominent government official involved in this alleged passports-for-terrorists scheme. El Aissami, the son of Syrian-Lebanese Druze, is an ardent supporter of Hezbollah and has used his political prominence in Venezuela to establish conduits to several Islamic governments. He has helped create a criminal-terrorist pipeline, funneling illicit funds and drugs to the Middle East and facilitating the movement of Islamists into the Western Hemisphere.[11] One intelligence report cited by the CNN documentary estimates that at least 173 Islamist and other militants from the Middle East received identification documents from the government of Venezuela. These militants capitalized on a sophisticated, multi-layered money-laundering network established by El Aissami and his family while he was the Interior Minister from 2008-2012.[12]

El Aissami's partner in this immigration scheme is alleged to be the former Venezuelan diplomat Ghazi Nassereddine. The

Nassereddines are a prominent Lebanese family in Venezuela with close ties to Hezbollah. They are believed to have facilitated travel to, and logistical support in, Venezuela for Hezbollah operatives for several decades, establishing a real estate footprint on Margarita Island in the Caribbean.[13] Ghazi Nasserredine, who is also wanted by the FBI, and Tareck El Aissami are both sanctioned by the U.S. Treasury Department's Office of Financial Assets and Control.[14]

Walid Makled Garcia, a noted Syrian-Venezuelan drug kingpin incarcerated in 2011, identified Tareck El Aissami and his brother Feras as former clients.[15] Makled claimed that the El Aissami brothers would pay him to create spaces for the Venezuelan armed forces to move illicit products from Venezuela to the Middle East and West Africa. Claiming to have more than 40 Venezuelan generals on his payroll, Makled had strategic access to ports, airports, national airlines, and fertilizer plants, to cover and conceal the movement of illicit narcotics and launder the funds for several Drug Trafficking Organizations, including Hezbollah.[16]

These accusations were formalized by the Department of Justice on May 27, 2020, when a former member of Maduro's political party, the PSUV, was charged with an alleged "cocaine-for-weapons" conspiracy between Iran, Syria, Hezbollah, Hamas, the FARC, and the Maduro regime-controlled drug network, the Cartel de Los Soles, named after the military insignia of the Venezuelan generals.[17] Adel El Zebayar, the former Venezuelan legislator, traveled in 2013 and 2014 to Syria to supposedly fight alongside forces defending dictator Bashar Al-Assad. According to the indictment, while in Syria and after, Zebayar helped the Maduro-regime controlled Cartel de Los Soles serve as an intermediary to transfer multi-ton shipments of cocaine from Colombia's the FARC to Hezbollah and Hamas, in exchange for military-grade weapons, including AK-47s and AT4 rocket launchers.[18]

Islamism and Society

For more than 150 years, waves of mass migration arrived from Lebanon, Syria, Armenia, and other countries in the Middle East, to Venezuela. In the early 20th century, a second wave of mass migration arrived in Venezuela from Lebanon who settled largely in Margarita Island, Puerto Cabello, Punto Fijo, and La Guaira.[19] It is via this mass migration that Venezuela's small Muslim population began to grow.

According to the conservative estimate of the U.S. State Department in its 2017 *International Religious Freedom Report*, there are more than 100,000 Muslims in Venezuela. They are primarily of Lebanese and Syrian descent and concentrated on Margarita Island, Punto Fijo, and in the country's capital, Caracas.[20] One of the largest and most established Muslim communities in Venezuela is on Margarita Island in the Nueva Esparta state. Around 12,000 Lebanese call the island their home, and there a growing Muslim population is increasingly involved in real estate and tourism.[21]

While Margarita Island's Muslim population is almost entirely Lebanese Shi'a, there are Sunni Muslims elsewhere in the country. For example, Caracas has a Sunni population of 15,000 that is served by one of the largest and tallest mosques in Latin America, built by the Saudi government as a sister mosque to the Sheikh Ibrahim Al-Ibrahim mosque in Gibraltar.[22] Venezuela's deteriorating economy, however, has pushed Muslim immigrants out of the country. This is apparent as the community ebbs and flows from Margarita Island, to Caracas, to Punto Fijo, along Venezuela's Caribbean coast, until it reaches the country's northwest border with Colombia in La Guaira. Across the border, the city of Maicao, Colombia, has become one of the most prominent destinations for Venezuelan migrants and refugees escaping the harsh conditions of the humanitarian crisis. This border town is home to Colombia's largest Sunni population, with approximately 5,000 Muslims.[23]

For the time being no mass conversion to Islam is taking place in Venezuela. This is not to say that efforts have not been made, especially among indigenous and Creole groups whose Christianity has never been especially solid. To the contrary, in the past 150 years of immigration from the Middle East to the New World, the opposite trend has held sway. Many prominent *turcos* (immigrants and their descendants from the Middle East) originally were Muslim but have been genuine *conversos* (converts to Christianity) for generations.

The presence in Caracas of the second largest mosque in Latin

America reflects Venezuela's cosmopolitan self-image more than it serves as evidence of an Islamic trajectory. Nonetheless, one should not dismiss the larger fact that Islam does play a significant—if not central—role in Venezuela's anti-globalist and anti-hegemonic culture, which post-colonial critic Robert Young notes incarnates a "tricontinental counter-modernity" that combines diaspora and local cultural elements, and blends Arab, Islamic, black and Hispanic factors to generate "a revolutionary black, Asian and Hispanic globalization, with its own dynamic counter-modernity... constructed in order to fight global imperialism."[24]

Islamism and the State

Ever since Hugo Chavez took his first trip to Iran in 2001, close relations with the Islamic Republic have been a cardinal tenet of Venezuela's foreign policy. During Iran's 2009 elections, Chavez offered "total solidarity" to Iranian president Mahmoud Ahmadinejad, equating attacks on him as an assault by "global capitalism,"[25] and condoned the brutal tactics of Iran's domestic militia, the *Basij*, in their crackdown on opposition protesters.[26] Iran reciprocated these friendly feelings when Hugo Chávez was decorated with the Higher Medal of the Islamic Republic of Iran in 2008, Mahmoud Ahmadinejad called Chávez "my brother… a friend of the Iranian nation and the people seeking freedom around the world. He works perpetually against the dominant system. He is a worker of God and servant of the people."[27]

In terms of concrete policy implementation, these have included joint nuclear science and technology pacts,[28] delegation and diplomatic visits,[29] promises of oil exchanges,[30] the launch of a binational bank to illicitly channel funds,[31] suspected industrial levels of support for Iran's WMD program,[32] and distributed lines of credit used to fund medical research.[33]

In 2017, street protests and social uprisings spread throughout Venezuela. Amid the domestic political and economic crisis, the spokesperson for Iran's Foreign Ministry stated "the continuation of instability in Venezuela does not benefit anyone but could only serve to heighten the pressure felt by citizens. The stability and security of Latin America, especially that of our friend Venezuela, is of great importance to Iran."[34] This show of solidarity was followed by pledge of military support from Iran's Defense Minister Brigadier General Hossein Dehqan, who met with Venezuela's Defense Minister Vladimir Padrino López at the Moscow International Security Conference.[35]

In 2018, Iran's Vice Minister of Foreign Affairs Morteza Sarmadi called for "closer cooperation" with Venezuela in standing against the Trump administration.[36] For his part, President Maduro reassured his Iranian allies that Venezuela will remain steadfast in partnership with the Islamic Republic against "U.S. aggression," stating that "[Iran and Venezuela] must firmly stand against U.S. patronizing policies in OPEC and coordinate the policies of OPEC and non-OPEC members against Washington."[37]

Concurrently, as Caracas strengthened its relationship with Tehran, it has reached out to Ankara. In 2018, Turkey announced plans to start the construction of a new mosque in Caracas at the behest of the Maduro regime,[38] although that project still has not materialized. That same year, the Venezuelan government began a complex gold-for-food scheme with Turkey's President Recep Tayyip Erdogan.[39] The scheme was built off an existing trade-based money laundering network run by Colombian Lebanese businessman, Alex Saab, and tapped into Venezuela's gold-rich Arco Minero and the regime's military-run food distribution program known as the CLAP system.[40]

In 2020, Saab was named as Maduro's special envoy to Tehran. He subsequently aimed to build a gold-for-gas scheme similar to the previous successful efforts with Turkey. With fuel shortages rampant throughout Venezuela, Saab and the Maduro regime arranged for no fewer than nine oil tankers from Iran, only five of which arrived in late May delivering approximately 1.5 million barrels of gasoline to various ports in Venezuela.[41] Prior to the tankers, 17 flights from the Iranian airline, Mahan Air, also arrived in Venezuela beginning in April, to deliver technicians and parts to help repair some of the country's oil refineries.[42]

Saab was arrested on June 13, 2020, in Cape Verde, off the coast of West Africa, off an Interpol Red Notice for money-laundering charges by the U.S. Southern District of Florida.[43] Saab was traveling to Iran at the time, and his arrest set off a diplomatic tug-of-war between the Trump administration and the Maduro regime. While as of August 2020 the matter is unresolved, Cape Verde authorities have so far accepted the extradition request from the United States and denied various appeals by Saab's lawyers, dealing a blow to the Tehran-Ankara-Caracas relationship.[44]

Iran and Venezuela increasingly unite using trade and humanitarian assistance as a cover for potential military transfers.[45] The nature of the flights by the Islamic Revolutionary Guard Corps' (IRGC) preferred airline, Mahan Air, stopping in Algeria and arriving at the Paraguana peninsula in Venezuela with contents unknown, suggest the return of "Aero Terror." This is a reference to a similar flight between Iran and Venezuela almost a decade ago.[46] Moreover, in addition to the five tankers with Iranian flags that arrived in early June, an additional four Liberian re-flagged tankers from Iran were in route to Venezuela before being stopped due to U.S. economic pressure on Greece, where the tankers were registered and insured. The U.S. then seized 1.1 million barrels of fuel reportedly on board these Liberian-flagged tankers, the largest U.S. seizure of Iranian fuel to date.[47] A civil forfeiture complaint in the District of Columbia by the Justice Department implies that these fuel shipments to Venezuela were arranged by the IRGC through the National Iranian Oil Company.[48]

The fuel shipments were followed by another Iranian-flagged general cargo ship, the Golsan, bringing food to Venezuela in June.[49] Shortly after, the *Wall Street Journal* reported that Iran's first supermarket recently inaugurated in Caracas, Megasis, was owned by a military conglomerate, Etka, that is known to cooperate with the IRGC.[50]

The blending of commercial with military activity, has provided Iran and the Maduro regime a degree of plausible deniability for potential covert military transfers. Fuel, food, technicians, and technology between Tehran and Caracas are layered with Iranian state-owned entities sanctioned specifically for its dual-use activity with the revolutionary guards. This concern culminated in early August 2020, when Colombian President Ivan Duque openly stated in a virtual event that the Maduro regime is seeking to acquire medium-to-long range missiles from Iran, a claim initially denied by the Venezuelan regime but now acknowledged by Nicolás Maduro as a "good idea."[51]

Endnotes

1. Alberto Garrido, *Las Guerras de Chavez* (Rayuela: Taller de Ediciones, 2006), 17.
2. Paul D. Taylor, ed., "Latin American Security Challenges: A Collaborative Inquiry from North and South," Naval War College *Newport Paper* no. 21, 2004.
3. U.S. Department of the Treasury, "Treasury Designates Islamic Extremist, Two Companies Supporting Hizballah in the Tri-Border Area," June 10, 2004, https://www.treasury.gov/press-center/press-releases/Pages/js1720.aspx
4. Emanuele Ottolenghi, "Hezbollah Operative Assad Ahmad Barakat Extradited to Paraguay." Foundation for Defense of Democracies. July 22, 2020, https://www.fdd.org/analysis/2020/07/22/hezbollah-operative-extradited-to-paraguay/
5. "Confirman detección de redes financieras vinculadas a Hezbolá en Chile" *Emol*, November 8, 2001, https://www.emol.com/noticias/nacional/2001/11/08/70757/
6. Author interview with Carlos Papparoni, Washington, DC, February 3, 2020. Papparoni was appointed by Venezuela's Interim President, Juan Guaido, as a representative in the Guaido government's "Office of Regional Cooperation against Money Laundering and Corruption."
7. U.S. Department of the Treasury, "Treasury Designates Islamic Extremist, Two Companies Supporting Hezbollah in Tri-border Area."
8. Antonio María Delgado, "Régimen chavista otorgó ilegalmente 10,000 pasaportes venezolanos a sirios, iraníes," *El Nuevo Herald*, April 16, 2017, https://www.elnuevoherald.com/noticias/mundo/america-latina/venezuela-es/article144934809.html.
9. The documentary, titled "Passports in the Shadows" aired simultaneously on AC360° and Conclusiones of CNN en Español on Feb. 14, 2017, https://www.cnn.com/videos/world/2017/02/14/fraudulent-venezuelan-passports-griffin-dnt-ac.cnn.
10. Misael Lopez-Soto identified Palestinian-Venezuelan dual na-

tional Hakim Diab Fattah in his investigations. This was verified by documents submitted by retired Venezuelan General Marcos Ferreira to José Pernalete of *Diario de Las* Americas in Miami, Florida, published in an article "Pruebas revelan que Venezuela occulta a sospechoso de terrorismo" on January 11, 2016. It is available at https://www.diariolasamericas.com/pruebas-revelan-que-venezuela-oculta-sospechoso-terrorismo-n3553685

11. "Passports in the Shadows," AC360.
12. "Passports in the Shadows," AC360.
13. Emili J. Blasco, *Boomerang Chavez: The Fraud that Led to Venezuela's Collapse* (CreateSpace Independent Publishing Platform, June 2016).
14. US Department of Treasury, "Treasury Sanctions Prominent Venezuelan Drug Trafficker Tareck El Aissami and his Primary Frontman Samark Lopez Bello," February 13, 2017, https://www.treasury.gov/press-center/press-releases/Pages/as0005.aspx.
15. Joseph Humire, "Chapter 8 - Venezuela: Trends in Organized Crime," in Bruce M. Bagley, Jonathan D. Rosen, and Hanna S. Kassab, eds., *Re-conceptualizing Security in the Americas in the 21st Century* (Lexington Books, 2016).
16. See Interview with Walid Makled on the "Aqui y Ahora" news program on Spanish-language network *Univision*, March 31, 2011, https://www.univision.com/shows/aqui-y-ahora/exclusiva-con-walid-makled-el-narcotraficante-que-quieren-extraditar-eu-y-venezuela
17. Southern District of New York, U.S. Attorney's Office, Department of Justice, "Former Member of Venezuelan National Assembly Charged with Narco-Terrorism, Drug Trafficking, and Weapons Offenses," May 27, 2020, https://www.justice.gov/usao-sdny/pr/former-member-venezuelan-national-assembly-charged-narco-terrorism-drug-trafficking-and
18. Alma Keshavarz and Robert J. Bunker, "Hybrid Criminal Cartel Note 1: Former Venezuelan National Assembly Member Adel El Zebayar Indicted on Charges of Narcoterrorism and Links to Hezbollah." *Small Wars Journal*, July 1, 2020, https://smallwarsjournal.com/jrnl/art/hybrid-criminal-cartel-note-1-former-venezuelan-national-assembly-member-adel-el-zabayar
19. Ignacio Klich and Jeffrey Lesser, "Introduction: 'Turco' Immigrants in Latin America," *The Americas* 53.1 (1996), 1–14.
20. U.S. Department of State, Bureau of Democracy, Human Rights

and Labor, "Venezuela," *2011 Report on International Religious Freedom*, September 2011, https://www.state.gov/j/drl/rls/irf/2011/wha/193009.htm.

21. Michael Smith and Monte Reel, "Venezuela's Trade Scheme With Turkey Is Enriching a Mysterious Maduro Crony," *Bloomberg*, April 25, 2019, https://www.bloomberg.com/news/features/2019-04-25/venezuela-turkey-trading-scheme-enriches-mysterious-maduro-crony
22. U.S. Department of State, Bureau of Democracy, Human Rights and Labor, "Venezuela."
23. Marco Rotunno, "Venezuelans living in the streets find safety at new reception centre in Colombia," United Nations Human Rights Coalition, April 15, 2019, https://www.unhcr.org/en-us/news/stories/2019/4/5cb48f934/venezuelans-living-streets-find-safety-new-reception-centre-colombia.html
24. Robert Young, *Postcolonialism: An Historical Introduction* (London: Blackwell Publishers, 2001), 2.
25. "Iran-Venezuela Ties Serve Strategic Aims," United Press International, August 14, 2009, http://www.upi.com/Top_News/Special/2009/08/14/Iran-Venezuela-ties-serve-strategic-aims/UPI-91201250266165.
26. Ibid.
27. "Chávez decorated in Iran; initials cooperation pacts," *El Universal* (Caracas), July 31, 2006, http://english.eluniversal.com/2006/07/31/en_pol_art_31A756133.shtml.
28. Roger F. Noriega, "Chávez's Secret Nuclear Program" *Foreign Policy*, October 5, 2010, http://www.foreignpolicy.com/files/fp_uploaded_documents/101004_0_Acuerdos_Ciencia_y_Tecnologia.pdf.
29. "Iranian Delegation in Venezuela," *Mathaba* (London), November 17, 2008, http://mathaba.net/news/?x=611701; "Zarif, Rodriguez stress expansion of Iran-Venezuela ties," MEHR News Agency (Iran), August 16, 2016, https://en.mehrnews.com/news/118959/Zarif-Rodr%C3%ADguez-stress-expansion-of-Iran-Venezuela-ties.
30. Robert M. Morgenthau, "The Emerging Axis Of Iran And Venezuela," *Wall Street Journal*, September 8, 2009, http://online.wsj.com/article/SB10001424052970203440104574400792835972018.html.
31. Ibid.; "Iran Raises Profile In Latin America," *Washington Post*, November 22, 2008.
32. United Nations, "Security Council Toughens Sanctions Against Iran, Adds Arms Embargo, With Unanimous Adoption of Reso-

lution 1747," March 24, 2007, https://www.un.org/press/en/2007/sc8980.doc.htm; U.S. Department of Treasury, "Treasury designates Iranian proliferation Individuals, Entities," July 8, 2008, http://www.treasury.gov/press-center/press-releases/Pages/hp1071.aspx; "Treasury designates Iranian proliferation Individuals, Entities," July 8, 2008; "The mysterious Venezuelan-Iranian gunpowder plant," *Univision News*, January 13, 2012, http://news.univision.com/article/2012-01-13/the-mysterious-venezuelan-iranian-gunpowder-plant-casto-ocando; U.S. Department of State, "U.S. Relations With Venezuela," August 31, 2016, https://2009-2017.state.gov/r/pa/ei/bgn/35766.htm.

33. Aditya Tejas, "Venezuela, Iran Sign Economic Cooperation Deals; Venezuela Signs $500M Credit Line With Iran," *International Business Times,* June 2015, http://www.ibtimes.com/venezuela-iran-sign-economic-cooperation-deals-venezuela-signs-500m-credit-line-iran-1986665.
34. Correo del Orinoco, "Irán rechaza cualquier intervención extranjera en los asuntos internos de Venezuela," *Apporea* (Venezuela), April 14, 2017, https://www.aporrea.org/internacionales/n307038.html.
35. "Iran discusses Defense Ties with Serbia, Venezuela," Tasnim News Agency (Iran), April 26, 2017, https://www.tasnimnews.com/en/news/2017/04/26/1390155/iran-discusses-defense-ties-with-serbia-venezuela.
36. "Iran, Venezuela need closer joint cooperation against Trump's policies," MEHR News Agency (Iran), July 1, 2018, https://en.mehrnews.com/news/135272/Iran-Venezuela-need-closer-joint-coop-against-Trump-s-policies.
37. Ibid.
38. "Turkey to build mosque in Caracas upon Venezuela's request," *Daily Sabah*, December 3, 2018, https://www.dailysabah.com/religion/2018/12/03/turkey-to-build-mosque-in-caracas-upon-venezuelas-request
39. Smith and Reel, "Venezuela's Trade Scheme with Turkey is Enriching a Mysterious Maduro Crony."
40. Joseph Humire, "Iran, Turkey, and Venezuela's Super Facilitator: Who is Alex Saab?" Center for a Secure Free Society (SFS) *Situation Report*, June 30, 2020, https://www.securefreesociety.org/research/who-is-alex-saab/
41. Mehdi Jedinia, Carolina Valladares Perez, and Sirwan Kajjo, "What's Behind Iran's Fuel Shipment to Venezuela?" *Voice*

of America, May 31, 2020, https://www.voanews.com/extremism-watch/whats-behind-irans-fuel-shipment-venezuela

42. Emanuele Ottolenghi, "Iran is Airlifting Supplies to Venezuela," *The Dispatch*, May 1, 2020, https://thedispatch.com/p/iran-is-airlifting-supplies-to-venezuela
43. U.S. Department of Justice, Office of Public Affairs, "Two Colombian Businessmen Charged With Money Laundering in Connection With Venezuela Bribery Scheme," July 25, 2019, https://www.justice.gov/opa/pr/two-colombian-businessmen-charged-money-laundering-connection-venezuela-bribery-scheme
44. Antonio Maria Delgado, "Cape Verde approves extradition to U.S. of Venezuelan regime's financial whiz," *Miami Herald*, July 14, 2020, https://www.miamiherald.com/news/nation-world/world/americas/venezuela/article244212727.html
45. Christina Armes, "Iran's military network comes out of the shadows in Venezuela," *PanAm Post*, July 25, 2020.
46. José R. Cárdenas, "Sanctioning Venezuela's 'aero-terror,'" *Foreign Policy*, June 23, 2011, https://foreignpolicy.com/2011/06/23/sanctioning-venezuelas-aero-terror/
47. U.S. Department of Justice, Office of Public Affairs, "Largest U.S. Seizure of Iranian Fuel from Four Tankers," August 14, 2020, https://www.justice.gov/opa/pr/largest-us-seizure-iranian-fuel-four-tankers
48. Ibid.
49. "Iran ship reaches Venezuelan waters with cargo of food." Reuters, June 21, 2020, https://www.reuters.com/article/us-venezuela-iran/iran-ship-reaches-venezuelan-waters-with-cargo-of-food-idUSKBN23S0WW
50. Ian Talley and Benoit Faucon, "Iranian Military-Owned Conglomerate Sets Up Shop in Venezuela," *Wall Street Journal*, July 5, 2020, https://www.wsj.com/articles/iranian-military-owned-conglomerate-sets-up-shop-in-venezuela-11593972015
51. "Maduro dice que "no es mala idea" comprar misiles a Irán," *DW*, August 22, 2020, https://www.dw.com/es/maduro-dice-que-no-es-mala-idea-comprar-misiles-a-ir%C3%A1n/a-54661914

Middle East and North Africa

9 Algeria

Quick Facts

Population: 40,969,443 (July 2017 est.)
Area: 2,381,741 sq km
Ethnic Groups: Arab-Berber 99%, European less than 1%
Government Type: Presidential republic
GDP (official exchange rate): $175.5 billion (2017 est.)

Source: CIA World FactBook (Last Updated April 2018)

Introduction

Since Algeria declared its independence from France in 1962, the country has seen many opposition groups. However, Islamist parties and armed groups have made up the major opposition to successive Algerian governments. Between 1991 and 1999, civil strife between violent Islamist extremists and security forces plagued Algeria and claimed over 150,000 lives. The majority of those killed were civilians. However, conservative Islamism continues to hold appeal for many in Algeria to this day. The Algerian government's attempts at reconciliation in 1994, 1999 and 2005 aided the decline of violent extremist groups, but unwittingly legitimized and empowered political Islamism, at least for a time. While Islamic parties have diminished in stature and appeal, as evidenced by their dwindling power and dismal electoral results in recent years, their ideas and underlying social conservatism remain.

Due to publishing constraints, this chapter is provided here only in summary form. To view the full study, please visit the online edition of the Almanac at almanac.afpc.org.

10 Bahrain

Quick Facts

Population: 1,505,003 (July 2020 est.)
Area: 760 sq km
Ethnic Groups: Bahraini 46%, Asian 45.5%, other Arab 4.7%, African 1.6%, European 1%, other 1.2% (includes Gulf Co-operative country nationals, North and South Americans, and Oceanians) (2010 est.)
Government Type: Constitutional monarchy
GDP (official exchange rate): $35.33 billion (2017 est.)

Source: CIA World FactBook (Last Updated July 2020)

Introduction

Bahrain is anomalous among the Arab states of the Persian Gulf. Islamism in Bahrain is traditionally domestically focused, directed at confronting economic and morality issues through nonviolent political action. Although it has never even remotely qualified as "free," Bahrain offers a relatively high degree of social and cultural openness compared to other Gulf states. Unfortunately, freedom of the press, operational latitude for NGOs, and what elements of democracy existed in the past have been degraded in recent years, particularly since the Arab Spring-inspired protests of 2011. Bahrain is now considered one of the region's most repressive states.[1]

There are some indications, however, that Bahraini Islamism is becoming violent: while in the past only a few Bahrainis traveled abroad to join in jihad or supported al-Qaeda either financially or logistically, a number of citizens are known to have joined ISIS, received combat training, and attempted to form local terrorist cells in the recent past.[2] *Further, some observers believe that the regime's emphasis on sectarian divisions helps to spur Salafi jihadism, which is particularly hostile to Shi'a Islam.*[3] *Although today the regional focus on Syria may have receded, both anti-Shi'a sentiment and loyalist tendencies remain.*

At present, Bahrain remains locked in an uneasy stasis. Both the Sunni and Shiite residents of the country are now so cynical that it is difficult to imagine how it can pretend to run a functional democracy – especially since opposition blocs were prohibited from participating in the November 2018 polls.[4] *Bahrain's domestic impasse, along with the intensifying regional conflict between the Iran-led Shiite bloc and the Sunni one led by Saudi Arabia, may in turn strengthen Sunni and Shia Islamist forces in the country.*

Islamist Activity

While as much as 70 percent of Bahrain's citizens are Shiites,[5] this majority is significantly poorer than its Sunni counterpart. As a result, it complains of facing discrimination in employment (particularly with regard to senior-level government and security-service jobs), housing, immigration policy, and government services. Accordingly, the Shiite opposition seeks to redress these inequalities while rhetorically mentioning more traditional Islamist goals. Its political and economic goals include:

- Genuine democracy, a system that would benefit the country's majority Shiite population.[6]
- The dismantling (or substantial weakening) of Bahrain's internal-security apparatus and the release of political prisoners.
- Economic justice, including equal access to employment and government services.
- An end to Bahrain's policy of facilitating Sunni immigration.
- Traditional Islamist beliefs like the elimination of alcohol, prostitution, and other evils from the kingdom and the application of *sharia* law.

Most Bahraini Shiites adhere to the Akhbari school of Twelver Shiism. Akhbaris believe that, while clerics should advise political leaders, they should not have direct power. Akhbaris traditionally claimed loyalty to the state and to its ruling family, seeking to change the system rather than overthrow it.[7] While the Bahraini Shiite community does not have its own *marja* (source of emulation) that represents a threat to the legitimacy of the Bahraini establishment, the Bahraini government's heavy-handed response to Shiite protests and political activism has radicalized Shiite political discourse.[8]

Despite the Shiite community's past assertions of loyalty to Bahrain and its governing family, many Bahraini Sunnis are suspicious that the country's Shiites maintain close cultural and political ties to Iran. The fact that Bahraini Shiite clerics are often trained in Iran adds credibility to this accusation, even though this arrangement is due at least partially to the lack of Shi'a clerical training facilities in Bahrain. The ongoing repression of Bahraini Shiites, as well as Bahrain's participation in the Saudi-led campaign against the Shiite Houthis in Yemen, have only increased the community's identification with Iran, and vice versa.[9]

The Bahraini government and others in the regional Sunni elite, as well as outside commentators concerned about Iranian influence, have repeatedly claimed that Shiite unrest in Bahrain is the product of Iranian scheming. Such accusations are plausible: Iran has a history of meddling in the internal affairs of other countries, and Iranian officials occasionally reassert their country's historical claim on Bahrain.[10] Further, the use of more sophisticated explosives in recent Shiite attacks does strengthen the case for Iranian involvement, if not instigation.[11] However, these claims are circumstantial in nature, and neutral observers point out that Bahraini Shiite unrest can likewise be explained by genuine domestic grievances.[12]

Even if Bahrain's Shi'a are sincere in their patriotism, Iran may attempt to gain their allegiance in the unlikely event that they achieve significant political power.[13] In any case, the Bahraini government seems intent on disintegrating any loyalty the country's Shiites may have to the Iranian regime, particularly as tensions between Iran and Saudi Arabia have risen in recent years.

Jam'īyat al-Wifāq al-Watanī al-Islāmīyah

The most prominent Bahraini Shiite political "society" is Jam'īyat al-Wifāq al-Watanī al-Islāmīyah (the al-Wefaq National Islamic Society, also known as the Islamic National Accord Association), officially led by Qom-educated "mid-level" cleric Sheikh Ali Salman. Bahrain's most prominent Shi'a cleric, Ayatollah Isa Qassim, a disciple of Iraqi Grand Ayatollah Ali al-Sistani, is generally considered al-Wefaq's unofficial spiritual leader.[14] Al-Wefaq has at least 1,500 active members.[15]

After boycotting the 2002 elections to protest the new constitution's failure to adopt fully democratic values, al-Wefaq candidates competed in the 2006 elections. They won big; out of 17 candidates fielded by the group, 16 won their districts in the first round of voting and the 17th candidate won in a second-round run-off. This group represented the largest single-political bloc in the elected lower house of the Bahraini legislature between 2006 and 2011, making it a target of government crackdown after these same representatives participated in the Arab Spring protests.[16] It aimed to unite "all the Shi'a Islamic currents under one banner" within Bahrain, eventually converting the country into a constitutional monarchy.[17] The group repeated this success in the 2010 elections, winning all 18 seats it contested. Were the Bahraini electoral system not gerrymandered to favor Sunni candidates, al-Wefaq would have easily won a commanding majority of the Council's 40 seats.[18]

Until the Arab Spring protests of 2011 and the government's violent response to them, al-Wefaq positioned itself as a loyal opposition. It worked to achieve equality for Bahraini Shiites while maintaining allegiance to the monarchy. However, this stance has largely evaporated. All 18 al-Wefaq members of the Council of Representatives resigned in protest in early 2011, and the group's leaders initially refused to enter a dialogue with the government until Prime Minister Khalifa al-Khalifa was replaced.[19] Al-Wefaq, partly in response to American and British persuasion, agreed to participate in a government-organized "national consensus dialogue" that began in July 2011; however, the group's representatives walked out when the opposition was allotted only 25 out of 300 seats and by the failure to address Shiite grievances.[20]

Al-Wefaq, along with the rest of the opposition, boycotted the 2011 and 2014 elections.[20] The vast majority of Shiite voters obeyed calls to boycott the vote,[21] and protests were violently suppressed with the help of Saudi GCC forces in March.[22] With no opposition representation, the Council of Representatives could no longer claim even a skewed representation.

In 2016, the government significantly escalated its conflict with al-Wefaq. It first suspended its activities and froze al-Wefaq's funds; then, in July, the government ordered al-Wefaq dissolved and its assets turned over to the national treasury.[23] Ayatollah Isa Qassim was accused of financial misdeeds[24] and stripped of his citizenship,[25] and Sheikh Ali Salman and other leaders of the group were imprisoned.[26] Al-Wefaq appealed this decision, but in February 2017 its appeal was rejected.[27] Ali Salman, already serving a nine-year prison sentence for "inciting hatred, promoting disobedience and insulting public institutions"[28] (later changed to "inciting hatred and calling for forceful regime change,"[29]) was accused of colluding with Qatar to carry out "hostile acts" and "damage Bahrain's prestige" in November 2017.[30]

The U.S. and other Western powers have condemned the suppression of al-Wefaq, but Bahraini authorities remain unmoved.[31] In May 2017, Ayatollah Qassim was convicted, fined, and given a one-year suspended sentence alongside two aides;[32] two days later, a raid on his home town of Diraz to "maintain security and public order" resulted in the killing of at least five protestors and the arrest of several hundred.[33] The government promised an investigation of these killings;[34] but it is unlikely that security forces will be held accountable. Meanwhile, "security and public order" in the town have not improved.[35] In May 2018, ahead of November's election, parliament approved a bill to bar members of al-Wefaq from contesting the polls, "due to their serious violations of the constitution and laws of the kingdom."[36] Since that time, the group continues to voice its opinions about the government, primarily online and from abroad, yet is largely inactive within Bahrain.

Haq Movement for Liberty and Democracy

Al-Wefaq's main competition for the loyalty of Bahraini Shiites, prior to its dissolution, was the Haq Movement for Liberty and Democracy. The Haq Movement was founded in 2005, largely by al-Wefaq's more radical leaders, who objected to al-Wefaq's participation in the 2006 elections. Haq specifically hopes to institute full democracy and is less concerned with morality issues or Shiite sectarianism. One of *Haq*'s leaders, Sheikh Isa Abdullah al-Jowder (who died in September 2011), was a Sunni cleric, and another founder (who eventually left the movement),[37] Ali Qasim Rabea, is a secular leftist nationalist.[38] Nonetheless, Haq is considered both Shi'a and Islamist (despite receiving no endorsements from any senior Bahraini Shiite cleric) due to its support base.[39]

Haq has unquestionably benefited, in terms of popular support, from the breakdown of the relationship between the Bahraini government and Bahraini Shiites. Indeed, unlike al-Wefaq, Haq never invested its credibility in a political process which it considered inherently unequal. In fact, Haq has consistently refused to register as an official "political society."[40] While al-Wefaq spent four years in the Council of Representatives ineffectively working for the Shiite community's interests, Haq (or, at least, groups of young Shiites inspired by Haq) threw rocks at the police.[41] The group submitted petitions to the United Nations and the United States condemning the Bahraini government.[42] While the rocks and petitions accomplished no more than al-Wefaq's political maneuvering, they did establish Haq as a genuine opposition force. The fact that Haq leaders Hasan Mushaima and Abdeljalil al-Singace were among the opposition leaders imprisoned after the 2011 protests only reinforced the movement's credibility; both leaders have been sentenced to life in prison for plotting to overthrow the monarchy.[43] Following these arrests, Haq, like Wafa' (discussed in detail below), both of which refused to register officially under the Political Associations Law of 2005, were effectively dissolved.[44]

As part of the Bahraini government's efforts to confront *Haq*, officials have accused the organization's leaders of being in the pay of Iran, either directly or through Hezbollah intermediaries. While it is very difficult to prove that such a relationship does exist, and many in the Sunni community truly believe that Bahraini Shiites are more loyal to Iran than to Bahrain, observers have pointed out that no convincing evidence has ever been produced to back these accusations.[45]

Wafa' (Loyalty)

Wafa' was founded in early 2009 by Abdulwahab Hussain, a cleric and leading Shi'a activist in the 1990s and a co-founder of al-Wefaq. Unlike Haq, Wafa' is backed by senior cleric (and rival of Ayatollah Isa Qassim) Sheikh Abduljalil al-Maqdad. Wafa' has also resisted participating in Bahrain's quasi-democratic government.

Despite the fact that Wafa' has clerical backing and credible, experienced leadership, it never managed to gain much traction among Bahraini Shiites. Now that Hasan Mushaima has returned to Bahrain (where he is in prison) and al-Wefaq has quit the Council of Representatives, it will be difficult for Wafa' to find a meaningful niche in Bahraini Shiite politics.[46] It is unlikely that Wafa' will have a domestic political future with Abdulwahab Hussein, its leader, in prison for life and with the organization charged with housing a terrorist wing.[47]

Amal ("Islamic Action Society," Jam'iyyat al-Amal al-Islami, or "the Shirazi faction")

Amal is "the non-violent heir to the defunct Islamic Front for the Liberation of Bahrain (IFLB), which launched a failed uprising in 1981 inspired by Iran's Islamic revolution."[48] In 1981, 60 members of the IFLB were accused of plotting against the ruling family and was accused of attempting similar attacks in the 1990s.[49] Amal refused to register for the 2002 election, won no seats in the 2006 election,[50] and did not participate in the 2010 election. The society's Secretary General, Sheikh Mohammed al-Mahfoodh, did not participate because Amal "[does not] want to just be employees... the members of parliament are just employees who get a big salary."[51] Amal was effectively shut down in July 2012 after some 200 of its members were arrested.[52]

Sunni organizations

Bahrain's Sunni community is not overwhelmingly Islamist in its beliefs. Indeed, Sunni Islamist groups compete with secular organizations and independent candidates for voter support. Moreover, because Sunnis are a relatively wealthy, privileged minority, Sunni Islamists do not join in calls for genuine democratic reform (which would effectively disempower Sunni politicians and their supporters). While they may aspire to "increase the standard of living for Bahrainis; strengthen political, social and economic stability; and enhance financial and administrative oversight of the government and industry,"[53] they do not agitate for a fully democratic system. Because the American military presence contributes to Bahrain's economy and rebuffs supposed Iranian influence, mainstream Sunni Islamist groups do not oppose the presence of the American Fifth Fleet on Bahrain's territory.

In short, Bahrain's organized Sunni Islamist groups (including the two principal Sunni-Islamist political societies in Bahrain, al-Menbar al-Islami – the political wing of the al-Eslah Society and what is generally considered Bahrain's branch of the Muslim Brotherhood – and the al-Asala Political Society – the political wing of al-Tarbiya al-Islamiya, a conservative Salafist organization) – are seen as pro-government parties that work to incrementally modify the *status quo* while not advocating full democracy or other large-scale, disruptive changes.

The government, however, has used Sunni Islamists to counter Shiite agitation, even fostering cross-Sunni Islamist cooperation among the Muslim Brotherhood and Salafis to provide a counterweight to Shiite influence.

Al-Menbar's association with al-Eslah, which was founded in 1948 and runs a network of mosques, gives it a support base among Bahraini Sunnis (especially those from the merchant elites). Furthermore, al-Eslah (and, by extension, al-Menbar) benefits from the official patronage of the Bahraini ruling family (its former President was Sheikh Isa bin Mohammed al-Khalifa), as well as from some of Bahrain's largest businesses.[54] While charitable contributions to al-Eslah do not necessarily provide direct support for al-Menbar's political activity, they unquestionably contribute to al-Eslah's standing in society, and thus to al-Menbar's credibility. Indeed, al-Menbar, through its connections to the ruling family and elite merchant families, enjoys preferential access to the security apparatus, judiciary, royal court, and ruling family.[55]

Al-Asala takes a harder line than al-Menbar on various social issues and is allegedly supported by the poorer and more tribal Sunni population. The group is, in general, opposed to Bahrain's comparatively socially liberal character. It has opposed U.S. military action in Iraq. Despite their differences, however, al-Menbar and al-Asala cooperate; and, like al-Menbar, al-Asala cannot be accurately described as an opposition "society" even though it dissents from some Bahraini government policies.

In the 2006 elections, al-Menbar and al-Asala intentionally

divided the Sunni electoral districts between them.[56] Each group won seven seats.[57] In 2010, however, they failed to organize a similar arrangement: the two groups ran against each other in many districts and subsequently lost most. Al-Menbar won only two seats in the Council of Representatives, and al-Asala received just three.[58] Furthermore, the Sunni Islamist "societies" lost two seats in the 2014 election, perhaps in part as a result of government redistricting.[59] Al-Menbar, in the November 2018 election and for the first time since its creation in 2002, failed to win a single seat in parliament; meanwhile, al-Asala won three seats, the cross-Sunni Islamist bloc National Unity Gathering (NUG), whose creation was aided by the government, won a single seat. That left four seats to Sunni Islamists. Weeks after the elections, Al-Asala MPs called for crackdowns on "gay sheesha havens," suggesting that their agenda may focus on social policies they view as objectionable.[60]

Indeed, in 2006 Al-Menbar's Council of Representatives helped prevent Bahrain from ratifying the International Covenant on Civil and Political Rights because the Covenant would mean "that Muslims could convert to another religion, something against the Islamic law."[61] Al-Menbar promised to field female candidates for the 2006 election, but this pledge was dropped as part of an electoral pact with al-Asala, which does not approve of women participating in politics. Further, al-Menbar's parent organization ("supported" by the Islamic Education Society) held a 2008 workshop opposing government efforts to promote gender equality.[62] This is in direct opposition to Al-Menbar's historic support for women's rights.[63]

Unsurprisingly, Bahraini Sunni Islamist organizations have not participated in any anti-government demonstrations. If anything, they may have been one of the pro-government forces behind several rallies that took place while Bahrain's Shiites were holding their own anti-government demonstrations.[64] While these pro-government rallies were not openly acknowledged as al-Menbar or al-Asala events, there is no question that Bahrain's Sunnis consider Shiite protests to be a threat to their privileged situation.

However, as protests have slowed and outside pressure has continued, it appears the relationship between local Sunni Islamists and Bahrain's government is becoming more tense. The Muslim

Brotherhood, which has a branch in Bahrain, is increasingly considered antagonistic by *status quo* Sunni-dominated states. In 2014, Saudi Arabia and the United Arab Emirates, both key allies for Bahrain, designated the Muslim Brotherhood a terrorist organization.[65] Given its dependency on Saudi and Emirati support, official Bahrain policy can do little other than toe the line or create anti-Brotherhood atmospherics.[66]

There is now concern that Bahrainis drawn to fight for ISIS and other Sunni extremist groups in Syria may return to their country radicalized against both Shiites and the societal *status quo*.[67] The government's policy of recruiting foreign Sunnis to join the security forces could ultimately backfire, as some of these recruits may be easily (or already) radicalized while they lack loyalty to the al-Khalifa family.[68] One irony in this situation is that, while Bahrain is officially part of the international coalition fighting ISIS, native-born Bahrainis joining the organization are typically from social strata close to the al-Khalifa monarchy.[69] But at the same time, the Bahraini government has failed to consistently counter Sunni radicalization, preferring to attempt to focus on Shiites.[70] The more the Shi'a population is smeared as an Iranian outgroup, the likelier radical Sunni Islamism will emerge.

Islamism and Society

In addition to political activities, many of the established Islamist groups in Bahrain engage in conventional charitable and outreach work: supporting widows, orphans, and the poor, operating mosques and providing religious education, and proselytizing for their particular brand of Islam both at home and abroad. Al-Eslah runs a large charitable enterprise, supported by corporate *zakat* (charity) as well as private contributions. Al-Eslah has also made a number of prominent humanitarian contributions to the Gaza Strip, funding a building construction project at the Islamic University in 2005 and sending five ambulances to Gaza in 2009.[71]

Shi'a and Sunni Islamists in Bahrain are not comfortable cooperating even when they agree, especially following the events of the Arab Spring. However, there are some issues upon which

Shiite and Sunni leaders have joined forces:

- While they have been unsuccessful in banning the sale and consumption of alcohol in Bahrain, Islamists have done what they can to impose limits on them. Islamist organizations supported a government move to close bars in two-star hotels in 2009 and three star hotels in 2014;[72] however, "viral" social-media rumors suggesting that the ban would be imposed on all hotels, along with a ban on hotel discos and night clubs, appear—at least as of the end of 2019—to be false.[73]
- Islamists have attempted to eliminate prostitution—either by banning female entertainers in cheap hotels or by attempting to prevent the issuance of visas to women from Russia, Thailand, Ethiopia, and China. (The latter measure, proposed by the Salafist al-Asala, fell flat; even other Islamists in the Council of Representatives pointed out that it would cause diplomatic damage if passed, and probably would not be very effective.)[76]
- In late 2012, between 50 and 100 "hardline" Islamists protested U.S. celebrity Kim Kardashian's visit to Bahrain to open a milkshake shop. Among the signs at the protest was one asserting that: "[n]one of our customs and traditions allow us to receive stars of porn movies." The government responded with tear gas.[75] There were no reports of Islamist pro-Kardashian demonstrations.

Traditionally, Bahraini Sunnis and Shiites lived and worked together with minimal friction. However, over the past several years Shi'a protests and the Sunni government's response to them (including, in at least some cases, Sunni vigilante participation)[76] have damaged this relationship. Within a week of the February

14, 2011 onset of Shiite protests, for instance, Sunnis mounted counter demonstrations (often encouraged by the government).[77] As the crisis continued, confrontations between Sunni and Shiite groups became more frequent and more violent. Some Sunni groups explicitly opposed the government-Shiite dialogue, preferring the *status quo* to a resolution they felt would favor Shiites over their own community.[78] Although the political environment in Bahrain today is far more placid than it was eight years ago, largely due to repression of protests, large numbers of political arrests, and restrictions placed on opposition organizations, even assuming if a political settlement is someday reached, it is difficult to imagine that Bahrain's social atmosphere will quickly return to the *status quo*.[79]

Islamism and the State

After a turbulent period during the 1990s, the country's new king, Hamad bin Isa al-Khalifa, restored Bahrain to a constitutional government in 2002. In accordance with the 2002 constitution, elections with universal suffrage are held every four years (most recently in November 2018) for the lower chamber of the National Assembly, the Majlis an-Nuwab (Council of Representatives); all members of the upper chamber, the Majlis al-Shura (Consultative Council), are appointed by the King. Both chambers must approve legislation, giving each one effective veto power over proposed laws. As a result, since the one national body that is democratically elected has such limited ability to accomplish anything against the wishes of the ruling establishment, the extent of public participation in politics has been unsatisfactory for many Bahrainis since 2002. Even the Council of Representatives' ability to block legislation does not constrain the ruling family's power; the King retains the right to rule by royal decree and can therefore bypass the legislature entirely.[80]

Real power is concentrated with the ruling al-Khalifa family; its members occupy the most important governmental positions, including 20 of the country's 25 Cabinet seats.[81] The Prime Minister, Prince Khalifa ibn Sulman al-Khalifa, has held office since the country was granted independence in 1971. He is currently the world's longest-serving Prime Minister, the uncle of King Hamad, and is thought to be one of the wealthiest people in Bahrain.[82]

While the Shiite unrest in Bahrain in the early 2010s has eclipsed most other news about Bahraini Islamism, earlier news stories paint a picture of a government willing to work with Islamists to achieve its goals, but equally willing to take strong measures to limit their actions and influence. The Bahraini government generally rejects Islamism; however, it is not above weaponizing Sunni Islamists against the Shiite community. The government, for instance, has in the past reportedly paid a number of individuals and NGOs, including both al-Islah/al-Menbar and the Islamic Education Society/al-Asala; in return those groups would operate "websites and Internet forums which foment sectarian hatred," as well as "Sunni Conversion" and "Sectarian Switch" projects.[83] More recently, however, the Bahraini government has sought to stymie the role of religion in politics: in May 2016, for instance, legislation was introduced to ban preachers from joining any political society or engaging in political activities.[84]

The foreign policy implications of Islamism can sometimes create problems for the Bahraini government. Indeed, as part of the so-called "blockade" of Qatar in recent years, regional states have vociferously rebuked Sunni Islamists – something that has perhaps spurred the Bahraini government to encourage the separation of religion and politics. Further, anti-Zionism continues to unite Bahraini Sunnis and Shiites: in the midst of the government's dissolution of al-Wefaq, the Shiite organization's Deputy Secretary General, Sheikh Hussein al-Daihi, condemned the government's permission for an Israeli delegation to attend an international conference of the world soccer association, FIFA, held in Manama in May 2017.[85]

Nevertheless, Bahrain is not usually considered a major source of terrorists or financial/logistical support for overseas *jihad*, likely because Sunni Bahrainis are not especially impoverished, exposed to more radical forms of *Wahhabbi* Islamic fundamentalism, or especially numerous. Still, a very small number of Bahrainis (estimated at 24 as of 2016, the last date for which comprehensive statistics were availabe) have indeed participated in foreign *jihad*.[86]

Inside Bahrain itself, the government has targeted individuals supporting al-Qaeda, ISIS, and other radical Sunni organizations. Concern about both Sunni and Shiite terrorism is often used as an excuse for political repression, particularly of nonviolent Islamist organizations. Indeed, in the months leading up to the country's 2010 elections, Bahrain's government targeted political organizations and news outlets, suppressing demonstrations and civil unrest.[87] The ostensible justification was that Shiite opposition leaders were planning to lead a revolt against the government. In February 2011, Bahrain experienced a new and significant round of demonstrations and rioting by Shiite citizens, triggered by this apparent rollback of democratic reforms, and by regional "Arab Spring" unrest. The mass demonstrations also coincided with the February 14th anniversary of the restoration of constitutional government in 2002 and the 2001 referendum that approved the new constitution.[88]

The government's initial reaction to these demonstrations was a vacillation between brutal suppression and attempts at conciliation. But after seven demonstrators were killed and many more injured, Bahrain's rulers backed down from lethal confrontation; on February 19th it began a concerted effort, led by Crown Prince Salman bin Hamad al-Khalifa, to de-escalate the crisis and promote a solution-oriented "national dialogue."[89] However, the talks ended with no accomplishments; they were clearly not intended to facilitate a genuine resolution of Bahrain's problems and Shiite leaders demanded substantial concessions before talks could begin.[90] Calls for dialogue are still occasionally made but nearly a decade later it still seems impossible for the factious ruling family, the disparate opposition, and loyalist groups to agree on conditions.[91] Clearly, even if negotiations do begin at some point, they will be difficult; after years of protests, repression, killings, torture,[92] mass dismissal of Shiites from their jobs,[93] revocation of citizenship,[94] and demolition of Shiite mosques,[95] there is very little good will or trust between Bahrain's Shiites and their government.[96]

In the meantime, the Bahraini government has a number of factors in its favor as it attempts to maintain the *status quo*:

- It is supported by almost all members of the country's Sunni minority, which holds most economic power and controls Bahrain's security forces.

- It is supported by neighboring Sunni states—particularly Saudi Arabia, which is concerned about unrest or even rebellion by its own large Shiite minority and has a history of intervening to preserve Bahrain's Sunni regime.
- It is backed by the United States. Although the U.S. has in the past been critical of the Bahraini government's more extreme measures to confront unrest and has called for more democratic rule and better protection of human rights, Bahrain's importance as a naval base and the dangers a regime collapse would pose to other Persian Gulf governments give Washington little real maneuvering room.[97] In the words of one anonymous U.S. official, Bahrain is "just too important to fail."[98]

Nonetheless, the Bahraini government has done tremendous damage to its own perceived legitimacy. While it would appear unlikely that the regime faces any real danger of being overthrown in the near future, it is equally true that, unless it can regain the trust of the country's Shiite community, Bahrain's ruling class will have a difficult time maintaining long-term stability. Lastly, as the regional Sunni-Shia conflict has intensified, particularly with rising tensions between Iran and Saudi Arabia in the Gulf, Bahrain's rulers may face greater tensions among Sunni and Shia populations within their borders.

Endnotes

1. "Bahrain," Freedom House, 2017, https://freedomhouse.org/report/freedom-world/2017/bahrain; "Bahrain 2016/2017," Amnesty International, n.d., https://www.amnesty.org/en/countries/middle-east-and-north-africa/bahrain/report-bahrain/.
2. "Bahrain jails 24 for forming ISIS cell," *Daily* Star (Lebanon), June 23, 2016, http://www.dailystar.com.lb/News/Middle-East/2016/Jun-23/358553-bahrain-jails-24-for-forming-isis-cell.ashx.

3. Marc Valeri, "Islamist Political Societies in Bahrain: Collateral Victims of the 2011 Popular Uprising," in Hendrik Kraetzschmar and Paola Rivetti, eds., *Islamists and the Politics of the Arab Uprisings: Governance, Pluralisation and Contention* (Edinburgh: Edinburgh University Press, 2018), 178.
4. "Bahrain is still hounding its Shia," *The Economist,* January 19, 2017, https://www.economist.com/news/middle-east-and-africa/21715023-protesters-are-cowed-repression-carries-bahrain-still-hounding-its.
5. Geneive Abdo, "The Arab Uprisings and the Rebirth of the Shia-Sunni Divide," Brooking Doha Center *Analysis Paper* 29, April 2013, 5, https://www.brookings.edu/wp-content/uploads/2016/06/sunni-shia-abdo.pdf.
6. Mahjoob Zweiri and Mohammed Zahid, "The victory of Al Wefaq: The rise of Shiite politics in Bahrain," Research Institute for European and American Studies (RIEAS) *Research Paper* no. 108, April 2007, http://rieas.gr/images/rieas108.pdf; "Bahrain Split by Electoral Boundaries," *The National*, June 3, 2010, https://www.thenational.ae/uae/bahrain-split-by-electoral-boundaries-1.482037; "Bahrain Opposition Representation: Was it a Silent Majority or is it now a Loud Minority?" n.p., n.d., http://www.scribd.com/doc/49888133/Bahrain-Opposition-Representation.
7. "Bahrain Shiites Eye Easing of Sunni Grip," Agence France Presse, October 23, 2010, http://www.arabtimesonline.com/NewsDetails/tabid/96/smid/414/ArticleID/161106/reftab/73/t/Bahrain-Shiites-eye-easing-of-Sunni-grip/Default.aspx.
8. Joost Hiltermann and Toby Matthiesen,"Bahrain Burning," *New York Review of Books*, August 18, 2011, http://www.tobymatthiesen.com/wp/newspaper_articles/bahrain-burning/.
9. Imran Khan, "Inside Friday prayer in Tehran," *Al Jazeera* (Doha), May 18, 2012, http://blogs.aljazeera.com/blog/middle-east/inside-friday-prayer-tehran.
10. "Bahrain WikiLeaks Cables: Bahrain as 'Iran's Fourteenth Province,'" *Telegraph* (London), February 18, 2011, http://www.telegraph.co.uk/news/wikileaks-files/bahrain-wikileaks-cables/8334785/GENERAL-PETRAEUS-VISIT-TO-BAHRAIN.html.
11. United States of America. Department of State. Overseas Security Advisory Council. *Bahrain 2019 Crime & Safety Report.* February 28, 2019. Accessed July 9, 2020. https://www.osac.gov/Country/Bahrain/Content/Detail/Report/28e1fc1e-9aeb-4d2c-85f5-15f4aeabbc38.

12. Christopher Hope, "WikiLeaks: Bahrain Opposition 'Received Training from Hezbollah,'" *Telegraph* (London), February 18, 2011, http://www.telegraph.co.uk/news/worldnews/wikileaks/8333686/WikiLeaks-Bahrain-opposition-received-training-from-Hizbollah.html; "US Embassy Cables: Bahrainis Trained by Hezbollah, Claims King Hamad," *Guardian* (London), February 15, 2011, http://www.guardian.co.uk/world/us-embassy-cables-documents/165861.
13. Jonathan Spyer, "Gulf Regimes: The Real Game – Saudi Arabia," *Jerusalem Post*, March 11, 2011, http://www.jpost.com/Features/FrontLines/Article.aspx?id=211679. According to Spyer, "Iran... is adept, however, at turning political chaos into gain... If the Gulf regimes fail to effectively navigate the current unrest, Iran is fair set to begin to apply these practices in this area."
14. "US Embassy Cables: Guide to Bahrain's Politics," *Guardian* (London), February 15, 2011, http://www.guardian.co.uk/world/us-embassy-cables-documents/168471; "Bahrain WikiLeaks Cables: Wafa': A New Shia Rejectionist Movement," *Telegraph* (London), February 18, 2011, http://www.telegraph.co.uk/news/wikileaks-files/bahrain-wikileaks-cables/8334607/WAFA-A-NEW-SHIA-REJECTIONIST-MOVEMENT.html.
15. Zweiri and Zahid, "The Victory of Al Wefaq," 9.
16. Valeri, "Islamist Political Societies in Bahrain: Collateral Victims of the 2011 Popular Uprising," 168.
17. Laurence Louer, as quoted in Valeri, "Islamist Political Societies in Bahrain: Collateral Victims of the 2011 Popular Uprising," 168.
18. Al Wefaq National Islamic Society, "Bahrain Split by Electoral Boundaries." Note that in addition to having district lines that separate Sunni and Shia populations in order to create Sunni-majority districts, the population size of the districts drawn varies widely: some Sunni-majority districts have as few as 1,000 voters, while some Shiite-majority districts have as many as 15,000 voters.
19. "MPs Urge Al Wefaq to Rethink Resignation," *Gulf Daily News*, March 9, 2011, http://www.gulf-daily-news.com/NewsDetails.aspx?storyid=301425; Adrian Bloomfield, "Bahrain King under Pressure to Sack Prime Minister Uncle," *Telegraph* (London), February 20, 2011, http://www.telegraph.co.uk/news/worldnews/middleeast/bahrain/8336934/Bahrain-king-under-pressure-to-sack-prime-minister-uncle.html.
20. Sara Sorcher, "What's The State of Play In Bahrain's Protests?" *National Journal*, July 18, 2011, http://www.nationaljournal.com/nationalsecurity/what-s-the-state-of-play-in-bahrain-s-pro-

tests--20110718; Hiltermann and Matthiesen, "Bahrain Burning."

21. Andrew Hammond, "UPDATE 1-Fewer than 1 in 5 vote in Bahrain by-elections," Reuters, September 25, 2011, http://www.reuters.com/article/2011/09/25/bahrain-vote-results-idUSL5E7KP13G20110925; "Bahrain opposition groups announce elections boycott", *BBC*, October 11, 2014, http://www.bbc.com/news/world-middle-east-29583378.
22. Ethan Bronner, "Bahrain Vote Erupts in Violence," *New York Times*, September 24, 2011, http://www.nytimes.com/2011/09/25/world/middleeast/bahrain-protesters-and-police-clash-during-election.html.
23. "Bahrain court orders Shia opposition group to be dissolved," Associated Press, July 17, 2016, https://www.theguardian.com/world/2016/jul/17/bahrain-al-wefaq-shia-opposition-group-sunni; "Bahrain regime to auction Al-Wefaq's seized assets," *Al Masdar News,* October 22, 2016, https://www.almasdarnews.com/article/bahrain-regime-auction-al-wefaqs-seized-assets/.
24. "Bahrain's leading Shia cleric charged with corruption", *Middle East Eye*, July 18, 2016, http://www.middleeasteye.net/news/bahrain-s-leading-shias-religious-leader-charged-corruption-1212082735.
25. "Bahrain strips Sheikh Isa Qassim of nationality," *Al Jazeera* (Doha), June 21, 2016, http://www.aljazeera.com/news/2016/06/bahrain-strips-religious-leader-nationality-160620122338238.html.
26. "Bahrain court orders Shia opposition group to be dissolved."
27. "Bahrain opposition loses appeal against dissolution," *Al Araby*, February 6, 2017, https://www.alaraby.co.uk/english/news/2017/2/6/bahrain-opposition-loses-appeal-against-dissolution.
28. Kate Kizer and Michael Payne, "Bahrain's five-year plan of repression," *Middle East Eye,* February 14, 2016, http://www.middleeasteye.net/columns/bahrain-s-five-year-plan-repression-1903103504.
29. "Bahrain court overturns jail term of opposition chief," *Middle East Eye,* October 17, 2016, http://www.middleeasteye.net/news/bahrain-court-overturns-jail-term-opposition-chief-215996772.
30. "Bahrain charges opposition leader with 'spying,'" *Al Jazeera* (Doha), November 1, 2017, http://www.aljazeera.com/news/2017/11/bahrain-charges-opposition-leader-spying-171101182543073.html.
31. U.S. Department of State, "Closure of Opposition Political Society Al-Wefaq in Bahrain," June 14, 2016, http://www.state.gov/r/pa/prs/ps/2016/06/258464.htm; "Bahrain snubs Western allies' condemnation of opposition ban," *Middle East Eye,* July 19, 2016, http://www.middleeasteye.net/news/bahrain-rejects-us-and-uk-condemnation-op-

position-ban-517968328.

32. "Bahrain's top Shi'ite cleric gets one year suspended jail sentence", Reuters, May 21, 2017, https://www.reuters.com/article/us-bahrain-security-trial/bahrains-top-shiite-cleric-gets-one-year-suspended-jail-sentence-idUSKBN18H07C.
33. Jon Gambrell, "Bahrain Raid on Shiite Cleric's Town: 5 Killed, 286 Arrested," Associated Press, May 23, 2017, https://www.bloomberg.com/news/articles/2017-05-24/bahrain-raid-on-shiite-cleric-s-town-5-killed-286-arrested; Kareem Fahim, "After assurances by Trump, Bahrain mounts deadliest raid in years on opposition," *Washington Post,* May 24, 2017, https://www.washingtonpost.com/world/after-assurances-by-trump-bahrain-mounts-deadliest-raid-in-years-on-pro-opposition-shiite-neighborhood/2017/05/24/6995e954-4067-11e7-9851-b95c40075207_story.html.
34. Sami Aboudi, "Bahrain says five died during raid on Shi'ite Muslim leader's hometown," Reuters, May 25, 2017, http://www.reuters.com/article/us-bahrain-security/bahrain-says-five-died-during-raid-on-shiite-muslim-leaders-hometown-idUSKBN18L0T2.
35. Celine Aswad, "Suspects arrested over Bahrain blast in village of Shi'ite cleric: ministry," Reuters, June 20, 2017, http://www.reuters.com/article/us-bahrain-security/suspects-arrested-over-bahrain-blast-in-village-of-shiite-cleric-ministry-idUSKBN19B0ED.
36. Aziz El Yaakoubi, "Bahrain Bars Members of Opposition Groups from Standing in Elections," Reuters, May 13, 2018, https://www.reuters.com/article/us-bahrain-security/bahrain-bars-members-of-opposition-groups-from-standing-in-elections-idUSKCN1IE0QA.
37. "Bahrain WikiLeaks Cables: Wafa': A New Shia Rejectionist Movement."
38. "Shaikh Isa Al Jowder and the Haq Movement," *Chan'ad* Bahraini blog, May 31, 2006, https://peoplepill.com/people/isa-al-jowder/
39. "Bahrain WikiLeaks Cables: Wafa': A New Shia Rejectionist Movement."
40. "US Embassy Cables: Guide to Bahrain's Politics."
41. "Bahrain – Political Parties," globalsecurity.org, n.d., http://www.globalsecurity.org/military/world/gulf/bahrain-politics-parties.htm.
42. "US Embassy Cables: Guide to Bahrain's Politics."
43. "Bahrain Appeal Court Upholds Activists' Convictions," *BBC*, September 4, 2012, http://www.bbc.co.uk/news/world-middle-east-19474026.
44. Justin Gengler, *Group Conflict and Political Mobilization in Bahrain and the Arab Gulf* (Bloomington: Indiana University Press, 2015),

79.

45. “US Embassy Cables: Guide to Bahrain’s Politics.”
46. “Bahrain WikiLeaks Cables: Wafa’: A New Shia Rejectionist Movement”; “Wafa’ (‘loyalty’),” globalsecurity.org, n.d., http://www.globalsecurity.org/military/world/gulf/bahrain-politics-parties-wafa.htm.
47. Habib Toumi, “Bahrain Busts 10-Member Terror Cell,” *Gulf News*, August 24, 2017, https://gulfnews.com/world/gulf/bahrain/bahrain-busts-10-member-terror-cell-1.2079681.
48. “US Embassy Cables: Guide to Bahrain’s Politics.”
49. Valeri, “Islamist Political Societies in Bahrain: Collateral Victims of the 2011 Popular Uprising,” 168.
50. “US Embassy Cables: Guide to Bahrain’s Politics.”
51. Zoi Constantine, “Opposition Party Votes against Bahrain Election,” *The National* (UAE), August 26, 2010, https://www.thenational.ae/world/mena/opposition-party-votes-against-bahrain-election-1.537990.
52. “The Opposition Parties: The Decision to Dissolve Amal Society is a Deliberate Attack on Political Activity in Bahrain,” *Al Wefaq*, July 12, 2012, http://162.241.167.148/cms/2012/07/12/6664/
53. “US Embassy Cables: Guide to Bahrain’s Politics.”
54. National Bank of Bahrain, “Social Responsibility,” n.d., http://www.nbbonline.com/default.asp?action=category&id=6;
55. Courtney Freer and Giorgio Cafiero, “Is the Bahraini Muslim Brotherhood’s ‘Special Status’ Over?” *The New Arab*, August 7, 2017, https://www.alaraby.co.uk/english/comment/2017/8/7/is-the-bahraini-muslim-brotherhoods-special-status-over.
56. Kenneth Katzman “Bahrain: The Political Structure, Reform and Human Rights,” *Eurasia Review*, February 28, 2011, http://www.eurasiareview.com/28022011-bahrain-the-political-structure-reform-and-human-rights/.
57. Kenneth Katzman “Bahrain: The Political Structure, Reform and Human Rights,” *Eurasia Review*, February 28, 2011, http://www.eurasiareview.com/28022011-bahrain-the-political-structure-reform-and-human-rights/.
58. Kenneth Katzman “Bahrain: The Political Structure, Reform and Human Rights,” *Eurasia Review*, February 28, 2011, http://www.eurasiareview.com/28022011-bahrain-the-political-structure-reform-and-human-rights/; Habib Toumi, “Al Asala, Islamic Menbar Join Forces in Bahrain,” *Gulf News*, October 29, 2010, http://gulfnews.com/news/gulf/bahrain/al-asala-islamic-menbar-join-forces-in-bahrain-1.703600.

59. Habib Toumi, "Bahrain's political societies lose big in polls", *Gulf News,* November 30, 2014, http://gulfnews.com/news/gulf/bahrain/bahrain-s-political-societies-lose-big-in-polls-1.1420042.
60. Mohammed Al-A'Ali, "Islamist MPs Seek Nationwide Clamp on 'Gay Sheesha Havens,'" GDN Online, December 16, 2018, http://www.gdnonline.com/Details/456060/Islamist-MPs-seek-nationwide-clamp-on-gay-sheesha-havensâ%C2%80%C2%99.
61. Zweiri and Zahid, "The Victory of Al Wefaq," 7.
62. Magdalena Karolak, "Bahraini Women in the 21st Century: Disputed Legacy of the Unfinished Revolution", Bridgewater State University, October 2012, https://vc.bridgew.edu/cgi/viewcontent.cgi?article=1002&context=jiws.
63. Zweiri and Zahid, "The Victory of Al Wefaq," 7.
64. Michael Slackman and Nadim Audi, "Protests in Bahrain Become Test of Wills," *New York Times*, February 22, 2011, http://www.nytimes.com/2011/02/23/world/middleeast/23bahrain.html; Nancy Youssef, "Huge Bahraini Counter-Protest Reflects Rising Sectarian Strife," McClatchy, February 21, 2011, https://www.mcclatchydc.com/news/nation-world/world/article24612922.html.
65. "Who is Targeting the Muslim Brotherhood?," Reuters, May 3, 2019, https://www.reuters.com/article/us-usa-trump-muslimbrotherhood-explainer/explainer-who-is-targeting-the-muslim-brotherhood-idUSKCN1S90YX.
66. Alex MacDonald, "Sunni Islamists could face uphill struggle in Bahrain elections," *Middle East Eye,* February 13, 2015, http://www.middleeasteye.net/in-depth/features/sunni-islamists-could-face-uphill-struggle-bahrain-elections-1404489268; "Bahrain FM: Muslim Brotherhood is a terrorist group", *Al Jazeera* (Doha), July 6, 2017, http://www.aljazeera.com/news/2017/07/bahrain-fm-muslim-brotherhood-terrorist-group-170706140931861.html.
67. Husain Marhoon, "Bahraini Salafists in Spotlight," *Al-Monitor,* June 18, 2013, http://www.al-monitor.com/pulse/originals/2013/06/bahrain-jihadists-syria-salafism.html.
68. Bill Law, "Bahrain: The Islamic State threat within," *Middle East Eye,* October 14, 2014, http://www.middleeasteye.net/columns/bahrain-islamic-state-threat-within-884335108.
69. Sayed Ahmed Alwadaei, "The Islamic State's Bahraini Backers," *New York Times,* November 25, 2015, http://www.nytimes.com/2015/11/26/opinion/the-islamic-states-bahraini-backers.html.
70. Giorgio Cafiero and Daniel Wagner, "Bahrain's Daesh Dilemma," *The World Post*, January 15 / March 17 2015, http://www.huffington-

post.com/giorgio-cafiero/bahrains-daesh-dilemma_b_6462998.html.

71. Aniqa Haider, "Society Sends Five Ambulances," *Gulf Daily News*, January 15, 2009, http://www.gulf-daily-news.com/Print.aspx?storyid=240214.
72. Habib Toumi, "Bahraini Islamist Societies Press for Closure of Bars, Discos," *Gulf News*, April 22, 2009, https://archive.globalgayz.com/middle-east/bahrain/ay-bahrain-news-and-reports/#article13.
73. "Liquor ban in Bahrain rumours go viral", *DT News / News of Bahrain*, November 14, 2017, http://www.newsofbahrain.com/viewNews.php?ppId=39521&TYPE=Posts&pid=21&MNU=2&SUB=2.
74. Habib Toumi, "Bahraini Islamist Societies Press for Closure of Bars, Discos"; Alexandra Sandels, "BAHRAIN: Islamists Seeking to Curb Prostitution Fail in Bid to Ban Women From 4 Countries," *Los Angeles Times Babylon & Beyond* blog, December 15, 2009, http://latimesblogs.latimes.com/babylonbeyond/2009/12/bahrain-conservatives-seeking-to-curb-prostitution-fail-in-bid-to-ban-visas-for-women-from-russia-thailand-ethiopia-and-china.html.
75. "Bahrain Police Deploy Teargas at anti-Kim Kardashian Protest," *USA Today*, December 1, 2012, http://www.usatoday.com/story/life/people/2012/12/01/bahrain-kardashian-protest/1739609/; Robert Mackey, "Bahrain's Embrace of Kim Kardashian," *New York Times*, December 3, 2012, http://thelede.blogs.nytimes.com/2012/12/03/bahrains-embrace-of-kim-kardashian/.
76. "Bahrain Protesters March on Palace as Gates Visits," Associated Press, March 12, 2011, http://www.washingtonpost.com/wp-dyn/content/article/2011/03/12/AR2011031201563.html.
77. Youssef, "Huge Bahraini Counter-Protest Reflects Rising Sectarian Strife."
78. "Bahrain's Sunni party rejects dialogue, calls for end to street violence," *Global Times* (China), December 27, 2012, http://www.globaltimes.cn/content/752643.shtml; Justin Gengler, "Look Who's Boycotting Dialogue Now," *Religion and Politics in Bah*rain, March 25, 2012, http://bahrainipolitics.blogspot.co.il/2012/03/look-whos-boycotting-dialogue-now.html.
79. "Bahrain is still hounding its Shia," *The Economist,* January 19, 2017, https://www.economist.com/news/middle-east-and-africa/21715023-protesters-are-cowed-repression-carries-bahrain-still-hounding-its.
80. "Bahrain Opposition Representation."
81. "Factsheet: Bahrain Protests Feb. 2011," Canadians for Justice and Peace in the Middle East *CJPME Factsheet Series* no. 114, February

22, 2011, http://www.cjpme.org/fs_114.
82. Bloomfield, "Bahrain King under Pressure to Sack Prime Minister Uncle."
83. "'Al Bander Report': Demographic Engineering in Bahrain and Mechanisms of Exclusion," Bahrain Center for Human Rights, September 30, 2006, http://www.bahrainrights.org/node/528.
84. Habib Toumi, "Bahrain MPs Ban Mixing of Politics and Religion," *Gulf News*, May 18, 2016, https://gulfnews.com/world/gulf/bahrain/bahrain-mps-ban-mixing-of-politics-and-religion-1.1830097.
85. "Al-Wefaq: Bahrain will always support Palestine", *Press TV,* October 19, 2016, http://presstv.ir/Detail/2016/10/19/489831/wefaq-bahrain-fifa-israeli.
86. Sandeep Singh Grewal, "UAE Releases Suspected Al Qaeda Militant of Bahraini Origin," *NewsBlaze*, June 12, 2009, https://newsblaze.com/world/middle-east/uae-releases-suspected-al-qaeda-militant-of-bahraini-origin_9582/.
87. "The Guantanamo Docket: Sheikh Salman Ebrahim Mohamed Ali al Khalifa," *New York Times*, n.d., http://projects.nytimes.com/guantanamo/detainees/246-sheikh-salman-ebrahim-mohamed-ali-al-khalifa/documents/2/pages/1781.
88. Canadians for Justice and Peace in the Middle East, "Factsheet: Bahrain Protests Feb. 2011"; Simeon Kerr, Robin Wigglesworth and Abigail Fielding-Smith, "Arab Regimes Brace for 'Days of Rage,'" *Financial Times*, February 3, 2011, https://ftalphaville.ft.com/2011/02/03/477981/arab-regimes-brace-for-fresh-protests/.
89. "Bahrain King Orders Release of Political Prisoners," Associated P*ress*, February 22, 2011, http://www.independent.co.uk/news/world/middle-east/bahrain-king-orders-release-of-political-prisoners-2222371.html.
90. See Note 22.
91. Shahira Salloum, "Bahrain: A Return to Dialogue?" *Al-Akhbar*, December 14, 2012, https://www.jadaliyya.com/Details/27650; Bill Law, "Bahrain Minister Plays Down Dialogue Calls," *BBC*, December 17, 2012, http://www.bbc.co.uk/news/world-middle-east-20757862.
92. Kristen Chick, "Bahrain Rights Activist's Wife Details Torture, Unfair Trial," *Christian Science Monitor*, May 16, 2011, http://www.csmonitor.com/World/Middle-East/2011/0516/Bahrain-rights-activist-s-wife-details-torture-unfair-trial.
93. Kristen Chick, "Amid Unrest, Bahrain Companies Fire Hundreds of Shiites," *Christian Science Monitor*, April 7, 2011, http://www.

csmonitor.com/World/Middle-East/2011/0407/Amid-unrest-Bahrain-companies-fire-hundreds-of-Shiites.

94. Human Rights Watch, "Bahrain – Events of 2015", n.d., https://www.hrw.org/world-report/2016/country-chapters/bahrain. See also Amnesty International, "Bahrain 2015/2016," n.d., https://www.amnesty.org/en/countries/middle-east-and-north-africa/bahrain/report-bahrain/.
95. "Mosques Under Construction Re-Demolished by Authorities in Bahrain," Bahrain Center for Human Rights, December 9, 2012, http://www.bahrainrights.org/en/node/5550.
96. Roy Gutman, "U.S. Warns Bahrain's Society 'Could Break Apart,'" McClatchy, November 20, 2012, https://truthout.org/articles/us-warns-bahrains-society-could-break-apart/.
97. Thomas Fuller, "Bahrainis Fear the U.S. Isn't Behind Their Fight for Democracy," *New York Times*, March 5, 2011, http://www.nytimes.com/2011/03/05/world/middleeast/05bahrain.html.
98. Adam Entous and Julian E. Barnes, "U.S. Wavers on 'Regime Change,'" *Wall Street Journal*, March 5, 2011, http://online.wsj.com/article/SB10001424052748703580004576180522653787198.html?mod=WSJEUROPE_hpp_MIDDLETopNews.

11 Egypt

Quick Facts

Population: 104,124,440 (July 2020 est.)
Area: 1,001,450 sq km
Ethnic Groups: 99.7%, other 0.3% (2006 est.)
GDP (official exchange rate): $236.5 billion (2017 est.)

Source: CIA World FactBook (Last Updated June 2020)

Introduction

Egypt has played a central role in the history of Islamism. In 1928, an Egyptian teacher named Hassan al-Banna (1906-1949) founded the Muslim Brotherhood, the world's first modern Islamist social and political movement, and the most prominent Islamist force in Egypt. The Brotherhood soon created an ideological framework that would become the main political opposition to future Egyptian governments. From the time of President Gamal Abdel Nasser and through the era of his successor, Hosni Mubarak, the Brotherhood was outlawed but tolerated to varying extents.

Mubarak's ouster in 2011 marked a turning point for Islamists in the country, with several Islamic groups establishing legal political parties to participate in post-uprising politics. In the parliamentary elections held between November 2011 and January 2012, Islamists and Salafis won nearly three-quarters of all seats in the new Egyptian parliament. Mohammed Morsi (1951-2019), a Muslim Brotherhood leader, was elected Egypt's president on June 30, 2012 in the country's first democratic presidential election. However, in the wake of mass protests against Morsi's increasingly authoritarian and incompetent government in the summer of 2013, the Egyptian military ousted Morsi and replaced him with an interim government tasked with drafting and passing a new constitution. That government severely repressed the group and imprisoned tens of thousands of its leaders and members – a trend that has continued under the tenure of its current President, General Abdel Fatah el-Sisi, who has held power since 2013. But the Sisi government has been forced to deal not only with the perceived internal threat posed by the Brotherhood; since Morsi's overthrow, Egypt has had to contend with a significant upsurge in jihadist violence in the Sinai Peninsula, which has impacted the country's internal security situation as well as its relations with neighboring Israel.[1]

Islamist Activity

The Muslim Brotherhood (Al-Ikhwan al-Muslimun, or MB)
The Muslim Brotherhood, founded in 1928 by Hassan al-Banna, is now the most prominent Egyptian Islamist movement. Its ideology states that a true "Islamic society" is one in which state institutions and the government follow the principles of the Quran, and in which laws follow *sharia* (Islamic law).[2] Al-Banna, a teacher from a modest background, was heavily influenced by Syrian-Egyptian thinker Mohammed Rashid Rida, who believed that a return to 7th and 8th century Islamic practices was the only way for Muslim societies to regain strength and to escape Western colonialism and cultural hegemony.[3] Al-Banna viewed Islam as an "all-embracing concept," meant to govern every aspect of life, and he constructed the MB to advance this totalitarian interpretation within Egypt from the grassroots up. Specifically, he sought to "reform" the individual through the Brotherhood's multi-year indoctrination process, those individuals would then form families, and the families would then spread the message within Egyptian society. Once Egyptian society was "Islamized," an Islamic state would emerge, and, once this happened throughout the Muslim world, the states would unify under a new *caliphate*.

Muslim Brotherhood cells spread rapidly throughout Egypt in the late 1920s and the 1930s. Amid episodic government crackdowns, the Brotherhood formed a violent "secret apparatus," which was implicated in multiple assassinations and terrorist attacks. Al-Banna was assassinated in February 1949, and, while the Brotherhood initially cooperated with Egypt's military following the July 1952 Free Officers' revolution, the government cracked down on the group following an attempt on President Gamal Abdel Nasser's life. During this period, the Brotherhood's chief ideologue, Sayyid Qutb, authored the famous Islamist manifesto *Ma'alim fi-l-Tariq* (*Milestones Along The Way*) while in prison in 1964. In *Milestones*, Qutb claims that all non-Muslim societies, and indeed those societies that are only Muslim in name but not in practice, are in a state of *jahiliyya* (ignorance). *Jahili* societies are those that do not strictly follow revelation, and Qutb called on Muslims to wage offensive *jihad* against *jahiliyya* until a global, united Islamic community was established. This was interpreted as a call to arms against the Egyptian state, and Qutb was executed in 1966.[4]

Following Nasser's death in 1970, his successor, Anwar al-Sadat, lifted restrictions on Islamist activism, viewing Islamists as a useful counter to the leftists and the Nasserist old guard who challenged his authority. During this period, a wide variety of Islamist groups emerged on Egyptian campuses. As the Egyptian government liberated Brotherhood leaders throughout the 1970s, the organization integrated many of these young Islamists as it rebuilt itself.

The Brotherhood has adopted political tactics that favor activism and elections rather than revolution and/or violence. This process began following the execution of Sayyid Qutb in 1966. Members of the movement began questioning the relevance of *jihad* as a way to combat the government, and many chose to reject violence. During the late 1970s and early 1980s, the Brotherhood increasingly disavowed *jihad* in favor of political participation on campuses, in labor unions, and in the general elections. The process began with the release of a text entitled *Preachers, Not Judges* in 1969, which was likely written by multiple individuals but has been attributed to supreme guide Hassan al-Hudaybi. In this tract, al-Hudaybi developed a series of theological counterarguments to Qutb's radical views.[5] Under the leadership of al-Hudaybi and his successor, Umar al-Tilmisani, the Brotherhood officially and unequivocally distanced itself from armed action, gave an oath to Sadat not to use violence against his regime, and even named the President a "martyr" after he was killed in 1981. Under Mubarak, the Brotherhood participated in most parliamentary elections, either in partnership with legal parties, including non-Islamist ones, or as independent candidates. However, it remained a barely tolerated illegal organization, and the government could use its illegality as a pretext for cracking down on the the Brotherhood whenever it appeared to be gaining strength – such as during the run-up to the 1995 elections, and following its success in the 2005 elections (when it won 88 of 444 contested seats).

Notably, the group's renunciation of violence was limited to the domestic sphere. The Brotherhood otherwise continued to praise terrorist acts conducted by Hamas, its Palestinian off-shoot, as well as by the Iranian-backed Shi'a militia Hezbollah.

In late April of 2011, the Brotherhood announced the creation of its "Freedom and Justice Party" (FJP). The FJP's policies would be grounded in Islamic principles but would be non-confessional and tolerant, including to both women and Christians in its ranks. In June 2011, the FJP received official recognition as a political party, enabling it to run candidates in the 2011-2012 parliamentary elections. This pragmatic positioning within the Egyptian political system, however, drew condemnation from other Islamist groups, most notably the al-Qaeda-affiliated Islamic Jihad and its commander Ayman al-Zawahiri, who criticized the Brotherhood's reorientation in a book entitled *The Bitter Harvest: The Muslim Brotherhood in Sixty Years* (*Al-Hisad al-Murr: Al-Ikhwan al-Muslimun fi Sittin 'Aman*).[6] Zawahiri wrote:

> The Muslim Brotherhood, by recognizing the tyrants' legitimacy and sharing constitutional legitimacy with them, has become a tool in the tyrants' hands to strike *jihadist* groups in the name of [fighting] extremism and disobeying *sharia* [Islamic law]. There should be no doubt that we are proud to be outside of this "legitimacy of disbelief," which the Muslim Brotherhood has accepted and approved.[7]

In the wake of the coup, the organization gathered is members and allies in northern Cairo's Rabaa al-Adawiya Square and Giza's al-Nahda Square. Protesters denounced the interim government installed to replace Morsi as illegitimate. After negotiations between it and the new government broke down, security forces violently cleared these protests on August 14, 2013 and killed at least 800 civilians.[8] The new government arrested tens of thousands of Brotherhood leaders and supporters and, following a terrorist incident in December 2013, the government labeled the organization a terrorist group.[9] Ultimately, the government's crackdown on the group appears to have been decapitated, rendering it incapable of executing a nationwide strategy in Egypt.[10]

Meanwhile, the Muslim Brotherhood faces a significant internal crisis pitting younger members, who want to fight the current government with violence, against older leaders who fear that violence will legitimize the regime's crackdown. The organization's youth wing seemingly won internal elections that in 2014, which explains a January 2015 statement from the Brotherhood calling for *jihad* and martyrdom in fighting the regime. For a time, the group's "revolutionary" wing was led by a senior leader, Mohamed Kamal, who endorsed and encouraged violence against Egyptian security forces and state infrastructure. Kamal commissioned a *sharia* body within the organization to draft an Islamic legal defense of his faction's violence, deemed acts of "self-defense," entitled *The Jurisprudence of Popular Resistance to the Coup*.[11] This pitted him and his faction against the group's "old guard," nominally headed by deputy supreme guide Mahmoud Ezzat.[12] The rift deepened after several "old guard" leaders who had remained in hiding in Egypt in mid-2015 were arrested, as the "old guard" blamed the "revolutionary" wing's violence for endangering senior leaders. For a brief period, however, the "revolutionary" wing appeared to have the upper hand, and took control of the organization's main web portal. However, when Kamal was killed during a raid in October 2016, the "old guard" retook control. This did little to dampen the rift, however, and in early 2017, the "revolutionary" wing launched a series of online pamphlets criticizing the "old guard" leaders' conduct since the 2011 uprising and calling for new group power structures.[13]

When Morsi died while imprisoned in June 2019, the Brotherhood called for funerals paying tribute to the former president. However, people in Egypt didn't pay vigil, whether due to fear of a crackdown on protest, low media coverage of the event, a decline in the Brotherhood's popularity and of Morsi himself since his term, or the state's successes in its efforts to delegitimize the group.[14]

Today, due to these internal disagreements as well as effective government pressure, the group no longer represents a significant threat to the current regime. The Egyptian government, in turn, has sought to press its advantage by shutting down the Brotherhood's social and educational services, freezing much of its finances and instituting strict restrictions on mosque preaching.

The Islamic Group (Al-Gama'a al-Islamiyya)

For years, the Islamic Group recruited on university campuses, in Egyptian prisons, and in the country's poor urban and rural areas. It was involved in a series of attacks during the 1980s and 1990s that were aimed at deposing Egypt's government and replacing it with an Islamic theocracy. These attacks included the 1997 killing of Western tourists in Luxor, the attempted assassination of President Hosni Mubarak in Ethiopia in 1995, the Cairo bombings of 1993, and several other armed operations against Egyptian intellectuals and Coptic Christians. The movement's spiritual leader, Umar Abd al-Rahman, was connected to Ramzi Yusuf, the perpetrator of the first World Trade Center bombing in 1993.[15] Rahman and nine followers were subsequently arrested and convicted of plotting to blow up the United Nations headquarters in New York, the New York Federal Reserve Building, the George Washington Bridge, and the Holland and Lincoln Tunnels.

In July 1997, during a military tribunal, one of the group's activists, Muhammad al-Amin Abd al-Alim, read a statement signed by six other Islamist leaders that called on their affiliates to cease all armed operations in Egypt and abroad.[16] While it elicited considerable controversy within the movement, the statement heralded the beginning of the group's renunciation of violence. In March 1999, the group's leadership launched an "Initiative for Ceasing Violence" and declared a unilateral ceasefire. Ideologues and leaders were mostly successful in convincing their base to renounce armed struggle and support a non-violent approach by authoring a series of texts to provide the ideological justification for their rejection of violence. Later that year, the Islamic Group declared a unilateral ceasefire in its longstanding struggle against the Egyptian government. This declaration marked a major ideological shift and, eventually, a complete end to violent behavior in 2002. Islamic Group leaders published four books in January 2002 under the title of *Correcting Conceptions* (*Silsilat Tashih al-Mafahim*), addressing the reasons behind its ideological reorientation and explaining why *jihad* in Egypt had failed. Twelve other books followed, developing a critique of al-Qaeda's extreme ideology.[17] Islamic Group members have not claimed responsibility for any armed attack since.[18]

Another notable example of this dynamic was the interaction between the Islamic Group and the smaller, more radical Islamic Jihad that began in the 1990s and culminated in 2007, when the latter embraced non-violence to some degree. These efforts were led by the movement's former leader, Sayyid Imam al-Sharif—also known as Abd al-Qadir Ibn Abd al-Aziz, or "Dr. Fadl." His *Document for the Right Guidance of* Jihad *in Egypt and the World* (*Tarshid al-'Amal al-Jihadi fi Misrwa-l-'Alam*) had an enormous impact within the country's prisons and led numerous inmates to reject violent *jihad*.[19]

These moves to diminish radicalism within the party drove a faction of the Islamic Group's more violent adherents to join al-Qaeda in 2006.[20] In the 2011-2012 parliamentary elections, the Islamic Group ran under the banner of *Hizb al-Bina'wa-l-Tanmiya* (the Building and Development Party) and won thirteen seats in the lower house.[21] Members of the Islamic Group have protested the Egyptian military's decision to depose Morsi and dissolve his government, but in February 2014 the organization announced it was ready to engage with the interim government to end Egypt's political impasse.[22]

Islamic Jihad (Al-Jihad)

Active since the 1970s, *Al-Jihad* was officially formed in 1980 from the merger of two Islamist cells led by Karam Zuhdi and Muhammad Abd al-Salam Faraj, respectively. Faraj's famous manifesto, *Al-Farida al-Ghayiba* (The Absent Duty), outlined the new movement's ideology.[23] Like those affiliated with the Islamic Group, members of Al-Jihad represent a relative minority within Egypt's Islamist spectrum and are mostly former members of the MB, some of whom allegedly fought alongside the Afghan *mujahideen* in the 1980s. The organization's stated objective was to overthrow the Egyptian "infidel" regime and establish an Islamic government in its place. The Islamic Jihad also sought to attack U.S. and Israeli interests in Egypt and abroad. The group is infamous for assassinating President Anwar Sadat in 1981 and for additional attacks on Egyptian government officials in the early 1990s. It also allegedly attacked Egypt's embassy in Pakistan in 1995 and was involved in planning bombings against U.S. embassies in Kenya and Tanzania in 1998. In June 2001, the group merged with al-Qaeda to form a new entity, called Gama'a Qa'idat al-Jihad, headed by Osama bin Laden's second-in-command, Ayman al-Zawahiri.[24]

Salafists

Salafists have had a presence in Egypt since the early 20th century. The first Salafist association, the "*Sharia* Assembly," was created in 1912 (before the formation of the Muslim Brotherhood). Another group, named the "Supporters of the Sunna" (Ansar al-Sunna), was founded by Sheikh Mohammed Hamid al-Fiqi in 1926. Its members focused on protecting monotheism and fighting practices and beliefs they considered against Islam.

Salafism became more visible in Egypt during the 1970s and 1980s, for two reasons. First, as previously mentioned, President Sadat permitted Islamists greater freedom during this period to counter leftists and Nasserists domestically. Second, Egyptians working abroad in Saudi Arabia and other Persian Gulf states returned home carrying with them Salafi-influenced ideas, allowing these religious tenets to spread. Further, both the Saudi religious establishment and private donors propagated Salafi ideology in Egypt by way of financial investment.

Although few Egyptians openly identified as Salafists under the Mubarak regime, there were signs that their puritanical interpretation of Islam was nonetheless gaining ground. This was, for instance, evidenced by the growing number of women wearing the *niqab* (full veil) and men growing their beards. Beyond the traditional role of radical *imams* in mosques, satellite television channels also adopted explicitly Salafist rhetoric, widening their audience in the process.[25]

Radical Islamists have, for years, openly targeted religious minorities in an attempt to provoke sectarian warfare in Egypt. Coptic Christians, a community that represents an estimated 10 percent of the population, has been a special target of Salafist bigotry. Militant Salafists commonly portray Christians as "infidels" who conspire against Islam, and have regularly called for violent attacks on them.[26] The rise of Islamists following Mubarak's ouster brought these attitudes to the fore, as radical preachers called minorities "heretics" and threatened to expel them if they did not pay the *jizya,* a tax levied on non-Muslims, in certain instances.[27]

Since the 2011 uprising, Salafists have engaged in a massive anti-Coptic hate campaign. As a result, many Egyptian Christians fled the country, fearing for their future under Islamist rule.[28] In 2012, several Salafists accused Copts of being "traitors" for voting against Islamists in the presidential polls.[29] Following Morsi's ouster, dozens of churches were torched nationwide. Unfortunately, these types of attacks have continued under the rule of President Abdel Fattah el-Sisi, despite the president's close relationship with the Coptic Orthodox Church.

Salafists have also targeted other sects of Islam, such as the Shi'a, Baha'i, and Sufis, viewing them as inauthentic.[30] Before 2011, Salafists banned the *dhikr* (a devotional act of Sufi orders) and continued to call for the prohibition of all Sufi ceremonies. Salafists further accuse Sufi community members of encouraging sin and debauchery by mixing the sexes at shrines and during their rituals. They have, for example, regularly pointed to the mosque of Ahmad al-Badawi in Tanta – where the founder of the Sufi Ahmadiyya order is buried – which does not enforce segregation between men and women except during prayers. Salafists also view ancient Egyptian monuments as idolatrous; following Mubarak's overthrow, various Salafist groups threatened to cover the pyramids in wax.[31]

Salafists have increasingly targeted Egyptian women. Because Egyptian law requires that at least one candidate from each party be a woman, the Salafist Al-Nour party (see below) has run female candidates; however, it replaced their pictures with either a rose or a logo. On multiple occasions, Salafist leaders who have appeared on political talk shows insisted that female hosts either wear a veil or that they be separated from them by a screen.[32]

The Salafist Call is the preeminent Salafi organization in Egypt, and in the past has focused primarily on preaching and social service. However, the group has recently shifted to focus on politics, establishing Hizb al-Nour (Light Party), led by Imad Abd al-Ghaffour.

Insurgencies and Jihadist Groups

Several little-known violent groups, like the *jihadist* "Abdallah Azzam Brigades in Egypt" or the "Holy Warriors of Egypt,"[33] emerged in the 2000s, spreading radical and extremist ideologies, conducting anti-regime activity, and accusing society and state institutions of "apostasy."[34] Another group calling itself *Tawhid wa-l-Jihad* (Monotheism and Holy War), which was connected to al-Qaeda, emerged during this period in the Sinai. It targeted the country's tourism sector in a wave of bombings that first hit the town of Taba in 2004 and then the resort towns of Sharm al-Sheikh and Dahab in 2005 and 2006.

When Mubarak was ousted following Egypt's 2011 "Arab Spring" uprising, Islamic extremist activities assumed a new intensity. On multiple occasions, armed fighters attacked Egyptian security forces, police stations, and the al Arish-Ashkelon pipeline exporting natural gas to Israel and Jordan. Other operations targeted Israeli patrols and soldiers.[35] New *jihadist* groups emerged, such as Ansar al-Jihad (Supporters of Holy War).[36] The most prominent of these was Ansar Beit al-Maqdis (Supporters of Jerusalem, or ABM), which swore allegiance to the Islamic State in November 2014 and renamed itself Wilayat Sinai (Sinai Province).[37] Since then, the Egyptian military has engaged in a broad, multi-year offensive campaign against these groups.[38] Egyptian authorities have recently declared victory in this campaign,[39] but the government's tight control over news regarding its operations in the Sinai make it difficult to assess the military's performance.

As mentioned, ABM is the most significant *jihadist* group in Egypt. ABM started its violent operations immediately following Mubarak's ouster in 2011, targeting Israel and Israeli interests in Egypt, such as the al Arish-Ashkelon natural gas pipeline, which has been bombed repeatedly since 2011. Since the 2013 coup, however, the Egyptian military has been the organization's primary target and, as previously mentioned, the Egyptian military has been actively fighting ABM since September 2013.[40] Another *jihadist* group is Ajnad Misr ("Soldiers of Egypt"), which emerged in late January 2014, saying that it was targeting "criminal" elements of the regime. As of early February 2014, the group has claimed responsibility for seven attacks in Cairo.[41] Ansar Bayt al-Maqdis has referred to Ajnad Misr as "brothers" and suggested[42] that the two organizations have cooperated on attacks in the past, although neither the extent nor the nature of the collaboration is currently known.

Some young people affiliated with the Muslim Brotherhood have formed a variety of low-level insurgency groups, such as the Molotov Movement, Revolutionary Punishment, Liwaa al-Thawra, and Hasm. These groups focus their attacks on state infrastructure and security forces. At the same time, Sinai-based *jihadists* used the 2013 coup as a pretext for escalating their attacks on security forces. These groups also benefitted from regional instability: state breakdown in Libya, for instance, has made additional weapons available. These groups have also aligned to varying extents with groups in Gaza, such as Hamas, in trying to destabilize the Egyptian government.

The Sinai Peninsula has been a hotbed for Islamic extremism for years. During the 2000s, a mix of state neglect and insufficient local security enabled groups active in the territory to develop smuggling networks, plan attacks, and develop local support there. A number of militant groups have even expressed the goal of creating an independent Islamic Emirate on the Peninsula. It also provides hideouts for *jihadist* networks and has become increasingly unstable since the July 3, 2013 military coup that ousted President Morsi from power.[43]

Islamic State (IS)

As mentioned, in November 2014, ABM pledged allegiance to the Islamic State and its former leader Abu Bakr al-Baghdadi and rebranded into Wilayat Sinai (WS). Following the November 2019 death of al-Baghdadi, WS was the first province to swear allegiance to Abu Ibrahim al-Hashemi al-Quraishi, the new leader of IS.[44] This close connection between WS and IS explains how the Islamic State expanded its Jihadist threat to Sinai and Egypt. WS sought full ideological identification with the Islamic State and began to shift from a mainly local dimension (Sinai and Egypt) to a more global/transnational *jihadist* one. At the same time, WS adopted strict new measures towards local populations and created new mechanisms to control the territory, such as a morality police that monitors communities and punishes those it considers to be informants. This strict oversight antagonizes some Sinai tribes, in particular the Sawarka and Tarabin, and has encouraged them to cooperate with the regime in response. However, ABM's affiliation with the Islamic State has split the organization into two wings, with the Nile Valley leaders remaining loyal to al-Qaeda. While WS operations are limited almost entirely to the Sinai, al-Qaeda has remained inside Egypt, operating mainly in the territory between the Libyan border crossing and Egypt's Western Desert.[45]

The increasing number of attacks in the Sinai has forced the Egyptian regime to embark upon a series of military operations against WS. Nevertheless, attacks have continued unabated in the peninsula, taking a steep human toll. Most attacks have been perpetrated in northern Sinai, including the infamous November 2017 attack on the al-Rawda mosque in Bir al-'Abd, in which over 300 people were killed in what was called "the worst bloodshed of its kind in Egypt's modern history."[46]

El-Sisi's strategy in the Sinai has undergone changes over the past years. In February 2018, the Egyptian government launched "Operation Sinai 2018," a mission intended to kill Islamic State fighters and reinforce army units already there.[47] Despite this escalation of Egypt's military operations in Sinai, two years later WS still enjoys high tactical and operational capacity and continues to pose a serious daily threat in the Sinai peninsula. While the Egyptian campaign against terrorism in the Sinai succeeded in eliminating many terrorists and senior leaders and reducing the overall number of attacks, deadly attacks in the Northern Sinai are still reported weekly. With the collapse of ISIS in Syria and Iraq, the Sinai has become a frontline in the global war against *jihadist* extremism and a possible new hub for foreign fighters. The Sinai offers IS a position of strategic significance. The group is also relatively sheltered there, forced to contend at present mainly with the Egyptian state, rather than external intervention or coalition airstrikes. WS operations conducted from the Sinai, in turn, illustrate the ongoing strength of the group and the relative ineffectiveness of the Egyptian regime's counter-terrorism efforts.[48]

El-Sisi's government, however, appears to be formulating a new regional counterterror strategy. LE175 ($10 million) has been allocated toward development projects in the Sinai, including in "the electricity sector, roads, improving the environment, strengthening local units, and strengthening security, traffic, and fire department services."[49] In June 2019, the President opened the tunnels under the Suez canal as part of the state's efforts to develop the Sinai and enhance regional investment opportunities.[50] The Egyptian Planning Ministry announced in August 2019 it would invest 5.23 billion Egyptian pounds ($315 million) in the Sinai Peninsula in fiscal year 2019-2020.[51] The el-Sisi government hopes that the regional buildup of infrastructure and local rule of law will strengthen the regime's grip on the notoriously challenging region and further consolidate el-Sisi's power.

Since the ABM's declaration of allegiance to the Islamic State in November 2014 and its subsequent transformation into Wilayat Sinai, there is also an intensifying ideological battle between the Egyptian regime and its Islamist rivals. The Grand Mufti of Egypt, Shawqi Allam, ruled that the *caliphate* was not a holy institution derived from religious texts, and that the Prophet Muhammad had not commanded it at all. According to his narrative, Islam is not a static religion that demands the restoration of a fixed form of government and a return to the Middle Ages; rather, flexibility is the soul of Islam, and there is no religious objection to the definition of Egypt as a modern nation state.[52] Simultaneously, since 2014, the el-Sisi regime has embarked on an ongoing campaign regarding the Egyptian identity and focusing on the contrast between Egyptian citizens who are loyal to their homeland and Islamists who seek to undermine the legitimacy of the nation state. As his government became more established, el-Sisi began formulating a positive identity discourse to serve as an alternative to competing Islamist debates. The identity that the regime ascribes to its citizens is composed of a mosaic of historic (Pharaonic, Coptic, Islamic, and

Greco-Roman) and geographic (Arab, Mediterranean, and African) layers, which together comprise the Egyptian personality. The Islamic layer is conceptualized by emphasizing the continuity of the nonviolent meetings between religions in Egypt that has taken place since the initial days of Islam and extending to the coexistence that prevails between them today. Similar continuity was attributed to the historic educational standing of the al-Azhar institution, due to its role in resuming religious discourse and in preaching moderate interpretations that are helpful to the global ideological battle against terrorism and Islamic radicalism.[53]

Islamism and Society

Since the 1950s, failures in governance, economic stagnation, and political exclusion have provided opportunities for reactionary Islamists to expand their influence in Egyptian society. Islamists have used their politicized interpretation of Islam as a source of legitimacy, and they have set up a number of informal institutions (charities, educational organizations, health services) to advance their ideology within various sectors.[54] While some extremist groups, including some in the official leadership of the Muslim Brotherhood, began to renounce violence in the 1970s, this rejection almost always catalyzed the emergence of violent groups that rejected the renunciations. As a result, radical discourse perpetuated within Islamist circles even when groups were technically non-violent. For example, a strong Qutbist faction formed and persisted within the Brotherhood, including among people who were jailed with him. The Brotherhood thus continued to read and teach Sayyid Qutb's works, even while claiming to have disavowed them. As a result, prominent contemporary leaders have been influenced by parts of the Qutbist ideology.[55]

Meanwhile, political stagnation and poor economic conditions under Mubarak generated sympathy for the Brotherhood and Salafist groups, which offered social services and religious education.[56] Salafists inherit their name from the Arabic term "*al-salaf al-salih,*" meaning the "righteous ancestors," a phrase referring to the first generations of Muslims after the Prophet Mohammed's death who sought to emulate his practices and maintained a literalist reading of the Qur'an and the *hadith* (the sayings of the Prophet). Salafists regard deviations from this literalist approach as *bid'a* (innovation), and therefore tantamount to *kufr* (apostasy). Under Mubarak, Salafists were strictly prohibited from political activities – in stark contrast to the Muslim Brotherhood, which was at times tolerated. Salafis, therefore, focused almost exclusively on social work and spiritual development and were permitted to launch television networks dedicated to preaching.

Islamism and the State

From the 1970s until the overthrow of Mubarak, the Egyptian state tolerated other Islamist groups at certain points while repressing or fighting them at others. The Muslim Brotherhood in particular used moments of tolerance to build its nationwide organization and win parliamentary seats while advocating for every day social causes. Similarly, it garnered public sympathy when the regime cracked down on it.

In 2005, the Brotherhood fielded approximately 150 candidates in the country's parliamentary elections and won 88 of 444 contested seats, making it the largest opposition bloc. The regime viewed these gains as threatening, and it responded with a series of constitutional amendments that limited the political participation of religious groups in 2007. The following year, more than 800 Brotherhood members were barred from standing as candidates for local council elections as a result of these restrictions. Subsequently, during the November 2010 parliamentary elections, the repression worsened: hundreds of Brotherhood members were arrested, and none of the organization's parliamentary candidates were elected in one of the most fraudulent elections in Egypt's contemporary history.[57]

While the fraudulence of the late 2010 parliamentary elections contributed to the January 2011 uprising, the Brotherhood and Salafi groups stayed largely on the sidelines during its earliest days. However, after massive protests on January 25, 2011, the Brotherhood endorsed the pivotal January 28th "Friday of Rage" protests, during which protesters overwhelmed the police and forced the military to take control of the streets. The group attempted to negotiate with the regime on at least two occasions during the uprising, but faced criticism from its youth members and revolutionary factions for doing so. It ultimately called for Mubarak's overthrow on February 7, 2011, four days before the Egyptian president was forced from power.[58]

Egypt's Islamist groups were the only political forces capable of mobilizing their members nationwide after the overthrow of Mubarak and the collapse of the National Democratic Party. Non-Islamist groups, by contrast, were weakened after decades of mostly working within the regime's legal constraints. So, when the Supreme Council of the Armed Forces (SCAF) took control of the country on February 11, 2011 and opened Egypt's political arena, many of these Islamist groups quickly established legal political parties.

The new Salafist end of the political spectrum – including the Building and Development Party and the Light Party – included smaller movements such as the ultraconservative *Al-Asala Party* founded by Adil Abd al-Maqsoud Afifi. This marked a considerable departure for Salafist groups, which had previously always been apolitical. Members of the groups generally refused to work with secular state institutions, dismissing the concept of democracy as "alien."[59] But under the guidance of charismatic preachers, Salafist movements opted for participation because it was an opportunity to implement *sharia* and feared that their failure to participate would lead to secularization.[60] Salafists also sought to provide ideological justification for their entry into politics. One important concern for leaders was to intertwine entrance into the political arena and religious principles for its members. That hinged on pointing to the duty incumbent on Muslims to try and implement *sharia* law wherever possible. Given the contested political environment of post-Mubarak Egypt, the alternative (namely, a secular regime) would constitute negligence.

Islamist political parties did extremely well in the parliamentary elections of late 2011 and early 2012: the FJP-led Democratic Alliance for Egypt won 47 percent of the seats, while the Light Party dominated Islamic Bloc, which included the Islamic Group's Building and Development Party, won 24 percent. The Wasat Party, an offshoot of the Muslim Brotherhood, gained an additional two percent of its seats in parliament.[61] However, the Salafists' electoral gains were by far the most unanticipated development of the election.[62]

Yet the Assembly was not the Brotherhood's last attempt to use its dominance in parliament. The group attempted to undermine the SCAF's political legitimacy, including trying to use the parliament to declare no confidence in the SCAF-backed government. In response, the SCAF issued a statement that tacitly threatened the group with a major crackdown.[63]

In 2011, former Brotherhood leader Abdel Moneim Abou el-Fotouh emerged as a dominant candidate in the then-upcoming 2012 presidential elections. The organization had banished el-Fotouh from its ranks for declaring his intention to run for president, despite the group's orders not to do so.

Just before the collapse of Mubarak's regime, the Brotherhood had promised not to run a presidential candidate, but it still did so. The group's initial candidate was disqualified due to his incarceration during the Mubarak regime (as were several other leading candidates). The Brotherhood eventually nominated FJP chairman Mohammed Morsi.[64] The final list of candidates included thirteen people, including members of former governments. Morsi won with 24 percent of the vote,[65] and then won the run-off election against former Prime Minister Ahmed Shafiq with 51.7 percent of the vote.

In June of 2012, a court disbanded the FJP-controlled parliament on the grounds that its election was unconstitutional, because the electoral format did not give political independents an equal opportunity to win. Also in June, on the eve of the declaration of Morsi's victory in the elections, the SCAF issued a constitutional declaration that protected the military from the elected president's oversight and granted itself legislative authority, to prevent Morsi from gaining power. In response, the Brotherhood and its allies occupied Cairo's Tahrir Square and threatened mass protests if Morsi did not become Egypt's president.

The constitutional declaration had a significant impact. When Morsi was sworn in on June 30, 2012, there was no parliament and no new constitution, and his exact powers were poorly defined.[66] On August 12, however, Morsi used a major attack in the Sinai that had taken place the previous week as a pretext for firing the SCAF's leaders, promoting director of military intelligence Abdel Fatah el-Sisi to defense minister, and granting himself legislative power until a new parliament was sworn in.[67]

This made Morsi the undisputed power holder in Egypt, at least in legal terms. But in November 2012, it appeared as though a second Constituent Assembly (which parliament had appointed before it was disbanded) was going to be nullified by the courts. Morsi responded by issuing another constitutional declaration that protected the Constituent Assembly from the courts, but also placed his own edicts above judicial oversight. When mass protests broke out in response, Morsi rammed through the ratification of a theocratic constitution.[68]

While the new constitution passed by 64 percent via referendum with a mere 30 percent turnout,[69] the political crisis persisted for months and protests against Morsi grew more violent and more regular. Meanwhile, the economy declined, lines for gas extended around city blocks, and power outages lasted for hours.[70] As a result, on June 30, 2013, millions of Egyptians took to the streets to demand early presidential elections. When Morsi refused to compromise, the military responded by ousting his government on July 3, 2013.

In March 2018, President el-Sisi won reelection with a reported 97% of the vote.[71] El-Sisi has continued targeting the Brotherhood as well as other religious opponents of his rule. On July 5, 2018, 14 alleged members of the Brotherhood were sentenced to life in prison for their association with the now-outlawed organization.[72] Three weeks later, on July 28, 2018, an Egyptian court sentenced 75 people to death for their role in the 2013 protests. Despite the continued crackdown, however, signs seemed to indicate the Brotherhood and el-Sisi's regime could reconcile; thus, in July 2018, amid the legal sentencing of Brotherhood members and demonstrators, an Egyptian appeals court overturned a verdict that placed 1,500 Brotherhood members on the national terror list.[73] However, as of this writing, a broader reconciliation has yet to materialize, despite repeated overtures.

To be sure, these efforts have not always resonated with Islamists. While Islamic Jihad leaders have publicly abandoned violence, some affiliated factions continue to advocate *jihad*, sometimes even leaving the movement to join other groups more closely aligned with their beliefs. One cell of Islamic Jihad, for example, joined al-Qaeda in the early 2000s and was likely involved in the wave of attacks that hit Egypt after 2003. The Islamic Group faced similar difficulties. In a 2010 interview, Nagih Ibrahim, one of its former ideologues, emphasized that although the group's formal rejection of violence had obviously helped limit the spread of violent Islamism in Egypt, such ideological revisions had had less impact on the younger generations, especially those sympathetic toward or active within hardline *jihadist* groups such as al-Qaeda.[74]

In September 2019, el-Sisi faced a severe public crisis over videos circulated widely on Facebook, and aired by Brotherhood-backed satellite channels, that accused Egypt's top military and political echelons of corruption and encouraged the public to demonstrate against the President. The videos were described by the President and state media as baseless rumors aimed at diminishing the regime's achievements, driving a wedge between the military and the citizenry, and threatening the stability of the homeland. He also alleged that they were part of a plot by the MB and its regional allies, Turkey and Qatar. However, only a few thousand people answered the call to demonstrate throughout Egypt on September 20, 2019; even fewer turned out on September 27th. Some television reports from the protests aired on Brotherhood-backed satellite channels were found to be fake.

The 2020 COVID-19 pandemic presented the Egyptian government and military with intertwining problems of combatting the virus a persistently challenging relationship with the Muslim Brotherhood. Government leadership was presented in state media outlets as efficiently social and economic systems. Meanwhile, the Brotherhood was reportedly the source of rumors suggesting higher contagion rates in prisons, the army, and the upper echelons of the administration. These rumors proliferate in an attempt to erode trust in government, encourage public disobedience, and ultimately present themselves as a viable alternative to the current administration.[75]

The government's repression of the Muslim Brotherhood has deterred other Islamist organizations from escalating their activities, and many of the group's initial allies in the "Coalition for Legitimacy" have either been imprisoned or resigned from the coalition. For this reason, those Islamists who have not joined *jihadist* movements have deferred their political ambitions until the current regime falls. They seek power in the long run, but are currently prioritizing their personal survival. However, the November 2017 attack by the Islamic State is a stark reminder of the limits of the regime's ability to contain all Islamist groups operating in and around its borders, particularly in Northern Sinai.

Endnotes

1. "Who are Egypt's militant groups?" BBC News, November 24, 2017, https://www.bbc.com/news/world-middle-east-34751349.
2. For an overview of the Muslim Brotherhood's formative ideology, see Hassan al-Banna's writings and memoirs, among which the *Letter To A Muslim Student* posits the core principles of the movement. For the English translation, see http://www.jannah.org/articles/letter.html.
3. For a detailed biography, see "Muhammad Rashid Rida," Encyclopedia Britannica online, n.d., http://www.britannica.com/EBchecked/topic/491703/Rashid-Rida.
4. Sayyid Qutb, *Milestones* (Kazi Publications, 2007).
5. Barbara Zollner, *The Muslim Brotherhood: Hasan al-Hudaybi and Ideology* (London: Routledge, 2008).
6. This book was first published in 1991 and attacked the Brotherhood for its "betrayal" after "recognizing the legitimacy of secular institutions" in Egypt and "helping the Tyrants [the government]" repress *jihadists*. Ayman al-Zawahiri, *The Bitter Harvest: The Muslim Brotherhood in Sixty Years*, trans. Nadia Masid, (Egypt: n.p., 1991).
7. Ayman al-Zawahiri, *The Bitter Harvest: The Muslim Brotherhood in Sixty Years*, trans. Nadia Masid, (Egypt: n.p., 1991).
8. Eric Trager, *Arab Fall: How the Muslim Brotherhood Won and Lost Egypt in 891 Days* (Washington: Georgetown University Press, 2016), 32-25.
9. Ali Omar, "Muslim Brotherhood responds to NCHR Rabaa report," *Daily News Egypt*, March 8, 2014, http://www.dailynewsegypt.com/2014/03/08/muslim-brotherhood-responds-nchr-rabaa-report/.
10. Salma Abdelaziz and Steve Almasy, "Egypt's interim Cabinet officially labels Muslim Brotherhood a terrorist group," *CNN,* December 25, 2013, http://www.cnn.com/2013/12/25/world/africa/egypt-mus-

lim-brotherhood-terrorism/.

11. Eric Trager, *World Almanac of Islamism 2017* (Rowman & Littlefield/American Foreign Policy Council, 2017).
12. Mohktar Awad, "The Rise of the Violent Muslim Brotherhood," *Current Trends in Islamist Ideology*, July 27, 2017, https://www.hudson.org/research/13787-the-rise-of-the-violent-muslim-brotherhood.
13. Trager, *World Almanac of Islamism 2017.*
14. Orit Perlov and Ofir Winter, "Mohamed Morsi: Martyr or Traitor?," Tel Aviv University Institute for National Strategic Studies *INSS Insight* no. 1183, July 1, 2019, https://www.inss.org.il/publication/mohamed-morsi-martyr-traitor/
15. "The Trial Of Omar Abdel Rahman," *New York Times*, October 3, 1995, http://www.nytimes.com/1995/10/03/opinion/the-trial-of-omar-abdel-rahman.html.
16. Omar Ashour, "Lions tamed? An inquiry into the causes of de-radicalization of armed Islamist movements: the case of the Egyptian Islamic Group," *Middle East Journal* 61, no. 4, 2007, 596-597; Rohan Gunaratna and Mohamed Bin Ali, "De-Radicalization Initiatives in Egypt: A Preliminary Insight," *Studies in Conflict & Terrorism* 32, no. 4, 2009, 277-291.
17. Among these are Karam Zuhdi, *The Strategy and the Bombings of Al-Qaeda: Mistakes and Dangers* (*Istratijiyyatwa Tajjirat al-Qa'ida: Al-Akhta' wa-l-Akhtar*) (Cairo: Al-Turath al-Islami, 2002); Nagih Ibrahim and Ali al-Sharif, *Banning Extremism in Religion and the Excommunication of Muslims* (*Hurmat al-Ghuluw fi-I-Din wa Takfir al-Muslimin*) (Cairo: Al-Turath al-Islami, 2002).
18. Holly Fletcher, "Jamaat al-Islamiyya," Council on Foreign Relations (CFR) *Backgrounder*, May 30, 2008, https://www.cfr.org/backgrounder/jamaat-al-islamiyya.
19. On this interactional process, see Omar Ashour, "De-Radicalization of Jihad? The Impact of Egyptian Islamist Revisionists on Al-Qaeda," *Perspectives on Terrorism* II, no. 5, 2008, http://www.terrorismanalysts.com/pt/index.php?option=com_rokzine&view=article&id=39&Itemid=54; See also Lawrence Wright, "The Rebellion Within: An Al Qaeda mastermind questions terrorism," *New Yorker*, June 2, 2008, http://www.newyorker.com/reporting/2008/06/02/080602fa_fact_wright?currentPage=all.
20. J. Dana Stuster, "Egyptian political party wants off U.S. terrorist list," *Foreign Policy*, May 14, 2013, https://foreignpolicy.com/2013/05/14/egyptian-political-party-wants-off-u-s-terrorist-list/ .
21. "Egypt: 2011/2012 People's Assembly elections results," Electoral

Institute for Sustainable Democracy in Africa, January 2013, https://www.eisa.org.za/wep/egy2012results1.htm

22. Raja Abdulrahim, “Egypt Islamist party proves savvy, pragmatic, analysts say,” *Los Angeles Times*, September 8, 2013, https://www.latimes.com/world/la-xpm-2013-sep-08-la-fg-egypt-islamists-20130908-story.html; Ahmed Rahim, “Islamic Group in Egypt Not Demanding Morsi’s Return,” *Al Monitor,* August 20, 2013, https://www.al-monitor.com/pulse/politics/2013/08/egypt-morsi-alliance-brotherhood-legitimacy.html#ixzz6IZkNcbQK.
23. Youssef H. Aboul-Enein, “Al-Ikhwan Al-Muslimeen: the Muslim Brotherhood,” *Military Review*, July-August 2003, 26-31, http://www.ikhwanweb.com/print.php?id=5617.
24. “Bin Laden, Osama,” in Olivier Roy and Antoine Sfeir, eds., *The Columbia World Dictionary of Islamism* (New York: Columbia University Press, 2007), 79-87.
25. On the media dimension, see Nathan Field and Ahmed Hamam, “Salafi Satellite TV In Egypt,” *Arab Media & Society* no. 8, Spring 2009, http://www.arabmediasociety.com/?article=712.
26. Jason Brownlee, “Violence Against Copts in Egypt,” Carnegie Endowment for International Peace, November 2013, https://carnegieendowment.org/files/violence_against_copts3.pdf.
27. NYer, “Coptic (Catholic) priest: We will resist reimposition of jizya to the point of martyrdom,” Free Republic, January 2, 2012, http://www.freerepublic.com/focus/f-religion/2827874/posts. (Reported from the source cited by author)
28. André Aciman, “After Egypt’s Revolution, Christians Are Living in Fear,” *New York Times*, November 19, 2011, http://www.nytimes.com/2011/11/20/opinion/sunday/after-egypts-revolution-christians-are-living-in-fear.html?pagewanted=all.
29. “Islamists in Egypt Blame Christians for Voting,” *Assyrian International News Agency (AINA)*, May 29, 2012, http://www.aina.org/news/20120528191505.htm.
30. See Baher Ibrahim, “Salafi Intolerance Threatens Sufis,” *Guardian* (London), May 10, 2010, http://www.guardian.co.uk/commentisfree/belief/2010/may/10/islam-sufi-salafi-egypt-religion.
31. See Sarah Sheffer, “Salafi group reaffirms call to set Egypt’s Pharaonic relics in wax,” bikyarmasr.com, December 6, 2011, http://www.masress.com/en/bikyamasr/50394.
32. Raymond Ibrahim, “Calls to Destroy Egypt’s Great Pyramids Begin,” *Counter Jihad Report*, July 10, 2012, http://counterjihadreport.com/2012/07/10/calls-to-destroy-egypts-great-pyramids-begin/.

33. Mohammad Mahmoud, "Islamic Group theorist: al-Qaeda's ideology in a state of decline," Al-Shorfa.com, August 2, 2010, http://www.al-shorfa.com/cocoon/meii/xhtml/en_GB/features/meii/features/main/2010/08/02/feature-01.
34. "Who are the Abdullah Azzam Brigades?" Reuters, August 4, 2010, http://uk.reuters.com/article/idUKTRE6733QJ20100804; Hugh Roberts, "Egypt's Sinai Problem," *The Independent* (London), April 26, 2006, http://www.crisisgroup.org/en/regions/middle-east-north-africa/egypt-syria-lebanon/egypt/egypts-sinai-problem.aspx.
35. "Egypt army dispatches team to Sinai following Eilat attack," *Ahram Online* (Cairo), April 17, 2013, http://english.ahram.org.eg/News/69484.aspx; Jodi Rudoren, "Sinai Attack Tests New Egyptian President's Relationship With Israel," *New York Times*, August 6, 2012, http://www.nytimes.com/2012/08/07/world/middleeast/sinai-attack-a-test-for-israel-egypt-and-gaza.html; "Pipeline Supplying Israel Is Attacked," Agence France Presse, February 4, 2012, http://www.nytimes.com/2012/02/05/world/middleeast/egyptian-pipeline-supplying-israel-is-attacked.html?_r=0.
36. See Bill Roggio, "Ansar al Jihad swears allegiance to al Qaeda's emir," *Long War Journal*, January 24, 2012, http://www.longwarjournal.org/archives/2012/01/ansar_al_jihad_swear.php; Gilles Kepel, *Muslim extremism in Egypt: The Prophet and Pharaoh* (Berkeley and Los Angeles: University of California Press, 2003), 72 – 77; Abigail Hauslohner, "What Scares the Sinai Bedouin: the Rise of the Radical Islamists," *Time*, August 10, 2011, http://content.time.com/time/world/article/0,8599,2087797,00.html.
37. Hauslohner, "In Egypt's Sinai, insurgency taking root"; Stephanie McCrummen, "Car bombs hit military site in Egypt's Volatile Sinai Peninsula," *Washington Post*, September 11, 2013, http://www.washingtonpost.com/world/middle_east/car-bombs-hit-military-sites-in-egypts-volatile-sinai-peninsula/2013/09/11/53f6d30e-1ae3-11e3-80ac-96205cacb45a_story.html.
38. Jacob Wirtschafter, "Egypt's Operation Sinai 2018 is an all-out war on militants," *The National*, February 10, 2018, https://www.thenational.ae/world/mena/egypt-s-operation-sinai-2018-is-all-out-war-on-militants-1.703394.
39. Jack Clause, "IS-Sinai Peninsula Hit by Egyptian Raids," Center for Security Policy, August 6, 2018, https://www.centerforsecuritypolicy.org/2018/08/06/is-sinai-peninsula-hit-by-egyptian-raids/.
40. These pamphlets are accessible at https://vision-28.com; Trager, *World Almanac of Islamism 2017*; "Profile: Egypt's militant Ansar

Beit al-Maqdis group," *BBC News*, January 24, 2014, http://www.bbc.com/news/world-middle-east-25882504.

41. David Barnett, "Ajnad Misr claims 7th Cairo area attack, 6 wounded," *Long War Journal*, February 7, 2014, http://www.longwarjournal.org/threat-matrix/archives/2014/02/ajnad_misr_claims_7th_cairo_ar.php.
42. Hamdi Alkhshali and Nadeem Muaddi, "Egyptian court sentences 75 people to death over 2013 demonstration," *CNN*, July 29, 2018, https://www.cnn.com/2018/07/28/middleeast/egypt-muslim-brotherhood-death-sentences/index.html.
43. Giuseppe Dentice, "The Geopolitics of Violent Extremism. The Case of Sinai," *EuroMeSCo*, February 2018, 22-28, https://www.euromesco.net/publication/the-geopolitics-of-violent-extremism-the-case-of-sinai/.
44. "Egypt's Sinai Province Swears Allegiance to New Daesh Leader," *Middle East Monitor*, November 3, 2019, https://www.middleeastmonitor.com/20191103-egypts-sinai-province-swears-allegiance-to-new-daesh-leader/
45. Dentice, 37-39.
46. Yursi Mohamed and Mahmoud Mourad, "Islamic State raises stakes with Egypt mosque attack," Reuters, November 26, 2017, https://www.reuters.com/article/us-egypt-security-mosque/islamic-state-raises-stakes-with-egypt-mosque-attack-idUSKBN1DQ0K0.
47. Zvi Mazel, "Five years after the revolution: Is Egyptian President El-Sisi winning the battle?" *Jewish News Syndicate*, July 15, 2018, https://www.jns.org/opinion/five-years-after-the-revolution-is-egyptian-president-al-sisi-winning-the-battle/.
48. Tobias J. Burgers and Scott N. Romaniuk, "Islamic State After Syria: A Dangerous New Stronghold in the Sinai," Jamestown Foundation *Terrorism Monitor* 16, iss. 10, May 18, 2018, https://www.refworld.org/docid/5b728d41a.html
49. Al-Masry Al-Youm, "Govt allocates LE174.5 mn for this year's North Sinai development projects," *Egypt Independent*, March 22, 2018, https://www.egyptindependent.com/govt-allocates-le174-5-mn-years-north-sinai-development-projects/.
50. Mohamed Gamal, "Egypt opens new corridors to connect Sinai," *Daily News Egypt*, June 15, 2019, https://wwww.dailynewssegypt.com/2019/06/15/egypt-opens-new-corridors-to-connect-sinai/.
51. "Egypt Raises Sinai Investment by 75% in 2019-20", Reuters, August 22, 2019, https://www.reuters.com/article/egypt-economy-sinai-investments/egypt-raises-sinai-investment-by-75-in-2019-20-

idUSL4N25I2FO

52. Ofir Winter, "The Islamic Caliphate: A Controversial Consensus," in Yoram Schweitzer and Omer Einav, eds., *The Islamic State: How Viable Is It?* (Tel-Aviv: INSS, 2016), 27-35.
53. Ofir Winter and Assaf Shiloah, "Egypt's Identity during the El-Sis-iEra: Profile of the 'New Egyptian,'" *Strategic Assessment* 21, iss. 4, January 2019, 65-78.
54. See Samir Amin, "Egypt: Muslim Brotherhood - Revolutionary or Anti-Revolutionary?" *Pambazuka News*, July 4, 2012, http://www.pambazuka.org/en/category/features/83202.
55. Samir Doha, "The Muslim Brotherhood's Generational Gap in the Post –Revolutionary Era" *Al-Muntaqa* 1, no. 2 August 2018, 37.
56. On the rise and spread of Salafism in Egyptian society, see Nathan Field and Ahmed Hamem, "Egypt: Salafism Making Inroads," Carnegie Endowment for International Peace *Arab Reform Bulletin*, March 9, 2009, https://carnegieendowment.org/sada/22823; Saif Nasrawi, "Egypt's Salafis: When My Enemy's Foe Isn't My Friend," *Al-Masry al-Youm* (Cairo), April 27, 2010, https://ww.egyptindependent.com/egypts-salafis-when-my-enemys-foe-isnt-my-friend/.
57. Amro Hassan and Jeffrey Fleishman, "Egyptian Police Crack down on Muslim Brotherhood before Elections," *Los Angeles Times*, November 23, 2010, https://www.latimes.com/archives/la-xpm-2010-nov-23-la-fg-egypt-brotherhood-20101123-story.html.
58. "Egyptian Elections Watch: Al-Nour Party," *Ahram Online* (Cairo), December 4, 2011, http://english.ahram.org.eg/NewsContentPrint/33/0/26693/Elections-/0/AlNour-Party.aspx.
59. See Omar Ashour, "The unexpected rise of Salafists has complicated Egyptian politics," *Daily Star* (Beirut), January 6, 2012, http://www.dailystar.com.lb/Opinion/Commentary/2012/Jan-06/159027-the-unexpected-rise-of-salafists-has-complicated-egyptian-politics.ashx#ixzz1iz2mHPKa.
60. The Islamic Group declared: "We believe that the suffering we endured during the past years was due to neglecting religion and putting those who don't fear [God] in power (…) Islam can contain everyone and respects the freedom of followers of other religions to refer to their own Sharia in private affairs." See "Al-Gamaa Al-Islamiya calls for unity, says minority rights guaranteed," *Daily News Egypt*, September 1, 2011, http://www.dailynewsegypt.com/2011/09/01/al-gamaa-al-islamiya-calls-for-unity-says-minority-rights-guaranteed/.
61. Salafist cleric Yasser Burhami, who was instrumental in the estab-

lishment of the al-Nour party, declared that, "Islam must become involved of all aspects of life, even the political, and the Islamic movement must unite." See Hani Nasira, "The Salafist movement in Egypt" (*Al-Salafiyya fi Misr*), Al-Ahram Center for Political and Strategic Studies *Strategic Note* no. 46, 2011.

62. Jasmine Coleman, "Egypt election results show firm win for Islamists," *Guardian* (London), January 21, 2012, https://www.theguardian.com/world/2012/jan/21/egypt-election-clear-islamist-victory.
63. Sherif Tarek, "El-Katatni: From prisoner to speaker of parliament," *Ahram Online* (Cairo), January 24, 2012, http://english.ahram.org.eg/NewsContent/1/0/32600/Egypt//ElKatatni-from-prisoner-to-speaker-of-parliament.aspx.
64. Trager, *Arab Fall: How the Muslim Brotherhood Won and Lost Egypt in 891 Days*, 129-130.
65. "Ten Egyptian candidates barred from elections," BBC, April 14, 2012, https://www.bbc.com/ncws/world-middlc-cast-17717268.
66. Although some contest the electoral results. See Borzou Daragahi, "Egypt nervously awaits election results," *Financial Times*, June 22, 2012, http://www.ft.com/cms/s/0/a17de564-bc5b-11e1-a470-00144feabdc0.html#axzz21WobfdCf.
67. Trager, *Arab Fall: How the Muslim Brotherhood Won and Lost Egypt in 891 Days*, 145; Trager, *World Almanac of Islamism 2017*.
68. Trager, *Arab Fall: How the Muslim Brotherhood Won and Lost Egypt in 891 Days*, 157-160; Trager, *World Almanac of Islamism 2017*.
69. Trager, *Arab Fall: How the Muslim Brotherhood Won and Lost Egypt in 891 Days*, 175-177; Trager, *World Almanac of Islamism 2017*.
70. Trager, *Arab Fall: How the Muslim Brotherhood Won and Lost Egypt in 891 Days*, 186-187; Trager, *World Almanac of Islamism 2017*.
71. John Davison and Ahmed Tolba, "Egypt's Sisi wins 97 percent in election with no real opposition," Reuters,April 2, 2018, https://www.reuters.com/article/us-egypt-election-result/egypts-sisi-wins-97-percent-in-election-with-no-real-opposition-idUSKCN1H916A.
72. "Egypt sentences 14 to life for belonging to banned Islamists," Associated Press, July 5, 2018, https://apnews.com/2df0735a66804de5b8e46e6fd25d5874/Egypt-sentences-14-to-life-for-belonging-to-banned-Islamists.
73. "Egypt's top appeals court overturns 'terror list' ruling on Morsi," *Al Jazeera* (Doha), July 4, 2018, https://www.aljazeera.com/news/2018/07/egypt-top-appeals-court-overturns-terror-list-ruling-morsi-180704171711654.html.
74. See "Another Salafi-Jihadi Cell Arrested in Egypt," Middle East Me-

dia Research Institute *MEMRI TV* no. 5017, January 4, 2010, http://www.memritv.org/report/en/4193.htm.

75. Winter, Ofir, and Tzvi Lev. "The Institute for National Security Studies." *The Institute for National Security Studies*. Tel Aviv University, April 22, 2020. https://www.inss.org.il/publication/egypt-coronavirus-test/.

12 Israel

Quick Facts

Population: 8,675,475 (includes populations of the Golan Heights or Golan Sub-District and also East Jerusalem, which was annexed by Israel after 1967) (July 2020 est.)
Area: 21,937 sq km
Ethnic Groups: Jewish 74.4% (of which Israel-born 76.9%, Europe/America/Oceania-born 15.9%, Africa-born 4.6%, Asia-born 2.6%), Arab 20.9%, other 4.7% (2018 est.)
Government Type: Parliamentary democracy
GDP (official exchange rate): $350.7 billion (2017 est.)

Source: CIA World FactBook (Last Updated July 2020)

Introduction

Although there was a strong Islamist current in the Palestinian national movement of the British Mandate Period, the Israeli War of Independence (1947–49) and subsequent policies adopted by the Israeli government kept Islamism largely at bay until the 1970s. Islamism regained popularity in the wake of Iran's 1979 Islamic Revolution, spreading to the Palestinian Territories and even into Israel itself as Israeli Arabs over time have shown increasing identification with their Palestinian cousins in the West Bank and Gaza Strip. Israeli preoccupation with secular Arab nationalist groups in the 1970s and 80s enabled Islamism to metastasize unfettered. In recent years, the phenomenon is manifested most concretely in the Islamic Movement of Israel. Today, the lack of strong governmental oversight in the Sinai Peninsula has led to militant Islamist infiltration of the area and poses significant threats to Israeli national security.

Islamist Activity

Hamas

The Islamist group known by the acronym HAMAS ("the Islamic resistance movement" in Arabic) is the premier Islamist faction in the Palestinian Territories, and the principal extremist threat to the state of Israel. Its precursor was an Islamist group known as Mujama al-Islamiya. In the 1970s, over the objections of moderate Palestinians,[1] the Israeli government permitted Sheikh Ahmed Yassin, the leader of the Muslim Brotherhood in the Gaza Strip, to register Mujama al-Islamiya first as a charity and then, in 1979, as an association.[2] At first, the group devoted itself primarily to building schools, clinics, and libraries. Mujama al-Islamiya refrained from anti-Israel violence in its early years, but when the First Intifada erupted in December 1987, Yassin and some of his Mujama al-Islamiya colleagues founded Hamas. Hamas promotes fundamentalist Islamic norms, such as requiring women to wear the *hijab* and permitting polygamous unions. Furthermore, Hamas has committed itself to waging an armed struggle to obliterate Israel and to establish an Islamic state governed by *sharia* law "from the Jordan River to the Mediterranean Sea."[3] To that end, Hamas has engineered dozens of suicide bombings that killed hundreds of Israelis. Hamas carried out almost 40 percent of suicide attacks during the Second Intifada (2000-2005), far more than any other group.[4]

Hamas, despite being a Sunni movement, benefits significantly from Iranian support. Iran has provided military assistance to Hamas since the early 1990s. It has also provided both rhetorical and logistical support to the group in its operations. In a now-infamous 2002 incident, Israel captured the *Karine A,* a ship destined for the Gaza Strip and carrying 50 tons of advanced weaponry on board. The ship had been stocked in Iranian waters.[5] Iran has also provided substantial financial aid to Hamas. In December 2006, Hamas reported on its website that Iran had provided the organization with $250 million.[6] After Operation Cast Lead in 2008–2009, Iran provided Hamas with a variety of weapons, including Grad rockets with range of 20–40 km, anti-tank missiles and others. Along with the military aid, Iran has provided advanced training for Hamas operatives with instructors from the Iranian Revolutionary Guards, as well as propaganda support.[7]

The Syrian civil war initially proved detrimental to the relationship between Hamas and Iran. Hamas refused to support Syrian dictator Bashar al-Assad, one of Iran's key allies.[8] In response, Tehran cut off

Hamas's funding, which amounted at that time to about $23 million per month.[9] This move forced Hamas to seek out alternative sources of funding, including from wealthy Sunni states such as Qatar[10] and Saudi Arabia. However, Hamas and Iran eventually reconciled, and in 2015 Iran began supplying Hamas anew with military technology, helping it repair tunnels destroyed in the 2014 conflict with Israel, and hosting Hamas delegations in Iran.[11]

Like many militant groups, Hamas has secured popular support among Palestinians and pursued recruitment through community service and engagement. Hamas provides schools, hospitals, and other necessary social services. Hamas guarantees to the family of its suicide bombers economic assistance, including education, healthcare, and funeral expenses. This financial support—especially in impoverished communities—serves as a continuing recruitment driver.[12]

Though Hamas is more active and powerful in Palestinian communities, Israeli Arabs have also been involved with the organization. In May 2011, the Haifa District Court sentenced an Israeli Arab to five years in prison for conspiring with his brother-in-law to gather an arms cache in Israel for Hamas.[13] The same year, Israeli authorities arrested two Arab residents of East Jerusalem holding Israeli citizenship who were planning to attack Jerusalem's Teddy Stadium during a Premier League soccer match. Authorities divulged that the two men had longstanding ties with Hamas.[14]

In the face of international pressure, Hamas cosmetically modified its charter in 2017 to make it appear more moderate. The amended charter still refuses to relinquish the claim to every part of British Mandate Palestine. However, it acknowledges "the establishment of a fully sovereign and independent Palestinian state, with Jerusalem as its capital along the lines of the 4th of June 1967, with the return of the refugees and the displaced to their homes from which they were expelled, to be a formula of national consensus."[15]

Islamic Movement in Israel

The Islamic Movement in Israel is a Sunni group founded by Abdullah Darwish that advocates for the vital role of Islam in public life in Israel. Much like Hamas, the Islamic Movement courts favor from local populations through providing social services. During the First Intifada, the Islamic Movement established the Islamic Relief Committee, the stated purpose of which was to provide assistance to injured Palestinians. In 1993, the Islamic Movement split in response to internal discord over the Oslo Accords. Darwish supported accepting the Accords, while more hardline members, such as Sheikh Ra'ed Salah and Sheikh Kemal Khatib, did not. The hardline faction became known as the Northern Branch (as the majority of its leaders came from northern Israel).[16] Darwish led the more moderate Southern Branch. The Northern Branch played a part in inciting the Second Intifada in 2000. Specifically, incitement by the group helped instigate clashes between Israeli Arabs and police in the Wadi Ara region in October 2000—clashes that left 13 protesters dead.[17]

Most of the Islamic Movement's support within Israel comes from the Bedouin community (discussed further below). In November 2015, the Israeli government designated the Northern Branch of the Islamic Movement and its 17 affiliated charities as illegal, and jailed its leader, Ra'ed Salah. To circumvent the ban, members of the Northern Branch of the Islamic Movement founded a new group, the Trust and Reform Party, in 2016. The head of the party, Husam Abu Leil, was the second deputy head of the Islamic Movement's Northern Branch.[18]

The group has sporadically reasserted its presence in Israeli politics and shown signs of life. In November 2016, for instance, Israel's internal security service, the Shin Bet, arrested two Israeli Arabs who were planning an attack on Israeli Defense Forces (IDF) troops in retaliation for the Northern Branch's proscription.[19] Subsequently, in 2018, nine people were convicted of being affiliated with a banned terrorist movement and conspiracy to commit a crime after they admitted their association with the Islamic Movement's northern branch.[20]

Palestinian Islamic Jihad (PIJ)

Palestinian Islamic Jihad emerged in Gaza in 1981 as a fusion of the Islamism advocated by Omar Abdel-Rahman, the spiritual leader of the Egyptian Islamic Jihad, with Palestinian nationalism. Its founders included Fathi Shaqaqi and Abd al-Aziz al-Awda, who were affiliated with the Egyptian Islamic Jihad until their expulsion from Egypt after President Anwar Sadat's assassination,[21] as well as several members of the secular Popular Liberation Forces. PIJ quickly became one of the most violent Palestinian factions, assassinating the commander of the Israeli military police in the Gaza Strip in August 1987 and launching a wave of suicide bombings.[22]

Israel deported Shaqaqi and al-Awda to southern Lebanon in 1988, and in 1989 Shaqaqi decided to relocate the organization's official command to Damascus.[23] According to the U.S. State Department, PIJ's high-ranking leadership is located in Syria while some leaders live in Lebanon, though most of its affiliates live in Gaza.[24] After the Mossad killed Shaqaqi in 1995, Ramadan Shallah, previously a professor at the University of South Florida, became head of the organization.[25] In recent years, Shallah was sidelined by chronic illness, and his deputy, Ziad al-Nakhalah, has served as the group's leader since 2018. Shallah died in June of 2020.[26]

PIJ is much smaller than Hamas and, according to IDF estimates, consists of around 15,000 members.[27] Like Hamas, it is ardently committed to the violent destruction of Israel,[29] but unlike Hamas spends little time on social services for Palestinians in Gaza and the West Bank, where it is active today. The organization's armed wing is called the al-Quds Brigades and, despite its small size, was responsible for more than a quarter of the suicide bombings during the Second Intifada.[30] In recent years, the organization has intensified its firing of rockets from Gaza into Israel.[31]

Though the group is Sunni, PIJ is nonetheless strongly influenced by the model of Islamic political activism embodied by Iran's 1979 Revolution.[32] As a result, Iran has historically provided extensive support to the group via funding, as well as military equipment and training. In 1998, it was revealed that Iran had allocated $2 million to PIJ's annual budget. Since then, the Iranian support to PIJ has been much higher. In 2013, PIJ sources stated that they received from Iran around $3 million per month.[33] According to Ali Nourizadeh, director of the Center for Iranian Studies in London, Iran at the time was transferring to the organization $100–150 million every year.[34] However, in 2015, tensions between the group and Iran began to appear, due to PIJ's refusal to condemn the Sunni Gulf state attacks, led by Saudi Arabia, against the Houthi rebels in Yemen.[35] In 2015, a senior PIJ leader acknowledged that the organization was suffering from the worst financial catastrophe since its founding as a result of Iran curtailing its financial support.[36] According to various reports in 2016, Iran cut its support for the organization by 90 percent.[37] In 2018, reports estimated that PIJ receives 30 million dollars a year from Iran. This figure appears to have remained static over the past two years.[38]

Hezbollah

Hezbollah is a Shi'a Muslim militia that engages in terrorist activity while maintaining a robust political/social-welfare wing.[39] The organization was founded in 1982 during the Lebanese Civil War with significant support from Iran's Islamic Revolutionary Guard Corps (IRGC).[40] In its founding statement,[41] Hezbollah professed its loyalty to Iran's Supreme Leader, the Ayatollah Ruhollah Khomeini; called for the establishment of an Islamic regime; and demanded the removal of the United States, France, and Israel from Lebanon, in addition to the annihilation of Israel.[42] Iran regards Hezbollah as a proxy and vehicle for spreading its influence through the region. The Islamic Republic provides extensive financial support, training, and advanced weaponry to Hezbollah. In total, Iran's support is estimated at between 700 to 800 million dollars per year, including weaponry, training, and logistical support.[43] In addition, Iran funds Hezbollah's television channel *Al-Manar*, providing approximately $15 million annually.[44]

Hezbollah coalesced following the 1982 Israeli invasion of Lebanon to oust the Palestinian Liberation Organization (PLO). Soon after the PLO evacuated Beirut for Tunis, Shi'a militias began attacking the IDF. Hezbollah was formed through the amalgamation of some of the aforementioned Shi'a militias and launched a guerilla war to expel the IDF from Lebanon. In 1985, the IDF withdrew to the "security belt" in southern Lebanon, where it proceeded to fight a 15-year war against Hezbollah. Then-Israeli Prime Minister Ehud Barak attempted to alter this equation in 2000 by removing Israel's remaining forces from Lebanon following Israel's withdrawal. However, Hezbollah quickly became the dominant political force in the country.[45] Hezbollah officially entered politics in the 1992 parliamentary elections and has continued to grow in influence and power since, to the point that it is now represented in the Lebanese cabinet.

According to Israeli Security Agency (ISA) assessments, following Israel's withdrawal from Lebanon in 2000, Hezbollah began to focus on penetrating the Israeli Arab population. Hezbollah sees Israeli Arabs as valuable operatives because they have the advantage of being Israeli citizens who enjoy freedom of movement and accessibility to targets.[46] While the majority of its activities are affiliated with Fatah's al-Aqsa Martyrs Brigades, Hezbollah also cooperates with Hamas, PIJ, and the Popular Front for the Liberation of Palestine (PFLP).[47] Hezbollah uses its international presence to recruit Israeli Arabs when they travel outside of Israel.[48]

Hezbollah is known for its cross-border operations in addition to extensive terrorist activities abroad, such as attacks in Argentina targeting the Israeli embassy in Buenos Aires and the Jewish community center there, in 1992 and 1994, respectively,[49] as well as an attack against a bus carrying Israeli tourists in Burgas, Bulgaria, in 2012. Hezbollah maintains a large presence of supporters and operatives all around the world, including North and South America, Africa, Asia, and Europe.[50] Some of the attacks carried out by the organization were initiated and directed by Iran, such as the Khobar Towers bombing in Saudi Arabia in 1996 and the attacks in Argentina.[51]

After Hezbollah operatives killed eight Israeli soldiers and captured two more in 2006, Israel and Hezbollah descended into a 33-day war.[52] During the conflict, Hezbollah launched thousands of rockets into Israel.[53] Although the war ended in a stalemate,[54] given Israel's overwhelming military advantage, Hezbollah could portray the outcome as a victory. Since 2006, the northern border has seen relatively little terrorist activity.[55] In February 2017, Hezbollah leader Hassan Nasrallah threatened to attack Israel's nuclear reactor in Dimona and has previously threatened to attack ammonia supplies in Haifa.[56]

Along with Iran, Syria has historically been a key supporter of Hezbollah. When the Arab Spring threatened the stability of the Assad dictatorship, both Iran and Hezbollah intervened to support the regime. Nearly a decade on, Iran (and Hezbollah's) help has been instrumental in turning the tide of the conflict away from the Assad regime's domestic opposition, and back toward Damascus. In turn, as Assad and his allies have consolidated power, Israeli fears have grown that the country could become more vulnerable to Hezbollah terrorism.[57] This has come at a high cost, however. At the peak of its commitment to Syria's war, Hezbollah dedicated 40% (some 8,000 fighters) of its personnel and capabilities to Syrian battlefields in 2018, according to IDF assessments.[58] Hezbollah sustained some 2,000 casualties and 10,000 injuries by 2018, according to those same assessments.

Over the past two and a half years, Israel's campaign to target Hezbollah forces and Iranian entrenchment in Syria has continued full steam. Former IDF Chief of Staff Lt. Gen. (ret.) Gadi Eisenkot confirmed in 2019 that Israel struck thousands of targets in Syria, some of which, it is safe to assume, involved Hezbollah's own attempts to create an offensive and terrorist infrastructure in Syria.[59] Israel's campaign has also targeted the Iranian-Hezbollah program to assemble and deploy precision guided missiles across Lebanon.[60]

Al-Qaeda and the Islamic State

Israel has more often been a rhetorical target of al-Qaeda than an actual one.[61] In almost every one of his public statements between 1990 and 2011, Osama bin Laden referenced the Palestinian issue. A 2001 Treasury Department report reveals that the group's Iraqi *emir*, Abu Musab al-Zarqawi, had received more than $35,000 for training Jordanian and Palestinian operatives in Afghanistan and enabling their travel to the Levant with assurances that he would receive more funding for attacks against Israel.[62] However, nothing came of these attacks and "[al-Qaeda's] plotting against Israel has never matched its anti-Israel propaganda."[63]

However, there have been some exceptions. In 2010, four Israeli Arabs were among those charged by Israeli authorities with establishing a terror cell and killing a taxi driver.[64] Two of the plaintiffs had trained at an al-Qaeda camp in Somalia.[65] Subsequently, in January 2014, Israeli officials revealed an al-Qaeda plot in Israel with a direct involvement of senior leaders of the organization. According to the reports, an al-Qaeda operative in Gaza run by Zawahiri recruited three men (two from East Jerusalem and one from the West Bank) through Skype and Facebook. All four operators were arrested.[66]

More recently, the Islamic State (ISIS) has likewise emerged as a threat to Israeli security. An offshoot of al-Qaeda,[67] in 2014 ISIS managed to occupy vast areas in the region of Iraq and Syria and to take control over the population in its territory. However, American and European airstrikes completely cleared ISIS from Iraq while reducing its domain in Syria to less than 5% of the nation's territory,[68] forcing the organization to expand into secondary territories, such as in Libya and the Sinai.[69]

The affiliate that proves most dangerous for Israel is the Sinai Province of the Islamic State, formerly known as Ansar Bayt al-Maqdis. The organization is located in the Sheikh Zweid area in the northern Sinai Peninsula, near the border with Israel,[70] and commands approximately 1,500 members.[71] The group pledged allegiance to ISIS on November 2014 with an emphasis on the importance of fighting the Jews:

> After decades... Allah ordered the flag of jihad to be raised in our land and gave us the honor of being the soldiers [Allah] chose to fight the nation's most bitter enemies... the Jews... Our swords will be extended against them until Allah is victorious.[72]

The Sinai Province affiliate has launched several attacks against Israel over the past few years, including a combined attack that was carried out against a bus in Eilat in August 2011, several rocket attacks on Eilat, and attacks against the gas pipeline between Egypt and Israel in north Sinai.[73]

Israeli Arabs have not proven immune to ISIS's appeal. As of 2017, at least 60 Israelis, including two Jewish converts to Islam, were known to have traveled to Syria or Iraq to fight with *jihadist* groups, leading Israel to revoke the citizenship of the 19 known to be fighting with ISIS.[74] In 2019, Israeli security forces announced the arrest and prosecution of two Israeli Arabs from the northern town of Tamra for plotting ISIS-linked terror attacks.[75] And in March 2020, an Israeli Arab doctor was killed in battle while fighting within ISIS ranks in Syria, the Shin Bet said. His brother was arrested.[76]

Uncoordinated Terrorism

Greater security cooperation between Israel and the Palestinian Authority since the end of the Second Intifada has greatly diminished the number of bombings and other coordinated attacks. Today, lone wolf attacks predominate. In recent years, there have been several spikes in lone wolf attacks, mostly committed by Palestinian residents of East Jerusalem. One spike was in the summer of 2014 after the murder and immolation of a Muslim teenager, Mohammad Abu Khdeir, by Jewish terrorists in retaliation for the kidnapping and murder of three Jewish teenage hitchhikers at Alon Shvut.[77] The violence took the form of vehicular assault, stabbings, stone throwing, and arson. The use of firecrackers was particularly prominent.[78] Rioters also targeted East Jerusalem infrastructure, destroying three light rail stations.[79]

Another spike in terrorism occurred during the 2017 Temple Mount Crisis. Accusations that Israel will annul the Supreme Muslim Council's control of the Temple Mount often provoke violence. On July 14, 2017, three Israeli Muslims from Umm al-Fahm who were affiliated with the Northern Branch of the Islamic Movement murdered two policemen at the Temple Mount. The Israeli government responded by placing metal detectors at the entrances to the site. The security measure elicited a furious reaction, expressed through terrorism. One particularly gruesome attack involved the fatal stabbing of three people during a Shabbat dinner in Halamish. After the attack, police found the perpetrator's suicide note, which explicitly cited the Temple Mount controversy as justification for the murders.[80] Ultimately, the Israeli Cabinet voted to remove all security measures introduced at the Temple Mount after the 14 July attack.

The Palestinian Authority exacerbated the violence by calling for a "day of rage" in East Jerusalem and the West Bank in response to the metal detectors,[81] approving demonstrations organized by the Fatah affiliated Tanzim militia against the Israeli security measures,[82] and offering free university tuition to students participating in the subsequent rioting.[83] PA incitement against Israel stretches back to its establishment, when it assumed responsibility for the Palestine Mujahidin and Martyrs Fund, renamed the Palestinian Authority

Martyrs Fund, which pays stipends to families of Palestinians imprisoned, injured, or killed for terrorism against Israelis. In 2017, the fund paid terrorists and their families over $347 million, according to PA records.[84] In 2019, the PA increased its "pay to slay" program by some 11%, giving over $65 million to imprisoned terrorists and their families between January and May of that year.[85]

Islamism and Society

Israel's population numbers nearly 8.6 million people, of which 74.6 percent is Jewish[86] and 17.7 percent is Muslim.[87] Within this body politic, however, deep divisions exist over the future of the state. According to a 2015 study by the Pew Research Center, 76 percent of Israeli Jews believe that Israel can simultaneously be a Jewish state and a democracy, whereas only 27 percent of Israeli Arabs agree with this sentiment. However, 60 percent of Israeli Arabs have a positive view of the state and 49 percent of Israeli Muslims do.[88]

The tension between Israel and its Arab citizens is also evident in the traditionally nomadic Bedouin community. Official Israeli neglect of the Bedouin communities in the Negev and difficulty transitioning from a nomadic to a sedentary lifestyle has spawned increasing alienation from the state among that community—an alienation that the Northern Branch of the Islamic Movement is exploiting. Thus, when the military planned a parade through Rahat, Israel's largest Bedouin town, to celebrate Israel's 63rd Independence Day in 2011, the town's mayor, Faiz Abu Sahiban, who belongs to the Islamic Movement, objected, preferring to commemorate the 1948 exodus of the Palestinian refugees instead.[89] This came in the wake of violent resistance to the Israeli government demolishing a mosque built illegally on public land in 2010 by the Northern Branch of the Islamic Movement.[90]

Concerns that Bedouin alienation might breed violence increased when two Bedouin from the Negev, Mahmoud Abu Quider, aged 24, and his 21-year-old brother Samah, confessed in January 2013 to planning to fire rockets, mount a suicide bombing at the Beer Sheba Central Bus Station, and launch other attacks. Before their arrest, the brothers built several explosive devices and traded drugs for an

IDF soldier's rifle.[91] In another incident in 2015, Bedouin teachers from the South were suspected of promoting the ideology of the Islamic State in a local school.[92] The perpetrator of a deadly terrorist attack in Beer Sheba in October 2015 attended the same school.[93] Then, in December 2017, two Bedouin stabbed to death an Israeli soldier at an Arad bus stop.[94]

The Northern Branch is increasingly penetrating the Negev and successfully discouraging Bedouin from joining the IDF, where a high percentage of Bedouin have historically served, mainly in scouting or tracking capacities. Furthermore, as the Islamic Movement has gained control of more town councils in Bedouin areas, they have been able to use their authority to obstruct the hiring of Bedouin who serve in the military.[95] There has been a public debate over whether young Arab Israelis should be perform mandatory military or national service. In this case, opinions are significantly divided between Jewish and Arab respondents; the majority of the Jews polled support this requirement (74.1 percent) while the majority of Arabs oppose it (71.8 percent).[96]

Despite the growth of the Islamic Movement, the Israeli Muslim community remains less religious than the Palestinians of the West Bank and Gaza. According to a 2016 Pew survey, 68 percent of Israeli Muslims say religion is very important in their lives, while the corresponding number among Palestinians is 85 percent.[97] Likewise, support for terrorism is much lower among Israeli Muslims. A 2014 Pew Research Center poll found that while 46 percent of Palestinians in the West Bank and Gaza believe suicide bombings can be justified to defend Islam "often" or "sometimes," only 16 percent of Israeli Muslims feel that way.[98] In 2018, a poll showed that the percentage of Palestinians who support "armed resistance" against Israel was 35%, up from 30% the preceding year.[99]

Islamism and the State

Israel has struggled with Islamism and Islamist sentiment both internally and externally. Officially, Israel sees the political-legal status of Israeli Arabs as a purely domestic matter without strategic implications. At the same time, however, it has traditionally refused to recognize Israeli Arabs as a national minority possessing collective rights apart from specific cases (such as in the education system and family law, each religious community being subject to its own clerics). This opening in the education system has enabled Israeli Arabs to cultivate a separate national identity—and created an ideological space in which Islamism can increasingly take root.

The country's Education Ministry has attempted to counter Islamism by banning the teaching of the *Nakba* ("catastrophe," the common Arabic reference for the establishment of Israel in 1948) in schools, by forcing students to sing *Hatikva* (the Israeli national anthem) and by rewarding schools that encourage military and national service. Many Israeli Arab leaders have voiced opposition to the campaign to promote Israeli Arab participation in national service, terming it a veiled attempt by the government to erode the community's sense of unity.[100]

Externally, Israel's national security was deeply and negatively impacted by the Arab Spring of 2011. First and foremost, the overthrow of the Mubarak regime in Egypt in February 2011 undermined law and order in the Sinai Peninsula, enabling al-Qaeda to develop a base there. As of May 2011, senior Egyptian security officials estimated that over 400 al-Qaeda militants were operating in the Sinai Peninsula.[101] The growing Islamist presence in the Sinai resulted in increasing terrorism originating from the territory. In August 2011, eight Israelis were killed in a cross-border attack by militants belonging to the Mujahideen Shura Council from the Environs of Jerusalem, an al-Qaeda affiliate founded in 2011 and operational in Gaza and Sinai. The Mujahideen Shura Council launched rocket attacks on Sderot in August 2012[102] and March 2013, during President Obama's visit to Israel,[103] as well as to Eilat in April 2013.[104] However, today, the main threat to Israel from its southern border emanates from the Sinai.

From the end of the Mubarak regime until June 2012, there was a significant increase in the number of attacks against the gas pipelines in the region and terrorist infiltration to Israel.[105] Salafi-*jihadists* see the pipelines as an instance of an Islamic resource sold to the Zionist enemy.[106]

Smuggling is another issue of concern to the Israeli security forces. Israel's withdrawal from the Gaza Strip significantly increased the smuggling of weapons, food and fuel to Gaza.[107] This was much intensified after Hamas takeover of Gaza in 2007.[108] Alongside the smuggling, the organization created an extensive network of tunnels contributing to the Gazan economy $230 million per month.[109] During 2014's Operation Protective Edge, one of Israel's goals was to terminate cross border tunnels, which were widely used for smuggling arms and people. The IDF destroyed of 32 tunnels. Unfortunately, Israel has not yet fully succeeded in developing technology to deal with the tunnels.[110] IDF officials and residents living near the Gazan border have expressed worry that Hamas is reconstructing its tunnels demolished in 2014.[111] The Israeli-Egyptian border (around 230 kilometers in length) is also characterized by extensive smuggling of people, drugs, weapons, and goods. After the Israeli disengagement, the Israeli-Egyptian border has also become a transit point of two types of terrorists: specialists in the manufacture of weapons and terrorists on their way to attack Israel.[112]

There are today several looming threats to Israel's security. The first is a more powerful Hezbollah, which gained valuable battlefield experience in Syria and may entrench itself on the Syrian-Israeli border after the Assad regime regains control of the area. The second is the deteriorating economic situation in Gaza, where more than 60% of the population is dependent on humanitarian aid,[113] increases the likelihood of another war between Israel and Hamas, which desperately wants to break the naval blockade of the Strip. The recent Hamas-orchestrated demonstrations along the Gaza-Israel border wall, which resulted in notable Palestinian fatalities, also risked igniting another war.[114] Lastly, Israel must confront greater radicalization of its Arab citizens, particularly the Bedouin, long the country's poorest group by several orders of magnitude.[115]

Endnotes

1. Anat Kurz and Nahman Tal, "Hamas: Radical Islam in a National Struggle," Tel Aviv University Jaffee Center for Strategic Studies *Memorandum* no. 48, July 1997.

2. Andrew Higgins, "How Israel Helped to Spawn Hamas," *Wall Street Journal*, January 24, 2009, http://online.wsj.com/article/SB123275572295011847.html.
3. Khaled Mash'al, "We Will Not Relinquish an Inch of Palestine, from the River to the Sea," speech, *Al-Aqsa TV*, December 7, 2012, https://www.memri.org/tv/hamas-leader-khaled-mashal-we-will-not-relinquish-inch-palestine-river-sea/transcript.
4. Efraim Benmelech and Claude Berrebi, "Human Capital and the Productivity of Suicide Bombers," *Journal of Economic Perspectives* 21, no. 3, Summer 2007, 227.
5. Rachel Brandenburg, "Iran and the Palestinians," United States Institute of Peace *Iran Primer*, 2010, http://iranprimer.usip.org/resource/iran-and-palestinians.
6. Intelligence and Terrorism Information Center at the Israel Intelligence Heritage & Commemoration Center (IICC), "Iranian Support of Hamas," January 12, 2008, http://www.terrorism-info.org.il/data/pdf/PDF_09_019_2.pdf.
7. Ibid.
8. Matthew Levitt, "Iran's Support for Terrorism Under the JCPOA," Washington Institute *Policywatch* 2648, July 8, 2016, http://www.washingtoninstitute.org/policy-analysis/view/irans-support-for-terrorism-under-the-jcpoa.
9. Harriet Sherwood, "Hamas and Iran Rebuild Ties Three Years After Falling out over Syria," *Guardian* (London), January 9, 2014, https://www.theguardian.com/world/2014/jan/09/hamas-iran-rebuild-ties-fa....
10. Brandenburg, "Iran and the Palestinians."
11. Levitt, "Iran's Support for Terrorism Under the JCPOA."
12. *"Dawa" – Hamas' Civilian Infrastructure and its Role in Terror Financing*, Israeli Security Agency, n.d., https://www.shabak.gov.il/SiteCollectionImages/english/TerrorInfo/dawa-en.pdf
13. "Israeli Arab Gets 5 Years for Hamas Plot," UPI, May 11, 2011, http://www.upi.com/Top_News/World-News/2011/05/11/Israeli-Arab-gets-5-ye....
14. Ibid.
15. "Hamas in 2017: The Document in Full," *Middle East Eye*, May 1, 2017, http://www.middleeasteye.net/news/hamas-charter-1637794876.
16. Hillel Frisch, "Israel and Its Arab Citizens," in Raphael Cohen-Almagor, ed., *Israeli Democracy at the Crossroads* (Routledge, 2005), 216.

17. Jonathan Lis, "Salah Calls for 'Intifada' against Temple Mount Excavation," *Ha'aretz* (Tel Aviv), February 16, 2007, https://www.haaretz.com/news/salah-calls-for-intifada-against-temple-mou....
18. Ariel Ben Solomon, "Israel's Islamic Movement: Overcoming Obstacles," *Jerusalem Post,* May 15, 2016, http://www.jpost.com/Arab-Israeli-Conflict/Israels-Islamic-Movement-Overcoming-obstacles-453861.
19. Gili Cohen and Almog Ben Zikri, "Shin Bet: Two Israelis Plotted Attack Against Soldiers," *Ha'aretz* (Tel Aviv), December 27, 2016, https://www.haaretz.com/israel-news/.premium-1.761709.
20. Yael Freidson, "7 people, 2 associations convicted of affiliation with terrorist group," *Yediot Ahronot* (Tel Aviv), February 2, 2018, https://www.ynetnews.com/articles/0,7340,L-5079803,00.html.
21. Monte Palmer and Princess Palmer, *Islamic Extremism: Causes, Diversity, and Challenges* (Rowman & Littlefield, 2008), 142.
22. [22] Holly Fletcher, "Palestinian Islamic Jihad," Council on Foreign Relations, April 10, 2008, http://www.cfr.org/israel/palestinian-islamic-jihad/p15984.
23. Ibid.
24. U.S. Department of State, *Country Reports on Terrorism 2013*, April 30, 2014, https://2009-2017.state.gov/j/ct/rls/crt/2013/224829.htm.
25. Susan Aschoff, "Jihad Leader Emerged from Shadows of USF," *St. Petersburg Times*, February 21, 2003, https://www.meforum.org/campus-watch/8287/jihad-leader-emerged-from-shadows-of-usf.
26. "Former Longtime Palestinian Islamic Jihad Leader Dies," Associated Press, June 6, 2020, https://apnews.com/ed29c16b3189ecd81ebb52605d61f05a.
27. "Palestinian Islamic Jihad Agitates for Violence in the Gaza Strip," The Begin-Sadat Center for Strategic Studies, November 6, 2019, https://besacenter.org/perspectives-papers/palestinian-islamic-jihad-violence-gaza-strip/.
28. "Palestinian Islamic Jihad," The Counter Extremism Project, 2017, https://www.counterextremism.com/threat/palestinian-islamic-jihad#overview.
29. The Meir Amit Intelligence and Terrorism Information Center, "The Palestinian Islamic Jihad," n.d., https://www.terrorism-info.org.il/en/c/the-palestinian-islamic-jihad/.
30. Efraim Benmelech and Claude Berrebi, "Human Capital and the Productivity of Suicide Bombers," 227.
31. Raymond Ibrahim, Jonathan Schanzer, David Barnett, and Grant

Rumley, "Palestinian Territories," *World Almanac of Islamism 2017*, http://almanac.afpc.org/palestinian-territories.

32. Fletcher, *Palestinian Islamic Jihad*.
33. Hazem Balousha, "Islamic Jihad May Respond If Israel Enters Syria War," *Al-Monitor*, September 2, 2013, http://www.al-monitor.com/pulse/originals/2013/09/islamic-jihad-syria-us-strike.html.
34. Joshua Levitt, "Expert: Hamas Received $2 Billion from Iran; Islamic Jihad Gets $150 Million Annually," *Algemeiner*, February 11, 2014, http://www.algemeiner.com/2014/02/11/expert-hamas-received-2-billion-from-iran-islamic-jihad-gets-150-million-annually/.
35. Brandenburg, "Iran and the Palestinians."
36. Hazem Balousha, "Islamic Jihad's Coffers Run Dry," *Al-Monitor*, June 2, 2015, http://www.al-monitor.com/pulse/originals/2015/06/palestine-islamic-jihad-financial-crisis-money-iran-hezbolla.html.
37. "Iran cuts 90% of support for Palestinian Islamic Jihad," *Middle East Monitor*, January 11, 2016, https://www.middleeastmonitor.com/20160111-iran-cuts-90-of-support-for-palestinian-islamic-jihad/.
38. Elior Levy, "Iran's $100 million aid to Hamas and Islamic Jihad," *Yediot Ahronot* (Tel Aviv), August 3, 2018, https://www.ynetnews.com/articles/0,7340,L-5321985,00.html.
39. Matthew Levitt, "Hezbollah Finances: Funding the Party of God," The Washington Institute, February 2005, http://www.washingtoninstitute.org/policy-analysis/view/hezbollah-finances-funding-the-party-of-god.
40. Matthew Levitt, "Hezbollah Finances: Funding the Party of God," The Washington Institute, February 2005, http://www.washingtoninstitute.org/policy-analysis/view/hezbollah-finances-funding-the-party-of-god.
41. "The Hizballah Program - An Open Letter," *The Jerusalem Quarterly*, January 1, 1988, https://www.ict.org.il/Article.aspx?ID=294#gsc.tab=0.
42. Jonathan Masters and Zachary Laub, "Hezbollah," Council on Foreign Relations, January 3, 2014, https://www.cfr.org/backgrounder/hezbollah.
43. Briefing by Lt. Colonel (res.) Sarit Zehavi, CEO of the Alma Research and Education Center, July 22, 2020.
44. Levitt, "Hezbollah Finances: Funding the Party of God."
45. Robert F. Worth, "Hezbollah's Rise Amid Chaos," *New York Times*, January 15, 2011, https://www.nytimes.com/2011/01/16/weekinreview/16worth.html.

46. Israel Ministry of Foreign Affairs, "Iranian efforts to recruit extensive network of agents uncovered," July 24, 2019, https://mfa.gov.il/MFA/ForeignPolicy/Terrorism/Pages/Iranian-efforts-to-recruit-extensive-network-of-agents-uncovered-24-July-2019.aspx
47. Research and Information Center, "Terrorist Organizations fighting Israel," July 2004, https://www.knesset.gov.il/mmm/data/pdf/m01057.pdf. (in Hebrew)
48. Israel Ministry of Foreign Affairs, "Iranian efforts to recruit extensive network of agents uncovered."
49. "Hezbollah Archives," *Terrorism Archives*, n.d., http://www.terrorism-info.org.il/en/Hezbollah.
50. Matthew Levitt, "Hezbollah," *The World Almanac of Islamism 2017*, http://almanac.afpc.org/Hezbollah.
51. Levitt, "Hezbollah Finances: Funding the Party of God."
52. "2006: Lebanon war," *BBC News,* May 6, 2008, http://news.bbc.co.uk/2/hi/middle_east/7381389.stm.
53. Dov Leiber and Alexander Fulbright, "Hezbollah Chief Threatens Israel's Dimona Nuclear Reactor," *Times of Israel*, February 16, 2017, http://www.timesofisrael.com/hezbollah-chief-threatens-israels-dimona-nuclear-reactor/.
54. "2006: Lebanon war," *BBC News*.
55. "Hezbollah Archives," *Terrorism Archives*.
56. Leiber and Fulbright, "Hezbollah Chief Threatens Israel's Dimona Nuclear Reactor."
57. "IDF: Clandestine Hezbollah unit operating on Golan," *Israel Hayom*, March 13, 2019, https://www.israelhayom.com/2019/03/13/clandestine-hezbollah-unit-operating-on-golan-idf-reveals.
58. Yaakov Lappin, "Israeli Military Chief Outlines Hizbullah's Syria Commitment," *IHS Janes*, January 4, 2018, https://ausa.inloop.com/en/article/108610/israeli-military-chief-outlines-hizbullahs-syria-commitment.
59. "Outgoing IDF chief: Israel has struck 'thousands' of Iranian targets in Syria," *Times of Israel,* January 12, 2019. Accessed August 5, 2020. https://www.timesofisrael.com/outgoing-idf-chief-israel-struck-thousands-of-iranian-targets-in-syria/
60. Jonathan Schanzer, "The New Rocket Threat to Israel," *Commentary*, January 2020, August 5, 2020, https://www.commentarymagazine.com/articles/jonathan-schanzer/the-new-rocket-threat-to-israel/
61. Matthew Levitt, "Zawahiri Aims at Israel," *Foreign Affairs*, February 3, 2014, https://www.foreignaffairs.com/articles/israel/2014-02-03/zawahiri-aims-israel.

62. Ibid.
63. Ibidem.
64. Eli Ashkenazi, "Israeli Arabs 'Inspired by Global Jihad' Charged with Taxi Driver Murder," *Ha'aretz* (Tel Aviv), June 28, 2010, https://www.haaretz.com/israel-news/israeli-arabs-inspired-by-global-jih....
65. "Shin Bet Arrests Eight Israeli Arabs for Illicit Arms Trading," *Ha'aretz* (Tel Aviv), July 15, 2010, https://www.haaretz.com/israel-news/shin-bet-arrests-eight-israeli-arabs....
66. Levitt, "Zawahiri Aims at Israel."
67. Hassan Hassan, "The True Origins of ISIS," *The Atlantic*, November 30, 2018, https://www.theatlantic.com/ideas/archive/2018/11/isis-origins-anbari-zarqawi/577030/.
68. "Less Than 5 Percent of Syria Under ISIS Control, Russia Says," *Ha'aretz* (Tel Aviv), October 24, 2017, https://www.haaretz.com/middle-east-news/syria/less-than-5-percent-of-syria-under-isis-control-russia-says-1.5459980.
69. Eitan Azani, Jonathan Fighel, and Lorena Atiyas Lvovsky, "The Islamic State's Threat to Israel: Challenges and Coping Mechanisms," The International Institute for Counter-Terrorism (ICT), February 17, 2016, https://www.ict.org.il/Article/1612/The-Islamic-States-Threat-to-Israel
70. Borzou Daragahi, "Sinai Jihadi Group Emerges at Forefront of Egypt Violence," *Financial Times*, January 31, 2014. http://www.ft.com/cms/s/0/b5ad40d0-8a7b-11e3-9c29-00144feab7de.html#axzz3RfJCfft2
71. Taylor Luck, "Why Sinai mosque attack is seen as a major ISIS miscalculation," *Christian Science Monitor*, November 27, 2017, https://www.csmonitor.com/World/Middle-East/2017/1127/Why-Sinai-mosque-attack-is-seen-as-a-major-ISIS-miscalculation.
72. "ISIS: Portrait of a Jihadi Terrorist Organization," The Meir Amit Intelligence and Terrorism Information Center (ITIC), November 2014, https://www.terrorism-info.org.il/en/20733/.
73. "A History of Terrorism in Egypt's Sinai," Middle East Institute, n.d., http://www.mei.edu/sinai-terrorism.
74. Anna Ahronheim, "19 Israelis to have citizenship revoked for fighting with ISIS," *Jerusalem Post*, August 22, 2017, http://www.jpost.com/Arab-Israeli-Conflict/19-Israelis-to-have-citizenship-revoked-for-fighting-with-ISIS-503145.
75. Siryoti, Daniel, Lilach Shoval et al., "2 Israeli Arabs indicted for allegedly planning ISIS-inspired terrorist attack," *Israel Hayom*,

https://www.israelhayom.com/2019/08/22/2-israeli-arabs-indicted-for-allegedly-planning-isis-inspired-terrorist-attack/

76. "Israeli Arab doctor killed fighting for ISIS: Shin Bet," *Al-Arabiya*, October 20, 2014, https://english.alarabiya.net/en/News/middle-east/2014/10/20/Israeli-Arab-doctor-killed-fighting-for-ISIS-Shin-Bet.html
77. Ruth Eglash and Griff Witte, "Clashes in East Jerusalem After Teen's Burial Revive Intifada Fears for Middle East," *Washington Post*, July 5, 2014, https://www.washingtonpost.com/world/2014/07/05/a9f5c538-d2a8-463d-b5cb-ec5f4fa0ab37_story.html?utm_term=.ed34ce5d8249.
78. Nir Hasson, ""Firecrackers: The Newest Popular Weapon, and the Newest Threat, in Jerusalem," *Ha'aretz* (Tel Aviv). November 4, 2014, https://www.haaretz.com/israel-news/.premium-1.624446.
79. Daniel K. Eisenbud and Lahav Harkov, "Minister of Public Security Blasts Barkat for Blaming Ministry for 'Silent Intifada,'" *Jerusalem Post*, October 5, 2014, http://www.jpost.com/Israel-News/Minister-of-Public-Security-blasts-Barkat-for-blaming-ministry-for-silent-intifada-378102.
80. Rotem Elizera, Yoav Zitun, Shahar Hay, and Elior Levy, "Deadly Halamish Attack Hits Family Celebrating Grandson's Birth," *Yediot Ahronot* (Tel Aviv), July 22, 2017, https://www.ynetnews.com/articles/0,7340,L-4992716,00.html.
81. "Abbas' Fatah party calls for 'day of rage' following Temple Mount clashes," Jewish Telegraphic Agency, July 18, 2017, https://www.jta.org/2017/07/18/news-opinion/israel-middle-east/abbas-fatah-party-calls-for-day-of-rage-following-temple-mount-clashes.
82. Avi Issacharoff, "Mobilizing militia, Abbas approves mass protests Friday over Temple Mount," *Times of Israel*, July 26, 2017, http://www.timesofisrael.com/mobilizing-militia-abbas-orders-mass-protests-friday-over-temple-mount/.
83. David Rosenberg, "Report: Mahmoud Abbas funding Jerusalem riots," *Israel National News,* July 30, 2017, http://www.israelnationalnews.com/News/News.aspx/233175.
84. Lahav Harkov, "Palestinian Authority paid terrorists nearly $350 million in 2017," *Jerusalem Post*, January 9, 2018, http://www.jpost.com/Arab-Israeli-Conflict/Palestinian-Authority-paid-terrorists-nearly-350-million-in-2017-533227.
85. Maayan Joffe-Hoffman, "PA Doubles Pay-For-Slay Salary to Murderer of 3 Israeli Teenagers," *Jerusalem Post,* July 11, 2019, https://www.jpost.com/Arab-Israeli-Conflict/PA-ups-pay-for-slay-salary-

to-murderer-of-3-Israeli-teenagers-in-2014-595302; Yonah Jeremy Bob, "Shin Bet Chief Argaman: We Thwarted 560 Terror Attacks This Year," *Jerusalem Post*, January 20, 2020, https://www.jpost.com/Israel-News/Shin-Bet-chief-Argaman-We-thwarted-560-terror-attacks-this-year-614723.

86. Lidar Gravé-Lazi, "Ahead of Jewish New Year, Israel's Population Stands at 8.585 Million," *Jerusalem Post*, September 27, 2016, http://www.jpost.com/Israel-News/Ahead-of-Jewish-New-Year-Israels-population-stands-at-8585-million-468809.
87. Ahiya Raved, "Central Bureau of Statistics Reports Muslim Growth Rate Still Highest in Israel," *Yediot Ahronot* (Tel Aviv), August 30, 2017, https://www.ynetnews.com/articles/0,7340,L-5009798,00.html.
88. Ben Lynfield, "Survey: 60% of Arab Israelis Have Positive View of State," *Jerusalem Post*, September 27, 2017, http://www.jpost.com/Israel-News/Survey-60-percent-of-Arab-Israelis-have...
89. Ilana Curiel, "Rahat objects to IDF Independence Day exhibit," *Yediot Ahronot* (Tel Aviv), May 9, 2011, http://www.ynetnews.com/articles/0,7340,L-4066563,00.html.
90. Yaakov Lappin, "Israel Lands Authority Demolishes Illegal Rahat Mosque," *Jerusalem Post*, November 7, 2010, https://www.jpost.com/Israel/Israel-Lands-Authority-demolishes-illegal-Rahat-mosque.
91. Yoav Zitun, "2 Bedouins Confess to Plotting Terror Attacks," *Yediot Ahronot* (Tel Aviv), January 20, 2013, http://www.ynetnews.com/articles/0,7340,L-4334793,00.html.
92. "Promoting the 'Islamic State' ideology in the educational system," Knesset Committee on Education, Culture and Sport, November 10, 2015, http://main.knesset.gov.il/Activity/committees/Education/Conclusion/161115.pdf#search=%D7%91%D7%93%D7%95%D7%90%D7%99%D7%9D.
93. Ibid.
94. Judah Ari Gross, "2 Bedouin Israelis suspected of killing soldier in terror attack," *Times of Israel*, December 4, 2017, https://www.timesofisrael.com/2-bedouin-israelis-suspected-of-killing-soldier-in-terror-attack/.
95. Donna Rosenthal, *The Israelis: Ordinary People in an Extraordinary Land*, 2nd ed. (Free Press, 2008), 300.
96. Tamar Hermann, Chanan Cohen, Ella Heller, and Dana Bublil, *The Israeli Democracy Index 2015* (Israel Democracy Institute, 2016), http://en.idi.org.il/analysis/idi-press/publications/english-books/

the-israeli-democracy-index-2015/.
97. Pew Research Center, "Israel's Religiously Divided Society," March 8, 2016, http://www.pewforum.org/2016/03/08/israels-religiously-divided-society/.
98. Frida Ghitis, "A Spark of Good News from the Middle East," *CNN*, July 10 2014, https://www.almendron.com/tribuna/a-spark-of-good-news-from-the-mideast/.
99. Khaled Abu Toameh, "Palestinians becoming more extreme in their positions – poll," *Times of Israel*, February 25, 2018, https://www.timesofisrael.com/palestinians-becoming-more-extreme-in-their-positions-poll/
100. Gil Shefler, "Israeli Arab Volunteers Rising," *JTA*, August 27, 2009, http://www.jta.org/news/article/2009/08/27/1007492/israeli-arab-voluntee....
101. Ilan Berman, "Al-Qaeda's Newest Outpost," *Forbes*, December 29, 2011, http://www.forbes.com/sites/ilanberman/2011/12/29/al-qaedas-newest-outpost/.
102. Elad Benari, "Salafi Terrorists: Jihad Against Criminal Jews is a Duty," *Israel National News*, August 27, 2012, http://www.israelnationalnews.com/News/News.aspx/159309.
103. Yaakov Lappin, "IDF Decreases Gazan Fishing Zone after Rockets," *Jerusalem Post*, March 21, 2013, https://www.jpost.com/Breaking-News/IDF-decreases-Gazan-fishing-zone-in-response-to-rockets-307339.
104. Aaron Kalman, "Gazan Salafist Vows to Keep Attacking Israel," *Times of Israel*, April 18, 2013, http://www.timesofisrael.com/gazan-salafist-vows-to-keep-attacking-israel/.
105. Holly Cramer, Tim Harper, Samantha Moog, and Eric Spioch, *A History of Terrorism in Egypt's Sinai*, Middle East Institute, n.d., http://www.mei.edu/sinai-terrorism.
106. Zach Gold, *Security in the Sinai: Present and Future*, International Center for Counter-Terrorism, March 2014, http://www.icct.nl/download/file/ICCT-Gold-Security-In-The-Sinai-March-2014.pdf.
107. Zack Gold, *Sinai Security: Opportunities for Unlikely Cooperation Among Egypt, Israel, and Hamas*, Saban Center for Middle East Policy at Brookings *Analysis Paper* no. 30, October 2013, https://www.brookings.edu/wp-content/uploads/2016/06/22-sinai-hamas-egypt-israel-gold.pdf.
108. Cramer, Harper, Moog, and Spioch, *A History of Terrorism in Egypt's Sinai.*
109. Zachary Laub, *Security in Egypt's Sinai Peninsula*, Council of

Foreign Relations, December 11, 2013, http://www.cfr.org/egypt/egypts-sinai-peninsula-security/p32055.

110. Efraim Inbar, "The Gaza Tunnels Get Too Much Attention," BESA Center *Perspectives Paper* no. 369, October 6, 2016, https://besa-center.org/wp-content/uploads/2016/10/Inbar-Efraim-Gaza-Tunnels-Get-Too-Much-Attention-PP-369-6-Oct-2016a.pdf.
111. "Netanyahu Threatens to Eclipse 2014 War to Destroy Gaza Tunnels," *Times of Israel*, January 31, 2016, http://www.timesofisrael.com/netanyahu-threatens-to-eclipse-2014-war-to-destroy-gaza-tunnels/.
112. "Smuggling through Israel-Egypt border," The Knesset Research and Information Center, 2006, https://www.knesset.gov.il/mmm/data/pdf/m01667.pdf (in Hebrew).
113. Beverly Milton-Edwards, "Gaza protests highlight humanitarian crisis and lack of political progress to peace," Brookings Institution, April 5, 2018, https://www.brookings.edu/opinions/gaza-protests-highlight-humanitarian-crisis-and-lack-of-political-progress-to-peace/.
114. Hazem Balousha and Peter Beaumont, "Palestinian death toll mounts as thousands protest on Gaza border," *Guardian* (London), April 6, 2018, https://www.theguardian.com/world/2018/apr/06/israel-warned-un-protesters-head-for-gaza-demonstrations.
115. Meirav Arlosoroff, "Settling the Bedouin Question," *Ha'aretz* (Tel Aviv), December 27, 2012, https://www.haaretz.com/.premium-meirav-arlosoroff-bitter-lives-of-the-bedouin-1.5282742

13 Iran

Quick Facts

Population: 84,923,314 (July 2020 est.)
Area: 1,648,195 sq km
Ethnic Groups: Persian, Azeri, Kurd, Lur, Baloch, Arab, Turkmen and Turkic tribes
Religions: Muslim (official) 99.4% (Shia 90-95%, Sunni 5-10%), other (includes Zoroastrian, Jewish, and Christian) 0.3%, unspecified 0.4% (2011 est.)
Government Type: Theocratic Republic
GDP (official exchange rate): $430.7 billion (2017 est.)

Quick Facts Courtesy of the CIA World Factbook (Last Updated June 2020)

Introduction

Since its founding in February of 1979, the Islamic Republic of Iran has consistently ranked as the world's most active state sponsor of terrorism, according to the estimates of the United States government. Iran's support for terrorism is both pervasive and ideological, encompassing a vast array of official and quasi-official institutions, individuals and policies. It finds its roots in the ideas of the Ayatollah Ruhollah Khomeini, the founder of the Islamic Revolution, who espoused the need to "export" Iran's successful religious model the world over. More than four three decades after Khomeini's death, that priority continues to animate Iran's leaders and guide their sponsorship of instability, both in Iran's immediate geographic neighborhood and far beyond.

Today, Iran's capabilities to do so have expanded significantly. In the decade between 2003 and 2013, the Iranian regime's persistent pursuit of a nuclear capability engendered escalating pressure from the United States and international community in the form of economic sanctions and diplomatic isolation. Over time, these measures took their toll, progressively isolating the Islamic Republic and severely impacting its economic fortunes. However, the successful conclusion of a nuclear deal between Iran and the P5+1 powers in July of 2015 fundamentally altered this dynamic, providing the Islamic Republic *with massive economic relief, totaling upward of $100 billion,*[1] *and laying the groundwork for a surge in post-sanctions trade with a range of international partners. The Iranian regime, in turn, used this dividend to strengthen its strategic capabilities; in the wake of the JCPOA's passage the Islamic Republic significantly increased its defense budget, with the country's defense expenditures rising from 4.3 percent of GDP ($19.5 billion) in 2015 to 6.1 percent of GDP ($27.3 billion) in 2018.*[2] *The fruits of the JCPOA also served to greatly expand the resources available to the Islamic Republic to support terror proxies in the region and beyond, and breathed new life into Tehran's longstanding efforts to reshape the global order in its own image.*

The advent of the Trump administration ushered in a new, more robust U.S. approach toward Iran. Following its withdrawal, in May 2018, from the 2015 Iran nuclear deal, the Trump administration has reimposed a range of primary and secondary sanctions on the Iranian regime. This "maximum pressure" campaign has had a pronounced effect on Iran's economic fortunes, precipitating an exodus of international commerce from the Islamic Republic and causing a massive devaluation of Iran's national currency, the rial.[3] *The advent, in early 2020, of the coronavirus pandemic has had a further deleterious effect on the Iranian economy, and on political stability within the Islamic Republic.*[4] *As of yet, however, these factors have not caused a significant, sustained change in Iran's regional behavior, its nuclear ambitions, or its persistent sponsorship of terrorism, both in its immediate neighborhood and more globally.*

Islamist Activity

The Iranian regime's support for international terrorism predates the establishment of the Islamic Republic itself. In the 1960s and 1970s, while in exile in Iraq and in France, the Ayatollah Ruhollah Khomeini formulated his ideas about the need for a radical Islamic transformation in his home country, Iran, and of subsequently "exporting" this system of government throughout the Middle East and beyond.[5] In keeping with this thinking, Khomeini's political manifesto, *Islamic Government*, extolled the virtues of "a victorious and triumphant Islamic political revolution" that would go on "to unite the Moslem nation, [and] to liberate [all] its lands."[6]

When the Ayatollah and his followers subsequently swept to power in Tehran in the spring of 1979, this principle became a cardinal regime priority. The preamble of the country's formative constitution, adopted in October 1979, outlines that the country's military would henceforth "be responsible not only for guarding and preserving the frontiers of the country, but also for fulfilling the ideological mission of *jihad* in God's way; that is, extending the sovereignty of God's law throughout the world."[7] These words were backed by concrete regime action, with Khomeini consolidating the country's various radical religious militias into an ideological army known as the Islamic Revolutionary Guard Corps (IRGC, or Pasdaran), tasked with promoting his revolutionary message abroad, with violence if necessary.

The four-plus decades since have seen a consistent regime commitment to international terrorism. In the early years of the Islamic Republic, Iran is known to have ordered, orchestrated or facilitated a series of terrorist attacks in the Middle East, among them the 1983 U.S. Embassy and Marine Barracks bombings in Beirut, Lebanon, as well as abortive coup attempts and bombings in Bahrain, the United Arab Emirates and Kuwait.[8] These activities, and the rationale behind them, were reinforced by the outcome of the country's bloody eight-year war with Iraq, which strengthened the Iranian government's belief that radical proxies could serve as an attractive, low-cost substitute for direct military action. As a result, the principle of "exporting the revolution" remained a vibrant element of regime policy after the death of Khomeini in 1989. In the decade that followed, the Islamic Republic continued to bankroll assassinations and terrorist acts on foreign soil, aided the infiltration of countries in Europe, Africa and Latin America by radical Islamic groups, and assisted irregulars in various international conflict zones.[9]

In the aftermath of the September 11, 2001 terrorist attacks, the Islamic Republic chose to dramatically strengthen its links to international terrorism, redoubling its support for Lebanon's Hezbollah militia and Palestinian rejectionist groups, expanding its footprint in the Palestinian territories, maintaining at least low-level links to the al-Qaeda network, and becoming heavily involved in the bankrolling of radical Shiite militias and activities aimed at hindering the U.S.-led Coalition in post-Saddam Iraq.

This support for terrorism, while ideologically driven, was and remains rooted in pragmatism. While Khomeini's Islamic Revolution was a distinctly Shi'a one, in the forty-one years since its establishment, the Islamic Republic has embraced a more universalist conception of its international role, aspiring to serve as the vanguard of Islamic revolution worldwide.[10] The Iranian regime today funds a broad range of both Sunni and Shi'a groups throughout the greater Middle East and beyond. The critical determinant appears to be the degree to which these movements and organizations can reinforce Iran's leading role in the "Shi'a revival" taking place in the Muslim world, and their shared animosity toward the West, most directly Israel and the United States.

The scope of Iran's support of violent Islamism is global in nature, and so is its reach. In the decade that followed the 9/11 attacks, it encompassed: ongoing support for Hezbollah in Lebanon and a reconstitution of the Shiite militia's strategic capabilities;[11] extensive involvement in post-Saddam Iraq, first through the provision of arms and materiel to the country's various Shi'a militias and later through political and strategic support of various forces both inside and outside of the government of Iraqi Prime Minister Nouri al-Maliki;[12] the provision of significant military and operational assistance to the insurgency in Afghanistan, increasing the lethality of forces arrayed against the government of President Hamid Karzai and Coalition authorities there;[13] exerting influence in the Palestinian arena through financial aid and support to Palestinian rejectionist groups, chief among them Hamas and the Palestinian Islamic Jihad[14] and; bankrolling terrorist and subversive activities in various countries, including Egypt.[15]

The onset of the Arab Spring in early 2011 marked a turning point for Iranian activities—and for its regional standing. In the early stages of the "Spring," Iranian officials sought to take credit for the anti-regime sentiment sweeping the region, depicting it as the belated product of the Ayatollah Khomeini's successful Islamic revolution in 1979 and heralding an "Islamic awakening" in which Iran would inevitably play a leading role.[16] Iran's stance was not simply rhetorical; the Islamic Republic became a political supporter of various regional insurgent causes, from protests by Bahrain's majority-Shiite population against the country's ruling al-Khalifa family[17] to the successful struggle by Yemen's al-Houthi rebellion against the central government in Sana'a.[18]

Iran's most conspicuous initiative, however, was to assume the role of a lifeline for the regime of Syrian dictator Bashar al-Assad. Shortly after the eruption of anti-regime unrest in Syria in March 2011, Iran took on a major role in bolstering and strengthening Assad's hold on power. It did so through extensive financial assistance, as well as the provision of forces to augment Syria's military in its fight against the country's disparate opposition elements. Over time, this effort led to the creation of what has been termed the "Shiite Liberation Army" (SLA), a cadre of as many as 200,000 Shi'a irregulars drawn from Afghanistan, Yemen, Pakistan, Iraq and elsewhere, trained and equipped by the IRGC, and deployed to foreign theaters.[19] Through this effort, Iranian-sponsored Shiite militants eclipsed the Sunni militancy in Iraq and Syria in both size and scope.; as of April 2018, the SLA's presence in the country was estimated at around 80,000[20], or twice the size of the foreign fighter contingent believed to have been mobilized up to that point by the Islamic State terrorist group.[21]

Iran's objectives in this effort are two-fold. Most immediately, Iran's aid is intended to shore up the stability of the Assad regime, its most important regional partner. More broadly, however, Iran sees its involvement in Syria as a direct blow against the "Great Satan," the United States. "Since Syria was and continues to be part of the Islamic resistance front and the Islamic Revolution, it provokes the anger of the Americans," IRGC commander Mohammad Ali Jafari explained on Iranian television in April of 2014.[22] That view has remained constant in the years since. Additionally, Iranian leaders view the Islamic State and its exclusionary, aggressive Sunni interpretation of the Islamic faith, as something approaching an existential threat to the Islamic Republic, and accordingly marshalled massive resources to eliminate the group.[23]

Broadly construed, Iran's regional efforts have been massively successful. The Iranian regime can now be said to control four regional capitals in the Middle East. The first is Damascus, where Iranian (as well as Russian) support has been instrumental to keeping the Assad regime in power. The second is Baghdad, where Iran continues to wield extensive influence among the country's political elites while simultaneously supporting an extensive network of powerful Shi'a militias, collectively known as the Hashd al-Shaabi. The third is Lebanon, where the group's principal terrorist proxy, Hezbollah, maintains a commanding grip on national politics. The fourth is Sana'a, Yemen, where since the spring of 2015, Iranian-supported rebels have succeeded in taking over the national government, precipitating a pitched civil war that – five years on – has created what is considered by many to be the world's worst humanitarian catastrophe.

The financial scope of these activities is enormous. In the past, U.S. officials have estimated that the Islamic Republic boasts "a nine-digit line item in its budget for support to terrorist organizations."[24] In the summer of 2015, in the aftermath of the conclusion of the JCPOA, the Congressional Research Service estimated that the Islamic Republic was spending between $3.5 billion and $16 billion annually on support for terrorism and insurgency worldwide.[25]

This funding remains pervasive. In August 2018, Brian Hook, the Trump administration's Special Representative for Iran, estimated that "Iran provides Lebanese Hezbollah about $700 million per year," and that the Iranian regime had spent "at least $16 billion on supporting its proxies in Syria, Iraq and Yemen" to that point.[26] Additionally, Hook stressed, "Iran has historically provided over $100 million per year to Palestinian groups, including Hamas and Palestinian Islamic Jihad."[27] Accordingly, Trump administration efforts are focused in large part on curtailing the funds available to the Iranian regime to engage in terror sponsorship—albeit without significant results so far.

Islamism and Society

While "exporting the revolution" was and remains a persistent regime objective, involvement and investment on the part of the Iranian population in this pursuit is far from universal. There is little empirical data to suggest that ordinary Iranians share the depth of their regime's commitment to the exportation of radical Islam. To the contrary, terrorism funding in Iran remains an elite—rather than popular—undertaking, directed through state institutions rather than non-governmental organizations, and overseen at an official, not a grassroots, level.

At times, Iran's involvement in the support of radical groups abroad has served as a significant bone of contention between the Iranian regime and its population. In the wake of Hezbollah's summer 2006 war with Israel, for example, Iran's extensive financial support for Lebanon's Shiites became a domestic flashpoint, with ordinary Iranians publicly questioning—and condemning—their government's skewed strategic priorities.[28] More recently, the Iranian regime's foreign adventurism – and its support for radical proxies – has emerged as prominent anti-regime narrative in the persistent protests that have taken place throughout the Islamic Republic since late 2017.

Support for radical Islamic causes is eroded by Iran's complex ethno/religious composition. Although the country is overwhelmingly (98 percent) Muslim and predominantly (89 percent) Shi'a, experts estimate that Iran's current population of more than eighty-five million is made up of some forty-two million Persians, an estimated twenty-seven million Azerbaijanis, and roughly eight million Kurds, five million Arabs, two million Turkmen, and one-and-a-half million Baluch.[29] Many of these minorities are systematically discriminated against by the Islamic Republic and feel little or limited allegiance to it. The base of support for Islamic radicalism—and other governmental priorities—in Iranian society is further weakened by the regime's persecution of religious minorities, which, according to the U.S. State Department, has created "a threatening atmosphere for nearly all non-Shi'a religious groups" in the Islamic Republic.[30]

Social and economic malaise has historically served to dilute identification with regime ideals and principles, something that was encapsulated in the mass uprising (colloquially known as the "Green Movement") that emerged in Iran in mid-2009. Back then, the protests were successfully quashed by the Iranian regime, but the underlying factors that propelled the uprising – including unemployment, poverty and widespread regime corruption – remain potent drivers of domestic politics. This has been evident since late 2017, which has seen Iran convulsed by persistent protests that have presented its leaders with the greatest challenge to their legitimacy since the 1979 Islamic Revolution. The initial period that followed the passage of the JCPOA in 2015 was greeted with considerable euphoria by ordinary Iranians, who were hopeful that the agreement would be accompanied by an economic "peace dividend" of sorts.[31] This, however, did not materialize, notwithstanding a surge in trade and investment into the Islamic Republic. The Iranian regime chose not to parlay the economic benefits of JCPOA-enabled trade into meaningful, sustained investments in infrastructure and prosperity within the Islamic Republic.

To the contrary, conditions within the Islamic Republic have continued to deteriorate. According to the World Bank, as of December 2019 unemployment within the country stood at 10.6 percent.[32] It is also endemic in nature, and in the past has been estimated to reach as high as 60 percent in some cities.[33] Youth unemployment is particularly widespread, measuring nearly 26 percent by the end of 2019,[34] with nearly half of all university graduates now unemployed.[35] Poverty within the Islamic Republic remains pervasive as well, with some 40 percent of the country's population classified as destitute even before the coronavirus hit.[36] Moreover, the Islamic Parliament Research Center (IPRC) recently estimated that between 2.8 million and 6.4 million people are expected to be added to the unemployment numbers as a result of the coronavirus pandemic and government policies surrounding it.[37]

Yet, rather than focus on the country's deleterious domestic conditions, Iran's leaders systematically prioritized guns over butter. In recent years, Iran has significantly expanded its foreign activism in places like Bahrain, Yemen and (most conspicuously) Syria, and done so at considerable cost to the regime. In 2018, for instance, the Islamic Republic's ongoing campaign in Syria was estimated to be costing the country between $15-$20 billion annually – roughly equivalent to Iran's total national healthcare budget of $16.3

billion.[38] In all, since the start of the Syrian civil war in 2011 it is now estimated that the Iranian regime has invested about $30 billion into preserving President Bashar al-Assad's regime.[39]

This combination of domestic neglect and foreign adventurism has generated a massive domestic backlash within Iran. Prominent among the slogans in the current cycle of protests within the Islamic Republic have been calls of "Leave Syria, think about us!" and "Death to Hezbollah!"[40] – chants that reflect a fundamental dissatisfaction with, and rejection of, the prevailing priorities of the Iranian regime.

Islamism and the State

Iran's support for Islamism is channeled through an elaborate infrastructure of institutions and governmental bodies tasked with the promotion of radical Islamic thought and action. These include:

The Islamic Revolutionary Guard Corps (IRGC, or Pasdaran)
At home, the IRGC, in addition to its professional military duties, has become the guardian of the regime's ballistic missile and weapons of mass destruction programs.[41] Founded at the start of the Islamic Revolution, the Guards were envisioned from the outset as the expeditionary arm of Khomeini's version of radical political Islam. The agenda of Iran's ideological army, however, is global in scope,[42] and so is its reach. Over the past four decades, the IRGC has emerged as the shock troops of Iran's Islamic Revolution, training terrorist organizations both within Iran and in specialized training camps in places like Lebanon and Sudan, as well as providing assistance to radical movements and terrorist proxies throughout the Middle East, Africa, Europe and Asia via specialized paramilitary units.[43] The most notorious of these is the Quds Force, a crack military battalion formed in 1990 and dedicated to carrying out "extra-regional operations of the Islamic Revolutionary Guard Corps"—namely, terrorism and insurgency in the name of the Islamic Republic.[44] The head of the Qods Force, until his death at the hands of the United States in January 2020, was Iran's most prominent military leader, Major-General Qassem Soleimani.

The IRGC also boasts a dedicated intelligence service, the Protection and Intelligence Department, or *H*efazat va Ettelaat-e Sepah-e Pasdaran. Founded in 1980, it encompasses three main functions: intelligence in support of IRGC military operations; political operations at home and abroad; and support to thc foreign terrorist operations of the Quds Force.[45]

The IRGC is far more than simply a military force, however. It also represents one of Iran's most powerful political and economic actors. IRGC-controlled and -affiliated entities now permeate every sector of the formal Iranian economy,[46] and are known to wield extensive influence over the country's gray- and black- market activities (including smuggling, illicit financial transfers and proliferation).

Ministry of Intelligence and Security (MOIS)

Controlled directly by Supreme Leader Ali Khamenei, the MOIS is used by Iran's ruling clergy to quash domestic opposition and carry out espionage against suspect members of the Iranian government.[47] Abroad, the MOIS plays a key role in planning and carrying out terrorist operations on foreign soil, using Iranian embassies and diplomatic missions as cover.[48] MOIS operatives are also known to operate abroad under unofficial identities—for example, as employees of Iran Air, Iran's official airline.[49] The MOIS conducts a variety of activities in support of the operations of Tehran's terrorist surrogates, ranging from financing actual operations to intelligence collection on potential targets. The Ministry also carries out independent operations, primarily against dissidents of the current regime in Tehran living in foreign countries, at the direction of senior Iranian officials.[50]

Ministry of Foreign Affairs

Iran's Foreign Ministry serves as an important enabler of the Iranian regime's international terrorist presence. Agents of the IRGC and MOIS often operate out of Iranian missions abroad, where they are stationed under diplomatic cover, complete with blanket diplomatic immunity. These agents—and through them Iranian foreign proxies—use the Ministry's auspices to untraceably obtain financing, weapons and intelligence from Tehran (for example, via diplomatic pouch).[51]

Cultural Affairs Ministry

Supplementing the role of the Foreign Affairs Ministry in exporting terrorism is Iran's Ministry of Culture and Guidance. Tasked with overseeing the cultural sections of Iranian foreign missions, as well as free-standing Iranian cultural centers, it facilitates IRGC infiltration of—and terrorist recruitment within—local Muslim populations in foreign nations.[52] The Ministry is particularly influential among majority Muslim countries like the former Soviet Republics, many of which share substantial cultural, religious and ideological bonds with Tehran. Between 1982 and 1992, the official in charge of the Ministry—and of its role in support of Iranian terror abroad—was Mohammed Khatami, Iran's subsequent "reformist" president.

Basij

Formed during the early days of the Islamic Republic and trained by the Pasdaran, this militia represents the Iranian regime's premier tool of domestic terror. During the eight years of the Iran-Iraq war, the organization's cadres were the Islamic Republic's cannon fodder, selected to clear minefields and launch "human wave" attacks against Iraqi forces.[53] With the end of the conflict with Iraq, the role of the Basij was reoriented, and the organization became the watchdog of Iranian society. Today, it is used by the ayatollahs to quell domestic anti-regime protests and eradicate "un-Islamic" behavior. Their role ranges from enforcing modest dress to gathering intelligence on university students, which is handed over to the regime's undercover police.[54] The Basij played a significant role in suppressing domestic dissent through violence and intimidation in the aftermath of the fraudulent reelection of Mahmoud Ahmadinejad to the Iranian presidency in June of 2009.[55] More recently, amid growing protests in and around Tehran and other urban centers beginning in December 2017, the Basij has played an instrumental role in regime repression, including by carrying out mass arrests of demonstrators.[56]

There are reported to be as many as 10 million registered Basij members, though not all are on active service.[57] The Basij also plays an important supporting role in Iran's state sponsorship of terror. It is known to be active in training anti-Israeli forces, including carrying out maneuvers designed to ready Hezbollah and assorted Palestinian militants for guerrilla warfare.

Domestic paramilitaries (guruh-I fishar)

Supplementing the role of the *Basij* are the numerous vigilante or "pressure" groups that are harnessed by the Iranian government. Though officially independent, these gangs actually operate under the patronage of government officials, the IRGC or the MOIS, and target internal opposition to the clerical regime.[58] The most famous is the Ansar-i Hezbollah, which was responsible for fomenting the July 1999 crisis at Tehran University that led to the bloody governmental crackdown on student opposition forces.

Bonyads

These sprawling socio-religious foundations, which are overseen only by Iran's Supreme Leader, serve as conduits for the Islamic Republic's cause of choice. Arguably the most important is the Bonyad-e Mostazafan (Foundation of the Oppressed), a sprawling network of an estimated 1,200 firms created in 1979 with seed money from the Shah's coffers.[59] Another is the Bonyad-e Shahid (Martyrs' Foundation), an enormous conglomerate of industrial, agricultural, construction and commercial companies with some 350 offices and tens of thousands of employees.[60] As recently as 2018, Iranian *bonyads* were believed to make up approximately 30% of Iran's GDP, consisting of more than 120 foundations[61] and accounting for as much as two-thirds of the country's non-oil GDP.[62] And while many of their functions are legitimate, they are also used by Iran's religious leaders to funnel money to their pet causes, from financing domestic repression to arming radical groups abroad.

Notably, however, even as Iran remains complicit in the pervasive sponsorship of international terrorism, it is itself the target of violent activity from a number of quarters.

Most pronounced has been the threat to Iran posed in recent years by the Islamic State. Following its ascent to regional prominence in mid-2014, ISIS targeted Shi'a Muslim communities throughout the Middle East, and made Iran a key target of its animus. The organization repeatedly attempted to breach Iran's common border with Iraq, and identified the Iranian regime as a principal adversary in its communiques and writings. ISIS likewise proved adept at exploiting Iran's latent ethnic cleavages, and in the past found fertile soil for recruitment among disenfranchised communities, such as Iran's Kurds, who are repressed and/or marginalized by the state.[63] Since then, however, the destruction of the physical ISIS caliphate in Iraq and Syria in early 2019 has led to a significant diminution in the threat posed by the group to the integrity and security of the Islamic Republic.

Nevertheless, Iran continues to face sporadic pockets of insurgency tied to the country's various restive ethnic minorities. For instance, in Sistan-Baluchistan, which borders Pakistan, a low-grade insurgency has been simmering since the middle of the last decade. There, attacks carried out by militant Sunni Baluch groups like Jundullah and Jaish ul-Adl against regime targets have persisted despite a 2014 understanding between Iran and Pakistan[64] under which both countries committed to stepped-up counterterrorism cooperation along their common border.

Similarly, Iran's eastern province of Khuzestan is the site of significant separatist activity on the part of the country's Arab minority. The region has a long history of social activism dating back to the 1920s, but in recent years the situation has become more heated, in part as a result of the activities of an insurgent group known as the Arab Struggle Movement for the Liberation of Ahvaz (ASMLA).

Most prominent of all, however, has been the resistance in Iran's majority Kurdish regions of West Azerbaijan, Kordestan and Kermanshah, where the Free Life Party of Kurdistan, or PJAK, operates. Led by Iranian-born German national Abdul Rahman Haji Ahmadi, PJAK is a violent Kurdish nationalist group that has carried out attacks on Iran from strongholds in neighboring Iraq since its formation in 2004. PJAK, which maintains an affiliation with Turkey's larger Kurdistan Workers Party (PKK), claims to seek "democratic change" and characterizes its actions as a "defense" against Iranian state repression of its Kurdish minority.[65] Iranian regime forces clashed repeatedly with members of PJAK between 2008 and 2011, successfully arresting and killing numerous group members as part of ongoing counterterrorism operations.[66] A major counterterrorism campaign against the group by Iranian security forces followed in the fall of 2011, culminating in a ceasefire between the two parties.[67] This ceasefire held until 2013, when clashes between the group and Tehran began anew,[68] and have continued sporadically until the present day.

Endnotes

1. See, for example, Guy Taylor, "Iran is Banking Billions More Than Expected Thanks to Obama's Deal," *Washington Times*, February 3, 2016, http://www.washingtontimes.com/news/2016/feb/3/iran-claims-100-billion-windfall-from-sanctions-re/.
2. U.S. Department of Defense, Defense Intelligence Agency, *Iran Military Power: Ensuring Regime Survival and Securing Regional Dominance* (Washington, DC: U.S. Government Printing Office, 2019), https://www.dia.mil/Portals/27/Documents/News/Military%20 Power%20Publications/Iran_Military_Power_LR.pdf
3. "Iran's Statistical Center Reports 7.6 Percent Decline in GDP," *Radio Farda*, February 10, 2020, https://en.radiofarda.com/a/iran-s-statistical-center-reports-7-6-percent-decline-in-gdp/30427214.html; Davide Barbuscia, "Iran Recession to Deepen, Reserves to Fall to $73 Billion by March: IIF," Reuters, January 15, 2020, https:// www.reuters.com/article/us-iran-economy-iif/iran-recession-to-deepen-reserves-to-fall-to-73-billion-by-march-iif-idUSKB-N1ZE139.
4. For an in-depth analysis, see Ilan Berman, "Will Iran's Regime Survive Coronavirus?" *National Review,* March 12, 2020, https://www.nationalreview.com/2020/03/will-irans-regime-survive-coronavirus/
5. Emmanuel Sivan, *Radical Islam: Medieval Theology and Modern Politics* (New Haven: Yale University Press, 1985), 188–207.
6. Ruhollah Khomeini, *Islamic Government* (New York: Manor Books, 1979).
7. Preamble of the Constitution of the Islamic Republic of Iran, http://www.oefre.unibe.ch/law/icl/ir00000_.html.
8. Robin Wright, *Sacred Rage: The Wrath of Militant Islam* (New York: Simon & Schuster, 1986), 111–21.
9. "Iranian Terrorism in Bosnia and Croatia," *Iran Brief*, March 3, 1997, http://www.lexis-nexis.com; Mike O'Connor, "Spies for Iranians Are Said to Gain a Hold in Bosnia," *New York Times*, November 28, 1997, 1.
10. Vali Nasr, *The Shi'a Revival: How Conflicts within Islam will Shape*

the Future (New York: W.W. Norton & Company, 2006), 137.

11. "Hezbollah has 50,000 Rockets: Report," Agence France Presse, December 7, 2010, http://www.spacewar.com/reports/Hezbollah_has_50000_rockets_report_999.html.
12. Joseph Felter and Brian Fishman, "Iranian Strategy in Iraq: Politics and 'Other Means,'" Combating Terrorism Center at West Point *Occasional Paper*, October 13, 2008, http://ctc.usma.edu/Iran_Iraq/CTC_Iran_Iraq_Final.pdf; Ned Parker, "Ten Years After Iraq War Began, Iran Reaps the Gains," *Los Angeles Times*, March 28, 2013, http://articles.latimes.com/2013/mar/28/world/la-fg-iraq-iran-influence-20130329.
13. "Chapter 3. State Sponsors of Terrorism," in *Country Reports on Terrorism 2012* (Washington, DC: U.S. Department of State, May 2013), http://www.state.gov/j/ct/rls/crt/2012/209985.htm.
14. "Chapter 3. State Sponsors of Terrorism," in *Country Reports on Terrorism 2012* (Washington, DC: U.S. Department of State, May 2013), http://www.state.gov/j/ct/rls/crt/2012/209985.htm.
15. The historically tense relations between Iran and Egypt deteriorated precipitously during 2008-2010, spurred in large part by Egyptian fears of Iranian internal meddling. These worries were showcased in spring of 2009, when Egyptian authorities arrested a total of twenty-six individuals suspected of carrying out espionage for Hezbollah, and of plotting to carry out terrorist attacks within Egypt. The suspects were subsequently formally charged with plotting subversion against the Egyptian state. "Egypt Charges 26 'Hizbullah Spies,'" *Jerusalem Post*, July 26, 2009, http://www.jpost.com/servlet/Satellite-cid=1248277893866&pagename=JPost%2FJPArticle%2FShowFullz
16. See, for example, "Lawmaker: Uprisings in Region Promising Birth of Islamic Middle-East," Fars News Agency (Tehran), February 5, 2011, http://english.farsnews.com/newstext.php?nn=8911161168.
17. "Iran's Support for Bahrain Protesters Fuels Regional Tensions," *Deutsche Welle*, April 15, 2011, http://www.dw.de/irans-support-for-bahrain-protesters-fuels-regional-tensions/a-6504403-1.
18. See, for example, Eric Schmitt, and Robert F. Worth, "With Arms for Yemen Rebels, Iran Seeks Wider Mideast Role," *New York Times*, March 15, 2012, http://www.nytimes.com/2012/03/15/world/middleeast/aiding-yemen-rebels-iran-seeks-wider-mideast-role.html.
19. For a detailed analysis of the SLA, see Nader Uskowi, *Temperature Rising: Iran's Revolutionary Guards and Wars in the Middle East* (Lanham, MD: Rowman & Littlefield, 2019).
20. Seth J. Franzman, "Who Are Iran's 80,000 Shi'ite Fighters in Syria?"

Jerusalem Post, April 28, 2018, https://www.jpost.com/Middle-East/Who-are-Irans-80000-Shiite-fighters-in-Syria-552940

21. Richard Barrett, *Beyond The Caliphate: Foreign Fighters and the Threat of Returnees* (The Soufan Center, October 2017), 5, http://thesoufancenter.org/wp-content/uploads/2017/10/Beyond-the-Caliphate-Foreign-Fighters-and-the-Threat-of-Returnees-TSC-Report-October-2017-v2.pdf.
22. "Iranian Revolutionary Guard Corps Commander Jafari: We Support Resistance to U.S. and Israel in Syria and Elsewhere in the Region," Middle East Media Research Institute *Clip* no. 4272, April 21, 2014, http://www.memritv.org/clip/en/4272.htm.
23. See, for example, Dina Esfandiary and Ariane Tabatabai, "Iran's ISIS Policy," *International Affairs* 91, iss. 1 (2015), https://www.chathamhouse.org/sites/default/files/field/field_publication_docs/INTA91_1_01_Esfandiary_Tabatabai.pdf.
24. Under Secretary of the Treasury for Terrorism and Financial Intelligence Stuart Levey, Remarks before the 5th Annual Conference on Trade, Treasury, and Cash Management in the Middle East, Abu Dhabi, United Arab Emirates, March 7, 2007, http://uae.usembassy.gov/remarks_of_stuart_levey_.html.
25. Carla Humud, Christopher Blanchard, Jeremy Sharp and Jim Zanotti, "Iranian Assistance to Groups in Yemen, Iraq, Syria, and the Palestinian Territories," Congressional Research Service *Memorandum*, July 31, 2015, http://www.kirk.senate.gov/images/PDF/Iran%20Financial%20Support%20to%20Terrorists%20and%20Militants.pdf.
26. Brian Hook, Remarks before the Foundation for Defense of Democracies, Washington, DC, August 28, 2018, http://www.defenddemocracy.org/content/uploads/documents/FDD-Summit-Brian-Hook.pdf.
27. Brian Hook, Remarks before the Foundation for Defense of Democracies, Washington, DC, August 28, 2018, http://www.defenddemocracy.org/content/uploads/documents/FDD-Summit-Brian-Hook.pdf.
28. See, for example, Azadeh Moaveni, "The Backlash against Iran's Role in Lebanon," *Time*, August 31, 2006, http://www.time.com/time/world/article/0,8599,1515755,00.html.
29. Brenda Shaffer, as cited in Ilan Berman, "Iran's Imperial History Overshadows Its Future," *The National Interest*, December 16, 2019, https://nationalinterest.org/blog/middle-east-watch/irans-imperial-history-overshadows-its-future-105652.
30. U.S. Department of State, Bureau of Democracy, Human Rights and Labor, *International Religious Freedom Report 2008*, n.d., http://www.state.gov/g/drl/rls/irf/2008/108482.htm.

31. See, for example, Ebrahim Mohseni, Nancy Gallagher and Clay Ramsey, *Iranian Public Opinion on the Nuclear Agreement*, Center for International & Security Studies at Maryland, September 2015, http://www.cissm.umd.edu/sites/default/files/CISSM-PA%20Iranian%20Public%20Opinion%20on%20the%20Nuclear%20Agreement%20090915%20FINAL-LR.pdf.
32. The World Bank. "Islamic Republic of Iran Overview," May 1, 2020, https://www.worldbank.org/en/country/iran/overview.
33. "Iran Worried as Unemployment Reaches 60% in Some Cities," *Radio Farda*, October 2, 2017, https://en.radiofarda.com/a/iran-unemployment-60-percent/28768226.html.
34. "Islamic Republic of Iran Overview," May 1, 2020. https://www.worldbank.org/en/country/iran/overview.
35. Ahmad Alavi, "Iran's Official Figures Indicate Alarming Unemployment Rate Later This Year," *Radio Farda*, January 9, 2019, https://en.radiofarda.com/a/iran-official-figures-alarming-unemployment-2019/29698225.html.
36. Lawrence Goodman, "COVID-19 Ravages Iran," *BrandeisNOW*, May 14, 2020, https://www.brandeis.edu/now/2020/may/iran-virus-kahalzadeh.html.
37. "Iran Statistical Center Claims Unemployment Dipped Last Year," *Radio Farda*, May 3, 2020, https://en.radiofarda.com/a/iran-statistical-center-claims-unemployment-dipped-last-year/30590549.html.
38. Amir Basiri, "Iran Increases its Military Budget in Response to Nationwide Protests," January 30, 2018, https://www.washingtonexaminer.com/iran-increases-its-military-budget-in-response-to-nationwide-protests.
39. "Report: Iran Spent $30 Billion on Propping up Syria's Assad," *Israel Hayom*, May 26, 2020, https://www.israelhayom.com/2020/05/26/report-iran-spent-30-billion-on-propping-up-syrias-assad/.
40. Philip Issa, "Iran Protests put Spotlight on Military's Vast and Shadowy War in Syria," Associated Press, January 5, 2018, https://www.thestar.com/news/world/2018/01/05/iran-protests-put-spotlight-on-militarys-vast-and-shadowy-war-in-syria.html.
41. Mohammad Mohaddessin, *Islamic Fundamentalism: The New Global Threat* (Washington: Seven Locks Press, 1993), 132-136.
42. Richard Horowitz, "A Detailed Analysis of Iran's Constitution," World Policy Institute, October 12, 2010, https://worldpolicy.org/2010/10/12/a-de- tailed-analysis-of-irans-constitution/.
43. See, for example, Michael Eisenstadt, *Iranian Military Power: Capabilities and Intentions* (Washington: Washington Institute for Near

East Policy, 1996), 70-72.
44. Mohaddessin, *Islamic Fundamentalism*, 102.
45. "Rev. Guards Intelligence," *Iran Brief*, January 6, 1997, http://www.lexis-nexis.com.
46. Bijan Khajehpour, "The real footprint of the IRGC in Iran's economy," *Al-Monitor*, August 9, 2017, https://www.al-monitor.com/pulse/origi- nals/2017/08/iran-irgc-economy-footprint-khatam-olanbia.html#ixzz6Ev- JxvvbX.
47. "Ministry of Intelligence and Security [MOIS]: "Vezarat-e Ettela'at va Amniat-e Keshvar VEVAK," globalsecurity.org, February 19, 2006, http://www.globalsecurity.org/intell/world/iran/vevak.htm.
48. Eisenstadt, *Iranian Military Power*, 70.
49. Federation of American Scientists, "Ministry of Intelligence and Security [MOIS]: Organization," n.d., http://www.fas.org/irp/world/iran/vevak/org.htm.
50. See, for example, "Khamene'i Ordered Khobar Towers Bombing, Defector Says," *Iran Brief*, August 3, 1998, http://www.lexis-nexis.com; American intelligence officials have long maintained that Iranian terrorism is authorized at the highest official levels. See, for example, CIA Director R. James Woolsey, "Challenges to Peace in the Middle East," remarks before the Washington Institute for Near East Policy's Wye Plantation Conference, Queenstown, Maryland, September 23, 1994, http://www.washingtoninstitute.org/templateC07.php?CID=66.
51. Eisenstadt, *Iranian Military Power*, 71.
52. Eisenstadt, *Iranian Military Power*, 71.; Mohaddessin, *Islamic Fundamentalism*, 101-102.
53. Drew Middleton, "5 Years of Iran-Iraq War: Toll May Be Near a Million," *New York Times*, September 23, 1985, 4.
54. Geneive Abdo, "Islam's Warriors Scent Blood," *Observer* (London), July 18, 1999, 26.
55. "Basij Commander Admits Forces Shot at 2009 Protesters," International Campaign for Human Rights in Iran, January 6, 2014, https://www.iranhumanrights.org/2014/01/basij-shot/.
56. See, for example, "Six People Said Killed, 300 Arrests at Sufi Protest in Iran," *Radio Farda*, February 20, 2018, https://www.rferl.org/a/iran-sufi-gonabadi-protests-tehran-deaths/29050268.html.
57. Angus McDowall, "Tehran Deploys Islamic Vigilantes to Attack Protesters," *Independent* (London), July 11, 2003, 12.
58. For more on the *guruh-i fishar*, see Michael Rubin, *Into the Shadows: Radical Vigilantes in Khatami's Iran* (Washington: Washington

Institute for Near East Policy, 2001).

59. Robert D. Kaplan, “A Bazaari’s World,” *Atlantic Monthly 277*, iss. 3 (1996), 28.
60. Wilfried Buchta, *Who Rules Iran? The Structure of Power in the Islamic Republic* (Washington: Washington Institute for Near East Policy – Konrad Adenauer Stiftung, 2000), 75.
61. “Iranian Bonyads Make up Approximately 30% of Iran’s GDP,” *IF-MAT*, March 26, 2018, https://www.ifmat.org/03/26/iranian-bonyads-make-30-iran-gdp/.
62. “Iranian Bonyads Make up Approximately 30% of Iran’s GDP,” *IF-MAT*, March 26, 2018, https://www.ifmat.org/03/26/iranian-bonyads-make-30-iran-gdp/; See also Kenneth Katzman, Statement before the Joint Economic Committee of the United States Congress, July 25, 2006.
63. See, for example, Fuad Haqaqi, “ISIS Boasts Rising Number of Recruits Among Iranian Kurds,” *Rudaw*, November 12, 2014, http://www.rudaw.net/english/middleeast/iran/101220141.
64. “Pakistan-Iran agree for joint Anti-Terrorist and Anti-Drug operations,” IANS, May 6, 2014, http://news.biharprabha.com/2014/05/pakistan-iran-agree-for-joint-anti-terrorist-and-anti-drug-operations/.
65. “Tehran Faces Growing Kurdish Opposition,” *Washington Times*, April 3, 2006, http://www.washingtontimes.com/news/2006/apr/3/20060403-125601-8453r/.
66. See, for example, “4 Members of PJAK Terrorist Group Arrested in Iran,” Fars News Agency (Tehran), November 30, 2010, http://english.farsnews.com/newstext.php?nn=8909091200; See also “Iranian Troops Attack Kurdish PJAK Rebel Bases in Iraq,” BBC (London), July 18, 2011, http://www.bbc.co.uk/news/world-middle-east-14189313.
67. “Iran Deploying Troops, Tanks to Kurdistan Border,” *World Tribune*, July 19, 2013, http://www.worldtribune.com/2013/07/19/iran-deploying-troops-tanks-to-kurdistan-border/.
68. “Five IRGC Soldiers Killed in Clash with ‘Terrorists’ in Western Iran,” Xinhua, October 11, 2013, http://news.xinhuanet.com/english/world/2013-10/11/c_125510936.htm.

14 Iraq

Quick Facts

Population: 38,872,655 (July 2020 est.)
Area: 438,317 sq km
Ethnic Groups: Arab 75-80%, Kurdish 15-20%, other 5% (includes Turkmen, Yezidi, Shabak, Kaka'i, Bedouin, Romani, Assyrian, Circassian, Sabaean-Mandaean, Persian)
Government Type: Federal parliamentary republic
GDP (official exchange rate):$192.4 billion (2017 est.)

Map and Quick Facts courtesy of the CIA World Factbook (Last Updated August 2020)

Introduction

Iraq's contemporary history is replete with both secular and Islamist political currents. Shi'a and Sunni Islamist movements in Iraq formed in response to Saddam Hussein's secular nationalist Ba'athist regime, and as part of the regional political Islam movement. Most of these Islamist parties existed in exile or in hiding for much of 1980s and 1990s, emerging after the fall of Saddam Hussein's regime in 2003. Since that time, both Sunni and Shi'a Islamist parties have played an important role in Iraq's political system. Although the 2010 parliamentary election saw the rise of secular political coalitions, rising sectarianism gave new life to Islamist currents. One extreme example was the Islamic State, which took Iraqi towns and cities in early 2014; another is the presence of certain Shi'a paramilitary groups within the Popular Mobilization Units (PMU, also known as the Popular Mobilization Forces, or PMF), an umbrella armed organization formed as a response to the Islamic State.

Sunni and Shi'a Islamist militant groups active in Iraq continue to fuel sectarian violence throughout the country. In 2015, the Iraqi Security Forces, supported by the PMUs, began re-taking territory from the Islamic State. By the end of 2017, Iraqi forces had retaken most of the territory that had been lost, including Mosul, the country's second largest city. Currently, in the so-called post-ISIS context, the question of Shi'a militant groups remains. Some have sought a more prominent political and economic role in Iraqi society, yet remain unwilling to integrate into the state apparatus or be held accountable under the rule of law. As Iraq's nascent democratic system evolves, both secular and Islamist forces will continue to vie for influence and power.

Islamist Activity

Islamist activity in Iraq today takes three distinct forms based along ethno-sectarian lines. Because Iraq's Shi'a population is significantly larger than that of the country's Sunnis, there is a wider array of Shi'a militant groups, ranging from sectarian to nationalist orientations. Salafi-*jihadi* Sunni groups, such as the Islamic State, continue to pose a significant threat to the Iraqi state. Additionally, among the country's Kurdish population, Islamic activity does exist – some Kurds have joined Salafi-*jihadi* groups, and others have joined the PMU – but remains relatively minimal.

Shi'a Groups

Since 2003, the main Shi'a political factions in Iraq have been the Ḥizb al-Daʿwa al-Islamiyya (Islamic *Dawa* Party), al-Tayyar al-Sadri (the Sadrist Trend), and al-Majlis al-A'ala al-Islami al-Iraqi (the Islamic Supreme Council of Iraq, or ISCI). During Iraq's first post-invasion elections, in 2005, the main Shi'a Islamist groups registered under one political bloc, known as the al-Itilaf al-Iraqi al-Muwahhad (United Iraq Alliance, or UIA). Since then, both ISCI and *Dawa* have suffered internal ruptures. In 2010, the Badr Organization, an armed faction, split from ISCI. Then, in the summer of 2017, ISCI leader Ammar al-Hakim split from the group to form the Tayar al-Hikmah al-Watani (National Wisdom Movement). Since 2003, *Dawa* has also suffered internal divisions and, as a result, lost the prime minister's office following the 2018 elections. Ahead of this vote, Abadi decided to form a new electoral list, the Tahaluf al-Nasr (Victory Alliance) to compete against his *Dawa* compatriot Nouri al-Maliki, who headed the Itilaf Dawlat al-Qanun (State of Law Coalition). During this election, Shi'a Islamist groups competed in separate electoral coalitions, some of which included groups and officials who were not Islamist or not Shi'a. These coalitions included Tahaluf al-Nasr (Haider al-Abadi's Victory Alliance), Nouri al-Maliki's Itilaf Dawlat al-Qanun (State of Law Coalition, or SOL), Hadi al-Ameri's Tahaluf al-Fateh (Conquest Alliance) and Muqtada al-Sadr's Tahaluf al-Sairoon (Revolutionaries for Reform Alliance).

Today, the main Shi'a military factions fall under the al-Hashd al-Shaabi (Popular Mobilization Units, or PMUs), including the Badr Organization, Asaib ahl al-Haq, Kataib Hezbollah, and others. Many of these paramilitaries have their own political identities. In early 2018, the PMU leadership formed an electoral list named the Tahaluf al-Fatah (Conquest Alliance), which includes non-armed Shi'a Islamist groups such as ISCI.[1] Groups to which these people belong include Kataeb Hezbollah, the Imam Ali Brigades, Sayed al-Shuhada, the al-Badr Organization, and Asaib ahl al-Haq (League of the Righteous).[2] Smaller Islamist groups include the National Reform Trend (led by former Prime Minister Ibrahim al-Jaafari) and the Fadhila (Islamic Virtue) Party.

Iraq's *Atabat* units are paramilitary groups affiliated with Shia Muslim shrines. These so-called "shrine units" are made up of four main groups — Liwa Ansar al-Marjaiya, Liwa Ali al-Akbar, Firqat al-Abbas al-Qitaliyah, and Firqat al-Imam Ali al-Qitaliyah — and have no links with Iran's Islamic Revolutionary Guard Corps (IRGC). Instead they are affiliated with the Ayatollah Ali Sistani, the Iraqi Shi'a leader whom they regard as their source of religious emulation. In total, the *Atabat* have around 18,000 active soldiers and tens of thousands of reserves.[3]

On January 3, 2020, Major General Qassim Soleimani, commander of the Quds Force of the IRGC, as well as Jamal Jafar Muhammad Ali- al-Ibrahim (also known as Abu Mahdi al-Muhandis), deputy chairman and *de facto* leader of Iraq's Popular Mobilization Forces/ Units, were killed in an American drone strike. The PMU has since faced significant challenges in its organization and leadership succession. This has led to a rivalry between the pro-Iran faction of the PMU and those loyal to Iraq's Grand Ayatollah Ali al-Sistani.[4]

The Islamic Dawa Party

The *Dawa* Party is the oldest Shi'a Islamist party in Iraq, and enjoyed executive power from 2005 to 2018 under three prime ministers: Ibrahim al-Jaafari, Nouri al-Maliki, and Haider al-Abadi. The party emerged in the late 1950s in response to the spread of socialist and communist movements in Iraq.[5] Grand Ayatollah Mohammed Baqir al-Sadr, a distinguished Shi'a scholar, is widely credited as *Dawa's* founder.[6] *Dawa* emphasized the promotion of Islamic values and ethics, and believed that the right to govern was distinct from the juridical function of religious authorities and that both should be subsumed under constitutional mechanisms.[7]

In the 1980s, Sadr split from *Dawa* due to tensions with the Shi'a *hawza* (seminary) in Najaf. *Dawa* remained the leading Shi'a Islamist opposition party of the 1970s and 1980s, suffering fierce persecution from Saddam Hussein's Ba'athist regime. Its members remained active and hid, either within Iraq or in exile. The main exiled *Dawa* branches were located in Iran, Syria, and the United Kingdom.

Dawa emerged as one of the main Shi'a political groups in Iraq in 2003 after the Iraq war and during the time of the Coalition Provisional Authority, the U.S.-administered transitional government that lasted from March 2003 until April 2004. Since power was handed back to Iraqi authorities, all of Iraq's Prime Ministers had been members of *Dawa* – with the exception of the current Prime Minister, Mustafa Al- Kadhimi, who was elected in May 2020. Al-Kadhimi is the first PM not to hail from a Shiite political movement.[8] Consequently, Kadhimi's appointment has caused concern in Tehran, due to his desire to limit Iran's influence in Iraq.[9]

The Sadrist Trend

The Sadrist Trend is a nationalist populist religious movement founded by Shi'a cleric Mohammed Sadeq al-Sadr in the 1990s. Across southern Iraq and in Baghdad, the movement gained widespread support from poor Shi'a communities drawn to its emphasis on economic and social relief, along with its focus on traditional Islamic law and customs.[10] The Sadrists believe that religious leaders should be politically and socially active, but oppose the Khomeinist notion of *wilayat al-faqih* (government of the jurists).

The Sadrists are distinguished by their desire for technocratic ministers and their opposition to any external interference in Iraqi domestic affairs.[11]

In 1999, Saddam Hussein ordered the assassination of Sadeq al-Sadr and his two oldest sons, forcing much of the movement's leadership into hiding. After the 2003 invasion of Iraq, the Sadrist Trend reemerged under the leadership of Sadeq's youngest son, Muqtada al-Sadr. The Sadrists vehemently opposed the presence of U.S. forces in Iraq. They also opposed Baghdad's new elite, who had spent decades exiled from the country, referring to these leaders as "foreigner Iraqis."[12] Muqtada al-Sadr was able to derive considerable legitimacy by making the claim that he was the only leader who had lived in Iraq under Hussein's dictatorship. The Sadrist Trend and its *Jaysh al-Mahdi* (JAM) militia were a powerful force during the height of sectarian violence in Iraq from 2004 to 2007.

The movement lost significant influence as U.S. and Iraqi forces degraded the JAM during offensives in 2007 and 2008. Nouri al-Maliki's *Saulat al-Fursan* (Operation Knights Charge) drove out Sadr, who disbanded the JAM and went into exile in Iran.

In 2011, Sadr returned from exile. His time in Iran had turned his sympathies back toward Iraq and against Iran, and his public discourse reflected this change in sentiment. He restructured the movement to emphasize political and social programs and a need to combat ineffective governance.[13]

Despite opposing the existence of the PMU, the Sadrists continue to maintain a militant wing, called Sarayat al-Salam (the Peace Brigades). The Peace Brigades have fought alongside Sunni tribes in Anbar, and remain skeptical of the better-funded, Iranian-backed Shi'a paramilitaries – particularly Asaib ahl al-Haq and Hezbollah. Like *Dawa*, the Sadrist Trend supports a strong central Iraqi government, but opposes American or Iranian presence in Iraq. It also opposes the current elite are corrupt and unrepresentative of the people.

In 2018, the Sadrists formed the Tahaluf al-Sairoon (Revolutionaries for Reform Alliance), which included Islamists and secularists linked to the Iraqi Communist Party, running on an anti-corruption platform. While al- Sadr was not an official political leader for the Alliance, he put his support behind the six- party coalition.[14] The list won 54 of 329 seats in the May 2018 elections, giving Sadr the chance to play kingmaker in the future. In March 2020, a new groups calling themselves Usbat al Tha'ireen (League of Revolutionaries) and Ashab al-Kahf (people of the Cave) emerged and have since been claiming responsibility for attacks and attempts against U.S. targets.[15] It is widely believed that these groups were created to serve as front organizations and allow Iran- backed PMF unites to continue to plan and carry out attacks against the United States without legal and/or political repercussions.[16]

The Islamic Supreme Council of Iraq

The third significant Islamist political actor in post-2003 Iraq is ISCI, previously known as the Supreme Council for the Islamic Revolution in Iraq (SCIRI). SCIRI was founded in Iran in 1982 and worked closely with the Iranian government during the Iran-Iraq War to support Shi'a activism against the Saddam regime. It had a militia called the Badr Corps. However, of all the Shi'a Islamic groups, ISCI has been affected the most by fragmentation. In the country's 2018 national elections, it only managed to secure two seats.

SCIRI became a dominant political force in the country's post-Coalition Provisional Authority government while maintaining its close relationship with Iran. In the mid 2000s, many Badr members were incorporated into the Iraqi Security Forces.[17] In an effort to distance itself from Iran, SCIRI changed its name to ISCI in 2007.[18] The group began to focus more heavily on Iraqi nationalism and shifted its primary religious allegiance away from Iran's Supreme Leader, the Ayatollah Ali Khamenei, to Grand Ayatollah Ali Sistani, who believes religious leaders should not be involved in state affairs. Sistani is the head of the Najaf Shi'a *hawza* and as such is the head of the Shi'a *marjai'ya* (religious establishment).

After the death of ISCI leader Abd al-Aziz al-Hakim in August 2009, his son, Ammar al-Hakim, assumed control of the movement. ISCI has suffered from two key defections. In March 2012, ISCI split from the Badr Organization, partly due to leadership squabbles in the wake of a poor performance in the 2010 parliamentary elections.[19] More importantly, the two organizations disagreed over whether to support Maliki as the incumbent prime minister. The Badr organization, under the leadership of Hadi al-Ameri, split off from Hakim's ISCI. Then, in 2017, Hakim left ISCI to form the National Wisdom Trend. As justification for his departure, Hakim cited internal power struggles within ISCI's senior leadership.[20]

After the Islamic State's defeat in 2017, PMUs resigned from their militia posts in order to run in the 2018 elections. Since its defeat the various Shia parties and militias, including ISCI, are no longer a cohesive group. These factions have subsequently turned on each other, using violence at times.[21]

The ideological concept of *wilayat al-faqih* (leadership by clerics) divides ISCI from *Dawa* and the Sadrists. While ISCI is closer to the belief that clergy should lead society, *Dawa* and the Sadrists, due to the influence of Mohammad Baqir al-Sadr, believe in *wilayat al-umma* (leadership by community).

The Popular Mobilization Units (PMU)

Following the emergence of the Islamic State, which began taking over Iraqi towns and cities in early 2014, Maliki established the PMU commission. The commission was further legitimized by Grand Ayatollah Ali al-Sistani's *fatwa*, which called on Iraqis to voluntarily fight against the group. It is notable that Sistani did not intend for the volunteers to join militias, preferring them to join state institutions. However, the collapse of the state's armed forces led many volunteers to prefer the militias.

The PMU is a conglomerate of roughly 50 militias, some of which are loyal only to Sistani (known as the Shrine militias). The most powerful, better funded, and better equipped PMUs are particularly loyal to and backed by Iran. Hadi al-Ameri's Badr Organization, Abu Muhandis' *Kataib Hezbollah* (KH), and Qais Khazali's Asaib ahl al-Haq (AAH) are all known to directly coordinate with Iran.

The second group includes paramilitaries closer to Sistani. The Ali al-Akbar Brigades and the *Abbadiyah* Brigades are part of this group. The third contingent is made up of militias that represent wings of political parties. ISCI militias or Sadr's *Sarayat al-Salam* fall into this category.[22]

In November 2016, the Iraqi parliament passed a law that will transform the PMUs into a legal and separate military corps alongside state forces.[36] Both Sadr and Sistani remain opposed to the politicization of the PMUs, and both call for the provision of greater state power. Sadr, despite being a militia leader, has claimed he is willing to disband if all other paramilitaries are also disbanded and the government monopoly on legitimate violence is restored.

In March 2019, the PMU continued its pursuit of state legitimacy, this time via the Iraqi national budget, which for the first-time recognized pay parity for PMU fighters with fighters in the MOD and MOI.

In a post-ISIS context, the PMU is redefining its identity. As the frontier has dried up, PMU groups are now competing with each other for access to territory, which brings with it access to revenues (checkpoints, taxation, etc.). Part of this process has thus included internal power struggles and arrests of potential dissidents.[23] Moving forward, the PMU are expanding their political and economic role in Iraq while maintaining their security responsibilities. They collectively hope to develop national guard style of presence, manning major roads connecting cities around southern and central Iraq.

Hikmah

As discussed above, in 2017 Ammar al-Hakim broke away from ISCI to form Tayar al-Hikmah al-Watani, or the National Wisdom Movement. In the 2018 election, *Hikmah* secured 19 seats. Hakim's ideas, the foundation for *Hikmah*'s ideology, argues for a bottom-up Islamism in tune with wider Iraqi society and is not solely based on Shi'ism. The faction also argues in favor of greater independence from Iran.

Sunni groups

The Sunni political landscape has recently shifted dramatically in Iraq. The major ideological debate among the Sunni Islamist community, however, remains the question of cooperating with Baghdad.[24] Many Sunni Islamists have chosen to reject the central government, which they perceive to be a Shi'a-Iranian dictatorship. However, during the Anbar Awakening and subsequent period of comparatively good governance in Iraq (2008-2010), Sunni Islamists participated in the political process.

The Iraqi Islamic Party

The Iraqi Islamic Party (IIP) is the only Sunni Islamist political party in Iraq, although it is not a unified organization and lacks the institutional capacity of most political parties. It is currently led by Ayad al-Samarraie. The IIP has its roots in the mid-1940s or early 1950s, when Mohammed al-Sawwaf, an Iraqi studying in Egypt, met Muslim Brotherhood founder Hassan al-Banna.[25] Upon his return to Iraq, al-Sawwaf and another activist, Amjad al-Zahawi Mahmood, founded an Iraqi organization modeled on the Muslim Brotherhood, known as the Islamic Brotherhood Society.[26] Later, in 1960, the IIP was formally established after Abdul-Karim Qassem's government allowed political parties to form in Iraq.[27] When the Ba'ath Party overthrew Qassem's government in 1963, the IIP was violently suppressed but continued clandestine operations in exile.[28] Ayad al-Samarraie, who had been the Secretary General of the IIP, fled Iraq in 1980.[29]

Following the fall of Saddam Hussein's Ba'athist regime in 2003, many IIP leaders, including al-Samarraie, returned to Iraq and the party re-emerged. The IIP ran as part of a Sunni coalition known as *Tawafuq* (Iraqi Accord Front), which won 44 seats in the 275-member parliament in the December 2005 parliamentary election. *Tawafuq* was the dominant Sunni political presence in the parliament, though it was seen by many as an exile party that did not represent their interests. By early 2009, *Tawafuq* began to disintegrate as its constituent parties left the coalition during the debate over the selection of the parliamentary speaker.[30]

In 2009 and 2010, as a result of a decline in membership, the IIP lost a considerable portion of its electorate to the secular nationalist coalition of former Prime Minister Allawi's *al-Iraqiyya* grouping, also called the Iraqiyah list. Even IIP leader Tariq al-Hashimi left the group to join *al-Iraqiyya*. IPP was the only party to run under the *Tawafuq* banner. At the start of the Arab Spring, IIP sought to build its support network by appealing to Sunnis through demonstrations, where the party used Islamist clerics to rally support of the party's Islamist messaging.[31] In 2014, the party lost credibility amongst its Sunni members due to its alliance with the Shiite Prime Minister, Haider al-Abadi. On May 12, 2018, the country held its first parliamentary elections since the defeat of ISIS, where many IIP candidates ran individually of as part of the party – winning 14 seats in the country's 329 seat parliament.[32]

The Association of Muslim Scholars

Hay'at al-'Ulama' al-Muslimeen (The Association of Muslim Scholars) was formed immediately after the U.S.-led invasion in April of 2003. It is a group of influential Sunni clerics and scholars seeking to represent the Sunni voice in Shi'a-dominated Baghdad. It was initially led by Harith al-Dhari, a cleric who called on Iraqis to boycott the U.S.-led attempts to rebuild the Iraqi government in a *fatwa* that also called for a "national insurgency."[33] Such sentiments, along with the Iraqi people's fear of retaliation if they participated in the political process, combined to significantly suppress voter turnout. For example, Anbar Province, which is 90% Sunni and has often suffered from violence and high levels of insurgency, had a 1% voter turnout in the January 2005 parliamentary interim elections.[34] However, by the December 2005 elections, national voter turnout rose to 77%.[35] The group was an important driving force of Sunni insurgency in 2006. However, it came into conflict with AQI and its leader, Abu Musab al-Zarqawi, particularly on the question as to the type and scope of acceptable violence. Following Harith's death, his son Muthanna took over the organization, which continues to claim to speak on behalf of disenfranchised Sunnis and attempts to stoke Iraqi nationalism.

Other groups seek to represent Sunni interests as well. Waqf al-Sunni (the Sunni Endowment) is a government-recognized body tasked with managing holy sites and distributing resources to the population. It is led by Abdul Latif al-Humayim, who was appointed by Prime Minister Haider al-Abadi. Majma al-Faqih al-Iraqi (the Fiqih Council of Iraq) and Dar al-Iftah al-Iraqi are other groups seeking to represent Sunnis. Finally, Hayat al-Iftah al-Salafi is a small Salafi organization opposed to the government in Baghdad.

The Islamic State (formerly al-Qaeda in Iraq - AQI)

The Islamic State initially grew out of an al-Qaeda offshoot, al-Qaeda in Iraq (AQI). AQI members included native Sunni Iraqis, members of the Kurdish Islamist group Ansar Al-Islam, and some foreigners, including its leader Abu Musab al-Zarqawi.[36] AQI was responsible for some of the deadliest car bombs and suicide bomb attacks in Iraq, as well as a surge in sectarian violence. AQI became the Islamic State of Iraq (ISI) in 2006. The organization had lost many of its strongholds in northern and western Iraq following the security offensives that began in 2007, but continued to operate in areas of northern Iraq, especially Mosul, in areas of Diyala, Salah ad-Din, Anbar, and Baghdad. Though AQI leaders pledged their allegiance to al-Qaeda in 2004, the group was no longer able to retain operational links with al-Qaeda leaders based in the tribal areas of Pakistan in the years that followed.[37]

ISI's subsequently transformed into the Islamic State in Iraq and the Levant (ISIL) in 2014. The group maintained a largely passive presence in Iraq but grew in numbers as Maliki began suppressing and attacking Iraqi Sunnis. It began taking over Iraqi territory, beginning in Fallujah and leading to Mosul which in early 2014. ISIL formally declared a caliphate and changed its name to the Islamic State after claiming Mosul in June 2014. By 2017, the group suffered defeats at the hands of the Iraqi security forces, the PMU, and the Kurdish *peshmerga*, reversing a trend of steady territorial gains and political growth. In 2019, the group faced a disastrous reality – it faced a massive decimation by Coalition forces, and lost control over several major cities, including Mosul (which it claimed as its capital), Ramadi, Fallujah, and Tikrit. In response, the group altered its tactics, reverting to AQI-style guerilla warfare and attacks on civilians in the Kirkuk, Diyala, Salahadeen, and Anbar provinces. Most of its attacks were against security forces, including checkpoints manned by police or PMU groups. As of this writing, ISIL fighters are seen to be ramping up terror activities anew, claiming responsibility for the surge of attacks across Iraq in the last six months.[38] These new attacks are low-tech, low-cost, but deadly[39] and exploit security gaps in Iraq's security sector caused by the coronavirus pandemic.[40]

Kurdish groups

Political Islam has also developed extensively in Iraqi Kurdistan, also called the Kurdistan Region, an autonomous region in northern Iraq run by the Kurdistan Regional Government (KRG). It is particularly strong in the city of Halabja, but occurs in other major areas as well. The largest Kurdish Islamist political groups are the Kurdistan Islamic Union (KIU) and the Kurdistan Islamic Group (KIG).[41]

The Kurdistan Islamic Union

The KIU, also known as *Yekgirtu*, was established in 1994. Principally an adherent to Sunni Islam, the group was closely aligned with the Muslim Brotherhood. The group describes itself as "an Islamic reformative political party that strives to solve all political, social, economic and cultural matters of the people in Kurdistan from an Islamic perspective which can achieve the rights, general freedom, and social justice."[42] It is currently led by Secretary General Sheikh Salah ad-Din Muhammad Baha-al-Din. The KIU has no armed forces of its own, and is most active in charity work.

The Kurdistan Islamic Group

The KIG was established in 2001 as a splinter faction of the KIU. It is led by Mala Ali Bapir. The KIG maintains close ties with extremist Islamist armed groups, such as *Ansar al-Islam*, which has been involved in attacks against leaders of the predominant political parties in Kurdistan, the Kurdistan Democratic Party (KDP) and the Patriotic Union of Kurdistan (PUK).[43] Bapir, however, claims his group has abandoned violence.

Nevertheless, the political influence of the KIU and KIG cannot compete with that of the KDP, PUK, and *Gorran* (Change List), which dominate Kurdish political and social life. Of the 111 seats in the Kurdish parliament, the KIU and KIG have only four.[44] At the national level, Kurdish Islamist parties are even less influential. The KIU and KIG collectively hold six seats in the 325-seat Iraqi parliament. The emergence of *Gorran* shifted the balance of power and gave the KIU and KIG another ally in the KRG parliament with which to challenge the dominant Kurdish parties. However, Kurdish Islamist parties remain only marginal actors in Iraqi political life.

Islamism and Society

97 percent of the Iraqi population is Muslim, and of that group, 60-65 percent are Shi'a.[45] Iraqi Shi'a primarily live in central and southern Iraq, though there are Shi'a communities in the north. 32-37 percent of Iraqi Muslims are Sunnis, and they are concentrated mainly in central and northern Iraq.[46] Of Iraq's more-than-30 million citizens, 75-80 percent are Arabs; 15-20 percent are Kurds; and Turkmen, Chaldean, Assyrian, Armenians, and other minority groups comprise the remainder.[47] Religious minorities, such as Christians, Mandeans, and Yazidis comprise the remaining three percent of Iraq's population; however, these non-dominant ethnic and religious populations have declined significantly since 2003.[48]

According to the U.S. military, more than 77,000 Iraqis were killed during the height of sectarian violence between 2004 and 2008. Iraqi government statistics put the number higher, at over 85,000.[49] The emergence of the Islamic State in Iraq led to "staggering violence," with some 18,800 killed between January 1, 2014 and October 31, 2015.[50] The United Nations Assistance Mission to Iraq estimated that approximately 6,878 Iraqi civilians were killed in 2016 in total, primarily by the Islamic State.[51]

Following the fall of Saddam Hussein's secular regime in 2003, both Sunni and Shi'a Iraqis were able to openly express their Islamic faith. The Shi'a population, for the first time in decades, could take part in the religious pilgrimages to the holy cities of Najaf and Karbala in southern Iraq. Exiled Sunni and Shi'a Islamist parties and movements returned to Iraq, where they played key roles in shaping Iraq's emerging political system. Iraqi politics, after 2003, became defined by identities – making political Islam an important tool for legitimacy.

Some places in northern Iraq have, at various times, fallen under strict Salafi-*jihadi* rule. From 2004 to 2007 and again from 2014 to 2017, as the security situation deteriorated and the Iraqi state proved unable to capably govern, Sunni Islamist militant groups (namely, AQI, and subsequently the Islamic State) grew in strength and violently imposed their strict interpretations of Islamic law on the population. They established strongholds in the predominantly Sunni areas of northern and western Iraq, brutally enforcing harsh societal rules.[52]

Shi'a militia groups have also at times enforced strict rules in the areas of Baghdad and southern Iraq under their control. During the 2005-2007 civil war, sectarian violence soared as Shi'a militia groups violently attacked mixed areas of Baghdad.

At other times, however, sectarianism has been rejected. Sunni tribal leaders in Anbar province rejected AQI rule and took up arms against Sunni extremists in 2006 during what became known as the Anbar Awakening. This, coupled with the U.S.-led security offensive that cleared first Baghdad and later the provinces surrounding the capital, significantly degraded AQI's capabilities and networks. During the Surge, Iraqi forces also targeted Shi'a militia groups in Baghdad and throughout central and southern Iraq. Iraqi-led operations in Basra and Baghdad dealt a significant blow to JAM and culminated in Sadr's announcement to disband his once-fearsome militia.[53] By mid-2008, when the last Surge forces left Iraq, violence had plummeted by more than 60 percent.[54]

By 2017, however, the shift from identity to issue-based politics reappeared, as internal Shi'a, Kurdish, and Sunni struggles outweighed the sectarian narrative. An NDI poll that year found that most Iraqis blamed corruption and their own leaders, rather than sectarianism, for the rise of groups like ISIS. Moreover, the poll also revealed that Shi'a leaders such as Abadi or Sadr enjoy considerable popularity in Sunni areas.[55]

In 2018, protests erupted in Basra as the summer's heat and the state's lack of services (electricity and water) became unbearable for the many in the province, where the poverty level is highest in the country. Unlike previous years, however, this time the protesters also began targeting the Islamist groups that previously enjoyed legitimacy, including the headquarters of PMU groups. Many activists argued against the Islamists who had governed them since 2003. In response, the PMU and state forces repressed protesters.[56]

Iraqi society remains heavily fragmented and sectarian divisions still exist, providing an opening for the possible re-emergence of the Islamic State.[57] Iraq's leading Shi'a parties, *Dawa* and the Sadrist Trend, retain their Islamist character and have emphasized this identity to shore up support. On October 25, 2019, mass anti-corruption protests spread throughout the country. Protesters demanded that the government be held accountable for its actions and halt Iran's influence within Iraq. The government failed to respond to the demands, instead it made noncommittal promises of reform and instructed its security forces to crack down with brutal force - leading to hundreds dead and tens of thousands injured.[58] In January 2020, the largely Shiite protests, which challenged the political *status quo* established after Saddam Hussein's demise, were crushed after Sadr announced that the protests had taken the wrong path and he was withdrawing his support.[59] Following the formation of a new Iraqi government in early May, protesters returned to the streets, clashing with security forces. The summer months have brought the expansion of protests to the southern provinces over a lack of clean water and electricity.[60] As of late July, security forces have continued to use force to try and contain ongoing anti-corruption demonstrations.[61]

Islamism and the State

Iraq is a parliamentary democracy, unlike its neighbor Iran. The Iraqi Constitution guarantees the democratic rights of all Iraqi citizens as well as "full religious rights to freedom of religious belief and practice of all individuals."[62] Yet the Iraqi Constitution stipulates Islam as the official religion of the state and makes clear that no law may be enacted that contradicts the provisions of Islam. The ambiguities inherent in these provisions have led to challenges in interpretation and meaning. In some areas of Iraq, local governments have adopted stricter interpretations of Islamic law. The provincial councils in Basra and Najaf, for instance, have banned the consumption, sales, or transit of alcohol.[63] In November 2010, the Baghdad provincial council used a resolution from 1996 to similarly ban the sale of alcohol.[64] There have been occasional violent raids or attacks on venues believed to be selling alcohol.[65]

The Iraqi government's response to Islamist militant groups has varied. Islamist parties dominated provincial and national governments from 2004 to 2008. During that time, the state was both unwilling and unable to challenge the Islamist militant groups that threatened the state's legitimacy. Shi'a militia groups penetrated elements of the Iraqi Security Forces, and certain paramilitary and police units were accused of perpetrating brutal sectarian violence.[66] The threat from extremist groups ultimately jeopardized the functioning of the Iraqi state by late 2006 and, in early 2007, U.S. forces announced a change of strategy in Iraq and the deployment of 20,000 additional troops in what became known as the Surge. As the counterinsurgency offensives of the Surge unfolded, the Iraqi state became more willing and able to challenge Sunni and Shi'a extremist groups as their influence and capability waned.[67] U.S. support during this time was critical in giving the Iraqi Security Forces and Iraq's political leadership the confidence to challenge extremist groups. U.S. and Iraqi leaders also worked to professionalize the Iraqi Security Forces, expand their capabilities, and root out corrupt or sectarian elements.[68] U.S. and Iraqi operations from 2007 to the present significantly degraded both Sunni and Shi'a extremist groups and reduced violence by over 90 percent.[69]

Today, Iraqi security forces are struggling to target the Islamic State in Iraq amid the coronavirus pandemic. Despite the growing influence of the PMU, which Amnesty International and Human Rights Watch have both criticized for committing war crimes, the former government of Adil Abdul-Mahdi did not act against Shi'a militant groups.[70] Through grassroots activism, the Iraqi people demanded the removal of the corrupt central government, specifically Abdul-Mahdi, who allowed Iranian leadership to play a significant role in Iraq's politics. The current PM, Mustafa al-Kadhimi, was thrust into a dysfunctional central government, and it is unclear whether the Iraqi state can maintain the will or muster the ability to sufficiently check Shi'a militant groups (some of which continue to receive Iranian assistance), or whether political interests will enable such groups to expand.

Endnotes

1. Alissa J. Rubin and Falih Hassan, "Iraqi Prime Minister Tries to Rein in Militias, and Their Grip on Economy," New York Times, July 1, 2019, https://www.nytimes.com/2019/07/01/world/middleeast/iraq-

armed-groups-prime-minister.html.
2. "AP Explains: Who are Iraq's Iran-backed militias?" Associated Press, December 31, 2019, https://apnews.com/57a346b17d6da07ae-732ba1437520fd2
3. Michael Knights, Hamdi Malik, and Aymenn Jawad al-Tamimi, "The Future of Iraq's Popular Mobilization Forces," Washington Institute for Near East Policy Policywatch 3321, May 28, 2020, https://www.washingtoninstitute.org/policy-analysis/view/the-future-of-iraqs-popular-mobilization-forces.
4. Ali Alfoneh, "Succession Crisis in Iraq's Popular Mobilization Forces," Arab Gulf States Institute in Washington, April 3, 2020, https://agsiw.org/succession-crisis-in-iraqs-popular-mobilization-forces/.
5. Vali Nasr, The Shi'a Revival: How Conflicts within Islam will Shape the Future (New York: Norton, 2006), 117.
6. Patrick Cockburn, Muqtada (New York: Scribner, 2008), 31; Faleh Abdul-Jabar, The Shiite Movement in Iraq (London: Saqi, 2003).
7. Jamar, The Shi'ite Movement in Iraq, 78-80; Islamic Dawa Party, "Party History," n.d., http://www.islamicdawaparty.com/?module=home&fname=history.php&active=7&show=1.
8. Simona Foltyn, "Will Iraq's Old Divisions Undermine Its New Prime Minister?" Foreign Policy, February 5, 2019, https://foreignpolicy.com/2019/02/05/iraqs-prime-minister-faces-old-challenges-to-deliver-on-reform/.
9. "Instability in Iraq During Leadership Transition," The Cipher Brief, May 11, 2020, https://www.thecipherbrief.com/column_article/instability-in-iraq-during-leadership-transition.
10. Jabar, The Shi'ite Movement in Iraq, 272-273.
11. Marisa Cochrane Sullivan, "The Fragmentation of the Sadrist Movement," Institute for the Study of War Iraq Report 12, January 2009, http://www.understandingwar.org/files/Iraq%20Report%2012.pdf.
12. Kanan Makiya, The Rope (New York: Pantheon Books, 2016).
13. Ibid.
14. F. Brinley Bruton, "Muqtada Al-Sadr Recasts Himself Ahead of Iraq Elections," NBC News, May 11, 2018, https://www.nbcnews.com/news/world/muqtada-al-sadr-recasts-himself-ahead-iraq-elections-n872921.
15. Isabel Coles, "Pompeo Urges Iraq to Act Against Killers of Top Security Analyst," Wall Street Journal, July 8, 2020, https://www.wsj.com/articles/pompeo-urges-iraq-to-act-against-killers-of-top-security-analyst-11594242303.
16. Crispin Smith, "Iraq's Raid on Iran-Backed Militias: Is the

New Prime Minister Ready to Rein Them In?" Just Security, July 16, 2020, https://www.justsecurity.org/71438/iraqs-raid-on-iran-backed-militias-is-the-new-prime-minister-ready-to-rein-them-in/.

17. Faleh Abdul Jabar, "The Iraqi Protest Movement: From Identity Politics to Issue Politics," LSE Middle East Centre Paper Series 25, June 2018, https://eprints.lse.ac.uk/88294/1/Faleh_Iraqi%20Protest%20Movement_Published_English.pdf
18. "Shiite Politics in Iraq: The Role of the Supreme Council," International Crisis Group Middle East Report Number 70, November 15, 2007.
19. "URGENT...SIIC, Badr Organization announce their official split," All Iraq News, March 11, 2012, http://www.alliraqnews.com/en/index.php?option=com_content&view=article&id=5847:urgentsiic-badr-organization-announce-their-official-split&catid=35:political&Itemid=2.
20. "Hakim announces the establishment of the National Wisdom Movement," Al-Sumaria News, July 24, 2017, https://www.alsumaria.tv/news/210878/%D8%A7%D9%84%D8%AD%D9%83%D9%8A%D9%85-%D9%8A%D8%B9%D9%84%D9%86-%D8%AA%D8%A3%D8%B3%D9%8A%D8%B3-%D8%AA%D9%8A%D8%A7%D8%B1-%D8%A7%D9%84%D8-%AD%D9%83%D9%85%D8%A9-%D8%A7%D9%84%D9%88%D8%B7%D9%86%D9%8A/ar
21. Ibrahim Al-Marashi, "Breaking Badr: Iraq's Divisive Shia Politics," TRT World, March 8, 2019, https://www.trtworld.com/opinion/breaking-badr-iraq-s-divisive-shia-politics-24768.
22. Mustafa Habib, "Taming The Beast: Can Iraq Ever Control Its Controversial Volunteer Militias?" Niqash, n.d., http://www.niqash.org/en/articles/security/5323/
23. Renad Mansour, "Why are Iraq's Paramilitaries Turning on their own ranks?" Washington Post, February 18, 2019, https://www.washingtonpost.com/news/monkey-cage/wp/2019/02/18/why-are-iraqs-paramilitaries-turning-on-their-own-ranks/
24. Renad Mansour, "The Sunni Predicament in Iraq," Carnegie Endowment for International Peace, March 2016, http://carnegieendowment.org/2016/03/03/sunni-predicament-in-iraq-pub-62924.
25. Basim Al-Azami, "The Muslim Brotherhood: Genesis and Development," in Faleh A. Jabar, ed., Ayatollahs, Sufis and Ideologues: State, Religion and Social Movements in Iraq (London: Saqi, 2002), 164.
26. Ibid.; Graham Fuller and Rend Rahim Francke, The Arab Shi'a : The Forgotten Muslims (Basingstoke, UK: Palgrave Macmillan, 2000);

"Iraqi Islamic Party," globalsecurity.org, n.d., http://www.globalsecurity.org/military/world/iraq/iip.htm; Iraqi Islamist Party, "History," n.d., http://www.iraqiparty.com/page/who-are-we/.

27. Thabit Abdullah, A Short History of Iraq: From 636 to the Present (London: Longman, 2003).
28. "Iraqi Islamic Party"; Iraqi Islamic Party, "History."
29. Ibid.
30. Jeremy Domergue and Marisa Cochrane Sullivan, "Balancing Maliki," Institute for the Study of War Iraq Report 14, June 26, 2009, http://understandingwar.org/files/IraqReport14.pdf.
31. Mustafa al-Kadimi, "Iraq Protests Present Muslim Brotherhood With Opportunity," Al Monitor, January 9, 2013, http://www.al-monitor.com/pulse/originals/2013/01/muslim-brotherhood-iraq.html.
32. Muhanad Seloom, "An Unhappy Return: What the Iraqi Islamic Party Gave Up to Gain Power," Carnegie Middle East Center, November 19, 2018, https://carnegie-mec.org/2018/11/19/unhappy-return-what-iraqi-islamic-party-gave-up-to-gain-power-pub-77747.
33. Roel Meijer, "The Association of Muslim Scholars in Iraq," MERIP Middle East Report 237, Winter 2005, http://www.merip.org/mer/mer237/association-muslim-scholars-iraq
34. "Irakische Streitkräfte starten Rückeroberung Ramadis," Deutsche Welle, May 26, 2015, http://www.dw.com/de/irakische-streit-kr%C3%A4fte-starten-r%C3%BCckeroberung-ramadis/a-18477575.
35. Edward Wong, "Turnout in the Iraqi Election is Reported at 70 Percent," New York Times, December 22, 2005, http://www.nytimes.com/2005/12/22/world/middleeast/turnout-in-the-iraqi-election-is-reported-at-70-percent.html; Anthony H. Cordesman, Iraq's Evolving Insurgency and the Risk of Civil War, Center for Strategic and International Studies, 2006, 8, http://reliefweb.int/sites/reliefweb.int/files/resources/1B26E4C64879415AC125715D002C49E3-csis-irq-26apr.pdf.
36. United States Forces-Iraq, "The Insurgency," July 31, 2009, http://www.usf-iraq.com/?option=com_content&task=view&id=729&Itemid=45.
37. Kenneth Katzman, "Al Qaeda in Iraq: Assessment and Outside Links," Congressional Research Service, August 15, 2008, http://www.fas.org/sgp/crs/terror/RL32217.pdf; DoD News Briefing with Commander, U.S. Forces-Iraq Gen. Raymond Odierno from the Pentagon, June 4, 2010.
38. Mark Tarallo, "After Setbacks, ISIS Ramps Up Attacks," ASIS International, August 1, 2020, https://www.asisonline.org/securi-

ty-management-magazine/articles/2020/08/after-setbacks-isis-ramps-up-attacks/.

39. Alissa J. Rubin, Lara Jakes, and Eric Schmitt, "ISIS Attacks Surge in Iraq Amid Debate on U.S. Troop Levels," New York Times, June 10, 2020, https://www.nytimes.com/2020/06/10/world/middleeast/iraq-isis-strategic-dialogue-troops.html.
40. United Nations Analytical Support and Sanctions Monitoring Team, "Twenty-Sixth Report of the Analytical Support and Sanctions Monitoring Team Submitted Pursuant to Resolution 2368 (2017) Concerning ISIL (Da'Esh), Al-Qaida and Associated Individuals and Entities," July 23, 2020, https://undocs.org/S/2020/717.
41. Rafid Fadhil Ali, "Kurdish Islamist Groups in Northern Iraq," Jamestown Foundation Terrorism Monitor 6, iss. 22, November 25, 2008, http://www.jamestown.org/single/?no_cache=1&tx_ttnews[tt_news]=34176.
42. Qassim Khidhir Hamad, "Kurdish Election Lists," Niqash (Baghdad), June 30, 2009.
43. Kathleen Ridolfo, "A Survey of Armed Groups in Iraq," Radio Free Europe/Radio Liberty Iraq Report 7, no. 20, June 4, 2004.
44. Kurdistan Regional Government, "The Kurdistan Parliament," n.d., http://www.krg.org/articles/detail.asp?rnr=160&lngnr=12&smap=04070000&anr=15057; Kurdistan Parliament, "The Members of the Parliament for Third Term 2009," n.d., http://www.perleman.org/Default.aspx?page=Parliamentmembers&c=Presidency-Member2009&group=40.
45. Ibid.
46. Ibidem.
47. "Iraq," CIA World Factbook, April 6, 2011, https://www.cia.gov/library/publications/the-world-factbook/geos/iz.html; U.S. Department of State, "Background Note: Iraq," September 17, 2010, http://www.state.gov/r/pa/ei/bgn/6804.htm.
48. Ibid.
49. "US military says 77,000 Iraqis killed over 5 years," Associated Press, October 15, 2010, http://www.post-journal.com/page/content.detail/id/120540/US-military-says-77-000-Iraqis-killed-over-5-years-.html?isap=1&nav=5030.
50. "Iraq Conflict: Civilians suffering 'staggering' violence – UN," BBC News, January 19, 2016, http://www.bbc.com/news/world-middle-east-35349861
51. Bethan McKernan, "Scale of Iraqi civilian casualties inflicted by Isis revealed by UN," Independent (London), January 3, 2017, http://

www.independent.co.uk/news/world/middle-east/iraq-isis-casualties-civilian-islamic-state-un-figures-united-nations-middle-east-mosul-a7507526.html.

52. Rod Nordland, "Despite Gains, Petraeus Cautious About Iraq," Newsweek, August 21, 2008, http://www.newsweek.com/2008/08/20/avoiding-the-v-word.html; "Marriages split al Qaeda alliance," Washington Times, August 31, 2007, http://www.washingtontimes.com/news/2007/aug/31/marriages-split-al-qaeda-alliance/?page=all#pagebreak; "Severe Islamic law which banned suggestive cucumbers cost Al Qaeda public support in Iraq," Daily Mail (London), August 10, 2008, http://www.dailymail.co.uk/news/worldnews/article-1043409/Severe-Islamic-law-banned-suggestive-cucumbers-cost-Al-Qaeda-public-support-Iraq.html.
53. Marisa Cochrane Sullivan, "The Fragmentation of the Sadrist Movement," Institute for the Study of War Iraq Report 12, January 2009, 37-38, http://www.understandingwar.org/files/Iraq%20Report%2012.pdf.
54. Viola Gienger, "Iraq Civilian Deaths Drop for Third Year as Toll Eases After U.S. Drawdown," Bloomberg, December 29, 2010, http://www.bloomberg.com/news/2010-12-30/iraq-civilian-deaths-drop-for-third-year-as-toll-eases-after-u-s-drawdown.html.
55. National Democratic Institute, Improved Security Provides Opening for Cooperation in Iraq: March to April 2017 Survey Findings, June 7, 2017, https://www.ndi.org/publications/improved-security-provides-opening-cooperation-iraq-march-april-2017-survey-findings.
56. Author Renad Mansour's interviews with protesters and analysts in Basra, Iraq, February 2019.
57. Marisa Cochrane Sullivan and James Danly, "Iraq on the Eve of Elections," Institute for the Study of War Backgrounder, March 3, 2010, http://www.understandingwar.org/files/IraqEveofElections.pdf.
58. Alissa J. Rubin, "Iraq in Worst Political Crisis in Years as Death Toll Mounts From Protests," New York Times, December 21, 2019, https://www.nytimes.com/2019/12/21/world/middleeast/Iraq-protests-Iran.html.
59. Jane Arraf, "Iraq's Protests Shook The Government. Now The Movement Is Nearly Crushed," NPR, February 21, 2020, https://www.npr.org/2020/02/21/807725624/iraqs-powerful-protests-forced-political-change-now-they-re-nearly-crushed.
60. Hassan Ali Ahmad, "Iraqi Protests Resume as New Government Builds Support for Reform," Al- Monitor, May 21, 2020, https://www.al-monitor.com/pulse/originals/2020/05/iraq-kadimi-protests.

html.

61. Amina Ismail, "Two Protesters Die after Clashes with Police in Baghdad, Medics and Security Sources Say," Reuters, July 27, 2020, https://www.reuters.com/article/us-iraq-protests/two-protesters-die-after-clashes-with-police-in-baghdad-medics-and-security-sources-say-idUSKCN24S1FA.
62. Iraqi Constitution, Section One, Article Two.
63. "Alcohol Banned in Iraq holy Shiite City of Najaf," Middle East Online, October 11, 2009, http://www.middle-east-online.com/english/?id=34869.
64. John Leland, "Baghdad Raids on Alcohol Sellers Stir Fears," New York Times, January 15, 2011, http://www.nytimes.com/2011/01/16/world/middleeast/16iraq.html.
65. Ibid.; "Kurdish Club Scene Booming as Baghdad Bans Alcohol," Associated Press, January 11, 2011.
66. Lionel Beehner, "Shiite Militias and Iraq's Security Forces," Council on Foreign Relations Backgrounder, November 30, 2005, http://www.cfr.org/iraq/shiite-militias-iraqs-security-forces/p9316; "Iraq death squad caught in act" BBC, February 16, 2006, http://news.bbc.co.uk/2/hi/middle_east/4719252.stm; Steve Inskeep, "Riding Herd on the Iraqi Police's Dirty Wolf Brigade,'" National Public Radio, March 28, 2007, http://www.npr.org/templates/story/story.php?storyId=9170738.
67. Sullivan, "The Fragmentation of the Sadrist Movement."
68. For more information on the growth and professionalization of the Iraqi Security Forces during the Surge, see LTG James Dubik, "Building Security Forces and Ministerial Capacity: Iraq as a Primer," Institute for the Study of War Best Practices in Counterinsurgency Report 1, August 2009, http://www.csmonitor.com/World/Middle-East/2011/0208/US-reports-20-percent-drop-in-Iraq-violence.
69. Scott Peterson, "US reports 20 percent drop in Iraq violence," Christian Science Monitor, February 8, 2011, http://www.csmonitor.com/World/Middle-East/2011/0208/US-reports-20-percent-drop-in-Iraq-violence.
70. "Iraq: End irresponsible arms transfers fuelling militia war crimes," Amnesty International, January 5, 2017, https://www.amnesty.org/en/latest/news/2017/01/iraq-end-irresponsible-arms-transfers-fuelling-militia-war-crimes/; "Iraq: Possible War Crimes by Shi'a Militia," Human Rights Watch, January 31, 2016, https://www.hrw.org/news/2016/01/31/iraq-possible-war-crimes-Shi'a-militia.

15 Jordan

Quick Facts

Population: 10,820,644 (July 2020 est.)
Area: 89,342 sq km
Ethnic Groups: Jordanian 69.3%, Syrian 13.3%, Palestinian 6.7%, Egyptian 6.7%, Iraqi 1.4%, other 2.6% (includes Armenian, Circassian) (2015 est.)
Government Type: Parliamentary constitutional monarchy
GDP (official exchange rate): $40.13 billion (2017 est.)

Source: CIA World FactBook (Last Updated August 2020)

Jordan

Jordan has faced a growing challenge to its stability in recent years from violent Islamist groups. The Kingdom has weathered the collapse of order in neighboring nations, first in Iraq and more recently in Syria, as well as the accompanying rise of the Islamic State terrorist group in both countries. These developments were accompanied by large-scale refugee flows, which have upset the Kingdom's demographic balance and which could still destabilize its social structure.

For its part, the Jordanian regime has long waged a wide-ranging and determined ideological struggle against radical Islamic organizations on its soil. In this contest, the Kingdom has sought to de-legitimize Salafi-jihadi ideology while disseminating a brand of moderate traditional Islam. Nevertheless, the large and easily radicalized Palestinian component of the country's population, the influence of the Muslim Brotherhood offshoot in the country, and Salafi jihadi trends from Iraq and Syria all pose real and imminent threats to the stability of the Kingdom.

Islamist Activity

Islam has been a part of the political life of Jordan for the country's entire modern history. In 1921, the British crafted the Emirate of Transjordan, with King Abdallah I as the new nation's king. Abdallah's Islamic identity, as well as the Hashemite family's connections to the Prophet Muhammad's tribe, was and continues to be a central source of the monarchy's legitimacy. Abdallah and his grandson Hussein presented themselves as deeply religious Muslims, publicly praying, taking part in rituals, and preforming the *Hajj* pilgrimage. In 1952, the Jordanian constitution made Islam the kingdom's official religion and stipulated that the king must be a Muslim, born of Muslim parents. The constitution also established *sharia* as a key legal framework of the kingdom. Notably, however, *sharia* was never considered the sole source of legal legitimacy.[1]

The radical Islamic camp in Jordan is composed of two separate – though frequently overlapping – wings. The first is the main body of Jordanian Islamists, which has been affiliated with the Muslim Brotherhood (MB). The second is the radical Salafi-*jihadi* movement, traditionally embodied by al-Qaeda and more recently also by supporters of the Islamic State (IS).

The radical Islamic camp in Jordan largely draws its strength from a diverse array of sources and circumstances within Jordanian society. Foremost among them are: its own significant organizational infrastructure inside the country; the indirect influence and public sympathy from the wider activities of the MB; the inflammatory influence of the wars in Iraq and Syria; the ongoing Arab conflict with Israel; and the rise of Islamism across the region following the Arab Spring.

The Muslim Brotherhood

The Muslim Brotherhood is deeply rooted in Jordan, and is one of the country's largest Islamic collectives, currently counting more than 10,000 members among its various factions.[2] The group's (formerly) healthy relationship with the central government and the crown allowed it to establish a broad *dawa* (proselytization) network of civil society organizations and charities,[3] operating via the social welfare services of the Islamic Center Charity Society (ICCS).[4] Since the emergence of the Jordanian Brotherhood in 1946, which formally adopted the name "Muslim Brotherhood Group" (MBG) in 1953, internal fissures and disarray over the direction of the organization have marred the its efforts.

Much of the Brotherhood's Jordan branch's formal politics has been channeled through the Islamic Action Front (IAF). Today the party and its bloc hold 15 seats – 10 of which are held by the IAF – in Jordan's 130-person parliament,[5] making it the largest opposition party in Jordanian government. This relative position of authority follows two cycles of IAF restraint, as the group boycotted the 2010 and 2013 elections in protest over allegedly biased referendum laws.[6]

Before the 2016 elections, the IAF updated its political platform to encompass a more secular and pragmatic narrative: IAF elections chairman Murad Adayle was quoted in an interview with the *Jordan Times* (which has since been removed from the outlet's website) that the party's 'main challenge would be to outperform former municipal leaders, which "cannot be achieved through ideologies."'[7] The decision is in keeping with the National Coalition for Reform (NCR), an electoral body comprised of Jordanian religious and ethnic minority groups, of which the IAF is a member.[8] Despite the recent decision by the Jordanian Court of Cassation to dissolve the country's Muslim Brotherhood branch (described in detail below), the IAF has been permitted to exist – at least so far.[9]

Platform changes of this variety, which have brought the IAF further into the Jordanian political mainstream, continued after the 2016 elections; in January 2017, for instance, both the Muslim Brotherhood and the IAF declared an end to their boycott of the U.S.[10] Subsequently, in June 2019, the IAF adopted political positions that, unlike previous ones, did not perpetuate demands for constitutional amendments to undermine the authority of the King. The IAF's published opinion deemed the Jordanian constitution to be "very important and advanced," and also said that "Extremism and radicalization are rejected and are condemned at the moral and human levels."[11]

In October 2012, internal fissures within the Muslim Brotherhood led to the formation of the Zam Zam Initiative. When the new entity was announced, its stated goals were encapsulated in five "phases." These included: the recruitment of new cadres and membership, including youth; launching a manifesto and laying down internal laws; a new political project, and; the pursuit of participation in national institutions and partnership with the government.[12] In 2013, the Zam Zam Initiative entered formal politics with the formation of the National Congress Party, otherwise known as Zamzam, and would go on to win 5 seats in the 2016 elections.[13] In April 2014, ten of the Initiative's leading members were expelled from the Muslim Brotherhood Group's ranks after calling for then-MBG Secretary General Hammam Saeed's removal.[14]

Zamzam is currently chaired by Dr. Rahil al Gharaibeh, one of several prominent Muslim Brotherhood figures identified by former Wilson Center visiting journalist Tarq Alnaimat as part of the organization's "pragmatic doves," calls for a domestic focus, allegiance to Jordan's crown government, and cooperation with the country's other political parties.[15]

Among those expelled by the Muslim Brotherhood Group was Abdul Majid Thuneibat, who would go on to form the Muslim Brotherhood Society (MBS, also known as the Muslim Brotherhood Association) in 2015.[16] Due to its stated goal of greater allegiance to the Jordanian Crown, Thuneibat's faction received a license to operate in Jordan, while the MBG did not. As pointed out by the Counter Extremism Project, "The move also restricted the MBG from holding public events, prompting the group to cancel a May 2015 rally that would have marked its 70th anniversary.... That July, the Jordanian Department of Land and Survey seized seven MBG properties and transferred them to the MBS."[17]

The MBG was formally dissolved by the Jordanian judicial system in July 2020.[18] However, the legal decision - made by the country's Court of Cassation – was not sudden; rather, it represented the culmination of a years-long back-and-forth between the Jordanian Brotherhood and the government. In a January 2013 interview with *The Atlantic*, Jordan's king, Abdullah II, referred to the MBG as a "wolf in sheep's clothing."[19] Although the MBG had made public overtures suggesting its willingness to comply with the established *status quo* – including renouncing ties to the global Muslim Brotherhood organization, secularizing its slogan,[20] and engaging in internal debates about the acceptability of a "civil state" model[21] – none of these steps prompted the government to adopt a more permissive attitude. Beginning in 2014, the government launched an anti-Brotherhood campaign that involved taking over various social charities and the removal of Brotherhood-aligned sheikhs from the traditional roles they held in mosques.[22] The government prevented the MBG from holding internal elections in March 2016 (a right given only to officially recognized groups) and shut down the MBG headquarters that April.[23]

Explanations for the Crown's focus on the MBG, effectively legislating it out of legal existence, are fundamentally twofold; poor standing with King Abdullah II, and declining public relevance. As Hana Jaber, a former Senior Fellow with the Arab Reform Initiative, opined for the *Fondation pour la Recherche Stratégique*, Adullah II's reign has been marked by "hard, ultraliberal policies which increased inequalities and after a few years led to an unrestrained business culture." Anything that conflicted with this vision (including the Brotherhood) was judged "as obsolete and jarring with his vision of modernity."[24] Also worthy of note are a series of incendiary comments leveled by senior members of the MBG condemning the Jordanian government and its foreign alliances, including condemnation of the UAE, an important regional ally for Amman, [25] and praise for the radical Hamas movement in the Palestinian Territories.[26]

At the same time, the MBG had lost footing among the Jordanian public in recent years. In 2018, for instance, Muslim Brotherhood-supported groups were defeated in the elections at the flagship Jordan University.[27] The group also lost control of the main teachers' union, and, after 26 years lost its dominance of the Engineers Union.[28]

Salafi jihadism

The Muslim Brotherhood has played a pivotal role in the dissemination and acceptance of Salafi-*jihadi* messaging, especially among younger Jordanian citizens. Outbreaks of violence between Israel and the Palestinians, particularly in the Gaza Strip, and the wars in Iraq, Syria and Afghanistan, have all served to strengthen Salafi sentiment in Jordan.

The ebb and flow of *jihadist* activity in Iraq profoundly affected Islamist organizations in Jordan. The 2006 killing of Abu Musab al-Zarqawi and coalition successes against al-Qaeda (which were aided by Jordan) created fissures in the Jordanian *jihadist* movement. The resulting product was a more "pragmatic" wing of the movement, led by the prominent Salafi cleric Abu Muhammad al-Maqdisi. Al-

Maqdisi has consistently criticized the school of thought epitomized by al-Zarqawi (and more recently by Abu Bakr Al-Baghdadi's ISIS), which sanctions intra-Muslim conflict due to ideological and political differences. Al-Maqdisi did not change the principles of *takfir*. However, he made the case against *jihadist* attacks inside Jordan, revising his own views about the permissibility of collateral casualties among Muslims.[29]

Another prominent figure in the Jordanian scene is Abu Qatada, who has for many years been considered a spiritual leader of a European Salafi-*jihadi* group. In August 2017, Abu Qatada said on a TV program:

> Our rivals accept only extermination – it's either us or them. If we raise and adopt the true banner of Islam – rather than the forged version of Islam in which the Muslims surrender to non-Muslims – we will be upholding Islam of glory and of an Islamic state, an Islam that implements the noble prophecies about the dominance of the banner of the Muslims in the world, about Islam raiding each and every home, about Islam invading Rome... This would be the glorious Islam. If we accept and believe in that [true] version of Islam, there can only be one outcome: confrontation.[30]

Both al-Maqdisi and Abu Qatada fell out of favor with radical groups following the rise of the Islamic State. However, both remain influential and live freely in Jordan after years of sporadic incarceration, disseminating messages and communicating with their followers via social media (primarily Telegram) on a near-daily basis.[31]

Many Jordanians have joined *jihadi* groups in Iraq and Syria, such as al-Qaeda and its affiliate Jabhat Fath Al-Sham (formerly Jabhat Al-Nusra), or the Islamic State. The most recent available publicly figures from the International Centre for the Study of Radicalisation and Political Violence, published in 2018, estimated thst between 3,000-3,950 Jordanian nationals had left Jordan to join the Islamic State, and only 250 had returned. Similar numbers are corroborated by a senior Jordanian security official.[32] However, as one October 2019 article in *Small Wars* notes, Jordan's process of managing the flow of returning foreign fighters is incredibly opaque. While Amman has "touted" its effectiveness in addressing the issue, only the most basic information about detained returnees, such as length of prison sentences, is released. Thus, estimates of how many *jihadists* have in actuality returned to Jordan can only reasonably phrased as "more than 250."[33]

Islamism and Society

Strict Islamic codes enjoy popular support among both the country's Trans-Jordanian and Palestinian people. In recent years, Islamic dress – particularly for women – has become more ubiquitous. Islamic bookstores selling radical tracts can now be found near almost any mosque in Amman. Polls have found widespread support in Jordan for the enactment of *sharia* law; a March 2019 study by Rice University's Baker Institute reveals that approximately 75 percent of people surveyed "expressed support for a constitution that emphasizes *sharia* law in some capacity." What's more, "approximately 90 percent of Jordanians expressed support for a legal system that maintains the importance of Islamic law."[34] It is important to note, however, that support for Islamic law does not translate into support for leaders of Islam influencing state politics. The same survey asked respondents whether or not Jordan would be better off if clerics of Islam could influence government decisions or elections. "Between 70 and 85 percent of respondents opposed clerics interfering in electoral politics…and nearly 80 percent also opposed the use of mosques for campaigning." What's more, "[s]light majorities also felt that it would be harmful for religious leaders to influence government decisions."[35]

Overall support for Salafi-*jihadi* groups appears to be declining. This is true both in the case of IS, as already demonstrated, as well as in the case of al-Qaeda, which in 2014 was supported by only 13 percent of the population.[36] In a series of surveys conducted three times between 2015 and 2017, 79-86 percent answered that they considered IS a terrorist organization and a national security threat.[37] (More recent polling is not publicly available at present). Nevertheless, Salafi-*jihadi* attitudes have multiple outlets, including popular mosques not under the regime's supervision and bookstands that propagate a radical, exclusionary religious worldview, as well as the many websites of global *jihadist* groups.

Islamism and the State

Per Chapter 1, Article 2 of the Constitution of Jordan, Islam is the official religion of the state.[35] What's more, in an October 2016 speech titled "Rule of Law and Civil State," King Abdullah II highlighted publicly that "[i]n a civil state, religion is a key contributor to the value system and social norms."[38] However, in the same speech, King Abdullah highlighted his (and, by extension, the state's) approach to governance and Islam when he said "we will not allow anyone to manipulate religion to serve political interests or gains for a specific faction."[39]

In practice, this has meant the propagation of a "state sanctioned" brand of Islam. This takes the form of the "Amman Message," a philosophy within Islamic thought dictated in a sermon by King Abdullah II on the eve of Ramadan in 2004. The Amman Message revolves around three central "points": 1) that all *Mathhabs* (legal schools) of Sunnia, Shi'a, and Ibadhi Islam are legitimate, that 2) *takfir* (declarations of apostasy) between Muslims were forbidden, and 3) standardizing the subjective and objective requirements to issue, meet, and violate a *fatwa* (a ruling issued by a religious authority).[40] Since its rollout in 2005, the Amman Message has been endorsed in various capacities by over 550 secular and Islamic government officials from 82 different countries, according to Jordanian government sources.[41]

The Amman Message has provided the Crown with significant latitude in its relationship with Islamic groups. By using the legal measures afforded to it, the regime of Abdullah II and the government of Jordan are able to dictate which Islamist groups are permissible or impermissible based on the parameters set forth in the Amman Message, which authorities have wielded to great effect.

In an anonymous interview with Scott Williamson, the

researcher of the aforementioned Baker Institute study, one Jordanian described his country's Grand Mufti as more afraid of King Abdullah II than he is of God.[42] This anecdote, as well as the state's selectively permissive dynamic with Muslim Brotherhood-aligned groups, demonstrates a larger trend within the government's relationship with Islam. As of 2014, Jordan was "demanding that preachers refrain from any speech against King Abdullah II and the royal family, slander against leaders of neighboring Arab states, incitement against the United States and Europe, and sectarianism and support for jihad and extremist thought." It also began providing a suggested list of acceptable Friday sermon topics, which were then made mandatory two years later, in 2016. Those religious figures who comply with state standards are provided a salary, invitations to workshops, and travel assistance for pilgrimage; all paid for by the government. [43] By contrast, Zaki Bani Irshaid, a prominent member of the MBG, was sentenced to 18 months in prison in 2015 after making Facebook posts deemed harmful to Jordan's relationship with the UAE.[44]

The Jordanian government has also partnered with prominent *imams* in the pursuit of a policy agenda that might overlap with Islam. In 2002, the government formed the Higher Population Council (HPC), which oversees the country's family planning-related programs. When the HPC published its 2005 Contraceptive Security Strategy, the Ministry of Awqaf was one of the three central coordinating bodies for the plan's implementation.[45] In February 2017, the Crown recommended that parliament repeal Article 308 of the national penal code, which allowed rapists to avoid punishment if they married their victims. Those offices worked with activists and religious leaders to pressure parliament in this effort. The article was repealed in April of that year.[46]

Jordan has been a member of the U.S.-led coalition to battle IS since 2014. In retaliation for the execution of Mu'ath Safi Yousef al-Kaseasbeh, who was captured by the Islamic State in December 2014 and immolated on camera in January 2015, anti-ISIS protests swept the country and were attended by the country's matriarch, Queen Rania. In response, officials claimed the country was "upping the ante" against the terror group with "dozens" of air strikes against

IS targets.[47]

March 2016 saw the first incident of Jordan's General Intelligence Department (GID) coming into direct domestic confrontation with the Islamic State during a raid in Irbid. Seven ISIS members, as well as one state security officer, were killed in the fighting. Prior to the incident, 13 people linked to the cell were detained in earlier raids.[48] In December 2016, 10 people were killed and 34 others were wounded in an attack by Islamic State-affiliated gunman at a tourist destination in Karak.[49] In August 2018, Jordanian security forces killed "several" ISIS fighters at its border with Syria.[50] Two weeks later, four state security officers were killed in an explosion triggered by three people subscribing the Islamic State ideology.[51]

The issue of fighters returning to Jordan returning home after the fall of the ISIS *caliphate* is especially pressing, given the proximity of the Kingdom to both Syria and Iraq. As already stated, at least 250 Jordanians are known to have left the battlefields in Iraq and Syria and returned home. Official government policy states that any returning fighters will be sentenced to prison and must enter deradicalization and reintegration programs before they can reenter society.[52] Researchers at George Washington University's Program on Extremism found, through a series of anonymous semi-structured interviews, that much of Jordan's state deradicalization program is jointly managed by the GID and the Community Peace Center (CPC), an extension of the country's Public Security Department and Ministry of Interior.[53] This assessment was reinforced by Dr. Saud Al-Sharafat, a former Brigadier General of the GID, who elaborated that returning fighters from Syria will "remain captive to the secretive and sensitive" GID, and that dealing with those "terrorists" and their families is perceived to be "entirely a security and military matter, not a humanitarian one" by Jordanian authorities.[54]

Endnotes

1. See Shmuel Bar, "The Muslim Brotherhood in Jordan," Moshe Dayan Center for Middle Eastern and African Studies Data and Analysis, June 1998, http://www.dayan.tau.ac.il/d&a-jordan-bar.pdf.
2. "Muslim Brotherhood in Jordan," Counter Extremism Project, n.d., https://www.counterextremism.com/content/muslim-brotherhood-jor-

dan

3. These were widely referred to and named in Ibrahim Gharaybah, *Jamaat Al-Ikhwan Al-Muslimin fi-l-Urdun 1946-1996* (Amman: Markaz al-Urdun al-Jadid lil-Dirasat: Dar Sindibad lil-Nashr, 1997), 169-185; Quintan Wiktorowicz, *The Management of Islamic Activism* (State University of New York Press, 2001), 83-92
4. Colin Powers, "Run the country like a business? The economics of Jordan's Islamic action front," *Critical Research on Religion*, Vol. 7 (1) 2019. p. 42. https://journals.sagepub.com/doi/abs/10.1177/2050303218823244
5. "Islamic Action Front wins 15 seats, making it the largest bloc in Jordan parliament," *al-Bawaba*, September 23, 2016, https://www.albawaba.com/news/islamic-action-front-wins-15-seats-making-it-largest-bloc-jordan-parliament-885880
6. Kirk H. Sowell, "Takeaways From Jordan's Elections," Carnegie Endowment for International Peace. September 30, 2016, https://carnegieendowment.org/sada/64749
7. Sarah Timreck, "The Islamist Spectrum – Jordan's Mosaic," Woodrow Wilson International Center for Scholars. December 13, 2017, https://www.wilsoncenter.org/article/the-islamist-spectrum-jordans-mosaic
8. Bar, "The Muslim Brotherhood in Jordan," 50-52.
9. Mohammad Ersan, "Jordan court affirms Muslim Brotherhood 'does not exist' in latest twist over rival groups," *Middle East Eye*, July 23, 2020, https://www.middleeasteye.net/news/jordan-muslim-brotherhood-dissolution-ruling-king-abdullah-arab-spring?fbclid=I-wAR1Q16ll6b613I2YjN5b37al8gAdb1z7oxUgRX67X9UFBnhF-Cpeh2HT8gs4
10. "The Jordanian Brotherhood officially decides to end its boycott on the US," *Quds Press*, January 22, 2017, http://www.qudspress.com/index.php?page=show&id=27780.
11. Mohammed Kheir al-Rawashida, "Islamic Movement in Jordan Unveils Political Credentials," *Asharq Al-Awsat* (London), June 18, 2019, https://aawsat.com/english/home/article/1772576/islamic-movement-jordan-unveils-political-credentials
12. Larbi Sadiki, "Jordan: Arab Spring Washout?" *Al-Jazeera* (Doha), January 12, 2013, http://www.aljazeera.com/indepth/opinion/2013/01/201319134753750165.html
13. Sowell, "Takeaways From Jordan's Elections."
14. Taylor Luck, "Former Brotherhood leader faces disciplinary measures," *Jordan Times*, June 7, 2014, http://www.jordantimes.com/

news/local/former-brotherhood-leader-faces-disciplinary-measures
15. Tareq Alnaimat, "The Continued Fragmentation of the Jordanian Brotherhood," Carnegie Endowment for International Peace, October 18, 2018, https://carnegieendowment.org/sada/77531
16. "Abdul Majid Thuneibat," Counter Extremism Project, n.d., https://www.counterextremism.com/extremists/abdul-majid-thuneibat
17. "Muslim Brotherhoood in Jordan," Counter Extremism Project.
18. Jeffrey Goldberg, "The Modern King in the Arab Spring," *The Atlantic*, April 2013, https://www.theatlantic.com/magazine/archive/2013/04/monarch-in-the-middle/309270/
19. Taylor Luck, "Reinvention of Jordan's Muslim Brotherhood involves women – and Christians," *Washington Post*, September 20, 2016, https://www.washingtonpost.com/world/middle_east/a-rebranded-muslim-brotherhood-attempts-a-comeback-in-jordan/2016/09/19/b9be80a6-7deb-11e6-ad0e-ab0d12c779b1_story.html
20. Fathi Khattab, "Restructuring the Jordanian MB to accompany the concept of 'civil state,'" *Al-Ghad,* October 30, 2017, http://www.alghad.tv/%D8%A5%D8%B9%D8%A7%D8%AF%D8%A9-%D9%87%D9%8A%D9%83%D9%84%D8%A9-%D8%A5%D8%AE%D9%88%D8%A7%D9%86-%D8%A7%D9%84%D8%A3%D8%B1%D8%AF%D9%86-%D9%84%D9%85-%D9%88%D8%A7%D9%83%D8%A8%D8%A9-%D9%85%D9%81/
21. Tareq Al Naimat, "The Jordanian regime and the Muslim Brotherhood: a tug of war," Woodrow Wilson Center *Viewpoints* no. 58 (July 2014), https://www.wilsoncenter.org/sites/default/files/jordanian_regime_muslim_brotherhood_tug_of_war.pdf.
22. "Muslim Brotherhoood in Jordan," Counter Extremism Project.
23. Hana Jaber, *The Jordanian Muslim Brotherhood Movement: from Pillar of Monarchy to Enemy of the State*, Fondation Pour la Recherche Stratégique, July 17, 2017, https://www.frstrategie.org/en/programs/observatoire-du-monde-arabo-musulman-et-du-sahel/jordanian-muslim-brotherhood-movement-pillar-monarchy-enemy-state-2017?fbclid=IwAR0I2awDtnwavDLeIAL1JYKMGpgu-oUuXB7KMT2lNOylPID6EgFENs7282hE
24. Rana F. Sweis, "Jordan Gives Prison Term for Criticism on Facebook," *New York Times*, February 15, 2015, https://www.nytimes.com/2015/02/16/world/middleeast/jordan-sentences-muslim-brotherhood-leader-for-facebook-post.html
25. Suleiman Al-Khaildi, "Jordanian stage pro-Gaza rally near Israeli embassy," Reuters, July 20, 2014, http://www.reuters.com/

article/2014/07/20/us-palestinian-israel-jordan-idUSKBN0F-P0UY20140720.

26. Sean Yom and Wael Al-Khatib, "Islamists are losing support in Jordan," *Washington Post*, May 17, 2018, https://www.washingtonpost.com/news/monkey-cage/wp/2018/05/17/islamists-are-losing-support-in-jordan/?utm_term=.3a462fd85339.
27. Daoud Kuttab, "Jordan's Muslim Brotherhood loses control of powerful union after 26 years," *Arab News*, May 6, 2018. http://www.arabnews.com/node/1297276/middle-east
28. See al-Maqdisi's website, http://www.tawhed.ws/, and the subsequent debate with other jihadi authorities such as Ma'asari. For a summary of these debates, see Joas Wagemakers, "Reflections on Maqdisi's Arrest," *Jihadica*, October 2, 2010, http://www.jihadica.com/reflections-on-al-maqdisis-arrest/.
29. "Salafi Jordanian Cleric Abu Qatada Al-Filastini: True Islam Leads to Raiding Rome and Confrontation," Middle East Media Research Institute, August 12, 2017, https://www.memri.org/tv/salafi-jordanian-cleric-abu-qatada-true-islam-means-confrontation/transcript.
30. Cole Bunzel, "Abu Qatada al-Filastini: 'I am not a Jihadi, or a Salafi,'" *Jihadica*, October 26, 2018. http://www.jihadica.com/abu-qatada-al-filastini-i-am-not-a-jihadi-or-a-salafi/
31. Saud Al-Sharafat, "Assessing Jordan's National Strategyto Combat Violent Extremism," Washington Institute for Near East Policy *Fikra Forum*. August 10, 2018, https://www.washingtoninstitute.org/fikraforum/view/assessing-jordans-national-strategy-to-combat-violent-extremism
32. Scott Williamson, „*Separating Islam From Politics But Not the State: Implications for Religious Authority in Jordan*, Baker Institute, March 2019, https://www.bakerinstitute.org/media/files/files/a65139aa/cme-pub-luce-williamson-030719.pdf
33. Alia Awadallah, "Transparency Needed: The Prosecution, Detention, and Deradicalization of Foreign Fighters," *Small Wars Journal*, October 1, 2019, https://smallwarsjournal.com/jrnl/art/transparency-needed-prosecution-detention-and-deradicalization-foreign-fighters
34. Williamson, *Separating Islam From Politics But Not the State*.
35. Jacob Poushter, "Support for al Qaeda was low before (and after) Osama bin Laden's death," Pew Research Center, May 12 2014. http://www.pewresearch.org/fact-tank/2014/05/02/support-for-al-qaeda-was-low-before-and-after-osama-bin-ladens-death/
36. "Survey of Jordanian Public Opinion, National Poll #15," Center for

Insights in Survey Research (CISR), May 22-25, 2017, http://www.iri.org/sites/default/files/2017-7-12_jordan_poll_slides.pdf
37. Hashemite Kingdom of Jordan, *Constitution of the Hashemite Kingdom of Jordan*, n.d., https://www.refworld.org/docid/3ae6b53310.html
38. Hashemite Kingdom of Jordan, Office of King Abdullah II, *Rule of Law and Civil State.* By Abdullah II Ibn Al-Hussein. October 16, 2016. Accessed August 2, 2020. https://kingabdullah.jo/en/discussion-papers/rule-law-and-civil-state.
39. Hashemite Kingdom of Jordan. Office of King Abdullah II, *Rule of Law and Civil State,* October 16, 2016, https://kingabdullah.jo/en/discussion-papers/rule-law-and-civil-state.
40. "The Three Points of the Amman Message V.1," n.d., https://ammanmessage.com/the-three-points-of-the-amman-message-v-1/
41. Hashemite Kingdom in Jordan, *The Amman Message*, n.d., https://ammanmessage.com/grand-list-of-endorsements-of-the-amman-message-and-its-three-points/
42. Williamson, *Separating Islam From Politics But Not the State.*
43. William Booth and Taylor Luck, "To counter rise of Islamic State, Jordan imposes rules on Muslim clerics," *Washington Post*, November 9, 2014, https://www.washingtonpost.com/world/middle_east/to-counter-rise-of-the-islamic-state-jordan-imposes-rules-on-muslim-clerics/2014/11/09/4d5fce22-5937-11e4-bd61-346aee66ba29_story.html?tid=ss_tw&utm_term=.db4ce00caa06; Jacob Burns, "Dictating sermons by SMS, Jordan hopes to clamp down on 'extremism'" *Middle East Eye*, April 28, 2017, https://www.middleeasteye.net/news/dictating-sermons-sms-jordan-hopes-clamp-down-extremism
44. "Jordan: 18 Months for Criticizing UAE," Human Rights Watch, February 15, 2015, https://www.hrw.org/news/2015/02/19/jordan-18-months-criticizing-uae
45. Hashemite Kingdom of Jordan, Higher Population Council General Secretariat, *Contraceptive Security Strategy*, November 2005, https://www.rhsupplies.org/uploads/tx_rhscpublications/DOC48.pdf
46. Zena Tahhan, "'Historic day' as Jordanian parliament repeals rape law," *Al-Jazeera* (Doha), August 1, 2017, https://www.aljazeera.com/indepth/features/2017/08/day-jordanian-parliament-repeals-rape-law-170801103929836.html
47. "Islamic State Crisis: Thousands rally in Jordan," *BBC*, February 6, 2015, https://www.bbc.com/news/world-middle-east-31158919

48. "Jordan Raid: Eight killed in Irbid as forces 'foil IS plot,'" *BBC*, March 2, 2016, https://www.bbc.com/news/magazine-35701841
49. Maria Abi-Habib, "Islamic State Claims Responsibility for Jordan Attack," *Wall Street Journal*, December 20, 2016, https://www.wsj.com/articles/islamic-state-claims-responsibility-for-jordan-attack-1482239654
50. "Jordan army says several ISIL fighters killed in border clashes," *Al-Jazeera* (Doha), August 2, 2018, https://www.aljazeera.com/news/2018/08/jordan-army-isil-fighters-killed-border-clashes-180802135231069.html
51. "Jordan: Four security officers killed after storming building," *Al-Jazeera* (Doha), August 13, 2018, https://www.aljazeera.com/news/2018/08/jordan-4-security-officers-killed-storming-building-180812080610180.html
52. Adam Hoffman and Marta Furlan, *Challenges Posed by Returning Foreign Fighters,* George Washington University Program on Extremism, March 2020, https://extremism.gwu.edu/sites/g/files/zaxdzs2191/f/Challenges%20Posed%20by%20Returning%20Foreign%20Fighters.pdf.
53. Mohammed Abu Dalhoum, , Duran Delgadillo, Hamza Elanfassi, and Shannon Walker, "Deradicalization of Returnees to Jordan and Morocco: Limitations, Strengths, and Lessons for the Region," George Washington University Program on Extremism, May 2020, https://cpb-us-e1.wpmucdn.com/blogs.gwu.edu/dist/6/1613/files/2020/05/Deradicalization-of-Returnees-to-Jordan-and-Morocco.pdf
54. Saud Al-Sharafat, "How Jordan Can Deal with Jordanian ISIS Fighters Still in Syria," Washington Institute for Near East Policy *Fikra Forum*, August 9, 2019, https://www.washingtoninstitute.org/fikraforum/view/How-Jordan-Can-Deal-with-Jordanian-ISIS-Fighters-Still-in-Syria.

16 Kuwait

Quick Facts

Population: 2,993,706 (July 2020 est.)
Area: 17,818 sq km
Ethnic Groups: Kuwaiti 30.4%, other Arab 27.4%, Asian 40.3%, African 1%, other .9% (includes European, North American, South American, and Australian) (2018 est.)
GDP (official exchange rate): $289.7 billion (2017 est.)
Source: CIA World Factbook (Last Updated September 2020)

Introduction

Although Kuwaiti soldiers, civilians, and U.S. forces have been the targets of sporadic attacks by radical religious elements in the past – most notably in June 2015, when a suicide bombing killed 27 people in a Kuwait City Shi'a mosque (an attack claimed by an Islamic State affiliate) – the phenomenon of global jihad is less prevalent in Kuwait than in many of its Gulf neighbors.[1] *Rather, ISIS and other terrorist groups have more commonly used Kuwaiti soil for logistical activities, such as the recruitment of fighters, and as a hub through which funds, operatives, and equipment are transferred to other countries. Counterterrorism measures have been successful in preventing fatal attacks in Kuwait itself, and, since 2015 in particular, efforts against facilitation networks involved in the global jihad have improved markedly.*

Kuwait preserves a delicate political balance by permitting Islamists a presence in the nation's parliament but vesting large amounts of power in the nation's Emir. For their part, Kuwait's Islamists (who include Shi'as, Salafis, and a Muslim Brotherhood affiliate) exhibit a pragmatic gradualist approach, working to expand the role of sharia law within the day-to-day life of Kuwaitis while remaining loyal to the country's constitution. Kuwait's Sunni Islamists have also increasingly become key players in the country's cross-ideological opposition, while the country's Shi'a Islamists are widely considered government loyalists.

Endnotes

1. "Kuwait Shia mosque blast death toll 'rises to 27,'" *BBC*, June 25, 2015, http://www.bbc.com/news/world-middle-east-33287136; Scott Neuman, "ISIS Claims Responsibility For Suicide Attack At Kuwait Mosque," *National Public Radio*, June 26, 2015, http://www.npr.org/sections/thetwo-way/2015/06/26/417708840/isis-claims-responsibility-for-suicide-attack-at-kuwait-mosque.

Due to publishing constraints, this chapter is provided here only in summary form. To view the full study, please visit the online edition of the Almanac at almanac.afpc.org.

17 Lebanon

Quick Facts

Population: 5,469,612 (July 2020 est.)

Area: 10,400 sq km

Ethnic Groups: Arab 95%, Armenian 4%, other 1%

Government Type: Parliamentary republic

GDP (official exchange rate): $54.18 billion (2017 est.)

Source: CIA World FactBook (Last Updated October 2020)

Introduction

Lebanon's unique demographic and political composition has had a profound influence on the trajectory of Islamism in the country. The coexistence of large Sunni and Shi'a Muslim populations (with neither constituting a national majority) alongside a comparably sized multidenominational Christian community and smaller minority groups has meant that few Islamists of either sectarian persuasion have aggressively pursued a theocratic state. Hezbollah, the dominant Shi'a Islamist group in Lebanon, has carved out a heavily armed state-within-a-state. As a result of the country's October 2019 protests, Hezbollah leader Hassan Nasrallah now holds a place in society that is de facto parallel and equal to that of the Lebanese government leadership.

Once revered across the Arab world for its armed "resistance" to Israel, the group's blind obedience to Iran and willingness to turn on other Muslims has helped transform it into a pariah. Sunni Islamist groups, meanwhile, are numerous, ideologically varied, politically marginalized, and surprisingly unwilling to work together in pursuit of common objectives. Radicalization in impoverished Sunni areas has been growing steadily but has not been effectively channeled by Islamist leaders.

The Syrian civil war has progressively drawn both Shi'a and Sunni Lebanese Islamists into direct conflict with one another while causing an influx of more than a million (mostly Sunni) Syrian refugees into neighboring Lebanon. In turn, terror attacks in Lebanon committed by local Nusra Front and Islamic State branches—and the first ever Lebanese-on-Lebanese suicide bombing of civilian targets – have served to renewed support for the Lebanese Army.[1]

Endnotes

1. Kareem Chehayeb and Megan Specia, "Lebanon's Parliament Confirms State of Emergency, Extending Army Power," *New York Times*, August 13, 2020, https://www.nytimes.com/2020/08/13/world/middleeast/lebanon-parliament-emergency.html.

Due to publishing constraints, this chapter is provided here only in summary form. To view the full study, please visit the online edition of the Almanac at almanac.afpc.org.

18 Libya

Quick Facts

Population: 6,890,535 (July 2020 est.)
Area: 1,759,540 sq km
Ethnic Groups: Berber and Arab 97%, other 3% (includes Egyptian, Greek, Indian, Italian, Maltese, Pakistani, Tunisian, and Turkish)
GDP (official exchange rate): $30.57 billion (2017 est.)

Source: CIA World FactBook (Last Updated August 2020)

Introduction

The North African nation of Libya is a failed state that is home to a wide array of Islamist and Salafi-jihadi groups. Muammar Qaddafi ruled the oil-rich country for four decades. The 2011 Arab Spring, the resulting Libyan revolution and a subsequent NATO intervention toppled the dictator's centralized state. The country devolved into a battleground for an array of ideologically diverse groups. The fall of the Qaddafi regime created the possibility for Libya's long suppressed Islamists to wield political power, but they failed to achieve even temporary political gains. Successive transitional governments likewise faltered, and the country spiraled into a complex civil war shaped by localized grievances, regional power struggles, ideological divides, and a zero-sum competition for power and resources.

*Several Salafi-jihadi groups took advantage of the regime's fall and subsequent instability to establish and expand safe havens in Libya. These groups include the al-Qaeda–linked Ansar al-Sharia Libya and the Islamic State (IS). Salafi-*jihadi *groups in Libya have recruited and trained militants, governed populations, and prepared attacks on other states in the Maghreb and in Europe. Islamist militants in Libya, including Salafi-jihadis, remain a destabilizing force and threat despite significant losses.*

Islamist Activity

Political Islam appeared in Libya in the mid-20th century, when King Idris I welcomed asylum-seekers from the Egyptian Muslim Brotherhood. This sanctuary period ended in 1969, when Colonel Muammar Qaddafi overthrew the Libyan monarchy. Qaddafi violently suppressed all political opposition during his forty-year rule, including the country's Islamist element. Islamist organizations challenged the regime through both peaceful and violent means from the 1970s to the 1990s. State oppression fostered the development of Libyan Islamist networks in the country's prisons and beyond its borders, including in Afghanistan and England. Qaddafi later sought to co-opt Islamist organizations through a policy of negotiation and de-radicalization spearheaded by his son, Sayf al-Islam, in the early 2000s.

The 2011 Arab Spring protests rallied Islamists and secularists alike against the Qaddafi regime. Qaddafi's brutal response led to a civil war, a NATO intervention, and ultimately the dictator's death. Various groups vied for influence in the resulting power vacuum, yielding chronic instability. Libya's transitional government struggled to establish order and rebuild state institutions. Militias and non-state actors proliferated and strengthened in the three years after the revolution.

Rivalries exploded into a full-scale civil war by 2014, when Khalifa Haftar, a former regime officer, launched Operation Dignity with the goal of defeating Islamist groups in Libya.[1] An alliance of western Libyan militias, including Islamist ones, launched Operation Dawn to counter Haftar's offensive in August 2014, seizing Tripoli's airport and other parts of the capital and causing a split in the country's transitional government.[2] Outside actors, such as the United Arab Emirates (UAE), Egypt, Russia, and Saudi Arabia supporting Haftar's Libyan National Army (LNA) and Qatar and Turkey bolstering the Government of National Accord (GNA) have since backed various proxies. Ongoing factional conflict has even mobilized a growing number of formerly nonviolent "quietist" Salafists to join the fray to defend their interests in opposition to both the Muslim Brotherhood and violent Salafi groups.[3]

Post-revolution Libya became a hotbed for transnational Salafi-

jihadi organizations. For example, Ansar al-Sharia, a Salafi-*jihadi* group formed by members of al-Qaeda and the Libyan Islamic Fighting Group (LIFG), is likely responsible for the September 2012 attack on U.S. government facilities in Benghazi that killed four Americans, including Ambassador J. Christopher Stevens.[4] IS took root and grew rapidly in 2014, establishing the first branch of its *caliphate* outside of Iraq and Syria. IS's Libyan branch has also supported terrorist attacks in Europe, notably the May 2017 Manchester bombing.[5]

Islamist and Salafi-*jihadi* armed groups in Libya, ranging from Islamist-leaning militias in the Libya Dawn coalition to Ansar al-Sharia allies and the Islamic State, have lost significant ground in the past five years, but remain a threat to the country's stability.[6] The establishment of the UN-backed GNA in late 2015 widened a split between hardline and moderate Islamists in the Operation Dawn coalition, marginalizing the former. In December 2016, GNA-allied forces, with U.S. support, ousted IS from its stronghold in Sirte.[7] Subsequent U.S. airstrikes have hindered, but not stopped, IS's efforts to reconstitute. Haftar's forces made significant gains against Islamists and Salafi-*jihadis* in eastern and central Libya from 2016 to 2019, including retaking Benghazi and claiming victory in Derna. Islamist and Salafi-*jihadi* armed actors remain key players in the Libya conflict, however. They will regain and likely retain power as long as Libya lacks effective governance and security structures. Nonviolent Islamist political actors also remain active in Libya, but are less influential than more organized armed factions.

Despite Islamist and Salafi-*jihadi* losses, ongoing conflict in Libya holds opportunities for such groups to regain strength. Haftar's forces attempted to seize the capital, Tripoli, in April 2019, kicking off more than a year of fighting in the capital region. A Turkish-backed intervention helped GNA forces, including Libyan Islamist militias and Syrian fighters, defeat Haftar's forces in Tripoli despite significant support from Russia, Egypt, and the UAE.[8] As of August 2020, the focus of the conflict has shifted to central Libya and the country's oil resources.

The Muslim Brotherhood

The Muslim Brotherhood seeks to establish sharia as the foundation for state and society in Libya. The organization came to Libya in 1949, when King Idris I allowed Egyptian Brotherhood members fleeing political persecution to settle in Benghazi.[9] Egyptian asylum-seekers and clerics founded the Libyan Muslim Brotherhood as a branch of the original Egyptian organization. The group, allowed relative freedom to spread its ideology, attracted local adherents.

Colonel Muammar Qaddafi overthrew the Libyan monarchy in 1969 and promptly cracked down on the Brotherhood, arresting some members and returning others to Egypt.[10] The crackdown continued until 1973, when Brotherhood members agreed to dissolve the organization, effectively silencing themselves for the remainder of the 1970s.

The Brotherhood reorganized in the early 1980s and revived its aspirations to replace the Qaddafi regime with one governed by sharia law. It renamed itself al-Jama'a al-Islamiyya al-Libiyya (Libyan Islamic Group), and gained popular support among Libyan students who met exiled members in the U.S. and UK. These students subsequently spread the Brotherhood's ideology and joined its covert cells inside of Libya.[11] The Brotherhood won popular appeal through charitable and welfare work and recruited members of the Libyan middle class to its cause. The Brotherhood was strongest in eastern Benghazi, where major tribes historically opposed Qaddafi's rule.[12] The regime either imprisoned or executed most Brotherhood members remaining in Libya by the mid-1980s.[13]

The Brotherhood began to regenerate in 1999 as a result of dialogue with the Qaddafi regime. The talks gained momentum in 2005-2006, when Qaddafi's son, Sayf al-Islam, assumed an active role in the talks in an effort to co-opt and neutralize opposition groups (especially Islamists). The Brotherhood is known to have had roughly 1,000 members within Libya and 200 more in exile on the eve of the 2011 Libyan uprising.[14]

After the fall of Qaddafi, the Muslim Brotherhood re-emerged and claimed a place in Libyan civil society. However, in the 2012 parliamentary elections that followed Qaddafi's ouster, a Brotherhood-affiliated party performed poorly[15] and support for the Libyan

Brotherhood remained limited in the subsequent parliamentary elections two years later.[16] The public's rejection of the movement reflects the legacy of Qaddafi's demonization of the organization, as well as the growth of anti-Brotherhood sentiment surrounding the presidency of Mohammad Morsi in Egypt. Resentment toward the Brotherhood also stems from perceptions that it is anti-democratic as well as accusations of ties to more radical groups like al-Qaeda and Ansar al-Sharia.[17]

Nevertheless, the Brotherhood remains a player in Libyan politics. It formally announced its support for the UN-backed GNA in March 2016.[18] However, the Brotherhood's influence is limited by the fragmentation of the Libyan Islamist movement and the rise of anti-Islamist militia commander Khalifa Haftar.[19] Haftar's rise—backed by anti-Islamist leadership in Egypt, the UAE, and Russia, as well as Saudi Arabia—has made life even more difficult for the group. The decision by a notable number of Islamist politicians to leave the Brotherhood in order to gain broader support in early 2019 reflects the challenges facing the group in a highly polarized political environment.[20]

The Libyan Islamic Fighting Group (LIFG)

The LIFG formed as an underground movement in 1982 that sought to overthrow the Qaddafi regime through an assassination campaign.[21] Authorities captured many LIFG members, including its founder Iwad al-Zawawi, after failed attempts to overthrow the regime in 1986, 1987, and 1989.[22]

LIFG members fled to Afghanistan and Pakistan where, supported by al-Qaeda, they built training camps to reinvigorate the organization and expand military capabilities. LIFG tested their military prowess while conducting *jihad* against the Soviet occupation of Afghanistan in the 1980s.[23] Influential Salafi-*jihadi* clerics, such as Abdullah Azzam, also indoctrinated Libyan recruits.[24]

LIFG reinvigorated its efforts to overthrow the Qaddafi regime in the 1990s following the Afghan *jihad*. LIFG members established cells or traveled to London to obtain logistical and financial support from al-Qaeda and (allegedly) the British government.[25] They also sought to establish the group's structure and develop leadership capabilities in this period.[26] LIFG established a base of operations in Sudan in 1993.[27] The group then sent delegations from Sudan to Algeria to continue training. LIFG's interlude in Sudan was independent of the plans of al-Qaeda leader Osama bin Laden, who spent five years there in the 1990s.[28]

A LIFG raid on a hospital in Benghazi sparked a crackdown by security forces that compelled the group to announce its existence publicly in October 1995.[29] The Libyan regime pressured the Sudanese regime to eject the LIFG at the time. Many LIFG members returned to Libya, while others escaped to England. Pressured by exposure, the LIFG conducted a series of attacks on the Libyan regime throughout the 1990s, including several failed attempts to assassinate Qaddafi. The Libyan regime fought the LIFG into the late 1990s and killed several of its leaders.[30]

The LIFG declared an official ceasefire in 2000 though its Libyan insurgency and terror campaign effectively ended by 1998.[31] Many members returned to Afghanistan. Those who fled included LIFG *emir* Abdelhakim Belhaj (aka Abu 'Abd Allah al-Sadiq), its chief religious official, Abu al-Mundhir al-Sa'idi, and Abu Anas al-Libi, an al-Qaeda operative involved in the 1998 bombing of two U.S. embassies in East Africa.[32]

The LIFG had a complicated relationship with al-Qaeda and its ideology. The U.S. Treasury Department designated members of the LIFG as Specially Designated Global Terrorists in 2001 for their ties to al-Qaeda.[33] Senior al-Qaeda leaders Ayman al-Zawahiri and Abu Yahya al-Libi announced a merger between the LIFG and al-Qaeda in 2007, but some LIFG senior leaders refused to swear allegiance to al-Qaeda.[34] Likewise, the LIFG did not demonstrate significant support for al-Qaeda's attacks on the West.[35] The group did not limit its activities to Libya, however, and the U.S. State Department listed it as a Foreign Terrorist Organization for its ties to the 2003 bombings in Casablanca, Morocco.[36]

Several LIFG members also went on to become senior figures in al Qaeda.[37] In 2005, the Libyan regime began a reconciliation and de-radicalization process overseen by Sayf al-Islam Qaddafi.[38] The LIFG revised its definition of *jihad* to exclude violence against the state in 2009, producing a new code titled "Corrective Studies" that permitted *jihad* only in the cases of the invasion of Muslim lands.[39] The LIFG officially disbanded in 2010. While the regime subsequently released many LIFG members, others, such as former LIFG member turned parliamentarian Abd al-Wahab Qa'id, were not released until the uprising against the Qaddafi regime in March 2011.[40] The U.S. State Department delisted the LIFG in 2015[41] and the UK Home Office did the same in 2019.[42]

The LIFG's extensive network of former members has played a prominent role in the swell of Islamist activity that began with the Arab Spring and the overthrow of the Qaddafi regime. Elements of the LIFG human network established branches of the al-Qaeda associate Ansar al-Sharia.[43] Other former LIFG members now lead political parties and militias. Among these figures are the group's former *emir*, Belhaj, who founded the Libyan Islamic Movement for Change and sought to rehabilitate his image by providing social services and youth activities. Belhaj formed the Alwattan Party ("Homeland Party) to compete in the 2012 parliamentary elections (it won no seats) and backed the Libya Dawn coalition in 2014.[44] Khalid al-Sharif, an LIFG deputy *emir*, served as deputy defense minister in two post-Qaddafi governments and remains a key political figure. Al-Sharif endorsed a new political movement formed by Islamist political leaders in western Libya in July 2020.[45]

Ansar al-Sharia in Libya (ASL)

The 2011 revolution created an opportunity for new Salafi-*jihadi* groups to fill the vacuum created by the LIFG's renunciation of military operations. Al-Qaeda *emir* Ayman al-Zawahiri charged senior operatives, including Abu Anas al-Libi, with forming a Libyan affiliate in 2011.[46] Former LIFG operatives formed branches of Ansar al-Sharia in the eastern Libyan cities of Benghazi and Derna.[47] Muhammed al-Zahawi, a former LIFG member and regime prisoner, led Ansar al-Sharia Benghazi until his death in late 2014 or early 2015.[48] ASL is a Sunni Islamist organization that pursued strict adherence to *sharia* law in Libya.[49] ASL opposed the democratic system, considering it an immoral structure that unduly gives power to man instead of God.[50]

ASL remains the primary suspect in the 2012 attack on the U.S. consulate in Benghazi.[51] Ansar al-Sharia Benghazi later changed its name to Ansar al-Sharia in Libya – an attempt by the organization to rebrand itself as a national movement rather than a local rebel force.[52] Ansar al-Sharia developed affiliates and established training camps throughout Libya, including in Sirte and Ajdabiya.

Ansar al-Sharia Benghazi was a separate organization from Ansar al-Sharia Derna, despite some crossover in membership and political goals. Former Guantanamo Bay inmate Abu Sufyan bin Qumu led the Derna group.[53] Bin Qumu's status is unknown following rumors that he defected to ISIS.[54] Both Ansar al-Sharia branches sought to establish *sharia* law in Libya.[55]

ASL built popular support in Libya and abroad through *dawa* and charity campaigns.[56] Its most effective method was the provision of social services, including infrastructure repair and development projects, the provision of security, and general aid.[57] One of the group's most successful projects was its anti-drug campaign in Benghazi, coordinated with a local hospital, a soccer club, and telecom and technologies companies.[58]

The ASL branches used local support bases to advance a global violent *jihad*. They formed an important cog within the global Salafi-*jihadi* movement and trained militants to fight in Syria, Mali, and elsewhere in North Africa.[59] The UN listed both Ansar al-Sharia Benghazi and Ansar al-Sharia Derna as terror organizations associated with al-Qaeda in November 2014.[60]

ASL developed battlefield relationships with other Libyan fighting forces to enhance its legitimacy, spread its ideology, and mask its affiliation to al-Qaeda. ASL has known ties to several smaller Salafi-*jihadi katibas* (battalions) in Libya, including Katibat Abu 'Ubaydah al-Jarah and Saraya Raf Allah al-Sahati.[61] These alliances were a force multiplier for ASL, which had only a few hundred members in 2012.[62] Since then, however, ASL has exploited the chaos and instability in Libya in order to strengthen its presence in Libyan communities and spread its ideology.[63]

In 2014, ASL transitioned almost exclusively to military operations in order to defend its position in Benghazi. Former Libyan Army commander Khalifa Haftar began Operation Dignity to defeat terrorists—broadly defined as all Islamists—in eastern Libya, with ASL among his priority targets.[64] ASL launched a counteroffensive that caused high civilian and military casualties.[65]

It joined with other Islamist militias fighting Haftar to form the Benghazi Revolutionaries Shura Council (BRSC) in June 2014.[66] Shortly thereafter, the new umbrella organization overran several bases in Benghazi, seized a large cache of weapons, and declared the city an Islamic *emirate*.[67]

The BRSC has since lost most of its military strength. This is due, in part, to Haftar's foreign-backed forces fighting the BRSC's own fighters. The BRSC cooperated with ISIS militants in a last-ditch effort to preserve its strongholds in 2017.[68] Ansar al-Sharia officially dissolved in May 2017 due to heavy casualties and leadership attrition.[69] Haftar declared victory in Benghazi in July 2017.[70] ASL and other al-Qaeda linked militants fled the city to safe havens elsewhere in Libya.[71]

Ansar al-Sharia Derna controlled Derna city as part of the Mujahideen Shura Council of Derna (MSCD) starting in December 2014. The MSCD drove Islamic State fighters out of Derna in June 2015.[72] Haftar's forces seized most Derna from the MSCD in mid-2018 following a yearlong blockade.[73]

Islamic State (IS)

IS took advantage of Libya's persistent chaos in the wake of the 2011 revolution to establish its first *wilayat* (province) in North Africa. The group's aspirations for a Libyan franchise began in 2013, when Islamic State in Iraq and the Levant (ISIL) leader Abu Bakr al-Baghdadi sent an emissary to Derna, which has longstanding Islamist militant networks.[74] ISIS leadership sought to establish a potential fallback for its base in the Levant.[75] Libyan militants and ideologues with ties to the conflicts in Iraq and Syria began pledging their allegiance to the Islamic State in Iraq and Syria (ISIS) by late 2014.[76] The establishment of three ISIS *wilayats* in Libya provided the group strategic proximity to Europe and a logistical hub for Africa.

ISIS first took root in Derna through an affiliate called the Shura Council of Islamic Youth, later known as ISIS *Wilayat Barqah* (Cyrenaica). ISIS simultaneously developed outposts elsewhere in Libya, notably in Sirte, Sabratha, and various Benghazi neighborhoods. ISIS lost its first Libyan position when the Mujahideen Shura Council of Derna (MSCD), which included

Ansar al-Sharia and other LIFG-linked militias, fought back against ISIS in response to its extreme ideology, brutal methods, and the assassination of a MSCD leader.[77] The MSCD ousted ISIS from Derna in June 2015.

ISIS tempered its loss in Derna with its takeover of Sirte on the central Libyan coast in spring 2015. The group conducted a *dawa* and intimidation campaign in the city, where it also co-opted pre-existing ASL networks.[78] ISIS propaganda soon featured the Libyan city alongside Raqqa, Syria, and Mosul, Iraq as a demonstration of the expanding caliphate.[79] ISIS *Wilayat Tarablus* governed Sirte with the same harshness as its Levantine counterparts, enforcing corporal punishments and violently quashing dissent. ISIS gradually expanded to the east and west of Sirte, controlling a 150-mile stretch of coastline at its peak. It also conducted a campaign of attacks on oil infrastructure in eastern Libya in an effort to deprive the Libyan state of revenue.[80]

Experts estimate that ISIS had 3,000 fighters in Sirte at the height of its presence there, although other reports estimated as many as 6,000 drawn from Libya, the broader Maghreb, and sub-Saharan Africa.[81] ISIS did not gain significant support from Libyan communities, which view the group as foreign. Claims of strong ties between pro-Qaddafi groups and ISIS in Libya, akin to those between former Ba'athists and ISIS in Iraq, are overstated.[82]

ISIS in Libya seeks to attack neighboring states and Europe. Katibat al-Battar, a seasoned ISIS unit compromised mainly of Libyan and European fighters, deployed from Iraq and Syria to Libya to coordinate attacks in Europe and Tunisia.[83] Libya-based militants conducted the 2015 Bardo and Sousse attacks that devastated Tunisia's tourism economy. ISIS also used Libya as a launchpad to try and expand the *caliphate* to the Tunisian city of Ben Guerdane in March 2016.[84] Members of Katibat al-Battar met in Tripoli with Salman al-Abedi, the British suicide bomber who killed 22 people at a concert in Manchester, England in May 2017.[85]

Between 2016 and 2017, ISIS suffered a series of defeats that significantly reduced its strength in Libya. Khalifa Haftar's Operation Dignity forces, with some Western assistance, drove ISIS *Wilayat Barqah* from its posts in Benghazi. American airstrikes supported an offensive that ousted ISIS from Sabratha, near the Tunisian border. Sirte and surrounding small towns remained the group's primary stronghold until mid-2016, when ISIS overreached into terrain controlled by forces from the western Libyan city-state of Misrata. Misratan militias, aligned with the UN-backed government and backed by American air power, launched a grueling campaign to recapture Sirte that culminated in December 2016. Many ISIS fighters left the city, but the group still suffered significant casualties.[86]

ISIS in Libya remains a potent threat despite its territorial losses. Former CIA Director John Brennan warned in June 2016 that the branch was ISIS's most developed and dangerous, citing its influence in Africa and ability to stage attacks in Europe.[87] ISIS is reconstituting in central and southwestern Libya, where it has access to lucrative smuggling routes.[88] Intermittent U.S. airstrikes have interrupted the group's resurgence, but it is not defeated. Hundreds of ISIS militants—if not more—remain active as a network of cells and military units—termed "Desert Brigades"—throughout the country.[89] The previously dormant ISIS *Wilayat Fezzan* has become the group's most active in Libya, claiming regular guerrilla attacks in Libya's remote southwest.[90] The group has also conducted several high-profile attacks intended to disrupt the formation of a functioning Libyan government in Tripoli, including a May 2018 attack on the High National Election Commission and a September 2018 attack on the National Oil Corporation.[91]

Al-Qaeda in the Islamic Maghreb (AQIM)

AQIM was first established in 1998 in Algeria as a Salafi-*jihadi* organization with the goal of establishing an Islamic Caliphate in the Maghreb that would enforce *sharia* law. The instability in North Africa that followed the Arab Spring in 2011 created a conducive environment for the group's expansion throughout the region. As a result, a number of fighters left the Sahara and Sahel region to fight in the growing conflict in Libya, allowing the group to expand east.[92] AQIM fighters transited southwestern Libya with the help of locals toward coastal Ansar al-Sharia networks.[93]

The fall of Qaddafi in 2011 gave AQIM the means to easily acquire weapons and recruit more fighters, especially amongst the experienced Tuaregs, who were supported by Qaddafi.[94] In post-

Qaddafi Libya, AQIM took advantage of the security vacuum and opened training camps, like the Ubari camp in the Southwest.[95]

In 2012, reports indicated that al-Qaeda sought to create a clandestine network in Libya to be used in the future to destabilize the government and offer logistical support to the branch's activities in the region.[96] AQIM has supported Ansar al-Sharia since its establishment in 2011. In return, Ansar al- Sharia in Libya has provided AQIM affiliates with fighters in Mali.[97]

AQIM has shifted its focus to the Sahel region of West Africa since coopting the Tuareg rebellion in Mali in 2012, with AQIM's prioritization of the Mali theater intensifying with the formation of an AQIM-affiliated umbrella group (Jama'at Nusrat al Islam wa al Muslimeen) in 2017. AQIM has retained a senior leadership haven in southwestern Libya. The United States carried out a series of drone strikes against al-Qaeda in southern Libya in 2018, begining on March 24 and ending on November 30, the last of which killed 11 suspected members of AQIM in southwest Libya near the town of al Uwaynat.[98] The US denied involvement in a strike targeting al-Qaeda in southwest Libya in February 2019. The GNA released a statement confirming a join US- Libyan operation, which allegedly hit an al-Qaeda cell in near Ubari.[99] The State Department reported in June 2020 that, since 2016, forces aligned with the LNA have conducted operations against both AQIM and ISIS in southern Libya, where terrorist groups are known to operate freely.[100] However, it must be mentioned that LNA operations in the Fezzan have also been criticized for targeting civilians.[101]

Islamism and Society

Libya has over six and a half million citizens, roughly 97 percent of whom are Sunni Muslim. The dominant school of Sunni thought in Libya is Malikism, often considered the most moderate of the four traditional schools of Islamic jurisprudence.[102] Non-Sunni Muslims in Libya are primarily Ibadi Muslims in the native Amazigh community or foreigners, including Christians, Buddhists, Hindus, and Jews.[103]

Islam permeates everyday life for most Libyans. Religious

instruction in Islam is compulsory in all public schools. *Sharia* governs matters like inheritance, divorce, and the right to own property.[104] Libya's draft constitution designates Islam as the official state religion and *sharia* as the principal source of legislation.[105] The constitution bars non-Muslims from Libya's parliament and presidency, per a July 2017 draft; however, the country's interim laws protect the rights of non-Muslims to practice their faiths.[106] A protracted and fierce debate over *sharia* has revealed cleavages over the role of Islam in contemporary Libyan society.[107]

Islamist political ideology in Libya has surged since the fall of the Qaddafi regime, but still lacks broad support. Libyans responded enthusiastically to Islamist political parties following Qaddafi's ouster because they promoted a sense of identity and pledged to maintain order.[108] Many Libyans remain skeptical of Islamism, but years of failed political transition have emboldened various Islamist factions and militias.[109] Islamist organizations have filled the governance gap left by the collapse of the Libyan state by providing valuable social and governmental services, including health care, youth activity planning, and religious organization. This allowed groups like ASL and the LIFG, in limited cases, to gradually move away from their image as global *jihadi* organizations and gain some domestic support.

Islamism has become increasingly divisive. The 2017 Gulf crisis, which pitted Saudi Arabia and the UAE against Qatar over the latter's support for political Islamists, has produced increasingly polarized media treatment of Islamism in Libya. Anti-Islamist media outlets and officials tend to portray all political Islamists as terrorists, even though the majority of Islamist politicians and armed groups oppose, and often fight against, Salafi-*jihadis*.

Islamism and the State

Libya won its independence from Italy in the aftermath of World War II. It became a constitutional monarchy in 1951 under King Idris I, the head of eastern Libya's Sufi Senussi order. Colonel Muammar Qaddafi overthrew the monarchy in a military *coup d'état* in September 1969 and established the *Jamahiriyah* (state of the masses), an Arab nationalist regime based on an ideology of Islamic socialism. Qaddafi outlawed all political parties and organized political dissent, including Islamist groups.[110]

The Qaddafi regime suppressed challenges to its rule, including the Muslim Brotherhood. The Brotherhood's failure to launch set conditions for the emergence of the LIFG. The LIFG launched several failed efforts to topple the regime and assassinate Qaddafi in the 1980s and 1990s. The regime decimated the Islamist opposition by 1998, leaving only fragmented resistance by the early 2000s.[111]

Sayf al-Islam Qaddafi began negotiations with Islamists on behalf of his father in the mid-2000s. He brokered a deal to free imprisoned Islamists if they agreed to recognize the legitimacy of Qaddafi's government, renounce violence, and formally revise their doctrines. These negotiations led to the release of more than 100 Brotherhood members in 2006 and hundreds of LIFG members by 2008.[112] The LIFG also renounced violence against the state. The regime brought quietest Salafi clerics from Saudi Arabia to Libya during this period to foster religious discourse that condemned anti-state rebellion.[113]

The Arab Spring protests upended Libya in February 2011. The regime cracked down violently on protesters, plunging the country into civil war. The conflict and additional prisoner releases allowed Islamist networks to reconstitute in Libya. Qaddafi's fall sent Libya into a turbulent democratic transition and set the stage for a power struggle in the resulting vacuum.

Political Islamists participated in parliamentary elections in 2012. The Muslim Brotherhood-affiliated Justice and Construction Party (JCP) faced off against the liberal National Forces Alliance (NFA).[114] The JCP, led by former political prisoner Mohammed Sawan, won 17 of 80 available seats to the NFA's 39.[115] The JCP failed to achieve post-Arab Spring electoral success like that of its model and inspiration, Egypt's Brotherhood-backed Freedom and Justice Party.

Two political factions of the LIFG – the Hizb al-Watan (HW) and Hizb al-Umma al-Wasat (HUW) also participated in the 2012 legislative elections. Former LIFG *emir* and Tripoli militia leader Abdelhakim Belhaj led the HW, which ran as a broad-based moderate party. Former LIFG religious official Sami al-Sa'adi led the HUW, which included most former LIFG figures and ran as a more conservative Islamic party.[116] The HW failed to win any seats in the election, while the HUW won a single seat, allocated to Abdul Wahhab al-Qa'id, brother of the late senior al-Qaeda official Abu Yahya al-Libi. Other small Islamist parties also failed to garner significant support. These parties include the Salafi party al-Asala, which won no seats, and the Hizb al-Islah wa-l-Tanmiyya, led by former member of the Muslim Brotherhood Khaled al-Werchefani.

Islamist parties and candidates won some seats the June 2014 legislative elections as political polarization increased. Low voter turnout and political violence between secular and Islamist forces marred the elections, and Libya collapsed into open war.[117] Operation Dignity and the subsequent political crisis split the government in half between the two transitional parliaments: the General National Congress (GNC, elected 2012) and the House of Representatives (HoR, elected 2014). Islamist militias affiliated with the GNC ousted the HoR from Tripoli, further hardening the divisions.

Libya has two primary political blocs as of March 2019: one in the west and one in the east. The United Nations-backed Government of National Accord (GNA), established in December 2015, controls the Libyan capital of Tripoli as of June 2020. The GNA was meant to bring together the warring GNC and HoR into a unity government. In practice, it divided and weakened the GNC's support base, though GNC leadership and armed allies remain potential spoilers. The HoR, whose leadership is aligned with Haftar, refuses to endorse the GNA.[118] Haftar has maintained international acceptance and territorial control since 2017, raising his profile as a prospective strongman despite weaknesses in his fighting force and opposition from rival factions.

Haftar and his external backers, especially Egypt, the UAE and Russia, seek to eradicate political Islam and crush Islamist armed groups in Libya. He has courted religious conservatives by empowering followers of Madkhalism, a form of quietist Salafism that enshrines loyalty to a political leader and opposes more activist Islamist strains.[119] Haftar's campaign mirrors that of Egyptian President Abdel Fatah el-Sisi. Sisi's crackdown on political Islam benefited Salafi-*jihadi* groups that argue for violence as the only meaningful force for change.[120] Islamism will remain a powerful current in Libya for the foreseeable future, however, as Libya is a key front in a regional struggle over future of political Islam.[121]

The future role of Islamist parties in Libya remains uncertain. As of June 2020, the GNA and its allies pushed the LNA out of Tripoli, ending Haftar's fifteen month attempt to occupy the city.[122] This development is likely to escalate the conflict after the Egyptian parliament authorized the possible deployment of troops to Libya. The European Union took the opportunity to call for a ceasefire, hoping to defuse the situation, just as GNA forces were planning to attack the resource-rich city of Sitre.[123] While how the situation will unfold depends heavily on the influence of external actors, it is unlikely that plans for peace negotiations will bear fruit.[124]

Islamist politicians and militia leaders have prominent roles in the Tripoli area. At the local level, quietist Salafi militias are taking on increasingly important security and governance roles in Libyan cities. The Salafi Rada Special Deterrence Force in Tripoli, for example, controls the city's one functioning airport and provides security in the name of the UN-backed GNA.[125] Salafi militias in Benghazi are also a powerful bloc within the LNA coalition.[126] Islamists will undoubtedly play a key role in shaping a future Libyan state, whether by participating in a democratic process, taking up arms for a local or national cause, or waging violent *jihad*.

Endnotes

1. Camille Tawil, "Operation Dignity: General Haftar's Latest Battle May Decide Libya's Future," Jamestown Foundation *Terrorism Monitor* 12 iss. 11, May 30, 2014, https://jamestown.org/program/operation-dignity-general-haftars-latest-battle-may-decide-libyas-future/.
2. Chris Stephen and Anne Penketh, "Libyan capital under Islamist control after Tripoli airport seized," *Guardian* (London), August 24, 2014, https://www.theguardian.com/world/2014/aug/24/libya-capital-under-islamist-control-tripoli-airport-seized-operation-dawn; Ala' Alrababa'h and Frederic Wehrey, "Taking On Operation Dawn: Creeping Advance of the Islamic State in Western Libya," Carne-

gie Middle East Center, June 24, 2015, https://carnegie-mec.org/diwan/60490.

3. Frederic Wehrey, "Quiet No More?" *Diwan*, October 13, 2016, http://carnegie-mec.org/diwan/64846; Frederic Wehrey and Anouar Boukhars, "As Their Influence Grows, the Maghreb's 'Quietist' Salafists are Anything but Quiet," *World Politics Review*, December 11, 2018, https://www.worldpoliticsreview.com/articles/26962/as-their-influence-grows-the-maghreb-s-quietist-salafists-are-anything-but-quiet.
4. Emily Estelle and Katherine Zimmerman, "Backgrounder: Fighting Forces in Libya," American Enterprise Institute Critical Threats Project, March 3, 2016, https://www.criticalthreats.org/analysis/backgrounder-fighting-forces-in-libya.
5. Rukmini Callimachi and Eric Schmitt, "Manchester Bomber Met With ISIS Unit in Libya, Officials Say," *New York Times*, June 3, 2017, https://www.nytimes.com/2017/06/03/world/middleeast/manchester-bombing-salman-abedi-islamic-state-libya.html.
6. Aaron Y. Zelin, "The Islamic State in Libya Has Yet to Recover," Washington Institute for Near East Policy *Policywatch* 3222, December 6, 2019, https://www.washingtoninstitute.org/policy-analysis/view/the-islamic-state-in-libya-has-yet-to-recover; Cameron Glenn, "Libya's Islamists: Who They Are – And What They Want," Woodrow Wilson International Center for Scholars, August 8, 2017, https://www.wilsoncenter.org/article/libyas-islamists-who-they-are-and-what-they-want
7. Hani Amara, "Libyan forces clear last Islamic State holdout in Sirte," Reuters, December 6, 2016, http://www.reuters.com/article/us-libya-security-sirte/libyan-forces-clear-last-islamicstate-holdout-in-sirte-idUSKBN13V15R.
8. Bethan McKernan, "Gaddafi's Prophecy Comes True as Foreign Powers Battle for Libya's Oil," *Guardian* (London), August 2, 2020, https://www.theguardian.com/world/2020/aug/02/gaddafis-prophecy-comes-true-as-foreign-powers-battle-for-libyas-oil.
9. Omar Ashour, "Libyan Islamists Unpacked: Rise, Transformation, and Future," Brookings Institution, July 28, 2016. https://www.brookings.edu/research/libyan-islamists-unpacked-rise-transformation-and-future/.
10. Allison Pargeter, "Political Islam in Libya," Jamestown Foundation *Terrorism Monitor* 3, iss. 6, May 5, 2005, http://www.jamestown.org/single/?no_cache=1&tx_ttnews[tt_news]=306.
11. Ibid.

12. Ibidem.
13. Omar Ashour, "Libya's Muslim Brotherhood faces the future," *Foreign Policy*, March 9, 2012, https://foreignpolicy.com/2012/03/09/libyas-muslim-brotherhood-faces-the-future/.
14. Ibid.
15. Mary Fitzgerald, "Introducing the Libyan Muslim Brotherhood," *Foreign Policy*, November 2, 2012, https://foreignpolicy.com/2012/11/02/introducing-the-libyan-muslim-brotherhood/.
16. Glenn, "Libya's Islamists: Who They Are - And What They Want."
17. Mary Fitzgerald, "Libya's Muslim Brotherhood Struggles to Grow," *Foreign Policy*, May 1, 2014, http://www.foreignpolicy.com/articles/2014/05/01/the_rise_of_libyas_muslim_brotherhood_justice_and_construction_party.
18. "Libya's Justice and Construction Party Announces Support for National Unity Government," Ikhwan Web, March 30, 2016, http://www.ikhwanweb.com/article.php?id=32490.
19. Emily Estelle, "The General's Trap in Libya," American Enterprise Institute Critical Threats Project, August 1, 2017, https://www.criticalthreats.org/analysis/the-generals-trap-in-libya.
20. Matthew Reisener, "What Khaled Al-Meshri Thinks About the Future of Libya," *The National Interest*, February 28, 2019, https://nationalinterest.org/blog/middle-east-watch/what-khaled-al-meshri-thinks-about-future-libya-45857.
21. Camille Tawil, *Brothers in Arms: The Story of al-Qa'ida and the Arab Jihadists* (London: Saqi Books, 2010), 33.
22. Ibid., 93-94.
23. Evan F. Kohlmann, "Dossier: Libyan Islamic Fighting Group," NEFA Foundation, October 2007, 3, https://web.archive.org/web/20121004030826/http://www.nefafoundation.org/miscellaneous/nefalifg1007.pdf
24. Ibid., 4.
25. "Libyan Islamic Fighter Group," Mapping Militant Organizations, March 4, 2017, http://stanford.edu/group/mappingmilitants/cgi-bin/groups/print_view/675#note24; "The British government allegedly helped support the LIFG's campaign against the Qaddafi regime, though there has not been independent confirmation of these claims." Gary Gambill, "The Libyan Islamic Fighting Group (LIFG)," Jamestown Foundation *Terrorism Monitor* 3, iss. 6, March 24, 2005.
26. Tawil, *Brothers in Arms*, 93-94.
27. James Astill, "Osama: The Sudan Years," *Guardian* (London),

October 16, 2001, https://www.theguardian.com/world/2001/oct/17/afghanistan.terrorism3.

28. Kohlmann, "Dossier: Libyan Islamic Fighting Group," 8.
29. Tawil, *Brothers in Arms*, 65.
30. Kohlmann, "Dossier: Libyan Islamic Fighting Group," 8-11.
31. Tawil, *Brothers in Arms*, 140.
32. Ibid., 179.
33. U.S. Department of the Treasury, "Three LIFG Members Designation for Terrorism," November 30, 2008, https://www.treasury.gov/press-center/press-releases/Pages/hp1244.aspx.
34. "Libyan Islamic Fighting Group," Mapping Militant Organizations.
35. Ibid.
36. Ibidem.
37. Three LIFG members, Abu Yahya al-Libi, Atiyah Abd al-Rahman and Abu Laith al-Libi, would go on to become senior members of al-Qaeda. All were killed in U.S. Predator drone attacks in Pakistan. Peter Bergen and Alyssa Sims, "Airstrikes and Civilian Casualties in Libya Since the 2011 NATO Intervention," New America Foundation, June 20, 2018, https://www.newamerica.org/international-security/reports/airstrikes-and-civilian-casualties-libya/the-jihadist-environment-in-libya-today/
38. Omar Ashour, "Post-Jihadism: Libya and the Global Transformations of Armed Islamist Movements*," Studies in Conflict and Terrorism* 23, iss. 3, 2011, 384.
39. Ibid., 385. According to Ashour, there were several challenges: "the six leaders in Abu Selim Prison wanted the decision to be unanimous so as to maximize the impact on the middle-ranks, the grassroots, and the sympathizers, and thus guarantee successful organizational de-radicalization. They thus demanded the involvement of the LIFG leaders abroad in the dialogue with the regime. Those leaders included two Shura Council members (Abu Layth al-Libi and 'Urwa al-Libi) and two influential members of the LIFG's legitimate (theological) committee: Abu Yahya al-Libi, currently believed to be the third person in al-Qaida, and Abdullah Sa'id, who was killed in December 2009 by a U.S. drone strike in Pakistan. All four rejected the offer."
40. David D. Kirkpatrick, "Political Islam and the Fate of Two Libyan Brothers," *New York Times*, October 6, 2012, https://www.nytimes.com/2012/10/07/world/africa/political-islam-and-the-fate-of-two-libyan-brothers.html?searchResultPosition=1.
41. United States Department of State, "Foreign Terrorist Organiza-

tions," n.d., https://www.state.gov/foreign-terrorist-organizations/.
42. United Kingdom Home Office, "Proscribed Terrorist Groups or Organisations," February 28, 2020, https://assets.publishing.service.gov.uk/government/uploads/system/uploads/attachment_data/file/896006/20200228_Proscription.pdf.
43. Estelle and Zimmerman, "Backgrounder: Fighting Forces in Libya."
44. Sudarsan Raghavan, "These Libyans Were Once Linked to al-Qaeda. Now They are Politicians and Businessmen," *Washington Post*, September 28, 2017, https://www.washingtonpost.com/world/middle_east/these-libyan-ex-militiamen-were-once-linked-to-al-qaeda-now-they-wield-power-in-a-new-order/2017/09/27/8356abf8-97dd-11e7-af6a-6555caaeb8dc_story.html.
45. "Renewing His Support for the Extremist Current .. Al-Sharif: Abu Sahmain is Walking with Steady Steps," *Akhbar Libya 24*, July 25, 2020, https://akhbarlibya24.net/2020/07/25/198233/.
46. Estelle and Zimmerman, "Backgrounder: Fighting Forces in Libya."
47. Aaron Y. Zelin, "Know Your Ansar al-Sharia," *Foreign Policy*, September 21, 2012, http://www.washingtoninstitute.org/policy-analysis/view/know-your-ansar-al-sharia.
48. "Libyan militant group says its leader, Mohamed al-Zahawi, was killed," Associated Press, January 24, 2015, https://www.nytimes.com/2015/01/25/world/africa/libyan-militant-group-says-its-leader-mohammed-al-zahawi-was-killed.html
49. Faisal Irshaid, "Profile: Libya's Ansar al-Sharia," *BBC News*, June 13, 2014; Zelin, "Know Your Ansar al-Sharia."
50. "Ansar Al-Sharia in Libya (ASL)," Counter Extremism Project, 2015.
51. Mary Fitzgerald, "It Wasn't Us," *Foreign Policy*, September 18, 2012, http://www.foreignpolicy.com/articles/2012/09/18/it_wasn_t_us.
52. Aaron Y. Zelin, "Libya Beyond Benghazi," *Journal of International Security Affairs* no. 25, Fall/Winter 2013, http://www.securityaffairs.org/sites/default/files/issues/archives/fw2013covertocover_small.pdf.
53. Zelin, "Know Your Ansar al-Sharia."
54. "Abu Sufyan Bin Qumu," Counter Extremism Project, n.d., https://www.counterextremism.com/extremists/abu-sufyan-bin-qumu.
55. Zelin, "Libya Beyond Benghazi."
56. Ibid.
57. Ibidem.
58. Zelin, "Know Your Ansar al-Sharia."

59. Aaron Y. Zelin, Testimony before the House of Representatives Committee on Foreign Affairs, Subcommittee on Terrorism, Nonproliferation, and Trade and Subcommittee the Middle East and North Africa, July 10, 2013, https://www.washingtoninstitute.org/uploads/Documents/testimony/ZelinTestimony20130710-v2.pdf.
60. "U.N. Blacklists Libya's Ansar al-Sharia, Involved in Benghazi Attack," Reuters, November 19, 2014, http://www.reuters.com/article/2014/11/19/us-libya-security-un-idUSKCN0J32KX20141119.
61. These battalions participated in ASL's first "annual conference" on June 6, 2012. Other participants included, the Islamic Foundation for Da'wa and Islah, The Supreme Commission for the Protection of Revolution of February 17, Liwa Dara' Libya, Katibat Shuhada Libya al-Hurrah, Katibat Faruq (Misrata), Katibat Thuwar Sirte, Katibat Shuhada al-Khalij al-Nawfaliya, Katibat Ansar al-Huriyya, Katibat Shuhada al-Qawarsha, Katibat al-Shahid Muhammad al-Hami, Katibat al-Jabal, Katibat al-Nur, Katibat Shuhada Abu Salim, Katibat Shuhada Benghazi, the Preventative Security Apparatus, Katibat al-Shahid Salih al-Nas, and other brigades from Darnah, Sabratha, Janzur, and Ajdabiya. Pictures of the conference can be accessed at https://www.facebook.com/media/set/?set=a.373188266078865.86838.156312127766481&type=1.
62. Zelin, "Know Your Ansar al-Sharia."
63. Aaron Zelin, "Libya's jihadists beyond Benghazi," *Foreign Policy*, August 12, 2013, http://foreignpolicy.com/2013/08/12/libyas-jihadists-beyond-benghazi/.
64. "Profile: Libya's military strongman Khalifa Haftar." BBC, September 15, 2016, http://www.bbc.com/news/world-africa-27492354.
65. "Ansar al-Sharia in Libya (ASL)," Counter Extremism Project, n.d., https://www.counterextremism.com/threat/ansar-al-sharia-libya-asl.
66. Glenn, "Libya's Islamists: Who They Are - And What They Want."
67. Ansar al-Sharia in Libya (ASL)," Counter Extremism Project.
68. "ISIS in Action," *Eyes on ISIS in Libya*, June 6, 2017, http://eyeonisisinlibya.com/isis-in-action/31-may-6-june-misratas-security-forces-release-isis-confession-video/.
69. "Libyan Islamist group Ansar al-Sharia says it is dissolving," Reuters, May 27, 2017, http://www.reuters.com/article/us-libya-security-idUSKBN18N0YR.
70. "Libya eastern commander Haftar declares Benghazi 'liberated,'" BBC, July 6, 2017, http://www.bbc.com/news/world-africa-40515325.
71. "Militants Find Sanctuary in Libya's Wild South," Associated Press,

July 13, 2017, https://www.voanews.com/a/militants-find-sanctuary-in-libya-wild-south/3942381.html.

72. Estelle and Zimmerman, "Backgrounder: Fighting Forces in Libya."
73. Glenn, "Libya's Islamists: Who They Are - And What They Want"; "Spokesperson says Haftar forces seized most of Libya's Derna," Associated Press, June 8, 2018, https://www.news24.com/Africa/News/spokesperson-says-haftar-forces-seize-most-of-libyas-derna-20180608.
74. Geoff D. Porter, "How Realistic Is Libya as an Islamic State "Fallback"?" Combating Terrorism Center at West Point, March 16, 2016, https://ctc.usma.edu/how-realistic-is-libya-as-an-islamic-state-fallback/
75. Ibid.
76. Tarck Kahlaoui, "The rise of ISIS in Libya, explained," *Newsweek*, May 29, 2016, http://www.newsweek.com/understanding-rise-islamic-state-isis-libya-437931.
77. Ibid.
78. Aaron Y. Zelin, "The Islamic State's Burgeoning Capital in Sirte, Libya," Washington Institute for Near East Policy *Policywatch* 2462, August 6, 2015, https://www.washingtoninstitute.org/policy-analysis/view/the-islamic-states-burgeoning-capital-in-sirte-libya
79. "IS Spokesman Rallics Fightcrs, Blasts U.S.-Led Campaign Against IS," SITE Intelligence Group, May 21, 2016, https://news.siteintelgroup.com/Jihadist-News/is-spokesman-rallies-fighters-blasts-u-s-led-campaign-against-is.html
80. "How the Islamic State Rose, Fell, and Could Rise Again in the Maghreb," International Crisis Group, July 24, 2017, https://www.crisisgroup.org/middle-east-north-africa/north-africa/178-how-islamic-state-rose-fell-and-could-rise-again-maghreb.
81. Patrick Wintour, "Isis loses control of Libyan city of Sirte." *Guardian* (London). December 5, 2016, https://www.theguardian.com/world/2016/dec/05/isis-loses-control-of-libyan-city-of-sirte
82. "How the Islamic State Rose, Fell, and Could Rise Again in the Maghreb," International Crisis Group.
83. Callimachi and Schmitt, "Manchester Bomber Met With ISIS Unit in Libya, Officials Say."
84. Emily Estelle, "Desknote: ISIS's Tunisian attack cell in Libya," American Enterprise Institute Critical Threats Project, March 8, 2016, https://www.criticalthreats.org/analysis/desknote-isiss-tunisian-attack-cell-in-libya.
85. Callimachi and Schmitt, "Manchester Bomber Met With ISIS Unit

in Libya, Officials Say."
86. Patrick Wintour, "Isis loses control of Libyan city of Sirte."
87. John Brennan, Statement before the Senate Select Committee on Intelligence, June 16, 2016, https://www.cia.gov/news-information/speeches-testimony/2016-speeches-testimony/statement-by-director-brennan-as-prepared-for-delivery-before-ssci.html.
88. Jason Pack, Rhiannon Smith, and Karim Mezran, "The Origins and Evolution of ISIS in Libya," Atlantic Council, June 20, 2017, https://www.atlanticcouncil.org/publications/reports/the-origins-and-evolution-of-isis-in-libya
89. Thomas Joscelyn, "How Many Fighters Does the Islamic State Still Have in Libya?" *Long War Journal*, July 20, 2017, http://www.longwarjournal.org/archives/2017/07/how-many-fighters-does-the-islamic-state-still-have-in-libya.php; Frederic Wehrey, "When the Islamic State Came to Libya," *The Atlantic*, February 10, 2018, https://www.theatlantic.com/international/archive/2018/02/isis-libya-hiftar-al-qaeda-syria/552419/; 'Turkey sends hundreds of mercenaries to Libya; national army arrested "the most dangerous ISIS,"' *Hawar News*, May 25, 2020. Accessed July 24, 2020. http://www.hawarnews.com/en/haber/turkey-sends-hundreds-of-mercenaries-to-libya-national-army-arrested-the-most-dangerous-isis-h16713.html
90. Zelin, "The Islamic State in Libya Has Yet to Recover"; Emily Estelle and Samuel Bloebam, "Africa File: Egypt Threatens Military Intervention in Libya," American Enterprise Institute Critical Threats Project, June 25, 2020, https://www.criticalthreats.org/briefs/africa-file/africa-file-egypt-threatens-military-intervention-in-libya.
91. Sudarsan Raghavan, "ISIS suicide bombers attack Libyan electoral commission, killing at least 12," *Washington Post*, May 2, 2018, https://www.washingtonpost.com/world/isis-suicide-bombers-attack-libyan-electoral-commission-killing-12/2018/05/02/e39d4cf4-4e28-11e8-85c1-9326c4511033_story.html?utm_term=.153cc9a31717; Ahmed Elumami, "Gunmen attack headquarters of Libya's state oil firm, two staff killed," Reuters, September 10, 2018, https://www.reuters.com/article/us-libya-security/gunmen-attack-headquarters-of-libyas-state-oil-firm-two-staff-killed-idUSKCN1LQ0SH.
92. Zachary Laub and Jonathan Masters, "Al-Qaeda in the Islamic Maghreb (AQIM)," Council on Foreign Relations, March 27, 2015, https://cisac.fsi.stanford.edu/mappingmilitants/profiles/

aqim#_ftn11
93. Arturo Varvelli, "Islamic State's Reorganization in LIbya and Potential Consequences with Illegal Trafficking," George Washington University, November 2017, 5, https://extremism.gwu.edu/sites/g/files/zaxdzs2191/f/Varvelli IS Reorganization in Libya and Trafficking.pdf.
94. Dalia Ghanem, "Why Is AQIM Still a Regional Threat?" *Al-Araby*, March 23, 2016, https://carnegie-mec.org/2016/03/23/why-is-aqim-still-regional-threat-pub-63121
95. "Samuel Laurent: "Le désert libyen est devenu un haut lieu de la contrebande et du terrorisme," *Radio France Internationale*, June 9, 2013, https://www.rfi.fr/fr/afrique/20130609-le-sud-libye-nouveau-sanctuaire-le-terrorisme-islamique
96. United States Library of Congress, Federal Research Division, "Al Qaeda in Libya: A Profile," August 2012, https://fas.org/irp/world/para/aq-libya-loc.pdf.
97. Lydia Sizer, "Libya's Terrorism Challenge: Assessing the Salafi-Jihadi Threat," Middle East Institute, 2017, 24-30, www.jstor.org/stable/resrep17568.12.
98. "Libya," Woodrow Wilson International Center for Scholars, n.d., https://www.wilsoncenter.org/libya
99. "Who bombed Al Qaeda in southwest Libya?" *The National*, February 17, 2019, https://www.hstoday.us/subject-matter-areas/counterterrorism/who-bombed-al-qaeda-in-southwest-libya/; Umberto Profazio, "Push for southern Libya tests ethnic ties and regional alliances," The International Institute for Strategic Studies, March 15, 2019, https://www.iiss.org/blogs/analysis/2019/03/southern-libya.
100. Christopher M. Blanchard, "Libya: Conflict, Transition, and U.S. Policy," Congressional Research Service, June 26, 2020, 23, https://fas.org/sgp/crs/row/RL33142.pdf.
101. "Government in Libya's Capital Condemns Deadly Air Strikes," Reuters, December 2, 2019, https://www.reuters.com/article/us-libya-security/government-in-libyas-capital-condemns-deadly-air-strikes-idUSKBN1Y62AT.
102. Manal Omar, "The Islamists are Coming," Woodrow Wilson International Center for Scholars, n.d., https://www.wilsoncenter.org/program/the-islamists
103. U.S. Department of State, Bureau of Democracy, Human Rights and Labor, *International Religious Freedom Report for 2013*, n.d., http://www.state.gov/j/drl/rls/irf/religiousfreedom/index.htm?year=2013&dlid=222303#sthash.IH9pgQVJ.dpuf; "Libya," Central

Intelligence Agency *World Factbook*, January 12, 2017, https://www.cia.gov/library/publications/the-world-factbook/geos/ly.html.

104. U.S. Department of State, *International Religious Freedom Report for 2013*.
105. Ragab Saad, "A Constitution That Doesn't Protect Rights and Freedoms: Libya Writes Its Constitution," Atlantic Council, August 3, 2017, https://www.atlanticcouncil.org/blogs/menasource/a-constitution-that-doesn-t-protect-rights-and-freedoms-libya-writes-its-constitution/.
106. U.S. Department of State, *International Religious Freedom Report for 2013*.
107. Ragab Saad, "A Constitution That Doesn't Protect Rights and Freedoms: Libya Writes Its Constitution."
108. Omar, "The Islamists are Coming."
109. Mohamed Eljarh, "In Post-Qaddafi Libya, It's Stay Silent or Die," *Foreign Policy*, September 24, 2014, https://foreignpolicy.com/2014/09/24/in-post-qaddafi-libya-its-stay-silent-or-die/
110. Pargeter, "Political Islam in Libya."
111. Ibid.
112. Manal Omar, "Libya: Rebuilding From Scratch," Woodrow Wilson International Center for Scholars, n.d., https://www.wilsoncenter.org/article/libya-rebuilding-scratch
113. Frederic Wehrey, "Quiet No More?"
114. Ashour, "Libya's Muslim Brotherhood faces the future."
115. Mary Fitzgerald, "A Current of Faith," *Foreign Policy*, July 6, 2012, http://www.foreignpolicy.com/articles/2012/07/06/a_current_of_faith.
116. Camille Tawil, "Tripoli's Islamist Militia Leader Turns to Politics in the New Libya," Jamestown Foundation *Terrorism Monitor* 10, iss. 11, June 1, 2012, http://www.jamestown.org/single/?no_cache=1&tx_ttnews%5Btt_news%5D=39450.
117. "Libya Publishes Parliamentary Election Results," BBC, June 26, 2014, https://www.bbc.com/news/world-africa-28005801.
118. Wolfgang Pusztai, "The Failed Serraj Experiment of Libya," Atlantic Council, March 31, 2017, http://www.atlanticcouncil.org/blogs/menasource/the-serraj-experiment-of-libya.
119. Frederic Wehrey, "Whoever Controls Benghazi Controls Libya," *The Atlantic*, July 1, 2017, https://www.theatlantic.com/international/archive/2017/07/benghazi-libya/532056/.
120. Estelle, "The General's Trap in Libya."
121. Karim Mezran and Elissa Miller, "Libya: From Intervention to

Proxy War," Atlantic Council, July 2017, https://www.atlanticcouncil.org/publications/issue-briefs/libya-from-intervention-to-proxy-war

122. Martin Chulov, "End of Tripoli siege raises fears of full-scale proxy war in Libya," *Guardian* (London), June 26, 2020, https://www.theguardian.com/world/2020/jun/26/libyan-standoff-risks-dragging-egyptian-military-into-regions-cold-war
123. Dorian Jones, "Turkey Faces Pressure as Libyan Conflict Widens," *Voice of America*, July 21, 2020, https://www.voanews.com/europe/turkey-faces-pressure-libyan-conflict-widens
124. "Libya slams Egypt parliament's authorization of military intervention," *Daily Sabah*, July 22, 2020, https://www.dailysabah.com/politics/libya-slams-egypt-parliaments-authorization-of-military-intervention/news; Alaeddin Saleh, "Erdogan's Libya Campaign Puts Africa on the Brink of War," *Modern Diplomacy*, July 21, 2020, https://moderndiplomacy.eu/2020/07/21/erdogans-libya-campaign-puts-africa-on-the-brink-of-war/
125. Mary Fitzgerald and Mattia Toaldo, "A quick guide to Libya's main players," European Council on Foreign Relations, 2017, http://www.ecfr.eu/mena/mapping_libya_conflict#.
126. Wehrey, "Whoever Controls Benghazi Controls Libya."

19 Mauritania

Quick Facts

Population: 4,005,475 (July 2020 est.)
Area: 1,030,700 sq km
Ethnic Groups: Black Moors (Haratines - Arab-speaking slaves, former slaves, and their descendants of African origin, enslaved by white Moors) 40%, white Moors (of Arab-Berber descent, known as Beydane) 30%, Sub-Saharan Mauritanians (non-Arabic speaking, largely resident in or originating from the Senegal River Valley, including Halpulaar, Fulani, Soninke, Wolof, and Bambara ethnic groups) 30%
GDP (official exchange rate): $4.935 billion (2017 est.)

Source: CIA World FactBook (Last Updated October 2020)

Introduction

Mauritania has historically avoided the path of radical Islamism. Rather, Islam helped unify Mauritania's Arab and African populations when the country earned its independence in 1960.[1] *Nevertheless, dynamics that fostered support for Islamist movements in other Middle Eastern and North African countries – among them poverty, unemployment, and a frustrated, largely urban population seeking improved material conditions and an ideological sense of direction – have led to an increased Islamist political presence in Mauritania in recent years. By and large, however, these groups have so far steered clear of using violence to achieve their objectives.*

According to the U.S. government, "Mauritania is not a safe haven for terrorists or terrorist groups, although regions in the interior are imperfectly monitored as a result of their geographic isolation from population centres and inhospitable desert conditions."[2] *However, research indicates that Mauritania has produced a significant number of jihadist ideologues and high-ranking terrorist operatives per capita.*[3] *Many Mauritanians have left home to join global Islamist groups. As a result, while there have been no terrorist attacks in Mauritania since 2011, the U.S. government maintains a standing travel advisory to the country.*[4]

Endnotes

1. See "l'Islamisme en Afrique du Nord IV: Contestation Islamiste en Mauritanie: Menace ou Bouc Émissaire?" International Crisis Group *Middle East/North Africa Report* no. 41, May 11, 2005, https://www.crisisgroup.org/middle-east-north-africa/north-africa/mauritania.
2. U.S. Department of State, Bureau of Counterterrorism, *Country Reports on Terrorism 2015*, 2016, https://www.state.gov/j/ct/rls/crt/2015/257514.htm.
3. See Anouar Boukhars, "As Threats Mount, Can Mauritania's Fragile Stability Hold?" *World Politics Review*, June 16, 2016, http://www.worldpoliticsreview.com/articles/19084/as-threats-mount-can-mauritania-s-fragile-stability-hold
4. See U.S. Department of State, "Mauritania Travel Advisory," n.d., https://travel.state.gov/content/travel/en/traveladvisories/traveladvisories/mauritania-travel-advisory.html.

Due to publishing constraints, this chapter is provided here only in summary form. To view the full study, please visit the online edition of the Almanac at almanac.afpc.org.

20 Morocco

Quick Facts

Population: 35,561,654 (July 2020 est.)
Area: 446,550 sq km
Ethnic Groups:Arab-Berber 99%, other 1%
GDP (official exchange rate): $109.3 billion (2017 est.)

Source: CIA World FactBook (Last Updated June 2020)

Use of maps of Morocco does not represent a judgement regarding the legal status of the Western Sahara by either the chapter author or the editors of the Almanac.

Introduction

Unlike many other Arab and majority-Muslim states, Morocco has integrated Islamist political movements that oppose violence and support the constitutional order into its political process. Its government relentlessly prosecutes adherents to Salafist and other extremist ideologies. Not surprisingly, the U.S. State Department's most recent report on global terrorism trends lauded the country's "comprehensive counterterrorism strategy that includes vigilant security measures, regional and international cooperation, and counter-radicalization policies."[1] The reformist course charted by King Mohammed VI has enabled Moroccans to avoid both the revolutionary tumult and violent repression characterizing their neighbors' experiences with the so-called Arab Spring; however, the North African kingdom endured jihadist *attacks and still confronts an Islamist movement that openly calls for the overthrow of the monarchy and creation of an Islamic state. The crown must also manage an Algerian-backed separatist group increasingly linked to al-Qaeda's regional affiliate. Thus, it remains to be seen whether the "Moroccan exception" is ultimately sustainable and, if so, what implications this might have for the region and the wider Arab and Muslim world.*

Islamist Activity

A number of Islamist groups and movements, either indigenous or foreign, are currently active in Morocco. Unlike in many other Arab or majority-Muslim nations, however, Islamism in Morocco is quite fragmented.

Ash-Shabiba al-Islamiyya ("Islamic Youth")

Founded in 1969, Shabiba (sometimes known by the French acronym AJI) was the first organization in the Maghreb region with the explicit objective of advancing Islamist politics.[2] The group also opposed the political leftism then in vogue in many Arab countries. Led by Abdelkarim Mouti, a former education ministry inspector, the group attracted support among university and high school students through vacation camps where they received training in propaganda and protest techniques. Shabiba also cultivated ties with clandestine Algerian organizations in the early 1970s.

Mouti fled into exile in 1975, following the murder of two prominent leftist political figures that authorities blamed on Shabiba. The investigation of the assassinations revealed that Shabiba had built up a secretive military arm, known as the al-Mujahidun al-Maghariba ("Moroccan Holy Warriors"), which was headed by a onetime law student named Abdelaziz Naamani. Sentenced to death *in abstentia*, Mouti spent time in both Saudi Arabia and Libya, but settled in Belgium where he continued to agitate against the Moroccan government. He published a small magazine, *Al-Mujahid* ("The Holy Warrior"), which garnered a modest following among the immigrant communities of Europe. After the Moroccan government discovered arms caches near the Algerian border in 1985, however, authorities set in motion a crackdown that all but shut down the group.

Al-Islah wa't-Tajdid ("Reform and Renewal") / At-Tawhid wa'l-Islah ("Unity and Reform")

The Movement for Reform and Renewal was created in 1992 by former Shabiba members who came to reject the group's embrace of violence and sought instead to advance their objectives within Morocco's existing political system; in 1996, they changed the organization's name to *at-Tawhid* (the Association for Unity and Reform).[3] While King Hassan II tolerated at-Tawhid, he did not accord it legal recognition. Consequently, Abdelilah Benkirane and other at-Tawhid leaders negotiated an arrangement with a longstanding but minor political party, the Democratic Constitutional Movement, that enabled them to participate in elections under the aegis of the latter. The merger took place in 1997, and the new political party changed its name the following year to the Justice and Development Party (generally known by its French acronym, PJD).[4]

Al-Adl Wal-Ihsan ("Justice and Charity")

Al-Adl, (JCO), formed in 1988, has been the most virulent Islamist political and religious movement in Morocco. Considered illegitimate and barely tolerated by the Moroccan government, JCO has gained adherents through its role as the sole indigenous Islamist movement challenging the king's political and religious roles. The Moroccan government refuses to recognize JCO as a political party.[5]

JCO advocates a restoration of *sharia* law, but asserts allegiance to democratic principles to differentiate itself from what it considers to be Morocco's authoritarian political system. JCO's leader and founder, Sheikh Abdessalam Yassine, has openly challenged the legitimacy of the Moroccan monarchy since the 1970s. For that stance, he was tried in 1984 and sentenced to house arrest — a sentence that remained in force until 1989.[6] JCO was officially outlawed in 1990 until the ban was modified by the current king, Mohammed VI, in 2004. Sheikh Yassine's daughter, Nadia Yassine, increasingly emerged as JCO's chief political organizational leader after her father died in 2012.

JCO is committed to the dissolution of the country's current constitutional system and its replacement by an Islamic republic. Nevertheless, JCO has publicly renounced the use of violence and armed struggle; it instead relies on protests and occasional civil disobedience to advance its goals. JCO's scope of support is a closely guarded secret, both by the organization itself and by the Moroccan government (some observers consider its support substantial given its extensive charitable and social network).[7] The JCO demonstrated some of this support during state unrest in June 2017: it organized an estimated 10,000 protestors for a march in solidarity with poor living conditions in the country's northern Rif region.[8]

JCO's leadership began exporting their movement to Europe beginning roughly in 1996, when it created the Muslim Participation and Spirituality (MPS) Association.[9] MPS has established chapters in various European cities, which are headed by JCO Islamist activists who have fled Morocco. The goal of MPS is to generate opposition to Morocco's king and government through political activities, eventually winning legal status for the JCO inside Morocco.[10] The French and Belgian MPS branches often organize demonstrations against Morocco.

The Party of Justice and Development (PJD)

In order to co-opt Islamist movements in Morocco, King Hassan II permitted new political movements that incorporated Islamist orientations — the most significant being the Justice and Development Party (PJD). While PJD draws on Islamic values and inspiration from Turkey's Justice and Development Party (AKP), they share no official connection.

As previously discussed, the Islamist-inspired *at-Tawhid* fused with the Constitutional Democratic Popular Movement and emerged as the PJD. The PJD brought together a coalition of small, moderate Islamist organizations, including conservative Islamist, pro-monarchial political figures, and has competed in Morocco's parliamentary elections since 1997. In 2002, the PJD emerged as the country's leading opposition party and third-largest group in the national legislature with 42 of the 325 seats in Morocco's parliament. The PJD won the largest percentage of the popular vote (10.9 percent on the local and 13.4 percent on the national lists) garnered by any single party in the 2007 election.[11]

Unlike JCO, the PJD is non-revolutionary and does not call for the overthrow of the monarchy; consequently, it does not directly challenge Morocco's constitutional system. PJD does not advocate the creation for an Islamist state, or caliphate, in Morocco; instead it intentionally downplays any religious agenda while adhering to Islamic political values. It views itself as the guardian of Morocco's Muslim identity, opposing further westernization of Moroccan society but pragmatically recognizing the importance of Morocco's ties to the West. The PJD also regards itself as a bulwark against radical Islamic groups such as JCO.

Since 1997, the PJD has gradually gained popular support throughout Morocco, and has become quite entrenched in Morocco's political process. PJD legislators have won plaudits for focusing their attention on ameliorating Morocco's significant social and economic challenges. During its period in opposition, the party had only marginal ability to translate its agenda into meaningful programs that would garner greater popular support. Nevertheless, once they became the governing party (see below), their failure to deliver on those promises dissatisfied voters and led to a resurgence of support for other parties.

The PJD's agenda in parliament has occasionally taken it into pure *sharia* territory — including calling for prohibition against alcohol distribution and consumption, and challenging media that it views as defamatory of Islamic principles. On other occasions, however, the PJD has trended in the opposite direction. In 2004, the party actively participated in the adoption of the *Moudawana*, a new, more liberal version of the country's code regulating marriage and family life.[12] The revision of the *Moudawana* greatly improved the social status of women in Morocco, and was ridiculed by more conservative Islamists. The PJD's leader at the time, Saad Eddine el-Othmani, defended his party's approval of the code's revision, asserting in 2006 that it had been approved by religious leaders, aided families, and was consistent with Islamic traditions.[13]

In the November 25, 2011 elections — the first held under the new constitution proposed by King Mohammed VI and approved by direct vote earlier that year — the PJD came away with 107 seats, making it by far the single largest party in the new legislature. Since the new charter stipulates that the monarch should appoint the prime minister from the largest party in parliament, the mandate to form a government was given to the PJD's Benkirane, who formed a coalition government with support from the venerable conservative nationalist Independence Party – Istiqlal – and two left-leaning parties. The new government was sworn in on January 3, 2012, with the PJD holding 11 of 30 ministerial portfolios.[14]

In the October 7, 2016 parliamentary elections, the PJD again emerged as the largest single party in parliament, with 125 seats. However, widespread dissatisfaction with the PJD's management of the government also manifested itself in an even stronger rally behind the Party of Authenticity and Modernity (PAM) which surged from a fourth-place finish in the previous election to second place with 102 seats in the legislature.

The 2016 election results led to five months of parliamentary deadlock, which ended when Benkirane, unable to reconcile with the USFP, failed to form a coalition government and was subsequently dismissed by the King. Saad Eddine el-Othmani, who was most recently serving as the PJD's secretary-general, was appointed Prime Minister on March 17, 2017, and quickly conceded 17 ministries to the bloc of parties led by conservative National Rally of Independents leader Aziz Akhannouch, including the powerful economy, finance, commerce, and agricultural portfolios. The PJD was left with eleven of 39 ministerial positions, which has stirred ire within the party, generated criticism within Othmani's leadership, weakened the PJD, and called its future into question.[15]

Salafist Jihadism

Morocco has "numerous small 'grassroots' extremist groups" that collectively adhere to Salafi-*jihadi* ideology.[16] Spanish anti-terror judge Baltazar Garzon stated in 2007 that "Morocco is the worst terrorist threat to Europe."[17] At that time, he estimated that al-Qaeda-linked cells in Morocco numbered more than 100 and that at least 1,000 terrorists were being actively sought by Moroccan authorities.[18] Al-Qaeda's regional offshoot, al-Qaeda in the Islamic Maghreb (AQIM), has been recently successful in bringing these disparate groups (which number less than 50 members per grouping, on average) under its umbrella. In March 2017, four regional militant groups, including Ansar Dine and other elements of AQIM, merged to form the Group for the Support of Islam and Muslims (GSIM).[19]

AQIM formed from the reconstitution of the Salafist Group for Preaching and Combat (GSPC) AQIM in early 2007. Its goal has been to integrate all of the North African radical movements, including the small Moroccan Islamic Combatant Group (GICM). On September 11, 2013, AQIM released an unprecedented 41-minute video "documentary" attacking Moroccan domestic and foreign policy, especially its counterterrorism efforts. Analysts believe that the production was the result of the terrorist organization's frustration that, while it had recruited some Moroccans, it had largely failed to successfully target the country or compromise its institutions.[20] AQIM, like its counterpart al-Qaeda in the Arabian Peninsula (AQAP), constitutes a potent regional terrorist threat not only to Morocco but to Algeria, Burkina Faso, Mauritania, Mali, Niger, and Tunisia.

Salafi *jihadis* as a whole remain a globally significant threat – one with high Moroccan participation. Scores of young Moroccans traveled to Iraq and Afghanistan to fight Americans in the first decade of the "War on Terror,"[21] and more recently Morocco's Central Bureau for Judicial Investigations estimated that over 1,600 Moroccans had joined ISIS.[22] If European citizens of Moroccan descent are included, the figure rises to between 2,000 and 2,500.[23] There also have been reports of considerable numbers of Moroccans traveling to Mali and Algeria to receive training from AQIM elements.[24] With the collapse of the ISIS "caliphate" in Iraq and Syria, Moroccan authorities anticipate a potentially significant number of extremists to return to the Kingdom in the years ahead.[25]

Salafis also represent a challenge to the Moroccan state, as underscored by a number of incidents over the past decade. For instance, on April 28, 2011, 17 people (among them 12 foreigners) were killed and at least 20 wounded in the bombing of a popular tourist café in Marrakech.[26] The government accused AQIM of the attack. More recently, in December 2018, two Danish tourists were murdered in the Atlas Mountains region.[27] Although Moroccan authorities determined that the incident was not directly coordinated by a terrorist group, the main suspects had pledged allegiance to ISIS.[28]

Islamism and Society

Under Moroccan law, the country's monarch traces his lineage back to the Prophet Mohammad. Consequently, the majority of Moroccans take great pride in their nation's embrace of moderate, tolerant Islam. It is worth noting that the reformed Moroccan constitution of 2011 explicitly acknowledges that the country's national culture is "enriched and nourished by African, Andalusian, Hebrew, and Mediterranean influences."[29]

However, social and economic conditions, including institutional neglect, play a role in Islamist sentiment. Morocco's high youth unemployment rate and an influx of Europe-bound migrants from sub-Saharan Africa has transformed northern cities like Tangier, Tetouan, or Al Houcema into smuggling centers feeding criminal elements and opponents of the regime.[30] Following a Berber rebellion against his rule in the early 1980s, King Hassan II largely abandoned the northern tier of Morocco to its own devices. The King rarely visited the north during his reign. Consequently, government services were severely cut, and Islamists filled the void with a social and charitable network offering food and medical treatment to the local population. While King Mohammed has reversed his father's policy of abandonment of the north (and even conducted an ancient traditional ceremony of mutual allegiance there[31]), the region is still relatively underdeveloped and deeply dependent on charitable networks, some with extremist links, for services not provided by the government.

Despite the current king's efforts to promote a legislative agenda to modernize Islamic laws governing civil society in Morocco (detailed below), the continued growth of political parties such as the PJD, as well as the continued activities of the JCO both inside Morocco and in Europe, highlight fractures in Moroccan society between those who favor a more moderate, tolerant Islam and significant elements that prefer stronger Islamic control over the nation's society and its political system.

The impoverished slums in Morocco's inner cities and northern regions have produced many extremists, and many Moroccan extremist groupings are composed of family members and friends from the same towns and villages. Indeed, the north of Morocco has become an especially fertile ground for Salafists who favor *Wahhabbism* and other extremist creeds over Morocco's more tolerant version of Islam.[32]

Islamism and the State

Following the 2003 Casablanca bombings, the Moroccan government focused on modernizing Islamic teaching and Islamic infrastructure and adopted laws liberalizing civil marriage and the role of women in Morocco's society. The Ministry of Endowments and Islamic Affairs was provided with new funding and authority to train more moderate Islamic clerics and to expand its programs in Morocco's educational system.

In 2004, King Mohammed VI pushed through a reform of the family code (*Moudawana*), overcoming conservative opposition and mass demonstrations in part by invoking his religious authority as Commander of the Faithful. Among other provisions, the legislation significantly advanced women's rights by elevating the minimum age of marriage to 18, limiting polygamy, granting couples joint rights over their children, and permitting women to initiate divorce proceedings.[33]

One incident in particular points to Morocco's more aggressive stance against ultra-conservative Muslim clerics who oppose the government's efforts to modernize Morocco's Islamic infrastructure and its religious teachings. In September 2008, Sheikh Mohamed Ben Abderrahman Al Maghraoui issued a highly provocative *fatwa* legitimizing the marriage of underage women as young as nine years old.[34] The Moroccan government sought to discredit the *fatwa* and ordered the immediate closure of 60 Koranic schools under his control. The government also launched an inquiry into Sheikh Al Maghraoui's competence as an Islamic scholar, and the public prosecutor's office initiated a criminal case against him for encouraging pedophilia.[35]

Following the incident, King Mohammed unveiled his "proximity strategy," which represented a modernization program for Islamic institutions in Morocco. Under the program, 3,180 mosques were designated to be "modernized," (essentially a wholesale replacement of *imams* deemed by the regime to be opponents of moderate Islamic principles). 33,000 new *imams* were to be trained and the number of regional *ulama* councils (charged with overseeing Islamic teaching and the competency of *imams*) was increased from 30 to 70. Exceptionally for the Arab world, women also have a place in Morocco's official religious establishment with *mourchidates*, or female religious guides, trained alongside more traditional male *imams*.[36]

To counter violent Islamist extremist ideologies, Morocco has developed a national strategy to reaffirm and further institutionalize Moroccans' historically widespread adherence to Sunni Islam's Maliki school of jurisprudence and its Ashari theology, as well as to the mystical spirituality of Sufism.

Unlike his father, the King has largely refrained from playing an activist role in Middle East diplomacy; rather, Mohammed VI focuses his diplomatic efforts closer to home in Africa, which the monarch has repeatedly characterized as the "top priority" of his country's foreign policy. He emphasizes that "this multi-dimensional relationship puts Morocco in the center of Africa" and "Africa holds a special place in the heart of Moroccans."[37] On January 30, 2017, Morocco joined the African Union, more than three decades after leaving its predecessor organization. Complimenting extensive partnerships with African countries on a variety of political and economic issues, Morocco's efforts to train religious leaders and preachers from across the continent—and, indeed, even some from Europe and beyond—in the kingdom's moderate form of Islam are increasingly visible. The Mohammed VI Institute for the Training of Imams, Morchidines, and Morchidates, established in 2015, has enrolled hundreds of students from Mali, Tunisia, Guinea, Côte d'Ivoire, and France.[38]

For many years, Morocco has permitted mainstream Islamic political parties that do not condone extremism and violence to exist and indeed, to participate in elections, although it continues to deny legal status to the JCO. The aborted terrorist plot in 2007 and the continuing threat of *jihadi* sentiment in the country's north only briefly arrested the pace of King Mohammed's reform agenda with respect to rights of women and the judiciary, including enacting legislation in 2014 to end the use of military tribunals to try civilians.

Since the Casablanca bombings in 2003, Moroccan authorities have maintained a vigilant and aggressive stance against any *jihadist* movement. Between 2002 and 2018, according to authorities, over 3,000 people have been arrested as part of the Kingdom's counterterrorism efforts.[39] As of 2018, the Moroccan Central Bureau for Judicial Investigations said it had broken up 57 militant cells, including 51 with connection to ISIS, since 2015.[40] Fighting with terrorist groups in other countries already constituted a crime under the Moroccan penal code, but authorities also adopted specific legislation criminalizing traveling abroad with intent to join terrorist groups like ISIS.[41]

At the same time, the Moroccan government for years has permitted Islamist parties that embrace more moderate Islamic principles and do not condone extremism and violence (such as the PJD) to exist and to participate in elections. The Moroccan government has demonstrated ingenuity in its "divide and conquer" strategy against Islamists who challenge the state. In addition to adopting the above-referenced "proximity strategy" to replace recalcitrant *imams*, authorities have established a grassroots police operation to report on any suspicious activities.[42]

The Moroccan government has also implemented the National Initiative for Human Development (INDH), a concerted, multibillion-dollar social development program aimed at generating employment, fighting poverty, and improving infrastructure in both rural areas as well as the urban centers susceptible to charities nurturing radicalism. In the largest *bidonvilles* (shantytowns) in Morocco's cities, significant social welfare, health and education programs have been instituted and many families have been relocated to new affordable housing units.[43] Overall, the U.S. State Department has applauded Morocco for having "a comprehensive strategy for countering violent extremism that prioritizes economic and human development goals in addition to tight control of the religious sphere and messaging."[44]

Even the historically touchy issue of Moroccan sovereignty over the former Spanish Sahara has seen forward movement amid recent reforms.[45] In 2007, the government advanced a proposal to break the longstanding impasse over the issue by offering generous autonomy to the area (including not only an elected local administration but also ideas about education and justice and the promise of financial support). Under the plan, the only matters that would remain in Rabat's control would be defense, foreign affairs, and the currency. The regional authority, meanwhile, has broad powers over local administration, the economy, infrastructure, social and cultural affairs, and the environment. Then-Secretary of State Hillary Rodham Clinton described the autonomy proposal in 2011 as "serious, credible, and realistic."[46]

Nevertheless, now well into its fourth decade, the "question of Western Sahara," as it is termed in United Nations nomenclature, is one of those challenges which has defied multiple efforts by the international community to facilitate its "solution." Former UN Secretary-General Bank Ki-moon and others have warned that "the rise of instability and insecurity in and around the Sahel" and the risk of "spillover" from the fighting in Mali requires "an urgent settlement" of this "ticking time bomb."[47] Secretary-General António Guterres reiterated these concerns in January 2018, after tensions escalated near Guerguerat.[48] Yet the "question" remains unanswered.

Supported by Algeria, the Frente Popular de Liberación de Saguía el Hamra y Río de Oro ("Popular Front for the Liberation of Saqiet al-Hamra and Río del Oro," commonly known as the Polisario Front) demands territorial independence, even though the armed conflict of the late 1970s and early 1980s left Morocco in control of more than 85 percent of it. The Moroccan government constructed a "sand berm" (a defensive shield consisting of a series of barriers of sand and stone completed in 1987) and the UN deployed a monitoring force to the Western Sahara. Both have largely confined the Polisario Front to a small zone around Tindouf in southwestern Algeria. Tens of thousands of Sahrawi refugees in squalid camps have recently been the object of former UN Secretary-General Ban Ki-Moon's concerns about conflict spillover.[49]

For most of its history, the Polisario Front has been avowedly secular and, indeed, leftist in its political orientations; many of its leaders studied in the Soviet bloc and fighters received training in Cuba well into the 1990s. However, there are worrisome indications of growing linkages with AQIM and other Islamist groups in the Maghreb and the Sahel, including providing AQIM's allies in northern Mali with both fighters and, in one notorious case, Western hostages to trade for ransom.[50] Morocco cut diplomatic ties with Iran in May 2018, accusing the Iranian-backed Hezbollah of providing weapons, training, and financial support to Polisario fighters.[51] Should these trends continue, they will not only heighten the challenge of Islamist violence for Morocco, but also exacerbate an already volatile security situation for the entire region.

Endnotes

1. U.S. Department of State, Office of the Coordinator for Counterterrorism, "Country Reports: Middle East and North Africa Overview," in *Country Reports on Terrorism 2017*, September 2018, https://www.state.gov/documents/organization/283100.pdf.
2. John P. Entelis, "Political Islam in the Maghreb," in John P. Entelis, ed., *Islam, Democracy, and the State in North Africa* (Bloomington: Indiana University Press, 1997), 52-53.
3. Amr Hamzawy, "Party for Justice and Development in Morocco: Participation and Its Discontents," Carnegie Endowment for International Peace *Carnegie Paper* no. 93, July 2008, 7-8, http://www.carnegieendowment.org/publications/index.cfm?fa=view&id=20314.
4. Amr Hamzawy, "Party for Justice and Development in Morocco: Participation and Its Discontents," Carnegie Endowment for International Peace *Carnegie Paper* no. 93, July 2008, 8, http://www.carnegieendowment.org/publications/index.cfm?fa=view&id=20314.
5. Samir Amghar, "Political Islam in Morocco," Center for European Policy Studies *CEPS Working Document* No. 269, June 2007.
6. Samir Amghar, "Political Islam in Morocco," Center for European Policy Studies *CEPS Working Document* No. 269, June 2007.
7. National Democratic Institute, *Final Report on the Moroccan Legislative Elections*, September 7, 2007.
8. Samia Errazzouki, "Led by Islamists, Thousands of Moroccans Rally in Support of Northern Protests," Reuters, June 11, 2017, https://www.reuters.com/article/us-morocco-protests/led-by-islamists-thousands-of-moroccans-rally-in-support-of-northern-protests-idUSKBN1920X8.
9. Amghar, "Political Islam in Morocco."
10. Amghar, "Political Islam in Morocco."
11. Daniel Williams, "Morocco Parliament May be Controlled by Islamic Party," Bloomberg, December 30, 2009, http://www.bloomberg.com/apps/news?pid=newsarchive&sid=aLXRR7EuJeEo.
12. Hamzawy, "Party for Justice and Development in Morocco: Participation and Its Discontents."
13. See Mona Yacoubian, "Engaging Islamists and Promoting Democracy: A Preliminary Assessment," in Daniel Brumberg and Dina Shehata, eds. *Conflict, Identity and Reform in the Muslim World: Challeng-*

es for U.S. Engagement (Washington: U.S. Institute of Peace Press, 2009), 420.

14. "Morocco: Islamist Party Takes over New Government," *Al Bawaba*, January 3, 2012, http://www.albawaba.com/news/morocco-islamist-party-takes-over-new-government-407621.
15. Imad Stitou, "Morocco Finally Gets New Government, but at What Cost?" *Al-Monitor*, April 12, 2017, https://www.al-monitor.com/pulse/originals/2017/04/morocco-government-islamist-party-majority.html.
16. U.S. Department of State, Office of the Coordinator for Counterterrorism, *Country Reports on Terrorism 2017* (Washington, DC: U.S. Department of State, September 2018), 148-149, https://www.state.gov/wp-content/uploads/2019/04/crt_2017.pdf.
17. Olivier Guitta, "Morocco Under Fire," *Washington Examiner*, March 29, 2007, https://www.washingtonexaminer.com/weekly-standard/morocco-under-fire.
18. Olivier Guitta, "Morocco Under Fire," *Washington Examiner*, March 29, 2007, https://www.washingtonexaminer.com/weekly-standard/morocco-under-fire.
19. Caleb Weiss, "Analysis: Merger of al-Qaeda Groups Threatens Security in West Africa," *Long War Journal*, March 18, 2017, https://www.longwarjournal.org/archives/2017/03/analysis-merger-of-al-qaeda-groups-threatens-security-in-west-africa.php.
20. Mawassi Lahcen, "AQIM Lashes Out at Morocco," *Morocco World News*, September 17, 2013, https://www.moroccoworldnews.com/2013/09/105233/aqim-lashes-out-at-morocco/.
21. Rogelio Alonso and Marcos García Rey, "The Evolution of Jihadist Terrorism in Morocco," *Terrorism and Political Violence* 19, no. 4 (August 2007), 571–92, https://doi.org/10.1080/09546550701606580; Bahija Jamal, "Moroccan Counter-Terrorism Policy: Case of Moroccan Female Migrants to ISIS," *International Annals of Criminology* 56, no. 1-2 (May 2018), 145–56, https://doi.org/10.1017/cri.2018.12.
22. Saad Eddine Lamzouwaq, "As ISIS Weakens, Morocco Faces Threat of Returning Fighters," *Morocco World News*, July 12, 2017, https://www.moroccoworldnews.com/2017/07/222883/as-isis-weakens-morocco-faces-threat-of-returning-fighters/.
23. Mohammed Masbah, "Moroccan Foreign Fighters," German Institute for International and Security Affairs (SWP) *Comments* no. 46 (October 2016), https://www.swp-berlin.org/fileadmin/contents/products/comments/2015C46_msb.pdf.

24. U.S. Department of State, *Country Reports on Terrorism 2008.*
25. Tamba François Koundouno, "Prospect of ISIS Fighters Returning Rings Alarm Bells in Morocco", *Moroccan World News*, December 31, 2019, https://www.moroccoworldnews.com/2018/12/262082/isis-fighters-morocco/.
26. "Morocco: Marrakesh bomb strikes Djemaa el-Fna square," *BBC*, April 28. 2011, https://www.bbc.com/news/world-africa-13226117.
27. "Morocco says suspects in Scandinavian tourists' murder are linked to Islamic State", Reuters, December 20, 2018, https://www.reuters.com/article/us-morocco-crime-idUSKCN1OJ0V1.
28. Mohammed Hikal, "Official: Scandinavian Tourists' Murder Wasn't a Coordinated ISIS Attack," *Moroccan World News*, December 24, 2018, https://www.moroccoworldnews.com/2018/12/261356/scandinavian-tourists-murder-isis/.
29. Preamble, Moroccan Constitution of 2011, https://www.constituteproject.org/constitution/Morocco_2011.pdf.
30. "Morocco Targets Migrant Smuggling Mafia," *The New Arab*, August 31, 2018, https://www.alaraby.co.uk/english/news/2018/8/30/morocco-targets-migrant-smuggling-mafia; "Morocco Dismantles a Migrant-smuggling Network in Tangier," *Yabiladi,* January 3, 2019, https://en.yabiladi.com/articles/details/72915/morocco-dismantles-migrant-smuggling-network-tangier.html.
31. Erlanger and Mekhennet, "Islamic Radicalism Slows Moroccan Reforms."
32. Constantine Eckner, "The Fear of Radicalisation: Moroccan Security Strategy post-2011," Human Security Centre, November 9, 2018, http://www.hscentre.org/counter-extremism/the-fear-of-radicalisation-moroccan-security-strategy-post-2011/.
33. Francesco Cavatorta and Emanuela Dalmasso, "Liberal Outcomes through Undemocratic Means: The Reform of the *Code du statut personnel* in Morocco," *Journal of Modern African Studies* 47, no. 4 (2009), 487-506.
34. U.S. Department of State, *Country Reports on Terrorism 2008.*
35. U.S. Department of State, *Country Reports on Terrorism 2008.*
36. Fatima Zahra Salhi, Ilham Chafik, and Nezha Nassi, "The Mourchidates of Morocco," in Maureen E. Fiedler, ed., *Breaking through the Stained Glass Ceiling: Women Religious Leaders in Their Own Words* (New York: Seabury Press, 2010), 28-30.
37. "S.M. le Roi adresse un discours à la Nation à l'occasion du 63ème anniversaire de la Révolution du Roi et du Peuple," Maghreb Arabe Presse, August 2016, http://www.mapnews.ma/fr/discours-messag-

es-sm-le-roi/sm-le-roi-adresse-un-discours-%C3%A0-la-nation-%C3%A0-loccasion-du-63-%C3%A8me.

38. Kamailoudini Tagba, "Morocco Sets Up New Foundation for African Ulemas," *North Africa Post*, June 8, 2016, http://northafricapost.com/12452-morocco-sets-new-foundation-african-ulemas.html.
39. "Abdelhak Khiame fait le bilan du BCIJ", *TelQuel*, October 12, 2018, https://telquel.ma/2018/10/12/nombre-de-cellules-demantelees-personnes-arretees-attentats-dejoues-le-patron-du-bcij-fait-le-point_1614135.
40. "Abdelhak Khiame fait le bilan du BCIJ", *TelQuel*, October 12, 2018, https://telquel.ma/2018/10/12/nombre-de-cellules-demantelees-personnes-arretees-attentats-dejoues-le-patron-du-bcij-fait-le-point_1614135.
41. "Morocco expands laws against militant seekers", *Al-Arabiya* (Riyadh), September 19, 2014, http://english.alarabiya.net/en/News/middle-east/2014/09/19/Morocco-expands-laws-against-militant-seekers.html.
42. Tossa, "Morocco's Fight Against Terrorism."
43. Tossa, "Morocco's Fight Against Terrorism."
44. U.S. Department of State, *Country Reports on Terrorism 2015*.
45. See J. Peter Pham, "Morocco's Momentum," *The Journal of International Security Affairs* 22 (Spring 2012), 13-20; See J. Peter Pham, "Not Another Failed State: Towards a Realistic Solution of the Western Sahara," *Journal of the Middle East and Africa* 1, no. 1 (Spring 2010), 1-24.
46. Secretary of State Hillary Rodham Clinton, Remarks with Moroccan Foreign Minister Taieb Fassi Fihri, March 23, 2011, archived at https://2009-2017.state.gov/secretary/20092013clinton/rm/2011/03/158895.htm.
47. "Corcas," Royal Advisory Council for Saharan Affairs, April 9, 2013, http://www.corcas.com/Western-Sahara/Ban-Ki-moon-stresses-urgency-of-settlement-in-Sahara,-calls-for-opening-borders-between-Morocco-and-Algeria-1055-2171-17271.aspx.
48. "Western Sahara: UN Chief Urges Morocco and Polisario Front to De-escalate Tensions in Buffer Strip," UN News Center, February 25, 2017, http://www.firstpost.com/world/un-secretary-general-antonio-guterres-expresses-concerns-over-spike-in-tensions-in-disputed-western-sahara-4291023.html.
49. Tim Witcher, "Ban says Western Sahara Risks being Drawn into Mali War," Agence France-Presse, April 9, 2013, http://www.google.com/hostednews/afp/article/ALeqM5iOnupKvBuc81_.

50. See J. Peter Pham, "The Dangerous 'Pragmatism' of Al-Qaeda in the Islamic Maghreb," *Journal of the Middle East and Africa* 2, no. 1 (January-June 2011), 15-29; See "Rebels: $18.4 Million Paid for Hostage Release," Associated Press, July 20, 2012, https://www.foxnews.com/world/rebels-18-4-million-paid-for-hostage-release.
51. "Morocco cuts ties with Iran over Sahara weapons dispute," Associated Press, May 1, 2018, https://apnews.com/3aebb7da756940c99434b420a45aa84b.

21 The Palestinian National Authority

Quick Facts

Population: *West Bank*: 2,900,034 (July 2020 est.), *Gaza Strip*: 1,918,221 (July 2020 est.)
Area: *West Bank*: 5,860 sq km *Gaza Strip*: 360 sq km
Ethnic Groups: *West Bank*: Palestinian Arab, Jewish, other *Gaza Strip*: Palestinian Arab
Religions: *West Bank*: Muslim 80-85% (predominately Sunni), Jewish 12-14%, Christian 1-2.5% (mainly Greek Orthodox), other, unaffiliated, unspecified <1% *Gaza Strip*: Muslim (predominately Sunni) 98-99%, Christian<1%, other, unaffiliated, unspecified <1%
Government Type: PLO/Fatah (contested)
GDP (official exchange rate): *West Bank*: $9.828 billion (2014 est.), *Gaza Strip*: $2.938 billion (2014 est.)

Map and Quick Facts derived in part from the CIA World Factbook (Last Updated November 2020)

Introduction

The Palestinian National Authority (PA or PNA) was created in accordance with the 1993 Oslo Accords. Under the subsequent "Oslo Process," the PA assumed the responsibilities of Israeli military administration in parts of the West Bank and Gaza Strip ("Area A"), and was expected to expand that territory through final status negotiations. The PA includes a Palestinian Legislative Council (PLC), a legislative body with 132 seats elected from the West Bank and Gaza. As a result of the Palestinian legislative elections in 2006, Hamas became the largest faction in the PLC with 72 seats. However, the rival Fatah faction, backed by Western governments concerned with Hamas' continued militancy, undermined the rule of subsequent Hamas-dominated governments. After more than a year of tension, Hamas forcibly seized control of Gaza in 2007. The two territories remained under separate rule for seven years. In June 2014, Hamas and Fatah forged an interim unity government to reunify through formal elections. Conflict between Gaza and Israel erupted soon thereafter, however, and it became clear that Hamas fully controlled the territory. A follow-up reconciliation agreement in October 2017 failed to end the division, as – so far – have reconciliation talks between the two sides in the Fall of 2020. Fatah maintains an iron grip on the West Bank, while Hamas remains the true power broker in Gaza.

Islamist Activity

Hamas

"Hamas" means "zeal" in Arabic, and is an Arabic acronym for Ḥarakat al-Muqāwamah al-ʾIslāmiyyah (the Islamic Resistance Movement). The group is primarily concentrated in the Gaza Strip, but has support in pockets of the West Bank. The group was founded as a splinter group of the Muslim Brotherhood in December 1987, during the early days of the *intifada* (uprising) against Israel. The Brotherhood refused to engage in violence against Israel, but Hamas' founders believed that it was a duty to "resist." According to one insider's account, the secretive organization's founders included Sheikh Ahmad Yassin, Hassan Yousef, Ayman Abu Taha, Jamil Hamami, Mahmud Muslih, Muhammed Jamal al-Natsah, and Jamal Mansour.[1]

In addition to its immediate goal of destroying the State of Israel, Hamas' 1988 *mithaq* (founding charter) illustrates the organization's commitment to universal Islamist principles, demonstrated by its slogan: "Allah is its goal [theocratic rule], the Prophet is its model [importance of the Sunna], the Qur'an its Constitution [sharia], *Jihad* [violence] is its path and death for the sake of Allah is the loftiest of its wishes."[2] While most Hamas members are Palestinian Sunni Arabs, the charter welcomes Muslims who: "embraces its faith, ideology, follows its program, keeps its secrets, and wants to belong to its ranks and carry out the duty."[3]

The Hamas charter conveys the conviction that Palestine is *waqf*, or land endowed to Muslims by Allah because it was "conquered by the companions of the Prophet."[4] Hamas also clearly defines nationalism as "part of the religious creed,"[5] thereby universalizing the notion of "nationalism" to include the entire Muslim *umma* (community).[6]

To achieve its immediate goal of an Islamic Palestinian state, Hamas has steadfastly denounced the 1993 Oslo Accords, the 2007 Annapolis conference, and all other diplomatic efforts to establish a lasting peace in the region as a "contradiction to the principles of the Islamic Resistance Movement."[7] However, when addressing Western audiences, Hamas leaders such as Gaza-based Ismail Haniyeh and politburo chief Khaled Meshal have stated that they are willing to recognize Israel along pre-1967 borders.[8] Yet other senior Hamas officials, such as Mahmoud al Zahar, bluntly state that no Hamas leaders are willing to acknowledge the pre-1967 borders or to live at peace with Israel.[9]

Hamas gained the support of a significant portion of the Palestinian people by providing social and welfare services and by presenting itself as Israel's implacable foe, as well as a pious opponent of the more corrupt and ossified Fatah faction, whose officials comprise most of the leadership of the Palestine Liberation Organization (PLO) and the PA. Indeed, Hamas candidates ran under the name "Change and Reform List" in the 2006 legislative elections.[10] Since its violent takeover of Gaza in 2007, Hamas has taken steps to Islamize society there. However, there are indications that this may have only served to undermine the movement's authority, curtailing social and cultural freedoms that had previously existed in the territory.[11] Additionally, press reports indicate that Hamas has been losing popularity due to its poor management of Gaza's festering economic and social problems, among other issues.[12]

Following September 11, 2001, the United States made efforts to cut the flow of cash to countless terror groups, including Hamas. Funds from Saudi Arabia, long identified as a top sponsor of Hamas, slowed following the Kingdom's decision to cut back on funding *jihadi* groups after suffering attacks by an al-Qaeda affiliate in 2004.[13]

Iran soon became Hamas' primary state sponsor, with hundreds of millions of dollars pledged and delivered.[14] This revenue stream was significantly and adversely impacted over time as U.S.-led sanctions sapped the Islamic Republic's cash reserves, and Tehran cut most (if not all) financial assistance when tension arose between it and Hamas over attitudes toward the Assad regime in Syria. The Iranians strongly supported the embattled Syrian leader, while Hamas did not, and vacated its headquarters in Damascus in protest. However, following the regional decline of the Muslim Brotherhood in 2013, the victory of the Assad regime in the Syrian civil war, and its own economic troubles, Hamas has recently restored its ties with Iran.[15] In the interim, Hamas reportedly expanded its ties with Turkey and Qatar, who at present are the group's – and the Gaza Strip's – primary state sponsors; indeed, by one count, Qatar alone has funneled $1 billion into Hamas-controlled Gaza since 2012.[16]

Hamas augments its funds from state sponsors with donations from private charities (the most notorious being the now-defunct Texas-based Holy Land Foundation, which channeled $12 million to the organization before it was proscribed[17]) and deep-pocketed donors around the world. Hamas has also extracted significant tax revenues from the subterranean tunnels connecting the Gaza Strip to the Sinai Peninsula. For years the tunnels supported black market trade; however, since the overthrow of Mohammed Morsi in July 2013, Egyptian authorities have shut down hundreds of smuggling tunnels along the Egypt-Gaza border. According to officials in Gaza, this has slashed approximately $230 million per month from the Gaza economy.[18] As a result, Hamas authorities have greatly increased local taxes in an effort to make up the budgetary shortfall.[19] Nevertheless, these steps have not been enough to ameliorate the group's financial distress stemming from ongoing Israeli, Egyptian and (more recent) PA curbs on economic activity inside Gaza.[20]

Hamas, along with other like-minded violent factions, has fired more than 15,000 rockets and mortars into Israel since 2001.[21] Evidence suggests that the military wing of Hamas, the Izz ad-Din al-Qassam Brigades, killed over 500 people in more than 350 separate terrorist attacks and suicide bombings from 1993 to 2012. This estimate is conservative, and the number of attacks has only grown in more recent years.[22]

The group draws a distinction between its political activities and its paramilitary attacks; however, this is a false distinction as all of the movement's component parts contribute to "resistance" activities.[23] The group's late founder, Sheikh Ahmad Yassin, is known to have remarked that "We cannot separate the wing from the body. If we do so, the body will not be able to fly."[24] In recent years Israeli authorities foiled numerous Hamas terror plots emanating from the West Bank.[25] Israeli officials identified Gaza-based Hamas official

Fathi Hamad[26] and Turkey-based Hamas leader Saleh al-Aruri[27] as key catalysts for many of these plots.[28] Meanwhile Hamas maintains a significant arsenal, primarily via Iran, which gives the faction the ability to fire deep into Israeli territory from the Gaza Strip.

After the 2014 war, Hamas continued to build tunnels into Israel and attempt to replenish its rocket supply.[29] Hamas regularly uses items meant for humanitarian aid to construct rockets.[30] The group has also carried out attacks across the West Bank, such as the fatal shooting of an Israeli rabbi in early 2018.[31] The group has also in the past planned attacks against Palestinian Authority leader Mahmoud Abbas[32] Hamas was also known to cooperate with an ISIS affiliate in Sinai, originally known as Ansar Beit al-Maqdis, which escalated tensions with the Egyptian government between 2014-2017.[33] Hamas regularly trained and treated Islamic State fighters before sending them back into the Sinai Peninsula.[34] However, more recently, Hamas-ISIS ties have reportedly eroded as a result of pressure from the Egyptian government and the group's efforts to repair relations with Cairo.[35]

With economic, humanitarian, and social conditions continuing to deteriorate in Gaza, Hamas began supporting protest marches on the Israeli border in March 2018.[36] The goal of the marches was nominally the "right of return" for Palestinians who had been evicted or fled from their lands in 1948; however, Hamas' real goal was increased international awareness for Gaza's plight in order to end the Israeli and Egyptian blockade.[37] Beginning in May 2018, weekly clashes on the border led to periodic escalations between Hamas (rocket fire) and the Israeli military (airstrikes and tank fire) which Egyptian and international mediators quickly reigned in. Hamas fired over 400 rockets and mortars at southern Israel over the course of two days in November 2018.[38] After months of weekly demonstrations and periodic escalations, during which over 200 Gazan civilians and militants were killed due to Israeli fire,[39] Hamas extracted additional funds, primarily from Qatar (with Israeli approval) to pay for civil servant salaries, fuel imports, and humanitarian projects.[40] Yet Hamas' objective of additional relief and an end to the blockade via a long-term truce with Israel remained elusive. By February 2019, Israeli military intelligence assessed that

Hamas could capably escalate conflict in an attempt to gain further concessions from Israel.[41]

Palestinian Islamic Jihad (PIJ)

Harakat al-Jihād al-Islāmi fi Filastīn (Palestinian Islamic Jihad, or PIJ) was founded sometime between 1979 and 1981 by several Muslim Brotherhood members who, like the members of Hamas, felt that the Brotherhood was too moderate and its commitment to the principle of *jihad* and a Palestinian state governed according to *sharia*. The founding members were also inspired by the 1979 Iranian Revolution.[42] Founders Fathi Shikaki and Abd al-Aziz Awda forged an organization whose ultimate aim was to destroy Israel through *jihad*. Unlike Hamas, which is amenable to a *hudna* (tactical truce) with Israel, PIJ explicitly rejects any compromise with the Jewish State.[43]

The exact size of PIJ, a highly secretive organization, is unknown. Most estimates suggest that membership ranges from a few hundred to a few thousand.[44] The ethnic make-up of the group is overwhelmingly Palestinian Sunni, though there have been reports of increasing Shi'a presence due to Iranian support.[45]

While PIJ was known for its suicide bombing attacks during the second *intifada* (2000-2005), the group has recently focused on rocket and sniper attacks and cross-border attack tunnel construction. The IDF has tried to thin PIJ's ranks through targeted killings and arrests in recent years; the effectiveness of these actions is unclear.

In January 2014, the U.S. State Department designated Ziyad al Nakhalah, the Deputy Secretary General of Palestinian Islamic Jihad (PIJ), as a Specially Designated Global Terrorist (SDGT).[46] Other group leaders have yet to be designated. Like Hamas, PIJ's activity against Israel from Gaza declined in 2013. However, it continued to plot and carry out attacks from the West Bank.[47] It subsequently played a significant role in the rocket war of July 2014, firing Iranian-made or Iranian-furnished rockets deep into Israeli territory.

PIJ was also a strong supporter of the wave of violence (known as the "knife *intifada*" by some) that swept across Israel for nearly a year in 2015-2016. In May 2016 Iran renewed its financial support of PIJ after nearly two years.[48] In Tehran, PIJ leader Ramadan Shallah praised Iran for its support of the "Palestinian *intifada*."[49]

When municipal elections were initially announced in the West Bank and Gaza in August 2016, PIJ boycotted the elections, as it had done on all previous occasions, unsuccessfully urging Palestinians to escalate the violence instead.[50]

PIJ plays an integral role in the Gaza marches on the Israel border, with several of its members reported killed by Israeli fire during the months of unrest that began in March 2018.[51] More recently, PIJ was held responsible for rocket and mortar fire from Gaza into southern Israel—a sign, according to some, of renewed Iranian influence on Palestinian politics.[52] This trend continued with two major incidents from Gaza – a rocket barrage into southern Israel in October 2018[53] and sniper fire on Israeli forces in January 2019.[54] By April 2019, Israeli security sources were warning of a major cross-border PIJ attack meant to scuttle Egypt's mediation efforts between Israel and Hamas.[55]

PIJ's pursuit of a policy ostensibly independent of Hamas was attributed in part to Ziad al-Nakhaleh's promotion to secretary-general (replacing the infirm Shallah).[56] Reports indicate that al-Nakhaleh is more militant than Shallah, and may seek to solidify his authority and continue currying favor with Iran by adopting hardline policies.[57]

Popular Resistance Committees

The Popular Resistance Committees (PRC) is made up of "former armed activists of different factions," and is likely the third largest violent group in the Palestinian Authority, after Hamas and PIJ.[58] According to the IDF, the PRC often "acts as a sub-contractor" for Iran, and is heavily influenced by Hezbollah.[59]

In recent years, the group has become increasingly Salafi in outlook and reportedly begun working with Salafi jihadist groups operating in the Sinai Peninsula abutting Gaza.[60] In February 2014, the Israeli Air Force targeted a PRC operative known to work with the Sinai-based *jihadist* group Ansar Bayt al-Maqdis.[61]

However, in light of Hamas' attempts to prevent unauthorized rocket attacks against Israel, the group has at times found itself at odds with Hamas. In July 2013, for example, the PRC demanded Hamas stop its arrest of the mujahideen in the Gaza Strip.[62] The PRC maintained a low profile during the 2014 rocket war, although its personnel are still active when trying to provoke Israeli retribution against Hamas. Israel holds Hamas responsible for militant activity emanating from Gaza. An improvised explosive device (IED) detonated on the Israel-Gaza border targeting Israel Defense Forces (IDF) personnel was deemed to be a PRC operation.[63] More recently, the PRC's military wing issued a public call for Bitcoin donations, highlighting the group's financial distress and its continued militant activities.[64]

Al Aqsa Martyrs Brigades

The Al Aqsa Martyrs Brigades (AAMB) is the military wing of the secular Fatah faction, and has adopted Islamist symbols and slogans.[65] The group was formally designated as a Foreign Terrorist Organization by the United States in March 2002, largely due to its responsibility for suicide bombings and small arms attacks targeting Israel during the second *intifada*.[66]

While the AAMB has primarily operated out of the Gaza Strip, with a handful of operations in the West Bank, the group has largely remained dormant over the past few years.[67] According to the U.S. Department of State, "Iran has exploited al-Aqsa's lack of resources and formal leadership by providing funds and guidance, mostly through Hezbollah facilitators."[68] The primary acts of violence carried out by the group in recent years have been rocket attacks from Gaza into southern Israel.[69] In recent years, however, press reports have suggested that the group may seek a comeback in the West Bank.[70] In March 2016, thirteen Palestinians were injured in firefights between the Palestinian Authority and members of the Aqsa Martyrs in Nablus.[71] As clashes escalated in August 2016, the PA arrested a local AAMB leader, Ahmed Izz Halawa, and beat him to death.[72] Halawa's death sparked mass protests in the West Bank.[73] Gunfights between PA security forces and local gangs erupt sporadically in the wake of PA arrest operations into Nablus' Balata refugee camp, as was the case in February 2018.[74]

Group members have taken part in (and been killed during) the "March of Return" border protests of 2018.[75] Training for attacks against Israel is ongoing. AAMB has publicly stated that, during any future conflict, it would fight alongside Hamas, PIJ and the other Gaza-based factions.[76]

Jaysh al-Islam (JI)

Jaysh al-Islam (JI), or "Army of Islam," is closely linked to the Dughmush clan of Gaza, and it is believed to have several hundred members.[77] Founded in 2005, JI is similar to other Palestinian Islamist splinter groups due to its global *jihadist* objectives and suspected ties to al-Qaeda in its early days.[78]

The group's affinity for al-Qaeda is widely documented. Days after the death of Osama bin Laden, JI released a eulogy for the fallen al-Qaeda leader.[79] In May 2011 the group was designated as a terrorist group by the U.S. Department of State. The accompanying press release noted that JI "worked with Hamas and is attempting to develop closer al Qaeda contacts."[80] In 2006, the group sent a letter to senior al-Qaeda leaders, asking whether it was permissible to accept money from other groups in Gaza that did not share their ideology, specifically nationalists or Iranian-backed factions.[81] Israeli officials also noted in 2006, "alleged efforts by Mumtaz Dughmush to make contact with Global Jihad sources, possibly to include those responsible for the bombing of the USS Cole."[82]

During Israel's Operation Pillar of Defense in November 2012, the Mujahideen Shura Council in the Environs of Jerusalem, a consolidation of Salafi *jihadist* groups in Gaza, and JI conducted joint rocket attacks against Israel.[83] According to Israeli officials, JI operated training camps in Gaza for jihadists (with the blessing of Hamas) who subsequently went to fight in Yemen, Syria, and Egypt's Sinai Peninsula, among other locations.[84] According to one JI leader, however, the group is not officially allied with either al-Qaeda or the Islamic State.[85]

Recently Hamas has cracked down on Salafist groups operating from Gaza, including JI, in a bid to rehabilitate its relationship with the Egyptian government and curb rocket fire against Israel.[86]

Jaysh al-Ummah (JU)

Ideologically affiliated with al-Qaeda, Jaysh al-Ummah (JU), or the "Army of the Nation," believes that "the sons of Zion are occupiers and they must be uprooted completely… We will fight them as we are ordered by God and the Prophet Mohammad."[87] The Salafi *jihadist* group was formed in either 2006 or 2007, and is led by Abu Hafs al-Maqdisi. While the group's membership number is kept secret, it lacks the capability to strike targets outside of Gaza, suggesting it is small in size.[88]

JU has historically been critical of Hamas. Most notably, it has criticized Hamas for arresting its members as they attempted to carry out terrorist operations.[89] Hamas appears to allow JU to conduct *dawa*-related activity in the Gaza Strip, however.[90]

JU has warned against the increasing influence of Iran and its proxy PIJ in the Gaza Strip. While the group has denied an operational connection to al-Qaeda, it maintains a similar ideological outlook as the bin Laden network.[91] We are "connected to our brothers in Al Qaeda by our beliefs, we and they are following the great Prophet. Osama bin Laden is our brother and we appreciate him very much," a JU official stated.[92]

Since 2013, the group has issued a number of statements and videos that belie its Salafi beliefs. In January 2013, the *jihadist* group issued a video urging "all the mujahideen all over Earth to target Iranian interests everywhere."[93] In a separate message released in January 2013, JU called for greater support for *jihadists* in Mali: "[W]e will support and be loyal and aid our mujahideen monotheist brothers in Mali without limits."[94] In August 2013, Abu Hafs al Maqdisi, JU's leader, called on Egyptians to wage jihad against Egyptian army chief General Abdel Fattah el-Sisi.[95] In November 2013 the group issued a eulogy for Hakeemullah Mehsud, the former emir of the Movement of the Taliban in Pakistan.[96] JU supposedly fought alongside other militant factions against Israel during the 2014 Gaza War.[97] As of June 2018, JU was still launching fundraising appeals to supporters via various social media platforms.[98]

Hizb-ut-Tahrir (HuT)

The Palestinian "Party of Liberation" is a local affiliate of the larger international HuT movement. The group's immediate aim is to establish a caliphate and implement *sharia* law throughout the Muslim world.[99]

Despite HuT's well-documented enmity toward Israel, the group does not directly engage in terrorism, nor do its branches maintain an armed wing. Rather, HuT seeks to "agitate and educate."[100] While no reliable figures can be found regarding HuT's membership in the Palestinian Authority, it is widely considered to be small, despite its organic base of support.

HuT organized a demonstration with over 2,500 attendees in Hebron, dissenting against the PLO's participation in the 2007 Annapolis peace summit; in the aftermath, one protestor was killed by PA police.[101] Over 10,000 HuT supporters gathered in Al-Bireh under the slogan: "the caliphate is the rising force."[102] In July 2010, PA security forces arrested thousands of HuT supporters at a rally in Ramallah.[103]

HuT members were arrested by the Palestinian Authority after PA forces disrupted an HuT rally in the West Bank.[104] In August 2011, Palestinian Authority President Mahmoud Abbas drew fire from HuT when Abbas suggested that NATO may have a presence in a future Palestinian state.[105]

HuT has continued to hold events in the West Bank despite intermittent security crackdowns.[106] In February 2014, HuT accused Palestinian Authority security forces in the West Bank of arresting its members for criticizing President Abbas.[107] The group was represented during the unrest in the Jerusalem neighborhood of Shuafat following the murder of a Palestinian teenager by Israeli extremists.

In recent years, HuT activities have been confined primarily to West Bank universities.[108] However, the group still maintains an elaborate media outreach and education arm online, issuing constant press releases on current developments in PA politics, international politics and Israeli actions.[109]

Mujahideen Shura Council in the Environs of Jerusalem (MSC)

The MSC, a Salafi *jihadist* group, was formed in the Gaza Strip in 2012. The group is a consolidation of Ansar al-Sunnah and the Tawhid and Jihad Group in Jerusalem.[110] In November 2012, one MSC leaders stated that the group aims to "fight the Jews for the return of Islam's rule, not only in Palestine, but throughout the world."[111]

While the exact size of the group is unknown, it claims responsibility for a number of rocket attacks against Israel, some of which have been carried out with Jaysh al Islam.[112] MSC took responsibility for a June 2012 bombing and shooting attack that killed one Israeli civilian.[113] According to a video released by the

MSC, the June attack was “a gift to our brothers in Qaedat al Jihad [al-Qaeda] and Sheikh [Ayman al-] Zawahiri” and a retaliation for the killing of Osama bin Laden.[114]

Several Israeli air strikes targeted MSC operatives in 2012. After those attacks, *jihadi* groups such as al-Qaeda in the Arabian Peninsula (AQAP) and leaders like al-Qaeda head Ayman al-Zawahiri posted eulogies online.

The MSC was one of several Salafi *jihadi* groups that took part in the November 2012 conflict with Israel. Following the ceasefire, the group said that “[W]e truly are not a party to the signing of this truce between the Palestinian factions and the Jews.”[115] Throughout 2013, the MSC promoted the *jihad* in Syria as well as the efforts of the Sinai-based jihadist group Ansar Bayt al Maqdis through its media wing.[116] In November 2013, three MSC operatives were reported killed by Israeli security forces in Yatta ahead of planned terrorist attacks.[117]

MSC attacks peaked in 2013 with several instances of rocket fire on Israeli towns, including in April and August of that year on the southern city of Eilat (likely emanating from the Sinai Peninsula). MSC also declared its support for the Islamic State in February 2014. In response, the U.S. State Department declared MSC a Specially Designated Global Terrorist entity.[118] Prominent MSC leaders have recently been targeted for arrest by Hamas authorities in Gaza (as part of broader crackdowns on Salafist groups), likely explaining the organization’s diminished profile.[119]

Harakat as-Sabirin Nasran li-Filastin

Harakat as-Sabirin Nasran li-Filastin (as-Sabirin), or “The Movement of the Patient Ones for the Liberation of Palestine” is a new, Iran-sponsored terror group in Gaza.[120] Founded in early 2014, the group burst onto the scene when one of its fighters, Nizar Saeed Issa, died in a mysterious explosion in the Gaza refugee camp of Jabalya.[121] Since then, As-Sabirin has lost two fighters in apparent clashes with Israel.

As-Sabirin is a Shiite group in a predominantly Sunni territory. Its flag and logo are inspired by Hezbollah, and its fighters are pulled from another Iranian proxy: PIJ. Its charter states that “jihad is the way of Allah to open doors to paradise… and in particular our journey faces the might enemies of the racist Zionist body and on its head America the great Satan."[122]

As-Sabirin is headed by Hisham Salem, a former PIJ commander from a prominent family in Gaza.[123] During the second *intifada,* Salem was placed on Israel's most wanted terrorist list.[124] He has run several charities in the Gaza Strip, one of which, al-Baqiyat al-Salihat, was shut down by Hamas for spreading Shi'ism.[125]

The Iranian proxy group receives approximately $10 million per year from Tehran typically smuggled through tunnels into Gaza.[126]

In February 2016, the Palestinian Authority broke up an as-Sabirin cell in Bethlehem attempting to convert families in the West Bank to Shiism.[127] In January 2018, the U.S. State Department announced that as-Sabirin was now a "Specially-Designated Global Terrorist Group."[128]

Islamism and Society

Evidence suggests that Hamas has been, at several points in the past, more popular among Palestinians than its secular rival, Fatah. Some analysts contend that such support is attributable more to a rejection of Fatah's alleged corruption rather than sincere support for Hamas' Islamism and militancy.[129] However, it may also be tied to the dwindling popular support, for the PLO's peace negotiations with Israel. An April 2019 poll from the Palestinian Center for Policy and Survey Research found that 50 percent of Palestinians now oppose a two-state solution; 58 percent do not believe it is feasible due to Israeli settlement expansion. More indicative, Palestinians were evenly split over the question of negotiations versus armed resistance vis-à-vis Israel.[130]

Since Hamas' takeover of Gaza in 2007, anecdotal evidence suggests that the daily challenges of governance have eroded some of the popular support Hamas garnered through its resistance of Israel.[131] In other words, it is hard to maintain popular support as a revolutionary movement when saddled with mundane problems. As one senior Hamas leader in the West Bank acknowledged in 2014, "the sovereign loses."[132] Most telling, opinion polls in late 2018 showed a slight increase in support for Hamas (relative to the PLO/ Fatah) due primarily to the lack of a diplomatic process with Israel, concessions wrung for Gaza from the "March of Return" protests, and Abbas's long rule.[133] By early 2019, those numbers dropped due to Hamas's violent suppression of internal protests,[134] as well as the adverse consequences of its escalation of hostilities with Israel. Under both Hamas rule in Gaza and PLO rule in the West Bank, evidence suggests that Christian minorities suffer discrimination and persecution, including religiously-motivated attacks on churches, destruction of crosses and altars, and the kidnapping and forced conversion of Christian girls.[135] Admittedly, Christians live with significantly more freedom in the West Bank relative to Gaza since Hamas took control of the coastal territory.[136]

Islamism and the State

The active role of violent Islamist groups in the West Bank has dropped precipitously since the 2007 Palestinian civil war. Fearing a Hamas takeover in the West Bank, the United States and other Western states have been furnishing the Palestinian Authority government in the West Bank with military training, weaponry, financing, and intelligence in order to more efficiently battle Hamas and other factions. Close security coordination between the PA and Israel has remained intact in the battle against perceived common Islamist enemies. Indeed, Hamas marches in the West Bank in December 2018, on the anniversary of the group's founding, were violently suppressed by PA security forces.[137] This approach has undoubtedly been successful; the West Bank has been relatively stable over the past decade compared to preceding years.[138]

With Hamas entrenched in Gaza, Israel will not likely neutralize the group with stand-off military power alone. The 2014 conflict made this clear; even as Israel pounded hundreds of Hamas targets, long-range rockets continued to strike deep into Israeli territory. Some propose that Israel should enter into negotiations with its long-time foe. Others contend that, because Hamas is at one of its historically weakest political and economic points, now may be the time to cripple the group.

The question of who controls Gaza after Hamas has prompted the Israelis to opt for the former approach. The threat of a bloody ground campaign to reoccupy the territory, in addition to potential anarchy afterwards, has counseled for a policy of restraint, at least so far.[139] As of early 2019, Israeli Prime Minister Benjamin Netanyahu had clearly chosen to enter into talks with Hamas via mediation from Egypt, funneling economic relief into Gaza and stating that "Leaders need to find a way…to return security [to southern Israel], to avoid humanitarian collapse and avoid needless wars."[140]

The shift in Israel's Gaza policy can be attributed in part to the collapse of the reconciliation process between Hamas and Fatah. Under the terms of multiple agreements that were never fully implemented, Fatah/PA would retake civilian control over Gaza, sparing Hamas the financial and political burdens of governance. Yet a major sticking point for PA President Mahmoud Abbas remains Hamas's unwillingness to disarm, which he has termed the "Hezbollah model."[141] As of 2019, real reconciliation and unity between Gaza and the West Bank, and between Hamas and Fatah, is unlikely – including with respect to the holding of open PA elections. Absent this unity, both political systems will likely remain separate even after Abbas exits the stage.[142]

Endnotes

1. Mosab Hassan Yousef and Ron Brackin, *Son of Hamas: A Gripping Account of Terror, Betrayal, Political Intrigue, and Unthinkable Choices* (Carol Stream: Tyndale House, 2010), 253-255.
2. "Hamas Covenant 1988," *The Avalon Project*, n.d., http://avalon.law.yale.edu/20th_century/hamas.asp.
3. "Hamas Covenant 1988," The Avalon Project, n.d.
4. "Hamas Covenant 1988," The Avalon Project, n.d.
5. "Hamas Covenant 1988," The Avalon Project, n.d.
6. See, for example, "Hamas MP and Cleric Yunis Al-Astal: The Jews Were Brought to Palestine for the "Great Massacre" Through Which Allah Will "Relieve Humanity of Their Evil"," *Middle East Media Research Institute*, May 11, 2011, http://www.memri.org/clip/en/0/0/0/0/0/0/2934.htm.
7. "Hamas Covenant 1988."
8. Amira Hass, "Haniyeh: Hamas Willing To Accept Palestinian State With 1967 Borders," *Ha'aretz*, September 11, 2008, http://www.haaretz.com/news/haniyeh-hamas-willing-to-accept-palestinian-state-with-1967-borders-1.256915; "Meshal: Hamas Seeks Palestinian State Based on 1967 Borders," *Ha'aretz*, May 5, 2009, http://www.haaretz.

com/news/meshal-hamas-seeks-palestinian-state-based-on-1967-borders-1.275412.

9. Shlomi Eldar, "Hamas Official Says 'Abbas Doesn't Represent Anyone'," *Al Monitor*, February 20, 2014, http://www.al-monitor.com/pulse/originals/2014/02/mahmoud-al-zahar-hamas-recognizing-israel-mahmoud-abbas.html.
10. "Who's Who in the Palestinian Elections," BBC News, January 16, 2006. http://news.bbc.co.uk/2/hi/middle_east/4601420.stm
11. Jonathan Schanzer, "The Talibanization of Gaza: A Liability for the Muslim Brotherhood," Hudson Institute *Current Trends in Islamist Ideology* 9, August 19, 2009, http://www.currenttrends.org/research/detail/the-talibanization-of-gaza-a-liability-for-the-muslim-brotherhood; Abeer Ayyoub, "Hamas Pushes Islamization of Gaza," *Al Monitor*, February 4, 2013, http://www.al-monitor.com/pulse/originals/2013/02/hamas-islamization-gaza.html.
12. Rasha Abou Jalal, "Hamas Sinks in Polls After Cutting Salaries to Public Servants," *Al Monitor*, February 20, 2014, http://www.al-monitor.com/pulse/originals/2014/02/hamas-gaza-salaries-payments-siege.html.
13. Matthew Levitt, "A Hamas Headquarters in Saudi Arabia," Washington Institute for Near East Policy *Policy Watch* 521, September 28, 2005, http://www.washingtoninstitute.org/policy-analysis/view/a-hamas-headquarters-in-saudi-arabia.
14. Nidal al-Mughrabi, "Hamas Gaza Leader Heads for Iran," Reuters, January 30, 2012, http://uk.reuters.com/article/2012/01/30/uk-palestinians-hamas-iran-idUKTRE80T14P20120130.
15. Adnan Abu Amer, "What Is Behind the Hamas-Iran Rapprochement," *Al Jazeera* (Doha), July 26, 2018, https://www.aljazeera.com/indepth/opinion/hamas-iran-rapprochement-180725150509789.html
16. Yaniv Kubovich, "With Israel's Consent, Qatar Gave Gaza $1 Billion Since 2012," *Ha'aretz* (Tel Aviv), February 10, 2019, https://www.haaretz.com/middle-east-news/palestinians/.premium-with-israel-s-consent-qatar-gave-gaza-1-billion-since-2012-1.6917856; Yoni Ben Menachem, "Turkey Embraces Hamas," Jerusalem Center for Public Affairs, February 22, 2018, http://jcpa.org/turkey-embraces-hamas/
17. "Five US Men Jailed for Allegedly Funding Hamas," Ma'an News Agency (Ramallah), May 28, 2009, http://maannews.net/eng/ViewDetails.aspx?ID=210849.
18. "Tunnel Closure 'Costs Gaza $230 Million Monthly,'" Agence France Presse, October 27, 2013, http://www.google.com/hostednews/afp/article/ALeqM5gj2-72tPr4jJFBW_e52ASHwGfy8g?do-

cId=aa97be5f-8a83-45b7-9fdd-cf4bc0ec6d74.

19. "Hamas Taxation Is Pushing Gaza's Residents to the Brink," Coordination of Government Activities in the Territories, March 16, 2017, http://www.cogat.mod.gov.il/en/Our_Activities/Pages/hamas-taxation.aspx
20. Nidal al-Mughrabi, "Anger As Palestinian Authority Cuts Gaza Salaries and Pays Late," Reuters, May 3, 2018, https://www.reuters.com/article/us-palestinians-gaza-salaries/anger-as-palestinian-authority-cuts-gaza-salaries-and-pays-late-idUSKBN1I41LM
21. "Rocket Attacks on Israel From Gaza," *IDF Blog*, n.d, http://www.idfblog.com/facts-figures/rocket-attacks-toward-israel/; "2010 Annual Summary," Israel Security Agency, n.d., http://www.shabak.gov.il/SiteCollectionImages/english/TerrorInfo/reports/2010summary2-en.pdf.
22. Bryony Jones, "Q&A: What is Hamas?" CNN, November 24, 2012, http://www.cnn.com/2012/11/16/world/meast/hamas-explainer/.
23. Matthew Levitt, *Hamas: Politics, Charity and Terrorism in the Service of Jihad* (New Haven: Yale University Press, 2006).
24. U.S. Department of the Treasury, "U.S. Designates Five Charities Funding Hamas and Six Senior Hamas Leaders as Terrorist Entities," August 22, 2003, http://www.treasury.gov/press-center/press-releases/Pages/js672.aspx.
25. See, for example, Yoav Zitun, "Shin Bet Foils Hamas-Planned Bombing in Israel," Hamas-Planned Bombing in Israel," *Yediot Ahronot* (Tel Aviv), November 22, 2018, https://www.ynetnews.com/articles/0,7340,L-5412061,00.html.
26. David Barnett, "Hamas Interior Minister Behind Terror Group's Activities in West Bank," *Long War Journal – Threat Matrix*, March 13, 2013, http://www.longwarjournal.org/threat-matrix/archives/2013/03/hamas_interior_minister_behind.php.
27. Amos Harel, "Hamas is Alive and Kicking in the West Bank – But in Remote Control," *Ha'aretz* (Tel Aviv), December 21, 2013, http://www.haaretz.com/weekend/week-s-end/.premium-1.564568.
28. Israel Security Agency, "2013 Annual Summary," n.d., http://www.shabak.gov.il/English/EnTerrorData/Reports/Pages/2013AnnualSummary.aspx.
29. "Hamas Says it Continues to Build Tunnels to Attack Israel," *Huffington Post,* January 29, 2016, http://www.huffingtonpost.com/huffwires/20160129/ml-gaza-tunnels/?utm_hp_ref=world&ir=world.
30. "Israel Intercepts Materials for Building Tunnels, Rockets on their Way to Hamas," *The Tower,* May 27, 2016, http://www.thetower.

org/3430oc-israel-intercepts-materials-for-building-tunnels-rockets-on-their-way-to-hamas/.

31. Yaniv Kubovich and Jack Khoury, "In Raid, Israel Security Forces Kill Murderer of West Bank Rabbi," *Ha'aretz* (Tel Aviv), February 6, 2018, https://www.haaretz.com/middle-east-news/palestinians/israel-security-forces-kill-murderer-of-west-bank-rabbi-in-raid-1.5791086
32. Mitch Ginsburg, "Abbas Orders Probe into Hamas Coup Plot Revealed by Israel," *Times of Israel,* August 19, 2014, http://www.timesofisrael.com/abbas-orders-investigation-into-hamas-coup-plot-revealed-by-israel/.
33. Ehud Yaari, "Hamas and the Islamic State: Growing Cooperation in the Sinai," Washington Institute for Near East Policy *Policywatch* 2533, December 15, 2015, http://www.washingtoninstitute.org/policy-analysis/view/hamas-and-the-islamic-state-growing-cooperation-in-the-sinai.
34. "IDF General: IS Fighters Training with Hamas in Gaza," *Times of Israel,* May 13, 2016, http://www.timesofisrael.com/idf-general-is-fighters-entered-gaza-to-train-with-hamas/.
35. Iyad Abuheweila and Isabel Kershner, "ISIS Declares War on Hamas, and Gaza Families Disown Sons in Sinai," *New York Times*, January 10, 2018, https://www.nytimes.com/2018/01/10/world/middleeast/isis-hamas-sinai.html.
36. Elior Levy and Yoav Zitun, "Situation in Gaza Approaches Critical Point," *Yediot Ahronot* (Tel Aviv), February 5, 2018, https://www.ynetnews.com/articles/0,7340,L-5090907,00.html.
37. Shlomi Eldar, "Hamas Focused on Ending the Blockade," *Al Monitor*, May 18, 2018. https://www.al-monitor.com/pulse/originals/2018/05/israel-palestinians-hamas-fatah-mahmoud-abbas-idf-border.html
38. Neri Zilber, "Israel and Gaza Go to War Despite Themselves," *The Daily Beast*, November 13, 2018, https://www.thedailybeast.com/israel-and-gaza-go-to-war-despite-themselves
39. Anna Ahronheim, "B'tselem Says 290 Palestinians Killed by IDF Fire in 2018," *Jerusalem Post*, January 17, 2019, https://www.jpost.com/Arab-Israeli-Conflict/BTselem-says-290-Palestinians-killed-by-IDF-fire-in-2018-577752
40. Alex Fishman, "Second Installment of Qatari Funds to Enter Gaza This Week," *Yediot Ahronot* (Tel Aviv), December 3, 2018, https://www.ynetnews.com/articles/0,7340,L-5419049,00.html
41. Judah Ari Gross, "IDF Warns Hamas Likely to Spark War in Gaza in Bid for International Support," *Times of Israel*, February 14, 2019, https://www.timesofisrael.com/idf-warns-hamas-likely-to-spark-war-

in-gaza-in-bid-for-international-support/

42. Asmaa al-Ghoul, "Palestinian Islamic Jihad: Iran Supplies All Weapons in Gaza," *Al Monitor*, May 14, 2013, http://www.al-monitor.com/pulse/originals/2013/05/gaza-islamic-jihad-and-iranian-arms.html.
43. Holly Fletcher, "Palestinian Islamic Jihad," Council on Foreign Relations, April 10, 2008, http://www.cfr.org/israel/palestinian-islamic-jihad/p15984.
44. "Chapter 6. Foreign Terrorist Organizations," in U.S. Department of State, *Country Reports on Terrorism* 2011, July 31, 2012, http://www.state.gov/j/ct/rls/crt/2011/195553.htm; Abeer Ayyoub, "Iran Top Backer of Palestinian Islamic Jihad," *Al Monitor*, January 9, 2013, http://www.al-monitor.com/pulse/originals/2013/01/palestinian-islamic-jihad.html; Crispian Balmer and Nidal al-Mughrabi, "Single-Minded Islamic Jihad Grows in Gaza's Shadows," Reuters, November 12, 2013, http://www.reuters.com/article/2013/11/12/us-palestinians-islamicjihad-idUSBRE9AB08720131112.
45. Avi Issacharoff, "Hamas Brutally Assaults Shi'ite Worshippers in Gaza." *Ha'aretz* (Tel Aviv), January 17, 2012, http://www.haaretz.com/news/middle-east/hamas-brutally-assaults-shi-ite-worshippers-in-gaza-1.407688.
46. David Barnett, "US Designates Deputy Secretary-General of Palestinian Islamic Jihad," *Long War Journal*, January 23, 2014, http://www.longwarjournal.org/archives/2014/01/us_designates_deputy.php.
47. See, for example, David Barnett, "Palestinian Islamic Jihad Operatives Behind Recent Bus Bombing Near Tel Aviv," *Long War Journal – Threat Matrix*, January 3, 2014, http://www.longwarjournal.org/threat-matrix/archives/2014/01/palestinian_islamic_jihad_oper.php.
48. Maayan Groisman, "Iran to Renew Financial Support for Islamic Jihad After Two-Year Hiatus," *Jerusalem Post,* May 25, 2016, http://www.jpost.com/Middle-East/Reembracing-Islamic-Jihad-Iran-to-renew-financial-aid-for-Palestinian-terror-group-454968.
49. Maayan Groisman, "Iran to Renew Financial Support for Islamic Jihad After Two-Year Hiatus," *Jerusalem Post,* May 25, 2016, http://www.jpost.com/Middle-East/Reembracing-Islamic-Jihad-Iran-to-renew-financial-aid-for-Palestinian-terror-group-454968.
50. Adam Rasgon, "Islamic Jihad Calls to Escalate Intifada and Boycott Palestinian Elections," *Jerusalem Post,* August 9, 2016, http://www.jpost.com/Arab-Israeli-Conflict/Islamic-Jihad-calls-to-escalate-intifada-as-it-boycotts-Palestinian-elections-463651.
51. Judah Ari Gross, "Hamas Official: 50 of the 62 Gazans Killed in Border Violence Were Our Members," *Times of Israel*, May 16, 2018,

https://www.timesofisrael.com/hamas-official-50-of-the-people-killed-in-gaza-riots-were-members/.

52. Yaniv Kubovich, "Iran's Fighting Force in Gaza, Calling and Firing the Shots: This Is Islamic Jihad in Palestine," *Ha'aretz* (Tel Aviv), June 17, 2018, https://www.haaretz.com/middle-east-news/iran/.premium-what-is-islamic-jihad-in-palestine-iran-s-fighting-force-in-gaza-calling-and-firing-the-shots-1.6158730.
53. "Islamic Jihad Claims Gaza Rocket Fire; IDF Says Iran, Syria Responsible," *Times of Israel*, October 27, 2018, https://www.timesofisrael.com/islamic-jihad-claims-gaza-rocket-fire-idf-says-iran-syria-responsible/
54. Elior Levy, Yoav Zitun and Inbar Tvizer, "Islamic Jihad Releases Footage of IDF Officer Being Shot in Head," *Yediot Ahronot* (Tel Aviv), February 3, 2019, https://www.ynetnews.com/articles/0,7340,L-5457259,00.html
55. Elior Levy, "Islamic Jihad Planning Major Attack to Scupper Gaza Deal, IDF Believes," *Yediot Ahronot* (Tel Aviv), April 1, 2019, https://www.ynetnews.com/articles/0,7340,L-5487781,00.html
56. Jack Khoury, "Islamic Jihad Names New Chief to Replace Ill Long-Time Leader," *Ha'aretz* (Tel Aviv), September 28, 2018, https://www.haaretz.com/middle-east-news/palestinians/islamic-jihad-names-new-chief-to-replace-ill-long-time-leader-1.6513542
57. Muhammad Shehada, "Iran Is Declaring War on Israel – From Gaza," *Ha'aretz* (Tel Aviv), March 29, 2019, https://www.haaretz.com/middle-east-news/.premium-iran-is-declaring-war-on-israel-from-gaza-1.7065348
58. "Who is the Palestinian Group Blamed for the Attacks?" Reuters, August 19, 2011, http://www.haaretz.com/news/diplomacy-defense/who-is-the-palestinian-group-blamed-for-the-attacks-1.379509.
59. "What Is The Popular Resistance Committee?" *IDF Blog*, March 10, 2012, http://www.idfblog.com/2012/03/10/popular-resistance-committee/; "Who is Organizing the PRC," *Walla*, June 28, 2006, http://news.walla.co.il/?w=//931483.
60. Category Archives: Nāṣir Ṣalāḥ ad-Dīn Brigades (PRC)," Jihadology, n.d., http://jihadology.net/category/na%E1%B9%A3ir-%E1%B9%A3ala%E1%B8%A5-ad-din-brigades-prc/.
61. David Barnett, "Israel Targets Gaza Terror Operative Linked to Sinai-Based Ansar Jerusalem," *Long War Journal – Threat Matrix*, February 9, 2014, https://www.longwarjournal.org/archives/2014/02/israel_targets_gaza_terror_ope.php
62. David Barnett, "Popular Resistance Committees Calls on Hamas

to Stop Arrests of 'Mujahideen,'" *Long War Journal – Threat Matrix*, July 22, 2013, http://www.longwarjournal.org/threat-matrix/archives/2013/07/popular_resistance_committees.php.

63. Shlomi Eldar, "Hamas' Grip on Gaza Weakens," *Al Monitor*, February 20, 2018. https://www.al-monitor.com/pulse/originals/2018/02/israel-idf-gaza-hamas-popular-resistance-committees-war.html
64. Meir Amit Intelligence and Terrorism Information Center, "Hamas and the Popular Resistance Committees Called on Their Supporters to Donate Money Using the Virtual Currency Bitcoin," February 4, 2019, https://www.terrorism-info.org.il/en/hamas-popular-resistance-committees-called-supporters-donate-money-using-virtual-currency-bitcoin/
65. Israel Ministry of Foreign Affairs, "The Involvement of Arafat, PA Senior Officials and Apparatuses in Terrorism against Israel: Corruption and Crime," May 6, 2002, http://www.mfa.gov.il/MFA/MFAArchive/2000_2009/2002/5/The+Involvement+of+Arafat-+PA+Senior+Officials+and.htm.
66. Holly Fletcher, "Al-Aqsa Martyrs Brigade," Council on Foreign Relations, April 2, 2008, http://www.cfr.org/israel/al-aqsa-martyrs-brigade/p9127.
67. See, for example, Ethan Bronner, "Israeli Military Kills 6 Palestinians," *New York Times*, December 26, 2009, http://www.nytimes.com/2009/12/27/world/middleeast/27mideast.html.
68. "Chapter 6. Foreign Terrorist Organizations."
69. See, for example: "Militant Group Claims Responsibility for Projectile," Ma'an News Agency (Ramallah), December 28, 2011, http://www.maannews.net/eng/ViewDetails.aspx?ID=448358.
70. "In Photos: Al-Aqsa Brigades Hold Military Parade in Qalandiam," Ma'an News Agency (Ramallah), November 17, 2013, http://www.maannews.net/eng/ViewDetails.aspx?ID=648178; Naela Khalil, "Is Fatah's Armed Wing Making Comeback?," *Al Monitor*, September 25, 2013, http://www.al-monitor.com/pulse/originals/2013/09/hebron-israeli-soldiers-killed-fatah-intifada.html.
71. Daniel Douek, "13 Injured as Palestinian Police Clash with Gunmen in Nablus," *Times of Israel,* March 29, 2016, http://www.timesofisrael.com/13-injured-as-palestinian-police-clash-with-gunmen-in-nablus/.
72. Adam Rasgon, "PA Official: Top Suspect in Killing of Two PA Officers Arrested and Beaten to Death," *Jerusalem Post,* August 23, 2016, http://www.jpost.com/Arab-Israeli-Conflict/Top-suspect-in-killing-of-two-PA-officers-arrested-and-beaten-to-death-464841.
73. "Mass Protests in West Bank City After Palestinian Detainee Dies,"

Reuters, August 23, 2016, http://uk.reuters.com/article/uk-palestinians-nablus-death-idUKKCN10Y1FM.

74. Adam Rasgon, "Suspected Palestinian Drug Trafficker Killed in Gunfight with PA Forces," Jerusalem Post, February 1, 2018, https://www.jpost.com/Middle-East/Suspected-Palestinian-drug-trafficker-killed-in-gunfight-with-PA-forces-540449
75. Meir Amit Intelligence and Terrorism Information Center, "Examination of the List of Fatalities in the 'Return Marches' Reveals That Most of Them Are Operatives of Terrorist Organizations," January 21, 2019, https://www.terrorism-info.org.il/en/examination-list-fatalities-return-marches-reveals-operatives-terrorist-organizations-half-affiliated-hamas/
76. Middle East Media Research Institute *Special Dispatch* No. 7322, "Al-Aqsa Martyrs Brigades Establish 'Yasser Arafat' Military Base in Gaza, Announces: No One Will Take the Weapons of Resistance From Us, Fatah is True Path of Armed Struggle," February 8, 2018, https://www.memri.org/reports/%20al-aqsa-brigades-establish-%27yasser%20arafat%27-base-in-gaza
77. "Chapter 6. Foreign Terrorist Organizations."
78. Jonathan Dahoah Halevi, "Al Qaeda Affiliate Jaish al-Islam Receives Formal Sanctuary In Hamas-Ruled Gaza," Jerusalem Center for Public Affairs *Jerusalem Issue Brief* 8, no. 7, August 20, 2008, http://jcpa.org/article/al-qaeda-affiliate-jaish-al-islam-receives-formal-sanctuary-in-hamas-ruled-gaz/.
79. Bill Roggio, "US Designates Palestinian Salafist Group as a Foreign Terrorist Organization," *Long War Journal*, May 19, 2011, http://www.longwarjournal.org/archives/2011/05/us_designates_palest.php.
80. Roggio, "US Designates Palestinian Salafist Group as a Foreign Terrorist Organization."
81. "SOCOM-2012-0000008," Combating Terrorism Center, n.d., http://www.ctc.usma.edu/posts/socom-2012-0000008-english.
82. Wikileaks, "Frances Townsend's November 12 Meeting With Isa Chief Diskin Focuses On The Palestinians," November 24, 2006, http://wikileaks.org/cable/2006/11/06TELAVIV4603.html.
83. David Barnett, "Gaza-Based Salafi Jihadists Conduct Joint Rocket Attacks, Sinai Jihadists Suppressed," *Long War Journal – Threat Matrix*, November 22, 2012, http://www.longwarjournal.org/threat-matrix/archives/2012/11/salafi-jihadist_groups_in_gaza.php.
84. David Barnett, "Report Provides Insight on Israeli View of Salafi Jihadists in Sinai," *Long War Journal*, August 20, 2013, http://www.longwarjournal.org/archives/2013/08/report_provides_insi.php.;

Barak Ravid, "Shin Bet Forms New Unit to Thwart Attacks on Israel by Sinai Jihadists," *Ha'aretz* (Tel Aviv), August 20, 2013, http://www.haaretz.com/news/diplomacy-defense/.premium-1.542417.

85. Aymenn Jawad Al-Tamimi, "Jaysh al-Islam in Gaza: Exclusive Interview," aymennjawad.org, January 25, 2019, http://www.aymennjawad.org/2019/01/jaysh-al-islam-in-gaza-exclusive-interview
86. Amos Harel, "Hamas Arrests and Tortures Salafi Militants to Curb Gaza Rocket Fire Into Israel," *Ha'aretz* (Tel Aviv), December 19, 2017. https://www.haaretz.com/israel-news/.premium-hamas-tortures-salafis-militants-to-curb-rocket-fire-into-israel-1.5629017.
87. "Pro Al-Qaeda Fighters Train in Gaza Strip," Reuters, September 1, 2008, http://www.alarabiya.net/articles/2008/09/01/55828.html.
88. Yoram Cohen, Matthew Levitt, and Becca Wasser, *Deterred but Determined: Salafi-Jihadi Groups in the Palestinian Arena* (Washington, DC: Washington Institute for Near East Policy, January 2010),; "Radical Islam in Gaza," International Crisis Group, March 29, 2011, http://www.crisisgroup.org/~/media/Files/Middle%20East%20North%20Africa/Israel%20Palestine/104%20Radical%20Islam%20in%20Gaza.ashx; Jaysh Al-Ummah Official: Expect Military Operation In South Lebanon Directed At Israel," *NOW Lebanon*, April 11, 2010, https://now.mmedia.me/lb/en/nownews/jaysh_al-ummah_official_expect_military_operation_in_south_lebanon_directed_at_israel.
89. "Jaish Al Ummah To Hamas: 'Whose Side Are You On?'" *CBS News*, May 27, 2009, http://www.cbsnews.com/news/jaish-al-ummah-to-hamas-whose-side-are-you-on/.
90. "Al-Rāyyah Foundation for Media Presents New Pictures From Jaysh al-Ummah: 'The Arrival of Goodness #3'," *Jihadology*, October 13, 2013, http://jihadology.net/2013/10/13/al-rayyah-foundation-for-media-presents-new-pictures-from-jaysh-al-ummah-the-arrival-of-goodness-3/.
91. "Jaysh Al-Ummah Official: Expect Military Operation In South Lebanon Directed At Israel."
92. "Al Qaeda Conducted Attack Against Israel from Gaza," *Ma'ariv* (Tel Aviv), September 2, 2008, http://www.nrg.co.il/online/1/ART1/781/681.html.
93. "Palestinian Faction Urges Help to Sunnis in Ahvaz, Iran, in Audio," SITE Intelligence Group, January 17, 2013, https://news.siteintelgroup.com/index.php/19-jihadist-news/2658-palestinian-faction-urges-help-to-sunnis-in-ahvaz-iran-in-audio.
94. "Palestinian Faction Supports Malian Jihadists, Calls for Attacks on

West," SITE Intelligence Group, January 22, 2013, http://news.siteintelgroup.com/index.php/19-jihadist-news/2678-palestinian-faction-supports-malian-jihadists-calls-for-attacks-on-west.

95. David Barnett, "Gaza Jihadists Call for 'Jihad' Against Egypt's El Sisi," *Long War Journal*, August 15, 2013, http://www.longwarjournal.org/archives/2013/08/gaza_jihadists_call.php.
96. David Barnett, "Gaza-Based Jaish al Ummah Praises Hakeemullah Mehsud," *Long War Journal – Threat Matrix*, November 13, 2013, http://www.longwarjournal.org/threat-matrix/archives/2013/11/gaza-based_jaish_al_ummah_prai.php.
97. "Mapping Palestinian Politics: Jaysh al-Umma (Gaza)," European Council on Foreign Relations, https://www.ecfr.eu/mapping_palestinian_politics/detail/jaysh_al_umma_gaza
98. "Jihad and Terrorism Threat Monitor (JTTM) Weekend Summary," Middle East Media Research Institute, June 9, 2018, https://www.memri.org/reports/jihad-and-terrorism-threat-monitor-jttm-weekend-summary-305
99. "About Us," Hizb Ut Tahrir, n.d., http://english.hizbuttahrir.org/index.php/about-us.
100. Jonathan Spyer, "Hizb ut-Tahrir: A Rising Force In Palestinian Territories," *Global Politician*, December 14, 2007, https://web.archive.org/web/20120202204241/http://globalpolitician.com/23871-palestine.
101. Isabel Kershner, "Palestinian Is Killed in Hebron as Police Disperse Protest Over Mideast Peace Talks," *New York Times*, November 27, 2007, http://www.nytimes.com/2007/11/28/world/middleeast/28palestinians.html.
102. Jonathan Spyer, "A 'Rising Force," *Ha'aretz* (Tel Aviv), June 12, 2007, http://www.haaretz.com/hasen/spages/932087.html.
103. "Hizb Ut-Tahrir: PA Attempts Arrest Of Member," Ma'an News Agency (Ramallah), December 17, 2009, http://www.maannews.net/eng/ViewDetails.aspx?ID=247723; "Hizb Ut-Tahrir: PA Arrests Thousands," Ma'an News Agency (Ramallah), July 17, 2010, http://www.maannews.net/eng/ViewDetails.aspx?ID=300222.
104. "PA Arrests 13 Islamists in Crackdown," Ma'an News Agency (Ramallah), July 15, 2011, http://www.maannews.net/eng/ViewDetails.aspx?ID=405427.
105. "Hizb ut-Tahrir Accuses PLO of Betrayal," Ma'an News Agency (Ramallah), August 13, 2011, http://www.maannews.net/eng/ViewDetails.aspx?ID=412772.
106. Khaled Abu Toameh, "Radical Islam Arrives in Ramallah," Gates-

tone Institute, June 5, 2013, http://www.gatestoneinstitute.org/3751/radical-islam-ramallah; "Hizb al-Tahrir Holds West Bank

107. Festival," Ma'an News Agency (Ramallah), June 17, 2012, http://www.maannews.net/eng/ViewDetails.aspx?ID=496157.
108. "Group Says PA Arrested Dozens of Its Members Over Abbas Criticism," Ma'an News Agency (Ramallah), February 9, 2014, http://www.maannews.net/eng/ViewDetails.aspx?ID=672063.
109. "Mapping Palestinian Politics: Hizb ut-Tahrir," European Council on Foreign Relations, https://www.ecfr.eu/mapping_palestinian_politics/detail/hizb_ut_tahrir; Hizb ut-Tahrir Central Media Office, http://www.hizb-ut-tahrir.info/en/index.php/press-releases/palestine.html
110. David Barnett, "Mujahideen Shura Council is Consolidation of Salafi-Jihadist Groups in Gaza: Sources," *Long War Journal*, October 14, 2012, http://www.longwarjournal.org/archives/2012/10/mujahideen_shura_cou.php.
111. David Barnett, "Mujahideen Shura Council Leader Slams Hamas, Calls for Public Dialogue," *Long War Journal – Threat Matrix*, November 9, 2012, http://www.longwarjournal.org/threat-matrix/archives/2012/11/mujahideen_shura_council_leade.php.
112. Ibid.; David Barnett, "Gaza-Based Salafi Jihadists Conduct Joint Rocket Attacks, Sinai Jihadists Suppressed," *Long War Journal – Threat Matrix*, November 22, 2012, http://www.longwarjournal.org/threat-matrix/archives/2012/11/salafi-jihadist_groups_in_gaza.php.
113. Thomas Joscelyn, "Al Qaeda-Linked Group Claims Responsibility for Attack in Israel," *Long War Journal*, June 19, 2012, http://www.longwarjournal.org/archives/2012/06/al_qaeda-linked_grou.php.
114. Bill Roggio, "Mujahideen Shura Council Calls Attack in Israel a 'Gift' to Zawahiri and Al Qaeda 'Brothers,'" *Long War Journal*, July 30, 2012, http://www.longwarjournal.org/archives/2012/07/egyptian_jihadist_gr.php.
115. David Barnett, "Mujahideen Shura Council: We Are Not Truly a Party to the Ceasefire with Israel," *Long War Journal*, November 27, 2012, http://www.longwarjournal.org/archives/2012/11/mujahideen_shura_cou_2.php.
116. David Barnett, "Jihadist Media Unit Urges Fighters to Strike Egyptian Army," *Long War Journal – Threat Matrix*, September 23, 2013, http://www.longwarjournal.org/archives/2013/09/jihadist_media_unit.php; David Barnett, "Jihadist Media Unit Releases Posters for Palestinian Fighters Killed in Syria," *Long War Journal – Threat Matrix*, October 1, 2013, http://www.longwarjournal.org/threat-matrix/archives/2013/10/jihadist_media_unit_releases_p.php.

117. Lihi Ben Shitrit & Mahmoud Jaraba, "The Threat of Jihadism in the West Bank," Sada: Carnegie Endowment for International Peace, February 6, 2014. http://carnegieendowment.org/sada/54455.
118. "Terrorist Designation of the Mujahidin Shura Council in the Environs of Jerusalem (MSC)," U.S. Department of State, August 19, 2014, https://www.state.gov/j/ct/rls/other/des/266549.htm
119. David Barnett, "Popular Resistance Committees Calls on Hamas to Stop Arrests of 'Mujahideen,'" *Long War Journal – Threat Matrix*, July 22, 2013, http://www.longwarjournal.org/threat-matrix/archives/2013/07/popular_resistance_committees.php.
120. Jonathan Schanzer and Grant Rumley, "Iran Spawns New Jihadist Group in Gaza," *Long War Journal,* June 18, 2014, http://www.longwarjournal.org/archives/2014/06/by_jonathan_schanzer.php.
121. "Gaza Militant Dies in Apparent Explosives Accident," *Times of Israel,* May 26, 2014, http://www.timesofisrael.com/gaza-militant-dies-in-apparent-explosives-accident/.
122. Al-Sabireen, "Our Charter," n.d., http://alsabireen.ps/ar/page/4/%D9%87%D9%88%D9%8A%D8%AA%D9%86%D8%A7
123. Ehud Yaari, "Replacing Hamas," *Foreign Affairs,* September 28, 2015, https://www.foreignaffairs.com/articles/palestinian-authority/2015-09-28/replacing-hamas.
124. Ehud Yaari, "Replacing Hamas," *Foreign Affairs,* September 28, 2015, https://www.foreignaffairs.com/articles/palestinian-authority/2015-09-28/replacing-hamas.
125. Adnan Abu Amer, "Why Hamas Closed Down Iranian Charity in Gaza," *Al Monitor,* March 22, 2016, http://www.al-monitor.com/pulse/originals/2016/03/gaza-hamas-shut-down-iran-affiliated-charity.html.
126. Yaari, "Replacing Hamas"; "Middle East: Iran Back Into Gaza," *Amad*, October 25, 2015, http://www.amad.ps/ar/?Action=Details&ID=95441
127.Khaled Abu Toameh, "Analysis: Iran Infiltrates the West Bank," *Jerusalem Post,* February 9, 2016, http://www.jpost.com/Arab-Israeli-Conflict/Analysis-Iran-Infiltrates-the-West-Bank-444352.; "Palestinian Security Sources: The "Patient" Movement Seeks to Stretch from Gaza to the West," *Amad*, May 2, 2016, http://www.amad.ps/ar/?Action=Details&ID=109775
128. Grant Rumley, "Trump Administration Designates Iranian-Spawned Jihadist Faction in Gaza," *Long War Journal*, January 31, 2018, https://www.longwarjournal.org/archives/2018/01/trump-administration-designates-iranian-spawned-jihadist-faction-in-gaza.php
129. Khaled Abu Toameh, "'Corruption Will Let Hamas Take W. Bank,'"

Jerusalem Post, January 29, 2010, http://www.jpost.com/Middle-East/Corruption-will-let-Hamas-take-W-Bank.

130. Palestinian Center for Policy and Survey Research, "Palestinian Public Opinion Poll No (71)," April 2019, https://www.pcpsr.org/sites/default/files/Poll%2071%20English%20full%20text%20March%20 2019.pdf
131. Hazem Balousha, "Gazans Unimpressed By Hamas Military Parades," *Al Monitor*, November 20, 2013, http://www.al-monitor.com/pulse/originals/2013/11/hamas-islamic-jihad-military-parade-gaza-crisis.html.
132. Neri Zilber, "Hamas on the Ropes," *Foreign Policy*, June 26, 2016, http://foreignpolicy.com/2014/06/26/hamas-on-the-ropes/.
133. Palestinian Center for Policy and Survey Research, "Palestinian Public Opinion Poll No (70)," December 18, 2018, http://www.pcpsr.org/sites/default/files/Poll%2070%20English%20full%20text%2024%20 Dec%202018.pdf
134. Palestinian Center for Policy and Survey Research, "Palestinian Public Opinion Poll No (71)," April 2019, https://www.pcpsr.org/sites/default/files/Poll%2071%20English%20full%20text%20March%20 2019.pdf
135. Jonathan Schanzer, *Hamas vs. Fatah: The Struggle for Palestine* (New York: Palgrave Macmillan, 2008), 110-111.
136. Miriam Berger and Heidi Levine, "Christians Under Siege: Gaza's Christians Blocked From Visiting Birthplace of Jesus," *The National*, December 23, 2018, https://www.thenational.ae/world/mena/christmas-under-siege-gaza-s-christians-blocked-from-visiting-birthplace-of-jesus-1.805691
137. "Abbas's Security Forces Use Batons to 'Brutally Beat' Hamas Protestors in Hebron," *Times of Israel*, December 14, 2018, https://www.timesofisrael.com/pa-security-forces-use-batons-to-beat-hamas-protesters-in-west-bank/
138. Neri Zilber and Ghaith al-Omari, *State with No Army, Army with No State: The Evolution of the Palestinian Authority Security Forces 1994-2018* (Washington Institute for Near East Policy, March 2018), pp. 57-59, http://www.washingtoninstitute.org/uploads/Documents/pubs/PolicyFocus154-ZilberOmari.pdf.
139. Peter Beaumont, "No Obvious Alternative to Hamas in Gaza, Says Top Israeli General," *Guardian* (London), May 12, 2015, https://www.theguardian.com/world/2015/may/12/idf-no-alternative-to-hamas-in-gaza-top-israeli-general-turgeman-war.
140. Neri Zilber, "Israel and Gaza Go to War Despite Themselves," *The*

Daily Beast, November 13, 2018, https://www.thedailybeast.com/israel-and-gaza-go-to-war-despite-themselves

141. Neri Zilber, "How Gaza Became Hell on Earth," *The Daily Beast*, May 15, 2018, https://www.thedailybeast.com/how-gaza-became-hell-on-earth

142. "Abbas Swears In New PA Government Led By His Fatah Ally, Mohammad Shtayyeh," *Times of Israel,* April 13, 2019, https://www.timesofisrael.com/abbas-swears-in-new-pa-government-led-by-his-fatah-ally-mohammad-shtayyeh/

22 Qatar

Quick Facts

Population: 2,444,174 (July 2020 est.)
Area: 11,586 sq km
Ethnic Groups: Non-Qatari 88.4%, Qatari 11.6% (2015 est.)
Religions: Muslim 67.7%, Christian 13.8%, Hindu 13.8%, Buddhist 3.1%, folk religion <.1%, Jewish <.1%, other 0.7%, unaffiliated 0.9% (2010 est.)
Government Type: Absolute monarchy
GDP (official exchange rate):$166.9 billion (2017 est.)

Map and Quick Facts derived in part from the CIA World Factbook (Last Updated July 2020)

Introduction

Qatar represents a study in contradictions. It is the only country other than Saudi Arabia to espouse Wahhabbism *as its official state religion, its authoritarian tribal rulers brook no internal opposition (Islamic or otherwise), and its leaders fund the popular and controversial satellite television network Al-Jazeera. Moreover, while Qatar hosts Al Udeid air base, the regional home of U.S. Central Command, it also provides money and diplomatic support to anti-Western Islamists.*

Wahhabbism *is especially influential among the al-Thani clan, which has ruled Qatar since the beginning of the nineteenth century. However, in contrast to other regional nations, Sunni Qatar has close relations with Shiite Iran. In the wake of the June 2017 diplomatic crisis with Saudi Arabia and several other Gulf states, that alliance has steadily grown.*

Islamist Activity

Qatar is an exceptionally wealthy country where the government subsidizes everything from petrol to education. Due to the government's commitment to public services, Qatar so far has lacked serious challenges to the legitimacy of its government. Likewise, there have been very few reported incidents of anti-

Western terrorism in Qatar in the past two decades. Incidents like the 2001 shooting at Al Udeid air base, the forward headquarters for U.S. Central Command, and the attempted ramming of the base's gates in 2002 are thought to have been perpetrated by lone wolf attackers.[1] In March 2005, Omar Ahmed Abdallah Ali, an expatriate Egyptian, blew himself up outside a theater in Doha. The attack, which killed a British school teacher, was the first suicide bombing of its kind in Qatar. Ali was believed to have had ties to al-Qaeda in the Arabian Peninsula, whose leader issued a communiqué two days before the attack.[2]

In the aftermath of this attack, a *Sunday Times* report alleged that Qatar's rulers were paying protection money to al-Qaeda. It described an agreement between the Qatari government and al-Qaeda prior to the 2003 Iraq War, as a result of which millions of dollars were paid annually to the terror network to keep Qatar off of its target list.[3] After the attack in Doha, the agreement was renewed, according to the *Times*' source, "just to be on the safe side."[4] This money was likely channeled via religious leaders sympathetic to al-Qaeda and supported its activities in Iraq.

The report highlights the fine line that Qatar treads in its relations with the U.S. and its powerful neighbors. Because it hosts the Al Udeid air base and Camp As Sayliyah, a pre-positioning facility for U.S. military equipment, Qatar represents an attractive target for terrorists. While officially these are Qatari bases, there are reportedly some 10,000 U.S and coalition personal stationed at Al Udeid.[5] Nevertheless, the Qatari government appears invested in these ties; in 2018, the country's defense minister expressed his government's desire to expand the base, which the U.S. government authorized the following year.[6]

Yet, while Qatar enjoys a close relationship with Washington, this proximity is balanced by the government's ties to regional Islamist groups. A 2009 State Department cable deemed Qatar's counterterror efforts "the worst in the region."[7] In the report, Qatar's security service was described as "hesitant to act against known terrorists out of concern for appearing to be aligned with the U.S. and provoking reprisals."[8]

The Qatari government has a reputation as a financial backer of Islamist causes abroad, including funding terrorist organizations. Qatar also shelters known Islamists, providing safe haven to members of the Muslim Brotherhood, the Palestinian Hamas movement, and Afghanistan's Taliban. The government's activities have not gone unnoticed, and the *emirate* has faced international consequences from its activities, most notable in the form of the diplomatic crisis that erupted between it and the other Gulf states beginning in 2017.

Backing Terrorist Entities Abroad

Qatar has backed and funded a host of Islamist groups abroad, including Hamas in the Palestinian Territories, the Muslim Brotherhood in Egypt, and al-Qaeda in Syria. At the start of the Arab Spring, the Qatari government supported Islamist protest movements throughout North Africa and the Middle East, and played a major role in almost all regional conflicts. Qatar was the first Arab country to recognize Libya's rebels and contributed six Mirage fighter jets to depose Muamar Qadhafi. Its financial support of the Libyan revolution may have reached as much as $2 billion in 2012 alone, channelled through various Islamist, anti-Western opposition figures.[9] Qatar continues to support Libya's ongoing internal conflict, with Qatari-Turkish joint venture BMC providing armored vehicles to the Libya's Government of National Accord (GNA) as of December 2019.[10] The Qatari government is also known to have provided financial aid to Islamist militants fighting in the Sahel.

In the Palestinian arena, The Qatari government has long been the primary financial and ideological sponsor of Hamas and has hosted senior Hamas officials. In October 2012, the Qatari *emir* became the first head of state to visit the Gaza Strip since Hamas took full control of the territory in 2007. At that time, the *emir* pledged $400 million for infrastructure projects. This visit took place just after the upgrading of the Palestinian Authority's (PA) status at the United Nations, and appears to have designed to boost Hamas's standing against its political rivals in the PA's secular Fatah faction.[11]

More recently, Qatar coordinated with Israel and the PA to pay the salaries of Hamas' employees, and to import construction materials into the Gaza Strip.[12] In 2018, Qatar launched a new payments program for families needing assistance in the Strip, to a tune of $330 million, for fuel, electricity, and civil servant salaries. In August 2019, Qatar's envoy to Gaza noted that over $150 million had been spent as part of that effort.[13] However, Axios reported in June 2020 that Qatar planned to suspend these payments beginning the following month, due to Israel's pending plans to annex parts of the West Bank. Notably, though, this story conflicts with Qatari state media, which stated that the country will continue payments.[14]

In July 2017, Qatari envoy Mohammed El-Amadi reaffirmed support for development projects in the Hamas-ruled Gaza Strip.[15] In October 2017, Qatar announced that it would fund a new headquarters for the PA in Gaza as part of a reconciliation deal between Hamas and Fatah.[16] As of early 2019, Israeli sources calculated that Qatar had donated more than $1.1 billion to projects on the Gaza Strip between 2012-2018.[17] Reportedly, 44% of Qatari funding went to infrastructure projects and 40% to medical and educational services, while the rest went to Hamas and other groups.[18]

Furthermore, in 2013, the Taliban were permitted to open an official office in Qatar.[19] Turkey, Saudi Arabia, and the UAE were also considered potential locations. Turkey was rejected since it was a NATO member, while Saudi Arabia and the UAE were seen as too close to the U.S. The Taliban ultimately preferred Qatar, seeing it as a neutral option. Qatar likely saw the Taliban office as yet another avenue for building its geopolitical clout.[20] The office closed shortly after opening because Taliban representatives flew the Taliban flag at the office,[21] an act that enraged then-Afghan President Hamid Karzai, but the facility reopened in 2015.[22]

While Qatari jets have provided symbolic participation in the airpower mission against the Islamic State, Qatar has become a significant financial sponsor of the Islamist elements arrayed against Syrian President Bashar al-Assad. For example, Qatar has provided funding and weapons to Ahrar al-Sham (Free Men of Syria). Khalid al-Attiyah, then-Qatari foreign minister, praised this movement as "purely" Syrian[23] and the U.S. State Department's 2014 *Country Reports on Terrorism* highlighted Qatar's offer to "host a train-and-equip program for moderate Syrian opposition forces."[24] However, Ahrar al-Sham fought alongside another Qatar-backed group, the al-Qaeda-linked Jabhat al-Nusra. Qatar has funded *Jabhat al-Nusra* since 2013. Much of *al-Nusra*'s funding comes from "ransoming" hostages from Western countries.[25] This is in addition to the large sums of money channeled to the group via Qatari charity organizations and individuals, who operate freely in the country.[26]

Al-Nusra ostensibly split from al-Qaeda in mid-2016, rebranding itself as Jabhat Fateh al-Sham (JFS) and later as Hayat Tahrir al-Sham. However, the "split" was in name only; the organization's leader did not renounce ties to its parent group.[27] Qatar, meanwhile, was essential to this rebranding; Qatari intelligence officials met several times with *al-Nusra* leader Abu Mohammed al-Jolani, spurring him to abandon al-Qaeda and even promising funding.[28]

Hundreds of fighters have left *al-Nusra* to join the Islamic State within the last few years.[29] These defections have led to the transfer of Qatari-supplied weapons and funds to ISIS, a fact that even Qatar's allies acknowledge. A leaked email published by Wikileaks in October 2016 singled out Qatar and Saudi Arabia for "providing clandestine financial and logistic support to ISIL [ISIS] and other radical Sunni groups in the region."[30] Two months earlier, in August 2016, two rebels disclosed to the *Financial Times* that Qatar and Saudi Arabia were consistently sending cash and supplies to Aleppo via Turkey, in order to aid Nusra's offensive against Assad forces in that city.[31] The Nordic Research Monitoring Network, a Sweden-based non-profit dedicated to tracking extremist trends, corroborated this information in December 2019.[32]

Means of Funding

Simultaneously maintaining good relations with both Islamist factions and with the West has facilitated Qatar's role as a regional mediator. This strategy has allowed the Qatari government to openly bankroll *jihadi* groups through the payment of ransoms for Western hostages.[33] The Qatari government negotiated the release of captive U.S. servicemen in Afghanistan in exchange for prisoners held by the U.S. in 2014 and, in April 2017, may also have paid the largest ransom in history – over $1 billion – to secure the release of a Qatari hunting party taken hostage in Iraq. The sum was delivered to an array of Sunni and Shia militias, including Hayat Tahrir al-Sham, Kataib Hezbollah in Iraq, and the Iranian Revolutionary Guards' Quds Force.[34]

Qatari charities represent another means of providing financial support to terror groups; several have been accused of actively financing al-Qaeda and other terrorist organizations. In the wake of the 2017 Gulf blockade of Qatar, Saudi Arabia, the UAE, and other Gulf states designated several Qatari charities as terror financiers. These included the Eid Charity, Qatar Charity, and the RAF Foundation. While Qatar Charity was set up and operated by an employee of the Qatari government,[35] the RAF Foundation is implicated in funneling money to Jabhat al-Nusra.[36] Eid Charity, cofounded by known terror financier Abdulrahman al-Nuaimi, is accused of funding projects and supporting individuals associated with al-Qaeda.[37]

Islamists and Islamist Extremists in Qatar

Qatar has, in the past, granted asylum to exiled Islamists, Islamic extremists, and radical preachers from other countries.[38] Following the 1979 attack on the Grand Mosque in Mecca by an Islamist extremist group, Qatar housed a number of radical exiles from Saudi Arabia, including *Wahhabbi* scholar Sheikh Abdallah bin Zayd al-Mahmud, who subsequently was appointed Qatar's most senior cleric.[39]

During the 1980s, many *Wahhabbi* exiles were appointed to senior and mid-level positions in Qatar's Interior Ministry, which controls both the civilian security force and the *Mubahathat* (secret police office). The following decade, a number of al-Qaeda leaders – including Osama bin Laden and Abu Mus'ab al-Zarqawi, the future leader of al-Qaeda in Iraq – reportedly travelled through Qatar under the protection of members of the country's ruling clan.[40] Chechen leader Zelimkhan Yandarbiyev, who was killed in Doha in 2004, also found refuge for several years in Qatar.

Among the political exiles who have sought refuge in Qatar are prominent Muslim Brotherhood figures, many of whom fled persecution at the hands of Gamal Abdel Nasser's government in Egypt during the 1950s. Some of these exiles reportedly laid the foundations for the Qatari Education Ministry and taught at various levels until the early 1980s.[41] The dean of the College of Islamic Studies at Qatar's flagship Hamad bin Khalifa University is Emad al-Din Shahin, a member of the Egyptian Muslim Brotherhood.[42]

One of the most influential – and controversial – voices in Islamist circles is Egyptian Sheikh Yusuf al-Qaradawi, who has lived in Qatar since 1961. Al-Qaradawi enjoyed worldwide exposure through his weekly television program on *Al Jazeera*, "Sharia and Life" (*al-Shari'a wa-al-Hayat*). Until 2010, he also oversaw the Islamist Web portal IslamOnline, which he founded in 1999 in Qatar with backing from the royal family.[43] Many consider Sheikh al-Qaradawi to be the most influential Islamic scholar alive today, and he is viewed as the spiritual leader of the Muslim Brotherhood.[44] Among some audiences, however, his comparatively moderate views on the acceptability of Muslim participation in Western democracies have brought him both praise and condemnation.[45] Al-Qaradawi is one of the founders of the *wasatiyya* ("Middle Way") movement, which attempts to bridge the various interpretations of Islam.[46] Al-Qaradawi's influence also played a role in the Arab Spring; his protégés emerged as new leaders, financial backers, religious authorities and politicians.[47]

Al-Qaradawi has sparked considerable controversy in the West for supporting suicide bombings in Israel and the killing of American citizens in Iraq. He is also a founder of *Itilaf al-Khayr* (Union of the Good), a coalition of European Islamic charities designated by the United States Treasury in 2008 as a channel for transferring funds to Hamas.[48] Three Qatari charities were part of the Union's network.[49]

In May 2013, he urged Sunni Muslims to join the *jihad* in Syria against the Assad regime and against Hezbollah.[50] Qaradawi's many pronouncements have made him a frequent point of strife between Qatar and its Gulf neighbors. In 2014, the UAE summoned Qatar's ambassador to Abu Dhabi to formally protest al-Qaradawi inveighing against the UAE.[51] In June 2017, Saudi Arabia, the UAE, Egypt, and Bahrain designated al-Qaradawi a terrorist.[52]

Investing for Islamism

Qatar's policies are consistent with two strategic objectives: to buy foreign influence through a variety of means while playing off its stronger neighbors — particularly Saudi Arabia and Iran. Uppermost on Qatar's agenda is the need to protect its sovereignty and natural gas wealth. This has motivated Qatar's historical spending spree in Europe, where Qatar invested billions of dollars in real estate, tourist venues, sports, and media sectors.[53] These are tools of both foreign and domestic policy; by investing heavily abroad, the al-Thanis are, effectively, buying insurance against a domestic uprising. This practice caused a stir when a 2012 *New York Times* article revealed that the Qatari government pledged 150 million Euro [$199 million] to investments in French suburbs inhabited by a Muslim majority. While Qatari officials insisted that the move was "just business," critics claimed that the Qataris were pushing an Islamist agenda. Such allegations have also dogged the spending of Qatari charities in European countries.[54]

Similar concerns have been voiced about donations received in the U.S.; Qatar Foundation International (QFI) has delivered large donations and grants to both K-12 and higher education institutions.[55] The Qatar Foundation (QF), QFI's parent organization, has donated billions to U.S. universities; some of those schools– such as Georgetown, Northwestern, Texas A&M, and Carnegie Mellon, among others – have built campuses in Doha.[56] Both QFI and the Qatar Foundation are effectively controlled by the al-Thani.[57]

QFI also develops curricula and education materials for Arabic-language programs in the U.S. with Qatari pro-Islamic influence. Their "Arabic Advocacy Kit" lays out several reasons for learning Arabic, particularly noting that learning the language will encourage Americans to hold warmer feelings towards Arabs and Muslims. *Al-Masdar*, QFI's online curriculum development resource, offers lesson plans and other teaching resources to aid Arabic language learning, including a lesson plan on "Express Your Loyalty to Qatar" and another on "Whose 'Terrorism'?" about the moral relativity around some definitions of terrorism.[58]

International Consequences

Qatar's role in playing off regional actors against one another, as well as its support of radical groups, has periodically brought it into conflict with its neighbors. In March 2014, Saudi Arabia, the UAE, and Bahrain withdrew their ambassadors due to the Qatar's sponsorship of the Muslim Brotherhood and other Islamist groups.[59] After then-Egyptian president Mohamed Morsi was overthrown in 2013, several Brotherhood members were asked to leave Qatar as part of a rapprochement agreement signed between Gulf countries.[60]

In December 2016, however, Egypt accused Qatar of being indirectly responsible for the bombing of a Coptic church which killed 24 people, due to its facilitation of the Muslim Brotherhood branch that had instructed the attacker to act.[61]

Tensions between Qatar and the Gulf states erupted anew at the end of May 2017, when *Emir* Sheikh Tamim bin Hamad al-Thani was quoted by Qatari state media as claiming, "there is no wisdom in harboring hostility towards Iran." Qatar later denied the *emir* had made the statements, claiming the state media website and Twitter accounts had been hacked. The statements—whether real or fabricated—provided Qatar's neighbors the excuse they needed to openly strike out against Qatari policies. Saudi Arabia and the UAE quickly blocked access to *Al Jazeera*'s website.[62]

On June 5, 2017, Saudi Arabia, Bahrain, Egypt and the UAE broke off relations and cut off all air, sea, and land routes with Qatar. Yemen, Mauritania, and the Maldives followed. Qatari citizens were given 14 days to leave Saudi Arabia, Bahrain, and the UAE, and those countries also banned their own citizens from entering Qatar. Saudi Arabia, which leads the coalition fighting Iran-backed Houthi rebels in Yemen, expelled Qatar from the coalition.[63]

On June 22, Saudi Arabia, the UAE, and Egypt issued a 13-point list of demands to restore relations and gave Doha 10 days to comply.[64] The demands include Qatar severing ties with *jihadist* groups, shutting down news outlets (including *Al Jazeera*), limiting ties with Iran, and expelling Turkish troops stationed in the country. Among the Islamist groups mentioned in the list were the Muslim Brotherhood, Hezbollah, al-Qaeda, and ISIS. As of July 2020, the dispute appears stalemated, despite repeated U.S. efforts to broker a resolution.[65] By all perceptions, Qatar is has claimed the upper hand, having proven resilient to financial and supply chain pressures caused by the early days of the blockade. Qatar has deepened links with other Middle Eastern countries, most notably Turkey and Iran, in a bid to cultivate new allies. The Trump administration, meanwhile, has backed off on finding a comprehensive solution to the blockade, and has of late narrowly focused on airspace.[66]

Qatar's continued support of Islamist elements, despite the negative diplomatic impact of this policy, reflects a clear ideological outlook.[67] At times, this support has been a matter of personal relations. According to U.S. intelligence officials, Abdallah bin Khalid al-Thani, a member of the Qatari royal family, helped wanted al-Qaeda chief Khaled Sheikh Mohammed elude capture in 1996. Abdallah bin Khalid, then Qatar's Minister of Religious Affairs, reportedly sheltered the wanted man on one of his farms.[68] Mohammed was supposedly employed in Qatar's Department of Public Water Works for some time before fleeing the country on a Qatari passport.[69]

Abdallah bin Khalid was hardly alone in his sympathies to al-Qaeda. U.S. officials have said that other Qatari royal family members similarly provided safe haven for al-Qaeda leaders.[70] In late 2013, the U.S. Treasury Department imposed sanctions on several prominent Qataris for providing funds to al-Qaeda and Islamic extremists in Syria.[71] One year later, one of those sanctioned people was still employed by the Qatari Interior Ministry.[72] In this way, more than twenty people under U.S. or UN sanctions have benefitted from Qatari negligence or support.[73]

Qatar made some progress toward accountability in the initial months of the Gulf crisis, including the expulsion of Hamas operative Saleh al-Arouri in June 2017.[74] In July 2017, Qatar signed a memorandum of understanding on terror finance with the U.S., and followed that with an agreement to impose further curbs on terror financing that October.[75] Al-Arouri, Hamas' military commander in the West Bank and the founder of its Izz al-Din al-Qassam Brigades, was behind the 2014 murder and kidnapping of three Israeli teenagers. Since then, however, Qatar seems to have returned to its old ways: in April 2018, Abdullah bin Nasser bin Khalifa al-Thani, Qatar's then-prime minister, attended the wedding of the son of a noted terror financier, Abdulrahman al-Nuaimi. Al-Nuaimi has been designated by both the U.S. and the UN for funding al-Qaeda in Iraq, and was even placed on Qatar's terror watch list.[76] In January 2020, an American citizen filed a lawsuit against a main Qatari bank, alleging that the bank facilitated funding operations for the Nusra Front and Ahrar al-Sham.[77] In June 2020, another lawsuit was filed in the U.S. against Qatar, alleging that Qatari charities funneled money to Hamas and Palestinian Islamic Jihad, which have both carried out attacks against Americans.[78]

Islamism and Society

Among the tribes that adopted the *Wahhabbi* interpretation of Islam in the late 19th century was the al-Thani – in contrast to the ruling al-Khalifas of Bahrain, who rejected it. When the al-Khalifas attempted to invade the peninsula of Qatar in 1867, the al-Thani and their followers, with the help of the British, repelled the invasion. This victory established the al-Thani family as Qatar's ruling clan. Thereafter, Qatar became the only country other than Saudi Arabia to espouse *Wahhabbism* as its official state ideology.[79] Further, the al-Thani claim to be descended from the Banu Tamim tribe, the same clan as Mohammed ibn Abd al-Wahhab, *Wahhabbism*'s progenitor.[80] Sympathy for Islamist causes has therefore traditionally been high among many members of the country's ruling clan.

However, *Wahhabbi* tenets are not officially enforced or strictly adhered to in most public settings; Qatari society is generally moderate, and, among Arab countries, its ranks second only to Lebanon in terms of civil liberties.[81] While instances of overt religious discrimination have been rare, anti-Semitic motifs are common in the mainstream media.[82] Extensive examples can be found in publicly available sermons and state-sponsored educational materials – the latter of which has also glorified *jihad*.[83]

Non-citizens constitute a majority of Qatar's residents; most are from Southeast Asia or from other Muslim majority countries.[84] Sunni Muslims constitute the overwhelming majority of the population, while Shi'a Muslims account for less than five percent.[85] As a result, the main drivers for Islamist opposition are less salient in Qatar; the government espouses a distinctly Islamist ideology, while social inequities and cultural frictions have been kept to a minimum.

Qatar's government sees to its citizens' health, educational, and other social service needs. This has decreased the opportunity for Islamic opposition groups to use traditional pathways to increase influence in Qatari society.[86] While many Qatari citizens express support for *jihadists* fighting in Syria and Iraq, relatively few have joined the fighting. This is somewhat surprising because a 2014 study found that, of all social media posts originating in Qatar, 47% were supportive of ISIS.[87]

Islamism and the State

Islamic jurisprudence is the basis of Qatar's legal system and civil courts have jurisdiction only over commercial law.[88] Qatar's governmental structure, despite a written constitution, conforms closely to traditional Islamic constraints, with tribal and family allegiance remaining an influential factor in the country's politics. There is no provision in Qatar's constitution for political parties, and hence there is no official political opposition.[89] Professional associations and societies, which in other Muslim countries play the role of unofficial political parties, are under severe constraints in Qatar and are forbidden from political activity.[90] Religious institutions are carefully monitored by the Ministry of Islamic Affairs, which oversees mosque construction and Islamic education. The Ministry appoints religious leaders and previews the content of mosque sermons on an *ad hoc* basis, but does not require clerics to receive approval for their sermons.[91] Comparatively, authorities are considerably lenient toward Qataris accused of funding Islamist activities abroad. The U.S. government has described this behavior as a "permissive" environment for terror finance.[92]

Marginal Reforms

In June 2013, Hamad bin Khalifa al-Thani abdicated in favor of his son, British-educated Tamim bin Hamad al-Thani. Now 40 years old, *Emir* Tamim is the youngest head of state in the region and has promised to modernize the country's governmental system and reduce his family's presence in the government. The need to keep pace with global social and economic development has pushed Qatar to gradually shift its political structure to one based on more formal institutions. Qatar's constitution institutionalized the hereditary rule of the al-Thani family, but it also mandated that two-thirds of the Advisory Council, its national legislative body, be directly elected. The Council would have the power to remove ministers from office, to approve the national budget, and to draft and vote on proposed legislation.[93] Still, elections have been repeatedly delayed. The *emir* announced in 2017 that the government was preparing for the polls, noting "there are legal shortcomings and legal issues" that need addressed.[94] While formally accountable to no one, the *emir* is still bound by the checks and balances of traditional Muslim Arab societies; all decisions must be in accordance with *sharia* and must not arouse the opposition of the country's leading families.[95]

In 2016, when Qatar posted its first budget deficit in 15 years, *Emir* Tamim reduced the number of government ministries, slashed state institutions' budgets, and put various social welfare schemes on hold. This was accompanied by hikes in utility rates, gas prices, government fines and service costs.[96] The *emir* has since reversed course in the wake of the Gulf crisis, repatriating some assets to cushion the economy and implementing a stimulus package to aid private sector businesses.[97] *Emir* Tamim has also loosened strictures on expressions of foreign culture, including state-owned sales of alcohol and pork to the country's foreign residents and supporting limited religious freedom for non-Muslims. These measures have not been universally popular. Some have accused the *emir* of forsaking his own citizens in favor of the migrant workers who make up some 90% of the population.

Using Al Jazeera to Proselytize Islamism

Though the Qatari press may be free from official censorship, self-censorship is the norm. Defense and national security matters, as well as stories related to the royal family, are considered strictly out of bounds. The country's major radio and television stations, Qatar Radio and Qatar Television, are both state-owned.[98] Although newspapers in Qatar are all privately owned in principle, many board members and owners are either government officials or have close ties to the government. For example, the chairman of the influential daily *Al-Watan*, Hamad bin Sahim al-Thani, is a member of the royal family.[99] Meanwhile, Qatar's former Foreign Minister, Hamed bin Jasem bin Jaber al-Thani, owns half of the newspaper.[100]

When then-*Emir* Hamad bin Khalifa al-Thani launched the *Al Jazeera* satellite network in 1996, the station initially offered the kind of free and unfettered discussion of issues not usually broadcast in the Muslim world. *Al Jazeera* is directly funded by the Qatari government, and Sheikh Hamid bin Thamer, a member of the royal family, has been the network's chairman since its inception.[101] In recent years, many of *Al Jazeera*'s more secular staff have been replaced by Islamists.[102] This process has been accompanied by a shift away from its ideologically diverse origins to a more populist—and more Islamist—approach.[103]

Al Jazeera's Arabic channel has actively promoted the Muslim Brotherhood as a viable player in Egypt and its Arabic channels reflect Doha's official policies.[104] Many leading figures at *Al Jazeera* news are Egyptians affiliated with the Brotherhood and Brotherhood guests, and loyalists dominate most of the channel's programs on Egyptian political affairs.[105] *Al Jazeera*'s Islamist shift was a matter of design as much as evolution, reflecting the interests of the Qatari ruling family, and seeking to influence events rather than just reporting on them.[106] Government control over the channel's reporting was so direct that the channel's output is a subject of bilateral discussions between Washington and Doha. An American diplomatic dispatch from July 2009 noted that *Al Jazeera* could be used as a bargaining tool to repair Qatar's relationships with other countries and called the station "one of Qatar's most valuable political and diplomatic tools."[107]

Al Jazeera rarely criticizes Qatar's ruling family.[108] This has not only infuriated those Arab governments on the receiving end of the station's critical coverage, but also raised the question of Qatari complicity in the destabilization of its neighbors. Libya and Saudi Arabia have both withdrawn their ambassadors to Doha in the past in response to *Al Jazeera* reportage, while Jordan and Lebanon have both accused the station of actively working to undermine their governments, while uncritically supporting their opposition Islamist movements.[109]

Al Jazeera's influence reflects the reality of an increasingly media-driven Middle East. The station's rivalry with the newer Saudi-backed, Dubai-based *Al Arabiya* satellite channel is indicative of a deeper competition for regional influence. While the Saudi-led coalition demanded, amongst other things, that *Al Jazeera* be shuttered to end the blockade, the attempt at silencing Qatar's regional *dawa* (missionary activity) seems to have only upped the ante; both Qatar and its opponents have funneled billions of dollars into PR efforts.[110]

In recent years, *Al Jazeera* is facing a pressure campaign to register under the Foreign Agent Registration Act (FARA).[111] In 2018, a bipartisan group of lawmakers led by Representatives Josh Gottheimer and Lee Zeldin published a letter urging the Department of Justice to enforce FARA against the network.[112] In June 2019, a group of lawmakers led by Senators Chuck Grassley and Tom Cotton sent another letter to the Department of Justice, asking why it has not mandated *Al Jazeera* to register.[113]

In addition to *Al Jazeera,* Qatar is purported to fund several other outlets, including *Middle East Eye, Al-Araby al-Jadeed,* and the now-defunct *HuffPost Arabi.*[114] Saudi Arabia, meanwhile, funds *Asharq al-Awsat* and *Arab News*, as well as the afore-mentioned *Al Arabiya*, while the UAE funds *Sky News Arabia*, a joint-venture between Britain's Sky and the Abu Dhabi Media Investment Corporation.[115] Twitter is another arena where this electronic warfare plays out, with both sides deploying an army of bots and smear accounts.[116] In effect, these governments vie to monopolize digital reporting.

While the initial onset of the Gulf crisis held hopes that the Saudi-Emirati pressure would push Doha to course correct, Qatar's success in withstanding the embargo has likely emboldened it. Instead of curbing its involvement with bad actors, Doha continues to fund and shelter Islamist groups while reaching out to the Iranian and Turkish governments.

Endnotes

1. Oxford Analytica, "The Advent of Terrorism in Qatar," *Forbes*, March 25, 2005, http://www.forbes.com/2005/03/25/cz_0325ox-an_qatarattack.html.
2. Oxford Analytica, "The Advent of Terrorism in Qatar."
3. Uzi Mahnaimi, "Qatar buys off al-Qaeda attacks with oil millions," *Sunday Times* (London), May 1, 2005, http://www.timesonline.co.uk/tol/news/world/article387163.ece.
4. Ibid.
5. Ben Brimelow, "Qatar wants the US military permanently in the country with a bigger air base," *Business Insider*, January 31, 2018,

https://www.businessinsider.com/qatar-al-udeid-us-air-base-middle-east-permanent-2018-1

6. Josh Lederman, "Seeking closer ties, Qatar to expand base used by US troops," Associated Press, January 31, 2018, https://www.militarytimes.com/news/your-military/2018/01/31/seeking-closer-ties-qatar-to-expand-base-used-by-us-troops/; Matthew Lee, "Pompeo signs off on al-Udeid Air Base expansion, but says Qatar diplomatic crisis 'has dragged on too long,'" Associated Press, January 13, 2019. https://www.militarytimes.com/flashpoints/2019/01/13/pompeo-signs-off-on-al-udeid-air-base-expansion-but-says-qatar-diplomatic-crisis-has-dragged-on-too-long/.
7. Elizabeth Weingarten, "Qatar: 'Worst' on Counterterrorism in the Middle East?" *The Atlantic*, November 29, 2010, http://www.theatlantic.com/international/archive/2010/11/qatar-worst-on-counterterroism-in-the-middle-east/67166/.
8. Scott Shane and Andrew W. Lehren, "Leaked Cables Offer Raw Look at U.S. Diplomacy," *New York Times*, November 28, 2010, http://www.nytimes.com/2010/11/29/world/29cables.html?_r=1.
9. "Qatar Sends Billions, Hoping for an Islamic Regime in Libya," *El-Khabar* (Algeria), August 3, 2012, as translated in *Al-Monitor*, August 3, 2012, http://www.al-monitor.com/pulse/security/01/08/report-warns-about-a-serious-thr.html.
10. Aykan Erdemir and Varsha Koduvayur, "Brothers in Arms: The Consolidation of the Turkey-Qatar Axis," Foundation for the Defense of Democracies, December 11, 2019. https://www.fdd.org/analysis/2019/12/11/brothers-in-arms/; Adam Nathan, "Cargo ship loaded with Turkish military vehicles arrives in Tripoli," *Al Arabiya*, May 19, 2019, https://english.alarabiya.net/en/News/north-africa/2019/05/19/Cargo-ship-loaded-with-Turkish-military-vehicles-arrives-in-Tripoli.
11. Acil Tabbara, "Qatar Emir in Gaza: Doha pushes Islamist Agenda to Detriment of Palestinian Unity," *Middle East Online*, October 23, 2012, http://www.middle-east-online.com/english/?id=55066.
12. Adam Rasgon, "Qatar coordinated payment to Hamas employees with Israel, PA," *Jerusalem Post,* July 24, 2016, http://www.jpost.com/Middle-East/Qatar-to-pay-salaries-of-Hamas-public-sector-employees-in-Gaza-462209.
13. "Qatari envoy says funds for Hamas helping prevent new Gaza war," *Times of Israel*, August 25, 2019, https://www.timesofisrael.com/qatari-envoy-says-funds-for-hamas-helping-prevent-new-gaza-war/.

14. Barak Ravid, "Qatar to Suspend Gaza Payments to Pressure Israel over Annexation," *Axios*, June 23, 2020, https://www.axios.com/qatar-payments-gaza-hamas-israel-annexation-36a77f27-57ef-4c70-83a6-c1afef00b662.html; Simone Foxman, "Qatar Says Gaza Payents to Continue as Annexation Date Nears," *Bloomberg*, June 28, 2020, https://www.bloomberg.com/news/articles/2020-06-28/qatar-says-gaza-payments-to-continue-as-annexation-date-nears.
15. "Inking anti-terror deal with US, Qatar vows backing for Hamas-ruled Gaza," *Times of Israel.* July 11, 2017, https://www.timesofisrael.com/inking-anti-terror-deal-with-us-qatar-vows-backing-for-hamas-ruled-gaza/
16. "After unity deal, Qatar to fund new Palestinian government HQ in Gaza," *Times of Israel,* October 27, 2017, https://www.timesofisrael.com/after-unity-deal-qatar-to-fund-new-palestinian-govt-hq-in-gaza/.
17. Stuart Winer, "Qatar gave over $1.1 billion to Gaza Strip from 2012-18, ministers told," *Times of Israel*, February 11, 2019, https://www.timesofisrael.com/qatar-gave-over-1-1-billion-to-gaza-strip-over-six-years-report/.
18. Ibid.
19. Matthew Rosenberg, "Taliban Opening Qatar Office, and Maybe Door to Talks," *New York Times*, January 3, 2012.
20. Shirin Jaafari, "Why negotiations between the US and Taliban mostly take place in Qatar," *PRI,* September 18, 2019, https://www.pri.org/stories/2019-09-17/why-negotiations-between-us-and-taliban-mostly-take-place-qatar.
21. Amena Bakr and Jibran Ahmed, "Afghan talks agree on reopening Taliban political office," Reuters, May 3, 2015, https://www.reuters.com/article/us-qatar-afghanistan/afghan-talks-agree-on-reopening-taliban-political-office-idUSKBN0NO0M920150504.
22. "Taliban reaffirms authority of its Qatar 'political office," *Dawn* (Karachi), January 25, 2016, http://www.dawn.com/news/1235165.
23. David Blair and Richard Spencer, "How Qatar is Funding the Rise of Islamist Extremists," *Telegraph* (London), September 20, 2014, http://www.telegraph.co.uk/news/worldnews/middleeast/qatar/11110931/How-Qatar-is-funding-the-rise-of-Islamist-extremists.html.
24. U.S. Department of State, Bureau of Counter-Terrorism, *Country Reports on Terrorism 2014*, 2015.
25. "Funding al-Nusra through Ransom: Qatar and the Myth of the 'Humanitarian Principle,'" CATF Reports, December 10, 2015,

https://web.archive.org/web/20171011091003/http://stopterrorfinance.org/stories/510652383-funding-al-nusra-through-ransom-qatar-and-the-myth-of-humanitarian-principle

26. David Weinberg, "Qatar is still negligent on terror finance," *Long War Journal*, August 19, 2015, http://mobile.businessinsider.com/qatar-is-letting-2-notorious-terror-financiers-operate-in-the-open-2015-8.
27. Thomas Joscelyn, "Analysis: Al Nusrah Front rebrands itself as Jabhat Fath Al Sham," *Long War Journal*, July 28, 2016. http://www.longwarjournal.org/archives/2016/07/analysis-al-nusrah-front-rebrands-itself-as-jabhat-fath-al-sham.php|.
28. Mariam Karouny, "Insight- Syria's Nusra Front may leave Qaeda to form new entity," Reuters, March 4, 2015, https://uk.reuters.com/article/uk-mideast-crisis-nusra-insight-idUKKBN0M00G620150304
29. Mariam Karouny "U.S.-led strikes pressure al Qaeda's Syria group to join with Islamic State," Reuters, September 26, 2019, http://uk.reuters.com/article/uk-syria-crisis-nusra-insight-idUKKCN0HL11520140926.
30. Email from John Podesta to Hillary Clinton dated September 27, 2014, https://wikileaks.org/podesta-emails/emailid/3774.
31. Erika Solomon, "Outside help behind rebel advances in Aleppo," *Financial Times* (UK), August 8, 2016, https://www.ft.com/content/da076830-5d77-11e6-a72a-bd4bf1198c63.
32. Abdullah Bozkurt, "US Defense Intelligence Agency Says Turkey, Qatar Supported Al-Nusra Front," *Nordic Monitor*, December 10, 2019, https://www.nordicmonitor.com/2019/12/us-defense-intelligence-agency-says-turkey-qatar-supported-al-nusra-front/.
33. Rukmini Callimachi, "Paying Ransoms, Europe Bankrolls Qaeda Terror," *New York Times,* July 29, 2014, https://www.nytimes.com/2014/07/30/world/africa/ransoming-citizens-europe-becomes-al-qaedas-patron.html; See also Ellen Knickmeyer, "Al Qaeda-Linked Groups Increasingly Funded by Ransom," *Wall Street Journal*, July 29, 2014, http://online.wsj.com/articles/ ransom-fills-terrorist-coffers-1406637010.
34. Paul Wood, "'Billion dollar ransom:' Did Qatar pay record sum?" *BBC,* July 17, 2018, https://www.bbc.com/news/world-middle-east-44660369; "Qatar Reportedly Paid 'Billion Dollar Ransom' to Terrorists- Largest in History," *Ha'aretz* (Tel Aviv), July 19, 2018, https://www.haaretz.com/middle-east-news/did-qatar-pay-the-biggest-ransom-in-history-to-terrorist-groups-1.6290726
35. Steven Emerson, Testimony before the House of Representatives

Committee on Financial Services, Subcommittee on Oversight and Investigations, February 12, 2002, 8-9, https://www.investigative-project.org/documents/testimony/14.pdf.
36. Jonathan Schanzer, Testimony before the House of Representatives Committee on Foreign Affairs, Subcommittee on Middle East and North Africa, July 26, 2017, 8, https://docs.house.gov/meetings/FA/FA13/20170726/106329/HHRG-115-FA13-Wstate-SchanzerJ-20170726.pdf.
37. bid.; "43 new designations specifically address threats posed by Qatar linked and based Al Qaida Terrorism Support Networks," Emirates News Agency, June 9, 2017, http://wam.ae/en/details/1395302618259
38. Oxford Analytica, "The Advent of Terrorism in Qatar."
39. Michael Knights and Anna Solomon-Schwartz, "The Broader Threat from Sunni Islamists in the Gulf," Washington Institute for Near East Policy *PolicyWatch* no. 883, July 25, 2004, http://www.washingtoninstitute.org/templateC05.php?CID=1761.
40. Barry Rubin, ed., *Guide to Islamist Movements* (London: M.E. Sharpe, 2009), 308-310.
41. Ehud Rosen, *Mapping the Organizational Sources of the Global Delegitimization Campaign Against Israel In the UK* (Jerusalem, Israel: Jerusalem Center for Public Affairs, December 24, 2010), http://www.jcpa.org/text/Mapping_Delegitimization.pdf.
42. Oren Litwin, "Islamist Qatar Buys American Teachers," *National Review*, March 2, 2018, https://www.nationalreview.com/2018/03/qatar-educational-foundation-spreads-islamist-propaganda-to-us-schools/
43. "Sheikh Yusuf al-Qaradawi: Theologian of Terror," Anti-Defamation League, May 3, 2013.
44. Samuel Helfont, "Islam and Islamism Today: the Case of Yusuf al-Qaradawi," Foreign Policy Research Institute *E-Notes*, January 2010, http://www.fpri.org/article/2010/01/islam-and-islamism-today-the-case-of-yusuf-al-qaradawi/.
45. Ibid.
46. Ibidem.
47. Steinberg, "Qatar and the Arab Spring," 4.
48. U.S. Department of the Treasury, "PRESS RELEASE HP-1267: Treasury designates the Union of Good," November 12, 2008, http://www.treasury.gov/press-center/press-releases/Pages/hp1267.aspx.
49. Erdemir and Koduvayur, "Brothers in Arms: The Consolidation of

the Turkey-Qatar Axis."
50. "Syria conflict: Cleric Qaradawi urges Sunnis to join rebels," *BBC*, June 1, 2013, http://www.bbc.com/news/world-middle-east-22741588.
51. "UAE summons Qatar envoy over Qaradawi remarks," *Al-Jazeera* (Doha), February 2, 2014, https://www.aljazeera.com/news/middleeast/2014/02/uae-summons-qatar-envoy-over-qaradawi-remarks-20142215393855165.html.
52. "43 new designations specifically address threats posed by Qatar linked and based Al Qaida Terrorism Support Networks," Emirates News Agency (UAE), June 9, 2017, http://wam.ae/en/details/1395302618259.
53. Nadina Shalaq, "Qatar's European Strategy," *As-Safir* (Lebanon), December 26, 2012, as translated in *Al-Monitor*, December 27, 2012, http://www.al-monitor.com/pulse/politics/2012/12/qatari-investments-in-greece-highlight-soft-power-strategy.html.
54. Daniel Rickenbacher, "The Qatar Papers: How Qatar Charity inserts itself in European Muslim Affairs," *European Eye on Radicalization,* January 21, 2020, https://eeradicalization.com/the-qatar-papers-how-qatar-charity-inserts-itself-in-european-muslim-affairs/.
55. Oren Litwin, "Qatari Soft Power: Doha Miseducates America," Middle East Forum, January 30, 2019, https://www.meforum.org/57695/qatar-soft-power?utm_source=Middle+East+Forum&utm_campaign=32c704ca54-LITWIN_CAMPAIGN_2019_02_01_02_33&utm_medium=email&utm_term=0_086cfd423c-32c704ca54-33735413&goal=0_08 6cfd423c-32c704ca54-33735413; https://www.qf.org.qa/about#section-5; "Elite Universities Hide Information on Funding from Ultraconservative Nation of Qatar," Zachor Legal Institute, January 28, 2019, https://zachorlegal.org/2019/01/28/elite-universities-hide-information-funding-ultraconservative-nation-qatar/
56. Nick Anderson, "Texas university gets $76 million each year to operate in Qatar, contract says," *Washington Post*, March 8, 2016, https://www.washingtonpost.com/news/grade-point/wp/2016/03/08/texas-university-gets-76-million-each-year-to-operate-in-qatar-contract-says/?noredirect=on&utm_term=.80bd8f3d7095
57. Litwin, "Qatari Soft Power: Doha Miseducates America."
58. Litwin, "Islamist Qatar Buys American Teachers."
59. Abigail Hauslohner, "Rift Deepens Between Qatar and Its Powerful Arab Neighbors," *Washington Post*, March 8, 2014.
60. "Qatar-Gulf deal forces expulsion of Muslim Brotherhood leaders,"

Guardian (London), September 16, 2014, https://www.theguardian.com/world/2014/sep/16/qatar-orders-expulsion-exiled-egyptian-muslim-brotherhood-leaders.

61. "Egypt Blames Muslim Brotherhood in Qatar for Involvement in Cairo Cathedral Attack," *Egyptian Streets*, December 13, 2016, https://egyptianstreets.com/2016/12/13/egypt-blames-muslim-brotherhood-in-qatar-for-involvement-in-cairo-cathedral-attack/.
62. "Al Jazeera blocked by Saudi Arabia, Qatar blames fake news," *CNN*, May 24, 2017, http://money.cnn.com/2017/05/24/media/al-jazeera-blocked-saudi-arabia-uae/index.html.
63. "Qatar denounces 'unjustified' cut of Gulf ties," *Times of Israel,* June 5, 2017, http://www.timesofisrael.com/qatar-denounces-unjustified-cut-of-gulf-ties/
64. "Qatar given 10 days to meet 13 sweeping demands by Saudi Arabia," *Guardian* (London), https://www.theguardian.com/world/2017/jun/23/close-al-jazeera-saudi-arabia-issues-qatar-with-13-demands-to-end-blockade
65. Dion Nissenbaum and Stephen Kalin, "Trump Makes Fresh Attempt to Resolve Saudi, Qatar Feud," *Wall Street Journal*, June 3, 2020, https://www.wsj.com/articles/trump-makes-fresh-attempt-to-resolve-saudi-qatar-feud-11591201000.
66. Ibid.
67. Guido Steinberg, "Qatar and the Arab Spring: Support for Islamists and New Anti-Syrian Policy," SWP Stiftung Wissenschaft und Politik German Institute for International and Security Affairs, February 2012, 4.
68. Terry McDermott, Josh Meyer and Patrick J. McDonnell, "The Plots and Designs of Al Qaeda's Engineer," *Los Angeles Times*, December 22, 2002, http://articles.latimes.com/2002/dec/22/world/fg-ksm22.
69. Brian Ross and David Scott, "Qatari Royal Family Linked to Al Qaeda," *ABC News*, February 7, 2003.
70. Ibid.
71. U.S. Department of the Treasury, "Press Release: Treasury Designates Al-Qa'ida Supporters in Qatar and Yemen," December 18, 2013, https://www.treasury.gov/press-center/press-releases/pages/jl2249.aspx.
72. Robert Mendick, "Al-Qaeda Terror Financier Worked for Qatari Government," *Telegraph* (London), October 12, 2014, http://www.telegraph.co.uk/news/11156327/Al-Qaeda-terror-financier-worked-for-Qatari-government.html.

73. David Andrew Weinberg, *Qatar and Terror Finance – Part I: Negligence* (FDD Press, December 2014), https://s3.us-east-2.amazonaws.com/defenddemocracy/uploads/publications/Qatar_Part_I.pdf.
74. "Senior Hamas leader spotted in Beirut for first time since Qatar expulsion," *Times of Israel*, August 2, 2017, https://www.timesofisrael.com/senior-hamas-leader-spotted-in-beirut-for-first-time-since-qatar-expulsion/
75. "U.S., Qatar agree to further curbs on terrorist financing," Reuters, October 30, 2017, https://www.reuters.com/article/us-qatar-usa-security/u-s-qatar-agree-to-further-curbs-on-terrorist-financing-idUSKBN1CZ2I7.
76. Damien McElroy, "Qatar's top terror suspect hosts prime minister at wedding," *The National*, April 17, 2018, https://www.thenational.ae/world/mena/qatar-s-top-terror-suspect-hosts-prime-minister-at-wedding-1.722398.
77. See "Complaint" in *Matthew Schrier v. Qatar Islamic Bank*, U.S. District Court, Southern District of Florida, January 2020, https://www.courthousenews.com/wp-content/uploads/2020/01/qatar-islamic-bank-1.pdf
78. "Lawsuit: Qatar Secretly Gave Funding for Terror Attacks That Killed Americans, Israelis," *JNS*, June 15, 2020, https://www.algemeiner.com/2020/06/15/lawsuit-qatar-secretly-gave-funding-for-terror-attacks-that-killed-americans-israelis/.
79. "Qatar: Wahhabi Islam and the Gulf," country-data.com, n.d., http://www.country-data.com/cgi-bin/query/r-11031.html.
80. "Qatar: Governance, Security, and U.S. Policy," Congressional Research Service, February 11, 2019. https://fas.org/sgp/crs/mideast/R44533.pdf
81. "Qatar: Political Forces," *The Economist*, March 11, 2009, http://www.economist.com/node/13216406.
82. U.S. Department of State, Bureau of Democracy, Human Rights and Labor, *International Religious Freedom Report 2010*, Washington, DC: U.S. Department of State, November 17, 2010, http://www.state.gov/g/drl/rls/irf/2010/index.htm.
83. "Qatari Backing for Extremist Preachers and Anti-Semitic Incitement," Anti-Defamation League, April 10, 2018, https://www.adl.org/blog/qatari-backing-for-extremist-preachers-and-anti-semitic-incitement; David Andrew Weinberg, "Qatari Government Promotes Textbook Teaching that Jews Seek World Domination," Anti-Defamation League, February 7, 2019, https://

www.adl.org/blog/qatari-government-promotes-textbook-teaching-that-jews-seek-world-domination; "Review Of Qatari Islamic Education School Textbooks—Part I: Encouraging Jihad and Martyrdom," Middle East Media Research Institute, February 6, 2019, https://www.memri.org/reports/review-qatari-islamic-education-school-textbooks-first-half-2018-2019-school-year

84. U.S. Department of State, Bureau of Near Eastern Affairs, "Background Note: Qatar," September 22, 2010.
85. U.S. Department of State, *International Religious Freedom Report 2010.*
86. David Roberts, "Qatar and the Muslim Brotherhood: Pragmatism or Preference?" *Middle East Policy* XXI, no. 3, Fall 2014, https://www.mepc.org/qatar-and-muslim-brotherhood-pragmatism-or-preference
87. "La social-mappa del sostegno all'ISIS nel mondo arabo: più alto in Europa (ma non in Italia) che in Medio Oriente," *Voices from the Blogs*, November 29, 2014, https://sentimeter.corriere.it/2014/11/28/la-social-mappa-del-sostegno-allisis-nel-mondo-arabo-in-europa-piu-alto-che-in-medio-oriente/ 9
88. U.S. Department of State, "Background Note: Qatar."
89. "Qatar: Political Forces."
90. U.S. Department of State, *International Religious Freedom Report 2010*, https://www.state.gov/j/drl/rls/irf/2010/148841.htm.
91. U.S. Department of State, *International Religious Freedom Report 2017*, https://www.state.gov/documents/organization/281246.pdf
92. U.S. Department of the Treasury Press Center, "Remarks of Under Secretary for Terrorism and Financial Intelligence David Cohen before the Center for a New American Security on 'Confronting New Threats in Terrorist Financing,'" March 4, 2014, https://www.treasury.gov/press-center/press-releases/Pages/jl2308.aspx; See also Taimur Khan, "US names two Qatari nationals as financiers of terrorism," *The National*, August 6, 2015, http://www.thenational.ae/world/americas/us-names-two-qatari-nationals-as-financiers-of-terrorism.
93. "Qatar: Governance, Security, and U.S. Policy," Congressional Research Service, February 11, 2019, https://fas.org/sgp/crs/mideast/R44533.pdf
94. "Qatar to hold Shura Council elections for first time in country's history," *The New Arab*, November 14, 2017, https://www.alaraby.co.uk/english/news/2017/11/14/qatar-to-hold-first-elections-for-shura-council

95. U.S. Department of State, "Background Note: Qatar."
96. Azhar Unwala, "The young emir: Emir Tamim and Qatar's future," *Global Risk Insights*, September 18, 2016, http://globalriskinsights.com/2016/09/emir-tamim-and-qatars-future.
97. "Qatar orders aid to private sector as sanctions hurt economy," Reuters, October 7, 2017, https://www.reuters.com/article/us-gulf-qatar-economy/qatar-orders-aid-to-private-sector-as-sanctions-hurt-economy-idUSKBN1CC0OZ
98. Jennifer Lambert, "Qatari Law Will Test Media Freedom," Carnegie Endowment for International Peace *Arab Reform Bulletin*, December 1, 2010, http://carnegieendowment.org/sada/?fa=42049.
99. Kristen Gillespie, "The New Face of Al Jazeera," *The Nation*, November 9, 2007.
100. "Arab Media Review: Anti-Semitism and Other Trends," *Anti-Defamation League*, July-December 2010, https://web.archive.org/web/20120119200951/http://www.adl.org/Anti_semitism/arab/arab-media-review-July-December2010.pdf.
101. Jonathan Schanzer and Varsha Koduvayur, "Qatar's Soft Power Experiment," in Ilan Berman, ed., *Digital Dictators: Media, Authoritarianism, and America's New Challenge* (Lanham, MD: Rowman & Littlefield, 2018)
102. Kristen Gillespie, "The New Face of Al Jazeera," *The Nation*, November 9, 2007; Oren Kessler, "The Two Faces of Al Jazeera," *Middle East Quarterly,* Winter 2012, 47-56, http://www.meforum.org/3147/al-jazeera ; Sultan Sooud Al Qassemi, "Qatar's Brotherhood Ties Alienate Fellow Gulf States," *Al-Monitor,* January 23, 2013, http://www.al-monitor.com/pulse/originals/2013/01/qatar-muslim-brotherhood.html ; see also http://foreignpolicy.com/2013/07/12/al-jazeeras-awful-week/.
103. Schanzer and Koduvayur, "Qatar's Soft Power Experiment."
104. Sultan Sooud Al Qassemi, "Morsi's Win Is Al Jazeera's Loss," *Al-Monitor*, July 1, 2012, http://www.al-monitor.com/pulse/originals/2012/al-monitor/morsys-win-is-al-jazeeras-loss.html#ixzz2I3awUthS; Adel Iskandar, co-author of *Al-Jazeera: The Story Of The Network That Is Rattling Governments And Redefining Modern Journalism*, quoted in "Why Arab states want to shut down Al-Jazeera," *CBC Radio,* July 6, 2017, https://www.cbc.ca/radio/thecurrent/the-current-for-july-6-2017-1.4191665/why-arab-states-want-to-shut-down-al-jazeera-1.4191668.
105. Mohammad Hisham Abeih, "Qatar on Defense over Meddling in Egypt," *As-Safir* (Lebanon), January 10, 2013, as translated in

Al-Monitor, January 10, 2013, http://www.al-monitor.com/pulse/politics/2013/01/qatars-media-and-political-influence-over-egypt.html#ixzz2I36FW8C4.

106. Zvi Bar'el, "Is Al Jazeera Trying to Bring Down the Palestinian Authority?" *Ha'aretz* (Tel Aviv), February 2, 2011, http://www.haaretz.com/print-edition/features/is-al-jazeera-trying-to-bring-down-the-palestinian-authority-1.340716.
107. "Qatar Uses Al-Jazeera as Bargaining Chip: WikiLeaks," *Economic Times* (India), December 6, 2010, http://economictimes.indiatimes.com/tech/internet/qatar-uses-al-jazeera-as-bargaining-chip-wikileaks/articleshow/7051690.cms.
108. U.S. Department of State, "Background Note: Qatar."
109. Bar'el, "Is Al Jazeera Trying to Bring Down the Palestinian Authority?"
110. Hassan Hassan, "Qatar Won the Blockade," *Foreign Policy,* June 4, 2018, https://foreignpolicy.com/2018/06/04/qatar-won-the-saudi-blockade/.
111. Ephrem Kossaify, "Pressure grows for Al Jazeera to register as foreign agent in US," *Arab News*, April 6, 2020, https://www.arabnews.com/node/1654406/media
112. United States House of Representatives, Office of Representative Josh Gottheimer, "Gottheimer, Zeldin, Cruz, Colleagues Demand DOJ Investigation Into Qatar's Al Jazeera Network." News release, March 6, 2018, https://gottheimer.house.gov/news/documentsingle.aspx?DocumentID=611.
113. United States Senate, Office of Senator Tom Cotton, "Lawmakers Seek FARA Evaluation of Qatari-owned Al Jazeera." June 19, 2019, https://www.cotton.senate.gov/?p=press_release&id=1161
114. Schanzer and Koduvayur, "Qatar's Soft Power Experiment."
115. Sam Bridge, "Sky News Arabia adds to top-level appointments with new CEO," *Arabian Business*, July 24, 2018, https://www.arabianbusiness.com/media/401412-sky-news-arabia-adds-to-top-level-appointment-with-new-ceo; Rory Jones, Benoit Faucon and Keach Hagey, "Saudi Arabia Sought Vice's Help to Build a Media Empire," *Wall Street Journal*, February 8, 2019, https://www.wsj.com/articles/saudi-arabia-sought-vices-help-to-build-a-media-empire-11549621800
116. "Online trolls and fake accounts poison Arab social media," *BBC Monitoring,* August 31, 2018, https://www.bbc.com/news/technology-45372272

23 Saudi Arabia

Quick Facts

Population: 34,173,498 (July 2020 est.)
Area: 2,149,690 sq km
Ethnic Groups: Arab 90%, Afro-Asian 10%
Religions: Muslim (official; citizens are 85-90% Sunni and 10-15% Shia), other (includes Eastern Orthodox, Protestant, Roman Catholic, Jewish, Hindu, Buddhist, and Sikh) (2012 est.)
Government Type: Absolute Monarchy
GDP (official exchange rate): $686.7 billion (2017 est.)

Map and Quick Facts courtesy of the CIA World Factbook (Last Updated May 2020)

Introduction

Saudi Arabia has exported Wahhabism, *its puritanical creed of Islam, for decades. Born in the 18th century,* Wahhabism *was mostly confined to the Arabian Peninsula until the 1960s, when Saudi Arabia politicized the ideology to reject both pan-Arabism and communism in the Middle East. This behavior became more frequent during the oil boom of the 1970s.*

However, domestic politics in Saudi Arabia have changed significantly of late, including the official approach to extreme interpretations of Islam. When King Abdullah bin Abdulaziz Al Saud died in 2015, his younger brother Salman bin Abdulaziz Al Saud ascended the throne. Controversially, King Salman named his nephew, Mohammed bin Nayef, Crown Prince of Saudi Arabia and his own son, Mohammed bin Salman (commonly known as MbS), as Deputy Crown Prince. However, a subsequent power struggle between bin Nayef and MbS led to Nayef's eventual (forced) abdication.[1] *MbS's subsequent anti-corruption and modernization efforts have attracted international attention, but doubts remain regarding their extent and nature, as well as whether the Kingdom has truly ended its long-standing practice of exporting* Wahhabism *around the world.*

Islamist Activity

The dominant interpretation of Islam in Saudi Arabia is *Wahhabism*, a "puritanical form of Sunni Islam" that "seeks to purify Islam of any innovations or practices that deviate" from the teaching of the Prophet Muhammad.[2] It has roots in the Najd region of Saudi Arabia, and was named for Muhammad ibn Abd al-Wahhab, an eighteenth-century scholar of Islam.[3] Roughly 85-90% of Saudi citizens are Sunni; the other 10-15% belong to the country's Shi'a minority.[4] *Wahhabism* opposes several popular Islamic practices that Abdel Wahhab considered "idolatrous," including the veneration of saints, most Shi'ite traditions, some Sufi practices, and the celebration of the Prophet's birthday.[5]

Islamism in Saudi Arabia is characterized by competing intellectual traditions which, while all conservative, hold significantly different, sometimes evolving ideas about the relationship between Islam and society.

The Rejectionists

The "rejectionists" are a pious, lower-class Islamic intellectual movement that emerged in the mid 20th century and categorically rejects the legitimacy of the state and its institutions.[6] Rejectionists also oppose any role or voice for themselves in national political discourse, choosing to withdraw from society, repudiating all schools of *fiqh* (Islamic jurisprudence), and relying solely on the unmediated sayings of the Prophet Muhammad, or *hadith*. They live in isolated, orthodox communities where they educate their children and pursue their distinctive lifestyle. However, they are not monolithic, and some have formed their own socio-political protest movements in spite of the trend's original doctrine.

One of these movements is the al-Jama'a al-Salafiyya al-Muhtasiba (JSM), which emerged in the 1970s and was inspired by the Syrian religious scholar Nasr al-Din al-Albani.[7] In 1979, the JSM, led by Juhayman al-Utaybi, orchestrated an armed takeover of the Grand Mosque in Mecca. The Saudi government was initially reluctant to use force in one of Islam's holiest sites but eventually raided the Mosque and ended the siege. After the Grand Mosque incident, the remaining members of JSM fled to Kuwait, Yemen, and the northern Saudi desert. However, Juhayman's ideas remained influential. The JSM's views allegedly influenced three men involved in the 1995 bombing in Riyadh, as well as "senior militants" who were part of al-Qaeda's 2003 campaign against the kingdom.[8]

The Sahwa

Another intellectual tradition that became prominent in the 1950s and 1960s is the *Sahwa* (Awakened), a pragmatic, political, elitist movement. *Sahwa* clerics trace their roots back to the rise of the Muslim Brotherhood, whose members were well educated and established in Saudi Arabia's new education and media sectors. As a result, the *Sahwa* clerics synthesized Salafi-*Wahhabbi* theological teachings with the Brotherhood's political activism.[9] However, the *Sahwa* is an extremely diverse faction that includes religious scholars, scientists, doctors, and academics.

Sahwa members commonly fall into two main camps: those who follow Hassan al-Banna, the founder of the Brotherhood, and those who follow Sayyid Qutb, al-Banna's more extreme ideological successor. Their ability to address issues traditionally outside the purview of the official Saudi religious establishment – like politics – made the *Sahwa* more appealing.[10]

For a number of years, the *Sahwa* rarely criticized the Saudi regime.[11] That began to change in early 2011, however, when several reform-focused petitions were signed by prominent *Sahwa* clerics.[12] When the *Sahwa* community condemned Saudi government support for the deposition of then-Egyptian President Mohammed Morsi, the Saudi government decreed that supporting formally categorized extremist or terrorist organizations is punishable by imprisonment.[13] Al-Odah and fellow Saudi cleric Aidh al-Qarni were arrested in September 2017 after backing reconciliation between Qatar and the other Gulf states.[14] Another *Sahwa* scholar, Safar al-Hawali, was arrested in 2018 for writing literature that criticized the Saudi royal family for its connections to Israel.[15]

The jihadists

A *jihadist* trend embodied by the rise of Osama bin Laden's al-Qaeda network has long existed in Saudi society. However, it has faced considerable challenges in recent years as the Islamic State

(IS) became more prominent, both regionally and globally.

From 1999 through 2001, conflicts in the Muslim world and a powerful Saudi recruiting network enabled bin Laden to attract people to al-Qaeda's Afghan-based training camps. Al-Qaeda's operations, in turn, were well-funded by Saudi individuals and organizations. The 9/11 Commission reported that bin Laden created a network of charities that allowed Saudi and Gulf financiers to fund al-Qaeda and fighting in Afghanistan.[16]

Two independent cells formed after Saudi al-Qaeda members returned to the country in early 2002. These operatives began stockpiling weapons, renting safe houses, setting up training camps, and recruiting other "Afghan Arabs."[17] The cells consisted principally of Saudis as well as a small percentage of foreign nationals. The majority of al-Qaeda members were not from typically impoverished or religiously conservative regions; rather, the overwhelming majority were urbanites from Riyadh with experience in Afghanistan.[18]

The Saudi government's aggressive counterterrorism efforts eventually forced al-Qaeda's local branch to relocate to Yemen. In January 2009, the Saudi and Yemeni branches of al-Qaeda merged to become al-Qaeda in the Arabian Peninsula (AQAP). A number of Saudis assumed leadership positions in that franchise.[19] Later that year, the organization nearly assassinated then-Saudi Deputy Interior Minister Prince Muhammad bin Nayef at his home in Jeddah.[20] Then, only months later, AQAP attempted to blow up a flight traveling from Yemen to Detroit on Christmas day.[21]

In 2014, after AQAP attacked a remote Saudi-Yemeni border checkpoint, the State Department stated that the organization has "continued… to inspire sympathizers to support, finance, or engage in conflicts outside of Saudi Arabia and encouraged individual acts of terrorism within the Kingdom."[22] Since then, the Saudi government has increasingly prevented Saudis from traveling abroad to support extremist groups like al-Qaeda and IS. Al-Qaeda leader Ayman al Zawahiri condemned the Saudi government in May 2016 after it executed a number of people with suspected ties to al-Qaeda.[23]

In August 2018, an Associated Press investigation revealed that the Saudi-led coalition in Yemen had negotiated a series of agreements with al-Qaeda militants. These deals involved paying some al-Qaeda militants to leave cities quietly, allowing al-Qaeda militants to leave cities with their equipment and assets, and recruiting militants to join the Saudi-led coalition itself.[24] In early 2019, a CNN investigation revealed that U.S.-made arms had been transferred to al-Qaeda linked fighters in Yemen, sometimes ending up in the hands of Iran-backed Houthi rebels.[25]

By his own account, current Saudi Crown Prince Mohammed Bin Salman, or MbS, remains deeply concerned with Sunni *jihadists*. During an April 2018 visit to the United States, MbS referred to Turkey, Iran, and radical Islamist groups as the "triangle of evil."[26] Subsequently, in March 2019 Saudi Arabia revoked the citizenship of bin Laden's heir and ostensible successor, Hamza.[27] (Hamza has since been determined to have been killed in Afghanistan or Pakistan sometime during the first two years of the Trump administration.[28])

The Shi'a

Saudi Shi'a have been marginalized and branded as *kuffar* (unbelievers) since the time of Muhammad ibn Abd al-Wahhab.[29] While Shi'a Islamists have never been as organized as the *Sahwa*, or even the *jihadists* in Saudi Arabia, political expressions of Shi'a Islam historically play a significant role in Saudi society. After the 1979 Islamic Revolution in Iran, *Radio Tehran's* Arabic channel broadcasted anti-Saudi regime propaganda to the Shi'a population, sparking a riot in Qatif in which citizens attacked the town's central market.[30] Since that time, the Saudi government has been extremely wary of Iran's influence in Saudi domestic affairs.

For a brief period, the Arab Spring rekindled opposition from Saudi Arabia's Shi'a population. Shortly after the outbreak of protests in Tunisia in December 2011, Saudi Shi'a Islamists organized through social media platforms, issuing petitions for political and social reforms. Violent protests erupted in July 2012 in the Eastern Province—home to not only most of the Shi'a population but also much of the country's oil—after security forces shot and arrested popular Shi'ite cleric Nimr al-Nimr for instigating "sedition."[31] Anger within the Shi'a population spread after Nimr's arrest and was exacerbated when Saudi authorities fatally shot two men during the demonstrations.[32] The protests in the Eastern Province escalated in October 2012, when tens of thousands of angry mourners carried the bodies of three young Shi'a men, slain by Saudi security forces, through the streets of Awwamiya while chanting "Death to al-Saud."[33] (In 2017, Saudi authorities destroyed Awwamiya's old quarter to quell dissent in the restive region. As of January 2019, the government had spent upwards of $200 million to rebuild destroyed parts of the town, with plans to broaden investments in the Qatif region as a means to stamp out violence.[34])

Al-Nimr was put on trial in March 2013 for "sowing discord" and "undermining national unity."[35] On October 24, when al-Nimr was sentenced to death along with his nephew, protests broke out.[36] On January 2, 2016, al-Nimr was executed along with 46 other people that the Saudi government labeled as terrorists.[37] Protests erupted in the Eastern Province, in Bahrain, and across the Middle East.[38] Iranian activists attacked and set fire to the Saudi Embassy in Tehran and the consulate in Mashhad, rupturing diplomatic ties between the two countries.[39] Saudi Shi'a have since made some gains – anti-Shi'a rhetoric has been excised from school textbooks, for example – and violence in the Eastern Province has died down.[40] Overall, however, the reason for this relative quiet, in the words of one Saudi watcher, is that "frustration and fatigue" have worn down the region's Shi'a and led to less unrest.[41]

Islamism and Society

Islamist opposition or reformist movements to the House of Saud have generally failed to garner significant support. This is largely due to the government's use of oil wealth to provide a robust welfare state for its citizens.[42] Furthermore, the Saud family has promoted *Wahhabism* as part of the basis of its power. Since the rise of the Islamic State and MbS's efforts to modernize the Saudi economy, there has been a renewed internal debate over the future of *Wahhabism*. Cole Bunzel of the Carnegie Endowment for International Peace has argued that there is a subtly emerging "correctionist" strain that is now more tolerated by the Saudi religious establishment.[43]

Information technologies, meanwhile, have influenced how Sahwa clerics engage with society, expanding their influence beyond the traditional Salafi-*Wahhabbi* international network. In 2011,

Forbes Middle East ranked Salman al-Odah fourth on its list of top 100 "Twitterati"; today, al-Odah has 11 million followers on Twitter, and almost 7 million on Facebook.[44] Fellow Saudi clerics Muhammad al-Arife and Aidh al-Qarni have been even more successful than al-Odah on social media. Al-Arefe has 20 million Twitter followers—three times as many as King Salman's own Twitter account.[45] Likewise, al-Qarni has 14.5 million.[46] After delivering a lecture in the Philippines in March 2016, al-Qarni was shot and injured in the shoulder. His notoriety, however, only increased as a result.[47]

These clerics can significantly influence Saudi public opinion and attitudes toward the West. On the eve of the 2004 American siege of Fallujah, 26 prominent clerics signed an "Open Sermon to the Militant Iraqi People" that legitimized joining the Iraqi insurgency as part of a "defense jihad" against the "aggressor" coalition.[48] Shortly thereafter, the number of Saudis who went to Iraq to fight against Western forces peaked.[49] In June 2012, a number of prominent clerics organized a fundraising campaign for Syrian rebels fighting against President Bashar al-Assad's regime. One of the organizations facilitating donations was the Revival of Islamic Heritage Society of Kuwait, a charity previously designated as a terrorist entity by the United States and UN for arming and financing al-Qaeda.[50] In 2015, 53 clerics and academics issued a call for "all those who are able, and outside of Saudi Arabia, to answer the calls of jihad" and fight against Russian forces and the Syrian government in Syria." This was in spite of the government's decree forbidding Saudis from fighting against ISIS outside Saudi Arabia.[51]

Several influential clerics have been arrested or newly restricted as part of MbS' crackdown on dissent. As already referenced, al-Odah and al-Qarni were arrested in 2017. A year later, Saudi Arabia's public prosecutor announced that he is seeking the death penalty for al-Odah.[52] Authorities arrested Safar al-Hawali in July 2018 after he published a book criticizing the royal family.[53] A Saudi Twitter account posted that authorities have stopped Mohammed al-Arefe – best known for his lecture series on how a man should properly beat his wife – from conducting dawa (outreach) activities and from preaching in mosques.[54] However, it is worth noting that al-Arefe remains at large. Thus, despite statements from MbS on returning to moderate Islam, Saudi authorities appear to lack a tangible strategy to achieve this aim.

Cracking down on terror finance remains a lingering problem for the Saudi state. The 9/11 Commission determined that there was no evidence that the Saudi government as an institution, or the Saudi leadership as individuals, provided support to al-Qaeda. However, the Commission noted that al-Qaeda raised money directly from individuals and through "charities with significant government sponsorship" in Saudi Arabia.[55] In 2007, then-Undersecretary of the Treasury for Terrorism and Financial Intelligence Stuart Levey said that, "If I could somehow snap my fingers and cut off funding from one country, it would be Saudi Arabia."[56] Implicating wealthy Saudis in terrorist financing cases with exact dollar amounts has been difficult largely because of cash transactions and anonymous donations.

A leaked 2008 cable from the U.S. State Department Consulate in Lahore showcases how financiers are able to conduct their operations. The cable alleged that financiers in Saudi Arabia and the UAE were sending nearly $100 million annually to Deobandi and Ahl-i-Hadith clerics in southern Punjab. In turn, those clerics were targeting families with multiple children and severe financial difficulties for recruitment under the initial pretense of charity. Next, a Deobandi or Ahl-i-Hadith maulana would offer to educate the children in his school and "find them employment in the service of Islam." During the education phase, the clerics would indoctrinate the children and assess their inclination "to engage in violence and acceptance of jihadi culture." Parents then received cash payments of $6,500 for each son chosen for "martyrdom" operations.[57]

Partially in response to the Justice Against Sponsors of Terrorism Act (JASTA) – U.S. legislation that narrows the abilities of 9/11 victims' families to make civil claims against a foreign state – Saudi Arabia aggressively pursued the issue of illicit financing throughout 2016. That summer, the former assistant secretary for terrorist financing at the U.S. Department of Treasury, Daniel Glaser, testified before Congress that Saudi Arabia had emerged as a "regional leader in targeted [terrorism sanctions] designations."[58] A spokesperson for Saudi Arabia's Ministry of the Interior claimed that the country had prosecuted more than 240 suspects and froze or investigated over 117 internal accounts.[59]

These Saudi government actions were also taken in response to the growing regional threat posed by IS. According to polling data taken in 2015, about 5% of Saudi Arabia's population—or over half a million people—support the Islamic State.[60] A cache of IS documents dated 2013-2014, which were leaked in 2016, revealed that 759 Saudis had joined the terror group as foreign fighters.[61] In July 2016, three suicide bombing attacks bearing the Islamic State hallmarks were conducted across Saudi Arabia; former CIA Director John Brennan described the event as "unprecedented."[62]

Islamism and the State

Islamism has always been a core tenet of the Saudi state. The Saudi king is customarily also known as the "Custodian of the Two Holy Mosques," a title introduced by King Faisal that denotes the monarchy's oversight of Mecca and Medina.[63] While an absolute monarchy, the government derives its legitimacy from sharia and from the 1992 Basic Law, which "sets out the system of governance, rights of citizens, and powers and duties of the government."[64] The Basic Law also states that the "Qur'an and the Traditions (Sunna) of the Prophet Muhammad serve as the country's constitution."

Saudi Arabia has long supported Islamic activities abroad, beginning under King Faisal's reign. To bolster his legitimacy and to counter the threat of secular governance sweeping the Middle East, Faisal established a policy of supporting Islamic institutions abroad in the 1960s. In 1962, he created the Muslim World League (MWL) to spread *Wahhabbi* ideology abroad. The Saudis also helped develop other religious organizations, including the World Assembly of Muslim Youth (WAMY), the Al Haramain Foundation, and the International Islamic Relief Organization (IIRO), among others.

In the face of dramatic political events in 1979 – including the seizure of the Grand Mosque in Saudi Arabia by Islamic radicals, the overthrow of the Iranian monarchy by the Ayatollah Ruhollah Khomeini's Islamic Revolution, the targeting of Saudi Arabia's Eastern Province by Shi'a protestors, and the invasion of Afghanistan by the Soviet Union – the House of Saud took drastic measures to assert its leadership in the Islamic world and to appease extremists at home. It did so by further weaponizing *Wahhabism* and ramping up its exportation as a foreign policy tool.[65] The policy included a distinct internal component; exporting *Wahhabism* abroad placated the Kingdom's domestic extremists, thereby neutralizing the threat they posed to the regime.[66]

From 1973-2002, the Saudi government donated more than $80 billion to Islamic institutions and other activities in the non-Muslim world alone, contributing to some 1,500 mosques, 150 Islamic centers, 202 Muslim colleges, and 2,000 Islamic schools.[67] The Saudis donate generous sums to American universities and elite institutions, preempting criticism from academia and hindering research on the consequences of the exportation of *Wahhabism*.[68] However, since 9/11, Islamic institutions in the U.S. have faced increasing scrutiny, and several organizations and institutions (including the MWL, WAMY, the Al Haramain Foundation, the SAAR Foundation, the International Institute of Islamic Thought, and the School of Islamic and Social Sciences) have been raided, shut down, or had their assets frozen because of suspected links to terrorism in the aftermath of the terrorist attacks on New York and Washington.[69]

Since late 2010, the Saudi government has sought to preempt demands for national reforms. King Abdullah rushed to avert a crisis of power by issuing a $130 billion aid package, creating a Facebook page for the population to air their grievances, and increasing the salaries of government workers. This aid package funded 60,000 jobs at the Ministry of the Interior, 500,000 new houses, and a public sector minimum wage higher than the minimum wage in the private sector, amongst other projects.[70] The government also injected $10.7 billion into its development fund, which offers Saudis interest-free loans to build homes, marry, and start small businesses. An additional $4 billion was earmarked for the healthcare sector.[71]

The Saudi government also sought help from pro-state clergy. On March 6, 2011, the country's highest religious body, the Council of Senior Ulema, called on "everybody to exert every effort to increase solidarity, promote unity and warn against all causes giving rise to the opposite."[72] It further warned Saudis about "deviant intellectual and partisan [Shi'a] tendencies" that could threaten Saudi stability.[73] Other clerics threatened potential protesters with violence. Saad al-Buraik, a member of the government's counseling program for re-educating extremists, called for "smashing the skulls of those who organize demonstrations or take part in them."[74]

When King Salman bin Abdulaziz rose to power in early 2015, he immediately asserted his authority. He released thousands of prisoners, increased public sector salaries, dismissed two influential officials who had opposed *Wahhabbi* clerics, and, in a nod to ultraconservative clerics, fired the Kingdom's only female Cabinet member. He also stripped the religious police of their ability to arrest. King Salman upset the traditional succession order, divesting his brother Muqrin bin Salman from the post of crown prince and filling that position with his nephew in 2015 and MbS (his son) in 2017.[75] Also in 2017, the king lifted a national ban that prevented women from driving, which came into effect in the summer of 2018.[76]

King Salman's approach to geopolitical changes has been both ideological and practical. Even as he has relied on the traditional cleric establishment to maintain legitimacy, he and MbS have also moved to restructure the Saudi economy to meet the shifting global energy landscape driven by U.S. oil independence.[77] The Saudi government has recently pursued a more aggressive foreign policy defined by its opposition to the pro-Iranian Assad regime in Syria and to Brotherhood-aligned governments in Turkey and Qatar, as well as its military campaign in Yemen.[78]

During his visit to the United States in April 2018, MbS professed previously unheard-of reformist opinions. In a landmark interview with Jeffrey Goldberg of The Atlantic, MbS stated that "the Palestinians and the Israelis have the right to have their own land."[79] MbS' statement was unprecedented for a Saudi official, given that the kingdom does not recognize Israel. MbS likewise expressed a desire to modernize the Saudi economy while preserving its culture and remaining anxious about the "triangle of evil" (Iran, the Muslim Brotherhood, and Sunni terrorist groups). However, some of his reformist zeal – at least as regards a change in Saudi Arabia's traditionally intolerant interpretation of Islam – was called into question. When asked by Goldberg about the pernicious influence of *Wahhabbi* ideology, MbS rejected the premise entirely, saying that he wasn't familiar with the concept at all. "No one can define [*Wahhabism*]," he said. "There is no [*Wahhabism*]. We don't believe we have [*Wahhabism*]. We believe we have, in Saudi Arabia, Sunni and Shiite…"[80]

Other public statements from MbS suggest that he hopes to return Saudi Arabia to a "moderate Islam." According to the Crown Prince, "what happened in the last 30 years is not Saudi Arabia… Now is the time to get rid of it."[81]

Other Saudi officials have noted the young royal's change in tone and supported it with their own. Sheikh Mohammad al-Issa, the leader of MWL, has publicly supported MbS.[82] Twice now, al-Issa has issued public letters on Holocaust Remembrance Day expressing his "great sympathy with the victims of the Holocaust" and noting that "Muslims around the world have a responsibility to learn" the Holocaust's lessons.[83] Al Issa's remarks are a historical milestone given the history of anti-Semitism from kingdom officials; King Faisal once lauded the cruel hoax known as the Protocols of the Elders of Zion as a fact.[84]

This change in direction has extended to the Kingdom's economic strategy as well. In April 2016, MbS announced "Vision 2030," an energy independence plan that seeks to boost women's participation in the workforce, trim the unemployment rate, privatize some state-owned assets, and diversify state assets. However, according to The Economist, the modest workforce participation goals – increasing the number of women with jobs from 22% to 30 % over 15 years – suggests resistance from the *Wahhabbi* clerical establishment.[85]

Vision 2030's successes so far have been mixed. On the one hand, Saudi Arabia has begun partially privatizing some state assets, deepened its capital markets, enacted pro-business reforms including passing a landmark bankruptcy law, and allowed some foreign ownership in certain sectors. As a result of its reforms, the Saudi stock exchange has been upgraded to emerging-markets status by both the MSCI and FTSE Russell indices, a move which could net the kingdom $10 billion of inflows.[86] In addition, societal reforms are implicit in Vision 2030. In addition to granting women the right to drive, Saudi Arabia passed a sexual harassment law in 2018, and in February 2019 announced it would review its controversial guardianship system.[87]

But these positive moves have been marred by a series of unforced errors under MbS' watch, culminating in the horrific murder of opposition journalist Jamal Khashoggi in October 2018. Even before that, however, in 2017, Saudi Arabia had begun a far-reaching crackdown on clerics, powerful businessmen, royals, and rights activists, which still continues today. In November 2017, the kingdom launched a widespread purge on the grounds of countering corruption. Saudi police arrested over 200 people, many of them wealthy and influential, and placed them in the Ritz-Carlton Hotel in Riyadh. Some reports suggest that the subsequent interrogations of the detainees included significant physical abuse.[88] Detainees had to pay a large sum of money and sign a non-disclosure agreement in order to leave.[89] The Saudi government claimed to have regained over $100 billion in the operation.[90] While MbS may have claimed anti-corruption as the motivation for the roundup, it was likely intended to remove potential political rivals. Among those arrested was Prince Miteb bin Abdullah, the head of the national guard. This left MbS in command of all three of branches of the Saudi military.[91] As of March 2019, 64 people (including an American citizen) were still detained.[92]

Shortly before removing the ban on women driving, the kingdom began detaining several rights activists. The Saudi public prosecutor had announced that investigations into the detained activists—whom Saudi media frequently portrayed as foreign agents, and many of whom had been tortured in Saudi prisons—had concluded, and that nine activists, unnamed, would stand trial.[93]

Saudi Arabia has often been critiqued for its human rights record and its state executions. Saudi Arabia executed at least 540 people between 2014 and 2017, according to human rights organizations (figures are difficult to verify due to the closed nature of the Saudi judicial system).[94] Crimes in Saudi Arabia that warrant death sentences include drug offenses, adultery, and "sorcery." Confessions to such crimes are repeatedly elicited through torture.[95] The Saudi regime has, at times, invoked "national security" as a catch-all defense for its execution policies.[96]

Moving forward, the scope and authenticity of current reforms will undoubtedly become clearer, as will the commitment of the country's leadership to those goals. For the moment, it all hinges on the stewardship of MbS, provided the young royal can cease his pattern of making repeated unforced errors that damage his credibility and the kingdom's reform efforts. That said, it remains unclear whether the Saudi government has plans to pursue this "moderate Islam" in earnest; further, there are few indications that Riyadh is stoppering the flow of Saudi money, preachers, and educational materials to mosques and madrassas abroad.[97]

ENDNOTES

1. Dexter Filkins, "A Saudi Prince's Quest to Remake the Middle East." The New Yorker, April 9, 2018. https://www.newyorker.com/magazine/2018/04/09/a-saudi-princes-quest-to-remake-the-middle-east.
2. Christopher M. Blanchard, "The Islamic Traditions of Wahhabism and Salafiyya," Congressional Research Service, updated January 24, 2008, https://fas.org/sgp/crs/misc/RS21695.pdf.
3. David Dean Commins, Wahhabi Mission and Saudi Arabia (IB Tauris, 2016).
4. U.S. Central Intelligence Agency, World Factbook, 2019, https://www.cia.gov/library/publications/the-world-factbook/geos/sa.html
5. Blanchard, "The Islamic Traditions of Wahhabism and Salafiyya."
6. Thomas Hegghammer and Stephane Lacroix, "Rejectionist Islamism in Saudi Arabia: The Story of Juhayman Al-'Utaybi Revisited," International Journal of Middle East Studies 39 (2007), 117, https://doi.org/10.1017/S0020743807002553
7. Stephane LaCroix, "Al-Albani's Revolutionary Approach to Hadith," ISIM Review, Spring 2008, https://openaccess.leidenuniv.nl/bitstream/handle/1887/17210/ISIM_21_Al-Albani-s_Revolutionary_Approach_to_Hadith.pdf?sequence=1.
8. Hegghammer and Lacroix, "Rejectionist Islamism in Saudi Arabia: The Story of Juhayman Al-'Utaybi Revisited."
9. Ondrej Beranek, "Divided We Survive: A Landscape of Fragmentation in Saudi Arabia," Brandeis University Crown Center for Middle East Studies Middle East Brief 28, January 2009, 3, http://www.brandeis.edu/crown/publications/meb/MEB33.pdf .
10. Madawi al-Rasheed, Contesting the Saudi State (Cambridge: Cam-

bridge University Press, 2007).

11. When al-Qaeda on the Arabian Peninsula attacked three foreign housing complexes in Riyadh in May 2003, killing 34 and injuring 200, al-Odah and al-Hawali issued a statement with nearly 50 other clerics, condemning the attacks and declaring the perpetrators ignorant, misguided young men. See "Saudi bombing deaths rise," BBC (London), May 13, 2003, http://news.bbc.co.uk/2/hi/middle_east/3022473.stm; Then, in December 2004, al-Odah, Aidh al-Qarni, and 33 other sheikhs signed a statement denouncing London-based Saudi dissident Saad al-Faqih's attempts to organize demonstrations against the regime. See Toby Craig Jones, "The Clerics, the Sahwa and the Saudi State," Center for Contemporary Conflict Strategic Insights, March 2005, 4, http://www.nps.edu/Academics/centers/ccc/publications/OnlineJournal/2005/Mar/jonesMar05.pdf. Subsequently, in January 2005, in response to a failed attack on the Ministry of Interior in Riyadh the previous month, 41 clerics issued a statement on al-Odah's website, Islam Today, warning against actions and discourse targeting the Saudi regime.
12. Stephanie Lacroix, "Saudi Arabia's Muslim Brotherhood predicament," Washington Post, March 20, 2014, https://www.washingtonpost.com/news/monkey-cage/wp/2014/03/20/saudi-arabias-muslim-brotherhood-predicament/?noredirect=on&utm_term=.a85d5d899d73.
13. Stephanie Lacroix, "Saudi Arabia's Muslim Brotherhood predicament," Washington Post, March 20, 2014, https://www.washingtonpost.com/news/monkey-cage/wp/2014/03/20/saudi-arabias-muslim-brotherhood-predicament/?noredirect=on&utm_term=.a85d5d899d73.
14. "Saudi Arabia arrests prominent cleric-social media," Reuters, September 11, 2017, https://af.reuters.com/article/commoditiesNews/idAFL5N1LR18G.
15. "Sheikh Safar al-Hawali had been a prominent critic of American influence in Saudi Arabia," Middle East Eye, July 12, 2018, https://www.middleeasteye.net/news/top-islamist-cleric-detained-saudi-authorities-1156314858.
16. "The 9/11 Commission Report," National Commission on Terrorist Attacks Upon the United States, July 22, 2004, http://govinfo.library.unt.edu/911/report/911Report.pdf.
17. Thomas Hegghammer, "Islamist Violence and Regime Stability in Saudi Arabia," International Affairs 84 (2008) 4, https://www.jstor.org/stable/25144872?seq=1#page_scan_tab_contents.

18. Thomas Hegghammer, "Islamist Violence and Regime Stability in Saudi Arabia," International Affairs 84 (2008) 45, https://www.jstor.org/stable/25144872?seq=1#page_scan_tab_contents.
19. "Al-Qaeda in the Arabian Peninsula," Al Jazeera (Doha), December 29, 2009, http://english.aljazeera.net/news/middleeast/2009/12/2009122935812371810.html.
20. Margaret Coker, "Assassination Attempt Targets Saudi Prince," Wall Street Journal, August 29, 2009, http://online.wsj.com/article/SB125144774691366169.html.
21. Anahad O'Connor and Eric Schmitt, "Terror Attempt Seen as Man Tries to Ignite Device on Jet," New York Times, December 25, 2009, http://www.nytimes.com/2009/12/26/us/26plane.html.
22. U.S. Department of State, Country Reports on Terrorism 2013, April 2014, https://2009-2017.state.gov/j/ct/rls/crt/2013/224823.htm.
23. "Al Qaeda Chief Tells Jihadist Fighters in Syria: Unite or Die," Reuters, May 8, 2016, http://www.reuters.com/article/us-mideast-crisis-syria-qaeda-idUSKCN0XZ0OA.
24. Maggie Michael, Trish Wilson, and Lee Keath, "AP Investigation: US allies, al-Qaida battle rebels in Yemen," Associated Press, August 7, 2018, https://apnews.com/f38788a561d74ca78c77cb43612d50da/Yemen:-US-allies-don%27t-defeat-al-Qaida-but-pay-it-to-go-away?utm_medium=AP&utm_campaign=SocialFlow&utm_source=Twitter.
25. Nima Elbagir, Salma Abdelaziz, Mohamed Abo El Gheit, and Laura Smith-Spark, "Sold to an ally, lost to an enemy," CNN, February 2019, https://www.cnn.com/interactive/2019/02/middleeast/yemen-lost-us-arms/.
26. Filkins, "A Saudi Prince's Quest."
27. "Hamza bin Laden loses Saudi citizenship after US offers $1m reward," Associated Press, March 1, 2019, https://www.theguardian.com/world/2019/mar/01/us-offers-1m-reward-for-help-finding-osama-bin-laden-son.
28. Sarah Westwood, Evan Perez and Ryan Browne, "Trump confirms Osama bin Laden's son Hamza killed in US counterterrorism operation," CNN, September 14, 2019, https://edition.cnn.com/2019/09/14/politics/hamza-bin-laden-al-qaeda-dead/index.html.
29. Ahmad Moussalli, "Wahhabism, Salafism, and Islamism: Who is the Enemy?" American University of Beirut, January 2009, 6, http://conflictsforum.org/briefings/Wahhabism-Salafism-and-Islamism.pdf.
30. Rachel Bronson, Thicker Than Oil: America's Uneasy Partnership with Saudi Arabia (New York: Oxford University Press, 2006), 147-

148.

31. "Two Die During Saudi Arabia protest at Shia Cleric Arrest," BBC (London), July 9, 2012, http://www.bbc.co.uk/news/world-middle-east-18768703.
32. Toby Matthiesen, "Saudi Arabia's Shiite Escalation," Foreign Policy, July 10, 2012, http://mideast.foreignpolicy.com/posts/2012/07/10/sable_rattling_in_the_gulf.
33. For videos of the protests in Awwamiya, see http://www.youtube.com/watch?v=dPLF5fGvYNA&feature=youtu.be and http://www.youtube.com/watch?v=JQsgTEBoH_E&feature=youtu.be.
34. Stephen Kalin, "Saudi Arabia pumps money into restive Shi'ite quarter it once flattened," Reuters, January 17, 2019, https://www.reuters.com/article/us-saudi-security-awamiya/saudi-arabia-pumps-money-into-restive-shiite-quarter-it-once-flattened-idUSKCN1PB1TZ.
35. "Saudi Arabia: Cleric Who Backed Protests on Trial for His Life," Human Rights Watch, May 11, 2013, http://www.hrw.org/news/2013/05/10/saudi-arabia-cleric-who-backed-protests-trial-his-life .
36. Leila Fadel, "Saudi Cleric's Death Sentence Focuses Shia Anger on Ruling Family," NPR, October 18, 2014, http://www.npr.org/2014/10/18/357108117/saudi-clerics-death-sentence-focuses-shia-anger-on-ruling-family.
37. "Sheikh Nimr al-Nimr: Saudi Arabia executes top Shia cleric," BBC News, January 2, 2016, (https://www.bbc.com/news/world-middle-east-35213244)
38. "Sheikh Nimr al-Nimr: Saudi Arabia executes top Shi'a cleric," BBC News, January 2, 2016, (https://www.bbc.com/news/world-middle-east-35213244)
39. Ben Hubbard, "Iranian Protesters Ransack Saudi Embassy After Execution of Shiite Cleric," New York Times, January 2, 2016, http://www.nytimes.com/2016/01/03/world/middleeast/saudi-arabia-executes-47-sheikh-nimr-shiite-cleric.html.
40. "Shias are doing better in Saudi Arabia," The Economist, August 30, 2018, https://www.economist.com/middle-east-and-africa/2018/08/30/shias-are-doing-better-in-saudi-arabia.
41. Kalin, "Saudi Arabia pumps money into restive Shi'ite quarter it once flattened."
42. Adel Abdel Ghafar, "A New Kingdom of Saud?" The Brookings Institution, February 14, 2018, https://www.brookings.edu/research/a-new-kingdom-of-saud/.
43. Cole Bunzel, "The Kingdom and the Caliphate: Duel of the Islamic

States," Carnegie Endowment for International Peace, February 18, 2016, http://carnegieendowment.org/2016/02/18/kingdom-and-caliphate-duel-of-islamic-states-pub-62810.

44. For Forbes Middle East's List, see www.forbesmiddleeast.com/arabic/ رثكا-100-ةيصخش-ةيبرع-اروضح-ىلع-رتيوت/; For Al-Odah's English Twitter Page, see http://twitter.com/Salman_Al_Odah; For his Arabic page, see www.facebook.com/DrSalmanAlOadah; For his Facebook Arabic page, see www.facebook.com/SalmanAlodah.
45. For al-Arefe's Twitter page, see http://twitter.com/MohamadAlarefe; For his Facebook page, see www.facebook.com/3refe; For King Salman's Twitter page, see https://twitter.com/KingSalman.
46. For al-Qarnee's Twitter page, see https://twitter.com/Dr_alqarnee; For his Facebook page, see www.facebook.com/dralqarnee?sk=wall.
47. "Philippine Gunman Attacks and Injures Saudi Preacher," Al Arabiya (Riyadh), March 1, 2016, http://english.alarabiya.net/en/News/2016/03/01/Saudi-preacher-injured-after-gun-attack-in-Philippines.html.
48. "The House of Saud: The Fatwa of the 26 Clerics: Open Sermon to the Militant Iraqi People," PBS Frontline, February 8, 2005, http://www.pbs.org/wgbh/pages/frontline/shows/saud/etc/fatwa.html.
49. Thomas Hegghammer, "Saudis in Iraq: Patterns of Radicalization and Recruitment." Revues.org, June 12, 2008, http://conflits.revues.org/index10042.html.
50. Jonathan Schanzer and Steven Miller, "Saudi Clerics Funnel Cash to Syrian Rebels through Terror Group," Weekly Standard, June 12, 2012, https://www.weeklystandard.com/jonathan-schanzer-and-steven-miller/saudi-clerics-funnel-cash-to-syrian-rebels-through-terror-group.
51. Huda Al-Saleh, "52 Saudi clerics, scholars call to battle Russian forces in Syria," Al-Arabiya (Riyadh), October 5, 2015, http://english.alarabiya.net/en/News/middle-east/2015/10/05/Fifty-two-Saudi-clerics-scholars-call-for-fight-against-Russian-forces-in-Syria.html.
52. Ben Hubbard, "Saudi Arabia Seeks Death Penalty in Trial of Outspoken Cleric," New York Times, September 4, 2018, https://www.nytimes.com/2018/09/04/world/middleeast/saudi-arabia-salman-al-awda.html.
53. "Saudi Arabia arrests prominent cleric Safar al-Hawali: activists," Reuters, July 12, 2018, https://www.reuters.com/article/us-saudi-arrests/saudi-arabia-arrests-prominent-cleric-safar-al-hawali-activists-idUSKBN1K22PQ.
54. @m3takl_en, "We confirm the news that Saudi authorities have

stopped the famous Saudi cleric Dr. Mohammad al-Arifi (#دمحم_يفيرعلا) from preaching in mosques and from all the other forms of Da'wah (preaching about Islam)," via Twitter, September 7, 2018, (https://twitter.com/m3takl_en/status/1038097020253286400); Benjamin Weinthal, "Switzerland bans cleric for anti-Semitic rhetoric," Jerusalem Post, May 28, 2013, https://www.jpost.com/International/Switzerland-bans-cleric-for-anti-Semitic-rhetoric-314665.

55. Christopher Blanchard and Alfred Prados, "Saudi Arabia: Terrorist Financing Issues," Congressional Research Service Report, December 8, 2004, http://fas.org/irp/crs/RL32499.pdf.
56. Christopher Blanchard and Alfred Prados, "Saudi Arabia: Terrorist Financing Issues," Congressional Research Service Report, December 8, 2004, http://fas.org/irp/crs/RL32499.pdf.
57. Qurat ul ain Siddiqui, "Saudi Arabia, UAE Financing Extremism in South Punjab," Dawn (Karachi), May 22, 2011, http://www.dawn.com/2011/05/22/saudi-arabia-uae-financing-extremism-in-south-punjab.html.
58. Kristina Wong, "Treasury Official: the Gulf states moving to cut off terrorist financing," The Hill, June 6, 2016, http://thehill.com/policy/defense/282989-treasury-official-gulf-remains-important-source-of-terrorist-financing.
59. Kristina Wong, "Treasury Official: the Gulf states moving to cut off terrorist financing," The Hill, June 6, 2016, http://thehill.com/policy/defense/282989-treasury-official-gulf-remains-important-source-of-terrorist-financing.
60. "Is Saudi Arabia to Blame for the Islamic State?" BBC, December 19, 2015, http://www.bbc.com/news/world-middle-east-35101612.
61. Abdullah bin Khaled Al-Saud, "Saudi Foreign Fighters: Analysis of Leaked Islamic State Entry Documents," Institute for the Study of Radicalisation, February 5, 2019, https://icsr.info/wp-content/uploads/2019/02/ICSR-Report-Saudi-Foreign-Fighters-Analysis-of-Leaked-Islamic-State-Entry-Documents.pdf.
62. "Attacks in Saudi Arabia bear hallmarks of Islamic State," Reuters, July 14, 2016, http://www.reuters.com/article/us-usa-saudi-idUSKCN0ZT2CL.
63. Galal Fakkar, "Story behind the king's title," Arab News, January 27, 2015, https://www.arabnews.com/saudi-arabia/news/695351.
64. "Saudi Arabia," in U.S. Department of State, 2010 Country Reports on Human Rights Practices, April 8, 2011, https://2009-2017.state.gov/j/drl/rls/hrrpt/2010/nea/154472.htm.
65. "Attacks in Saudi Arabia bear hallmarks of Islamic State," Reu-

ters, July 13, 2016, https://www.reuters.com/article/us-usa-saudi-idUSKCN0ZT2CL.

66. Scott Shane, "Saudis and Extremism: 'Both the Arsonists and the Firefighters,'" New York Times, August 25, 2016, https://www.nytimes.com/2016/08/26/world/middleeast/saudi-arabia-islam.html.
67. Alexander Alexiev, "The Wages of Extremism: Radical Islam's Threat to the West and the Muslim World." Hudson Institute, March 2011, 44, https://www.hudson.org/content/researchattachments/attachment/875/aalexievwagesofextremism032011.pdf.
68. Shane, "Saudis and Extremism."
69. Alexander Alexiev, "The End of an Alliance," National Review, October 28, 2002, https://www.unz.com/print/NationalRev-2002oct28-00038/.
70. Steffen Hertog, "The Costs of Counter-Revolution in the GCC," Foreign Policy, May 31, 2011, http://mideast.foreignpolicy.com/posts/2011/05/31/the_costs_of_counter_revolution_in_the_gcc.
71. Jonathan Schanzer and Steven Miller, "How Saudi Arabia Has Survived – So Far," The Journal of International Security Affairs, May 14, 2012, https://www.fdd.org/analysis/2012/05/14/how-saudi-arabia-has-survived-so-far/.
72. Jonathan Schanzer and Steven Miller, "How Saudi Arabia Has Survived – So Far," The Journal of International Security Affairs, May 14, 2012, https://www.fdd.org/analysis/2012/05/14/how-saudi-arabia-has-survived-so-far/.
73. Jonathan Schanzer and Steven Miller, "How Saudi Arabia Has Survived – So Far," The Journal of International Security Affairs, May 14, 2012, https://www.fdd.org/analysis/2012/05/14/how-saudi-arabia-has-survived-so-far/.
74. Madawi al-Rasheed, "Preachers of Hate as Loyal Subjects," New York Times, March 14, 2011, http://www.nytimes.com/roomfordebate/2011/03/14/how-stable-is-saudi-arabia/preachers-of-hate-as-loyal-subjects.
75. Filkins, "A Saudi Prince's Quest."
76. Ben Hubbard, "Saudi Arabia Agrees to Let Women Drive," New York Times, September 26, 2017, https://www.nytimes.com/2017/09/26/world/middleeast/saudi-arabia-women-drive.html.
77. Matt Clinch and Hadley Gamble, "Saudi Arabia unveils 15-year plan to transform its economy," CNBC, April 25, 2016, https://www.cnbc.com/2016/04/25/saudi-arabias-government-officially-unveils-long-term-economic-plan.html.
78. "Saudi Arabia launches air strikes in Yemen," BBC, March 26, 2015,

http://www.bbc.com/news/world-us-canada-32061632.

79. Jeffrey Goldberg, "Saudi Crown Prince: Iran's Supreme Leader 'Makes Hitler Look Good,'" The Atlantic, April 2, 2018, https://www.theatlantic.com/international/archive/2018/04/mohammed-bin-salman-iran-israel/557036/.
80. Jeffrey Goldberg, "Saudi Crown Prince: Iran's Supreme Leader 'Makes Hitler Look Good,'" The Atlantic, April 2, 2018, https://www.theatlantic.com/international/archive/2018/04/mohammed-bin-salman-iran-israel/557036/.
81. Martin Chulov, "I Will Return Saudi Arabia to Moderate Islam, Says Crown Prince," Guardian (London), October 24, 2017, https://www.theguardian.com/world/2017/oct/24/i-will-return-saudi-arabia-moderate-islam-crown-prince.
82. David Ignatius, "Are Saudi Arabia's reforms for real? A recent visit says yes," Washington Post, March 1, 2018, https://www.washingtonpost.com/opinions/global-opinions/are-saudi-arabias-reforms-for-real-a-recent-visit-says-yes/2018/03/01/a11a4ca8-1d9d-11e8-9de1-147dd2df3829_story.html?noredirect=on&utm_term=.0e07ccb361b3.
83. Mohammad Al-Issa, "Why Muslims from around the world should remember the Holocaust," Washington Post, January 25, 2019, https://www.washingtonpost.com/opinions/2019/01/25/why-muslims-around-world-should-remember-holocaust/?utm_term=.1b65879a8ff0; Mohammad Al-Issa, "Statement on Holocaust Remembrance from Head of Saudi-Based Muslim World League," Washington Institute for Near East Policy, January 25, 2018, https://www.washingtoninstitute.org/press-room/view/statement-on-holocaust-remembrance-from-head-of-saudi-based-muslim-world-le.
84. Robert Satloff, "A Historic Holocaust Awareness Awakening in Saudi Arabia, of All Places," New York Daily News, January 26, 2018, https://www.washingtoninstitute.org/policy-analysis/view/a-historic-holocaust-awareness-awakening-in-saudi-arabia-of-all-places.
85. "Saudi Arabia's Post-Oil Future," The Economist, April 30, 2016, http://www.economist.com/news/middle-east-and-africa/21697673-bold-promises-bold-young-prince-they-will-be-hard-keep-saudi-arabias.
86. Natasha Turak, "Inclusion in MSCI index is a 'big milestone' for Saudi market, stock exchange boss says," CNBC, June 21, 2018, https://www.cnbc.com/2018/06/21/inclusion-in-msci-index-is-a-big-milestone-for-saudi-market.html.
87. Noor Nugali, "'Justice for all': How Saudi Arabia's sexual harass-

ment law will work," Arab News, June 3, 2018, http://www.arabnews.com/node/1314546/saudi-arabia.

88. Ben Hubbard et al., "Saudis Said to Use Coercion and Abuse to Seize Billions," New York Times, March 11, 2018, https://www.nytimes.com/2018/03/11/world/middleeast/saudi-arabia-corruption-mohammed-bin-salman.html.
89. Filkins, "A Saudi Prince's Quest."
90. "Saudi Arabia claims anti-corruption purge recouped $100bn,"Guardian (London), January 30, 2018, https://www.theguardian.com/world/2018/jan/30/anti-corruption-purge-nets-more-than-100bn-saudi-arabia-claims.
91. Filkins, "A Saudi Prince's Quest."
92. David D. Kirkpatrick, "Saudi Arabia Is Said To Have Tortured an American Citizen," New York Times, March 2, 2019, https://www.nytimes.com/2019/03/02/world/middleeast/saudi-arabia-torture-american-citizen.html.
93. Linda Givetash and Associated Press, "Saudi Arabia women's rights activists to face trial, prosecutors say," NBC, March 2, 2019, https://www.nbcnews.com/news/world/saudi-arabia-women-s-rights-activists-face-trial-prosecutors-say-n978511.
94. Hubbard, "Iranian Protesters Ransack Saudi Embassy."; "China, Iran, Saudi Arabia executed most people in 2016," Al Jazeera (Doha), April 10, 2017, https://www.aljazeera.com/news/2017/04/death-penalty-2016-170410230144434.html; Human Rights Watch, "Saudi Arabia: Events of 2017," World Report 2018, 2018, https://www.hrw.org/world-report/2018/country-chapters/saudi-arabia.
95. Amnesty International, "Saudi Arabia 2017/2018," June 6, 2017, https://www.amnesty.org/en/countries/middle-east-and-north-africa/saudi-arabia/report-saudi-arabia/.
96. Amnesty International, "Saudi Arabia: 14 protesters facing execution after unfair trials," June 6, 2017, https://www.amnesty.org/en/latest/news/2017/06/saudi-arabia-14-protesters-facing-execution-after-unfair-trials/.
97. David Andrew Weinberg, "Teaching Hate and Violence: Problematic Passages from Saudi State Textbooks for the 2018-2019 School Year," Anti-Defamation League, November 2018, https://www.adl.org/media/12180/download

24 Tunisia

Quick Facts

Population: 11,721,177 (July 2020 est.)
Area: 163,610 sq km
Ethnic Groups:Arab 98%, European 1%, Jewish and other 1%
GDP (official exchange rate): $39.96 billion (2017 est.)

Source: CIA World FactBook (Last Updated June 2020)

Introduction

Tunisia is perhaps best-known as the site of protests that sparked the 2011 Arab Spring. The ensuing revolution ended the decades-long reign of authoritarian leader Zine el-Abedine Ben Ali (who died in exile in September 2019), thus terminating the restrictive one-party political structure that had been the norm in the country since 1956. Since the revolution, previously suppressed opposition movements, formerly exiled politicians, new political groups, and politicians from the old regime have coexisted in this newly opened field.

The Tunisian government has often been referred to as the only successful democratic transition in the region; one influenced not only by state action, but also civil society. Indeed, while the country's new constitution includes various references to Islam, it also includes sections that outline secular democratic principles. The transition has not been without difficulties, however. The country's economic and security situation has worsened since 2011, as it has faced political assassinations as well as both attempted and successful terrorist attacks. Non-violent Salafism has attracted many, primarily young, people who are frustrated and have become disillusioned with the new post-revolutionary order's failure to improve employment, the economy, and social justice conditions.[1] In part as a result of this ferment, Tunisia has emerged as a major source of foreign fighters that have mobilized to support Islamic extremist groups on the region's battlefields.[2]

Islamist Activity

Political Parties

Hizb Ennahda (The Renaissance Party)

Ennahda is one of the major Tunisian political parties. Founded as the "Movement of Islamic Tendency" (MTI) in 1981, it was inspired by Egypt's Muslim Brotherhood (MB) and is still considered associated with the Brotherhood, although Ennahda has tried to distance itself from the MB since 2011.[3]

When Prime Minister Zine el-Abedine Ben Ali ousted then-President Habib Bourguiba in a bloodless palace coup in November 1987, he launched a series of reforms that included granting a pardon to MTI founder Rached Ghannouchi, who had been imprisoned under Bourguiba's regime. Ghannouchi, in turn, signed Ben Ali's "National Pact," which was essentially a social contract between the government and civil and political groups.[4] But Ben Ali soon changed course and, among other measures, prohibited any party's name from using the words "Islam" or "Islamic" (the prohibition of religiously-identified parties remains in place to this day). Even though MTI renamed itself Hizb Ennahda, it was not allowed to enter the elections as a recognized political party, and could only field "independent" candidates.

Yet the unexpectedly strong performance of Islamists within the opposition, coupled with Ennahda's increasingly strident political rhetoric, caused the regime to deny the group's second request for recognition. An escalating cycle of protest and repression ensued and Ghannouchi fled, first to Algiers then to Khartoum and finally to London, where he was granted political asylum in 1993.[5] By 1992, virtually all of Ennahda's leadership had been imprisoned and its organizational capabilities within the country were destroyed. Although it was commonly understood that Ennahda had been effectively dismantled by the early 1990s, many Tunisians, including

Ben Ali, nonetheless believed the group maintained a "sleeping" presence in the country.[6]

Ennahda's ideology is rooted in Ghannouchi's philosophy, which views the Quran and the Hadith as "an anchor for political thought and practice."[7] However, he appears to contextualize Quranic texts through Western political thinking and freedoms; namely the dignity of human beings, human rights, and Quranic prohibitions against Muslim dictators.[8] Ghannouchi is a "literalist" and believes that it is the duty of Muslims to establish Islamic government where achievable.[9] He does not advocate government by clerics and has said that, "[t]he state is not something from God but from the people... the state has to serve the benefit of the Muslims."[10]

However, once in power following the October 2011 elections (during which Ennahda secured 90 of the 217 seats in the Tunisian parliament), the Ennahda-led government governed in much the same way as the Egyptian Muslim Brotherhood would in Cairo – namely, it seemingly tolerated the disruptive and sometimes violent actions of Salafi elements while cracking down on secular demonstrations. In a widely-cited example of these allegations, police allowed the Salafist "occupation" of Manouba University to drag on for several weeks, but quickly used force to break up peaceful anti-Ennahda demonstrations in April 2012.

The issue came to a head with the assassination of two leftist politicians in 2013, which was widely seen as the work of Salafists emboldened by Ennahda sympathies. Popular demonstrations against the government grew and the "National Salvation Front" – a collective of opposition parties – called for the dissolution of the National Constituent Assembly and new elections. Compounding the situation, the economy at the time was far from robust and the social environment was one of public frustration and pessimism. Ennahda leaders realized that some sort of national compromise was necessary, lest they meet the same fate as the Muslim Brotherhood-dominated government of President Mohammed Morsi in Egypt. Various compromises were suggested and Ennahda offered concessions to its political opponents. Popular demonstrations and civil disobedience waned in the fall of 2013, and the two sides negotiated a way forward. Finally, a national dialogue led by

Tunisia's labor union federation brokered a compromise in early January 2014, under which the Ennahda-led government would step down in favor of an interim, technocratic administration that would lead the country to new elections, while the Constituent Assembly (about 42% Islamist) would remain and finish the constitution.

By the end of January 2014, the new constitution was drafted and approved by the Constituent Assembly. Serious unrest was avoided, the new constitution was widely accepted, and the country appeared to be moving ahead. During this time, Ennahda may have been more inclined to encourage pluralism in Muslim politics in order to better govern a politically diverse country.[11] Further, the party indicated that it would accept the outcome of prospective power-sharing. Ghannouchi told a Washington, DC audience in February 2014 that:

> the Tunisian experience has proven to those doubting the intentions of Islamists that Islam and democracy are compatible and that victims of decades of repression, marginalization, and exclusion are not carrying hatred or the desire for revenge, but rather an enlightened modernist civil project as embodied in the new Tunisian constitution, which has been adopted with the widest possible consensus.[12]

In the October 2014 parliamentary elections, Ennahda gathered 27.79% of the votes, 69 seats in the Assembly, and a junior partnership in a coalition government. The readiness of Essebsi, the newly elected President, and Ghannouchi to compromise and govern together marks the Tunisian government's transition to democracy. Results in subsequent elections have been mixed for Ennahda. The local elections of May 2018 were a victory for the party; it earned 29.68% of the votes behind independent lists and Ennahda's Souad Abderrahim became Tunis's first elected mayor in July 2018. In the September 2019 presidential elections, Ennahda named Abdelfattah Mourou its first ever presidential candidate. However, Mourou did not progress to the second round of voting.

In the past, analysts pointed to ambiguity in the relationship between Ennahda and Salafi-*jihadists*, especially in the immediate aftermath of the revolution.[13] However, since 2013, Ennahda has acted more decisively against Salafi-*jihadists*. In April 2013, it declared *Ansar al-Sharia*, the largest Salafi group in Tunisia, a terrorist organization.[14] Ennahda has adopted a security-oriented approach to Salafi-*jihadism*, going so far as to force Salafists to register their religious affiliation with the police. While many members of Ennahda are uncomfortable with these measures, as well as with police brutality,[15] the global rise of Salafi-*jihadism* has made it difficult to criticize these policies.[16]

In May 2016, during the group's 10th party congress, 93.5 percent of *Ennahda*'s delegates voted to separate religious and political activities into different branches. Ennahda thus called itself a Muslim Democratic party rather than an Islamic one. This decision means that elected officials can no longer hold positions both in the party and in broader society. That includes mosques and Islamic organizations. Ghannouchi won reelection as party leader and had a major hand in crafting the policy shift that divided Ennahda's social and political wings.[17] For some analysts, this split, which deepened internal divisions, is largely cosmetic and has already experienced setbacks.[18]

Jebahat el-Islah (JI, or "Reform Front") and al-Rahma ("Mercy")

After the revolution ended in 2011, participating in politics rapidly became a fault-line within the Salafi movement.[19] In May 2012, the Tunisian government granted a license to JI to operate as a party under the Political Parties Law, which requires respect for the "civil principles of the state". It was the first Salafist group to be recognized as such.[20] JI claims that it rejects violence and supports democratic governance.[21]

While JI remains unswervingly dedicated to bringing *sharia* law into Tunisia, younger Salafi-*jihadis* consider legislating *sharia* unwieldy and unappealing.[22] Furthermore, most JI members are older men as the group has failed to attract younger Tunisians to its cause.[23] In fact, young JI members of the JI ran as independent candidates in past elections.[24] Al-Rahma, was legalized in July 2012. Its stated goal is to establish *sharia* law. Like JI, al-Rahma is not particularly popular.[25]

Hizb ut-Tahrir (HuT, or the Islamic Liberation Party)
HuT established a presence in Tunisia in 1973, but has historically had only a few dozen members in the country.[26] The group emerged publicly after the 2011 revolution, seeking to offer an "alternative constitution" to the Constituent Assembly, and was officially recognized in 2012.[27] While it claims to renounce violence, HuT does not rule out rebellion and civil disobedience to achieve its goal of establishing an Islamic state. Furthermore, HuT has developed a reputation as a pipeline for radicalization.[28] Many Tunisians believe that, if it seized power, HuT would ban other parties and implement "one man, one vote, one time."[29] Indeed, in April 2017, HuT's politburo chief, Abderraouf Amri, publicly stated that, "Democracy no longer attracts anyone… It is time to announce its death and work to bury it."[30]

In September 2016, the Tunisian government requested that a military court ban HuT, on the grounds that the group had been accused repeatedly of "undermining public order" since 2012.[31] Tunisian judicial authorities implemented a one-month long ban a year after the party successfully appealed the original decision.[32] However, the party continues to operate. HuT held a congress in March 2019, renewing its plea for the creation of a caliphate.[33]

Jihadist Groups
Ansar al-Sharia Tunisiyya (Supporters of Islamic Law, or AST)
Ansar al-Sharia Tunisiyya was established in April 2011. Though there are many groups throughout the world that go by the name of Ansar al-Sharia, these organizations are not part of a unified chain of command. Terrorism analyst Aaron Zelin writes: "(Ansar al-Sharia groups) are fighting in different lands using different means, but all for the same end, an approach better suited for the vagaries born of the Arab uprisings."[34]

AST's founder, Saifallah Ben Hassine (also known as Abu Ayyad al-Tunisia), was a *jihadist* who fought in Afghanistan and was subsequently arrested and deported to Tunisia in 2003. He was freed with many other prisoners after the country's 2011 revolution.[35] AST has claimed responsibility for the 2012 attack on the U.S. Embassy in Tunis, and the assassinations of liberal politicians, Chokri Belaid and Mohamed Brahmi, in February and July 2013.[36] Its most recent attack occurred in 2014, AST militants attacked Tunisian soldiers at checkpoints near the Algerian border. Fourteen people were killed in that incident.[37]

AST has also devoted energy to *dawa* (proselytization) and community service.[38] In this manner, AST has entrenched itself and won support in a nation that feels abandoned by political elites and disappointed in the outcome of the 2011 revolution.[39] In 2013, AST was designated as a terrorist organization, which limited its ability to publicly proselytize.[40]

In July 2014, an AST spokesman declared the group's allegiance to Islamic State in Syria and Levant (ISIS/ISIL) *emir* Abu Bakr Al-Baghdadi.[41] AST has recruited heavily for ISIS in Tunisia and encourages many young Tunisians to make the journey to Syria.[42]. The State Department's 2016 report on terrorist groups indicated that AST's strength and numbers, as well as its foreign aid and financing, remain unknown, although analysts agree that its capacities have decreased over time.[43] More recent reports suggest that AST has disbanded and its members have joined other groups.[44] In February 2019, French forces around *El Aklé, Mali, c*laimed to have killed Seifallah Ben Hassine, one of the founders of AST.[45]

Al-Qaeda in the Islamic Maghreb (AQIM)

AQIM only established an active recruiting base in Tunisia comparatively recently. After the fall of Ben Ali, the Okba Ibn Nafaâ brigade was created and supported by Abdelmalek Droukdal (a.k.a. Abu Mossab Abdel Wadoud, the supreme leader of AQIM). According to a Tunisian official, the brigade has never had more than 200-300 men and operates through networks and cells.[46]

AQIM has not carried out suicide bomb-type terrorist operations in Tunisia; however, its "conventional" forces, armed with weapons looted from Libyan arsenals, have fought Tunisian security forces in the past. In 2014, AQIM claimed responsibility for an attack on the home of interior minister, Lotfi Ben Jeddou.[47] Okba Ibn Nafaâ is also responsible for the March 2015 Bardo museum attack, although the incident was claimed by ISIS. AQIM has historically considered Tunisia as a support zone and employs more defensive operations than offensive strikes.[48]

The group has been weakened in recent years. Some AQIM

members have defected to ISIS and ISIS has co-opted some of AQIM's support cells along Tunisia's border with Algeria, taking supplies for themselves.[49] In 2015, Tunisian counterterrorism operations eliminated much of the group's leadership. Subsequently, in 2017, the group's leader, Murad Sha'ib, was killed, and a year later, on January 2018, his successor, Bilal Kobi, was also eliminated.[50] The group's activity in Tunisia has radically diminished since then.[51]

The Islamic State in Syria and Levant

As mentioned above, ISIS' growth in Tunisia partly derives from defections from AST and Okba Ibn Nafaâ. ISIS also features Tunisians prominently in its own propaganda, often lauding the efforts and martyrdom of Tunisian foreign fighters.[52] The main ISIS affiliated organization in Tunisia is known as Jund Al Khilafa (Soldiers of the Caliph).[53] ISIS has launched a number of notable attacks in Tunisia to date. In November 2014, ISIS claimed responsibility for the bombing of a presidential guard bus. The blast killed 12 presidential guards.[54] The Islamic State also took responsibility for the 2015 Sousse shooting that killed 39 and wounded 36. In March 2016, 50 gunmen affiliated with ISIS, many of whom were part of sleeper cells, coordinated attacks on "security installations and security personnel in the border town of Ben Guerdane." Security forces killed 49 of the militants, while 17 security officials and seven civilians were killed.[55] In November 2016, the Islamic State claimed responsibility for killing a Tunisian Air Force soldier who was found dead in his home.[56] In June 2019, two suicide attacks targeted police forces. ISIS claimed responsibility through its Amaq News Agency.[57] *Jund Al Khilafa* remains active to this day, although it is less impactful. Its latest attacks have been against military targets and have been mainly concentrated in the Western part of Tunisia.[58]

The main threat, arguably, does not come from local organizations, but rather from foreign fighters.[59] Between 3,000 and 7,000 of ISIS's foreign fighters come from Tunisia, according to various sources.[60] While not all of those people fought on behalf of ISIS, most eventually changed allegiances. Over time, however, these allegiances have proved fluid; many have moved to the south of the Sahel, seeking to continue their fight.[61] Recent reports highlight the increasing number of fighters that have now become associated with AQIM and its branches.[62]

Islamism and Society

Ninety-eight percent of Tunisia's 11 million person population is Sunni Muslim.[63] Shi'ites number perhaps in the thousands, and most converted to the sect after the 1979 Iranian Revolution.[64] Tunisians tend to be moderate in their views and behavior. Habib Bourguiba, the country's first president following its independence from France in the 1950s, was supported by the public and set a moderate political course. Guerrilla warfare and terrorism did not characterize the struggle back then, and there were no violent purges. This trend has largely continued; Tunisian society is not used to violent extremism and has demonstrated its unity in condemning it. After the 2013 murder of politician Chokri Belaid, one million people participated in the "country's biggest demonstrations since the 2011 revolution" to protest the killing.[65] However, the sense that the revolution has not fulfilled all expectations and the lack of opportunities for the youth, in particular from poorer southern interior regions, have challenged this unity and made violent extremism more attractive for some disenfranchised segments of the population.

Islamism and the State

The Tunisian state was hostile to Islamism from its independence in 1956 through to the end of the Ben Ali regime in 2011. Habib Bourguiba, the hero of Tunisian liberation and president for over 30 years, ignored the country's Arab/Islamic history and connected modern Tunisia directly to a pre-Islamic past – its Carthaginian heritage – while simultaneously secularizing the state and weakening traditional Islamic institutions.[66] When the regime's social and economic development failed, it adapted and instituted programs focused on public education and literacy, economic mobility, and the position of women in society.

The 2003 anti-terrorism law allowed the government to jail anyone threatening national security, though it primarily targeted Islamist-leaning young people using the Internet "illegally" (i.e., blogging or visiting *jihadist* websites).[67] At the same time, the Ben Ali regime used religion to support government policies.[68] This state-facilitated Islam was designed to counter the threat of extremism and terrorism by preaching the values of moderation and tolerance and, at the same time, claiming ownership of Tunisians' Islamic identity.[69] The state also controlled mosque construction, sermon content, religious education, and appointment and remuneration of imams.

There were heated debates in the process of drafting the 2014 Constitution between Islamic political groups and secular movements over the role of Islamic law in the Tunisian Constitution, the prohibition of blasphemy, and the rights of women. However, Islamic groups showed self-restraint overall.[70] Ennahda announced its opposition to including *sharia* in the constitution. The only reference to Islam repeated the 1959 Constitution's Article 1 and states: "Tunisia is a free, independent and sovereign state. Its religion is Islam, its language is Arabic, and its type of government is the Republic. This article cannot be amended."[71] However, the document includes language that outlines the primacy of civil law as referenced in Article 2, as well as the freedom of conscience, the values of moderation and tolerance, and commitments to peace and stability, per Article 6.[72]

The state of Tunisia has vigorously fought against violent extremism over the last several years at the encouragement of foreign partners. While the Ministry of Religious Affairs has claimed that it has regained control over mosques controlled by Salafi groups, the 2017 National Risk Assessment (NRA) shows that terrorist groups have been backed through "non-profitable organizations, mosques, and smuggling."[73] When 10kg of explosive substances were found in a mosque near Tunis in July 2019, the subsequent seizure reflected the government's difficulty in controlling the estimated 5000 mosques around the country. [74]

Despite a heated debate on reintegration vs. punitive measures to deal with the estimated 1000 *jihadists* that have returned to Tunisia and the adoption of the National Strategy for Counter Terrorism in 2016 that promotes a holistic approach, the estimated 1000 people that have returned to Tunisia from fighting for *jihadist* causes abroad[75] are largely considered a security threat, leading to repressive policies.[76] Such a strategy is problematic in that "[t]he country's overcrowded prisons continue to serve as a breeding ground for *jihadists*."[77] The country's subsequent 2015 anti-terrorism law expanded the definition of terrorism and offered a legislative basis to suspend civic associations and reinforce social controls.[78] The result has been a constriction of civil society. Between 2014 and 2017, around "150 civil associations [were] suspended and 157 closed for alleged links to terrorism."[79] The Ministry of Religious Affairs has likewise enforced new administrative measures to "register and monitor religious institutions and their workers, including preachers, and to impose fixed opening hours," in addition to the closure of mosques outside their supervision.[80] More recently, in July 2019, Tunisian authorities also banned the wearing of the *niqab* in public institutions, justifying the measure on the basis of security concerns, as a response to a June 2019 terrorist attack that targeted security forces in the center of Tunis.

ENDNOTES:

1. Anouar Boukhars, "In the Crossfire: Islamists' travails in Tunisia," Carnegie Endowment for International Peace, January 2014, 13.
2. Haim Malka and Margot Balboni, "Tunisia: Radicalism Abroad and at Home," Center for Strategic and International Studies, June 2016, http://foreignfighters.csis.org/tunisia/why-tunisia.html.
3. Aiden Lewis, "Profile: Tunisia's Ennahda Party," *BBC*, October, 2011, http://www.bbc.com/news/world-africa-15442859; "Ennahda Party Of Tunisia," *Global Muslim Brotherhood Daily Watch*, 2019, https://www.globalmbwatch.com/ennahda-party-of-tunisia/; Youssef Cherif, "Ennahda and Morsi's Eulogy," Carnegie Endowment for International Peace, July 2019, https://carnegieendowment.org/sada/79420.
4. Cherif, "Ennahda and Morsi's Eulogy."
5. Jennifer Noyon, *Islam, Politics and Pluralism Theory and Practice in Turkey, Jordan, Tunisia and Algeria* (London:

Royal Institute for International Affairs/Chatham House, 2003), 103.

6. Correspondence of previous chapter author, Larry Velte, with Tunisian academic and lawyer, September 2009.
7. Noyon, *Islam, Politics, and Pluralism*, 99.
8. Mohamed Elhachmi Hamdi, *The Politicization of Islam: A Case Study of Tunisia* (Boulder, CO: Westview Press, 1998), 107.
9. Noyon, *Islam, Politics, and Pluralism*, 101.
10. As cited in John L. Esposito and Francois Burgat, eds., *Modernizing Islam* (Rutgers University Press, 2003), 78.
11. Aaron Zelin, "Who is Jabhat al-Islah?" Carnegie Endowment for International Peace, July 2015, http://carnegieendowment.org/sada/?fa=48885.
12. Posted by the Center for the Study of Islam and Democracy, Washington, DC, March, 2014. https://www.csidonline.org/post/washington-celebrates-landmark-new-tunisian-constitution
13. Monica Marks, "Tunisia's Ennahda: Rethinking Islamism in the context of ISIS and the Egyptian coup," Brookings Institution *Project on U.S. Relations with the Islamic World Working Paper*, August 2015, https://www.brookings.edu/wp-content/uploads/2016/07/Tunisia_Marks-FINALE.pdf.
14. Monica Marks, "Tunisia's Ennahda: Rethinking Islamism in the context of ISIS and the Egyptian coup," Brookings Institution *Project on U.S. Relations with the Islamic World Working Paper*, August 2015, https://www.brookings.edu/wp-content/uploads/2016/07/Tunisia_Marks-FINALE.pdf.
15. [15] Monica Marks, "Tunisia's Ennahda: Rethinking Islamism in the context of ISIS and the Egyptian coup," Brookings Institution *Project on U.S. Relations with the Islamic World Working Paper*, August 2015, https://www.brookings.edu/wp-content/uploads/2016/07/Tunisia_Marks-FINALE.pdf.
16. Monica Marks, "Tunisia's Ennahda: Rethinking Islamism in the context of ISIS and the Egyptian coup," Brookings Institution *Project on U.S. Relations with the Islamic World Working Paper*, August 2015, https://www.brookings.edu/wp-

content/uploads/2016/07/Tunisia_Marks-FINALE.pdf.

17. Sarah Souli, "What is left of Tunisia's Ennahda Party?" *Al Jazeera* (Doha), May 26, 2016, http://www.aljazeera.com/news/2016/05/left-tunisia-ennahda-party-160526101937131.html.
18. Fabio Mérone, "Politicians or Preachers? What Ennahda's Transformation Means for Tunisia," Carnegie Middle East Center, January, 2019, https://carnegie-mec.org/2019/01/31/politicians-or-preachers-what-ennahda-s-transformation-means-for-tunisia-pub-78253; Cherif, "Ennahda and Morsi's Eulogy."
19. Theo Blanc, "Salafisme: Le Cas Tunisien," *Les Clés Du Moyen-Orient*, March 11, 2017, https://www.lesclesdumoyenorient.com/Salafisme-3-le-cas-tunisien.html.
20. Houda Trabelsi, "Tunisia Approves First Salafist Party," *Magharebia*, May 17, 2012.
21. Houda Trabelsi, "Tunisia Approves First Salafist Party," *Magharebia*, May 17, 2012.
22. Anouar Boukhars, "In the Crossfire: Islamists' Travails in Tunisia," Carnegie Endowment for International Peace *Paper*, January 27, 2014, http://carnegieendowment.org/2014/01/27/in-crossfire-islamists-travails-in-tunisia-pub-54311.
23. Aaron Zelin, "Meeting Tunisia's Ansar al-Sharia," *Foreign Policy,* March 8, 2013, http://foreignpolicy.com/2013/03/08/meeting-tunisias-ansar-al-sharia/.
24. Zelin, "Who Is Jabhat Al-Islah?"
25. Stefano M. Torelli, Fabio Merone and Francesco Cavatorta, "Salafism in Tunisia: Challenges and Opportunities for Democratization," *Middle East Policy* XIX, no. 4, Winter 2012.
26. Alaya Allani, "The Islamists in Tunisia between Confrontation and Participation, 1980-2008," The Journal of North African Studies 14, iss. 2, 2009, 258.
27. Interview by previous chapter author, Larry Veldte, with Tahrir spokesman Ridha Belhaj, Assarih, Tunis, March 11, 2011; "Hizb ut-Tahrir Tunisia Spokesman: 'Our Appeal for a License has Been Accepted'," Hizb-ut Tarhir website, July 2012, http://www.hizb.org.uk/news-watch/hizb-ut-tahrir-tunisia-

spokesman-our-appeal-for-a-license-has-been-accepted.

28. "Hizb-ut Tahrir," American Foreign Policy Council *World Almanac of Islamism,* January 2017, http://almanac.afpc.org/hizb-ut-tahrir.
29. Interview with an-Nahda official Abdelfattah Mourou, *Al-Jazeera* (Doha), March, 2011.
30. "Tunisian Islamist party says time to 'bury' democracy," Agence France Presse:, April 15, 2017, http://al-monitor.com/pulse/afp/2017/04/tunisia-politics-religion.html.
31. "Tunisia calls for a ban on radical Islamist party," *Al Arabiya* (Riyadh), September 7, 2016, http://english.alarabiya.net/en/News/middle-east/2016/09/07/Tunisia-calls-for-ban-on-radical-Islamist-party-.html.
32. "Tunisia radical Islamist party banned for one month," *News 24*, June 7, 2017, https://www.news24.com/Africa/News/tunisia-radical-islamist-party-banned-for-one-month-20170607
33. "Tunisie – Hizb-Ut-Tahrir prone la Califat et la Chariâa, et organize une manifestation avec la participation d'enfants," *Tunisie Numerique*, March 30, 2019, https://www.tunisienumerique.com/tunisie-hizb-ut-tahrir-prone-la-califat-et-la-chariaa-et-organise-une-manifestation-avec-la-participation-denfants/
34. Zelin, "Know Your Ansar al-Sharia."
35. Torelli, Merone and Cavatorta, "Salafism in Tunisia: Challenges and Opportunities for Democratization."
36. "Ansar al-Sharia in Tunisia (AST)," Counter Extremism Project, 2016, http://www.counterextremism.com/threat/ansar-al-sharia-tunisia-ast.
37. "Ansar al-Shariah (Tunisia),", Stanford University, August 2016, http://web.stanford.edu/group/mappingmilitants/cgi-bin/groups/view/547#note3.
38. Zelin, "Meeting Tunisia's Ansar al-Sharia."
39. Christine Petré, "Tunisian Salafism: the rise and fall of Ansar al-Sharia," ETH Zurich *Policy Brief* 209, October 2015, https://css.ethz.ch/en/services/digital-library/publications/publication.html/194178.
40. Christine Petré, "Tunisian Salafism: the rise and fall of Ansar

al-Sharia," ETH Zurich *Policy Brief* 209, October 2015, https://css.ethz.ch/en/services/digital-library/publications/publication.html/194178.
41. Jamel Arfaoui, "Tunisia: Ansar Al-Sharia Spokesman Backs Isis," *AllAfrica*, July 8, 2014, http://allafrica.com/stories/201407090299.html.
42. "AST," Counter Extremism Project.
43. "Chapter Six: Foreign Terrorist Organizations – Ansar al-Shari'a in Tunisia," in U.S. Department of State, *Country Reports on Terrorism 2016*, 2017, https://www.state.gov/j/ct/rls/crt/2016/272238.htm.
44. Djallil Lounnas, "The Tunisian Jihad: Between al-Qaeda and ISIS", *Middle East Policy* 26, iss. 1, Spring 2019, https://onlinelibrary.wiley.com/doi/full/10.1111/mepo.12403.
45. MENASTREAM. (2019). *Exclusive: End of the run for Tunisian Ansar al-Sharia founder Abu Iyadh al-Tunisi - MENASTREAM.* [online] Available at: http://menastream.com/exclusive-tunisian-ansar-al-sharia-founder-abu-iyadh-al-tunisi-killed-in-mali/ [Accessed 5 Nov. 2019].
46. Djallil Lounnas, "The Tunisian Jihad: Between al-Qaeda and ISIS", *Middle East Policy* 26, iss. 1, Spring 2019, https://onlinelibrary.wiley.com/doi/full/10.1111/mepo.12403.
47. "Foreign Terrorist Organizations – Al-Qa'ida in the Islamic Maghreb," in U.S. Department of State, *Country Reports on Terrorism, 2015*, 2016, https://www.state.gov/j/ct/rls/crt/2015/257523.htm.
48. Jaclyn Stutz, "AQIM and ISIS in Tunisia: Competing Campaigns," AEI Critical Threats Project, 2016, http://www.criticalthreats.org/al-qaeda/stutz-aqim-isis-tunisia-competing-campaigns-june-28-2016.
49. Jaclyn Stutz, "AQIM and ISIS in Tunisia: Competing Campaigns," AEI Critical Threats Project, 2016, http://www.criticalthreats.org/al-qaeda/stutz-aqim-isis-tunisia-competing-campaigns-june-28-2016.
50. Aaron Zelin, "Not Gonna Be Able To Do It: al-Qaeda in Tunisia's Inability to Take Advantage of the Islamic State's Setbacks," *Perspectives on Terrorism*, 13(1), 2019, 63-77.

51. “Al-Qaeda in the Islamic Maghreb (AQIM),” Counter Extremism Project, 2019, https://www.counterextremism.com/threat/al-qaeda-islamic-maghreb-aqim.
52. “AST*,”* Counter Extremism Project.
53. Lounnas, “The Tunisian Jihad: Between al-Qaeda and ISIS.”
54. Lounnas, “The Tunisian Jihad: Between al-Qaeda and ISIS.”
55. Lounnas, “The Tunisian Jihad: Between al-Qaeda and ISIS.”
56. “Tunisia Takes on Extremism with New ‘Terrorism’ Strategy,” *The New Arab*, November 8, 2016, https://www.alaraby.co.uk/english/news/2016/11/8/tunisia-takes-on-extremism-with-new-terrorism-strategy.
57. “Tunisia: Extremism & Counter-Extremism,” Counter Extremism Project, 2019, https://www.counterextremism.com/countries/tunisia.
58. Charlotte Bozonnet, *«La plus grande menace des djihadistes de l’Ouest tunisien est leur capacité de résilience,». Le Monde*, July 10, 2018, https://www.lemonde.fr/afrique/article/2018/07/10/la-plus-grande-menace-des-djihadistes-de-l-ouest-tunisien-est-leur-capacite-de-resilience_5329184_3212.html.
59. Lounnas, “The Tunisian Jihad: Between al-Qaeda and ISIS.”
60. Haim Malka and Margot Balboni, “Tunisia: Radicalism Abroad and at Home,” Center for Strategic and International Studies, June 2016, http://foreignfighters.csis.org/tunisia/why-tunisia.html.
61. Lisa Watanabe and Fabian Merz; “Tunisia’s Jihadi Problem and how To deal with it,” *Middle east Policy* XXiV, no. 4, 2017, 141.
62. U.S. Central Intelligence Agency, *CIA World Factbook*, 2019, https://www.cia.gov/library/publications/the-world-factbook/.
63. Zelin, “Not Gonna Be Able To Do It: al-Qaeda in Tunisia’s Inability to Take Advantage of the Islamic State’s Setbacks.”; Bozonnet, *«La plus grande menace des djihadistes de l’Ouest tunisien est leur capacité de résilience.»*.
64. “Tunisia Islamist Trends back to the Forefront,” *Al-Arabiya* (Riyadh), January 20, 2011, http://www.alarabiya.net/articles/2011/01/20/134294.html.

65. "Tunisia: Extremism & Counter-Extremism," Counter Extremism Project, 2019.
66. Noyon, *Islam, Politics, and Pluralism*, 96.
67. Hugh Roberts, address before the Center for Strategic and International Studies, Washington DC, March 21, 2007.
68. Kristina Kausch, "Tunisia: The Life of Others," Project on Freedom of Association in the Middle East and North Africa, *Documentos de Trabajo FRIDE* No. 85, 2009.
69. Correspondence of previous chapter author, Larry Velte, with Tunisian academic and lawyer, September 2009.
70. "The Role of Islamic Law in Tunisia's Constitution And Legislation Post-Arab Spring," 2019, https://www.loc.gov/law/help/role-of-islamic-law/tunisia-constitution.php.
71. Duncan Picard, "The Current Status of Constitution Making in Tunisia," Carnegie Endowment for International Peace, April 2012.
72. "Freedom of opinion/thought/conscience: The state is the guardian of religion. It guarantees freedom of conscience and belief, the free exercise of religious practices and the neutrality of mosques and places of worship from all partisan instrumentalisation. The state undertakes to disseminate the values of moderation and tolerance and the protection of the sacred, and the prohibition of all violations thereof. It undertakes equally to prohibit and fight against calls for Takfir and the incitement of violence and hatred" https://www.constituteproject.org/constitution/Tunisia_2014.pdf
73. *Tunisia National Risk Assessment of Money Laundering and Terrorism Financing*, April 2017, 62.
74. Aaron Y. Zelin and Katherine Bauer, "The Development of Tunisia's Domestic Counter-Terrorism Finance Capability," *CTC Sentinel*, November 28, 2019; *Tunisia National Risk Assessment of Money Laundering and Terrorism Financing*, April 2017, https://ctaf.bct.gov.tn/ctaf_f/userfiles/files/NRA_REPORT_Vf.pdf.
75. Thomas Renard, ed., "Returnees in the Maghreb: Comparing Policies on Returning Foreign Fighters in Egypt, Morocco, and Tunisia," Egmont Institute *Egmont Paper* 107, April 2019,

37, http://www.egmontinstitute.be/content/uploads/2019/04/EP107-returnees-in-the-Maghreb.pdf.

76. Richard Barrett, "Beyond the Caliphate: Foreign Fighters and the Threat of Returnees," The Soufan Center, October 2017, 47, http://thesoufancenter.org/wp-content/uploads/2017/11/Beyond-the-Caliphate-Foreign-Fighters-and-the-Threat-of-Returnees-TSC-Report-October-2017-v3.pdf.
77. Aaron Y. Zelin and Jacob Walles, "Tunisia's Foreign Fighters," Washington Institute for Near East Policy *Policy Watch* 3053, December 17 2018, https://www.washingtoninstitute.org/policy-analysis/view/tunisias-foreign-fighters.
78. Lounnas, "The Tunisian Jihad: Between al-Qaeda and ISIS."
79. Watanabe and Merz, "Tunisia's Jihadi Problem and how To deal with it."
80. Watanabe and Merz, "Tunisia's Jihadi Problem and how To deal with it."

25 United Arab Emirates

Quick Facts

Population: 9,992,083 (July 2020 est.)
Area: 83,600 sq km
Ethnic Groups: Emirati 11.6%, South Asian 59.4% (includes Indian 38.2%, Bangladeshi 9.5%, Pakistani 9.4%, other 2.3%), Egyptian 10.2%, Philippine 6.1%, other 12.8% (2015 est.)
Government Type: Federation of monarchies
GDP (official exchange rate): $382.6 billion (2017 est.)

Source: CIA World FactBook (Last Updated June 2020)

Introduction

In the wake of the September 11, 2001 terrorist attacks on the United States, citizens of the UAE were found to be significantly involved in Islamic terrorism. Two of the 9/11 hijackers were UAE residents, while another had lived there.[1] *Nearly two decades on, the UAE remains outwardly calm. The interpretation, practice, and religious leadership of Islam in the UAE have evolved in the country since its independence in 1971. The founding father and 33-year leader of the UAE promoted a conservative (but moderate) interpretation of Islam, which helped legitimize government efforts to contain Islamic extremism. Since 9/11, the UAE has seriously attempted to counter Islamic terrorism, the extreme forms of belief that promote it, and the financial support that facilitates it.*

The country's continued forceful responses to Islamic extremism have minimized the possibility of terrorist plots being carried out from or through the UAE. However, it seems clear that the arrests and convictions of Islamists stem more from the government's fear of popular attraction to political Islam than from evidence of an explicit plot to overthrow the government. Since 2011, the Emirati government has energetically suppressed any dissent, criticism, or calls for political reform.[2] *The UAE considers Iran and its Arab world proxies, as well as the Muslim Brotherhood (MB) and its affiliates, to be existential threats, and has pursued an increasingly assertive policy to counter them, as reflected in its leading role (in concert with Saudi Arabia, Bahrain, and Egypt) in efforts to isolate Qatar, as well as the country's intervention in Yemen.*

Islamist Activity

Islamists in the UAE have historically been constrained by several factors. First, Islam in the UAE is generally moderate and apolitical in nature, and the government closely monitors Muslim organizations (especially political ones). Furthermore, the largest segment of Muslims in the country is South Asian expatriates, who are drawn there by job opportunities and subject to expulsion for any politically threatening behavior. Finally, astute government distribution of national wealth has been effective in blunting any discontent that challenges the state.

The Muslim Brotherhood

The Muslim Brotherhood (MB) has maintained a presence in the UAE since before the country's independence in 1971. During the 1960s and 1970s, MB members fleeing Egypt found public and private sector jobs in the Emirates, especially in educational and judicial institutions. The MB thus gained significant influence in the UAE in subsequent years.[3] By the 1990s, however, that influence dissipated as the UAE government forced MB members employed by the Ministry of Education to renounce the Brotherhood or be fired. In 1994, al-Islah, the UAE branch of the MB, was formally outlawed. In 2003, Mohammed bin Zayed Al Nahyan, the Crown Prince of Abu Dhabi (and *de facto* ruler of the UAE), failed to strike a deal with senior MB leaders which would have permitted the group to operate in the UAE in exchange for a cessation of its political activities. Later the same year, UAE authorities forced MB associated teachers out of the education system, and, after 2006, hundreds of expatriate MB members were deported from the country.[4] An Islamist commentator observed at the time that "despite some interesting developments among the cadres and the youth of the MB, intense security obstacles prevented them from doing much by way of renewing their thought or engaging in popular actions."[5] The UAE government outlawed the Brotherhood as a political entity because of its perceived intention to establish a theocracy.[6] In the aftermath of the 2011 Arab Spring, the UAE felt threatened by the MB's attempts to incite Islamist activity in the UAE. While Mohammed Morsi was president of Egypt (2011-2013), relations between the two countries were strained due to the Egyptian government's prevailing Brotherhood sympathies. However, the UAE began giving financial aid to Egypt anew after Morsi was overthrown.[7]

In November 2014, the UAE released a list of approximately 83 designated terrorist groups (the exact number varies slightly in various reports), some of which were allegedly linked to the MB. Among these were two U.S. groups, the Council on American-Islamic Relations (CAIR) and the Muslim American Society (MAS). UAE action against CAIR and MAS was meant to support U.S. government officials who wished to designate the MB as a terrorist organization.[8] In June 2016, the UAE Federal Supreme Court convicted a group of Emiratis and Yemenis of setting up a branch of the MB. While sentences for the offenders were light, one report suggested that the government continues to feel challenged by the MB.[9]

On June 5, 2017, the UAE joined Saudi Arabia, Bahrain, and Egypt in isolating Qatar by denying it territorial access, citing Qatar's support for the MB and its constituent movements. Qatar maintains that MB engagement can defuse extremism, while the UAE sees the MB and other Islamists as undercutting their embrace of tolerance and modernity.[10] Qatar-UAE tensions heated up when U.S. intelligence revealed that the UAE government had hacked Qatari government news and social media sites in order to post controversial, false quotes attributed to the emir of Qatar.[11] At the same time, the UAE announced that a former MB member had confessed that the Qatari government supported UAE destabilization.[12] For the U.S., this dispute unfortunately reduces counterterrorism cooperation in the Gulf.[13] The UAE eased trade restrictions on Qatar in February 2019, following complaints from the World Trade Organization (WTO) and increased political tensions.[14]

Al-Islah

Al-Islah is the largest and best-organized opposition group in the UAE. It was founded in 1974 as a non-governmental organization dedicated to promoting sports, cultural activity, and charitable work. In recent years, the government has curbed its influence by prohibiting al-Islah members from holding public office and other prominent positions. The government now views al-Islah as a security threat.[15] By 2012, some 20,000 UAE residents were estimated to be affiliated with al-Islah.[16]

From December 2011 and throughout 2012, UAE officials arrested a number of Al-Islah members, convinced that the group was actively working with the MB to challenge the UAE's political system.[17] The crackdown culminated in the arrest of MB "spy ring" members allegedly collecting secret information and plotting to overthrow the Emirati regime. The forceful reaction of the government reflected its fear that Egypt's then-Brotherhood-dominated government was seeking to destabilize the Gulf monarchies by spreading its populist form of political Islam.[18]

The UAE government's subsequent November 2014 list of terrorist organizations, together with its continued arrests of suspected extremists, suggest that the UAE perceives al-Islah as a continuing political threat.[19] However, the UAE lacks internal consensus about al-Islah; analysts cannot agree on whether it is a chapter of the MB, a group that embraces a similar ideology without organizational links, or is simply an entity deeply influenced by the Brotherhood.[20] The Emirati government fears that al-Islah could become an analog to the MB, though it is probably more accurate to characterize the organization as focused on non-revolutionary governmental reform. Al-Islah's base is located in the northern emirates, where resentment of the wealth and opportunities found in Abu Dhabi and Dubai has fueled social grievances.[21]

Shortly after the appearance of news media reports in late 2018 that the UAE had hired a team of American and Israeli mercenaries to assassinate senior members of Yemen's al-Islah branch, the Crown Prince of Abu Dhabi, Mohammed bin Zayed, met with *al-Islah* leaders to establish a rapprochement. To some extent, the rapprochement reflects U.S. pressure on the UAE and Saudi Arabia to seek a negotiated peace with their opponents in Yemen.[22] At the same time, al-Islah's public split with the MB is meant to secure protection for it in southern Yemen.[23] However, given the ideological differences between the UAE government and al-Islah, a long-term consensus seems destined to fail.

Al-Qaeda

The terrorist attacks of September 11, 2001 highlighted links between the UAE and al-Qaeda. Two of the operatives who carried out the attacks were Emiratis; another resided in the UAE during the planning of the attacks. Furthermore, the UAE was one of only three countries to recognize the Taliban regime in Afghanistan.

Since 9/11, there have been no al-Qaeda attacks carried out in the UAE or launched from its soil, but numerous threats of varying credibility have been reported. Additionally, the presence of al-Qaeda operatives in the country has been established conclusively. In November 2002, the suspected ringleader of the October 12, 2000 attack on the USS Cole in Aden, Yemen, was captured in Dubai. The same year, a considerable number of al-Qaeda fighters who were captured in Afghanistan were discovered to be UAE nationals. Welfare associations in Dubai and Fujairah encouraged young men to join terrorist groups and were accused of funding radical groups in South Asia. Arrests occurring in 2004 suggested that Dubai continued to serve as a waypoint for al-Qaeda operatives.[24] In July 2005, a new group calling itself "The al-Qaeda Organization in the Emirates and Oman" demanded that UAE rulers immediately dismantle U.S. military installations located in the country.[25]

In 2008, the British government warned of possible terrorist attacks in the UAE, likely connected to threats from al-Qaeda.[26] In 2009, UAE authorities broke up a major terrorist ring which had been plotting against targets in Dubai.[27] In September of the same year, a Saudi tip led to the interception in Dubai of explosives which al-Qaeda in the Arabian Peninsula (AQAP) operatives had placed on UPS and FedEx flights.[28] However, no reports of al-Qaeda activity in the UAE have been issued in years.

Some *jihadi* internet forum discussants have suggested that al-Qaeda's failure to strike the UAE reflects a lack of popular local support for such an action. This is due, in part, to the non-militant nature of Emirati fundamentalists.[29] The government has likewise taken measures to counter extremism, including launching a public awareness campaign about the dangers of violent extremism.[30]

The UAE, in partnership with the U.S., is combating AQAP in southern Yemen through military, economic, and humanitarian support (the U.S. intelligence community has regarded AQAP as the most dangerous al-Qaeda affiliate since that organization's 2009 attempt to bomb an airliner *en route* to Detroit). The UAE has focused its efforts in southern Yemen, while Saudi forces have concentrated their efforts on the anti-Houthi campaign in the north of the country. The UAE has a unique rapport with the tribes in southern Yemen, as many southern Yemenis fled the civil war in the 1960-70s and settled in the UAE, and a significant number of those migrants subsequently joined the UAE's security forces.[31]

Since 2016, the UAE has aligned itself with U.S. counterterrorism aims. As U.S. drone attacks against AQAP increased, the UAE expanded its military activities in southern Yemen. UAE troops, or forces trained by them, took control of ports, airfields, and bases along Yemen's southern coast. By August 2018, the UAE had trained 60,000 Yemeni soldiers, half of whom were engaged in counterterrorist actions.[32]

The Islamic State (IS)

The UAE has been an active partner in the struggle against IS. UAE contributions to the anti-IS coalition were dramatically underscored in 2014, when a female Emirati pilot flew in the first wave of U.S.-led air attacks against IS targets in Syria.[33] In response, IS promised retaliation against Dubai and Abu Dhabi.

In the years since, Emirati authorities have moved against manifestations of IS in the country. In January 2016, the self-proclaimed leader of ISIS in the UAE, Mohammed al Habashi al-Hashemi, was put on trial in the UAE Federal Supreme Court, charged with planning several terrorist plots, including an attack on the November 2014 Formula One race in Abu Dhabi. In May 2016, he was sentenced to life in prison.[34] In March 2016, the same court sentenced 38 defendants to prison terms of varying length for association with terrorist groups and for plotting terrorist attacks, in the UAE. The court also ordered the dissolution of the Shabab al Manara group, with which the defendants had been linked.[35]

The Emirates also play an important role in the "war of ideas" against IS, and – in coordination with the U.S. – the UAE's Sawab Center counters ISIS propaganda efforts online.[36] As with threats from al-Qaeda, the UAE seems reasonably protected from IS due to vigilance and general financial prosperity.

However, threats do exist. In February 2016, an ISIS sympathizer was detained for allegedly planning to detonate a grenade in a Dubai restaurant.[37] In August 2017, Lebanese-Australian ISIS operatives unsuccessfully attempted to place an explosive device on a flight from Sydney to Abu Dhabi.[38] Furthermore, money has been smuggled through Dubai to IS.[39]

In November 2018, the UAE and Saudi Arabia reportedly sent military advisers and troops to northeast Syria to support the Kurdish YPG as it battled IS (although neither government confirmed the reports). This reflects fears shared by the UAE and Saudi Arabia of Turkish action against the Kurds and the extension of Turkish influence into post-war Syria.[40] On December 27, 2018, the UAE announced the reopening of its embassy in Damascus. With the prospect of unchecked Turkish and Iranian influence after President Trump announced the withdrawal of U.S. troops from Syria, the UAE and other Arab states have begun to reengage with the Assad regime.[41]

The Taliban and Haqqani Network

The U.S. government believes that the Taliban and affiliated Haqqani Network are funded in part by donors in the UAE, drawing support from the local Pashtun community there.[42] The Taliban is known to extort money from Afghan businessmen based in the UAE.[43] The size of both voluntary contributions and forced aid is still unknown at this time. However, Mullah Akhtar Mohammad Mansour, the former Afghan Taliban leader who was killed in a U.S. drone strike in May 2016, is known to have frequently visited the UAE to raise funds for Taliban operations.[44]

The Haqqani Network and the Pakistani Taliban are both on the UAE's list of banned terrorist organizations.[45] However, evidence suggests that these classifications do not seriously impede the groups' movements in the country, even though these elements remain an indirect threat to the Emirates. In February 2017, the UAE ambassador to Afghanistan died of wounds sustained in a terrorist attack in Kandahar the preceding month. The provincial police chief blamed the attack on the Haqqani Network.[46] In April 2018, Afghanistan accepted an offer from the UAE to boost its small troop presence to train Afghan recruits and to participate in operations against insurgents. Such operations would comprise actions against the Haqqani Network, its Taliban allies, and the IS.[47] As the U.S. pursued peace talks with the Taliban starting in late 2018, the UAE sought to play a helpful role. In December 2018, Abu Dhabi hosted talks between U.S. and Afghan Taliban officials, including Pakistani participants.[48]

Lashkar-e-Taiba (LeT)

LeT developed out of the Ahl-e-Hadith movement, which has roots in both the Middle East and the Indian Subcontinent.[49] LeT reportedly receives large amounts of money from Gulf-based networks, including funders in the UAE. Additionally, funds have apparently been sent from the UAE to LeT operatives in India.[50] There likewise appears to be a link between the UAE and LeT's terrorist activities carried out in India; an investigation of the 2003 Mumbai bombings revealed a connection between UAE LeT operatives and cells in India. Other urban terrorist attacks in India revealed a similar link. The November 2014 list of terror organizations outlawed by the UAE included LeT, and the UAE has worked closely with India to counter terrorist groups, notably the Indian Mujahedeen, which is closely linked with LeT. Intelligence sharing between the two countries led to the UAE turning over to the Indian government key Mujahedeen operatives who had been hiding in the Emirates. Among the Gulf countries, the UAE is prominent for the number of LeT and other terrorist suspects that have been extradited to India.[51]

The Houthi Movement

A leading risk assessment organization has asserted "there is a moderate risk of terrorist attacks against Emirati airports, ports and energy infrastructure" after a Houthi operative attacked an airport in Dubai with a drone in July 2018.[52] Beyond these dangers, the UAE perceives Yemen's Houthis to be a serious national security threat, fearing that they might provide Iran, which is currently supporting Houthi-led forces throughout the southern Gulf, with a greater opportunity to destabilize the Arabian Peninsula.[53]

ISLAMISM AND SOCIETY

Population estimates for the UAE in 2019 vary somewhat, but the World Bank's figure of 9,682.000 appears to align more accurately than others with the UAE's official figures from 2017.[54] Native Emiratis represent only 11.6 % of the total population. South Asians account for 59.4%, with Indians alone accounting for 38.2% of the country's people.[55] Citizens are overwhelmingly Muslim, with Sunnis representing 85% of Emiratis, while Shias comprise the remaining 15%, and Islam is the religion of 76% of the population.[56] Most Sunni Emiratis adhere to the Maliki school of Islamic law, which is officially recognized in Abu Dhabi and Dubai. The Hanbali school predominates elsewhere, except in Fujairah, where the Shafi'i school holds sway.[57]

The UAE constitution guarantees freedom of worship and declares all persons equal without discrimination on the basis of religious belief. The State Department has reported that "Christian churches and Hindu and Sikh temples operated on land donated by the ruling families. During the year 2017, construction was underway on multiple houses of worship. Other minority religious groups conducted religious ceremonies in private homes without interference." The report added that "Within society there was tolerance for non-Muslims, including for holiday celebrations and traditions, although there was pressure discouraging conversion from Islam." Religious groups have reported a "high degree of acceptance and tolerance for diverse religious views." At the same time, anti-Semitic publications continued to be available.[58] In May 2017, a multi-faith government sponsored group, the Forum for Promoting Peace, received an American Caravan for Peace delegation, comprising Muslim, Christian, and Jewish clergy, to discuss fostering tolerance and the role of religion in public life.[59] Since 2008, Dubai's small Jewish community has maintained a (previously secret) synagogue.

The synagogue went public in December of 2018; this, as well as the diplomatic visits made by high profile Israeli officials (including Prime Minister Benjamin Netanyahu) to Oman and the UAE in the preceding months, represented a thawing of relations between Israel and the Gulf states.[60] The UAE featured a dramatic visit by Pope Francis in February 2019, during which he celebrated Mass for more than 100,000 congregants.[61] Attitudes toward Islamic groups in the UAE are difficult to discern since there is no significant, direct popular participation in government. While the constitution mandates freedom of speech, public assembly and association are still subject to government approval. Although the Emirati press is among the freest in the Arab world, it exercises self-censorship on sensitive issues, and the broadcast media are government-owned. Thus, attitudes concerning Islamic groups must be assessed mainly by inference, rather than by consideration of explicit expressions of opinion.[62]

Islamic Groups Supporting Emirati populations

The Mohammed bin Rashid Al Maktoum Foundation was launched in 2007 by the prime minister and ruler of Dubai, who also serves as vice president of the UAE, with a personal donation in the form of a $10 billion endowment. The Islamic component of the foundation's mission is not explicit, but is nonetheless significant. A central element of the foundation is the *Bayt ul-Hikma*, named for the House of Knowledge that represented Islamic science and learning in the Abbasid Empire of the Middle Ages.[63] In 2017, the Foundation's name was changed to Mohammad bin Rashid Al Maktoum Knowledge Foundation.[64]

In Abu Dhabi, the Sheikh Zayed bin Sultan Al Nahyan Charitable and Humanitarian Foundation was established in 1992 with a $100 million endowment. Its mission is overtly aimed at advancing Islamic goals: it includes support for mosques and educational and cultural institutions and financing for both Emiratis and other Muslims in performing the Hajj. The foundation also supports humanitarian projects, including a camp and hospital for Syrian refugees in Jordan, and assists low income Emiratis and others in building, refurbishing, and maintaining housing.[65]

The Tabah Foundation is a non-profit institution that seeks

to promote a more effective contemporary Islamic discourse, to advance Islamic values, and to counter negative images of Islam. Funded by various institutions and individuals in the UAE, Tabah entered into an agreement with the *Diwan* (Council of State) of the Crown Prince of Abu Dhabi to develop the Zayed House for Islamic Culture. It also established a media department with a television and documentary film division.[66] In 2015, the Foundation's Tabah Futures Initiative established a partnership with Zogby Research Services to explore the attitudes of millennials in the Arab world toward religion and religious leadership. During 2017 and 2018, the foundation supported programs focused on the junction of religion, the public space, and regional and global affairs. Projects included studies of Islamic education in the UAE, religious identity and Egyptian youth, and the experiences of American Muslim youth.[67]

Islamism and the State

The UAE government funds or subsidizes the majority of Sunni mosques in the country (about 5% are privately endowed). It employs all Sunni *imams* and provides guidance to both Sunni and Shi'ite clergy. Shi'ite mosques are considered private, but may receive funds from the government upon request.

While no evidence suggests that Shi'ite (or Sunni) mosques have any connection with political or extremist motives, in 2012 a Khoja Shi'ite *madrassa* in Dubai was closed by the government with no explanation. These events followed numerous deportations of Shias from the UAE, who were forced to leave over possible connections to Hezbollah.[68]

The UAE has historically supported moderate, apolitical Islamic activities while opposing any politically threatening ones. Shaikh Zayed bin Sultan Al Nahyan embodied that philosophy. He was generous in his support of religious leaders, arming himself and the state against attacks from secular or religious quarters. The chief threat to the UAE in the first years of its independence was regional secular radicalism.

Following the September 11th terrorist attacks, the government reacted promptly (albeit cautiously) to the threat posed by al-Qaeda.

While the generally moderate nature of Islam in the UAE precluded broad support for al-Qaeda and other extremist groups, popular antipathy for some U.S. government actions in the Middle East complicated the government's cooperation with the United States.[69] In 2002, a contingent of Emirati troops was deployed to Afghanistan to help in the struggle to unseat the Taliban, whose government the UAE had recognized before 9/11. Also in 2002, UAE authorities announced that they had arrested Abd al-Rahim al-Nashri, the apparent mastermind behind the October 12, 2000 attack on the USS Cole in Aden.[70]

The UAE has won praise from the U.S. governments for its efforts to counter Islamic terrorism. While the general tendency of the UAE's rulers has been to co-opt potential troublemakers, the U.S. State Department noted that the UAE's preferred approach was to deny extremists a foothold rather than to permit their political participation.[71] Crown Prince Muhammad bin Zayed sought to counter Islamic politics in the educational system by devoting considerable resources to modernizing curricula. While UAE funds given for house construction and humanitarian programs in Gaza may have previously ended up supporting Hamas, there is evidence that the UAE's position on the group has dramatically shifted. The UAE had forewarning of Israel's 2014 offensive against Gaza and pushed for action against the group because of its close ties with the Muslim Brotherhood. Recent UAE support for housing in Gaza has been coordinated with the UN Relief and Works Agency (UNRWA).[72] A strained relationship between the crown prince, who allegedly called the Palestinian Authority (PA) a "hodgepodge of failure and corruption," and PA President Mahmoud Abbas led, in 2016, to the UAE's withholding of hundreds of millions of dollars of aid to the PA. The estrangement is reflected in Abbas's expulsion of former senior Fatah senior official, Mohammed Dahlan, in 2011. This violated a promise to the crown prince, who had urged Abbas to heal his rift with Dahlan. The latter then moved to the UAE, where he has developed a close relationship with the crown prince and undertaken activities that suggest an ambition to become head of the PA.[73]

The UAE-U.S. partnership in combating Islamist extremists in

Yemen has been extended to Somalia, the Balkans, and Afghanistan. The UAE's military reach has likewise been greatly expanded through the construction of bases in Africa.[74] The UAE, drawn by the struggle against al-Qaeda in the Horn of Africa, has become one of several regional contenders for military and commercial positioning. It competes with Saudi Arabia, Qatar, Turkey, and China.[75]

Aspects of the UAE's initiatives combating Islamic extremism can be problematic for the U.S., however. For example, the UAE has embraced autocratic rulers such as General Khalifa Haftar in Libya, to whom it has given military support in contravention of a UN arms embargo.[76] Yemeni President Abed Rabbi Mansour Hadi is currently prevented from leaving Saudi Arabia at the UAE's request after Hadi resisted Emirati efforts to establish areas of permanent influence in southern Yemen.

The UAE has built its own military bases in Hadramawt and it has carried out military operations without coordinating with Yemen's national government.[77] The UAE continues to purchase weapons from non-American sources (especially Chinese armed drones).[78] Further, the UAE (and Saudi Arabia) have transferred American-made weapons to militias linked to AQAP in an effort to buy their loyalty, breaking the terms of their arms sales agreements. Abu al-Abbas, a Yemeni warlord, fundraiser for al-Qaeda, and possible IS member, revealed that the UAE had provided him with support. The UAE reportedly works with Islamic fundamentalists in southern Yemen as a counterweight to its opponents; however, this potentially opens the way for AQAP to infiltrate UAE forces.[79] In early 2019, General George Votel, then head of U.S. Central Command, called for an investigation into weapons transfers after CNN discovered that U.S. weaponry provided to the UAE and Saudi Arabia was being used by Iran-linked militias and al-Qaeda.[80] The resulting information has led to congressional opposition for the UAE-Saudi coalition, as reflected by legislation passed by the U.S. Senate. This legislation was passed in the House as well, but is expected to meet a presidential veto.[81]

There is also concern that the UAE does not have a proactive strategy for dealing with a terrorist threat.[82] Since 2015, however, UAE counter-terrorism measures have been robust. U.S. State

Department reports observed that "the UAE has arrested senior *al-Qaeda* operatives; denounced terror attacks; improved border security; instituted programs to counter violent extremism; investigated suspect financial transactions; criminalized use of the Internet by terrorist groups; and strengthened its bureaucracy and legal framework to combat terrorism."[83] In mid-2016, the UAE accepted 15 detainees from the Guantanamo Bay prison, the largest such transfer during Barack Obama's presidency. The released detainees were put in a de-radicalization and rehabilitation program.[84]

The U.S. and UAE have cooperated on several initiatives to prevent radicalization and to counter violent extremism. UAE Foreign Minister Sheikh Abdullah bin Zayed Al Nahyan opened the International Center for Excellence in Countering Violent Extremism (ICECVE), also called the "Hedayah" (Guidance) Center, in 2012.[85] The center's establishment stemmed from the Global Counter Terrorism Forum (GCTF) created by the U.S. Department of State in September 2011. The GCTF promotes cooperation between its thirty member countries, performs subject matter research, and assists members in countering threats.[86] In May 2015, Hedayah initiated the Strengthening and Resilience to Violence and Extremism program (STRIVE), funded by the EU and aimed at increasing the capacity of state and non-state actors to challenge violent extremism.[87] In March 2019, STRIVE joined ICECVE and the Institute for Strategic Dialogue (ISD) in launching the Counter Extremism Hub, a global CVE web portal designed to bring together all relevant actors in the field of CVE.[88]

The "Sawab" (Correctness) Center, a joint UAE-U.S. initiative to combat online extremist Islamist propaganda, has sponsored more than 30 social media campaigns since its founding in July 2015.[89] The center has more than four million social media account followers.[90]

The UAE remains concerned about a possible threat from resident Shias, especially those from Lebanon. This will continue as long as Hezbollah and Iran actively support the Assad government in Syria, and as the Sunni-Shia divide grows more pronounced and dangerous.[91] This has led the UAE and Saudi Arabia to seek cooperation with Israel in opposing Iran and its affiliates. The UAE has purchased considerable military equipment from Israel and agreed to establish an Israeli diplomatic mission in Abu Dhabi, accredited to the International Renewable Energy Agency (IRENA).[92] In July 2018, the Israeli Air Force hosted a UAE military delegation to review operations of the IAF's F-35 fighter jets, which the UAE seeks to purchase.[93] In early 2019, at UAE-funded camps in the Negev Desert, Israeli officers trained foreign mercenaries, including Colombians and Nepalese, to participate in the fighting in Yemen.[94]

At the same time, the UAE has pursued ties with Iraq and the powerful Iraqi Shi'ite cleric Moqtada al-Sadr, who maintains independence from Iran, in hopes of diminishing Iran's influence on Iraq's Shi'a community.[95] In November 2018, Iraqi President Barham Salih visited the UAE to discuss improved bilateral ties. The UAE has committed $50.4 million to rebuild the Grand Al Nuri Mosque in Mosul which was destroyed by ISIS in 2017.[96]

Another area of concern is the flow of money from private donors to support extremist Sunni groups fighting in Syria, like IS, Jabhat al-Nusra, and Ahrar al-Sham. While some of the funds are specifically given to assist militias, much of the money is raised under the guise of humanitarian assistance. A Gulf-based organization, the Ummah Conference, recruits volunteers for Syria. Former senior UAE military officers lead the UAE branch of the organization.[97]

The U.S. has closely scrutinized UAE financial institutions and, in 2012, pursued two financial service companies with ties to Iran for sanctions violations.[98] In July 2012, the UAE Central Bank issued regulations that made *hawala* registration mandatory with sanctions for non-compliance. Moreover, the public has been cautioned against dealing with unlicensed charities.[99] In presenting a joint financial counter-terrorism task force between the U.S. and the UAE, then U.S. Undersecretary of Treasury for Terrorism and Financial Intelligence David Cohen stated that the U.S. has "a very good close relationship with the Emiratis in combating terrorist financing…"[100]

However, concerns about the UAE serving as a haven for illicit funds remain. The UAE's main financial hub, Dubai, has garnered a reputation for housing Taliban money leaving Afghanistan.[101] The city's large Free Trade Zone facilitates criminal and terrorist activities through front companies, fraud, smuggling, and banking system exploitation. In March 2018, the UAE enacted new regulations to raise the standards of exchange house operations and to restrict trade-related and other transactions in an effort to mitigate illicit financial behavior.[102] In May 2018, American and Emirati officials sanctioned several Iranian companies and officials who were operating an illegal financial network in the UAE through the Quds Force and regional Iranian proxies.[103]

The UAE has perceived Islamism in two ways—as the terrorist threat of al-Qaeda and ISIS and as the broad populism represented by the Brotherhood and Iranian influence. Cooperation with the U.S. in combating terrorism and terror financing has been increasingly close and effective. There have been no reports of terrorist incidents in the UAE for the past several years. While some concerns remain, the UAE's success in countering terrorism has been impressive. The greater concern in the UAE today is with the impact of the Arab Spring and the events it set in motion. The rise to power of the MB in Egypt was alarming to the Emirates, especially because of domestic Brotherhood and al-Islah influence. This accounts for the increased crackdown on dissent and the wide-ranging government identification of terrorist organizations. At the same time, fear of Iranian actions and influence, given the UAE's proximity to Iran and its considerable Shi'ite minority, has led to harsh treatment of expatriate Shi'as because of possible links to Hezbollah. These perceived threats have also led to a more assertive role in the Middle East, including active cooperation with the U.S. against ISIS, *al-Qaeda*, and the Houthi-led forces in Yemen.

The expanded and more aggressive UAE efforts to counter Islamist threats may bring enhanced risk of retaliatory terrorist attacks. Additionally, the UAE's push against Qatar has split the Gulf Cooperation Council, potentially compromising the effectiveness of regional cooperation against the threats of Islamic extremists.

Endnotes

1. *The 9/11 Commission Report* (New York: W.W. Norton & Company, Inc., 2004), 162, 231, and 168.
2. Lori Plotkin Boghardt, "The Muslim Brotherhood on Trial in the UAE," Washington Institute for Near East Policy *Policywatch* no. 2064, April 12, 2013, http://www.washingtoninstitute.org/policy-analysis/view/the-muslim-brotherhood-on-trial-in-the-uae.
3. Sultan Al Qassemi, "The Brothers and the Gulf," *Foreign Policy*, December 14, 2012, https://foreignpolicy.com/2012/12/14/the-brothers-and-the-gulf/.
4. Sultan Al Qassemi, "Qatar's Brotherhood Ties Alienate Fellow Gulf States," *Al-Monitor*, January 23, 2013, http://www.almonitor.com/pulse/originals/2013/01/qatar-muslim-brotherhood.html; Rachel Ehrenfeld and J. Millard Burr, "The Muslim Brotherhood Deception & Education," American Center for Democracy, April 18, 2013, http://acdemocracy.org/the-muslim-brotherhood-deception-education.
5. As cited in Marc Lynch, "MB in the Gulf," Abu Aardvark blog, June 10, 2008, http://abuaardvark.typepad.com/abuaardvark/2008/06/mb-in-the-gulf.html (site removed).
6. Samir Salama, "Muslim Brotherhood is Political and not Religious," *Gulf News*, September 22, 2008.
7. "The UAE and Saudi War on the Muslim Brotherhood Could Be Trouble for the U.S.," *Geopolitical Diary*, November 18, 2014, https://www.stratfor.com/geopolitical-diary/uae-and-saudi-war-muslim-brotherhood-could-be-trouble-us.
8. Members of the U.S Congress have, on multiple occasions, failed to pass legislation designating the MB as a foreign terrorist organization. Donald Trump had promised to do so during his presidential campaign, but so far failed to do so. "The UAE and Saudi War," *Geopolitical Diary;* and Adam Taylor, "Why the UAE is calling 2 American groups terrorists," *Washington Post*, November 17, 2014; Freer, "The Muslim Brotherhood and the Emirates" and "The UAE and Saudi War;" Julian Hattem, "Cruz bill would designate Muslim Brotherhood as terrorist group," *The Hill*, November 4, 2015, http://thehill.com/policy/national-security/259099-cruz-bill-would-designate-muslim-brotherhood-as-terrorist-group; Nahal Toosi, "Activists poke Trump to move faster on Muslim crackdown," *Politico*, January 24, 2017, http://www.politico.com/story/2017/01/trump-muslim-crackdown-234128.
9. "Verdict on 'Yemeni Muslim Brotherhood,' Group was accused of setting up a branch of the Muslim Brotherhood," *Emirates 24/7*

News, June 13, 2016, http://www.emirates247.com/news/emirates/verdict-on-yemeni-muslim-brotherhood-2016-06-13-1.632926.

10. David Ignatius, "Political Islam in the Modern World," *Washington Post*, July 14, 2017, A19.
11. James M. Dorsey, "The Gulf Crisis: fake news shines spotlight on psychological warfare," July 17, 2017, 1, https://mideastsoccer.blogspot.com/2017/07/the-gulf-crisis-fake-news-shines.html.
12. "He affirmed that Qatar's government is clearly aiding and abetting the terrorist Muslim Brotherhood," *Khaleej Times*, July 15, 2017, 1, https:/www.khaleejtimes.com/region/qatar-crisis/qatar-plotted-to-destabilize-use-ex-muslim-brotherhood-member.
13. Maria Abi-Habib and Gordon Lubold, "Pentagon Rebukes Gulf Allies," *Wall Street Journal*, October 7-8, 2017, A8.
14. "UAE eases Qatar shipping ban amid continuing Gulf dispute," *Al Jazeera* (Doha), February 20, 2019, https://aljazeera.com/news/2019/02/uae-eases-qatar-shipping-ban-continuing-gulf-dispute-190220152356122.html.
15. Pekka Hakala, "Opposition in the United Arab Emirates," European Parliament, Directorate General for External Relations, Policy Department, November 15, 2012, www.europarl.europa.eu/RegData/... EXPO-AFET_SP%282012%29491458_EN.pdf.
16. Jenifer Fenton, "Al-Islah in the UAE," *Arabist*, August 4, 2012, http://www.arabist.net/blog/2012/.../4/crackdown-on-islamists-in-the-uae.html.
17. Human Rights Watch, "UAE: Crackdown on Islamist Group Intensifies," July 18, 2012, http://hrw.org/news/2012/07/18/uae-crackdown-islamist; Ali Rashid al-Noaimi, "Setting the Record Straight on al-Islah in the UAE," *Middle East Online*, October 17, 2012, http://www.middle-east-online.com/english/?id=54950.
18. Jouini, Hassen. "'Egypt-UAE Relations Worsen with 'Brotherhood' Arrests,'" *Morocco World News*, January 3, 2013. https://www.moroccoworldnews.com/2013/01/72662/egypt-uae-relations-worsen-with-brotherhood-arrests/.
19. Freer, "The Muslim Brotherhood and the Emirates"; Amnesty International, "UAE: Ruthless crackdown on dissent exposes 'ugly reality' beneath facade of glitz and glamour," November 18, 2014, https://www.amnesty.org/en/latest/news/2014/11/uae-ruthless-crackdown-dissent-exposes-ugly-reality-beneath-fa-ade-glitz-and-glamour/.
20. Al Qassemi, "The Brothers and the Gulf"; Yara Bayoumy, "UAE Imprisons Islamist coup plotters," *Daily Star* (Beirut), July 3, 2013;

"UAE sentences 69 suspects to prison in mass coup plot trial," Associated Press, July 2, 2013.

21. Boghardt, "The Muslim Brotherhood on Trial in the UAE."
22. Khalil Dewan, "UAE and Yemen's al-Islah: Meeting of enemies doesn't mean peace," *Middle East* Eye, November 16, 2018, https://www.middleeasteye.net/opinion/uae-and-yemens-al-islah-meeting-enemies-doesnt-mean-peace;
23. Elana de Lozier, "The UAE and Yemen's Islah: A Coalition Coalesces," Washington Institute for Near East *Policy Watch* 3046, December 6, 2018, https://www.washingtoninsitute.org/policy-analysis/view/the-use-and-yemens-islah-a-coalition-coalesces.
24. Christopher M. Davidson, "Dubai and the United Arab Emirates: Security Threats," *British Journal of Middle Eastern Studies* 36, no. 3, December 2009, 444.
25. Davidson, "Dubai and the United Arab Emirates: Security Threats," 446; Reacting to the berthing of U.S. aircraft carriers in Dubai, after their planes had carried out missions to "bombard the Muslims in Iraq and Afghanistan," the organization stated that the UAE's ruling families would "endure the fist of the mujahideen in their faces" if their demand was not met.
26. Abdul Hamied Bakier, "An al-Qaeda Threat in the United Arab Emirates?" Jamestown Foundation *Terrorism Focus* 5, iss. 25, July 1, 2008, http://www.jamestown.org/single/?no_cache=1&tx_ttnews%5Btt_news%5D=5025.
27. "Terror Network Dismantled in U.A.E.," *Global Jihad*, September 17, 2009; "AQAP Unlikely behind UPS Plane Crash - US Officials," Reuters, November 11, 2010, http://in.reuters.com/article/2010/11/11/idINIndia-52846520101111.
28. Hamied Bakier, "An al-Qaeda Threat in the United Arab Emirates?"
29. "United Arab Emirates," in U.S. Department of State, *International Religious Freedom Report 2011*, July 30, 2012, http://www.state.gov/j/drl/rls/irf/2011religiousfreedom/index.htm?dlid=192911#wrapper.
30. Sudarasan Raghavan, "Still Fighting al-Qaeda," *Washington Post*, July 7, 2018.
31. Kyle Monsees, "The UAE's Counterinsurgency Conundrum in Southern Yemen," Arab Gulf States Institute in Washington, August 18, 2016, http://www.agsiw.org/the-uaes-counterinsurgency-conundrum-in-southern-yemen/.
32. Rawan Shaif and Jack Watling, "How the UAE's Chinese-Made Drone is Changing the War in Yemen," *Foreign Policy*, April 27,

2018, http://foreignpolicy.com./2018/04/27/drone-wars-how-the-uaes-chinese-made-drone-is-changiong-the-war-in-yemen.

33. Ian Black, "UAE's leading role against ISIS reveals its wider ambitions," *Guardian* (London), October 30, 2014, https://www.theguardian.com/world/2014/oct/30/uae-united-arab-emirates-leading-player-opposition-isis-middle-east.
34. Brandon Turkus, "Man charged with plot to bombAbu Dhabi F1 race,: *Autoblog*, December 30, 2015, https://www.autoblog.com.2015/12/30/abu-dhabi-f1-terrorist-trial; *AlArabiyya English*, "Self-proclaimed ISIS 'emir' on trial in UAE," January 26, 2016, https://english.alarabiyya.net/en/News/middle-east/2016/01/26/Emirati-on-trial-was-self-proclaimed-ISIS-emir-html; and U.S. Department of State, "Country Reports on Terrorism 2016-United Arab Emirates, July 19, 2017, https://www.refworld.org/docid/5981e40913.html.
35. U.S. Department of State, "Country Reports on Terrorism 2016-United Arab Emirates."
36. "U.S., U.A.E. launch anti-ISIS messaging center in Dubai," *CBS News,* July 8, 2015, http://www.cbsnews.com/news/us-uae-launch-anti-isis-messaging-center-dubai/.
37. "UAE court gives four death sentence for supporting ISIS," *Al-Arabiyya* (Riyadh), February 14, 2016, http://english.alarabiya.net/en/News/middle-east/2016/02/14/UAE-Federal-Supreme-Court-sentences-defendants-for-joining-ISIS.html.
38. Jack Moore, "Lebanon Foiled ISIS Barbie Doll Bomb Plot on Flight from Australia to Abu Dhabi," Newsweek, p.1, August 21, 2017, accessed on November 15, 2017.
39. Paul Tilsley, "Jihadist couriers? Suspects nabbed at Johannesburg airport with $6M were ISIS-bound, say cops," *Fox News,* September 21, 2015, http://www.foxnews.com/world/2015/09/21/5-suspects-stopped-at-johannesburg-airport-with-6m-cash-headed-for-isis.html.
40. Leith Aboufadel, "Saudi Arabia, UAE allegedly deploy troops to Syria, AMN (*Al-Masdar News*), citing Turkish publication *Yeni* Safak, November 21, 2018, https://www.almasdarnews.com/article/saudi-arabia-uae-allegedly-deploy-troops-to-syria-turkish-media.
41. Marc Daou, "Thaw in relations between Arab leaders and Syria's Assad," *France 24*, January 4, 2019, https://www.france24.com/en/20190104-syria-bashar-al-assed-diplomacy-uae-russia-iran-raab-league-saudi-arabia.
42. "US Embassy Cables: Afghan Taliban and Haqqani Network Using

United Arab Emirates as Funding Base," *Guardian* (London), December 5, 2010, http://www.guardian.co.uk/world/us-embassy-cables-documents/242756.

43. "US Embassy Cables: Afghan Taliban and Haqqani Network Using United Arab Emirates as Funding Base," *Guardian* (London), December 5, 2010, http://www.guardian.co.uk/world/us-embassy-cables-documents/242756.
44. Eltaf Najafizada, "Taliban Says Ex-Leader Often Visited United Arab Emirates, Iran," Bloomberg, May 26, 2016, http://www.bloomberg.com/news/articles/2016-05-26/taliban-says-ex-leader-often-visited-united-arab-emirates-iran.
45. "UAE bans five Pakistan-based outfits among terror groups," *Economic Times*, November 16, 2014, http://articles.economictimes.indiatimes.com/2014-11-16/news/56137274
46. "UAE ambassador dies of wounds from Afghanistan bombing," *The New Arab*, February 16, 2017, 1, https://www.alaraby.co.uk/english/news/2017/2/16/uae-mbassador-dies-of-wounds-from-afghanistan-bombing.
47. "UAE to boost troop presence in Afghanistan for training: officials," Reuters, June 8, 2018 https://www.reuters.com/article//us-afghanistasn-emirates/uae-to-boost-troop-presence-in-afghanistan-for-training-officials-idUSKCN1J41E7.
48. "UAE to deposit $3bn. in Pakistan central bank to help ease economic turmoil," *Middle East Eye*, December 21, 2018, https://www.middleeasteye.net/news/uae-deposit-3bn-pakistan-central-bank-amid-balance-payments-crisis-1786728775..
49. Animesh Roul, "Lashkar-e-Taiba's Financial Network Targets India from the Gulf States," Jamestown Foundation *Terrorism Monitor* 7, iss. 19, July 2, 2009, https://jamestown.org/program/lashkar-e-taibas-financial-network-targets-india-from-the-gulf-states/.
50. Animesh Roul, "Lashkar-e-Taiba's Financial Network Targets India from the Gulf States," Jamestown Foundation *Terrorism Monitor* 7, iss. 19, July 2, 2009, https://jamestown.org/program/lashkar-e-taibas-financial-network-targets-india-from-the-gulf-states/; Qazi Faraz Ahmad, "NIAA Arrests 2 Hawala Operators from UP's Muzaffarnagar on Terror Funding Charges," *News 18*, February 5, 2018, https://www.news18.com/news/india/nia-arrests-2-hawala-operators-from-ups-muzzafarnagar-on-terror-funding-charges-1650535.html.
51. Think Chowdury, "India and the UAE: A Partnership Against Terrorism," *Swarajya*, August 25, 2015, http://swarajyamag.com/

world/India-and-uae-a-partnership-against-terrorism; Rajeesh Ahuja and Jayanth Jacob, "Of 24 terror suspects turned in by Gulf countries to India since 2012, 18 are from UAE and Saudi," *Hindustan* Times, August 24, 2018, https://www.hindustantimes.com/india-news/of-24-terror-suspects-tu…-2012-18-are-from-uae-and-saudi/story-225ND6ilOaWrD9mYZYRFLL.html.

52. "Terrorism risks rising in the United Arab Emirates," JLT Specialty, October 31, 2018, https://www.jltspecialty.com/our-insights/thought-leadership/cps/terrorism-risks-rising-in-the-united-arab-emirates.
53. Sigurd Neubauer, "Gulf States See Guantanamo Detainees As Policy Asset," Arab Gulf States Institute in Washington, September 9, 2016, http://agsiw.org/gulf-states-see-guantanamo-detainees-as-policy-asset.
54. GMI Blogger, "United Arab Emirates Population Statistics (2019," January 30, 2019, https://www.globalmediainsight.com/blog/uae-population-statistics/.
55. *Countries of the World, United Arab Emirates PEOPLE 2019*, https://theodora.com/wfbcurrent/united-arab-emirates-people.html; U.S. Department of State, Bureau of Democracy, Human Rights and Labor, "United Arab Emirates," *International Religious Freedom Report for 2017*, https://www.state.gov/i/drl/ris/irf/rcligiousfreedom/index.htm#wrapper.
56. Fanack, "Population of the UAE," updated January 23, 2019, https://www.uae-embassy.org/about/uae/travel-culture/7-emirates.
57. Malcolm C. Peck, *The United Arab Emirates: A Venture in Unity* (Boulder, CO: Westview Press, 1986),60.
58. "United Arab Emirates" in United States Department of State, *2017 Report on International Religious Freedom.*
59. Asa Fitch, "U.A.E. Slowly Loosens Constraints on Religious Freedom, *Wall Street Journal,* January 28, 2019, A7.
60. Yaniv Pohoryles, "Dubai synagogue comes out of the shadows," *Jewish World*, December 10, 2018, https://www.ynetnews.com/articles/0,7340,L-5422429,00.html; Miriam Herschlag, "For the first time, Dubai's Jewish community steps hesitantly out of the shadows," *Times of Israel*, December 5, 2018, https://www.timesofisrael.com/for-the-first-time-dubais-jewish-community-steps-hesitantly-out-of-the-shadows/.
61. Francis X. Rocca and Nicolas Parasie, "Pope Francis Acknowledges Nuns Were Abused," *Wall Street Journal*, February 6, 2019.
62. In the fall of 2010, through an agreement with the Crown Prince

Court of Abu Dhabi, the Gallup Organization opened a new research center in Abu Dhabi to conduct inquiries into attitudes of Muslims around the world. While the initial report it issued looked broadly at the state of Muslim-West relations, the Abu Dhabi Gallup Center was set up to perform research specifically on attitudes in the UAE. Most of the UAE polling, focused on non-controversial topics like healthcare access, although a poll on factors hindering women's entrepreneurship in the UAE and other GCC countries was conducted. However, the center was closed down in March 2012, when the UAE government ordered the closure of foreign NGOs, including the U.S.-based National Democratic Institute. Gallup reported that it "made the strategic decision to bring its efforts in Abu Dhabi back to its headquarters in Washington, DC" and that it "will continue to conduct research and publish findings about the region, and will maintain a presence in Dubai." See "Abu Dhabi and Gallup Establish New Research Center," *PRNewswire*, October 25, 2010, http://www.prnewswire.com/new-releases/abu-dhabi-and-gallup-establish-new-research-center-105668138.html; Vivian Nereim, "Gallup and think tank leave Abu Dhabi," *The National*, March 29, 2012, http://www.thenational.ae/news/uae-news/gallup-and-think-tank-leave-abu-dhabi. See also Shibley Telhami, *The World Through Arab Eyes* (New York: Basic Books, 2013), which presents some interesting results of polling done in the UAE.

63. "Mohammed bin Rashid Al Maktoum Foundation," *Revolvy*, N.D. (presumably 2015), https://www.revolvy.com/main/index.php?s=Mohammed%20bin%20Rashid%20AI%20Maktoum%20Foundation&item_type=topic
64. "Mohammad bin Rashid Al Maktoum Foundation renamed," *Gulf News*, February 15, 2017, 1, http://gulfnews.com/news/uae/government/mohammad-bin-rashid-al-maktoum-foundation-renamed-1.1978954.
65. "Zayed bin Sultan Al Nahyan Charitable and Humanitarian Foundation: A 26-year journey of humanitarian giving," WAM, August 6, 2018, http://wam.ae/en/details/1395302702517.
66. See Tabah's newsletter, *Clarity*, iss. 1, Fall 2010, for a discussion of its programs, http:/www.tabahfoundation.org/newsletter/pdfs/1/TabahNewsEn_201009.pdf.
67. "Tabah Futures Initiative," *Medium*, November 19, 2018, https://medium.com/@futuresinitiative.
68. Esperance Ghanem, "What is behind UAE deportation of Lebanese nationals?" *Al Monitor*, April 17, 2015, http://www.al-monitor.com/

pulse/originals/2015/04/lebanon-nationals-deportation-uae-decision-html#ixzz40DFzmDtB; "Over 4000 Shiites deported from UAE," *Shia World News Facebook*, February 13, 2013, https://. facebook.com/newsshia/posts/337686526342852.

69. See Malcolm C. Peck, *Historical Dictionary of the Gulf Arab States*, 2nd ed. (Lanham, MD: The Scarecrow Press, Inc. 2008), 144.
70. Sultan Al Qassemi, "The Sacrifice of Our Troops and a Need for Civil Society," *The National* (Abu Dhabi), February 28, 2010, http://www.thenational.ae/news/the-sacrifice-of-our-troops-and-a-need-for-civil-society; Mohammed Nasser, "Military Expert: Al Qaeda Present in the Gulf... but not Active," *Al-Sharq al-Awsat* (London), December 29, 2010, http://www.aawsat.com/english/news.asp?section=1&id=23598.
71. "US Embassy Cables: Abu Dhabi Favours Action to Prevent a Nuclear Iran," *Guardian* (London), November 28, 2010, http://www.guardian.co.uk/world/us-embassy-cables-documents/59984.
72. "UAE, Israel have secret meeting, UAE 'offered to fund Israel's Gaza offensive,' *The Peninsula*, July 19, 2014, http://freedmanreport.com/?p=1651; and "600 UAE-funded housing units given to refugees in Gaza," *Middle East Monitor*, December 7, 2015, https://www.middleeastmonitor.com/20151207-600-uae-funded-housing-units-given-to-refugees-in-gaza/.
73. Rori Donaghy, "REVEALED: How Palestinian president made an enemy of the UAE," *Middle East Eye*, July 18, 2016, http://www.middleeasteye.net/news/revealed-how-palestinian-president-made-enemy-uae.
74. U.S. Embassy Abu Dhabi, "Scenesetter for Counterterrorism Coordinator."
75. Matina Stevis-Gridneff, "Mideast Power Struggle Plays Out on New Stage," *Wall Street Journal*, June 2-3, 2018, A1.
76. Kareem Fahim and Missy Ryan, "In the UAE, U.S. finds an ally and a headache."
77. Kareem Fahim, "As Yemen increasingly splinters, U.S. policy is challenged," *Washington Post*, September 23, 2018.
78. Rawan Shaif and Jack Watling, "How the UAE's Chinese-Made Drone Is Changing War in Yemen," *Foreign Policy*, April 27, 2018.
79. Emily Ferguson, "Al-Qaeda armed with US WEAPONS: Fears Bin Laden's terrorists using weapons from Washington," *Express* (London), February 23, 2019, https://www.express.com.uk/news/world/1091444/al-qaeda-return-us-weapons-saudi-arabia; "Re-

port Claims UAE arms Al-Qaeda and Daesh in Yemen," *Middle East Monitor*, January 2, 2019, https://www.middleeastmonitor.com/20190102-report-claims-use-arms-al-qaeda-and-daesh-in-yemen/.

80. "U.S. general calls for probe into alleged Saudi-UAE arms-links with Al-Qaeda," *The New Arab*, February 5, 2019, https://www.a;araby.com.uk/english/news/20129/2/5/us-general-says-probe-saudi-uae-arms-links-with-al-qaeda.
81. Sudarasdan Raghavan, "Study: U.S., British bombs killed 203 civilians in Yemen," *Washington Post*, March 7, 2019; Karoun Demirjian, "Senate votes to end military support for operation in Yemen led by Saudis," *Washington Post*, March 14, 2019.
82. Cited in Kenneth Katzman, *The United Arab Emirates (UAE): Issues for U.S. Policy*, Congressional Research Service, November 28, 2016.
83. Jess Bravin and Carole E. Lee, "U.S. Transfers 15 Guantanamo Bay Detainees," *Wall Street Journal*, August 15, 2016, http://www.wsj.com/articles/u-s-transfers-15-guantanamo-bay-detainees-1471303872.
84. Government of the UAE, "Centres for countering extremism," updated May 6, 2019, https://government.ae/en/about-the-uae/culture/tolerance/centers-for-countering-extremism.
85. U.S. Department of State, "Global Counterterrorism Forum Co-chair's Fact Sheet=About thebGCTF," September 23, 2014, https://2009-2017.state.gov/r/pa/prs/ps/2014/09/232018.htm.
86. United Nations Consultant Research Projects," Hedayah Background," May 2, 2018, https://uncareer.net/vacancy/consultant-research-projects-168080.
87. MENAFN-Emirates News Agency," UAE-Counter Extremism Hub launched to reduce threat of violent extremism," March 4, 2019, https://menafn.com/1098203995/UAE-Counter-Extremism-Hub-launched-to-reduce-threat-of-violent-extremism?src=Rss.
88. "UAE Interact, "Sawab Center warns against Daesh youth recruitment," May 1, 2017, https://www.uaeinteract.com/news/default3.asp?ID=534.
89. "Sawab Centre highlights values of tolerance," *Gulf Today*, November 19, 2018, http://gulftoday.ae/portal/1ea526e8-20fe-446f-bd63-49e3327d45750.aspx; "Sawab Centre celebrates third anniversary, *Gulf News*, July 28, 2018, https://gulfnews.com/uae/government/sawab-centre-celebrates-third-anniversary-1.2258042.-
90. Hair Nayouf, "Iran has "sleeper cells" in the Gulf: Ex-diplomat,"

Al Arabiya, October 30, 2007, https://english.alarabiya.net/articles/2007/10Abdul H/30/41005.html; Abdul Hameed Bakier, "Sleeper Cells and Shi'a Secessionists in Saudi Arabia: A Salafist Perspective," Jamestown Foundation *Terrorism Monitor* 7, iss. 18, June 25, 2009, http://www.jamestown.org/single/?no_cache=1&tx_ttnews%5Btt_news%5D=35182.; On fears of Iran and possible "fifth column" activities by UAE residents of Iranian origin, see Katzman, *The United Arab Emirates*, 16.

91. James M. Dorsey, "All the UAE's Men: Gulf Crisis Opens Door to Power Shift in Palestine," *HuffPost*, July 9, 2017, https://www.huffpost.com/entry/all-the-uaes-men-gulf-crisis-opens-door-to-power_b_59619923e4b085e766b5135f.
92. "IDF Press release: A New Age in the IAF," *i24 News*, July 9, 2018, https://www.i24news.tv/en/news-israel/178686-180704-sorces-tell-124news-israel-hosted-uae-military-delegation-to-review-f-35s.
93. "Israel training mercenaries for Yemen war in UAE camps in Negev: Haaretz," *Press TV*, February 16, 2019, https://www.presstv.com/DetailFr/2019/02/16/588694/Israel-Saudi-Srabia-Yemen.
94. Maher Chmaytelli, "UAE pushes for better ties with cleric Sadr amid efforts to contain Iran," Reuters, August 14, 2017, https://www.reuters.com/article/us-mideast-crisis-iraq-emirates.
95. Mina Aldroubi, "UAE reaches out to Iraq to counter Iranian influence in the Levant," *The National*, December 26, 2018, https://www.thenational.ae/world/mena/uae-reaches-out-to-counter-iranian-influence-in-the-levant-1.806541.
96. Joby Warrick, "Donors boost Islamists in Syria," *Washington Post*, September 22, 2013.
97. See Peck, *Historical Dictionary of the Gulf Arab States*, 297; Steve Barber, "The 'New Economy of Terror:' The Financing of Islamist Terrorism," *Global Security Issues* 2, iss. 1, Winter 2011, 5, 9.
98. Gregor Stuart Hunter, "U.S. official to focus on illicit finance and sanctions in UAE talks," *The National* (Abu Dhabi), January 27, 2013, http://www.thenational.ae. The two financial service companies were HSBC and Standard Chartered.
99. Celina B. Realuyo, "Combating Terrorist Financing in the Gulf," The Arab Gulf States Institute in Washington, January 26, 2015.
100. Taimur Khan, "Joint US-UAE task force to choke off ISIL funding," *The National* (Abu Dhabi), October 27, 2014, http://www.thenational.ae/world/middle-east/joint-us-uae-task-force-to-choke-off-isil-funding.
101. Said Salahuddin and Erin Cunningham, "Taliban video purports to

show captives' pleas to Trump," *Washington Post*, January 11, 2017.
102. Katherine Bauer, "Grading Counterterrorism Cooperation with GCC States," Testimony before the House Foreign Affairs Committee, Subcommittee on the Middle East and North Africa, April 21, 2018.
103. Ian Talley, "U.S. Raises Pressure on Iran," *Wall Street Journal,* May 11, 2018.

26 Yemen

Quick Facts

Population: 29,884,405 (July 2020 est.)
Area: 527,968 sq km
Ethnic Groups: Predominantly Arab; but also Afro-Arab, South Asian, European
GDP (official exchange rate): $31.27 billion (2017 est.)

Source: CIA World FactBook (Last Updated August 2020)

Introduction

Yemen is home to multiple militant Islamist organizations as well as Salafi-jihadi groups. Both al-Qaeda and the Islamic State have exploited the conditions created by Yemen's protracted civil war and collapse over the past several years. The Zaydi Shia Houthi movement, which receives Iranian support, has also been empowered through the conflict, and now controls much of northern and central Yemen.

Multiple Islamist groups have taken advantage of Yemen's instability to advance their political agendas. At the extreme end of the spectrum, Salafi-jihadi groups have established safe-havens within the country's borders. The Yemeni government and Emirati-backed Yemeni militias, for their part, have coordinated with the United States on counterterrorism operations to target leaders of al-Qaeda, which expanded its influence at the beginning of the civil war but has receded in recent years. The Islamic State likewise maintains a modest foothold in Yemen.

The economic, social, and security issues plaguing the Yemeni state, coupled with a drawn-out civil war, have paralyzed the government, leaving it unable to provide effective governance and security to much of the country. This has added to historical internal challenges facing the nation, including political and economic instability, declining oil reserves, severe water shortages, internally displaced persons (IDPs), and regional and tribal tensions. The

UN has ranked Yemen as the world's worst humanitarian crisis due to the staggering rates of malnutrition and starvation, the world's largest cholera outbreak, and more than 24 million people in need of humanitarian assistance in the country.[1]

ISLAMIC ACTIVITY

In the three decades since the unification of traditionalist North Yemen and the Marxist South, Yemen has suffered from frequent instability and weak governance. This has made it an ideal safe haven for opposition and terrorist groups of varying political stripes. Prior to 1990, local authorities in the Marxist South supported and harbored an array of Palestinian terrorist organizations. Tacit support for subversive groups continued in Yemen after unification, but extremist Islamist organizations, especially those opposed to the Saudi monarchy, replaced radical Palestinian and leftist ones.[2]

The accessibility of weapons through Yemen's underground market has compounded the country's insecurity; estimates suggest that three guns exist for every one person in Yemen.[3] The Yemeni political and social landscape has historically been replete with tribal leaders and Islamist groups that had the arms and power to operate outside the constraints of the Yemeni government, creating conditions for piracy, smuggling, and Salafi-*jihadi* activity.[4]

The ouster of the country's longtime autocratic president, Ali Abdullah Saleh, in 2011 after widespread anti-government protests and the political transition that followed his departure transformed Yemeni politics. A U.S.-backed, Gulf Cooperation Council (GCC)-brokered transition agreement led to a referendum electing former vice president Abd Rabu Mansour Hadi as Saleh's replacement. A National Dialogue Conference, presided over by Hadi, laid the groundwork for a new Yemeni Constitution and included a number of opposition groups and Islamist factions, including Zaydi Shiite Houthi rebels.[5]

Opposition groups denounced the transition process for not fully shifting power away from the established elite. In 2014, The Houthis left the negotiating table and militarized, advancing from their northern stronghold towards Sana'a, Yemen's capital, with

Saleh's support.[6] They forced the Hadi government to sign an agreement giving opposition groups—including *Hirak* (the Southern Movement), an umbrella group for southern opposition factions—greater power in the government.[7] The Houthi coup culminated in the winter of 2015, when the Hadi government fled the country. Thereafter, civil war broke out between the Houthi-Saleh faction and those opposed to it, including the Southern Movement, the Sunni party al-Islah, local tribal militias, and al-Qaeda. An Arab coalition, led by Saudi Arabia, intervened in Yemen in March 2015 in support of the Hadi government.[8] Most of Saleh's coalition split with the Houthis in December 2017, following Saleh's death at the hands of Houthi forces.[9] New groups opposed to the Houthis have also emerged since the start of the civil war, including the UAE-backed Transitional Political Council for the South (STC), which formed in May 2017 as a hardline splinter of the Southern Movement.[10] Radical actors on both sides of the war are actively promoting sectarianism in parts of Yemen where it was not previously prevalent.

Islamist and Salafi-jihadi actors

Yemen hosts a diverse array of Islamist actors, ranging from establishment political parties like al-Islah, a Muslim Brotherhood-influenced organization, to Salafi-*jihadi* insurgents like al Qaeda and the Islamic State at the extreme end of the spectrum. Within Yemen's Shi'a community, the Houthi movement is the most dominant Islamist actor.

Al-Qaeda

From its founding until the late 1990s, al-Qaeda maintained training camps in various locations in the country.[11] In 1997, bin Laden reportedly sent an envoy to Yemen to explore the possibility of establishing a base there in the event the Taliban expelled him from Afghanistan.[12] Additionally, Ayman al-Zawahiri - Osama bin Laden's successor as the head of al-Qaeda - and several of his companions from Egyptian Islamic Jihad briefly established a base of operations in the country in the 1990s.[13] Yemenis trained in camps in Afghanistan and Pakistan, including under al-Qaeda's high command, through a pipeline facilitated by the Yemeni government throughout the 1980s and 1990s.[14] The Saleh regime integrated many of these militants into existing state security and political organizations, directing them against socialists and separatists in the south.

In the immediate aftermath of 9/11, the Yemeni government implemented stiff counterterrorism measures and cooperated with the United States to eliminate senior al-Qaeda operative Abu Ali al-Harithi.[15] By the end of 2003, however, Sana'a began to lag in its counterterrorism efforts, and in February 2006 23 al-Qaeda terrorists, including the mastermind of the 2000 *USS Cole* bombing, escaped from a Yemeni prison.[16] An October 2009 report by the American Enterprise Institute (AEI) asserted that the escapees were likely assisted by members of the Yemeni security apparatus. [17]

Capitalizing on Yemen's instability of the late 2000s, the group has subsequently emerged as a major insurgent actor in Yemen, where it seeks to mobilize the country's Sunnis against the Yemeni state. Significantly, it does not demand ideological support. The group instead operates within local customs and develops relations based on pragmatic lines of support and by providing locals with basic goods and services.[18] AQAP has found a particularly favorable political climate in the aggrieved south.[19]

The number of Yemenis aligned with AQAP is unknown. Membership estimates range from the low hundreds to several thousand, and numbers have fluctuated over the last decade.[20]

Fighters are known to have travelled to Yemen from conflict zones in Syria and Iraq in recent years, bringing with them new skills and tactics.[21] Even before the 2011 anti-government protests swept through Yemen, AQAP was on a path to establish links with the country's eastern tribes.[22]

In the wake of the 2011 uprisings, AQAP sought to capitalize on the political transition, increasing attacks against government targets. The group's insurgent arm, Ansar al-Sharia, was powerful enough to seize key cities in the south at the time; it held the capital of Abyan province, Zinjibar, from May 2011 till June 2012.[23] The group controlled al Mukalla, a major port city in southeast Yemen, from April 2015 to April 2016, and expanded its influence behind the frontlines.[24]

AQAP uses asymmetrical attacks—such as complex attacks

involving vehicle-borne improvised explosive devices (VBIEDs) and small tactical teams—to degrade the military capabilities of opposing forces. The group has assassinated military and government leadership, intelligence officers, and government-aligned local powerbrokers. AQAP has also kidnapped individuals for ransom and political leverage over foreign powers. The 2012 kidnapping of Saudi deputy consul Abdallah al-Khalidi is one example.[25]

AQAP has historically conducted significant international outreach, although recent counterterrorism operations have disrupted its media capabilities. Anwar al-Awlaki, the late American-born Muslim cleric who became a leading figure within AQAP, ran an online campaign from Yemen to recruit and aid Muslims in foreign countries to carry out attacks.[26] Al-Qaeda's English-language magazine, *Inspire*, which provides radicalizing literature and instructions for planning and conducting terrorist attacks, has been produced in Yemen since 2010, although there has not been a new issue since 2017.[27] AQAP released a shorter "Guide to Inspire," designed for potential recruits, after the June 2016 Orlando shooting and the July 2016 attack in Nice.[28] AQAP has also directly supported al-Qaeda affiliates in other theaters.[29]

AQAP has also repeatedly attempted to attack the U.S. homeland. Most recently, AQAP played a significant role in the attack on the U.S. naval air station in Pensacola, Florida by Saudi pilot Mohammad al Shamrani in December 2019. The FBI assessed that the Saudi had been in touch with AQAP since 2015 and had joined the Royal Saudi Air Force with the intention of carrying out an attack.[30] AQAP has also claimed responsibility for the January 2015 assault on the Paris offices of the satirical French magazine *Charlie Hebdo*.[31]

In recent years, a sustained UAE-led and U.S.-backed counterterrorism campaign in Yemen has worn down AQAP leadership and reduced the group's safe haven. The group's first two leaders both perished in U.S. airstrikes—first Nasir al-Wuhayshi in 2015 and then Qasim al-Raymi in January 2020. Several other prominent AQAP officials have also been killed in U.S. operations, including the infamous bomb maker Ibrahim al-Asiri.[32] AQAP's current *emir*, the Saudi-born Khaled Batarfi, was named as Raymi's replacement in February 2020. He inherits a weakened organization that suffers from internal divisions and controls only a portion of the territory it could once claim.[33]

The Islamic State (IS)

Since its emergence as an independent entity in 2013, IS has competed with al-Qaeda for leadership of the global Salafi-*jihadi* movement. Yemen is key to this contest, due to both its religious significance and the presence of AQAP in the country.[34] To this end, IS's late military commander, Omar al-Shishani, mentioned Yemen in the Islamic State's celebratory June 2014 video calling for the end of borders that separate Muslims.[35]

Initial support for IS materialized in Yemen immediately after the group declared its caliphate in Iraq in June 2014, culminating in the creation of a dedicated IS branch in the country – known as *Wilayat al-Yaman* – later that year. IS *emir* Abu Bakr al-Baghdadi formally recognized the Yemeni branch alongside four others in a November 2014 video.[36] The group reaffirmed its pledge to Baghdadi in July 2019 as part of an IS media campaign across many of its global affiliates.[37]

IS claimed its first attack in Yemen on March 20, 2015, simultaneously bombing two mosques in Sana'a. The attack was at that time the deadliest terrorist incident in Yemen, and targeted Zaydi Shi'a.[38] In October 2015, the group shifted its primary focus from targeting the Houthis to targeting the Arab coalition in Yemen, and thereafter the coalition-backed Yemeni military and government. It attacked the government in al-Mukalla after an April 2016 Emirati-led offensive wrested control of the city from AQAP.[39] IS then expanded into al-Bayda governorate in central Yemen, claiming small-scale attacks against Houthi and Houthi-aligned tribal forces beginning in the fall of 2016. It also established training camps in the governorate, but these were later destroyed by U.S. airstrikes.[40]

Both AQAP's strong presence as well as the nature of IS's strategy has limited the latter's expansion to date. The targeting of non-combatants - a practice generally absent in Yemen, but common for IS — has alienated the group from the Yemeni people. In the first years of its existence, the group used a top-down leadership approach, working with a primarily non-Yemeni leadership body that generally rejected Yemeni tribal customs.

By 2017, IS was severely weakened, but it retained its presence in al-Bayda and regenerated an attack capability in Aden that fall.[41] In February 2018, IS again claimed an attack in Aden, killing fourteen people in an assault on a local counterterrorism force's headquarters.[42] In August 2019, IS claimed a bombing of an Aden police station that killed eleven officers.[43] The group may have maintained a cell in eastern Yemen in 2019 as well. U.S.-backed Saudi and Yemeni counterterrorism forces captured the alleged leader of the Islamic State in Yemen, Abu Osama al-Muhajir, and the group's chief financial officer in the al-Mahrah capital, al-Ghaydah, in June of that year.[44]

IS focused most of its attacks in Yemen between September 2018 and January 2019 against AQAP rather than the Houthis or Yemeni counterterrorism forces, according to data compiled by Elisabeth Kendall of Oxford University.[45] IS escalated its campaign against AQAP in March 2019, using suicide vests in multiple attacks. Fighting between the two groups continued throughout that summer, though the pace of attacks declined in the autumn. The last significant skirmish between the groups occurred in February 2020.[46] However, the rivals have continued their fight online, posting a litany of grievances, accusations, and taunts against each other in *jihadi* chat rooms. IS has repeatedly accused AQAP of collaborating with Yemeni security forces and urged its fighters to defect while AQAP propaganda has featured IS defectors who testify regarding the group's cruelty.[47]

IS's enduring presence in al-Bayda since 2016 may reflect a newfound pragmatism that allows the group to better navigate local rivalries. In a January 2020 report, UN investigators documented instances of collaboration between IS and the Houthis in al-Bayda, including "prisoner exchanges and [the] handover of military camps to ISIL under Houthi supervision."[48] The Houthis likely seek to prolong the IS-AQAP conflict as a means of securing their own presence in the governorate. Kendall has gone further and speculated that other actors within Yemen's civil war, and possibly regional powers, have coopted AQAP and IS or factions thereof in order to advance their own interests within the country.[49]

The Houthi Movement

The Houthis are a Zaydi Shi'a movement that maintains a stronghold in northern and central Yemen. They were the most direct threat to the Yemeni state from 2004–2010, engaging in an on-again, off-again guerrilla war with the Yemeni government that led to the death and displacement of thousands. The Saleh regime accused the Houthis of receiving support from Iran and of, "trying to reinstate the clerical *imamate*" (Shiite Islamic government) that ruled northern Yemen for roughly 1,000 years.[50] However, the Houthis contended that they were merely advocating for "freedom of worship and social justice".[51]

Currently led by Abdul Malik al-Houthi, the younger brother of the group's late founder, the group accused the Saleh government of "widespread corruption, of aligning itself too closely with the United States, of allowing too much [*Wahhabbi*]... influence in the country, and of economic and social neglect in predominantly Shi'a parts of the country."[52] Though the Houthis based their challenge to Saleh's rule on religious grounds – Saleh was not of Hashemite descent, making him illegitimate to rule in strict Zaydi practice – the roots of the conflict were political. It began in 2003 when followers of the Zaydi revivalist group "Believing Youth" shouted anti-American and anti-Israeli rhetoric inside a Sa'ada mosque where Saleh was attending service.

In the years that followed, the Yemeni government and Abdul Malik al-Houthi expressed their readiness for dialogue on a number of occasions. However, the resulting ceasefire agreements always proved short-lived. The Yemeni government and Houthis fought six small wars in the decade after 2004. In the fall of 2009, the conflict spilled over the Saudi border as Houthi fighters seized areas within southern Saudi Arabia. The Saudi military retaliated with airstrikes and ground forces.[53]

After Saleh was ousted from power in 2011, the reconciliation process under the supervision of President Hadi granted the Houthis political recognition with 35 of 565 seats at the National Dialogue Conference (NDC).[54] The Houthis, however, rejected the outcome and continued to use military force to expand their influence. The decision to divide Yemen into six administrative districts would have isolated the Houthi stronghold and forced the Houthis to compete with another powerful Zaydi family, the Sanhan, in Sana'a.[55]

The Houthis decided to overlook their historical animosity towards Saleh and developed a partnership of convenience with the former President and his allies in 2014. This allowed the Houthis to unseat the Hadi government from Sana'a in early 2015. The Houthi-Saleh bloc sought to negotiate a political settlement to the civil war but repeatedly rejected the terms put forward by the international community, which favored the Yemeni government. Today the Houthis possess an outsized level of influence over national politics compared to the movement's small size. Saleh and the Houthis cut a power-sharing agreement in July 2016, establishing a political council to govern the country that was split between Saleh's General People's Congress (GPC) party and the Houthis' Ansar Allah party.[56] However, the Houthis gradually sidelined this council and expanded their control over the state's security and political apparatus at the expense of Saleh and his allies.

The Houthis' relationship with Saleh's bloc soured in 2017 as Saleh sought to privately broker a political resolution with the Saudi-led coalition to serve his interests while the Houthis expanded their control of Sana'a government ministries.[57] These tensions sparked a conflict in late November 2017. After roughly three days of clashes, Houthi forces killed Saleh in early December, parading his body around the streets of Sana'a.[58] Many members of the pro-Saleh wing of the GPC split from the Houthis at this time, including the influential commander Tareq Saleh, nephew of the late president, who has since commanded thousands of troops in operations against the Houthis.[59] Some GPC members remained aligned with the Houthis, however, and continue to hold positions in Sana'a government.[60]

The al-Houthi movement has grown closer to Tehran over the course of the civil war and the Iranian regime appears to be elevating the group to a more prominent position within its proxy and partner network. Iran's Supreme Leader Ayatollah Ali Khamenei received a Houthi delegation for the first time on August 13, 2019, an honor that is generally reserved for world leaders or Iran's closest non-state partners.[61] The Houthis formally appointed an ambassador to Tehran a few days later.[62]

The Iranian regime has armed the Houthis with a wide range of weaponry over the course of the civil war. Houthi IEDs have been found to contain components that originate in Iran while Lebanese Hezbollah appears to have transferred even deadlier explosively formed penetrators to the group.[63] The UN Yemen Panel of Experts has cited Iran for violating the arms embargo on Yemen by providing the Houthis with short-range ballistic missiles and suggested that Iran has supported the Houthis' drone program.[64] The Houthis have modified Iranian ballistic missiles – a capability also likely learned from Hezbollah – enabling them to strike as far as Riyadh.[65]

The Houthis initiated a campaign of drone and missile attacks against Saudi Arabia in May 2019 in tandem with Iranian and Iranian proxy actions in the Persian Gulf.[66] During this campaign, the Houthis shot down two U.S. surveillance drones in June and August 2019, respectively. U.S. Department of Defense officials assessed that the Houthis used an Iranian surface-to-air missile in the first incident and implied that Iran was linked to the second.[67] Saudi Arabia repeatedly blamed Iran for directing Houthi drone and missile attacks over the course of 2019, but Houthi leadership denied taking orders from Tehran and framed the attacks as either retaliatory or as part of a deterrence strategy.[68]

On September 14, 2019, the Houthis claimed a massive drone and missile attack on Saudi ARAMCO facilities in Abqaiq and Khurais. U.S. officials assessed that the incident originated in Iran and that the Houthi claim was intended to provide Tehran with plausible deniability.[69] Shortly after the September attacks, Saudi Arabia and the Houthis began backchannel talks over a potential ceasefire. The Houthis consequently ceased large-scale cross-border attacks that month while the Saudis reciprocated by limiting airstrikes. The Houthis resumed some missile attacks on Saudi Arabia in the spring of 2020—albeit at a lower tempo than in the summer of 2019—likely as a means of maintaining diplomatic pressure.[70]

Saudi Arabia, once confident in its ability to defeat the Houthis militarily, now seeks a face-saving exit from Yemen that secures its vital interests. In February 2020, Saudi Arabia conceded to a long-standing Houthi demand and allowed a UN medical flight from Sana'a airport.[71] Subsequently, in March, the Saudi ambassador to

Yemen invited Houthi and Hadi government representatives to the Kingdom for in-person talks, although a Houthi official claimed that Riyadh would not be a suitable venue. Then, in early April, Saudi Arabia announced a two-week ceasefire in response to the COVID-19 pandemic, which has further strained Saudi resources by precipitating a steep decline in global oil prices. Saudi Arabia subsequently extended the ceasefire by a month.[72] The negotiations with Saudi Arabia have not stopped the Houthis from continuing the fight within Yemen, however.[73] The Houthis appear confident—perhaps overly so—in their favorable military balance within Yemen and seem to believe that they can sideline the weak Hadi government in any peace talks. The Houthis' latest proposal for ending the war, published in April 2020, insists for the first time that any comprehensive peace settlement be signed between the Houthis and the Saudi-led coalition rather than with the Hadi government.[74]

Al-Islah

Al-Islah is Yemen's most notable Sunni Islamist party and is entrenched in the country's political landscape. In the years following unification, the party had considerable support in the former Marxist South, where a strong anti-socialist movement favored Islamist candidates and platforms over the dominant Yemeni Socialist Party.

Al-Islah gained power in the immediate post-Arab Spring reforms in Yemen. During the transition and in the NDC under President Hadi, al-Islah and the Yemeni Socialist Party were the two major factions in the Joint Meeting Parties (JMP), a coalition of parties opposing Saleh's GPC. Al-Islah shared power with the former ruling GPC party and held 50 seats in the NDC.[75] The addition of the Houthis' party, Ansar Allah, to the NDC negotiations added to the list of Islamist groups represented in the post-Saleh government. However, it also put President Hadi at odds with many Sunni clerics, including the prominent Salafi Abd al-Majid al-Zindani—who had recruited many Yemenis to the anti-Soviet *jihad* in the 1980s[76]—and some within al-Islah.[77]

Today al-Islah remains an important ally of the Hadi government. Hadi's Vice President since 2016, General Ali Mohsen al-Ahmar, has historically had close ties with senior Islahis. However, as with many other factions in Yemen, the party is itself not a particularly unified or coherent organization.[78]

Saudi Arabia has close relationships with senior members of al-Islah despite the fact that many Islahis have strong ties to the Muslim Brotherhood, which Saudi Arabia and the UAE consider a terrorist organization.[79] Saudi Arabia is in competition with its coalition partner in Yemen and sees al-Islah as a counterweight to Emirati influence. The UAE has sought to weaken al-Islah and is allegedly behind several assassination attempts on its officials.[80] The UAE signaled a desire for rapprochement in November 2018, when Crown Prince Mohammed bin Zayed hosted the group's leaders in Abu Dhabi. The UAE has since expressed that it maintains good relations with all Hadi government parties.[81] However, The UAE-backed STC remains openly hostile to al-Islah and characterizes the group as a terrorist organization that controls the Hadi government. When the STC temporarily seized Aden from the Yemeni government in August 2019, it called for the expulsion of al-Islah's members from Hadi's cabinet.[82] Islah-linked militias may have participated in clashes with STC-aligned forces in the weeks thereafter.[83] Saudi Arabia eventually brokered a power-sharing agreement between the STC and Hadi government in November 2019, but it quickly stalled. In April 2020 the STC declared "self-rule" in several southern provinces. Then in June, clashes between the STC and Hadi government-aligned forces briefly flared up again.[84]

While creating opportunities for new partnerships, the war has also put al-Islah under strain, as evidenced by a spate of recent unclaimed assassinations of Islah-affiliated imams in southern Yemen, particularly Aden.[85] Many Islahis appear to have fled the country along with some of the more moderate Salafi voices since the war began. Yemen's "southern question" is unlikely to be resolved anytime soon, suggesting that the bad blood between al-Islah and the STC will persist for some time.

Islamism and Society

Yemen holds religious significance in Islam. Two *hadiths* (accounts of the sayings of the Prophet Muhammad) directly reference the area. The first prophesies that an army of 12,000 men will rise from

Aden and Abyan in southern Yemen to give victory to Allah. The second states that two religions could not co-exist on the Arabian Peninsula, implying that Islam would overcome the other. Yemen's status in Islam makes it important to transnational Islamist groups, particularly Salafi-*jihadi* ones.

Historically, Yemeni society has been comprised of two main religious identities: the Zaydi Shi'a sect common in the north and northwest, and the Shafa'i Sunni sect popular in the south and southeast. Sunnis are believed to represent the majority sect among Yemen's population of 26 million; Zaydis claim around 35 percent.[86]

In his studies of Islamism in Yemen, Laurent Bonnefoy of the Institut Français du Proche-Orient found that "despite episodes of violent stigmatization orchestrated by certain radical groups, the vast majority of the population is at times indirectly (and most of the time passively) involved in the convergence of the once-distinct Sunni and Zaydi religious identities."[87] For example, former president Saleh was of Zaydi origin but did not initially refer to this as his primary identity. However, as anti-government protests threatened his presidency, Saleh drew on his Zaydi identity "in an attempt to rally Zaydi tribal solidarity against what he also allegedly framed as a Shafa'i led protest movement." In response, Saleh was accused of exacerbating sectarian divisions.[88]

While Yemeni Salafi-*jihadism* predates the civil war, sectarian tensions, as noted by Bonnefoy, were not particularly widespread prior to the conflict. However, this has changed in recent years. Reports indicate that Yemenis of different sects are less likely today to worship in the same mosques than they were before the war.[89] Al-Qaeda and the Islamic State portray the civil war in starkly religious terms. The Houthis also employ sectarian rhetoric, having long accused Saudi Arabia of attempting to export *Wahhabbism* to northern Yemen. The Houthis have also begun appropriating certain symbols, rhetoric, and celebrations associated with the Islamic Republic of Iran and/or Twelver Shi'ism, such as celebrations of Ashura and Quds Day. However, there is no evidence to support the claims made by some of the Houthis' detractors that the group's leadership has converted to Twelver Shi'ism.[90]

Islamism and the State

Islam is the official religion of the Yemeni state according to its constitution, and *sharia* law rests at the center of the country's legal system.[91] Under the constitution it is illegal to convert from Islam, political parties cannot oppose the religion, and penalties for violating blasphemy laws are steeper if the offense is committed against Islam than if it is committed against other religions. To become the president of Yemen, one must be Muslim.[92]

However, because of the fractured nature of modern Yemen and its weakened central government, state administration is not merely top-down. In a 2009 article for *The Middle East Review of International Affairs*, Bonnefoy pointed to the "presence of a strong traditional 'civil society' in the form of tribal and religious groups, most of them armed or capable of opposing the state" as a source in "undermining the regime's capacity to monopolize all the levers of power and fulfilling any totalitarian dreams."[93] For years, the Saleh regime maintained power-sharing arrangements with these groups as a way of coopting and dividing any potential opposition. As part of these arrangements, numerous Islamist groups were integrated into the state apparatus throughout the 1990s and 2000s, gaining important posts in the army and security forces. As a result, repression of Islamist groups was limited, allowing easy access to political and tribal elites for Salafists, Sufis, Zaydi revivalists, Muslim Brothers, and some individuals sympathetic to *jihadist* doctrines (see Islamic Activity).[94]

The practice of religions other than Islam can be significantly restricted in Yemen. Individuals and institutions ascribed to the Baha'i faith – a religion considered heretical by some Islamic countries – have, for years, been targeted by the Yemeni government and Houthi groups.[95] On January 2, 2018, Hamed bin Haydara, a Baha'i man, was sentenced to death for his religious beliefs.[96] Haydara had been first detained in 2013; according to James Samimi Farr of the U.S. Baha'i Office of Public Affairs, Haydara was 'beaten and electrocuted, forced to sign documents while blindfolded, accused of being a "destroyer of Islam and religion" and of being a spy for Israel. while in custody.[97] Haydara's sentencing was upheld in court in March 2020, but Yemen's Houthi authority leader Mahdi al-Mashat called for the release of Haydara – as well as the release of all Baha'i "political prisoners." Haydara, as well as other Baha'i prisoners, have since been released.[98]

Endnotes

1. "Humanitarian crisis in Yemen remains the worst in the world, warns UN," *UN News*, February 14, 2019, https://news.un.org/en/story/2019/02/1032811
2. Shaul Shay, *The Red Sea Terror Triangle* (R. Liberman, trans.) (New Brunswick: Transaction Publishers, 2005), 113-114
3. "Yemen Stems Weapons Trade," Saba Net, September 23, 2008, http://www.sabanews.net/en/news164686.htm; See also "Yemen Moves to Control Arms Trade," *Al-Motamar* (Sana'a), April 25, 2007, http://www.almotamar.net/en/2463.htm.
4. Ginny Hill, "Yemen: Fear of Failure," Chatham House *Briefing Paper*, November 2009, https://www.chathamhouse.org/sites/default/files/public/Research/Middle%20East/bp1108yemen.pdf.
5. Katherine Zimmerman, "Yemen's Pivotal Moment," AEI Critical Threats Project, February 12, 2014, http://www.criticalthreats.org/yemen/zimmerman-yemens-pivotal-moment-february-12-2014.
6. Alexis Knutsen, "Yemen's Counter-Terrorism Quandary," AEI Critical Threats Project, June 26, 2014, http://www.criticalthreats.org/yemen/knutsen-houthi-counterterrorism-quandary-june-26-2014.
7. Alexis Knutsen, "Sana'a Under Siege: Yemen's Uncertain Future," AEI Critical Threats Project, September 25, 2014, http://www.criticalthreats.org/yemen/knutsen-sanaa-under-siege-yemens-uncertain-future-september-25-2014.
8. Peter Salisbury, "Yemen: Stemming the Rise of a Chaos State," Chatham House, May 25, 2016, https://www.chathamhouse.org/sites/files/chathamhouse/publications/research/2016-05-25-yemen-stemming-rise-of-chaos-state-salisbury.pdf.
9. Noah Browning, "The last hours of Yemen's Saleh," Reuters, December 8, 2017, https://www.reuters.com/article/us-yemen-security-saleh-insight/the-last-hours-of-yemens-saleh-idUSKBN1E20YY.
10. "Banished Aden governor forms independent "South Yemen" council," *The New Arab*, May 11, 2019, https://www.alaraby.co.uk/english/News/2017/5/11/Governor-turned-president-Adens-Al-Zubaidi-announces-council-to-govern-South-Yemen.
11. Lawrence E. Cline, "Yemen's Strategic Boxes," *Small Wars Jour-*

nal, January 2, 2010, http://smallwarsjournal.com/blog/journal/docs-temp/339-cline.pdf; Jonathan Schanzer, Testimony before the House of Representatives Committee on Foreign Affairs, February 3, 2010, https://foreignaffairs.house.gov/2010/2/yemen-brink-implications-us-policy.

12. Jason Burke, *Al-Qaeda: The True Story of Radical Islam* (London: Penguin Books, 2004), 215.
13. Thomas Joscelyn, "Resolving the Conflict in Yemen: U.S. Interests, Risks, and Policy," *The Long War Journal*, March 10, 2017, https://www.longwarjournal.org/archives/2017/03/resolving-the-conflict-in-yemen-u-s-interests-risks-and-policy.php.
14. Hill, "Yemen: Fear of Failure"; Martin Jerrett and Mohammed al-Haddar, "Al Qaeda in the Arabian Peninsula: From Global Insurgent to State Enforcer," Hate Speech International, March 2017, 6-7, https://www.hate-speech.org/wp-content/uploads/2017/03/From-Global-Insurgent-to-State-Enforcer.pdf.
15. Gregory Johnsen, "Waning Vigilance: Al-Qaeda's Resurgence in Yemen," Washington Institute for Near East Policy *Policywatch* 1551, July 14, 2009, http://www.washingtoninstitute.org/templateC05.php?CID=3088.
16. Ibid.; See also "USS Cole Bombing Fast Facts," *CNN*, September 18, 2013, https://www.cnn.com/2013/09/18/world/meast/uss-cole-bombing-fast-facts/index.html; Harnisch, "Denying Al-Qaeda a Safe Haven in Yemen."
17. Harnisch, "Denying Al-Qaeda a Safe Haven in Yemen."
18. Katherine Zimmerman, "AQAP: A Resurgent Threat," Combating Terrorism Center at West Point *CTC Sentinel*, September 11, 2015, https://www.ctc.usma.edu/posts/aqap-a-resurgent-threat.
19. Katherine Zimmerman, "AQAP Post-Arab Spring and the Islamic State," in Aaron Y. Zelin, ed., *How al-Qaeda Survived Drones, Uprisings, and the Islamic State* (Washington Institute, June 2017), http://www.washingtoninstitute.org/policy-analysis/view/how-al-qaeda-survived-drones-uprisings-and-the-islamic-state.
20. Yemeni Foreign Minister Abu Bakr al-Qirbi claimed in late 2008 that Yemen was playing host to more than 1,000 jihadist fighters and al-Qaeda affiliates. See Hill, "Yemen: Fear of Failure." Most Yemeni officials reported only 200-300 AQAP members as of 2010, but U.S. estimates rose by 2015. See Ian Black, "Al-Qaida in the Arabian Peninsula: Renegades or Rising Threat?" *Guardian* (London), January 24, 2010, https://www.theguardian.com/world/2010/jan/24/al-qaida-yemen-jihad-training; "AQAP Fast Facts," CNN, August 5,

2015, http://www.cnn.com/2015/06/16/middleeast/aqap-fast-facts/index.html; and Maggie Michael, Trish Wilson, and Lee Keath, "AP Investigation: US allies, al-Qaida battle rebels in Yemen," Associated Press, August 6, 2018, https://apnews.com/f38788a561d74ca78c-77cb43612d50da; Katherine Zimmerman, "AQAP: A Resurgent Threat."

21. Rania El Gamal, "Saudis Hardened by Wars in Syria, Iraq Join Al Qaeda in Yemen," Reuters, March 14, 2014, http://www.reuters.com/article/2014/03/14/us-yemen-security-qaeda-idUS-BREA2D0XO20140314.
22. Gregory D. Johnsen, "The Expansion Strategy of Al-Qa'ida in the Arabian Peninsula," Combating Terrorism Center at West Point *CTC Sentinel* 2, iss. 9, September 2009, 8-11, https://ctc.usma.edu/the-expansion-strategy-of-al-qaida-in-the-arabian-peninsula-2/.
23. Jeremy Binnie, "Yemen Overruns Al-Qaeda Enclave," *Jane's Defence Weekly*, June 28, 2012; See also Katherine Zimmerman, "Al Qaeda's Gains in South Yemen," AEI Critical Threats Project, July 8, 2011, http://www.criticalthreats.org/yemen/al-qaedas-gains-south-yemen-july-8-2011#_edn2; Ahmed Al-Haj, "Yemen Recaptures Center of Al-Qaida-Held City," Associated Press, April 24, 2011; For a chronology of attacks by AQAP in Yemen, visit the "AQAP and Suspected AQAP Attacks in 2010, 2011 and 2012," AEI Critical Threats Project, n.d., http://www.criticalthreats.org/yemen/aqap-and-suspected-aqap-attacks-yemen-tracker-2010.
24. Katherine Zimmerman, "2016 Yemen Crisis Situation Report, May 2," AEI Critical Threats Project , May 2, 2016, http://www.criticalthreats.org/yemen/yemen-crisis-situation-reports-may-2-2016; See also "AQAP Expanding behind Yemen's Frontlines," AEI Critical Threats Project, February 17, 2016, http://www.criticalthreats.org/yemen/zimmerman-aqap-expanding-behind-yemens-frontlines-february-17-2016.
25. Kristin Deasy, "Abdullah al-Khalidi, Saudi diplomat, abducted in Yemen," *PRI The World*, March 28, 2012, https://www.pri.org/stories/2012-03-28/abdullah-al-khalidi-saudi-diplomat-abducted-yemen
26. Eric Schmitt, Mark Mazzetti, and Robert F. Worth, "American-Born Qaeda Leader Is Killed by U.S. Missile in Yemen," *New York Times*, September 30, 2011, http://www.nytimes.com/2011/10/01/world/middleeast/anwar-al-awlaki-is-killed-in-yemen.html.
27. Thomas Joscelyn, "Al Qaeda in the Arabian Peninsula Releases 12th Issue of Inspire Magazine," *Long War Journal*, March 17, 2014, http://www.longwarjournal.org/archives/2014/03/al_qaeda_in_the_

arab.php.
28. Available on www.jihadology.net.
29. Rukmini Callimachi, "Yemen terror boss left blueprint for waging jihad," Associated Press, August 9, 2013, https://www.pulitzer.org/files/2014/international-reporting/callimachi/08callimachi2014.pdf; Katherine Zimmerman, "AQAP: A Resurgent Threat," *CTC Sentinel* 8, iss. 9, September 2015, https://ctc.usma.edu/aqap-a-resurgent-threat/.
30. Katie Benner and Adam Goldman, "F.B.I. Finds Links Between Pensacola Gunman and Al Qaeda," *New York Times,* May 18, 2020, https://www.nytimes.com/2020/05/18/us/politics/justice-department-al-qaeda-florida-naval-base-shooting.html.
31. Catherine E. Shoichet and Josh Levs, "AQAP: Charlie Hebdo attack was years in the making," *CNN*, January 21, 2015, https://www.cnn.com/2015/01/14/europe/charlie-hebdo-france-attacks/index.html.
32. Michael Crowley, "Trump Confirms 2017 Killing of Feared Bomb Maker for Al Qaeda," *New York Times,* October 10, 2019, https://www.nytimes.com/2019/10/10/world/middleeast/qaeda-bomber-death-trump.html.
33. Gregory D. Johnsen, Khalid Batarfi and the Future of AQAP," *Lawfare*, March 22, 2020, https://www.lawfareblog.com/khalid-batarfi-and-future-aqap; Jessica Kocan, "Yemen File – May 21, 2020," AEI Critical Threats Project, May 21, 2020, https://www.criticalthreats.org/briefs/yemen-file/yemen-file-aqap-did-more-than-just-inspire-the-pensacola-attack.
34. See Katherine Zimmerman, "Province Ties to the Islamic State Core: Islamic State in Yemen," in Katherine Bauer, ed., *Beyond Syria and Iraq: Examining Islamic State Provinces* (Washington Institute, November 2016).
35. "Islamic State Video Promotes Destruction of Iraq-Syria Border Crossing," SITE Intelligence Group, June 29, 2014, English translation available online at www.siteintelgroup.com.
36. "IS Leader Abu Bakr Al-Baghdadi Rallies Fighters, Welcomes New Pledges," SITE Intelligence Group, November 13, 2014, www.siteintelgroup.com.
37. "IS' Yemen Province Boasts of its Military Operations Since Pledge, Renews Allegiance in Video," SITE Intelligence Group, July 27, 2019, English translation available at www.siteintelgroup.com.
38. Alexis Knutsen, "ISIS in Yemen: Fueling the Sectarian Fire," AEI Critical Threats Project, March 20, 2015, http://www.criticalthreats.org/yemen/knutsen-isis-yemen-fueling-sectarian-fire-march-20-2015.

39. Jon Diamond and Katherine Zimmerman, "Challenging the Yemeni State: ISIS in Aden and al Mukalla," AEI Critical Threats Project, June 9, 2016, http://www.criticalthreats.org/yemen/zimmerman-diamond-challenging-yemeni-state-isis-in-aden-al-mukalla-june-9-2016.
40. Maher Farrukh and Hamsa Fayed, "Yemen Situation Report," AEI Critical Threats Project, November 22, 2016, https://www.criticalthreats.org/briefs/yemen-situation-report/2016-yemen-crisis-situation-report-november-22; Maher Farrukh, "Yemen Situation Report," AEI Critical Threats Project, October 30, 2017, https://www.criticalthreats.org/briefs/yemen-situation-report/2017-yemen-crisis-situation-report-october-30; Maher Farrukh, Coy Ozias, and Tyler Parker, "Yemen Situation Report," AEI Critical Threats Project, August 11, 2017, https://www.criticalthreats.org/briefs/yemen-situation-report/2017-yemen-crisis-situation-report-august-11; Barbara Starr and Zachary Cohen, "First US Airstrike Targeting ISIS in Yemen Kills Dozens," *CNN*, October 16, 2017, https://www.cnn.com/2017/10/16/politics/us-isis-training-camp-strike-yemen/index.html.
41. Maher Farrukh, "Yemen Situation Report," AEI Critical Threats Project, November 22, 2017, https://www.criticalthreats.org/briefs/yemen-situation-report/2017-yemen-crisis-situation-report-november-22; Maher Farrukh and Katherine Zimmerman, "Yemen Situation Report," AEI Critical Threats Project, March 1, 2018, https://www.criticalthreats.org/briefs/yemen-situation-report/2018-yemen-crisis-situation-report-march-1; "Yemen's Islamic State affiliate claims responsibility for deadly attack on Aden police station the previous day," Associated Press, August 2, 2019, https://www.apnews.com/ca4bd73adfed44d5b852183f90b23b05.
42. Mohammed Mukhashaf, "At least six killed in Yemen suicide bombing claimed by the Islamic State," Reuters, November 14, 2017, https://www.reuters.com/article/us-yemen-security/at-least-six-killed-in-yemen-suicide-bombing-claimed-by-islamic-state-idUSKBN1DE0LP; "At least 14 killed in attack on Yemen counter-terrorism base, Islamic State claims responsibility," *ABC* (Australia), February 25, 2018, http://www.abc.net.au/news/2018-02-25/14-dead-in-attack-in-yemen-islamic-state-claims-responsibility/9482912.
43. "Yemen's Islamic State affiliate claims responsibility for deadly attack on Aden police station the previous day," Associated Press, August 2, 2019, https://www.apnews.com/ca4bd73adfed44d5b852183f90b23b05; "Dozens killed in attacks on security forces in Yemen's Aden," *France 24*, August 1, 2019, https://www.france24.com/en/20190801-yemen-aden-two-deadly-attacks-police-jihad-

ists-shiite.

44. Kareem Fahim and Missy Ryan, "Saudi Arabia announces capture of an ISIS leader in Yemen in U.S.-backed raid," *Washington Post*, June 25, 2019, https://www.washingtonpost.com/world/saudi-arabia-announces-capture-of-islamic-state-leader-in-yemen-in-us-backed-raid-backed/2019/06/25/79734ca2-976a-11e9-9a16-dc551ea5a43b_story.html.
45. Elisabeth Kendall, "The Failing Islamic State Within the Failed State of Yemen," *Perspectives on Terrorism* vol. 13, iss. 1, February 2019, pp. 78-87.
46. Sudarsan Raghavan, "With the ISIS Caliphate Defeated in Syria, an Islamist Militant Rivalry Takes Root in Yemen," *Washington Post*, April 14, 2019; "AQAP Focuses Attacks Solely on IS in al-Bayda', Claims 3 Strikes on SBF in Abyan," SITE Intelligence Group, August 27, 2019, English translation available at www.siteintelgroup.com; "ISIS in Yemen: Caught in a Regional Power Game," Center for Global Policy, July 21, 2020, https://cgpolicy.org/articles/isis-in-yemen-caught-in-a-regional-power-game/.
47. See Elisabeth Kendall, "The Failing Islamic State"; Posting on Twitter, August 14, 2019, https://twitter.com/Dr_E_Kendall/status/1161676408743190528; "AQAP-affiliate Releases 3rd Installment in Video Series Documenting IS' Torture of Own Fighters in Prison," SITE Intelligence Group, July 18, 2019, English translation available at www.siteintelgroup.com; Jessica Kocan, "Yemen File – May 21, 2020," AEI Critical Threats Project, May 21, 2020, https://www.criticalthreats.org/briefs/yemen-file/yemen-file-aqap-did-more-than-just-inspire-the-pensacola-attack.
48. UN Security Council, "Twenty-fifth report of the Analytical Support and Sanctions Monitoring Team submitted pursuant to resolution 2368 (2017) concerning ISIL (Da'esh), Al-Qaida and associated individuals and entities," January 20, 2020, 8, https://undocs.org/S/2020/53.
49. Kendall, "ISIS in Yemen."
50. Hamida Ghafour, "Rebel Without A Clear Cause," *The National* (Abu Dhabi), August 21, 2009, http://www.thenational.ae/apps/pbcs.dll/article?AID=/20090822/WEEKENDER/708219838/1306; See also Christopher Harnisch, A Critical War in a Fragile Country: Yemen's Battle with the Shiite al Houthi Rebels," AEI Critical Threats Project, August 31, 2009, http://www.criticalthreats.org/yemen/critical-war-fragile-country-yemens-battle-shiite-al-houthi-rebels#_edn3.
51. Bonnefoy, "Varieties of Islamism In Yemen."

52. "Yemeni Government Steps Up Assault On Shiite Rebels," *Wall Street Journal*, August 12, 2009, http://online.wsj.com/article/SB125007847389825757.html?mod=googlenews_wsj.
53. Katherine Zimmerman and Steve Gonzalez, "Tracker: Saudi Arabia's Military Operations Along Yemeni Border | Critical Threats," AEI Critical Threats Project, January 4, 2010, https://www.criticalthreats.org/briefs/saudi-arabia.
54. "Representations in the National Dialogue Conference," *Yemen Observer*, March 18 2013, http://www.yemenobserver.com/national-dialogue/227-representations-in-the-national-dialogue-conference.html.
55. Katherine Zimmerman, "A New Model for Defeating al Qaeda in Yemen," AEI Critical Threats Project, September 10, 2015, http://www.criticalthreats.org/yemen/zimmerman-new-model-for-defeating-al-qaeda-in-yemen-september-10-2015, 7.
56. "Signing of the National Political Agreement Between the General People's Congress and its Allies and Ansar Allah and its Allies," SABA.ye, July 28, 2016, http://www.saba.ye/ar/news434879.htm.
57. Maher Farrukh and Katherine Zimmerman, "President Saleh is Dead. What's Next for Yemen?" AEI Critical Threats Project, December 4, 2017, https://www.criticalthreats.org/analysis/president-saleh-is-dead-whats-next-for-yemen.
58. Ibid.
59. "Yemen's Hodeidah braces for blitzkrieg as Tareq Saleh seeks prominence," *Middle East Eye*, June 13, 2018, https://www.middleeasteye.net/fr/news/yemen-s-hodeida-braces-blitzkrieg-saleh-seeks-win-prominence-1414877896.
60. Sama'a Al-Hamdani, "Understanding the Houthi Faction in Yemen," *Lawfare*, April 7, 2019, https://www.lawfareblog.com/understanding-houthi-faction-yemen; "Where does Yemen's GPC stand two years after the death of Saleh?" *The New Arab*, December 5, 2019, https://english.alaraby.co.uk/english/indepth/2019/12/5/where-does-yemens-gpc-stand-two-years-after-saleh; Ibrahim Jalal, "A fight for survival in a new landscape: Can Yemen's GPC recover after Saleh?" Middle East Institute, February 4, 2020, https://www.mei.edu/publications/fight-survival-new-landscape-can-yemens-gpc-recover-after-saleh; "Rethinking Peace in Yemen," International Crisis Group, July 2, 2020, https://www.crisisgroup.org/middle-east-north-africa/gulf-and-arabian-peninsula/yemen/216-rethinking-peace-yemen.
61. Amir Toumaj, Twitter, August 13, 2019, https://twitter.com/AmirToumaj/status/1161324395412897792.
62. Mohammed Hatem, "Yemen Shiite Rebels Appoint an Ambassador

to Iran for First Time," *Bloomberg*, August 18, 2019, https://www.bloomberg.com/news/articles/2019-08-18/yemen-shiite-rebels-appoint-an-ambassador-to-iran-for-first-time; "In an operation that is the largest of its kind .. The Air Force targeting a field and an oil refinery on the Saudi-UAE border," *Al Masirah*, August 17, 2019, https://almasirah.net/details.php?es_id=43704&cat_id=3; "Yemen severs diplomatic ties with Iran," Reuters, October 2, 2015, https://www.reuters.com/article/us-yemen-security-iran/yemen-severs-diplomatic-ties-with-iran-state-media-idUSKCN0RW1A220151002.

63. "Mines and IEDs employed by Houthi forces on Yemen's west coast," Conflict Armament Research, September 2018, https://www.conflictarm.com/dispatches/mines-and-ieds-employed-by-houthi-forces-on-yemens-west-coast/; Michael Knights, "Defeating Iran's Roadside Bombs in Yemen," March 26, 2018, https://www.washingtoninstitute.org/policy-analysis/view/defeating-irans-roadside-bombs-in-yemen.
64. Final Report of the UN Panel of Experts on Yemen, January 26, 2018, http://www.un.org/en/ga/search/view_doc.asp?symbol=S/2018/68; Final Report of the UN Panel of Experts on Yemen, January 25, 2019, https://reliefweb.int/sites/reliefweb.int/files/resources/S_2019_83_E.pdf.
65. Ibid.
66. "Threat Update – June 27, 2019," AEI Critical Threats Project, June 27, 2019, https://www.criticalthreats.org/briefs/threat-update/double-suicide-bombing-in-tunisia-iran-poised-to-violate-nuclear-deal.
67. Chad Garland, "CENTCOM confirms Yemen rebels shot down US drone," *Stars and Stripes*, June 16, 2019, https://www.stripes.com/news/middle-east/centcom-confirms-yemen-rebels-shot-down-us-drone-1.586257; Lucia I. Suarez Sang, "US military drone shot down over Yemen, official confirms," *Fox News*, August 21, 2019, https://www.foxnews.com/world/us-military-drone-shot-down-over-yemen-official-confirms.
68. Salma Al Wardany, "Saudi Prince Says Iran Ordered Pipeline Attack as Tensions Rise," *Bloomberg*, May 16, 2019, https://www.bloomberg.com/news/articles/2019-05-16/saudi-prince-iran-ordered-houthi-attacks-on-aramco-facilities; "Gulf of Aden Security Review – August 19, 2019," AEI Critical Threats Project, August 19, 2019, https://www.criticalthreats.org/briefs/gulf-of-aden-security-review/gulf-of-aden-security-review-august-19-2019; "In an operation that is the largest of its kind .. The Air Force targeting a field and an oil refinery on the Saudi-UAE border," *Al Masirah*, August 17, 2019,

https://almasirah.net/details.php?es_id=43704&cat_id=3.

69. This is not unprecedented. For past occurrences, see Nicholas Carl and James Barnett, "Iran Hit the West Where it Hurts: At the Pump," AEI Critical Threats Project, September 2017, 2019, https://www.criticalthreats.org/analysis/iran-hit-the-west-where-it-hurts-at-the-pump; Isabel Coles and Dion Nissenbaum, "U.S.: Saudi Pipeline Attacks Originated From Iraq," *The Wall Street Journal*, June 28, 2019, https://www.wsj.com/articles/u-s-saudi-pipeline-attacks-originated-from-iraq-11561741133.
70. Ahmed Al-Haj and Maggie Michael, "Saudi Arabia, Yemen's Houthi rebels in indirect peace talks," *Associated Press*, November 13, 2019, https://apnews.com/cb393079f7be48d2951b3ae3f2d4361b; and Jessica Kocan, "Yemen File – April 10, 2020," AEI Critical Threats Project, April 10, 2020, https://www.criticalthreats.org/briefs/yemen-file/yemen-file-al-houthi-movement-offensive-targets-oil-in-northern-yemen.
71. "Yemen's first 'mercy flight' departs from Sana'a airport to Jordan," *Al Masdar*, February 4, 2020, https://al-masdaronline.net/national/304.
72. Ibrahim Jalal, "Saudi Arabia eyes the exit in Yemen, but Saudi-Houthi talks alone won't resolve the conflict," Middle East Institute, April 15, 2020, https://www.mei.edu/publications/saudi-arabia-eyes-exit-yemen-saudi-houthi-talks-alone-wont-resolve-conflict; "Saudi-led coalition announces one-month extension of Yemen ceasefire," Reuters, April 24, 2020, https://www.reuters.com/article/us-yemen-security-saudi/saudi-led-coalition-announces-one-month-extension-of-yemen-ceasefire-idUSKCN2261GS.
73. Jessica Kocan, "Yemen File – April 10, 2020," AEI Critical Threats Project, April 10, 2020, https://www.criticalthreats.org/briefs/yemen-file/yemen-file-al-houthi-movement-offensive-targets-oil-in-northern-yemen.
74. "Rethinking Peace in Yemen," International Crisis Group, July 2, 2020, https://www.crisisgroup.org/middle-east-north-africa/gulf-and-arabian-peninsula/yemen/216-rethinking-peace-yemen.
75. "Representations in the National Dialogue Conference."
76. Zindani was designated by the U.S. as a Specially Designated Global Terrorist for his role in support al Qaeda in Yemen. U.S. Department of the Treasury, "United States Designates bin Laden Loyalist," press release, February 24, 2004, https://www.treasury.gov/press-center/press-releases/Pages/js1190.aspx.
77. Ashraf Al-Muraqab, "Yemeni Clerics Disapprove of their Exclusion

From the National Dialogue," *Yemen Times*, July 4, 2012, http://www.yementimes.com/en/1587/news/1092/Yemeni-clerics-disapprove-of-their-exclusion-from-the-National-Dialogue.htm; "Yemen President Offers Conditional Dialogue With Al Qaeda," Reuters, September 26, 2012, http://www.reuters.com/article/2012/09/26/yemen-qaeda-idUSL5E8KQ5LF20120926.

78. "Rethinking Peace," International Crisis Group.
79. Neil Patrick, "Saudi Arabia's Problematic Allies against the Houthis," *Cairo Review of Global Affairs*, February 14, 2016, https://www.thecairoreview.com/tahrir-forum/saudi-arabias-problematic-allies-against-the-houthis/.
80. Aram Roston, "A Middle East Monarchy Hired American Ex-Soldiers to Kill Its Political Enemies. This Could Be the Future of War." *Buzzfeed*, October 16, 2018, https://www.buzzfeednews.com/article/aramroston/mercenaries-assassination-us-yemen-uae-spear-golan-dahlan.
81. "UAE and Yemen's Al-Islah: An alliance of convenience only," *The New Arab*, November 20, 2018, https://www.alaraby.co.uk/english/comment/2018/11/20/uae-and-yemens-al-islah-an-alliance-of-convenience-only.
82. Sune Engel Rasmussen and Saleh al-Batati, "Yemen Separatists Storm Presidential Palace in Aden," *Wall Street Journal*, August 7, 2019, https://www.wsj.com/articles/yemen-separatists-storm-presidential-palace-in-aden-11565207321.
83. "A campaign of arrests by the forces of the first military zone," *Hadramout*, August 16, 2019, https://www.7adramout.net/golden-news/7127249.html.
84. Mohammed Mukhashat, "Yemen separatists seize remote Socotra island from Saudi-backed government," Reuters, June 21, 2020, https://www.reuters.com/article/us-yemen-security-separatists/yemen-separatists-seize-remote-socotra-island-from-saudi-backed-government-idUSKBN23S0DU; Abdullah Ahmad, "Yemeni government, STC agree to ceasefire: coalition," *Anadolu Agency*, June 23, 2020, https://www.aa.com.tr/en/middle-east/yemeni-government-stc-agree-to-ceasefire-coalition/1886366.
85. Ahmed al-Haj, "Fear Grips Yemen's Aden as Deadly Attacks Target Clerics," Associated Press, April 5, 2018, https://apnews.com/cb514ded6f284e81b3776575db3ebcd2/Fear-grips-Yemen's-Aden-as-deadly-attacks-target-clerics.
86. "Yemen," Central Intelligence Agency *World Factbook*, April 15, 2014, https://www.cia.gov/library/publications/the-world-factbook/

geos/ym.html; Bernard Haykel, *Revival and Reform: The Legacy of Muhammad al-Shawkani* (Cambridge: Cambridge University Press, 2003), 151.

87. Laurent Bonnefoy, "Les identités religieuses contemporaines au Yémen: convergence, résistances et instrumentalisations," *Revue des mondes musulmans et de la Méditerranée* 121-122, April 2008, 201-15; See also Bonnefoy, "Varieties Of Islamism In Yemen."
88. "Popular Protests in North Africa and the Middle East (II)."
89. Katherine Zimmerman's conversations with NGO workers in Yemen, fall 2016.
90. Mohammed Almahfali and James Root, "How Iran's Islamic Revolution Does, and Does Not, Influence Houthi Rule in Northern Yemen," Sana'a Center for Strategic Studies, February 13, 2020, https://sanaacenter.org/publications/analysis/9050.
91. Freedom House, "Yemen," n.d., https://freedomhouse.org/country/yemen/freedom-world/2020
92. April Artrip, "State Department: Yemen Faces Obstacles To Religious Freedom," Yemen Peace Project, August 21, 2017, https://www.yemenpeaceproject.org/blog-x/2017/8/21/state-department-yemen-faces-obstacles-to-religious-freedom
93. Laurent Bonnefoy, "Varieties of Islamism In Yemen: The Logic of Integration Under Pressure," Middle East Review of International Affairs, 2009, 13 (1), 11.
94. Ibid.
95. "The Bahá'í Community in Yemen: A brief history of the recent persecution: August 2019," Bahá'í International Community, August 2019, https://www.bic.org/situation-in-yemen/background
96. Ibid.
97. Baha'I National Center, "News Release: Electrocutions, beatings and mass arrests: Houthis' Iran-inspired campaign against the Yemeni Baha'is," February 24, 2020, https://www.globenewswire.com/news-release/2020/02/24/1989050/0/en/Electrocutions-beatings-and-mass-arrests-Houthis-Iran-inspired-campaign-against-the-Yemeni-Baha-is.html
98. Amnesty International, "News Release: Yemen: huthi authorities' decision to release Baha'i prisoners is 'positive signal,'" March 26, 2020, https://www.amnesty.org/en/latest/news/2020/03/yemen-huthi-authorities-decision-to-release-bahai-prisoners-is-positive-signal/; "Yemen's Houthis release Bahai leader sentenced to death over apostasy," *Middle East Eye*, July 30, 2020, https://www.middleeasteye.net/news/yemen-bahai-faith-released-houthi-prison-

sanaa.

Sub-Saharan Africa

27 Ethiopia

Quick Facts

Population: 108,113,150 (July 2020 est.)
Area: 1,104,300 sq km
Ethnic Groups:Oromo 34.4%, Amhara (Amara) 27%, Somali (Somalie) 6.2%, Tigray (Tigrinya) 6.1%, Sidama 4%, Gurage 2.5%, Welaita 2.3%, Hadiya 1.7%, Afar (Affar) 1.7%, Gamo 1.5%, Gedeo 1.3%, Silte 1.3%, Kefficho 1.2%, other 8.8% (2007 est.)
GDP (official exchange rate): $80.87 billion (2017 est.)

Source: CIA World FactBook (Last Updated June 2020)

Introduction

The U.S. Department of State has described Ethiopia as "a strategic partner in the Global War on Terrorism" and welcomed "Ethiopia's dedication to maintaining security in the region."[1] The country has received high-level visits from then-U.S. President Barack Obama and then-Secretary of State Rex Tillerson, both of whom lauded the partnership between the two countries in addressing governance issues, economic growth, and regional security concerns. Tillerson, speaking from the Ethiopian capital of Addis Ababa in 2018, highlighted the "many touch points where [the United States and Ethiopia] share a common interest of security, stability for the region...and opportunities for economic prosperity."[2] This cooperation was strengthened in 2017, when Ethiopia joined the Global Coalition to Defeat ISIS – one of only twelve African states to do so.

The encomia are more than merited, both for the Ethiopian government's actions abroad and for the challenges it faces at home. As the State Department noted in 2017, "Ethiopia also focused its counterterrorism strategy on pursuing potential threats from armed opposition groups often based in neighboring countries. The Ethiopian Federal Police (EFP) and the U.S. Federal Bureau of Investigation (FBI) shared information on counterterrorism matters pursuant to a memorandum of understanding."[3]

Endnotes

1. United States. Department of State. *Ethiopia: Background Note.* January 2009. Accessed March 5, 2019. https://2009-2017.state.gov/outofdate/bgn/ethiopia/110843.htm; United States. Department of State. Bureau of African Affairs. *U.S. Relations with Ethiopia.* June 20, 2016. Accessed March 5, 2019. https://2009-2017.state.gov/r/pa/ei/bgn/2859.htm.
2. United States. Department of State. Bureau of Public Affairs. *Remarks – Secretary of State Rex Tillerson and Ethiopian Foreign Minister Workneh Gebeyehu at a Joint Press Availability.* March 8, 2018. Accessed March 5, 2019. https://translations.state.gov/2018/03/08/remarks-secretary-of-state-rex-tillerson-and-ethiopian-foreign-minister-workneh-gebeyehu-at-a-joint-press-availability/.
3. United States. Department of State. Bureau of Counterterrorism. *Country Reports on Terrorism 2017.*September 2018. Accessed March 5, 2019. https://www.state.gov/documents/organization/283100.pdf, p. 22.

Due to publishing constraints, this chapter is provided here only in summary form. To view the full study, please visit the online edition of the Almanac at almanac.afpc.org.

28 Mali

Quick Facts

Population: 19,553,397 (July 2020 est.)
Area: 1,240,192 sq km
Ethnic Groups: Bambara 33.3%, Fulani (Peuhl) 13.3%, Sarakole/Soninke/Marka 9.8%, Senufo/Manianka 9.6%, Malinke 8.8%, Dogon 8.7%, Sonrai 5.9%, Bobo 2.1%, Tuareg/Bella 1.7%, other Malian 6%, from member of Economic Community of West Africa .4%, other .3% (2018 est.)
GDP (official exchange rate): $15.37 billion (2017 est.)

Source: CIA World FactBook (Last Updated August 2020)

Introduction

The Malian government and international forces continue to struggle to adequately police the plethora of Islamist and non-Islamist armed groups active in the north and center of the country. Instability can be traced back to the 2012 Tuareg rebellion, itself a product of longstanding cleavages between the government in Bamako and aggrieved northern Tuareg tribes. In January 2012, Tuareg separatists began an offensive that overran Malian forces in the north, destabilizing the country and fomenting a military coup d'état. In the ensuing turmoil, Islamist groups wrested control of the country's north and threatened an invasion of the south, prompting an international intervention.

While intervention forces, led by the French and assisted by Malian and international troops, have regained control of major northern towns, large swathes of northern Mali remain unstable and insurgent groups launch frequent attacks. More recently, jihadist groups have spread to Mali's central Mopti region, exploiting rifts and fueling deadly conflicts between the Fulani (Peul), Bambara, and Dogon ethnic communities, which has led to a precipitous decline in the security situation therein.[1]

Absent a major strategic shift in the country and wider Sahel region, the marked increase of Islamist activity is likely to continue unabated. Deadly attacks on Malian military personnel, United Nations (UN) peacekeepers, and civilians persist in both the northern and central regions of the country, including the January 2017 suicide bombing in the city of Gao that killed 47 people, the January 2019 attack in Aguelhok that killed 10 UN peacekeepers, and five major attacks from November 2019 to June 2020 that killed at least 145 Malian soldiers.[2] *Furthermore, the October 2017 attack that killed four American soldiers stationed in Niger occurred near the Malian border. The attack was eventually claimed by a group that has pledged bayat (allegiance) to the Islamic State.*[3]

Meanwhile, public trust in the Malian government continues to be undermined by the extrajudicial torture and murder of civilians by its forces and allied militias.[4] *The government of Mali has recognized this problem and has begun to reform the country's security sector to prevent abuses.*[5] *However, the March 2019 massacre of at least 160 Fulani herders—reportedly perpetrated by the government-supported Dan Na Ambassagou militia—and subsequent resignation of the Malian government illustrates the difficult road ahead.*[6] *Similarly, the government has not been able to implement the June 2015 Algiers Accord, which would theoretically begin the process of reconciling moderates and countering extremist groups.*[7] *In February 2020, the Malian government acknowledged that initial contact had been established with leaders of al Qaeda affiliate Jama'at Nasr al-Islam wal Muslimin (JNIM) to explore options for peace, a significant shift in six years of policy.*[8]

Elections in the summer of 2018, though deemed credible by observers, were beset by violence, boycotts, and poll closures in the center and north.[9] *After disputed parliamentary elections in the spring of 2020, protests against the administration of President Ibrahim Boubacar Keïta erupted in Bamako that June. Protesters led by the president's former electoral opponents and popular imam Mahmoud Dicko accused the Keïta administration of corruption, economic mismanagement, and a failure to resolve the security crisis in the country.*[10] *As of July 2020, the Malian government had responded to the protests with both deadly violence and concessions that fell short of protestor demands for Keïta's resignation. There are now fears that further instability in Mali will exacerbate an already deteriorating situation in the country.*[11] *Without significant reforms, a durable peace in Mali will remain elusive, and Salafi-jihadi groups will continue to use the country as a base to further destabilize the region.*

Islamist Activity

Since Mali declared itself independent in 1960, Tuaregs (a Berber ethnic group) who live in the north have repeatedly launched secessionist rebellions. One such separatist group, the National Movement for the Liberation of Azawad (MNLA), was formed in October 2011. The MNLA is nominally secular but has allied with Islamist organizations at different points in its history. Armed with weapons and experience gained from the Libyan Civil War, MNLA-led rebellions in the north began early in 2012 and quickly handed the Malian military a string of defeats.[12] A group of disgruntled soldiers called the Green Berets attacked the presidential palace in Bamako and deposed President Amadou Toumani Touré out of frustration and a perceived lack of support from the government.

The National Council for the Recovery of Democracy and the Restoration of the State (CNRDRE), formed by the Green Berets after taking power, suspended Mali's constitution and dissolved its institutions, promising to restore civilian rule.[13] The coup caused enough chaos to benefit the MNLA's cause. On April 2, 2012, the MNLA seized several major cities in the country's north, including Gao, Kidal, and Timbuktu.[14] The MNLA announced a ceasefire on April 6th of that year, claiming that they had enough land to form their own state of Azawad.[15] The country was split in two, with Bamako in control of the south and the rebels holding the north.

The MNLA sought the assistance of Islamist groups in its rebellion. These groups included al-Qaeda in the Maghreb (AQIM), Ansar Dine, and the Movement for Unity & Jihad in West Africa (MUJAO). In May 2012, the MNLA and Ansar Dine agreed to merge to form an Islamist state.[16] Within less than a week, however, the two groups clashed over the degree to which *sharia* law would be enforced. MUJAO similarly united with the MNLA, and similarly fell out. Thereafter, MUJAO and Ansar Dine worked together to push the MNLA out of Gao in June 2012.[17]

In early December 2012, representatives of *Ansar Dine* and the MNLA agreed to a ceasefire with the government.[18] However, Ansar Dine suspended this arrangement just one month later, accusing the government of using the reprieve to prepare for war.[19] The Islamist militants then began aggressively moving south towards Bamako. By January 10th, Islamist rebels attacked and took control of Konna, a town less than 40 miles from Mopti, where the Malian army maintains a strategic base.[20]

The French government responded by announcing Operation Serval, in which the French military would support Mali in rebuffing Islamist forces. With French support and deployed troops from the Economic Community of West African States (ECOWAS), the Malian army regained control of Konna.[21] French, Malian, and ECOWAS troops quickly retook northern cities and towns in the weeks that followed. However, after military forces retook Gao, the Islamists regrouped and launched an insurgency.[22] In August 2014, *Operation Serval* was replaced by Operation Barkhane. With a mandate focused more on counterterrorism, the Barkhane force is headquartered in Chad and operates across Western and Central Africa. Operation Barkhane was reinforced in January 2020 and is still active as of this writing.[23]

The Malian government has signed ceasefires with several groups, including the Coordination of Azawad Movements (CMA), which functions as an umbrella group for Tuareg and Arab separatists, among them the MNLA. The most recent, known as the Algiers Accord, was signed in June 2015. The agreement included provisions for former separatist fighters to be integrated into northern Malian security forces, better representation for northern regions in central government institutions, and the right for people in the north to form local institutions.[24] Implementation of the agreement has stagnated however, due to insecurity in the northern regions and lingering distrust between the government and the MNLA.[25]

Islamist groups initially did not participate in the peace process, remaining active in the north and increasingly the south and center of the country. Roughly 1,350 to 3,160 Salafi-*jihadi* fighters were active in Mali as of 2018, and *jihadist* activities have only increased since.[26] While there are several distinct Islamist groups, membership between them tends to be fluid. The March 2017 creation of Jama'at Nasr al-Islam wal Muslimin (JNIM) from four disparate Islamist groups into a single al-Qaeda franchise has significantly escalated the threat posed by radical Islamists in the region.[27]

Ansar Dine ("Defenders of the Faith")

Iyad ag Ghaly formed Ansar Dine in 2011, with the group expanding its reach and power in northern Mali throughout 2012. As previously noted, the group initially worked with the MNLA to take over the north, but differing positions on the imposition of *sharia* caused the relationship between the two to deteriorate. *Ansar Dine*, in partnership with other Islamist groups such as MUJAO, expelled the MNLA and took control of Timbuktu, Kidal, and Gao in June 2012.[28]

As Ansar Dine took control of more and more of northern Mali, it increasingly pushed a radical interpretation of Islam. On July 10, 2012, its militants destroyed two tombs at Timbuktu's ancient Djingareyber mud mosque, angering the city's residents and drawing international condemnation.[29] The Islamist group banned alcohol, smoking, Friday visits to cemeteries, and watching soccer, and required women to wear veils in public.[30] The group whipped and beat those who did not adhere to its strict interpretation of *sharia* law.[31]

In June 2016, ag Ghaly released his first video in almost two years, issuing new threats against the West and commending recent attacks against French forces and UN peacekeepers.[32] On October 31, 2016, Mahmoud Dicko, president of Mali's High Islamic Council, told reporters that he has brokered a truce with Ag Ghaly.[33] Ansar Dine immediately denied the report, calling the claim "completely baseless."[34] In March 2017, Ansar Dine joined JNIM and pledged allegiance to al-Qaeda, retaining its leader Iyad ag Ghaly atop the new organization.[35] As part of JNIM, Ansar Dine militants remained active through 2019, conducting attacks in Mali with allied Islamist organizations such as the Macina Liberation Front.[36]

Movement for Unity and Jihad in West Africa (MUJAO) and Al-Mourabitoun ("The Sentinels")

MUJAO is a West Africa-based militant Islamist organization that is allied with and has ties to AQIM.[37] Soon after its first public statement in December 2011, MUJAO reportedly concluded an agreement with both Ansar Dine and AQIM to pursue a common goal of spreading Islamism across the region.[38] The group appears to target West Africa more than other terror groups, and identifies itself as "an alliance between native Arab, Tuareg and Black African tribes and various *muhajirin* ("immigrants," i.e. foreign *jihadists*) from North and West Africa."[39] The group appears to fund itself through kidnapping activities.[40]

Like Ansar Dine, MUJAO initially had a truce with the MNLA as they jointly fought to take control of Mali's north from Bamako.[41] While Ansar Dine appeared to have taken control of Timbuktu with AQIM, Gao was held by MUJAO.[42] During its advance on Gao, MUJAO reportedly sacked Algeria's consulate and kidnapped seven Algerian diplomats.[43] Once in control of the city, MUJAO imposed a draconian interpretation of sharia law on Malians.[44] In August 2013, a significant faction of MUJAO merged with a militant group formerly associated with AQIM to form a new group called al-Mourabitoun, leaving MUJAO largely defunct.[45]

Al-Mourabitoun

Al-Mourabitoun was formed in August 2013 following a merger between a breakaway segment of AQIM led by Algerian commander Mokhtar Belmokhtar and a faction of MUJAO.[46] The group aims to unite Islamic movements and Muslims across Africa against secular influences, with a particular focus on attacking French interests and allies across the region.[47] Belmokhtar's faction, known as the al-Mulathamun Battalion ("the Masked Battalion"), had previously been part of AQIM, but split into a separate organization in late 2012 after an ongoing dispute with AQIM's *emir*, Abdelmalek Droukdel.[48] Under Belmokhtar's command, the group claimed responsibility for the January 2013 Tiguentourine gas facility attack, which killed 39 civilians.

Al-Mourabitoun's unified front may belie greater internal turmoil. In May 2015, al-Mourabitoun co-founder Adnan Abu

Walid al Sahrawi pledged allegiance to the Islamic State and Abu Bakr al Baghdadi in an audiotape that was released to the *Al Akhbar* news agency.[49] Several days later, however, Belmokhtar dismissed the pledge, a move that indicated a split between al Sahrawi and al-Mourabitoun's *shura* council.[50] In the weeks that followed, local Malian media reported clashes between factions loyal to Belmokhtar and those loyal to al Sahrawi.[51] Al Sahrawi's faction continued to launch attacks in the region, including on a military outpost in Burkina Faso near the border with Mali and on a high-security prison in Niger thought to house militants from Nigeria's Boko Haram and AQIM.[52]

Questions about al-Mourabitoun's leadership persist. Founder Belmokhtar was reportedly killed by U.S. forces in Libya three separate times, the latest in 2016. Since then, it is rumored (though unsubstantiated) that Belmokhtar remains alive and at large. Irrespective of its leader's status, reports indicated that al-Mourabitoun reunited with AQIM following the Radisson Blu attack in November 2015.[53] This reconciliation was formalized by the March 2017 merger of multiple West African al-Qaeda affiliated groups to form JNIM.[54] In January 2017, al-Mourabitoun claimed responsibility for a suicide car bombing at a military camp in Gao that killed 47 people.[55]

Al-Mourabitoun has been involved in several high-profile attacks against foreigners in central and southern Mali, including three attacks in Sévaré and Bamako in 2015 that collectively killed 37 people.[56] The group has also launched attacks outside of Mali, including collaborating with AQIM on an attack on the Splendid Hotel in Ouagadougou, Burkina Faso, in January 2016 as well as on the March 2016 attack on the Grand Bassam beach resort in Côte d'Ivoire.

Macina Liberation Front (FLM)

The FLM emerged in January 2015 and is led by Amadou Koufa, an ethnically Fulani radical Islamic preacher. Koufa rose to prominence after he led a joint AQIM, Ansar Dine, and MUJAO offensive against the town of Konna in early January 2013, the capture of which triggered the French intervention in Mali. The term "Macina" refers to the 19th century Fulani-led Islamic Macina Empire that stretched across central Mali, and Koufa has proven adept at capitalizing on the sense of victimization among ethnic Fulani in this region.

FLM ideology blends Islamic extremism with a local ethnic radicalism that is a product of increased insecurity and competition between central Malian ethnic groups.[57] The group targets young Fulanis for recruitment through local radio stations. Koufa's Fulani-language sermons draw on a narrative of a mythical time when Fulani were the masters of a prosperous Islamic faith in West Africa.[58] However, far from heralding prosperity, Fulani–FLM collaboration has prompted significant reprisals against Fulani communities by ethnic neighbors and government forces in central Mali.[59]

FLM membership is estimated to be a few hundred fighters, often recruiting from the Fulani pastoral community; the small numbers have thus far prevented the group from independently conducting anything more than small-scale attacks using improvised explosive devices (IEDs).[60] However, the FLM often collaborates with other Islamist groups to launch high profile attacks on United Nations peacekeepers and civilian targets. The FLM claimed a role in the November 2015 attack on the Radisson Blu hotel in Bamako and in the July 2016 attack on the Malian military base in the central Segou Region.[61] The FLM also exploits the government's continual human rights abuses, such as extrajudicial executions and arrests, to curry favor with the Malian population.[62] Rumors of the death of FLM leader Amadou Koufa in a November 2018 raid by French forces proved to be premature after Koufa reappeared in a video that circulated in March 2019.[63] Koufa was subsequently designated a Specially Designated Global Terrorist by the U.S. Department of State in November 2019.[64]

Along with assisting the establishment of Ansarul Islam in December 2016, the FLM joined with other al-Qaeda affiliated groups in the Sahel to form JNIM in March 2017.[65]

Al-Qaeda in the Islamic Maghreb (AQIM)

Over time, AQIM has evolved from a local terrorist group seeking to replace Algeria's government with an Islamic one to an al-Qaeda group preaching global *jihad*. Formerly known as the Group Salafiste Pour la Predication et Combat (GSPC), AQIM has its roots in the Algerian Civil War of the 1990s. In Mali, the group has taken advantage of the country's sparsely populated, poorly governed northern regions to conduct operations. Mali's three northern regions—Timbuktu, Gao, and Kidal—contain only 10 percent of the population, while accounting for two-thirds of the country's land.[66] As noted by analysts, the group has periodically turned to smuggling and criminality to raise funds. At its core, it has remained a highly resilient and pragmatic Islamist insurgency.[67]

GSPC/AQIM, like many Islamist terrorist groups, finances itself through crime. Prior to its merger with al-Qaeda, the group achieved international notoriety when it ransomed 15 European tourists in Algeria in early 2003, receiving a reported sum of 5 million Euro.[68] Between 2007 and 2017, there were a number of additional, high profile kidnappings that illustrated the group's continued ability to operate in northern Mali. The kidnappings serve a dual purpose for AQIM; the activity itself drove foreign investment away from the region, while the ransom payments brought AQIM cash needed for weapons and supplies.[69] In addition to kidnapping, AQIM also engages in profitable smuggling operations with routes going through northern Mali.

According to the *Long War Journal*, AQIM affiliates launched 276 attacks in West Africa in 2017.[70] This marked a slight increase from 2016, and a nearly 150 percent increase from 2015.[71] After the merger of AQIM into JNIM, attacks claimed exclusively by AQIM have become more difficult to separate and define. However, the pace of attacks continues to increase: in April 2018, AQIM claimed an attack that killed a United Nations peacekeeper and wounded seven French soldiers, and indicated that the strike was a retaliation against French operations that had killed AQIM members.[72] In 2019, AQIM and its affiliates conducted two-thirds of the 800 attacks carried out by Salafi-*jihadist* groups in the Sahel, inflicting hundreds of casualties.[73] AQIM itself claimed responsibility for an attack that killed 10 UN peacekeepers in January of that year.[74]

These attacks seem to underscore the group's ability to recalibrate its strategy and tactics in the face of ongoing counterterrorism efforts. Nevertheless, its influence has waned as a result of competition from other Islamist groups.[75] While AQIM remains loyal to al-Qaeda, the group's roots in the Maghreb and leadership have proven a hurdle in the Sahel, when compared to its locally-affiliated rivals.[76] Indeed, since 2015, the group has faced increasing competition from the Islamic State, which was a potential impetus for AQIM's Sahara branch to merge with Ansar Dine, al-Mourabitoun, and the FLM to form JNIM in March 2017.[77] AQIM faced a devastating setback when French forces killed its leader Abdelmalek Droukdel and several close associates in a gunfight on June 3, 2020.[78] This setback will certainly not erase AQIM as an acute threat to peace in Mali, but will likely hasten the group's decline in favor of locally-led groups such as Ansar Dine, Ansarul Islam, FLM, and Islamic State Greater Sahara (ISGS).

Jama'at Nasr al-Islam wal Muslimin (JNIM, "Group for the Support of Islam and Muslims")

In March 2017, JNIM was founded through the merger of four al-Qaeda affiliated Salafi-*jihadist* groups in Mali and the greater Sahel region—Ansar Dine, AQIM, al-Mourabitoun, and the FLM. The group aims to impose *sharia* law in West Africa and expel Western forces (particularly the French). Ansar Dine leader ag Ghaly pledged *bayat* to al-Qaeda leader Ayman al-Zawahiri on behalf of JNIM, cementing JNIM as the central al-Qaeda affiliate in the region.[79] JNIM was designated a foreign terrorist organization by the U.S. Department of State on September 5, 2018.[80]

JNIM is estimated to number 2,000 fighters.[81] The merger has increased available resources and coordination, thereby improving the group's operational capacity despite increased pressure from security forces, which have inflicted significant losses among JNIM's leadership, including Abdelmalek Droukdel himself.[82] In Mali, JNIM was responsible for the April 2018 attack on a French and UN base in Timbuktu that wounded seven French soldiers. The group has also claimed a number of attacks against Malian, French, and UN forces as well as opposing militias and civilians, using tactics ranging from conventional assaults with light and heavy weapons, to IEDs and SVBIEDs (Suicide Vehicle-borne IEDs).[83] JNIM also conducts assassinations and kidnappings, and extorts resources from local people.[84] In the first half of 2020, JNIM claimed responsibility for multiple attacks, killing 69 Malian soldiers in just three particularly large assaults on military bases and convoys across central and northern Mali.[85] JNIM is also suspected of carrying out the June 2020 ambush that killed 24 Malian soldiers.[86]

In February 2020, the Malian government admitted to contacting senior JNIM leadership, including Amadou Koufa and Iyad ag Galy. While no concrete dialogue has yet been established, JNIM nonetheless acknowledged talks with the government and issued demands for the withdrawal of French forces as a prerequisite to more serious peace discussions.[87] JNIM's present demands may not seem politically viable, but opposition leader and *imam* Mahmoud Dicko firmly believes in dialogue with Islamist groups, and Mali may yet adopt a policy of reconciliation with the al-Qaeda affiliate.

A potential consequence of talks with the Malian government was the breakdown of the *de facto* peace that had existed between al-Qaeda and Islamic State affiliates in the Sahel since 2015. In the spring of 2020, remote clashes devolved into open warfare among the two Islamist factions.[88] While neither group has gained supremacy, fierce attacks from ISGS can only decrease JNIM's capabilities to act against security forces, but threatens to inflict even more civilian casualties.

Ansarul Islam

Ansarul Islam is an Islamist group founded in Burkina Faso, but which reportedly maintains bases and has conducted attacks in northern Mali.[89] The first such group native to Burkina Faso, Ansarul Islam announced its presence shortly after it conducted its first attack in December 2016.

Ansarul Islam was founded by Malam Ibrahim Dicko, allegedly with the backing of FLM leader Amadou Koufa, and reportedly numbers 150-200 fighters.[90] Dicko allegedly passed due to natural causes in mid-2017 and Ansarul Islam is reportedly led by his brother Jafar as of early 2019.[91] Ansarul Islam appears closely linked to Malian al-Qaeda affiliated *jihadist* groups and has received training from JNIM operatives.[92] It also reportedly participates in JNIM operations in Mali: the two groups claimed involvement in the March 2017 attack on a Malian military base in Boulikessi that killed eleven Malian soldiers.[93] Ansarul Islam has also been ascribed responsibility for a number of IED and conventional attacks in Mali, such as one that killed a French soldier in April 2017.[94] The group has demonstrated its ability to grow as Sahelian states have been increasingly destabilized by Islamist violence. While many of its attacks occur in Burkina Faso, in October 2019 suspected Ansarul Islam fighters carried out a sophisticated attack on two Malian military outposts, killing at least 25 soldiers.[95]

The Islamic State Greater Sahara (ISGS)

After the loss of core territory and power in Iraq and Syria, the Islamic State has broadened its territorial scope and interests to the Sahel region of North Africa.[96] The creation of an IS affiliate in the Sahel has been attributed to *jihadi* leader Adnan Abu Walid al Sahrawi, who was formerly affiliated with MUJAO and al-Mourabitoun.[97] While Sahrawi left al-Qaeda and pledged allegiance to the Islamic State in May 2015, the depth of the connection remains obscure. Nevertheless, the Islamic State's official media channels acknowledged the group's *bayat* in 2016. In mid-2019, Islamic State incorporated its Sahelian affiliate into Islamic State West Africa Province (ISWAP).[98]

ISGS has demonstrated a high operational tempo since its founding in 2015, conducting a number of sophisticated attacks in Mali, Niger, and Burkina Faso.[99] In October 2017, ISGS killed four U.S. Special Forces soldiers, as well as four Nigerien soldiers. The attack occurred in Tongo Tongo, near Niger's border with Mali.[100] As a result of this attack, ISGS and al-Sahrawi received a terrorist designation from the U.S. State Department in May 2018.[101] ISGS has come under increasing pressure by security forces, particularly through the French Operation Barkhane. This pressure possibly facilitated the surrender of veteran *jihadist* Sultan Ould Bady to Algerian authorities in August 2018 and led to the capture of senior ISGS commander Mohamed Mrabat by French forces in May 2020.[102]

ISGS' core strength has been estimated at around 200 to 300 fighters, but it is believed that it can call upon or hire upward of 1,000.[103] The group has risen to become the primary enemy of French forces and its Sahelian allies operating in the region. In a period of less than two months in late 2019, for instance, ISGS attacks killed over 300 people across the Sahel.[104]

Despite controversy between Belmokhtar and al Sahrawi

after ISGS' split from Al-Mourabitoun, the Islamic State and al Qaeda-affiliated groups refrained from open hostilities from 2015 until 2020.[105] While there are likely many facets to the conflict, *Al Naba*, Islamic State's central news agency, has accused JNIM of initiating hostilities and betraying the Islamist cause by speaking to the Malian government.[106] The fighting remains inconclusive as of mid-2020, but JNIM maintains a larger force, which may blunt the rising power of ISGS in Mali and the Sahel, but the latter will likely remain a major threat.

Islamism and Society

Mali has a significant Muslim majority, with nearly 94 percent of the population adhering to the Islamic faith as of 2018.[107] While the northern and central regions have experienced a significant uptick in radical Islamist activity, it is not clear that this reflects the broader sentiments of the Malian people. Islamists, their radical teachings, and their harsh imposition of justice have reportedly not been embraced by northerners, many of whom have fled into refugee camps in neighboring Mauritania, Burkina Faso, and Niger.[108] One reason may lie in the practice of Malian Islam, which is not typical of other Islamic nations. Malian religious practices incorporate animist traditions from the region, including "absorbing mystical elements [and] ancestor veneration."[109] Mali's lengthy history figures prominently in the country's contemporary culture; Malians "regularly invoke Muslim rulers of various pre-colonial states and empires and past Muslim clerics, saints, and miracle-workers from the distant and more recent colonial and post-colonial past."[110] Islam and animism, in other words, have coexisted in Mali for centuries, which is counter to many Islamist's strict interpretation of the religion.[111]

Since Islamists took over the north, several French MPs have received reports that Qatar was financing the MNLA, Ansar Dine, and MUJAO.[112] Iran has also attempted to peddle influence in Mali.[113] Malian officials, however, have disparaged such efforts. Before his ouster, President Touré commented that: "Mali is a very old Islamic country where tolerance is part of our tradition."[114]

When Islamists were in control of the north, they sought to impose their beliefs on the region and purge any dissonant practices. There have been several instances of Islamist militants destroying shrines and mausoleums in the north, particularly in Timbuktu, claiming that the veneration of Sufi saints and scholars was sacrilegious. Sixteen of the mausoleums destroyed as part of this effort were listed as UNESCO World Heritage Sites.[115] The destruction of these historic shrines was recently ruled a war crime by the International Criminal Court, which sentenced one fighter involved, Ahmad al-Mahdi, to nine years in prison for his participation.[116]

While people in the north initially welcomed French intervention, frustrations have grown as the French and UN peacekeepers struggle to effectively provide security. There has also been discontent regarding certain provisions of the 2015 Algiers Accord. In July 2016, three people were killed and dozens wounded when the Malian military opened fire on protestors demonstrating against the nomination of former militants to government positions, as specified by the Algiers Accord.[117]

Young people between the ages of 18 and 35 form the largest number of recruits for armed non-state actors in Mali.[118] Over 19 million people live in Mali, and nearly 70 percent of the population is under the age of 24.[119] A potential draw to militant groups for young people is a "governance vacuum," in which most rural communities feel ignored or abandoned by their government while militant groups are seen as potentially better sources of protection.[120] Islamist recruitment, in turn, is bolstered by increasing insecurity in the northern and central regions of the country, as well as abuses by security forces. As of mid-2020, the UNHCR estimated that 141,000 Malian refugees have been forced to flee the country, while an additional 250,998 were classified as Internally Displaced Persons.[121]

Islamism and the State

Religion in Mali "is understood as private and confessional."[122] The Malian constitution, adopted in 1992, mandates a secular state. However, the 1990s saw a dramatic increase in the number of Islamic associations throughout the country, each with varying motivations and religious interpretations.[123] The government formed the High Islamic Council (Haut Conseil Islamique) in 2002.[124] While religious political parties are banned under the constitution, Mali's government supports the High Islamic Council as an "official and unique interlocutor of political authorities for all questions relative to the practice of Islam."[125]

The Bush administration began the Pan Sahel Initiative in October 2002 to train African security forces in counterterrorism.[126] In June 2005, the program expanded to include more countries from the region, becoming the Trans-Saharan Counter-Terrorism Partnership (TSCTP).[127] The Partnership's Operation Flintlock provides anti-insurgency training to the armies of the seven participating states, which includes Mali.[128] Operation Flintlock has been reprised on several occasions, most recently in February 2020.[129] However, a shift in U.S. military priorities and increasing concerns over abuses by security forces active in the region may jeopardize future aid.[130] In 2020, the U.S. appointed a new special envoy for the Sahel to address the aggressive expansion of extremist Islamist groups in the region.[131]

Mali and its neighbors have made efforts to coordinate their counterterrorism activities. Algeria held a conference in March 2010 inviting leaders from some West African countries to build a joint counter-*jihad* security plan.[132] Subsequently, Algeria, Mauritania, Niger, and Mali established a joint military base in Tamanrasset, southern Algeria.[133] In 2014, Burkina Faso, Chad, Mali, Mauritania, and Niger founded the Group of Five (G5) Sahel, a regional institution aimed at coordinating development and security policies. The joint force for the G5 Sahel (FC-G5S) was formed in 2017, with the objective of countering regional Islamist militant activities. However, while the FC-G5S has secured a modicum of international financial support in the interim, it is relatively new and unproven in the fight against Islamists in the Sahel region.[134]

From March 27 to April 2, 2017, Mali held a Conference of National Understanding, as part of the requirements of the 2015 peace agreement. The conference participants recommended that the Malian government should open negotiations with *jihadists*.

The Malian government initially indicated interest, but its French allies were not as enthusiastic.[135] Nothing conclusive has emerged from initial contact with *jihadist* groups but the desire of Malians to negotiate have been expressed by Mahmoud Dicko, who represents the large body protestors who have called for the government's removal.[136]

Under Operation Barkhane, France has continued its regional counterterrorism operations and support. The over 5,000-member force has had successes in the killing of AQIM leader Abdelmalek Droukdel and the capture of senior ISGS commander Mohamed Mrabat. MINUSMA, the UN mission to Mali, renewed its mandate for another year in June 2020, maintaining over 15,000 military and police personnel in Mali.[137]

Overall, the government response to Islamist groups has focused heavily on security solutions and building policing capacity. This has catalyzed two problems. The heavy-handed practices of Malian security forces have exacerbated local grievances, risking increasing support for Islamist groups. This has already happened with Mali's Fulani populations, and groups like the FLM have found success recruiting among young Fulani people aggrieved by abuses.[138] Nevertheless, these abuses continue.[139]

Second, Mali's focus on security solutions has come at the expense of addressing local social and economic issues in the north. Unfortunately, despite a close relationship between the Malian government and its international partners, President Keïta's tenure has been hampered by allegations of corruption and his administration's inability to solve the security crisis, which has boiled over into popular protest.[140] As increasing unrest wracks Mali's capital and southern regions, Islamist groups expand their reach and carry out attacks in the country's north and south. Without improving trust in state institutions, service delivery mechanisms, and accountability, it will be difficult for the Malian government to effectively protect against the allure of Islamist groups, which will continue to capitalize on local crises and insecurity.[141]

Endnotes

1. Ibrahim Yahaya Ibrahim and Mollie Zapata, "Regions at Risk: Preventing Mass Atrocities in Mali," United States Holocaust Memorial Museum, April 2018, https://www.ushmm.org/m/pdfs/Mali_Report_English_FINAL_April_2018.pdf; "Mali Villagers Killed in Armed Raid in Mopti Region," BBC, January 1, 2019, https://www.bbc.com/news/world-africa-46732703.
2. Angela Dewan, "Mali suicide bombing: Al Qaeda-linked group claims responsibility," *CNN*, January 19, 2017, https://www.cnn.com/2017/01/19/africa/mali-military-bombing/index.html; "Mali: Ten UN peacekeepers killed in 'jihadist' attack," *BBC*, January 20, 2019, https://www.bbc.com/news/world-africa-46941711; "Militants kill 54 in attack on Mali army post; IS claims responsibility," Reuters, November 1, 2019, https://www.reuters.com/article/us-mali-security/militants-kill-54-in-attack-on-mali-army-post-is-claims-responsibility-idUSKBN1XB4W7; "Mali army loses 24 soldiers in Niger border attack," *BBC*, November 19, 2019, https://www.bbc.com/news/world-africa-50466025; "At least 20 Mali soldiers killed in JNIM attack on Sokolo camp," *The Defense Post*, January 27, 2020, https://www.thedefensepost.com/2020/01/27/mali-soldiers-killed-jnim-sokolo-segou/; Baba Ahmed, "25 soldiers killed in attack in Mali's north, army says," Associated Press, April 7, 2020, https://apnews.com/ab5e933f95c2ce435469c81e504b23be; "24 Malian soldiers killed in ambush near Mauritania border," Associated Press, June 15, 2020, https://apnews.com/ba3e87fb3fa8e257c82555f01807c6ce.
3. Rukmini Callimachi, "ISIS Affiliate Claims October Attack on U.S. Troops in Niger," *New York Times*, January 13, 2018, https://www.nytimes.com/2018/01/13/world/africa/niger-isis-green-berets-attack.html.
4. "Mali: Deaths, Torture in Army Detention," Human Rights Watch, April 9, 2018, https://www.hrw.org/news/2018/04/09/mali-deaths-torture-army-detention.
5. "Mali's Prime Minister and Foreign Minister Discuss Security Sector Reform," Atlantic Council, March 27, 2019, https://www.atlanticcouncil.org/events/past-events/mali-s-prime-minister-and-foreign-minister-discuss-security-sector.
6. "Insider Insight: Explaining the Mali Massacre," *African Arguments*, March 26, 2019, https://africanarguments.org/2019/03/26/insiders-insight-explaining-the-mali-massacre/; "Mali Government Resigns After Massacre," *Voice of America*, April 18,

2019, https://www.voanews.com/a/mali-government-resigns-after-massacre/4882666.html?utm_source=Media+Review+-for+April+19%2C+2019&utm_campaign=Media+Review+-for+April+19%2C+2019&utm_medium=email.

7. J. Peter Pham, "After Mali's Runoff, Challenges Remain," *Africa-Source*, August 13, 2018, http://www.atlanticcouncil.org/blogs/africasource/after-mali-s-runoff-challenges-remain.
8. Aïssatou Diallo, "Mahmoud Dicko: "The dialogue with the jihadists must hold," *The Africa Report*, March 24, 2020, https://www.theafricareport.com/24932/mahmoud-dicko-the-dialogue-with-the-jihadists-must-hold/.
9. "Freedom in the World 2018: Mali Profile," Freedom House, 2018, https://freedomhouse.org/report/freedom-world/2018/mali; Clair MacDougall, "Keïta Gets 2nd Term as Mali President with Runoff Victory," *New York Times*, August 16, 2018, https://www.nytimes.com/2018/08/16/world/africa/keita-mali-election.html.
10. Diallo, "Mahmoud Dicko: "The dialogue with the jihadists must hold."
11. "Mali's President Keïta dissolves constitutional court amid unrest," *BBC*, July 12, 2020, https://www.bbc.com/news/world-africa-53378433; Paul Melly, "Mahmoud Dicko: Mali imam challenges President Keïta," *BBC*, June 28, 2020, https://www.bbc.com/news/world-africa-53176083.
12. Xan Rice, "Mali Steps Up Battle Against Tuareg Revolt," *Financial Times*, February 19, 2012, https://www.ft.com/content/056fc1e8-5ae4-11e1-a2b3-00144feabdc0#axzz1n4Z8DUN6.
13. Adam Nossiter, "Soldiers Overthrow Mali Government in Setback for Democracy in Africa," *New York Times*, March 22, 2012, https://www.nytimes.com/2012/03/23/world/africa/mali-coup-france-calls-for-elections.html.
14. Neal Conan and Ofeibea Quist-Arcton, "Turmoil in Mali Deepens After Military Coup," *National Public Radio*, April 5, 2012, http://www.npr.org/2012/04/05/150072681/a-military-coup-cre-ates-political-crisis-in-mali.
15. "Mali Rebels Announce Ceasefire," *ABC News*, April 6, 2012, http://www.abc.net.au/news/2012-04-06/mali-rebels-announce-ceasefire/3936824.
16. "Mali Tuareg and Islamist Rebels Agree on Islamist State," *BBC*, May 27, 2012, http://www.bbc.co.uk/news/world-africa-18224004?print=true.
17. "Mali: Islamists Seize Gao from Tuareg Rebels," *BBC*, June 27,

2012, https://www.bbc.com/news/world-africa-18610618.

18. Monica Mark, "Mali Rebel Groups Agree Ceasefire," *Guardian* (London), December 5, 2012, http://www.guardian.co.uk/world/2012/dec/05/malian-rebel-groups-agree-ceasefire.
19. "Mali Islamist Group 'Suspends' Ceasefire," *VOA News*, January 4, 2013, https://www.voanews.com/a/mali-islamist-group-suspends-ceasefire/1577693.html.
20. Afua Hirsch, "French Troops Arrive in Mali to Stem Rebel Advance," *Guardian* (London), January 11, 2013, http://www.guardian.co.uk/world/2013/jan/11/france-intervene-mali-conflict.
21. Ibid.; Christopher Isiguzo and Damilola Oyedele, "Nigeria: Air Force Sends War Planes to Mali Thursday," *ThisDay*, January 17, 2013, http://allafrica.com/stories/201301170615.html.
22. David Lewis, "In Mali Town, Counter-Insurgency Task Ties Down French," Reuters, February 14, 2013, https://www.reuters.com/article/us-mali-rebels-gao/in-mali-town-counter-insurgency-task-ties-down-french-idUSBRE91D1EV20130214?feedType=RSS&feedName=worldNews.
23. Fergus Kelly, "Barkhane: France to deploy 220 experienced troops 'accustomed to operating in the Sahel,'" *The Defense Post*, January 17, 2020, https://www.thedefensepost.com/2020/01/17/france-220-troops-sahel-barkhane/.
24. "Malian rivals sign peace deal," *Al Jazeera* (Doha), June 21, 2015, http://www.aljazeera.com/news/2015/06/malian-rivals-sign-peace-deal-150620173301883.html.
25. "Briefing by the Former Executive President of the Coordination of Azawad Movements," Atlantic Council, January 11, 2018, https://www.atlanticcouncil.org/events/past-events/briefing-by-the-former-executive-president-of-the-coordination-of-azawad-movements.
26. Seth G. Jones et. al., "The Evolution of the Salafi-Jihadist Threat: Current and Future Challenges from the Islamic State, Al-Qaeda, and Other Groups," Center for Strategic and International Studies, November 2018, https://csis-prod.s3.amazonaws.com/s3fs-public/publication/181221_EvolvingTerroristThreat.pdf.
27. U.S. Department of State, Office of the Spokesperson, "State Department Terrorist Designation of Jama'at Nusrat al-Islam wal-Muslimin (JNIM)," September 5, 2018, https://www.state.gov/r/pa/prs/ps/2018/09/285705.htm.
28. "'Lion of the Desert': Ex-Partner of Germany Leads Malian Islamists," *Der Speigel* (Hamburg), January 13, 2013, http://www.

spiegel.de/international/world/leader-of-malian-isla-mists-once-helped-german-government-a-878724.html.

29. "Ansar Dine Destroy More Shrines in Mali," *Al Jazeera* (Doha), July 10, 2012, http://www.aljazeera.com/news/africa/2012/07/201271012301347496.html.
30. Michael Lambert and Jason Warner, "Who is Ansar Dine?" *CNN*, August 14, 2012, http://globalpublicsquare.blogs.cnn.com/2012/08/14/who-are-ansar-dine/.
31. Adam Nossiter, "Burkina Faso Official Goes to Islamist-Held Northern Mali in Effort to Avert War," *New York Times*, August 7, 2012, https://www.nytimes.com/2012/08/08/world/africa/burkina-faso-official-visits-mali-in-effort-to-avert-war.html.
32. Conor Gaffey, "Who is Iyad Ag Ghaly, Mali's Veteran Jihadi?" *Newsweek*, June 29, 2016, http://www.newsweek.com/who-iyad-ag-ghaly-malis-veteran-jihadi-475473.
33. Idriss Fall, "Mali: Insurgent Group Accepts Cease-fire but With Conditions," *Voice of America*, October 31, 2016, http://www.voanews.com/a/mali-insurgent-group-ansar-dine-accepts-cease-fire/3573301.html.
34. "Mali Islamists Still Waging War, Dismiss Ceasefire Report," *Voice of America*, November 2, 2016, http://www.voanews.com/a/mali-dicko-ansar-dine/3576634.html.
35. "Backgrounder: Jama'at Nasr al-Islam wal Muslimin (JNIM)," Center for Strategic and International Studies, September 25, 2018, https://csis-prod.s3.amazonaws.com/s3fs-public/180927_JNIM_Backgrounder.pdf?CXpU5VJRYdLDg819YAoD_NA0WgloBybV.
36. Pauline Le Roux, "Confronting Central Mali's Extremist Threat," Africa Center for Strategic Studies, February 22, 2019, https://africacenter.org/spotlight/confronting-central-malis-extremist-threat/; Fergus Kelly, "Mali: UN Peacekeeper Injured in Attack on Kidal MINUSMA Base," *The Defense Post*, April 4, 2019.
37. Nossiter, "Burkina Faso Official Goes to Islamist-Held Northern Mali in Effort to Avert War."
38. "Some Things We May Think About MUJWA," *The Moor Next Door*, May 30, 2012, https://reliefweb.int/sites/reliefweb.int/files/resources/20120718_Report%20on%20Northern%20Mali.pdf.
39. Andrew McGregor, "Islamist Groups Mount Joint Offensive in Mali," Jamestown Foundation *Militant Leadership Monitor* XI, iss. 1, January 10, 2013, https://jamestown.org/wp-content/uploads/2013/01/TM_011_Issue01_01.pdf.
40. Sanders and Moseley, "A Political, Security and Humanitarian Cri-

sis: Northern Mali."
41. "'Dozens killed' in Northern Mali Fighting," *Al Jazeera* (Doha), June 28, 2012, http://www.aljazeera.com/news/africa/2012/06/201262891738152474.html.
42. Nossiter, "Burkina Faso Official Goes to Islamist-Held Northern Mali in Effort to Avert War."
43. "Some Things We May Think About MUJWA," *The Moor Next Door*.
44. Serge Daniel, "North Mali Residents Ready to Resist Islamist Groups," American Free Press, August 14, 2012, https://www.egyptindependent.com/north-mali-residents-ready-resist-islamist-groups/.
45. Bill Roggio, "Al Qaeda Group Led by Belmokhtar, MUJAO Unite to Form Al-Murabitoon," *Long War Journal*, August 22, 2013, https://www.longwarjournal.org/archives/2013/08/al_qaeda_groups_lead_by_belmok.php.
46. Ibid.
47. Government of Australia, "Australian National Security: Al-Murabitun," November 5, 2014, https://www.nationalsecurity.gov.au/Listedterroristorganisations/Pages/Al-Murabitun.aspx.
48. U.S. Department of State, Office of the Coordinator for Counterterrorism, *Country Reports on Terrorism 2013*, April 2014, http://www.state.gov/documents/organization/225886.pdf.
49. Thomas Joscelyn, "Confusion Surrounds West African Jihadists' Loyalty to Islamic State," *Long War Journal*, May 17, 2015, https://www.longwarjournal.org/archives/2015/05/confusion-surrounds-west-african-jihadists-loyalty-to-islamic-state.php.
50. "Sahara Islamist Leader Belmokhtar Dismisses Islamic State Pledge: Report," Reuters, May 17, 2015, https://www.reuters.com/article/us-sahara-militants/sahara-islamist-leader-belmokhtar-dismisses-islamic-state-pledge-report-idUSKBN0O20R020150517.
51. Thomas Joscelyn and Caleb Weiss, "Islamic State Recognizes Oath of Allegiance from Jihadists in Mali," *Long War Journal*, October 31, 2016, https://www.longwarjournal.org/archives/2016/10/islamic-state-recognizes-oath-of-allegiance-from-jihadists-in-west-africa.php.
52. Conor Gaffey, "Niger Repels Attack on Prison Holding Jihadis from Mali and Nigeria," *Newsweek*, October 17, 2016, https://www.newsweek.com/niger-repels-attack-prison-holding-jihadis-mali-and-nigeria-510618.
53. "Mali Extremists Join with Al-Qaeda-linked North Africa Group,"

Associated Press, December 4, 2015, http://www.cnsnews.com/news/article/mali-extremists-join-al-qaida-linked-north-af-rica-group.

54. "Backgrounder: Jama't Nasr al-Islam wal Muslimin," Center for Strategic and International Studies.
55. Angela Dewan, "Mali suicide bombing."
56. "Mali Hotel Siege: Several Killed in Sevare, Four UN Workers Saved," *BBC*, August 9, 2015, http://www.bbc.com/news/world-af-rica-33833363; "Al-Qaeda-Linked Group Claims Mali Restaurant Attack," *Al Jazeera* (Doha), March 9, 2015, http://www.aljazeera.com/news/2015/03/al-qaeda-linked-group-claims-mali-restaurant-at-tack-150309072613760.html; "Two Arrested in Connection with Bamako Hotel Attack," *Guardian* (London), November 27, 2015, https://www.theguardian.com/world/2015/nov/27/two-arrest-ed-in-connection-with-bamako-hotel-attack.
57. Michael Shurkin, "How to Defeat a New Boko Haram In Mali," *Newsweek*, September 7, 2015, http://www.newsweek.com/how-de-feat-new-boko-haram-mali-369430.
58. "Mali Islamists Armed Group Push Fighting Beyond Conflict-hit North," *Telegraph* (London), September 23, 2015, https://www.tele-graph.co.uk/news/worldnews/africaandindianocean/mali/11884570/Mali-Islamists-armed-group-push-fighting-beyond-conflict-hit-north.html; Yvan Guichaua and Dougoukolo Alpha Oumar Ba-Konaré, "Central Mali Gripped by a Dangerous Brew of Jihad, Revolt and Self-Defence," *The Conversation*, November 13, 2016, https://theconversation.com/central-mali-gripped-by-a-dangerous-brew-of-jihad-revolt-and-self-defence-67668.
59. "'I Have Lost Everything': In Central Mali, Rising Extremism Stirs Inter-communal Conflict," IRIN News, September 4, 2018, https://www.thenewhumanitarian.org/news-feature/2018/09/04/mali-fu-lani-dogon-extremism-stirs-intercommunal.
60. Rida Lyammouri, "Attack Highlights Poor Resources of Malian Army and Underscores Collaboration between Islamist Militants," IHS Jane's *Terrorism and Insurgency Monitor* 16, iss. 8, September 2016.
61. "Mali: Une Seconde Revendication de L'attaque de L'hôtel Radisson," *Radio France Internationale Afrique*, November 23, 2015, http://www.rfi.fr/afrique/20151123-mali-revendication-attaque-ho-tel-radisson-front-liberation-macina-bamako; Lyammouri, "Attack Highlights Poor Resources of Malian Army and Underscores Collaboration between Islamist Militants."

62. Sperber, "What Can Save Mali?"
63. "'Dead' Mali Jihadist Amadou Koufa Reappears in Video," *BBC*, March 2, 2019, https://www.bbc.com/news/world-africa-47428246.
64. U.S. Department of State, Office of the Spokesperson, "State Department Terrorist Designation of Amadou Kouffa," November 17, 2019.
65. Katherine Zimmerman, "Salafi-Jihadi Ecosystem in the Sahel," AEI Critical Threats Project, April 2020, https://www.criticalthreats.org/wp-content/uploads/2020/04/Salafi-Jihadi-Ecosystem-in-the-Sahel.pdf
66. William B. Farrell and Carla M. Komich, "USAID/DCHA/CMM Assessment: Northern Mali," Management Systems International, June 17, 2004.
67. J. Peter Pham, "The Dangerous 'Pragmatism' of Al-Qaeda in the Islamic Maghreb," *Journal of Middle East and Africa* no. 2, 2011, 15-29.
68. Stephen Harmon, "From GSPC to AQIM: The Evolution of an Algerian Islamist Terrorist Group into an Al-Qa'ida Affiliate and its Implications for the Sahara-Sahel Region," *Concerned African Scholars Bulletin* no. 85, Spring 2010, 17, http://concernedafricascholars.org/docs/bulletin85harmon.pdf; Raffi Khatchadourian, "Pursuing Terrorists in the Great Desert," *The Village Voice*, January 12, 2006, http://www.villagevoice.com/2006-01-17/news/pursuing-terrorists-in-the-great-desert/.
69. Michael Petrou, "Al-Qaeda in North Africa," *Maclean's*, May 11, 2009.
70. Caleb Weiss, "Al Qaeda maintains operational tempo in West Africa in 2017," *Long War Journal*, January 5, 2018, https://www.longwarjournal.org/archives/2018/01/al-qaeda-maintains-operational-tempo-in-west-africa-in-2017.php.
71. Caleb Weiss, "Al Qaeda linked to more than 250 West African attacks in 2016," *Long War Journal*, January 8, 2017, http://www.longwarjournal.org/archives/2017/01/over-250-al-qaeda-linked-attacks-in-west-africa-in-2016.php.
72. "Al-Qaida claims deadly attack on French, UN forces in Mali," Associated Press, April 20, 2018, https://www.foxnews.com/world/al-qaida-claims-deadly-attack-on-french-un-forces-in-mali.
73. "Africa's Active Militant Groups," Africa Center for Strategic Studies, January 2020, https://africacenter.org/wp-content/uploads/2020/01/Threat-from-African-Militant-Islamist-Groups-Expanding-Diversifying-printable.pdf.

74. "Mali: Ten UN peacekeepers killed in 'jihadist' attack," *BBC*, January 20, 2019, https://www.bbc.com/news/world-africa-46941711.
75. Anoar Boukhars, "How West Africa Became Fertile Ground for AQIM and ISIS," *World Politics Review*, November 29, 2016, http://www.worldpoliticsreview.com/articles/20556/how-west-africa-became-fertile-ground-for-aqim-and-isis.
76. Peter Tinti, "Al-Qaida and ISIS Turn On Each Other in the Sahel, With Civilians in the Crossfire," *World Politics Review,* June 15, 2020, https://www.worldpoliticsreview.com/articles/28838/al-qaida-isis-turn-on-each-other-in-the-sahel-with-civilians-in-the-crossfire.
77. Sergei Boeke, "Al Qaeda in the Islamic Maghreb: Terrorism, Insurgency, or Organized Crime?" *Small Wars & Insurgencies* 27, no. 5, 2016, 914-936, https://www.tandfonline.com/doi/full/10.1080/09592318.2016.1208280.
78. Caleb Weiss, "AQIM confirms leader's death," *Long War Journal,* June 18, 2020, https://www.longwarjournal.org/archives/2020/06/aqim-confirms-leaders-death.php.
79. "Backgrounder: JNIM," Center for Strategic and International Studies.
80. U.S. State Department, "State Department Terrorist Designation of Jama'at Nusrat al-Islam wal-Muslimin."
81. "Backgrounder: Jama'at Nasr al-Islam wal Muslimin (JNIM)," Center for Strategic and International Studies, September 25, 2018, https://csis-prod.s3.amazonaws.com/s3fs-public/180927_JNIM_Backgrounder.pdf?CXpU5VJRYdLDg819YAoD_NA0WgloBybV; Jacob Zenn, "Negotiating With Jihadists in the Sahel and Nigeria," *Lawfare,* June 14, 2020, https://www.lawfareblog.com/negotiating-jihadists-sahel-and-nigeria.
82. Caleb Weiss, "JNIM Confirms Death of Co-founder, Senior Leaders in French Raids," *Long War Journal*, March 4, 2018, https://www.longwarjournal.org/archives/2018/03/jnim-confirms-deaths-of-co-founder-senior-leaders-in-french-raids.php; Caleb Weiss, "AQIM Emir Confirms Death of Jihadist Commander in Mali," *Long War Journal*, https://www.longwarjournal.org/archives/2018/12/aqim-emir-confirms-death-of-jihadist-commander-in-mali.php.
83. Caleb Weiss, "Al Qaeda's JNIM Claims Suicide Assault in Timbuktu," *Long War Journal*, April 20, 2018, https://www.longwarjournal.org/archives/2018/04/al-qaedas-jnim-claims-suicide-assault-in-timbuktu.php.
84. Rida Lyammouri, "Mali – Sahel: June 2017 Violent Incidents Relat-

ed to As-Qaeda Affiliate JNIM, Ansaroul islam, and Other Security Incidents," *Sahel Memo*, August 2, 2017, http://www.sahelmemo.com/wp-content/uploads/2017/08/June-2017-Monthly-Tracker-Mali-Sahel.pdf

85. Caleb Weiss, "JNIM targets military bases in central Mali," *Long War Journal*, January 27, 2020, https://www.longwarjournal.org/archives/2020/01/jnim-targets-military-bases-in-central-mali.php; "Mali: JNIM claims responsibility for April 6 attack in Bamba (Gao region)," *GardaWorld*, April 11, 2020, https://www.garda.com/crisis24/news-alerts/331511/mali-jnim-claims-responsibility-for-april-6-attack-in-bamba-gao-region-update-1; Caleb Weiss, "JNIM kills dozens in Mali base attack," *Long War Journal,* March 22, 2020, https://www.longwarjournal.org/archives/2020/03/jnim-kills-dozens-in-mali-base-attack.php.
86. Tiemoko Diallo, "Mali says 24 soldiers killed in ambush on Sunday," Reuters*,* June 15, 2020, https://www.reuters.com/article/us-mali-security/mali-says-24-soldiers-killed-in-ambush-on-sunday-idUSKBN23M2O0.
87. "Mali's president admits to holding talks with senior jihadist leaders," *France24*, February 10, 2020, https://www.france24.com/en/20200210-exclusive-mali-s-president-acknowledges-dialogue-with-jihadist-leaders; Thomas Joscelyn, "Al Qaeda's West African branch seeks French withdrawal, then negotiations,"
88. Peter Tinti, "Al-Qaida and ISIS Turn On Each Other in the Sahel, With Civilians in the Crossfire," *World Politics Review,* June 15, 2020, https://www.worldpoliticsreview.com/articles/28838/al-qaida-isis-turn-on-each-other-in-the-sahel-with-civilians-in-the-crossfire.
89. Héni Nsaibia and Caleb Weiss, "Ansaroul Islam and the Growing Terrorist Insurgency in Burkina Faso," Combatting Terrorism Center at West Point *CTC Sentinel* no. 11, March 2018, 3, https://ctc.usma.edu/app/uploads/2018/03/CTC-Sentinel-Vol11Iss3.pdf.
90. Morgane Le Cam, "Burkina Faso : confessions d'un ancient djihadiste," *Le Monde*, December 10, 2017, https://www.lemonde.fr/afrique/article/2017/12/10/confessions-d-un-djihadiste-du-burkina-vu-ce-que-font-les-forces-de-securite-a-nos-parents-je-ne-regretterai-jamais-leur-mort_5227587_3212.html; "Mali-Burkina Faso : Une vaste operation de ratissage de soldats français, Burkinabès et Maliens est en cours dans la province de Soum," *Nord Sud Journal*, April 4, 2017, https://www.nordsudjournal.com/mali-burkina-faso-une-vaste-operation-de-ratissage-de-soldats-francais-burkinabes-et-maliens-est-en-cours-dans-la-province-de-soum/.

91. Nsaiba and Weiss, "Ansaroul Islam"; Morgane Le Cam, "Comment est né Ansaroul Islam, premier groupe djihadiste de l'Histoire du Burkina Faso," *Le Monde Afrique*, April 11, 2017, https://www.lemonde.fr/afrique/article/2017/04/11/comment-est-ne-ansaroul-islam-premier-groupe-djihadiste-de-l-histoire-du-burkina-faso_5109520_3212.html.
92. Ibid.
93. Ibidem; "Critical Threats Today: March 13, 2017," *Critical Threats*, March 12, 2017, https://www.criticalthreats.org/briefs/critical-threats-today/critical-threats-today-march-13-2017; "Soldiers Killed in Mali Attack as Violence Surges," *Al Jazeera* (Doha), March 6, 2017, https://www.aljazeera.com/news/2017/03/soldiers-killed-mali-attack-violence-surges-170306043203675.html.
94. Nsaiba and Weiss, "Ansaroul Islam."
95. "At least 25 killed in Mali militant attack," *BBC*, October 2, 2019, https://www.bbc.com/news/world-africa-49904226.
96. Kersten Knipp, "'Islamic State' seeks new foothold in Africa,'" *Deutsche Welle*, January 2, 2018, http://www.dw.com/en/islamic-state-seeks-new-foothold-in-africa/a-41977922.
97. "Islamic State affiliate claims deadly attack on U.S. troops in Niger," Reuters, January 13, 2018, https://www.reuters.com/article/us-niger-security/islamic-state-affiliate-claims-deadly-attack-on-u-s-troops-in-niger-idUSKBN1F20L3.
98. "Islamic State replaces al-Qaeda as Enemy No. 1 in Sahel," *France24*, January 15, 2020, https://www.france24.com/en/20200115-islamic-state-replaces-al-qaeda-as-enemy-no-1-in-sahel.
99. "Militant Islamic Group Activity in the Sahel Rises," Africa Center for Strategic Studies, October 29, 2018, https://africacenter.org/spotlight/militant-islamist-group-activity-sahel-rises/.
100. Callimachi, "ISIS Affiliate Claims October Attack on U.S. Troops in Niger."
101. U.S. Department of State, Office of the Spokesperson, "State Department Designations of ISIS in the Greater Sahara (ISIS-GS) and Adnan Abu Walid al-Sahrawi," May 16, 2018, https://www.state.gov/r/pa/prs/ps/2018/05/282168.htm.
102. Caleb Weiss, "Veteran Jihadist Surrenders to Algeria," *Long War Journal*, August 12, 2018, https://www.longwarjournal.org/archives/2018/08/veteran-malian-jihadist-surrenders-to-algeria.php; "Al-Qaeda chief in north Africa Abdelmalek Droukdel killed – France," *BBC*, June 5, 2020, https://www.bbc.com/news/world-afri-

ca-52943692.

103. Jacob Zenn, "Negotiating With Jihadists in the Sahel and Nigeria," *Lawfare,* June 14, 2020, https://www.lawfareblog.com/negotiating-jihadists-sahel-and-nigeria; "Islamic State replaces al-Qaeda as Enemy No. 1 in Sahel," *France24*, January 15, 2020, https://www.france24.com/en/20200115-islamic-state-replaces-al-qaeda-as-enemy-no-1-in-sahel.
104. "Militants kills 54 in attack on Mali army post; IS claims responsibility," Reuters, November 1, 2019, https://www.reuters.com/article/us-mali-security/militants-kill-54-in-attack-on-mali-army-post-is-claims-responsibility-idUSKBN1XB4W7.
105. Peter Tinti, "Al-Qaida and ISIS Turn On Each Other in the Sahel, With Civilians in the Crossfire," *World Politics Review,* June 15, 2020, https://www.worldpoliticsreview.com/articles/28838/al-qaida-isis-turn-on-each-other-in-the-sahel-with-civilians-in-the-crossfire.
106. Mina Al-Lami. "Africa's Sahel becomes latest al-Qaeda-IS battleground, *BBC*, May 11, 2020, https://www.bbc.com/news/world-africa-52614579.
107. "Mali," *CIA World Factbook*, January 2020, https://www.cia.gov/library/publications/the-world-factbook/geos/ml.html.
108. Kate Thomas, "In Limbo: Malian Refugees in Burkina Faso," *Refugees Deeply*, April 20, 2016, https://www.newsdeeply.com/refugees/community/2016/04/20/in-limbo-malian-refugees-in-burkina-faso.
109. Lisa Anderson, "Democracy, Islam share a home in Mali," *Chicago Tribune*, December 15, 2004, http://articles.chicagotribune.com/2004-12-15/news/0412150328_1_mali-islamic-cinq.
110. Soares, "Islam in Mali in the Neoliberal Era," 212.
111. Robert Pringle, "Democratization in Mali: Putting History To Work," United States Institute of Peace *Peaceworks* no. 58, October 2006, 27, https://www.usip.org/publications/2006/10/democratization-mali-putting-history-work.
112. Ségolène Allemandou, "Is Qatar Fuelling the Crisis in North Mali?" *France 24*, January 23, 2013, http://www.france24.com/en/20130121-qatar-mali-france-ansar-dine-mnla-al-qaeda-sunni-islam-doha.
113. Willy Stern, "Moderate Islam, African-Style," *Weekly Standard*, August 4, 2008, https://www.weeklystandard.com/willy-stern/moderate-islam-african-style.
114. Anderson, "Democracy, Islam Share a Home in Mali."
115. Joshua Hammer, "The Race to Save Mali's Priceless Artifacts," *Smithsonian Magazine*, January 2014, http://www.smithsonianmag.

com/history/Race-Save-Mali-Artifacts-180947965/.

116. "ICC: Mali Fighter Jailed for Destroying Timbuktu Sites," *Al Jazeera* (Doha), September 27, 2016, http://www.aljazeera.com/news/2016/09/icc-mali-fighter-jailed-destroying-timbuk-tu-sites-160927093507739.html.
117. Kamissa Camara, "Violent Protests Have Erupted in Mali. Here's What is Driving Them," *Washington Post*, August 15, 2016, https://www.washingtonpost.com/news/monkey-cage/wp/2016/08/15/whats-the-role-for-malis-youth-after-the-2015-peace-accord-not-enough-protesters-say/.
118. Anthony Morland, "Why Some Malians Join Armed Groups," *IRIN News*, January 25, 2018, http://www.irinnews.org/analy-sis/2018/01/25/why-some-malians-join-armed-groups.
119. "Mali," *CIA World Factbook*, May 2018, https://www.cia.gov/li-brary/Publications/the-world-factbook/geos/ml.html.
120. Morland, "Why Some Malians Join Armed Groups."
121. "Sahel Crisis," *R4Sahel*, June 30, 2020,https://r4sahel.info/en/situa-tions/sahelcrisis; United Nations High Commissioner for Refugees, "Mali" December 31, 2019, https://reporting.unhcr.org/mali.
122. Soares, "Islam in Mali in the Neoliberal Era," 214.
123. Nicolas Colombant, "Mali's Muslims Steer Back to Spiritual Roots," *Christian Science Monitor*, February 26, 2002, http://www.csmonitor.com/2002/0226/p08s02-woaf.html.
124. Colombant, "Mali's Muslims Steer Back to Spiritual Roots."
125. Soares, "Islam in Mali in the Neoliberal Era," 215.
126. Harmon, "From GSPC to AQIM," 22.
127. Ibid., 23.
128. Ibidem.
129. Emanuelle Landais, "US led Flintlock counter-terrorism exercises end in Senegal, " *Deutsche Welle*, February 29, 2016, http://www.dw.com/en/us-led-flintlock-counter-terrorism-exercis-es-end-in-sen-egal/a-19083235; U.S. Africa Command, "Press Release: Flintlock 2019 Announced," January 28, 2019, https://www.africom.mil/me-dia-room/pressrelease/31465/flintlock-2019-announced.
130. Lara Seligan and Robbie Gramer, "U.S. Officials Worry Looming Military Cuts in Africa Are 'About Politics'" *Foreign Policy*, January 28, 2020, https://foreignpolicy.com/2020/01/28/us-offi-cials-worry-military-cuts-africa-political-sahel/; "U.S. warns aid at risk unless alleged abuses in West Africa's Sahel region addressed," Reuters, July 9, 2020, https://www.reuters.com/article/us-sahel-se-curity-usa/us-warns-aid-at-risk-unless-alleged-abuses-in-west-afri-

cas-sahel-region-addressed-idUSKBN24A223.

131. Humeyra Pamuk, "U.S. creates new envoy position to counter rising terrorism in Sahel," Reuters, March 6, 2020, https://www.reuters.com/article/us-usa-sahel/u-s-creates-new-envoy-position-to-counter-rising-terrorism-in-sahel-idUSKBN20T2ZJ.
132. "Al-Qaida Digs in to Resist Region's Armies," United Press International, July 6, 2010, https://www.upi.com/Al-Qaida-digs-in-to-resist-regions-armies/14121278441085/.
133. "Brief: Saharan Countries' Cooperation Against AQIM," *Stratfor*, April 21, 2010, https://worldview.stratfor.com/article/brief-saharan-countries-cooperation-against-aqim.
134. Matthieu Fernandez, "Looking for Unity in the Sahel," *Africa-Source*, December 10, 2018, https://www.atlanticcouncil.org/blogs/africasource/looking-for-unity-in-the-sahel.
135. Alex Thurston, "Speaking with Jihadists: Mali Weighs Its Options," *The Global Observatory*, May 25, 2017, https://theglobalobservatory.org/2017/05/jihadism-mali-al-qaeda-france-keita/.
136. Paul Melly, "Mahmoud Dicko: Mali imam challenges President Keïta," *BBC*, June 28, 2020, https://www.bbc.com/news/world-africa-53176083.
137. "UN renews Mali peacekeeping force MINUSMA without personnel cuts," *Al-Jazeera* (Doha), June 29, 2020, https://www.aljazeera.com/news/2020/06/renews-mali-peacekeeping-force-minusma-personnel-cuts-200629202039321.html.
138. Boukhars, "How West Africa Became Fertile Ground for AQIM and ISIS."
139. "Mali" Deaths, Torture in Army Detention," Human Rights Watch, April 9, 2018, https://https://www.hrw.org/news/2018/04/09/mali-deaths-torture-army-detention.
140. Grégory Chauzal, "A Snapshot of Mali Three Years After the 2012 Crisis," Netherlands Institute of International Relations, June 8, 2015, https://www.clingendael.nl/publication/snapshot-mali-three-years-after-2012-crisis; Paul Melly, "Mahmoud Dicko: Mali imam challenges President Keïta," *BBC*, June 28, 2020, https://www.bbc.com/news/world-africa-53176083.
141. Boukhars, "How West Africa Became Fertile Ground for AQIM and ISIS."

29 Nigeria

Quick Facts

Population: 214,028,302 (July 2020 est.)
Area: 923,768 sq km
Ethnic Groups:Hausa 30%, Yoruba 15.5%, Igbo (Ibo) 15.2%, Fulani 6%, Tiv 2.4%, Kanuri/Beriberi 2.4%, Ibibio 1.8%, Ijaw/Izon 1.8%, other 24.7% (2018 est.) note: Nigeria, Africa's most populous country, is composed of more than 250 ethnic groups
GDP (official exchange rate): $376.4 billion (2017 est.)

Source: CIA World FactBook (Last Updated June 2020)

Introduction

Since its independence in 1960, Nigeria has been plagued by a number of organized militant groups. Among them are Niger Delta militants in southeastern Nigeria, whose grievances have been based on extreme environmental degradation, as well as political and economic disenfranchisement, although these groups have been pacified through government amnesty programs in recent years. Additionally, there are ethnic-based militants in Nigeria's Middle Belt, where the predominantly Muslim northern region and predominantly Christian southern region meet. There are also often conflicts among ethnic groups of different religions over land use. In recent years, Muslim Fulani herders moving southward from northern Nigeria and even Niger have increasingly armed themselves and clashed with Christian villagers in unprecedented numbers, albeit without any centralized coordination. Finally, there are Islamist militants in northern Nigeria, such as the extremely violent Boko Haram and the potentially militant, pro-Iranian, Shiite Islamic Movement in Nigeria (IMN), which has become embattled after a series of crackdowns by the central government in Abuja. These two groups seek to establish Islamic governance in Nigeria (for Boko Haram, a Sunni-Salafi state, and for the IMN a Khomeinist Shi'a one), to institutionalize Islamic law and an Islamic identity for the country, to pry Nigeria out of its alliances with Western countries, and to reorient it toward the Islamic world.

Since September 2010, Boko Haram has become the greatest threat to Nigeria's unity, and is responsible for more violence than any other militant movement in the country. More than 30,000 people have been killed to date in Boko Haram-related violence, but that number may be a low estimate given that many deaths go unreported. Millions more have been displaced and need food assistance due to Boko Haram's disruption of the local economy and destruction of villagers.[1] *Notably, however, Boko Haram is divided internally between two factions. One is loyal to, and recognized as an affiliate by, the Islamic State. It is known as the Islamic State's West Africa Province, or ISWAP, and has recently become more lenient toward the local population in order to better win "hearts and minds."*[2] *The other faction is Jama'atu Ahlis Sunna Lidda'awati wal-Jihad (The Group for Preaching the Prophet's Teachings and Jihad, or JAS), which is loyal to Islamic State* caliph *Abu Bakr al-Baghdadi but is not recognized by the Islamic State as one of its affiliates. It remains exceedingly violent and harsh toward civilians. Both factions are referred to as "Boko Haram" by the media and government, although neither group refers to itself as such. A third faction, Ansar al-Muslimina Fi Biladis Sudan (Vanguards for the Protection of Muslims in Black Africa, or "Ansaru") also exists, but it only reemerged from dormancy in 2020 after five years of little activity.*

Islamist Activity

In addition to ISWAP, JAS, and Ansaru, which are northern Nigeria's most violent Salafist-*jihadist* groups, there are hundreds of other Islamist groups in Nigeria, including millenarian *mahdists*. The numbers of those actors, however, have declined in recent decades due to proselytization by Salafists and Shi'a militants. There are also many religiously moderate, albeit socially conservative, Sufi groups of the Qadiriyya and Tijaniyya orders, as well as Jama'atu Nasril Islam (JNI), a northern Nigerian Muslim umbrella organization led by the Sultan of Sokoto. In contrast to violent Islamist leaders, JNI has called on Muslims to "pray fervently for peaceful co-existence in Nigeria and for Allah to put to shame those who are bent on chaos and unrest."[3] The former emir of Kano has similarly attempted to dampen Islamist rhetoric by promoting coexistence with Christians, including accepting them as "indigenes" in a historically Muslim city like Kano.[4]

Nigerian universities have long served as hotbeds of Islamist activity, especially by the Lagos-founded Muslims Students Society, whose branches are found at various Nigerian universities.[5] Most activists at the forefront of Islamic extremism in northern Nigeria have their roots in the universities, where they have been able to spread radical ideas and use academic platforms to influence students. Two noteworthy trends in Nigeria, which are consistent with the rest of the Islamic world, are that youth are the primary demographic group susceptible to radicalization, and that men gravitate toward radicalization more than do women.

This section describes four of the most prominent Islamist groups in northern Nigeria: JAS and ISWAP (both commonly referred to as "Boko Haram" in media and government discourse); Maitatsine/ Kala Kato; Jama't Izalat al Bid'a Wa Iqamat as Sunna (Izala); and the Islamic Movement in Nigeria (IMN).

JAS and ISWAP (Boko Haram)

JAS traces its lineage to Mohammed Yusuf, a Nigerian preacher who maintained his headquarters in northeastern Nigeria's Borno State. Yusuf primarily taught that Western education and influence were impermissible in Islam because they contradicted the Quran, and that service in the Nigerian government was unacceptable since Nigeria was not an Islamic State. Various Saudi clerics and Salafi-*jihadi* ideologues and groups, including the Taliban, were influential on Yusuf's worldview, and prompted his adoption of a strain of Salafi-jihadi ideology that, in his own words, emulated that of the Taliban and al-Qaeda, although Yusuf did not explicitly cite al-Maqdisi and other major al-Qaeda ideologues, such as Abu Basir al-Tartusi, in his sermons.[6] As Yusuf gained in popularity in the late 2000s, his teachings began to generate opposition from mainstream Salafists who had previously mentored him; one such scholar argued that if Muslims follow Yusuf's advice, then "pagan policemen [who serve in government] will kill and injure Muslims, and when taken to hospitals pagan doctors and nurses [with Western education] will attend to them."[7]

However, although Yusuf began urging his followers (who numbered in the thousands and hailed from Nigeria, Niger, Chad and Cameroon) to prepare for conflict with the Nigerian government, he did not start out as a *jihadist* – or, at least, he seemed to have a long-term project for *jihad*, which meant he initially did not *appear* to be a *jihadist* to outsiders.[8] During his leadership of the organization (2002 to 2009), Yusuf's followers did not engage in coordinated violence against the state, although occasional clashes with Nigerian security forces did occur. According to Yusuf's son, he once explained that his "[*dawa*] was for [*jihad*], and all who have thought it is [*dawa*], or education, or teaching, or a call without identity ... have not understood the [*dawa*]. It is [*dawa*] and a [*jihadi*] movement, a fighting group, and not only a group for [*dawa*]."[9]

Yusuf was killed along with several hundred of his followers in a four-day series of clashes with the Nigerian government in northeastern Nigeria in July 2009. Afterward, Yusuf's deputy, Abubakar Shekau, and other followers announced a *jihad* against the Nigerian government and security forces, Christians, and assorted moderate Muslim religious and political figures. This was the first time the group claimed a formal name: JAS. Its first attack took place on September 7, 2010, when approximately 50 fighters attacked Bauchi Prison and freed fellow members who had been detained in the July 2009 clashes, making good on the organization's promise that these prisoners would not spend the holiday of Eid al-Fitr behind bars. Since then, JAS has carried out thousands of attacks and killed in excess of 20,000 people. Its area of operations initially ranged from its hub of operations in northeastern Borno State to Kogi State in the geographic south of Nigeria, to Sokoto in northwestern Nigeria. However, since 2013, due to a security crackdown as well as grassroots opposition from local populations, JAS has concentrated predominantly in southern Borno and along the Nigerian-Cameroonian borderlands, while ISWAP has dominated the Nigerian-Niger borderlands and the region around Lake Chad.[10] Only in 2019 did the weaker JAS establish cells around Lake Chad, which have begun to contest ISWAP for predominance in that area.[11]

At a minimum, JAS's main objectives are to strip religious authority from traditional Muslim leaders and place it in the hands of JAS's religious leaders, and to create an Islamic state in some or all of Nigeria. After 2009, some members might have accepted prosecution of the security officers who killed Mohammed Yusuf, amnesty for all JAS members in prison, and compensation for mosques and homes destroyed in clashes with the government, as grounds for a cessation of conflict. However, too much time has passed since then for such measures to resonate among the group's members, who now will settle for nothing less than an Islamic state. JAS mostly carries out *sharia* punishments, and holds hundreds of captives, including a reported 700 women.[12] In addition, while many JAS members remain in prison, some hostage exchanges, including for 23 and 82 Chibok schoolgirls in late 2016 and early 2017, respectively, have led to the release of several key JAS members.[13]

Despite some of JAS's successes, its killings of innocent Muslims during attacks on the government and security forces—both as collateral damage and as a means to intimidate the broader population—has bred dissent among the movement's members. In January 2012, the more internationally oriented faction of the group, which called itself *Jama'atu Ansaril* Muslimina Fi Biladis Sudan (Vanguards for the Protection of Muslims in Black Africa, or "Ansaru"), announced its formation in a video statement and in fliers distributed in Kano.[14] This occurred after Boko Haram's January 20, 2012 attacks left more than 170 civilians dead.[15] Ansaru has since been proscribed as a terrorist group by the United Kingdom for its alleged involvement in the kidnapping and killing of two British and Italian men in Sokoto State in March 2012, and for being "broadly aligned" with al-Qaeda.[16] Ansaru began raising its online media profile in November 2012, around the same time that its fighters carried out a prison break in Abuja.[17] In December 2012 *Ansaru* kidnapped a Frenchman in Katsina, 30 miles from the border with Niger, and warned France that the prisoner's fate would be contingent on France rescinding the law banning the Islamic veil and ceasing its planned attack on the Islamic state in northern Mali (the Frenchman later escaped captivity).[18] In January 2013, Ansaru also kidnapped seven foreigners in Bauchi State. The hostages were subsequently killed after the group alleged that the UK and Nigeria were preparing to conduct a rescue attempt, as one of the seven captives was British.[19] Furthermore, Ansaru jointly claimed a kidnapping with the larger JAS in December 2013 of a French priest in Cameroon, who was later released for a multi-million dollar sum of money as well as the release of JAS militants imprisoned in Cameroon.[20]

By 2014, however, Ansaru was virtually defunct operationally, although it continued to issue statements. Despite initially offering itself as a more "humane" alternative to JAS, three factors led to its demise: the French-led intervention in northern Mali in 2012-13, which separated Ansaru from its AQIM patrons; the arrests of key members by Nigerian special forces, including those who had received funding from AQIM; and JAS's assassinations of Ansaru commanders who had defected from JAS. Some Ansaru members (partly out of desperation) rejoined JAS and brought with them skills in kidnapping and media manipulation, especially in the Lake Chad region. Nevertheless, in January 2020 Ansaru proved it still was a threat when it ambushed an emir's convoy in Kaduna State, although it seems Ansaru was biding time before formally reannouncing its presence.[21]

After Shekau pledged allegiance to Abu Bakr al-Baghdadi and the Islamic State in March 2015, JAS officially became known as the Islamic State's West Africa Province (ISWAP). However, the move prompted Nigeria, under new president Muhammadu Buhari, to launch a large-scale military offensive against ISWAP, causing the group to lose control of much of the territory in northeastern Nigeria that JAS had previously controlled.[22] These battlefield reversals, as well as lingering ideological disputes between Shekau and former Ansaru members as well as some of his own former loyalists over tactics, ultimately led to a fracturing of ISWAP. Under the leadership of Muhammed Yusuf's son, Abu Musab al-Barnawi, a large contingent of fighters left Shekau's camp and successfully appealed to the Islamic State to recognize their faction, which it did in August 2016.[23] Shekau, meanwhile, was compelled to leave ISWAP with a relatively small contingent of his loyalist fighters, and subsequently announced in August 2016 that he was reverting to the name JAS.[24]

Both ISWAP and JAS remain active today, with the former fielding around 4,000 fighters and largely operating in scattered territory in the Lake Chad region, while the latter's force around 2,000 fighters is scattered in disparate territories in Borno State. For the most part, the groups remain at odds. While some militants in JAS have reportedly offered to negotiate with the Nigerian government, JAS and ISWAP remain responsible for almost all of the Islamist violence in northern Nigeria, and as a result any truce with other factions would be inconsequential and difficult to envision.[25]

Maitatsine/Kala Kato

Kala Kato, which means "mere man," in reference to the Prophet, is an offshoot of the Maitatsine sect of the 1980s led by the Cameroonian Mohammed Marwa.[26] Marwa claimed to be a new Prophet of Islam and was known as the "Maitatsine," meaning "the one who damns." More eccentric than Boko Haram founder Mohammed Yusuf, Marwa condemned anyone who read any book other than the Quran or used products which reflected Western life, such as watches, cars, bicycles, televisions, buttons, or cigarettes. An antecedent not only to Kala Kato but also to Boko Haram, Marwa and his thousands of followers clashed with Nigerian authorities in a battle in Kano in 1980 in which Marwa was killed. Subsequent battles to suppress his followers took place in Borno State in 1982; in Gongola State (present-day Gombe State) in 1984; and in Bauchi State in 1985. In December 2009, Kala Kato engaged in a series of riots and clashes with Nigerian security forces in Bauchi State, resulting in the death of 70 people, including soldiers, policemen, women and 15 children.[27] The cause of the clashes was Kala Kato's violation of an ordinance against preaching outdoors, which was imposed following the Boko Haram clashes of July 2009.[28]

Kala Kato remains one of the most obscure Islamist groups in northern Nigeria. Its leader, Mallam Salisu, maintains that it "has no link with the Boko Haram followers."[29] It is also a small group of approximately 2,000 members, and likely will not hold out appeal to future generations of Islamists or *jihadists*, who will be inclined to see Boko Haram as a more "legitimate" option because of the recognition it has received from the Islamic State and its greater adherence to general Salaf-*jihadi* ideology. Nonetheless, Kala Kato and similar groups can be placed on a spectrum of heterodox forms of Islamic extremism that, for the time being, pose little threat of violence directed against the state, Muslims who disagree with them, or Christians.

Jama't Izalat al Bid'a Wa Iqamat as Sunna (Society of Eradication of Innovation and Implementation of the Sunna, or Izala)

The Izala movement in Nigeria is an anti-Sufi Salafist movement that opposes *bid'a* (innovation) and seeks a literal interpretation of the Quran. It was established with funding from Saudi Arabia in the late 1970s, in part as an effort to quell then growing pro-Khomeinist leanings among northern Nigerian Muslims and also to oppose Sufism. Many Izala clerics have lamented the "Westernization" of Nigerian society, albeit while accepting modern technology and sciences and embracing women's education and financial self-sufficiency. With many institutions all over the country and influence at the local, state and even federal levels, Izala has become one of the largest Islamist societies not only in Nigeria, but also in the neighboring countries of Chad, Niger, and Cameroon. The implementation of *sharia* law in twelve northern states since 2000 legitimized the Izala movement, which claims to have been the "vanguard" of the pro-*sharia* movement.[30] Even Ja'far Mahmud Adam (one of the most prominent Izala leaders in northern Nigeria) reduced his role in 2005, claiming that *sharia* was not properly implemented.[31] Nevertheless, Izala clerics' participation in democracy and friendly relations with Nigerian and even Western political leaders has led to Boko Haram labeling them as hypocrites and even assassinating Adam in 2007, which was a precursor to the *jihad* that was launched in 2010.[32]

Today, Izala's important contribution to the Nigerian Islamist landscape is that it presents a credible and non-violent option for Islamists even though in the early 2000s some Izala leaders had mentored Boko Haram leaders.[33] Nonetheless, the rising anti-Shi'a sentiment in Nigeria, coupled with broader anti-Iranian sentiment in Saudi Arabia and the Middle East, has positioned Izala also as a leading anti-Shi'a group in Nigeria.[34] Consequently, new members might embrace its new anti-Shi'a activism.

Islamic Movement in Nigeria (IMN)

The IMN is distinct from other Islamist groups in Nigeria because it historically received inspiration and backing from the Islamic Republic of Iran, whereas most other groups (like Izala) are supported by Saudi Arabia and other wealthy Sunni Muslim sponsors. The leader of the IMN, Shaykh Ibrahim el-Zakzaky, has alleged that the IMN is only an "Islamic Movement," rather than either "Shi'a" or "fundamentalist"; however, the common, and correct, perception of the IMN in Nigeria is that it is in fact a Shi'a movement.[35] Although the IMN's members are mostly Shi'a, the IMN resembles Izala and Boko Haram in that it believes secular authorities should not hold power and that an Islamic state is the solution for problems in northern Nigerian society.[36]

Throughout the 1980s and 1990s, Ibrahim el-Zakzaky and his followers sought to bring about an Islamic revolution similar to the 1979 Iranian revolution. When *sharia* law was instituted in twelve states of northern Nigeria in 2000, el-Zakzaky believed there was an over-emphasis on corporal punishments; that the northern governors were illegitimate since they did not come to power through Islamic parties; that the governors were dishonest people "who amputate the hands of poor people, who steal peanuts, while those who steal millions of tax-payers' money go scot-free"; and that anything short of Iran-style Islamic Revolution would be a failure.[37] Since 2001, the IMN has committed itself to involvement "in national or international issues that are of concern to Muslims, as well as in solidarity with oppressed sections of the Muslim Ummah such as the Palestinians and Iraqis." In 2012, el-Zakzaky said a U.S. or Israeli attack on Iran would impact not only Nigeria but the entire world.[38]

After years of steady growth in terms of followers, particularly around el-Zakzaky's base in Zaria, Kaduna State, the ranks of the group were thinned when the Nigerian army killed 300 IMN members during a violent crackdown in December 2015.[39] El-Zakaky himself was reportedly heavily wounded during the fighting and taken to a military hospital in Lagos.[40] The repression of IMN and el-Zakzaky, which has continued since 2015, has drawn criticism from international human rights watchdogs.[41] The Nigerian army—possibly with support from anti-Iran elements in the Arab World—

has justified action against the IMN because el-Zakzaky had created a quasi-state in parts of Zaria, with its own police, media, and schools reminiscent of and arguably modeled after Hezbollah in Lebanon. Although unproven, there are also rumors that Saudi Arabia encouraged the elimination of el-Zakzaky in an effort to blunt Iranian influence in Nigeria.[42] Ultimately, in August 2019, a court ruled that al-Zakzaky must be allowed to leave detention to receive medical treatment, and there were rumors he might seek refuge in exile in Iran.[43]

ISLAMISM AND SOCIETY

Nigeria's 190 million citizens are divided almost evenly between Muslims and Christians, with Muslims forming the majority of the population in the northern half of the country and Christians forming the majority in its southern half. With more than 90 million Christians and a roughly equal number of Muslims, Nigeria is both the most populous Christian country in Africa and the most populous Muslim one. The Hausa and Fulani (often referred to as the "Hausa-Fulani" because of their close cultural interaction for the past several centuries) constitute the largest single Muslim ethnic group in Nigeria, and about one-fourth of its total population. The Muslim Kanuri ethnic group predominates in Yobe and Borno States and is about 4% of Nigeria's total population. The Yorubas of southwest Nigeria are about 60% Christian, and one of the three largest ethnic groups in Nigeria along with the Hausa-Fulanis and the Igbos of southeast Nigeria. At an estimated 15 million, Yoruba Muslims are second only to the Hausa-Fulanis in terms of total population in an ethnic group. There are also dozens of other predominantly Muslim ethnic groups in Nigeria, including the Shuwa Arabs of Borno State, who trace their lineage to the Arab tribes who migrated into northeastern Nigeria from the Sudan centuries ago.

Most Muslims in Nigeria are Sunni Muslims. However, about five percent of Nigeria's Muslims are Shi'a, and they can be found throughout northern Nigeria, particularly in Zaria, Kaduna State but also in large numbers in Sokoto, Kano and Yobe and southern Nigeria. The number of Shi'a Muslims in the country has increased since the

Iranian Revolution of 1979, which brought an Islamic government to power in Iran. Ibrahim el-Zakzaky has served as the leader of Nigeria's Shi'a (via the IMN) with support – primarily ideological – from Iran, although factions have broken from al-Zakzaky and received support from Iran.[44] The rise of Shiism in Nigeria has led to a rivalry with the majority Sunni part of the Muslim population, and there Sunni-Shi'a clashes have been reported.[45] Iran's support of Shiism in Nigeria and West Africa more broadly suggests Shiism is likely to grow in future decades.[46]

Conflict is most frequent between Muslims and Christians, as each group competes for a greater share of political and economic power in Nigeria. Election season in the country has tended to generate the most tensions. Muslims, for example, believed that, since they often claim to constitute more than 70% of Nigeria's population, the 2011 victory of the Christian presidential candidate Goodluck Jonathan over Muslim candidate Muhammadu Buhari (by 58% to 32% of the vote) was likely fraudulent. Anger over this issue contributed to an increasing sense of marginalization among Nigerian Muslims, which has since been alleviated by Buhari's victory in the presidential elections in 2015 and 2019, and a smooth transfer of power. But Boko Haram has tended to exploit this tension by staging dozens of attacks on churches and Christians in northern Nigeria. Most recently, Muslim-Christian violence has emerged in the context of Muslim Fulani herdsmen, who are now armed with machine guns (as opposed to the clubs they traditionally carried), raiding farmlands owned by Christian Nigerians and sometimes killing them. This has, in turn, led to reprisals.[47]

Overpopulation contributes to religious tensions as Muslim groups from northern Nigeria migrate into Christian areas in the Middle Belt, prompting competition over land use and new member proselytization. The Sultan of Sokoto, who also leads the Jama'atu Nasril Islam (JNI), has said that "The rise of secularism and the increasing activities of western evangelical organizations have made it all the more urgent that the message of Islam shall be heard loud and clear and the JNI must play a leading role in this endeavor."[48]

Islamism and the State

Section 101 of the Nigerian constitution states that "The Government of the Federation or of a State shall not adopt any religion as State Religion." In practice, however, religion plays such a large role in the state that Nigeria cannot be considered not truly secular.[49]

Islam impacts the governmental sphere in several ways. The country observes Islamic holidays such as Eid el-Fitr, Eid al-Adha and Milad al-Nabi. Nigeria's government is involved in organizing the *Hajj* pilgrimage. Islamic slogans in the Arabic language are featured on the country's currency and army insignias. Islamic sermons are delivered in public places throughout the country. Most significant of all, twelve states in northern Nigeria have implemented *sharia* law since 2000.

This controversial step is inextricably linked to politics. Many northern governors seem to support *sharia* out of religious devotion, but also because of a desire to gain political advantage and shore up their support from mainstream Muslims by appealing to the religious sentiments of those people. Through at least a veneer of dedication to Islam, these politicians attempt to win the support of the masses and stifle criticism or, in many cases, investigations into their corrupt behavior. Some religious scholars have argued that the traditional rulers, including the sultans and *emirs* who have no formal authority but serve as political advisers and maintain influence through their social status, are opposed to *sharia* law because certain interpretations (especially Salafism) do not permit hereditary succession.[50] Izala, the IMN, and Boko Haram all believe that the Sultan and other traditional rulers are apostates for accepting a version of "half-*sharia*" in which secular institutions like elections and democracy exist side by side with Islam.

Although Islam is not formally a state institution in Nigeria, Muslims organizations play an important role in the country. With the advent of *sharia* law in twelve northern states starting between 1999 and 2001,[51] these groups have begun to challenge the secular nature of the country, although the struggle over implementing *sharia* has dampened the desire to completely replace the secular system for an Islamic one. Boko Haram, meanwhile, seeks to overthrow both the secular and the traditional Muslim establishment in Nigeria and create an Islamic state akin to the "caliphate" established by the Islamic State terrorist group in Iraq and Syria. In recent years, Boko Haram has achieved success in controlling territory in Borno State and removing the Nigerian government's presence altogether from certain areas. Although it is not likely to achieve this goal throughout Nigeria, Islamist insurgent groups are nonetheless gaining more traction in West Africa – suggesting that the secular nature of the Nigerian state will continue to face a challenge from regional Islamist forces. That, in turn, may erode support among Nigerian Muslims for secular national authorities. The saving grace for Nigeria may, paradoxically, be Boko Haram's violence, which has turned much of the Muslim citizenry away from *jihadism* compared to the period after 9/11.

One of the challenges in countering Boko Haram has been the government's consistent (and inaccurate) claims to have defeated the insurgency.[52] Moreover, the Nigerian government has been slow to report to families the status of fallen soldiers, which has led to demoralization in the army, especially when families learn about the fate of their loved ones through online Boko Haram propaganda videos.[53] The army has proven capable of securing Maiduguri, Borno's capital, and rural towns. However, the countryside is too vast for the army to patrol and soldiers come from throughout Nigeria and do not necessarily know local languages as well as Boko Haram fighters. This benefits to the insurgents, which can easily hide among the population.

In this fight, the Nigerian army has an obvious advantage in terms of weapons and materiel. However, it has also lost significant quantities of weaponry to Boko Haram[54] as a result of numerous successful Boko Haram ambushes and, in the case of ISWAP, growing capabilities imparted by the training of its members in places like Libya.[55]

The counter-insurgency has been characterized by excessive confidence by the army, an inability to outmaneuver the *jihadists* in the countryside (especially in Borno) and the lack of clear strategy to win beyond simply counting numbers of dead Boko Haram militants. At the same time, corruption in the military has led to accusations of wasted resources and poorly constructed bases. If the Nigerian army does not succeed in turning the situation around, there are now legitimate fears that parts of Borno will, in the long term, *de facto* secede from the larger state.

Endnotes

1. Martin Cuddihy, "Major famine imminent in Nigeria as Boko Haram attacks cripple economy," *ABC News,* December 1, 2016, http://www.abc.net.au/news/2016-12-02/nigeria-major-famine-imminent-boko-haram/8085946.
2. Colin Freeman, "Boko Haram adopts 'hearts and minds' strategy in Nigeria – inspired by Isil," *The Telegraph*, May 22, 2019, https://www.telegraph.co.uk/global-health/terror-and-security/boko-haram-adopts-hearts-minds-strategy-nigeria-inspired-isil/
3. "Ramadan: JNI Asks Muslims to Pray for Peaceful Co-Existence of Nigeria," *Sahara Reporters,* July 23, 2012, http://saharareporters.com/2012/07/23/ramadan-jni-asks-muslims-pray-peaceful-co-existence-nigeria.
4. Abdulmumin Murtala, "Nigeria: Every Nigerian a Living in Kano Is an Indigene, Emir Sanusi II Reaffirms," *AllAfrica*, July 1, 2019, https://allafrica.com/stories/201907010507.html
5. Adeyemi Balogun, "'When Knowledge Is There, Other Things Follow': The Muslim Students' Society of Nigeria and the Making of Yoruba Muslim Youths." *Islamic Africa* 10, no. 1-2 (June 12, 2019), 127–52, https://doi.org/10.1163/21540993-01001005.
6. "Ramadan: JNI Asks Muslims to Pray for Peaceful Co-Existence of Nigeria."
7. Muhammad S. Umar, "The Popular Discourses of Salafi Radicalism and Salafi Counter-radicalism in Nigeria: A Case Study of Boko Haram." *Journal of Religion in Africa* 42, no. 2, 2012, 118-144.
8. D.N. Danjibo, "Islamic Fundamentalism and Sectarian Violence: The 'Maitatsine' and 'Boko Haram' Crises in Northern Nigeria, University of Ibadan Institute of African Studies Peace and Conflict Studies Programme, 2010; Abdulbasit Kassim, Michael Nwankpa and David Cook, *The Boko Haram Reader: from Nigerian Preachers to the Islamic State* (New York: Oxford University Press., 2018), 327.
9. Aymenn Jawad Al-Tamimi, "The Islamic State West Africa Province vs. Abu Bakr Shekau: Full Text, Translation and Analysis," aymennjawad.org, August 5, 2018, http://www.aymennjawad.org/21467/the-islamic-state-west-africa-province-vs-abu

10. Jacob Zenn, "Boko Haram's Dangerous Expansion into Northwest Nigeria," Combating Terrorism Center at West Point *CTC Sentinel* 5, iss. 10, October 2012, https://www.ctc.usma.edu/posts/boko-harams-dangerous-expansion-into-northwest-nigeria; "Attacks by Boko Haram continue in Niger's Diffa region, forcing more people to flee," *United Nations: Africa Renewal Online,* June 6, 2016, http://www.un.org/africarenewal/news/attacks-boko-haram-continue-niger%E2%80%99s-diffa-region-forcing-more-people-flee-%E2%80%93-un; Vincent Ehiabhi, "Boko Haram Attacks Chad, Kills 10," *Naij.com,* 2016, https://www.naij.com/384576-breaking-boko-haram-attacks-chad-for-first-time.html.
11. Zenn, Jacob. "Islamic State in West Africa's Province's Factional Disputes and the Battle with Boko Haram," *Terrorism Monitor*, March 20, 2020.https://jamestown.org/program/islamic-state-in-west-africa-provinces-factional-disputes-and-the-battle-with-boko-haram/
12. *North-East Nigeria: Humanitarian Situation Update*, United Nations Office for the Coordination of Humanitarian Affairs, September 2017, https://reliefweb.int/sites/reliefweb.int/files/resources/20102017_ocha_nga_ne_sitrep_no_sept_2017.pdf; "Corps Member, Hundreds More Nigerians Rot in Boko Haram Custody," *Salkida*, March 3, 2019, https://salkida.com/corps-member-hundreds-more-nigerians-rot-in-boko-haram-custody/
13. Seun Opejobi, "Boko Haram mocks Army, calls Buhari 'a small ant' over Shekau," *Daily Post,* September 5, 2017, http://dailypost.ng/2017/09/05/boko-haram-mocks-army-calls-buhari-small-ant-shekau/.
14. "Boko Haram: Splinter Group, Ansaru Emerges," *Vanguard*, February 1, 2012, http://www.vanguardngr.com/2012/02/boko-haram-splinter-group-ansaru-emerges/.
15. Mike Oboh, "Islamist insurgents kill over 178 in Nigeria's Kano," Reuters, January 22, 2012, http://www.reuters.com/article/us-nigeria-violence-idUSTRE80L0A020120122.
16. Government of Great Britain, "Proscribed terror groups or organizations," November 2012, http://webarchive.nationalarchives.gov.uk/20130128103514/http://www.homeoffice.gov.uk/publications/counter-terrorism/proscribed-terror-groups/.
17. The group posted a series of videos online, but they were subsequently removed for violating YouTube Terms of Service.
18. Ibrahim Shuaibu, "Islamic Group Claims Responsibility for Kidnapping French Citizen," *ThisDay*, December 24, 2012.

19. "Extremist Group in Nigeria Says It Killed 7 Foreign Hostages," Associated Press, March 9, 2013, http://www.nytimes.com/2013/03/10/world/africa/extremist-group-in-nigeria-says-it-killed-7-foreign-hostages.html.
20. "Vandenbeusch Father Supporers Rally in Discretion," *RFI Africa,* December 14, 2013. http://www.rfi.fr/afrique/20131214-france-cameroun-soutiens-pere-vandenbusch-mobilisent-discretion-boko-haram.
21. Wahab, Bayo. "Police Arrest Ansaru Militants Who Attacked Emir of Potiskum in Kaduna." *Pulse*, February 9, 2020. https://www.pulse.ng/news/metro/police-arrest-ansaru-militants-who-attacked-emir-of-potiskum-in-kaduna/8x9pbne.
22. Thomas Joscelyn, "Jihadists argue over leadership of Islamic State," *Long War Journal,* August 4, 2016, http://www.longwarjournal.org/archives/2016/08/jihadists-argue-over-leadership-of-islamic-states-west-africa-province.php.
23. Aaron Y. Zelin, "New audio message from Abu Bakr al-Shekau: 'Message to the World,'" *Jihadology*, August 3, 2016, http://jihadology.net/2016/08/03/new-audio-message-from-abu-bakr-al-shekau-message-to-the-world/.
24. Aaron Y. Zelin, "New audio message from Abu Bakr al-Shekau: 'Message to the World,'" *Jihadology*, August 3, 2016, http://jihadology.net/2016/08/03/new-audio-message-from-abu-bakr-al-shekau-message-to-the-world/.
25. "Statement By Boko Haram's Spokesperson Debunking Reports Of Dialogue With The Nigerian Government," *Sahara Reporters*, August 23, 2012; Jacob Zenn, "Confronting Jihadist Factions in Nigeria: An Antidote to Defeatism," *War on The Rocks*, July 17, 2019, https://warontherocks.com/2019/07/confronting-jihadist-factions-in-nigeria-an-antidote-to-defeatism/
26. Muhammad S. Umar, "Education and Islamic Trends in Northern Nigeria: 1970s-1990s," *Africa Today*, 2001, 126-150.
27. Mohammed Abubakar and Ahmed A. Mohammed, "Kala-Kato crisis: How Latest Bauchi incident erupted," *The Daily Trust,* January 1, 2010, https://www.dailytrust.com.ng/kala-kato-crisis-how-latest-bauchi-incident-erupted.html.
28. Aminu Abubakar, "Death toll from Nigeria clashes climbs to 70," Agence France Presse, December 30, 2009.
29. Isa Sa'isu, "Kala-Kato: Meet group with yet another perception of Islam," *Weekly Trust*, August 15, 2009.
30. Amara, Ramzi Ben. "6 'We Introduced sharīʿa'—The Izala Movement in Nigeria as Initiator of sharīʿa-reimplementation in the North

of the Country: Some Reflections". In *6 'We Introduced sharīʿa'— The Izala Movement in Nigeria as Initiator of sharīʿa-reimplementation in the North of the Country: Some Reflections*, (Leiden, The Netherlands: Brill, 2014).

31. Thurston, Alex. "Salafism in Northern Nigeria Beyond Boko Haram." Council on Foreign Relations, January 27, 2017, https://www.cfr.org/blog/salafism-northern-nigeria-beyond-boko-haram.
32. "Council on Foreign Relations." *Council on Foreign Relations*, April 10, 2020. https://www.cfr.org/blog/case-not-quite-closed-assassination-nigerian-salafi-scholar-shaikh-jaafar-adam.
33. Jonathan N. C. Hill, "Sufism in Northern Nigeria: Force for Counter-Radicalization?" Strategic Studies Institute, U.S. Army War College, May 17, 2010; "The Volatility of Salafi Political Theology, the War on Terror and the Genesis of Boko Haram," *Diritto e Questioni Pubbliche* 15, no. 2, 174-201.
34. Feierstein, Gerald and Craig Greathead, "The Fight for Africa: The New Focus of The Saudi-Iranian Rivalry." *Middle East Institute*, 2017, 6. Accessed May 29, 2019. https://www.mei.edu/sites/default/files/publications/PF2_Feierstein_AfricaSaudiIran_web_4.pdf.
35. Feierstein, Gerald and Craig Greathead, "The Fight for Africa: The New Focus of The Saudi-Iranian Rivalry." *Middle East Institute*, 2017, 6. Accessed May 29, 2019. https://www.mei.edu/sites/default/files/publications/PF2_Feierstein_AfricaSaudiIran_web_4.pdf.
36. Hill, "Sufism in Northern Nigeria: Force for Counter-Radicalization."
37. Vincent Egunyanga, "El-Zakzaky Blasts Sharia Governors," *Daily Champion*, April 21, 2002.
38. Mark Lobel, "Sheikh Zakzaky: Why Nigeria Could Fear an Attack on Iran." *BBC*, May 8, 2012, https://www.bbc.com/news/world-africa-17908704.
39. Ludovica Laccino, "Nigeria Zaria killings: IMN releases names of 700 missing Shias as Zakzaky returns to Abuja," *International Business Times,* January 26, 2016, http://www.ibtimes.co.uk/nigeria-zaria-killings-imn-releases-names-700-missing-shias-zakzaky-returns-abuja-1540076.
40. Garba Muhammad, "Zakzaky, wife suffer life threatening injuries – IMN," *Premium Times*, July 25, 2016, http://www.premiumtimesng.com/news/top-news/207519-zakzaky-wife-suffer-life-threatening-injuries-imn.html.
41. Garba Muhammad and Abraham Achirga, "Nigerian Shi'ite Group Says 42 Killed When Security Forces Fired upon Protests." *Reuters*

(Kaduna/Mararaba, Nigeria), October 31, 2018, https://www.reuters.com/article/us-nigeria-security-shiites/nigerian-shiite-group-says-42-killed-when-security-forces-fired-upon-protests-idUSKCN1N51OL; Jacob Zenn, "A Shia 'Boko Haram' Insurgency or Iranian Proxy in Nigeria? Not So Fast," Jamestown Foundation *Terrorism Monitor* 17, no. 15, July 26, 2019, https://jamestown.org/program/a-shia-boko-haram-insurgency-or-iranian-proxy-in-nigeria-not-so-fast/.

42. Kit O'Connell, "Saudi Arabia Takes Proxy War With Iran To Nigeria As Shias Are Brutalized," *Mint Press News,* January 15, 2016, http://www.mintpressnews.com/saudi-arabia-takes-proxy-war-with-iran-to-nigeria-as-shias-are-brutalized/212629/.
43. "Montazeri urges Nigeria to send Sheikh Zakzaky to Iran for treatment," *Tehran Times*, July 20, 2019, https://www.tehrantimes.com/news/438360/Montazeri-urges-Nigeria-to-send-Sheikh-Zakzaky-to-Iran-for-treatment
44. Isa, Kabiru Haruna, and Sani Yakubu Adam. "A History of Shia and Its Development in Nigeria: the Case-Study of Kano." *Journal for Islamic Studies* 36 (August 28, 2018). https://www.ajol.info/index.php/jis/article/view/176698.
45. "Nigerian Shia base knocked down," *BBC*, August 1, 2007.
46. Yaroslav Trofimov, "With Iran-Backed Conversions, Shiites Gain Ground in Africa," *Wall Street Journal*, May 12, 2016, https://www.wsj.com/articles/with-iran-backed-conversions-shiites-gain-ground-in-africa-1463046768.
47. Jacob Zenn, "Leadership Analysis of Boko Haram and Ansaru in Nigeria," Combating Terrorism Center at West Point, February 24, 2014, https://www.ctc.usma.edu/posts/leadership-analysis-of-boko-haram-and-ansaru-in-nigeria.
48. Gow, James, 'Funmi Olonisakin, and Ernst Dijxhoorn. *Militancy and Violence in West Africa: Religion, Politics and Radicalisation.* London: Routledge, 2014.
49. "Nigeria is Not a Secular State," *Sun News Online*, August 25, 2011.
50. Mallam Lawan Danbazau, *Politics and Religion in Nigeria* (Kano: Tofa Commercial Press, 1991), vii.
51. Philip Ostien, *Sharia Implementation in Northern Nigeria* (Spectrum Books Limited, 2007), http://www.sharia-in-africa.net/pages/publications/sharia-implementation-in-northern-nigeria.php.
52. "Boko Haram is 'defeated,' Nigeria insists, blaming international jihadists for ongoing insurgency, *The Defense Post*, July 31, 2019, https://thedefensepost.com/2019/07/31/nigeria-boko-haram-defeated-iswap/

53. "My Father, Festus Oluwayi Is The Soldier Captured By Boko Haram" – Twitter User – Politics," *Beauty Milk,* n.d., https://beauty-milk.com/my-father-festus-oluwayi-is-the-soldier-captured-by-boko-haram-twitter-user-politics/
54. "Dangerous Developments: The Weaponry of IS West Africa (Pt 2)," *Calibre Obscura*, May 23, 2019, https://www.calibreobscura.com/dangerous-developments-the-weaponry-of-iswa-part-2/
55. *Survival and Expansion: The Islamic State's West African Province*, The Global Initiative For Civil Stabilisation, Abuja, Nigeria, April 2019, https://conflictstudies.gics.live/2019/04/23/gics-report-survival-and-expansion-the-islamic-states-west-african-province/. Accessed December 18, 2019.

30 Senegal

Quick Facts

Population: 15,736,368 (July 2020 est.)
Area: 196,722 sq km
Ethnic Groups: Wolof 37.1%, Pular 26.2%, Serer 17%, Mandinka 5.6%, Jola 4.5%, Soninke 1.4%, other 8.3% (includes Europeans and persons of Lebanese descent) (2017 est.)
GDP (official exchange rate): $21.11 billion (2017 est.)

Source: CIA World FactBook (Last Updated June 2020)

Introduction

Although the Republic of Senegal borders the Republic of Mali and the Islamic Republic of Mauritania, both of which have been plagued by violent Islamist activity, there have been minimal signs of jihadist terrorism in Senegal to date. Senegal is a participant in the United States-led Trans-Sahara Counterterrorism Partnership (TSCTP) and has won some praise for its efforts to counter regional extremism and terrorist financing while also promoting a localized Islam that is both moderate and tolerant. Geographically, however, Senegal presents a potential backdoor for radical, jihadist Islam, and although it has not yet been hit by a major terrorist attack, President Macky Sall has acknowledged that his country is not immune from the threat.

Due to publishing constraints, this chapter is provided here only in summary form. To view the full study, please visit the online edition of the Almanac at almanac.afpc.org.

31 Somalia

Quick Facts

Population: 11,757,124 (July 2020 est.)
Area: 637,657 sq km
Ethnic Groups: Somali 85%, Bantu and other non-Somali 15% (including 30,000 Arabs)
GDP (official exchange rate): $20.44 billion (2017 est.)

Source: CIA World FactBook (Last Updated August 2020)

Introduction

The U.S. State Department has noted that, despite experiencing significant military pressure in recent years, al-Shabaab has proven resilient. The group has "maintained control over large portions of the country" and "retained the ability to carry out high-profile attacks" aimed at both delegitimizing the Federal Government of Somalia (FGS) and weakening the resolve of the African Union Mission in Somalia (AMISOM). In pursuit of these goals, al-Shabaab uses asymmetric tactics against AMISOM and Somali security forces, as well as attacks soft targets in Somalia and in neighboring AMISOM troop-contributing countries, mainly Kenya.[1] *Nevertheless, the group has had to grapple with the death of several key leadership figures as a result of U.S. aerial strikes, the loss of strongholds in parts of south-central Somalia, and, in the view of U.S. authorities, increasing factionalism and defections "as the appeal of the Islamic State of Iraq and the Levant (ISIL) created divisions within al-Shabaab's core leadership."*[2] *One reason for the group's resilience is the weakness of the FGS, whose authority is not widely accepted by Somalis. Hampering the U.S. response to this threat is not only the absence of a capable partner government in Mogadishu but also Washington's failure to creatively engage effective Somali authorities, including those in the unrecognized Republic of Somaliland.*[3]

ISLAMIST ACTIVITY

Islamists active in Somalia fall roughly into one of seven principal groups:

Harakat al-Shabaab al-Mujahideen ("Movement of Warrior Youth," al-Shabaab)

Known colloquially as al-Shabaab, this movement arose out of the militant wing of the Islamic Courts Union. When the latter was defeated during a 2007 Ethiopian intervention, al-Shabaab broke with other Islamists who regrouped under the sponsorship of Eritrea, instead forming the Alliance for the Re-Liberation of Somalia (ARS) to oppose the Transitional Federal Government (TFG) then installed in Mogadishu.

Founded in large part due to the efforts of Aden Hashi Ayro, a militant who had trained with al-Qaeda in Afghanistan prior to September 11, 2001, al-Shabaab's schism with other Islamists reflects Ayro's adherence to a more radical *jihadist* ideology that does not cooperate with the non-Muslim Eritrean regime, even against a common enemy. Although divided into several factions even before Ayro was killed by a U.S. aerial strike in May 2008, al-Shabaab was an effective fighting force overall. Senior al-Shabaab leadership has included veteran *jihadists* with experience on battlefields abroad, including in Afghanistan, Bosnia, and Kashmir.[4] It seized large sections of southern and central Somalia, including parts of Mogadishu, where it has installed a strict Islamist regime that has carried out a number of harsh punishments—among them the stoning of a 13-year-old rape victim for the crime of "adultery" in 2008.[5]

Over time, al-Shabaab's leadership split into two principal currents. The first consists primarily of foreign or foreign-funded *jihadists* and follows a transnational *jihadist* agenda. It carried out the attack on Kenya's Westgate Shopping Mall in 2013, the subsequent April 2015 attack on Garissa University in Garissa, Kenya, and the January 2018 attack on Nairobi's DusitD2 hotel complex—incidents which collectively left over 200 people dead and scores injured. Ahmed Abdi Godane, also known as Mukhtar Abu Zubair, initially led this faction and proclaimed the group's formal allegiance to al-Qaeda and to Osama bin Laden's successor, Ayman al-Zawahiri, in February 2012. The other faction renamed itself the "Islamic Emirate of Somalia" in early 2011. It rejected al-Qaeda's branding and objectives while it focused primarily on domestic challenges with a "nationalist agenda."

Al-Shabaab's internal divisions facilitated its loss of control over Somalia. Since Kenyan and Ethiopian troops joined African Union Mission in Somalia (AMISOM) and Transitional Federal Government forces to expel al-Shabaab from major cities beginning in late 2011, the group has surrendered its strongholds in numerous regional capitals. Al-Shabaab defections have increased substantially. In December 2012, Godane admitted major defeats, but pledged to continue a guerrilla war against Somali and AMISOM forces.[6]

In 2013, Godane moved against the nationalist faction of the organization, killing or forcing into hiding most of its senior leadership.[7] While Godane himself was killed by a U.S. aerial strike in September 2014, al-Shabaab still adheres to transnational *jihadism*. Under the leadership of Godane's successor, Ahmed Omar, al-Shabaab focuses less on controlling territory and more on launching successful attacks both within Somalia and in neighbouring countries. Targets have included Ugandan and Kenyan-run AMISOM bases in the southern Somali towns of Janale and El Adde, hotels and FGS figures in Mogadishu, and soft targets in neighbouring AMISOM troop-contributing countries, including Kenya and Djibouti.

The rise of the Islamic State in the Middle East has created another challenge to the organizational unity of al-Shabaab. Several al-Shabaab factions in Puntland and Southern Somalia have pledged allegiance to the Islamic State, which sparked a crackdown on defectors in late 2015 by al-Shabaab's senior central leadership.[8] Nevertheless, the Islamic State's media offices continue to encourage *al-Shabaab*-affiliated fighters in Somalia and members of the Somali diaspora abroad to support the group.

Clashes between factions loyal to the Islamic State and those loyal to al-Qaeda escalated in 2018.[9] In October of that year, the deputy commander of the self-styled Islamic State in Somalia (ISS) was killed by a suspected al-Shabaab death squad and, in December, al-Shabaab launched an offensive to get rid of ISS militants in Somalia.[10] On November 3, 2017, the United States conducted its first airstrikes against Islamic State in Somalia, proving the group's resilience following the defeat of its parent organization in Iraq and Syria and underlining the ongoing challenge posed by ISS to al-Shabaab.[11]

Hizbul Islam ("Islamic Party")

Led by Hassan Dahir 'Aweys, previously the military commander of Somali Muslim Brotherhood offshoot al-Itihaad al-Islamiyya (AIAI, the "Islamic Union") and subsequently the chairman of the *shura* of the Islamic Courts Union, Hizbul Islam is the product of several groups. Hizbul Islam does not place as much emphasis on global *jihadist* objectives; rather, its two principal demands are the strict implementation of *sharia* as the law in Somalia, and the withdrawal of all foreign troops from the country.

Hizbul Islam draws its membership and support primarily from 'Aweys' Habar Gedir sub-clan.[12] By and large, Hizbul Islam has cooperated with al-Shabaab, although the two groups have come into occasional conflict over the division of spoils. Hizbul Islam lost control of Beledweyne to al-Shabaab in June 2010, retaining only some territory in the Bay and Lower Shabelle regions. Subsequently, during the Muslim holy month of Ramadan, the two groups cooperated on a joint offensive against TFG and AMISOM forces in Mogadishu. Reports of a merger between the two groups surfaced at the end of 2010; however, in September 2012, a spokesperson from Hizbul Islam announced its split with al-Shabaab, citing ideological differences and al-Shabaab's weakened regional position.[13]

Hizbul Islam's stance with respect to the Somali government is unclear, as is the current state of the group. While 'Aweys reportedly declared war against the regime after Sheikh Hassan Mohamud was elected president in September 2012, the group's spokesman, Mohamed Moalim, welcomed the new president and parliament as a "positive development."[14] In fact, 'Aweys came to Mogadishu in June 2013 for talks with government officials, but was arrested and reportedly roughed up.[15] With 'Aweys in custody since then, very little has been heard from his followers.

Mu'askar Ras Kamboni ("Ras Kamboni Brigades")

Founded by Hassan Abdullah Hersi ("al-Turki"), a former military commander for the Islamic Courts, the Ras Kamboni Brigades is based in Middle and Lower Jubba Valley, where it controlled towns with access to the Kenyan border. The group was aligned with *Hizbul Islam* until late 2009, when al-Shabaab took control of the port of Kismayo. A faction of Ras Kamboni, led by al-Turki, announced in early 2010 that it was joining forces with al-Shabaab and proclaimed its adhesion to "the international *jihad* of al-Qaeda."[16]

The rest of the Ras Kamboni Brigades follows Sheikh Ahmed Mohamed Islam (Sheikh Ahmed Madobe) who served as the governor of Kismayo from 2006 until the fall of the Islamic Courts Union.[17] Ras Kamboni played a key role in helping the AMISOM, Kenyan, and Somali government forces push al-Shabaab out of Kismayo in October 2012, although some Mogadishu-based Somali government officials denied cooperating with the "competing militants."[18] In 2013, while continuing to lead the Ras Kamboni Brigades against al-Shabaab forces in the region, Madobe was elected president of the newly established autonomous region of Jubaland.[19]

A spokesperson for the Somali government forces in Juba reported that Ras Kamboni allied with Ogaden National Liberation Front (ONLF) to fight for control of the port city, leading to clashes with government troops in February 2013.[20] However, in August 2013, Madobe signed an Ethiopian-brokered "national reconciliation agreement" with the FGS that allowed him to maintain control of Kismayo as the head of an "interim administration" that would preside over the police forces in Jubaland, while military forces were gradually integrated into the national army.[21]

Ahlu Sunna wal-Jama'a (roughly, "[Followers of] the Traditions and Consensus [of the Prophet Muhammad]")

The original Ahlu Sunna wal-Jama'a (ASWJ) was an umbrella group of traditional Somali Muslims organized by General Muhammad Farah 'Aideed as a counterweight to his *Wahhabbi*-inspired opponents in AIAI.[22] In mid-2009, the excesses of al-Shabaab led to a revival of the movement to oppose the al-Shabaab ideology. Loosely organized into armed militias, Ahlu Sunna wal-Jama'a fighters stopped the seemingly relentless surge of al-Shabaab forces in 2010. Trained and assisted by Ethiopian defense forces, Ahlu Sunna wal-Jama'a emerged as a force in southern and central Somalia. However, the group's opposition to al-Shabaab should not be confused with support of the TFG; the group's formal alliance with the TFG in 2010, formed under tremendous international pressure, has largely fallen apart.

Ahlu Sunna wal-Jama'a has its own Islamist agenda. The group has conducted operations against those who it felt were not properly observing the fast of Ramadan—something that may put it at odds with the more secular elements of Somali society.[23]

The group took control of several towns and villages in Galgadud and Hiran.[24] After assisting the Somali government fight al-Shabaab for two years, in December 2012, Ahlu Sunna wal-Jama'a troops were officially integrated into Somali government forces.[25] In February 2013, the chairman of the executive committee of Ahlu Sunna wal Jama'a, passed away in a hospital in Mogadishu; ever since, relations between the militia and the FGS have frayed.[26] ASWJ and Somali government forces clash sporadically, most notably in a February 2015 clash in Guricel that left nine dead.[27]

Al-Islah al-Islamiyya ("Islamic Movement")

Al-Islah emerged as an offshoot of the Somali Muslim Brothers alongside al-Itihaad al-Islamiyya (the Islamic Union) in 1978 and the early 1980s, respectively. In 2004, the U.S. Department of State described al-Islah as an "organized Islamic group whose goal is the establishment of an Islamic state," but termed it "a generally nonviolent movement that operates primarily in Mogadishu."[28] Largely displaced when the Islamic Courts Union rose to power, al-Islah underwent something of a revival in Mogadishu when Sharif Ahmed returned as the head of the TFG in 2009. al-Islah's chief role was as the administration of schools in the capital which were supported by the group's foreign benefactors. Given how spectacularly state institutions have collapsed in Somalia, it is not surprising that "this naturally promoted fundamentalist trends (such as al-Islah) in local Islam, which had previously been largely Sufi in character, and these were encouraged by financial support from Saudi Arabia and other Middle Eastern centers."[29] Hassan Sheikh Mohamed, who served as the elected head of the Somali government from September 2012 to February 2017, has links with al-Islah.[30]

Al-Qaeda

While its earlier foray into Somalia did not prove particularly successful, al-Qaeda remains interested in Somalia both as a theater of operations and as a jumping-off point for terrorist activities in the nearby Arabian Peninsula and elsewhere in Africa.[31] Osama bin Laden released an audio statement in 2009 praising the Islamist insurgency in Somalia and calling upon Muslims to support it.[32] More recently, Ayman al-Zawahiri, bin Laden's successor, endorsed Ahmed Omer as the current leader of al-Shabaab.[33]

Analysts who previously discounted al-Qaeda's involvement in Somalia now acknowledge that, since at least early 2008, al-Qaeda advisors have played a critical role in al-Shabaab operations.[34]

In September 2009, U.S. Special Operations Forces killed Saleh Ali Saleh Nabhan in Somalia. Nabhan was a Kenyan national wanted in connected with the 1998 bombings of the U.S. embassies in Dar es Salaam, Tanzania and Nairobi, Kenya. At the time of his death, Nabhan was running terrorist training camps while bringing in foreign trainers and fighters to support al-Shabaab on behalf of al-Qaeda.

In February 2012, al-Shabaab leadership formally pledged its allegiance to al-Qaeda leader Ayman al-Zawahiri.[35] That affiliation has persisted; in a statement claiming responsibility for the January 2019 attack on the DusitD2 hotel complex in Nairobi, Kenya, al-Shabaab referred to the guidance of Osama bin Laden and Ayman al-Zawahiri and justified the attack within the parameters of al-Qaeda's transnational vision of *jihad*.[36]

The Islamic State in Somalia (Islamic State of Iraq and the Levant, Daesh)

Although its success has been limited, the Islamic State has made efforts to co-opt al-Shabaab forces demoralized by their recent battlefield losses. Led by Abdulkadir Mumin, a group of fighters in Puntland broke away from al-Shabaab and pledged allegiance to the Islamic State, calling themselves the Islamic State in Somalia. Official recognition of ISS by the Islamic State has been limited, and Somalia has not been officially designated a province *(wilayat)* of the group.[37]

In March 2016, ISS claimed its first attack in Somalia (the bombing of an African Union vehicle in Mogadishu) and subsequently released a video showing what it claimed was its first Somali training camp. The group has reportedly attracted several hundred al-Shabaab defectors, as well as a number of prominent *imams*.[38] Islamic State activities in Somalia have spiked in recent years.[39] In May 2018, the Islamic State claimed an attack that killed five security officers in Puntland.[40] The Islamic State's growing influence in Somalia has posed a threat to al-Shabaab, which launched an offensive against Islamic State-affiliated groups in December 2018.[41]

Islam and Society

Somali people traditionally subscribe to Sunni Islam and follow the Shāfi'ī school (*mahdab*) of jurisprudence, which, although conservative, is open to a variety of liberal practical views.[42] Until Somalia's independence in 1960, there were different movements within the Sunni Islam in Somalia. The most dominant were the Sufi brotherhoods (sing., *tarīqa*, pl. *turuq*), especially that of the Qadiriyya order (although the Ahmadiyya order, introduced into Somali lands in the 19th century, was also influential).[43] While traditional Islamic schools and scholars (*ulamā*) played a role as focal points for rudimentary political opposition to colonial rule in Italian Somalia, historically their role in Somali clan politics was neither institutionalized nor particularly prominent. *Sharia* has never historically been especially entrenched in Somalia: being largely pastoralists, the Somali people relied more on customary law (xeer) than on religious prescriptions.[44] Hence, Somali Islamism was strengthened by the collapse of the state in 1991, the ensuing civil war, international intervention, external meddling, and efforts by Somalis themselves at political reconstruction. Absent this chain of events, it is doubtful that militant Islamism would be much more than a marginal force in Somali politics.

Although its adherents often appeal to the early 20th century anti-colonial fight of the "Mad Mullah" Sayyid Muhammad 'Abdille Hassan,[45] Somali Islamism is, at its origins, an import dating back at most to the 1950s. The 1953 establishment in Mogadishu of an Institute of Islamic Studies run by Egyptian scholars from Cairo's al-Azhar University introduced both Arabic language curriculum and contact with the Egyptian Muslim Brotherhood (al-Ikhwan al-Muslimoon). Unlike the Sufis who emphasize socialization, moral education, and spiritual preparation, the Muslim Brothers stress organization, activism, and the socio-political dimension of change directed toward the creation of a modern Islamic state. After Somalia's independence in 1960, Egyptians opened secondary schools in many of the country's towns. In the 1960s and 1970s, Saudi religious and educational institutions—especially the Islamic University of Medina, the Umm al-Qura University in Mecca, and the Imam Muhammad bin Saud Islamic University in Riyadh—joined al-Azhar in offering scholarships to graduates of these institutions. This development has parallels with the entrenchment of radical Islam in nearby Sudan via the establishment of the Sudanese Muslim Brotherhood, the precursor to the currently-ruling National Congress Party (formerly the National Islamic Front).

By the 1970s, the nascent Somali Muslim Brotherhood was so visible that the dictatorial regime of Siyad Barre took measures to suppress it, driving its adherents underground. When the group split into al-Islah and al-Itihaad, their memberships and leadership network overlapped considerably. The differences between them were, at least initially, largely circumstantial. Both sought an expansive "Islamic Republic of Greater Somalia" and eventually a political union embracing all Muslims in the Horn of Africa.[46]

When the Siyad Barre regime collapsed in January 1991, internecine warfare laid waste to Somalia. AIAI was forced to withdraw after heavy fighting, which allowed Somali Islamists to regroup in the Somali region of Ethiopia. AIAI tried to seize control of strategic assets like seaports and crossroads. Although it temporarily held the northern port of Bosaso and the eastern ports of Marka and Kismayo, the only area where it exercised long-term control was the economically vital intersection of Luuq, where it imposed harsh *sharia*-based rule from 1991 until 1996. From its base in Luuq, the Islamists of AIAI encouraged subversive activities among ethnic Somalis of Ethiopia and carried out a series of terrorist attacks.

The exasperated Ethiopian regime finally intervened in Somalia in August 1996, wiping out AIAI bases in Luuq and Buulo Haawa and killing hundreds of Somali extremists and scores of non-Somalis who flocked to the Horn of Africa under the banner of *jihad*. From this period emerged the cooperation between Somali Islamists and Ethiopian groups like ONLF, which continue to struggle against the newly established government of Ethiopia.

From its inception, AIAI rejected the non-confessional nature of the Somali state and sought to establish an Islamic regime based on a strict *Wahhabbi* interpretation. When it found the direct road to power blocked by Muhammad Farah 'Aideed, it adopted a subtler approach based on the establishment of economic and other social programs, together with Islamic courts.[47]

Some Somali people see Islam as an alternative to both the traditional clan-based identities and the emergent criminal syndicates led by so-called "warlords." The increased influence of religion has been largely a phenomenon of small towns and urban centers, although increased adherence to its normative precepts is a wider trend. Islamic religious leaders have helped organize security and other services; businessmen in particular were supportive of *sharia*-based court installation throughout the south, which was a precursor of the Islamic Courts Union established in June 2006. The Islamists attempted to fill certain voids left by state collapse; in doing so, they also made a bid to supplant other identities, offering a pan-Islamist one in lieu of other allegiances.[48]

Given their previous experiences with Somali Islamism, it was not surprising that, after many of the same extremists emerged in positions of authority in the Islamic Courts Union, the Ethiopians would intervene to support Somalia's internationally-recognized but weak TFG as they did in 2006.[49] Unfortunately, while the intervention ended the rule of the Islamic Courts Union, it also provoked an insurgency spearheaded by the even more radical al-Shabaab. Even after Ethiopian troops withdrew in early 2009, the al-Shabaab-led insurgency against the TFG has continued; AMISOM deployed to protect the transitional regime as the conflict drew longer; over time the number of AMISOM casualties increased. On September 17, 2009, seventeen peacekeepers were killed and forty others were wounded in a suicide car bombing.[50] On December 3, 2009, three TFG ministers and sixteen other people were killed while attending a graduation ceremony within the small enclave of Mogadishu.[51]

With the end of the TFG's mandate in August 2012, the Somali Federal Government (SFG) was formed. Depending on how one counts them, it is either the 15th or 16th interim regime since the collapse of the Siyad Barre dictatorship in 1991. Hassan Sheikh Mohamud, an educator and civil society activist with ties to al-Islah as well as the earlier Islamic Courts Union, was selected to head the new government, which was formally recognized by the United States in January 2013. It is the first Somali regime to be accorded that status in more than two decades. While the Federal Government of Somalia, with the help of AMISOM, has rolled back al-Shabaab territorial control in southern Somalia, the group strikes SFG-affiliated targets in Mogadishu; an attack on the Nasa Hablod hotel in June 2016 killed a serving government minister, among other victims. On October 14, 2017, al-Shabaab was blamed for a double truck-bombing that killed an unprecedented 512 civilians.

Somalia elected Mohamed Abdullahi Mohamed – better known as 'Farmajo' – president on February 8, 2017. Despite accusations of vote-buying and corruption in the run-up to the polls,[52] the election was marked by the peaceful transfer of power.[53] Despite some praise for Mohamed's previous experience in the Barre regime, the new Somali government has had difficulty in establishing legitimacy in the country and remains vulnerable to attacks by al-Shabaab.[54] The October 2017 attack highlighted the limitations of the Somali Federal Government and its international allies in countering Islamist terror groups on Somali soil.

Islamists within the state apparatus are becoming increasingly influential. Buoyed by financial support from outside backers such as Qatar and Turkey, who themselves are locked in competition with Gulf State rivals for bases and resources in the Horn of Africa, a cabal with an Islamist agenda has apparently pushed the Federal Government of Somalia into siding with more Islamist foreign allies.[55] The ascendancy of such a faction within the state would undermine its ability to counter the plethora of Islamist militants within Somalia's borders.

Islamism and the State

Somali governmental policy toward Islamism is muddled, compromised by the complicity of the government in Islamist thought and activity. While Somali Islamism was damaged by the military defeat dealt to the Islamic Courts Union following the Ethiopian military intervention in late 2006 and early 2007, Somali territories (outside Somaliland) sunk into chaos under the aegis of the TFG, especially given some of the historical linkages between Islamism and pan-Somali identity.[56] Consequently, Islamists will maintain a strong presence in Somali politics.

In March 2009, a unity government was established between the TFG and elements of the Alliance for the Re-Liberation of Somalia (ARS). The number of seats in the country's parliament expanded to 550, and former ICU leader Sharif Sheikh Ahmed was elected president. Both demonstrated the inclusion of a broader spectrum of Islamic ideology in government.[57]

The election of Hassan Sheikh Mohamud and Mohamed Abdullahi Mohamed to the presidency of the Federal Government of Somalia in September 2012 and February 2017, respectively, represents movement toward more moderate, albeit mildly Islamist, leadership.[58] Though Mohamud's tenure was characterized by slow improvement in Somali national security, events under the Mohamed administration prove that extremist elements in Somalia continue to influence and threaten political order. This situation is exacerbated by the withdrawal of AMISOM forces (due to the respective domestic security needs of contributing countries and a decrease in international support for their deployment in Somalia).

At the same time, two governmental response topics require elucidation and governmental response: those relating to 1) Somaliland and 2) piracy.

Somaliland

Although Somaliland's sovereignty has yet to be formally recognized by any other state, more than a decade and a half have passed since Somaliland proclaimed the dissolution of its voluntary union with the central government. Perhaps most important to the rising tide of Islamist militancy is Somaliland's reliance on the older political systems. Clan elders and the respect they command "has served as something of a mediating force in managing pragmatic interaction between custom and tradition; Islam and the secular realm of modern nationalism… Islam may be pre-empting and/or containing Islamism."[59]

The consequence of an organic relationship between Somali culture and tradition and Islam appears to play a stabilizing role for religion, society, and, particularly, politics. In Somaliland, for example, the population is almost exclusively Sunni Muslim. The *shahada*, the Muslim profession of the oneness of God and the acceptance of Muhammad as God's final prophet, is emblazoned on the flag. Yet *sharia* is only one of the three sources of the jurisprudence in the region's courts, alongside secular legislation and Somali traditional law. Unlike the rest of the Somali lands, the region is governed by a democratic constitution which was approved by 97 percent of the voters in a May 2001 referendum.

The constitution provides an executive branch of government, consisting of a directly elected president, a vice president, and appointed ministers; a bicameral legislature consisting of an elected House of Representatives and an upper chamber of elders, the *guurti*; and an independent judiciary. Somaliland has held presidential elections in 2003 and 2010 and parliamentary elections in 2005. All three were judged "free and fair" by international observers. Initially postponed due to drought, Somaliland held presidential elections on November 13, 2017, in which the incumbent Ahmed Mohamed Mahamoud did not seek a second term. In an election that the international community claimed, "preserved the integrity of the electoral process." Mahamoud's successor in the Peace, Unity, and Development Party (KULMIYE), Muse Bihi Abdi, was elected president with 55 percent of the vote."[60]

The relative success of Somaliland has drawn the ire of Islamists in southern and central Somalia. In 2008, on the same day that Shirwa Ahmed, a naturalized U.S. citizen from Minneapolis, Minnesota, blew himself up in an attack on the headquarters of the Puntland Intelligence Service in Bosaso, other suicide bombers from *al-Shabaab* hit the presidential palace, the UN Development Programme office, and the Ethiopian diplomatic mission in the Somaliland capital of Hargeisa.[61]

Since suffering defeats in south and central Somalia, al-Shabaab fighters have established footholds in Puntland, posing a major threat to the region's governing institutions and its overall stability.[62] In the past, semi-autonomous Puntland has criticized Somaliland for ignoring the threat posed by al-Shabaab militants in northern Somalia.[63] However, a number of developments—including the effective use of a small coast guard to keep Somaliland largely free of piracy, as well as the 2009 transfer of two Guantanamo Bay detainees to Hargeisa, rather than the less secure Mogadishu—indicate that Somaliland is seen as less vulnerable to militant Islam than south and central Somalia.[64] In February 2013, local authorities arrested approximately eighty al-Shabaab members, including the son of a Somaliland politician.[65]

Islamism and Piracy

Piracy has dramatically decreased since 2012 thanks to increased international patrols and maritime security improvements; however, there was no evidence of anything other than opportunistic cooperation between Somalia's Islamists and pirates. In early 2011, al-Shabaab reportedly reached a deal with one of the larger piracy syndicates; they would receive a 20% of all future ransoms from piracy. Al-Shabaab would even open an office to specifically liaise with the pirates in the port of Xarardheere where the Islamist group would permit hijackers to anchor seized ships while awaiting ransom payments.[66] A 2011 U.S. Congressional Research Service report cited testimony suggesting that Somali pirates were not directly allied with al-Shabaab, but did maintain many of these mutually beneficial financial arrangements.[67] Moreover, al-Shabaab's loss of control of key ports including Xarardheere, Marka, Baraawe, and Kismaayo, to the Somali military and AMISOM further limit opportunities for cooperation between the Islamists and piracy networks.

Endnotes

1. U.S. Department of State, Office of the Coordinator for Counterterrorism, "Country Reports: Africa," in *Country Reports on Terrorism 2017*, 2018, https://www.state.gov/j/ct/rls/crt/2017/282841.htm.
2. U.S. Department of State, Office of the Coordinator for Counterterrorism, "Country Reports: Africa," in *Country Reports on Terrorism 2015*, 2016, http://www.state.gov/j/ct/rls/crt/2015/257514.htm.
3. J. Peter Pham, "Peripheral Vision: A Model Solution for Somalia," *RUSI Journal* 154, no. 5 (October 2009), 84-90.
4. Roland Marchal, "A Tentative Assessment Of The Somali Harakat al-Shabaab," *Journal of Eastern African Studies* 3, no. 3 (2009), 389.
5. Chris McGreal, "Rape Victim, 13, Stoned To Death In Somalia," *Guardian* (London), November 2, 2008, http://www.guardian.co.uk/world/2008/nov/02/somalia-gender.
6. Claire Felter, Jonathan Masters and Mohammed Aly Sergie "Al-Shabab Backgrounder," Council on Foreign Relations, January 31, 2019, https://www.cfr.org/backgrounder/al-shabab
7. Matt Bryden, "The Reinvention of Al-Shabaab: A Strategy of Choice or Necessity?" Center for Strategic & International Studies, February 2014, https://csis-prod.s3.amazonaws.com/s3fs-public/legacy_files/files/publication/140221_Bryden_ReinventionOfAlShabaab_Web.pdf
8. "Somalia's Al-Qaeda branch warns members against joining IS," Agence France-Presse, November 24, 2015, https://www.yahoo.com/news/somalias-al-qaeda-branch-warns-members-against-joining-075418683.html?ref=gs
9. Stig Jarle Hansen, "Has Shabaab been weakened for good? The answer is 'yes' and 'no,'" *The Conversation,* October 17, 2016, http://theconversation.com/has-shabaab-been-weakened-for-good-the-answer-is-yes-and-no-67067
10. "Bloody Rivalry erupts between al-Shabaab, IS group in Somalia," Associated Press, December 6, 2018, https://www.apnews.com/1982417577f5465a97dc87352cb10152.
11. J. Peter Pham, "US Strikes on ISIS in Somalia Underscore Threat, Vulnerabilities," *New Atlanticist*, November 6, 2017, http://www.atlanticcouncil.org/blogs/new-atlanticist/us-strikes-on-isis-in-somalia-underscore-threat-vulnerabilities.
12. "Somalia: Hizbul Islam Group Withdraws Allegiance, Says 'Al Shabaab Is Weakened,'" *Garowe Online*, September 25, 2012, http://allafrica.com/stories/201209261141.html.
13. "Somali Islamists al-Shabab and Hizbul Islam 'to merge,'" *BBC*

News, December 10, 2010, http://www.bbc.co.uk/news/world-africa-12038556; "Kenyan Amisom soldier kills six Somali civilians," *BBC News*, September 24, 2012, http://www.bbc.co.uk/news/world-africa-19698348.

14. Ibid.
15. See "Somalia and its Shabab: Are the Islamists Truly on the Ropes," *The Economist*, July 6, 2013, http://www.economist.com/news/middle-east-and-africa/21580523-new-and-much-lauded-president-finding-it-hard-bury-old-divisions-are.
16. Abdi Sheikh and Abdi Guled, "Somali Rebels Unite, Profess Loyalty To Al Qaeda," Reuters, February 1, 2010, http://www.reuters.com/article/idUSTRE6102Q720100201.
17. "The smiling warlord who Controls Ras Kamboni," *The Daily Nation,* July 11, 2012, http://www.nation.co.ke/Features/DN2/The-smiling-warlord-who-Controls-Ras-Kamboni-/-/957860/1425264/-/12mrtirz/-/index.html
18. Abdul Kadir Khalif, "Somalia in row with militias in captured town," *The Daily Nation,* October 11, 2012, http://www.nation.co.ke/News/africa/-/1066/1530598/-/14pr6i0/-/index.html.
19. "Somalia: Kismayo Residents Fear New Clan Fighting," *Deseret News*, October 4, 2012, https://www.deseretnews.com/article/765609108/Somalia-Kismayo-residents-fear-new-clan-fighting.html
20. Abdul Kadir Khalif, "Somalia in row with militias in captured town," *The Daily Nation,* October 11, 2012, http://www.nation.co.ke/News/africa/-/1066/1530598/-/14pr6i0/-/index.html; "Gulf of Aden Security Review - February 25, 2013," American Enterprise Institute Critical Threats Project, February 25, 2013, http://www.criticalthreats.org/gulf-aden-security-review/gulf-aden-security-review-february-25-2013.
21. "Somali Government and Jubaland Strike Peace Deal," *The New Times*, August 29, 2013, http://www.africareview.com/News/Somali+government+and+Jubaland+strike+a+deal/-/979180/1972618/-/3a6xv7z/-/index.html.
22. Menkhaus, ""Somalia And Somaliland," 33.
23. "Ahlu Sunna Wal Jama," *Mapping Militant Organizations*, June 18, 2016, http://web.stanford.edu/group/mappingmilitants/cgi-bin/groups/view/109#ideology.
24. "Somalia's Shabaab seize third town this month after peacekeepers withdraw," Reuters, October 23, 2016, http://af.reuters.com/article/topNews/idAFKCN12N0JZ .

25. "Somalia: Ahlu Sunna Wal-Jamaa Forces to Join Somali National Army," *Sabahi,* November 30, 2012, http://allafrica.com/stories/201212040647.html.
26. "Somalia: A leader of Ahlu Sunna Wal Jama'a Dies," *AllAfrica,* February 14, 2013, http://allafrica.com/stories/201302141519.html.
27. "Sufi Militias Repel Somalia Army Counterattack on Town," *Hiraan Online*, February 12, 2015, http://www.hiiraan.com/news4/2015/Feb/98127/sufi_militias_repel_somalia_army_counter_attack_on_town.aspx.
28. United States Department of State, "International Religious Freedom Report 2004," 2004, http://www.state.gov/j/drl/rls/irf/2004/35382.htm.
29. Ioan M. Lewis, *A Modern History of the Somali*, 4th rev. ed. (Oxford: James Currey, 2002), 299.
30. "Hassan Sheikh Mohamud: Somalia's new president profiled," *BBC News,* September 11, 2012, http://www.bbc.co.uk/news/world-africa-19556383.
31. Kinfe Abraham, *The Bin Laden Connection and the Terror Factor in Somalia* (Addis Ababa: Ethiopia International Institute for Peace and Development, 2006).
32. J. Peter Pham, "Bin Laden's Somali Gambit," Foundation for Defense of Democracies, March 26, 2009, https://www.fdd.org/analysis/2009/03/26/bin-ladens-somali-gambit/.
33. Thomas Joscelyn, "Shabaab's Leadership Fights Islamic State's Attempted Expansion in East Africa," *Long War Journal*, October 26, 2015, http://www.longwarjournal.org/archives/2015/10/shabaab-leadership-fights-islamic-state-expansion.php.
34. Ken Menkhaus, "Somalia: What Went Wrong?" *RUSI Journal* 154, no. 4 (August 2009), 12.
35. Katherine Houreld, "Somali Militant Group al-Shabaab Formally Joins al-Qaida," Associated Press, February 9, 2012, https://www.theguardian.com/world/2012/feb/09/somali-al-shabaab-join-al-qaida.
36. "Al-Quds (Jerusalem) Will Never Be Judaized," *Al-Kataib*, January 16, 2019, https://www.longwarjournal.org/19-01-16-shabaab-al-quds-will-never-be-judaized-2.
37. Christopher Anzalone, "Black Banners in Somalia: The State of al-Shabaab's Territorial Insurgency and the Specter of Islamic State," *CTC Sentinel* 11, no. 3 (March 2018), https://ctc.usma.edu/app/uploads/2018/03/CTC-Sentinel-Vol11Iss3.pdf.
38. Heidi Vogt, "Islamic State in Africa Tries to Lure Members from al-Shabaab," *Wall Street Journal*, October 26, 2016, http://www.wsj.

com/articles/african-terror-franchise-now-has-competition-from-islamic-state-1477474200.

39. "Bloody Rivalry erupts between al-Shabab, IS group in Somalia", Associated Press, December 6, 2018, https://www.apnews.com/1982417577f5465a97dc87352cb10152; Jason Warner, Charlotte Hulme, "The Islamic State in Africa: Estimating Fighter Numbers in Cells Across the Continent," *CTC Sentinel* 7, no. 11 (August 2018), 21-27.
40. U.S. Department of State, Office of the Coordinator for Counterterrorism, "Country Reports: Africa," in *Country Reports on Terrorism 2017*, 2018, https://www.state.gov/j/ct/rls/crt/2017/282841.htm.
41. "Bloody Rivalry erupts between al-Shabab, IS group in Somalia."
42. Ioan M. Lewis, *Blood and Bone: The Call of Kinship in Somali Society* (Princeton, NJ: Red Sea Press, 1994), 167.
43. Ioan M. Lewis, *Saints and Somalis: Popular Islam in a Clan-Based Society* (Lawrenceville, NJ: Red Sea Press, 1998).
44. Michael van Notten and Spencer Heath MacCallum, eds., *The Law of the Somalis: A Stable Foundation for Economic Development in the Horn of Africa* (Trenton, NJ: Red Sea Press, 2006).
45. Robert L. Hess, "The 'Mad Mullah' And Northern Somalia," *Journal of African History* 5, no. 3 (1964), 415-433; see also Abdi Sheik-Abdi, *Divine Madness: Mohammed Abdulle Hassan (1856-1920)* (Atlantic Highlands, NJ: Zed, 1993).
46. Medhane Tadesse, *Al-Ittihad: Political Islam and Black Economy in Somalia. Religion, Money, Clan and the Struggle for Supremacy over Somalia* (Addis Ababa, 2002), 16-24.
47. Roland Marchal, "Islamic Political Dynamics in The Somali Civil War," in Alex de Waal, ed., *Islamism and its Enemies in the Horn of Africa* (Addis Ababa: Shama Books, 2004), 114-146.
48. Shaul Shay, *Somalia between Jihad and Restoration* (New Brunswick, NJ: Transaction Publishers, 2007), 93-127; see also Kenneth J. Menkhaus, "Somalia and Somaliland: Terrorism, Political Islam, and State Collapse," in Robert I. Rotberg, ed., *Battling Terrorism in the Horn of Africa* (Washington, DC: Brookings Institution Press, 2005), 23-47; and Jonathan Stevenson, "Risks and Opportunities in Somalia," *Survival* 49, no. 2 (Summer 2007), 5-20.
49. Ken Menkhaus, "The Crisis in Somalia: Tragedy In Five Acts," *African Affairs* 106, no. 204 (2007), 357-390.
50. "21 Killed In Suicide Attack On African Union Base In Somalia," CNN.com, September 18, 2009, http://edition.cnn.com/2009/WORLD/africa/09/18/somalia.suicide.attack/index.html.

51. Stephanie McCrummen, "Bombing Kills 19 In Somali Capital," *Washington Post*, December 4, 2009, A19.
52. Jeffrey Gettleman, "Fueled by Bribes, Somalia's Election Seen as Milestone of Corruption," *New York Times*, February 7, 2017, https://www.nytimes.com/2017/02/07/world/africa/somalia-election-corruption.html?mtrref=undefined&gwh=B1816BA4881DEA1BE161AAABEDDA11D5&gwt=pay.
53. Merrit Kennedy, "In Somalia's Presidential Election, A Surprise Victor Declared," *National Public Radio*, February 8, 2017, https://www.npr.org/sections/thetwo-way/2017/02/08/514089778/in-somalias-historic-presidential-election-a-surprise-victor-declared.
54. James Butty "New Somali Prime Minister's "Experience" Praised by Analyst," *Voice of America*, October 14, 2010, https://www.voanews.com/a/butty-somalia-new-pm-analysis-aligas-15october10-105009799/156109.html.
55. J. Peter Pham, "Somalia's Continuing Crisis Worsens with UAE Dispute," *AfricaSource*, April 23, 2018, https://www.atlanticcouncil.org/blogs/africasource/somalia-s-continuing-crisis-worsens-with-uae-dispute; Will Toddman, "The Gulf Scramble for Africa: GCC States' Foreign Policy Laboratory," *Center for Strategic and International Studies*, November 2018, https://csis-prod.s3.amazonaws.com/s3fs-public/publication/181120_Todman_Africa_layout_v3_0.pdf?x-gtwB2_gU7.SS8Z2zPX7DXb_5kw.gmoc.
56. See J. Peter Pham, "Somalia: Insurgency and Legitimacy in the Context of State Collapse," in David Richards and Greg Mills, eds., *Victory Among People: Lessons from Countering Insurgency and Stabilising Fragile States* (London: RUSI, 2011), 277-294.
57. Mohammed Ibrahim, "Moderate Elected President in Somalia," *New York Times,* January 30, 2009, http://www.nytimes.com/2009/01/31/world/africa/31somalia.html?_r=0
58. Gabe Joselow, "Somalia Elects New President," *Voice of America,* September 10, 2012, https://www.voanews.com/africa/somalia-elects-new-president.
59. Iqbal Jhazbhay, "Islam And Stability in Somaliland and the Geo-politics Of the War on Terror," *Journal of Muslim Minority Affairs* 28, no. 2 (2008), 198.
60. Abdiqani Hassan, "Somaliland Picks Ruling Party's Candidate as New President," Reuters, November 21, 2017, https://www.reuters.com/article/us-somaliland-election/somaliland-picks-ruling-partys-candidate-as-new-president-idUSKBN1DL1UH?il=0.
61. Andrew McGregor, "Somaliland Charges Al-Shabaab Extremists

with Suicide Bombings," Jamestown Foundation *Terrorism Monitor* 6, no. 23 (December 8, 2008), 7-9.

62. Yara Bayoumy, "Somalia's al Shabaab, squeezed in south, move to Puntland," Reuters, November 9, 2012, http://www.reuters.com/article/2012/11/09/somalia-puntland-shabaab-idUSL5E8M96UZ20121109.
63. Abdisamad Mooge, "Somaliland: Real terrorism threats in fictional State," *Horseed Media*, February 25, 2013, http://horseedmedia.net/2013/02/25/somaliland-real-terrorism-threats-in-fictional-state/.
64. J. Peter Pham, "The Somaliland Exception: Lessons on Postconflict State Building from the Part of the Former Somalia That Works," *Marine Corps University Journal* 3, no. 1 (2012), 27-28.
65. Mooge, "Somaliland: Real terrorism threats in fictional State."
66. Mohamed Ahmed, "Somali Rebels Agree to Ransom Deal with Pirate Leaders," Reuters, February 22, 2011, http://af.reuters.com/article/worldNews/idAFTRE71L1GO20110222.
67. Lauren Ploch et al., "Piracy off the Horn of Africa," Congressional Research Service, April 27, 2011, 16-17, http://fpc.state.gov/documents/organization/162745.pdf.

32 Tanzania

Quick Facts

Population: 58,552,845 (July 2020 est.)
Area: 947,300 sq km
Ethnic Groups: Mainland - African 99% (of which 95% are Bantu consisting of more than 130 tribes), other 1% (consisting of Asian, European, and Arab); Zanzibar - Arab, African, mixed Arab and African
Government Type: Presidential republic
GDP (official exchange rate): $51.76 billion (2017 est.)

Source: CIA World FactBook (Last Updated June 2020)

Introduction

The level of Islamist activity in Tanzania is currently low, especially as compared to regional neighbors Egypt, Somalia, Sudan, and Kenya. However, a number of factors—including the country's ongoing slide toward authoritarianism—have spurred some Muslims in Tanzania to adhere to Islamism as an ideological alternative.[1] *The character of Tanzania's internal politics as a one-party-dominated political system and historic grievances by the country's Muslim Zanzibari population further strain inter-religious relations and threaten to politicize what has historically been a localized (and moderate) practice of Islam. So, too, does a tendency by the central government on the use of unnecessary force and brutality in response to suspected incidents in Muslim communities.*

Tanzania's proximity to Somalia, inside of which both al-Qaeda and ISIS currently vie for influence, remains a risk factor, as does the emergence of Islamic militancy in nearby Mozambique. Similarly, the presence of foreign-funded mosques and universities within the country has increased in recent years. Tanzanian Muslims thus today experience competing forms of Islam, and more radical strains are becoming increasingly attractive as avenues for legitimate political expression continue to shrink.

Endnotes

1. Harvey Glickman, "The Threat of Islamism in Sub-Saharan Africa: The Case of Tanzania," Foreign Policy Research Institute *E-Notes,* April 2011, https://www.fpri.org/docs/media/201104.glickman.islamismsubsaha- ranafrica.pdf; "Baseline Evaluation of Katika Usalama Tunategemeana and Pamoja! Strengthening Community Resilience in Tanzania," Search for Common Ground, April 6, 2017, https://www.sfcg.org/wp-content/uploads/2017/07/Baseline-Report.Final_.Public.pdf, 16-19

Due to publishing constraints, this chapter is provided here only in summary form. To view the full study, please visit the online edition of the Almanac at almanac.afpc.org.

Europe

33 Albania

Quick Facts

Population: 3,074,579 (July 2020 est.)
Area: 28,748 sq km
Ethnic Groups: Albanian 82.6%, Greek 0.9%, other 1% (including Vlach, Romani, Macedonian, Montenegrin, and Egyptian), unspecified 15.5% (2011 est.)
Government Type: Parliamentary republic
GDP (official exchange rate): $13.07 billion (2017 est.)

Source: CIA World FactBook (Last Updated September 2020)

Introduction

Islamist trends in Albania parallel similar developments in other Balkan countries. These states share several important characteristics: a lack of employment and educational opportunities, especially for young people; indigenous Muslim populations; a transition from former autocratic socialist or communist governments, and; the entrenched presence of foreign Islamist forces attempting to educate local Muslims, build mosques, provide public services, make investments, and otherwise build influence. And, as in neighboring Kosovo, the attempts of the Vatican to bolster Catholicism in Albania have angered parts of the country's Muslim population.

While Albanians of all faiths have historically co-existed peacefully, the participation of Albanian fighters in ISIS—and subsequent foiled terrorist plots within Albania itself—indicate that Islamic radicalism has become an important future security challenge for the country. The foundations for radicalism were laid in the early 1990s, when foreign Islamic states and organizations sought to gain influence in a country then just emerging from 45 years of Communist dictatorship. While Islamism has never found mass appeal, Albania has always been a place of interest for both terrorist groups and those hunting them—as demonstrated by CIA operations targeting terrorist cells in the country beginning in August 1998.

The number of people leaving Albania to join ISIS and the al-Nusra Front over the past two years declined significantly in tandem with the strategic reversals experienced by both groups. However, as with other regional countries experiencing the same phenomenon, Albania's success in stemming the departure of foreign fighters has been offset by new problems. These include the need to deradicalize returning fighters or foil terrorist plots organized from the Middle East or Western European diasporas —the most high-profile of which, at least so far, was a failed plot to attack the Israeli soccer team in a match played in Albania in November 2016.[1]

In response to the challenges posed by growing radicalism, the Obama administration created a NATO Center of Excellence devoted to countering radicalization in what was then the Alliance's newest member state. As of this writing, the center has not yet become fully operational.[2] *However, then-U.S. Defense Secretary James Mattis complimented Albania in 2018 for "punching above its weight" as a NATO member, participating in anti-terrorism missions in Afghanistan, and being the first state to provide arms to the Trump administration's anti-ISIS coalition.*[3] *As with other regional nations, Albania's security cooperation against terrorism has been (and will be) conducted in cooperation the U.S., EU, and regional security partners.*

Endnotes

1. Lizzie Dearden, "Isis attack on Israeli football team foiled by police at World Cup qualifier in Albania," *Independent* (London), November 17, 2016, https://www.independent.co.uk/news/world/europe/isis-attack-israeli-israel-football-team-police-kosovo-terror-simultaneous-a7422696.html.
2. North Atlantic Treaty Organization, "Centres of Excellence," Last Updated January 24, 2019, https://www.nato.int/cps/en/natohq/topics_68372.htm; Fatjona Mejdini, "Albania to Host NATO Centre on Foreign Fighters," *Balkan Insight*, June 23, 2016, https://balkaninsight.com/2016/06/23/albania-will-host-nato-center-on-foreign-terrorist-fighters-06-23-2016/; "NATO sets up center in Albania to

counter radicalism," Associated Press, May 13, 2016, https://apnews.com/08f402bbe6134982a85348cfb93aa8bb.

3. U.S. Department of Defense, "Remarks by Secretary Mattis at an Enhanced Honor Cordon Welcoming Albania Defense Minister Olta Xhaçka to the Pentagon," April 17, 2018, https://dod.defense.gov/News/Transcripts/Transcript-View/Article/1496102/remarks-by-secretary-mattis-at-an-enhanced-honor-cordon-welcoming-albania-defen/.

Due to publishing constraints, this chapter is provided here only in summary form. To view the full study, please visit the online edition of the Almanac at almanac.afpc.org.

34 Denmark

Quick Facts

Population:5,869,410 (July 2020 est.)
Area: 43,094 sq km
Ethnic Groups: Danish (includes Greenlandic (who are predominantly Inuit) and Faroese) 86.3%, Turkish 1.1%, other 12.6% (largest groups are Polish, Syrian, German, Iraqi, and Romanian) (2018 est.)
Government Type: Parliamentary constitutional monarchy
GDP (official exchange rate): $325.6 billion (2017 est.)

Source: CIA World FactBook (Last Updated August 2020)

Introduction

The history of militant Islamism in Denmark dates back to the 1990s, when veterans of the Afghan jihad against the Soviet Union were granted political asylum in the country. Today, violent Islamists are few in number and vastly outnumbered by non-violent Islamist groups. Nevertheless, a majority of political parties in the Danish Parliament regard Islam and Muslims with suspicion.

Due to publishing constraints, this chapter is provided here only in summary form. To view the full study, please visit the online edition of the Almanac at almanac.afpc.org.

35 France

Quick Facts

Population: 67,848,156 (July 2020 est.)
Area: 643,801 sq km; 551,500 sq km (metropolitan France)
Ethnic Groups: Celtic and Latin with Teutonic, Slavic, North African, Indochinese, Basque minorities
GDP (official exchange rate): $2.588 trillion (2017 est.)

Source: CIA World FactBook (Last Updated August 2020)

Introduction

Muslims remain a distinct minority in France, accounting for less than 10 percent of the overall national population. However, French Muslims are significantly represented among the country's young – and politically active – cohort. While the state has created several institutions with the (at least declared) intention to invest in and engage with the Muslim community, issues surrounding inclusiveness, economic opportunity, and public dress have nonetheless fostered societal tension. This has contributed to the radicalization of a small minority of French Muslims, with the result that in recent years France has ranked as one of the most significant sources of the Islamic State's foreign fighters.

Domestically, several notable terrorist attacks, including the Charlie Hebdo shooting and Bastille Day truck massacre, have claimed over 250 lives since 2015, and in the process accentuated and accelerated a national conversation about the Islamic faith.[1] *Over the years, the Conseil Français du Culte Musulman (French Council of the Muslim Faith, or CFCM), which France created to represent the Muslim community, has experienced internal divisions among the constituent organizations that represent the many subgroups of France's Muslim population. As France cracks down on Islamic extremism and continues to debate the wearing of traditional Islamic clothing in public, communication and consensus with the Muslim community have emerged as critical elements of public policy. Insufficient official engagement by French authorities with the country's Muslims, however, have to date generated feelings of exclusion among that cohort and contributed to large scale protests and even riots.*

Endnotes

1. "France: Extremism & Counter-Extremism," Counter Extremism Project, n.d., https://www.counterextremism.com/countries/france

Due to publishing constraints, this chapter is provided here only in summary form. To view the full study, please visit the online edition of the Almanac at almanac.afpc.org.

36 Germany

Quick Facts

Population: 80,159,662 (July 2020 est.)
Area: 357,022 sq km
Ethnic Groups: German 87.2%, Turkish 1.8%, Polish 1%, Syrian 1%, other 9% (2017 est.)
Government Type: Federal parliamentary republic
GDP (official exchange rate): $3.701 trillion (2017 est.)

Map and Quick Facts courtesy of the CIA World Factbook (Last Updated September 2020)

Introduction

Germany, alongside France, has the highest number of Muslim citizens in Western Europe or among European Union member states. It is also a hotbed of Islamist activity. Most notably, the 9/11 attacks were organized in part in Germany by the Hamburg cell headed by Mohammed Atta.[1]

Islamism in Germany has deep roots stretching back to a symbiosis between the German state and radical religious elements during the First World War. However, in more recent years, the relationship between the two has been significantly more adversarial. Nonetheless, Islamism and jihadism are prevalent in today's Germany, with the first jihadist attack of note in Germany taking place less than half-a-decade ago, in December 2016.

Endnotes

1. *The 9/11 Commission Report: Final Report of the National Commission on Terrorist Attacks Upon the United States* (New York: WW Norton & Co., 2004).

Due to publishing constraints, this chapter is provided here only in summary form. To view the full study, please visit the online edition of the Almanac at almanac.afpc.org.

37 Italy

Quick Facts

Population: 62,402,659 (July 2020 est.)
Area: 301,340 sq km
Ethnic Groups: Italian (includes small clusters of German-, French-, and Slovene-Italians in the north and Albanian-Italians and Greek-Italians in the south)
Government Type: Parliamentary republic
GDP (official exchange rate): $1.939 trillion (2017 est.)

Source: CIA World FactBook (Last Updated June 2020)

Introduction

While Italy has experienced a surge in Muslim immigration over the past several years as a result of the Syrian civil war and a parallel wave of African migration, Islam - both radical and moderate – was already a significant presence in the country beforehand. The Union of Islamic Communities and Organizations of Italy (UCOII) has been at the forefront of the debate for the representation of the highly fragmented Italian Muslim community. Italy remained primarily a logistical base for jihadist *activities until 2009, when an attempted bombing by a Libyan radical in Milan shattered the popular belief that the country was safe from extremist attacks. The event sparked significant public debate and the Italian government has begun to strengthen anti-terrorism and surveillance laws in an effort to respond more effectively to radical Islamism.*

Due to publishing constraints, this chapter is provided here only in summary form. To view the full study, please visit the online edition of the Almanac at almanac.afpc.org.

38 Kosovo

Quick Facts

Population: 1,932,774 (July 2020 est.)
Area: 10,887 sq km
Ethnic Groups: Albanians 92.9%, Bosniaks 1.6%, Serbs 1.5%, Turk 1.1%, Ashkali 0.9%, Egyptian 0.7%, Gorani 0.6%, Romani 0.5%, other/unspecified 0.2% (2011 est.)
Government Type: Parliamentary republic
GDP (official exchange rate): $7.094 billion (2017 est.)

Source: CIA World FactBook (Last Updated June 2020)

Introduction

Islam's footprint in Kosovo dates back to the time of the Ottoman conquest. Although much of the ethnic Albanian-majority population practices a moderate form of Islam, the slow pace of social, political, and economic development since the 1999 NATO intervention has created fertile soil for Islamic radicalization. The post-intervention period (even after national independence in 2008) has seen amorphous and unaccountable UN and EU missions linger, with wide authority and influence. Kosovo Force (KFOR), a smaller NATO detachment led by the United States, also remains, though it has handed over most security duties to local governments.

While most Kosovars are still moderate, the highest number of foreign fighters per capita among European countries joining ISIS and al-Nusra Front have historically hailed from Kosovo.[1] *While numbers dropped sharply with ISIS' territorial defeat in 2018, homegrown terrorists continued to be arrested in Kosovo throughout that year. As such, the issue of countering violent extremism (CVE) and the potential for attacks by returning fighters are prominent concerns for the government and its Western backers today. While the Kosovar government has tended to downplay the threat, it continues to deal with radicalization, passing laws against foreign fighters and arresting terrorists with the help of European governments and Europol.*

In the long term, the development of education, health and work opportunities for local youth probably represents the greatest challenge Kosovo faces in countering violent extremism. However, throughout 2018, authorities admitted to media that chosen CVE strategies have not had the desired effect, and that re-orienting Islamic radicals has proven more difficult than expected. At the same time, ethnic linkages between Kosovars at home and those in Western European countries have resulted (and will result) in police actions elsewhere on the Continent against Kosovo-related terror cells linked to ISIS.

Endnotes

1. Joanna Paraszczuk, "Report Finds Alarming Outflow Of Kosovars To Islamic State," *Radio Free Europe/Radio Liberty*, April 15, 2015, http://www.rferl.org/content/islamic-state-kosovars-fighting-syria-iraq/26957463.html.

Due to publishing constraints, this chapter is provided here only in summary form. To view the full study, please visit the online edition of the Almanac at almanac.afpc.org.

39 The Netherlands

QUICK FACTS

Population: 17,280,397 (July 2020 est.)
Area: 89,342 sq km
Ethnic Groups: Dutch 76.9%, EU 6.4%, Turkish 2.4%, Moroccan 2.3%, Indonesian 2.1%, German 2.1%, Surinamese 2%, Polish 1%, other 4.8% (2018 est.)
Government Type: Parliamentary constitutional monarchy
GDP (official exchange rate): $832.2 billion (2017 est.)

Source: CIA World FactBook (Last Updated November 2020)

INTRODUCTION

Historically, the Netherlands has been renowned for its religious tolerance. In the Golden Age of the 17th and 18th centuries, the Republic of the United Provinces served as a haven for Jews and Protestants fleeing persecution in other parts of Europe. Muslim immigrants joined their ranks in the late 19th century. Decades later, as it sought cheap labor during the 1960s, the Dutch government encouraged immigration from Indonesia and Suriname, both Muslim-majority countries and former Dutch colonies. Such days, however, have long since passed; ideological conflicts abroad now serve as magnets for aspiring Dutch jihadists, while xenophobia, the refugee crisis of recent years, and the looming threat of Islamic terrorism have driven the adoption of increasingly restrictive immigration and asylum policies. Despite Dutch efforts to proactively counter radicalization and encourage integration, this social transformation has allowed Islamists to push the political envelope, exposing a values gap between the Dutch majority and its immigrant Muslim population and fomenting an ominous trend of polarization.

Due to publishing constraints, this chapter is provided here only in summary form. To view the full study, please visit the online edition of the Almanac at almanac.afpc.org.

40 North Macedonia

Quick Facts

Population: 2,125,971 (July 2020 est.)
Area: 25,713 sq km
Ethnic Groups: Macedonian 64.2%, Albanian 25.2%, Turkish 3.9%, Romani 2.7%, Serb 1.8%, other 2.2% (2002 est.)
Government Type: Parliamentary republic
GDP (official exchange rate): $11.37 billion (2017 est.)

Source: CIA World FactBook (Last Updated September 2020)

Introduction

Ethnically- and religiously-divided North Macedonia has seen significant turbulence since its 2015 political crisis, which was followed by the larger European migration crisis. North Macedonia has been affected by this latter trend, serving as a transit corridor for international migrants between Greece and Serbia, and the attendant threat of terrorists posing as migrants has been noted by government officials as a result. Yet even before these crises, security risks involving Islamism existed in North Macedonia, which has cooperated with U.S. counterterrorism efforts and joined the Global Coalition to Defeat ISIS.[1] According to the U.S. State Department's most recent Country Reports on Terrorism, Roughly 150 ethnic North Macedonians volunteered to join the al-Nusra Front and ISIS in Syria and Iraq.[2] In response to this trend, the North Macedonian government in September 2014 passed a "foreign fighters law," which criminalized participation in foreign terrorist groups among North Macedonian nationals. Subsequently, several alleged terrorist recruiters and fighters were arrested by local police as part of a large-scale law enforcement operation dubbed "Operation Cell." Then, in February 2018, a new government introduced an ambitious strategy for countering extremism and terrorism.[3] Evidence indicates that this approach has been effective.[4]

Some critics (such as officials in neighboring Kosovo) claim that the country's imams have been instrumental in preaching a radical agenda that has helped to indoctrinate fighters.[5] *Several radical imams have been arrested as a result, and the country's official Islamic Community has admitted that certain mosques operate outside of its control.*

The West's support for North Macedonian anti-terrorism efforts picked up following the creation of a new government in 2017, which controversially agreed to change the country's former name and constitution to please Greece in the so-called Prespa Agreement of June 2018. While supporters of the agreement hoped that Greece would thus drop its veto of North Macedonian NATO and EU membership, some Greek politicians vowed to never ratify the deal. Indeed, the Prespa Agreement was opposed by a majority of both Greeks and North Macedonians. Nevertheless (and despite a referendum in September 2018), North Macedonian leaders vowed to press ahead with unpopular constitutional changes. The political development has important implications for national cohesion and radicalism in the country, since fears have swirled for years that ethnic Albanian Muslims, who have no allegiance to the North Macedonian name or identity, could demand autonomy. Given the religious affiliation of this demographic, Islamism has always lurked in the background, even during amicable day-to-day relations between North Macedonia's different ethnic and religious groups.

Endnotes

1. "82 Partners United in Ensuring Daesh's Enduring Defeat," The Global Coalition, n.d., https://theglobalcoalition.org/en/partners/
2. U.S. State Department, "North Macedonia," *Country Reports on Terrorism 2019*, 2020, https://www.state.gov/reports/country-reports-on-terrorism-2019/north-macedonia/; United States Department of State, "Macedonia," in *Country Reports on Terrorism 2017*, 2018, https://www.refworld.org/docid/5bcf1f9620.html.
3. Government of the Republic of Macedonia, National Committee for Countering Violent Extremism and Countering Terrorism, "National Counterterrorism Strategy of the Republic of Macedonia (2018-2022)," February 2018, https://wb-iisg.com/wp-content/uploads/bp-attachments/6135/ct_national_strategy_eng_translation_sbu.pdf
4. U.S. Department of State, "North Macedonia," in *Country Reports*

on Terrorism 2019, 2020, https://www.state.gov/reports/country-reports-on-terrorism-2019/north-macedonia/

5. This consensus is based on comments to the author made by several senior Kosovo officials since 2015.

Due to publishing constraints, this chapter is provided here only in summary form. To view the full study, please visit the online edition of the Almanac at almanac.afpc.org.

41 Spain

Quick Facts

Population: 50,015,792 (July 2020 est.)
Area: 505,370 sq km
Ethnic Groups: Spanish 86.4%, Morocco 1.8%, Romania 1.3%, other 10.5% (2018 est.)
Government Type: Parliamentary constitutional monarchy
GDP (official exchange rate): $1.314 trillion (2017 est.)

Source: CIA World FactBook (Last Updated June 2020)

Introduction

Spain's location as the gateway of the Mediterranean has long rendered it a prime destination for Muslim immigrants from North Africa and the Middle East, but a small number of radical elements view the country with more nefarious objectives. To many would-be jihadists, al-Andalus – the territory of the Iberian Peninsula lost by Islam in the fifteenth century – is not simply an abstract cause, but rather a concrete objective.[1] After al-Qaeda-inspired militants first struck Spain in the Madrid train bombing of March 11, 2004, the country experienced a lull of more than ten years without a major terrorist attack. However, that fragile sense of security was shattered in August of 2017, when another group of militants staged a car attack in Barcelona and a subsequent attack days later in nearby Cambrils. In the wake of these attacks, the Spanish government has been forced to double down on its efforts to counter terrorism and radicalization, while Spanish society has been forced to manage impulses of isolationism and xenophobia.

Endnotes

1. In a post-9/11 broadcast, al-Qaeda leader Ayman al-Zawahiri termed the loss of Andalusia a "tragedy." For more, see Rafael L. Bardaji and Ignacio Cosidó, "Spain: from 9/11 to 3/11 and Beyond," in Gary J. Schmitt, ed., *Safety, Liberty, and Islamist Terrorism: American and*

European Approaches to Domestic Counterterrorism (Washington, DC: AEI Press, 2010).

Due to publishing constraints, this chapter is provided here only in summary form. To view the full study, please visit the online edition of the Almanac at almanac.afpc.org.

Eurasia

42 Azerbaijan

Quick Facts

Population: 10,205,810 (July 2020 est.)
Area: 86,600 sq km
Ethnic Groups: Azerbaijani 91.6%, Lezghin 2%, Russian 1.3%, Armenian 1.3%, Talysh 1.3%, other 2.4% (2009 est.)
Government Type: Presidential republic
GDP (official exchange rate): $40.67 billion (2017 est.)

Source: CIA World FactBook (Last Updated October 2020)

Introduction

Bordering both Russia and Iran, and with a close security relationship with both the United States and Israel, Azerbaijan occupies an important geostrategic position. As the former Soviet Union's only Shi'a Muslim majority country, the South Caucasus republic is even more unique. Azerbaijan's geographic location has led to a situation in which various domestic and international forces vie for influence; it has a population of over 9 million people, the majority of whom are closely linguistically and culturally related to the population of nearby Turkey, an extremely antagonistic relationship with neighboring Armenia, and proximity to restive Dagestan, a federal republic of Russia.

Since becoming an independent state in 1991, Azerbaijan has seen an upsurge in Islamist activity emanating from both Sunni and Shi'a organizations. Iranian-backed Shiite extremists have attempted attacks on targets deemed to be close to the U.S. and Israel, and Sunni jihadists have descended from hotbeds of radicalism in the North Caucasus. In addition, terrorist groups have attempted to exploit organized crime networks and smuggling routes to support their endeavors in the Middle East. The government of Azerbaijan, in its efforts to address the threats emanating from both Sunni and Shi'a radicals, has doubled down on secular governance.

ISLAMIST ACTIVITY

Like many of the post-Soviet states with Muslim populations, Azerbaijan saw a rekindled interest in Islam following its independence in 1991. With an end to state-enforced atheism, the stage was set for domestic and foreign actors to vie for spiritual access to the country's predominantly Muslim community. That community is estimated to be two-thirds Shi'a and one third Sunni.[1] This ratio nevertheless is in flux, given the growing role of various Sunni movements—with Shafi'i and Salafi missionaries coming from the Arab world, and Hanafi activists emanating from Turkey.[2]

Shi'a Radicalism and the role of Iran and Hezbollah

Azerbaijan is situated at the vital geostrategic nexus of Iran, Russia and Turkey. The oil- and gas-rich country shares historical, linguistic and economic ties with all three of these regional powers. Azerbaijan has close ties to both the U.S. and Israel, relationships neighboring Iran regards with deep suspicion. Furthermore, a quarter of the Iranian population (including Supreme Leader Ayatollah Ali Khamenei himself) is ethnically Azerbaijani. Azerbaijan, either by specific actions or simply through its very existence, has considerable potential to spark anti-Iranian ethnic nationalism in Iran's volatile northeastern provinces.[3] In an effort to counteract the threat emanating from Azerbaijani nationalist movements, Tehran has sought to promote religious movements in Azerbaijan and empower Shiite clergy to oppose the Azerbaijani state. The nationalist and autonomist ambitions within Iran's Azerbaijani minority are a sensitive issue – one which to date has not received the attention it deserves. The Azerbaijani government has on several occasions alluded to efforts by Tehran to undermine its authority by stirring up religious unrest at home. Officials in Baku alleged in 2002 that Iranian funding and support had contributed to major protests in the Baku suburbs. In mid-2002, then-President Heydar Aliyev made reference to "outside powers" which wished to turn Azerbaijan into an Islamic state, unquestionably a veiled reference to Iran.[4]

In 2006, Azerbaijani authorities foiled a major terror attack involving Iranian operatives and directed at Israeli and Western targets.[5] In the course of the investigation, 15 Azerbaijani citizens were found to have been trained by Iranian security forces. Follow-up investigations led to the prevention of a second attack in 2008 on the Israeli embassy. These plans appear to have been carried out by a secret cell operating on Azerbaijani soil, which had been mobilized by Tehran in collaboration with Hezbollah, in retaliation for the killing of Hezbollah military chief Imad Mughniyeh in Damascus. Prior to the attempted attack, Azerbaijani police apprehended two Hezbollah militants, while suspects of Lebanese, Iranian and Azerbaijani extraction fled across the border to Iran. During subsequent court trials in October 2009, evidence indicated that both Hezbollah and the Iranian Revolutionary Guard Corps were linked to plot against the Israeli embassy.[6]

Further conspiracies were uncovered in 2012, in the run-up to the Eurovision song contest, when several attempted attacks against perceived pro-Western and pro-Israeli targets were foiled. First, in January of that year, two men were arrested on charges of plotting to murder two teachers at a Jewish school in Baku. Then, in February 2012, another cell, allegedly trained by the Iranian secret service, came to the attention of Azerbaijani state security.[7] Soon afterward, 22 individuals were arrested on the grounds of planning attacks the embassies of the United States and Israel.

However, beginning in 2012, a rapprochement between Baku and Tehran led to a decrease of Iranian-linked subversive activity. The Obama administration's hostile attitude toward Azerbaijan and its parallel warming of relations with Iran led Tehran to decrease its pressure, and forced Baku to initiate its own outreach to Iran. Indeed, the Obama Administration strongly pushed for a Turkish-Armenian normalization process that ignored Azerbaijan's concerns over its unresolved conflict with Armenia. As Azerbaijan successfully contributed to halting that normalization process, relations between Washington and Baku soured considerably, with mutual public recriminations that risked undermining the strategic partnership between America and Azerbaijan. As a result, Baku sought to improve relations with other powers, including Iran. While Iranian representatives continued to put pressure on Baku over its close ties to Israel, the improvement of relations appeared to reduce state-sponsored Iranian Islamist activity.

By 2017, however, there were signs that the winds were shifting again. Azerbaijani authorities once more complained of increasingly hostile Iranian rhetoric toward the Azerbaijani government, targeted in particular at Azerbaijani pilgrims to holy sites in Iran.[8] This rise in Iranian activity mirrored a growing warmth in U.S.-Azerbaijan relations, as ties between the two countries have moved toward normalization under the Trump presidency, and as the Saudi-Iranian rivalry across the region has picked up speed.[9] Indeed, pro-Saudi news outlets have in recent years accorded increasing interest to Iranian activities in Azerbaijan.[10]

In particular, the curious case of the town of Nardaran continues to trouble Azerbaijani authorities. Only a dozen miles outside the capital, the town has been a hotbed of Shi'a radicalism since the mid-1990s, when it gave birth to the defunct Islamic Party of Azerbaijan. Nardaran has long been known for the presence of extremist Shi'a activists and as a hotbed of anti-state Islamism. Following the arrest of over a dozen Islamist activists, including Taleh Bagirov, the leader of the Muslim Unity Movement (MUM) of Azerbaijan, clashes erupted in November 2015 between security forces and local protestors that left seven dead.[11] Among these were two police officers and five alleged Shiite militants. The confrontations were followed by series of raids. Security forces surrounded Nardaran and cut off all roads into and out of the district, in order to sweep for weapons and literature, in an effort to head off alleged terrorist activities.

In 2017, the commemoration of Ashura (the death of Ali's son Hussain at Kerbala in 680 CE) saw the gathering of exceptionally large crowds in Baku. This was interpreted as a sign of the greater reach of Iranian propaganda in Azerbaijan, something the government had privately complained about for some time. In response, the government took steps to limit the participation of children in Ashura and other religious rites.[12]

The "Khawarij" and the Forest Brotherhood

Azerbaijan's radical Salafi Sunni community has historically revolved around populations in the country's north, bordering Dagestan, and the Abu Bakr Mosque of Baku, which has been seen as a hotbed of terrorist recruitment and violent extremism. While the majority of the congregation is not violent, several prominently connected terrorists, including former Guantanamo Bay inmate Polad Sabir Sirajov, had close ties to the community and served as vectors of radicalization.[13] These community members with extremist sympathies have broken with the leadership of the mosque, earning them the titles of Khawarij or "expelled ones."

These Khawarij believe they are justified in rebelling against the authority of religious leaders whom they view as having departed from a justified course of violence against civilians. One prominent example of such leadership is Gamat Suleymanov, the *imam* of the Abu Bakr Mosque, who has made statements against the use of violence against "infidels." Suleymanov was injured in a grenade attack on his congregation in 2008, an incident which killed two and left a further 17 people injured.[14] The attack was likely carried out by the Khawarij, who did not take kindly to the *imam*'s conciliatory attitude. Following an investigation of the attack, the Azerbaijani government made a statement in which two Azerbaijani nationals, Ilgar Mollachiyev and his brother-in-law Samir Mehtiyev, both with ties to Sunni radicals in the nearby Dagestan Republic of Russia, were named as suspects.

Both Mollachiyev and Mehtiyev were alleged to have illegally entered Azerbaijan from Dagestan and been involved with setting up the foundations for terrorist cells in Baku and the coastal town of Sumgait. Baku accused the pair of attempting to reestablish the Azerbaijani branch of the "Forest Brothers," a militant group active in the Northern Caucasus that Azerbaijan banned in 2007. Mollachiyev and Mehtiyev were charged with creating an illegal armed group.[15]

Insurgency in Dagestan and the Northern Caucasus

Against the backdrop of the ongoing insurgency in the North Caucasus, which to date has claimed hundreds of lives among both civilians and combatants, Azerbaijan's government has in recent years increased law enforcement efforts along the country's northern border.[16] In the wake of the collapse of the Soviet system, the North Caucasus became the scene of high levels of violence between Russian security forces and various opposition factions. Over time, resistance to Russian rule took an increasingly Islamist turn, with *jihadi* extremists coming to form the bulk of the resistance.[17] While Chechnya has become the focal point of this conflict in the imagination of many observers, the violence has not been confined to that unhappy republic, and spread throughout the region. Dagestan became a major center of unrest, playing host to the majority of clashes for several years.[18] From 2012 onward, however, the exodus of fighters to the Syrian conflict led to a relative reduction of violence across the North Caucasus. As of yet, however, the apparent destruction of the Islamic State terrorist group in Syria does not appear to have led to the return of these militants in significant numbers.

Located at the eastern end of the North Caucasus, the Republic of Dagestan shares a long border with Azerbaijan. The patchwork of ethnic groups that made up the former Soviet Union means that both states share ethnic minority communities, including Avars and Lezgins. Members of both these ethnic minority communities with Azerbaijani citizenship have crossed the Azerbaijani-Russian border to partake in the ongoing Islamist insurgency in the North Caucasus.[19] While the grievances of these groups are primarily directed against Moscow, the rise of Islamic radicalism in the North Caucasus has made extremist groups in the region part of the global *jihadi* movement, and as of 2014 an estimated 1,000 of its members had already traveled to fight in Syria.[20]

This has led to a far more significant and dangerous flow of people and *jihadi* ideology southward into Azerbaijan. Salafist ideological streams, funded in part by Islamic organizations in the Gulf States, began entering Azerbaijan from the North Caucasus in the 1990s.[21] Conflict on Russian soil has also repeatedly led to an influx of Chechen and Dagestani fighters, seeking refuge and the opportunity to regroup in Azerbaijan. Most of those crossing into Azerbaijan from the North Caucasus are adherents of Salafism, and this fact, combined with the efforts of missionary establishments funded by the oil rich Arab Gulf States, has led to a situation in which there is a significant Salafist population in Azerbaijan—estimated as of 2015 to number about 15,000.[22] In the capital, Baku, their focal point has been the Abubakr Mosque.

Though a majority of Salafists are not violent extremists but followers of the purist, nonviolent Salafi approach—such as the avowedly apolitical Imam Suleymanov—the potential for violence should not be underestimated. Much of Salafist thought is anchored in the belief that the Muslim community can and should be central to the structuring of government. Additionally, it rejects the tenets of multiculturalism and religious plurality. Considering the public priorities of Baku, that rejection sets its adherents on a collision course with state institutions.[23]

The Gülen/Hizmet movement

Another example of an Islamist group which successfully established itself in post-independence Azerbaijan is the network of the influential, if increasingly controversial, Turkish cleric Fethullah Gülen. Like other missionizing Islamic movements, the Gülen movement saw the end of Soviet state atheism as an opportunity to gain support and followers in the newly independent, and nominally Muslim, states of the Caucasus and Central Asia. Based in Turkey, Gülen's followers were able to leverage linguistic and cultural similarities with the Turkic populations of the former Soviet Union to establish networks of educational institutions in the 1990s to cultivate the new state elites.[24] This, in turn, provided them with a stepping stone to becoming a truly global movement, which is well-represented and headquartered in the United States.

Azerbaijan became the first state outside of Turkey to host Gülen schools. Well-funded, and garnering support from then President Heydar Aliyev, the movement quickly established itself on the Azerbaijani education scene, opening several high schools, a private school, the Qafqaz University and a host of regional centers to promote its activities. Mindful not to antagonize the Azerbaijani government, the movement emphasized shared Turkic identity and cultural values over religious tenets.[25]

Despite this cautious approach, the Gülen movement has suffered significant setbacks in recent years. The Azerbaijani state has been increasingly focused on training its own population rather than having foreign groups do so. The collapse of the political alliance between Fethullah Gülen and Turkish President Recep Tayyip Erdoğan in 2014 further undermined the position of Gülen supporters abroad, with the Turkish government putting pressure on Baku to curb the activities of the movement in Azerbaijan. Following the July 2016 coup attempt in Turkey, which Ankara was quick to ascribe to the Gülenists, Turkish officials put enormous pressure on Baku to dismiss people in government who were believed to be too close to the movement.[26] Only a small number of officials were dismissed, but the Azerbaijani government began to curtail the influence of the Gülen movement, including taking control of the schools that the movement previously ran in the country.

Islamism and Society

The majority of Azerbaijan's population of 9.7 million inhabitants self-identify as Muslim, about two thirds of whom are Shiites.[27] Sunni Islam is most established in the northern and western regions of the country, especially among the ethnic minorities who live closest to the Northern Caucasus regions of Russia. However, it is gathering strength in the country at the expense of Shi'a traditions, something noted by observers and visible through the influence, not least, of Turkish schools and popular culture.[28] Azerbaijan's south and east, the areas closest to Iran, have historically been dominated by Shiite Islam, though decades of Soviet state atheism resulted in Azerbaijanis in Azerbaijan being generally less observant than their co-ethnics across the border. Under the nationalities policy of the early Soviet period, Azerbaijanis were encouraged to think of Shiism as a marker of national identity rather than a guiding principle of spiritual life.[29]

However, following the end of the official state atheism, numerous Azerbaijanis have found new ways to express their religion. A new generation, for whom the Soviet experience is but a vague memory, has taken an interest in public expressions of religiosity. At the same time, both Shiite Iran and the Sunni monarchies of the Gulf have sought to encourage the revival of Islamic faith in Azerbaijan, and mold the religious experience of Azerbaijan's youth in a way that favors their own objectives and priorities.

Efforts to promote radicalism have, however, run up on the government's increasingly outspoken secularism, which is firmly entrenched in public discourse despite the quarter century since the demise of the Soviet ideology. The prominence of Islam has prompted debates about the role religion should play in the modern Republic of Azerbaijan, and there remains a deep-seated mistrust of Islamism among the Azerbaijani elite.[30] In a situation analogous to that of other post-socialist states with large Muslim populations, radical Islamism in Azerbaijan is fed by the quest for identity in a rapidly changing society, social ills such as corruption, and disappointment over the unfulfilled promises of modernization. Perhaps ironically, Azerbaijan has been subject to criticism from western governments and NGOs for its treatment of Islamist organizations within the country that have developed radical objectives in their criticism of the state.

Available polling suggests Azerbaijan is among the Muslim-majority societies least penetrated by Islamist ideology. For example, in a 2013 Pew poll, Azerbaijan had the lowest percentage of any country expressing support for *sharia* law, at eight percent. It also had the lowest percentage of respondents saying suicide bombing is justified (one percent), that religious leaders should have large influence on politics (two percent), and that tensions between devout and less devout are a big problem (one percent).[31]

Islamism and the State

The major influx of Arab, Iranian and Turkish missionaries into Azerbaijan, tolerated at first in the early 1990s, increasingly became a concern for officials in Baku. Perhaps surprised by the rapidity and scope of these well-funded newcomers on the scene, the government opted for a more decisive course of action. In 1996, the Azerbaijani parliament passed an amendment to the Law on Freedom of Religious Belief which proscribed the participation of "foreigners" in the propagation of "religious propaganda."[32] After deadly riots in the Baku suburb of Nardaran left one person dead and 16 injured in 2002, these measures were expanded to bar anyone who had received religious training abroad.[33]

Further measures to curtail the recruitment efforts of radical Islamists included requiring religious communities to refile their state registration and establishing the State Committee for Work with Religious Associations, which increased state control of religious institutions.[34] The state's efforts to curb the spread of radical Islam are also part of a larger initiative to combat Islamic terrorism. Azerbaijan's counterterrorism policy has included close cooperation with regional as well as international actors, specifically the United States. Baku granted overflight rights and permission for numerous refueling and supply landings to Coalition forces during the military intervention in Afghanistan. Azerbaijani troops themselves took part in operations in Afghanistan, helping in international attempts to stabilize the security situation in Central and South Asia.[35] Azerbaijani officials have also supported international law enforcement through information sharing and joint policing operations.

Following the drawdown of coalition troops from Afghanistan and the rise to prominence of the Islamic State, Baku has turned its attention to the struggle to contain terrorism emanating from Iraq and Syria. Azerbaijan's leadership has contributed to these international efforts by disrupting the flow of arms and supplies through its territory, by sharing information, apprehending suspected returnee foreign fighters and having state religious authorities, such as the Caucasus Muslim Board, counter the claims of the propaganda savvy organization.

A significant number of legal amendments added every year between 2009 and 2015 have been squarely aimed at tackling the extremist threat and preventing further radicalization. Among these, an amendment to the criminal code ensured that the punishment for "foreign fighters" traveling to Syria became a 15 year-long jail sentence. Similarly, the penalty for spreading religious propaganda has been increased to one to two years in prison.[36] Amendments added in 2014-2015 prevented clerics educated abroad (with the exception of those educated in state-approved educational institutions) from working in Azerbaijan, while a 2014 amendment led the State Committee for Work with Religious Organizations to monopolize religious education for the conduct of rites. To fill the need for training clerics, the State Committee expanded its own role and conducted more than 30,000 trainings in 2015-16. However, the amendments were not applied retroactively, which means that any previous training that existing clerics may have received has not been invalidated. Whereas the official state estimate is that 1,800 individuals have already received religious education abroad, the real number is probably higher.[37]

Endnotes

1. United States Department of State, *Country Reports on Terrorism 2011* (Washington, DC: U.S. Department of State, July 2012), http://www.state.gov/j/ct/rls/crt/2011/195543.htm
2. Fuad Aliyev, "The Gülen Movement in Azerbaijan," *Current Trends in Islamist Ideology* 14, 2013, 90, http://www.currenttrends.org/docLib/20130124_CT14Aliev.pdf.
3. Ilan Berman, *Tehran Rising: Iran's Challenge to the United States* (Lanham, MD: Rowman & Littlefield Publishers, 2005), 94-95; Emil Souleimanov and Josef Kraus, "Iran's Azerbaijan Question in Evolution," Central Asia-Caucasus Institute *Silk Road Paper*, September 2017, http://silkroadstudies.org/publications/silkroad-papers-and-monographs/item/13252.
4. Berman, *Tehran Rising*, 94-95.
5. Sebastian Rotella, "Azerbaijan Seen as a New Front in Mideast Conflict," *Los Angeles Times*, May 30, 2009, http://articles.latimes.com/2009/may/30/world/fg-shadow30.
6. "Cell Sent By Hezbollah To Attack Israeli Embassy," *Yediot Ahrono*t (Tel Aviv), July 7, 2009, http://www.ynetnews.com/articles/0,7340,L-3743694,00.html.
7. "Four jailed in Azerbaijan for Eurovision terror plot," *Jerusalem Post*, December 3, 2012, http://www.jpost.com/International/Article.aspx?id=294463.
8. Farkhad Mamedov, "Iran Invades Azerbaijan by the Weapon of Pilgrims," haqqin.az, December 1, 2017, https://haqqin.az/news/117537
9. James M. Dorsey, "Saudi Arabia and Iran Battle it Out in Azerbaijan," *Daily Star*, February 19, 2018, http://www.thedailystar.net/opinion/global-affairs/saudi-arabia-and-iran-battle-it-out-azerbaijan-1536553
10. Eg. Huda Alhusseini, "Will Iran turn Azerbaijan into another Iraq?" *Al Arabiya*, January 26, 2018, http://english.alarabiya.net/en/views/news/middle-east/2018/01/26/Will-Iran-turn-Azerbaijan-into-another-Iraq-.html
11. Paul Goble, "'A Syrian Echo in Azerbaijan?', Shiites, Police Clash

in Nardaran," Jamestown Foundation *Eurasia Daily Monitor* 12, no. 14, December 1, 2015, https://jamestown.org/program/a-syrian-echo-in-azerbaijan-shiites-police-clash-in-nardaran/.

12. Zaur Shiriyev, "Azerbaijan Wrestles with Rising Iranian Influence," *Eurasianet*, December 27, 2017, https://eurasianet.org/s/azerbaijan-wrestles-with-rising-iranian-influence.
13. The U.S. Department of Defense's assessment is available online. See Department of Defense, Headquarters, Joint Task Force Guantanamo, "JTF-GTMO Detaine Assessment", January 25, 2008, https://assets.documentcloud.org/documents/82446/isn-89-poolad-t-tsiradzho-jtf-gtmo-detainee.pdf
14. Elmir Guliev, *Central Asia 2008 Analytical Annual* (Sweden: Institute for Central Asian, Caucasian Studies & Institute of Strategic Studies of the Caucasus, 2009), 95, http://www.ca-c.org/annual/2008-eng/14.shtml.
15. "Ilgar Mollachiyev and his brother-in-law Samir Mehdiyev committed explosion in Abu Bakr Mosque," apa.az, September 2, 2008, http://en.apa.az/print/87964.
16. Mairbek Vatchagaev, "Azerbaijani Jamaat Cooperates with Caucasus Emirate," Jamestown Foundation *Eurasia Daily Monitor* 9, iss. 73, April 12, 2012, http://www.jamestown.org/single/?no_cache=1&tx_ttnews%5Btt_news%5D=39262.
17. Svante E. Cornell, "The 'Afghanization' of the North Caucasus: Causes and Implications of a Changing Conflict," in Stephen Blank, ed., *Russia's Homegrown Insurgency* (Carlisle, PA: U.S. Army War College, 2012).
18. John O'Loughlin et.al., "The Changing Geography of Violence in Russia's North Caucasus, 1999–2011: Regional Trends and Local Dynamics in Dagestan, Ingushetia, and Kabardino-Balkaria," *Eurasian Geography and Economics* 52, no. 5, 2011, 596-630.
19. Emil Souleimanov, "Jihadism on the rise in Azerbaijan," Central Asia Caucasus Institute *CACI Analyst*, May 2, 2012, http://www.cacianalyst.org/?q=node/5766.
20. Emil A. Souleimanov, "Globalizing Jihad? North Caucasians in the Syrian Civil War," *Middle East Policy* 21, no. 3, 2014.
21. Svante E. Cornell, *Azerbaijan since Independence* (Armonk: M.E. Sharpe. 2011), 277-279; Sofie Bedford, "Islamic Activism in Azerbaijan: Repression and Mobilization in a Post-Soviet Context," Doctoral thesis before the Stockholm University Department of Political Science, 2009, 104, http://su.diva-portal.org/smash/record.jsf?pid=diva2:200259.

22. Anar Valiyev, "The Rise of Salafi Islam in Azerbaijan," Jamestown Foundation *Terrorism Monitor* 3, no. 13, July 1, 2015, https://jamestown.org/program/the-rise-of-salafi-islam-in-azerbaijan/
23. Emil Souleimanov and Maya Ehrmann, "The Rise of Militant Salafism in Azerbaijan and its Regional Implications," *Middle East Policy* 20, no. 3, Fall 2013, http://www.mepc.org/journal/middle-east-policy-archives/rise-militant-salafism-azerbaijan-and-its-regional-implications.
24. "The Gulen Movement in Azerbaijan & a quid pro quo?" *The Perimeter Primate*, January 14, 2013, http://perimeterprimate.blogspot.com/2013/01/the-gulen-movement-in-azerbaijan-quid.html.
25. Eldar Mamedov, "Azerbaijan: Evaluating Baku's Attitude toward the Gulen Movement," *Eurasianet*, February 16, 2012, http://www.eurasianet.org/node/65013.
26. Altay Göyüşov, "The Gulen movement in Azerbaijan and Erdogan's intervention," *MeydanTV*, August 02, 2016, https://www.meydan.tv/en/site/society/16428/.
27. Souleimanov and Ehrmann, "The Rise of Militant Salafism in Azerbaijan and its Regional Implications"; Cornell, *Azerbaijan Since Independence;* International Crisis Group, "Azerbaijan: Independent Islam and the State," *Europe Report* no. 191, March 2008.
28. Yavuz Kerimoğlu, "Azerbaycan: Toplum ve Siyaset," *insamer*, April 5, 2016, http://insamer.com/tr/azerbaycan-toplum-ve-siyaset_275.html.
29. Bedford, "Islamic Activism in Azerbaijan," 90-91.
30. Svante E. Cornell, Halil Karaveli and Boris Ajeganov, "Azerbaijan's Formula: Secular Governance and Civic Nationhood," Central Asia-Caucasus Institute & Silk Road Studies Program *Silk Road Paper*, November 2016.
31. Pew Research Center, "The World's Muslims: Religion, Politics and Society", April 30, 2013, https://www.pewforum.org/2013/04/30/the-worlds-muslims-religion-politics-society-overview/.
32. State Committee of the Azerbaijani Republic for the work with Religious Organizations, The Law of the Republic of Azerbaijan "On Freedom of Religious Belief," August 20, 1992 (Contains changes and additions of 1996 and 1997), http://www.dqdk.gov.az/eng/zakon_svoboda_e.html.
33. "В Азербайджане запретят мулл, обучавшихся за границей" Oxu.az, December 2, 2015, http://ru.oxu.az/society/104949.
34. Svante E. Cornell, "The Politicization of Islam in Azerbaijan," Central Asia-Caucasus Institute *Silk Road Paper*, October 2006, https://

www.silkroadstudies.org/resources/pdf/SilkRoadPapers/2006_10_SRP_Cornell_Islam-Azerbaijan.pdf.

35. Madeleine Z. Bordallo, "Afghanistan Withdrawal Logistics and Capability of Azerbaijan to Support U.S. Military Requirements," The Sunlight Foundation, August 2012, http://capitolwords.org/date/2012/08/01/E1380-3_afghanistan-withdrawal-logistics-and-capability-of/.
36. U.S. Department of State, *Country Reports on Terrorism 2015* (Washington, DC: United States Department of State, 2016), https://www.state.gov/j/ct/rls/crt/2015/257516.htm.
37. Cornell et. al., "Azerbaijan's Formula: Secular Governance and Civic Nationhood."

43 Kazakhstan

Quick Facts

Population: 19,091,949 (July 2020 est.)
Area: 2,724,900 sq km
Ethnic Groups: Kazakh (Qazaq) 68%, Russian 19.3%, Uzbek 3.2%, Ukrainian 1.5%, Uighur 1.5%, Tatar 1.1%, German 1%, other 4.4% (2019 est.)
GDP (official exchange rate): $159.4 billion (2017 est.)

Source: CIA World FactBook (Last Updated August 2020)

Introduction

The issue of violent extremism did not feature prominently for Kazakhstan in the early years following its independence from the USSR in 1991. While the country did experience episodes of violent upheaval before and during the collapse of the Soviet system, these were primarily motivated by ethno-nationalist tensions or economic grievances, not Islamic fundamentalism, and Kazakhstan was spared the effects of radicalization. Kazakh security officials were more concerned with the threat of separatism, viewing violent Islamic extremism as a phenomenon inherent to the country's smaller minority communities concerned with events largely external to the country. Thus, in September 2000, when two police officers were killed in a shooting in Almaty,[1] the attack was quickly attributed to Uyghur extremists whose motivation was ending Chinese rule in nearby Xinjiang and ushering in some form of Islamist government.

Following a wave of terrorist attacks in 2011, however, officials and the public at large became aware of the changing reality of the country.[2] The rise in attacks coincided with jihadist organizations beginning to use new media to promote violent rhetoric and ideology, as well as to groom and recruit new followers for their causes. In 2016, another series of deadly attacks raised fears of a further escalation of religiously motivated violence within the country.[3] Authorities reacted with stricter controls over religious institutions and harsher counterterrorism measures, a response reminiscent of the approach of neighboring states. Yet attacks have persisted, and growing economic disparity has fueled anger and disaffection within the country, especially among young people. Issues like the repatriation of returnees from Syria and Iraq, as well as widespread public anger over the counterterrorism policies of neighboring China, where an extensive incarceration program has swept up ethnic Kazakhs, have further complicated policy responses.

Endnotes

1. "Four Chinese killed in Kazakhstan," *BBC*, September 28, 2000, http://news.bbc.co.uk/2/hi/asia-pacific/946089.stm.
2. "Six Suspects Arrested For Terror Attacks In Kazakhstan," *Radio Free Europe/Radio Liberty*, November 30, 2011, https://www.rferl.org/a/six_suspects_arrested_for_terror_attacks_in_kazakhstan/24407405.html
3. Catherine Putz, "After Aktobe Attacks, Many Questions Remain," *The Diplomat*, June 10, 2016, https://thediplomat.com/2016/06/after-aktobe-attacks-many-questions-remain/

Due to publishing constraints, this chapter is provided here only in summary form. To view the full study, please visit the online edition of the Almanac at almanac.afpc.org.

44 Kyrgyzstan

Quick Facts

Population: 5,964,897 (July 2020 est.)
Area: 199,951 sq km
Ethnic Groups: Kyrgyz 73.5%, Uzbek 14.7%, Russian 5.5%, Dungan 1.1%, other 5.2% (includes Uyghur, Tajik, Turk, Kazakh, Tatar, Ukrainian, Korean, German) (2019 est.)
GDP (official exchange rate): $7.565 billion (2017 est.)

Source: CIA World FactBook (Last Updated August 2020)

Introduction

Nearly three decades on from its independence from the Soviet Union, Kyrgyzstan's Islamic revivalism continues to shape the political, economic, and social landscape of the country. After decades of Soviet atheism and repression, people seem keen to connect with their spiritual past. This re-emergence of Islam is strengthened by the support provided by Islamic missionaries, which include Tablighi missions in Bangladesh, Pakistan and India, apart from missionaries in Saudi Arabia, Iran, Egypt and Turkey.[1] Islamism was institutionalized by these groups through the establishment of mosques and the translation of the Koran into Kyrgyzstan's local languages. In turn, the proliferation of mosques and other religious organizations in Kyrgyzstan in recent years reflects the success of these efforts.[2]

Kyrgyzstan has a checkered history in dealing with orthodox Salafism, blurring the lines between faith and extremism. The popularity of radical movements like the Hizb-ut Tahrir (HuT) and Kateebat Tawhid wal Jihad (KTJ) has redefined the way in which Islam is viewed in the secular Kyrgyz Republic. The presence, as of 2019, of more than 800 Kyrgyz citizens in the Islamic State (IS) reflects a growing trend of intolerant religious indoctrination.[3]

Governmental control over religious organizations and practices stands in contrast to Kyrgyzstan's traditionally vibrant religious tradition, and has on occasion proven counterproductive and resulted in increasing hostility toward the state. However, the country remains vulnerable to the spread of radical and extremist ideology on account of several factors, include its geographical proximity to extremist hotspots such as Afghanistan, Xinjiang, and the Ferghana valley, the appeal of the Islamic State to young Kyrgyz, the weakness of the state itself, and an internal environment conducive to criminality that supports terror.

Endnotes

1. Elmurat Ashiraliev, "Kyrgyzstan Attempts to Isolate Local Islam," *The Diplomat*, August 28, 2019, https://thediplomat.com/2019/08/kyrgyzstan-attempts-to-isolate-local-islam/
2. "We Live in Constant Fear," Human Rights Watch, September 17, 2018, https://www.hrw.org/report/2018/09/17/we-live-constant-fear/possession-extremist-material-kyrgyzstan; "Kyrgyzstan: A Taste of Secularism in Religious Schools," *Institute for War and Peace Reporting,* July 23, 2019, https://iwpr.net/global-voices/kyrgyzstan-taste-secularism-religious-schools.
3. "Kyrgyzstan 2019 Crime & Safety Report," *OSAC,* June 27, 2019, https://www.osac.gov/Country/Kyrgyzstan/Content/Detail/Report/ac8fa4f9-e878-4c0c-b059-161f682cc4e1.

Due to publishing constraints, this chapter is provided here only in summary form. To view the full study, please visit the online edition of the Almanac at almanac.afpc.org.

45 Russia

Quick Facts

Population: 141,722,205 (July 2020 est.)
Area: 17,098,242 sq km
Ethnic Groups:Russian 77.7%, Tatar 3.7%, Ukrainian 1.4%, Bashkir 1.1%, Chuvash 1%, Chechen 1%, other 10.2%, unspecified 3.9% (2010 est.)
GDP (official exchange rate): $1.578 trillion (2017 est.)

Source: CIA World FactBook (Last Updated June 2020)

Introduction

According to the most recent Russian national census, Muslims represent Russia's second largest confessional group, numbering 20 to 21 million souls, or roughly 14 percent of the country's overall population of approximately 146 million.[1] *It is also a group in ideological and societal transition. Although Islamic institutions were largely destroyed and believers forced underground under Soviet rule, Islam has experienced a quick and vibrant, if still ill-defined, revival since the collapse of the USSR, with various ideological tendencies competing for the support of society and state. Among Russia's Muslims, the explosion of ethno-nationalism sparked by the USSR's implosion in the late 1980s and early 1990s has given way to religious identification and the rise of faith-based politics.*

Nevertheless, to date, only a small portion of Russia's Muslims has manifested Islamist tendencies, and just a fraction of those have been drawn into violence—either within Russia itself or abroad. However, Russia's ongoing involvement in the Syrian civil war, the rise of exclusionary, ultranationalist identity politics under the government of President Vladimir Putin, and expanding repression and discrimination on the part of the Kremlin have all contributed to disenfranchisement and radicalization among Russia's Muslims. The result is a dangerous distance between the Russian government and the country's Muslim minority—a dynamic that extreme Islamist organizations such as the Islamic State have sought to exploit.

Islamist Activity

The Caucasus Emirate

The primary Islamist terrorist group in Russia is known as the Caucasus Emirate (CE), or Imarat Kavkaz. Encompassing a network of terrorist cells spread across the North Caucasus, the organization is an outgrowth of the radicalization of the Chechen national separatist movement that took place in the 1990s and early 2000s.

The CE evolved from the Chechen separatist movement that emerged amid the Soviet collapse of the early 1990s. Before then, although some radical Islamic political elements existed within Chechen society—and the region's first president, Dzhokar Dudaev, did implement elements of *sharia* law—the Chechen movement was predominantly nationalist in character. This state of affairs persisted through the first Russo-Chechen war (1994-1996), but following the 1996 Khasavyurt peace agreement signed between Russian President Boris Yeltsin and Dudaev's successor, Aslan Maskhadov, the quasi-independent Chechen Republic of Ichkeria (ChRI) devolved into a state of permanent chaos, criminality, and civil strife. The resulting political vacuum was used by a small number of local Islamists, as well foreign extremist elements (including al-Qaeda), to establish a beachhead in the area.

As early as 1996, Ayman al-Zawahiri, then al-Qaeda's second-in-command, attempted to visit incognito and establish a presence in Russia, but he was discovered and deported.[2] In a subsequently published book, he targeted Russia for violent *jihad* and the establishment of an expansive southern Eurasian caliphate.[3] At about the same time, Shamil Basaev, then a Chechen field commander, visited Afghanistan and received training there.[4] Omar Abu Ibn al-Khattab, an al-Qaeda operative, was in Chechnya then as well and, amid the inter-war lawlessness, established camps where perhaps as many as several hundred foreign fighters, as well as local militants, trained in terrorist tactics.[5] These units subsequently spearheaded the August 1999 invasion of the neighboring republic of Dagestan, which was organized jointly by Basaev and Khattab and aimed at creating an Islamist enclave there. It was this offensive that set off the second Chechen war.[6]

As during the first Chechen war, Russia deployed a brutal military response, and by 2002 had defeated the militants in conventional war, driving the bulk of the ChRI government and parliament into foreign exile, with many finding refuge in places like Washington, London, Istanbul, Baku, the United Arab Emirates, and Qatar. The more dedicated extremist elements retreated into the mountain forests in southern Chechnya and neighboring Georgia, where they began a classic guerilla insurgency campaign punctuated by occasional large-scale attacks. With national separatist forces isolated abroad, Islamists gradually consolidated power over the movement throughout the following half-decade.

In the summer of 2002, following the death of Khattab at the hands of Russian security forces, an expanded emergency meeting of the underground remnants of the ChRI government and armed forces convened in the mountains of Chechnya. The meeting served as a *coup d'etat* of sorts; as a result of the gathering, a *sharia*-based order was adopted, with the goal of expanding the insurgency across the North Caucasus.[7] Thereafter, Basaev began to travel across the Caucasus seeking out young radicals and establishing a network of combat cells in Ingushetia, Dagestan, Kabardino-Balkaria, and Karachaevo-Cherkessia.[8] The results produced a series of terrorist incidents in subsequent years, including the October 2002 Dubrovka Theater hostage-taking, a rash of suicide attacks in Moscow in 2003,[9] and the September 2004 seizure of School No. 1 in Beslan in early September—a terrorist incident in which 333 people, including 186 children, were killed. Subsequently, between 2006 and 2010, terrorist activity in Russia saw a significant uptick, rising from just 3 major terrorist attacks in 2006 to 22 in 2010.[10]

This radical activism continued for the next several years. The CE has been responsible for scores of high-profile attacks on Russian targets in the North Caucasus and beyond in recent years, including the March 2010 attack on the Moscow subway, the December 2013 bombing of the train station in Volgograd, near the site of the 2014 Olympic Games, and a coordinated December 2014 assault on historic landmarks in Chechnya's capital of Grozny that left at least 20 dead.[11] While the pace of CE activity has waned significantly in recent years, Stanford University's Mapping Militant Organizations project still classifies CE as an active terrorist organization.[12]

Russian officials have been quick to attribute the decline in the number of terrorist attacks carried out by the CE and its affiliates in Russia to the Kremlin's robust counterterrorism policies.[13] However, this characterization is deeply misleading, because it discounts the extensive mobilization that has taken place among Russia's Islamist cadres since the Kremlin's military intervention into the Syrian civil war in September 2015. In 2015, one-quarter of all foreign fighters that had joined the Islamic State in Iraq and Syria were estimated to have come from the territory of the former Soviet Union,[14] and Russian ranked as the third most frequently spoken language among fighters of the Islamic State.[15] This robust representation continued; in a 2017 report, the Soufan Group estimated that more than 8,700 foreign fighters from the territory of the former Soviet Union had by then traveled to join the ranks of the Islamic State. An estimated 3,417 of those fighters were from Russia itself, predominantly the North Caucasus region.[16] Rather than combatting this outflow of militants, however, Russian authorities did the opposite, with government agencies essentially facilitating the departure of terrorists as a way of "externalizing" the country's religious militancy problem.[17]

This, however, appears to have been only a temporary solution. As of 2017, the Soufan Group estimated that a total of 400 foreign fighters had returned home to Russia.[18] More recent authoritative estimates are currently unavailable, but it is clear that a large-scale influx of mobilized militants is a matter of significant concern for Kremlin officials. Since the large-scale territorial defeat of the Islamic State, the Russian government has sought to establish significantly stricter laws for prosecuting returnees in an effort to avert large-scale returnee flows.[19] A notable exception in this regard has been Russia's repatriation of women and children linked to the conflict, which has become a significant priority of the Kremlin. Russia now has "the most active program to return detainees from Iraq and Syria, notably children," according to human rights NGO Human Rights Watch.[20]

The CE functions as a decentralized network, consisting of local combat cells loosely tied together and subordinate to sectors, which are in turn subordinated to the CE's "provinces," referred to by its fighters as *veliyats*. The CE is known to have five such *veliyats*: Veliyat Nokchicho (Chechnya); Veliyat Gyalgyaiche (Ingushetia and Ossetia); Veliyat Dagestan; the United Veliyat of Kabardia, Balkaria, and Karachai (the KBR, the KChR, and probably Adygeya); and Veliyat of the Nogai Steppe (Krasnodar Krai and Stavropol Krai).[21]

The CE is composed of members from each of the Muslim ethnic groups in Russia, as well as members of non-Muslim ethnic groups. Chechens, Ingush and various Dagestani (Avars, Dargins, Kumyks, Nogais, Tabasarans, etc.) predominate, but the Muslim Alans (Karachais and Balkars) and Circassians (Kabards, Cherkess, and Adygs) are also well represented.[22] In short, the CE puts into practice the extremist principle that Islam is universal.

Publicly available information detailing CE's financial sources is limited. It remains likely that Arab and other foreign Islamic governments, businesses, and philanthropists still provide funds to the group, despite the efforts of Russian authorities to prevent it. The local population is known to provide limited financial support in the form of the Islamic *zakat* (charitable contributions), as well as considerable logistical and other material support, such as weapons, safe houses, and food provisions.[23] Support is also generated through criminal activity—something that represents a legacy of the first Russo-Chechen war and the turbulent period that followed, when the ChRI received funding from elements of the Chechen mafia, narcotics trafficking, illicit oil exports, and the lucrative hostage-taking industry.[24]

The size of the CE's network is extremely difficult to estimate. Official Russian estimates have tended to downplay the number of active members affiliated with the group,[25] but expert analysis suggests that it is reasonable to assume that there may be more than 1,000 CE fighters, and thousands of additional facilitators.[26] These figures have been affected by the Syrian civil war, which has drawn Russian Islamists to its cause in significant numbers. In the Fall of 2014, Russian security officials estimated that some 800 militants from the North Caucasus had traveled to Syria to take up arms against the Assad regime.[27] By September 2015, that number had swelled to an estimated 2,400—a threefold increase in less than a year.[28] It is unclear what percentage of these mobilized Islamists is made up of CE cadres, but the organization is believed to be heavily represented within the Islamic State.[29] (In turn, the collapse of the ISIS "caliphate" in Iraq and Syria since 2017 has seen at least some of these cadres begin to return to the Russian Federation, as outlined above.)

While the CE has long been a prominent part of the global *jihadist* movement, it has traditionally served as an affiliate of the bin Laden network, having formally pledged allegiance to al-Qaeda back in April of 2009. However, in 2015, elements of the group broke ranks and formally pledged allegiance to the Islamic State. *Emirs* in Dagestan were the first to formally pledge allegiance to IS,[30] followed by the CE's leading military commander, and Chechnya's *emir*, Aslan Buytukaev, who declared allegiance to IS leader Abu Bakr al-Baghdadi on behalf of all Chechen fighters that summer. Other CE *veliyats* followed soon after. The move created a rift within the organization, with a minority of *veliyat* remaining loyal to the CE (and therefore al-Qaeda). Those that joined the Islamic State, however, were incorporated into an ISIS "governate" encompassing Russia's restive majority-Muslim regions of Dagestan, Chechnya, Ingushetia, Kabardino-Balkaria and Karachayevo-Cherkessia.[31] Then-ISIS *emir* Abu Bakr al-Baghdadi subsequently named Abu Muhammad al-Kadari (Rustam Asilderov) leader of the newly declared Islamic State province, known as the Velayat Qawqaz.[32] Asilderov was killed in a December 2016 raid carried out by Russian authorities near Makhachkala, Dagestan.[33] No clear leader has emerged publicly since, which could signal the group's diminishing activity and a loss of morale among its fighters.[34] Al-Baghdadi, meanwhile, was killed in October of 2019 as part of a U.S. raid in Syria. He was succeeded by a little-known militant named Abu Ibrahim al-Hashemi.[35]

There is no indication as of this writing whether the leadership change has led to a change in the group's outlook on Russia. Historically, IS has made a point of targeting Russia, if not for its treatment of Muslims internally then certainly for its activities in

Syria. This has included high-profile attacks such as the October 2015 downing of a Russian commercial airliner flight from Sharm el-Sheikh to St. Petersburg (an attack that was orchestrated by the Islamic State)[36] and assorted terrorist incidents and plots on Russian soil.[37] IS has even threatened Russian President Vladimir Putin directly.[38] The Islamic State also leveled threats against the Summer 2018 World Cup Games, for which Russia was the host, but no attacks of note materialized.[39] In December 2019, the FBI shared information with Russia that aided in foiling a New Years' terror attack being planned by IS elements, for which Russian President Vladimir Putin expressed his appreciation to the Trump administration.[40] As of this writing, the most recent successful attack claimed by IS took place on December 31, 2019, in Ingushetia, when two men hit a police officer with their vehicle and attacked several more others with knives. One police officer was killed in the incident, and three others were wounded.[41]

The degree to which Islamist militants in the North Caucasus are currently split between IS-Vilayat Kavkaz and the remnants of CE remains unclear, but both factions are believed to retain significant operational capability.

Other Islamists

In the past, suspected al-Qaeda operatives such as Omar Abu Ibn al-Khattab have joined the ChRI/CE, but there is no open source evidence indicating that al-Qaeda or other foreign *jihadist* groups operate in Russia independently from the CE. Russian law enforcement occasionally claims that al-Qaeda operatives number among killed and captured CE fighters, but such claims are never documented. Moreover, al-Qaeda's position in Russia (and elsewhere in the "post-Soviet space") has been largely supplanted in recent years by the Islamic State.[42]

The only other Islamic extremist organization reported to be active in Russia is the Uighur-Bulgar Jamaat (UBJ). The group was established between 2006 and 2008 in Bashkortostan by Pavel Dorokhov, an ethnic Russian converted and trained by Taliban camps in Afghanistan.[43] It has sporadically engaged in militancy in Russia's Volga region (encompassing the republics of Tatarstan and Bashkortostan). In 2010, no fewer than 20 members of the UBJ attempted to blow up a gas line in Bashkortostan's Birsk district, and were subsequently killed in a shootout with Bashkir police.[44] In 2012, the group disrupted the long-time peace between religious groups in Tatarstan when they severely injured the region's Grand Mufti, Ilduz Fayzov, and killed his deputy, Valliulla Yakupov.[45] The UBJ also makes up part of the contingent of foreign fighters in Syria, and as of 2013 numbered around 200 in that theater.[46] The UBJ may or may not be one and the same organization as the apparently ethnic Tatar Bulgar Jamaat, which fought in Afghanistan around 2009.[47]

Despite being banned in Russia, Hizb ut-Tahrir (HuT) maintains a presence in the country as well. Many alleged HuT members are arrested annually, mostly in the republics of Tatarstan and Bashkortostan. By 2012, HuT and other Islamists had penetrated many autonomous mosques and official Islamic institutions in Tatarstan, carried out public demonstrations in tandem with nationalist groups, and organized several automobile caravans flying the HuT flag.[48] According to Memorial, a Russian human rights watchdog, HuT has become a non-violent organization in recent years.[49] Memorial considers 23 of the Muslims arrested in 2016 on charges associated with Hizb ut-Tahrir to be "political prisoners," a term it uses to refer to those who have been wrongfully arrested to meet political ends.[50]

Other domestic groups

Several small Tatar groups have Islamist tendencies but are at least equally or predominantly national separatist in nature, confining their activity to the republic of Tatarstan and, to a lesser degree, Bashkortostan. They include: Azatlyk, Ittifak, Mille Mejlis, and elements within the All-Tatar Public Center.[51] These organizations have historically confined themselves to occasional declarations, conferences, and small demonstrations, but now increasingly engage in those activities in partnership with Islamist elements such as HuT. Some of their official statements and documents are sent to North Caucasus terrorist websites.[52] None, however, are at present believed to constitute a significant threat to the Russian state.

Islamism and Society

Since the collapse of the Soviet Union, Islam has undergone a revival among its traditionally Muslim ethnic groups. According to Russia's leading mufti, Chairman of the Council of Muftis of Russia (CMR) Ravil Gainutdin, the number of mosques in Russia grew from 150 in 1991 to some six thousand by October 2005.[53] From 2000 to 2015, mosque construction averaged just over one per day, according to expert estimates.[54] In 2019, Chechnya inaugurated the latest such structure; billed as "Europe's biggest mosque," the facility boasts capacity for more than 30,000 worshippers and is located outside the regional capital of Grozny.[55]

This explosive growth has been propelled by the size of Russia's Muslim minority itself. While Russia's Muslims remain a distinct minority in Russia, differences in communal behavior—including fewer divorces, less alcoholism and a greater rate of reproduction—have given them a more robust demographic profile than their ethnic Russian counterparts.[56] Thus, according to the United Nations, the fertility of Russia's Muslims, at 2.3, is significantly higher than the overall Russian national fertility rate of 1.7.[57] Other estimates peg the reproductive rate of Russia's Muslims higher still.[58] As a result, a variety of projections have suggested that Russia's Muslims will account for a fifth of the country's total population by the end of this decade, and may make up a majority of Russians by as early as mid-century.[59] Russian religious authorities have more or less confirmed these estimates; in a 2019 interview, Russia's chief *mufti*, Ravil Gainutdin, stated that the Muslim population in Russia is expected to increase to 30 percent of the overall total over the next decade-and-a-half.[60]

Moreover, migrants (the majority of them Muslim) continue to enter the Russian Federation in search of employment and economic opportunity. In 2019, the total number of migrant workers present on Russian soil was estimated to be approximately 11.6 million, some 8 percent of the country's total population.[61] This second cohort helps to augment the size and political reach of Russia's indigenous Muslim community.

Russia's Muslims are divided by geography, history, ethnicity, and divergent confessional movements (Sufis, Sunnis, and Shi'ites) and legal schools (*maskhabs*). The overwhelming majority of Russia's Muslims, however, are Sunni. Although Muslim communities can be found all across the length and breadth of the vast federation, the largest concentrations of ethnic Muslims (ethnic groups that traditionally have adhered in overwhelming numbers to the Islamic faith) are found in the North Caucasus's Muslim republics—Chechnya, Ingushetia, Dagestan, Adygeya, Kabardino-Balkaria (KBR), and Karachaevo-Cherkessia (KChR)—and in the Volga and Urals republics of Tatarstan and Bashkortostan. There are also large Muslim populations in Moscow and St. Petersburg, but these are more Russified, urbanized, and secularized than those in other regions, especially the North Caucasus. The Muslims of the North Caucasus remain largely rural, traditionally religious, and indigenously ethnic or clan-oriented.

Russia's other main ethnic Muslim groups, Tatars and Bashkirs, are concentrated to a great extent in the Tatarstan and Bashkortostan Republics. As of the 2010 Russian census, Tatars make up a slim majority in Tatarstan, while ethnic Russians outnumber Bashkirs in Bashkortostan. Both Tatars and Bashkirs are better integrated into Russian life than are the North Caucasians. Some historically non-Muslim ethnic groups are seeing some of their members convert to Islam, including ethnic Russians.[62]

In terms of political ideology, Russia's Muslims, much like ethnic Slavs, are divided among democrats, conservatives, Eurasianist and Islamist reactionaries. Since, under Russian law, political parties based on any communal identification are forbidden from participating in elections, it is difficult to attain a detailed picture of Muslims' distribution on Russia's political spectrum. Political Islam, however, is in evidence at both the official and unofficial levels. Media controlled by official Islamic structures carry numerous articles on introducing elements of *sharia* law in Russia, including the introduction of Islamic banking and insurance.[63] Also, there are strong anti-American, anti-Western, anti-Israeli, and even anti-Semitic tendencies, not just among Russia's Islamists but among Russia's traditional Muslims as well.[64]

Generally, however, there is only limited support for violent Islamism in both Russia's Muslim and non-Muslim populations.

The country's Islamic clergy feels threatened and virulently opposes manifestations of political Islam, and Islamists have found limited support in the Muslim community. That said, many young Muslims are increasingly fascinated by—and sympathetic toward—radical trends, including Islamism as represented by the charismatic fighters of the Caucasus Emirate and, more recently, by the Islamic State.

The Russian government is ill-equipped to deal with this trend. In recent years, the Kremlin has done precious little of substance to address the needs of the country's growing Muslim minority. To the contrary, the ultranationalist identity erected by the government of Vladimir Putin over the past decade has systematically shut Russia's Muslims out of contemporary politics and society, leaving them vulnerable to the lure of alternative ideologies—Islamism chief among them.[65]

Islamism and the State

Russia's *Freedom of Religion Law of 1997* establishes Islam, along with Orthodox Christianity, Buddhism, and Judaism, as one of the four "traditional" faiths.[66] As of the 2010 Russian census, Muslims make up the second largest group of these (after Orthodox Christianity).

Russia's Muslims are not strongly self-organized. Rather, they are well organized "from above" by the Islamic clergy and the Russian state. Muslim communities must be registered with the government, and each is then incorporated into a regional Muslim Spiritual Administration (MSA), every one of which in turn is included under one of the three main Muslim umbrella organizations: the Council of Muslims of Russia (CMR), the Central Muslim Spiritual Administration (CMSA), and the Coordinating Council of the Muslims of the North Caucasus (CCMNC). The CMR at present is the most influential of the umbrella organizations, with its leader, the ethnic Tatar *mufti* Ravil Gainutdin, on good terms with the Kremlin. Two smaller umbrella organizations—the MSA of the European part of Russia and the MSA of the Asian part of Russia—are subordinated to two of the abovementioned. In all, there are known to be approximately 60 regional MSAs, all of which are included under one or another of the umbrella organizations.[67] These various structures help organize the travel of Muslims to the *hajj* and to study abroad, support Islamic schools and universities in Russia, and recruit and train Islamic clergy. The various Muslim spiritual councils (Dukhovnyie Upravlenii Musulman, or DUM in Russian) receive state funding for muftis' salaries, university and school development, and the building of mosques. Independent Muslim communities and mosques persist but are illegal and are usually discovered by the authorities and incorporated into the official administrations. Typically, these have manifested Islamist tendencies, and some have produced terrorist organizations, leaders, and cadres.[68]

Both the Russian state and official Islamic clergy are strongly opposed to and greatly fear any manifestation of Islamism. As a result, the state has banned political parties based on religion (as well as on ethnicity and gender), and the Islamic clergy cooperates closely with the state apparatus in combating independent Islamic or Islamist groups and supporting reformist, Euro-Islamic, and other more secularized Islamic trends as an antidote to Islamism. Ravil Gainutdin, as well as the leadership of the Republic of Tatarstan, has led in this effort.[69]

Past experience has taught Russian authorities to treat Islamists severely, and they move quickly and often illegally to imprison them for long terms. Arrests of Islamists belonging to non-violent but illegal organizations such as HuT and Tablighi Jamaat are often accompanied by official charges of conspiracy to commit terrorist attacks and claims that searches produced not only extremist literature but also weapons and explosives.[70]

The extent to which these policies and practices lead to significant violations of Muslims' civil, political, and human rights, in turn, creates a catalyst for extremist recruitment. Putin-era amendments to Russia's laws "On Extremism" and "On Combating Terrorism" give the Federal Security Service (FSB), the Ministry of Internal Affairs (MVD), Justice Ministry, and General Prosecutor's Office broad leeway in holding suspects and determining what constitutes "extremist literature." In June of 2020, for instance, a Russian journalist was put on trial for the infraction of airing criticism of state policy relating to terrorism during an interview; she faces up to 7 years in prison.[71] Searches are frequently conducted on questionable pretexts, detention can often result in torture, and some convictions are based on exaggerated charges. These practices are more prevalent in the North Caucasus, especially in Chechnya under regional president Ramzan Kadyrov, where authorities have even carried out extra-judicial retribution against the families of suspected and actual terrorists, including the abductions of relatives and the burning of homes.

Imprisonment and detention on charges of extremism also continue in Russian-occupied Crimea.[72] Since Russia's annexation of the peninsula in 2014, Crimean Tatars have been prosecuted for alleged affiliation with Hizb ut-Tahrir.[73] Many of those arrested are activists who openly oppose Russian occupation. Moreover, Russia's Supreme Court has deemed the *Mejlis*, the "self-governing body of Crimean Tatars," to be an extremist group and banned its operation,[74] despite protests from the international community.

Federal counterterrorism policy has in recent years increasingly focused on "soft power" approaches. Moscow has increased federal contributions to the budgets of republics hardest hit by the CE. In 2014, the Russian central government was still funding the majority of the budget for the North Caucasus in return for the loyalty of local officials and businessmen.[75] As of 2016, the support percentage of the republic's budgets ranged from 46.7% (Kabardino-Balkaria) to 82% (Ingushetia).[76] As of 2016, some of those youth programs came in the form of media schools that taught students how to promote Russian interests and "standards in journalism."[77]

Russian support to the North Caucasus region has shifted in recent years. What began as a focus on socioeconomic conditions and infrastructure project support has increasingly shifted toward increasing investment opportunities and decreasing unemployment in the region under the label of "post conflict reconstruction."[78] One thing that has remained unchanged, however; the Kremlin's continued support to the North Caucasus. Even in the aftermath of U.S. and international sanctions imposed following the 2014 annexation of Crimea, Moscow continued and even expanded its support to regional republics, particularly Chechnya.[79]

These funding efforts have been supplemented by increasingly broad federal authorities to curb perceived terrorist activities. In 2016, Russia passed a series of laws, cumulatively referred to as the "Yarovaya Packet," which expand the definition of "extremism," allowing the criminalization of a highly subjective range of acts and authorizing the prosecution of any person or financier of an act that harms Russians worldwide.[80] The law further tightens the aforementioned organizational structure, requiring official permits for religious activities, including praying, that take place outside of officially recognized religious buildings. It targets outreach and missionary work, confining it to churches and other specific areas, and usually requiring permits. The "Yarovaya Packet" defines "failure to report crime" as a criminal act and sets the accountable age at 14 years for this and other "extremism" charges.[81]

Perhaps most notably, the "Packet" provides the Kremlin with broad oversight over the Internet domain. Under the law's provisions, individuals can now be charged for inciting or justifying terrorism, as well as proselytizing on social media and in emails. "Yarovaya" likewise grants security agencies full access to private communications, as well as requiring telecommunications companies to store all data for at least six months, including conversations and text messages. Meanwhile, "organizers of information distribution" are required to store data for one year and help decrypt information, if necessary.[82]

These "soft power" efforts have been mirrored by a more concrete organizational reconfiguration. In 2016, Russia created a new super-security service known as the National Guard, ostensibly to help the Kremlin better fight terrorism and organized crime.[83] This body encompasses the country's riot police (OMON) and SWAT teams (SOBR), as well as other relevant units, and will work "in close cooperation" with the country's Ministry of Interior Affairs.[84] However, experts note that this new, militarized structure will likely have little actual role fighting terrorism, because its forces are predominantly public security forces, trained to control and deter.[85]

Each of the North Caucasus Muslim republics has carried out its own, and often very different, policies to counter violent Islamism. Chechnya's strongman, Ramzan Kadyrov, has traditionally suppressed Islamist groups with heavy-handed tactics, while simultaneously seeking to co-opt Islamist rhetoric and push Islamist social policies, such as imposing *sharia* law on the province as a method of reducing support for Islamist groups.[86] By contrast, Ingushetia's former President Yunus bek Yevkurov, pioneered a continuous amnesty or "adaptation" policy that sought to draw fighters out of the forest and back to their families and civilian life by offering reduced or suspended sentences and educational and work opportunities.[87] Yevkurov resigned in July of 2019, and was succeeded as regional President by Mahmud-Ali Kalimatov, who previously served as a functionary in Russia's Samara Oblast.

In 2010, Dagestan established an adaptation commission, which engages in the same work, and in 2011 Kabardino-Balkariya followed suit. In 2012, in an effort to isolate, divide, and rule radical Muslims, Dagestan's authorities helped establish a dialogue between the official Sufi-oriented Muslim Spiritual Administration of Dagestan and the republic's growing Salafi community, the main recruiting pool for the CE. These local policies are aimed at blunting the recruitment efforts of the CE and other radicals.

Nevertheless, recent years have seen a marked uptick in the radicalization and mobilization of elements of Russia's Muslim minority. This is attributable to a number of factors, ranging from a lack of economic integration and opportunity to rising state xenophobia to the growing prevalence of Islamist groups and ideas within the Russian Federation.[88] This mobilization has been exacerbated by the Russian intervention into the Syrian civil war, which has made the country itself the target of various extremist groups. Al-Qaeda's Syrian affiliate, Jabhat al-Nusra (now rebranded as Jabhat Fateh al-Sham), has called for terrorist attacks within Russia as a retaliatory measure.[89] So, too, has the Islamic State.[90] These threats have been followed by concrete incidents of terrorist violence within Russia (detailed above).

These statements highlight the risks inherent in Russia's current foreign policy. By wading into the Syrian civil war on the side of the Assad regime, Russia's government has effectively exacerbated the mobilization—and the radicalization—of its own Muslims. Despite Moscow's increasingly draconian and invasive counterterrorism laws, and notwithstanding continued financial support from the Kremlin to areas of the country affected by radicalization, the Russian Federation is likely to face a growing jihad problem for years to come.

Endnotes

1. The last official census of the Russian population was taken in 2010, and it tallied the national population at 142.9 million. See *Vserosiiskii Perepis Naselenie 2010*, http://www.perepis-2010.ru/. Since then, various numbers have been floated for the overall size of the Russian population – as well as the proportional size of its Muslim minority. The figures cited above are estimates deemed credible by the authors, but are subject to revision. On Russia's overall population (incorporating that of the annexed Crimean Peninsula), see Marlene Laruelle, "How Islam Will Change Russia," in S. Enders Wimbush and Elizabeth Portale, *Russia in Decline* (Jamestown Foundation, 2017). The estimated size of Russia's Muslim minority is drawn from the author's conversations with Russian officials in Washington, DC in the Fall of 2015.
2. Andrew Higgins and Alan Cullison, "A Terrorist's Odyssey," *Wall Street Journal*, July 2, 2002; See also Yurii Tyssovskiy, "Terrorist No. 2 Al-Zawahiri spent time in Makhachkalinsky Prison," *VEK*, July 19, 2002.
3. Faisal Devji, *Landscapes of Jihad: Militancy, Morality, and Modernity* (Ithaca, NY: Cornell University Press, 2005), 130-131; Dore Gold, *Hatred's Kingdom: How Saudi Arabia Supports the New Global Terrorism* (Washington, DC: Regnery, 2003), 137; and Gordon M. Hahn, *Russia's Islamic Threat* (New Haven and London: Yale University Press, 2007), 36-37.
4. Michael Reynolds, "False Comfort on Afghanistan," *Middle East Strategy at Harvard*, August 31, 2009; Mike Bowker, "Western Views of The Chechen Conflict," in Richard Sakwa, ed., *Chechnya: From Past to Future* (London: Anthem Press, 2005), 235.
5. Declassified DIA report NC 3095345, October 16, 1998. http://www.judicialwatch.org/cases/102/dia.pdf; See also Lorenzo Vidino, *Al-Qaeda in Europe* (Prometheus Books, 2006).
6. Hahn, *Russia's Islamic Threat*, 37-39 and 104-110.
7. "Aslan Maskhadov: 'My sozdadim polnotsennoe Islamskoe Gosudarstvo," *Kavkaz-Tsentr*, March 8, 2010, www.kavkazcenter.com/

russ/content/2010/03/08/71101.shtml; See also "Prezident ChRI Sheik Abdul-Khalim. Kto On?" *Kavkaz-Tsentr*, March 12, 2005, www.kavkazcenter.com/russ/content/2005/03/12/31285.shtml; "Abdallakh Shamil Abu-Idris: 'My oderzhali strategicheskuyu pobedu,'" *Kavkaz-Tsentr*, January 9, 2006, www.kavkazcenter.net/russ/content/2006/01/09/40869.shtml; Paul Murphy, *The Wolves of Islam: Russia and the Faces of Chechen Terrorism* (Dulles, VA: Brassey's Inc., 2004), 171-75.

8. Hahn, *Russia's Islamic Threat*, 43, 158; Vadim Rechkalov, "'Pochemu spetssluzhby ne mogut poimat' Shamilya Basaeva," *Izvestiya* (Moscow), December 6-10, 2004; "Shamil Basaev: 'Segodnya voyuet ves chechenskii narod,'" *Kavkaz-Tsentr*, August 17, 2005, www.kavkazcenter.net/russ/content/2005/08/17/36759.shtml; Aleksandra Larintseva, Timur Samedov, and Olga Allenova, "Koltso kavkazskoi natsionalnosti," *Kommersant-Vlast* (Moscow), September 29-October 5 2003, 20; Valerii Khatazhukov, "Kabardino-Balkariya Crackdown on Islamists," IWPR'S *Caucasus Reporting Service* no. 199, August 2003; Mayrbek Vachagaev, "Evolution of the Chechen Jamaat," Jamestown Foundation *Chechnya Weekly* VI, iss. 14, April 6, 2005; Timur Samedov, "Podozrevaemyie iz 'Yarmuka'," *Kommersant Daily* (Moscow), December 15, 2004, 4.
9. A detailed discussion of the 2003 suicide bombing campaign can be found in Yossef Bodansky, *Chechen Jihad: Al Qaeda's Training Ground and the Next Wave of Terror* (New York: Harper, 2007).
10. See Robert Johnston, "Terrorist Attacks in Russia." May 22, 2015, http://www.johnstonsarchive.net/terrorism/terr-russia.html.
11. Andrew E. Kramer and Neil McFarquhar, "Fierce Attack by Islamist Militants in Chechen Capital Kills at Least 20," *New York Times*, December 4, 2014, https://www.nytimes.com/2014/12/05/world/europe/grozny-chechnya-attack.html?_r=0.
12. "Caucasus Emirate," *Mapping Militant Organizations*, April 11, 2014, http://web.stanford.edu/group/mappingmilitants/cgi-bin/groups/view/255.
13. Daria Garmonenko, "FSB Sbila v Rossii Terroristichiskoyu Activnost (The FSB has Diminished Terrorist Activity in Russia)," *Nezavisimaya Gazeta* (Moscow), November 11, 2015, http://www.ng.ru/politics/2015-11-11/100_fsbter.html.
14. Garmonenko, "FSB Sbila v Rossii Terroristichiskoyu Activnost."
15. Interview with Evgenia Albats, *Ekho Moskvy*, November 17, 2015, http://echo.msk.ru/programs/personalno/1659708-echo/.
16. "Report: Russia, Former Soviet Region Largest Source For Foreign

Fighters in Syria, Iraq," *Radio Free Europe/Radio Liberty*, October 24, 2017, https://www.rferl.org/a/soufan-report-iraq-syria-russian-fighters/28813611.html.

17. Michael Weiss, "Russia is Sending Jihadis to Join ISIS," *The Daily Beast*, August 23, 2015, http://www.thedailybeast.com/articles/2015/08/23/russia-s-playing-a-double-game-with-islamic-terror0.html.
18. Richard Barrett, "Beyond the Caliphate: Foreign Fighters and the Threat of Returnees," *The Soufan Center*, October 2017, http://thesoufancenter.org/wp-content/uploads/2017/11/Beyond-the-Caliphate-Foreign-Fighters-and-the-Threat-of-Returnees-TSC-Report-October-2017-v3.pdf.
19. "Section IX Crimes Against Public Safety and Public Order," *The Criminal Code of the Russian Federation*, March 1, 2017, http://www.uk-rf.com/glava24.html.
20. "Putin Shows Rare Soft Spot to Rescue Russia's ISIS Children," Bloomberg, February 1, 2019, https://www.themoscowtimes.com/2019/02/01/putin-shows-rare-soft-spot-to-rescue-russias-isis-children-a64363.
21. On the structure of the CE, see Hahn, *Russia's Islamic Threat*, 63-64.
22. Gordon Hahn, *The Caucasus Emirate Mujahedin: Global Jihadism in Russia's North Caucasus and Beyond.* (McFarland and Company, Inc., 2014).
23. "Khazbiev: chinovniki Ingushetii soderzhat boevikov," *Kavkaz uzel*, July 24, 2009, www.kavkaz-uzel.ru/articles/157053; Alexei Malashenko, "The Kremlin's Violent Underbelly," *The Moscow Times*, July 29, 2009.
24. Pavel Khlebnikov, *Razgovor s Varvarom: Besedy s chechenskim polevym komandirom Khozh-Akhmedom Nukhaevym o banditizme i islame* (Moscow: Detektiv-Press, 2004); Paul Klebnikov, *Godfather of the Kremlin: The Decline of Russia in the Age of Gangster Capitalism* (Orlando, FL: Harcourt, 2001); A. Khinshtein, *Berezovskii i Abramovich: Oligarkhi s bol'shoi dorogi* (Moscow: Lora, 2007).
25. "MVD RF: na Severnom Kavkaze deistvuyut okolo 500 boevikov," *Kavkaz uzel*, March 26, 2010, www.kavkaz-uzel.ru/articles/167037/; "Yedelev: v Chechnye deistvuyut do 500 boevikov," *Kavkaz uzel*, January 21, 2009, www.kavkaz-uzel.ru/articles/148344; "MVD: v Chechnye deistvuyut ne menee 400 boevikov," *Kavkaz uzel*, February 6, 2008, www.kavkaz-uzel.ru; and "IMARAT KAVKAZ. Moskva pereschitala modzhakhedov. Ikh okazyvaetsya 1500 boitsov," *Kavkaz-Tsentr*, May 20, 2009, www.kavkazcenter.com/russ/con-

tent/2009/05/20/65749.shtml.

26. Hahn, *Russia's Islamic Threat*, 67-68.
27. "Russia Calls for Joint Effort With U.S. to Fight Islamic State," *The Moscow Times*, September 29, 2014, http://www.themoscowtimes.com/article.php?id=507990.
28. "Moscow Says About 2,400 Russians Fighting With Islamic State: RIA," Reuters, September 18, 2015, http://news.yahoo.com/moscow-says-2-400-russians-fighting-islamic-state-...
29. Ivan Petrov, "MVD: Up to 3,500 Russians are fighting for the terrorists in Syria and Iraq," *Rossiyskaya Gazeta*, March 17, 2016. https://rg.ru/2016/03/17/mvd-na-storone-terroristov-v-sirii-i-irake-voiuiut-do-35-tys-rossiian.html.
30. Ekaterina Sokirianskaya, "Russia's North Caucasus Insurgency Widens as ISIS Foothold Grows," *World Politics Review*, April 12, 2016, http://www.worldpoliticsreview.com/articles/18466/russia-s-north-caucasus-insurgency-widens-as-isis-foothold-grows.
31. "Islamic State Declares Foothold in Russia's North Caucasus," *The Moscow Times*, June 24, 2015, https://themoscowtimes.com/news/islamic-state-declares-foothold-in-russias-north-caucasus-47666.
32. "Треугольник Имарат Кавказ, Исламское Государство, аш-Шишани," МКРУ Дагестан, July 27, 2016, http://mkala.mk.ru/articles/2016/07/27/treugolnik-imarat-kavkaz-islamskoe-gosudarstvo-ashshishani.html.
33. Alikhan Mamsurov, "Death of Rustam Asilderov triggered experts' debate," *Caucasian Knot*, December 5, 2016, http://www.eng.kavkaz-uzel.eu/articles/37737/.
34. Neil Hauer, "The Current State and Future of Caucasian Groups in Syria," Atlantic Council, April 19, 2018, http://www.atlanticcouncil.org/blogs/syriasource/the-current-state-and-future-of-caucasian-groups-in-syria.
35. "Islamic State group names its new leader as Abu Ibrahim al-Hashemi," *BBC*, October 31, 2019, https://www.bbc.com/news/world-middle-east-50254785.
36. Lizzie Dearden, "ISIS Plane Attack," *Independent* (London), February 24, 2016, http://www.independent.co.uk/news/world/africa/isis-plane-attack-egypt-terrorists-downed-russian-metrojet-flight-from-sharm-el-sheikh-islamic-state-a6893181.html.
37. Lizzie Dearden, "Isis claims responsibility for first terror attack in Russia after men try to kill police with gun and axes near Moscow," *Independent* (London). August 19, 2016, http://www.independent.co.uk/news/world/europe/isis-terror-attacks-news-latest-russia-mos-

cow-balashikha-police-gun-axe-allegiance-video-chechen-a7198731.html; Russian Federal Security Service, "Press Release: Russian FSB and MVD disrupt plans of IS conspirators in Dagestan," December 29, 2016. http://www.fsb.ru/fsb/press/message/single.htm%21id%3D10438055%40fsbMessage.html; Ivan Nechepurenko and Rukmini Callimachi, "Website with Qaeda Ties Publishes Claim on St. Petersburg Bombing," *New York Times*, April 25, 2017, https://www.nytimes.com/2017/04/25/world/europe/st-petersburg-metro-al-qaeda.html; David Filipov and Andrew Roth, "Russia arrests possible accomplices of presumed St. Petersburg bomber," *Washington Post*, April 6, 2017, https://www.washingtonpost.com/world/europe/russia-arrests-possible-accomplices-of-presumed-st-petersburg-bomber/2017/04/06/ea63ec9a-1a2c-11e7-8598-9a99da559f9e_story.html?utm_term=.4de355c63942; Andrew E. Kraemer, "ISIS Claims Deadly Attack on Church in Russian Region of Dagestan", *New York Times*, February 18, 2018, https://www.nytimes.com/2018/02/18/world/europe/russia-dagestan-attack.html.

38. Dmitri Trenin, "Is Russia Safe From Extremist Attacks Like Those In Europe?" *Newsweek*, August 12, 2016, http://www.newsweek.com/russia-really-safe-deadly-attacks-isis-france-belgium-germany-488262.
39. See, for example, Henry Hollaway, "World Cup 2018: ISIS Threatens Massacre 'Like you have NEVER Seen' to get REVENGE on Putin," *Daily Star* (London), June 14, 2018, https://www.dailystar.co.uk/news/world-news/709358/world-cup-2018-terrorist-isis-russia-saudi-arabia-jihad-luzhniki-stadium-football-putin.
40. "Putin hails US for helping prevent terror attack in Russia," Associated Press, February 20, 2020, https://apnews.com/3fd2ef0f02ff0c494e51415c2d4e74af.
41. "Islamic State Claims Responsibility For Deadly Attack In Ingushetia," *Radio Free Europe/Radio Liberty*, January 2, 2020, https://www.rferl.org/a/islamic-state-claims-responsibility-for-deadly-attack-in-ingushetia/30356052.html.
42. Jonah Goldberg. "Al-Qaeda's out. ISIS is in!" *National Review*, June 12, 2015, http://www.nationalreview.com/article/419657/al-qaedas-out-isis-jonah-goldberg.
43. "Member of Extremist Organization, Uyghur-Bulgar Jamaat was Sentenced to 15 Years in a Camp." *Kommersant* (Moscow), July 20, 2009, http://www.kommersant.ru/doc/1207571.
44. Vladislav Maltsev, "Bashkirian Jihad," *Nezavisimaya Gazeta* (Moscow), September 1, 2010, http://www.ng.ru/society/2010-09-01/4_ji-

had.html.

45. Leon Aron, "Russia is New Front for Militant Islam," *Washington Post*, November 13, 2015, https://www.washingtonpost.com/opinions/russias/2015/11/13/3f456156-887c-11e5-9a07-453018f9a0ec_story.html?utm_term=.c9f678c640bf.
46. "Separatists in Tatarstan announce support of Islamist fighters in Syria," *Regnum*, June 13, 2013, https://regnum.ru/news/polit/1670767.html.
47. "Special Agents of the FSB try to fight the UBJ," *Komsolmoskaya Pravda*, October 26, 2012, http://www.centrasia.ru/newsA.php?st=1351234020. For the *Bulgar Jamaat*'s Russian-language website, see http://tawba.info orhttp://jamaatbulgar.narod.ru.
48. See Gordon M. Hahn, *Islam, Islamism and Politics in Eurasia Report* nos. 43, 45, 47, 48, 58 and 60, available at https://csis.org/node/33013/publication. On the HuT's penetration of official Islamic structures, demonstrations, and automobile caravans in 2012 see, for example, Rais Suleimanov, "Al'yans vakhkhabizma n national-separtizma v Tatarstane i 'russkii vopros' v regione," RISI, May 2, 2012, http://www.gumilev-center.ru/alyans-vakhkhabizma-i-nacional-separatizma-v-tatarstane-i-russkijj-vopros-v-regione/ and Rais Suleimanov, "Islamskii terrorizm v sovremennom Tatarstane: vakhkhabizm na praktike," *Agentsvo politicheskikh novostei*, July 25, 2012, www.apn.ru/publications/article26923.htm; See also "V Kazani islamisty proekhali avtokolonnoi s razvernutymi flagami," Regnum.ru, October 26, 2012, www.regnum.ru/news/fd-volga/1586886.html.
49. Memorial, "Persecution of Hizb ut-Tahrir," October 13, 2015, http://memohrc.org/special-projects/presledovanie-organizacii-hizb-ut-tahrir.
50. Memorial, "Memorial recognizes 23 Muslims from Bashkotostan as political prisoners," April 26, 2016. http://memohrc.org/news/memorial-priznal-23-h-musulman-iz-bashkortostana-politzaklyuchennymi.
51. Hahn, *Russia's Islamic Threat*, 213-214.
52. For such contacts before 2005, see Hahn, *Russia's Islamic Threat*, 205-206.
53. Neil Buckley, "Russia's Islamic Rebirth Adds Tension," *Financial Times*, October 28, 2005.
54. Paul Goble, "7500 Mosques Have Been Erected Since Putin Became President," *The Interpreter*, December 4, 2014, http://www.interpretermag.com/7500-mosques-have-been-erected-in-russia-since-putin-became-president/.
55. "Chechnya Inaugurates 'Europe's Biggest Mosque,'" Reuters,

August 23, 2019, https://www.themoscowtimes.com/2019/08/23/chechnya-inaugurates-europes-biggest-mosque-a67006.

56. Abdullah Rinat Mukhametov, "Russian Muslims Face Challenges of Demography and Migration," *New Eastern Europe*, August 14, 2015, http://www.neweasterneurope.eu/articles-and-commentary/1690-russian-muslims-face-challenges-of-demography-and-migration.
57. Pew Forum on Religion and Public Life, "The Future of the Global Muslim Population: Projections for 2010–2030," January 27, 2011, http://www.pewforum.org/future-of-the-global-muslim-population-russia.aspx.
58. "Muslim Birthrate Worries Russia," *Washington Times*, November 20, 2006, http://www.washingtontimes.com/news/2006/nov/20/20061120-115904-9135r/?page=all.
59. Jonah Hull, "Russia Sees Muslim Population Boom," *Al-Jazeera* (Doha), January 13, 2007, http://english.aljazeera.net/news/europe/2007/01/2008525144630794963.html; "Cherez polveka Musulmani v Rossii Mogut Stat Bolshenstvom - Posol MID RF [In Half a Century, Muslims in Russia Could Become the Majority - Russia's OIC Ambassador]," Interfax (Moscow), October 10, 2007, http://www.interfax-religion.ru/islam/print.php?act=news&id=20767.
60. "Russia Will Be One-Third Muslim in 15 Years, Chief Mufti Predicts," *The Moscow Times*, March 5, 2019, https://www.themoscowtimes.com/2019/03/05/russia-will-be-one-third-muslim-in-15-years-chief-mufti-predicts-a64706.
61. United Nations Population Division, "International Migrant Stock 2019: Country Profiles," n.d., https://www.un.org/en/development/desa/population/migration/data/estimates2/countryprofiles.asp.
62. Although there are no exact figures on the number of converts, it is clear that a Russian/Slavic Islamic community is emerging. According to one report, almost 50 thousand people, mostly ethnic Russians and young women, converted to Islam in the city of Moscow alone from January 2002 to October 2004. This figure comes from a posting on a Qatar-based website IslamOnLine citing an anonymous source from the Council of Muftis of Russia cited in "S 2002 Islam v Moskve prinyali pochti 50 tys. chelovek," Islam.ru, October 7, 2004, www.islam.ru/press/rus/2004/10/07/. An ethnic Russian Muslim community emerged in Omsk in 2004. Aleksei Malashenko, "Shadow of Islam over Europe," *International Affairs* (Moscow) 50, no. 5 (September-October 2004), 70.
63. See, for example, Rinat Bekkin, "Esly by ne krizis… R. Bekkin o roste interesa k islamskim finansam v Rossii," Islam.ru, n.d., www.

islam.ru/pressclub/gost/esbikaznu/. Islam.ru is affiliated with the MSA of Dagestan and frequently carries articles and interviews on the subject, in particular those of a key lobbyist for the introduction of Islamic financing in Russia, Rinat Bekkin.

64. Gordon M. Hahn, "Anti-Americanism, Anti-Westernism, and Anti-Semitism Among Russia's Muslims," *Demokratizatsiya* 16, no. 1 (Winter 2008), 49-60.
65. David M. Herszenhorn, "Russia Sees a Threat in Its Converts to Islam," *New York Times*, July 1, 2015, https://www.nytimes.com/2015/07/02/world/russia-sees-a-threat-in-its-converts-to-islam.html.
66. Russian Federation, *Federal Law on Freedom of Religion and Religious Unity*, 1997, http://pravo.gov.ru/proxy/ips/?docbody=&nd=102049359.
67. Shireen Hunter, *Islam in Russia: The Politics of Identity and Security* (Armonk, NY: M.E. Sharpe, 2002), 54-55.
68. A. Zhukov, "Kabardino-Balkariya: Na puti k katastrofe," *Kavkaz-uzel*, n.d., www.kavkaz-uzel.ru/analyticstext/analytics/id/1231255.html.
69. Ravil Gainutdin, *Islam v sovremennoi Rossii* (Moscow: Fair Press, 2004), 264-297; Hahn,*Russia's Islamic Threat*, 183-186.
70. "Rodnym obvinyaemykh v chlenstve v 'Khizb ut-takhrir' prishlos' proryvat'sya v zal suda," Islam.ru, February 27, 2009, www.islam.ru/rus/2009-02-27/; "V Chelyabinskoi oblasti predstanut pered sudom 5 'khizb ut-takhrirovtsev,'" Islam.ru, August 17, 2009, www.islam.ru/rus/2009-08-17/#27984.
71. Maria Vasilyeva, "Russian journalist charged with justifying terrorism calls her trial a sham," Reuters, June 22, 2020, https://www.reuters.com/article/us-russia-journalist-court/russian-journalist-charged-with-justifying-terrorism-calls-her-trial-a-sham-idUSKBN23T22A.
72. Human Rights Watch, "Ukraine: Escalating Pressure on Crimean Tatars," April 2, 2019, https://www.hrw.org/news/2019/04/02/ukraine-escalating-pressure-crimean-tatars#.
73. "Russia-Imposed Authorities In Crimea Search More Crimean Tatars' Homes," *Radio Free Europe/Radio Liberty*, June 19, 2019, https://www.rferl.org/a/russia-imposed-authorities-in-crimea-search-more-crimean-tatars-homes/30008149.html.
74. "Kyiv Protests Russian Ruling That Bans Crimean Tatars' Mejlis," *Radio Free Europe/Radio Liberty*, September 29, 2016, https://www.rferl.org/a/russia-court-upholds-ban-crimean-tatar-mejlis/28022600.

html.

75. Valery Dzutsati. "Russian Expert Warns North Caucasus Faces Economic Recession." Jamestown Foundation *Eurasia Daily Monitor* 12, iss. 6, January 12, 2015, https://jamestown.org/program/russian-expert-warns-north-caucasus-faces-economic-recession-2/.
76. Liz Fuller, "Kadyrov's Chechnya Appears Exempt From Russian Funding Cuts," *Radio Free Europe/Radio Liberty*, July 30, 2017, https://www.rferl.org/a/caucasus-report-kadyrov-chechnya-exempt-funding-cuts/28648698.html.
77. Orysia Lutsevych, "The Long Arm of Russian "Soft" Power," The Atlantic Council, May 4, 2016, http://www.atlanticcouncil.org/blogs/ukrainealert/the-long-arm-of-russian-soft-power.
78. Fuller, "Kadyrov's Chechnya Appears Exempt from Russian Funding Cuts."
79. Liz Fuller, "Moscow Amends North Caucasus Development Program Yet Again," *Radio Free Europe/Radio Liberty*, June 16, 2016, https://www.rferl.org/a/caucasus-report-development-program-amended-moscow/27803510.html.
80. "The Yarovaya Packet has been accepted into law," *Meduza*, June 24, 2016, https://meduza.io/feature/2016/06/24/paket-yarovoy-prinyat-i-eto-ochen-ploho.
81. Russian Federation, *Federal Law #1039101-6 on Changing the Criminal Code of the Russian Federation and Criminal Procedural Code of the Russian Federation and Establishing Extra Counter-Terrorism Measures and Public Safety Guarantees*, March 6, 2016.
82. Russian Federation, *Federal Law #1039149-6 on Changing Legislative Acts of the Russian Federation and Establishing Extra Counter-Terrorism Measures and Public Safety Guarantees*, March 6, 2016.
83. Russian Federation, *Federal Order on Questions of Federal Service of a National Guard*, April 5, 2016.http://kremlin.ru/acts/news/51648.
84. Mark Galiotti, "Putin's New National Guard," *In Moscow's Shadows*, April 5, 2016, https://inmoscowsshadows.wordpress.com/2016/04/05/putins-new-national-guard-what-does-it-say-when-you-need-your-own-personal-army/.
85. Mark Galiotti, "Putin's New National Guard," *In Moscow's Shadows*, April 5, 2016, https://inmoscowsshadows.wordpress.com/2016/04/05/putins-new-national-guard-what-does-it-say-when-you-need-your-own-personal-army/.
86. Fred Weir, "Kremlin frets as Russia's once restive Islamist region

takes up political Islam," *Christian Science Monitor*, September 20, 2017, https://www.csmonitor.com/World/Europe/2017/0920/Kremlin-frets-as-Russia-s-once-restive-Islamist-region-takes-up-political-Islam.

87. Robert Coalson, Terrorist Wave Raises Doubts About Moscow's North Caucasus Strategy," *Radio Free Europe/Radio Liberty*, February 16, 2011, http://www.rferl.org/a/doubts_about_moscow_north_caucasus_strategy/2311376.html.
88. See generally Ilan Berman, *Implosion: The End of Russia and What it Means for America* (Regnery Publishing, 2013).
89. Martin Chulov, "Syrian War's Al-Qaida Affiliate Calls for Terror Attacks in Russia," *Guardian* (London), October 13, 2015, https://www.theguardian.com/world/2015/oct/13/syria-al-qaida-group-jabhat-al-nusra-terror-attacks-russia.
90. Malia Zimmerman, "ISIS Coming for the Kremlin, New Video Warns," *Fox News*, November 12, 2015, http://www.foxnews.com/world/2015/11/12/new-isis-video-says-jihadis-coming-for-kremlin/.

46 Tajikistan

Quick Facts

Population: 8,873,669 (July 2020 est.)
Area:144,100 sq km
Ethnic Groups: Tajik 84.3% (includes Pamiri and Yagnobi), Uzbek 13.8%, other 2% (includes Kyrgyz, Russian, Turkmen, Tatar, Arab) (2014 est.)
Government Type: Presidential republic
GDP (official exchange rate): $7.144 billion (2017 est.)

Source: CIA World FactBook (Last Updated August 2020)

Introduction

The poorest of Central Asia's former Soviet republics, Tajikistan is precariously situated along the lawless northeastern border of Afghanistan and straddles the southern and western ends of the restive Ferghana Valley. The end of official Soviet state atheism led to a reemergence of political Islam. However, uniquely among the former Soviet bloc, Tajikistan was the site of all-–out civil war that pitted former communists against opposition forces that included Islamists.

Sporadic violence persisted after the civil war's end in the late 1990s, and some fear that Tajikistan could once again become unstable. Economic stagnation, a precarious geopolitical position, and poor political management are factors that could fuel a sudden revival of Islamist militancy. Despite measures aimed at curbing jihadists and other anti-state movements, both have persisted. Tajikistan may well prove to be a springboard for further Islamic militancy should authorities continue serving corporate interests, keep the government closed to public control, and fail to hold officials accountable for their misdeeds.

Tajikistan

Due to publishing constraints, this chapter is provided here only in summary form. To view the full study, please visit the online edition of the Almanac at almanac.afpc.org.

47 Turkey

Quick Facts

Population: 82,017,514 (July 2020 est.)
Area: 783,562 sq km
Ethnic Groups: Turkish 70-75%, Kurdish 19%, other minorities 7-12% (2016 est.)
Government Type: Presidential republic
GDP (official exchange rate): $851.5 billion (2017 est.)

Source: CIA World FactBook (Last Updated August 2020)

Introduction

While Turkey remains a nominally secular republic, political Islam has been ascendant in the country since the military coup of 1980. The consolidation of power by Recep Tayyip Erdogan's Justice and Development Party in the past 15 years, however, has led to the gradual weakening of secularism and the promotion of political Islam in Turkish public life. Political Islam has become increasingly visible at the grassroots level, as pious Turks enjoy growing representation in the political process.

In parallel, the mounting authoritarian tendencies of the Turkish government have stifled political opposition. The transformation of Turkey from a parliamentary to a presidential system of government in a 2017 referendum has ensured, for the time being, that Erdogan's political agenda faces no serious domestic challenges. That said, following the fallout with the Gülen Movement with whose support Erdoğan came to power, he has been forced into an uneasy alliance with domestic ultra-nationalists. This has not diminished Erdoğan's Islamism, however, but rather injected it with greater doses of Turkish nationalism.

Turkey's foreign policy has been transformed accordingly. Following the 2011 Arab Spring uprisings, Turkey actively intervened to secure the victory of political Islam across the Middle East and North Africa, lending support especially to the Muslim Brotherhood and affiliated organizations. Turkey's efforts came to naught in both Egypt and Syria, however, and led to Ankara's growing isolation on the regional scene. But rather than reverse course, Turkey doubled down on this approach in Libya, where it has had some success to date in propping up the Brotherhood-aligned Tripoli government against the forces of the Libyan National Army.

Islamist Activity

Islamist forces in Turkey generally take one of three shapes: (1) Islamic brotherhoods and their offshoots; (2) formally incorporated civil society organizations and business entities; and (3) Islamist militant and terrorist groups. The Turkish government has historically had an ambiguous relationship with Islamism: secularist tendencies seeking to limit the role of religion in state and society have coexisted with efforts to harness and control Islamism for official purposes. The latter tendency has grown since the 1980 military coup, and in particular after the AKP came to power in 2003.

Religious Orders and Communities[1]

Religious brotherhoods have been the key focus of Turkish Islamic life since Ottoman times. These orders differed in terms of their focus on spiritual matters as opposed to participation in public life, and several jostled for influence in the Ottoman bureaucracy. They were nevertheless seriously weakened in the second half of the nineteenth century, as the modernization and secularization of the Ottoman state progressed. Thereafter, the Kemalist revolution forced them underground, but also made them increasingly political. With the introduction of multi-party democracy in the 1950s, they have gradually re-emerged as powerful forces in Turkish society and politics.

While Sufi orders are known for their esoteric and mystical nature, one diverges from this tendency: the Naqshbandi, which stands out for its compatibility with orthodox, official Islam. Tracing its chain of spiritual transmission to the first Sunni *caliph*, Abu Bakr, it is firmly rooted in the orthodox Sunni tradition and in adherence to *sharia*.[2] The branch most influential in Turkey traces to Khalid-i-Baghdadi, a sheikh of Kurdish descent from present-day northern Iraq, who developed a new branch of the order known as Khalidiyya. This new branch built on earlier political activist practices, and added a powerful rejection of foreign rule and non-Islamic ideas. From the 1920s onward, the Khalidiyya became a leading element seeking to restore the supremacy of *sharia* law in reaction to secularization reform.[3] When this failed, the order grew increasingly opposed to Ottoman leadership.[4]

This opposition continued into the Republican era, during which the Khalidi order generated a number of lodges, as well as offshoot communities not formally Naqshbandi-Khalidi, but which were created by individuals steeped in the order's tradition. Examples of formal lodges include the influential Iskender Paşa and Menzil; offshoot groupings include most prominently the Fethullah Gülen community, as well as smaller groups such as the Süleymancılar.

In political terms, it is hard to overstate the role of the Iskender Paşa lodge. Its leader from 1958 until his death in 1980, Mehmet Zahid Kotku, was the informal leader of Turkish political Islam. Kotku adapted to the new environment of democratic politics, in which he pushed an anti-colonial agenda intent on unshackling Turkey from foreign "economic slavery." Kotku's followers successfully ensconced themselves in a number of state agencies, most notably the State Planning Organization, where they began to exert influence both on policy and on personnel appointments.[5] As Turkish scholar Birol Yeşilada has noted, the Naqshbandis "always emphasized the need to conquer the state from within by aligning themselves with powerful sources of capital and political actors."[6] This influenced the strategy of many religious communities in the decades to come.

Kotku formally approved the creation of the first major Islamist political party in 1969: Necmettin Erbakan's National Order Party. Thereafter, Kotku's followers in the Iskender Paşa lodge reached unprecedented positions in Turkey. Besides Erbakan, Turgut Özal became Prime Minister and President of Turkey, as did Recep Tayyip Erdogan. In addition, over a dozen followers reached ministerial positions—suggesting an enormous influence for a small religious lodge. Today, the religious influence of the Iskender Paşa lodge is no longer an important factor, yet it formed a generation of Turkish Islamist politicians, making an outsize imprint on Turkish politics.

The Menzil lodge, based in Adıyaman, is a branch of the Khalidiyya that has risen to prominence in recent decades. The lodge is very large, having branched out to Turkey's major cities, particularly Ankara. It grew to prominence in the aftermath of the 1980 military coup, partly because of its support for the state and its proximity to Turkish nationalist groups, including the late founder of the National Unity Party, Muhsin Yazıcıoğlu. In the AKP government, former Energy Minister Taner Yıldız and Health Minister Recep Akdağ are known for their allegiance to Menzil. The lodge controls a business association, TÜMSIAD, which boasts 15,000 members, and whose leader, Hasan Sert, spent two terms as an AKP member of parliament.

The Nurcu movement is often termed a religious brotherhood, but rejects that notion: it terms itself a school of exegesis. Its founder was the preacher Said-i Nursi, who hailed from Erzurum in Kurdish-dominated eastern Turkey. Nursi was strongly influenced by Naqshbandi-Khalidi sheikhs: he studied in Naqshbandi schools, and was formally initiated into the order. Nurcu communities—including the Gülen groups, in turn an offshoot from the Nurcu—all share the common characteristic of seeking to raise new generations trained simultaneously in religious education and modern science.

During the 1960s, Nursi's followers spread all over Turkey, where they set up circles to study his Risale-i Nur, a multi-volume exegesis in which Nursi expounded on the meaning of the Quran. After his death, Nursi's movement split over methods for teaching his work. There are a dozen influential Nurcu groups today, the largest and most important of which is the Gülen group. Nursi's teaching urged his followers to remain aloof from politics; most Nurcu groups did so until the creation of the AKP. Yet, they indirectly tended to provide electoral support for center-right parties, and importantly, not the Islamists under Erbakan.

The Gülen movement is an offshoot from the *Nurcu* community. Over the years, it established its own place—not only by its sheer size, but by emphasizing Gülen's role as spiritual leader over that of Nursi.[7] Gülen, who began his activities in Izmir in the 1960s, refers to the movement as the Hizmet movement, literally meaning "service," a term taken from Nursi's concept of *hizmet-i imaniye ve kur'aniye*, or service to the faith and Quran.

The Gulen movement stands out by its focus on education, developing a network of schools that particularly attracted children of conservative families who sought a culturally conservative education.

In the early 1990s, the collapse of the Soviet Union provided an opportunity to export this model to the newly independent Turkic-speaking states. From there on, the movement developed a global presence, with its epicenter in the Poconos mountains in Pennsylvania, where Gülen resides since moving into self-imposed exile in 1998. At its peak, the movement ran an astounding 1,200 schools in 140 countries.[8] Before its fallout with Erdoğan in 2013, the movement controlled substantial financial institutions, a large business association, TUSKON, Turkey's largest-circulation newspaper, *Zaman*, and a number of charitable organizations.

Compared to most religious communities in Turkey, the Gülen movement stands out by abstaining from the anti-western attitudes that dominate Turkey's Islamic milieus. Because Gülen is a resident of the United States, the movement is effectively run from his compound in the Poconos. Perhaps, as a result of this, it is generally pro-American and eschews the anti-Israeli rhetoric of the Islamist groups of Turkey. Thus, the Gülen movement diverges considerably from its roots in the Naqshbandi-Khalidi movement. While the movement stayed away from electoral politics, it focused on increasing its presence in the state bureaucracy in ways that were fully clear only in the aftermath of the July 2016 failed military coup. The movement's considerable success in this regard initially made it Erdoğan's main partner, but subsequently his most powerful enemy.

Similar to the Nurcu movement, the Süleymanci movement has its roots in the Naqshbandi order, but is not technically a lodge of its own. Its founder, Süleyman Hilmi Tunahan, received religious education in the Naqshbandi-Khalidi order. After the suppression of religious schools following the Kemalist revolution, Tunahan developed a network for teaching the Quran in small groups. The movement then spread when Quranic classes were once again allowed in 1947. It is present not only in Turkey, but particularly in Europe, having set up several hundred mosques and Quranic schools in Germany.

Tunahan died in 1959, but his son-in-law, Kemal Kaçar, took over leadership of the movement. The Süleymanci tended to support Süleyman Demirel's Justice Party, and Kaçar served in parliament for the party for many years. However, the movement was divided when Kaçar died in 2000 and a struggle for leadership broke out between two of Tunahan's grandsons. The two wings ended up supporting different political parties: one faction leader, Mehmet Denizolgun, became a founding member of the AKP, while his brother Ahmet shifted political affiliations. He first joined Erbakan's Welfare Party, then switched allegiance to the Motherland Party (ANAP). In 2007, he ran on the ill-fated Democrat Party ticket, but in 2011 and 2015, he supported the nationalist MHP.[9]

Charities/Organizations

In their efforts to better organize and expand their reach, Turkish Islamists have expanded their activity from orders and brotherhoods to NGOs and business groups. Nearly every lodge or religious community has formed affiliated formal organizations.

The most well-known of these may be the Foundation for Human Rights and Freedoms and Humanitarian Relief (IHH), which organized the May 2010 humanitarian aid flotilla to the Gaza Strip that resulted in a raid by Israeli forces that left nine dead.[10] The IHH is not considered a terrorist group by Turkey. The group operates as a humanitarian relief organization, and has close ties both to the unreformed Saadet (Islamist Felicity) Party and to the ruling Justice and Development Party (AKP).[11] Formed to provide aid to Bosnian Muslims in the mid-1990s,[12] it has held "Special Consultative Status" with the United Nations Economic and Social Council since 2004.[13] However, French counterterrorism magistrate Jean-Louis Bruguière has accused the group of helping *mujahideen* to infiltrate the Balkans in the mid-1990s, and alleges that the IHH is affiliated with al-Qaeda.[14] IHH continues to undertake broad humanitarian activities in emergency-stricken areas around the globe, placing a larger emphasis on countries with a Muslim population while appearing to use these activities as a cover for relations with global *jihadist* networks.[15] It has been particularly active in Syria.

Established in 1990, MÜSİAD (the Independent Industrialists and Businessmen's Association) appears to have originally been formed as a more religious counterpart to the country's predominant business group, the Turkish Industry and Business Association (TUSIAD).[16] The group's main function appears to be to extend the reach of Islamist capital – what is called *yeşil sermaye* (green money) in Turkey. Green money is money from wealthy Islamist businessmen and Middle Eastern countries that, through careful investment, is funneled into legitimate businesses that end up serving as an engine for Islamist parties.[17] MUSIAD and TUSKON differ in the nature of their members, with MUSIAD's members coming from AKP's Milli Görüş tradition, while those close to Gülen's *cemaat* were organized under TUSKON until that organization was also closed down following the coup.[18]

Terrorist Organizations

The İslami Büyük Doğu Akıncılar (Islamic Great Eastern Raiders, or IBDA) was founded in 1970 as a peripheral youth faction of Erbakan's Millî Selamet Partisi (National Salvation Party, or MNP). This group, known as Akıncılar, saw a splinter group develop under the leadership of Salih Mirzabeyoğlu, known as IBDA-C, the "C" standing for "cephe" or "front." It became the first group in the history of modern Turkey to advocate armed struggle in the service of an Islamic revolution. Its ideology, notable and perhaps unique among modern Islamist groups, is a mixture of Sunni Islam, Trotskyism, and Platonic idealism. IBDA-C adheres to this ideology, but differs from the mainstream currents due to its use of violence, including terrorism, to achieve its goals—something that has made the group marginal in political terms. No precise estimate of the size of its membership exists. Members organize independently, without any defined hierarchy or central authority, and both its legal and illegal actions are carried out via autonomous local "front" groups that cooperate with other opposition elements in Turkey when necessary.[19]

IBDA-C joined al-Qaeda in claiming responsibility for the November 2003 bombings in Istanbul.[20] In the summer of 2008, a front staged an armed attack on the United States General Consulate in Istanbul, killing three police officers who had been defending it. Turkish police claimed to have dismantled several *cephe* the following year. On October 7, 2014, the group formally pledged its support to the Islamic State.[21] Its leader, Salih Izzet Erdiş, was released that year after a decade-and-a-half in prison. Upon his release, Erdoğan met with him and, following his death in 2019, senior AKP leaders including Defense Minister Hulusi Akar visited his grave.[22]

Turkish Hezbollah is a Kurdish Sunni extremist organization founded in the 1980s by Hüseyin Velioğlu, an ethnic Kurd and former student activist, in the southeastern city of Diyarbakır. The organization, which is unrelated to the Lebanese Shiite militia of the same name (but shares its sympathy for Iran) seeks to establish an Islamic state in three distinct phases: (1) a period of propaganda and indoctrination, known as *tebliğ* (communication); (2) the consolidation of a popular base, known as *cemaat* (community); and (3) a *jihad* to overthrow the secular order and establish an Islamic state.[23] It is vehemently hostile to the Marxist Kurdistan Workers' Party (PKK). Beginning in the mid-1990s, Turkish Hezbollah expanded its activities from killing PKK militants to conducting low-level bombings against liquor stores and other establishments that the organization considered *haram* (forbidden).[24] Turkish Hezbollah is known for cleaver-assaults, kidnappings, beatings, acid attacks on women not dressed in an Islamic manner, and assassinations. Consecutive Turkish governments have accused Iran of using Hezbollah in Turkey in a similar manner as its counterpart in Lebanon.[25]

The Turkish government initially ignored Hezbollah, hoping that its Islamism might provide an ideological bulwark against the rival PKK's atheistic Marxism. But by the late 1990s, Turkish authorities acknowledged that Hezbollah had become a major threat in its own right, and moved against the group.[26] Leader Huseyin Velioğlu was killed in a shootout with Turkish forces in January 2000. The incident touched off a series of counterterrorism operations against the group, resulting in some 2,000 detentions and the arrests of several hundred on criminal charges. Turkish Hezbollah has not conducted a major operation since it assassinated the popular Diyarbakır police chief in 2001.[27] In January 2010, five members of the group were freed in accordance with a new national law restricting the amount of time suspects can be held while awaiting the final verdict in their cases.[28]

Hüda-Par ("Free Cause Party") is a Kurdish Sunni radical party that emerged from Turkish Hezbollah. It is reported to be sympathetic to ISIS. Following a decision to end its armed struggle in 2002, sympathizers of Turkish Hezbollah founded the Solidarity with the Oppressed Association, Mustazaflar ile Dayanışma Derneği or Mustazaf Der.[29] In 2010, Mustazaf Der held a celebration of the Prophet Muhammad's birthday estimated to have been attended by 120,000 people. A Diyarbakir court then ordered the closure of Mustazaf Der on the grounds that it was a front for Hezbollah. Societies associated with *Hüda-Par* operate under the umbrella organization Peygamber Sevdalıları ("Lovers of Prophet," or in "Evindarên Pêyxamber" in Kurdish).[30]

The "*Caliphate* State", also known as the Kaplan group and ICB-AFID, is a terrorist group that operates in Germany and seeks to overthrow the secular Turkish government and establish an Islamic state modeled after Iran. The group was founded by Cemalettin Kaplan, following his parting with the Millî Görüş movement in Turkey, and subsequently led by his son Metin after the elder Kaplan's death in 1995. Its immediate purpose is to gather the Muslim masses living in Europe under an Islamic banner to reject democracy and Western culture. Its ultimate goal is to establish a federative Islamic state on Anatolian soil based on Shari'a by overthrowing the constitutional state and the secular order. The group, organized as Verband der Islamischen Vereine und Gemeinden e.V. (*Islami Cemaat ve Cemiyetler Birliği/ ICCB*) with 1,200 members in Germany and an estimated membership of 5,000 around Europe, was outlawed by the German authorities in 2002.[31] Despite the increasingly Islamist nature of Turkey, the Kaplan group has not changed its attitude toward the Turkish government.

Kudüs Ordusu (also known as Tevhid-Selam or "The Army of Jerusalem") is an illegal organization which emerged in 1985. Using the publication of several magazines, including Tevhid and Selam, as a cover, the group often collaborated with other organizations and received its inspiration from the Qods Force, a paramilitary unit of Iran's Islamic Revolutionary Guard Corps.[32] In 2000, twenty-four members were indicted for attempting to overthrow the country's secular regime and establish a state based upon religious law, and for their involvement in the assassinations of several pro-secular journalists and academics during the 1990s. Fifteen of them were subsequently convicted in 2002, with three receiving a death sentence (the death penalty has since been abolished in Turkey).[33]

Al-Qaeda remains active in Turkey as well. In 2003, a Turkish chapter of the bin Laden network surfaced, possibly in collaboration with IBDA-C members, to conduct terrorist attacks against two synagogues, an HSBC bank, and the British consulate.[34] Richard Barrett, the head of the UN's Al Qaeda and Taliban monitoring group, estimated in 2010 that there were over 100 Turkish-speaking al-Qaeda members along the Pakistan-Afghanistan border.[35] Unfortunately, knowledge about al-Qaeda's current size and capabilities within Turkey is undercut by a chronic lack of proper study. Turkish police have been generally successful at thwarting al-Qaeda's attacks, and thwarted attacks rarely receive significant media attention. Furthermore, Turkey does not seem a natural target for al-Qaeda, given that its government is heavily influenced by Islamic ideals.[36] In fact, at least some tactical collaboration between the Turkish state and the bin Laden network appears to have taken place in the past. In January 2015, leaked Turkish military documents indicated that the Turkish national intelligence service (MIT) was shipping weapons to al-Qaeda in Syria. Erdogan insisted these deliveries were destined for Syrian Turkmen groups. The veracity of the account is hard to establish—as is the veracity of much reported about Turkey since the fallout between Erdogan and Gülen. Media outlets have been officially banned from reporting on the incident, however.[37]

The Muslim Brotherhood and Hamas are not domestic Turkish organizations, but have nonetheless become an increasingly prominent part of the Islamist scene in Turkey. Erdoğan's government proclaimed its support for Hamas as early as 2006, when it won elections in Gaza and proceeded to violently grab total power in the territory.[38] Following the Arab upheavals of 2011, Turkey moved to support the bid for power of the Muslim

Brotherhood (Hamas's parent organization) across the Middle East and North Africa. In particular, Turkey supported the short-lived Brotherhood-affiliated government of Mohammad Morsi in Egypt. When Morsi's government was overthrown and the Brotherhood banned, the movement relocated its headquarters to Turkey and Qatar. By 2014, pressure from Gulf states led Qatar to ask a number of prominent Brotherhood figures to leave the country.[39] This led the Brotherhood to concentrate in Turkey, and the country has for practical purposes become the organization's global center. Several Brotherhood-aligned television stations today operate from there.[40] Upward of 20,000 Egyptian exiles, mostly attached to the Brotherhood, also now reside in Turkey, and are recipients of the Erdoğan's government's support.[41]

Hizb ut-Tahrir, founded in 1953, made its way to Turkey in 1978, espousing its aim of establishing an Islamic *caliphate* and introducing *sharia* law. The Turkish police have frequently detained members of the organization, which was formally outlawed by a Turkish court in 2004.[42] The latest raid came in 2009, with authorities detaining 165 suspected Hizb ut-Tahrir members.[43] Though the exact size and breadth of the group's Turkish branch is not known, documents and maps confiscated during the 2009 raids have exposed the organization's plans to establish a *caliphate* across large portions of the globe.[44] Hizb ut-Tahrir is active in Turkey, despite having been formally banned, and boasts an organizational office in the capital city of Ankara, as well as a dedicated website under the name of Türkiye Vilayeti ("Turkish province.")[45] From 2013 to 2016, the organization held yearly meetings and demonstrations in support of the reinstatement of the *caliphate*, without encountering government intervention. In March 2017, however, its attempt to hold a conference in support of the *caliphate* was denied, and Hizb ut-Tahrir leaders were briefly detained. However, they were released within several days, in contrast to secularist and Kurdish activists who have lingered in jails for months to years.[46] Still, the Turkish Information Technology and Communications Board banned access to the organization's sites in April 2017.[47] Lower courts and Turkish court of Cassation had determined that Hizb-ut Tahrir is a terrorist organization, a decision upheld as recently as 2017. However, in

2018, the Erdoğan-controlled Constitutional Court overturned these findings, determining that there is insufficient evidence to classify it as a terrorist group.[48] As a result, in March 2019, it organized a "Caliphate Conference" in Ankara ahead of local elections, in which speakers called for the immediate abolition of the democratic republic.[49] The organization has continued to develop openly in Turkey: it operates a highly active publishing house called Köklü Değişim (Comprehensive Change) and organized a conference with hundreds of attendees in Istanbul in March 2020 entitled "From Family to the State – Building an Islamic Society."[50]

For several years, Turkey was an important logistical and financial base for the Islamic State (IS, or ISIS). However, as the group began targeting interests in Turkey, the government gradually altered its *laissez-faire* attitude to one of greater efforts to limit the group's presence in the country. The basic logic behind Turkey's approach to ISIS was that it was a lesser danger to Turkey than either the Kurdish forces in Syria or the Assad regime. ISIS's strategy, on the other hand, was at first to lay low in Turkey. But when the group was unable to operate unhindered in the country, it began to seek to create a division between increasingly extremist Sunnis and others in society by carrying out acts of violence that increase the already-significant tensions along Turkey's sectarian, ethnic, and political fault lines. It moreover sought to raise the price of Turkey's involvement in the anti-ISIS coalition by targeting its tourism industry. For example, on January 12, 2016, an ISIS suicide bomber attacked Istanbul's historic Sultanahmet Square, killing 12 people. All of the victims killed were foreign tourists. In response, the Turkish Army launched tank and artillery strikes on ISIS positions in Syria and Iraq.

ISIS sought to radicalize Islamist youth who have become alienated from their communities and encourage them to radical action.[51] Polling showed that only about 1.3% of Turkey's population sympathized with ISIS, which translates to roughly a million potential ISIS sympathizers in the country.[52] The most fertile recruiting grounds have been the poorest areas in Turkey's Kurdish southeast, where unemployment is roughly six times higher than elsewhere in the country.[53] The Dokumacılar (Weavers) was a branch of ISIS that specifically targeted the Kurdish People's Protection Units (YPG) during the Syrian Civil War. Estimates of the group's Turkish membership range from 60 to 400.[54]

Turkey's relationship to ISIS militants is the subject of much controversy. Ankara has armed and trained opposition fighters, hosted Syrian dissidents, and backed radical groups like Ahrar al-Sham, which worked with Jabhat al-Nusra, Syria's al-Qaeda franchise.[55] Cengiz Candar, a Turkish journalist, has argued that Turkey's intelligence service, MIT, helped "midwife" the Islamic State, as well as other *jihadi* groups.[56] However, from 2015 onward, Turkey gradually become far tougher on foreign fighters attempting to travel to Syria via Turkey, and launched a broad crackdown on militants streaming across its territory.

In March 2016, the *Washington Post* reported that Turkey had deported nearly 3,200 people suspected of foreign-fighter-related activities since the war in Syria began in 2011. An additional 3,000 were awaiting deportation in "returnee centers." But even these numbers are but a small percentage of the total who traveled to Syria since 2011, the vast majority of whom entered Syria through Turkey.[57] (More recent figures detailing the scope of Turkey's foreign fighter problem are not currently available.)

One reason the Turkish government was slow to target ISIS is that most of ISIS's operations in Turkey targeted political opposition parties and Kurdish activists. This included the Dokumacılar bombings in 2015, and a massive suicide bombing in Ankara that October which killed 109 people. Evidence has come to light that Ankara's anti-terror department received intelligence of these attacks before the bombings, but did not inform its superiors or the unit responsible for protecting the rally. Ankara police advised its agents to protect themselves against a potential suicide attack during the October 10th rally, but did not take any measures to protect the rally attendees.[58] The attack had a major impact on Turkish voters, and swung their votes in favor of AKP in the November 1st election.[59]

From August 2016 onward, Turkey launched a series of military operations in northern Syria. This began with the 2016-2017 Operation Euphrates Shield, which was initially supported by western powers. Over time, however, tensions arose as Turkey pushed deeper into Syria.[60] Turkey continued to secure a "de-escalation zone" in northern Syria in the fall of 2017, with Russian acquiescence. It then established a presence in northern Syria for the long haul. In October 2019, Turkey launched Operation Peace Spring, which aimed to establish Turkish-controlled territories in northeastern Syria – areas thus far controlled by the Syrian Kurds – into which Turkey planned to relocate Syrian refugees in Turkey. Aside from its own military presence in northern Syria, Turkey has organized Arab and Turkmen militias into an umbrella force called the Syrian National Army, which is estimated to have some 25,000 fighters. These forces are bankrolled by Turkey, effectively functioning as Turkish-supported mercenaries. However, these various groups never gelled into a coherent force, and instances of infighting between them are numerous. Still, in 2019-20, the Pentagon Inspector General estimates that Turkey deployed up to 3,800 troops from the SNA into Libya, where they played a key role in fighting the Libyan National Army's offensive against the Tripoli government supported by Turkey.[61]

Islamism and Society

Turkey's population of nearly 80 million is over 99 percent of Muslim heritage. About 80 percent are Sunni, primarily of the Hanafi school, although the Shafi'i school is also represented primarily among Turkey's Kurds. Some 15-20 percent of Turks are Alevis—an indigenous religious tradition nominally belonging to Shia Islam, but with strong syncretic elements drawing on Christian and neo-Platonic traditions. The Bektaşi order is strongly wedded to Alevi beliefs.[62] In addition, 2-3 million adhere to the Twelver Jafari Shiism practiced in Iran—chiefly among Azerbaijani Turks in eastern Turkey—while several hundred thousand Nusairis exist in southern Turkey, near the Syrian border.

During the time of the Ottoman Empire, religious communities were allowed to govern themselves under their own *millet* (system)—*sharia* for Muslims, Canon Law for Christians and Halakha for Jews. In the millet system, people were defined by their religious affiliations, rather than their ethnic origins.[63] After the demise of the Ottoman Empire following the First World War, the Republic of Turkey was founded on the ideals of modernism and secularism.[64] The founders of the modern republic considered the separation of religion and politics an essential step for adopting Western values and secularism, and a mandatory condition for its success as a Muslim nation.[65] The new regime therefore abolished the Ottoman sultanate in 1922 and the *caliphate* in 1924, replacing laws based on *sharia* with European legal codes.[66] Additionally, it switched from the Arabic alphabet to the Latin one, and from the Islamic calendar to the Gregorian while restricting public attire associated with religious affiliations (outlawing the fez and discouraging women from wearing the veil).

With the abolition of the *caliphate*, Islam no longer constituted the basis for the Turkish legal system. However, vestiges remained: despite the abolition of *Şeyhülislam*, the superior authority in the matters of Islam, and the Ministry of Religious Affairs and Pious Foundations,[67] Islam was still preserved as the state religion by the country's 1924 Constitution, but this clause was abolished in 1928.[68] Meanwhile, the Directorate for Religious Affairs, Diyanet, was established to oversee the organization and administration of religious affairs. The Unification of Instruction, *Tevhid-i Tedrisat*, brought all educational establishments under the control of the state.[69] Hence, the transformation from an imperial-religious entity to a national entity—from an *ummah* to a modern nation-state—was initiated.

Since the start of multi-party democracy in 1946 and the ensuing victory of the *Demokrat Parti* (the Democratic Party) four years later, Islamic groups have managed to take advantage of political parties pandering for votes. This is in part because they are capable of delivering considerable block votes to political parties. These orders and communities have increasingly become powerful players in Turkish politics, exploiting the deficiencies of the nation's young democratic system.

The emergence of political Islam in Turkey was connected to the emergence of political Islam elsewhere in the Muslim world, particularly the rise of the Egyptian Muslim Brotherhood. Numerous scholars have noted the influence of key Brotherhood ideologists on former Prime Minister Necmettin Erbakan and the *Milli Görüş* movement.[70] While the Brotherhood is in principle opposed to Sufi orders, this does not appear to apply to the Naqshbandi-Khalidi order, which has deep Sunni roots.

In today's Turkey, indigenous Islamist groups imitate the strategies of foreign ones. Political sociologists and commentators have long recognized this phenomenon. For example, in a 1999 letter to then-Prime Minister Bulent Ecevit, political scientist Gürbüz Evren warned about the importation of ideas and strategy from the Muslim Brotherhood, and that a new party based on this model was most likely to be founded out of a cadre of the Islamist *Refah Partisi* (Welfare Party) and *Fazilet Partisi* (Virtue Party). As predicted, the AKP—which contains former members of both *Refah* and *Fazilet*—was founded on August 14, 2001, and went on to win the country's November 2002 parliamentary elections.[71]

Grassroots Islamism in Turkey is also strengthened by the infusion of "green money" from Middle Eastern states. These vast financial flows, estimated by government officials and Turkish economists to annually be worth billions,[72] have given both imported and domestic interpretations of Islamism considerable voice in Turkish society. Moreover, extremist groups active in Turkey appear to be financed not only through domestic methods (including donations, theft, extortion, and other illicit activity), but also through funds from abroad that contribute to the cost of training and logistics. The amount and origin of such funding is not fully known, but is understood to be substantial. For example, documents recovered in the January 2000 raid against Turkish Hezbollah in Istanbul helped to expose the significant financial and logistical support Iran has provided the group. Since such raids by the security forces often disrupt group activity, foreign support serves as a much-needed lifeline in terms of sanctuary, training, arms, ammunition, food and clothing.[73]

Turkish society in general does not appear as susceptible to radical Islamism as that of other Muslim nations or the Muslim communities in Europe. Traditionally, Turks have tended toward relatively liberal schools of thought in Islam, such as the Hanafi school of jurisprudence and Maturidi tradition, which grant considerable flexibility to the interpretation of religious law. Arab and Kurdish Islam, however, have tended toward the Hanbali and Shafi'i schools of thought, based on the Ashari tradition, which is much stricter.

When surveyed in 2007, 42 percent of Turks reported that they consider themselves unreligious or slightly religious, 37 percent are somewhat religious, and 21 percent identify themselves as very religious or extremely religious (with only 1.6 percent falling into the latter category).[74] Subsequent polls, such as the 2013 Eurobarometer survey, showed that the number of self-reported atheists had doubled.[75] A 2019 Konda poll confirms the tendency: compared to 2008 figures, the number of self-reported "religious conservatives" declined from 32 to 25 percent, and the percentage who fast during Ramadan went from 77 to 65 percent. Similarly, the percentage who agreed that a woman needs her husband's permission to work declined dramatically, from 69 to 55 percent.[76]

However, Islamist groups in the form of "Islamic holdings" have been known to prey on religious communities in Anatolian Turkey and the religious Turkish population in Germany, borrowing directly from lenders without using any financial intermediaries and accumulating large sums of capital.[77] The support for Islamist terror groups by Turkish society, on the other hand, has been negligible and is restricted to the extreme minority.

Islamism and the State

Since the founding of the Turkish Republic, the Turkish state has made an effort to separate Islam from Islamism. In its attempt to erect a tradition of "state Islam," the government has regulated religious affairs via the *Diyanet* (the Directorate of Religious Affairs established in 1924). The *Diyanet,* directly tied to the Office of the Prime Minister, coordinates the building of mosques, trains and appoints *imams*, and determines the topics for weekly Friday sermons by imams. Thus, in contrast with other regional states—where governments finance, certify, and supervise mosques but underground radical mosques, Koranic schools, and *imams* successfully compete with government establishments more or less unchecked—state Islam in Turkey has enjoyed a near-monopoly on legitimate expression of the Muslim faith.[78]

Over the years, the formally secular nature of the Turkish state has led to constraints on political participation. Article 2 of the Turkish Constitution, which states, "The Republic of Turkey is a democratic, secular and social state governed by the rule of law,"[79] has served as the basis for the closure of four political parties—the *Milli Nizam Partisi*, *Milli Selamet Partisi*, *Refah Partisi* and *Fazilet Partisi*—each of which was charged with violating the secular nature of the Republic. Twenty-two other parties have been banned for various reasons.[80]

Turkey's transition to a multi-party system and the evolution of Turkish democracy has been marked by friction between the competing pulls of modernization and traditional societal norms. Successful collective political action by tribal leaders, in combination with the appeasement policies of political leaders, has given tribal entities a disproportionate voice in Turkish politics, allowing the more traditional minority to dominate the country's political scene.[81] As a result, even the *Diyanet*, established to control the religious exploitation common in an earlier age, has ended up being dominated by one of the Islamist bodies it was intended to control, namely the Nakşibendi order. The outcome has been the further "Sunni-ization" of Turkey over the years, despite the supposed neutrality of the state toward all religions and their branches.

The behavior of the governing AKP since consolidating its power has exposed new approaches of imposing Islamism on Turkish society. The 2010 Constitutional Referendum weakened the separation of powers that previously existed in the Turkish political system, essentially giving the governing party the power to control all three branches of the government.[82] Nearly all state institutions have been inundated with AKP cadres; any opposition is largely insignificant and has been silenced.

Education reforms in 2012-14 led to an Islamization of the public schooling system. The age limit preventing students under 12 years from attending Qur'an courses was lifted, and a program for the introduction of Qur'an courses for preschoolers was introduced. Qur'anic schools are now also allowed to have dormitories, enabling them to fully immerse students in a religious environment.

Public schools saw an extension of compulsory religious education, as well as the introduction of courses on the Life of Muhammad and on the Qur'an, bringing religious education to a possible total of six hours per week. While these courses are nominally elective, in many schools there is considered practically or socially mandated.[83]

Erdoğan's rhetoric continues to express support for a particular brand of Islamism – both at home and abroad. He has severely castigated Saudi Arabia's reforms, rejecting the notion of "moderate Islam" advanced by Crown Prince Muhmmad Bin Sultan in recent years. Erdoğan stated that this is a "trap to weaken Islam," while AKP mouthpieces like the daily *Yeni Şafak* called Saudi reforms a "very dangerous game," purportedly instigated by the United States and Israel, an "American plan whose final aim is to occupy Islam's holy sites, Mecca and Medina."[84] Similarly, Erdoğan threatened to cut ties with the UAE following Abu Dhabi's summer 2020 announcement it would normalize ties with the Jewish State – despite Turkey's continued relations with Jerusalem.[85]

Domestically, Erdoğan has made symbolic gestures that suggest a greater Islamization of society. These include, most prominently, the conversion of the landmark Hagia Sophia cathedral into a mosque in July 2020. This was followed by the similar conversion of another medieval Greek Orthodox church in Istanbul into a museum the following month. While those actions cannot be separated from the growing tensions between Turkey and Greece over maritime issues in the Aegean and Mediterranean, they nevertheless point to Erdoğan's growing Islamist populism.

Endnotes

1. For a fuller analysis of the brotherhoods, see Svante E. Cornell and M.K. Kaya, "The Naqshbandi-Khalidi Order and the Evolution of Political Islam in Turkey," *Current Trends in Islamist Ideology*, no. 19, 2015.
2. Albert Hourani, *The Emergence of the Modern Middle East* (Oakland, CA: University of California Press, 1981), p. 78.
3. Şerif Mardin, "The Nakshibendi Order of Turkey" in Martin E.

Marty and R. Scott Appelby, eds., *Fundamentalisms and the State* (Chicago: University of Chicago Press, 1993), 213.

4. Ibid., 214-215; Itzchak Weismann, *The Naqshbandiyya: Orthodoxy and Activism in a worldwide Sufi Tradition* (London: Routledge Press, 2007).
5. Esen Kirdiş, *Between Movement and Party: Islamic Political Party Formation in Morocco, Turkey and Jordan* (St. Paul: University of Minnesota Press, 2011), p. 129.
6. Birol Yeşilada, "The Refah Party Phenomenon in Turkey," in Birol Yeşilada, ed., *Comparative Political Parties and Party Elites: Essays in Honor of Samuel J. Eldersveld* (Ann Arbor: University of Michigan Press, 1999), 137.
7. Isa Tatlıcan, "Nurculuk ile Gülen Cemaatı arasında 8 fark," *Milat*, January 6, 2014, http://www.yazaroku.com/guncel/isa-tatlican/06-01-2014/nurculuk-ile-gulen-cemaati-arasinda-ki-8-fark/659454.aspx.
8. "World's Most Powerful Imam to Rise?" Turkishnews.com, June 18, 2012, http://www.turkishnews.com/en/content/tag/gulen/page/7/.
9. Yalçın Bayer, "MHP'yi Baraj altından Sÿleymancılar mı kurtardı?" *Hürriyet*, June 15, 2011, http://www.ilkehaber.com/haber/mhpyi-baraj-altindan-suleymancilar-mi-kurtardi-17278.htm.
10. Yaakov Katz, "Nine Dead in Vicious conflict Aboard 'Mavi Marmara,'" *Jerusalem Post*, June 1, 2010, http://www.jpost.com/Israel/Nine-dead-in-Vicious-conflict-aboard-Mavi-Marmara.
11. Damien McElroy et al., "Gaza flotilla: Turkey Accused of Behaving like Iran by Israel," *Telegraph* (London), June 3, 2010, http://www.telegraph.co.uk/news/worldnews/europe/turkey/7801641/Gaza-flotilla-Turkey-accused-of-behaving-like-Iran-by-Israel.html.
12. "Factbox: Turkish Charity Group Behind Gaza-Bound Convoy," Reuters, May 31, 2010, http://www.reuters.com/article/2010/06/01/us-palestinians-israel-turkey-group-fact-idUSTRE64U4SO20100601.
13. The list of non-governmental organizations in consultative status with the Economic and Social Council as of September 2009 is available at United Nations Economic and Social Council, E/2009/INF/4, September 1, 2009, http://esango.un.org/paperless/content/E2009INF4.pdf.
14. "Turkey's Radical Drift," *Wall Street Journal*, June 3, 2010, http://online.wsj.com/article/SB10001424052748703561604575282423181610814.html.
15. "The Turkish organization IHH provides humanitarian assistance to the famine-stricken regions of Somalia," Meir Amit Intelligence and

Terrorism Information Center, May 11, 2011, http://www.terrorism-info.org.il/en/article/17827.

16. Eylem Türk, "Ömer Cihad Vardan. Son dönemin yükseleni muhafazakâr dernekler," [The rising conservative associations of the recent era] *Milliyet*, August 1, 2009, http://www.milliyet.com.tr/Ekonomi/HaberDetay.aspx?aType=HaberDetay&ArticleID=1123854&Date=20.03.2011&Kategori=ekonomi&b=Son%20donemin%20yukseleni%20muhafazak%C3%A2r%20dernekler; TUSIAD US, "Mission Statement," n.d., http://www.tusiad.us/about.cfm?TEMPLATE=1.
17. Michael Rubin, "Green Money, Islamist Politics in Turkey," *Middle East Quarterly*, Winter 2005, 13-23, http://www.meforum.org/684/green-money-islamist-politics-in-turkey.
18. Mustafa Sönmez, "TUSKON'la MUSIAD birbirine girecek (TUSKON and MUSIAD will clash)," *Odatv* (Istanbul), February 20, 2012, http://www.odatv.com/n.php?n=tuskonla-musiad-birbirine-girecek-2002121200.
19. Yoni Fighel, "Great East Islamic Raiders Front (IBDA-C) – A Profile," International Institute for Counter-Terrorism, January 12, 2003, http://www.ict.org.il/Articles/tabid/66/Articlsid/565/currentpage/19/Default.aspx.
20. "Turkey Buries Latest Bomb Victims," CNN, November 21, 2003, http://articles.cnn.com/2003-11-21/world/turkey.blast_1_attacks-on-british-interests-bomb-attacks-qaeda?_s=PM:WORLD.
21. "İstanbul'da IŞİD'cilerden 'iç savaş' toplantısı," *Ileri Haber,* November 30, 2014, http://ilerihaber.org/istanbulda-isidcilerden-ic-savas-toplantisi/3807/.
22. "Turkish court censors articles on minister's visit to cemetery of Islamist leader," *Ahval*, August 18, 2020, https://ahvalnews.com/press-freedom/turkish-court-censors-articles-ministers-visit-cemetery-islamist-leader.
23. Gareth Jenkins, "Back with a Vengeance: Turkish Hezbollah," Jamestown Foundation *Terrorism Monitor* 6, iss. 2, January 25, 2008, http://www.jamestown.org/programs/gta/single/?tx_ttnews%5Btt_news%5D=4684&tx_ttnews%5BbackPid%5D=167&no_cache=1.
24. Department of State, "Appendix C: Background Information on Other Terrorist Groups," n.d., http://www.state.gov/documents/organization/31947.pdf.
25. "Huda-Par's emergence," *The Economist,* November 23, 2013, http://www.economist.com/news/europe/21590595-islamist-par-

ty-turkeys-kurds-huda-pars-emergence.

26. Jenkins, "Back with a Vengeance."
27. Department of State, "Appendix C: Background Information on Other Terrorist Groups."
28. İzgi Güngör, "Release of Turkish Hizbullah members sparks controversy over its future strategy," *Hürriyet* (Istanbul), January 9, 2010, http://www.hurriyetdailynews.com/n.php?n=release-of-turkish-hizbullah-members-sparks-controversy-over-its-future-strategy-2011-01-09.
29. Ismail Güney Yılmaz, "Hizbullah: Tebliğ, Cemaat, Cihat," *Biamag,* April 13, 2013, http://bianet.org/biamag/toplum/145800-hizbullah-teblig-cemaat-cihat.
30. "Peygamber Sevdalıları Platformu kuruldu," [The Prophet Lovers Platform was Founded] *Milli Gazete,* April 12, 2009.
31. "Kaplancılar'ın itirazı kabul edilmedi," [Kaplan Objection was not Accepted] *Mynet Haber*, November 28, 2002, http://haber.mynet.com/detay/dunya/kaplancilarin-itirazi-kabul-edilmedi/32157.
32. "Keleş: Mumcu cinayeti çözüldü," [Keleş: Mumcu's Murder Solved] *NTVMSNBC*, July 11, 2000, http://arsiv.ntvmsnbc.com/news/16885.asp.
33. "Ugur Mumcu anılıyor," [Ugur Mumcu Remembered] *Hurriyet* (Istanbul), January 24, 2002, http://webarsiv.hurriyet.com.tr/2002/01/24/79593.asp.
34. Emrullah Uslu, "Was Alleged al-Qaeda Attack a Failed Attempt to Occupy the U.S. Consulate in Istanbul?" Jamestown Foundation *Terrorism Monitor* 5, iss. 27, July 23, 2008, http://www.jamestown.org/programs/gta/single/?tx_ttnews[tt_news]=5073&tx_ttnews[backPid]=246&no_cache=1.
35. Tolga Tanış, "En az 100 Turk El Kaideci," [More than 100 Turkish al-Qaeda Hands] *Hurriyet* (Istanbul), October 10, 2010, http://www.hurriyet.com.tr/dunya/16004291.asp.
36. Karen Hodgson, "The al Qaeda threat in Turkey," *Long War Journal,* July 8, 2013, http://www.longwarjournal.org/archives/2013/07/the_al_qaeda_threat_1.php.
37. Fehim Taştekin, "Turkish military says MIT shipped weapons to al-Qaeda," *Al Monitor,* January 15, 2015, http://www.al-monitor.com/pulse/originals/2015/01/turkey-syria-intelligence-service-shipping-weapons.html#ixzz4NZ2vMCrh.
38. Soner Çagaptay, "Hamas Visits Ankara: The AKP Shifts Turkey's Role in the Middle East," Washington Institute for Near East Policy *Policywatch* 1081, February 16, 2006, https://www.washingtoninsti-

tute.org/policy-analysis/view/hamas-visits-ankara-the-akp-shifts-turkeys-role-in-the-middle-east.
39. "Prominent Muslim Brotherhood figures to leave Qatar," Reuters, September 13, 2014, https://in.reuters.com/article/uk-egypt-qatar-brotherhood-idUKKBN0H807T20140913.
40. Murat Sofuoglu, "Istanbul: A haven for Egyptian journalists in exile" *TRT World*, March 31, 2018, https://www.trtworld.com/magazine/istanbul-a-haven-for-egyptian-journalists-in-exile-16358.
41. Abdelrahman Ayyash, "The Turkish Future of Egypt's Muslim Brotherhood," Century Foundation, August 17, 2020, https://tcf.org/content/report/turkish-future-egypts-muslim-brotherhood/?agreed=1.
42. Patrick Wrigley, "Turkey Hems in its Islamist Fringe," *Asia Times*, August 7, 2009, http://www.atimes.com/atimes/Middle_East/KH07Ak02.html.
43. "Turkey Detains 165 Suspected Members of Radical Islamist Group Hizb ut-Tahrir," *Fox News*, July 27, 2009, http://www.foxnews.com/story/0,2933,534927,00.html.
44. \"Hizb-ut Tahrir'in "Hilafet Devletinin toprakları," [Hizb-ut Tahrir's "Caliphate State Lands"] *Radikal* (Istanbul), July 27, 2009, http://www.radikal.com.tr/Radikal.aspx?aType=RadikalDetayV3&ArticleID=946898&Date=28.07.2009&CategoryID=77.
45. "Hizb-ut Tahrir Türkiye Vilayeti," n.d., http://turkiyevilayeti.org/html/iltsm/iltsm.html.
46. Pınar Tremblay, "Next in Line on Erdoğan's Warpath: Naughty Islamists", *Al-Monitor*, March 9, 2017, https://www.al-monitor.com/pulse/originals/2017/03/turkey-erdogan-begins-taking-revenge-non-conformist-islamists.html
47. "Hizb-ut Tahrir'e Yasaklama," *Odatv*, April 1, 2017, https://odatv4.com/hizb-ut-tahrire-yasaklama-0104171200.html.
48. "AYM'den Hizb-ut Tahrir kararı!" *Habertürk*, October 26, 2018, https://www.haberturk.com/aym-den-hizb-ut-tahrir-karari-2193604.
49. "Jihadist Hizb ut-Tahrir calls for 'destroying the Republic' before Turkey's local elections," *Sol International*, March 31, 2019, https://news.sol.org.tr/jihadist-hizb-ut-tahrir-calls-destroying-republic-turkeys-local-elections-175778.
50. "Hizb ut Tahrir Wilayah Turkey Holds Huge Khilafah Conference in Istanbul," Khilafah.com, March 8, 2020, http://www.khilafah.com/hizb-ut-tahrir-wilayah-turkey-holds-huge-khilafah-conference-in-istanbul/.
51. Metin Gürcan, "Atatürk Havalimanı saldırısı: IŞİD ne yapmaya çalışıyor?" *T24*, July 1, 2016, http://t24.com.tr/yazarlar/metin-gur-

can/ataturk-havalimani-saldirisi-isid-ne-yapmaya-calisiyor,14930.

52. Tülin Daloğlu, "Turks rumored to be joining the Islamic State," *Al-Monitor*, October 1, 2014, http://www.al-monitor.com/pulse/tr/contents/articles/originals/2014/10/turkey-syria-isis-coalition-polls.html.
53. Michael Kaplan, "Kurds Joining Islamic State? ISIS Finds Unlikely Supporters Among Turkey's Disgruntled Kurds," *International Business Times*, July 15, 2015, http://www.ibtimes.com/kurds-joining-islamic-state-isis-finds-unlikely-supporters-among-turkeys-disgruntled-2029924.
54. Mahmut Bozarslan, "Unraveling Islamic State's Turkish recruitment scheme," *Al Monitor,* October 23, 2015, http://www.al-monitor.com/pulse/en/originals/2015/10/turkey-syria-isis-adiyaman-suicide-bomber-arsenal.html; "Diyarbakır ve Suruç bombacıları Tel Abyad'da birlikte savaştı'," *Radikal,* July 22, 2015, http://www.radikal.com.tr/turkiye/diyarbakir-ve-suruc-bombacilari-tel-abyadda-birlikte-savasti-1401886/.
55. Michael Weiss, "Syrian Rebels Say Turkey Is Arming And Training Them," Information Clearing House, May 22, 2012, http://www.informationclearinghouse.info/article31399.htm.
56. Cengiz Candar, "Will Turkey Midwife Independent Kurdistan?," *Al-Monitor*, July 14, 2014, http://www.realclearworld.com/2014/07/17/will_turkey_midwife_independent_kurdistan_160143.html.
57. Greg Miller and Souad Mekhennet, "Undercover teams, increased surveillance and hardened borders: Turkey cracks down on foreign fighters," *Washington Post,* March 6, 2016, https://www.washingtonpost.com/world/national-security/undercover-teams-increased-surveillance-and-hardened-borders-turkey-cracks-down-on-foreign-fighters/2016/03/06/baa4ba3a-e219-11e5-8d98-4b3d9215ade1_story.html.
58. Kadri Gursel, "How Turkish police could have prevented IS massacre in Ankara," *Al Monitor,* April 18, 2016, http://www.al-monitor.com/pulse/originals/2016/04/turkey-isis-police-can-prevented-ankara-attack.html.
59. Gursel, "How Turkish police could have prevented IS massacre in Ankara."
60. "Russian and Turkish jets 'bomb ISIL,' in Syria's Al Bab," *Al Jazeera* (Doha), January 18, 2017, http://www.aljazeera.com/news/2017/01/russian-turkish-jets-bomb-isil-syria-al-bab-170118130233894.html.

61. "Pentagon: Turkey sent up to 3,800 fighters to Libya," *Gulf News*, July 18, 2020, https://gulfnews.com/world/mena/pentagon-turkey-sent-up-to-3800-fighters-to-libya-1.72667083.
62. Erik Cornell, "A Surviving Neoplatonism: On the Creed of the Bektashi Order," *Islam and Christian-Muslims Relations* 17, no. 1, 2006, 1-20, http://www.tandfonline.com/doi/abs/10.1080/09596410500399078?journalCode=cicm20.
63. Ilber Ortaylı, *Son İmparatorluk Osmanlı* [The End of the Ottoman Empire] (Istanbul: Timas Yayinlari, 2006), 87–89.
64. Kemal Karpat, "Modern Turkey," in P.M. Holt et al., eds. *The Cambridge History of Islam* vol. 1 (Cambridge: Cambridge University Press, 1970), 528; Yael Navaro-Yashin, *Faces of the State: Secularism and Public life in Turkey* (Princeton: Princeton University Press, 2002).
65. Stanford J. Shaw and Ezel K. Shaw, *History of the Ottoman Empire and Modern Turkey: Reform, Revolution and Republic* vol. 2 (Cambridge: Cambridge University Press, 1977), 384.
66. M. Winter, "The Modernization of Education in Modern Turkey," in Jacob M. Landau, ed., *Atatürk and the Modernization of Turkey* (Leiden: Brill, 1984), 186.
67. Karpat, "Modern Turkey," 533-4.
68. Shaw and Shaw, *History of the Ottoman Empire and Modern Turkey*, 385.
69. Republic of Turkey Presidency of Religious Affairs, "The State and Religion in Modern Turkey," n.d., http://www.diyanet.gov.tr/english/weboku.asp?id=795&yid=31&sayfa=10.
70. Svante E. Cornell and M. K. Kaya, "The Naqshbandi-Khalidi Order and Political Islam in Turkey," Hudson Institute *Current Trends in Islamist Ideology*, September 3, 2015, http://hudson.org/research/11601-the-naqshbandi-khalidi-order-and-political-islam-in-turkey#footNote15.
71. Claire Berlinski's interview with Gürbüz Evren, Ankara, Turkey, August 2007. See World Almanac of Islamism, "Turkey", 2011, (http://almanac.afpc.org/sites/almanac.afpc.org/files/Turkey_1.pdf)
72. Rubin, "Green Money, Islamist Politics in Turkey," 13-23.
73. Turkish National Police, "Terör Örgütlerinin Finans Kaynakları," n.d., http://www.egm.gov.tr/temuh/terorizm10_makale5.htm.
74. KONDA Research, "Religion, Secularism and the Veil in Daily Life Survey," September 2007."
75. Ulaş Dikmen, "Türkiye'deki Ateist Nüfus Hızla Artıyor," *Onedio,* March 10, 2015, https://onedio.com/haber/turkiye-deki-ateist-nu-

fus-hizla-artiyor-468344.
76. KONDA, "Lifestyle Survey," 2018, https://interaktif.konda.com.tr/en/HayatTarzlari2018/#firstPage.
77. Gül Berna Özcan & Murat Çokgezen, "Trusted Markets: The Exchanges of Islamic Companies," *Comparative Economic Studies* (2006), http://pure.rhul.ac.uk/portal/files/778768/Trust%20and%20Islamic%20companies.pdf.
78. Soner Çağaptay, Düden Yeğenoğlu, and Ekim Alptekin, "Turkey and Europe's Problem with Radical Islam," Washington Institute for Near East Policy *PolicyWatch no.* 1043, November 2, 2005, http://www.washingtoninstitute.org/templateC05.php?CID=2391.
79. *Constitution of the Republic of Turkey*, Article 2, http://www.anayasa.gov.tr/images/loaded/pdf_dosyalari/THE_CONSTITUTION_OF_THE_REPUBLIC_OF_TURKEY.pdf.
80. "Fazilet, kapatılan 25. Parti," [Virtue, 25th Party Closed] *Hurriyet* (Istanbul), June 22 2001, http://dosyalar.hurriyet.com.tr/hur/turk/01/06/22/turkiye/85tur.htm.
81. Mancur Olson, *The Logic of Collective Action: Public Goods and the Theory of Groups* revised edition (Boston: Harvard University Press, 1971).
82. Okan Altıparmak, "Is Turkey really a 'vibrant democracy'?" *P.J Media*, September 30, 2011, http://pjmedia.com/blog/is-turkey-really-a-vibrant-democracy/.
83. Svante E. Cornell, "The Islamization of Turkey: Erdoğan's Education Reforms," *Turkey Analyst*, September 2, 2015, https://www.turkeyanalyst.org/publications/turkey-analyst-articles/item/437.
84. Svante E. Cornell, "Turkish-Saudi Rivalry: Behind the Khashoggi Affair," *The American Interest*, November 9, 2018, https://www.the-american-interest.com/2018/11/06/behind-the-khashoggi-affair/.
85. "Erdogan: Turkey may suspend ties with UAE over Israel deal," *Al Jazeera* (Doha), August 15, 2020, https://www.aljazeera.com/news/2020/08/erdogan-turkey-suspend-ties-uae-israel-deal-200815064313281.html.

48 Turkmenistan

Quick Facts

Population: 5,528,627 (July 2020 est.)
Area: 488,100 sq km
Ethnic Groups: Turkmen 85%, Uzbek 5%, Russian 4%, other 6% (2003)
Religions: Muslim 89%, Eastern Orthodox 9%, unknown 2%
Government Type: presidential republic; authoritarian
GDP (official exchange rate): $37.93 billion (2017 est.)

Map and Quick Facts derived in part from the CIA World Factbook (Last Updated August 2020)

Introduction

Islam in Turkmenistan is comprised of an unusual blend of Sufi mysticism, orthodox (Sunni) Islam, and shamanistic Zoroastrian practices. The cult of ancestors is still observed, and reverence for members of the owlat, or four holy tribes, is still strong. Popular or "folk" Islam is centered around Sufism, the mystical dimension of Islam that originated in Central Asia. The veneration of holy places (generally tombs connected with Sufi saints), mythical personages, and tribal ancestors continue to play an active role in the preservation of religious feeling among the population.

Folk Islam, together with the Soviet-era repression of religion and the authoritarian nature of the country's political system, act as barriers to the growth of Islamism in Turkmenistan. Thus, the country's leadership has sought to capitalize on the popularity of Sufism in order to encourage religious beliefs to conform to local popular practices as a way of combating the emergence of Islamism. As in other parts of Central Asia, the distinction between religious and "national" rituals is blurred in Turkmenistan. Since the perestroika period of the late 1980s, the Turkmen leadership has attempted to co-opt Islam as a fundamental component of its overarching nation-building campaign.

Due to publishing constraints, this chapter is provided here only in summary form. To view the full study, please visit the online edition of the Almanac at almanac.afpc.org.

49 Syria

Quick Facts

Population: 19,398,448 (July 2020 est.)
Area: 187,437 sq km
Ethnic Groups: Arab ~50%, Alawite ~15%, Kurd ~10%, Levantine ~10%, other ~15% (includes Druze, Ismaili, Imami, Nusairi, Assyrian, Turkoman, Armenian)
GDP (official exchange rate): $24.6 billion (2014 est.)

Source: CIA World FactBook (Last Updated October 2020)

Introduction

The history and demography of Syria, its governmental structure as a hereditary dictatorship, and the political staying power of clans from among the Alawis, a sect regarded by most Muslims as beyond the bounds of the faith, has made Syria uniquely fertile ground for Islamist and jihadist opposition.[1] *The Islamic State (IS), in its various forms dating back to its affiliation with Al Qaeda, received support from the Assad regime to wage war on the Iraqi government and Coalition forces after the overthrow of Saddam Hussein.*[2] *The Assad regime has also provided shelter and support to various Islamist movements, including Lebanese Hezbollah and the Palestinian Hamas movement. After the outbreak of the country's popular uprising in March 2011, the government worked with allied extremist groups to help destroy the rebellion – a conflict which continues, in more muted form, to this day.*

Islamist Activity

The Syrian Muslim Brotherhood (SMB)

The SMB is the oldest and most prominent of the country's oppositional Islamist movements. The Syrian chapter of the Brotherhood was established in 1946 under the leadership of Mustafa al-Siba'i.[3] Emboldened by the French departure from Syria, and influenced by his time spent in Cairo with Muslim Brotherhood founder Hassan al-Banna, Al-Siba'i openly identified his network as that group's Syrian chapter.[4] Like the Brotherhood's original branch in Egypt, the SMB promoted an anti-imperialist ideology.

This does not mean, however, that the SMB was a carbon copy of its parent organization at its founding; rather, the SMB retained its unique identity as a conglomeration of indigenous Sufi Islamic societies.[5] Moreover, the Syrian branch of the Brotherhood was a small, elitist, and parliamentary institution. The SMB was always careful to stress its subordination to the Brotherhood's Supreme Guide (the organization's spiritual leader) in Cairo, but the operational significance of this allegiance appears to have been minimal, and the SMB has always been almost entirely autonomous.[6]

The SMB had always been careful to present a non-sectarian image, even as it worked for a Sunni empowerment that would in practice have meant a reduction in the status of Syria's minorities.[7] With Ba'athist rule beginning in 1963 (something that is, to date, uninterrupted), the societal dynamics in Syria became less accommodating for the SMB. The group was banned in 1963 and membership was deemed punishable by death in 1980.[8] In response, the group went into systemic opposition and became a powerful element of the Islamist current that would dominate the anti-Ba'athist movement between 1963 and 1982.[9]

Following the 1982 Hama uprising, in which the military, under the direction of Hafez al-Assad, killed as many as 40,000 people in that city in less than a month,[10] some members ceased opposition activity altogether and disaffiliated from the SMB. After a period of dormancy, in 1996 Ali Sadredeen al-Bayanuni took over the SMB, which was by then headquartered in Jordan. Al-Bayanuni sought to distance the SMB from violence and sectarianism, reinventing the group as a moderate conservative force that was committed to parliamentary democracy and rights for religious minorities—even going to far as to say a Christian or an Alawi would be acceptable as president,[11] and renouncing violence in 2001.[12]

Al-Bayanuni worked assiduously in the early 2000s to strengthen the Brotherhood's ties to the secular opposition, and signed onto the October 2005 Damascus Declaration alongside a broad spectrum of

Syrian oppositionists. The statement called on the Assad regime - weakened after its assassination of Lebanese prime minister Rafiq al-Hariri, which prompted a rebellion in Lebanon that ended the Syrian occupation there and generated global condemnation and isolation - to permit a "peaceful, gradual" democratic reform process.[13]

The Declaration did little to mobilize internal resistance to Assad, however. In 2006, the SMB formed an alliance with Abd al-Halim Khaddam, a prominent regime defector and Sunni ex-Ba'athist who had once served as vice-president. This union went nowhere, however. In 2009, after Israel's Operation CAST LEAD against Hamas in Gaza, the SMB under Al-Bayanuni changed direction again: publicly embracing a militant posture, attempting to defuse tensions with the Assad regime, using its support for Hamas to suspend opposition activities, and trying to have Qatar and Turkey mediate with Damascus. However, Assad did not bite and, in 2010, Al-Bayanuni and his Aleppine supporters lost the internal elections, being replaced by a Hamawi faction led by Muhammad Riad al-Shaqfa and his deputy, Mohammed Faruq Tayfur.[14]

In March 2011, the Arab revolutionary wave arrived in Syria in the form of mass anti-regime protests. In the latter months of 2011, after six months of mostly peaceful demonstrations, protesters began to pick up weapons to defend themselves from the regime's onslaught and Syria spiraled into an armed rebellion.

Both the protests and subsequent violence took the Brotherhood and its affiliates by surprise. The group's standard operating procedure is to work within systems to change them in directions it finds congenial, rather than fomenting revolution.[15] In the peripheral towns, where the Ba'ath party was more influential and where more economically disenfranchised people lived, people resorted to violence earlier. This class division—with the city-dwellers "bristl[ing] at the idea that they would be led by provincials"—was one of many cleavages Assad would seek to inflame to prevent a united front against his government.[16] The Brotherhood had no infrastructure of its own to contend with these events, so, for the purposes of distributing resources within the rebellion, it created a Civilian Protection Commission (CPC) in late 2011. By March 2012, the Brotherhood had openly endorsed violent resistance against the

Assad regime.[17]

In January 2013, the SMB formed the Shields of the Revolution Council, an alliance of militarized anti-government factions.[18] However, by August of the following year, the group dissolved, and its constituent parts were either absorbed by the Syrian Revolutionary Command Council[19] or absorbed into the so-called Sham Legion with other groups not previously affiliated with the SMB.[20]

Meanwhile, in November 2013, the SMB announced the formation of the National Party for Justice and the Constitution (otherwise known as the "Waad" or "Promise" Party). Waad's abilities to mobilize and organize have proven lacking; although years in the making, the party's founding and beginnings were tumultuous.[21] It formally launched in March 2014 from Istanbul, where some SMB members, including current leader Dr. Mohamed Hikmat Walid, had been in exile during the civil war.[22] Like other Brotherhood-linked parties, Waad has attempted to distance itself from its Islamist links in favor of a nationalist platform.[23] However, this has not stymied speculation that it simply serves as an instrument of the Brotherhood's will in Syrian politics; in November 2014, the then-head of Waad resigned to assume leadership of the SMB. Moreover, the organization still funds much of the party's operations.[24]

Currently fractured among several countries – including Syria itself after 2015, when hundreds of SMB members began to return despite membership in the organization being a capital offense[25] – the Syrian Brotherhood remains politically weak. Despite continued backing from the Turkish government, the SMB is not affiliated with any current member of the UN-guided post-civil war constitutional assembly.[26] While the official excuse was that the process was not sufficiently independent and therefore illegitimate, the real reason has more to do with the group's marginalization; the only constituent to the assembly affiliated with the SMB, Ahmad Sayyed Yousef, was forced out of the process days before any official stance by the Brotherhood was taken.[27]

Hezbollah

Hezbollah, a key Iranian proxy designated a terror group by the U.S. State Department,[28] has been active in Syria in various capacities for decades. In 1982, the Assad regime allowed Iran's Islamic

Revolutionary Guards Corp (IRGC) to set up a training camp within Syria's borders, in the Beqaa Valley. The activity was driven by Iran and Syria's shared adversarial relationship with Israel, whom the IRGC planned to target with the new fighters. Hezbollah's inaugural class was formed from this cadre.[29] However, the relationship fell apart due to infighting in the latter half of the decade, when the two countries began to compete for influence. The rift would last until 1990, when Iran and Syria agreed to cease their conflict and cooperate strategically.[30]

The 1990s and 2000s marked a shift in the relationship between Hezbollah and the Syrian government. While the two were previously hostile, they now complimented one another, working toward mutual goals. When Syrian-Israeli peace talks ultimately failed in January 2000 and the latter unilaterally withdrew from Lebanon that May, the relationship between Syria and Iran, a historic adversary of Israel, was preserved.[31] Between June 2000, when Bashar al-Assad ascended to head the Syrian government, and the outset of the Arab Spring in March 2011, the relationship between the Syrian government and the Iranian proxy assumed a more equal footing. In 2006, when Hezbollah and Israel engaged in a summer of conflict, Syria supplied Hezbollah with weaponry.[32] In January 2011, Hezbollah party members and their allies, then in positions of authority within the Lebanese government, precipitated its constitutional collapse by simultaneously withdrawing from their posts.[33] This followed failed efforts by the Syrian and Saudi governments to jointly mediate tensions between Hezbollah and Lebanon's unity government after the latter permitted UN investigations into the assassination of Prime Minister Rafic Hariri, of which Hezbollah was suspected.[34]

After the onset of the Syrian civil war in March 2011, the Syrian regime was increasingly propped up and defended by both Iran and Hezbollah.[35] For Hezbollah, the decision to do so was a strategic one; the group hoped to increase its foothold in Syria as a result of its involvement. In 2016, during an interview with Iranian state TV, retired General Mohammad Ali Al Falaki stated that Hezbollah had formed a new branch, the "Shia Liberation Army," the primary objective of which "would be to fight in Arab countries and would recruit heavily from non-Iranian Shia Muslims across the world."[36]

Estimates from the Syrian Observatory for Human Rights place the number of Hezbollah fighters killed in the conflict at 1,697 as of March 2020.[37] This figure has likely increased since due to ongoing fighting involving Hezbollah.[38] Death at such a scale reflects that a significant contingent of the Hezbollah fighters has been dispatched to Syria over the conflict. In September 2017, one commander of the group claimed that as many as 10,000 Hezbollah members had been dispatched to Syria at the height of the group's involvement.[39] While other estimates place the figure lower, at 7,000,[40] it nonetheless represents the largest deployment of Hezbollah fighters outside Lebanon to take place in the group's history.

The cost to Hezbollah has not been solely human. In May 2020, an Iranian parliamentarian told state media that the country – Hezbollah's largest financial backer – likely spent roughly $20-30 billion in Syria since the onset of the civil war.[41] However, this figure could be higher than reported. Sources within the Lebanese security apparatus estimated in 2013 that Iran, by way of Hezbollah, was spending roughly $600-700 million per month in Syria.[42] Notably, this estimate was provided before fighting in Syria reached its peak intensity.

With the effective end of the Syrian civil war and the victory of the Assad regime, Hezbollah has begun withdrawing fighters from that front.[43] Multiple sources told *al-Arabiya* in September 2020 that roughly 2,500 Hezbollah fighters remained in Syria – a significant decrease in numbers over years past.[44] However, this drawdown has not precluded the group from continuing to fight Israeli forces and their allies in the country.[45]

Jihadi organizations

Sunni Islamism is an opposition movement in Syria, but the picture is complicated by the ruling regime's attempts to coopt and weaponize it. Many *jihadists* that have fought the Syrian government over the last decade can trace their roots, in some way, to March-May 2011, when the Assad regime released hundreds of political prisoners in an attempt to placate anti-regime protestors.[46] Among the list of previous detainees were members of *Al-Nusra* and the Islamic State, as well as those who would go on to become the leaders of Jaysh al-

Islam, Liwa al-Haq, Ahrar al-Sham, and Suqur al-Sham – some of the most formidable Islamist units in the insurgency.[47] Simultaneously, the Assad dynasty has used terrorism of every ideological shade as an instrument of its foreign policy since its foundation, as Western statesmen who have engaged the regime continually find.[48]

Today, despite the end of the Syrian civil war, the situation remains complicated. While the Islamic State's physical *caliphate* has been eliminated, the terror group has not ceased violent activity in Syria, and has given clear indications that it is attempting a resurgence. According to the Counter Extremism Project, Islamic State militants "carried out at least 35 attacks, killing at least 76 pro-Assad regime fighters in the Homs, Deir Ez Zor, Raqqa, Hama, and Aleppo governorates" in August 2020 alone.[49] The following month, they carried out at least 32 attacks, killing as many pro-regime fighters, as well as 12 civilians, in the same regions.[50] Meanwhile, al-Nusra has been absorbed by, and morphed into, Hay'at Tahrir al-Sham (HTS), which has gradually transitioned into a Turkish proxy organization[51] in the face of U.S. drone strikes and Syrian government forces.[52] Ahrar al-Sham, meanwhile, has seemingly endorsed HTS as the leading resistance organization,[53] suggesting that it might soon fall under the HTS banner. As for Hamas, it is is currently on the outs with the Syrian regime, but receiving backing from Turkey and Russia and appears to be hoping to use these latter relationships to repair the former.[54]

The Islamic State (IS, formerly ISIS) and Al-Nusra Front

Ahmad al-Shara (Abu Muhammad al-Jolani) was dispatched to Syria in the summer of 2011 as part of the Islamic State's advance team, which sought to expand the group's reach from Iraq into Syria. In doing so, it established satellite organization Jabhat al-Nusra (now Hay'at Tahrir al-Sham, or HTS).[55] When ISIS's then-leader, Abu Bakr al-Baghdadi, tried to publicly take ownership of *Al-Nusra* in 2013, Al-Shara refused and instead swore allegiance to al-Qaeda, which soon expelled ISIS.[56] The Assad regime's role in supporting ISIS is something the group itself has since documented in its newsletter.[57] This support included freeing imprisoned *jihadists* to disrupt anti-government forces and protestors,[58] transporting Islamic State fighters to Idlib to fight,[59] and buying oil from ISIS-controlled territory.[60]

One of the key leaders that enabled the group to expand in Syria—and to nearly destroy Al-Nusra by secretly recruiting many of its *emirs* and foreign fighters—was Amr al-Absi (Abu al-Atheer). Al-Absi was arrested in 2007, during one of the Assad regime's periodic crackdowns on *jihadists*, but was subsequently released by the Syrian government, along with hundreds of other hardened radicals, in May or June of 2011.[61] The jail cells at the infamous Sednaya prison had been emptied of *jihadists* within a few months of the start of the uprising, and those cells were instead filled with peaceful protesters.[62] "The regime did not just open the door to the prisons and let these extremists out," explained one military defector, "it facilitated them in their work, in their creation of armed brigades." In January 2017, the al-Nusra Front announced that it dissolved and formed Hay'at Tahrir al-Sham (HTS) in its place.[63]

By December 2017, the Islamic State presence in Syria was drastically reduced as a result of coordinated counterterror efforts between global governments and local forces. This included Raqqa, a city designated as the capital of the *caliphate*.[64] In March 2019, the U.S.-aligned Syrian Democratic Forces (SDF) officially declared victory over the Islamic State after the battle of Baghouz.[65] Now, the terror group is involved in what the Center for International Security and Cooperation refers to as "a decentralized, guerilla-style insurgency" that continues to "carry out attacks through sleeper cells" in, among other places, Syria.[66] Meanwhile, dozens of governments from all over the world are currently grappling with how to manage the thousands of men, women, and children who travelled to Syria from their homes – some of whom swore allegiance to the Islamic State and fought on its behalf – and are now returning to their countries of origin.[67]

Hay'at Tahrir al-Sham (HTS, or "Organization for the Liberation of the Levant")

HTS was formed in January 2017 as an amalgamation of other *jihadist* organizations, including Jabhat Fatah al-Sham, Jabhat al-Nusra), Harakat Nour al-Din al-ZInki, Liwa al-Haq, Jaysh al-Sunna, and Jabhat Ansar al-Din.[68] Jabhat Fatah Al-Sham's public ideological separation from al-Qaeda – the catalyst for its rebranding – carried over when it evolved into HTS as a collective. Ayman al-Zawahiri, the *emir* of al-Qaeda, publicly denounced HTS's formation as an unsanctioned "violation of the covenant."[69]

Led by Abu Mohammad al-Jolani, a veteran *jihadist* with ties to Abu Musab al-Zarqawi, the late leader of the Islamic State's precursor group,[70] HTS has evolved into one of the leading resistance forces fighting the Syrian government. Like other *jihadist* factions involved, HTS's focus is domestic; it seeks to form an Islamic *caliphate* specific to Syria by "toppling the criminal regime and expelling the Iranian militias."[71] It has also, at various times during its struggle, fought the Islamic State and the National Liberation Front (NLF) for control or primacy.[72] In its conflict with the latter, HTS would gain territory in the Idlib governorate and cease fighting in 2019, thereafter turning its attention toward the Syrian regime.[73] Today, the remainder of the anti-Assad resistance, including HTS, continues fighting the regime in Idlib. This does not, however, mean that the resistance is unified; in June 2020, HTS was involved in fighting different defector factions, including Hurras al-Deen, which has become al-Qaeda's newest Syrian surrogate.[74] HTS itself "insists it is independent, but the UN and the US both regard it as associated with al-Qaeda."[75]

Ḥarakat al-Muqāwamah al-ʾIslāmiyyah (Hamas, or "Islamic Resistance Movement")

Hamas, a Sunni fundamentalist, anti-Israel paramilitary organization that now most notably serves as the *de facto* governing body of the Gaza Strip in the Palestinian territories, has had a tumultuous relationship with the Syrian regime. Hamas established military ties to Damascus beginning in 1993, and opened its central office in Damascus in 1999.[76] When Bashar al-Assad ascended to the Syrian presidency in 2000, he adopted staunch anti-Israeli stances and allowed Hamas to propagate in the country's Palestinian refugee camps. In turn, the organization provided social services and gained grassroots support among that constituency.[77]

However, the dynamic between Hamas and the Syrian government shifted dramatically during the Arab Spring and subsequent Syrian civil war. The shift was largely a product of the Syrian government's widespread, fatal abuse of protestors, thousands of whom were refugees from the Palestinian territories. (According to one prominent Syria-focused human rights organization, the Syrian government has, as of summer 2020, killed nearly 3,200 Palestinian refugees, nearly 500 of whom were tortured to death. Over 2,600 others "disappeared" into state intelligence prisons.[78]) Facing significant pressure from its support network in the Palestinian territories, and after months of silence out of fear that the party would draw the ire of the Assad regime,[79] Hamas officially endorsed ongoing open armed rebellion against the Syrian government in February 2012.[80]

Now that the Syrian civil war is effectively over, and the Assad regime is reestablishing control over the country, Hamas is attempting to repair this damaged relationship. So far, however, the Assad regime has proved unwilling to reconcile. In June 2019, the *Jerusalem Post* reported that Iran and Hezbollah were mediating discussions between Hamas and the Syrian government. However, at the time, the office of Bashar al-Assad released public statements that reiterated its accusations that Hamas supported terrorism in Syria.[81] Later that year and continuing into 2020, Hamas was reportedly engaged in high level conversations with the Russian government (an ally and supporter of the Assad regime). In March 2020, Ismail Haniyeh, Hamas' political leader, supported Assad's sovereignty over Syria while attending a conference in Moscow.[82]

Harakat Ahrar al-Sham al-Islamiyya (Otherwise known as Ahrar al-Sham, or "The Islamic Movement of the Free Men of the Levant")[83]

Ahrar al-Sham formed after Hassan Abboud and other anti-Assad political prisoners were released by the regime during the Arab Spring between March and May of 2011. The group announced itself in Idlib in January 2012.[84] Over time, Ahrar al-Sham has grown in size and stature, proving itself capable of absorbing Jaysh al-Islam and Suqur al-Sham, as well as Kateeb Thawar al-Sham, Jaysh al-Mujahideen, Tajamo Fastaqim Kama Umirat, and al-Jabha al-Shamiya.[85]

Ahrar's start-up funders were linked to al-Qaeda networks on the Gulf. Among its founders was Muhammad al-Bahaya (Abu Khaled al-Suri), a veteran *jihadist* and the personal emissary to Syria of al-Qaeda leader Ayman al-Zawahiri.[86] Institutionally, Ahrar's decision to work in lockstep with Al-Nusra was the single most important factor in the latter's empowerment.[87] The group spent years attempting to differentiate itself from al-Qaeda.[88] One way in which it sought to do so is through the definition of its goals and ideology; while, like other Sunni-*jihadi* organizations, it seeks to establish an Islamic state, its efforts are domestic in nature, focused entirely on Syria.[89]

In 2018, Ahrar al-Sham merged with the Nour al-Din al-Zenki Movement, another Sunni Islamist rebel group, to form the Syrian Liberation Front (SLF), which, in turn, would join the National Liberation Front (NLF) along with other anti-Assad groups. This was due, in part, to increasing tension between those groups with HTS.[90] However, fighting between the two factions ended in 2019, after the NLF lost most of its control over Idlib and agreed to recognize HTS' dominion. The two now coordinate anti-regime efforts.[91]

Islamism and Society

As of October 2020, an estimated 87% of the people in Syria identify as Muslim, according to the CIA World Factbook. More specifically, roughly 74% of the country identifies as Sunni, while the other 13% identifies as Alawi, Ismaili, or Shia.[92] However, it is currently not fully clear how the Syrian civil war has impacted religious demographics inside the country. According to the United Nations, as of mid-October 2020 there are roughly 5.57 million registered Syrian refugees in other countries, including Turkey, Lebanon, Jordan, Iraq, and Egypt.[93] There are also roughly 6.1 million internally displaced persons (IDPs) still living in Syria, according to U.S. intelligence estimates.[94]

In the decades leading up to the Syrian civil war, several smaller cities in the country grew in population and economic prosperity. As a result, mosques grew in prominence, assuming the role of community centers. While approval by the central government was still required to serve as an *imam* in Syria (see the section on "Islamism and the State"), because mosques increasingly depended on local (rather than federal) funding, this dynamic had the effect of making religious identity and political Islam more localized. With the outbreak of the Syrian civil war, cities became more isolated from one another, and this localization accelerated.[95]

Because Syria's religious landscape was now almost entirely decentralized by the regionalization of the country, mosques both became 1) more prominent in the local *milleu*, and 2) increasingly under the control of opposition groups like Ahrar al-Sham and Jaysh al-Islam, whose Salafi ideologies were antithetical to the Assad regime's Alawite Shi'ism.[96] Thus, propagation of Salafism in those isolated areas became more common, while Sufism and more moderate interpretations of the religion were pushed out.[97]

Some attribute this Islamic awakening to the fact that donations from the Arab Gulf states and private Arab donors outpaced assistance from the West. According to such "resource mobilization" explanations,[98] the influx of cash from Salafi donors not only strengthened *jihadist* forces vis-à-vis the FSA, but also led relatively secular groups within the FSA to adopt Salafi dress and customs.[99] Many rank and file fighters of Salafi-*jihadi* militias are devout Sunnis with no firm extremist convictions. Rather, in the words of one expert, "[s]ize, money and momentum are the things to look for in Syrian insurgent politics—ideology comes fourth, if even that."[100]

As of writing, Syrian people are reconciling with, among countless other things, residual sentiment for *jihadist* organizations. Whether these groups have been able to recruit people in Idlib hased on Islamic principles or because of anti-government sentiment, however, is unclear. In October 2020, the United States Institute of Peace (USIP) described some of the current and looming challenges of releasing individuals from al-Hol, a notorious refugee camp in what once was IS-controlled territory. According to USIP analysts, al-Hol residents still harbor deep sympathies for the Islamic State, making a conflict between them and local Kurdish communities in Northeast Syria inevitable.[101] Other Islamist groups still fighting the Syrian government in Idlib maintain popular support as well; the Washington Institute for Near East Policy has found that HTS and its cohorts have successfully recruited new fighters in and around Idlib as recently as February 2020.[102]

Islamism and the State

In the early years of the regime of Bashar al-Assad, there was some talk of liberalization. Assad tried to maintain open lines of communication with the country's religious opposition and even attempted to court their support. He made religion a topic of his speeches,[103] and state universities held Qur'an recitation competitions.[104] There were even prisoner releases for Islamists who had been imprisoned during the rule of his father, Hafez. The ban on women wearing the headscarf in public schools was likewise lifted,[105] and mosques were permitted to remain open between prayer times.[106] However, within a year of taking power in 2000, Bashar was already moving to restrict the space for opposition elements, and religious institutions remained under firm state control.[107]

A key element of the Assad regime's public messaging after the civil war began in 2011 revolved around its purported efforts to protect religious minorities. Realistically, however, Syria's governance is focused on controlling religious discourse to orient it toward pro-state attitudes.[108] The Assad regime has now succeeded in creating a unified Sunni clerical establishment that is under firm state control. However, as previously mentioned, this centralization appears brittle, with those clerics serving the system discredited by the association, and the extreme pressure brought to bear by the regime has succeeded in creating a unified opposition establishment.

Assad's Syria has long served as a state sponsor of terrorism. According to the State Department's 2019 *Country Reports on Terrorism*:

> Syria continued its political and military support to various terrorist groups... The Assad regime's relationship with [Hezbollah] and Iran grew stronger in 2019 as the regime became more reliant on external actors to fight opponents and secure areas. The Islamic Revolutionary Guard Corps (IRGC) remains present and active in the country with the permission of President Bashar al-Assad... Over the past two decades, the Assad regime's permissive attitude towards AQ and other terrorist groups' FTF facilitation

> efforts during the Iraq conflict fed the growth of AQ, ISIS, and affiliated terrorist networks inside Syria. The Syrian government's awareness and encouragement for many years of terrorists' transit through Syria to Iraq for the purpose of fighting U.S. forces before 2012 is well documented. Those very networks were among the terrorist elements that brutalized the Syrian and Iraqi populations in 2019.[109]

Iran's support for the Assad regime is framed by, among other things, ideological motivations. Although the historically secular Syrian state and the Shi'a Islamic Republic of Iran may not have similar end goals, the Iranian regime saw the opportunity to confront *takfiri* (non-believers – in this case the Islamic State, Sunni terror opposition groups, and Israel) on Syrian soil.[110] What's more, keeping the Alawite Assad regime in power furthers Iran's goals of establishing a "Shi'a crescent" and extending its own influence throughout the region and presented an opportunity to put its own troops on the Israeli border.[111] The Assad regime has acquiesced to Iran's intrusion because it has, in recent years, required near-comprehensive support in order to maintain its hold on power – something the Iranian government provided via equipment, Shi'a militia groups and other fighters, intelligence support, guidance from the Islamic Revolutionary Guard Corps (IRGC), and financial assistance.[112]

Endnotes

1. Nibras Kazimi, *Syria Through Jihadist Eyes: A Perfect Enemy* (Hoover Press, 2010).
2. Kyle Orton, "The Assad Regime's Collusion With ISIS and al-Qaeda: Assessing The Evidence," personal blog, March 24, 2014, https://kyleorton1991.wordpress.com/2014/03/24/assessing-evidence-collusion-assad-isis-qaeda/
3. "Egyptian Muslim Brotherhood, The," Harvard Divinity School *Religion and Public Life*, n.d., https://rpl.hds.harvard.edu/faq/egyptian-muslim-brotherhood.
4. Raphael Lefevre, *Ashes of Hama: The Muslim Brotherhood in Syria*

(Oxford University Press, 2013), 23-4.
5. Ibid., 9.
6. Joshua Teitelbaum, "The Muslim Brotherhood in Syria, 1945-1958: Founding, Social Origins, Ideology," *Middle East Journal* 65, no. 2, Spring 2011, https://www.jstor.org/stable/23012146?seq=1.
7. Ibid.
8. "Muslim Brotherhood in Syria," Counter Extremism Project, n.d., https://www.counterextremism.com/content/muslim-brotherhood-syria
9. Lefevre, *Ashes of Hama*, 44.
10. "Bashar Assad Teaches Visiting Members of U.S. Congress How to Fight Terrorism," Middle East Media Research Institute, January 16, 2002, https://www.memri.org/reports/bashar-assad-teaches-visiting-members-us-congress-how-fight-terrorism
11. Aron Lund, "The Syrian Brotherhood: On the Sidelines," Middle East Institute, September 24, 2013, https://www.mei.edu/publications/syrian-brotherhood-sidelines
12. Yehuda Blanga, "The Role of the Muslim Brotherhood in the Syrian Civil War," *Middle East Policy* XXIV, no. 3, Fall 2017, https://mepc.org/journal/role-muslim-brotherhood-syrian-civil-war
13. "Damascus Declaration in English," *Syria Comment*, November 1, 2005, http://faculty-staff.ou.edu/L/Joshua.M.Landis-1/syriablog/2005/11/damascus-declaration-in-english.htm.
14. Lund, "The Syrian Brotherhood: On the Sidelines."
15. Hassan Hassan, "In Syria, the Brotherhood's Influence Is on the Decline," *The National*, April 1, 2014, https://www.thenational.ae/in-syria-the-brotherhood-s-influence-is-on-the-decline-1.274365
16. Fouad Ajami, *The Syrian Rebellion* (Hoover Institution Press, 2012), 88-91.
17. Aron Lund, "Struggling to Adapt; the Muslim Brotherhood in a New Syria," Carnegie Endowment for International Peace *Paper*, May 7, 2013, https://carnegieendowment.org/2013/05/07/struggling-to-adapt-muslim-brotherhood-in-new-syria-pub-51723
18. Raphaël Lefevre and Ali El Yassir, "Militias for the Syrian Muslim Brotherhood?" Carnegie Endowment for International Peace, October 29, 2013, https://carnegieendowment.org/sada/?fa=53452
19. Cedric Labrousse, "EXCLUSIVE – 18 Syrian revolutionary factions advancing toward a One Army project," *The Arab Chronicle*, August 26, 2014, https://web.archive.org/web/20140826115620/http://the-arab-chronicle.com/exclusive-18-syrian-revolutionary-factions-advancing-toward-one-army-project/

20. Ryan O'Farrell and Cody Roche, "Syrian Opposition Factions in the Syrian Civil War," Bellingcat, August 13, 2016, https://www.bellingcat.com/news/mena/2016/08/13/syrian-opposition-factions-in-the-syrian-civil-war/
21. Raphaël Lefèvre, "The Belated Birth of the Waad Party," Carnegie Middle East Center, December 16, 2013, https://carnegie-mec.org/diwan/53926
22. Raphaël Lefèvre and Yezid Sayigh, "Uncertain Future for the Syrian Muslim Brotherhood's Political Party," Carnegie Middle East Center, December 9, 2013, https://carnegie-mec.org/2013/12/09/uncertain-future-for-syrian-muslim-brotherhood-s-political-party/gvot
23. Ibid.
24. Raphaël Lefèvre, "Islamism within a civil war: The Syrian Muslim Brotherhood's struggle for survival," Brookings Institution, August 2015, https://www.brookings.edu/wp-content/uploads/2016/07/Syria_Lefevre-FINALE.pdf
25. Dasha Afanasieva, "Banned in Syria, Muslim Brotherhood members trickle home," Reuters, May 7, 2015, https://www.reuters.com/article/us-syria-crisis-brotherhood/banned-in-syria-muslim-brotherhood-members-trickle-home-idUSKBN0NR20Y20150507
26. Sami Moybayed, "Why Has the Syrian Muslim Brotherhood Stayed Out of the Constitutional Assembly," *European Eye on Radicalization*, November 21, 2019, https://eeradicalization.com/why-has-the-syrian-muslim-brotherhood-stayed-out-of-the-constitutional-assembly/
27. Ibid.
28. U.S. Department of State, "Hizballah," in *Country Reports on Terrorism 2019*, 2020, https://www.state.gov/reports/country-reports-on-terrorism-2019/#Hizballah.
29. Mohanad Hage Ali, "Power Points Defining the Syria-Hezbollah Relationship," Carnegie Middle East Center, March 29, 2019, https://carnegie-mec.org/2019/03/29/power-points-defining-syria-hezbollah-relationship-pub-78730
30. Nicholas Blanford, *Warriors of God: Inside Hezbollah's Thirty-Year Struggle Against Israel* (New York: Random House, 2011), 92.
31. Mohanad Hage Ali, "Power Points Defining the Syria-Hezbollah Relationship," Carnegie Middle East Center, March 29, 2019, https://carnegie-mec.org/2019/03/29/power-points-defining-syria-hezbollah-relationship-pub-78730
32. Anthony H. Cordesman, George Sullivan and William D. Sullivan, *Lessons of the 2006 Israeli-Hezbollah War* (Washington,

DC: Center for Strategic and International Studies, 2007), https://csis-prod.s3.amazonaws.com/s3fspublic/legacy_files/files/publication/120720_Cordesman_LessonsIsraeliHezbollah.pdf.

33. Nada Bakri, "Resignations Deepen Crisis for Lebanon," *New York Times*, January 12, 2011, https://www.nytimes.com/2011/01/13/world/middleeast/13lebanon.html; "Lebanese government collapses," *al-Jazeera* (Doha), January 13, 2011, https://www.aljazeera.com/news/2011/01/13/lebanese-government-collapses/
34. Ronen Bergman, "The Hezbollah Connection," *The New York Times Magazine*, February 10, 2015, https://www.nytimes.com/2015/02/15/magazine/the-hezbollah-connection.html
35. "The Text of Sayyid Nasrallah's Speech on the Ayoub Drone and Other Matters on Al-Manar Television" [in Arabic], *Al-Manar*, October 12, 2012, archive.almanar.com.lb/article.php?id=324599.
36. Tallha Abdulrazaq, "Iran's 'Shia Liberation Army' is par for the course," *al-Jazeera* (Doha), August 21, 2016, https://www.aljazeera.com/opinions/2016/8/21/irans-shia-liberation-army-is-par-for-the-course/
37. Syrian Observatory for Human Rights, "Syrian Revolution NINE years on: 586,100 persons killed and millions of Syrians displaced and injured," March 15, 2020, https://www.syriahr.com/en/157193/?__cf_chl_jschl_tk__=3e4f3d0e90392ede-b603646167ef961ee4e1e144-1603286310-0-AdBQxJsT1bm lvNqi6jXCBzAHCMOHJZrK3YKaz-P6eyEdwgeXCvomjZd6yt-MinXjQSjLg0-V_VmxYTYg_wM1i_szLJJhJk6shH0362hFoIV-Vwys89nMzyoTcvBDbPEcn7NjQvjgBZ_iwDZeJeTfRNwcu81l-Frn4KOIEAhtkiyIAqhopcaqLr2ee2zvNWewzI6JeGO6G_Rx-4tLrDPgvA4Zuu7pJumSUpin_M5Nqu3zR2Toshq8IplVkewKB-vSzEZMyN-tpPsLaA0uO7tBIyCqFzRhZzOPfY330g7Q4nIvVgFOy
38. See, for example, Isabel Kirshner, "Israel Says It Hit Bombers on Syrian Boundary," *New York Times*, August 3, 2020, https://www.nytimes.com/2020/08/03/world/middleeast/israel-syria-border.html ; "Israel 'thwarts Hezbollah infiltration from Lebanon," *BBC News*, July 27, 2020, https://www.bbc.com/news/world-middle-east-53511336 ; Jack Khoury, "Israel Reportedly Strikes Targets in Southern Syrian in First Since mid-September," *Ha'aretz* (Tel Aviv), October 21, 2020, https://www.haaretz.com/israel-news/.premium-israel-struck-military-positions-in-southern-syria-report-says-1.9250324
39. "Syrian rebels near Israel border ordered to surrender by regime forces," *Times of Israel*, December 27, 2017, https://www.time-

sofisrael.com/syrian-rebels-near-israel-border-ordered-to-surrender-by-regime-forces/

40. Seth G. Jones, "The Escalating Conflict with Hezbollah in Syria," Center for Strategic & International Studies, June 20, 2018, https://www.csis.org/analysis/escalating-conflict-hezbollah-syria.
41. Yaghoub Fazeli, "Iran has spent $30 billion in Syria: Prominent MP," *al-Arabiya* (Riyadh), May 20, 2020, https://english.alarabiya.net/en/News/middle-east/2020/05/20/Iran-has-spent-30-billion-in-Syria-Prominent-MP
42. Samia Nakhoul, "Special Report: Hezbollah gambles all in Syria," Reuters, September 26, 2013, https://www.reuters.com/article/us-syria-hezbollah-special-report/special-report-hezbollah-gambles-all-in-syria-idUSBRE98P0AI20130926.
43. Nader Uskowi, *Temperature Rising: Irans Revolutionary Guards and Wars in the Middle East* (Lanham: Rowman & Littlefield, 2019); Jack Khoury, "Hezbollah's Nasrallah: Israel's Actions in Syria Not Reason for Withdrawing Forces," *Ha'aretz* (Tel Aviv), May 13, 2020, https://www.haaretz.com/middle-east-news/syria/.premium-hezbollah-s-nasrallah-israel-s-actions-in-syria-not-reason-for-withdrawing-forces-1.8844480
44. Johnny Fakhry, "What is going on? Hezbollah withdraws more than 2,500 personnel from Syria," *al-Arabiya* (Riyadh), September 3, 2020, [in Arabic] https://www.alarabiya.net/ar/arab-and-world/2020/09/03/%D8%AD%D8%B2%D8%A8-%D8%A7%D9%84%D9%84%D9%87-%D8%AD%D8%B2%D8%A8-%D8%A7%D9%84%D9%84%D9%87-%D9%8A%D8%B3%D8%AD%D8%A8-%D8%A3-%D9%83%D8%AB%D8%B1-%D9%85%D9%86-2500-%D8%B9%D9%86%D8%B5%D8%B1-%D9%85%D9%86-%D8%B3%D9%88%D8%B1%D9%8A%D8%A7-%D9%85%D8%A7%D8%B0%D8%A7-%D9%8A%D8%AC%D8%B1%D9%8A%D8%9F.
45. "Israel's Netanyahu warns Hezbollah after Syria attack," *al-Arabiya* (Riyadh), August 4, 2020, https://www.aljazeera.com/news/2020/8/4/israels-netanyahu-warns-hezbollah-after-syria-attack; Mona Alami, "Hezbollah, Israel jostle in Syria, Lebanon," *al-Monitor*, July 31, 2020, https://www.al-monitor.com/pulse/originals/2020/07/lebanon-hezbollah-south-syria-escalation.html.
46. Leila Fadel, "Syria's Assad moves to allay fury after security forces fire on protesters," *Washington Post*, March 26, 2011, https://www.

washingtonpost.com/world/syrias-assad-moves-to-allay-fury-after-security-forces-fire-on-protesters/2011/03/26/AFFoZDdB_story.html

47. Phil Sands, Justin Vela, and Suha Maayeh, "Assad Regime Abetted Extremists to Subvert Peaceful Uprising, Says Former Intelligence Official," *The National* (UAE), January 21, 2014, https://www.thenational.ae/world/assad-regime-abetted-extremists-to-subvert-peaceful-uprising-says-former-intelligence-official-1.319620
48. Margaret Thatcher, *The Downing Street Years* (HarperCollins, 1993), 823.
49. Gregory Waters, "ISIS Redux: The Central Syria Insurgency in August 2020," Counter Extremism Project, September 1, 2020, https://www.counterextremism.com/blog/isis-redux-central-syria-insurgency-august-2020
50. Ibid.
51. Charles Lister, "Assad Hasn't Won Anything," *Foreign Policy*, July 11, 2019, https://foreignpolicy.com/2019/07/11/assad-hasnt-won-anything-syria/
52. Sultan al-Kanj, "'Guardians of Religion' extremist group under siege in Syria's Idlib," *al-Monitor*, September 28, 2020, https://www.al-monitor.com/pulse/originals/2020/09/syria-idlib-jihadist-guardians-of-religion-us-drone-strikes.html.
53. Jason Ditz, "Infighting Threatens to Tear Syria's Ahrar al-Sham Rebels Apart," *Antiwar*, October 13, 2020, https://news.antiwar.com/2020/10/13/infighting-threatens-to-tear-syrias-ahrar-al-sham-rebels-apart/.
54. Ahmad Abu Amer, "Hamas in Moscow to mend ties with Syrian regime," *al-Monitor*, March 16, 2020, https://www.al-monitor.com/pulse/originals/2020/03/international-diplomacy-hamas-damascus-relations-moscow.html
55. "Al-Nusra Front (Hayat Tahrir al-Sham)," Counter Extremism Project, n.d., https://www.counterextremism.com/threat/al-nusra-front-hayat-tahrir-al-sham
56. Ibid.
57. Kyle Orton, "Islamic State Admits to Colluding with the Syrian Regime," personal blog, April 20, 2018 https://kyleorton1991.wordpress.com/2018/04/20/isis-assad-collusion-al-naba/
58. Maayeh, Suha, Phil Sands, and Justin Vela, "Assad regime abetted extremists to subvert peaceful uprising, says former intelligence official," *The National* (UAE), January 21, 2014, https://www.thenational.ae/world/assad-regime-abetted-extremists-to-sub-

vert-peaceful-uprising-says-former-intelligence-official-1.319620; Roy Gutman, "Assad Henchman: Here's How We Built ISIS," *The Daily Beast*, April 13, 2017, https://www.thedailybeast.com/assad-henchman-heres-how-we-built-isis; https://www.newsweek.com/how-syrias-assad-helped-forge-isis-255631

59. "Regime transfers 400 Daesh fighters to Idlib," Agence France-Presse, September 25, 2018, https://gulfnews.com/world/mena/regime-transfers-400-daesh-fighters-to-idlib-1.2282506; "Syria war: Army takes full control of Damascus after ousting IS," *BBC News*, May 21, 2018, https://www.bbc.co.uk/news/world-middle-east-44198304
60. Anne Speckhard and Ahmet Yayla. "ISIS's Revenues Include Sales of Oil to the Al- Assad Regime." *ICSVE Brief Reports*, April 27, 2016. https://www.researchgate.net/publication/301676661_ISIS's_Revenues_include_Sales_of_Oil_to_the_al-_Assad_Regime.; Benoit Faucon and Ahmed Al Omran, "Islamic State Steps Up oil and Gas Sales to Assad Regime," *Wall Street Journal*, January 19, 2017, https://www.wsj.com/articles/islamic-state-steps-up-oil-and-gas-sales-to-assad-regime-1484835563
61. Kyle Orton, "Death of a Caliphate Founder and the Role of Assad," personal blog, March 10, 2016, https://kyleorton1991.wordpress.com/2016/03/10/obituary-the-islamic-states-amr-al-absi-abu-al-atheer/
62. "Syria: Human Slaughterhouse," Amnesty International, February 7, 2017, https://www.amnesty.org/en/documents/mde24/5415/2017/en/
63. "Al-Nusra Front, (Hayat Tahrir al-Sham)," Counter Extremism Project, n.d., https://www.counterextremism.com/threat/al-nusra-front-hayat-tahrir-al-sham.
64. "Timeline: the Rise, Spread, and Fall of the Islamic State," Wilson Center, October 28, 2019, https://www.wilsoncenter.org/article/timeline-the-rise-spread-and-fall-the-islamic-state
65. Phillip Issa, Andrea Rosa, and Maya Alleruzzo, "US-allied Syrian force declares victory over Islamic State," Associated Press, March 23, 2019, https://apnews.com/article/ced0b1d5bd9b4447a3d36039213c8b3b
66. "The Islamic State," Mapping Militant Organizations, Center for International Security and Cooperation, n.d., https://cisac.fsi.stanford.edu/mappingmilitants/profiles/islamic-state#text_block_18356
67. H.J. Mai, "Why European Countries Are Reluctant To Repatriate Citizens Who Are ISIS Fighters," *National Public Radio*, December 10, 2019, https://www.npr.org/2019/12/10/783369673/europe-remains-reluctant-to-repatriate-its-isis-fighters-here-s-why; "The

Debate Around Returning Foreign Fighters in the Netherlands," *Clingendael Magazine*, January 13, 2020, https://www.clingendael.org/publication/debate-around-returning-foreign-fighters-netherlands; Brian Michael Jenkins, "Options for Dealing with Islamic State Foreign Fighters Currently Detained in Syria," *CTC Sentinel* 12, iss. 5, May/June 2019, https://ctc.usma.edu/options-dealing-islamic-state-foreign-fighters-currently-detained-syria/

68. Thomas Joscelyn, "Al Qaeda and allies announce 'new entity' in Syria," *Long War Journal*, January 28, 2017, https://www.longwarjournal.org/archives/2017/01/al-qaeda-and-allies-announce-new-entity-in-syria.php; Danika Newlee, "Hay'at Tahrir al-Sham," Center for Strategic & International Studies Transnational Threats Project *Terrorism Backgrounder*, 2018, https://www.csis.org/programs/transnational-threats-project/terrorism-backgrounders/hayat-tahrir-al-sham-hts
69. Ayman al-Zawahiri, "Let Us Fight Them with a Solid Structure," As-Sahab Media Foundation, released November 2017; See also SITE Intelligence Group, "AQ Leader Zawahiri Gives First Public Rejection of Nusra Front Split," November 28, 2017, https://news.siteintelgroup.com/Jihadist-News/aq-leader-zawahiri-gives-first-public-rejection-of-nusra-front-split.html.
70. Abdul-Zahra and Zeina Karam, "Elusive Al-Qaeda leader in Syria stays in shadows," *Times of Israel*, November 4, 2013, https://www.timesofisrael.com/elusive-al-qaeda-leader-in-syria-stays-in-shadows/
71. "HTS Condemns U.S. Terror Designation, Demands Evidence of AQ Link," Site Intelligence Group, June 1, 2018, https://ent.siteintelgroup.com/Statements/hts-condemns-u-s-terror-designation-demands-evidence-of-aq-link.html.
72. "Syria: Extremism & Counter-Extremism," Counter Extremism Project, n.d., https://www.counterextremism.com/countries/syria#radicalization_and_foreign_fighters; Danika Newlee, "Hay'at Tahrir al-Sham," Center for Strategic & International Studies Transnational Threats Project.
73. "Syria: Extremism & Counter-Extremism," Counter Extremism Project, n.d., https://www.counterextremism.com/countries/syria#radicalization_and_foreign_fighters
74. Harun al-Aswad, "Civil war within civil war: HTS battles rival militants, defectors in Syria's Idlib," *Middle East Eye*, June 27, 2020, https://www.middleeasteye.net/news/syria-idlib-hts-operations-room-rival-militants ; "Hurras al-Din," Counter Extremism

Project, n.d., https://www.counterextremism.com/threat/hurras-al-din

75. Zulfiqar Ali, "Hamza Bin Laden: Is al-Qaeda still a threat?" *BBC News*, August 1, 2019, https://www.bbc.com/news/world-asia-48056433
76. Valentina Napolitano, "Hamas and the Syrian Uprising: A Difficult Choice," *Middle East Polic*y 20, no. 3, https://mepc.org/hamas-and-syrian-uprising-difficult-choice
77. Valentina Napolitano, "Hamas and the Syrian Uprising: A Difficult Choice," Middle East Policy Council, Volume 20, Number 3, n.d., https://mepc.org/hamas-and-syrian-uprising-difficult-choice
78. Syrian Network for Human Rights, "3,196 Syrian Palestinians Were Killed by Syrian Regime Fores, including 491 Due to Torture, Between March 2011 and July 2020, and 49 Appeared in Caesar Photos," July 29, 2020, http://sn4hr.org/blog/2020/07/29/55316/; Harun al-Aswad, "Palestinians' homes stolen once again as Assad eyes Syria's Yarmouk camp," *Middle East Eye*, August 4, 2020, https://www.middleeasteye.net/news/syria-palestinians-assad-homes-stolen-yarmouk-camp
79. Nidal al-Mughrabi, "Assad puts Hamas in corner over Syrian assault," Reuters, August 17, 2011, https://www.reuters.com/article/us-palestinians-syria-hamas/assad-puts-hamas-in-corner-over-syrian-assault-idUSTRE77G3ZF20110817; Napolitano, "Hamas and the Syrian Uprising: A Difficult Choice."
80. Nidal al-Nughrabi, "Hamas ditches Assad, backs Syrian revolt," Reuters, February 24, 2012, https://www.reuters.com/article/us-syria-palestinians/hamas-ditches-assad-backs-syrian-revolt-idUSTRE81N1CC20120224
81. Khaled Abu Toameh, "Syria says no to restoring ties with 'terrorist-supporting' Hamas," *Jerusalem Post*, June 12, 2019, https://www.jpost.com/middle-east/syria-no-to-restoring-ties-with-terrorist-supporting-hamas-592149
82. Ahmad Abu Amer, "Hamas in Moscow to mend ties with Syrian regime," *al-Monitor*, March 16, 2020, https://www.al-monitor.com/pulse/originals/2020/03/international-diplomacy-hamas-damascus-relations-moscow.html
83. "Ahrar al-Sham," Mapping Militant Organizations, n.d., https://web.stanford.edu/group/mappingmilitants/cgi-bin/groups/view/523
84. Ibid.; Bill Roggio, "Al Nusrah Front claims suicide attack in Syria," *Long War Journal*, February 26, 2012, https://www.longwarjournal.org/archives/2012/02/al_nusrah_front_clai.php

85. Mariya Petkova, "Syrian opposition factions join Ahrar al-Sham," *al-Jazeera* (Doha), January 26, 2017, https://www.aljazeera.com/news/2017/01/syrian-opposition-factions-join-ahrar-al-sham-170126133928474.html
86. Kyle Orton, "Ahrar al-Sham and Al-Qaeda," personal blog, August 12, 2016, https://kyleorton1991.wordpress.com/2016/08/12/ahrar-al-sham-and-al-qaeda/
87. Charles Lister, *Profiling Jabhat al-Nusra* (Brookings Institution, July 2016), 26-9, https://www.brookings.edu/wp-content/uploads/2016/07/iwr_20160728_profiling_nusra.pdf
88. Ali El Yassir, "The Ahrar al Sham Movement: Syria's Local Salafists," Wilson Center, August 23, 2016, https://www.wilsoncenter.org/article/the-ahrar-al-sham-movement-syrias-local-salafists-0 ; Sam Heller, "Ahrar Al-Sham's Revisionist Jihadism," *War on the Rocks*, September 30, 2015, https://warontherocks.com/2015/09/ahrar-al-shams-revisionist-jihadism/
89. "Ahrar al-Sham," Mapping Militant Organizations, n.d., https://web.stanford.edu/group/mappingmilitants/cgi-bin/groups/view/523
90. Ahmed Hamza, "Increasing popular unrest against "Tahrir al-Sham" in Idlib, *Alraby*, February 4, 2018, https://www.alaraby.co.uk/%D8%A7%D8%AD%D8%AA%D9%82%D8%A7%D9%86-%D8%B4%D8%B9%D8%A8%D9%8A-%D9%85%D8%AA%D8%B2%D8%A7%D9%8A%D8%AF-%D8%B6%D8%AF-%22%D8%AA%D8%AD%D8%B1%D9%8A-%D8%B1-D8%A7%D9%84%D8%B4%D8%A7%D9%85%22-%D9%81%D9%8A-%D8%A5%D8%AF%D9%84%D8%A8; Tamer Osman, "Syrian Islamist factions join forces against Hayat Tahrir al-Sham," *al-Monitor*, February 28, 2018, https://www.al-monitor.com/pulse/originals/2018/02/syria-liberation-front-battes-against-hayat-ahrar-al-sham.html
91. "Syria: Extremism & Counter-Extremism," Counter Extremism Project, n.d., https://www.counterextremism.com/countries/syria#radicalization_and_foreign_fighters
92. Central Intelligence Agency World Factbook, "Syria," Last Updated October 16, 2020, https://www.cia.gov/library/publications/the-world-factbook/geos/sy.html.
93. United National High Commissioner on Refugees, "Syrian Regional Refugee Response," Last Updated October 14, 2020, http://data2.unhcr.org/en/situations/syria
94. Central Intelligence Agency World Factbook, "Syria."
95. Kheder Khaddour, "Localism, War, and the Fragmentation of Sunni

Islam in Syria," Carnegie Middle East Center, March 28, 2019, https://carnegie-mec.org/2019/03/28/localism-war-and-fragmentation-of-sunni-islam-in-syria-pub-78714.

96. Thomas Pierret (Francesco Cavatorta and Fabio Merone, eds.), *Salafism After the Arab Awakening: Contending With People's Power* (London: Hurst, 2017), https://www.research.ed.ac.uk/portal/files/45620332/Thomas_Pierret_Syran_Salafists_at_war_final_draft_1_.pdf
97. Khaddour, "Localism, War, and the Fragmentation of Sunni Islam in Syria."
98. Zach Goldberg, "Syria's Salafi Awakening: Existential Psychological Primers (Part 1/2)," *Fair Observer*, July 15, 2014, http://www.fairobserver.com/region/middle_east_north_africa/syrias-salafi-awakening-existential-psychological-primers-01474/
99. Aron Lund, "Syria's Salafi Insurgents: The Rise of the Syria Islamic Front," Swedish Institute of International Affairs *Occasional Paper* Number 17, March 2013, https://www.ui.se/globalassets/ui.se-eng/publications/ui-publications/syrias-salafi-insurgents-the-rise-of-the-syrian-islamic-front-min.pdf
100. Aron Lund, "Islamist Groups Declare Opposition to National Coalition and US Strategy," *Syria Comment*, September 24, 2013, https://www.joshualandis.com/blog/major-rebel-factions-drop-exilcs-go-full-islamist/
101. Chris Bosley, Leanne Erdberg Steadman and Mona Yocubian, "Can Syrians Who Left ISIS Be Reintegrated into Their Communities?" United States Institute of Peace, October 21, 2020, https://www.usip.org/publications/2020/10/can-syrians-who-left-isis-be-reintegrated-their-communities; Ashish Kumar Sen, "ISIS Determined to Make a Comeback – How Can it Be Stopped?" United States Institute of Peace, August 13, 2020, https://www.usip.org/publications/2020/08/isis-determined-make-comeback-how-can-it-be-stopped
102. Aymenn Jawad Al-Tamimi, "Idlib and Its Environs: Narrowing Prospects for a Rebel Holdout," Washington Institute for Near East Policy, February 2020, https://www.washingtoninstitute.org/uploads/Documents/pubs/PolicyNote75-Tamimi.pdf
103. Andrew Tabler, *In the Lion's Den: An Eyewitness Account of Washington's Battle With Syria* (Lawrence Hill Books, 2011), 118.
104. Ibid., 134.
105. Eyal Zisser, "Syria, the Ba'ath Regime and the Islamic Movement: Stepping on a New Path?" *The Muslim World* 95, 2005, 54.

106. Sami Moubayed, "The Islamic Revival in Syria," *Mideast Monitor* 1, no. 3, September-October 2006, http://www.nabilfayad.com/%D9%85%D9%82%D8%A7%D9%84%D8%A7%D8%AA/335-the-islamic-revival-in-syria.html
107. Zisser, "Syria, the Ba'ath Regime and the Islamic Movement," 45.
108. U.S. Department of State, "Syria," in *2019 International Religious Freedom Report*, 2019, https://www.state.gov/wp-content/uploads/2020/05/SYRIA-2019-INTERNATIONAL-RELIGIOUS-FREEDOM-REPORT.pdf
109. U.S. Department of State, "Syria," in *Country Reports on Terrorism 2019*, 2020, https://www.state.gov/reports/country-reports-on-terrorism-2019/syria/
110. Aniseh Bassiri Tabrizi and Raffaello Pantucci, "Understanding Iran's Role in the Syrian Conflict," Royal United Services Institute, August 2016, https://rusi.org/sites/default/files/201608_op_understanding_irans_role_in_the_syrian_conflict_0.pdf
111. Nader Uskowi, "The Evolving Iranian Strategy in Syria: A Looming Conflict with Israel," Atlantic Council, September 2018, https://www.atlanticcouncil.org/wp-content/uploads/2019/09/The_Evolving_Iranian_Strategy_in_Syria.pdf
112. Tabrizi and Pantucci, "Understanding Iran's Role in the Syrian Conflict."

50 Uzbekistan

Quick Facts

Population: 30,565,411 (July 2020 est.)
Area: 447,400 sq km
Ethnic Groups: Uzbek 83.8%, Tajik 4.8%, Kazakh 2.5%, Russian 2.3%, Karakalpak 2.2%, Tatar 1.5%, other 4.4% (2017 est.)
GDP (official exchange rate): $48.83 billion (2017 est.)

Source: CIA World FactBook (Last Updated September 2020)

Introduction

Uzbekistan's struggles with Islamism predate the formation of the country, as several Islamist groups were active in the former Soviet state before the collapse of the USSR. Uzbek militant groups hold sway and significance throughout the wider theater of Central Asia, most notably the Islamic Movement of Uzbekistan (IMU). Prior to his death in 2016,[1] *President Islam Karimov attempted to control Islamists in Uzbekistan, with growing success. Karimov was succeeded by former Prime Minister Shavkat Mirziyoyev,*[2] *who has taken a more proactive stance in the field of religion, seeking to counter extremism by advancing an "Enlightened Islam." While Central Asia has been a prominent source of foreign fighters traveling to Iraq and Syria to join the Islamic State and other jihadi groups, the majority are recruited as labor migrants in Russia, not in the region.*

Islamist Activity

For most of the quarter-century since it declared independence from the USSR, Uzbekistan has been an active arena for a range of Islamist groups. These groups vary in their ideologies, objectives and methods. All, however, share the broad goal of transforming Uzbekistan from its current status as a secular authoritarian regime into a state based upon, and governed by, *sharia* law. Most, however, operate outside the country's boundaries.

Islamic Movement of Uzbekistan (IMU)

The Islamic Movement of Uzbekistan (IMU) is one of the most important militant groups in Central Asia. The IMU grew out of an amalgam of Islamist groups that were active in the late 1980s and early 1990s, most notably the Adolat (Justice) group, which was formed by Tahir Yuldashev and Jumabai Khojiyev (also known as Juma Namangani). Adolat, formed in 1991 in the city of Namangan in the Ferghana Valley, had the aim of building an Islamic state in Uzbekistan.[3] During the slow decay of Soviet power, Islamist militias in Namangan sought to effectively replace Soviet authorities, and began to enforce Islamic dress code and close down establishments serving alcohol. On December 8, 1991, Adolat organized a violent takeover of regional power structures, subsequently levying an ultimatum at Uzbek authorities and demanding President Islam Karimov proclaim the establishment of an Islamic state.[4] The resulting government clampdown a few months later led to thousands of arrests, prompting an exodus of Islamic radicals from Uzbekistan to Tajikistan.[5] In 1992, Karimov formally banned Adolat. Yuldashev and Namangani fled to Tajikistan, and subsequently to Afghanistan and Pakistan.[6]

In total, about two thousand Uzbeks are estimated to have left the country during the 1990s, with many of them subsequently taking part in Tajikistan's civil war on the side of the United Tajik Opposition (UTO).[7] In Tajikistan, the Namangan Battalion (NB) was formed in 1992 (named after the majority of the group's members, who hailed from the city of Namangan). Namangani became the commander of this militia, which established a network of military bases and training camps for the IMU in northern Tajikistan, mostly in the Jirgatal and Garm regions. The Namangan Battalion was well-armed and developed a special system of training, focusing on guerrilla warfare, sabotage and terrorist activities. Uzbek instructors as well as instructors from Islamic organizations in Afghanistan, Pakistan, Kashmir, and some Middle Eastern countries worked at the NB's Tajik bases. Many of them collaborated with foreign intelligence services, most prominently Pakistan's spy agency, the Directorate for Inter-Services Intelligence (ISI).[8]

During the 1990s, Yuldashev and others traveled to Afghanistan, where they made contact with alumni of the Afghan *jihad* and established training camps for Uzbek militants.[9] These contacts created an avenue for further radicalization, and the following years saw a number of Uzbek militants pass through Afghan training camps before returning to Uzbekistan with the aim of destabilizing the country. By 1998, Yuldashev and Namangani had officially formed the IMU,[10] with Yuldashev serving as the IMU's political leader, or *emir*, and Namangani heading its military wing. The organization's headquarters were established in Peshawar, Pakistan, but later relocated to Taliban-controlled Kabul, Afghanistan.

Militants trained in IMU camps in Tajikistan and abroad, mostly in Afghanistan and Pakistan, in camps belonging to Islamist organizations such as al-Qaeda, Harkat-ul-Ansar, Hezb-e-Islami, Harkat-ul-Mujahideen, and the Taliban. However, in most cases, instructors were Uzbek Islamists affiliated with the bin Laden network, as well as specialists from Pakistan's ISI.[11] In total, during the 1990s more than a thousand militants of the Islamic Movement of Uzbekistan received military training in training camps in these two countries.[12]

Notably, creating a militia between 500 to several thousand fighters, including all the necessary support, equipment, and arms, posed a significant financial challenge. Accordingly, analysts presume that significant foreign funding aided the effort.[13] Thereafter, the IMU financed its activities in Central Asia, as well as in other regions, primarily through involvement in narcotics trafficking[14] and support from international Islamist organizations as well as wealthy members of the Uzbek diaspora in Afghanistan, Turkey and Saudi Arabia. Beginning in the mid-1990s, Uzbek Islamist opposition leaders bolstered this aid with active fundraising activities, with the aim of generating support for a powerful military-political structure.

In 1999, the IMU commenced an organized insurgent campaign against the Uzbek state.[15] Given its lack of capability to seize power through large-scale violence, the IMU's tactics were to destabilize the Ferghana Valley by armed incursions on the territory of both Kyrgyzstan and Uzbekistan. These incursions continued until U.S. counterterrorist operations in Afghanistan in 2001 weakened the

Taliban and al-Qaeda, and inflicted heavy losses on the IMU itself, including killing Namangani near Mazar i-Sharif in November 2001.

The IMU survived by relocating to the Waziristan area of northwest Pakistan, and merging with a number of like-minded groups. Yuldashev was reportedly killed in August 2009 in South Waziristan as a result of a U.S. Predator drone strike.[16] His death appears to have resulted in a downturn of the group's militant activities, with the last large-scale attack by the IMU being the September 19, 2010 ambush on a convoy of government troops in the Kamarob valley of Tajikistan – an operation that killed 25.[17]

Nevertheless, elements of the IMU have remained active, particularly in Afghanistan. In 2012, the International Security Assistance Force and the Afghan armed forces conducted 26 raids against the IMU in eight Afghan provinces—Badakhshan, Baghlan, Faryab, Logar, Helmand, Kunduz, Takhar and Wardak—with eight of them occurring in Kunduz province alone.[18]

However, the emergence of the Syrian civil war and the rise of the Islamic State changed matters. Many Uzbek and other Central Asian militants were attracted by the prospect of *jihad* in the core Middle East, where some joined ISIS and others the al-Qaeda-aligned Nusra Front. In 2015, the IMU formally broke away from the Taliban and al-Qaeda and pledged allegiance to the Islamic State. This was made official on August 6, 2015, when the IMU released a video depicting its leader, Usman Ghazi, pledging allegiance to IS.[19] The IMU statement declared that the Taliban "cannot be trusted," and accused the Afghan militant group of collaboration with Pakistan's ISI.[20]

The IMU's pledge to the Islamic State placed the organization in conflict with Taliban. In December 2015, pro-Taliban Sabiq Jihadmal declared the death of Ghazi in a Twitter message that claimed to show Ghazi's corpse. A pro-IMU fighter, known as Tahir Jan, recounted the group's collapse. Jan alleged that the Taliban and Afghan government cooperated to destroy the remainder of the IMU. The Taliban's forces quickly laid siege to the organization's bases, slaughtering hundreds of IMU partisans, and effectively spelling the end of the organization.[21] As Jan described it:

> The former Islamic Movement of Uzbekistan has almost been completely destroyed unfortunately, and

> maybe less than 10% of those who were in the fronts or on other assignments remain after the events of Zabul.[22]

Akramiyya

The founder of Akramiyya, Akram Yuldashev, was born in 1963 in Andijan, Uzbekistan.[23] A teacher by profession, his 1992 treatise "Lymonga Yul" emphasized that the ultimate goal of his organization is the assumption of power and the creation of an Islamic state.[24] Members of Akramiyya called themselves *birodarami*, or brothers. There were in the late 2000s several thousand adherents.[25] The organization first appeared in the Ferghana Valley in 1998, where—motivated by the ideology of Hizb ut-Tahrir—it espoused a selective reading of the Quran, arguing in favor of *sharia* as the answer to the modern, "unfavorable" period for Muslims in Central Asia. Yuldashev is said to have structured the activities of his group in five phases, beginning with the indoctrination of new members, extending to the accumulation of wealth for charitable Islamic works, and culminating in the gradual, "natural transition" to Islamic rule in Uzbek society.[26]

Ideologically, Akramiyya is an outgrowth of the Ahl al-Quran movement which existed in the 1940s in Uzbekistan. Members of this movement categorically refused to recognize the teachings of other Sunni schools (*mad'hab*). They adhered to very austere views, rejected the "Soviet way of life" and did not recognize official clergy. Members of Akramiyya believe only in Allah, and do not worship the Prophet Mohammed; they also do not recognize any nation in the world. They ignored state laws, renounce their parents, and subjected themselves exclusively to the direction of the group's leaders.[27] Most Akramiyya members were of Uzbek ethnicity. Its members were mostly businessmen with small agricultural enterprises, funds and industrial warehouses. The organization was known to control dozens of commercial firms, which did business under a unified leadership.

Authorities in Tashkent took an ambivalent approach to Akramiyya. But gradually, they began to see the movement as a threat and crack down on it. Yuldashev was sentenced in 1998 to two-and-a-half years in prison for violating Article 276 (drug possession) of the Uzbek Criminal Code.[28] In late December of the same year, he received amnesty, only to be arrested again the day after a bombing in Tashkent in February 1999 that sought to assassinate President Karimov. In May 1999, Yuldashev was sentenced to 17 years in prison on charges of terrorism, incitement of religious hatred, possession of weapons and drugs, among others.[29] During the same period (1998-1999), 22 other young members of Akramiyya were given varying terms in prison.[30] However, members of the group continued to exist and to thrive, including in the Ferghana Valley city of Andijan, where they established a working relationship with the local authorities. President Karimov, usually no friend of Islamist organizations, even went so far as to praise the group's charitable activities in 2004.[31]

The organization continued to exist until the Andijan uprising of 2005, which occurred after the group had a falling out with a newly-appointed governor in Andijan and two dozen of its members were jailed. This appears to have led to a rapid radicalization of the group, which attacked an interior ministry compound, freed prisoners at the Andijan jail, stormed a national security service headquarters, and took over the provincial capitol building. The group took human shields, resulting in a standoff and an armed confrontation with security forces, which led to some 200 deaths.[32] In the aftermath, many members of fled from Uzbekistan through Kyrgyzstan to the West, leading to the gradual dissolution of the group. In 2016, Uzbek authorities announced Yuldashev had died of tuberculosis in prison in 2011.[33]

Hizb ut-Tahrir (HuT)

Unlike the IMU, HuT is a truly transnational movement that enjoys considerable support among young Muslims in Western Europe and has a broad organizational base in London. HuT was founded in 1952 by Sheikh Taqiuddin al-Nabhani in Jordanian-ruled East Jerusalem, who died in 1977.[34]

The main goal of HuT is to recreate the *caliphate*, the Islamic state formally brought to an end in 1924 following the collapse of the Ottoman Empire. Although it claims to be nonviolent, HuT acknowledges that violence may eventually be necessary in order to overthrow the regimes standing in the way of the *caliphate*. It is anti-Semitic and anti-American, and disseminates a radical ideology fundamentally opposed to democratic capitalism and to Western concepts of freedom. While HuT as an organization does not engage in terrorist activities, it does operate as an ideological vanguard that supports and encourages terrorist acts.[35]

HuT ideology was imported to Uzbekistan in 1955 by a Jordanian named Atif Salahuddin. That same year, the organization was founded in the city of Tashkent, and subsequently in the Andijan, Samarkand, Tashkent and Fergana provinces of Uzbekistan. HuT cells were mostly composed of local youth. Members of HuT were distinguished not so much by their desire for strict adherence to Islamic norms, but by their religious and political activities. HT acquired adherents first in Uzbekistan, and then migrated to the neighboring former Soviet republics of Kyrgyzstan, Tajikistan and Kazakhstan. In these countries, the party first recruited its followers among ethnic Uzbeks, but gradually young ethnic Kyrgyz, Tajiks and Kazakhs became involved in HT, causing a rapid expansion of the group during the late 1990s.

HuT activities did not attract the attention of Uzbek authorities until May 1998, when party members began to distribute leaflets in public places. The response was rapid; between August and November of 1998, at least 15 members of the Tashkent branch of the movement were arrested. Mass arrests of members throughout Uzbekistan began the following year. According to the State Department, "approximately 6,800 to 7,300 persons were arrested between 1999 and 2001 on suspicion of Islamic extremism or terrorism."[36]

Following the events of September 11, 2001, many members of HT in Uzbekistan went underground, fearing large-scale retaliation. The group has largely continued to operate covertly to this day, as a result of unprecedented (and often violent) persecution on the part of Uzbek authorities. This led it gradually to reduce its presence in the country, and in recent years it can be deemed to have effectively been neutralized in Uzbekistan. In recent years, the group has exhibited only nominal activity, although experts caution that this lull may be temporary in nature.[37] In May 2020, Uzbek authorities rounded up HT supporters in the Ferghana valley.[38] Elsewhere in the region, however, HT expanded its activities. As authorities in Uzbekistan ratcheted up their counterterrorism efforts, party activists were forced to seek refuge among Uzbek communities in neighboring countries, primarily in Kyrgyzstan, to where its focus appears to have moved.

Islamism and Society

Although the majority (88 percent) of Uzbekistan's population of more than 30 million is Muslim,[39] most of them Sunni, this population appears to be broadly supportive of a secular state system. Muslim leaders in Uzbekistan have been very critical of Islamist organizations, and have argued that these movement are essentially political rather than religious organizations.

While most moderate Muslims in Uzbekistan reject the goals and ideology of both the IMU and Hizb-ut-Tahrir, the latter had some success in drawing attention to official corruption. HuT leaflets highlighting corruption, inequality and oppression tended to find a receptive ear, especially among more disadvantaged members of society. Nevertheless, neither the IMU nor HuT can claim widespread support anywhere in Central Asia. Both organizations appeal only to a small fraction of the regional population—and even then this support was localized, strongest in parts of the Fergana Valley, possibly in south Uzbekistan, and in some areas of Tajikistan.

In the decade between the violence in Andijan and the death of President Karimov, there was a noticeable decrease in Islamist activity in Uzbekistan. The limited data available also suggests that Islamist ideology had little appeal to the country's population. A Pew poll conducted worldwide in 2013 was not allowed to ask questions on the most sensitive questions, such as support for *sharia*. However, results in Uzbekistan are in line with findings in other Central Asian states, with one exception: only 39 percent of Uzbeks – the lowest number in the sample – felt they were "very free" to practice their faith, compared to between 60 and 70 percent in other regional states. However, on social issues, Uzbeks were as liberal or more compared to regional states. For example, two-thirds of Uzbeks thought women themselves should decide whether to wear the veil – more than in Tajikistan or Kyrgyzstan, but less than in Azerbaijan or Turkey. Only three percent see tensions between devout and less devout Muslims, whereas only 18 percent – the lowest number in Central Asia – think there is a conflict between religion and science. Uzbeks appear slightly more conservative in many of their values than Kazakhs or Azerbaijanis, but more liberal than Tajiks, and certainly than the average Middle Eastern or South Asian Muslim society.[40]

Islamism and the State

In September 2016, Uzbekistan underwent a political sea change with the death of its longtime president, Islam Karimov. Karimov, the leader of the Uzbek Communist Party during the Soviet era, became president after the country's independence from the Soviet Union in 1991.[41]

Virtually from its formation, Karimov's government strived to control the Uzbek population, and temper political and religious activism in the country. In the early 1990s, the government launched a series of measures to marginalize secular opposition groups, and thereafter directed its attention toward Islamic associations. The government feared that any form of religious expression not controlled by the state could serve as a vehicle for alien, Islamist ideology to enter the country and jeopardize the delicate process of nation- and state-building that was taking place after the collapse of the Soviet Union. This pattern continued for two decades; state intelligence agencies worked to eliminate and marginalize those Islamic leaders who deviate from the official state-sponsored Hanafi Sunni Islam. Uzbek security forces, meanwhile, routinely utilized repressive methods against Islamic organizations indiscriminately, often failing to differentiate between terrorist groups like the IMU and non-violent groups. Adherents to all of these organizations were subject to arbitrary arrest, based upon suspicions of extremism.[42]

The Uzbek government continues to take a hostile approach toward anyone engaged in unregulated religious activity. This, however, has increasingly been coupled with a subtle and surprisingly sophisticated "soft power" approach to combating Islamist ideology. This approach finds its roots in the nature of Central Asian Islam itself, where the dominant branch of Sunni Islam is the Hanafi school—one of the most tolerant and liberal of the faith. Hanafi Islam was, nevertheless, considerably suppressed during the Soviet period, as Communist authorities sought to apply a divide-and-rule approach which included tolerating, if not encouraging, the influx of more radical theological approaches that undermined the compact, Hanafi tradition in the region.[43]

This approach leverages an asset shared by the Central Asian states: a strong knowledge base with which to fight radical Islamists. Since gaining independence, the countries of the region have managed to educate considerable numbers of knowledgeable experts in Islam. Moreover, in these countries, the Quran and Hadith have been translated into local languages, and many academics and *imams* are applying their knowledge on a practical level. By necessity, Central Asian governments, especially those in Uzbekistan and Kyrgyzstan, have created and developed an extensive educational system—spanning from kindergarten to university level—that inculcates the moral norms and social principles of tolerant Islam, and which respects the value of human life (be it Muslim, Christian, Jewish, or other). The system provides textbooks for schools, cartoons for children, education for imams of local mosques, a network of counselors in Islamic affairs for central and local administrations, and television and radio talk shows that challenge the intolerant Salafi interpretation of the Quran and *Hadith* and provide listeners with a religious alternative.[44]

Since coming to power, Uzbek President Shavkat Mirziyoyev has doubled down on this approach. He has increased the state's emphasis on promoting the tolerant Islamic tradition indigenous to the region, something he has termed "Enlightened Islam." This has included a state policy that now embraces public expressions of religion, including the holding of competitions in Quran recital and the building of roadside mosques. Mirziyoyev has, importantly, announced the creation of several new institutions in the religious field. This includes an Islamic Academy of Uzbekistan, as well as an Islamic Culture Center that is specifically designed to "fight religious ignorance and promote Islam's true values."[45] In addition, an Imam Bukhari International Scientific Research Center was created at the Imam Al-Bukhari Academy in Samarkand to focus both on religious and scientific research.

The government has also removed 16,000 of 17,000 names registered as "religious radicals" from a state-held list, and has encouraged the return of religious dissidents to the country. The government has also begun to engage with international bodies promoting the freedom of religion, including UN agencies as well as NGOs such as Human Rights Watch.[46] In September 2020, legislation was introduced that further relaxed restrictions on religious freedom. While strict guidelines for the registration of religious organizations remained, the changes will allow the wearing of religious garb in public for people other than clerics, and allow parents to teach children the basics of religion at home and for minors to attend mosque services. In a sign that the government remains wary of alien religious influences, the censorship of religious materials will remain, as will the prohibition of private religious education.[47]

Mobilization of Foreign Fighters

Central Asian and Russian foreign fighters make up as much as a third of the total *jihadis* that traveled to Iraq and Syria between 2011-2016, according to some estimates.[48] The exact number of Uzbek fighters is difficult to gauge, especially when considering the intricacies of the divide between ethnicity and nationality, and the close linguistic ties between Uzbeks and China's Uighurs. In October 2017, the Soufan Group estimated that fewer than 1,500 Uzbeks had become foreign fighters.[49] Meanwhile, the Uzbek government's approach to repatriation of families of foreign fighters suggests a confidence that the Uzbek government and society can handle their reintegration. In 2019, the government arranged for the repatriation of over 400 individuals, almost exclusively women and children, stranded in camps in Syria and Iraq.[50]

Uzbek authorities are according great attention to strengthening their police and internal security agencies in order to counter the internal extremist Islamic terrorist organizations. Yet it should be noted that the vast majority of Uzbek nationals, as well as other Central Asians, who have joined the ranks of *jihadi* groups in the

Middle East have been recruited while labor migrants in Russia, and not in Uzbekistan itself. Leon Aron of the American Enterprise Institute estimates that over 80 percent of Islamic State fighters from Kyrgyzstan, Tajikistan, and Uzbekistan were recruited in Russia.[51] Uzbekistan, however, is vulnerable to this trend, as individuals radicalized in Russia may return to Uzbekistan to spread their ideology there. This problem will remain until the country's domestic economic development—which President Mirziyoyev is trying to kick-start—reduces the appeal of labor migration.

Endnotes

1. "Islam Karimov: Uzbekistan president's death confirmed," *BBC,* September 2, 2016, http://www.bbc.com/news/world-asia-37260375.
2. "Uzbekistan's new leader promises major government reshuffle," Reuters, December 14, 2016, http://www.reuters.com/article/us-uzbekistan-president-idUSKBN1431LN?feedType=RSS&feedName=worldNews.
3. Igor Rotar, "The Islamic Movement of Uzbekistan: A Resurgent IMU?" Jamestown Foundation, *Terrorism Monitor* 1, iss. 8, December 17, 2003, http://www.jamestown.org/single/?no_cache=1&tx_ttnews[tt_news]=26187.
4. Orozbek Moldaliyev, *Islam i Politika: Politizatsiya Islama ili Islamizatsiya Politiki? (Islam and Politics: The Politicization of Islam of the Islamization of Politics?)* (Bishkek: n.p., 2008), 269; See also A. Starkovsky, "Armia Izgnanikov, Chast I" (Army of Outcasts, Part I) freas.org, January 18, 2004, http://freeas.org/?nid=2367; Vitaly Ponomarev, *Ugroza "Islamskovo Ekstremisma" v Uzbekistane: Mifui i Realnosti (The "Islamic Extremist" Threat in Uzbekistan: Myth and Reality)* (Moscow: Memorial, 1999).
5. Moldaliyev, *Islam i Politika*; See also *Res Publica,* September 15-21, 1998.
6. Thomas M. Sanderson, Daniel Kimmage, and David A. Gordon, *From the Ferghana Valley to South Waziristan: The Evolving Threat of Central Asian Jihadists,* 2010, CSIS Transnational Threats Project, pg 6, https://csis.org/files/publication/100324_Sanderson_FerghanaValley_WEB_0.pdf.
7. Michael Falkov, "Islamic Movement of Uzbekistan (IMU): History, financial base and a military structure," *Nezavisimaya Gazeta* (Moscow), August 24, 2000.

8. Ibid.
9. Moldaliyev, *Islam i Politika*, 271.
10. Sanderson, Kimmage, and Gordon, *From the Ferghana Valley to South Waziristan*, 6.
11. Moldaliyev, *Islam i Politika*, 271.
12. Ibid.
13. Author's interview with former IMU member, Osh, Kyrgyzstan, August 11, 2004; See also Alex Alexiev, "Oil Dollars to Jihad: Saudi Arabia Finances Global Islamism," *Internationale Politik* 1 (2004), 31.
14. Svante E. Cornell, "The Islamic Movement of Uzbekistan," in Svante E. Cornell and Michael Jonsson, eds., *Conflict, Crime and the State in Postcommunist Eurasia* (Philadelphia: University of Pennsylvania Press, 2013), 68-81.
15. Sanderson, Kimmage, and Gordon, *From the Ferghana Valley to South Waziristan*, 7.
16. Bill Roggio, "Tahir Yuldashev Confirmed Killed In U.S. Strike In South Waziristan," *Long War Journal*, October 4, 2009, http://www.longwarjournal.org/archives/2009/10/tahir_yuldashev_conf.php
17. U.S. Department of State, "Islamic Movement of Uzbekistan," *Country Reports on Terrorism 2010,* 2011, www.state.gov/j/ct/rls/crt/2010/170264.htm.
18. "Afghanistan: IMU leader detained in Kunduz," *Fergana News Agency*, August 14, 2012, http://www.fergananews.com/news.php?id=19262&print=1, 08.14.2012
19. Margaret Foster, "2015 Retrospective: How the Fall of the IMU Reveals the Limits of IS' Expansion," *INSITE on Terrorism*, n.d., https://news.siteintelgroup.com/blog/index.php/submissions/21-jihad/4498-2015-retrospective-how-the-fall-of-the-imu-reveals-the-limits-of-is-expansion
20. Merhat Sharipzhan, "IMU Declares It Is Now Part Of The Islamic State," *Radio Free Europe/Radio Liberty*, August 6, 2015, http://www.rferl.org/a/imu-islamic-state/27174567.html.
21. Foster, "2015 Retrospective: How the Fall of the IMU Reveals the Limits of IS' Expansion."
22. Sharipzhan, "IMU Declares It Is Now Part Of The Islamic State."
23. Bakhtiyar Babadjanov, "Akramia: A Brief Summary," Carnegie Endowment for International Peace, May 2006,http://www.carnegieendowment.org/files/Akramiya.pdf
24. Ibid.
25. Author interview with Uzbek expert on Islam B. Babadzhanov, Tash-

kent, Uzbekistan, September 14, 2009.
26. Ibid.
27. Author interview with Uzbek expert on Islam I. Mirsaidov, Tashkent, Uzbekistan, September 16, 2009
28. Moldaliyev, *Islam i Politika*, 286.
29. Ibid., 286-287.
30. Ibidem, *Islam i Politika* , 286-287.
31. Jeffry Hartman, "The May 2005 Andijan Uprising: What We Know," Washington: Central Asia-Caucasus Institute & Silk Road Studies Program *Silk Road Paper* 2016, 20. https://silkroadstudies.org/publications/silkroad-papers-and-monographs/item/13204.
32. Ibid.; Shirin Akiner, "Violence in Andijan, 13 May 2005: An Independent Assessment," Washington: Central Asia-Caucasus Institute & Silk Road Studies Program *Silk Road Paper*, July 2005, https://www.silkroadstudies.org/resources/pdf/SilkRoadPapers/2005_akiner_violence-in-andijan-13-may-2005.pdf.
33. "Akram Yuldashev is Dead," *Radio Free Europe/Radio Liberty*, January 12, 2016. (https://www.rferl.org/a/akram-yuldashev-is-dead-uzbekistan-andijon/27483648.html.
34. Ahmed Rashid, *Jihad: The Rise of Militant Islam in Central Asia* (New Haven: Penguin Books, 2003), 119.
35. Zeyno Baran, "Radical Islamists in Central Asia," *Current Trends in Islamist Ideology* 2, 2005, http://www.hudson.org/content/researchattachments/attachment/1175/20060130_current_trends_v2.pdf
36. US Department of State, Bureau of Democracy, Human Rights, and Labor, "Country Reports on Human Rights Practices" 2002, March 31, 2003, https://2009-2017.state.gov/j/drl/rls/hrrpt/2002/18400.htm
37. Author Evgueuni Novikov interview with Uzbek expert on Islam M.P., Tashkent, Uzbekistan, September 11, 2009.
38. "Uzbekistan keeps up heat on marginal Islamic groups," *Eurasianet,* May 29, 2020, https://eurasianet.org/uzbekistan-keeps-up-heat-on-marginal-islamic-groups.
39. Central Intelligence Agency World Factbook, "Uzbekistan," October 1, 2020, https://www.cia.gov/library/publications/the-world-factbook/geos/uz.html
40. Pew Research Center, *The World's Muslims*, April 30, 2013, 62, 105, 130, http://assets.pewresearch.org/wp-content/uploads/sites/11/2013/04/worlds-muslims-religion-politics-society-full-report.pdf.
41. Krishnadev Calamur, "Islam Karimov's Legacy," *The Atlantic,* September 2, 2016, http://www.theatlantic.com/news/archive/2016/09/

islam-karimov-dead/498533/.
42. See, for example, United Nations Human Rights Committee, "Human Rights Committee Concludes Consideration of Uzbekistan's Third Report," March 12, 2010, http://www.un.org/News/Press/docs/2010/hrct719.doc.htm.
43. Svante E. Cornell and Jacob Zenn, "Religion and the Secular State in Uzbekistan," Washington: Central Asia-Caucasus Institute & Silk Road Studies Program *Silk Road Paper*, June 2018, http://silkroadstudies.org/publications/silkroad-papers-and-monographs/item/13285.
44. For a detailed analysis of the "soft power" counterterrorism approaches of Central Asian states, see Evgueni K. Novikov, *Central Asian Responses to Radical Islam* (Washington, DC: American Foreign Policy Council, 2006).
45. "Leader Says Most of Uzbeks Listed As Extremists Rehabilitated," Ozbekistan Television 1530 GMT, September 1, 2017.
46. Cornell and Zenn, "Religion and the Secular State in Uzbekistan."
47. "Uzbekistan's new religion law promises limited change," *Eurasianet,* September 16, 2020, https://eurasianet.org/uzbekistans-new-religion-law-promises-limited-change
48. Uran Botokbekov, "ISIS and Central Asia: A Shifting Recruiting Strategy," *The Diplomat,* May 17, 2016, http://thediplomat.com/2016/05/isis-and-central-asia-a-shifting-recruiting-strategy/.
49. Richard Barrett, *Beyond the Caliphate: Foreign Fighters and the Threat of Returnees,* October 2017, http://thesoufancenter.org/wp-content/uploads/2017/11/Beyond-the-Caliphate-Foreign-Fighters-and-the-Threat-of-Returnees-TSC-Report-October-2017-v3.pdf.
50. Nodirbek Soliev, "Syria: Uzbekistan's Approach to IS Detainees," RSIS Commentary, October 9, 2019, https://www.rsis.edu.sg/rsis-publication/icpvtr/syria-uzbekistans-approach-to-is-detainees/#.X3W1VWgzY2w.
51. Leon Aron, "The Coming of the Russian Jihad, Part I," *War on the Rocks*, September 23, 2016; Zinaida Burskaya, "The Road to IGIL Passed Through Moscow" ["Doroga v IGIL Prolegla Cherez Moskvu"], *Novaya Gazeta*, January 18, 2016.

South Asia

51 Afghanistan

Quick Facts

Population: 36,643,815 (July 2020 est.)
Area: 652,230 sq km
Ethnic Groups: Pashtun, Tajik, Hazara, Uzbek, other (includes smaller numbers of Baloch, Turkmen, Nuristani, Pamiri, Arab, Gujar, Brahui, Qizilbash, Aimaq, Pashai, and Kyrghyz)
GDP (official exchange rate): $20.24 billion (2017 est.)

Source: CIA World FactBook (Last Updated July 2020)

Introduction

Afghanistan is among the nations most affected by Islamic militancy. A myriad of militant groups that vary in size, tactics, and political objectives perpetrate violent Islamist activity in the country. Key active groups include the Taliban and their splinter factions, of which the Haqqani Network is most prominent, as well as Lashkar-e Taiba, Lashkar-e Jhangvi (LeJ), al-Qaeda (AQ), the Islamic State (IS), and a host of others. The majority of these groups maintain a regional or global focus, and strategic military and political objectives. They either target relevant interests within Afghanistan or utilize the country as a base of operations. The groups generally support both the creation of an ultraconservative Islamic state in the region, the removal of perceived false governments, and the expulsion of U.S. and NATO forces from the region. The Taliban remain the largest and most influential group focusing solely on Afghanistan. Their campaign to remove the government of Afghanistan and enforce ultraconservative policies across the country receives the greatest amount of focus from the international community.

The Taliban emerged in 1994 in response to the Afghan civil war and the corruption of warlords countrywide. They seized Kabul and, by extension, power in Afghanistan in 1996 and continued to defeat warlords and capture territory until 2001, when their regime was ousted by a U.S.-led coalition in response to the September 11, 2001 terrorist attacks perpetrated by al-Qaeda, then headquartered in the country. In the nearly two decades since, the U.S.-led coalition and the Afghan government, under a succession of leaders, have struggled to subdue an insurgency waged by the Taliban and ideological affiliates which have enjoyed sanctuary in, and financial and military support from, neighboring Pakistan.

The ongoing peace process between the Taliban and the U.S. is fraught with hostile negotiations, shifting timelines, and increasing tension. The peace process between the Taliban and the Afghan government faces even steeper odds and harsher demands. While a tentative truce was concluded between the U.S. and the Taliban in February of 2020, enacting it has faced significant challenges in the face of continued Taliban aggression. The majority of other Islamist groups in Afghanistan, meanwhile, have no interest in the current peace process and will likely continue their operations regardless of the outcome.

Islamist Activity

The Taliban "Religious Students"

The Taliban is a Sunni Islamist fundamentalist militant group founded by Mohammed "Mullah" Omar in 1994, during the Afghan civil war. The Taliban, or "religious students" in Pashto, were primarily *madrassa* students whose education was rooted in the Deobandi reformist school of north India, and who were motivated to restore peace, eliminate corruption, and enforce *sharia* law in Afghanistan. The Deobandi school rejects modern interpretations of Islam and instead focuses on a literal interpretation of the Quran.[1] The Taliban mesh their religious ideology with their own brand of legal jurisprudence that mixes Pashtunwali tribal traditions and conservative *sharia* law. The groups strategic motivations tie directly into these ideological systems in an effort to create an Islamic state in Afghanistan.

The Taliban formed in Kandahar and initiated a military campaign against regional warlords to capture Afghanistan. The movement seized Kandahar in November 1994 and Kabul in September 1996, taking control of the Afghan government in the process. It then began to rely upon foreign extremist groups like al-Qaeda for financial support. Islamist *jihadi* groups gravitated to Afghanistan because of the Taliban's strict imposition of *sharia* law. Its influence was symbolized by the March 2001 destruction of the Buddhas of Bamyan, Afghanistan's greatest historical site, because they were deemed by the movement to be "heathen idols."[2]

After the September 2001 attacks, the Taliban refused to hand over Osama bin Laden to the United States government because of a strict interpretation of the Pashtun code of hospitality. In response, the U.S. and allied forces invaded Afghanistan and captured Kabul by November 2001, toppling the Taliban regime and leading to the group's flight to Quetta, Pakistan, where the Quetta Shura was formed. Taliban leadership directed their operations in Afghanistan from Quetta with the strategic goal of removing coalition forces from Afghanistan and the creation of an ultraconservative Islamic state in the country. Nineteen years after the U.S.-led intervention to defeat the Taliban and remove al-Qaeda from Afghanistan, the fight against an active Taliban-led insurgency in the country continues.

Originally, the Taliban would often attack in large groups and would thus lose many fighters in combat. Soon, though, the Taliban incorporated tactics developed by insurgent and *jihadist* groups in Iraq including suicide bombing. These new tactics supported a strategy designed not only to fragment Afghan forces but also to capture more territory. So far it has enabled the group to determine where and when to fight and to target weaknesses through ambushes. 29% of casualties caused by the Taliban are a result of ground engagements, 22% due to IEDs, 20% due to suicide-IEDs, 8% due to targeted killings, and 5% due to unexploded ordinance.[3]

Before the end of the U.S. combat mission in Afghanistan in 2014, the Afghan government and the Obama administration pushed for a negotiated settlement with the Taliban. In July 2013, the Taliban opened diplomatic offices in Doha, Qatar, with the intention of using the facility as a neutral base from which to enter peace negotiations with the United States and Afghanistan. Peace efforts quickly stalled when the Taliban staged a flag-hoisting ceremony thought by the Afghan government and its Western allies to have been a Taliban government in exile, and after they issued unreasonable preconditions for negotiations. A parallel track of engagement is purportedly being facilitated by Pakistan.

An unconditional peace agreement proposed by the Afghan government in February 2018 was rejected outright by the Taliban. Subsequently, in July 2018, the U.S. initiated secret negotiations that became public that October. The US, North Atlantic Treaty Organization (NATO), the Afghan government and the Taliban held regular negotiations to solidify the peace agreement over the course of 2018 and 2019; however, that time period was fraught with stalled or canceled negotiations as a result of continued Taliban combat operations and the deaths of U.S. soldiers. The U.S. and the Taliban signed a tentative peace agreement in February 2020, the terms of which included the immediate departure from Afghanistan of 5,000 of the approximately 13,000 troops previously stationed there, and the removal of all U.S. troops by May 2021. As of this writing, however, the fate of this agreement is in considerable question, with Taliban attacks surging and an intensification of the American military response.[4] The Taliban maintain an estimated 20,000 to 30,000 fighters in Afghanistan.[5]

The Haqqani Network (HQN)

The Haqqani Network is the Taliban's foremost subordinate network. Jalaluddin Haqqani, the founder of the organization, was originally a member of Hezb-e-Islami Khalis, but broke away with his network during the Soviet occupation of Afghanistan. The Haqqani Network actively fought the Soviets throughout the war. Jalaluddin Haqqani and his network were co-opted into the Taliban in 1996. Haqqani was allowed by Mullah Omar to operate his network as a subordinate under the auspices of the Taliban regime. Jalaluddin pledged allegiance to Mullah Omar, becoming the Minister of Tribal and Border Affairs, the Governor of Paktia, and eventually the Taliban's overall military commander. In 2003, Jalaluddin led the Taliban's strategy for the eastern zone. Jalaluddin handed control of the network to his son Sirajuddin in 2007, and the group has only increased in combat effectiveness since.

HQN is known for conducting extremely high profile and high impact suicide vehicle borne improvised explosive device attacks and raids against U.S., NATO, and Afghan military and government targets as well as economic and media institutions among other civilian targets. They are known for a complex assault on the US Embassy and ISAF Headquarters in September 2011, a June 2012 suicide bombing at FOB Salerno that wounded over 100 people, a May 2017 truck bomb that exploded near the Kabul Green Zone killing over 150 people, and a January 2018 ambulance bomb in Kabul that killed over 100 people.[6] They also target hotels frequented by Westerners and take hostages for ransom and political bargaining. The group maintains ties to the majority of Islamist groups in the region but is most closely affiliated with the Taliban. As of late 2019, the U.S. Department of Defense assessed that HQN maintained 3,000 to 5,000 members operating in Afghanistan.[7] HQN remains active as of 2020. In February of 2020, the *New York T*imes published an article by Sirajuddin Haqqani listing the demands of the organization to participate in the peace process.[8] Although the article outlines these conditions, the Haqqani Network will likely continue to operate semi-autonomously from the Taliban in the event a real peace is achieved.

The Afghan government's ongoing peace negotiations with the Taliban present further opportunities for Islamists to expand their political power and influence over policy. Should the Taliban and the government reach a lasting peace agreement, the Taliban will become a legitimate political party, maintain influence throughout the country and will likely be able to win parliament seats. Since 2004, the Taliban have actively attempted to disrupt the Afghan political process, attacking polling centers in 2018 and 2019.[9] A peace agreement would ideally prevent these attacks, but it would provide the group with a real political platform for the first time since 2001.

Al Qaeda (AQ) "The Base"

Al Qaeda (AQ) is a Salafi-*Jihadi* Sunni Islamist militant group founded by Osama bin Laden in 1988. The organization was formed in Afghanistan with the goal of extending the *jihad* against the Soviets globally to all oppressors of Muslims after the Soviets were defeated. AQ's strategic objectives have since expanded to include removal of U.S. and Western forces from Afghanistan and the wider Muslim world, the destruction of governments friendly to the West, and the creation of an Islamic state that mandates *sharia* law globally.[10] AQ's support for the Taliban stems from a shared desire to create such a state in Afghanistan. In practice, the group generally seeks to disrupt and destroy Western interests. Current AQ leadership is based in southern and northeastern Afghanistan.

AQ returned from Sudan to Afghanistan in 1996 as the Taliban grew more influential in the latter. While the Taliban and al-Qaeda do not occupy the same ideological space, Taliban commanders regularly comment favorably on al-Qaeda.[11] AQ's leadership has reciprocated this familiarity; in August 2015, for instance, al-Qaeda leader Ayman al-Zawahiri declared his support for the Taliban as he pledged allegiance to the new (now late) "commander of the faithful," Mullah Mansour.[12] AQ's primary aid to the Taliban comes in the form of shared battlefield tactics as well as the employment of sophisticated Internet and social media propaganda designed to promote and recruit.

Although AQ is globally focused, it conducts attacks in Afghanistan with strategic purpose. Tactically, AQ focuses on high profile suicide and non-suicide bombings, assassinations, and hostage taking.[13] Outside of the September 2001 attacks, AQ is most well-known for perpetrating bombings against the U.S. Embassies in Nairobi, Kenya and Dar es Salam, Tanzania in 1998 and the *USS Cole* bombing in Aden, Yemen in 2000.[14]

Beyond the Taliban, AQ maintains ties with the vast majority of Islamist groups in Afghanistan.[15] The group's regional branch, al-Qaeda in the Indian Subcontinent (AQIS), emerged in 2014 as the bulk of the organization decentralized and shifted away from direct attack planning. AQIS is responsible for conducting attacks regionally and within Afghanistan against U.S., NATO and Afghan government targets. AQ and AQIS act largely in an advisory role in the training of Taliban fighters in Afghanistan.[16] The U.S. Department of Defense has assessed that, as of 2020, AQ and AQIS are primarily attempting to survive and build capacity rather than conduct attacks.[17] The leader of AQIS had been killed in a drone strike in Helmand, Afghanistan in September the preceding year.[18] And as of late 2019, US DOD assessed that approximately 300 AQ and AQIS members remain in Afghanistan.[19]

Tehrik-i-Taliban Pakistan (TTP) "Taliban Movement in Pakistan"
Tehrik-i-Taliban Pakistan (TTP) is a coalition of Pakistani Deobani Sunni Islamist militant groups that formed in December 2007 in response to Pakistani military operations in Pakistan's Federally Administrated Tribal Area (FATA) and U.S. military operations across the border in Afghanistan. In keeping with its anti-state philosophy, TTP seeks to evict U.S. and NATO forces from the region and to implement *sharia* law in Pakistan, and maintains no aspirations for peace or political power in either Afghanistan or Pakistan short of the removal of the Pakistani government.[20] The coalition includes subordinate groups Jamaat ul-Ahrar (JuA), Lashkar-e-Islam, Hafiz Gul Bahadur, TTP Hafeez Ullah Kochwan, TTP Sanja, TTP Punjab, Tariq Gidar, and Majlis-e-Ahrar.[21] However, constant conflict has led to internal fissures; some regional commanders have pledged allegiance to the Islamic State, and now have close relations with that group's regional franchise. [22] The death of TTP leader Hakimullah Mehsud in November 2013 led to additional internal conflict and the emergence of splinter groups.[23]

TTP operates in Kunar, Nangarhar, and Paktika provinces along the Afghan-Pakistan border as well as the FATA region of Pakistan.[24] TTP supports Taliban operations in Afghanistan, but largely focuses on conducting high profile suicide bombings, assassinations, and raids against Pakistani government, military, and civilian targets.[25] It has attacked Shi'a mosques, schools, hospitals, and military bases in the region. TTP also conducts global missions. Most notably, TTP funded and directed the attempted New York City Time Square bombing in May 2010.[26] It is also responsible for an attempt to assassinate the Pakistani Prime Minister in 2007, and a subsequent attack against a school in Peshawar that killed over 140 people - mostly children. TTP remains active as of mid-2020 in both Afghanistan and Pakistan, with an estimated 3,000 to 5,000 members operating between the two countries.[27]

Islamic State Khorasan Province (ISKP)
The Islamic State's Afghanistan branch, Islamic State Khorasan Province (ISKP), is a Salafi-*jihadi* militant organization that emerged in Afghanistan in 2015. The Islamic State's existential rationale for its presence in Nangarhar, Kunar, Laghman, and Jowzjan provinces

is rooted in its interpretation of Islamic religious texts, which states that an army of true believers will convene in "Khorasan" Province, a historic region that encompasses Afghanistan, Pakistan, and parts of Central Asia, before the "apocalypse" or Day of Judgment. ISKP's strategic objectives include the creation of an Islamic state in Afghanistan and Central Asia, the removal of NATO and U.S. forces from the region, and the destruction of Shi'a Muslims.[28] ISKP harbors no aspirations for peace or political power short of the removal of the Afghan government and the implementation of an Islamic state.

Following the Islamic State's declaration of a *caliphate* in Iraq in June 2014,[29] IS began to gain support among *jihadist* groups in the "Khorasan" region, particularly in Pakistan. At the time of ISKP's emergence, U.S. commanders in Afghanistan said that this represented a rebranding of 'marginalized or renegade Taliban'[30] operating under a different name, flag, and a leader. In 2016, the United States designated ISKP a foreign terrorist organization in its own right.[31] ISKP regularly fights other Islamist groups, including the Taliban and IMU. ISKP also contends for recruits against other Islamist groups and actively steals their members.

Tactically, ISKP focuses on suicide bombings, assassinations, and kidnappings targeting Afghan and Pakistani government and military targets, Shi'a populations, and seemingly random civilian targets.[32] They launch high profile attacks including detonating a 1.5-ton truck bomb in central Kabul in May 2017 that killed over 150 people and another at a hospital in Kabul in March 2018 that left at least 49 people dead.[33] Over the last two years, ISKP was responsible for major attacks in Kabul. These included, among others, a coordinated multiple-suicide bombing targeting Afghan government employees in July 2019,[34] a suicide bombing of a wedding in August 2019,[35] an attack against a memorial service attended by Afghan government officials in March 2020,[36] a raid against a Sikh religious compound in March 2020,[37] and a suicide bombing at a hospital and maternity ward in May 2020.[38]

American, Afghan, and Taliban forces have increasingly targeted ISKP in recent years through both ground offensives and drone strikes. Joint operations have killed almost all of the group's founding leaders and taken out hundreds of its fighters, restricting ISKP's ability to operate freely in the country.[39] The group maintains an estimated 2,000 to 5,000 fighters in Afghanistan as of late 2019, though the majority have been ousted from Nangarhar by joint operations.[40] Nevertheless, the Islamic State's presence in Afghanistan is starting to gain global attention as a new vanguard of reinvigorated *jihadism* in the country.

Lashkar-e-Taiba (LeT), "Army of the Righteous"

Lashkar-e-Taiba (LeT) is an *Ahle Hadith* Sunni Islamist militant organization.[41] LeT was founded in 1990 as the military arm of Markaz ud Dawa ul-Irshad (MDI), a Sunni Islamist charitable organization founded in 1985 that actively supported the *jihad* against the Soviets in Afghanistan. LeT seeks to overthrow oppressors of Muslims globally, is strongly anti-Christian, anti-Jewish, and anti-Hindu, and has proclaimed the desire to destroy India and reunite the entire subcontinent under Islamic rule. The group seeks no political power, only desiring the removal of the Indian government, and has no interest in the Afghan peace process.

LeT is based in Pakistan but has focused on targets in Afghanistan and India. The organization's strategic objectives have evolved over time, but center on undermining Indian control of Jammu and Kashmir and reuniting the area with Pakistan.[42] The organization has also stated the intent to remove U.S. and NATO forces from Afghanistan. LeT is most well-known for conducting a terror attack in November 2008 in Mumbai, India that killed over 160 people.[43]

LeT utilizes the conflict in Afghanistan as a platform to train fighters and to conduct attacks against Indian, U.S., and NATO targets. LeT maintains strong ties to the Taliban and supports its efforts to remove U.S. and NATO forces from the country. It also maintains connections with AQ, TTP, and other Islamist groups in the region. LeT supports trafficking arms and fighters from Pakistan to Afghanistan.[44] It is also responsible for assassinating Afghan and Indian government officials and attacking government buildings. It operates primarily in Kunar and Nangarhar provinces, but has conducted attacks country wide. As of 2020, the group remains active and maintains an estimated 300 fighters in Afghanistan.[45]

Lashkar-e-Jhangvi (LeJ) "Army of Jhangvi"
Lashkar-e-Jhangvi (LeJ) is a Deobandi Sunni Islamist militant organization. LeJ was founded in 1996 as the military arm of Sipah-e-Sabaha, a Sunni Islamist organization focused on preventing Shi'a expansion in Pakistan.[46] LeJ operates in Afghanistan and Pakistan with a primary focus similar to that of its former parent organization – the establishment of a Sunni state in the latter country.[47] It also seeks to remove U.S. and NATO forces from the region. Over time, LeJ developed a subordinate faction, Al Alami, that has shifted toward attacking non-Sunni religious groups.[48]

LeJ is most well-known for attempting to assassinate the Pakistani Prime Minister in 1999 and 2007, an attempt on the life of the Pakistani President in 2003, and attacking Indian Parliament in 2001 alongside JeM.[49] The group provides logistical support – including safe houses, supplies and protection – to Afghan groups, including the Taliban, in Pakistan.[50] LeJ maintains strong ties to TTP, JEM, and SSP in Pakistan and ISKP in Afghanistan, other Islamist groups in the region, and remains active as of June 2020. LeJ maintains an unknown number of fighters in Afghanistan.[51]

Islamic Movement of Uzbekistan (IMU)
Founded in 1998 with the goal of overthrowing the President of Uzbekistan, the IMU is a Salafi-*jihadi* militant organization. The IMU is based in Afghanistan and operates out of Badakhshan, Jowzjan, Kunduz, and Faryab provinces.[52] It is regionally focused and conducts operations in Afghanistan, Uzbekistan, Kyrgyzstan, and Tajikistan. The organization's strategic objectives include the overthrow of the Uzbek government, the creation of an Islamic state in Central Asia, governance by *sharia* law, as well as the removal of U.S. and NATO forces from Afghanistan. It has no interest in supporting the peace process in Afghanistan or seeking political power.

Tactically, the IMU primarily conducts bombings against targets in Uzbekistan, NATO and U.S. military forces in Afghanistan, and has, on several occasions, attempted to attack U.S. embassies in the region.[53] The IMU also takes hostages for ransom purposes. The group maintains connections with ISKP and AQ.[54] IMU operations have slowed in Afghanistan since 2015, with a shift toward lone wolf attacks that require minimal resources and supporting ISKP objectives.[55] The IMU maintains a presence of approximately 300 fighters across Afghanistan.[56]

Islamic Jihad Union (IJU)

The Islamic Jihad Union (IJU) is a Salafi-*Jihadi* Islamist militant organization founded in 2002 as a globally focused offshoot of the regionally oriented IMU.[57] The IJU is based in Paktika and Nangarhar, Afghanistan but conducts operations in Central Asian states and is expanding operations globally to include the wider Middle East and Europe.[58] The organization's strategic objectives are the removal of U.S. and NATO forces from Afghanistan, overthrow of the government of Uzbekistan, the creation of an Islamic state in that country, and the targeting of Western interests globally.[59] The IJU exhibits no desire for political power in Afghanistan, and does not support the peace process there.

The IJU was responsible for the 2004 bombings of the U.S. and Israeli Embassies in Tashkent, Uzbekistan. It conducts attacks against Afghan, U.S. and NATO forces and also regularly supports the Taliban in their efforts to do the same.[60] Tactically, the majority of IJU attacks are suicide or non-suicide bombings.[61] The IJU conducted several large ambushes and bombings in Afghanistan throughout 2016 and 2017, but has since shifted efforts to Syria in support of al-Nusra in 2019 and 2020.[62] The IJU maintains connections with the Taliban, AQ, and the IMU. As of this writing, the IJU has not conducted an attack in Afghanistan in 2020, but is estimated to maintain 100 to 200 members in the country.[63]

Jaish-e-Mohammed (JeM) "Army of Mohammed"

JeM is a Deobandi Sunni Islamist militant organization. JeM was founded in 1999 and initiated offensive operations in early 2000, focusing on Afghan and Indian government targets in both countries, including the Indian Consulate in Mazar-i-Sharif in 2016.[64] It is based in Peshawar, Pakistan, but operates in Afghanistan and India.[65] The organization's strategic objectives are securing Pakistani control of Jammu and Kashmir, destroying Indian interests globally, and the removal of the U.S. and NATO presence from Afghanistan.[66] The organization is strongly anti-Indian and anti-Western in orientation.

JeM is most well-known for attacking the Indian Parliament in 2001, an assault it carried out in coordination with LeJ.[67] They have also attacked the Jammu and Kashmir Legislative Assembly.

JeM utilizes training camps in Afghanistan and smuggles goods from Pakistan into Afghanistan in support of local groups.[68] JeM also conducts attacks within Afghanistan targeting Indian interests, as well as occasionally carrying out attacks against U.S. and NATO forces there.[69] JeM maintains ties to AQ, the Taliban, LeJ, TTP, and SSP. They remain active as of 2020 though approximate numbers within Afghanistan are unknown.[70] JeM's focus remains conducting attacks in Jammu and Kashmir.[71]

Political parties

Islamist groups compete for control within the Afghan political system. Since the inception of the modern Islamic Republic of Afghanistan, a variety of Islamist political parties have operated legally within the country, including Hezb-i Islami (Islamic Party), Jamiat-e Islami (Islamic Society), Harakat-e Islami (Islamic Movement), Tanzim-e Dahwat-e Islami (Islamic Dawah Organization), and Etalaf-e Milli (National Coalition of Afghanistan).[72] While there is no outright legal ban on Islamist parties or Islamism in general, the Afghan Constitution does restrict political parties, mandating that they cannot contradict Islam or the constitution in principle, cannot have military branches or goals, cannot have connections to foreign entities, cannot be operated in biased manner in relation to tribe or language, cannot be operated in a sectarian manner, and must maintain transparent finances.[73] The constitution also protects the rights to free speech, individual human rights, and the equality of all people. The constitution likewise forces Islamist parties to renounce violence and military branches in order to participate politically. The majority of Islamist political parties are former insurgent groups that have followed these guidelines in an effort to pursue Islamist policies through peaceful political change. Hezb-i Islami and Jamiat-e Islami remain the most influential Islamist political parties as of 2020.

Jamiat-e Islami ("Islamic Society")

Jamiat-e Islami was founded in the 1970s by Burhanuddin Rabbani, originally as a Tajik political organization that became a militant organization before gradually transitioning back into a political one. Founded by university students opposing the progressive modernization of the Daoud regime and the expansion of communist ideology in Afghanistan,[74] it was driven to militancy by the subsequent Soviet occupation. Jamiat-e Islami subsequently served as a critical mujahedeen group in the fight against the Soviets.[75] It renounced violence after the occupation, and shifted back to pursuing peaceful political power in Afghanistan.

Jamiat-e Islami has contested every major election in the modern history of the current Islamic Republic of Afghanistan, and has actively participated in peace talks with the Taliban.[76] Politically, the party is focused on directing change across Afghan society to implement ultraconservative Islamic principles.[77] Jamiat-e Islami draws its ideology from Abul A'la Maududi, the founder of Jamaat-e Islami, the Indian precursor to the Afghan political party.[78] That ideology consists of literal interpretation and implementation of the Quran and the use of (preferably non-violent) *jihad* to expand the Muslim world.[79] Economically, it seeks to implement an Islamist economic system, combining capitalism and socialism under *sharia* law with minimal government intervention and an expansion of citizens' economic rights.[80] Socially, it advocates an extremely conservative social framework, including the banning of music and alcohol.[81]

Hezb-i Islami "Party of Islam"

Hezb-i Islami is predominantly Pashtun breakaway from Jamiat-e Islami and is a political party and Sunni Islamist militant organization. It was founded in 1976 by Gulbuddin Hekmatyar in Kunduz in response to Afghan leftist movements within government. The organization actively fought the Soviets throughout their occupation of Afghanistan and cooperated with other Afghan mujahideen groups.

During Hekmatyar's brief but controversial stint as Afghanistan's prime minister during the Afghan civil war in 1990s, Hizb-i Islami was accused of atrocities and war crimes.[82] He later fled to Iran in order to escape the Taliban once the group assumed power in 1996. His base of support within Afghanistan collapsed, and although he returned to Afghanistan in 2002, he has not been able to mobilize mass support among Afghans for the movement. Most of the fighters that belonged to HI operated in the northeastern parts of the country, close to the border with Pakistan, and many hailed from the Pashtun ethnic group. In February 2003, the U.S. Department of State declared Gulbuddin Hekmatyar a Specially Designated Foreign Terrorist (SDGT) for participating in and supporting acts of terror committed by al-Qaeda and the Taliban.[83] HI has never had a prominent battlefield presence and primarily conducted high profile assassinations and suicide bombings.[84]

In January 2010, Hekmatyar and the Karzai administration initiated reconciliation talks in Kabul, followed by an HI delegation's attendance at *Loya Jirga* ("grand assembly"), the tribally-appointed consultative body that ratified the Afghan constitution.[85] The two sides also met on two separate occasions in 2012.[86] In May 2016, the Afghan National Unity Government and Hekmatyar came close to finalizing a 25-point peace agreement; it was signed four months later, after the group agreed to cease hostilities in return for official recognition.[87] The United Nations Security Council Sanctions Committee subsequently removed Hekmatyar's name from its sanctions list in February 2017[88] and Hekmatyar was hosted at the Afghan presidential palace by President Ghani, alongside hundreds of his supporters and other political and *jihadi* leaders.[89] The deal reached between the Afghan government and HI is widely regarded as a model for future peace deals between authorities and other insurgent groups – although the agreement is still fragile and easily reversible.

Islamism and Society

Islamism in Afghanistan has origins in Islamist education systems abroad. Groups of Afghan students returning from educational opportunities abroad in the 1950s, primarily in Egypt, brought back Islamist ideas that spread widely throughout the country.[90] Returned students created groups like Jamiat-e Islami that remained non-violent while rejecting modernization and the dueling political ideologies of socialism and liberal democracy[91] and participating in the public discourse regarding the future of politics in the country. The communist People's Democratic Party in Afghanistan (PDPA) exacerbated tensions with Islamist groups after it seized power in 1978 and removed all political parties, leading to Islamist rebellion.[92] The PDPA's oppression of Islamists and the Soviet occupation directly led to a drastic expansion of Islamism in the country, and the creation of an array of militant Islamist groups.

The country remains deeply religious in nature. As of 2019, the Asia Foundation's annual "Survey of the Afghan People" found that over 57% of respondents believe religious leaders should be consulted on political matters. Support for violent Islamism, however, is far sparser. While nearly 90% of those polled supported Afghan government efforts to negotiate with the Taliban, 85.1% held absolutely no sympathy for the Islamist group. Indeed, the Taliban is seen by the Afghan population to be the greatest threat to security and stability in the country, with nearly 69% of respondents categorizing it as such (as compared to just 12.4% who said the same about ISIS).[93]

Islamism and the State

The central Afghan government's support for political Islam is reflected in Chapter 1, Article 2 of the Afghan Constitution, which reads: "The religion of the state of the Islamic Republic of Afghanistan is the sacred religion of Islam."[94] Traditional tribal support is reflected in the institution of the *Loya Jirga*.

In general, Islamists sought to portray the Mohammed Karzai government's 13 year reign (2001-2014) as reflecting subservience to the wishes of the United States and its Western allies, as well as being corrupt and un-Islamic.[95] Taliban propaganda, for example, routinely referred to President Karzai as the "new Shah Shuja," a reference to the Afghan king put on the throne by British invaders in the 19th century.

As part of the peace and reconciliation campaign, current President Ashraf Ghani's government established a Quadrilateral Coordination Group (QCG), which includes Afghanistan, Pakistan,

China and the United States. The QCG planned to meet several times in the spring of 2016, in hopes that Pakistan will end its "undeclared war" against Afghanistan and sincerely bring the Taliban to the negotiating table.[96] However, the Taliban delegation did not attend, causing such frustration among the Afghan delegation that it demanded the Taliban be declared irreconcilable.[97] In April 2016 - after a suicide attack outside Afghanistan's intelligence headquarters, the National Directorate of Security (NDS), claimed 64 lives and wounded almost 350 others[98] - President Ghani addressed the nation with the boldest declaration since the 1990s, stating that Afghanistan no longer wants Pakistan to facilitate negotiations with the Taliban. Ghani also declared that amnesty and a lenient approach would no longer define Afghan policy toward militancy, but that Afghanistan's doors would remain open to those who wish to lay down their weapons and reconcile.

In February 2018, President Ghani extended an unconditional invitation to negotiate to the Taliban. In his peace proposal, Ghani offered the Taliban generous peace terms, including recognizing the Taliban as a political group, providing them immunity, political office, security guarantees for Taliban fighters and their families, and removing Taliban leaders from blacklists. In response, the Taliban not only ignored Ghani's offer but instead announced their spring offensive. In June 2018, Ghani extended another olive branch to the Taliban by announcing a ceasefire opportunity during annual Eid celebrations. Accordingly, Ghani announced a unilateral ceasefire for eight days (from the 27th day of Ramadan to the 5th day of Eid) and ordered Afghan security forces to not conduct any offensive operations against the Taliban for the duration. In response, the Taliban also announced a 3-day ceasefire. The ceasefire proved successful and is likely to play an important role in building trust between the two warring parties.

The U.S., the Taliban, and the Afghan government spent the remainder of 2018 and 2019 in fitful negotiations, eventually resulting in a U.S.-Taliban "truce" signed in February of 2020 and aimed at forcing an eventual peace agreement between Kabul and the Taliban, and the inclusion of the group in the Afghan government. However, despite continued peace negotiations, violence involving the Taliban continues unabated, and civilian casualties remain an endemic problem.

Endnotes

1. "Deoband School" Encyclopedia Britannica, n.d., https://www.britannica.com/topic/Deoband-school
2. Barry Bearak, "Afghan Says Destruction of Buddhas is Complete," *New York Times*, March 12, 2001, http://www.nytimes.com/2001/03/12/world/afghan-says-destruction-of-buddhas-is-complete.html.
3. "Afghanistan: Protection of Civilians in Armed Conflict" United Nations, February 2020, https://unama.unmissions.org/sites/default/files/afghanistan_protection_of_civilians_annual_report_2019_-_22_february.pdf.
4. "U.S. forces conduct airstrikes on Taliban in Afghanistan" Reuters, June 2020, https://www.reuters.com/article/us-usa-afghanistan-taliban/u-s-forces-conduct-airstrikes-on-taliban-in-afghanistan-idUSKBN23C27W.
5. U.S. Department of Defense, "OPERATION FREEDOM'S SENTINEL LEAD INSPECTOR GENERAL REPORT TO THE UNITED STATES CONGRESS," November 2019, https://media.defense.gov/2019/Nov/20/2002214020/-1/-1/1/Q4FY2019_LEADIG_OFS_REPORT.PDF
6. U.S. Department of State, *Country Reports on Terrorism 2019*, June 2020, https://www.state.gov/reports/country-reports-on-terrorism-2019/.
7. U.S. Department of Defense, "OPERATION FREEDOM'S SENTINEL LEAD INSPECTOR GENERAL REPORT TO THE UNITED STATES CONGRESS."
8. Sirajuddin Haqqani, "What We, the Taliban, Want," *New York Times*, February 20, 2020, https://www.nytimes.com/2020/02/20/opinion/taliban-afghanistan-war-haqqani.html
9. U.S. Department of Defense, "OPERATION FREEDOM'S SENTINEL LEAD INSPECTOR GENERAL REPORT TO THE UNITED STATES CONGRESS."
10. U.S. Department of State, *Country Reports on Terrorism 2019*.
11. Former Taliban leader Mullah Dadullah famously explained: "We like the al-Qaeda organization. We consider it a friendly and brotherly organization, which shares our ideology and concepts. We have

close ties and constant contacts with it. Our cooperation is ideal." See Brian Glyn Williams, "Suicide Bombings in Afghanistan," *Jane's Islamic Affairs Analyst*, September 2007, http://www.brianglynwilliams.com/IAA%20suicide.pdf.

12. Noah Browning, Sami Aboudi and Mark Heinrich, "Al Qaeda Leader Zawahiri Pledges Allegiance to New Taliban Chief: Websites," Reuters, August 13, 2015, http://www.reuters.com/article/us-afghanistan-taliban-qaeda-idUSKCN0QI1FO20150813.
13. U.S. Department of State, *Country Reports on Terrorism 2019.*
14. United Nations, "Al-Qaida," n.d., https://www.un.org/securitycouncil/sanctions/1267/aq_sanctions_list/summaries/entity/al-qaida.
15. U.S. Department of State, *Country Reports on Terrorism 2019.*
16. "Al-Qaeda in the Indian Subcontinent," The Soufan Center, January 2019, https://thesoufancenter.org/wp-content/uploads/2019/01/Al-Qaeda-in-the-Indian-Subcontinent-AQIS.pdf
17. U.S. Department of Defense, "OPERATION FREEDOM'S SENTINEL LEAD INSPECTOR GENERAL REPORT TO THE UNITED STATES CONGRESS."
18. "Al-Qaeda's South Asia Chief 'Killed in Afghanistan'" *BBC*, October 8, 2019, https://www.bbc.com/news/world-asia-49970353
19. U.S. Department of Defense, "OPERATION FREEDOM'S SENTINEL LEAD INSPECTOR GENERAL REPORT TO THE UNITED STATES CONGRESS."
20. U.S. Department of State, *Country Reports on Terrorism 2019.*
21. United Nations, "UN Security Council Analytical Support and Sanctions Monitoring Team Report," May 2020, https://www.undocs.org/S/2020/415.
22. Matt Bradley, "ISIS Declares New Islamist Caliphate." *Wall Street Journal*, June 29, 2014, https://www.wsj.com/articles/isis-declares-new-islamist-caliphate-1404065263.
23. "Hakimullah Meshud Killed by Drone," *BBC*, November 2, 2013, https://www.bbc.com/news/world-asia-24776363
24. United Nations, "UN Security Council Analytical Support and Sanctions Monitoring Team Report."
25. "Tehrik-i-Taliban Pakistan" United Nations, n.d., https://www.un.org/securitycouncil/sanctions/1267/aq_sanctions_list/summaries/entity/tehrik-e-taliban-pakistan-%28ttp%29.
26. U.S. Department of State, *Country Reports on Terrorism 2019.*
27. U.S. Department of Defense, "OPERATION FREEDOM'S SENTINEL LEAD INSPECTOR GENERAL REPORT TO THE UNITED STATES CONGRESS."

28. U.S. Department of State, *Country Reports on Terrorism 2019.*
29. Bradley, "ISIS Declares New Islamist Caliphate."
30. Jamie Crawford, "Congress hears Afghanistan troop plans amid ISIS fears," *CNN*, February 12, 2015, http://www.cnn.com/2015/02/12/politics/isis-afghanistan-u-s-fears/.
31. Douglas Schorzman, "U.S. Lists Afghan Branch of ISIS as Terrorist Group," *New York Times,* January 15, 2016, https://www.nytimes.com/2016/01/15/world/asia/us-lists-afghan-branch-of-isis-as-terrorist-group.html?_r=0.
32. "ISIL-K" United Nations, n.d., https://www.un.org/securitycouncil/content/islamic-state-iraq-and-levant-khorasan-isil-k
33. Josh Smith, "Kabul truck-bomb toll rises to more than 150 killed: Afghan president," Reuters, June 6, 2017, https://www.reuters.com/article/us-afghanistan-blast/kabul-truck-bomb-toll-rises-to-more-than-150-killed-afghan-president-idUSKBN18X0FU.
34. Abdul Qadir Sediqi and Rupam Jaim "Bombs in Kabul Kill at least 11 as US steps up diplomacy in effort to end war" Reuters, July 25, 2019, https://www.reuters.com/article/us-afghanistan-blast/bombs-in-kabul-kill-at-least-11-as-u-s-steps-up-diplomacy-in-effort-to-end-war-idUSKCN1UK0BB
35. Rahim Faiez and Cara Anna, "Islamic State Claims Bombing at Kabul Wedding that killed 63" Associated Press, August 18, 2019, https://apnews.com/b5ceb0cfb33d4d73aaaadf5eee19fe9d
36. "Islamic State Claims Responsibility after gunmen kill 32 at Memorial Ceremony" *Market Watch*, March 6, 2020, https://www.marketwatch.com/story/islamic-state-claims-responsibility-after-gunmen-kill-32-at-memorial-ceremony-in-afghan-capital-2020-03-06
37. Abdul Qadir Sediqi, "Gunmen in Afghanistan kill 25 at Sikh Complex, Islamic State Claims Responsibility" Reuters, March 25, 2020, https://www.reuters.com/article/us-afghanistan-attack/gunmen-in-afghanistan-kill-25-at-sikh-complex-islamic-state-claims-responsibility-idUSKBN21C0IF
38. "US Says Islamic State Conducted Attack on Kabul Hospital" Reuters, May 14, 2020, https://www.reuters.com/article/us-afghanistan-attacks-usa/us-says-islamic-state-conducted-attack-on-kabul-hospital-idUSKBN22Q3QU
39. United Nations, "UN Security Council Analytical Support and Sanctions Monitoring Team Report."
40. U.S. Department of Defense, "OPERATION FREEDOM'S SENTINEL LEAD INSPECTOR GENERAL REPORT TO THE UNITED STATES CONGRESS."

41. Jasmin Lorch, "Trajectories of Political Salafism: Insights from the Ahle Hadith Movement in Pakistan and Bangladesh" Middle East Institute, October 30, 2018, https://www.mei.edu/publications/trajectories-political-salafism-insights-ahle-hadith-movement-pakistan-and-bangladesh
42. Sheikh Mushtaq, "Violence not only answer to Kashmir - Lashkar-e-Taiba," Reuters, January 19, 2009, https://in.reuters.com/article/idINIndia-37536220090119
43. U.S. Department of State, *Country Reports on Terrorism 2019.*
44. United Nations, "UN Security Council Analytical Support and Sanctions Monitoring Team Report."
45. U.S. Department of Defense, "OPERATION FREEDOM'S SENTINEL LEAD INSPECTOR GENERAL REPORT TO THE UNITED STATES CONGRESS."
46. Asif Farooqi, "Profile: Lashkar-e-Jhangvi" *BBC*, January 11, 2013, https://www.bbc.com/news/world-asia-20982987.
47. U.S. Department of State, *Country Reports on Terrorism 2019.*
48. "Lashkar-e-Jhangvi" United Nations, n.d., https://www.un.org/securitycouncil/sanctions/1267/aq_sanctions_list/summaries/entity/lashkar-i-jhangvi-%28lj%29
49. Sanjeev Miglani, "12 die in Indian parliament attack" *Guardian* (London), December 14, 2001, https://www.theguardian.com/world/2001/dec/14/kashmir.india.
50. U.S. Department of State, *Country Reports on Terrorism 2019.*
51. U.S. Department of Defense, "OPERATION FREEDOM'S SENTINEL LEAD INSPECTOR GENERAL REPORT TO THE UNITED STATES CONGRESS."
52. United Nations, "UN Security Council Analytical Support and Sanctions Monitoring Team Report."
53. "Islamic Movement of Uzbekistan" United Nations, n.d., https://www.un.org/securitycouncil/sanctions/1267/aq_sanctions_list/summaries/entity/islamic-movement-of-uzbekistan.
54. U.S. Department of State, *Country Reports on Terrorism 2019.*
55. "Islamic Movement of Uzbekistan," CISAC, August 2018, https://cisac.fsi.stanford.edu/mappingmilitants/profiles/islamic-movement-uzbekistan#_ftn11
56. U.S. Department of Defense, "OPERATION FREEDOM'S SENTINEL LEAD INSPECTOR GENERAL REPORT TO THE UNITED STATES CONGRESS."
57. U.S. Department of State, *Country Reports on Terrorism 2019.*
58. United Nations, "UN Security Council Analytical Support and Sanc-

tions Monitoring Team Report."

59. U.S. Department of State, *Country Reports on Terrorism 2019.*
60. Ibid.
61. "Islamic Jihad Group" United Nations, n.d., https://www.un.org/securitycouncil/sanctions/1267/aq_sanctions_list/summaries/entity/islamic-jihad-group.
62. U.S. Department of State, *Country Reports on Terrorism 2019.*
63. Ibid.
64. Bashir Ansari, "Afghan forces end siege near Indian consulate in Mazar-i-Sharif," Reuters, January 4, 2016, https://www.reuters.com/article/us-afghanistan-attack-india/afghan-forces-end-siege-near-indian-consulate-in-mazar-i-sharif-idUSKBN0UI0C020160104.
65. "Jaish-e-Mohammad" United Nations, n.d., https://www.un.org/securitycouncil/sanctions/1267/aq_sanctions_list/summaries/entity/jaish-i-mohammed
66. U.S. Department of State, *Country Reports on Terrorism 2019.*
67. Miglani, "12 die in Indian parliament attack."
68. United Nations, "UN Security Council Analytical Support and Sanctions Monitoring Team Report."
69. Office of the Director of National Intelligence, "Jaish-e-Mohammed (JeM)," September 2013, https://www.dni.gov/nctc/groups/jem.html
70. U.S. Department of State, *Country Reports on Terrorism 2019.* t
71. Pradeep Dutta, "Jammu Now on Terror Radar, Jaish-e-Mohammed and ISI Planning Attack in the Region" *Times Now*, June 20, 2020, https://www.timesnownews.com/india/article/jammu-now-on-terror-radar-jaish-e-mohammed-and-isi-planning-attack-in-the-region/609422
72. "Registered Political Parties" Afghan Ministry of Justice, n.d., https://moj.gov.af/index.php/en/registered-political-parties
73. "Afghanistan's Constitution of 2004" Constitute Project, n.d., https://www.constituteproject.org/constitution/Afghanistan_2004.pdf?lang=en
74. Himan Rights Watch, "Blood-Stained Hands Past Atrocities in Kabul and Afghanistan's Legacy of Impunity," June 2013, https://www.justice.gov/sites/default/files/eoir/legacy/2013/06/14/afghanistan0605.pdf
75. Husain Haqqani, "Afghanistan's Islamist Groups," Hudson Institute, June 2007, https://www.hudson.org/research/9772-afghanistan-s-islamist-groups#footNote10
76. Haseeba Atakpal, "Jamit-e-Islami Prepares Peace Plan with Taliban," *Tolo News*, December 9, 2018, https://tolonews.com/afghanistan/

jamiat-e-islami-prepares-peace-plan-taliban
77. Haqqani, "Afghanistan's Islamist Groups."
78. Ibid.
79. "Maulana Maududi Economic System of Islam" Australian Islamic Library, n.d., https://archive.org/stream/MaulanaMaududiEconomicSystemOfIslam#page/n203/mode/2up
80. Ibid.
81. Ibidem.
82. Greg Myre, "The 'Butcher Of Kabul' Is Welcomed Back In Kabul," *NPR*, May 4, 2017, http://www.npr.org/sections/parallels/2017/05/04/526866525/the-butcher-of-kabul-is-welcomed-back-in-kabul.
83. U.S. Department of State, "Designation of Gulbuddin Hekmatyar as a Terrorist," February 19, 2003, https://2001-2009.state.gov/r/pa/prs/ps/2003/17799.htm
84. Kenneth Katzman, "Afghanistan: Post-Taliban Governance, Security, and U.S. Policy," Congressional Research Service, June 2016, http://www.fas.org/sgp/crs/row/RL30588.pdf
85. Bill Roggio, "Hekmatyar's Peace Plan Calls for NATO Withdrawal by 2011," *Long War Journal*, March 22, 2010, https://www.longwarjournal.org/archives/2010/03/hekmatyars_peace_pla.php
86. Katzman, "Afghanistan: Post-Taliban Governance, Security, and U.S. Policy."
87. Rod Nordland, "Afghanistan Signs Draft Peace Deal With Faction Led by Gulbuddin Hekmatyar," *New York Times*, September 23, 2016, https://www.nytimes.com/2016/09/23/world/asia/afghanistan-peace-deal-hezb-i-islami.html
88. United Nations, "Security Council ISIL (Da'esh) and Al-Qaida Sanctions Committee Removes One Entry from Its Sanctions List," February 3, 2017, https://www.un.org/press/en/2017/sc12705.doc.htm.
89. "Afghan warlord Hekmatyar returns to Kabul after peace deal," BBC, May 2017, http://www.bbc.com/news/world-asia-39802833.
90. Arian Sharif, "Islamist Groups in Afghanistan and the Strategic Choice of Violence" U.S. Institute for Peace, November 2016, https://www.usip.org/publications/2016/11/islamist-groups-afghanistan-and-strategic-choice-violence
91. Ibid.
92. Ibidem.
93. Tabasum Askeer and John Rieger, eds., *Afghanistan in 2019: A Survey of the Afghan People* (The Asia Foundation, December 2019),

https://asiafoundation.org/wp-content/uploads/2019/12/2019_Afghan_Survey_Full-Report.pdf

94. "The Constitution of Afghanistan" The Constitute Project, May 2020, https://www.constituteproject.org/constitution/Afghanistan_2004.pdf?lang=en
95. "Taliban: Winning the War of Words?" International Crisis Group, July 24, 2008, http://www.crisisgroup.org/home/index.cfm?id=5589&l=1.
96. Ibid.
97. Ibidem.
98. Samimullah Arif, "Ashraf Ghani's New Plan to Win Afghanistan's Long War Against the Taliban," *The Diplomat*, April 2016, http://thediplomat.com/2016/04/ashraf-ghanis-new-plan-to-win-afghanistans-long-war-against-the-taliban/

52 Bangladesh

Quick Facts

Population: 162,650,853 (July 2020 est.)
Area: 148,460 sq km
Ethnic Groups: Bengali at least 98%, ethnic groups 1.1%
Government Type: Parliamentary republic
GDP (official exchange rate): $261.5 billion (2017 est.)

Source: CIA World FactBook (Last Updated August 2020)

Introduction

Islam exerts a profound influence on the society and politics of Bangladesh. Islamist activity in the country takes three broad forms: the traditional revivalism of grassroots movements such as the Hefazat-e-Islam, Ahl-i-Hadith, and Tablighi Jama'at; the incremental political Islam of Islamic political parties (most prominently the Bangladeshi Jama'at-i-Islami); and the more radical, subversive activism of jihadist organizations such as the Harkatul Jihad al-Islam (HUJIB) and Jagrato Muslim Janata Bangladesh (JMB), which seek to capture state power through unconstitutional or violent means.

Since 1988, Islam has served as the state religion, although Bangladesh's constitution allows for both freedom of religion and religiously-based politics. Terrorist attacks have been fairly uncommon in recent years, a credit to the government's vigilance. However, heavy-handed tactics to counter violent Islamic extremism, while effective, nonetheless carry the risk of radicalizing Islamist groups that currently wish to participate in legitimate political institutions.

Due to publishing constraints, this chapter is provided here only in summary form. To view the full study, please visit the online edition of the Almanac at almanac.afpc.org.

53 India

Quick Facts

Population: 1,326,093,247 (July 2020 est.)
Area: 3,287,263 sq km
Ethnic Groups: Indo-Aryan 72%, Dravidian 25%, Mongoloid and other 3% (2000)
Government Type: Federal parliamentary republic
GDP (official exchange rate): $2.602 trillion (2017 est.)

Source: CIA World FactBook (Last Updated November 2020)

Introduction

Few nations have felt the deadly consequences of Islamist extremism more acutely than has India. South Asia and nearby regions host numerous centers of Islamist militancy that have affected India, including Pakistan, which is a key sponsor and instigator of international Islamist terrorism; Iran, the principal driver of Shi'a militancy; Afghanistan and Bangladesh, where Sunni militancy has flourished; and the Arab states, where radical interpretations of Sunni Islam have affected expatriate Indian workers and their families.

However, India's Muslim community has, in large part, refused to yield to the call of militancy. A community of well over 189 million Muslims – the third largest in the world, after those of Indonesia and Pakistan – lives in relative harmony within India's multicultural, multi-religious, secular democracy.[1] This coexistence is not without points of friction, however: strife between the various religious communities has been a significant feature in India since the country's partition in 1947. However, the Indian Muslim community has largely rejected broader attempts at radicalization and indoctrination and remains integrated into the fabric of Indian society.

Islamist terrorism in India has most impacted the state of Jammu

& Kashmir, where a separatist movement has plagued the region for over two-and-a-half decades.[2] *Islamist terrorist attacks on a smaller scale by both foreign and indigenous groups, meanwhile, have occurred in many other parts of the country.*

Endnotes:

1. "Countries With The Largest Muslim Populations." World Atlas. April 19, 2018. https://www.worldatlas.com/articles/countries-with-the-largest-muslim-populations.html. (accessed February 25, 2019).
2. Swami, Praveen. *India, Pakistan and the Secret Jihad: The Covert War in Kashmir 1947–2004*. Asian Security Studies. Abingdon, Oxon: Routledge, 2007. Low-grade *jihadi* subversion and Pakistani incursions commenced almost from the moment of Partition.

Due to publishing constraints, this chapter is provided here only in summary form. To view the full study, please visit the online edition of the Almanac at almanac.afpc.org.

54 Maldives

Quick Facts

Population: 391,904 (July 2020 est.)
Area: 298 sq km
Ethnic Groups: Homogenous misture of Sinhalese, Dravidian, Arab, Australasian, and African
Government Type: Presidential republic
GDP (official exchange rate): $4.505 billion (2017 est.)

Source: CIA World FactBook (Last Updated July 2020)

Introduction

The Republic of Maldives, a tourist paradise in the Indian Ocean, has recently faced a number of internal challenges, ranging from economic and environmental concerns to political infighting and religious dissent. The Maldivian government does not allow freedom of worship, and its constitution denies non-Muslims citizenship rights. It has also struggled with Salafi-jihadi ideology, which has gained support among large swaths of the population (in particular the nation's youth). The Maldives has become a safe haven for radical strains of Islam and fertile ground for transnational jihadist recruitment and indoctrination. Simmering religious dissent, growing Islamic radicalization, and Maldivians returning from jihad hotspots like Syria, Iraq and Afghanistan remain major stumbling blocks to stability in the island nation.

Due to publishing constraints, this chapter is provided here only in summary form. To view the full study, please visit the online edition of the Almanac at almanac.afpc.org.

55 Pakistan

Quick Facts

Population: 233,500,636 (July 2020 est.)
Area: 796,095 sq km
Ethnic Groups: Punjabi 44.7%, Pashtun (Pathan) 15.4%, Sindhi 14.1%, Saraiki 8.4%, Muhajirs 7.6%, Balochi 3.6%, other 6.3%
GDP (official exchange rate): $305 billion (2017 est.)

Source: CIA World FactBook (Last Updated June 2020)

Introduction

Pakistan was established in 1947 as a homeland for South Asia's Muslims after British colonial rule ended in India. The majority of Pakistanis practice a moderate form of Sufi Islam, but Islamist political parties nonetheless exercise significant influence in the country, shaping political debates, foreign policy, and legislation. Moreover, throughout Pakistan's history, its military and intelligence services have developed ties with violent Islamist groups to achieve regional strategic objectives. The U.S. war in Afghanistan following the September 11, 2001 terrorist attacks, and Pakistan's role in fighting terrorism, have severely complicated the political landscape in Pakistan. The emergence of the Tehreek-i-Taliban Pakistan (TTP, or Pakistani Taliban)—an amalgam of anti-state militants that formed in reaction to the Pakistan military's storming of the notorious Red Mosque—destabilized the nation significantly between 2007 and 2014. The TTP conducted countless terrorist attacks, killing some 30,000 civilians and security forces, prompting a major Pakistan Army operation against the militants in 2014. While Pakistan has continued to be hit by terror attacks in the years since operations began, the number has fallen significantly. In the context of terrorism threats, Pakistan is much more stable now than it was in the period between 2007-2014.

Pakistan will continue to grapple with its status as a Muslim constitutional democracy, and with developing ways to channel

Islamist ideologies. While Islamist political parties are unlikely to take power in the near future, they will continue to influence the country's legal framework and political discourse. While societal attitudes will also shape Islamist trends in Pakistan, the military's posture and attitude toward violent Islamists may be a core factor in determining the country's future (i.e., whether it remains positively engaged with Western countries or takes a decisively Islamist turn that severs its alliance with the United States).

ISLAMIST ACTIVITY

The Afghan Taliban

Pakistan's military and intelligence services (particularly the Inter-Services Intelligence Directorate, or ISI) historically have had close ties with the Afghan Taliban. Before the September 11, 2001 terrorist attacks, the Pakistani government openly supported and recognized Taliban rule in Afghanistan. Pakistan continued to support the Taliban into the late 1990s, long after Osama bin Laden took refuge in Afghanistan in 1996 and despite the growing problems that it created for Islamabad's relations with Washington. Although Pakistani officials largely disagreed with the Taliban's harsh interpretation of Islam, the movement was considered the government's best chance to achieve its own strategic interests in the region, including denying India, Iran, and Central Asian countries a strong foothold in Afghanistan. Additionally, Pakistan hoped to ensure no territorial claims on Pashtun areas along the Pakistan-Afghanistan border were made.

Despite pledging to break ties with the Taliban after the U.S. invasion of Afghanistan in 2001, Islamabad failed to crack down forcefully on the group's leaders or to disrupt their activities. U.S. officials have acknowledged that ISI officials maintain relationships with Afghan Taliban leaders (some ISI officials believe that the Taliban will again play a role in Afghan politics).[1]

Hopes for a negotiated Afghan settlement were raised in July 2015, when Pakistan hosted talks between the Afghan government and Taliban leaders. Just before a second round of talks were to be held, however, reports surfaced that Taliban supreme leader Mullah Omar had died two years prior caused disarray within the movement. Pakistan helped install Omar's successor, Mullah Akhtar Mansour, who was subsequently killed in a U.S. drone strike on May 21, 2016.

Escalating Taliban violence in Afghanistan, as well as major Taliban gains on the battlefield closed the door on negotiations for much of 2016 and 2017. The Trump administration's South Asia strategy, unveiled by the president in August 2017, directs U.S. forces to increase fighting against the Taliban.[2] While President Trump didn't rule out talks, he indicated that they were a distant prospect.

Efforts to jumpstart reconciliation continued.[3] The United States, China, Pakistan, and Russia all attempted to bring the Taliban to the table in the last few years. Initially, the Taliban, which has little incentive to abdicate the battlefield given the major gains it has achieved there, has generally expressed muted interest in such a move. Eventually, however, the Afghan Taliban would agree to participate in peace talks between itself and Washington, rather than Kabul.[4] In September of 2019, those negotiations broke down amid a renewed series of attacks by the Taliban, which prompted President Donald Trump to scupper a planned peace summit.[5] However, the talks soon resumed, and the two sides reached a deal at the end of February 2020. But while that deal largely halted Taliban attacks on U.S. forces, it did not require the group to stop targeting the Afghan state. The Taliban continued to wage its fight into the summer of 2020, even as the Afghan and U.S. governments sought to launch a formal peace process.

Al-Qaeda

The unilateral 2011 U.S. raid in Abbottabad, Pakistan that eliminated Osama bin Laden exposed deep fissures in U.S.-Pakistan relations. Pakistanis were incensed that the U.S. did not take its leadership into confidence before the raid. U.S. officials, on the other hand, were incredulous that the world's most wanted terrorist could live in a Pakistani garrison town for years without the knowledge of officials within the military establishment. U.S. Senator Susan Collins said the bin Laden killing revealed the "double-game" Pakistan has been playing and called for stricter conditions on U.S. aid to the country.[6]

However, the CIA has said that top Pakistani military leaders did not know that bin Laden was in Pakistan.[7]

Pakistan's subsequent arrest of Dr. Shakil Afridi, a Pakistani doctor who helped the U.S. track bin Laden's whereabouts through a fake vaccination campaign, was a blow to bilateral relations. Afridi was initially sentenced to 33 years in prison on trumped-up charges of supporting a militant group. In August 2013, however, Afridi's sentence was overturned, and a retrial ordered.[8] Pakistani authorities privately acknowledged that the doctor was being punished for helping the CIA. In mid-December 2016, a senior Pakistani official indicated that Pakistan would be willing to discuss the release of Dr. Afridi with the Trump administration however, as of early 2019, nothing had materialized.[9] Pakistan may agree to exchange Afridi for Aafia Siddiqui, a Pakistani scientist and *cause célèbre* in Pakistan who is currently in a federal prison in Texas on terrorism charges.[10] However, the Trump administration is unlikely to agree to such an arrangement, given its hardline stance on Islamic terrorism.

The Obama administration's intensive drone campaign in Pakistan's tribal border areas hindered al-Qaeda's ability to plot and train for terrorist attacks across the globe. Pakistani officials and media outlets regularly criticize the drone missile strikes as a violation of Pakistani sovereignty, but the program appears to be at least tacitly accepted at the highest levels of the Pakistani government. Indeed, Mark Mazzetti of the *New York Times* reported that the ISI and CIA had an agreement authorizing the use of drones, so long as they were restricted to the tribal areas.[11] There have been roughly 400 drone strikes carried out in Pakistan since 2004, including the strike on Mansour in Baluchistan and one that the Trump administration carried out in Khyber-Pakhtunkhwa in 2017 (there have only been about a half dozen drone strikes carried out in Pakistan since 2017, with the last known one carried out in July 2018).[12] The hit on Mansour angered Pakistani officials, who called it a violation of national sovereignty.

Due in part to Pakistani public anger over the drone campaign and complaints from human rights organizations about civilian casualties, the U.S. administration has considerably reduced its reliance on drones. The United States has also eliminated all its key targets—which, at least as defined by the Obama administration, were senior al-Qaeda leaders, the Pakistani Taliban, and other terrorist groups that pose a threat to both Pakistan and the United States. There were only 10 drone strikes in Pakistan in 2015, down from a peak of 128 in 2010. According to the New America Foundation, there were 16 drone strikes since the start of 2016 and none since July 2018.[13]

To fend off ISIS, al-Qaeda leader Ayman al-Zawahiri has sought to strengthen relations with Pakistan-based terrorist groups and to make inroads with the Muslim populations in other parts of South Asia. In September 2014, Zawahiri made a video announcement launching an al-Qaeda wing in the Indian Subcontinent (AQIS). In the video, Zawahiri assured Muslims in India, Bangladesh, and Burma that the organization "did not forget you and that they are doing what they can to rescue you from injustice, oppression, persecution, and suffering."[14] Just two days after the launch of AQIS, the group attempted to attack a Pakistani navy frigate in order to target American naval assets in the Indian Ocean. Al-Qaeda remains resilient in Pakistan and the broader region despite drone strikes and other counterterrorism tactics. This can be attributed to the support it receives from powerful, local terror groups and its rebranding effort to seem like an ISIS alternative.[15]

Tehreek-e-Taliban Pakistan (TTP)

The TTP, a collection of Pakistani militant groups loosely affiliated with al-Qaeda and the Afghan Taliban, was formed in 2007. TTP's numerous suicide attacks since 2012 have killed over 9,000 Pakistani civilians and 2,400 Pakistani security forces.[16]

In the six weeks before the May 2013 Pakistani elections, the TTP took responsibility for attacks that killed scores of election workers and candidates, mainly from secular-leaning political parties. Nawaz Sharif's Pakistan Muslim League/Nawaz (PML/N) party ran on a campaign of supporting negotiations with the TTP and failed to denounce the attacks. Six months after winning the elections, the Nawaz Sharif government offered to negotiate with the TTP. Those talks officially started in January 2014, but did not last long. The TTP claims of instituting a cease-fire were undermined by attacks against civilians and security forces.

Talks broke down altogether following a major TTP attack on the Karachi airport in June 2014 that killed 36. One week later, the Pakistani military announced the launch of a new military offensive against TTP bases in North Waziristan called Zarb-e-Azb ("Strike of the Prophet's Sword"). The Pakistani Army intensified its counterterrorism operations following an attack on a military school in Peshawar in December 2014 that killed 130, mostly children. Military operations in the FATA reportedly contributed to a nearly 50 percent decline in terrorist attacks in the country between 2014 and 2015.[17] This decline continued into 2019. However, factions of the TTP have continued to stage sporadic attacks in Pakistan, mostly in the western provinces of Baluchistan and Khyber Pakhtunkhwa, from hideouts in Afghanistan.

The National Action Plan (NAP) to combat terrorism passed by the Pakistani parliament in January 2015 has attempted to lay the initial groundwork for delegitimizing extremist ideologies. The plan includes lifting the moratorium on the death penalty for terrorists, establishing special military courts to try terrorists, curbing the spread of extremist literature and propaganda on social media, freezing the assets of terrorist organizations, and forming special committees comprised of army and political leaders.

Still, Pakistan has a long way to go in reversing the tide of extremism and terrorism in the country, as evidenced by several major terrorist attacks that occurred in 2016 and 2017. On January 20, 2016, militants stormed a university in the Pakistani city of Charsadda, killing at least 20 students and teachers. Afghanistan-based TTP leader Omar Mansour claimed credit for the attack (Mansour's faction of the TTP was also behind the 2014 attack on the school in Peshawar).[18] A U.S. drone strike in eastern Afghanistan subsequently killed Mansour in July 2016.

Jamaat-ul-Ahrar, another splinter group of the TTP, was responsible for a suicide bombing at a park in Lahore on Easter Sunday 2016. The group said it directly targeted Christians and that the bombing was a message to the Pakistani government that "we will carry out such attacks until Sharia is imposed in the country."[19] Nevertheless, most victims were Muslim, and about half of the 72 killed were children.

In February 2017, Pakistan was convulsed by a series of attacks over a period of four days. Militants struck all four provinces and three major urban areas. The TTP claimed responsibility for a car bomb attack in the eastern city of Lahore in July 2017 that killed nearly 30 people. TTP attacks continued in 2018. An attack on an election campaign rally in Peshawar killed at least 20 people, including a senior politician named Haroom Bilour.

The Haqqani Network

The Haqqani Network has been a major facilitator of the Taliban insurgency in Afghanistan, and responsible for some of the fiercest attacks against U.S. and coalition forces there. Its founder Jalaluddin Haqqani—a powerful Afghan militant leader whose followers operate in the broder areas between Afghanistan and the FATA—was allied with the Afghan Taliban and Pakistani intelligence before his death in 2014. Jalaluddin's son, Sirajuddin, has taken over operational control of the militant network and currently serves as second in command of the Afghan Taliban.

Haqqani forces were responsible for four of the most dramatic and devastating terror attacks in Afghanistan between 2008 and 2017. The attacks targeted U.S., Indian, and Afghan government officials. Over 260 people were killed in the four attacks.

The source of the Haqqanis' power lies primarily in their relations with different terrorist groups (al-Qaeda, the Afghan Taliban, the Pakistani Taliban, and India-focused groups like the *Jaish-e-Muhammed*), while also maintaining links to Pakistani intelligence agencies. Pakistani military strategists view the Haqqani Network as their most effective tool for blunting Indian influence in Afghanistan.[20]

U.S. officials have appealed to Pakistani leaders to crack down on the Haqqani Network. During a press conference in Kabul in July 2017, Senator John McCain declared that if Pakistan doesn't change its position toward the Haqqani Network, then "maybe we should change our behavior toward Pakistan as a nation."[21] However, American authorities have been rebuffed with declarations that the Pakistani military is overstretched and incapable of taking on too many militant groups at once. The Zarb-e-Azb offensive, despite claims to the contrary by Pakistani authorities, did not target the

Haqqani Network. Many analysts contended that, after the operation began, the group simply relocated from the North Waziristan tribal agency to the Kurram tribal agency.[22]

On September 7, 2012, under pressure from Congress, the U.S. State Department listed the Haqqani Network as a Foreign Terrorist Organization (FTO), subjecting it to financial and immigration sanctions.[23] Since the designation, the U.S. has killed several Haqqani Network leaders in Afghanistan and in Pakistan's tribal border areas.[24]

The U.S. has periodically blocked military aid to Pakistan due to the latter's failure to crack down on the Haqqanis. The U.S. withheld $300 million in CSF payments to Pakistan in FY 2015 because the Obama administration could not certify that Pakistan's military offensive in the tribal border areas included operations against Haqqani bases.[25] Furthermore, Congress blocked U.S. funding for the transfer of F-16 aircraft to Pakistan in the first half of 2016 because of Islamabad's lack of action against the Haqqani sanctuary within its borders.[26] And in January 2018, the Trump administration froze all security aid to Pakistan until the country demonstrates action against the Haqqani Network on Pakistani soil.

The extent to which these punitive measures have affected the Haqqani Network is unclear. As of the summer of 2020, there was no evidence indicating that Islamabad has sought to sever its ties to what amounts to one of its most important militant assets.

Lashkar-e-Taiba (LeT) and Jaish-e-Mohammed (JeM)

Groups like LeT and JeM focused their attacks throughout the 1990s on Indian security forces in Jammu and Kashmir. Now, the groups conduct attacks throughout India and target both Indian and Western civilians. The Pakistani government's failure to shut down groups like JeM and LeT is thus creating instability in the region. In March 2010, Pakistani-American David Headley pleaded guilty to involvement in the Mumbai attacks and a plot to attack Danish newspaper offices for publishing caricatures of the Prophet Mohammed. In four days of testimony and cross-examination, Headley detailed meetings between himself and a Pakistani intelligence officer, a former Army major, and a Navy frogman, all of whom were among the key players orchestrating the assaults. Headley's revelations raised questions about whether there was official Pakistani involvement in the Mumbai attacks.[27]

Following the Mumbai attacks, Islamabad responded to U.S. and Indian pressure by arresting seven LeT operatives, including Zaki ur Rehman Lakhvi and Zarar Shah, whom India had identified as the ringleaders of the attacks. The Pakistani government also reportedly shut down some domestic LeT offices. Despite these actions, there are indications that the LeT continues to operate relatively freely in the country. Pakistan released LeT founder Hafez Muhammed Sayeed from detention in June 2009 when the Lahore High Court determined there was insufficient evidence to continue his detainment. Sayeed has taken an increasingly public role in Pakistan; he frequently speaks at political rallies and calls for jihad against India. In 2012, the U.S. issued a $10 million reward for information leading to his arrest and conviction.[28] As further evidence of its unwillingness to act against the LeT, Pakistan released Zaki ur Rehman Lakhvi from jail in April 2015, just days after the U.S. approved the sale of nearly $1 billion in military equipment to Pakistan.

The LeT has put down roots in Pakistani society through its social welfare wing, the Jamaat-ud-Dawa (JuD). The JuD runs schools and medical clinics and is especially active in central and southern Punjab. The headquarters of the LeT/JuD is a 200-acre site in Muridke. The JuD increased its popularity while helping victims of the October 2005 earthquake in Pakistani Kashmir. The U.S. government considers JuD a front organization of the LeT. The U.S. State Department designated the LeT as a FTO in December 2001, and later included the JuD on the Specially Designated Global Terrorist Designation list as an alias of the LeT.[29] On December 11, 2008, the United Nations Security Council designated JuD as a global terrorist group.[30]

There are well-known links between both the LeT and JeM and international terrorism. Shoe bomber Richard Reid apparently trained at a LeT camp in Pakistan; one of the London subway bombers spent time at the LeT complex in Muridke; and al-Qaeda leader Abu Zubaydah was captured from a LeT safe house in Faisalabad, Pakistan. The LeT signed Osama bin Laden's 1998 fatwa calling for Muslims to kill Americans and Israelis.

Reports indicate that a prime suspect in the 2006 London airliner bomb plot had family ties to Maulana Masood Azhar, the leader of JeM. The JeM has also been linked to the kidnapping and brutal murder of *Wall Street Journal* reporter Daniel Pearl in January 2002. Pakistan officially banned the JeM in 2002, but Azhar has never been formally charged with a crime. Indeed, reports indicate Masood Azhar addressed a large public rally in Pakistan via phone in early 2014 and called on his supporters to resume *jihad* against India. Furthermore, the JeM conducted a major attack on the Indian air base at Pathankot in early January 2016, just six days after Indian Prime Minister Narendra Modi had made a surprise goodwill visit to Lahore, where he met with Pakistani Prime Minister Nawaz Sharif. Efforts to have Azhar formally designated by the UN as a terrorist have repeatedly failed, as Pakistan's close ally China has used its Security Council veto to block such a move.

Indo-Pakistani tensions escalated further following a September 18, 2016, attack by Pakistan-based terrorists on an Indian military base in Kashmir that killed at least 18 Indian soldiers. New Delhi concluded that LeT was behind the attack. Ten days later, India launched surgical strikes across the Line of Control (LoC) to neutralize terrorist bases inside Pakistani territory. Shelling and firing across the LoC, which had become an almost-daily occurrence, decreased later in 2016 and into 2017, but rhetoric from both Pakistani and Indian officials remains heated. Cross-border firing surged during the first few months of 2018.[31]

The Pakistan-based anti-India terror groups at the heart of India-Pakistan tensions, like JeM and LeT, remain dangerous. In July 2017, New Delhi blamed LeT for a deadly attack that killed seven Hindu pilgrims in Kashmir. New Delhi again implicated LeT in a March 2018 attack in Kashmir, this time an assault on security forces that killed three Indian soldiers and two policemen.

In 2019, LeT went largely quiet, but JeM seemingly made a comeback. After being relatively passive for a long period of time, the group staged a series of attacks in Jammu and Kashmir. Its deadliest attack, which killed more than 40 Indian security forces in the town of Pulwama on Valentine's Day 2019, brought India and Pakistan to the brink of war. The crisis deescalated relatively quickly, but tensions remained high. In March 2019, China blocked a UN Security Council effort to designate Azhar as a terrorist for the fourth time.

While the surge in JeM-led attacks has injected more venom into India-Pakistan relations, it's worth noting that most of these attacks have been carried out by local JeM militants in Kashmir using local weaponry. There is no indication that the Pakistani state endorsed or assisted these attacks. However, for New Delhi, given that JeM is still based in Pakistan and still enjoys ties to the Pakistani state, Islamabad is guilty by association.

On August 5, 2019, the Indian government carried out its longstanding threat to repeal the special autonomous status of Jammu and Kashmir (J&K) and designated it as a union territory of India. For Pakistan, which has long claimed J&K as its own, the move was regarded as provocative and hostile. In the following weeks, Islamabad launched a major global diplomatic effort to convince key capitals, including Washington, to chastise India for affront. However, despite some comments criticizing New Delhi for the ensuing security lockdown and media blackout in J&K, the international community did not oppose India's decision.

The implications are stark. In order to push back against New Delhi, a frustrated Islamabad may encourage the non-state assets at its disposal – particularly LeM and JeM – to stage attacks in Kashmir and across India. However, this may be mitigated by pressure imposed upon Islamabad by the Financial Action Task Force (FATF), a terrorist financing watchdog, to curtail its ties to terror groups and their financial networks. Pakistan has not infiltrated nearly as many militants across the border in the last few years as it had done in the 1990s. One reason why is that Pakistan's involvement in the insurgency in Kashmir hasn't been necessary. In recent years, increasingly heavy-handed tactics from the Indian government in Kashmir have radicalized young Kashmiris, with some of the most recent mass-casualty attacks — including an assault on Indian security forces in Pulwama in February 2019 that sparked a major India-Pakistan crisis — organized and carried out by local residents. Still, a combination of factors — the Article 370 repeal, India's continued repressive acts in Kashmir, Islamabad's inability to attract international focus to the Kashmir issue, and a lack of clear Pakistani options to deter India — suggest that the threat of Pakistan deploying India-focused assets across the border remains a very real threat.

Additionally, the end of J&K's autonomous status increases the likelihood of conflict between India and Pakistan. Any major future attack on Indian forces in Kashmir – whether staged with assistance from Pakistan or not – will likely be blamed on Pakistan by India, inciting limited military retaliations.

The Islamic State (IS, or ISIS)

IS has sought the allegiance of various regional terrorist groups and, in January 2015, officially announced the formation of its Khorasan "province." Khorasan is an Islamic historical term used to describe the area encompassed by Afghanistan, parts of Pakistan, and parts of other countries bordering Afghanistan. According to the relevant *Hadith* (sayings attributed to the Prophet Muhammad), South-Central Asia plays a key role in establishing a global caliphate. The Hadith contains references to the Ghazwa-e-Hind (Battle of India), where the final battle between Muslims and non-Muslims before the end times will supposedly take place. One *Hadith* further says that an army with black flags will emerge from Khorasan to help the *Mahdi* (the prophesied redeemer of Islam) establish his caliphate at Mecca.[32]

A handful of TTP and Afghan Taliban leaders have pledged their allegiance to the group and its late leader, Abu Bakr al-Baghdadi. The Pakistan-based, anti-Shia sectarian outfit Jundullah reportedly pledged support to ISIS in late 2014.[33] In July 2015, a U.S. drone strike in the eastern Afghan province of Nangahar killed more than two dozen ISIS fighters, including Shahidullah Shahid, former spokesman for the Pakistani Taliban, who had defected to ISIS ranks the year before.[34]

ISIS' inability so far to make significant inroads into Pakistan is largely due to the well-established roots of al-Qaeda there; most terror groups in Pakistan and Afghanistan are al-Qaeda-aligned and openly hostile toward ISIS. ISIS' prospects in Pakistan are also constrained by sectarian issues. ISIS embraces the Salafi school of Islamic thought and rejects the Deobandi school, to which most South Asian militant groups adhere. There have been some operational marriages of convenience, however; several of the February 2017 attacks were claimed by both ISIS and factions of the Pakistani Taliban and Lashkar-e-Jhangvi. Additionally, an October 2017 report from the Soufan Center estimated that around 650 fighters had travelled from Pakistan to join the ranks of the group.[35]

The collapse of ISIS in the Middle East, set in motion by the loss of its physical caliphate and exacerbated by the death of Abu Bakr al-Baghdadi in Syria in October 2019, has raised concerns that the group's central leadership could attempt to redirect resources and activities to South Asia – a worry that was elevated by the 2019 attacks in Sri Lanka on Easter Sunday. Pakistan presents fertile soil for the group to do so; ISIS claimed several large-scale attacks on both state and civilian targets in Pakistan between 2016 and 2018 (there were none in 2019). These included the bombing of a civil hospital and a police training college in the city of Quetta, the provincial capital of Baluchistan, in 2016; an attack on a Sufi shrine in the city of Sehwan in Sindh province in 2017; and assaults on election targets in three different areas of Baluchistan province in 2018.

Islamism and Society

The strategic environment in South Asia and the Pakistani response to regional challenges has influenced Islamist trends in society and heightened religious-inspired violence. The war against the Soviets in Afghanistan (1979-1989) and the Islamization policies of Pakistani president General Zia ul-Haq during roughly this period strengthened Islamist political forces and puritanical sects over more moderate ones.[36] The influence of Sufism, dating back to the eighth and ninth century in South Asia, has a moderating influence on how most Pakistanis practice and interpret Islam.

Jamaat-e-Islami (JI) was founded by Islamic scholar Maulana Abul Ala Maududi in 1941. Maududi came of age as British colonial rule was ending on the Subcontinent and an Indian national identity was developing. Witness to Hindu-Muslim communal tensions, Maududi believed the only way Muslims could safeguard their political interests was to return to a pure and unadulterated Islam that would not accommodate Hindus. He denounced nationalism and secular politics and held that an Islamic state was a panacea for all the problems facing Muslims. He called on Muslims to mobilize against Hindus, breaking free of any Western influences.[37] Reflecting Maududi's early thought, modern Islamist extremist literature in Pakistan draws parallels between British colonial rule and U.S. ascendancy.[38]

In contrast with Maududi, Pakistan's founding father and leader of the Muslim League, Muhammed Ali Jinnah, supported the idea of Islam as a unifying force but envisioned the country as a largely secular and multiethnic democratic state. Thus, although the argument to establish a separate Pakistani state was based on religious exclusivity, Jinnah's ultimate goal was not to establish Pakistan as a theocracy.[39] Soon after the creation of Pakistan, however, debate about religion's role in the country's constitutional and legal systems was increasingly influenced by Islamic principles.[40]

Maududi's contrasting vision for Pakistan created problems during the early years after partition. Pakistani authorities questioned the allegiance of JI members to the state and even incarcerated Maududi for his controversial positions on the Indo-Pakistani dispute over Kashmir.[41] After spending time in jail, Maududi eventually stopped questioning the legitimacy of the Pakistani state and focused on encouraging Islamization of the government.

Today's *Jamaat-e-Islami* political party in Pakistan, led by Siraj-ul-Haq, draws most of its support from middle class urban Pakistanis. It has generally performed only marginally at the polls, capturing about five percent of the vote in most elections held during the last two decades. However, the party's influence on Pakistani politics and society outweighs its electoral performance because of its effectiveness in mobilizing street power, its ability to influence court cases, and its adeptness at using Pakistan's Islamic identity to pressure governments to adopt aspects of its Islamist agenda.[42] In the 2002 elections, the JI formed an alliance with five other religious political parties. The coalition garnered over 11 percent of the national vote. The resulting coalition of Islamist parties grabbed enough votes in Khyber Pakhtunkhwa (KPK) to form the government, marking the first time Islamists were charged with running a provincial government (see below).

The other major Islamist movement in South Asia is the Deobandi movement. This movement originated in 1866 in the city of Deoband in the Indian state of Uttar Pradesh with the establishment of the Dur ul-Ulum *madrassa*, (a Muslim religious school), which is still the largest operating Deobandi *madrassa*. Deobandism was a reformist movement developed in reaction to British colonialism and based on the belief among Muslim theologians that British influence was corrupting the religion of Islam. The Deobandis offered a puritanical perspective for South Asian Muslims, much as the *Wahhabbis* have done in present-day Saudi Arabia.[43]

Three wars and several military crises with India have also bolstered the influence of religious extremists with the backing of the Pakistani state. During the 1990s, the JI focused its agenda on supporting Kashmiri militants, while the Jamaat-e-Ulema Islam (JUI) turned most of its attention to supporting the Taliban in Afghanistan. More recently, both the JUI and JI have rallied their political supporters against U.S. policies in the region, taking advantage of high levels of anti-American sentiment fueled by the post 9/11 American and NATO military presence in Afghanistan and U.S. pressure on Pakistan to manage terrorists on its own soil. Most Pakistanis blame their country's counterterrorism cooperation with the U.S. for the incessant suicide bombings and attacks across the nation that have claimed more than 9,000 civilian lives since 2012.

The 2007 Red Mosque siege and the events that followed play a significant role in Pakistani society's current perception of Islamist movements. Students of the notorious Red Mosque in Islamabad and an adjacent *madrassa* for women launched a vigilante-like campaign to force their view of Islam on the local population. They burned CD and video shops, took over a local children's library, and kidnapped women whom they accused of running a brothel, as well as several policemen. In July 2007, military troops stormed the buildings. After two days of fierce fighting, the military gained control of the premises, but only after 19 soldiers and 62 militants were killed.

The Pakistani public reacted negatively to the military operation, with Islamist circles questioning the use of force against the country's own citizens and mosques. More liberal commentators faulted the government for allowing the situation to get out of hand in the first place, noting shared ties between Pakistani intelligence and the mosque. Some Islamist political parties faced a dilemma; they largely agreed with the policies of the Red Mosque leaders, but did not support the idea of violent confrontation with the government to meet these goals.[44] Following the military operation that ended the siege, then-JI leader Qazi Hussain held the state "wholly responsible" for the confrontation. Two Islamist parties hailed the Red Mosque militants as "mujahideen who fought for enforcing Islam in its true spirit."[45]

The incident's impact on Islamist extremism cannot be overstated. Numerous *jihadist* organizations, including al-Qaeda and Lashkar-e-Jhangvi, have staged attacks on the Pakistani military. The terrorist violence in Pakistan from 2007 until 2014 can be traced back to the Red Mosque offensive and the retaliatory attacks that followed it. The Pakistani Taliban – the most potent of Pakistan's anti-state terror actors during that period – was formally launched after the Red Mosque offensive. Before the offensive, it had been an umbrella group of anti-state forces but it was galvanized by the Red Mosque offensive and established a more unified movement against the Pakistani state.[46]

Tensions came to a head in April 2009, when pro-Taliban forces moved from the Swat Valley into the neighboring district of Buner. On April 24, 2009, under both Pakistani public and U.S. pressure, the Pakistan Army deployed paramilitary troops to the region, and then-Chief of Army Staff (COAS) General Ashfaq Kayani sent a warning to the militants that the Army would not allow them to "impose their way of life on the civil society of Pakistan."[47] The statement was a positive first step in clarifying Pakistani policy toward the militants and was followed by aggressive military operations.[48] By mid-summer, the Pakistani military had cleared the militants from the Swat Valley.

However, vestiges of extremism remain. The Pakistani public was outraged when Malala Yousafzai—a fifteen-year-old girl who openly advocated for the education of girls in the Swat Valley—

was shot by Taliban militants in early October 2012 as she boarded a school bus. Yousafzai survived the assassination attempt and continues to advocate for female empowerment and education from the United Kingdom, where she graduated from high school in 2017.[49] She is the youngest person ever to have won the Nobel Peace Prize.

The Army's resolve in fighting militants in the Swat Valley, and more recently in North Waziristan, signals greater understanding about the threat posed by the Pakistani Taliban. However, there are few signs that the Pakistani Army leadership is ready to accommodate U.S. requests to crack down on other groups that target U.S. and coalition forces in Afghanistan. The Pakistani state has also done little to combat India-focused militant groups on its soil.

The most troubling development involving Islam and Pakistani society in 2018 was the establishment of several new hardline religious political parties. One of them, known as the Milli Muslim League, is tied to the LeT. These groups were formed before the country's 2018 parliamentary elections, and credible evidence indicates that the Pakistani military supported their formation.[50] The idea was to give hardliners an opportunity to join the political mainstream in an effort to reduce the likelihood of violence. Some observers speculated that another reason the military supported these groups was their ability to cut into the vote bank of the Pakistan Muslim League-Nawaz (PML-N) party, the ruling party that had sparred with the army since taking office in 2013. These hardline religious parties contested the 2018 elections and some of them fared respectably. While the total number of votes for religious parties—less than 10 percent — was low, several performed well in a country where religious parties are typically more successful at mobilizing in the street than at the ballot box.[51] For example, the *Tehreek-e-Labbaik* party placed sixth in the national vote count and fourth in Punjab—Pakistan's most populous province.[52]

Unfortunately, efforts to "mainstream" these groups backfired when these new parties, emboldened by their newfound legitimacy, tried to impose their radical and extremist views on society. The most effective group in this regard is the *Tehreek-e-Labaik Pakistan* (TLP), which has called for the execution of religious minorities.

It has staged several extended protests that blocked traffic for days.[53] In the fall of 2018, Asia Bibi, a Christian woman on death row on charges of blasphemy, was acquitted by the Pakistani Supreme Court. The TLP took to the streets, calling on the judges who freed her to be executed and—in an unusual move for Islamist hardliners—threatened to attack the Pakistani military for the acquittal. To its credit, the Imran Khan-led government, facing an early test, quietly staged a series of arrests. Still, the TLP's ability to mobilize and to pressure the government with hardline Islamist demands is a troubling development to monitor in the months ahead. Equally concerning is the fact that the TLP earned more than two million votes in the 2018 parliamentary elections.[54] Admittedly, this represented only about 4 percent of the total number of votes, but it was still an impressive showing for a hardline religious party in Pakistan.

The erosion of respect for religious pluralism in Pakistan has also been facilitated by exclusionary laws and the proliferation of minority-hate material in public and private school curriculums. Several studies have documented a broad-based connection between *madrassa* education and the propensity toward gender, religious, and sectarian intolerance as well as militant violence in Pakistan.[55] *Madaris* (Islamic seminaries) are spread throughout Pakistan, but most analysts believe that only about 5–10 percent of Pakistani school children attend these institutions. A number of these schools are financed and operated by Pakistani Islamist parties, Pakistani expatriates, and other foreign entities, including many in Saudi Arabia. In a seminal study entitled "Islamic Education in Pakistan," South Asia scholar Christine Fair notes that while there is little evidence that *madaris* contribute substantially to direct recruitment of terrorists, they do create conditions that are conducive to supporting militancy.[56] Though Pakistan's National Action Plan—the strategy unveiled in early 2015 to combat extremism—highlights the importance of eliminating speech and literature deemed hateful, successful efforts to amend textbooks and other educational sources of extremist material largely remain elusive.[57]

Discrimination against religious minorities—including Christians, Hindus, Sikhs, Ahmadis, and Shia—has led to a threefold increase in religious and sectarian violence in the country over the last 30 years. The rising violence against the Shiite community (which makes up about 25 percent of Pakistan's total population) correlates with an upward trend in sectarian attacks. Between 2013 and 2015 attacks directed at the Shia population killed over 300 people. Many of the perpetrators of these attacks remain elusive. In an indication of the impunity that sectarian-minded hardliners enjoy in Pakistan, a group of religious protestors calling for the executions of Ahmadis—another vulnerable religious minority in Pakistan—held a two-week sit-in on a major highway outside of Islamabad in November 2017, snarling traffic for days. In May 2018, a young man with links to a religious political party that organized the November sit-in tried to assassinate Ahsan Iqbal, Pakistan's Interior Minister.[58] However, the Imran Khan-led government that took office in August 2018 arrested several top leaders from these religious groups after some of their members protested in Islamabad in October 2018 and called for the assassination of Supreme Court judges. Protestors took to the streets after the court ordered the acquittal of Asia Bibi, a Christian woman who had been on death row for eight years since being convicted on the bogus charge of blasphemy. In Pakistan, hardliners often exploit the country's far-reaching blasphemy laws and target religious minorities.[59]

In recent years, most of the attacks against Pakistani Shia have been carried out by the Lashkar-e-Jhangvi (LJ), a Sunni militant organization inspired and supported by al-Qaeda. The Pakistani government has begun to crack down, albeit modestly, on LJ and target its leadership. In July 2015, one week after his arrest, LJ Founder and Supreme Leader Malik Ishaq was killed in an encounter with police, alongside over a dozen of his followers.[60] At the same time, Lashkar-e-Jhangvi al-Alami, a particularly virulent faction of LJ, linked up with ISIS. Since then, the group has claimed several attacks in Pakistan.[61] Like ISIS, LJ is a sectarian-focused organization that seeks to eliminate Shia and members of any non-Sunni Muslim communities.

The minority Ahmadi community has also suffered severely from the growing culture of religious intolerance in Pakistan. In late May 2010, militants armed with hand grenades, suicide vests, and assault rifles attacked two Ahmadi mosques, killing nearly 100 worshippers.[62] Human rights groups in Pakistan criticized local authorities for their weak response to the attacks and for their failure to condemn the growing number of kidnappings and murders of members of the Ahmadi community. In December 2014, a member of the Ahmadi community in Gujranwala was shot and killed five days after an extremist cleric called Ahmadis "the enemy" in a rant on a popular Pakistani television show.[63] Ahmadis have been targeted in additional attacks in the period since.[64]

Christians likewise are increasingly bearing the brunt of rising Islamist extremism in Pakistan. There have been numerous incidents of violence against Christians and their worship areas. On September 22, 2013, 85 people were killed during Sunday services when dual suicide bombers attacked a church in Peshawar, Pakistan. The group responsible for the attack, a faction of the TTP said they were retaliating against U.S. drone strikes in Pakistan's tribal border areas.[65]

A TTP splinter group carried out a suicide attack against Christians celebrating the Easter holiday at a park in Lahore in March 2016.[66] In December 2017, nine were killed in an attack on a Methodist church in Quetta.[67] In April 2018, ISIS claimed an attack on a Christian family in Quetta that killed four people,[68] and, a few days earlier, a drive-by shooting that killed two Christians as they were leaving their church.[69] There were no reported terror attacks on Christians in Pakistan in 2019 and through June 2020.

There are some signs that the Pakistani government is slowly seeking to reverse extremist trends in society. The most notable was the government's follow-through with the execution of Mumtaz Qadri, the murderer of reformist politician Salman Taseer. Despite street protests in all of Pakistan's major cities, the government resisted intervention against the Supreme Court's decision; the death sentence for the 2011 killing was carried out on February 29, 2016.[70] The government further defended religious minorities in mid-December 2016 by belatedly renaming the National Center for Physics of Quaid-i-Azam University in Islamabad after Nobel Prize-winning physicist Abdus Salam, a member of the Ahmadi community.

One week after the government's gesture, however, Pakistani police raided an Ahmadiyya central office in Rabwah, where they beat up staffers, looted the office, and made arrests without a warrant.[71] That same week, a mob of more than 1,000 people descended on an Ahmadi place of worship in Chakwal, Punjab.[72] In a May 2018 decision that enraged Pakistani liberals and other supporters of minority rights, Pakistan's National Assembly passed a resolution to remove Salam's name from the National Center for Physics.[73] In September 2018, the brand new Imran Khan-led government ordered a prominent Pakistani economist, the Princeton-based Atif Mian, to step down from the Economic Advisory Council due to his Ahmadi identity. And in May 2020, Islamabad established a new National Commission for Minorities, but it forbids Ahmadis from serving as members (Hindus, Christians, and other religious minorities are represented on it).[74] These episodes highlight how small, recent gestures by Islamabad to demonstrate more tolerance are often overshadowed by the power and influence of religious hardliners.

Islamism and the State

The Pakistani Army's support for militancy as a foreign policy instrument has eroded religious tolerance and created strong links between the country's Islamist political parties and militant groups.[75] Pakistan has long relied on violent Islamist groups to accomplish its strategic objectives in Afghanistan and India. Pakistan's support for these groups remains undiminished, even as it has increased military operations in the tribal border areas against the TTP. There are around 150,000 Pakistani troops deployed along the Pakistan-Afghanistan border. Since 2002, the U.S. has provided nearly $14 billion to Pakistan in the form of Coalition Support Fund (CSF) reimbursements for Pakistan's military border deployments and operations.[76]

Following the 9/11 attacks, former Pakistani President Pervez Musharraf broke official ties with the Taliban, supported the U.S. invasion of Afghanistan, granted over-flight and landing rights for U.S. military and intelligence units, facilitated logistical supply to military forces in Afghanistan, and contributed substantially to breaking up the regional al-Qaeda network. Pakistan helped capture scores of senior al-Qaeda leaders, most notably 9/11 mastermind Khalid Sheikh Mohammed. However, the government's various relationships with Islamist groups were not entirely severed, and progress has been mixed. In addition to sporadic military operations, the Pakistani government in the past pursued several peace deals with the militants that further destabilized the Pakistani state and facilitated insurgent attacks against coalition forces in Afghanistan.

The first peace deal in March 2004, referred to as the Shakai Agreement, was interpreted by locals as a military surrender.[77] A February 2005 peace agreement with now-deceased TTP leader Baitullah Mehsud also backfired, emboldening Mehsud later to form the TTP. Mehsud directed a string of suicide attacks against both Pakistani security forces and civilians in 2008-2009. He was killed by a U.S. drone strike in August 2009 and was replaced by Hakimullah Mehsud, who was also killed by a drone strike in November 2013.[78] His successor, Mullah Fazlullah, met the same fate in June 2018. Fazlullah, unlike his predecessors, was killed in Afghanistan.[79] The TTP waged a horrific campaign of violence between 2007 (when it was formally established) and 2014. In more recent years, following a major Pakistani counterterrorism offensive in the North Waziristan tribal agency, it has been much quieter. The group has been badly degraded, and its main remaining vestiges—which include several splinter groups—are based in Afghanistan.

Pakistan's Islamist political parties performed poorly in the country's February 2008 and May 2013 elections. In 2008, the JI boycotted the election, and the other Islamist parties garnered only 2% of the national vote. In 2013, the JUI/F won 10 seats, and the JI only three seats in the National Assembly. Several new religious political parties—including one with ties to LeT – were established in 2017 as part of the political "mainstreaming" effort.

During its time in office, the Obama administration challenged the Pakistani government for its inconsistency in countering regional terrorist groups that threaten the U.S. and coalition mission in Afghanistan. The Kerry-Lugar bill passed by the Senate in September 2009 (formally known as the Enhanced Partnership with Pakistan Act of 2009) authorized $7.5 billion in civilian aid to Pakistan over a five-year period, but it also conditioned military assistance on Pakistani measures to address terrorist threats. Former U.S. Director of National Intelligence Admiral Dennis Blair testified before Congress on February 2, 2010, "Pakistan's conviction that militant groups are strategically useful to counter India are hampering the fight against terrorism and helping al-Qaeda sustain its safe haven."[80]

Additionally, the U.S. Congress has used its authority to block U.S. military aid for Pakistan in recent years. The National Defense Authorization Act (NDAA) for FY2015 stipulated that $300 million of the $1 billion in CSF funding appropriated for Pakistan could no longer be subject to Presidential waiver authority. Thus, when the Obama Administration failed to certify that the Pakistan military's operations in the tribal areas included attacking Haqqani Network bases, Congress blocked the transfer of $300 million in CSF payments to Pakistan. The NDAA for FY2016 authorized another $900 million in CSF funding for Pakistan, with $350 million being ineligible for waiver.

The military confrontation following the siege of the Red Mosque in 2007, the aggressive military operations in the Swat Valley in 2009, and the on-going Zarb-e-Azb operations in North Waziristan against the TTP all demonstrate that, in certain situations, the Pakistan military is prepared to confront extremists. The army's links to religious militants revolve more around regional strategic calculations than deep ideological sympathies with the ideology (though extremist views are known to be held by some within the Pakistani military, justifying concerns about sympathetic officers enabling infiltration of the military).

While it may take time to fully sever ties between elements of the military/ISI establishment and Islamist militant groups, this outcome is possible—albeit unlikely. So long as the Pakistani military projects India as an existential threat, the country will maintain its strategy of retaining links to terror groups—which at the end of the day is a strategy meant to target and intimidate India and to keep India at bay in Afghanistan (in the case of the Afghan Taliban and Haqqani Network). There is little reason to believe that Pakistan will change its position toward India any time in the foreseeable future.

The Trump administration took office vowing to take a harder line on Pakistan until the country cracked down on all Islamist terror groups, especially those that target U.S. troops in Afghanistan. However, this has not happened. When Pakistan did not change its policy toward Islamist terror groups, the Trump administration did not engage in the punitive steps it had promised. The only exception was cutting all security assistance to Pakistan in January 2018. However, this was nothing particularly new. U.S. policy has done this before—and it did not prompt Pakistan to change its policies. The Trump White House has opted to aggressively pursue peace talks with the Taliban which began in 2018 and are facilitated by Pakistan. As such, Washington cannot afford a harsher policy toward Islamabad. Furthermore, the administration cannot afford to take draconian measures that risk Pakistan retaliating by shutting down the NATO supply routes on its soil—one of Islamabad's few powerful tools of leverage to deploy against the United States. This U.S. policy continued through 2019, as Washington sought Islamabad's cooperation in an effort to secure a U.S. troop withdrawal deal with the Taliban and to launch a formal peace process.

Initially, this process stalled as the Taliban continued to attack civilian and military targets in order to leverage a better negotiating position.[81] However, momentum grew once the Trump administration agreed to hold formal talks with the Taliban that excluded the Afghan government. The present truce calls on the Taliban to begin formal peace talks with the Afghan government, and for the group to sever all ties to international terror groups on Afghan soil. If the Taliban upholds these commitments, according to the agreement, the United States will remove all its forces from Afghanistan by the end of April 2021.[82]

Islamabad is one of the big winners from this agreement, which calls for a peace process between the Taliban, the Afghan government, and other key stakeholders known as an intra-Afghan dialogue that could (in theory) end the war. Any political settlement that emerges would entail the Taliban sharing power in a post-war administration - a major boon for the Pakistani government. At the same time, if the peace process fails, Pakistan would not necessarily be a loser. To be sure, if U.S. forces leave Afghanistan and the peace process falls apart, resulting in heavy destabilization in Afghanistan, Pakistan would not benefit from a destabilized western neighbor, and the spillover effects — refugee flows, a greater drug trade, an increase in Afghanistan-based sanctuaries for anti-Pakistan terror groups like ISIS — would be deeply problematic for Pakistan. However, an increasingly destabilized Afghanistan would only make the Taliban stronger—meaning that Pakistan's most powerful asset in Afghanistan would grow more potent.

Endnotes

1. John R. Allen, Testimony before the Senate Armed Services Committee, March 22, 2012, http://www.rs.nato.int/images/20120322_sasc_hearing_allen_transcript.pdf.
2. White House, "Remarks by President Trump on the Strategy in Afghanistan and South Asia," August 21, 2017, https://www.whitehouse.gov/briefings-statements/remarks-president-trump-strategy-afghanistan-south-asia/.
3. Lynn O'Donnell, "The Taliban Now Hold More Ground in Afghanistan Than At Any Point Since 2001," Associated Press, June 16, 2016, http://www.militarytimes.com/story/military/pentagon/2016/06/16/afghanistan-nicholson-commander-pentagon-report-war/85972056/.
4. "Afghan Taliban Cool to Ghani Peace Offer While UN, 20 Countries Support It," *Radio Free Europe/Radio Liberty*, March 1, 2018, https://www.rferl.org/a/afghan-taliban-cool-ghani-peace-offer-while-20-countries-kabul-process-support-it/29069945.html.
5. "Blast Hits Kabul after Briefing on US-Taliban Deal to Withdraw 5,000 Troops." *Associated Press*. September 2, 2019. https://www.theguardian.com/world/2019/sep/03/blast-hits-kabul-after-briefing-us-deal-withdraw-5000-troops-afghanistan.
6. Stephanie Condon. "After Osama Bin Laden's Death, Congress Puts Pakistan on the Hot Seat." *CBS News*, May 3, 2011, http://www.cbsnews.com/news/after-osama-bin-ladens-death-congress-puts-pakistan-on-the-hot-seat/.
7. Jane Corbin, "Have We Been Told the Truth about Bin Laden's Death?" *British Broadcasting Corporation*, June 17, 2015, https://www.bbc.com/news/world-middle-east-33152315.
8. "Bin Laden Doctor Shakil Afridi to Be Retried." *BBC News*, August

29, 2013. http://www.bbc.com/news/world-asia-23882900.

9. Ayaz Gul, "Pakistan 'Willing' to Discuss Freedom for Doctor Who Helped Find Bin Laden," *VOA News,* December 16, 2016, http://www.voanews.com/a/pakistan-doctor-who-helped-find-bin-laden/3638778.html.
10. Saeed Shah, "U.S. and Pakistan Discuss Release of Doctor Who Helped Find Osama bin Laden," *Wall Street Journal*, May 16, 2017, https://www.wsj.com/articles/u-s-and-pakistan-discuss-release-of-doctor-who-helped-find-bin-laden-1494927000; Shamil Shams, "Is Pakistan Trying to Swap Bin Laden Doctor Afridi for Aafia Siddiqui?" *Deutsche Welle*, January 18, 2017, http://www.dw.com/en/is-pakistan-trying-to-swap-bin-laden-doctor-afridi-with-aafia-siddiqui/a-37178892.
11. Mark Mazzetti, *The Way of the Knife: The CIA, a Secret Army, and a War at the Ends of the Earth* (New York: Penguin Books, 2014).
12. The exact number is open to debate. While there have been 414 drone strikes according to the New America Foundation, there have been 404 according to the *Long War Journal*. Meanwhile, the Bureau of Investigative Journalism has recorded 424. See: Peter Bergen, David Sterman, Melissa Salyk-Virk, Alyssa Sims, and Albert Ford, "Drone Strikes: Pakistan," New America, n.d., https://www.newamerica.org/in-depth/americas-counterterrorism-wars/pakistan/; Phil Hegseth, "US Airstrikes in the Long War," *Long War Journal*, January 3, 2018, https://www.longwarjournal.org/us-airstrikes-in-the-long-war; "Naming the Dead," *Naming the Dead*, n.d., https://v1.thebureauinvestigates.com/namingthedead/?lang=en.
13. Peter Bergen, David Sterman, Melissa Salyk-Virk, Alyssa Sims, and Albert Ford, "Drone Strikes: Pakistan," New America, n.d., https://www.newamerica.org/in-depth/americas-counterterrorism-wars/pakistan/; Phil Hegseth, "US Airstrikes in the Long War," *Long War Journal*, January 3, 2018, https://www.longwarjournal.org/us-airstrikes-in-the-long-war; "Naming the Dead," *Naming the Dead*, n.d., https://v1.thebureauinvestigates.com/namingthedead/?lang=en.
14. Lisa Curtis, "Al-Qaeda Announces New Affiliate in South Asia," *Daily Signal*, September 4, 2015, http://dailysignal.com/2014/09/04/al-qaeda-announces-new-affiliate-south-asia/.
15. Daveed Gartenstein-Ross and Nathaniel Barr, "How al-Qaeda Survived the Islamic State Challenge," Hudson Institute report, March 1, 2017, https://www.hudson.org/research/12788-how-al-qaeda-survived-the-islamic-state-challenge; Ali Soufan, "The Resurgent Threat of al-Qaeda," *Wall Street Journal*, April 21, 2017, https://www.wsj.

com/articles/the-resurgent-threat-of-al-qaeda-1492786991.
16. "Fatalities in Terrorist Violence in Pakistan 2003-2016," South Asia Terrorism Portal, n.d., http://www.satp.org/satporgtp/countries/pakistan/database/casualties.htm.
17. *Pakistan Security Report 2015*, Pak Institute of Peace Studies, n.d., http://pakpips.com/downloads/293.pdf.
18. "Taliban faction releases video of four BKU attack militants," *Dawn* (Karachi), January 23, 2016, http://www.dawn.com/news/1234887/taliban-faction-releases-video-of-four-bku-attack-militants?utm_source=feedburner&utm_medium=feed&utm_campaign=-Feed%3A+dawn-news+(Dawn+News).
19. Shaiq Hussain and Erin Cunningham, "Taliban Splinter Group Claims Attack on Christians at Pakistan Park; 60 dead," *Washington Post*, March 27, 2016, https://www.washingtonpost.com/world/explosion-kills-at-least-15-at-park-in-pakistans-lahore-reports-say/2016/03/27/00e49d32-f42e-11e5-958d-d038dac6e718_story.html.
20. Mark Manzetti and Eric Schmitt, "Pakistanis Aided Attack in Kabul, U.S. Officials Say," *New York Times*, August 1, 2008, http://www.nytimes.com/2008/08/01/world/asia/01pstan.html.
21. "McCain Calls for Support of Pakistan to Eliminate Militancy in Afghanistan," Agence France-Presse, July 5, 2017, https://www.dawn.com/news/1343353.
22. Bill Roggio, "U.S. Drones Target 'Jihadist' Hideouts in Pakistan's Tribal Areas," *Long War Journal*, February 22, 2016, http://www.longwarjournal.org/archives/2016/02/us-drones-target-jihadist-hideouts-in-pakistans-tribal-areas.php.
23. Eric Schmitt, "White House Backs Blacklisting Militant Organization," *New York Times*, September 7, 2012, https://www.nytimes.com/2012/09/07/world/asia/white-house-backs-blacklisting-militant-organization.html?_r=1&emc=na&mtrref=undefined&assetType=REGIWALL&mtrref=www.nytimes.com&gwh=F7215D1436239ABADA1320436F8A2493&gwt=pay&assetType=REGIWALL.
24. Noor Zahid, "US Strike Reportedly Kills Haqqani Network Commander in Pakistan," *VOA News*, June 14, 2017, https://www.voanews.com/a/strike-reportedly-kills-haqqani-network-commander-pakistan/3899067.html.
25. Jamie Crawford, "US Holds up $300 Million for Pakistan over Terrorism." *CNN*, August 4, 2016.
26. Franz-Stefan Grady, "US Won't Subsidize Pakistan's Purchase of

F-16 Fighter Jets," *The Diplomat,* May 4, 2016, http://thediplomat.com/2016/05/us-wont-subsidize-pakistans-purchase-of-f-16-fighter-jets/.

27. Katherine Wojtecki, "Chicago Man Pleads Guilty to Terror Plots," *CNN*, March 18, 2010, http://www.cnn.com/2010/CRIME/03/18/headley.plea/index.html.
28. U.S. Department of State, Office of the Coordinator for Counterterrorism, *Country Reports on Terrorism 2008* (Washington, DC: U.S. Department of State, April 30, 2009), http://www.state.gov/s/ct/rls/crt/2008/122434.htm.
29. U.S. Department of State, "Rewards for Justice - Lashkar-e-Tayyiba Leaders Reward Offers," April 3, 2012.
30. Zahid Hussain and Eric Bellman, "Pakistan Says It May Outlaw Islamic Group," *Wall Street Journal,* December 11, 2008, http://online.wsj.com/article/SB122889700300394357.html.
31. Lisa Curtis, "Indian Strikes against Pakistani Terror Bases: U.S. Must Ensure No Further Escalation," *Daily Signal,* September 20, 2016, http://dailysignal.com/2016/09/30/india-strikes-across-line-of-control-to-neutralize-terrorist-bases-in-pakistan/.
32. Husain Haqqani, "Prophecy and the Jihad in the Indian Subcontinent," Hudson Institute *Current Trends in Islamist Ideology* 18 (2015), 6.
33. Farhan Zahid and Muhammad Ismail Khan, "Prospects for the Islamic State in Pakistan," Hudson Institute *Current Trends in Islamist Ideology* 20 (2016), 69.
34. Sudarsan Raghavan and Tim Craig, "Suspected U.S. drone strikes kill key Islamic State figures in Afghanistan," *Washington Post*, July 9, 2015, https://www.washingtonpost.com/world/us-drone-strike-kills-key-islamic-state-figure-in-afghanistan/2015/07/09/f4114ab2-2636-11e5-b621-b55e495e9b78_story.html.
35. Richard Barrett, "Beyond the Caliphate: Foreign Fighters and the Threat of Returnees," The Soufan Center, October 2017, http://thesoufancenter.org/wp-content/uploads/2017/11/Beyond-the-Caliphate-Foreign-Fighters-and-the-Threat-of-Returnees-TSC-Report-October-2017-v3.pdf.
36. For a discussion of the Barelvi school of Islamic thought, see Haider A.H. Mullick and Lisa Curtis, "Reviving Pakistan's Pluralist Traditions to Fight Extremism," Heritage Foundation *Backgrounder* no. 2268, May 4, 2009, http://www.heritage.org/Research/AsiaandthePacific/bg2268.cfm.
37. Haider A.H. Mullick and Lisa Curtis, "Reviving Pakistan's Pluralist

Traditions to Fight Extremism," Heritage Foundation *Backgrounder* no. 2268, May 4, 2009, http://www.heritage.org/Research/AsiaandthePacific/bg2268.cfm.
38. Husain Haqqani, "The Ideologies of South Asian Jihadi Groups," Hudson Institute *Current Trends in Islamist Ideology* 1 (2005), 12.
39. Stephen Philip Cohen, *The Idea of Pakistan* (Washington, DC: The Brookings Institution, 2004), 161.
40. Fatima Mullick and Mehrunnisa Yusuf, P*akistan: Identity, Ideology, and Beyond* (London: Quilliam, August 2009), 11.
41. Nasr, *The Vanguard of the Islamic Revolution*, 121.
42. White, *Pakistan's Islamist Frontier*, 38.
43. Mullick and Curtis, "Reviving Pakistan's Pluralist Traditions to Fight Extremism."
44. Joshua T. White, "Vigilante Islamism in Pakistan," Hudson Institute *Current Trends in Islamist Ideology* 7 (2008), 56.
45. Joshua T. White, "Vigilante Islamism in Pakistan," Hudson Institute *Current Trends in Islamist Ideology* 7 (2008), 59.
46. Aryn Baker, "At Pakistan's Red Mosque, A Return of Islamic Militancy," *Time*, April 17, 2009, http://content.time.com/time/world/article/0,8599,1892254,00.html.
47. "Pakistani Taliban Withdraw from Key Northwestern District," *Voice of America*, April 24, 2009.
48. Lisa Curtis, Testimony before the U.S. Senate Committee on Homeland Security and Governmental Affairs, Subcommittee on Federal Financial Management, Government Information, Federal Services, and International Security, July 7, 2009.
49. Daniel Victor, "Malala Yousafzai, Girls' Education Advocate, Finishes High School," *New York Times*, July 7, 2017, https://www.nytimes.com/2017/07/07/world/middleeast/malala-yousafzai-graduates.html.
50. Asif Shahzad, "Pakistan Army Pushed Political Role for Militant-Linked Groups," Reuters, September 15, 2017, https://www.reuters.com/article/us-pakistan-politics-militants/pakistan-army-pushed-political-role-for-militant-linked-groups-idUSKCN1BR02F.
51. Ramsha Jahangir, "Religious Parties Clinch over 9pc Share of Votes in National Assembly." *Dawn* (Karachi), August 1, 2018, https://www.dawn.com/news/1424235/religious-parties-clinch-over-9pc-share-of-votes-in-national-assembly.
52. For final election figures both nationally and in Punjab, based on Pakistan Election Commission data, see http://gallup.com.pk/wp-con-

tent/uploads/2018/07/Gallup-Pakistan-Exit-Poll-2018-Who-did-TLP-voters-vote-in-2013-GE-1.pdf.

53. Michael Kugelman and Adam Weinstein, "Prosecuting Pakistan's New Extremists," Lawfare, December 19, 2018, https://www.lawfareblog.com/prosecuting-pakistans-new-extremists.
54. For election data, see http://gallup.com.pk/wp-content/uploads/2018/07/Gallup-Pakistan-Exit-Poll-2018-Who-did-TLP-voters-vote-in-2013-GE-1.pdf.
55. Mullick and Curtis, "Reviving Pakistan's Pluralist Traditions to Fight Extremism."
56. C. Christine Fair, "Islamic Education In Pakistan," United States Institute of Peace, March 26, 2006, http://home.comcast.net/~christine_fair/index.html.
57. See "20 Points of National Action Plan," National Counter Terrorism Authority of Pakistan, http://nacta.gov.pk/NAPPoints20.htm.
58. Ashif Shahzad and Mubasher Bukhari, "Protests after Pakistan Frees Christian Woman Sentenced to Death over Blasphemy," Reuters, October 30, 2018, https://af.reuters.com/article/worldNews/idAFKCN1N42Y0.
59. Mubasher Bukhari and Asif Shahzad, "Pakistani Interior Minister Shot by Man Linked to New Religious Party: Report," Reuters, May 6, 2018, https://www.reuters.com/article/us-pakistan-attack/pakistani-interior-minister-shot-by-man-linked-to-new-religious-party-report-idUSKBN1I70J8.
60. "Malik Ishaq: Pakistan Sunni Militant Chief Killed by Police," *BBC*, July 29, 2015, http://www.bbc.com/news/world-asia-33699133.
61. Kunwar Khuldune Shahid, "An Alliance Between Islamic State and Lashkar-e-Jhangvi in Pakistan Was Inevitable," *The Diplomat*, November 15, 2016, http://thediplomat.com/2016/11/an-alliance-between-islamic-state-and-lashkar-e-jhangvi-in-pakistan-was-inevitable/.
62. Rizwan Mohammed and Karin Brulliard, "Militants Attack Two Ahmadi Mosques In Pakistan; 80 Killed," *Washington Post*, May 29, 2010, http://www.washingtonpost.com/wp-dyn/content/article/2010/05/28/AR2010052800686.html.
63. "Ahmadi Man Gunned Down in Gujrunwala," Reuters, December 27, 2014, https://www.dawn.com/news/1153496.
64. "Five Ahmedis Shot, Injured in Two Incidents," *Daily Times*, July 9, 2019, https://dailytimes.com.pk/264711/hate-crime-five-ahmedis-shot-injured-in-two-incidents/.
65. Ismail Khan and Salman Masood, "Scores Are Killed by Suicide

Bomb Attack at Historic Church in Pakistan," *New York Times*, September 22, 2013, https://www.nytimes.com/2013/09/23/world/asia/pakistan-church-bombing.html.

66. "Lahore Attack: Pakistan 'Detains 200' After Easter Blast", BBC, March 29, 2016, https://www.bbc.com/news/world-asia-35916578.
67. "Deadly Attack on Methodist Church in Pakistan," BBC, December 18, 2017, https://www.bbc.com/news/world-asia-42383436.
68. Bill Chappell, "ISIS Claims Murders Of 4 Christians In Pakistan." *National Public Radio*, April 3, 2018, https://www.npr.org/sections/thetwo-way/2018/04/03/599098645/isis-claims-murders-of-4-christians-in-pakistan.
69. Anum Mirza, "Christians Claim They Are Being Forced out of Pakistani City by Isil Violence," *Telegraph* (London), April 21, 2018, https://www.telegraph.co.uk/news/2018/04/21/christians-claim-forced-pakistani-city-isil-violence/.
70. "Thousands in Pakistan Protest Hanging of Governor's Killer Mumtaz Qadri," *Deutsche Welle*, March 27, 2016, http://www.dw.com/en/thousands-in-pakistan-protest-hanging-of-governors-killer-mumtaz-qadri/a-19145439.
71. Haroon Balogun, "Gunmen raid Ahmadiyya central office," *Vanguard*, December 9, 2016, http://www.vanguardngr.com/2016/12/gunmen-raid-ahmadiyya-central-office/.
72. Imran Gabol, "Mob 'besieging' Ahmadi place of worship in Chakwal dispersed by police," *Dawn* (Karachi), December 13, 2016, https://www.dawn.com/news/1302057.
73. "NA Passes Resolution to Rename QAU's Abdus Salam Centre," *Geo News*, May 3, 2018, https://www.geo.tv/latest/193941-na-passes-resolution-to-rename-qaus-abdus-salam-centre.
74. Niala Mohamad, "Pakistani Ahmadi Leaders Fear Backlash After New Minority Commission Formation," *Voice of America*, May 18, 2020, https://www.voanews.com/extremism-watch/pakistani-ahmadi-leaders-fear-backlash-after-new-minority-commission-formation.
75. Yusuf, "Prospects of Youth Radicalization in Pakistan: Implications for U.S. Policy," 19-20.
76. K. Alan Kronstadt, "Direct Overt U.S. Aid Appropriations for and Military Reimbursements to Pakistan, FY2002-FY2017, *Congressional Research Service Memo,* February 24, 2016, https://www.fas.org/sgp/crs/row/pakaid.pdf.
77. C. Christine Fair and Seth G. Jones, "Pakistan's War Within," *Survival* 51, no. 6 (December 2009–January 2010), 171.
78. Zahir Shah Sherazi, "Pakistani Taliban Chief Hakimullah Mehsud

Killed in Drone Strike," *Dawn*, November 1, 2013, https://www.dawn.com/news/1053410.

79. William Branigin and Sayed Salahudin, "Pakistani Taliban Leader Mullah Fazlullah Killed in U.S. Airstrike in Afghanistan." *Washington Post*, June 15, 2018, https://www.washingtonpost.com/world/asia_pacific/pakistan-taliban-leader-mullah-fazlullah-is-killed-in-a-us-airstrike-in-afghanistan/2018/06/15/9ea6cc56-70ab-11e8-b4d8-eaf78d4c544c_story.html.
80. Dennis C. Blair, "Annual Threat Assessment of the US Intelligence Community for the Senate Select Committee on Intelligence," February 2, 2010, http://intelligence.senate.gov/100202/blair.pdf.
81. Michael Crowley, "Trump visits Afghanistan and Says He Reopened Talks With the Taliban," *New York Times*, November 28, 2019, https://www.nytimes.com/2019/11/28/us/politics/trump-afghanistan.html.
82. Riley Beggin, "The US and Taliban Sign Agreement Meant to End America's Longest War," *Vox*, February 29, 2020, https://www.vox.com/world/2020/2/29/21158939/us-taliban-sign-peace-deal-troops-afghanistan.

56 Sri Lanka

Quick Facts

Population: 22,889,201 (July 2020 est.)
Area: 65,610 sq km
Ethnic Groups: Sinhalese 74.9%, Sri Lankan Tamil 11.2%, Sri Lankan Moors 9.2%, Indian Tamil 4.2%, other 0.5% (2012 est.)
GDP (official exchange rate): $87.35 billion (2017 est.)

Source: CIA World FactBook (Last Updated August 2020)

Introduction

Sri Lanka is a country tragically familiar with ethno-religious conflict, having fought a brutal civil war against the Liberation Tigers of Tamil Eelam (LTTE), the original pioneers of suicide bombing, for a quarter century between 1983 and 2009. The conflict claimed as many as 100,000 lives before the LTTE, comprising radical members of the country's Hindu Tamil minority, was decimated by a Sri Lankan military offensive in 2009 that also carried a heavy civilian toll. However, until recently the island's Muslim population was largely removed from communal tensions and religious violence and there was little history of violent Islamist groups operating in the country.

The island nation of roughly 25 million citizens off southeastern coast of India is majority Buddhist, with large Hindu, Muslim, and Christian minorities. The religious divide between Buddhist and Hindus largely parallels an ethnic divide between the majority Sinhalese and the minority Tamils more concentrated in the country's north. This has historically been the principal ethno-religious fault line in the nation, and the basis for the aforementioned civil war.

Though a small number of Sri Lankans were found to have

traveled to join the Islamic State in the Middle East, Sri Lankan Muslims are considered largely moderate, rejecting more fundamentalist interpretations of Islam with little history of violence or terrorism. Indeed, prior to 2019, there had never been a significant terrorist attack inside Sri Lanka perpetrated by an Islamist group. That changed dramatically on Easter Day, April 21, 2019, when a heinous multi-pronged terrorist attack largely targeting Sri Lanka's Christian minority claimed over 250 lives. It was not only the first terrorist attack since the country's civil war ended in 2009; it was the deadliest terrorist attack in Sri Lankan history—and indeed all of South Asian history.

Due to publishing constraints, this chapter is provided here only in summary form. To view the full study, please visit the online edition of the Almanac at almanac.afpc.org.

East Asia and Oceania

57 Australia

Quick Facts

Population: 25,466,459 (July 2020 est.)
Area: 7,741,220 sq km
Ethnic Groups: English 25.9%, Australian 25.4%, Irish 7.5%, Scottish 6.4%, Italian 3.3%, German 3.2%, Chinese 3.1%, Indian 1.4%, Greek 1.4%, Dutch 1.2%, other 15.8% (includes Australian aboriginal .5%), unspecified 5.4% (2011 est.)
GDP (official exchange rate):$1.38 trillion (2017 est.)

Source: CIA World FactBook (Last Updated July 2020)

INTRODUCTION

By global standards, the threat of Islamist violence in Australia is low. Generally, Australia has not proven fertile ground for global terrorist organizations, despite some attempts at recruitment and fundraising. The overwhelming majority of those convicted under the country's anti-terrorism laws belonged to small, independent, self-starting groups with no clear connection to established global terrorist organizations. The few individuals who had links to such organizations have long since left them and show little, if any, intention of undertaking large-scale terrorist acts in Australia. Notably, however, the threat of terrorism associated with the Islamic State (ISIS) has grown in recent years, as the group has gained strength in the Muslim world. That threat, and the organization's larger appeal, continues, despite the collapse of the ISIS caliphate in Iraq and Syria.

Due to publishing constraints, this chapter is provided here only in summary form. To view the full study, please visit the online edition of the Almanac at almanac.afpc.org.

58 China

Quick Facts

Population: 1,394,015,977 (July 2020 est.)
Area: 9,596,960 sq km
Ethnic Groups: Han Chinese 91.6%, Zhuang 1.3%, other (includes Hui, Manchu, Uighur, Miao, Yi, Tujia, Tibetan, Mongol, Dong, Buyei, Yao, Bai, Korean, Hani, Li, Kazakh, Dai, and other nationalities) 7.1% (2010 est.)
Government Type: Communist party-led state
GDP (official exchange rate): $12.01 trillion (2017 est.)

Source: CIA World FactBook (Last Updated July 2020)

Introduction

Prior to 1949, China's Nationalist government recognized Muslims as one of the "five peoples" constituting the Chinese nation – along with Manchus, Mongols, Tibetans and Han. The Communist Party of China (CPC) has maintained this recognition and continued to push Muslims toward integration. China, in the words of one official, "allows the practice of religion, but not at the expense of the state."[1] In all, Beijing recognizes ten separate Muslim nationalities, the largest being Uighurs, Hui, and Kazakhs.

The spread of Islam in China, particularly in the Xinjiang Uighur Autonomous Region—a sprawling western expanse of inhospitable deserts and mountains—has long been a source of official concern, resulting in numerous laws restricting assembly, as well as religious practices and teaching. These repressive measures have culminated in "reeducation" camps intended to Sinicize minority Muslim detainees. More subtly, the Chinese state has made efforts to dilute Uighur dominance demographically through the transplantation of Han Chinese to the region. This policy has resulted in a material shift in the demographics of the region; according to official estimates, Han Chinese, who made up just 6 percent of the overall population of Xinjiang in 1949, comprised over 30 percent of the provincial total as of 2018.[2]

In 2008, a New York Times journalist described life for Muslims in Xinjiang as living, "an intricate series of laws and regulations intended to control the spread and practice of Islam."[3] Eleven years later, the same outlet reported that "authorities in Xinjiang have detained hundreds of thousands of Uighurs, Kazakhs, and other Muslim minorities in internment camps."[4] Chinese officials ascribe rising social and political tensions in the region to the growing influence of radical Islam – rather than to repressive state policies. As such, they see radical Islam as an external threat to what would otherwise be a peaceful and happy Chinese religious minority.[5]

Islamist Activity

Chinese authorities collectively classify separatism, extremism, and terrorism as the "three forces" that represent a threat to the nation. Chinese authorities divide their struggle against these evils into five phases between 1990 and 2007.[6] During this period, religious radicalism metamorphized, culminating in the rise of groups such as East Turkestan Islamic Movement (ETIM), also known as the Turkistan Islamic Party (TIP), or al-Hizb al-Islami al-Turkistani, the East Turkestan Islamic Reform Party, the East Turkestan Democratic Reform Party, and the East Turkestan Justice Party.

The Xinjiang Autonomous Region is the epicenter of concerns about Islamic extremism, and the focal point of China's long-running anti-terror campaign. Xinjiang is China's largest territory, spanning more than 1.6 million square kilometers in the country's extreme west. According to official Chinese statistics in 2017, traditionally Muslim ethnic groups make up nearly 14 million of Xinjiang's population of 23 million. Of these, the largest ethnic bloc is the Uighur, who number over 11 million.[7]

Recently, the Chinese central government has sought to repress and control Xinjiang residents. This campaign is complex, since radical Islamism and Uighur separatism are inextricably linked in the minds of many Chinese officials and citizens. Han Chinese – even those with progressive attitudes toward democracy – often cannot see the difference between a politically active Uighur and a separatist, nor do they acknowledge meaningful differentiation between Muslim identity and extremism.[8]

Uighurs have long lived as *de facto* second class citizens within China, with many denied economic opportunity and political representation – and with little attention paid, at least until recently, to their living standards and economic conditions. Over time, a comparatively tiny fraction of Uighurs, what experts have defined as "a very small minority within the minority,"[9] has become politically active through illegal and/or militant groups. The goal of these organizations is the promotion of Uighur rights and separatist tendencies in Xinjiang.

In December of 2003, China's Ministry of Public Security released a list of organizations deemed to pose a threat to the state. The document listed four distinct groups – the ETIM/TIP, the (ETLO), the World Uighur Youth Congress, and the East Turkestan Information Center – as well as eleven individuals.[10] Of these, only ETIM/TIP and the World Uighur Congress (a merger of the World Uighur Youth Congress and the Eastern Turkestan National Congress)[11] remain active today. The U.S. Department of State designated ETIM as a Foreign Terrorist Organization in September 2002, but declined to designate the other organizations as such despite pressure from the Chinese government to do so. This resistance was due largely to suspicions that the Chinese government blacklisted these organizations because of political considerations, rather than as a result of legitimate security concerns.[12]

The state's increasingly tight controls on speech, movement, and the practice of Islam engendered widespread frustration and anger among Chinese Muslims. A growing resentment of heavy-handed state intervention in religious life solidified the separatist movement and strengthened its grassroots support. This, in turn, catalyzed large-scale and violent Uighur anti-government riots in 2008–2009, and has perpetuated sporadic instances of violence since. These have included, among others, an attack on a train station in Yunnan province in March 2014 in which Uighur militants killed 29 people,[13] a police raid in July 2015 that resulted in the deaths of three purported Uighur terrorists in Shenyang,[14] and an attack on a coal mine in September 2015 in which at least 50 people were killed by alleged separatists.[15]

Over time, this unrest has prompted a change in Xinjiang's Islamist groups – most directly, ETIM/TIP. Following 2009, groups such as Hizb ut-Tahrir and the al-Qaeda-linked Islamic Movement of Uzbekistan (IMU) began to exert greater influence over ETIM/TIP's ideology and tactics,[16] with the latter reportedly involved in the training of the group's militants.[17] ETIM/TIP ideology promotes Uighur independence and resistance against the suppression of Islam in Xinjiang. For example, one Uighur separatist publication, Turkistan al-Muslimah (Muslim Turkistan), regularly links Islam and separatism by claiming that ETIM/TIP is "seeking freedom and independence and to be ruled by God's *Sharia*."[18] The Media Center Islam Avazi reported in 2017 that hundreds of TIP Uighur militants trained not only in military tactics but also in *sharia* law.[19]

Information regarding ETIM/TIP is tightly controlled by the Chinese government, and little is known about the group's current size, strength, and sources of funding. Nevertheless, the organization's increasingly strident Islamist rhetoric in recent years, as well as its surge of attacks against Chinese targets, suggest that the organization continues to constitute a real—albeit limited—threat to Chinese security.

Over the past several years, both the Islamic State and al-Qaeda have begun targeting China with both threats and online propaganda.[20] Al-Qaeda leader Ayman al-Zawahiri has labeled China an enemy of the Muslim world; so has the leader of the al-Qaeda-affiliated TIP, Abdul Haq.[21] The Islamic State, meanwhile, released a propaganda video in March 2017 highlighting Chinese Uighurs living and training to fight in the Islamic State, as well as depictions of the torture Uighurs suffer at the hands of the Chinese government.[22]

Exact numbers of Uighur foreign fighters are hard to estimate, so verifying the precise figure proves challenging.[23] A 2016 study by the New America Foundation, a Washington, DC-based think tank, noted that ISIS fighters from China were overwhelmingly Uighur in ethnicity, and hailed from Xinjiang. Moreover, these fighters were more likely to be married than other fighters, and in many cases brought their families with them, suggesting that they intended to stay with the Islamic State for the foreseeable future.[24] With the collapse of the Islamic State in Iraq and Syria, China's worries turned to the effect that these fighters could have on the Chinese Muslim population if they returned home.[25] Given the emergence of new migratory routes flowing through Southeast Asia toward Syria, China has leaned hard on Thailand, Malaysia, and others to repatriate Uighurs back to the PRC. For many Uighurs traveling this path, they seek refuge and ultimately asylum in Turkey, which has introduced complexities to Beijing-Ankara relations.[26]

Islamism and Society

The largest segments of China's Muslim population are Uighurs, Hui, and Kazakhs, which have been formally recognized by the Chinese state since 1949. The Uighurs, a Turkic Muslim minority, populate the rugged, oil- and mineral-rich territory of Xinjiang that constitutes one-sixth of China's total land mass. Uighurs are the largest ethnic group in Xinjiang, accounting for approximately 45% of the region's total population of roughly 24 million as of 2017.[27] Over the past three years, this number has declined as a result of China's sterilization and birth control policies (see "Islamism and the State" section). Uighurs have practiced Sunni Islam since the 10th century, and the faith has experienced a revival among the community in recent years. More recently, in 2019, the Chinese government claimed that there were more than 35,000 mosques throughout the entire country. Recent evidence, however, suggests that provincial officials have partly or totally demolished over two dozen mosques in Xinjiang alone in the past three years.[28] In 2016, the Chinese government reportedly demolished 5,000 mosques throughout the country in the name of public safety.[29] In the midst of China's reeducation campaign of Muslims in Xinjiang, authorities have stripped Islamic crescents and domes from mosques, banned religious schools and Arabic classes, and barred Muslim children from participating in faith-based activities.[30]

The Uighur community has numerous grievances against the Chinese government: restrictions on their religion, language and culture; official policies that encourage Han emigration to Xinjiang to dilute the strength of the Uighur ethnic identity; and common

Han discrimination towards Uighurs. China's authorities reject the validity of these complaints, saying Uighurs should instead be grateful for Xinjiang's rapid economic development and targeted investment from the government. Beginning in 2008, these racial and religious tensions fueled Uighur protests against state restrictions on Islam. A simultaneous series of attacks by Uighurs against the authorities and their Han neighbors only precipitated increasingly restrictive countermeasures. Ultimately, this cycle culminated in the mob violence of July 2009 (see "Islamism and the State" section). Farming remains the primary source of income for approximately 80 percent of Uighurs in the poor southern portion of the region.[31] Many face discrimination in the job market, both over their ethnic and religious heritage. This discrimination is exacerbated by the linguistic barrier between the Uighurs and the rest of China.[32]

Since Uighurs have no real voice in national politics, their political interests are largely represented by the World Uyghur Congress (WUC). The WUC is the most well-known international Uighur political organization. It is an umbrella group of smaller Uighur nationalist organizations formed after the East Turkestan National Congress and the World Uyghur Youth Congress merged in April 2004.[33] The WUC claims to "peacefully promote the human rights, religious freedom, and democracy for the Uyghur people in East Turkistan."[34] Beijing, on the other hand, asserts that the WUC is a front through which Western nations clandestinely channel funds and weapons into Xinjiang and undermine the Chinese state.[35]

The Hui are China's second-largest Muslim ethnic group, with a population of over 10 million scattered throughout China.[36] They are most numerous in the Ningxia Hui Autonomous Region, Gansu, Qinghai, Henan, Hebei, Shandong, and Xinjiang. Over time, the Hui have lost their proficiency in Arabic and Central Asian languages and adopted Chinese as their native tongue. Today's Hui are best understood as Sinicised Muslims that (unlike other official Muslim groups) look Han and speak Mandarin or other local dialects. Unlike the Uighurs – whose claim to Xinjiang predates that of the Han – the Hui settled in areas already dominated by ethnic Hans.[37] The Hui today enjoy far more religious freedom than they did in the first decades of Communist rule, when all religion was repressed.

However, greater religious freedom has also increased mosque attendance among Hui—a tendency that many Han interpret as clannish.

Finally, approximately 1.6 million Kazakh Muslims[38] reside in the north of Xinjiang, on the border with the Central Asian republic of Kazakhstan. Unlike the Hui, Kazakhs feel a close connection to clans in neighboring Kazakhstan and speak Kazakh rather than the mainstream Mandarin. In Kazakh society, rituals are generally performed in accordance with Islamic tradition, and include prayers, fasting, observance of the Hajj (pilgrimage to Mecca), and adherence to Islamic burial rites. Similarly, Kazakhs supplement their official legal marriages with traditional ceremonies. Historically, Kazakh Muslims enjoy a comparatively better relationship with the Han.[39] However, in November 2017, the Chinese government increased pressure on Kazakhs by detaining and investigating several hundred of them[40] as part of the government's larger crackdown on ethnic minorities.[41] Government officials in Kazakhstan have downplayed this issue and have suggested that a mere 33 Kazakh citizens were detained in camps, 20 of which the Chinese government returned.[42]

It appears that the Uighur community (rather than the Hui or Kazakhs) is the primary domestic constituency and support base for Islamist movements that call for Xinjiang's independence. *Turkistan al-Muslimah*, for instance, publishes articles on government persecution of Uighurs, but does not mention the plight of Hui or Kazakh Muslims in Xinjiang.[43] The magazine publishes only the names of "martyred" Uighurs, and in its first issue, the journal stated its aim as exposing "the real situation of our Muslim nation in East Turkistan, which is living under the occupation of the Communist Chinese."[44]

Islamism and the State

The Chinese state maintains an intricate system of control over its Muslim minorities. The regional Commission on Religious and Ethnic Affairs (CREA) closely monitors China's Islamic educational institutions, which span grades one through 12. Its teachers and clergy are thoroughly vetted by the parallel Islamic Association to ensure they do not harbor extremist ideas or tendencies. In practice, this has created a series of state-sponsored and tightly-controlled religious schools for Chinese Muslims.[45] This has included the underwriting of academic efforts to "reinterpret" Islamic scriptures so that they are more in keeping with Chinese society and values, as well as the promotion of communist ideas and integration among different ethnic groups (namely, the Uighur and the Han, with intermarriage actively encouraged by authorities). It has also advocated bilingual education (both Uighur and Mandarin) for the region's residents.[46] China currently has 10 Islamic institutes nationwide, the most prominent being the Islamic Institute of Xinjiang in Urumqi. Now some three decades old, the Institute has 450 students and turns out between 40 and 80 graduates per year. As of September 2016, it had graduated roughly 750 alumni, all of whom have gone on to become *imams*, mostly within China.[47]

Currently, curriculum at the facility is 30 percent academic and 70 percent religious (including Quranic recitation, the study of the hadith, and other subjects). The average course of study lasts five years, and students are nominated to attend the institution by their local communities, with candidacies considered by regional authorities to ensure they are in keeping with the larger ideological bent of religious policy.[48]

Funding for the Institute comes from the country's Islamic Association. This investment is part of a strategy to reduce the exposure of local Muslims to radical ideas and teachings. However, China's Muslims are not hermetically sealed off from divergent ideological strains of the religion. Notably, a small minority receives additional religious education abroad at institutions in Libya or Pakistan, or at Egypt's famed Al-Azhar University.[49] That said, according to local Chinese officials and administrators in Xinjiang, China has developed long-term relationships with these intuitions and they have yet to experience adverse consequences from sending students to these schools.[50]

Limits on religious activity abound. Prior to 2009, propaganda and education controls, coupled with an ample security presence, appeared to suppress Islamist activity within China's Muslim communities. However, as previously discussed, in July of 2009,

Xinjiang's capital of Urumqi became the site violent clashes between the local Uighur and Han communities – a culmination of months of simmering regional ethnic and communal tensions. The initial demonstrations and armed counter-protests, left more than 150 dead, marking the largest instance of public violence in China since the 1989 Tiananmen Square massacre.[51]

The government response to the Urumqi riots was sharp and swift. Among its numerous policies, it suspended all text messaging and Internet services in Xinjiang between July 2009 and January 2010.[52] Authorities in Yining "smashed two violence gangs, and arrested more than 70 suspects," according to Jiao Baohua, secretary of the Yining city CPC committee.[53] Since then, thousands of armed police, special police, and public security personnel began patrolling the Uighur sections of Urumqui and carry out raids.[54] The government issued new ordinances calling on local businesses and residents to register guests with the authorities[55] and temporarily restricting travel after dark.[56]

The state also expanded its propaganda efforts, and increased its control over legal and information services. The former included implementing a "political education" campaign to promote "new model citizens with a modern attitude."[57] The latter encompassed new restrictions on—and warnings to—lawyers,[58] as well as death sentences for some rioters and harsh prison sentences for others.[59] Other policies include limits on the length of sermons, prohibitions on prayer in public areas, and outlawing the teaching of the Quran in private. Muslims are now only permitted to attend mosques in their hometowns and government workers are now prevented from attending mosques.[60]

Two of Islam's five pillars—the sacred fasting month of Ramadan and the *Hajj* pilgrimage—are also restricted. Authorities use propaganda and control of passports to compel Muslims to join government-run *Hajj* tours that deliberately reduce exposure to Islamist teachings.[61] The government has also banned fasting during Ramadan,[62] and indicated that parents or guardians who "encourage or force" their children to be religious should be reported to the police. Though China claims to allow religious freedom, minors are not allowed to participate in religious expression, and there have been crackdowns on covert *madrassas*.[63] The Chinese government has applied a variety of other invasive measures to weaken Uighur communities, including explicitly ordering Muslim restaurant and store owners to sell alcohol and cigarettes, and promote them in "eye-catching displays."[64] Xinjiang has even expanded its policies to encompass bans against traditional names and clothing. In 2017, local authorities banned parents from giving their children names like "Muhammed" and "Medina"[65] and passed a law that bans veils and "abnormal" beards.[66]

In 2014, a massive contingent of 200,000 Communist Party officials visited 8,000 villages in Xinjiang. During visits they worked to establish a vast network of informers designed to keep tabs on villages throughout Xinjiang.[67] Following the uptick in inter-ethnic violence and terror later in 2014, 3,000 former members of the People's Liberation Army were deployed to Xinjiang communities.[68] The following year, the government enacted an anti-terrorism law. The statute requires that telecommunications and internet providers provide "technical and support and assistance including decryption," bans the dissemination of information about terrorist activities and the fabrication of stories about fake terror incidents, and allows the military to conduct counter-terrorism operations overseas.[69]

Xinjiang's security became even tighter after Chen Quanguo became Party Secretary of Xinjiang in August 2016 following his posting in Tibet. In the first half of 2017, Xinjiang spent $6 billion on security there, which included placing police stations every 500 meters within cities.[70] Shop owners have been forced to use their own money to install metal detectors and security cameras in their stores, and citizens report being stopped on the streets and forced to install an app on their phones called "web cleaning soldier," which checks their phones for illicit files.[71] Between February and June 2017, all drivers in the region were required to install a satellite navigation system in their cars that will allow the authorities to track vehicles' whereabouts.[72] Initially, citizens interviewed by foreign reporters in 2017 claimed that these measures made them safer, but also complained about the extra hassle and expense they cause.[73] In 2019, Han residents in Xinjiang began exiting the territory as the pervasive technological surveillance dampened economic growth and opportunity. In the words of one small businessman in Korla, a large metropolis in Xinjiang, "When you go into a shopping centre you have to scan your face, scan your ID, scan your bag, store your bag in a locker. You have to hand over your ID just to buy something."[74]

In the past several years, the government – in the name of counterterrorism and counterextremism – has embarked on a hardline reeducation program designed to transform Muslim ethnic minorities into a population that is largely secular, integrated into mainstream Chinese culture, and compliant with the Communist Party.[75] The program hinges on barbed wire-ringed compounds and factories labeled as "reeducation" camps by the Chinese government. These camps house possibly more than a tenth of Xinjiang's Uighur population, as well as Huis and Kazakhs,[76] the majority of whom pose no violent threat.[77] Estimating the precise number of interned individuals is difficult, but the United Nations announced in August 2018 that China was reeducating 1 million ethnic Uighurs.[78]

In these camps, Muslims are forced to denounce Islam and pledge allegiance to the officially atheist ruling Communist Party.[79] Leaked Chinese government documents published by the *New York Times* reveal that prisoners are assessed on a scoring system that tracks their daily behavior in the camps and their attendance record at ideological sessions.[80] Reasons for arrest and internment run the gamut, from religious reasons like praying or wearing a headscarf, or for having overseas connections to places like Turkey,[81] to supposedly suspect actions like entering one's house through the backdoor.[82] Xinjiang's technological surveillance apparatus feeds these data into the Integrated Joint Operation Platform, an algorithm that, according to Human Rights Watch, "regularly 'pushes' information of interests and lists of names of people of interest to police, Chinese Communist Party, and government officials for further investigation."[83]

According to Uighurs who have escaped the camps, torture is constant and ranges from electric shocks and pulled fingernails to medical experiments and rape.[84] In June 2020, a report from the Jamestown Foundation revealed a systemic campaign organized and executed by PRC officials to reduce the Uighur population in

Xinjiang. Methods of population reduction included mandatory sterilization, forced abortion, and compulsory birth control.[85]

Beyond pacifying Muslims within China, officials in Beijing are also focused on the interpersonal and cultural influence of Muslims in neighboring Belt and Road (BRI) partner states, which could further incite "separatism." The economics of BRI and securing trade routes informs the PRC's policy of widescale Uyghur repression.[86] The PRC also has designs for Xinjiang as a BRI manufacturing hub, and is compelling interned Muslims there into forced labor. According to a report from the Center for Strategic and International Studies, a think tank in Washington, DC, China "is in the process of significantly increasing textile and apparel manufacturing in the region through a mix of company subsidies and underpaid workers. Xinjiang will then be an export hub for the Belt and Road Initiative."[87]

Endnotes

1. Interviews by American Foreign Policy Council scholars, Xinjiang, China, June 2008.
2. In 2017, there were 67.7% minorities in Xinjiang, leaving the other 32.3% to be the majority Han Chinese. "25-17 Administrative Division and Population of Ethnic Minority Autonomous Areas (2017)," *2018 China Statistical Yearbook*, National Bureau of Statistics of China, http://www.stats.gov.cn/tjsj/ndsj/2018/indexeh.htm.
3. Edward Wong, "Wary Of Islam, China Tightens A Vise Of Rules," *New York Times*, October 18, 2008, https://www.nytimes.com/2008/10/19/world/asia/19xinjiang.html?_r=3&hp&oref=slogin.
4. Austin Ramzy and Chris Buckley, "'Absolutely No Mercy': Leaked Files Expose How China Organized Mass Detentions of Muslims," *New York Times*, November 16, 2019, https://www.nytimes.com/interactive/2019/11/16/world/asia/china-xinjiang-documents.html.
5. Interviews by American Foreign Policy Council scholars, Xinjiang, China, September 2016.
6. Interviews by American Foreign Policy Council scholars, Xinjiang, China, June 2008.
7. Statistics Bureau of Xinjiang Uygur Autonomous Region, "3-8 主要年份分民族人口数" (3-8 Number of sub-nationalities in major years), March 15, 2017, http://www.xjtj.gov.cn/sjcx/tjnj_3415/2016xjtjnj/rkjy/201707/t20170714_539451.html.

8. Louisa Greve, Testimony before the Congressional-Executive Commission on China, February 13, 2009, https://www.govinfo.gov/content/pkg/CHRG-111hhrg48222/html/CHRG-111hhrg48222.htm.
9. Randal G. Schriver, Testimony before the U.S. House of Representatives Committee on Foreign Affairs, Subcommittee on International Organizations, Human Rights and Oversight, June 16, 2009, https://www.gpo.gov/fdsys/pkg/CHRG-111hhrg50504/pdf/CHRG-111hhrg50504.pdf.
10. "China identifies Eastern Turkestan Terrorist Organizations," *PLA Daily*, December 16, 2003, http://www.globalsecurity.org/wmd/library/news/china/2003/china-031216-pla-daily01.htm.
11. Who We Are, World Uighur Congress, Accessed December 12, 2017, https://www.uyghurcongress.org/en/introducing-the-world-uyghur-congress/.
12. Schriver, Testimony before the U.S. House of Representatives Committee on Foreign Affairs, Subcommittee on International Organizations, Human Rights and Oversight.
13. Beina Xu, Holly Fletcher, and Jayshree Bajoria, "The East Turkestan Islamic Movement (ETIM)," Council on Foreign Relations *CFR Backgrounder,* September 4, 2014 https://www.cfr.org/backgrounder/east-turkestan-islamic-movement-etim.
14. "Three 'Xinjiang terrorists' shot dead by police in China," *BBC,* July 14, 2015, http://www.bbc.com/news/world-asia-china-33517512.
15. "Death Toll in Xinjiang Coal Mine Attack Climbs to 50," *Radio Free Asia*, September 30, 2017, http://www.rfa.org/english/news/uyghur/attack-09302015174319.html.
16. Rodger Baker, "China and the Enduring Uighurs," *Stratfor Terrorism Intelligence Report*, August 6, 2008, https://www.stratfor.com/weekly/china_and_enduring_uighurs.
17. Murad Batal Al-Shishani, "Journal of the Turkistan Islamic Party Urges Jihad in China." Jamestown Foundation *Terrorism Monitor* 7, iss. 9, April 10, 2009, https://jamestown.org/program/journal-of-the-turkistan-islamic-party-urges-jihad-in-china/.
18. Al-Shishani, "Journal of the Turkistan Islamic Party Urges Jihad."
19. Uran Botobekov, "China and The Turkestan Islamic Party: From Separatism to World Jihad – Analysis," *Eurasia Review,* December 10, 2017, https://advance-lexis-com.go.libproxy.wakehealth.edu/api/document?collection=news&id=urn:contentItem:5V96-5BX1-F0YC-N0GM-00000-00&context=1516831.
20. Uran Botobekov, "Al-Qaeda and Islamic State Take Aim at China," *The Diplomat,* March 8, 2017, http://thediplomat.com/2017/03/al-

qaeda-and-islamic-state-take-aim-at-china/.

21. Ibid.
22. Ibidem.
23. Colin P. Clarke and Paul Rexton Kan, "Uighur Foreign Fighters: An Underexamined Jihadist Challenge," *ICCT Policy Brief,* November 2017, https://icct.nl/wp-content/uploads/2017/11/ClarkeKan-Uighur-Foreign-Fighters-An-Underexamined-Jihadist-Challenge-Nov-2017-1.pdf; Adam Taylor, "ISIS recruits from China don't fit a typical profile – and Beijing may be partially to blame," *New York Times,* July 20, 2016, https://www.washingtonpost.com/news/worldviews/wp/2016/07/20/how-isis-fighters-from-china-differ-from-other-foreign-fighters/?utm_term=.866747ec269b; Uran Botobekov, "China and The Turkestan Islamic Party: From Separatism to World Jihad – Analysis," *Eurasia Review,* December 10, 2017, https://advance-lexis-com.go.libproxy.wakehealth.edu/api/document?collection=news&id=urn:contentItem:5V96-5BX1-F0YC-N0GM-00000-00&context=1516831; Nate Rosenblatt, *All Jihad is Local: What ISIS' Files Tell Us About Its Fighters,* New America Foundation, July 2016, 23, https://na-production.s3.amazonaws.com/documents/ISIS-Files.pdf; Ben Blanchard, "Syria Says up to 5,000 Chinese Uighurs fighting in Militant Groups," Reuters, May 11, 2017, https://uk.reuters.com/article/uk-mideast-crisis-syria-china/syria-says-up-to-5000-chinese-uighurs-fighting-in-militant-groups-idUKKBN1840UP; Uran Botobekov, "China and the Turkistan Islamic Party: From Separatism to World Jihad," *Modern Diplomacy*, December 9, 2017, https://moderndiplomacy.eu/2017/12/09/china-and-the-turkestan-islamic-party-from-separatism-to-world-jihad/.
24. Rosenblatt, *All Jihad is Local.*
25. Colin P. Clarke and Paul Rexton Kan, "All That Could Go Wrong When Jihadists Return Home — to China," *Defense One*, September 28, 2017, https://cdn.defenseone.com/a/defenseone/interstitial.html?v=9.11.4&rf=https%3A%2F%2Fwww.defenseone.com%2Fideas%2F2017%2F09%2Fall-could-go-wrong-when-jihadists-return-home-china%2F141386%2F.
26. Mathieu Duchâtel, "China's Foreign Fighters Problem," *War on the Rocks,* January 25, 2019, https://warontherocks.com/2019/01/chinas-foreign-fighters-problem/.
27. "Uyghurs in China," Congressional Research Service, June 18, 2019, https://fas.org/sgp/crs/row/IF10281.pdf.
28. Lily Kuo, "Revealed: new evidence of China's mission to raze the mosques of Xinjiang," *Guardian* (London), May 6, 2019, https://

www.theguardian.com/world/2019/may/07/revealed-new-evidence-of-chinas-mission-to-raze-the-mosques-of-xinjiang.

29. Shohret Hoshur and Brooks Boliek, "Under the Guise of Public Safety, China Demolishes Thousands of Mosques," *Radio Free Asia*, December 19, 2016, http://www.rfa.org/english/news/uyghur/udner-the-guise-of-public-safety-12192016140127.html.
30. Sam McNeil and Yanan Wang, "Religion must obey Chinese law, paper says of mosque protest," Associated Press, August 11, 2018, https://apnews.com/e67c5b125e9a410d850f3fd2281fbbce.
31. Roberts, "China Tries to Bring Growth to Its Restless Xinjiang Region."
32. "Don't make yourself at home," *The Economist*, January 15, 2015, http://www.economist.com/news/china/21639555-uighurs-and-tibetans-feel-left-out-chinas-economic-boom-ethnic-discrimination-not.
33. "Introducing the World Uyghur Congress," Official Website of the World Uyghur Congress, n.d., https://www.uyghurcongress.org/en/introducing-the-world-uyghur-congress-2/.
34. "Introducing the World Uyghur Congress."
35. "Jiangdu, gai kongxi cilue," (Uighur separatists changed terrorism strategy) *Ta Kung Pao* (Hong Kong), August 11, 2008.
36. "25-19 Geographic Distributions and Population of Ethnic Minorities," *2017 China Statistical Yearbook*, National Bureau of Statistics of China, http://www.stats.gov.cn/tjsj/ndsj/2018/indexeh.htm.
37. Richard Baum, *China Watcher: Confessions of a Peking Tom* (Seattle: University of Washington Press, 2010), 204.
38. Statistics Bureau of Xinjiang Uygur Autonomous Region, "3-8 Number of sub-nationalities in major years."
39. Iraj Bashiri, *The Kazakhs of China* (n.p., 2002), https://www.academia.edu/10187200/The_Kazakhs_of_China.
40. Luisetta Mudie and Qiao Long, "China Carries Out 'Mass Detentions' of Ethnic Kazakhs in Xinjiang," *Radio Free Asia*, November 13, 2017, https://www.rfa.org/english/news/uyghur/kazaks-arrests-11132017130345.html.
41. Paul Eckert and Eset Sulaiman, "China Runs Region-wide Re-education Camps in Xinjiang for Uyghurs And Other Muslims," *Radio Free Asia,* September 11, 2017, https://www.rfa.org/english/news/uyghur/training-camps-09112017154343.html.
42. Reid Standish and Aigerim Toleukhanova, "Kazakhs Won't Be Silenced on China's Internment Camps," *Foreign Policy*, March 4, 2019, https://foreignpolicy.com/2019/03/04/961387-concentrationcamps-china-xinjiang-internment-kazakh-muslim/.

43. Al-Shishani, "Journal of the Turkistan Islamic Party Urges Jihad in China."
44. Ibid.
45. Interviews by American Foreign Policy Council scholars, Xinjiang, China, June 2008.
46. Ibid.
47. Ibidem.
48. Ibidem.
49. Interviews by American Foreign Policy Council scholars, Xinjiang, China, June 2008.
50. Ibid.
51. "The Riots In Xinjiang: Is China Fraying?" *The Economist*, July 9, 2009, http://www.economist.com/node/13988479.
52. Andrew Jacobs, "China Restores Text Messaging in Xinjiang," *New York Times*, January 17, 2010, https://www.nytimes.com/2010/01/18/world/asia/18china.html.
53. Zhu Jingzhao, "Xinjiang yining dadiao liangbaoli fanzui tuanhuo, zhuabu shean qishiyuren," (Yining, Xinjiang wiped out two groups of violent crime suspects, arrested more than 70 people) *Zhongguo Xinwen She* (Beijing), July 13, 2009.
54. "Jiehou Wulumuqi jianwen: wending yadao yiqie," (Life in Urumqi after the festival: Stability is everything), *Ta Kung Pao* (Hong Kong), July 18, 2009, http://www.takungpao.com/news/09/07/18/xjsl_xgbd-1113938.htm.
55. Government of the People's Republic of China, "Riot-Hit Urumqi To Tighten Migrant Population Administration," August 9, 2009 http://english.cctv.com/20090810/102405.shtml.
56. "China Imposes Curfew In Capital Of Xinjiang," *Kyodo News Agency* (Japan), September 7, 2009.
57. Xi Wang, "Ideological Campaign Launched in Xinjiang," *Radio Free Asia*, February 17, 2012 https://www.rfa.org/english/news/uyghur/campaign-02172012144813.html.
58. Human Rights Watch, "China: Xinjiang Trials Deny Justice, Proceedings Failed Minimum Fair Trial Standards," October 15, 2009, https://www.hrw.org/news/2009/10/15/china-xinjiang-trials-deny-justice.
59. Cui Jia, "Murderers in Urumqi riots will not appeal," *China Daily* (Beijing), October 27, 2009 http://www.chinadaily.com.cn/cndy/2009-10/27/content_8852664.htm.
60. Wong, "Wary of Islam, China Tightens A Vise Of Rules."
61. Ibid.

62. "China bans Muslims from fasting Ramadan in Xinjiang," *Al Jazeera* (Doha), June 18, 2015, http://www.aljazeera.com/news/2015/06/china-bans-ramadan-fasting-muslim-region-150618070016245.html.
63. "China's new rules for Xinjiang ban parents from encouraging or forcing children into religion," *South China Morning Post,* October 12, 2016, http://www.scmp.com/news/china/policies-politics/article/2027342/chinas-new-rules-xinjiang-ban-parents-encouraging-or.
64. Simon Denyer, "China orders Muslim shopkeepers to sell alcohol, cigarettes, to 'weaken' Islam," *Washington Post,* May 5, 2015, https://www.washingtonpost.com/news/worldviews/wp/2015/05/05/china-orders-muslim-shopkeepers-to-sell-alcohol-cigarettes-to-weaken-islam/?utm_term=.86b80fa76626.
65. Javier C. Hernández, "China Bans 'Muhammed' and 'Jihad' as Baby Names in Heavily Muslim Region," *New York Times*, April 25, 2017, https://www.nytimes.com/2017/04/25/world/asia/china-xinjiang-ban-muslim-names-muhammad-jihad.html?rref=collection%2Ftimestopic%2FUighurs%20(Chinese%20Ethnic%20Group).
66. Nectar Gan, "Ban on beards and veils – China's Xinjiang passes law to curb 'religious extremism,'" *South China Morning Post*, March 30, 2017, https://www.scmp.com/news/china/policies-politics/article/2083479/ban-beards-and-veils-chinas-xinjiang-passes-regulation.
67. Tom Phillips, "China launches massive rural 'surveillance' project to watch over Uighurs," *Telegraph* (London), October 20, 2014, http://www.telegraph.co.uk/news/worldnews/asia/china/11150577/China-launches-massive-rural-surveillance-project-to-watch-over-Uighurs.html.
68. Tom Phillips, "China sends thousands of troops to combat violence," *Telegraph* (London), November 28, 2014, http://www.telegraph.co.uk/news/worldnews/asia/china/11259959/China-sends-thousands-of-troops-to-combat-Xinjiang-violence.html.
69. "China Passes Controversial New Anti-Terror Laws," *BBC,* December 28, 2015, https://www.bbc.com/news/world-asia-china-35188137.
70. Rob Schmitz, "Wary Of Unrest Among Uighur Minority, China Locks Down Xinjiang Region," *NPR*, September 26, 2017, https://www.npr.org/sections/parallels/2017/09/26/553463964/wary-of-unrest-among-uighur-minority-china-locks-down-xinjiang-province.
71. Emily Feng, "Security clampdown bites in China's Xinjiang region," *Financial Times,* November 13, 2017, https://www.ft.com/content/ee28e156-992e-11e7-a652-cde3f882dd7b.
72. Edward Wong, "Western China Region Aims to Track People by Re-

quiring Car Navigation," *New York Times*, February 24, 2017, https://www.nytimes.com/2017/02/24/world/asia/china-xinjiang-gps-vehicles.html.

73. Rob Schmitz, "Wary of Unrest Among Uighur Minority, China Locks Down Xinjiang Region."
74. Yuan Yang, "Xinjiang security crackdown sparks exodus of Han Chinese."
75. Austin Ramzy, "China Targets Prominent Uighur Intellectuals to Erase an Ethnic Identity," *New York Times,* January 5, 2019, https://www.nytimes.com/2019/01/05/world/asia/china-xinjiang-uighur-intellectuals.html.
76. Ishaan Tharoor, "The Cone of Silence Around China's Muslim 'Gulags,'" *Washington Post,* January 9, 2019, https://www.washingtonpost.com/world/2019/01/09/cone-silence-around-chinas-muslim-gulags/.
77. Gerry Shih, "China's Mass Indoctrination Camps Evoke Cultural Revolution," Associated Press*,* May 17, 2018, https://apnews.com/6e151296fb194f85ba69a8babd972e4b.
78. Stephanie Nebehay, "U.N. says it has credible reports that China holds million Uighurs in secret camps," Reuters, August 10, 2018, https://www.reuters.com/article/us-china-rights-un/u-n-says-it-has-credible-reports-that-china-holds-million-uighurs-in-secret-camps-idUSKBN1KV1SU.
79. "China Passes Law to Make Islam 'Compatible with Socialism," *Al Jazeera* (Doha)*,* January 5, 2019, https://www.aljazeera.com/news/2019/01/china-passes-law-islam-compatible-socialism-190105185031063.html.
80. "'Absolutely No Mercy': Leaked Files Expose How China Organized Mass Detentions of Muslims," *New York Times*, November 16, 2019, https://www.nytimes.com/interactive/2019/11/16/world/asia/china-xinjiang-documents.html.
81. John Sudworth, "China Muslims: Xinjiang Schools Used to Separate Children from Families," *BBC,* July 4, 2019, https://www.bbc.com/news/world-asia-china-48825090.
82. Bethany Allen-Ebrahimian, "Exposed: China's Operating Manuals for Mass Internment and Arrest by Algorithm," International Consortium of Investigative Journalists, November 24, 2019, https://www.icij.org/investigations/china-cables/exposed-chinas-operating-manuals-for-mass-internment-and-arrest-by-algorithm/.
83. "China: Big Data Fuels Crackdown in Minority Region," Human Rights Watch, February 26, 2018, https://www.hrw.org/

news/2018/02/26/china-big-data-fuels-crackdown-minority-region#.

84. David Stavrou, "A Million People Are Jailed at China's Gulags. I managed to Escape. Here's What Really Goes on Inside," *Ha'aretz* (Tel Aviv), October 17, 2019, https://www.haaretz.com/world-news/.premium.MAGAZINE-a-million-people-are-jailed-at-china-s-gulags-i-escaped-here-s-what-goes-on-inside-1.7994216.
85. Adrian Zenz, "Sterilizations, Forced Abortions, and Mandatory Birth Control: The CCP's Campaign to Supress Uyghur Birthrates in Xinjiang," The Jamestown Foundation, June 2020, https://jamestown.org/wp-content/uploads/2020/06/Zenz-Internment-Sterilizations-and-IUDs.pdf?x60014.
86. Rebecca Warren, "Xinjiang and the Belt and Road Initiative," *Real Clear Defense*, June 17, 2019, https://www.realcleardefense.com/articles/2019/06/17/xinjiang_and_the_belt_and_road_initiative_114507.html.
87. Amy K. Lehr and Mariefaye Bechrakis, "Connecting the Dots in Xinjiang: Forced Labor, Forced Assimilation, and Western Supply Chains," CSIS, October 2019, https://csis-prod.s3.amazonaws.com/s3fs-public/publication/Lehr_ConnectingDotsXinjiang_interior_v3_FULL_WEB.pdf.

59 Indonesia

Quick Facts

Population: 267,026,366 (July 2020 est.)
Area: 1,904,569 sq km
Ethnic Groups: Javanese 40.1%, Sundanese 15.5%, Malay 3.7%, Batak 3.6%, Madurese 3%, Betawi 2.9%, Minangkabau 2.7%, Buginese 2.7%, Bantenese 2%, Banjarese 1.7%, Balinese 1.7%, Acehnese 1.4%, Dayak 1.4%, Sasak 1.3%, Chinese 1.2%, other 15% (2010 est.)
GDP (official exchange rate): $1.015 trillion (2017 est.)

Source: CIA World FactBook (Last Updated July 2020)

Introduction

Indonesia boasts the world's largest Muslim population and is the planet's largest Muslim-majority democracy. Indonesia is not, however, a Muslim state per se. *Rather, it can best be classified as a secular democracy with significant Islamic influences. It is guided by a state philosophy known as the* Pancasila, *or five principles (faith, humanity, national unity, citizenship and social equality). Indonesia is also one of the world's most pluralistic societies in terms of its population's ethnic, linguistic, cultural, and religious affiliations. Much of this diversity is attributable to the country's diffuse geography; the Indonesian archipelago consists of more than 17,800 islands and islets.*

While the virulent brand of Islamist activism epitomized by both jihadi *and paramilitary groups is undoubtedly a feature of the country's modern social-political terrain, it represents only a small fraction of the wider Muslim community resident in the Southeast Asian nation. Although religious conservatism does figure prominently in national politics and culture, this has not translated into significant support for Islamist agendas among Indonesian citizens. Indeed, just one of Indonesia's thirty-four provinces, Aceh, has formally enshrined* sharia *law. Nevertheless, there are concerns that other provinces could eventually follow suit if Islamic conservatism continues to spread, and because the Indonesian government has of late delegated more and more power to provinces and districts to adopt their own laws.*[1]

Islamist Activity

Since the nation's founding in 1945, the legal status of Islam has divided the nation. Issues such as incorporating *sharia* into the Indonesian Constitution and the establishment of an Islamic state are still hotly contested, but some Islamic political parties have attempted to adopt a more inclusive agenda. These groups promote a pluralistic ideology and focus on universal Islamic values. Yet, while many are pluralist and accommodating, some do adopt rigid, uncompromising positions.

Partai Keadilan Sejahtera – PKS ("Prosperous Justice Party")

The PKS was originally founded in 1998 as "Lembaga Da'wah Kampus" (LDK), or "University Students' Body for Islamic Predication"[2] at a time when Indonesia's political climate accommodated Islam and sought to educate the public on its moral principles.[3] It is the most organized of the Indonesian Islamist parties, with some 25, 000 core cadres and 400,000 carefully selected and well-trained supporting cadres.[4] It has cultivated an image of collective decision-making and power-sharing, wherein no individual leader stands out. Additionally, the PKS has, in the past, successfully contained its internal differences and prevented public schisms. The party is popular with the modernist Islamic constituency, especially among students and educated middle-class Muslims. The PKS has moderated its Islamic ideology in order to appeal to non-Islamic elites and to stitch together a widely representative ruling coalition. The PKS, generally speaking, represents its members' political aspirations, provides *tarbiyah* (educational) activities under the moral guidance of a teacher, and provides public services. For example, the PKS set up a *Pos Keadilan* (Justice Post) from which its members could assist communities affected by ethnic/religious conflicts or natural disasters. In December 1999, a year after the party's official founding, its social services were institutionalized into the Pos Keadilan Peduli Umat (Justice Post Concerning Muslim Society), and expanded to include assistance to farmers selling their under-priced crops.[5]

In Indonesia's 2004 and 2009 elections, the PKS secured 45 and 56 seats out of 550 in the country's parliament, respectively. The PKS captured 24 percent of the vote in Jakarta and its voter base extended to both the urban elite and poor migrants residing in the slums. Its success was due, in part, to a political agenda that emphasized the broadly popular theme of "clean and caring government" in opposition to incumbent Islamist and secularist parties, perceived by voters to be corrupt and elitist.[6] The party's most deft political move has been to adopt the secular state ideology of *Pancasila*,[7] which prioritizes democratic deliberations as well as *bhinneka tunggal ika* (unity in diversity).[8] From the PKS's perspective, democracy is a means to, in the long term, establish a Islam-inspired political ideology. In the 2019 elections, the PKS garnered 8.21 percent of votes cast[9] and won 50 seats in the House of Representatives.[10]

The *tarbiyah* movement and activism on college campuses are essential for the PKS's success.[11] The PKS engages members through hundreds of regular gatherings that are not only attended by the upper echelons of the party but also by ordinary people. Often, these meetings focus on religion and religious understanding; they are catalysts for member interaction, party discipline, and recruitment. This level of regular contact gives the PKS easy, meaningful access to thousands of its followers and helps it to mobilize members during elections.

However, the PKS's image as a party free of corruption has been undermined in recent years by a number of controversies. Muhammad Misbakhun, a PKS lawmaker, was imprisoned for fraud in 2010,[12] while another, Arifinto, was arrested for watching pornography during a parliamentary session in 2011.[13] In addition to these internal crises, the PKS lost influence in the ruling coalition in 2011 when then-President Susilo Bambang Yudhoyono replaced the party's research and technology minister, Suharno Surapranata, with environment minister Gusti Muhammad Hatta as part of a cabinet reshuffle. The move was purportedly a response to the Islamist party's departure from coalition positions on policy issues.

Despite these controversies, however, the party suffered only a one percent dip in support in the April 2014 parliamentary elections. Analysts have argued that strong campaigning, particularly by secretary-general Anis Matta, and efficient party machinery helped. In its 2019 election bid, the PKS promised to pass a bill that would protect Muslim clerics, religious figures, and symbols in lieu of what it portrayed as persecution of the *Ulema*.[14] The party gained 12 seats between 2014 and 2019.[15]

Partai Kebangkitan Bangsa – PKB ("National Awakening Party")
The PKB was established to contest the June 1999 parliamentary elections. Its membership overlaps considerably with that of the *Nahdlatul Ulama* (NU), which is currently the largest Islamist group in the world. The PKB is the most politically successful of Indonesia's Islamic parties, and commands roughly nine-and-a-half percent of the national vote as of the country's 2019 elections. The PKB is led now by Muhaimin Iskandar, whose term as chairman runs until 2024.[16] Notably, the NU believes that Muslims should be allowed to vote for non-Muslim political and administrative leaders[17] – something which has contributed to the PKB's success. The PKB also reflects the NU's thinking on the interplay between religion and politics; in 2015, the NU led a messaging campaign designed to counter the Islamic State terrorist group with tolerance and compassion.[18]

Partai Persatuan Pembangunan – PPP ("United Development Party")
The PPP emerged from a merger of four Islamic parties in 1973: the NU, the Indonesian Islamic Party, the United Islamic Party of Indonesia, and the Muslim Teachers' Party. From 1973 to 1998, the PPP was politically neutered, but nonetheless played an important role in helping to ensure that the country's military did not dominate the National Legislature. While the PPP has endured the post-Suharto political landscape as a result of support from modernist and traditionalist Islamic leaders,[19] the party's share of votes declined drastically between 1999 and 2019. In the 1999 elections, the PPP had enjoyed more than 10 percent of all votes[20]; in 2019, the PPP's voter share stood at less than half that figure, 4.6 percent.[21] The PPP officially states that its ideological basis rests in Islam, and that

religion has a vital role to play in the life of a nation. The PKS does not focus on the formal adoption of *sharia,* instead committing to *Pancasila* and the 1945 Constitution.

Partai Bulan Bintang – PBB ("Crescent Star Party")
The PBB, which claims to be the descendant of Masyumi, the largest Islamic party of the 1950s, was founded in July 1998. Masyumi was banned in the 1960s and its leaders were jailed. After they were released, former Masyumi leaders established the *Dewan Da'wah Islamiyah Indonesia* (DDII), a modernist Islamic organization with close relations with other similar bodies.[22] The PBB was eventually formed from a collective of those groups.

The PBB espouses a classic Islamist political agenda. Both the PBB and PPP advocated for *sharia* during the 2002 annual session of the People's Consultative Assembly. In July 2017, when Indonesian President Joko "Jokowi" Widodo forcibly disbanded the Hizb ut-Tahrir Indonesia (HTI) under a Presidential decree, PBB chairman Yusril Ihza Mahendra invited the former HTI members to join his party.[23] The PBB's influence, however, is limited; since the 2004 elections, it has never polled above 2.5 percent.

Front Pembela Islam – FPI ("Front of the Defenders of Islam")
The FPI was founded by Muhammad Rizieq Syihab, a young man of Hadrami descent born into a family of *sayyids* (reputed descendants of the Prophet Muhammad).[24] Sometimes mistakenly characterized as a Salafi group, the FPI is actually Sufi in orientation. Before establishing the FPI, Syihab was a prominent religious preacher and a teacher at an Islamic school in Central Jakarta.[25] Laskar Pembela Islam (LPI), the paramilitary division of the FPI, was a loosely organized entity with an open membership.[26] The majority of its members were from mosque youth associations and a number of Islamic schools (*madrassas*) in Jakarta. Other members were simply unemployed youths, some of whom were *preman* (thug) group members motivated by money. The FPI routinely targets nightclubs and bars that violate their interpretation of Islamic code as well as the Ahmadiya minority sect.[27] Members who were indoctrinated by Syihab were taught that they should "live nobly, or better, die in holy war as a martyr."[28] The LPI eventually succeeded in expanding its

network to cities outside Jakarta. It claims 68 provincial and district branches and tens of thousands of sympathizers.[29]

The LPI first made its presence felt on the national stage in a mass demonstration on August 17, 1998, where it denounced Megawati Soekarnoputri's presidential candidacy. It became "the most active group in conducting what it called *razia maksiat* (raids on vice)."[30] Moreover, the group demanded that the government repeal the "sole foundation" policy, which required all political and social organizations to accept *Pancasila*.[31] The group supported the Jakarta Charter, which would have given Islamic law constitutional status. On one occasion, the group reportedly ransacked the offices of the National Human Rights Commission, which it felt "had not been objective in its investigation of the Tanjung Priok massacre (where the army had shot hundreds of Muslim demonstrators)."[32] The FPI also threatened Americans in Indonesia in response to U.S. attacks on the Taliban in Afghanistan.[33]

In late 2016, the FPI was at the forefront of protests against gubernatorial candidate Basuki "Ahok" Tjahaja Purnama, who had allegedly broken laws against blasphemy. The first rally was attended by between 150,000 and 250,000 people, while the second was much larger, with attendance estimated at 500,000 to 750,000.[34] The successful mobilization against Ahok contributed to his eventual defeat as well as his subsequent conviction in May 2017. Syihab currently resides in Saudi Arabia (where he fled to escape imprisonment) and alleges that the Joko Widodo administration conspires with the Saudis to prevent him from returning home.[35]

The FPI has recently landed in legal trouble for questioning *Pancasila.* The Indonesian government has demanded that, in order to procure its organizational permit, it must remove words like 'Caliphate' and 'Islamic State' from its organizational principles. The group has been told it must also clearly specify its loyalty to *Pancasila*.[36]

Laskar Jihad – LJ ("Holy War Force")

LJ first captured the attention of the public in early 2000. It mobilized in response to purported Christian violence against Muslims in the Moluccas, an archipelago within Indonesia, as well as the apparent inability of the Indonesian central government to protect local Muslims. LJ was a paramilitary group established by Ja'far Umar Thalib and leading Salafi personalities such as Muhammad Umar As-Sewed, Ayip Syafruddin, and Ma'ruf Bahrun.

LJ was originally, for the most part, apolitical and quietist, though it was influenced by puritanical *Wahhabbi* Salafism.[37] Many of its members were educated, were at some point part of campus Islamic student movements, were in contact with *Darul Islam*, an Islamist militant group. They were influenced by Thalib, who spent years studying in conservative and radical circles in Saudi Arabia and Yemen after which he was dispatched to Afghanistan to take part in *jihad*.[38] From 1994 to 1999, the cadres of LJ contented themselves with teaching and preaching *Wahhabbi* Islam and operated within the transnational Salafi *dawa* movement.[39] However, it was the conflict in the Molucca Islands that propelled them into radical activism and violence. In fact, Thalib portrayed the Moluccas conflict as one instigated by Zionists and Christians.[40] Shortly after the conflict began, the group established a training camp in West Java and was dispatching thousands of its members – both as relief workers as well as fighters – to the Moluccas.[41]

LJ was militaristic in structure, with "one brigade divided into battalions, companies, platoons, teams and one intelligence section."[42] The group adopted the image of two crossed sabres under their creed ("La ilaha illa Allah, Muhammad Rasul Allah," or "there is no God but Allah and Muhammad is His messenger") as its symbol.[43]

LJ dismissed manmade laws in favor of its own interpretation of *sharia*. It rejected democracy and popular sovereignty, maintaining that they fundamentally contradict Islam. The group condemned Megawati Sukarnoputri's presidency on the grounds that she was a woman. While active, LJ repeatedly instigated violent street riots in the pursuit of *sharia*. Other acts of violence included attacks on cafes, brothels, gambling dens, and other places they considered representations of vice.

In the aftermath of the Bali bombings of October 2002, public opinion swung decidedly away from these local paramilitary groups as Indonesian Muslims expressed outrage at the targeting of co-religionists. At the same time, their patrons from security services withdrew support and endorsements because of the international attention. Both the FPI and LJ were quickly disbanded.

Majelis Mujahidin Indonesia–MMI ("Jihad Fighter Group of Indonesia")

The MMI "places a different emphasis on *sharia* discourse than does LJ and FPI, associating it with the Jakarta Charter and the historical struggle of the Darul Islam movement."[44] It appears to be a front for various groups that have some relation to Darul Islam. The group's key organizer is Irfan S. Awwas and its chief religious authority is Abu Bakar Ba'asyir. Ba'asyir is accused of having ties to al-Qaeda.

MMI is arguably one of the oldest militant organizations active in Indonesia's post-New Order era. According to observers:

> …it is a loose alliance of a dozen minor Muslim paramilitary organizations that had been scattered among cities such as Solo, Yogyakarta, Kebumen, Purwokerto, Tasikmalaya and Makassar. Notable member groups are Laskar Santri (Muslim Student Paramilitary Force), Laskar Jundullah (God's Army Paramilitary Force), Kompi Badar (Badr Company), Brigade Taliban (Taliban Brigade), Corps Hizbullah Divisi Sunan Bonang (God's Party Corps of the Sunan Bonang Division), Front Pembela Islam Surakarta (Front of the Defenders of Islam of Surakarta/FPIS) and Pasukan Komando Mujahidin (Holy Warrior Command Force).[45]

MMI members lobby for the incorporation of *sharia* into the country's constitution, particularly at the local and regional level, in former Darul Islam strongholds. One of the MMI's main objectives is to establish an Islamic *khilafah* (caliphate). The MMI has actively called for *jihad*, particularly in the Moluccas and other troubled spots. In contrast to the large-scale mobilization of LJ, however, MMI has preferred to operate in small, well-trained, well-armed units. On June 12, 2017, the U.S. Department of State formally designated MMI a terrorist organization under Executive Order 13224.[46] MMI's paramilitary wing is the Laskar Mujahidin Indonesia

(LMI). Its propaganda magazine, *Risalah Mujahidin*, lobbies Indonesian political officials to impose *sharia*. It has connections to Jemaah Islamiya's Muhammad Iqbal Abdurrahman. Muhammad Jibril Abdul Rahman, Abdurrahman's son, was arrested on charges of raising funds for the JI and the MMI. He was sentenced to five years in prison on June 29, 2010 for his role in the July 17, 2009 Jakarta terrorist attacks, in which seven people died.[47]

Hizb-ut-Tahrir (HuT, or "Party of Liberation")

It is unclear when HuT came to Indonesia, but some scholars trace the organization's presence as far back as the 1970s when suspected group members emigrated to Southeast Asia and established the group through social and familial networks. Before the fall of Suharto's regime, Hizb-ut-Tahrir Indonesia (HTI) remained underground, moving from one mosque to another and avoiding any public coverage or evidence that might reveal its existence and activities. During the subsequent era of *reformasi* (political reform), however, the group made its appearance through several public rallies and called for the establishment of a *sharia*-based caliphate. But, for fear of prosecution, HTI has never revealed the identity of the leader of its Indonesian branch. Its public representative, Ismail Yusanto, claims that he is just the group's spokesperson.

At present, the HTI is arguably one of the fastest growing Islamic movements in Indonesia, and exhibits a particularly strong presence on Indonesian Islamic universities. HTI advocates for *sharia* law, viewing Islam as a political system and way of life.[48] Like the MMI, its most important objective is to establish an Islamic *khilafah*.[49] The group lobbies for one global government for all Muslims. Therefore, it is not surprising that this group rejects the idea of nationalism or the nation-state. Unofficial estimates place its membership at one million[50] and the organization has been drawing new members established Islamic organizations. On July 10, 2017, President Joko Widodo signed a proposed amendment to the 2013 Law on Mass Organisations which would allow the state to ban any social or political group that did not pledge allegiance to the state ideology of *Pancasila*. HTI was outlawed under this decree and, in May 2018, state administrative courts rejected attempts to overturn the executive action.[51]

HTI successfully spread its ideas by focusing on discussions with the *ummah* on how to internalize Islamic teachings in daily life. Its strength is its ability to establish presence not only in Jakarta but also in distant provinces where basic needs go unfulfilled. HTI's ability to stay away from violence and instead utilize legal means to question its 2017 permit revocation has made the group more effective.

Darul Islam and Jemaah Islamiyah al-Jama'ah al-Islamiyyah (JI)
The Darul Islam movement led by S. M. Kartosoewirjo first emerged in the mid-1940s in West Java as part of the broader armed anti-colonial movement against the Dutch reoccupation after the Second World War. Kartosoewirjo declared the formation of an Indonesian Islamic State, Negara Islam Indonesia (NII), based on *sharia* in 1949. While the group closed its doors in 1962, its influence over armed movements on Indonesia's political periphery has proven to be long-lasting.[52]

JI was founded in 1993 by two former Darul Islam leaders, Abdullah Sungkar and Abu Bakar Ba'asyir. JI saw itself as the heir of Darul Islam, despite its militant methods, including the deliberate targeting of civilians. Many prominent members of JI were veterans of the *jihad* against the Soviet Union in Afghanistan during the 1980s and had been recruited through Darul Islam channels.[53]

The Bali bombings of October 2002, however, sparked an internal debate over the issue of killing of Muslims and whether the organization should focus its immediate attention on proselytization rather than bombings in order to advance its goals. This schism eventually forced a split within JI; a hardline faction led by two key Malaysian leaders—Noordin Top and Azahari Husin—broke away from the main organization and continued a reign of terror with attacks on embassies and hotels between 2003-2009.

JI has assumed a lower profile in recent years, in part because of the success of the Indonesian government's counter-terrorism operations, but also because of internal differences over how the group should engage in *jihad*—specifically, whether it should localize its activities to Indonesia or carry them out on a global scale. However, this shift should not be mistaken for inactivity. JI remains particularly active in Indonesian prisons, where incarcerated activists and militants enjoy easy excess to other prisoners because of the inadequacies of the under-resourced prison system.[54]

In a significant breakthrough, Indonesia arrested alleged JI chief Para Wijayanto and his wife in a Jakarta hotel in July 2019. Wijayanto had received military training in a camp in the Southern Philippines and had been instrumental in getting new JI recruits, sending some to train with the Islamic State in Syria.[55] In the same timeframe, 81-year-old Abu Bakr Bashir, the alleged mastermind behind the JI Bali bombings, was due for release from prison on account of his ill-health. However, in January 2019, President Joko Widodo stipulated that Bashir must publicly endorse *Pancasila* and the Indonesian state, as well as renounce radicalism.[56] Widodo initially granted Bashir early release on humanitarian grounds,[57] but rescinded the decision after it was met with objections from Australia and from the families of domestic terror victims.[58]

The Islamic State (IS)

Islamic *jihadi* extremism has found new expression in Indonesia in recent years through the growing appeal of the Islamic State. Since 2014, videos of Indonesians engaging in armed conflict in support of ISIS and other *jihadi* groups in Iraq and Syria have surfaced. Indonesia also became the target of the first ISIS-inspired attack in Southeast Asia when self-proclaimed followers of the group carried out coordinated several attacks across Jakarta in January 2016.[59] As of mid-2017, an estimated 500-700 Indonesians had made their way to Middle Eastern conflict zones.[60] Notably, a significant percentage of these people are believed to be women and children.[61] Indonesians form a large contingent of Katibah Nusantara, a Southeast Asian wing of ISIS.

The growing influence of ISIS, in turn, caused a split in the Indonesian *jihadi* community. Pro-ISIS elements include followers of the late Poso-based *jihadi* leader, Abu Wardah Santoso, as well as Aman Abdurrahman, who is currently incarcerated but has translated ISIS material into Indonesian for mass consumption while behind bars. Others, however, have also claimed the mantle of leadership for "ISIS Indonesia," including Bahrum Naim, the alleged mastermind behind a foiled 2016 terror plot on Singapore's Marina Bay Sands. Naim, a trained engineer, is known to have been instrumental in drawing Malaysian recruits to ISIS.[62] Naim was killed in a U.S. drone strike as he was riding a motorcycle in Ash Shafa, Syria.

A comparatively recent wave of violence triggered fresh concerns for the growing threat posed by pro-ISIS groups and individuals in Indonesia. On May 8, 2018, pro-ISIS detainees at a Jakarta detention center staged a riot in which five police officers were killed. Five days later, several members of one family launched coordinated attacks on three churches in Surabaya.[63] Troublingly, children – including one girl as young as nine – participated in the attack. That same evening, a mother and son were killed when their husband/father accidentally detonated an explosive device. A day later, another family attempted to bomb the police headquarters in Surabaya. The only survivor from that family was an eight-year-old girl. All three families were acquainted with each other and had studied under the same religious teacher who was deported from Turkey back to Indonesia for attempting to join the Islamic State.[64]

Another major problem is the issue of ISIS returnees. Indonesian counter-terrorism officials stated in 2019 that Indonesia would allow Indonesian ISIS members to return home on condition that they renounce radicalism.[65] In January 2020, however, Indonesia reversed this policy and will now no longer take back the 600 or more Indonesian ISIS members and their families.[66] The role of women in these activities is being scrutinized, as they are believed to have played a major role in radicalization.[67] Several Indonesian ISIS members are currently in Kurdish jails or in refugee camps.[68] ISIS returnees could be viewed as a security threat after eight ISIS-linked terrorists were arrested in a foiled bid to stage a series of bombings during the announcement of the April 2019 election results. The eight arrested are affiliated with to Jamaah Anshar Daulah, which had pledged allegiance to ISIS.[69]

Islamism and Society

During the global Islamic resurgence of the 1960s and 1970s, numerous Indonesian students made their way to the great Islamic learning centers of the Arab world. Locally, an Islamic *dawa* (proselytization) movement began in Bandung around the campus-based Salman mosque and soon spread across the country to other educational institutions. This movement was organized around study groups modeled after the Egyptian Muslim Brotherhood. The related *tarbiyah* movement began in the early 1980s at various university campuses.[70] The legacy of this process remains evident today in the increased social activism of the country's various Muslim communities. One of the lasting impacts of the *tarbiyah* movement was to involve itself in the institution of marriages, aiming to ensure that families and any children born within them would be guided by its tenets and perspective. Followers of this movement believe that Islam is a total way of life and the utilization of *usrah* (groups) for the spread of their ideology is key.[71]

A driving force behind the *dawa* movement was the suppression of Islamist intellectuals. The Suharto administration placed substantial restrictions on the political aspirations of popular, socially active Muslim groups, like the NU and Muhammadiyah, to the point that they were effectively de-politicized. More conservative Muslims were also concerned about the increasing assertiveness of what was thought to be "liberal" Islamic ideas in Indonesian society:

> "the general mass media, as another manifestation of the public sphere, tended to serve as the state ideological apparatus in championing modernization. The media was thus preconditioned to be sympathetic to the renewal movement. Realizing that the public sphere was hostile to their ideo-political aspirations, the Islamist intellectuals created a subtle and fluid social movement, which was relatively impervious to state control, as a new foundation for constructing collective solidarity and identity."[72]

The works of early prominent Brotherhood members focused on closed groups, networking, piety, and, ultimately, the establishment of an Islamic state based on *sharia*. However, it was not until the late 1970s that these ideas and organizational techniques began to win a sizeable following. Indonesian Islamist leaders learned these ideas mainly through Indonesian translations of books written by Ikhwan activists. Critically, Hasan al-Banna's ideas of beginning the

Islamization process by focusing on the family and removing non-Islamic influences from national society had a deep impact.

Meanwhile, an influx of financial support from Saudi Arabia beginning in the mid-1970s created an alternative strain of Salafism.[73] The College of Islamic and Arabic (more commonly known by its Indonesian acronym, LIPIA), formed in 1980, popularized this form. The curriculum in LIPIA hews closely to Saudi versions of Salafist theology and ideology, with an emphasis on the teachings of Ibn Abdul Wahab, Ibn Taymiyyah, and the Hanbali school of classical Islamic jurisprudence. LIPIA has strong institutional links to the Imam Muhammad ibn Saud Islamic University in Riyadh and is strictly monitored by the Saudi embassy in Jakarta. Its management has Saudi nationals in key positions. Alumni include Aman Abdurrahman, Islamic Defenders Front (FPI) leader Rizieq Syihab, and PKS leader Anis Matta, among other notables. Several leading Indonesian politicians have pursued higher Islamic education funded by Saudi money in the Islamic University of Madinah.[74] Saudi funding for Indonesian boarding schools has also increased in the last decade or so, enabling Indonesian students to study at, for instance, the Maududi Institute in Lahore, Pakistan.[75]

It was Indonesia's fifth Prime Minister, Mohammad Natsir, and his organization, the DDII, that was chiefly responsible for encouraging Islamic student activism in Indonesian universities.[76] While it is difficult to establish the extent of Natsir's relationship with *Ikhwan* and *Jamaat* leaders, it is clear that he helped facilitate the travel of Indonesian students to *Ikhwan* and *Jamaat*-dominated universities in the Middle East and Pakistan. He was also responsible for introducing the *Ikhwan*'s religio-political ideas and methods of organization to Muslim students on various campuses. It was these students who established the Lembaga Dakwah Kampus (LDK, or Campus Proselytising Network) and the Kesatuan Aksi Mahasiswa Muslim Indonesia, (KAMMI, or "Indonesian Muslim Undergraduate Action Association"). With the collapse of the New Order regime, KAMMI activists formed what would become the PKS. The PKS maintains strong links with the broader transnational Salafi network.

Wahhabbi ideology has made inroads into Indonesia since the 1960s via the building of mosques, paying preachers, and sending missionaries, as well as subsidizing generous scholarships and building a tuition-free university system. The followers of *Wahhabbism* believe that Muslim society must first be Islamized through a gradual evolutionary process that includes *tarbiyah* and *tasfiyyah* (purification) before *sharia* can be fully implemented. They are fervently committed to *dawa* activities, such as participating in the creation of *halaqah* (Islamic study groups) and *daurah* (Islamic courses).

Following the *Wahhabbi* tradition, the *tarbiyah* movement has organized Islamic teachings in schools and universities, the study of jurisprudence for women, tutorial study, and the translation of Islamic books. They study Islam intensively, proselytize, train proselytization coaches, and host intensive events focused on Islamization. In this fashion, the movement seeks to influence Indonesian youth by demonstrating growing piety in society.

The Saudi government has influenced Indonesian politics in a number of ways. It provides Indonesia's neighbours, such as Malaysia, with financial commitments like investing in Malaysia's oil and gas company, Petronas. This creates competition for Indonesia within its regional sphere. Further, its aforementioned funding for religious universities and scholarships for Indonesian students to study in Saudi Arabia has only become more generous over time.[77]

Alternative patterns of thinking were also emerging within the Indonesian Muslim community. During the late 1970s and early 1980, people—particularly younger intellectuals—sought to recalibrate Islam's role in Indonesian society. This phenomenon, initially called *gerakan pembaruan* (the "reform movement") and more recently, *Islam kultural* ("cultural Islam"), consciously rejected the aspirations of Islamist parties and sought to redefine Indonesian Islam as apolitical and cultural. Among the chief proponents of this movement were former president Abdurrahman Wahid and the late Nurcholish Madjid.[78]

Cultural Islam has been critical of political Islam (or Islamist activism) in several ways. The success experienced by Islamist parties is limited, and they have not been able to unite Muslims politically or garner a majority of votes in general elections; they also have not succeeded in getting Islamic laws implemented. Many proponents of cultural Islam repudiate the concept of an Islamic state, arguing that the Quran contains no prescription for the structure of the state. Instead, they support *Pancasila*, asserting that it is consistent with Islamic principles. They dispute the sentiment that Muslims should only support Islamic parties, arguing that pluralist, "deconfessionalized," parties were not less virtuous.[79] A 2013 Pew Research survey on Muslim belief in *sharia* revealed that, while 72 percent of polled Indonesians believed that *sharia* should be the law of the land, they wanted it limited to property and domestic disputes and were deeply divided on if it should apply to non-Muslims.[80]

The democratization of Indonesia was critical to expanding the space for Islamic discourse and activism. Along with the proliferation of faith-based political parties, Islamic civil society groups also emerged (including the aforementioned radical organizations). This included Muslim groups whose interpretations of Islamic scripture were deemed unorthodox by the mainstream. One such movement was the Liberal Islam Network, a movement that shunned received wisdom and encouraged critical thinking. Formed in early 2001, it has come under heavy criticism from fundamentalist quarters in the Indonesian Muslim intellectual community. At the same time, the movement has an uneasy relationship with more moderate organizations such as the NU.[81]

Instances of hostility and even violence perpetrated by more extremist Muslim groups against fringe organizations are also concerning. For example, on January 28, 2011, members of the FPI attacked an *Ahmadiyah* mosque in Makassar and forced the congregation to evacuate the premises before destroying their property.[82] Since then, attacks on *Ahmadiyah* places of worship and members by Muslim vigilante groups, such as FPI, have become more frequent. The last two presidential administrations have often proved unable or unwilling to stifle the violence; in 2017, the *Ahmadiyah* community in Manislor district protested against a local administrative rule that effectively required them to renounce their faith to get identification cards (the *Ahmadiyah* Islamic sect is not recognized as a religion according to Indonesia's 1965 blasphemy laws,[83] and the national ID form requires one to state their religion).

These cards are required to register marriages or to be treated at local hospitals.

It was in this climate that, at its annual convention in August 2015, the NU formally introduced the concept of "Islam Nusantara" or "Islam of the archipelago" into the discourse of Indonesian Islamic thought and practice. Islam Nusantara is predicated on the promotion of peace, moderation, and tolerance. Despite the ambiguity surrounding the concept, ambitious Indonesian leaders such as Said Aqil Siradj have suggested that Islam Nusantara could potentially take on a transnational character and be embraced and practiced by Muslims globally.

Islam Nusantara is itself not without controversy, however. Not only are the expansionist aspirations of its progenitors far too ambitious, the legitimacy of the concept itself remains debated within Indonesian circles, including among NU leaders themselves. Conservative critics of Islam Nusantara have dismissed it as *bida'a* (innovation), which is forbidden in Islam. Others have criticized it as the contamination of "pure" Islam by Indonesia's dominant Javanese culture.

However, while most observers consider the NU and Muhammadiyah to be the guardians of Islamic moderation in Indonesia, there are signs that these organizations are themselves coming under the influence of growing Islamic conservatism. Conservative clerics and activists took over the leadership of both organizations in 2005, forcing out progressive and moderate activists from positions of leadership. Even though moderates have since regained senior leadership posts in both movements, serious questions their future trajectories still abound. Tens of thousands of NU and Muhammadiyah activists joined the Defending Islam rallies in 2017, openly defying the senior leadership of both organizations, who urged them not to participate. Reports of young Muhammadiyah and NU members joining Islamist and Salafist groups are also frequently reported. Newly formed groups such as the 'True Path NU' (*NU Garis Lurus*), which was founded by young NU clerics who recently graduated from advanced Islamic studies programs in the Middle East, seek to remove any influence of 'liberal' and 'pluralist' teachings from the organization.[84]

Indonesia's reputation for religious tolerance suffered a notable blow in 2016. Radical groups staged two massive rallies calling for the conviction of Jakarta's incumbent governor, Basuki "Ahok" Tjahaja Purnama, for blasphemy against the Quran. Under pressure from this Muslim social movement, the Indonesian government made the decision to distance itself from "Ahok" and limited its intervention to calls for restraint.[85] "Ahok" was subsequently defeated in the election's second round by his political challenger, Anies Baswedan, a former education minister known to be a liberal but who nevertheless seized the opportunity to utilize these conservative Islamic forces. "Ahok" was later convicted of the crime of blasphemy and sentenced to two years imprisonment.[86] The Chairman of the ASEAN Parliamentarians for Human Rights (APHR), Charles Santiago, remarked at the time that, "Indonesia was thought to be a regional leader in terms of democracy and openness. This decision places that position in jeopardy and raises concerns about Indonesia's future as an open, tolerant, diverse society."[87]

The episode involving "Ahok" suggests that religious identity politics can be successful in Indonesia. In the 2019 general elections, Islam played a major role in deciding the winners. Incumbent president Jokowi won another term, not only because he boosted Indonesia's economy but also because he simultaneously developed closer relations with Muslim clerics.[88] Both instances suggest that there are segments of the Indonesian Muslim population for whom religious identity (in particular more conservative expressions of it) is playing an increasingly important role.

Islamism and the State

Indonesia's political and constitutional history reveals that divisive debates surround the formal role of Islam in the state and *sharia's* position in the constitution. Much of this debate focused on the Jakarta Charter, an agreement struck between Muslim and nationalist leaders on June 22, 1945 as part of the preparations for Indonesia's independence. The most controversial part of the charter was a seven-word clause: "with the obligation for adherents of Islam to practice Islamic law" (*dengan kewajipan menjalankan syari'at Islam bagi pemeluk-pemeluknya*). Further, Islamic leaders succeeded in having a stipulation inserted into the draft constitution that mandated the president be a Muslim. However, both this mandate and the seven-word clause were dropped from the constitution two months after the initial agreement.

The domestic resurgence of politically moderate Islam put greater pressure on the government. Suharto extended greater aid to the country's Muslim community in the late 1980s, increasing state subsidies for mosque building, Islamic education, Muslim television programming, the celebration of religious holidays, and preferential treatment for Muslim entrepreneurs in state contracts. He lifted a ban on the veil in state schools and imposed tighter restrictions on the activities of Christian missionaries. The president even went as far as to sponsor an Islamic faction in the armed forces, previously a bastion of conservative secular nationalism.[89] Perhaps most prominent among the slew of legislative and institutional concessions was "the expansion of the authority of religious courts in 1989, the establishment of the Indonesian Muslim Intellectuals association (ICMI) in 1990, lifting of the ban on female state school students wearing hijabs in 1991, the upgrading of government involvement in alms collection and distribution, the founding of an Islamic bank (BMI) in 1992, and the abolition of the state lottery (SDSB) in 1993."[90]

The end of Suharto's rule did not spell the end of efforts to exploit religious tensions for political advantage. After May 1998, in the wake of post-Suharto democratization, several politicians appealed to ethno-religious sentiments in order to enhance their credentials. The tactic had an especially bloody consequence in Maluku, Central Kalimantan, and Sulawesi, upsetting a delicate demographic balance between Christians and Muslims with the rise of sectarian paramilitaries and bloody campaigns of ethnic cleansing.

Sharia implementation appears to be gaining some traction at the regional level. In the north Sumatran province of Aceh, *sharia* was promulgated under special autonomy laws in early 2002. Yet there is intense debate within the local Islamic community over the scope of the laws and the details of their implementation. The *sharia* issue has also attracted strong support from Muslim groups in South

Sulawesi, West Sumatra and Banten, but is still far short of receiving majority support. In a number of districts in West Java, *sharia* has been implemented in a *de facto* fashion by local Muslim groups, often in concert with district government officials and Ulama.[91]

At least in the case of Aceh, it bears noting that the prevalence *sharia*-inspired laws and by-laws reflects a compromise between the Indonesian government and the separatist Free Aceh Movement, whereby *sharia* law was introduced as part of a deal to appease the latter.[92] However, there has been very little evidence to suggest that the Indonesian government intends to slow down – let alone stop – this gradual *sharia*-ization, despite multiple critics pointing out that it runs counter to the nation's secular constitution. There are also reports that radical Muslim elements have infiltrated Indonesia's bureaucracy and military and will bring pressure upon Jokowi to adopt more strict Islamic principles as part of its state philosophy in the future.[93]

Endnotes

1. Ana Salva, "Aceh Indonesia: When Dating Meets Sharia Law", *The Diplomat*, July 24, 2019,https://thediplomat.com/2019/07/aceh-indonesia-when-dating-meets-sharia-law/.
2. Anies Rasyid Baswedan, "Political Islam in Indonesia: Present and Future Trajectory," *Asian Survey* 44, no. 5 (October 2004), 675.
3. Noorhaidi Hasan, "Islamist Party, Electoral Politics, and Da'wa Mobilization among Youth: The Prosperous Justice Party (PKS) in Indonesia," RSIS Working Paper, no. 184, October 22, 2009, https://www.rsis.edu.sg/wp-content/uploads/rsis-pubs/WP184.pdf.
4. Masdar Hilmy, *Islamism and Democracy in Indonesia Piety and Pragmatism* (Singapore: Institute of Southeast Asian Studies, 2010), 183.
5. Baswedan, "Political Islam in Indonesia: Present and Future Trajectory," 677.
6. R. William Liddle and Saiful Mujani, "Indonesia in 2004: The Rise of Susilo Bambang Yudhoyono," *Asian Survey* 45, no. 1 (January 2005), 123.
7. Embassy of the Republic of Indonesia, Bucharest, Romania, "The Republic of Indonesia," n.d., http://www.indonezia.ro/republic.htm.
8. Embassy of the Republic of Indonesia, Bucharest, Romania, "The

Republic of Indonesia," n.d., http://www.indonezia.ro/republic.htm.
9. Beritasatu Team & Telly Nathalia, "Jokowi Wins Re-Election, PDI-P Wins Most Seats," *Jakarta Post*, May 21, 2019, https://jakartaglobe.id/context/jokowi-wins-reelection-pdip-wins-most-seats.
10. "The House of Representatives of the Republic of Indonesia," n.d., http://www.dpr.go.id/en/tentang/fraksi
11. Liddle and Mujani, "Indonesia in 2004," 121.
12. "Indonesia: Twitter Defamation Case Casts Shadow on Media Landscape," *Global Voices*, February 7, 2014, https://advox.globalvoices.org/2014/02/07/indonesia-twitter-defamation-case-casts-shadow-on-media-landscape/
13. "Anti-Porn Indonesian MP Watches Porn, Resigns," *CBS*, April 11, 2011, https://www.cbsnews.com/news/anti-porn-indonesian-mp-watches-porn-resigns/.
14. Karina M. Tehussijarana and Nurul Fitri Ramadhani, "PKS Campaign Pledge to Pass 'Ulema Protection' Bill Draws Criticism," *Jakarta Post*, January 21, 2019, https://www.thejakartapost.com/news/2019/01/21/pks-campaign-pledge-to-pass-ulema-protection-bill-draws-criticism.html.
15. John McBeth, "Complex Political Calculus behind Widodo 2.0," *Asia Times*, June 20, 2019, https://www.asiatimes.com/2019/06/article/complex-political-calculus-behind-widodo-2-0/.
16. "Muhaimim reelected as PKB Chairman," *Jakarta Post*, August 21, 2019, https://www.thejakartapost.com/news/2019/08/21/muhaimin-reelected-as-pkb-chairman.html.
17. "NU: Voting for non-Muslim leader is allowed," *Tempo*, March 13, 2017.
18. Joe Cochrane, "From Indonesia, A Muslim Challenge to the Ideology of the Islamic State," *New York Times*, November 26, 2015, https://www.nytimes.com/2015/11/27/world/asia/indonesia-islam-nahdlatul-ulama.html.
19. Stephen Sherlock, *The 2004 Indonesian Elections: How the System Works and What the Parties Stand For* (Canberra: Centre for Democratic Institutions, Research School of Social Sciences, Australian National University, 2004), 32.
20. Stephen Sherlock, *The 2004 Indonesian Elections: How the System Works and What the Parties Stand For* (Canberra: Centre for Democratic Institutions, Research School of Social Sciences, Australian National University, 2004), 17.
21. "Breaking the Cycle of Corruption," *Jakarta Post*, March 18, 2019, https://www.thejakartapost.com/academia/2019/03/18/break-

ing-the-cycle-of-corruption.html.

22. Anies Rasyid Baswedan, "Political Islam in Indonesia: Present and Future Trajectory," *Asian Survey* 44 no. 5 (September-October 2004), 669-690.
23. Erin Cook, "Indonesia's Hizbut Tahrir Debate Rages on Amid Election Fever," *The Diplomat*, May 12, 2018, https://thediplomat.com/2018/05/indonesias-hizbut-tahrir-debate-rages-on-amid-election-fever/.
24. Isthiaq Ahmed, ed., *The Politics of Religion in South and Southeast Asia* (London and New York, 2011), 144.
25. Isthiaq Ahmed, ed., *The Politics of Religion in South and Southeast Asia* (London and New York, 2011), 144.
26. Sherlock, *The 2004 Indonesian Elections,* 17.
27. Telly Nathalia and Olivia Rondonuwu, "Indonesian Police Detain Hardliners for Rally Attacks," Reuters, June 4, 2008, https://www.reuters.com/article/idUSJAK70423.
28. Noorhaidi, "Lashkar Jihad: Islam, Militancy and the Quest for Identity in Post-New Order Indonesia," June 14, 2005, 6, https://core.ac.uk/download/pdf/15601106.pdf.
29. Hesti Wulandari, "Religion Industrial Complex in Indonesia," Lulu.com, 2014, https://www.lulu.com/shop/hesti-wulandari/religion-industrial-complex-in-indonesia/paperback/product-21445229.html?ppn=1; Hesti Wulandari, *Religion Industrial Complex: Commodification through Religious Exploitation* (Critical Study of Religious Opportunist Group in Indonesia), University of Indonesia, 2012, updated 2014, http://lib.ui.ac.id/file?file=digital/20319767-S-Hesti%20Wulandari.pdf.
30. Noorhaidi, "Lashkar Jihad: Islam, Militancy and the Quest for Identity in Post-New Order Indonesia," 4.
31. M. Rizieq Syihab, *Kyai Kampung: Ujung Tombak Perjuangan Umat Islam* (Ciputat: Sekretariat FPI, 1999).
32. "Police Question Rights Body Over FPI Attack," *Jakarta Post*, May 26, 2010.
33. "Indonesia's Muslim militants," *BBC* (London), August 8, 2003, http://news.bbc.co.uk/2/hi/asia-pacific/2333085.stm.
34. Greg Fealy, "Bigger than Ahok: Explaining the 2 December Rally," Indonesia at Melbourne, December 7, 2016, http://indonesiaatmelbourne.unimelb.edu.au/bigger-than-ahok-explaining-jakartas-2-december-mass-rally/.
35. "FPI Leader Rizieq Shihab Claims Gov't is 'Blocking' Him from Returning to Indonesia, Gov't: Prove it," *Coconuts Jakarta*, August

26, 2019, https://coconuts.co/jakarta/news/fpi-leader-rizieq-shihab-claims-govt-is-blocking-him-from-returning-to-indonesia-govt-prove-it/.

36. Karina M. Tehusijarana, "FPI Finds Itself Out of Government Favor," *Jakarta Post*, August 14, 2019, https://www.thejakartapost.com/news/2019/08/13/fpi-finds-itself-out-of-government-favor.html.
37. Salafis are those who attempt to reform Islam by taking it away from its traditional association with syncretism and re-orienting it towards scripturalism. Henri Lauzière, *The Making of Salafism: Islamic Reform in the Twentieth Century* (New York: Columbia University Press, 2015).
38. Scott Helfstein, " Radical Islamic Ideology in Southeast Asia," Combating Terrorism Center at West Point, 2009, https://www.hsdl.org/?view&did=718972.
39. Noorhaidi, "Lashkar Jihad: Islam, Militancy and the Quest for Identity in Post-New Order Indonesia."
40. Christopher J. Van Der Krogt, "Lashkar Jihad: Islam, Militancy, and the Quest for Identity in Post-New Order Indonesia," *Journal of Religious History*, 36 no. 3 (September 2012), 459-461.
41. See Kirsten E. Schulze, "Laskar Jihad and the Conflict in Ambon," *Brown Journal of World Affairs* 9, iss.1 (Spring 2002).
42. Noorhaidi, *Laskar Jihad: Islam, militancy and the quest for identity in post-New Order Indonesia* (Utrecht: Utrecht University, 2005), 6, https://dspace.library.uu.nl/handle/1874/10280.
43. Noorhaidi, *Laskar Jihad: Islam, militancy and the quest for identity in post-New Order Indonesia* (Utrecht: Utrecht University, 2005), 6, https://dspace.library.uu.nl/handle/1874/10280.
44. See Martin van Bruinessen, "Genealogies of Islamic Radicalism in Post-Suharto Indonesia," in Joseph Chinyong Liow and Nadirsyah Hosen (eds.), *Islam in Southeast Asia* vol. IV (London: Routledge, 2009), 52-53.
45. Noorhaidi, "Lashkar Jihad: Islam, Militancy and the Quest for Identity in Post-New Order Indonesia," 7.
46. U.S. Department of State, "Chapter 16 Table of Contents," *Digest of United States Practice in International Law*, n.d, 650, https://www.state.gov/wp-content/uploads/2019/05/2017-Digest-Chapter-16.pdf.
47. United Nations Security Council, "Muhammad Jibril Abdul Rahman", August 12, 2011, https://www.un.org/securitycouncil/sanctions/1267/aq_sanctions_list/summaries/individual/muhammad-jibril-abdul-rahman.
48. Saiful Umam, "Radical Muslims in Indonesia: The case of Ja'far

Umar Thalib and the Laskar Jihad," *Explorations*, vol. 6, no. 1, 2006, 1-26, https://scholarspace.manoa.hawaii.edu/handle/10125/2255.

49. Saiful Umam, "Radical Muslims in Indonesia: The case of Ja'far Umar Thalib and the Laskar Jihad," *Explorations*, vol. 6, no. 1, 2006, 1-26, https://scholarspace.manoa.hawaii.edu/handle/10125/2255.
50. Alex Arifianto, "Banning Hizbut Tahrir Indonesia: Freedom or Security?" RSIS Commentaries, May 18, 2017. https://www.rsis.edu.sg/rsis-publication/rsis/co17099-banning-hizbut-tahrir-indonesia-freedom-or-security/#.WVNbrk2QyM8.
51. Kate Lamb, "Jakarta court rejects attempt by Hizb ut-Tahrir to reverse its ban," *Guardian* (London), May 7, 2018, https://www.theguardian.com/world/2018/may/07/indonesia-jakarta-court-rejects-hizb-ut-tahrir-attempt-to-reverse-ban.
52. Sydney Jones, "Darul Islam's Ongoing Appeal," *International Crisis Group*, August 18, 2010, https://www.crisisgroup.org/asia/south-east-asia/indonesia/darul-islam-s-ongoing-appeal.
53. Greg Fealy and Virginia Hooker, eds, *Voices of Islam in Southeast Asia: A Contemporary Source Book* (ISEAS Online Publication, 2006), https://bookshop.iseas.edu.sg/publication/317.
54. Niniek Karmani, "Study: Extremists Still Flourishing in Indonesia's Prisons," Associated Press, February 9, 2018, https://apnews.com/b1d8e7bf7c9f49448410f6ac0b7919cc/Study:-Extremists-still-flourishing-in-Indonesia's-prisons.
55. "Indonesia Arrests Alleged Jemaah Islamiah Terrorist Network Leader Para Wijayanto," *ABC News*, July 1, 2019, https://www.abc.net.au/news/2019-07-02/indonesian-police-arrest-jemaah-islamiyah-network-leader/11269286.
56. Abu Bakr Bashir Must Renounce Radicalism before Release, Says Indonesia", *Guardian* (London), January 22, 2019, https://www.theguardian.com/world/2019/jan/23/abu-bakar-bashir-must-renounce-radicalism-before-release-says-indonesia.
57. Angus Watson and Lauren Said-Moorehouse, "Alleged 'Spiritual Leader' of the Group Behind the 2002 Bali Bombings Will Be Freed," *CNN*, January 18, 2019, https://www.cnn.com/2019/01/18/asia/indonesian-cleric-released-intl/index.html.
58. Anne Barker, "Joko Widodo between a Rock and a Hard Place over Terrorist Abu Bakar Bashir's Release," *ABC*, January 22, 2019, https://www.abc.net.au/news/2019-01-23/joko-widodo-in-dilemma-after-touting-abu-bakar-bashir-release/10737900.
59. Sidney Jones, "Battling ISIS in *Indonesia*," *New York Times*, January 18, 2016, http://www.nytimes.com/2016/01/19/opinion/bat-

tling-isis-in-indonesia.html?_r=0.

60. *Foreign Fighters: An Updated Assessment of the Flow of Foreign Fighters into Syria and Iraq,* The Soufan Group, December 2015, 8, http://soufangroup.com/wpcontent/uploads/2015/12/TSG_Foreign-FightersUpdate4.pdf.
61. The respected observer of extremism in Indonesia, Sidney Jones, estimates that up to 40 percent of Indonesians in Syria and Iraq are women and children under the age of 15. See Sidney Jones, "The Shifting Extremist Threat in Southeast Asia," UBC School of Public Policy and Global Affairs, October 2017, https://sppga.ubc.ca/wp-content/uploads/sites/5/2017/10/16-Sidney-Jones.pdf.
62. Amy Chew, "Slain Indonesian IS Leader Bahrum Naim Recruited Malaysians to Launch Terror Attacks on Country," *Channel News Asia*, July 13, 2018, https://www.channelnewsasia.com/news/asia/indonesian-islamic-state-leader-bahrum-naim-recruited-malaysians-10528876.
63. Ben Otto and I Made Sentana. "Family of Suicide Bombers Attacks Churches in Indonesia," *Wall Street Journal*, May 13, 2018, https://www.wsj.com/articles/bomb-attacks-rock-three-indonesia-churches-1526177568.
64. Sidney Jones, "How ISIS has changed terrorism in Indonesia," *New York Times*, May 22, 2018.
65. John McBeth, "ISIS Headed Home to Indonesia," *Asia Times*, June 21, 2019, https://asiatimes.com/2019/06/isis-headed-home-to-indonesia/.
66. Wahyudi Soeriaatmadja, "Indonesia Refuses to let ISIS Fighters and their Families Return Home," *Straits Times*, February 11, 2020, https://www.straitstimes.com/asia/se-asia/indonesia-refuses-to-let-isis-fighters-and-their-families-to-return-home.
67. Ana P. Santos, "In Indonesia, Women are now a permanent part of the Jihadi Structure," *World Politics Review*, November 1, 2019, https://pulitzercenter.org/reporting/indonesia-women-are-now-permanent-part-jihadi-structure.
68. McBeth, "ISIS Headed Home for Indonesia."
69. "Indonesia Arrest 8 Suspects in ISIS-Linked Election Bomb Plot," *Defense Post*, May 7, 2019, https://thedefensepost.com/2019/05/07/indonesia-isis-bomb-plot-election/.
70. Andreas Ufen, "Mobilising Political Islam: Indonesia and Malaysia Compared," *Commonwealth & Comparative Politics* 47, no. 3 (2009), 316. For further reading on the *dakwah* movements and *tarbiyah* movements, see Yudi Latif, "The Rupture of Young Muslim

Intelligentsia in the Modernization of Indonesia," *Studia Islamika* 12, no. 3 (2005), 373-420, and Salman, "The Tarbiyah Movement: Why People Join This Indonesian Contemporary Islamic Movement," *Studia Islamika* 13, no. 2 (2006), 171-240.

71. Suaidi Asyani and M. Hasnul Abid, "Expanding the Indonesian Tarbiyah Movement through Ta'aruf and Marriage", *Al-Jāmi'ah: Journal of Islamic Studies* vol. 54, no. 2 (2016), 337-368, https://pdfs.semanticscholar.org/df31/be2b14e2fb457b4e6a5db64a3435fa6b0de1.pdf.
72. Latif, "The Rupture of Young Muslim Intelligentsia in the Modernization of Indonesia," 391. Some scholars refer to the renewal movement (*gerakan pembaharuan*) as reform movement (*gerakan pembaruan*).
73. Fred R. von der Mehden, *"Saudi Religious Influence in Indonesia," Middle East Institute*, December 1, 2014. http://www.mei.edu/content/map/saudi-religious-influence-indonesia.
74. Asmiati Malik and Scot Edwards, "Saudi Arabia's Influence in Southeast Asia: Too Embedded to be Disrupted?", *The Conversation*, November 8, 2018, https://theconversation.com/saudi-arabias-influence-in-southeast-asia-too-embedded-to-be-disrupted-106543.
75. Carolyn Nash, "Saudi Arabia's Soft Power Strategy in Indonesia," Middle East Institute, April 3, 2018, https://www.mei.edu/publications/saudi-arabias-soft-power-strategy-indonesia.
76. Any Muhammad Furkon, *Partai Keadilan Sejahtera: Ideologi dan Praksis Kaum Muda Muslim Indonesia Kontemporer* (Jakarta: Penerbit Terajau, 2004), 124.
77. Krithika Varagur," How Saudi Arabia's Religious Project Transformed Indonesia," *Guardian* (London), April 16, 2020, https://www.theguardian.com/news/2020/apr/16/how-saudi-arabia-religious-project-transformed-indonesia-islam.
78. Greg Fealy, "Divided Majority: Limits of Indonesian Political Islam," in Shahram Akbarzadeh and Abdullah Saeed, eds., *Islam and Political Legitimacy* (London: RoutledgeCurzon, 2003), 161.
79. Greg Fealy, "Divided Majority: Limits of Indonesian Political Islam," in Shahram Akbarzadeh and Abdullah Saeed, eds., *Islam and Political Legitimacy* (London: RoutledgeCurzon, 2003), 162.
80. Pew Research Center, "Chapter 1: Beliefs about Sharia," April 30, 2013, https://www.pewforum.org/2013/04/30/the-worlds-muslims-religion-politics-society-beliefs-about-sharia/; Michael Lipka, "Muslims and Islam: Key findings in the U.S. and around the world," Pew Research Center *FactTank*, August 9, 2017, https://www.pewre-

search.org/fact-tank/2017/08/09/muslims-and-islam-key-findings-in-the-u-s-and-around-the-world/.

81. Anita Rachman, "Fundamental differences to the fore at NU meeting," *Jakarta Globe*, March 25, 2010.
82. Hadianto Wirajuda, "Ahmadiyah attack a threat to Indonesia's democracy," *Jakarta Post*, February 10, 2011.
83. "Indonesia's Blasphemy Laws," *The Economist*, November 24, 2016, https://www.economist.com/the-economist-explains/2016/11/24/indonesias-blasphemy-laws.
84. "Islam Nusantara and its Critics: The Rise of NU's Young Clerics-Analysis," *Eurasia Review*, January 24, 2017, https://www.eurasiareview.com/24012017-islam-nusantara-and-its-critics-the-rise-of-nus-young-clerics-analysis/.
85. Greg Fealy, "Bigger than Ahok: Explaining the 2 December Rally," Indonesia at Melbourne, December 7, 2016, http://indonesiaatmelbourne.unimelb.edu.au/bigger-than-ahok-explaining-jakartas-2-december-mass-rally/.
86. Anggun Wijaya Callistasia, "Ahok guilty of blasphemy, sentenced to two years," *Jakarta Post*, May 9, 2017.
87. Fergus Jensen and Fransiska Nangoy, "Jakarta's Christian Governor Jailed for Blasphemy Against Islam," Reuters, May 8, 2017, https://www.reuters.com/article/us-indonesia-politics/jakartas-christian-governor-jailed-for-blasphemy-against-islam-idUSKBN1842GE.
88. Tripti Lahiri, "Another Big Democracy is Voting Amid a Deepening Divide Around Religion," *Quartz,* April 16, 2019, https://qz.com/1596853/indonesia-election-another-large-diverse-democracy-sees-religious-divides-deepen/.
89. Hefner, "State, Society, and Secularity in Contemporary Indonesia."
90. Fealy, "Divided Majority: Limits of Indonesian Political Islam," 163.
91. Fealy, "Divided Majority: Limits of Indonesian Political Islam," 164-165.
92. Dewi Kurniati, "Shariah in Aceh: Eroding Indonesia's secular freedoms," *Jakarta Globe*, August 18, 2010.
93. Konradus Epa, "At Least 12, 000 in Indonesian military 'back hardline Islam', *UCA News*, June 21, 2019, https://www.ucanews.com/news/at-least-12-000-in-indonesian-military-back-hard-line-islam/85469; Amy Chew, "Indonesia's Ma'ruf Amin to Fight Radicalisation that has spread from 'play groups to government," *South China Morning Post*, November 29, 2019, https://www.scmp.com/week-asia/politics/article/3039821/indonesia-appoints-vice-president-and-muslim-cleric-maruf-amin.

60 Malaysia

Quick Facts

Population: 32,652,083 (July 2020 est.)
Area: 329,847 sq km
Ethnic Groups: Bumiputera 62% (Malays and indigenous peoples, including Orang Asli, Dayak, Anak Negeri), Chinese 20.6%, Indian 6.2%, other 0.9%, non-citizens 10.3% (2017 est.)
Government Type: Federal parliamentary constitutional monarchy
GDP (official exchange rate): $312.4 billion (2017 est.)

Source: CIA World FactBook (Last Updated November 2020)

Introduction

Malaysia has long been viewed as a pro-Western, moderate Muslim-majority country. In recent years, however, it has experienced a shift toward Islamic conservatism, as evidenced by the increasing popularity of sharia law, the state-sanctioned suppression of civil rights and liberties, and moral policing by Islamic religious authorities. While a 2018 election victory for the country's then so-called Pakatan Harapan (PH) opposition coalition had initially raised hopes for a more inclusive, multicultural turn, political shifts since then, along with wider trends, have dampened such hopes.

Islam's increased visibility in Malaysian society and politics in recent years has been driven not only by the Islamist Parti Islam Se-Malaysia (Islamic Party of Malaysia, or PAS), but also by the United Malays National Organization (UMNO), whose members were also the architects of Malaysia's brand of progressive, moderate Islam.[1] *Likewise, alternative actors increasingly participate in Malaysia's politicization of Islam, at times eclipsing mainstream political parties. Islam in Malaysia is arguably fragmented and variegated in both substance and expression, with religious vocabulary and idioms being mobilized by the state, opposition forces, and a wide array of civil society groups. While Malaysian Islamists nominally operate within the boundaries of the country's mainstream political processes, they also work to define them. Moreover, even as the*

Muslim opposition attempts to shed its doctrine in pursuit of a reform agenda, the "moderate" UMNO-led government seeks to constrict the country's cultural and religious space. Many assumed that PH's recent electoral triumph signaled a greater willingness to promote a moderate, multicultural agenda. However, recent political upheavals have undermined the PH's efforts while promoting PAS to a position of power within a newly formed coalition.

ENDNOTES

1. Consider, for example, how former UMNO president and Malaysian prime minister Abdullah Badawi regularly made references to Islam in his public speeches, or how *Mingguan Malaysia [Malaysia Weekly*], a best-selling government-linked daily, has weekend columns offering advice on various matters pertaining to religion in everyday life. Malaysia has also regularly hit the country-level limit set by the Saudi government for *Hajj* pilgrims, and there is now a three-year waiting list for Malaysians wanting to make the pilgrimage.

Due to publishing constraints, this chapter is provided here only in summary form. To view the full study, please visit the online edition of the Almanac at almanac.afpc.org.

61 The Philippines

Quick Facts

Population: 109,180,815 (July 2020 est.)
Area: 300,000 sq km
Ethnic Groups: Tagalog 24.4%, Bisaya/Binisaya 11.4%, Cebuano 9.9%, Ilocano 8.8%, Hiligaynon/Ilonggo 8.4%, Bikol/Bicol 6.8%, Waray 4%, other local ethnicity 26.1%, other foreign ethnicity .1% (2010 est.)
GDP (official exchange rate): $313.6 billion (2017 est.)

Source: CIA World FactBook (Last Updated July 2020)

Intrroduction

Since 1972, the overwhelmingly Catholic nation of the Philippines has confronted long-running secessionist insurgencies from some portions of its Muslim community in the Southern islands of Mindanao and in the Sulu archipelago. A combination of endemic corruption, failing state institutions, socio-cultural marginalization, crippling poverty, and low levels of human development has fueled demands from some Muslim community members for an independent homeland. The three primary groups which supported such a separation, meanwhile, are themselves divided along tribal and ideological lines.

Since 2002, the United States has increased military assistance to the Philippine government and the Armed Forces of the Philippines (AFP). Furthermore, since 2004, the U.S. has deployed some 500 special forces personnel to the southern Philippines to provide intelligence support and training. That figure has more recently been reduced to just over 100 as a result of domestic successes by the country's security agencies in neutralizing key terrorist leaders and reining in various jihadist groups and insurgencies. Nevertheless, the AFP are hobbled by corruption, limited by outdated equipment, and often stretched too thin. These deficiencies have been ameliorated somewhat since the conclusion of the peace process with the Moro Islamic Liberation Front (MILF) in 2014, but the country still faces ongoing threats from other insurgent and radical groups.

Since 2015, the AFP has confronted Islamic State (IS) infiltration into Mindanao, as various local jihadist groups pledged allegiance to the transnational terror group. Meanwhile, Philippine President Rodrigo Duterte's almost single-minded focus on a controversial and bloody campaign against illegal drugs had served to distract his administration from the growing threat in the south, depleting finite security and intelligence community resources. As a result, the Philippines is today an increasingly weak link in Southeast Asia and a potential site for the establishment of an IS Wilayat (governorate).

Due to publishing constraints, this chapter is provided here only in summary form. To view the full study, please visit the online edition of the Almanac at almanac.afpc.org.

62 Thailand

Quick Facts

Population: 68,977,400 (July 2020 est.)
Area: 513,120 sq km
Ethnic Groups: Thai 97.5%, Burmese 1.3%, other 1.1%, unspecified <.1% (2015 est.)
GDP (official exchange rate): $455.4 billion (2017 est.)

Source: CIA World FactBook (Last Updated July 2020)

Introduction

An ethno-nationalist insurgency spearheaded by rebels representing the country's minority Malay-Muslim communities has been active in southern Thailand since January of 2004. With a history of separatist tendencies, the native Malay Muslims consider the majority Thai Buddhist government to be an occupying force. By 2017, as a result of this violent campaign, an estimated 7,000 people had died and over 10,000 people had suffered injuries.[1] *Violent incidents and fatalities have declined gradually since 2013, however, coinciding with peace dialogue and reconciliation efforts between Thailand's National Security Council and the five insurgent groups represented under a conglomerate called MARA Patani (Majlis Syura Patani or Patani Consultative Council). The MARA Patani includes several members of the most powerful Barisan Revolusi Nasional Melayu Patani (Patani-Malay National Revolutionary Front, or BRN). Despite these unofficial dialogues, however, factional violence has persisted, albeit on a more limited scale.*

After nearly two decades of conflict, prospects for a sustained and just peace remain elusive; the Buddhist-dominated national government emphasizes the indivisibility of the Thai nation-state, largely based on the values and principles of the Theravada School of Buddhism, while the Muslim minority insists on a measure of genuine political autonomy, if not self-determination.

ENDNOTES

1. "Death toll in Thailand's southern conflict hits record low," *Straits Times*, December 27, 2017, http://www.straitstimes.com/asia/se-asia/death-toll-in-thailands-southern-conflict-hits-record-low.

Due to publishing constraints, this chapter is provided here only in summary form. To view the full study, please visit the online edition of the Almanac at almanac.afpc.org.

GLOBAL MOVEMENTS

63 Al-Qaeda

Quick Facts

Geographical Areas of Operation: Afghanistan, Pakistan, Syria, Lebanon, Yemen, North Africa, and Somalia
Numerical Strength (Members): Exact numbers unknown
Leadership: Ayman al-Zawahiri
Religious Identification: Sunni Islam

Quick Facts State Department's Country Reports on Terrorism (2019)

Introduction

Born out of the anti-Soviet jihad in Afghanistan during the Cold War, al-Qaeda would grow over the ensuing decades to become one of the most prolific and consequential global terror groups to ever exist. Its mission – to form a global movement of Islamic sharia governance rooted in Wahhabi and Ikhwani religious philosophies and to wage war against the United States and its allies – has taken the cellular organization to South and Central Asia, North and Sub-Saharan Africa, North America, the South Pacific, and Europe. The organization has killed thousands of people, and instigated a now-decades old war with the events of September 11, 2001.

In contrast to its ideological progeny and current rival, the Islamic State (IS), al-Qaeda tries to blend in with the societies it eventually seeks to politically co-opt. This has led to the formation of several satellite organizations, each of which operate at various capacities and different capabilities. After a period of relative inactivity on the global jihad stage, al-Qaeda is now seemingly reemerging. The 2020 assassination of U.S. Navy servicemembers in Pensacola, Florida, the fall of the Islamic State's physical caliphate, and continued activity in both Afghanistan and North Africa all signal the group's continued viability, as well as its ongoing desire to reclaim the mantle of the world's preeminent Islamist extremist organization.

History and Ideology

Though the attacks of September 11, 2001 are the most profound symbol of al-Qaeda's notoriety, the group finds its roots in another, more conventional, war. al-Qaeda was formally created in the latter years of the Afghan-Soviet war (1979–1989) as the brainchild of Abdullah Azzam, an extreme Islamic theologian of Palestinian origin who provided the intellectual framework for the creation of a transnational militant Islamist organization to carry out global *jihad*.[1]

Among the most influential elements of Azzam's effort was the creation of a transnational Islamist cadre. The idea was brought to him and Osama Bin Laden, a Saudi-born financier who backed the Afghan *mujahideen* with money and equipment, by successful *jihadists* who had emerged out of the Afghan civil war.[2] The result was the founding, in October 1984, of the Services Bureau (*Maktab al-Khidamat*), a recruitment and fundraising network designed to supply funds and personnel to the Afghan *jihad*.[3] This network would provide the human and financial pool on which al-Qaeda subsequently relied. Thereafter, in October 1986, Bin Laden began construction of a military training camp near Jaji, a facility that would come to be known simply as "the military base" (*al-Qaeda al-Askariyya*).[4] Al-Qaeda the organization emerged out of these beginnings.[5]

Azzam was assassinated in Peshawar on November 24, 1989.[6] While no perpetrator was ever found, at least some evidence suggests Jordanian intelligence services were responsible. Analysts have speculated that the KGB, Israeli Mossad, Afghan intelligence or Ayman all-Zawahiri, then head of Egypt's Islamic Jihad, could also have been responsible.[7] Azzam's death exacerbated the fault lines of an already fractured Arab-Afghan community. Having preached against authority when deciding on *jihad*—governments, clerical institutions, even parents—Azzam had become a source of authority with no way to pass on the role. When he died, a vacuum of authority emerged, and al-Qaeda filled the void.[8]

Beginning in 1989, al-Qaeda began evolving into a truly global organization. When the Soviet Union began to implode, Bin Laden attributed this to his battlefield victories against the Russians – a position that would later become a motivator for the September 11th attacks.[9]

Saddam Hussein's annexation of Kuwait in August 1990 led to a schism between Bin Laden and the Saudi government. The U.S. intervened to defend the House of Saud, and in return was allowed to use Saudi territory to evict Saddam from Kuwait, then stay on to monitor the subsequent ceasefire.[10] Bin Laden easily exploited the question of the permissibility of non-Muslims in the Kingdom, and found a sympathetic ear among significant segments of the Saudi *ulema*.[11] As a result of the ensuing political tensions with Saudi authorities, Bin Laden was expelled from the Kingdom in 1992, and subsequently migrated to Sudan, which had begun to allow any Muslim into the country without a visa in a display of Islamic solidarity.[12] His Saudi citizenship was formally revoked in 1994.[13]

From its new perch in Sudan, AQ and its supporters conducted three bombings targeting U.S. troops in Aden, Yemen, in December 1992, and claimed responsibility for shooting down U.S. helicopters and killing U.S. soldiers in Somalia in 1993.[14] In February of that year, the World Trade Center was attacked for the first time when operatives detonated a bomb underneath the center's North Tower, intending to knock it into the South Tower. They failed to achieve their primary objective, but six people were killed and over 1,000 were injured. Ramzi Yousef, the man who carried out the failed 1993 World Trade Center attack (and who was the nephew of 9/11 architect Khalid Shaykh Muhammad, or KSM as he is commonly known), was arrested in Pakistan in February 1995.[15] When arrested, Yusuf and KSM were in the process of plotting Operation BOJINKA, a coordinated campaign to bring down eleven planes over the Pacific Ocean.[16] They also planned to assassinate the Pope and crash planes into U.S. federal government buildings.[17]

Al-Qaeda's campaign of violence continued. In November 1995, four Americans training the Saudi National Guard were killed,[18] and three dozen others were wounded, in a twin car bombing in Riyadh by Arab-Afghans inspired by Bin Laden.[19] Under intense U.S. pressure, the Sudanese regime expelled Bin Laden in May 1996, and he moved back to Afghanistan.[20]

The second major attack in Saudi Arabia occurred in June

1996. A housing complex in Khobar was bombed, killing nineteen Americans and wounded 500 people. Bin Laden endorsed the attack and issued his "Declaration of War against the Americans Occupying the Land of the Two Holy Place" in August 1996, but he had never actually claimed the attack.

In February 1998, Bin Laden declared that it was the "individual duty" for Muslims to "kill the Americans and their allies … in any country."[21] The subsequent August 1998 bombings of the American Embassies in Kenya and Tanzania, which killed hundreds and provoked U.S. cruise missile strikes in Afghanistan and Sudan, communicated that his organization was prepared to act upon this guidance.

On January 3, 2000, al-Qaeda tried to blow up the *USS Sullivan* with an explosive-laden skiff while the ship was in the port of Aden. The attack failed, but AQ salvaged the explosives and succeeded in its second attempt, this time against the *USS Cole,* on October, 12, 2000. Seventeen American sailors were killed and nearly 40 others were wounded in that attack.[22]

The culmination of this decade of sporadic attacks came on the morning of September 11, 2001, when coordinated airplane attacks on New York and Washington organized by al-Qaeda killed nearly 3,000 people from ninety countries and wounded more than 6,000.[23] In the aftermath of the 9/11 attacks, al-Qaeda lost its safe haven in Afghanistan as the United States, with the support of coalition partners, initiated a broad military campaign that – over the course of several weeks – ousted Afghanistan's ruling Taliban regime and decimated the Bin Laden network militarily.[24] These setbacks, in turn, led to the rise of AQ "franchises" through which the organization could continue its militancy in decentralized fashion. According to the Counter Extremism Project, "the group has established five major regional affiliates pledging their official allegiance to al-Qaeda: in the Arabian Peninsula, North Africa, East Africa, Syria, and the Indian subcontinent."[25]

Despite these developments, AQ remained committed to its anti-Western campaign of violence – albeit in more scattered fashion. The first few post-9/11 follow-on plots—the British "shoe bomber" Richard Reid, and the Brooklyn-born would be "dirty bomber"

José Padilla (Abdullah al-Muhajir)—were amateurish failures. Meanwhile, U.S. and allied counterterrorism operations continued to erode the organization's network and capabilities. For instance, KSM, the organization's *de facto* chief of external operations, was arrested in 2003 in a joint CIA and ISI effort. (He is currently detained at Guantanamo Bay and his death penalty trial for his involvement in the September 11 attacks is set for January 2021. Other prominent members of AQ leadership to have been detained or killed between 2003 and 2010 include Mustafa Hamid, who was arrested in 2003, Khalid al-Habib and Abu Musab al-Zarqawi, who were killed in 2006, and Saeed al-Masri, who was killed in 2010.[26]) Most notable, of course, was the death of Osama Bin Laden himself. The al-Qaeda founder and leader was killed at the hands of U.S. special forces on May 2, 2011 in an early morning raid in Abbottabad, Pakistan. Leadership of the organization subsequently passed to the group's second-in-command, Ayman al-Zawahiri.

Nevertheless, the years since 9/11 have borne witness to AQ's continued lethality and capacity for violence. Per the Counter Extremism Project, al-Qaeda and its affiliate organizations to date have killed over 2200 people and injured thousands more all over the world.[27] Particularly notable attacks linked to the organization include the March 2004 train bombings in Spain, in which 191 people were killed and more than 1800 injured, the March 2005 transit bombings that killed 56 people in England, the August 2007 fuel truck attacks in Iraq that killed more than 300, the Westgate Mall shootings of 2013 in Kenya that killed more than 60 people and injured 80 others, a series of attacks that targeted schools in Nigeria from January to February 2014, killing roughly 200 students, and a suicide bombing in Somalia that killed more than 500 people in October 2017.

Al-Qaeda's foundational *wahhabi* ideology, which endures to this day, evolved out of bin Laden's religious schooling at university[28] as well as the philosophies of the *Ikhwan*, a military force of nomadic Saudi tribesmen that are credited with the politicization of Islam during the early 20th century's colonial period.[29] The *Ikhwani* school of thought focuses on a notional "a pure Islam of the *aslaf*, and on the idea that individuals and societies that adhere to "true" Islam will prosper in this world,"[30] Today, al-Qaeda is a *jihadist* network that aims to purge the Muslim world of Western influence, destroy Israel, build an Islamic *caliphate* stretching from Spain to Indonesia, and impose a strict interpretation of Sunni *sharia* law.[31] The group seeks to overthrow corrupt "apostate" regimes in the Middle East, and, in turn, replace them with what it deems to be "true" Islamic governments.[32] This has been a source of conflict and contention within the organization, as there has been debate over what qualifies as corrupt "apostate" regimes. AQ's primary enemy is the United States, it ultimately strives to end U.S. support for these corrupted regimes and push America to withdraw from the region, something that would leave these client states – and perhaps even the U.S. itself – vulnerable.[33]

Global Reach

It would be fair to say that recent years have proved to be challenging ones for the Bin Laden network. Militarily, concerted coalition actions have helped to erode the group's ranks and jeopardize its various post-9/11 bases of operation. Ideologically, meanwhile, recent years have seen the emergence of fierce competition for the group in the "war of ideas," as its Iraqi offshoot transformed into the Islamic State and subsequently sought to challenge the group for leadership of the global *jihadi* movement.[34] At the same time, however, changes like the "Arab Spring" revolutions that swept over the Middle East and North Africa between 2010-2012, and the civil wars in Libya, Syria and Yemen all afforded the organization with new opportunities for relevance and permissive environments for operations.

As of March 2020, it is estimated that al-Qaeda and its subsidiary groups have between 30,000 and 40,000 fighters the world over. That figure includes as many as 20,000 in Syria, 2,000 in Africa's Sahel region (roughly 1,000 of whom belong to AQIM), 6,000 in Yemen, 7,000 in Somalia, and 600 in Afghanistan.[35] Today, the post-Afghanistan evolution of al-Qaeda can be said to be complete, and the organization – once a unitary movement – now operates predominantly via its various affiliated organizations, franchises and ideological fellow-travelers. These include:

Al-Shabaab ("the Youth")

Al-Shabaab started gaining ground in Somalia in early 2007, re-infiltrating Mogadishu and seizing neighborhoods of the capital by 2008,[36] then consolidating into control over larger tracts of territory in 2009.[37] In 2012, the group pledged allegiance to al-Qaeda.[38] As of this writing, al-Shabaab is estimated to have between 7,000 and 9,000 members.[39]

Funded by "taxes" extracted from the population and revenue from captured resources, al-Shabaab created a repressive Islamist polity.[40] In August 2011, while fighting a still ongoing civil war against the Somali government, al-Shabaab withdraw from Mogadishu entirely.[41] It then lost Baraawe, its final urban stronghold and the access point to the Indian Ocean, in October 2014.[42] Still, al-Shabaab holds territory and engages in violence, primarily targeting the Somali government, throughout the country.[43]

When the Islamic State challenge arrived in Somalia in 2015, al-Shabaab's intelligence and counter-intelligence service, the Amniyat,[44] was mobilized. The Amniyat arrested IS sympathizers and agents throughout 2016 and 2017. IS anointed a *wilayat* (province) in December 2017, and by December 2018 all-out war had been declared by al-Shabaab.[45]

In July 2019, Qatar was exposed as having sponsored an al-Shabaab attack against its Gulf rival, the UAE, in the port city of Bosaso three months earlier.[46] The former head of Somalia's main intelligence body, the National Intelligence and Security Agency (NISA), said Qatar is the "main sponsor [of al-Shabaab] and uses tricks such as … random deals" to channel money to them.[47] NISA itself stands accused of being entangled with elements of al-Shabaab and being behind some of the *jihadist* group's attacks in Kenya.[48] On December 28, 2019, a bomb went off at a checkpoint entering Mogadishu, killing 85. Al Shabaab would later claim responsibility for the attack.[49] In January 2020, al-Shabaab claimed its first ever attack on a U.S. base in Somalia,[50] and in Kenya a British base was attacked.[51]

Al-Qaeda in the Arabian Peninsula (AQAP)

AQAP was al-Qaeda's most active division in terms of foreign terrorist attacks in 2009 and 2010, but soon after shifted to a local focus. Within Yemen, the group seemed relatively weak, estimated at between 200 and 300 members, albeit with unofficial estimates approximately double that.[52] It was, therefore, somewhat surprising when AQAP conquered Ja'ar and Zinjibar in the Abyan governorate in the spring of 2011 and Shaqwa in the late summer of that year.[53] Security forces offered no resistance as AQAP advanced; many Yemenis believe the country's ruler, Ali Abdullah Saleh, allowed AQAP to run riot in order to try to rally support, domestic and foreign, for his regime as it faced down a popular uprising.[54]

Saleh was finally pushed out in February 2012 and within a few months AQAP was forced into a "strategic retreat" from Abyan province.[55] However, this defeat would prove short-lived. Under interim president Abd Rabbuh Mansur Hadi, a Saudi-facilitated national dialogue was initiated to bring the various sectors of Yemen together around a decentralized governing structure, leading to national elections. That process was interrupted in September 2014 by a coup from Ansar Allah, better known as the Houthis, supported by Iran.[56]

AQAP capitalized on power vacuums created by Houthi aggression and carved out another mini-*emirate*, conquering the city of al-Mukalla in April 2015. At best, the Saudi-led coalition was indifferent to AQAP's advances, with its focus drawn to the Houthi. Meanwhile, there are local reports that the Coalition prevented tribal fighters who wanted to resist the AQAP takeover of their city,[57] and the UAE has publicly admitted that AQAP operatives have been brought within the forces it supports.[58]

AQAP "further softened its approach by socializing with residents and refraining from draconian rules," as The International Crisis Group notes. It ruled through a local council and police drawn from city residents, did not display its black banner, and launched infrastructure projects alongside its provision of food and medical care. This governance method—with the emphasis on "Sunni" security against the "Shi'a" Houthi threat, stability, and economic activity—was reasonably popular.[59]

The coalition, nettled by accusations it was aligning with terrorists to conduct its mission, gradually began to go after Sunni *jihadists* in Yemen. In April 2016, the coalition ostensibly pushed AQAP out of al-Mukalla.[60] The fact that AQAP avoided fighting for the city meant it retained much of the popularity it had built up,[61] and there are accusations that end of AQAP's overt control in al-Mukalla was the result of a negotiated financial settlement.[62]

Any momentum for anti-AQAP operations was sapped entirely by the UAE's announced withdrawal from Yemen in July 2019. However, the onset of all-out war between AQAP and IS in Yemen in July 2018 has gravely weakened both groups. As a result, it is unclear how much advantage they can take of any political and security vacuums.[63]

The franchise's focus has not been solely internal, however. In 2012, AQAP attempted to recruit a Saudi national to carry out a suicide bombing attack on a plane bound for the United States. However, this attack was thwarted from the very beginning, as a result of the fact that the operative chosen was in fact an agent of the Saudi intelligence services.[64]

Subsequently, on January 7, 2015, Chérif and Saïd Kouachi, two brothers of Algerian descent, carried out the attack on the headquarters of the French satirical magazine *Charlie Hebdo*, which had published cartoons mocking Islam. The Kouachi brothers killed twelve of the magazine's staff, were themselves killed two days, and AQAP claimed direct responsibility for the attacks.[65] However, there are doubts that AQAP was in fact involved at all.[66]

AQAP announced a new leader, Khalid Batarfi, in February of 2020, following the death of the group's previous chief, Qasim al-Rimi, in a U.S. airstrike. As of the Spring of 2020, fighting has intensified in at least four provinces in Yemen, including in areas where both AQ and IS are present. In Bayda, AQAP and IS are now fighting over territory, recruits and influence, with an onset of frequent clashes and ambushes, as well as a propaganda war on social media and internet chat rooms.[67]

Al-Qaeda in the Islamic Maghreb (AQIM)

AQIM publicly announced itself in 2007 under the leadership of Abd al-Malek Droukdel (Abu Musab Abd al-Wadud), a colleague of IS founder Al-Zarqawi. AQIM evolved out of the Group for Preaching and Combat (GSPC), an anti-Algerian government terror faction that fought in that country's civil war of the 1990s and early 2000s.[68]

Amid the domestic instability in Mali in 2012, AQIM—having gained a foothold in nearby Libya and operating inside Mali through front-groups—occupied an area about the size of Texas in the country's north and administered it for a number of months.[69] By the time France intervened in January 2013, AQIM's territorial grip had been weakened, as Droukdel well knew, because the *jihadists* had tried to implement their program too quickly.[70] The main rival Droukdel had to deal with was the infamous one-eyed *jihadist*, Mokhtar Belmokhtar, whose wayward schemes often led to disaster—like the attack siege of the gas plant near Amenas in southeastern Algeria, which between Belmokhtar and Le Département du Renseignement et de la Sécurité (DRS), an Algerian state intelligence service, killed nearly 100 people in the days after the French intervention in Mali.

AQIM was the first al-Qaeda affiliate to reject IS and its *caliphate* in 2014,[71] but the problem in maintaining unity is structural: a vast geography that makes communication difficult, porous borders, revenue streams from drugs and other contraband that incentivize internal competition, and all in the shadow of the DRS. AQIM, while holding to al-Qaeda organizationally, lost important splinters to IS and also ceded control over groups it had nurtured, like Boko Haram in Nigeria.[72] In turn, in March 2017, Jama'at Nasr al-Islam wal Muslimin (Group to Support Islam and Muslims, or JNIM), a North African *jihadist* group formed from the merger of several local Salafi-*jihadi* groups, pledged allegiance to AQIM.[73] Since the beginning of 2020, the intra-*jihadi* competition in West Africa and the Sahel has intensified.[74]

On June 3, 2020, Droukdel was killed in Mali during a raid by French forces.[75] While the loss will likely hinder AQIM's operations, it is probably not a paralyzing blow, as Droukdel had, as of late, evolved into a symbolic figurehead. When asked about potential successors, sources within the French military named Iyad

Ag Ghali, head of JNIM, another North African al-Qaeda affiliate.[76] What's more, it is unlikely that any successor to Droukdel will enjoy the same legitimacy and authority as their predecessor.[77]

Hayat Tahrir al-Sham (HTS) and the al-Nusra Front

HTS was formed in January 2017 as a coalition effort between five Syrian *jihadist* groups, including the former-al-Qaeda affiliate, al-Nusra Front. Upon renouncing its formal affiliation with al-Qaeda in July 2016, al-Nusra Front renamed itself Jabhat Fath al-Sham (JFS) while continuing to operate under its founder and current leader, Ahmad al-Shara.[78] One of the largest HTS contingencies, JFS fighters make up a significant number of HTS members; though figures are inexact, it is estimated their numbers are in the thousands.[79]

In February 2018 a new *jihadist* organization, Tanzim Hurras al-Deen (HaD), publicly announced itself and its affiliation with al-Qaeda. As a branch of al-Qaeda, HaD's ideology matches that of its parent organization. The formation of the new group followed some public, if contained, disputes between HTS and open al-Qaeda loyalists in Idlib at the end of 2017 and a speech from Al-Zawahiri directly critical of Al-Shara. [80] However, while evidence exists of the two groups collaborating in their fight against the Syrian government,[81] an analytical consensus has emerged that HTS and Hurras al-Deen are functionally competitors and enemies. This is further evidenced by HTS's apparent June 2020 crackdown on HaD.[82]

Whether or not Hurras al-Deen represents a true existential threat to HTS' dominion in Syria has yet to be seen; HaD is functionally 1/10th the size of HTS, with roughly half of its fighters coming from other countries. What's more, U.S. airstrikes have killed several HaD senior leaders since the group's founding.[83] The U.S. Department of State has estimated that the al-Nusra Front possesses between 1,000 and 5,000 fighters.[84]

Al-Qaeda on the Indian Subcontinent (AQIS)

Established in 2014 by Asim Umar, a veteran of various south Asian *jihadist* movements, AQIS was designated as a Foreign Terrorist Organization by the U.S. State Department in 2016 and is today comprised of several hundred members. However, the group has not carried out or claimed an attack since 2014, much of its membership has been killed in drone strikes in tribal Pakistan, and Umar himself was killed in September 2019 in a joint U.S.-Afghan military raid.[85]

As a January 2019 report from the Soufan Center notes, AQIS maintains relationships with other violent Islamic extremist organizations in South Asia. These include Lashkar e-Taiba (LeT), the Taliban, Harkat ul Jihad e Islami, and Lashkar e Jhangvi.[86] Historic funding streams for the group have been charity donations, kidnappings, and individual donations, as well as resources provided by al-Qaeda's central authority.[87]

Recent Activity

In July 2019, Zawahiri called for extremists in Kashmir to attack Indian forces. On September 11, 2019, al-Zawahiri appealed to Muslims to attack U.S., European, Israeli, and Russian military targets in a video recording.[88]

On December 6, 2019, a 21-year-old Saudi Air Force officer, Second Lieutenant Mohammed Saeed al-Shamrani, was killed as he attacked fellow students at a training facility in at Naval Air Station Pensacola, Florida. Al-Shamrani murdered three people and wounded eight.[89] In an audio statement released on February 2, 2020, AQAP's leader, Qassem al-Raymi (who had been killed three days earlier in an American drone strike), claimed responsibility. Simultaneously, AQAP released Al-Shamrani's last will, written in September 2019, and copies of the correspondence Al-Shamrani had with AQAP over an encrypted application.[90] The FBI later accessed Al-Shamrani's mobile telephones, confirmed that these messages were real, that Al-Shamrani had been in contact with al-Qaeda, and planned the attack for years.[91]

The timing of al-Qaeda's first attack targeting the United States in more than a decade makes some sense. With the final destruction of the Islamic State's physical *caliphate* in Baghuz in March 2019, al-Qaeda can claim eminence, and try to wrestle back its *jihadist* leadership position. While the world was distracted with IS, al-Qaeda was quietly engaged in the groundwork to draw local Muslim communities closer to its worldview.[92]

FBI Director Christopher Wray offered this read on where al-Qaeda is two months before Pensacola. Whatever "desire" al-Qaeda "maintains… for large-scale, spectacular attacks", said Wray, "the near term" is "more likely to [see al-Qaeda] focus on building its international affiliates and supporting small-scale, readily achievable attacks in key regions such as east and west Africa". Regional prioritization makes sense—the point of the foreign attacks was driving the West out of the region so the non-*jihadist* governments could be toppled, after all. If possible, al-Qaeda "seeks to inspire individuals to conduct their own attacks in the U.S. and the West," said Wray, placing them nearer to the low-tech end of the spectrum, quite possibly because the "degraded" state of its leadership.[93]

While the departure of American forces from Afghanistan is currently looming as a product of ongoing peace negotiations between the U.S. and Afghan governments and the Taliban, a recent United Nations report suggests that al-Qaeda is growing stronger in the country.[94] Meanwhile, AQ's North and Sub-Saharan affiliates are likely to face less comparative pressure from local counterterror coalitions as the Pentagon continues to weigh ending support for ongoing operations in those subregions.[95]

Endnotes

1. See generally Thomas Hegghammer, *The Caravan: Abdallah Azzam and the Rise of Global Jihad* (Cambridge University Press, 2020).
2. Mustafa Hamid and Leah Farrell, *The Arabs at War in Afghanistan* (Hurst, 2015), 65-70; Daniel L. Byman, Testimony before the House Committee on Homeland Security Subcommittee on Counterterrorism and Intelligence, April 29, 2015, https://www.brookings.edu/testimonies/comparing-al-qaeda-and-isis-different-goals-different-targets/.
3. John Roth, Douglas Greenburg and Serena Wille, "Staff Report to the Commission: Monograph on Terrorist Financing," National Commission on Terrorist Attacks Upon the United States, 2004, https://www.9-11commission.gov/staff_statements/911_TerrFin_Monograph.pdf.
4. Assaf Moghadam, *Nexus of Global Jihad: Understanding Cooperation Among Terrorist Actors* (Columbia University Press, 2019).

5. Hegghammer, *The Caravan*, 350-52.
6. Thomas Hegghammer, "The Mysterious Assassination That Unleashed Jihadism," History News Network, November 24, 2019, https://historynewsnetwork.org/article/173697
7. "Abdullah Azzam," Investigative Project on Terrorism, n.d., https://www.investigativeproject.org/profile/103/abdullah-azzam; Bruce Riedel, "Abdullah Azzam, Spiritual Father of 9/11 Attacks: Ideas Live On," *The Daily Beast*, September 11, 2011, https://www.thedailybeast.com/abdullah-azzam-spiritual-father-of-911-attacks-ideas-live-on; "Abdullah Azzam," Counter Extremism Project. Counter Extremism Project, April 26, 2019, https://www.counterextremism.com/extremists/abdullah-azzam.
8. Hegghammer, 'The Mysterious Assassination That Unleashed Jihadism."
9. Bernard Lewis, *From Babel to Dragomans: Interpreting the Middle East* (Oxford University Press, 2004), 376.
10. Lawrence Wright, *The Looming Tower: Al-Qaeda and the Road to 9/11* (Vintage, 2007), 156-9.
11. For the fullest explanation of *Al-Sahwa al-Islamiyya*, see: Stephane Lacroix, *Awakening Islam: The Politics of Religious Dissent in Contemporary Saudi Arabia* (Harvard University Press, 2011).
12. Tim Weiner and James Risen, "Decision to Strike Factory in Sudan Based on Surmise Inferred From Evidence," *New York Times*, September 21, 1998, https://www.nytimes.com/1998/09/21/world/decision-to-strike-factory-in-sudan-based-on-surmise-inferred-from-evidence.html?searchResultPosition=8.
13. Patrick Tyler and Philip Shenon, "Call by Bin Laden Before Attacks Is Reported," *New York Times*, October 2, 2001, https://www.nytimes.com/2001/10/02/us/nation-challenged-investigation-call-bin-laden-before-attacks-reported.html.
14. U.S. Department of State, "Al Qaeda," *Country Reports on Terrorism 2019*, June 2020, https://www.state.gov/reports/country-reports-on-terrorism-2018/#AQ
15. Tina Kelley, "Suspect in 1993 Bombing Says Trade Center Wasn't First Target," *New York Times*, June 1, 2002, https://www.nytimes.com/2002/06/01/us/suspect-in-1993-bombing-says-trade-center-wasn-t-first-target.html
16. Matthew Brzezinski, "Bust and Boom," *Washington Post*, December 30, 2001, https://www.washingtonpost.com/archive/lifestyle/magazine/2001/12/30/bust-and-boom/1109903e-3762-4b78-90a6-d191efd39920/

17. "Bojinka Plot," Encyclopedia Britannica, n.d., https://www.britannica.com/event/Bojinka-Plot; "Suspect in Plot to Kill Pope in Custody, Police Say," Associated Press, January 1, 1996, https://apnews.com/acebf1db4522e9d234b737894b67ee47.
18. Elaine Sciolino, "Bomb Kills 4 Americans in Saudi Arabia," *New York Times*, November 14, 1995, https://www.nytimes.com/1995/11/14/world/bomb-kills-4-americans-in-saudi-arabia.html
19. Thomas Hegghammer, "Deconstructing the Myth about al-Qa'ida and Khobar," *CTC Sentinel*, February 2008, https://ctc.usma.edu/deconstructing-the-myth-about-al-qaida-and-khobar/
20. "Osama Bin Laden: A Chronology of His Political Life," Public Broadcasting Service, n.d., https://www.pbs.org/wgbh/pages/frontline/shows/binladen/etc/cron.html; James Astill, "Osama: the Sudan Years," *Guardian* (London), October 16, 2001, https://www.theguardian.com/world/2001/oct/17/afghanistan.terrorism3.
21. Paul Todd and Jonathan Bloch, "Back to the Future?" in Paul Todd and Jonathan Bloch, eds. *Global Intelligence: The World's Secret Services Today* (London: Zed Books, 2003), 90–91, https://books.google.com/books?id=0gZ7sjNakKEC&dq=In+February+1998,+Bin+Laden+declared+that+it+was+the+"individual+duty"+for+Muslims+to+"kill+the+Americans+and+their+allies+…+in+any+country."&source=gbs_navlinks_s.
22. Department of Defense, "U.S. Indicts Two Yemeni Nationals, Al Qaeda Members in USS Cole Attack," May 15, 2003, https://archive.defense.gov/news/newsarticle.aspx?id=28976
23. "September 11 Attack Timeline," 9/11 Memorial, n.d., https://timeline.911memorial.org/#Timeline/2
24. Bruce Riedel, "Al-Qaida today, 18 years after 9/11," The Brookings Institution, September 10, 2019, https://www.brookings.edu/blog/order-from-chaos/2019/09/10/al-qaida-today-18-years-after-9-11/; Wesley Morgan, "Whatever happen to Al Qaeda in Afghanistan?" *Politico*, August 15, 2018, https://www.politico.com/story/2018/08/15/al-qaeda-afghanistan-terrorism-777511
25. "Al Qaeda." Counter Extremism Project, n.d., https://www.counterextremism.com/threat/al-qaeda
26. Carol Rosenberg, "Trial for Men Accused of Plotting 9/11 Attacks Is Set for 2021," *New York Times*, August 30, 2019, https://www.nytimes.com/2019/08/30/us/politics/sept-11-trial-guantanamo-bay.html; "Al-Qaeda's remaining leaders" *BBC News*, June 16, 2015, https://www.bbc.com/news/world-south-asia-11489337; John F. Burns and Dexter Filkins, "At Site of Attack on Zarqawi, All That's Left Are

Questions," *New York Times*, June 11, 2006, https://www.nytimes.com/2006/06/11/world/middleeast/11scene.html?pagewanted=all; "Group: Al Qaeda says top leader in Afghanistan dies," *CNN*, May 31, 2010, https://afghanistan.blogs.cnn.com/2010/05/31/group-al-qaeda-says-top-leader-in-afghanistan-dies/

27. "Al Qaeda," Counter Extremism Project, n.d., https://www.counter-extremism.com/threat/al-qaeda
28. Rohan Gunaratna, "Al Qaeda's Ideology," Hudson Institute *Current Trends in Islamist Ideology*, May 19, 2005, https://www.hudson.org/research/9777-al-qaeda-s-ideology.
29. "Al-Ikhwan Al-Muslimeen: The Muslim Brotherhood," *Military Review*, July-August 2013, 26–31, https://www.hsdl.org/?view&did=455611.
30. Christopher Henzel, "The Origins of Al Qaeda's Ideology: Implications for US Strategy," *Parameters*, Spring 2005, 69–80. https://www.cia.gov/library/abbottabad-compound/AC/AC109E252F2BC6B9C7D32EB31C211AA9_henzel.pdf.
31. "Dreaming of a Caliphate," *The Economist*, August 6, 2011, https://www.economist.com/briefing/2011/08/06/dreaming-of-a-caliphate.
32. Byman, Testimony before the House Committee on Homeland Security Subcommittee on Counterterrorism and Intelligence.
33. Ibid.
34. J.M. Berger, "The Islamic State vs. al Qaeda," *Foreign Policy*, September 2, 2014, https://foreignpolicy.com/2014/09/02/the-islamic-state-vs-al-qaeda/.
35. Bruce Hoffman and Jacob Ware, "Al-Qaeda: Threat or Anachronism?" *War on the Rocks*, March 12, 2020, https://warontherocks.com/2020/03/al-qaeda-threat-or-anachronism/; U.S. Department of State, *Country Reports on Terrorism 2019*, June 2020, https://www.state.gov/reports/country-reports-on-terrorism-2019/#AQ
36. Jeffrey Gettleman and Mohamed Ibrahim, "Shabab Concede Control of Capital to Somalia Government," *New York Times*, August 6, 2011, https://www.nytimes.com/2011/08/07/world/africa/07somalia.html
37. Bohumil Dobos, "Shapeshifter of Somalia: Evolution of the Political Territoriality of Al-Shabaab," *Small Wars and Insurgencies*, August 5, 2016, https://www.tandfonline.com/doi/abs/10.1080/09592318.2016.1208282
38. "Al-Shabaab Joining Al Qaeda, Monitor Group Says," *CNN*, February 10, 2012, https://www.cnn.com/2012/02/09/world/africa/somalia-shabaab-qaeda/index.html.

39. U.S. Department of State, "Al Qaeda," *Country Reports on Terrorism 2019*, June 2020, https://www.state.gov/reports/country-reports-on-terrorism-2019/#AQ
40. Tom Keatinge, *The Role of Finance in Defeating Al-Shabaab*, Royal United Services Institute (RUSI), December 2014, 4, https://rusi.org/sites/default/files/201412_whr_2-14_keatinge_web_0.pdf
41. "Somalia's al-Shabab rebels leave Mogadishu," *BBC News*, August 6, 2011, https://www.bbc.com/news/world-africa-14430283
42. Christopher Anzalone, "The Resilience of al-Shabaab," *CTC Sentinel*, April 2016, https://ctc.usma.edu/the-resilience-of-al-shabaab/
43. Clair Felter, Jonathan Masters, and Mohammed Aly Sergie, "Al-Shabab," Council on Foreign Relations *Backgrounder*, January 10, 2020, https://www.cfr.org/backgrounder/al-shabab
44. "Somalia's frightening network of Islamist spies," *BBC News*, May 27, 2019, https://www.bbc.com/news/world-africa-48390166
45. Caleb Weiss, "Reigniting the Rivalry: The Islamic State in Somalia vs. al-Shabaab," *CTC Sentinel*, April 2019, https://ctc.usma.edu/reigniting-rivalry-islamic-state-somalia-vs-al-shabaab/
46. Ronen Bergman and David Kirkpatrick, "With Guns, Cash and Terrorism, Gulf States Vie for Power in Somalia," *New York Times*, July 22, 2019, https://www.nytimes.com/2019/07/22/world/africa/somalia-qatar-uae.html
47. Abuga Makori, "Somalia: Ex-NISA Boss Links Qatar to Financing of Al-Shabaab, Accuses Fahad Yasin of Being 'Middleman,'" *Garowe Online*, May 16, 2020, https://www.garoweonline.com/en/news/somalia/somalia-ex-nisa-boss-links-qatar-to-financing-of-al-shabaab-accuses-fahad-yasin-of-being-middleman
48. "Somali Intelligence Funding Shabaab to Attack Kenya — Report," *Star*, April 17, 2020, https://www.the-star.co.ke/news/2020-04-17-somali-intelligence-funding-shabaab-to-attack-kenya--report/
49. Harun Maruf, "Al-Shabab Claims Responsibility for Deadly Bombing in Somali Capital," *Voice of America*, December 30, 2019, https://www.voanews.com/africa/al-shabab-claims-responsibility-deadly-bombing-somali-capital
50. "Al-Shabaab kills three Americans in attack on US military base in Kenya," Associated Press, January 5, 2020, https://www.theguardian.com/world/2020/jan/05/al-shabaab-attack-us-military-base-kenya; Stig Jarle Hansen, "Al-Shabaab's attacks come amid backdrop of West's waning interest," *The Conversation*, January 15, 2020, https://theconversation.com/al-shabaabs-attacks-come-amid-backdrop-of-wests-waning-interest-129706

51. Duncan Miriri and Katharine Houreld, "Kenya arrests three men for trying to breach British army camp," Reuters, January 5, 2020, https://www.reuters.com/article/us-kenya-security/kenya-arrests-three-men-for-trying-to-breach-british-army-camp-idUSKBN1Z404G
52. "Western Counter-Terrorism Help 'Not Enough for Yemen,'" *BBC News*, December 29, 2009, http://news.bbc.co.uk/2/hi/8433844.stm
53. Grace Wyler, "Al Qaeda Declares Southern Yemeni Province An 'Islamic Emirate,'" *Business Insider*, April 1, 2011, https://www.businessinsider.com/al-qaeda-declares-southern-yemeni-province-an-islamic-emirate-2011-3?r=US&IR=T
54. "Yemen's al-Qaeda: Expanding the Base," The International Crisis Group, February 2, 2017, https://www.crisisgroup.org/middle-east-north-africa/gulf-and-arabian-peninsula/yemen/174-yemen-s-al-qaeda-expanding-base
55. Andrew Michaels and Sakhr Ayyash, "AQAP's Resilience in Yemen," *CTC Sentinel*, September 2013, http://www.ctc.usma.edu/posts/aqaps-resilience-in-yemen
56. Brian Bennett and Zaid al-Alayaa, "Iran-backed rebels in Yemen loot secret files about US spy operations," *Stars and Stripes*, March 25, 2015, https://www.stripes.com/news/middle-east/iran-backed-rebels-in-yemen-loot-secret-files-about-us-spy-operations-1.336632
57. "Yemen's al-Qaeda: Expanding the Base," The International Crisis Group.
58. Bel Trew, "Former al-Qaeda footsoldiers have been allowed into Yemen forces, admits UAE military," *Independent* (London), August 16, 2018, https://www.independent.co.uk/news/world/middle-east/yemen-civil-war-al-qaeda-soldiers-uae-military-emirati-a8494481.html
59. "Yemen's al-Qaeda: Expanding the Base," The International Crisis Group.
60. "Yemen conflict: Troops retake Mukalla from al-Qaeda," *BBC News*, April 25, 2016, https://www.bbc.co.uk/news/world-middle-east-36128614
61. "Yemen's al-Qaeda: Expanding the Base," The International Crisis Group.
62. Maggie Michael, Trish Wilson, and Lee Keath, "AP Investigation: US allies, al-Qaida battle rebels in Yemen," Associated Press, August 7, 2018, https://apnews.com/f38788a561d74ca78c77cb43612d50da/AP-investigation:-Yemen-war-binds-US,-allies,-al-Qaida
63. Elisabeth Kendall, "The Failing Islamic State Within The Failed

State of Yemen.

64. Sudarsan Raghavan, Peter Finn, and Greg Miller, "In foiled bomb plot, AQAP took bait dangled by Saudi informant," Washington Post, May 9, 2012, https://www.washingtonpost.com/world/in-foiled-bomb-plot-aqap-took-bait-dangled-by-saudi-informant/2012/05/09/gIQA9oXIEU_story.html
65. "Document: 'Message regarding the blessed battle of Paris,'" Terrorism.net, January 14, 2015, https://www.terrorisme.net/2015/01/14/document-message-regarding-the-blessed-battle-of-paris/
66. An attack by Al-Qaeda in a Western city in January 2015 would be diametrically at odds with AQC's strategy, and an attack in collaboration with IS is unthinkable (Amedy Coulibaly killed five people in two attacks in Paris around the same time as the Charlie Hebdo shooting. He was a close friend of the Kouachi brothers and had previously pledged allegiance to ISIS). Further, In the video of Coulibaly pledging allegiance to the Islamic State, Coulibaly says he "coordinated" with the brothers for the anuary 8th murder of policewoman Clarissa Jean-Philippe. What's more, Coulibaly said he supplied the money to the Kouachis for their weapons ("a few thousand euros") and coordinated his attack with their attack on the offices of Charlie Hebdo, staging them consecutively rather than simultaneously, protracted over three days rather than just a few hours on one day, "so that it'd have more impact". The Kouachis were, said Coulibaly, "brothers from our team". See Jane Onyanga-Omara, "Video shows Paris gunman pledging allegiance to Islamic State," *USA Today*, January 11, 2015, https://www.usatoday.com/story/news/world/2015/01/11/video-gunman-islamic-state/21589723/; Brian Rohan, Lori Hinnant, and Diaa Hadid, "Video of Paris gunman raises questions of affiliations," Associated Press, January 12, 2015, https://apnews.com/f953ca926b9f4fee86d241816668bd32.
67. Sudarsan Raghavan, "As Yemen's War Intensifies, an Opening for Al-Qaeda to Resurrect Its Fortunes," *Washington Post*, February 25, 2020, https://www.washingtonpost.com/world/middle_east/as-yemens-war-intensifies-an-opening-for-al-qaeda-to-resurrect-its-fortunes/2020/02/24/6244bd84-54ef-11ea-80ce-37a8d4266c09_story.html.
68. Lianne Kennedy Boudali, "The GSPC: Newest Franchise in al-Qaida's Global Jihad," Combatting Terrorism Center North Africa Project, April 2, 2007, https://www.ctc.usma.edu/the-gspc-newest-franchise-in-al-qaidas-global-jihad/
69. Zachary Laub and Jonathan Masters, "Al-Qaeda in the Islamic

Maghreb," Council on Foreign Relations, March 27, 2015, http://www.cfr.org/terrorist-organizations-and-networks/al-qaeda-islamic-maghreb-aqim/p12717

70. Charles Lister, "Jihadi Rivalry: The Islamic State Challenges al-Qaida," Brookings Institution, January 2016, 11, https://www.brookings.edu/wp-content/uploads/2016/07/en-jihadi-rivalry.pdf
71. Tore Refslund Hamming, "ISIS's charm offensive toward al-Qaeda in the Islamic Maghreb," Middle East Institute, December 13, 2018, https://www.mei.edu/publications/isiss-charm-offensive-toward-al-qaeda-islamic-maghreb
72. Jacob Zenn, "Demystifying al-Qaida in Nigeria: Cases from Boko Haram's Founding, Launch of Jihad and Suicide Bombings," *Perspectives on Terrorism*, 2017, www.terrorismanalysts.com/pt/index.php/pot/article/view/666/html
73. "Al Qaeda branch rallies jihadists to join forces after Mali merger," *Defence Web*, March 20, 2017, https://www.defenceweb.co.za/security/national-security/al-qaeda-branch-rallies-jihadists-to-join-forces-after-mali-merger/?catid=49%3ANational%20Security&Itemid=115
74. "Jihadist Competition and Cooperation in West Africa," European Eye on Radicalization, April 3, 2020, https://eeradicalization.com/jihadist-competition-and-cooperation-in-west-africa/
75. Benjamin Roger and Farid Alilat. "How AQIM Leader Abdelmalek Droukdel Was Killed in Mali," *The Africa Report*, June 8, 2020, https://www.theafricareport.com/29482/how-aqim-leader-abdelmalek-droukdel-was-killed-in-mali/.
76. Julie Coleman and Méryl Demuynck, "The Death of Droukdel: Implications for AQIM and the Sahel," International Centre for Counter-Terrorism - The Hague, June 9, 2020, https://icct.nl/publication/the-death-of-droukdel-implications-for-aqim-and-the-sahel/
77. Ibid.
78. "Al-Nusra Front (Hayat Tahrir al-Sham)," Counter Extremism Project, n.d., https://www.counterextremism.com/threat/al-nusra-front-hayat-tahrir-al-sham
79. Kyle Orton, "Did Assad Recruit the Leader of Al-Qaeda in Syria?" Counter Extremism Project, August 11, 2016, https://www.counterextremism.com/threat/al-nusra-front-hayat-tahrir-al-sham
80. Hassan Hassan, "Two Houses Divided: How Conflict in Syria Shaped the Future of Jihadism," *CTC Sentinel*, October 2018, https://ctc.usma.edu/two-houses-divided-conflict-syria-shaped-future-jihadism/

81. See Aaron Y. Zelin, "Huras al-Din: The Overlooked al-Qaeda Group in Syria," Washington Institute for Near East Policy *Policywatch* 3188, September 24, 2019, https://www.washingtoninstitute.org/policy-analysis/view/huras-al-din-the-overlooked-al-qaeda-group-in-syria; "The Best of Bad Options for Syria's Idlib," International Crisis Group, March 14, 2019, 18, https://d2071andvip0wj.cloudfront.net/197-the-best-of-bad-options%20.pdf; "Military Groups Calling Themselves 'The Finest Factions of the Levant' Form Joint Operations Room," *Syria Call*, October 15, 2018, http://nedaa-sy.com/en/news/9078.
82. Simon Hooper and Harun al-Aswad, "British aid worker Tauqir Sharif arrested by HTS in Idlib," *Middle East Eye*, June 23, 2020, https://www.middleeasteye.net/news/british-aid-worker-tauqir-sharif-syria-idlib-hts-arrest
83. "Hurras al-Din," Counter Extremism Project, n.d., https://www.counterextremism.com/threat/hurras-al-din
84. U.S. Department of State, "Al-Nusrah Front," *Country Reports on Terrorism 2019*. June 2020, https://www.state.gov/reports/country-reports-on-terrorism-2019/#ANF
85. Ibid.; Sajid Farid Shapoo, Colin P. Clarke, Meriem El Atouabi, et al, "Al-Qaeda in the Indian Subcontinent: The Nucleus of Jihad in South Asia," The Soufan Center, January 2019, https://thesoufancenter.org/wp-content/uploads/2019/01/Al-Qaeda-in-the-Indian-Subcontinent-AQIS.pdf
86. Ibid.
87. Ibidem.
88. U.S. Department of State, "Al-Qaeda," *Country Reports on Terrorism 2019*, June 2020, https://www.state.gov/reports/country-reports-on-terrorism-2019/#AQ
89. Katie Benner and Adam Goldman, "F.B.I. Finds Links Between Pensacola Gunman and Al Qaeda." *New York Times*, May 18, 2020, https://www.nytimes.com/2020/05/18/us/politics/justice-department-al-qaeda-florida-naval-base-shooting.html.
90. Declan Walsh, "Al Qaeda Claims It Directed Florida Naval Base Shooting," *New York Times*, February 2, 2020, https://www.nytimes.com/2020/02/02/world/middleeast/al-qaeda-claims-it-directed-florida-naval-base-shooting.html
91. U.S. Department of Justice, "Attorney General William P. Barr and FBI Director Christopher Wray Announce Significant Developments in the Investigation of the Naval Air Station Pensacola Shooting," May 18, 2020, https://www.justice.gov/opa/pr/attorney-general-wil-

liam-p-barr-and-fbi-director-christopher-wray-announce-significant

92. Katherine Zimmerman, Statement before the House Homeland Security Committee Subcommittee on Counterterrorism and Intelligence, July 13, 2017, https://www.criticalthreats.org/analysis/testimony-al-qaedas-strengthening-in-the-shadows
93. Christopher Wray, Statement before the House Homeland Security Committee, October 30, 2019, https://www.fbi.gov/news/testimony/global-terrorism-threats-to-the-homeland-103019.
94. United National Security Council, "Eleventh report of the Analytical Support and Sanctions Monitoring Team submitted pursuant to resolution 2501 (2019) concerning the Taliban and other associated individuals and entities constituting a threat to the peace, stability and security of Afghanistan," May 27, 2020, https://www.undocs.org/S/2020/415
95. Katherine Zimmerman, "Why the US should spend 0.3 percent of its defense budget to prevent an African debacle," *Military Times*, March 12, 2020, https://www.militarytimes.com/opinion/commentary/2020/03/12/why-the-us-should-spend-03-percent-of-its-defense-budget-to-prevent-an-african-debacle/

64 Boko Haram/Islamic State West Africa Province

Quick Facts

Geographical Areas of Operation:Nigeria, Cameroon, Niger, and Chad
Numerical Strength (Members): Several Thousand Fighters
Leadership: Abu Musab al-Barnawi
Religious Identification: Sunni Islam

Source: U.S. State Department's Country Reports on Terrorism (2019)

INTRODUCTION

Boko Haram is an Islamist militant group based in northern Nigeria and the Lake Chad region. In 2015, Boko Haram leader Abubakar Shekau pledged allegiance to Abu Bakr al-Baghdadi, the leader of the Islamic State, and Boko Haram became known as "Islamic State in West Africa Province" (ISWAP). In August 2016, the Islamic State ousted Shekau from his leadership position in ISWAP in favor of another candidate. Thereafter, Shekau revived Boko Haram as a separate entity. ISWAP now operates in the same general region of northeastern Nigeria as Boko Haram, although ISWAP operates near Lake Chad and the Niger border and Boko Haram is primarily found in Sambisa Forest in southern Borno. There are major ideological barriers to collaboration between the two factions.

Boko Haram traces its ideological origins to the Nigerian Salafi imam Mohammed Yusuf. Yusuf was killed during a Boko Haram uprising in 2009. Abubakar Shekau was Yusuf's deputy during the latter's lifetime, and his successor after his death. When the Islamic State demoted Shekau, the Islamic State named Abu Musab al-Barnawi, Yusuf's son, as Shekau's successor. Al-Barnawi led ISWAP until March 2019, when he was reportedly demoted to a "shura member" to lieu of Ba Idrisa, another follower of Yusuf.[1]

Under Yusuf, Boko Haram sought to create an Islamic state in northern Nigeria modeled after the Taliban in Afghanistan and the teachings of Saudi Salafi preachers. However, it was not until Shekau took power in 2009 that Boko Haram began to truly use the international connections with al-Qaeda that Yusuf had developed throughout his lifetime. Soon after, Boko Haram gained legitimacy in the international jihadist community.

In 2014, Boko Haram announced the establishment of an "Islamic State" in parts of northeastern Nigeria. This announcement heralded the group's departure from al-Qaeda over long-standing ideological differences between Shekau and the Bin Laden network's regional franchise, al-Qaeda in the Islamic Maghreb (AQIM), as well as with AQIM-trained Nigerian fighters. It also signaled growing ties between Boko Haram and the Islamic State—a relationship that would culminate with Shekau's public pledge of allegiance to the group's caliph, Abu Bakr al-Baghdadi, in March 2015. Al-Baghdadi accepted the pledge amid great fanfare among various Islamic State provinces. However, a combined Nigerian and regional military offensive subsequently forced Boko Haram to abandon territories it had conquered in northeastern Nigeria, causing Shekau's self-declared state and shift its focus to rural areas.

At the same time, the larger Islamic State also faced pressure from national armies, rival rebels, and international forces in Iraq, Syria, and Libya. That pressure initially limited the Islamic State's ability to support new provinces such as ISWAP. However, the Islamic State fully integrated ISWAP into its media operations and now considers ISWAP an "official" province. As a result of the Islamic State's territorial loss in Iraq and Syria in March 2019, the group has reprioritized ISWAP. ISWAP, for its part, has rebounded since 2016; Abu Musab al-Barnawi has refocused the group on military targets (rather than civilian ones), fighting the Nigerian army to a stalemate in northeastern Nigeria. The Islamic State, meanwhile, advertises ISWAP's successes and has claimed attacks by ISWAP more than any other subsidiary outside of Iraq and Syria since late 2018.

ISWAP under Abu Musab al-Barnawi has already evolved from being a local threat to a sub-regional threat, with attacks in Nigeria, Niger, Chad and Cameroon. There are signs that ISWAP has networks throughout Africa, as evidenced by its relationship with the larger

Islamic State, and that it coordinated with cells in Senegal and other West African countries.[2] *Meanwhile, Shekau's Boko Haram may not have the strong regional and global connections that al-Barnawi's ISWAP now has, but it nonetheless still operates throughout southern Borno and represents a significant threat in northeastern Nigeria.*

History and Ideology

As the leader of Boko Haram from 2002 to 2009, Mohammed Yusuf's foremost tenet was that Western education is sinful, which in Hausa translates to "Boko Haram" (*Boko* can mean "Book" or, more broadly, "Western education," and *Haram* means "sinful" or "forbidden"). Yusuf also taught that employment in the Nigerian government and participation in democracy was *haram* for Muslims, because Nigeria was not an Islamic State. He also preached that other activities, such as sports or listening to music, were *haram* because they could lead to idol worship.[3]

Yusuf's estimated 280,000 followers, who hailed from Nigeria, Niger, Chad, and Cameroon, either listened to his sermons in-person or on audiocassettes. They became known in northern Nigeria and abroad as the "Nigerian Taliban" because of their adherence to the theology of the Taliban in Afghanistan, which Nigerian Taliban members cited as a source of inspiration.[4] Yusuf's anti-Western and anti-education ideology appealed to many northern Nigerian Muslims who believed Nigeria was losing its Muslim identity to Western influence and Christianity, and who saw *sharia* as a panacea to the "corrupt" secular and democratic society they lived in.

Before the British colonial period (1850 – 1960), a large swath of northern Nigeria, southern Niger and Cameroon was under the rule of the Sokoto Caliphate (1804 – 1903), while Nigeria's Borno and Yobe States, parts of northern Cameroon, southeastern Niger and western Chad were under the rule of the Borno Empire (1380 – 1893). The British disbanded both of these Muslim empires and established the Northern Nigeria Protectorate in 1900, which later became part of colonial Nigeria in 1914, and then part of independent Nigeria in 1960. Colonization brought with it British education, including the English language, Western schools, and Christian missionaries.

By the time of Nigeria's independence in 1960, southern Nigeria, where British influence was strongest, was economically stronger and more highly educated than the country's north. Moreover, its population, which was largely animist before the arrival of the British, had become predominantly Christian. Northern Nigeria, on the other hand, was and remains predominantly Muslim; the influence of Islamic practices from Saudi Arabia and the Middle East, such as Salafism and Shiism, have become among the most prominent features of northern Nigerian Islam, and have heavily influenced the doctrines of Muhammed Yusuf and his followers.

When democracy was instituted in Nigeria in 1999 after several failed attempts at political liberalization, some northern Nigerian Muslims saw democracy as a byproduct of Western influence and a ploy that would lead to the marginalization of northern Nigerian Muslims or the dilution of the Islamic identity of the region.[5] As a result, twelve states in northern Nigeria have adopted *sharia* law to date. But Salafists like Boko Haram founder Mohammed Yusuf considered this to be only "half-*sharia*," because the framework was not imposed throughout the entire country and traditional Islamic leaders still mixed *sharia* with secular institutions like electoral democracy and co-educational schooling. Moreover, *sharia* was rarely actually employed; in cases where it was, only the poor ended up being punished.[6]

As a result of this perception of weakened Islamic identity and diluted Islam, Yusuf's rallying cry when he became the deputy of Boko Haram in 2002 was to advocate the creation of a true Islamic state and the elimination of all forms of Western influence and education.[7] According to Yusuf, for a short-lived period in 2003, several thousand members of the Nigerian Taliban, "left the city, which is impure, and headed for the bush, believing that Muslims who do not share their ideology are infidels."[8] They called their encampment, which was located two miles from Nigeria's border with Niger, "Afghanistan."

The local government ordered the Nigerian Taliban to leave "Afghanistan" in late 2003. Although it is unclear exactly what transpired at this time, it appears that the government cracked down on the camp after it learned that the camp was more than the "simple commune" it has often been portrayed to be.[9] Rather, key commanders at the camp had forged an alliance with al-Qaeda's external operations unit leader for Africa, Ibrahim Harun, to attack U.S. targets in Nigeria.[10] When one group member traveled to Pakistan to provide "coded messages… on how to carry out terrorist activities against American interests in Nigeria," he was intercepted by Pakistani intelligence and deported back to Nigeria.[11] Not only did the Nigerian government want to prevent attacks on U.S. targets; leading Nigerian Salafi scholars, who at least tacitly supported the camp, did as well. These scholars may have accepted some military training for fighting in the *jihads* in Iraq and Afghanistan, but opposed any violence in Nigeria. They believed local insurgency would ultimately lead to crackdowns that would harm Muslims. In this context, leading Salafi scholars are believed to have cooperated with the government in its crackdown on the camp, which occurred in early 2004. Several hundred members of the Nigerian Taliban, including its military leader Muhammed Ali, who had trained with *jihadists* abroad prior to 2003, were killed, while the residences of local government leaders, regional officials, and the divisional police were attacked.[12] Ultimately, security forces succeeded in destroying the entire "Afghanistan" camp.

In late 2004, Yusuf succeeded the late Muhammed Ali as leader of the Nigerian Taliban; subsequently, under Yusuf's leadership, the group would later become known as Boko Haram. Yusuf ascended after a year of exile in Saudi Arabia, only returning when northern Nigerian politicians assured him he would not be harmed if he came back. For the next five years, Yusuf's followers generally avoided conflict with the Nigerian government and security forces. However, Yusuf himself still preached against the government and declared that his group would launch a *jihad* once it had amassed enough power to succeed. This relative hiatus came to an end in July 2009, when Yusuf's followers and security forces engaged in battles in Borno and several other states in northeastern Nigeria over the span of four days. As a result, police captured Yusuf and executed him extra-judicially. More than 700 of his followers were also killed.[13]

While the government and Yusuf's followers blamed each other for instigating the clashes, conflict may have been inevitable given

Yusuf's rising popularity in northeastern Nigeria, his rejection of Nigerian state primacy, his sermons encouraging followers to hoard weapons in preparation for battle, and his establishment of training and financial contacts with al-Qaeda during the mid-2000s – all of which made Yusuf a credible and serious threat. The rapid expansion of the militant capabilities of Yusuf's followers beginning in 2010 also attested to the training they received from al-Qaeda. That training could not have taken place if Yusuf had not forged alliances with al-Qaeda, especially AQIM, throughout the mid-2000s. Shekau continued to strengthen those ties following Yusuf's death. He sent three of Yusuf's followers to meet with Abu Zeid, the AQIM commander for the Sahel, to discuss launching a guerilla war in Nigeria.[14] Following the meeting, Zeid requested financial and logistical support from the overall leader of AQIM, Abudelmalek Droukdel—a request which Droukdel granted.[15]

AQIM also connected Shekau with Osama bin Laden, then in Pakistan, so Shekau could explore the process of formally joining al-Qaeda and becoming an affiliate.[16] However, difficulties soon arose. AQIM-trained Nigerians, including Khalid al-Barnawi, complained to AQIM about Shekau's excessive violence, including his penchant for killing anyone—even Muslims—who did not join Boko Haram in the two years after 2009, something al-Qaeda's leadership attempted to raise unsuccessfully with him thereafter.[17]-As a result, AQIM stopped supporting Boko Haram and shifted its backing to a breakaway group called Ansaru when it was founded by al-Barnawi in 2012.[18] Al-Qaeda, therefore, never recognized Boko Haram as an affiliate during their two years of cooperation, although some splinter factions continued to cooperate with Shekau and other Boko Haram members.

Relations between Shekau and AQIM had soured by 2012, but by then Shekau had already accumulated a large enough following that he was able to maintain strength without AQIM's support. Many of Yusuf's followers went underground in Nigeria or took refuge in Niger, Chad and Cameroon, all of which border Nigeria's northeastern Borno State. In July 2010, Shekau, who Nigerian security forces believed had been killed in the July 2009 clashes, emerged via a video statement to declare himself Boko Haram's new leader. His video message was issued "on behalf of my mujahideen brothers in some African territory called Nigeria... to the soldiers of Allah in the Islamic State of Iraq in particular." It warned that: "Jihad has just begun... O America, die with your fury."[19] On October 2, 2010, AQIM's media wing, al-Andalus, also published a statement by Shekau to the Shumukh al-Islam *jihadist* web forum, which marked the first time that AQIM disseminated an official message from another militant leader or group. In the message, Shekau mourned the deaths of two al-Qaeda in Iraq leaders; he offered:

> "condolences on behalf of the Mujahideen in Nigeria to the Mujahideen in general, in particular to those in the "Islamic State of Iraq, Osama bin Laden, Ayman Al-Zawahiri, Abu Yahya Al-Libi, Abu Abdullah Al-Muhajir, the Emir of the Islamic State in Somalia, the Emir of Al-Qaeda in the Islamic Maghreb, the Emir of the Mujahideen in Pakistan, in Chechnya, Kashmir, Yemen, the Arabian Peninsula, and our religious clerics whom I did not mention."[20]

After Khalid al-Barnawi's meeting with Abu Zeid, AQIM published statements supporting Shekau in August 2009 and again in 2010. Furthermore, al-Qaeda in Iraq and al-Shabaab also issued condolences to Boko Haram on the one-year anniversary of Yusuf's death.

Shekau remained the leader of Boko Haram from 2010 through his pledge of allegiance to al-Baghdadi in March 2015. After this, he served as leader of ISWAP until August 2016. At that time, the Islamic State endorsed a rival faction under the leadership of Abu Musab al-Barnawi, and Shekau was deposed. The rival faction's criticism of Shekau mirrored Khalid al-Barnawi's complaints from 2011.[21] This transition of power was made public when the Islamic State announced that the new *wali* (governor) of ISWAP was Abu Musab al-Barnawi. Shekau, in turn, reverted back to his pre-ISWAP title of "imam" of Boko Haram (Jamaatu ahlis Sunna li'Dawati wal Jihad), while still maintaining his loyalty to Abu Bakr al-Baghdadi as *Caliph*. Since 2016, ISWAP and Boko Haram have maintained an active rivalry due to their disparate ideologies, although ISWAP itself has taken a more hardline turn since Abu Musab al-Barnawi was demoted and replaced by Ba Idrisa in March 2019. Cumulatively, however, the two comprise the main *jihadist* factions in Nigeria.

Global Reach

Boko Haram's attacks have largely been confined to the Lake Chad region of Africa, including attacks in northern Cameroon, Niger, and Chad. In Nigeria itself, Boko Haram's attacks have been concentrated in the country's north, especially in Borno State. Bombings in the wider Middle Belt region have become increasingly rare since the loss of AQIM support in 2012.

In April 2012, Boko Haram militants, including Shekau, were reportedly in northern Mali with the Movement for Unity and Jihad in West Africa (MUJWA), AQIM, and Ansar al-Dine when the Islamist militias established the "Islamic State of Azawad" in northern Mali.[22] Boko Haram fighters are said to have taken part in attacking the Algerian consulate in April 2012, but there is little evidence to corroborate that report.[23] A video issued by Mokhtar Belmokhtar and MUJWA after attacks in Arlit and Agadez in June 2013, however, featured a member of Ansaru—suggesting that it may have been Ansaru, rather than Boko Haram, which played the greater operational role in the original attack on the consulate.[24]

A French-led military intervention eventually expelled the Islamist militants, including Boko Haram and Ansaru fighters, from northern Mali in early 2013.[25] After the intervention, some Boko Haram members returned to northern Nigeria and used similar desert warfare tactics to overrun Nigerian military barracks throughout Borno State.[26] This allowed Boko Haram to become the de facto military power in large swathes of Borno State in 2014 and provided the basis for Shekau's announcement the same year that Boko Haram had succeeded in establishing an "Islamic State." The videos carried the same visual signatures of the Islamic State's own releases and hinted that a pledge from Shekau to al-Baghdadi was in the making.[27] Boko Haram's control over territory and its new tactics, such as kidnapping and enslaving more than 250 schoolgirls from Chibok, Nigeria, impressed the Islamic State and facilitated the eventual establishment of ISWAP. Boko Haram has also employed female suicide bombers more than other similar groups, in part because women are less likely to be considered a threat. Between 2014 and the end of 2019, Boko Haram deployed over 500 female suicide bombers (often in tandem or trios) in Nigeria, Niger, Chad and Cameroon.[28]

Coinciding with Boko Haram's merger with the Islamic State in March 2015, Nigeria and regional militaries from Niger, Chad and Cameroon launched incursions into northeastern Nigeria to oust the group from the territories it controlled. This, in turn, led Boko Haram to retaliate against all of these countries. In February 2015, Boko Haram sent male and female suicide bombers to attack Diffa, Niger. In June 2015, Boko Haram sent two suicide bombers to N'djamena, Chad to attack government buildings. The Islamic State later claimed responsibility for those operations.[29] Two other suicide attackers targeted markets in N'djamena, while other suicide bombers (often female) regularly targeted islands in Lake Chad. Cameroon had been a target of Boko Haram as early as 2014, even before the regional military offensive against the group. By 2015, Boko Haram was targeting Cameroon's northern region as frequently as northern Nigeria, again also primarily using women as suicide bombers.[30]

Cameroon's large-scale counterinsurgency efforts had rolled back Boko Haram attacks in the country by 2016. Chad, too, managed to mitigate further Boko Haram attacks in that country by 2016, in part through "non-aggression pacts" with Boko Haram in which the Chadian military would not attack the group across the border so long as Boko Haram did not attack Chad. Niger saw reduced Boko Haram attacks, but after the split between Abu Musab al-Barnawi and Shekau, al-Barnawi launched several large-scale ISWAP operations in Diffa and Bosso in the country's southeast. A June 2016 raid by more than 100 ISWAP militants, for example, destroyed military barracks in Bosso.[31] ISWAP filmed this attack in a video entitled "Invading Niger: Scenes from Liberating the Nigerien Apostate Army Camp in the Area of Bosso."[32] ISWAP released the video via the Islamic State's media channels in July 2016, and seems to have done so in anticipation of—and as a promotion for—Abu

Musab al-Barnawi's impending ascension to ISWAP's leadership position.

ISWAP established cells in Senegal in 2015 and 2016.[33] There were also approximately 100 Nigerians and several dozen Senegalese fighting with the Islamic State in Libya.[34] This presence gave the group a significant operational capability; with Abu Musab al-Barnawi's more internationally connected ISWAP faction now in charge of these regional relationships, ISWAP could activate cells of Nigerian and Senegalese ex-foreign fighters in Libya. Activating those cells would launch ISWAP's first attack outside of the Lake Chad region. However, ISWAP concentrated its attacks almost exclusively to Borno State and southern Niger from late 2016 to 2018. Because ISWAP fighters often know the northeastern Nigerian terrain and civilian population better than military soldiers, who may come from different parts of the country, ISWAP has become more powerful in the region.

There are no signs at this time that ISWAP is planting cells in Europe in preparation for attacks there. Rather, the Islamic State has used its Syrian and, increasingly, Libyan network to carry out this function.

Recent Activity

From the time of his pledge to al-Baghdadi in March 2015 until August 3, 2016, the formerly bombastic Shekau was not seen publicly in any video or propaganda material, although the Islamic State still recognized him as its *wali* (governor). During this time, Shekau and his former rival, Mamman Nur, were locked in a factional feud, with each publishing behind-the-scenes audios condemning the other.[35] Moreover, as Nur's ally, Abu Musab al-Barnawi, controlled the communications between the Islamic State and ISWAP, he was able to cut off Shekau—which explains the latter's absence from media even while he was "governor" of ISWAP.

After Abu Musab al-Barnawi's condemnations of Shekau, the latter was forced to back down and the Islamic State announced on August 3, 2016 that Abu Musab al-Barnawi had become the new *wali* of ISWAP.[36] In an audio clip released on YouTube just after his demotion, Shekau announced that he was reverting to his former position and declared himself *imam* of Boko Haram, thereby signaling that he had left ISWAP.[37] Several days later, Boko Haram released a video on YouTube for the first time since Shekau returned to his role as *imam*. In the video, Shekau declared that Boko Haram would refuse to follow Abu Musab al-Barnawi because he did not adhere to "authentic Salafism." In subsequent videos issued since September 2016, Shekau reiterated that Boko Haram was still loyal to al-Baghdadi and considers itself part of the Islamic State (even though the latter only recognized ISWAP, and not Boko Haram). Shekau also claimed that his militants would continue *jihad* regardless of their affiliation.[38] Furthermore, Shekau condemned the electoral victory of the "pagan" and "homosexual" Donald Trump over the "prostitute" Hillary Clinton in the November 2016 U.S. presidential election, making clear that the U.S. remains a target of his animus.[39] In the first months of 2017, Shekau's videos continued to feature Islamic State-style imagery, began to feature French-speaking fighters, and criticized Nigerian Salafis who—Boko Haram argues—chose the Nigerian government over "Muhammed Yusuf's blood."[40]

Shekau showed pragmatism in his decision to return 83 of the Chibok schoolgirls in May 2017 after a breakaway commander returned 21 girls in October 2016. Although the Nigerian government claimed that it only exchanged prisoners for the Chibok captives, one of the prisoners said in a Boko Haram video that the Nigerian government paid ransoms for the girls as well.[41] This demonstrates that Boko Haram still has a diversified messaging strategy and a level of pragmatism not often recognized as being one of its core characteristics.

The leadership change in August 2016 led to ISWAP becoming more regional than local in nature. Both Nur and Abu Musab al-Barnawi were more internationally connected than Shekau, and they became the top figures in ISWAP. However, they could not attack outside Nigeria or the Lake Chad region and may not have wanted to invite foreign pressure on their fighters by attacking Western targets. ISWAP could also maintain good relations with the civilian population; group leadership was accused of weakness, however, and Mamman Nur was purged and killed in September 2018 as a result. Abu Musab al-Barnawi was put under house arrest and Ba Idrisa replaced him as ISWAP leader in March 2019.[42] Shekau could benefit from hardliners leading ISWAP. but there is no indication that ISWAP seeks a relationship with him.

ISWAP's main strength remains its versatility in carrying out operations throughout the Lake Chad region, especially Niger. Shekau's Boko Haram, in contrast, has increasingly consolidated around Sambisa Forest since 2016.[43] Although ISWAP does not have Boko Haram's level of grassroots membership, it nonetheless maintains a significant contingent of skilled fighters, because many who were originally in Boko Haram defected to and remained in ISWAP. Because ISWAP fighters do not antagonize or torment the local population, civilians often avoid cooperating with the Nigerian military. Locals who do cooperate with authorities, however, are killed by ISWAP.[44] This has helped ISWAP control parts of Borno State with little popular revolt. The group has also established consistent funding streams via taxes levied on cattle herders, farmers, and fishermen in exchange for local stability.

One of the prototypical examples of how ISWAP differs from Boko Haram took place in February 2018, when a faction of ISWAP, which was likely comprised of defectors from Shekau's group, kidnapped 111 girls from a school in Yobe State. When they brought the girls to Abu Musab al-Barnawi's hideout near Lake Chad, he demanded the girls be returned to their families except for the one Christian girl who could only return to her family if she converted to Islam.[45] According to al-Barnawi, it was unacceptable to kidnap Muslims for religious reasons, but also because it could alienate the group from its broader Muslim support base in northeastern Nigeria.[46] He also reportedly contacted Islamic State leader Abubakar al-Baghdadi, who urged him to release the girls so long as they repented for receiving Western education and living with unbelievers. According to the Islamic State, it would hurt ISWAP's image if they were to enslave Muslim girls (Boko Haram, however, did enslave one kidnapped Christian girl).[47] When in March 2018 ISWAP delivered the 105 girls (all but the Christian girl and five others who had died during the kidnapping itself) back to their villages after coming to a "safe corridor" agreement with the Nigerian government, which was met with great fanfare from the villagers. This did not, however, presage a broader ceasefire with the government.

Although the Islamic State is weaker than al-Qaeda in the Sahel and increasingly struggling in Iraq, Syria, and Libya, ISWAP represents a highlight for the Islamic State. One additional reason for why Ba Idrisa replaced Abu Musab al-Barnawi may have to do with the trust the Islamic State's leaders place in his leadership. Because al-Barnawi maintained a relationship with al-Qaeda in the past, his loyalties remain suspect to some degree. Ba Idrisa, by contrast, does not have any such connections and as a result helps to ensure that ISWAP remains loyal to the Islamic State.

Endnotes

1. Kassim, Abdulbasit. Twitter post, March 11, 2019, 10:44 a.m. https://twitter.com/ScholarAkassi1/status/
2. Tamba Jean-Matthew, "3 imams charged with terrorism in Senegal," *Africa Review*, November 9, 2015, http://www.africareview.com/news/Senegalese-imams-charged-with-terrorism-/979180-2949060-dv12q3z/index.html; "Coup de Filet Anti Boko Haram Au Sénégal: La cellule de Abu Youssouf," Dakaractu, n.d., http://www.dakaractu.com/COUP-DE-FILET-ANTI-BOKO-HARAM-AU-SENEGAL-La-cellule-de-Abu-Youssouf-decimee_a115021.html; http://www.buzz.sn/news/boko-haram-attirerait-il-autant-de-senegalais-que-la-branche-libyenne-de-lei/34207; "Peer Raises Fears Over UK Charity's Alleged Links to Boko Haram," *Guardian* (London), September 9, 2012, https://www.theguardian.com/world/2012/sep/09/uk-charity-boko-haram.
3. Tamba Jean-Matthew, "3 imams charged with terrorism in Senegal," *Africa Review*, November 9, 2015, http://www.africareview.com/news/Senegalese-imams-charged-with-terrorism-/979180-2949060-dv12q3z/index.html; "Coup de Filet Anti Boko Haram Au Sénégal: La cellule de Abu Youssouf," Dakaractu, n.d., http://www.dakaractu.com/COUP-DE-FILET-ANTI-BOKO-HARAM-AU-SENEGAL-La-cellule-de-Abu-Youssouf-decimee_a115021.html; http://www.buzz.sn/news/boko-haram-attirerait-il-autant-de-senegalais-que-la-branche-libyenne-de-lei/34207; "Peer Raises Fears Over UK Chari-

ty's Alleged Links to Boko Haram," *Guardian* (London), September 9, 2012, https://www.theguardian.com/world/2012/sep/09/uk-charity-boko-haram.

4. Muhammad S. Umar, "The Popular Discourses of Salafi Radicalism and Salafi Counter-radicalism in Nigeria: A Case Study of Boko Haram," *Journal of Religion in Africa*, 2012.
5. Aminu Abubakar, "Nigerian Islamist sect threaten to widen attacks," Agence France Presse, March 29, 2010.
6. Simeon H.O. Alozieuwa, "Contending Theories on Nigeria's Security Challenge in the Era of Boko Haram Insurgency," *The Peace and Conflict Review*, 2012.
7. Karen Brulliard, "For Many, Nigeria's Moderate Form of Sharia Fails to Deliver on Promises," *Washington Post*, August 12, 2009.
8. Farouk Chothia, "Who are Nigeria's Boko Haram Islamists?" BBC, January 11, 2012/
9. Emmanuel Goujon and Aminu Abubakar, "Nigeria's 'Taliban' Plot Comeback from Hide□outs," Agence France□Presse, January 11, 2006.
10. Andrea Brigaglia, "A Contribution to the History of the Wahhabi Daʿwa in West Africa: The Career and the Murder of Shaykh Jaʿfar Mahmoud Adam (Daura, ca. 1961/1962-Kano 2007)," *Islamic Africa* 3, iss. 1, 2012, 1-23; Andrea Brigaglia, "The Volatility of Salafi Political Theology, the War on Terror and the Genesis of Boko Haram," *Diritto e Questioni Pubbliche* 15, iss. 2, 2015, 174-201.
11. Pervez Musharraf, *In the Line of Fire* (Free Press, 2008); Department of Justice, U.S. Attorney's Office Eastern District of New York, "Al Qaeda Operative Convicted Of Multiple Terrorism Offenses Targeting Americans Overseas,", March 16, 2017; Ikechukwu Nnochiri, "Danger Alert: Al□Qaeda boss in West Africa lives in Kano," Odili.net, April 8, 2012, http://www.nairaland.com/910534/mallam-adnan-ibrahimal-qaeda-boss-west; U.S. Department of State, Office of the Coordinator for Counterterrorism, *Country Reports on Terrorism 2007*, April 30, 2008, http://www.refworld.org/docid/48196c9a1a.html.
12. U.S. Department of State, Office of the Coordinator for Counterterrorism, *Country Reports on Terrorism 2007*, "Chapter 2 -- Country Reports: Africa Overview," April 30, 2008, http://www.state.gov/j/ct/rls/crt/2007/103705.htm; Ahmad Salkida, "Nigeria: Sect Leader Vows Revenge," *Daily Trust*, July 27, 2009, http://allafrica.com/stories/200907270879.html.
13. Benjamin Maiangwa and Ufo Okeke Uzodike, "The Changing

Dynamics of Boko Haram Terrorism," *Al-Jazeera* (Doha), July 31, 2012.

14. Human Rights Watch, "Spiraling Violence: Boko Haram Attacks and Security Force Abuses in Nigeria," Human Rights Watch, October 11, 2012, https://www.hrw.org/report/2012/10/11/spiraling-violence/boko-haram-attacks-and-security-force-abuses-nigeria.
15. Letter from 'Abdallah Abu Zayd 'Abd-al-Hamid Abu Mus'ab 'Abd-al-Wadud," *Bin Laden's Bookshelf – ODNI*, released January 2017, https://www.dni.gov/files/documents/ubl2017/english/Letter%20from%20Abdallah%20Abu%20Zayd%20Abd-al-Hamid%20to%20Abu%20Mus%20ab%20Abd-al-Wadud.pdf.
16. Abdallah Abu Zayd 'Abd-al-Hamid to 'our Shaykh and Emir, Abu Mus'ab 'Abd-al-Wadud' Subject: A letter from the Emir of the Nigeria group," *Bin Laden's Bookshelf – ODNI*, released January 2017, https://www.dni.gov/index.php/features/bin-laden-s-bookshelf.
17. Abubakr Shekau, "Praise be to God the Lord of all worlds," *Bin Laden's Bookshelf – ODNI*, released August 2016, https://www.dni.gov/index.php/features/bin-laden-s-bookshelf.
18. Chothia, Farouk. "Profile: Who Are Nigeria's Ansaru Islamists?" *BBC News*, March 11, 2013, https://www.bbc.com/news/world-africa-21510767.
19. Jacob Zenn, "Ansaru: Who Are They And Where Are They From?" *Africa in Transition*, July 1, 2013, https://www.cfr.org/blog-post/ansaru-who-are-they-and-where-are-they.
20. "Nigerian Islamist leader threatens US: monitors," Agence France Presse, July 14, 2010.
21. International Institute for Counterterrorism, "Periodical Review July 2010 – No. 2," August 2010.
22. "New Boko Haram Leader, al-Barnawi, Accuses Abukbakar Shekau of Killing Fellow Muslims, Living In Luxury," *Sahara Reporters,* August 5, 2016, http://saharareporters.com/2016/08/05/new-boko-haram-leader-al-barnawi-accuses-abubakar-shekau-killing-fellow-muslims-living.
23. Ely Karmon, "Boko Haram's International Reach," Universiteit Leiden Terrorism Research Initiative *Report* no. 1, 2014, http://www.terrorismanalysts.com/pt/index.php/pot/article/view/326/html.
24. "Dozens of Boko Haram in Mali's rebel-seized Gao: sources," *Bangkok Post,* April 10, 2012, https://www.bangkokpost.com/news/world/288208/dozens-of-boko-haram-in-mali-rebel-seized-gao-sources
25. "New Video Message From Ansar Ad-Din: The Conquest of

Azawad," *Jihadology*, January 6, 2013, https://jihadology.net/2012/07/10/new-video-message-from-an%E1%B9%A3ar-ad-din-the-conquest-of-azawad/

26. Jacob Zenn, "Nigerians in Gao: Was Boko Haram Really Active in Northern Mali?" *African Arguments*, January 20, 2014.
27. "Boko Haram Militants Shows Off Weapons 'Captured' From An Army Barack Raid," *Sahara TV,* April 29, 2013, https://www.youtube.com/watch?v=El-O37TNIm4; Jacob Zenn, *Boko Haram's Evolving Tactics and Alliance in Nigeria,* Combatting Terrorism Center, June 25, 2013, https://www.ctc.usma.edu/posts/boko-harams-evolving-tactics-and-alliances-in-nigeria; Kareem Ogori, "Boko Haram Raids Army Barracks, Kills 22," *Blueprint*, March 4, 2013.
28. "Boko Haram Militants Display Control Of Captured Towns In Northeastern Nigeria," *Sahara TV,* November 10, 2014, https://www.youtube.com/watch?v=77YwVoM7_JA.
29. "Boko Haram Widely Deploying Female Suicide Bombers," *The Clarion Project,* December 15, 2014, http://www.clarionproject.org/news/boko-haram-widely-deploying-female-suicide-bombers; "Boko Haram Turns Female Captives into Terrorists," *The New York Times,* April 7, 2016 http://www.nytimes.com/2016/04/08/world/africa/boko-haram-suicide-bombers.html; Jacob Zenn, Abdulbasit Kassim, Elizabeth Pearson, Atta Barkindo, Idayat Hassan, Zacharias Pieri, and Omar Mahmoud, *Boko Haram Beyond the Headlines: Analyses of Africa's Enduring Insurgency*, United States Military Academy Combatting Terrorism Center, May 2018, 33-52.
30. "Bloody Weekend as Boko Haram Strikes Chad, Nigeria," *Africa News*, February 5, 2016, http://www.africanews.com/2016/01/31/bloody-weekend-as-boko-haram-strikes-chad-nigeria/; "Chad Executes 10 Boko Haram Fighters over Deadly Attacks." *BBC News*, August 29, 2015, http://www.bbc.com/news/world-africa-34100484.
31. "A female suicide bomber killed by a poisoned arrow in Cameroon," Reuters, May 4, 2016, https://francais.rt.com/international/20091-femme-kamikaze-tuee-par-fleche.
32. "Boko Haram retakes Niger town of Bosso, says mayor," Reuters, June 6, 2016. http://www.reuters.com/article/us-nigeria-security-niger-idUSKCN0YS1TY.
33. "The Fight against Islamic State Is Moving to Africa." *The Economist*, July 14, 2018, https://www.economist.com/middle-east-and-africa/2018/07/14/the-fight-against-islamic-state-is-moving-to-africa.
34. "Terrorism: over 23 Senegalese joined Boko Haram," *Press Afrik,*

February 25, 2016, http://www.pressafrik.com/Terrorisme-plus-de-23-Senegalais-ont-rejoint-Boko-Haram_a146725.html; "Senegal arrests suspected Boko Haram recruiter, extremists," *Fox News*, April 12, 2017, https://www.foxnews.com/world/senegal-arrests-suspected-boko-haram-recruiter-extremists.

35. "Who are the Senegalese men joining the Islamic State group?" *The Observers,* February 1, 2016, http://observers.france24.com/en/20160201-senegal-jihadist-islamic-state; "Boko Haram may be sending fighters to Isis in Libya – US officials," *Guardian* (London), May 13, 2016, https://www.theguardian.com/world/2016/may/14/boko-haram-may-be-sending-fighters-to-isis-in-libya-us-officials; Ayorinde Oluokun, "DSS arrest members of Boko Haram, Ansaru terror groups in Kano, Kaduna, Edo," *TheNEWS,* August 22, 2016, http://thenewsnigeria.com.ng/2016/08/dss-arrest-members-of-boko-haram-ansaru-terror-groups-in-kano-kaduna-edo/.
36. Jacob Zenn, *Leadership Analysis of Boko Haram and Ansaru in Nigeria,* Combatting Terrorism Center, February 24, 2014, https://www.ctc.usma.edu/posts/leadership-analysis-of-boko-haram-and-ansaru-in-nigeria; "Nigeria Sets $175,000 Bounty For Mamman Nur, The Alleged UN Office Bomber," *Sahara Reporter,* September 18, 2011, http://saharareporters.com/2011/09/18/nigeria-sets-175000-bounty-mamman-nur-alleged-un-office-bomber; "New Boko Haram Leader, al-Barnawi, Accuses Abubakar Shekau Of Killing Fellow Muslims, Living In Luxury" *Sahara Reporters,* August 5, 2016, http://saharareporters.com/2016/08/05/new-boko-haram-leader-al-barnawi-accuses-abubakar-shekau-killing-fellow-muslims-living.
37. Islamic State, *al-Naba* Weekly Newsletter #41, August 2, 2016 available at: http://jihadology.net/2016/08/02/new-issue-of-the-islamic-states-newsletter-al-naba-41/; "Al-Urwah al-Wuthqa Foundation Presents a New Video Message from Boko Haram", *Jihadology*, January 27, 2015, http://jihadology.net/2015/01/27/al-urwah-al-wuthqa-foundation-presents-a-new-video-message-from-from-boko-ḥarams-jamaat-ahl-al-sunnah-li-dawah-wa-l-jihad-interview-with-the-official-spokesma/.
38. Video has been removed for violating YouTube's Terms of Service. Original URL is https://www.youtube.com/watch?v=AhY-R37fvB-k&feature=youtu.be.
39. "New video message from Jamā'at Ahl al-Sunnah li-l-Da'wah wa-l-Jih ād's Abū Bakr Shekau: 'Message to the World,'" *Jihadology,* September 24, 2016, http://jihadology.net/2016/09/24/new-video-message-from-jamaat-ahl-al-sunnah-li-l-dawah-wa-l-jihads-abu-

bakr-shekau-message-to-the-world/.

40. Video has been removed for violating YouTube's Terms of Service. Original URL is https://www.youtube.com/watch?v=AhY-R37fvB-k&feature=youtu.be.
41. Daniel Finnan, "Focus on Cameroon in Boko Haram's latest propaganda video, analysis," *RFI,* March 23, 2017, http://saharareporters.com/2017/05/12/chibok-girls-wielding-ak-47-rifles-appear-boko-haram-video-explain-refusal-return-home; Bello Husman, "Iqamat al-Hadud," April 3, 2017, https://www.youtube.com/watch?v=nrv-V7NZyMsI).
42. Finnan, "Focus on Cameroon in Boko Haram's latest propaganda video, analysis."
43. "Boko Haram Leader Mamman Nur 'Killed By His Closest Lieutenants' For Releasing Dapchi Girls." Nur, the brain behind the ties between Boko Haram and the Abu Bakr al-Baghdadi-led Islamic State, was said to have been killed by his closest lieutenants for releasing the Dapchi girls without demanding ransom, among other reasons. "Boko Haram Leader Mamman Nur Killed by His Closest Lieutenants for Releasing Dapchi Girls," *Sahara Reporters*, September 14, 2018, http://saharareporters.com/2018/09/14/boko-haram-leader-mamman-nur-killed-his-closest-lieutenants-releasing-dapchi-girls.
44. Ahmed Kingimi, "Man purporting to be Boko Haram leader denies Sambisa forest defeat," Reuters, December 29, 2016, http://www.reuters.com/article/us-nigeria-security-idUSKBN14I1J3.
45. "Three dead in Boko Haram 'collaboration' killing," *Vanguard*, March 27, 2017, http://www.vanguardngr.com/2017/03/three-dead-boko-haram-collaboration-killing/.
46. "Boko Haram Gives Reason For Release of Dapchi Girls, Denies Ceasefire Talks With FG," *Sahara Reporters,* April 09, 2018, http://saharareporters.com/2018/04/09/boko-haram-gives-reason-release-dapchi-girls-denies-ceasefire-talks-fg.
47. Jacob Zenn, "The Terrorist Calculus in Kidnapping Girls in Nigeria: Cases from Chibok and Dapchi," *CTC Sentinel,* March 2018, https://ctc.usma.edu/the-terrorist-calculus-in-kidnapping-girls-in-nigeria-cases-from-chibok-and-dapchi/; A Boko Haram faction, Islamic State West Africa Provence (ISWAP), has given the reason it released the girls kidnapped from the Government Girls' Technical College, Dapchi in Yobe State. The group, in an audio recording exclusively obtained by SaharaReporters, said the girls were freed because of its allegiance to the leadership of the Islamic State in Iraq and the Levant (ISIL). In the recording, the faction's head of Shura (high-

est decision body), Abu Bashir, urged its members to remain loyal to ISIL. "Boko Haram Gives Reason For Release Of Dapchi Girls, Denies Ceasefire Talks With FG." *Sahara Reporters*, April 9, 2018, http://saharareporters.com/2018/04/09/boko-haram-gives-reason-release-dapchi-girls-denies-ceasefire-talks-fg.

65 Fetullah Gülen Movement

Quick Facts

Geographical Areas of Operation: East Asia, Eurasia, Europe, Latin America, Middle East and North Africa, North America, South Asia, Sub-Saharan Africa, Australia
Numerical strength (members): There are somewhere between three and six million Gülen followers although exact numbers are impossible to offer because, as Ihsan Yilmaz stated, the boundaries of this "collectivity" are "extremely loose and difficult to specify."
Leadership: Fetullah Gülen
Religious identification: Mainstream Sufism

Quick Facts courtesy of Ihsan Yilmaz's, "Inter-Madhhab Surfing, Neo-Ijtihad, and Faith Based Movement Leaders" and Claire Berlinski's, "Who is Fethullah Gulen?" (Autumn 2012)

Introduction

Fethullah Gülen, a charismatic Turkish preacher, inspires and leads an eponymous Islamic revivalist movement. Unlike many other organizations in this compilation, the Gülen movement claims to be pacifist and focused on providing quality education to communities all over the world of which it is a part, ostensibly working toward the modernization and democratization of Turkey. However, there is compelling evidence to suggest that the Gülen movement is more focused more on cultivating its own social power than any other objective. Furthermore, the movement operates internally in an undemocratic and opaque fashion. Critics maintain that its vast network of charter schools illegally funnels millions of American taxpayer dollars to Turkish businesses. Detractors inside Turkey, meanwhile, have accused it of infiltrating the Turkish judiciary and security apparatuses, and blame the organization for staging a bloody failed coup against the government of President Recep Tayyip Erdoğan on July 15, 2016. On May 26, 2016, the Gülen movement was officially classified as a terrorist organization by the Turkish government under the name Fethullahist Terror

Organization (Fethullahçı Terör Örgütü, or FETÖ) or Parallel State Organization (Paralel Devlet Yapılanması, or PDY). Gülen continues to give weekly talks (Bamteli and Herkul Nağme), which are uploaded to Herkul.org and regularly downloaded by some 20,000–50,000 listeners. However, the movement's membership and influence continue to decline as the Turkish government targets their financial resources, both within Turkey and abroad.

History & Ideology

According to an article quoted on Fethullah Gülen's website, he is:

> ...an authoritative mainstream Turkish Muslim scholar, thinker, author, poet, opinion leader and educational activist who supports interfaith and intercultural dialogue, science, democracy and spirituality.[1]

The site notes that he was "the first Muslim scholar to publicly condemn the attacks of 9/11 (in an advertisement in the *Washington Post*)."[2] Yet, there is more to the story. At the height of his power, Gülen was an immensely powerful, controversial figure in Turkey, and has cultivated global influence through the networks established by his followers.

Although the two never met, Gülen is a follower of Said Nursî (1876-1960), one of the great charismatic religious personalities of the late Ottoman Caliphate and early Turkish Republic, and whose followers became known as the Nurcu Movement. As a young man, Nursî was greatly influenced by the Sufi brotherhoods, known as *tariqah* from the Arabic for "road" or "path," although he was never formally initiated into any of them. Nursî was a prolific writer, producing numerous pamphlets, letters, brochures, and Qur'anic commentaries, which were collected in what became known as the Risale-i Nur or "Epistles of Light."[3] As Nursî's following grew in size, the Risale-i Nur became the basis for the formation of reading circles known as *dershanes*. These evolved into so-called, "textual communities" devoted to reading and internalizing

Nursî's commentaries. Nursî argued strongly for the compatibility of modern science with the Qur'an and the collections of sayings and deeds of the Prophet Muhammed, known as the Hadith. He contended that any apparent contradictions between modern science and Islamic scripture were the product of a superficial or erroneous understanding of the sacred texts. He encouraged his followers to study mathematics and the sciences as they shaped their lives according to Islamic precepts. He maintained that they should follow a three-phase process: seeking first to Islamize individuals and then society, before moving onto the final stage of Islamizing the state and regulating it according to *sharia* (Islamic law).

The *dershanes* gradually spread throughout Anatolia. Hakan Yavuz, a Turkish political scientist at the University of Utah who was formerly sympathetic to Gülen, claims that the Nurcu movement:

> ...differs from other Islamic movements in terms of its understanding of Islam ... As a resistance movement to the ongoing Kemalist modernization process, the Nurcu movement is forward-looking and pro-active. Said Nursî offers a conceptual framework for a people undergoing the transformation from a confessional community (Gemeinschaft) to a secular national society (Gesellschaft)... Folk Islamic concepts and practices are redefined and revived to establish new solidarity networks and everyday-life strategies for coping with new conditions.[4]

Gülen's movement, which is frequently known as the *cemaat* (community), arose from roughly a dozen Nurcu textual communities. Unlike Nursî, who was Kurdish by origin, Gülen is an ethnic Turk, and his teachings have always a contained strong elements of Ottoman nostalgia, Turkish nationalism, and an emphasis on the Turkish language. As a result, although Kurds make up some of his followers, even at its height, the Gülen Movement struggled to establish a strong presence in predominantly Kurdish southeastern Turkey. Gülen's worldview has also been shaped by Sunni sectarianism, especially toward the Shia of Iran, whose historical predecessor, the Persian Empire, was one of the Ottomans' greatest rivals.

Born in 1941 in eastern Anatolia, Gülen was taught Arabic and the basic tenets of Islam by his father.[5] In 1958, he passed the entrance examination for the state-controlled Presidency of Religious Affairs, commonly known as the Diyanet, and was appointed as the resident preacher at a mosque in Edirne in northwest Turkey.[6] It was around this time that he became acquainted with Nursî's writings. In 1966, Gülen was transferred to the Aegean port of Izmir. He began to attract a growing following in 1971 while providing religious instruction at youth summer camps. During the factional fighting of the 1970s, Gülen was also involved in the anti-Communism movement.

Nursî's reputation was built on his notoriously complex writings, which are often criticized by outsiders for their obliqueness. However, his followers maintain that their difficulty is evidence of their complexity and profundity, and that discussions about their meaning draw readers deeper into the text. In contrast, the appeal of Gülen's writings and public utterances has been primarily emotional; during his sermons, Gülen frequently breaks down in tears while describing the sufferings of the Prophet Muhammed. Although his followers developed a rapidly expanding network of reading circles to study his writings in across much of Anatolia, Gülen was never regarded as a leading Islamic theologian by those outside his own cemaat. For Sufi brotherhoods such as the Naqshbandi—whose members undergo a rigorous training and initiation process before they are deemed worthy of being admitted into an esoteric tradition believed to stretch back to the Prophet Muhammed himself—Gülen is regarded as something of a theological parvenu, lacking the spiritual authority and pedigree of the *tariqah*.

Since he relocated to the U.S. in 1999, Gülen has presented himself as an advocate of tolerance, reconciliation and interfaith dialogue. However, his early career was notable for statements, sermons, and publications expressing intolerance toward those whom he considered enemies of Islam. In one sermon from 1979 Gülen energetically chides his flock for allowing infidels (*gâvur*) to take control of all the holy places of Islam. He declared, "Muslims should become bombs and explode, tear to pieces the heads of the infidels! Even if it's America opposing them." He further curses those who are indifferent to this cause.[7] In another, he says: "Until this day missionaries and the Vatican have been behind all atrocities. The Vatican is the hole of the snake, the hole of the cobra. The Vatican is behind the bloodshed in Bosnia. The Vatican is behind the bloodshed in Kashmir. They have lobby groups in America and Germany."[8]

In the first editions of books from his early career, such as *Fasıldan Fasıla* (From Chapter to Chapter) and *Asrın Getirdiği Tereddütler* (The Puzzles of the Age), Gülen called the West the "continuous enemy of Islam." Of Christians, he wrote: "After a while they perverted and obscured their own future." Gülen also wrote that Jews have a "genetic animosity towards any religion;" and have used "their guile and skills to breed bad blood… uniting themselves with Sassanids, Romans and crusaders." He averred that: "the Church, the Synagogue and Paganism form the troika that has attacked Islam persistently." "In any case," he wrote, "the Prophet considers Islam as one nation and the *Kuffar* as the other nation."[9]

Such references have been removed from the later editions of Gülen's books and from the copies of his writings available on the Gülen Movement's websites. He has never provided an explanation for the change, or disowned his previous statements. Many Turks, however, still view him as an archconservative *imam* with extremist views about women, atheists, and apostates.

Gülen maintains that Muslims and non-Muslims lived in harmony under the Ottoman Turks—even though, for nearly all of the Ottoman Empire's existence, non-Muslims were legally subordinated to Muslims in what amounted to a religious caste system. Gülen argues that, in order to ensure peaceful cohabitation between different faiths, Turks should become leaders in the promotion of religious tolerance. The authors Latif Erdoğan and Davut Aydüz, both of whom were sympathetic to Gülen at the time,[10] argued that the *cemaat*'s key goal was to help Turkey play a pivotal role in the international political environment. "Turkey will be the representative of justice in the world... Turkey should show the meaning of civilization to the world once more."[11]

Starting in the 1970s, Gülen sought to create a "Golden Generation" of committed male followers who, in addition to embodying Islamic values in their everyday lives, would form the leadership cadre of the *cemaat*.[12] Most were the children of pious, low income, families of first or second generation migrants from the countryside to the cities. Selected at an early age, they would have their education paid for by wealthy members of the *cemaat*. The benefactors would also arrange shared accommodation and a small stipend for those who were forced to relocate to attend university. The shared apartments —known as *ışık evleri* (lighthouses)—were single sex. Students would receive regular visits from older members of the *cemaat*, known as *abiler* (elder brothers) or *ablalar* (elder sisters), who would check on their welfare and lead discussions and readings of Gülen's works.

As the *cemaat* grew in size, it began to expand its educational and recruitment activities, particularly through specialized schools established by Gülen followers to prepare students for the nationwide high school and university entrance examinations. The *cemaat* would identify bright students from low income backgrounds and provide them with scholarships to attend private schools and universities. Gradually, the cemaat established dormitories and schools of its own.

In his writings, Gülen's theology differentiates between *tebliğ* (communication) and *temsil* (representation). He calls on his followers to avoid open proselytism, or *tebliğ*. He urges them instead to practice *temsil*—living an Islamic way of life at all times without uttering the word "Islam" or other "dangerous words." *Temsil* missionaries are to set a good example, embodying their ideals in their way of life. It is very visible that, within the *cemaat*, the embodiment of these ideals appears to involve a subordinate role for women.

Gülen frequently encouraged his followers to seek employment in the Turkish civil service on the grounds that it would enable them to serve the nation, although skeptics accused him of trying to take over the state by stealth. Those of his followers who went into the private sector created a rapidly growing network of companies, media organizations, and NGOs. In addition to creating employment for Gülen's followers, these commercial activities also provided a steady revenue stream for the *cemaat*. Members who could afford to donate were vigorously encouraged to do so with a portion of their salaries as *zakat*, the religiously required giving of alms, in order to support the *cemaat*'s activities.

The internal organization of the *cemaat* has always been extremely opaque and secretive. A small number of prominent organization members meet with Gülen once or twice a month, to assess the *cemaat*'s activities and determine strategic goals. Although some members of this inner circle have geographical responsibilities, such as overseeing activities in a particular country or region, there is no detailed hierarchical structure. Any decisions made resulting from meetings with Gülen is usually the result of ad-hoc cooperation between individual members under the supervision of one or more senior figures.

During his later years, Said Nursî was an outspoken supporter of the Democrat Party (DP) of Prime Minister Adnan Menderes (1899-1961), who was overthrown by a military coup in 1960 and hanged the following year. The DP was banned after the coup.

Over the next decade, Nursî's followers tended to vote for the Justice Party (AP) until the AP was outlawed following the 1980 coup, at which point those supporters tended to cast their votes for the True Path Party (DYP), the AP's natural successor.

In 1970, the Nurcus joined with the *tariqah* to support the foundation of an explicitly Islamist political party, the National Order Party (MNP), under the leadership of Necmettin Erbakan (1926-2011), who had close connections with the Istanbul-based İskenderpaşa lodge of the Naqshbandi *tariqah*.

The MNP was closed down after the 1971 coup and replaced by the National Salvation Party (MSP), which was also led by Erbakan and supported by the Nurcus. However, the Nurcus broke away from the MSP in 1974 after it entered a coalition government and supported an amnesty for leftists convicted of political offences. The majority of Turkish Islamists, including most of the *tariqah*, however, continued to back the MSP until it was banned; they would later support the MSP's successor, the Welfare Party (RP).

The situation changed in 1997, when the Turkish military launched a campaign to force an RP-led coalition government from office, and to purge what were seen as reactionary forces from the public and political spheres. On June 19, 1999, the *ATV* national television channel broadcast two videos of Gülen apparently instructing his followers to infiltrate critical parts of the government, biding their time by presenting a moderate image until they were strong enough to implement their agenda.[13] As state prosecutors began a judicial investigation into Gülen, he fled to the U.S., ostensibly for medical treatment.

In August 2001, after the RP was also outlawed and Erbakan banned from politics for five years, a younger generation of former RP members formed the Justice and Development Party (AKP), under the leadership of Recep Tayyip Erdoğan, the former mayor of Istanbul. Like Erbakan, Erdoğan had close connections to the İskenderpaşa lodge of the Naqshbandi *tariqah*. Despite their differences, Erdoğan and the Gülen Movement formed an alliance of convenience against what they regarded as a shared enemy: the secular Turkish establishment and the country's military. When the AKP came to power in November 2002, Erdoğan enabled the *cemaat* to rapidly expand its presence in the apparatus of state, especially in the Turkish National Police, the judiciary and the Education Ministry—both by employing large numbers of Gülen's followers and by fast-tracking them for promotion. In return, the *cemaat* mobilized its networks in support of Erdoğan and the AKP, both domestically and abroad. At the time, the AKP had no organized presence outside Turkey, and very few foreign language speakers. The *cemaat* filled the gap, particularly in Washington, where its members lobbied vigorously on Erdoğan's behalf and formed close relations with interest groups with ties to the administration.

Inside Turkey, Erdoğan and the *cemaat* were initially very cautious for fear of triggering a military intervention. The situation changed when the AKP reacted to a clumsy attempt by the military to prevent it from appointing then-Foreign Minister Abdullah Gül to the presidency by calling an early general election for July 2007, which the party won in a landslide. Unwilling to defy such a clear manifestation of public sentiment, the military remained silent as Gül was sworn in as president in August 2007.

Confident that he no longer needed to fear the military, Erdoğan began pursuing an increasingly overt pro-religion agenda. The *cemaat* used its presence in the police and judiciary to go on the offensive against its opponents and perceived rivals by various means, including initiating a series of highly politicized mass trials and leaking embarrassing wire-tapped private telephone conversations involving its more outspoken critics to the public. The most notorious of the trials involved hundreds of people who were arrested and charged with belonging to Ergenekon, a vast covert organization which prosecutors claimed had been responsible for almost every act of political violence in modern Turkish history. The investigation and the subsequent trials, spanning 2007 until August 2013, were extensively covered by the *cemaat*'s media organs. Lurid allegations against the accused were published and defamation campaigns targeted critics of the cases. "A noticeable number of those arrested in the case and in subsequent probes were nationalists or hardline Kemalists who had criticized or attacked the Gülen network over the years," wrote Turkish journalist Asli Aydintaşbaş.[14]

Supporters of the Ergenekon investigation claimed it was an attempt to unravel what Turks call the "Deep State"—a covert network with roots in the military that had manipulated political processes and was responsible for numerous acts of politically motivated violence, including death squads targeting leftists and Kurdish nationalists. Although its influence weakened from the late 1990s onwards, the Deep State was a reality. However, the Ergenekon investigation made no attempt to investigate the real Deep State; it instead opted to target opponents, rivals and critics of the *cemaat*.[15] As the latter were almost invariably hostile to Erdoğan, he actively supported the investigation. "I am the prosecutor of this case," he said; his supporters, meanwhile, ridiculed critics who claimed the *cemaat* had taken over the state.[16]

In 2009, a new round of mass arrests began, targeting Kurdish nationalists accused of being members of the Kurdistan Communities Union (KCK), an umbrella organization for all of the groups following the ideology of Abdullah Öcalan, the founder of the militant Kurdistan Workers' Party (PKK). The police and prosecutors overseeing the KCK investigation were all suspected members of the *cemaat*; in many instances the same officials were responsible for Ergenekon. Some of the thousands who were arrested and imprisoned in the KCK investigation were sympathetic to the PKK. Many others were not. The latter included staff at NGOs active in the predominantly Kurdish southeastern region of Turkey, where the *cemaat* was attempting to establish a presence for its own schools and NGOs.

In January 2010, pro-Gülen journalists published details of alleged plans to stage a military coup in 2003. The plans were supposedly drawn up by a cabal of high-ranking military officers in December 2002. According to *Taraf,* the newspaper where the journalists worked, the coup, codenamed Balyoz (or "Sledgehammer"), would start after the conspirators engineered the bombing of two mosques in Istanbul and the downing of a Turkish F-16 warplane over the Aegean, which would have been blamed on Greece. The cabal, it was alleged, would have used the resultant chaos to seize power, to establish an interim government, and to imprison its domestic enemies. *Taraf* handed the documents to pro-Gülen prosecutors, who launched an investigation that led to the arrest, trial, and imprisonment of hundreds of active-duty and retired members of the military.

However, it soon became clear that the Balyoz coup plan was flawed. Prosecutors claimed that some of the defendants had held a seminar at First Army Headquarters in Istanbul on March 5-7, 2003, to discuss bombing mosques in the city on February 28, 2003. A detailed analysis of the alleged coup plan by Harvard scholars Dani Rodrik and Pınar Doğan, the daughter of one of the defendants, revealed hundreds more anachronisms and contradictions. Forensic analysis by Turkish, U.S., and German experts of the CD on which the Balyoz plan was stored concluded that it had been forged and copied onto computers associated with the defendants.[17] Nevertheless, in September 2012, 325 serving and retired officers were sentenced to lengthy prison terms for their alleged role in the plot. As Dani Rodrik wrote:

> Today it is widely recognized that the coup plans were in fact forgeries. Forensic experts have determined that the plans published by Taraf and forming the backbone of the prosecution were produced on

> backdated computers and made to look as if they were prepared in 2003. A quasi-judicial United Nations body has slammed the Turkish government for severe violations of due process during the trial.[18]

As the number of cases brought by pro-Gülen prosecutors grew, they increasingly targeted those who had specifically criticized the *cemaat* itself, not opponents and critics that the *cemaat* shared with Erdogan. In 2006, Adil Serdar Saçan, former director of the Organized Crimes Unit of the Istanbul police, gave an interview to Kanaltürk TV in which he claimed that Gülen sympathizers had thoroughly penetrated the state's security apparatus:

> During my time at the [police] academy, those in the directorate who did not have ties to the [Gülen] organization were all pensioned off or fired in 2002 when the AKP came to power… Belonging to a certain *cemaat* has become a prerequisite for advancement in the force. At present, over 80 percent of the officers at supervisory level in the general security organization are members of the *cemaat*.[19]

In 2010, another former police chief, Hanefi Avcı, once thought sympathetic to the *cemaat*, published a devastating account of the manner in which Gülen's followers had established networks within the police and judiciary that were controlling cases against the *cemaat*'s perceived critics.[20] In 2011, it became known that the left-wing journalist Ahmet Şık was completing a book on the *cemaat*'s penetration of the Turkish state apparatus. All three men were arrested and imprisoned on charges of belonging to Ergenekon. Şık was arrested before his book was published.[21]

From prison, Şık sent a handwritten note to the journalist Justin Vela, who published part of it in *Foreign Policy:*

> The Ergenekon investigations are the most important part of allowing the *cemaat* to take power in the country. I must say that the deep state is still intact. Just the owner has changed. What I mean by this

> ownership ... is composed of the coalition of AKP and the *cemaat*.... 'Something' has come to power in Turkey, but not *sharia*. I can't name that 'thing' properly.[22]

Privately, members of the *cemaat* made little effort to conceal their personal disdain for Erdoğan, and were preparing for an eventual power struggle. However, Erdogan was convinced that the *cemaat* would not dare to challenge his authority. In November 2011, a listening device was found in Erdoğan's office. When Erdoğan was recuperating at home following an operation for intestinal cancer three months later, pro-Gülen prosecutors issued a summons for Hakan Fidan, the head of Turkey's main spy agency, the National Intelligence Organization (MİT). Fidan was charged with knowingly allowing MİT agents in the PKK to engage in terrorism. At the time, Fidan was regarded as one of Erdoğan's closest confidantes; the summons was seen as an attempt to weaken Erdoğan's grip on power while he was incapacitated. However, Erdoğan immediately ordered the Justice Minister to block the summons and to suspend the associated prosecutors.

During the following months, pro-Gülen companies and NGOs found themselves increasingly excluded from state contracts, disbursements, and access to cheap funding from Turkey's state-run banks. In November 2013, Erdoğan announced plans to abolish the crammer school system, thus effectively threatening to remove what had become the *cemaat*'s main means of recruitment and a primary source of income. In December–2013, pro-Gülen prosecutors hit back by issuing arrest warrants for nearly 100 associates of the AKP leadership, including Erdoğan's son Bilal. The allegations claimed that members of Erdoğan's inner circle had participated in a scheme operated by Turkish-Iranian businessman Reza Zarrab to circumvent U.S. sanctions on Iran by channelling funds through Turkey, sending gold to Tehran in exchange for oil.[23] Erdoğan eventually succeeded in quashing the investigation and having the prosecutors suspended, but not before four ministers implicated in the scandal were forced to resign.[24]

Erdoğan initiated a massive purge of suspected Gülenists from the police, sometimes suspending entire departments. Over the next three months, the *cemaat* reacted with daily internet postings (mostly from U.S.-based accounts). The posts were voice recordings of leading AKP members fixing state contracts and manipulating judicial procedures. The growing tensions between the *cemaat* and Erdoğan had descended into open warfare. The *cemaat* sought, with the release of the recordings, to damage Erdoğan in the run-up to local elections on March 30, 2014. Erdoğan hoped that a convincing victory would provide him with the momentum to stand as a candidate in the presidential elections scheduled for August 2014. On April 6, 2014, a week after Erdoğan and the AKP had comfortably won the local elections, the postings came to an abrupt halt. On August 10, 2014, Erdoğan was duly elected president.

Over the next two years, Erdoğan intensified efforts to purge suspected Gülenists from police departments. He also moved against Bank Asya, the *cemaat*'s bank, which operated according to Islamic financing rules. In February 2015, the state seized a majority stake in Bank Asya, and in July 2015 it took over the entire bank. In March 2016, the state seized control of *Zaman*, the *cemaat*'s flagship daily newspaper, and its English language affiliate *Today's Zaman*. One by one, politicized cases such as Ergenekon and Balyoz were all overturned on appeal. By late 2015, all of those who had been convicted had been released from custody.

In February 2014, the minutes of the Turkey's National Security Council (MGK) meetings began referring to the *cemaat* as an "organization that threatens national security." The phrase was repeated in the minutes of all subsequent MGK meetings until May 26, 2016, when the *cemaat* was officially included in the list of proscribed terrorist organizations as the *Fethullahçı Terör Örgütü* (Fethullahist Terror Organization, or FETO).

Cemaat members first infiltrated the Turkish military in the late 1980s. These efforts had intensified during the 1990s, when hundreds of suspected Gülen sympathizers were expelled from the officer corps. Those who confessed described how they were recruited into the *cemaat* as teenagers, told to take the entrance examinations for officer training school and then to pursue a military career while taking care to avoid showing any signs of piety, such as praying regularly or refraining from drinking alcohol.

Gülenists who succeeded in infiltrating the military did not network amongst themselves and were normally unaware of other members of the *cemaat* in the officer corps. Most remained in intermittent contact with Gülenist mentors outside the military through covert meetings. Others went for years without any contact at all, until they were approached and given tasks such as stealing documents or, particularly during the Ergenekon and Balyoz investigations, planting fabricated evidence in military installations.

Through early 2016, there were repeated rumors that there would be a purge of suspected Gülenist officers at the annual Supreme Military Council (YAŞ) at the beginning of August 2016. Some of the retired officers targeted by the Balyoz case circulated lists of officers they believed to be Gülenists.

On the evening of July 15, 2016, Turkey was rocked by an attempted coup, as military units tried to seize a handful of locations in Istanbul and Ankara. Erdoğan called on his supporters to confront the putschists. Around 250 civilians and an unknown number of military personnel were killed in the ensuing clashes. By 10am on July 16, 2016, the coup attempt had been crushed and virtually all of the 8,000 military personnel who had taken to the streets – most of them cadets and conscripts who had been told by their officers that they were participating in an exercise – were in custody.

Within minutes of the news of the attempted coup breaking, and long before the identities of officers involved were known, AKP officials were blaming the *cemaat*. These accusations intensified after it emerged that the names of some who had played an active role in the putsch were on lists drawn up by retired officers. A handful of the putschists even confessed to being Gülenists, although the vast majority vigorously denied any connection to the *cemaat*. Those who were aware they were participating in a coup maintained that they believed it was being staged by the military high command rather than the *cemaat*.

Many aspects of the coup attempt remain unclear, not least how the putschists expected to seize control of the country with such limited resources and what they would have done next if the coup had been successful. Erdoğan has refused to allow a transparent and comprehensive investigation into the events of July 15-16, 2016, which his opponents, including the *cemaat*, have used to claim that Erdoğan instigated the coup himself—something he has resolutely denied. It has also meant that the U.S. has repeatedly rebuffed Turkish requests for Gülen's extradition, citing a lack of evidence demonstrating that he was directly involved in the attempted putsch.[25] The refusal to extradite Gülen has added new tensions to the increasingly strained relationship between Washington and Ankara; it has fueled the widespread belief, both in government circles and amongst the Turkish public, that the U.S. was complicit in the putsch.[26]

Under normal circumstances, Turkish law makes it extremely difficult to dismiss state employees. However, on July 21, 2016, Erdoğan announced a State of Emergency, enabling him to suspend civil rights and to rule by presidential decree. Over the next year, the State of Emergency was used to imprison more than 50,000 people on charges of Gülenist sympathies and to dismiss 110,000 civil servants, mostly from the judiciary, police, military and Education Ministry. In addition, more than 2,000 NGOs, media outlets and educational institutions were closed down and nearly 1,000 private companies with total assets of $11 billion were seized by the state.[27] By December 2018, the *cemaat*'s networks in Turkey had been shattered and around 33,000 alleged members and sympathizers had been imprisoned in Turkey for terrorism-related crimes.[28]

Global Reach

There are believed to be somewhere between three and six million Gülen followers worldwide, although the exact figure is difficult to determine. As Gülen follower İhsan Yılmaz explains, the boundaries of the *cemaat*'s "collectivity" are "extremely loose and difficult to specify."[29] Skeptical observers note that Gülen's followers have long tended to deny their association with him. In 2006, for example, in a cable released by Wikileaks, U.S. consulate officers in Istanbul remarked that "[w]hile on the surface a benign humanitarian movement, the ubiquitous evasiveness of Gülenist applicants—coupled with what appears to be a deliberate management of applicant profiles over the past several years—leaves Consular officers uneasy, an uneasiness echoed within Turkey by those familiar with the Gülenists..."[30]

At its peak, the value of the institutions inspired by Gülen worldwide varied between $20 to $50 billion. According to researcher Hakan Yavuz, the movement had three coordinated tiers: businessmen, journalists, and teachers and students.[31] Financial support for its activities came largely from the so-called "Anatolian bourgeoisie," which funded hundreds of private high schools, universities, colleges, dormitories, summer camps, and foundations around the world. Although some of Gülen's followers established revenue-generating activities outside the country, most of its foreign operations were at least partly dependent on funding from Turkey. As a result, in addition to having a devastating impact on its activities inside Turkey, Erdoğan's crackdown on the *cemaat* has forced the group to severely reduce its global activities. Before the crackdown, the *cemaat* had established close relations with the ruling elites in many countries, who often sent their children to be educated in its schools. Until 2013, Turkish diplomats were under instruction from Ankara to support the activities of the *cemaat*'s schools and NGOs which were regarded as instruments of Turkish "soft power." In some countries, particularly ones in Africa, the *cemaat*'s local networks exerted more influence than the Turkish state.[32] But since 2013, and even more so since the failed coup of July 2016, the Turkish government has vigorously encouraged governments to close down the *cemaat*'s schools and NGOs—and, in several cases, threatened to withhold foreign aid unless they do so.

Gülen himself lives in the Pocono Mountains of northeast Pennsylvania, rarely leaving the sprawling rural complex he has inhabited since 1999. Before the split with Erdoğan, Gülen's supporters, Turkish politicians, and leading businessmen often visited him at his compound. Subsequently, his only visitors have been his committed followers and occasional journalists.

The Gülenist Schools

There are Gülen schools on every continent but Antarctica. To date, 95 countries with Gülen schools have been identified, although some speculate that there were as many as 140 host countries at the height of the movement.[33]

In 2001, Gülen was granted an immigrant visa as a "religious worker," and soon after received his green card.[34] During the years that followed, the *cemaat* was able to amass sufficient manpower and influence to woo countless U.S. lawmakers, becoming the largest operator of charter schools in America. Gülenist schools were funded with millions of taxpayer dollars, many of these issued in the form of public bonds. These schools have come under scrutiny by the FBI and the Departments of Labor and Education, which have been investigating their hiring practices, including H1-B visa process exploitation. Some schools would replace American teachers with uncertified Turkish ones hired at a higher salary.[35]

Academic cheating runs rampant; charges range from grade-changing schemes to accusations that some science fair projects have been completed by the teachers. The *cemaat* has also been credibly and frequently charged with channeling school funds to other Gülen-inspired organizations using the schools to generate political connections. In 2011, the *New York Times* reported that Gülen charter schools in Texas were funneling some $50 million in public funds to a network of Turkish construction companies, among them Atlas, which was identified with Gülen in a 2006 cable from the American Consul General in Istanbul that was subsequently released by WikiLeaks.[36]

Nevertheless, there have been no prosecutions and the network of *cemaat*-controlled charter schools has continued to operate.[37] The U.S. is the only country in the world where the Gülen Movement has been able to establish schools fully funded by the host country's taxpayers. The *Washington Post* reported in 2018 that 167 U.S. charter schools were tied to the Gülen movement.[38] Despite pressure from Ankara, the *cemaat* has also maintained an effective lobbying presence in Washington.

Unlike in Turkey, where religion dominates both curricular and extra-curricular activities, there is no evidence that Islamic proselytizing takes place at the *cemaat*'s schools in other countries, which are generally viewed positively by students and parents alike. Graduates perform reasonably well, and some perform outstandingly so. Despite continuing questions and concerns and the uncertainty about the Gülen movement's future, its schools and NGOs are currently still active in many countries all over the world.

Recent Activity

The Gülen Movement is largely in retreat. It has been crushed and discredited in Turkey, where the overwhelming majority of the public believe it was responsible for the July 2016 coup attempt. Its once vast networks have been dismantled and virtually all of its leading members have either been imprisoned or fled abroad. The possibility of Gülen restoring his public image or the *cemaat* ever recovering its former strength is low.

Even if many still cite a lack of concrete evidence for the Turkish government's narrative about the July 2016 coup attempt, the collapse of its alliance with Erdoğan has allowed enough evidence of its misdeeds—particularly in relation to the Ergenekon and Balyoz cases—to enter the public domain damaging its foreign reputation. Apart from its activities in the U.S., all of the *cemaat*'s foreign activities relied on financial support from businesses and NGOs inside Turkey. With these sources now severed, its global activities appear to have entered a long, inexorable decline. Most critically, Gülen himself has been in poor health and has no successor.

There are numerous credible reports that many of those arrested during Erdoğan's July 2016 crackdown have suffered torture and physical abuse. In addition to being dismissed from their jobs, a large proportion of those targeted by Erdoğan's purges have also been stripped of their homes, cars, bank accounts, pensions, and social security rights; in nearly every case, without ever being convicted of any crime. Gülen has counselled his followers to be patient, comparing their sufferings to those of the Prophet Muhammed in the early years of Islam. However, such statements have merely exacerbated unprecedented signs of discontent inside the *cemaat*. Dissidents argue that, as an elderly lifelong bachelor enjoying a comfortable secluded existence in the Poconos, Gülen does not face the same risks and hardships as his followers and their families. Although this discontent has yet to lead to any major public schisms, the number of new recruits is falling far short of the number of existing members drifting away from the organization.

Endnotes

1. Dehlvi, Ghulam Rasool. "Turkey Coup and Fethullah Gülen: Why Blame a Progressive Islamic Modernist?" *Firstpost*, July 18, 2016. Accessed February 11, 2019. https://www.firstpost.com/world/turkey-coup-and-fethullah-gulen-why-blame-a-progressive-islamic-modernist-2899204.html.
2. "Peace Advocate." *Gulen Movement*. Accessed February 11, 2019. http://www.gulenmovement.com/fethullah-gulen/fethullah-gulen-as-a-peace-advocate.
3. Nursi, Said. *The Risale-i Nur Collection*. Translated by Sukran Vahide. 6 vols. Istanbul: Sözler Publications, 2007.
4. Yavuz, M. Hakan. "Towards an Islamic Liberalism?: The Nurcu Movement and Fethullah Gülen." *Middle East Journal* 53, no. 4 (1999): 584-605.
5. Jenkins, Gareth. *Political Islam in Turkey: Running West, Heading East*. New York, NY: Palgrave MacMillan, 2008, 158.
6. Cıngıllıoğlu, Salih. *The Gülen Movement: Transformative Social Change*. New York: Palgrave Macmillan, 2017, 57.
7. "Fethullah Gülen's exemplary preaching," Haber 5, June 13, 2010, http://haber5.com/video/fethullah-Gülenden-ibretlik-vaaz.
8. "Fethullah Gülen'in İç Yüzü/ 3. Bölüm" YouTube video, April 2, 2007, http://www.youtube.com/watch?v=SRAyGkE1q50#t=4m51s; Berlinski, Claire. "Who is Fethullah Gülen?" *City Journal*, Autumn 2012. Accessed February 11, 2019. https://www.city-journal.org/html/who-fethullah-gülen-13504.html.
9. Gülen, Fethullah. *Asrin Getirdigi Tereddutler*. 4 vols. Izmir: Nil, 1994-5; Gülen, Fethullah. *Küçük Dünyam*. Istanbul: AD Yayıncılık, 1995. Gülen's early writings are out of print and hard to find, but digital copies are archived on various social media sites (see, for example, https://www.flickr.com/photos/eksib612/sets/72157631747801352/)
10. "Adil Öksüz›ün Hocası Davut Aydüz'e Hapis Cezası." *Posta*, April 13, 2018. Accessed February 11, 2019. https://www.posta.com.tr/adil-oksuz-un-hocasi-davut-ayduz-e-hapis-cezasi-1405138. Latif Erdoğan began to distance himself from the Gülen Movement before

the failed July 15, 2016, coup attempt, while Davut Aydüz continued to be regarded as being a member of the movement and, on April 13, 2018, was sentenced to a prison term of seven years and six months.

11. Bilir, Ünal. "'Turkey-Islam': Recipe for Success or Hindrance to the Integration of the Turkish Diaspora Community in Germany?" *Journal of Muslim Minority Affairs* 24, no. 2 (October 2004): 259-83.
12. Joshua D Hendrick, *Gülen: The Ambiguous Politics of Market Islam in Turkey and the World,* (New York: New York University Press, 2013), 90.
13. "Fethullah şoku" [Fethullah Shock]. *Hürriyet*, June 20, 1999. Accessed February 11, 2019. http://www.hurriyet.com.tr/gundem/fethullah-soku-39086583.
14. Aydintasbas, Asli. *"The Good, The Bad, and the Gülenists: The Role of the Gülen Movement in Turkey's Coup Attempt.* Essay. European Council on Foreign Relations. September 2016. Accessed February 11, 2019. https://www.ecfr.eu/page/-/ECFR_188_-_THE_GOOD_THE_BAD_AND_THE_GÜLENISTS.pdf.
15. Jenkins, Gareth H. *Between Fact and Fantasy: Turkey's Ergenekon Investigation.* Silk Road Paper. Silk Road Studies Program, Central Asia-Caucusus Institute. August 2009. Accessed February 11, 2019. http://isdp.eu/content/uploads/publications/2009_jenkins_between-fact-and-fantasy.pdf.
16. "Cemaat Devlete Sızmış, Buna Kargalar Güler." *NTV*, February 20, 2012. Accessed February 11, 2019. https://www.ntv.com.tr/turkiye/cemaat-devlete-sizmis-buna-kargalar-guler,FMxmUxV-JhUqKz-8NGPbZnQ.
17. "Evidence altered in Balyoz case, says expert," *Hürriyet Daily News*, November 29, 2011. Accessed February 11, 2019, http://www.hurriyetdailynews.com/default.aspx?pageid=438&n=evidence-altered-in-balyoz-case-says-expert-2011-11-29; "Balyoz lawyers complain about court to top board," *Hürriyet Daily News*, April 17, 2012. Accessed February 11, 2019. http://www.hurriyetdailynews.com/balyoz-lawyers-complain-about-court-to-top-board.aspx?pageID=238&nID=18577&NewsCatID=338.
18. Rodrik, Dani. "The Plot Against The Generals," June 2014. Accessed February 11, 2019. http://drodrik.scholar.harvard.edu/files/dani-rodrik/files/plot-against-the-generals.pdf.
19. Sharon-Krespin, Rachel. "Fethullah Gülen's Grand Ambition: Turkey's Islamist Danger." *Middle East Quarterly* 16, no. 1 (Winter 2009): 55-66. Accessed February 11, 2019. https://www.meforum.org/2045/fethullah-gulens-grand-ambition.

20. Avcı, Hanefi. *Haliç'te Yaşayan Simonlar: Dün Devlet Bugün Cemaat* [The Simons Living On The Golden Horn: Yesterday The State, Today The *Cemaat*]. Ankara: Angora Yayıncılık, 2010.
21. Şık, Ahmet. *İmamın Ordusu* [The Imam's Army] Istanbul: Kırmızı Kedi, 2017. It was eventually published several years later.
22. Vela, Justin. "Behind Bars in the Deep State." *Foreign Policy*, January 11, 2012. Accessed February 12, 2019. https://foreignpolicy.com/2012/01/11/behind-bars-in-the-deep-state/.
23. Christie-Miller, Alexander. "The Gulen Movement: A Self-exiled Imam Challenges Turkey's Erdogan." *The Christian Science Monitor*, December 29, 2013. Accessed February 12, 2019. https://www.csmonitor.com/World/Middle-East/2013/1229/The-Gulen-movement-a-self-exiled-imam-challenges-Turkey-s-Erdogan.
24. Jenkins, Gareth H. "Falling Facades: The Gülen Movement and Turkey's Escalating Power Struggle." *Turkey Analyst* 7, no. 1 (January 15, 2014). Accessed February 12, 2019. https://turkeyanalyst.org/publications/turkey-analyst-articles/item/81-falling-facades-the-gülen-movement-and-turkeys-escalating-power-struggle.html.
25. Gall, Carlotta. "U.S. Is 'Working On' Extraditing Gulen, Top Turkish Official Says." *The New York Times*, December 16, 2018. Accessed February 12, 2019. https://www.nytimes.com/2018/12/16/world/europe/fethullah-gulen-turkey-extradite.html.
26. Arango, Tim, and Ceylan Yeginsu. "Turks Can Agree on One Thing: U.S. Was Behind Failed Coup." *The New York Times*, August 2, 2016. Accessed February 12, 2019. https://www.nytimes.com/2016/08/03/world/europe/turkey-coup-erdogan-fethullah-gulen-united-states.html?mtrref=undefined.
27. Srivastava, Mehrul. "Assets worth $11bn Seized in Turkey Crackdown." *Financial Times*, July 7, 2017. Accessed February 12, 2019.
28. Gurcan, Metin. "Turkey Can't Build Prisons Fast Enough to House Convict Influx." *Al-Monitor*, December 4, 2018. Accessed February 12, 2019. https://www.al-monitor.com/pulse/originals/2018/11/turkey-overcrowded-prisons-face-serious-problems.html.
29. Yilmaz, Ihsan. "Inter-Madhhab Surfing, Neo-Ijtihad, and Faith-Based Movement Leaders." In *The Islamic School of Law: Evolution, Devolution, and Progress*, edited by Peri Bearman, Rudolph Peters, and Frank E. Vogel, 191-206. Cambridge, MA: Harvard University Press. 2005. Accessed February 12, 2019. https://www.academia.edu/333445/Inter-Madhhab_Surfing_Neo-Ijtihad_and_Faith-Based_Movement_Leaders.
30. "Fethullah Gülen: Why Are His Followers Traveling." Wikileaks.

August 30, 2011. https://wikileaks.org/plusd/cables/06ISTANBUL832_a.html.

31. Yavuz, M. Hakan. *Islamic Political Identity in Turkey*. New York, NY: Oxford University Press, 2003. Accessed February 12, 2019. http://citeseerx.ist.psu.edu/viewdoc/download?doi=10.1.1.468.2947&rep=rep1&type=pdf, p. 184.
32. Tee, Caroline. *The Gülen Movement in Turkey: The Politics of Islam and Modernity*. London: I. B. Tauris, 2016, p. 158.
33. "Every Continent but Antarctica: The Numbers." A Guide to the Gulen Movement's Activities in the US. October 2, 2011. Accessed February 12, 2019. https://turkishinvitations.weebly.com/every-continent-but-antarctica-the-numbers.html. A comprehensive list of estimates, drawing from various foreign sources, can be found here.
34. Hauslohner, Abigail, Karen DeYoung, and Valerie Strauss. "He's 77, Frail and Lives in Pennsylvania. Turkey Says He's a Coup Mastermind." *The Washington Post*, August 3, 2016. Accessed February 12, 2019. https://www.washingtonpost.com/national/hes-frail-77-and-lives-in-pennsylvania-turkey-says-hes-a-coup-mastermind/2016/08/03/6b1b2226-526f-11e6-bbf5-957ad17b4385_story.html?utm_term=.03a199345070.
35. Humaire, Joseph M. "Charter Schools Vulnerable to Controversial Turkish Movement." *The Hill*, March 10, 2016, Accessed February 12, 2019. http://thehill.com/blogs/congress-blog/education/272424-charter-schools-vulnerable-to-controversial-turkish-movement.
36. Saul, Stephanie. "Charter Schools Tied to Turkey Grow in Vegas." *The New York Times*, June 6, 2011. Accessed February 12, 2019. http://www.nytimes.com/2011/06/07/education/07charter.html.
37. Roebuck, Jeremey and Martha Woodall. "Poconos cleric denies involvement in Turkey coup attempt.." *The Inquirer*, July 15, 2016. Accessed February 12, 2019. https://www.philly.com/philly/news/20160716_Turkey_s_president_blames_Muslim_cleric_in_the_Poconos_for_military_coup.html-2
38. Ravitch, Diane. "Charter Schools Damage Public Education." *The Washington Post*, June 22, 2018. Accessed February 12, 2019. https://www.washingtonpost.com/opinions/charter-schools-are-leading-to-an-unhealthy-divide-in-american-education/2018/06/22/73430df8-7016-11e8-afd5-778aca903bbe_story.html?utm_term=.a1648c6c7fc3.

66 Hezbollah

Quick Facts

Geographical Areas of Operation: Europe, Latin America, Middle East and North Africa, North America, and Sub-Saharan Africa

Numerical Strength (Members): tens of thousands of supporters and members worldwide.

Leadership: Hassan Nasrallah

Religious Identification: Shi'a Islam
Quick Facts Courtesy of the U.S. State Department's Country Reports on Terrorism (2019)

Introduction

Hezbollah (the Party of God) is not just a major political party and provider of social services in Lebanon; it is also a militant organization that fields both a well-armed and well-trained militia in Lebanon and a terrorist wing combined with elements of Iranian intelligence services operating abroad. Even as the movement has undergone a process of "Lebanonization," through which it has successfully integrated itself into the Lebanese parliamentary political system, it remains committed not only to its Lebanese identity but also to revolutionary pan-Shi'a and pro-Iran ideas and sentiments.

History & Ideology

Founded in the wake of the Israeli invasion of Lebanon in 1982, Hezbollah was the product of a Shi'a awakening in Lebanon that followed the disappearance of Sayyid Musa al-Sadr in 1978 and the Iranian Revolution of 1979. Long neglected by the Lebanese government and underrepresented in the country's social and political institutions, Lebanese Shi'ite leaders empowered their disenfranchised community. Eager to follow in the footsteps of the Iranian revolution, young Lebanese Shi'a were driven to break with established parties like *Amal* and gravitated to Hezbollah because of the Israeli invasion and subsequent occupation of southern Lebanon. Iran, motivated to export its Islamic revolution to other Shi'a communities throughout the Middle East, was more than willing to help. Iranian assistance included financial backing and training from the Islamic Revolutionary Guard Corps (IRGC), backed by a Syrian regime seeking a proxy in Lebanon. It was the IRGC, however, that shaped Hezbollah's ideological foundations and informed its operational policies.

Hezbollah is simultaneously a Lebanese party, a pan-Shi'a movement and an Iranian proxy group. The group's multiple identities form the foundation and context for its radical ideology. The establishment of an Islamic republic in Lebanon was a central component of Hezbollah's original political platform, which was released publicly in 1985.[1] The document also prominently features the fight against "Western Imperialism" and the continued conflict with Israel. Hezbollah is ideologically committed to the Ayatollah Ruhollah Khomeini's revolutionary doctrine of *Velayat-e faqih* (Guardianship of the Jurist), creating tension between its commitments to the decrees of Iranian clerics, the Lebanese state, the sectarian Shiite community in Lebanon and its fellow Shi'a abroad. As a result, its objectives simultaneously include establishing an Islamic republic in Lebanon; promoting Shi'a communities worldwide; undermining Arab states with Shi'a minorities in an effort to export the Iranian revolution; eliminating the State of Israel; challenging "Western imperialism;" and serving as the long arm of Iran in coordination with the paramilitary wing of the IRGC, known as the Qods Force. The consequences of these competing ideological drivers became clear after Hezbollah dragged both Israel and Lebanon into a war neither wanted by crossing the UN-demarcated Israel-Lebanon border, killing three Israeli soldiers and kidnapping two more in July 2006.

Hezbollah receives significant financial support from supporters (particularly Lebanese nationals) living abroad. Over time, these communities developed into a global network available not only to raise funds but to provide logistical and operational support for Hezbollah operations as well. Such support networks have developed in Latin America, North America, Europe, Africa, and in

Middle Eastern countries with minority Shi'a populations, such as Saudi Arabia.

Global Reach

Hezbollah is well known for several international terrorist attacks, most notably the 1992 and 1994 bombings of the Israeli embassy and Jewish community center (AMIA), respectively, in Argentina, the 1995 Khobar Towers attack in Saudi Arabia, and the 2012 bombing of a bus full of Israeli tourists in Bulgaria.[2] These activities were facilitated by support networks that the organization maintains in Africa, Southeast Asia, the Americas, and Europe.

In Europe, Hezbollah has for decades leveraged local support networks to help operatives use the continent as a launching pad to conduct attacks or collect intelligence in Israel. The organization's most successful European operation to date took place on July 18, 2012, when it bombed a tour bus carrying Israelis in Bulgaria. Five tourists and the bus driver were killed and roughly 30 others were injured as a result.[3] (Notably, at least some countries in Europe are now attempting to make the continent a less permissive environment for Hezbollah. Thus, in February 2019, the UK moved to ban all wings of Hezbollah, classifying the movement as a whole as a terrorist organization.[4] In other parts of the EU, however, Hezbollah continues to possess extensive freedom of action.)

Hezbollah has maintained an active support network in Southeast Asia since the 1990s. Hezbollah has also conducted significant fundraising in Southeast Asia, nearly succeeded in bombing the Israeli embassy in Bangkok, Thailand in 1994, and collected intelligence on synagogues in Manila and Singapore throughout that decade.[5] Hezbollah members similarly are known to have procured and cached weapons in Thailand and the Philippines.[6] They collected intelligence on the Bangkok office of Israel's national airline, El Al, and on U.S. Navy and Israeli commercial ships in the Singapore Straits.[7] The network recruited South Asian Sunni Muslims and sent several to Lebanon for training.[8] Such contacts continue; in January 2012, Thai police arrested Hussein Atris, a Lebanese national carrying a Swedish passport, at Bangkok's Suvarnabhumi Airport.[9]

Atris led authorities to a three-story building containing a stockpile of 8,800 pounds of distilled chemicals used to make explosives.[10] Some of the explosives, disguised as cat litter, were intended to be shipped abroad. Bangkok had already been described as "a center for a [Hezbollah] cocaine and money-laundering network"; it was now clear that the city also served as a hub for explosives.[11]

In Africa, Hezbollah operatives have long helped finance the group's activities through their participation in local conflicts.[12] Hezbollah also raises funds in Africa from the continent's local Shi'a expatriate communities. In some cases, Shi'a donors are unwittingly conned into funding Hezbollah, while others are willing participants in the process.[13] The group likewise engages in operational activities and recruitment on the continent; in 2002, for instance, Ugandan officials disrupted a cell of Shi'a students who were recruited by Iranian intelligence agents and sent to study at the Rizavi University in Mashhad, Iran. Upon their return, one student recruit, Shafri Ibrahim, was caught, while another, Sharif Wadulu, is believed to have escaped to one of the Gulf States. The two were trained by the MOIS alongside new Lebanese Hezbollah recruits and sent home with fictitious covers to establish an operational infrastructure in Uganda.[14]

Hezbollah activity in South America has been well documented, including its frenetic activity in the tri-border region where Argentina, Paraguay and Brazil intersect. The group's activities received special attention in the wake of the 1992 bombing of the Israeli embassy in Buenos Aires, Argentina and the 1994 bombing of the AMIA Jewish community center there. What is less well known, however, is that Hezbollah is also active in Chile, Venezuela, Cuba, Panama and Ecuador as well.[15] Of particular concern to law enforcement officials throughout South America is Hezbollah's increased activity in free trade zones, especially under the cover of import-export companies.[16]

Finally, Hezbollah maintains a sizeable presence in North America. The U.S. Treasury Department has designated Hezbollah charities in the Detroit area, while individuals and cells have been prosecuted across the U.S. and Canada for raising funds and procuring weapons and dual use technologies like night vision goggles. The most prominent case to date occurred in Charlotte, North Carolina, where Hezbollah operatives smuggled cigarettes to raise funds for the group while maintaining direct contact with Sheikh Abbas Haraki, a senior Hezbollah military commander.[17] Charlotte cell members received receipts back from Hezbollah for their donations, including receipts from the office of then-Hezbollah spiritual leader Sheikh Mohammad Fadlallah. The Charlotte cell was closely tied to a sister network in Canada that was primarily engaged in procuring dual-use technologies. The Canadian network was under the direct command of Hajj Hassan Hilu Lakis, Hezbollah's chief military procurement officer, who is also known to procure material for Iran.[18]

Despite the crackdown on this network, support for Hezbollah in North America still lingers. In August 2016, a Michigan man admitted he had lied to authorities when he was arrested onboard a Lebanon-bound flight in 2014. Upon his arrest, he had insisted that he was traveling to see his dentist. In fact, he had intended to join Hezbollah.[19] Ali Kourani of New York and Samer el Debek of Michigan were arrested on charges related to alleged activities on behalf of Hezbollah in June 2017.[20] According to the U.S. Department of Justice, Kourani and el Debek had received "military-style" training from the group, including in the use propelled grenade launchers and machine guns. El Debek allegedly conducted missions in Panama to locate the U.S. and Israeli embassies there. As part of that mission, he assessed the vulnerabilities of the Panama Canal and ships transiting the waterway. Kourani allegedly also surveilled potential targets in the U.S., including military and law enforcement facilities in New York City.[21]

Hezbollah's most prominent international operations, however, have been those in support of the Assad regime in Syria. The organization assumed a key role in providing "training, advice and extensive logistical support to the Government of Syria" shortly after the outbreak of the Syrian civil war in 2011.[22] According to various reports, Hezbollah has had seven thousand fighters in Syria at any given time over the course of the conflict. These forces have redeployed throughout Syria when the group has carried out major offensives. Hezbollah's elite force — the Radwan Brigade — has been redeployed in Syria a number of times to participate in battles in places like Aleppo and Daraa. Hezbollah has also been involved in weapon production for Iran in Syria.[23]

With the winding down of the Syrian civil war over the past year, Hezbollah's strategy on Syrian soil has shifted. While its military operations have decreased in scope and operational tempo, the organization has become more deeply involved in "support" activities, which it has coordinated closely with its patron, Iran. This has included helping Iran to purchase land, invest money, and implement religious and cultural initiatives within Syria.[24] These activities suggest strongly that, like its patron, Hezbollah hopes to put down roots in Syria.

Hezbollah in Lebanon

May 2008 represented a turning point for Hezbollah in its home base of Lebanon. Starting in November 2007, an ongoing crisis surrounding a vacant national presidency set the backdrop for the most violent intrastate fighting in Lebanon since the end of the country's civil war in 1991. In early May of that year, the Lebanese government discovered a Hezbollah surveillance camera at the Beirut airport. Subsequent pro-Hezbollah protests throughout Beirut left nearly 100 dead and 250 wounded.[25] While the Lebanese Armed Forces (LAF) ultimately deployed and stopped the fighting, Hezbollah successfully leveraged its military strength for political advantage over the weakened Lebanese government. The result, after five days of Qatari mediation, was the Doha Agreement, under which Hezbollah secured a "blocking third's" worth of representation in a new national unity government, that could obstruct any government initiative.

The Doha Agreement left the issue of Hezbollah's weapons—maintained in blatant violation of UN Security Council resolutions 1559 and 1701—unresolved, leaving Hezbollah the only group in Lebanon with a private arsenal. A public relations coup within Hezbollah during the talks in Doha prevented serious discussion of the issue. Despite a more robust United Nations presence in southern Lebanon in the wake of the July 2006 war, Hezbollah successfully restocked its arsenal of missiles. Indeed, Hezbollah was by then believed to have amassed more rockets, with longer ranges and larger payloads, than it had prior to the 2006 war.[26] These political gains, however, were reversed in May 2009, when the German weekly *Der Spiegel* revealed that the UN special tribunal investigating former Lebanese Prime Minister Rafiq Hariri's assassination had implicated Hezbollah in the killing.[27]

In early January 2011, it became evident that the chief prosecutor of the Special Tribunal for Lebanon (STL) would submit a draft indictment to the pre-trial judge for review. While the actual contents of the indictment would be under seal for several months, Hezbollah preempted the indictment's release and withdrew its support for Saad Hariri's government, forcing its collapse.[28] Subsequently, aided by sympathetic leaders of Lebanon's Christian and Druze communities, Hezbollah raised Najib Mitaki to the premiership and cemented its control over Lebanon.[29]

In September 2018, the STL prosecution finally submitted its closing arguments with ample evidence to corroborate the link between Hezbollah's leadership and the perpetrators of the killing, including details on their movements and communications ahead of the attack.[30]

Subsequently, on September 16, 2019, The STL issued five new charges against Hezbollah cadre Salim Ayyash relating to the killings of three men, including former secretary-general of the Lebanese Communist Party George Hawi. Pre-trial judge Daniel Fransen, also issued warrants for the arrest of court fugitive Ayyash to the Lebanese government and international police organizations.

Nevertheless, Hezbollah's power over Lebanese state institutions has only grown. Capitalizing on the collapse of the pro-Western "March 14" coalition, Hezbollah and its Lebanese allies won the May 2018 parliamentary elections, and pressured Lebanon's political class to form a pro-Hezbollah majority cabinet.[31] However, Hezbollah now finds its position in Lebanon challenged, in large part due to its role in the Syrian civil war; despite heavy involvement in the conflict, Hezbollah could not deliver a decisive victory that would benefit the Shi'a community. To the contrary, growing Western sanctions on Iran have hurt Hezbollah's financial operations in Lebanon, leaving the broader Shi'a community more isolated.

Recent Activity

Hezbollah in the Middle East

The impact of the Syrian war on Hezbollah has been dramatic, shifting the group's focus from battling Israel and contesting the dynamics of its support base to engaging in conflicts beyond Lebanon. Hezbollah deployed a unit to Iraq to train Shiite militants during the Iraq War, where it worked in close cooperation with Iran. Its deep commitment to the war in Syria, visible to this day, underscores the group's new, regional, pan-Shi'a focus.

As Hezbollah became more involved in the war in Syria, its main priority was defending Damascus while protecting the surrounding suburbs and territory that links the Alawite coast to the Syria-Lebanon border. This initiative resulted in the major ethnic cleansing of Sunnis from strategically important areas. Hezbollah's leadership also prioritized controlling the Syria-Iraq border, and thereby securing the land bridge that would connect Iran to Lebanon through Iraq and Syria. Consequently, Hezbollah's weapons arsenal grew from 33,000 rockets and missiles before the 2006 war to an estimated 150,000 a decade later.[32] Similarly, it expanded from a few thousand members in 2006 to an estimated 20,000-plus as of 2017.[33]

However, Hezbollah has since lost many of its high-ranking commanders and well-trained fighters as a result of the conflict, with official fatalities number ranging between 1,200 and 1,400.[34] Many of its recruited replacements have not undergone the same training usually required by Hezbollah. Furthermore, Hezbollah's extensive military operations in the region have forced the group to cut certain budgets. As most resources are now allocated to military operations, Hezbollah was forced to shrink its available pool of social services.[35] This belt-tightening resulted in serious discontent within the Shi'a community, particularly in poor neighborhoods of Lebanon.[36]

Additional budget restrictions were introduced after the Trump administration imposed sanctions on Iran. Marshall Billingslea, assistant secretary for terrorist financing at the U.S. Department of the Treasury, said during his visit to Beirut on September 23, 2019, that the U.S. sanctions had drastically deprived Hezbollah of funds, especially those coming from Iran. He said Hezbollah used to receive around $700 million a year from Iran but, thanks to tough U.S. sanctions on Tehran, this cash flow had diminished considerably.[37]

Besides the group's significant interest in Syria, Hezbollah's regional reorientation is most obvious in its increased operational tempo in the Gulf region. In Yemen, a small number of Hezbollah operatives have been training Houthi rebels for some time; in early 2016, the Gulf-backed Yemeni government claimed to have physical evidence of "Hezbollah training the Houthi rebels and fighting alongside them in attacks on Saudi Arabia's border."[38] Three years earlier, the U.S. government revealed that Khalil Harb, a former special operations commander and a close adviser to Nasrallah, oversaw Hezbollah's activities in Yemen. Harb has also coordinated Hezbollah's operations in Yemen with Iran.[39] Former Hezbollah special operations commander in southern Lebanon Abu Ali Tabtaba has reportedly also been sent to Yemen.[40] Hezbollah has never been open about these deployments, but in April 2015 Hezbollah Deputy Secretary-General Naim Qassem warned that Saudi Arabia would "incur very serious losses" and "pay a heavy price" as a result of its Yemen campaign.[41]

Beyond Yemen, Hezbollah's support for Gulf region terror groups continues unabated. In August 2015, Kuwaiti authorities raided a terrorist cell of 26 Shi'a Kuwaitis accused of amassing "a large amount of weapons, ammunition, and explosives."[42] After media outlets reported alleged links between the cell, Iran, and Hezbollah, the public prosecutor issued a media gag order on the investigation.[43] Subsequently, in January 2016, authorities in Bahrain arrested six members of a terrorist cell with connections to Hezbollah for a July 2015 explosion outside of a girls' school in Sitra.[44]

In the first half of 2016, three people were found guilty of spying on behalf of Iran and Hezbollah on two unrelated occasions by Kuwait and Emirati courts.[45] In July 2016, a Kuwait court sentenced a Shi`a member of parliament in absentia for issuing statements deemed insulting to Saudi Arabia and Bahrain and for calling on people to join Hezbollah.[46]

Because of this aggressive activity in the Gulf, the Gulf Cooperation Council (GCC) formally labeled Hezbollah a terrorist group in March 2016. The Arab League and the OIC followed suit within weeks.[47] Since then, the Gulf States have cracked down on Hezbollah supporters and financiers within their borders.[48]

This seemingly rapid series of condemnations was actually years in the making. In May 2014, Saudi authorities withdrew the business license of a Lebanese national linked to Hezbollah, and a GCC offer to engage Iran in dialogue if Tehran changed its policy on Syria fell on deaf ears.[49] In January 2016, the Saudi government released a report on Iranian-sponsored terrorism that focused heavily on Hezbollah, spanning the group's militant activities from the 1980s to the present.[50]

In May 2018, the GCC states agreed to increase sanctions against Hezbollah's senior leadership as part of its cooperation with the U.S following the latter's withdrawal from the Joint Comprehensive Plan of Action (JCPOA), known colloquially as the "Iran Nuclear Deal."[51] Additional U.S. sanctions have targeted Hezbollah's top officials, including its leader Hassan Nasrallah and his deputy, Naim Qassem. Washington has also blacklisted members of Hezbollah's primary decision-making body, the Shura Council.

Hezbollah's involvement in the Gulf is a function of sustained geopolitical and sectarian tensions between Saudi Arabia and Iran. Pressure increased in January 2016 when Saudi Arabia executed Shiite Sheikh Nimr al-Nimr on charges of sedition and taking up arms against Saudi security forces; in Iran, two Saudi diplomatic compounds were stormed in protest. The Arab League and the OIC both condemned the attacks at Saudi Arabia's request. Lebanon, however, offered only "solidarity." This perceived slight prompted Saudi Arabia to cut off monetary support to Lebanon and pull funds from Lebanese banks.[52] Bahrain and the UAE fell in line with the Saudis, issuing travel warnings and travel bans, respectively, for Lebanon.[53] A month after the execution and protests, Saudi Arabia blacklisted four companies and three Lebanese businessmen, citing their relationships to Hezbollah.[54] The United States had designated these companies and individuals a year earlier, but Saudi actions indicated the kingdom's heightened focus on Hezbollah.[55]

Nasrallah has tried to deflect these actions as Israeli machinations, but Hezbollah and Iran have been recently increasingly active in the Gulf. Iranian, Hezbollah, and Saudi posturing all come against the backdrop of a Gulf concerned with life in the aftermath of the 2015 Iran nuclear deal known as the JCPOA. Gulf leadership was wary of an Iranian financial windfall resulting from the deal; Sunni Gulf states were thus particularly sensitive to Iranian and Hezbollah activity in the Gulf since the announcement of the JCPOA in 2015.

Nasrallah has tried to justify Hezbollah's presence in regional proxy wars by framing the issue as a Lebanese national security threat. In July 2016, Sheikh Nabil Qaouq, the deputy head of Hezbollah's Executive Council, derided Saudi Arabia for supporting terrorism in Lebanon and throughout the region. The terrorists "who staged bombings in Beirut, Hermel and the Bekaa, and who abducted and slaughtered the (Lebanese) servicemen are [al-Qaeda's] branch in Lebanon and Syria (Abdullah Azzam Brigades) and al-Nusra Front, and al-Nusra Front [are]… today fighting with Saudi weapons," Qaouq charged. Qaouq accused the Saudis of continuing to arm Jabhat al-Nusra "although it has murdered us, executed our servicemen and continued to occupy our land in the Bekaa," noting that Saudi sponsorship of terrorism "poses a real threat to Lebanese national security."[56]

Hezbollah was dealt a heavy blow in May 2016 with the loss of its most prominent military figure, Mustafa Badreddine. Badreddine was killed in an explosion in Damascus while acting as head of Hezbollah's External Security Organization and its forces in Syria, making him the most senior Hezbollah official killed since the death of former "chief of staff" Imad Mughniyah in 2008.

In the 1980s, Badreddine was involved in terrorist attacks in Lebanon and Kuwait, with targets including U.S. embassies and Marine barracks. He escaped from prison in Kuwait in the early 1990s during the Iraqi invasion there and fled back to Lebanon where he rose to power in Hezbollah, aided by his expertise and family ties to Mughniyah. The two men, Badreddine and Mughniyah, led Hezbollah's military activities for years and founded some of the organization's most infamous units. Describing Badreddine, one Hezbollah operative said he was "more dangerous" than Mughniyah, his longtime "teacher in terrorism."[57]

The assassination of Badreddine shocked Hezbollah; it lost

an especially qualified commander with a unique pedigree as the brother-in-law of Mughniyah and a confidant of Nasrallah. Yet most confounding to Hezbollah was that Israel, Hezbollah's arch enemy, was not the assassin. Though Hezbollah outlets quickly pinned the attack on Israel, Nasrallah soon personally announced that there was "no sign or proof leading us to the Israelis." Nasrallah quickly added that Hezbollah is "not afraid to blame Israel when necessary," but in this case, "our investigations led us to the [Sunni] terrorist groups." Nasrallah could not be clearer: "Within 24 hours we knew who killed Syed Mustafa, don't just try to point at Israel."[58]

Some within Hezbollah believe that the Saudis were likely acting behind the scenes, possibly supporting the Sunni rebels Nasrallah claims were behind the attack. Indeed, there would be historical precedent for this. The Saudis reportedly supported the Lebanese militants targeting Sheikh Mohammad Hussein Fadlallah in a failed assassination attempt in 1985.[59] In fact, the United States has been fairly open about its partnership with GCC countries and others to counter Hezbollah.[60]

Hezbollah's shift toward the Gulf should not be seen as a pivot away from Israel, however. To the contrary, Hezbollah sees a pernicious, budding alliance among the United States, Saudi Arabia, and Israel that directly benefits the Sunni "takfiri" militants it is fighting in the region. While Hezbollah is taking active measures to prepare for the next, eventual war with Israel, it is eager to avoid conflict at present. Despite the recent tensions between Hezbollah and Israel following a 2019 Israeli attack on a Hezbollah stronghold in Beirut, Hezbollah's response has been very calculated and demonstrated hesitancy and aversion to conflict.[61]

Hezbollah has invested heavily in the Syrian war with both personnel and resources; it desires not to give Israel a pretext to either enter that war on the side of the Sunni rebels or take advantage of Hezbollah's deployment there by targeting Hezbollah's military presence and rocket arsenal in south Lebanon.

Hezbollah is now working to strengthen its deterrence by transforming some rockets into precision missiles. When Israel targeted much of these missile facilities in Syria, Hezbollah moved them to Lebanon, thereby increasing the risk of a war with Israel.[62]

Moreover, Hezbollah has been trying to extend its reach into the Palestinian Territories. In August 2016, Israeli authorities busted several Hezbollah cells in the West Bank. The members, some of whom had been ordered to commit an imminent attack against Israeli Defense Forces (IDF) in the area, had been recruited online by Hezbollah operatives.[63]

Hezbollah beyond the Middle East

Hezbollah's international operations are not limited to its home region. Although the organization's military wing was formally added to the EU's list of banned terrorist groups in July 2013,[64] it has continued plotting attacks across Europe, including in Bulgaria in 2012 and in Cyprus in 2015. The organization also maintains a significant continental presence; Germany's domestic intelligence agency recently reported that Hezbollah maintains some 950 active operatives in the country.[65]

Hezbollah also continued procuring weapons and technology in Europe. In July 2014, the U.S. Treasury Department blacklisted a Lebanese consumer electronics business, Stars Group Holding, along with its owners, subsidiaries, and "certain managers and individuals who support their illicit activities." Together, they functioned as a "key Hezbollah procurement network" that purchased technology around the world—including in Europe—to develop the drones Hezbollah deploys over Israel and Syria.[66]

The Treasury Department has, over the years, targeted key individuals and companies facilitating Hezbollah's international misdeeds, with a focus on those with ties to the Islamic Jihad Organization, Hezbollah's terrorist arm.[67] President Barack Obama signed legislation in December 2015 designed to "thwart" the group's "network at every turn" by imposing sanctions on financial institutions that deal with Hezbollah or its television station, al Manar.[68]

Other nations have also responded negatively to Iran and Hezbollah's involvement in their affairs. In May 2018, Morocco severed relations with Iran, accusing it of providing funds, training and weapons to Polisario Front in the disputed Western Sahara.[69] The collaboration between the Polisario and Hezbollah appears to have intensified after Moroccan authorities arrested Lebanese businessman Kassim Tajeddine in March 2017.[70]

The group also continues to boast a durable presence in the Americas. In February 2016, the U.S. Drug Enforcement Administration (DEA) implicated Hezbollah in a multi-million-dollar drug trafficking and money laundering network that spanned four continents.[71] According to the DEA report, Hezbollah had relationships with South American drug cartels in an international cocaine-smuggling network. The proceeds funded a money laundering scheme known as the Black Market Peso Exchange and provided Hezbollah with "a revenue and weapons stream.[72]

Nasrallah dismissed the investigation's implication of Hezbollah, stating: "The criminal regimes are falsely accusing Hezbollah of corruption and money laundering in order to destabilize the party."[73] Regardless of Nasrallah's protests, Hezbollah's activities in South America have continued. Since at least the early 1980s, Iran has operated an intelligence network in Latin America – and Hezbollah soon followed suit.

These activities have increased significantly in recent years. In November 2014, Brazilian police reports revealed that Hezbollah helped a Brazilian prison gang, the First Capital Command (PCC), obtain weapons in exchange for the protection of prisoners of Lebanese origin detained in Brazil. The same reports indicated that Lebanese traffickers tied to Hezbollah reportedly helped sell C4 explosives that the PCC allegedly stole in Paraguay.[74]

Peruvian counterterrorism police arrested the Hezbollah operative in Lima in November 2014 after a months-long surveillance operation. Mohammed Amadar, a Lebanese citizen, arrived in Peru in November 2013 and married a dual Peruvian-American citizen two weeks later. When police raided Amadar's home after the arrest, they found traces of TNT, detonators, and other inflammable substances. They also found chemicals used to manufacture explosives in the garbage.[75]

In 2016, Brazilian authorities arrested former Hezbollah member Fadi Hassan Nabha. According to police, Nabha served in Hezbollah's special services and had weapons and explosives training.[76] The justice ministry has been seeking to expel him from the country. September 2016 saw two more arrests of key Hezbollah operatives in South America: Khalil Mohamed El Sayed and Mohammed Jalil. El Sayed, a Lebanese naturalized Paraguayan, was arrested while trying to enter Argentina using counterfeit documents. The U.S. has investigated El Sayed for six years for his involvement in Hezbollah, and Brazil has accused El Sayed of drug and arm trafficking. Jalil, also a Lebanese-Paraguayan attempting to enter Argentina on false papers, was arrested on similar charges. Jalil is wanted in the U.S., Brazil, and Paraguay.

In light of its international operations, Hezbollah's confidence is not entirely unfounded. In August 2016, Nasrallah expressed Hezbollah's international ambitions in no uncertain terms. "If Hezbollah emerged from the 2006 war a regional force," Nasrallah declared, "it will emerge from Syria crisis an international force."[77]

This confidence, however, has been bruised by severe financial pressure caused by the U.S. sanctions against Iran. Hezbollah's services are no longer catering for the whole community, the organization is having trouble paying salaries on time, and has had to laid off contractors and employees. As a result, people have started to criticize and question the organization, as well as its patron, Iran.[78] However, Hezbollah leadership is not worried on the long term. Its leaders know that as long as Iran survives the Trump administration's "maximum pressure" campaign and can hold on until a new U.S. president is elected, Hezbollah will regain its financial capabilities and restore its relations with its constituency.

Endnotes

1. Rafid Fadhil Ali, "New Hezbollah Manifesto Emphasizes Political Role in a United Lebanon," Jamestown Foundation *Terrorism Monitor* 7, iss. 38, December 15, 2009, http://www.jamestown.org/single/?no_cache=1&tx_ttnews[tt_news]=35830&tx_ttnews[backPid]=13&cHash=42a34967d2.
2. "Israelis Killed in Bulgaria Bus Terror Attack, Minister Says," CNN, July 18, 2012, http://www.cnn.com/2012/07/18/world/europe/bulgaria-israel-blast/index.html.
3. "Israelis Killed in Bulgaria Bus Terror Attack, Minister Says," CNN, July 18, 2012, http://www.cnn.com/2012/07/18/world/europe/bulgaria-israel-blast/index.html.

4. "Britain to expand ban on Lebanon's Hezbollah, calling it terrorist group," Reuters, February 25, 2019, https://ca.reuters.com/article/idCAKCN1QE1D2-OCATP
5. Ely Karmon, "Fight on All Fronts: Hizballah, the War on Terror, and the War in Iraq," Washington Institute for Near East Policy *Research Memorandum* no. 45, December 2003, http://www.washingtoninstitute.org/templateC04.php?CID=18; Zachary Abuza, "Bad Neighbours: Hezbollah in Southeast Asia," *Australia/Israel Review*, November 2006, http://www.aijac.org.au/review/2006/31-11/abuza31-11.htm
6. John T. Hanley, Kongdan Oh Hassig, and Caroline F. Ziemke, "Proceedings of the International Symposium on the Dynamics and Structures of Terrorist Threats in Southeast Asia, Held at Kuala Lumpur, Malaysia," Institute for Defense Analyses, September 2005.
7. John T. Hanley, Kongdan Oh Hassig, and Caroline F. Ziemke, "Proceedings of the International Symposium on the Dynamics and Structures of Terrorist Threats in Southeast Asia, Held at Kuala Lumpur, Malaysia," Institute for Defense Analyses, September 2005; "Hizbollah Recruited Singaporeans: The Muslims Were Recruited Through Religious Classes in Singapore to Aid a Plot to Blow Up US and Israeli Ships," *Straits Times* (Singapore), June 9, 2002; "Indonesian Government Expect Escalation in Terrorist Bombings; Hizballah Ops Out of Singapore Also Noted," *Defense & Foreign Affairs Daily* 20, no. 104 (2002).
8. Maria A. Ressa, *Seeds of Terror: An Eyewitness Account of Al-Qaeda's Newest Center of Operations in Southeast Asia* (New York: Free Press, 2003); Hanley, Hassig and Ziemke, "Proceedings of the International Symposium on the Dynamics and Structures of Terrorist Threats in Southeast Asia, Held at Kuala Lumpur, Malaysia."
9. Dudi Cohen, "Bangkok Threat: Terrorist's Swedish Connection," *Yediot Ahronot* (Tel Aviv), January 15, 2012, http://www.ynetnews.com/articles/0,7340,L-4175513,00.html; "Second Terror Suspect Sought, Court Issues Warrant for Atris's Housemate," *Bangkok Post*, January 20, 2012, http://www.bangkokpost.com/news/local/275914/second-terror-suspect-sought.
10. James Hookway, "Thai Police Seize Materials, Charge Terror-Plot Suspect," *Wall Street Journal*, January 17, 2012, http://online.wsj.com/article/SB10001424052970204555904577164632227644906.html; Sebastian Rotella, "Before Deadly Bulgaria Bombing, Tracks of a Resurgent Iran-Hezbollah Threat," *Foreign Policy*, July 30, 2012, http://www.foreignpolicy.com/articles/2012/07/30/be-

fore_deadly_bulgaria_bombing_tracks_of_a_resurgent_iran_hezbollah_threat?wp_login_redirect=0.

11. Thomas Fuller, "In Twisting Terror Case, Thai Police Seize Chemicals," *New York Times*, January 16, 2012, http://www.nytimes.com/2012/01/17/world/asia/thai-police-in-bangkok-seize-bomb-making-material.html.
12. "U.N. Prosecutor Accuses Taylor of Al Qaeda Links; More," United Nations Foundation *UN Wire*, May 15, 2003, http://www.unwire.org/unwire/20030515/33747_story.asp.
13. Douglas Farah, "Hezbollah's External Support Network in West Africa and Latin America," International Assessment and Strategy Center, April 15, 2009, http://www.strategycenter.net/research/pubID.118/pub_detail.asp.
14. Matthew Levitt, "Hizbullah's African Activities Remain Undisrupted," *RUSI/Jane's Homeland Security and Resilience Monitor*, March 1, 2004.
15. Matthew Levitt, "Hezbollah: A Case Study of Global Reach," Remarks to a conference on "Post-Modern Terrorism: Trends, Scenarios, and Future Threats," International Policy Institute for Counter-Terrorism, Herzliya, Israel, September 8, 2003, https://www.aclu.org/sites/default/files/field_document/ACLURM001616.pdf
16. Matthew Levitt, "Hezbollah Finances: Funding the Party of God," in Jeanne K. Giraldo and Harold A. Trinkunas, eds., *Terrorism Financing and State Responses: a Comparative Perspective* (Palo Alto: Stanford University Press, 2007).
17. *United States v. Mohamad Youssef Hammoud, et al.* United States Court of Appeals for the Fourth District, 381 F.3d 316, September 8, 2004; U.S. Department of the Treasury, "Twin Treasury Actions Take Aim at Hizballah's Support Network," July 24, 2007, http://www.treasury.gov/press-center/press-releases/Pages/20077241029461 3432.aspx.
18. *United States v. Mohamad Youssef Hammoud, et al.* United States Court of Appeals for the Fourth District, 381 F.3d 316, September 8, 2004; U.S. Department of the Treasury, "Twin Treasury Actions Take Aim at Hizballah's Support Network," July 24, 2007, http://www.treasury.gov/press-center/press-releases/Pages/200772410294613432.aspx.
19. Robert Snell, "Dearborn man lied about dental visit to join Hezbollah," *Detroit News*, August 15, 2016.
20. Department of Justice, "Two Men Arrested for Terrorist Activities on Behalf of Hizballah's Islamic Jihad Organization," June 8, 2017,

https://www.justice.gov/opa/pr/two-men-arrested-terrorist-activities-behalf-hizballahs-islamic-jihad-organization.

21. Department of Justice, "Two Men Arrested for Terrorist Activities on Behalf of Hizballah's Islamic Jihad Organization," June 8, 2017, https://www.justice.gov/opa/pr/two-men-arrested-terrorist-activities-behalf-hizballahs-islamic-jihad-organization.
22. U.S. Department of the Treasury, "Press Release: Treasury Designates Hizballah Leadership," September 13, 2012, http://www.treasury.gov/press-center/press-releases/Pages/tg1709.aspx; United Nations, Office of the High Commissioner for Human Rights, Independent International Commission of Inquiry on the Syrian Arab Republic established pursuant to United Nations Human Rights Council Resolutions S-17/1, 19/22 and 21/26, December 20, 2012, http://www.ohchr.org/Documents/Countries/SY/ColSyriaDecember2012.pdf.
23. David Kenner, "Why Israel Fears Iran's Presence in Syria," *The Atlantic*, July 22, 2018, https://www.theatlantic.com/international/archive/2018/07/hezbollah-iran-new-weapons-israel/565796/
24. Hanin Ghaddar, "U.S. Sanctions Are Hurting Hezbollah," The Washington Institute for Near East Policy *Policywatch* 3090, March 6, 2019, https://www.washingtoninstitute.org/policy-analysis/view/u.s.-sanctions-are-hurting-hezbollah
25. Nadim Ladki, "Lebanese Forces Pledge Crackdown; Force To Be Used to Quell Fighting That Has Killed 81," *Montreal Gazette*, May 13, 2008.
26. Israel Defense Forces, Strategic Division, Military-Strategic Information Section, "The Second Lebanon War: Three Years Later," July 12, 2009, http://www.mfa.gov.il/MFA/About+the+Ministry/Behind+the+Headlines/The-Second-Lebanon-War-Three-years-later-12-Jul-2009.
27. Erich Follath, "New Evidence Points to Hezbollah in Hariri Murder," *Der Spiegel* (Hamburg), May 23, 2009, http://www.spiegel.de/international/world/0,1518,626412,00.html.
28. Laila Bassam, "Hezbollah and Allies Resign, Toppling Lebanon Government," Reuters, January 12, 2011, http://www.reuters.com/article/2011/01/12/us-lebanon-hariri-resignation-idUSTRE70B26A20110112.
29. "Hezbollah-Backed Najib Mikati Appointed Lebanese PM," BBC, January 25, 2011, http://www.bbc.co.uk/news/world-middle-east-12273178.
30. Hanin Ghaddar, "Prosecution Highlights Hezbollah, Syrian Links to

Hariri Assassination," Washington Institute for Near East Policy *Policywatch* 3016, September 14, 2019, https://www.washingtoninstitute.org/policy-analysis/view/prosecution-highlights-hezbollah-syrian-links-to-hariri-assassination

31. Hanin Ghaddar, "What Does Hezbollah's Election Victory Mean for Lebanon?" Washington Institute for Near East Policy *Policywatch* 2966, May 8, 2018, http://www.washingtoninstitute.org/policy-analysis/view/what-does-hezbollahs-election-victory-mean-for-lebanon
32. "Hezbollah: Five ways group has changed since 2006 Israel war," BBC Monitoring, July 11, 2016, https://www.bbc.com/news/world-middle-east-36672803.
33. Hanin Ghaddar, "A War with Hezbollah would Essentially Mean War with Iran this time around," *The National*, September 4, 2017, https://www.thenational.ae/opinion/a-war-with-hizbollah-would-essentially-mean-war-with-iran-this-time-around-1.625530; Amos Harel and Gilli Cohen, "Hezbollah, From terror group to army," *Ha'aretz* (Tel Aviv), December 7, 2016, https://www.haaretz.com/st/c/prod/eng/2016/07/lebanon2/
34. Ran Elkayam, "Estimate of Hezbollah's fatalities during the Syrian civil war and the conclusions arising from the analysis of their identity," The Meir Amit Intelligence and Terrorism Information Center, November 3, 2019, https://www.terrorism-info.org.il/en/estimate-hezbollahs-fatalities-syrian-civil-war-conclusions-arising-analysis-identity/
35. Hanin Ghaddar, "Economic Alternatives Could Split Shiites from Hezbollah," Washington Institute for Near East Policy *Policywatch* 2711, October 18, 2016, http://www.washingtoninstitute.org/policy-analysis/view/economic-alternatives-could-help-split-shiites-from-hezbollah.
36. Hanin Ghaddar, "Shia Unrest in Hezbollah's Beirut Stronghold," Washington Institute for Near East Policy *Policywatch* 2880, October 30, 2017, http://www.washingtoninstitute.org/policy-analysis/view/shia-unrest-in-hezbollahs-beirut-stronghold.
37. Osama Habib, "No U.S. plan to target local banks: official," *Daily Star* (Beirut), September 24, 2019, http://www.dailystar.com.lb/Business/International/2019/Sep-24/492179-no-us-plan-to-target-local-banks-official.ashx?utm_campaign=20190924&utm_source=sailthru&utm_medium=email&utm_term=Middle%20East%20Minute
38. Angus McDowall, "Yemen government says Hezbollah fighting alongside Houthis," Reuters, February 24, 2016.
39. U.S. Department of the Treasury "Press Release: Treasury Sanctions

Hizballah Leadership," August 22, 2013.
40. Itamar Sharon, "'Six Iranians, including a general, killed in Israeli strike,'" *Times of Israel*, January 19, 2015.
41. Zeina Karam, "Hezbollah accuses Saudi Arabia of 'genocide' in Yemen," *Times of Israel*, April 13, 2015.
42. U.S. Department of State, Bureau of Counterterrorism and Countering Violent Extremism, "Country Reports on Terrorism 2015," June 2016.
43. U.S. Department of State, Bureau of Counterterrorism and Countering Violent Extremism, "Country Reports on Terrorism 2015," June 2016.
44. "Bahrain says it dismantled Iran-linked terror cell," Agence France-Presse, January 6, 2016.
45. Yara Bayoumy, "Kuwait court sentences two to death for spying for Iran, Hezbollah," Reuters, January 12, 2016; "UAE Jails Emirati Woman on Charges of Spying for Hezbollah," Agence France-Presse, June 28, 2016.
46. "Kuwait jails Shiite MP for insulting Saudi, Bahrain," Agence France-Presse, July 27, 2016.
47. "Arab League labels Hezbollah a 'terrorist' group," *Al-Jazeera* (Doha), March 12, 2016, https://www.aljazeera.com/news/2016/03/arab-league-labels-hezbollah-terrorist-group-160311173735737.html
48. "GCC declares Lebanon's Hezbollah a 'terrorist' group," *Al Jazeera* (Doha), March 2, 2016.
49. Fahd Al-Zayabi, "Saudi Arabia launches financial sanctions on Hezbollah," *Al Sharq Al-Awsat* (London), May 29, 2014; Sultan Al-Tamimi, "GCC: Hezbollah terror group," *Arab News*, June 3, 2013.
50. Royal Embassy of Saudi Arabia, "Fact Sheet: Iran's Record in Supporting Terrorism and Extremism," January 20, 2016.
51. "US and Gulf states impose more sanctions on Hezbollah leaders," *Middle East Eye,* May 17, 2018, http://www.middleeasteye.net/news/us-gulf-states-sanction-hezbollah-leaders-492203809.
52. Anne Barnard, "Saudi Arabia Cuts Billions in Aid to Lebanon, Opening Door for Iran," *New York Times*, March 2, 2016.
53. "Saudi and UAE ban citizens from travelling to Lebanon," *Al Jazeera* (Doha), February 23, 2016.
54. Rania El Gamal and Sam Wilkins, "Saudi Arabia blacklists four firms, three Lebanese men over Hezbollah ties," Reuters, February 26, 2016.
55. Rania El Gamal and Sam Wilkins, "Saudi Arabia blacklists four firms, three Lebanese men over Hezbollah ties," Reuters, February

26, 2016.

56. "Concerned over its terror labeling Hezbollah urges Saudis to review decision," *YaLibnan*, July 9, 2016.
57. Matthew Levitt, "Senior Hizballah Official Wanted for Murder," Washington Institute for Near East Policy *Policywatch* 1833, July 20, 2011, https://www.washingtoninstitute.org/policy-analysis/view/senior-hizballah-official-wanted-for-murder.
58. Matthew Levitt and Nadav Pollak, "Hizbullah Under Fire in Syria," Tony Blair Faith Foundation, June 9, 2016, https://www.washington-institute.org/policy-analysis/view/hizbullah-under-fire-in-syria.
59. Matthew Levitt, *Hezbollah: The Global Footprint of Lebanon's Party of God* (Washington: Georgetown University Press, 2013), 27.
60. At the release of the State Department's annual terrorist report in June 2016, a senior U.S. official highlighted these efforts. "Confronting Iran's destabilizing activities and its support for terrorism was a key element of our expanded dialogue with the countries of the Gulf Cooperation Council, following the leaders' summit at Camp David in May of [2015]. We've also expanded our cooperation with partners in Europe, South America, and West Africa to develop and implement strategies to counter the activities of Iranian-allied and sponsored groups, such as Hezbollah." U.S. Department of State, "Country Reports on Terrorism 2015 Special Briefing with Justin Siberell, Acting Coordinator for Counterterrorism," June 2, 2016.
61. Hanin Ghaddar, "How Will Hezbollah Respond to Israel's Drone Attack?" The Washington Institute For Near East Policy *Policywatch* 3171, August 28, 2019, https://www.washingtoninstitute.org/policy-analysis/view/how-will-hezbollah-respond-to-israels-drone-attack
62. Katherine Bauer, Hanin Ghaddar, and Assaf Orion, "Iran's Precision Missile Project Moves to Lebanon," Washington Institute for Near East Policy *Policy Notes* 56, December 2018, https://www.washingtoninstitute.org/policy-analysis/view/irans-precision-missile-project-moves-to-lebanon.
63. "Hezbollah cells in West Bank busted by Israeli security forces," *Jerusalem Post*, August 18, 2016.
64. Matthew Levitt, "Inside Hezbollah's European Plots," *The Daily Beast,* July 20, 2015, https://www.thedailybeast.com/inside-hezbollahs-european-plots.
65. Benjamin Weinthal, "Increase of Hezbollah members in German state, says intel report," *Jerusalem Post*, July 4, 2019, https://www.jpost.com/international/increase-of-hezbollah-members-in-german-state-says-intel-report-594481.

66. U.S. Department of the Treasury, "Treasury Sanctions Procurement Agents Of Hizballah Front Company Based In Lebanon With Subsidiaries In The UAE And China," July 10, 2014, https://www.treasury.gov/press-center/press-releases/Pages/jl2562.aspx.
67. Matthew Levitt, "The Crackdown on Hezbollah's Financing Network," *Wall Street Journal*, January 27, 2016, http://www.washingtoninstitute.org/policy-analysis/view/the-crackdown-on-hezbollahs-financing-network.
68. Matthew Levitt, "The Crackdown on Hezbollah's Financing Network," *Wall Street Journal*, January 27, 2016, http://www.washingtoninstitute.org/policy-analysis/view/the-crackdown-on-hezbollahs-financing-network.
69. Amira El Masaiti, "Morocco cuts ties with Iran over Sahara weapons dispute," *Chicago Tribune,* May 4, 2018, http://www.chicagotribune.com/news/nationworld/sns-bc-ml--morocco-iran-20180501-story.html.
70. Hanin Ghaddar and Sarah Feuer, "Will Morocco Extradite a Hezbollah Financier to the United States?" Washington Institute for Near East Policy *Policywatch* 2775, March 23, 2017, http://www.washingtoninstitute.org/policy-analysis/view/will-morocco-extradite-a-hezbollah-financier-to-the-united-states.
71. Matthew Levitt, "Don't Forget, or Deny, Hezbollah's Brutal Crimes," *National Post*, July 20, 2016, http://www.washingtoninstitute.org/policy-analysis/view/dont-forget-or-deny-hezbollahs-brutal-crimes.
72. United States Drug Enforcement Administration, "DEA and European Authorities Uncover Massive Hizballah Drug and Money Laundering Scheme," February 1, 2016, http://krwg.org/post/dea-and-european-authorities-uncover-massive-hizballah-drug-and-money-laundering-scheme.
73. Levitt, "Don't Forget, or Deny, Hezbollah's Brutal Crimes."
74. Kyra Gurney, Police Documents Reveal 'Hezbollah Ties' to Brazil's PCC, *InSight Crime*, November 10, 2014, https://www.insightcrime.org/news/brief/police-documents-hezbollah-ties-brazil-pcc/
75. Mitra Taj, "Lebanese Detainee in Peru Denies Hezbollah Link, Says Police Coerced Confession," *Ha'aretz* (Tel Aviv), November 14, 2014, https://www.haaretz.com/lebanese-in-peru-denies-hezbollah-link-1.5328779.
76. "Brazil nabs former Hezbollah member wanted for drug trafficking," Reuters, July 29, 2016, http://www.reuters.com/article/us-olympics-rio-security-idUSKCN1091V5.
77. "S. Nasrallah: Hezbollah Will Emerge from Syria War as an Inter-

national Force," *al-Manar*, August 19, 2016, http://archive.almanar.com.lb/english/article.php?id=282798.

78. Ghaddar, "U.S. Sanctions Are Hurting Hezbollah."

67 Hizb ut-Tahrir

Quick Facts

Geographical Areas of Operation: Global
Numerical Stregnth (Members): Unknown
Leadership: Ata Abu Rashta
Religious Identification: Sunni Islam

Source: Counter Extremism Project

Introduction

Hizb ut-Tahrir al-Islami or Hizb ut-Tahrir ("Party of Islamic Liberation," "Party of Liberation," HT, or HuT) is a complex pan-Islamist organization, with branches around the world. Hizb ut-Tahrir (HuT) is banned in numerous countries throughout the Middle East, South and Central Asia, and parts of Europe for its extremist beliefs.[1] The group ostensibly renounces violence, armed revolution, and political participation, and it does not fit the model of a terrorist organization, a political party, or a revolutionary movement. However, this is misleading.[2] In reality, its ideology sanctions military coups and the mass killing of innocents to achieve its desired political objectives, helping to inspire jihadist terrorism.[3] Currently, there is no proof of a working relationship between HuT and the activities or funding of more violent groups, but its ideology has influenced many in the West and elsewhere to join violent jihadist groups.[4] As such, Hizb ut-Tahrir occupies a unique space among global Islamist movements, becoming what has led many experts to believe that the group could act as a 'conveyor belt to terrorism'.[5]

History and Ideology

In 1953, an al-Azhar University-trained Palestinian Islamic scholar, Sheikh Muhammad Taqiuddin al-Nabhani, founded Hizb ut-Tahrir (HuT) in East Jerusalem (occupied by the Kingdom of Jordan at that time). While HuT alleges that Sheikh al-Nabhani had no prior political experience, he engaged with Muslim Brotherhood members during his time in Egypt although it is unclear whether he was a member.[6] Al-Nabhani continued to have extensive contact with the Muslim Brotherhood, and exchanged views with Sayyid Qutb, whose works later inspired al-Qaeda, as well as influential Palestinian Sheikh Izz al-Din al-Qassam. Al-Qassam spent time with Al-Nabhani during the latter's teens and twenties helping plan revolutionary activities against British colonial rule.[7]

HuT's structure as a modern political party was influenced by contemporary Middle Eastern pan-national identities and ideologies, such as Arab nationalism and Ba'athism. Like these parties, HuT adapted Leninist revolutionary vanguard concepts, such as the formation of a modern political party.[8] However, unlike Arab nationalism's embrace of a secular, pan-Arab identity to promote unity, al-Nabhani based his views and those of HuT on the centrality of Islam in politics. HT differentiated itself from other emerging Islamist organizations by implementing these elements into the organizational political structure.

Hizb ut-Tahrir has a well-defined platform and ideology, both rooted in Islam. It disavows nationalism, capitalism, and socialism as Western ideologies that are antithetical to Islam. Instead, the organization seeks to re-establish the *caliphate* that ruled Muslims following the death of the Prophet Muhammad.[9] HuT rejects the legitimacy of modern states – such as Saudi Arabia and Iran – that claim to be Islamic.[10] However, the group also denied the legitimacy of the Islamic State's claim that it had reestablished the *caliphate* under Abu Bakr al-Baghdadi.[11]

The modern *caliph* envisioned by al-Nabhani and HuT would control the religion, army, economy, foreign policy, and political system of the *caliphate*. The *caliphate*'s draft constitution considers *Aqeedah* (the Islamic belief system) as the foundation of the state. All legislation and the constitution itself must be based on the Quran,

Sunnah, the consensus of the companions of *ashab al-ijma* (the four righteous *caliphs*), and *qiyas* (analogy).[12] The *caliph* and his deputies interpret and apply these instructions and thereby solve all social, economic, and ethnic problems that the *ummah* (the Islamic community) may face. Should HuT succeed, Arabic would be the state language.

While HuT does welcome female members into its ranks, it would relegate them – as well as non-Muslims – to subordinate administrative positions, as only male Muslims can govern.[13] The *caliph* appoints an *emir* (commander) to prepare the people for and wage *jihad* (holy war/struggle) against non-believers, as well as mandates compulsory military service for all Muslim men over the age of 15.[14] While the *caliphate* is able to make treaties with friendly, non-Islamic countries, it is forbidden from participating in international organizations governed by non-Islamic rules, such as the United Nations. Furthermore, the *caliphate* cannot make treaties with Britain, America, France, and Russia, as those countries are considered "imperialist states." The *caliphate* remains in a state of war with Israel.[15]

HuT criticizes other Islamist parties for their use of democratic structures to gain political advantage. For example, the Islamic Revival Party of Tajikistan, the Muslim Brotherhood, and Hamas have all engaged with non-Islamic governments by holding ministerial posts or participating in elections in order to become influential.[16] HuT, in contrast, believes that all Muslims who adopt democracy reject *Allah* as the universe's sole legislator, and thus making apostates of those who accept democracy.[17] In this vein, al-Nabhani completely rejected the concept of gradualism as espoused by the Muslim Brotherhood. Instead, HuT favors peaceful, but radical, political change through the demolition of the existing state apparatus and the construction of a new Islamic state.

Nevertheless, HuT prefers to persuade society to gradually accept its ideas, which it believes will inevitably lead to regime change. As one expert explained: "Rather than slogging through a political process that risks debasing the Quran and perpetuating the *ummah*'s subjugation to the West, Hizb ut-Tahrir aims at global, grassroots revolution, culminating in a sudden, millenarian victory… when

Muslims have achieved a critical mass of Koranic rectitude."[18]

HuT's strategy consists of three stages.[19] The first is to recruit members and build a strong organization. Next is HuT's "interaction" with the *ummah* in an effort to impose its principles as the only legitimate version of Islam – one "stripped of all cultural accretions and purged of alien influences."[20] Finally, the ensuing grassroots revolution will re-establish the *caliphate*. HuT wants to bring one or more Muslim countries under its control to create a base and to convince others, generating a domino effect. The group seeks to use dispossessed populations to seize power in other states as a prelude to a broader *caliphate*, removing wayward Muslim regimes and eventually overthrowing non-Muslim ones as well. Thus, the organization welcomed the overthrow of Arab dictators during the Arab Spring revolutions.

HuT reportedly shuns violence; its justification for non-violence lies in the example of the Prophet, who criticized the Pagan leaders of Mecca, gathered followers around him, and initially resisted using force to establish his Islamic state.[21] According to one expert:

> The Party still thinks that it must follow the strategy of the Prophet: like Muhammad in Mecca, they must preach without violence. In practical terms, it means that when HT achieves a large following for its ideology, they could overthrow... regimes through peaceful demonstrations. Also, like Muhammad in his war against the Arab tribes in Mecca, they could get outside assistance or *nusrah* from the military to organize a coup.[22]

Emmanuel Karagiannis and Clark McCauley provide two arguments for the ideological complexities of HT's position on violent action: "The first is to say that they have been committed to non-violence for fifty years. The second is to say that they have been waiting fifty years for the right moment to begin violent struggle."[23]

The two perspectives are more similar than they first appear. Historically, few groups are unconditionally committed to nonviolence, and "Hizb ut-Tahrir is not exceptional but typical in this regard. Its commitment to nonviolent struggle is conditional and the condition sought is the declaration of *jihad* by legitimate authority," (i.e., the *caliph*).[24] HuT also endorses defensive *jihads*, where Muslims are required to fight if attacked. This position clearly has the potential for broad interpretation, and has already been applied to promote violence against coalition forces in Iraq and Afghanistan.[25] Moreover, the group was proscribed in Denmark after distributing pamphlets urging Muslims to "kill [Jews] wherever you find them, and turn them out from where they have turned you out."[26]

HuT has developed the concept of *nusrah* (seeking outside assistance) from other groups, such as the militaries of target states.[27] One could argue that HuT's preferred method of establishing the *caliphate* through political change is, in fact, a *coup d'état* by a military that has embraced Islam as its guiding politico-religious principle. HuT has been directly or indirectly linked to a number of unsuccessful coup attempts in Jordan, Bangladesh, Syria, and Egypt.[28] HuT infiltrated Tunisian politics, as well as the Syrian and Pakistani militaries; members of the latter, including a general, have been arrested or fired for their activities in service of the political party.[29] Hizb ut-Tahrir also attempted to persuade Libyan leader Moamar Ghaddafi, Iraqi President Saddam Hussein, and Iranian Supreme Leader Ruhollah Khomeini to assume the role of *caliph*.[30]

Radicalization of group members who then conduct violent acts as individuals without explicit direction remains a source of concern. According to Zeyno Baran, "Hizb ut-Tahrir is part of an elegant division of labor. The group itself is active in the ideological preparation of the Muslims, while other organizations handle the planning and execution of terrorist attacks… Hizb ut-Tahrir today serves as a *de facto* conveyor belt for terrorists."[31] Several known militants and *jihadists* associated with more radical Islamist groups were previously members of or radicalized by HuT. For example, Omri Bakri Muhammed, founder and former leader of Hizb ut-Tahrir-Britain, left the group to found al-Muhajiroun, which was later banned in the United Kingdom for funding and supporting terrorist organizations.[32] Another is Omar Sharif, in whose home British intelligence officials discovered a cache of HuT literature after Sharif blew himself up in a Tel Aviv bar in 2003.[33] Al-Qaeda's leader and 9/11 mastermind, Khaled Shaikh Mohammed, reportedly spent time with the group.[34] Abu Musab al-Zarqawi, who led the Islamic State's predecessor organization, al-Qaeda in Iraq, also spent time as a member.[35]

Hizb ut-Tahrir's strategy in the West raises concern among many observers as the group appears to pursue a disingenuous dual-track strategy: grassroots activism among Western Muslims on one hand and engagement with wider Western society on the other. According to Houriya Ahmed and Hannah Stuart of the London-based Centre for Social Cohesion, HuT activism in Britain consists of two messages and two complementary aims. One message is aimed at the UK's Muslim communities, and the other at intellectuals and opinion-makers such as journalists and politicians. Presenting itself as the vanguard of Islam, HuT works within the British Muslim community to promote identification with the global Muslim community and discourage any other political loyalties.[36] Within society, HuT presents Islamism, the *caliphate*, and its interpretation of *sharia* law as a tenable alternative to current thinking.[37] Despite this, the group rejects moderate clerics who embrace *al-Wasatiyyah*, or Islam as a religion of tolerance, arguing that it amounts to an attempt to secularize religion.[38]

Global Reach

Whatever the concerns and criticisms regarding HuT's goals and methods, the movement has a significant following in many parts of the world. Some even claim that "of all the banned Islamist groups in the former Soviet Union, Hizb ut-Tahrir is the only one that can be called a mass organization."[39] It is also a popular organization among young Muslims in Western Europe.[40] The group's major organizational center is said to be in London, where most of its literature is published and a good deal of its fundraising and training occurs.[41]

The global leader of HuT meets with regional leaders who distribute literature and funding to district leaders. In monthly meetings, the district leaders then redistribute these items and provide strategic direction to individual cells. For operational security, most cell members only know other members of their cell and are kept in the dark about any other cells operating locally, regionally, or nationally.[42] Ahmed and Stuart claim that:

> HT's ideology and strategy are centralized. HT global leadership issues strategy communiqués to the executive committees of national branches, which then interpret them into a localized strategic action plan… Whilst HT core ideology stressed the indivisibility of the Muslim '*ummah*' and rejects national identity, national strategies often reflect the ethnic origins of the various Muslim communities... National executives are encouraged to interpret strategy to best suit their localized needs.[43]

Because Hizb ut-Tahrir leadership and cells operate in secret, there is little reliable information on global membership numbers. Hizb ut-Tahrir's support in Central Asia grew in the 1990s. As of 2015, experts estimate that the group has some 25,000 members in Central Asia alone.[44] The group's support base consists of college students, the unemployed, factory workers, and teachers,[45] but it also seems to be making particularly strong headway among prison inmates.[46]

HuT's growth in Central Asia is significantly, though unintentionally, fueled by repressive tactics used by local regimes. With few exceptions, the states that emerged out of the Soviet Union smother – rather than engage – their political opponents. The anti-democratic policies adopted by these regimes unwittingly expand the influence of extremist groups (like HuT) from the margins of national political discourse to its center.[47] Despite efforts by Central Asian authorities to infiltrate and crack down on the group's local branches – often successfully disrupting the link between the party's international and local leadership – the group continues to maintain a sizeable presence in the region.[48]

South and Southeast Asia are often seen as strongholds of HuT activism. The group's recruitment in Pakistan relies on pamphlets, conferences, seminars, and *daroos* (religious lectures), as well as individual proselytization, mainly in urban centers. HuT Pakistan mainly targets the urban middle class and "opinion-makers" such as journalists, trade unionists, teachers, and lawyers. However, the party has failed to achieve a widespread presence in the country, due to both competition from other Islamist parties and its Pan-Islamist outlook on the Pakistani military.[49] In Indonesia, Hizb ut-Tahrir claims that it recruited "tens of thousands" of members there.[50] A 2007 HuT conference in Indonesia drew between 80,000 and 100,000 attendees from around the world.[51] HuT also holds regular public protests and demonstrations in Pakistan, Indonesia, and Bangladesh, and has a presence of unknown strength in Syria, Iraq, Turkey, Palestine, Lebanon, Egypt, Tunisia, Afghanistan, Malaysia, China, Canada, Australia, South Africa, Russia, Ukraine, and others.

In the West, Hizb ut-Tahrir's strategy uses Muslim identity and contemporary events in the organization's outreach. The party's 1998 strategy document instructs its Western national executives to "incorporate localized international incidents" – such as the Palestinian-Israeli confrontation, the Balkan wars, and ostensibly the War on Terror into a clash of civilizations narrative as part of an appeal to Western Muslims. HuT's objective is to "inflame and co-opt grievances" within Muslim communities in the West, and prevent their assimilation into Western society.[52] The organization specifically targets young, second-generation Muslims to exploit their alienation from both the Western society in which they live and the culture of their parents.[53] Through mosques, HuT-run schools, sports clubs, and workshops, the group works to proselytize vulnerable audiences.[54] Furthermore, members are encouraged to recruit through their existing social networks: "mother-and-baby groups, student unions, even a chat with the neighbors." As one former member notes, the group offers young Muslims "a single, simple solution to all the political, social and economic problems of the world, from a religious perspective."[55] The delegation of important duties at a young age provides for an "intoxicating" sense of power and community.[56]

Most of HuT's money is raised in Europe, the Middle East, and South Asia.[57] Members are expected to contribute to the operational costs of the organization, including mundane outlays like printing leaflets.[58] Most HuT members operate out of their own homes, and very few, if any, are paid.[59] A great deal of the organization's technology in Central Asia is funded and imported from abroad, reflecting both the international scope of the movement and potentially the complicity of at least some officials responsible for customs and border controls among local governments.[60]

Recent Activity

In recent years, HuT activity in Western countries has included organizing protests, sit-ins, and petitions. The group, for example, asked Muslims to abstain from the 2015 parliamentary elections in Great Britain.[61] It also staged a protest against the killing of civilians in Aleppo outside the Syrian embassy in London.[62] In March 2019, the group's Scandinavia branch organized a prayer and demonstration of several hundred at the Danish Parliament in Copenhagen, Denmark in response to the New Zealand Mosque shooting.[63] In the United States, the local branch organized two events about the siege of Aleppo by Syrian regime forces and pro-Iranian militias.[64]

The Australian HuT branch is increasingly active. In March 2015, a video emerged of Hizb ut-Tahrir's Australia leader Ismail Alwahwah calling for *jihad* against Jews at a rally in New South Wales.[65] In November 2015, the group organized a conference in Australia against "forced assimilation,"[66] and two years later it received criticism for releasing "Women of Hizb ut-Tahrir," a video that supported domestic violence against "disobedient" wives.[67] The group also publicly blamed the West for a June 2017 terror attack in Melbourne.[68]

In 2017, the group launched a campaign to exploit the plight of the Rohingya Muslims displaced from Myanmar in Bangladesh.[69] In the Bangladeshi port city of Chittagong, HT posted and distributed posters calling for "fellow Muslims to unite" to support the Rohingya and also for "devoted army officers" to dethrone the ruling Awami-League government of PM Sheikh Hasina.[70]

Hizb ut-Tahrir is banned in the Russian Federation after it was labelled an "extremist organization" by the country's Supreme Court.[71] Hizb ut-Tahrir members were arrested throughout Russia's

Muslim-populated areas in August 2012.[72] In 2017, the Russian FSB detained six Crimean locals on accusations of being members of the group.[73] In June 2019, a Russian court sentenced five Crimean Tatars to hard labor for their membership in the group in a move that was condemned by the Ukrainian and the United States missions to the Organization for Security and Co-operation in Europe (OCSE).[74] The FSB arrested another eight Tatars on charges of membership of the group during the same month.[75]

The group held a demonstration outside the Uzbek embassy in Brussels during Islam Karimov's January 2011 visit to the European Union and NATO, which was the first open manifestation of HuT in Belgium.[76] While the group appears to have scaled down its activities in Central Asia following the Arab Spring, it continues to face government persecution.

In 2017, the Kyrgyz government shut down more than a hundred websites alleged to be affiliated with extremism, including Hizb ut-Tahrir's regional language webpages.[77] Kyrgyz authorities also arrested eleven alleged HuT members, including a local leader of the organization in December 2017.[78]

Following the Arab Spring revolutions of 2010-2012, a renewed quest for religious identity in the Middle East and North Africa partly manifested itself in the pursuit of political Islam. Seeking to capitalize on this trend, HuT organized a much-publicized female conference in Tunisia in March 2012.[79] In April 2013, hundreds of women, including journalists, representatives of organizations and other female opinion- makers gathered at a critical press conference in Amman, Jordan, organized by Hizb ut-Tahrir to discuss the establishment of a Caliphate to protect the women and children in al-Sham from Bashar al-Assad and his regime.[80]

In the Palestinian Territories, where the group was founded, the movement has gained traction. In 2015, the group attempted to hold a caliphate conference in Ramallah despite Palestinian Authority (PA) opposition. In May 2015, the group incited protests against a Jordanian cleric's visit to the al-Aqsa Mosque in Jerusalem, prompting the PA to arrest several members.[81] In 2017, global HuT branches organized rallies calling for the destruction of Israel.[82] In June 2019, the group's Palestinian branch clashed with the PA's police after attempting to celebrate the Eid al-Fitr holiday in Hebron on the day declared by Saudi, Emirati, Qatari, and Kuwaiti religious clerics to be the end of Ramadan, rather than the day declared by clerics in Palestine, Egypt, and Jordan.[83]

The group also faced setbacks in the Middle East and the Arab World. In September 2016, the Tunisian government asked a military court to outlaw Hizb ut-Tahrir. A year later in July 2017, the Tunisian government successfully banned HuT for one month on the grounds of "inciting hatred."[84] Following the month, the party successfully appealed the original decision and continues to operate in Tunisia today.[85] In December 2017, Tunisian police arrested forty HuT members at a broader protest in Sidi Bouzid for carrying "banners hostile to the state."[86] In late 2016, the Jordanian government, arrested 15 senior members of Hizb ut-Tahrir for campaigning against changes to the school curriculum.[87] In Turkey, HuT and its annual conference are now outright banned after the government conflated it with the Gülen movement and imprisoned 58 of its members.[88]

After months of Hizb ut-Tahrir protesting against Jakarta's former Christian governor Basuki "Ahok" Tjahaja Purnama and accusing him of blasphemy, the Indonesian government banned HuT for opposing the state's secular ideology and "causing friction in society.[89] The public pressure by both HuT's organized campaign against Ahok and others involved in the increasing Islamist trend resulted in the former governor being sentenced to two years in prison on blasphemy charges.[90] In order to skirt the Indonesian government's ban on its activities, the group allegedly rebranded itself the Islamic Royatul Community (KARIM), which upheld the ideology, symbolism, and tactics of the group under a new name.[91] Beyond Indonesia, the BRICS countries – Brazil, Russia, India, China, and South Africa – agreed at their annual 2017 meeting to label the group a terrorist organization, along with several other violent South Asia-based groups.[92]

The ongoing Syrian crisis has allowed Hizb ut-Tahrir to mobilize Muslims living in Western countries. HuT has portrayed itself as a defender of Muslim populations in war zones. It will continue to appeal to these grievances, and to Muslim identity, in its recruitment across the Islamic world, and to minority Muslim communities in the West, where it can particularly capitalize on rising anti-Muslim, nationalist, and nativist sentiment. Finally, the group will likely attempt to increase its activities in Muslim-majority countries in South and South-East Asia. However, it will likely continue to meet resistance and be deemed a threat to ruling authorities in countries where it gains sufficient strength.

Endnotes

1. "Hizb Ut-Tahrir," Counter Extremism Project, n.d., https://www.counterextremism.com/threat/hizb-ut-tahrir.
2. "Understanding Islamism," International Crisis Group *Middle East/North Africa Report* no. 37, March 2, 2005, https://www.crisisgroup.org/middle-east-north-africa/understanding-islamism; Clark McCauley, "Some Hizb ut-Tahrir members have engaged in political violence, but this appears rare and not supported by Hizb ut-Tahrir leadership," University of Maryland START, n.d., https://www.start.umd.edu/research-projects/hizb-ut-tahrir-al-islami-challenge-non-violent-radical-islam; "Hizb ut-Tahrir claims to reject violence as a form of political struggle, and most of its activities are peaceful. In theory, the group rejects terrorism, considering the killing of innocents to be against Islamic law. However, behind this rhetoric, there is some ideological justification for violence in its literature, and it admits participation in a number of failed coup attempts in the Middle East." See "Radical Islam in Central Asia: Responding to Hizb ut-Tahrir," International Crisis Group *Europe and Central Asia Report* no. 58, June 30, 2003, https://www.crisisgroup.org/europe-central-asia/central-asia/uzbekistan/radical-islam-central-asia-responding-hizb-ut-tahrir
3. Houriya Ahmed and Hannah Stuart, "Profile: Hizb Ut-Tahrir in the UK," *Current Trends in Islamist Ideology* 10, August 17, 2010, https://www.hudson.org/research/9827-profile-hizb-ut-tahrir-in-the-uk-.
4. Sara Malm, "100 members of controversial Islamic group linked to radicalized British students including Jihadi John have 'joined forces with Al Qaeda in Syria," *Daily Mail*, April 11, 2015, https://www.dailymail.co.uk/news/article-3034733/100-members-controversial-Islamic-group-linked-radicalised-British-students-including-Jihadi-John-joined-forces-al-Qaeda-Syria.html

5. Elisa Orofino, "Extreme and Non-Violent? Exploring the Threat Posed by Non-Violent Extremists," *European Eye on Radicalization*, July 14, 2020, https://eeradicalization.com/extreme-and-non-violent-exploring-the-threat-posed-by-non-violent-extremists/
6. Taqiuddin an Nabahani, *The Islamic State* (CreateSpace Independent Publishing Platform, 2017).
7. "Taqiuddin al-Nabhani," *Le Parisien*, n.d., http://dictionnaire.sensagent.leparisien.fr/Taqiuddin_an-Nabhani/en-en/
8. "Radical Islam in Central Asia: Responding to Hizb ut-Tahrir," International Crisis Group *Asia Report* no. 58, June 30, 2003, https://www1.essex.ac.uk/armedcon/world/europe/commonwealth_of_independent_states/tajikistan/TajikistanRadicalIslam.pdf
9. "The Aim of Hizb Ut-Tahrir," Hizb ut-Tahrir, July 24, 2015. http://www.hizb-ut-tahrir.info/en/index.php/definition-of-ht/item/7982-the-aim-of-hizb-ut-tahrir.
10. Daniel J. Ruder, "The Long War in Central Asia: Hizb-ut-Tahrir's Caliphate," monograph, May 25, 2006, 22, https://www.globalsecurity.org/military/library/report/2006/ADA450614.pdf.
11. "Radical Islam in Central Asia," I; Mamdooh Abu Sawa Qataishaat, "Media Statement Regarding ISIS's Declaration in Iraq," Media Office of Hizb ut-Tahrir, Wilayah of Jordan, July 1, 2014, http://www.hizb.org.uk/current-affairs/media-statement-regarding-isiss-declaration-in-iraq
12. "A Draft Constitution of the Khilafah State," *Kilafah.com*, January 18, 2013, www.khilafah.com/a-draft-constitution-of-the-khilafah-state/
13. Ibid.
14. *The Method to Re-establish the Khilafah and Resume the Islamic Way of Life* (London, Al-Khilafah Publications, 2000), 67.
15. "A Draft Constitution of the Khilafah State."
16. Matthew Herbert, "The Plasticity of the Islamist Activist: Notes from the Counterterrorism Literature," *Studies in Conflict and Terrorism* 32 (2009), 399
17. Houriya Ahmed and Hannah Stuart, *Hizb ut-Tahrir: Ideology and Strategy* (Henry Jackson Society, 2009), 38-39, http://henryjacksonsociety.org/wp-content/uploads/2013/01/HIZB.pdf.
18. Olivier Roy, *Globalized Islam: The Search for a New Ummah,* (New York: Columbia University Press, 2004), 248.
19. Herbert, "The Plasticity of the Islamist Activist," 399.
20. Emmanuel Karagiannis and Clark McCauley, "Hizb ut-Tahrir al-Islami: Evaluating the Threat Posed by a Radical Islamic Group That

Remains Nonviolent," *Terrorism and Political Violence* 1, 2006, 328.

21. Zeyno Baran, *Hizb ut-Tahrir: Islam's Political Insurgency*, The Nixon Center, 2004, 11, https://www.hudson.org/content/researchattachments/attachment/448/eurasian_tahririslamspoliticalinsurgency.pdf.
22. Didier Chaudet, "An Islamist Threat to Central Asia?" *Journal of Muslim Minority Affairs* 26, no. 1, April 2006. 117.
23. Karagiannis and McCauley, "Hizb ut-Tahrir al-Islami," 328.
24. Rauert, "The Next Threat From Central Asia," 28; See also A. Elizabeth Jones, Testimony before the U.S. House of Representatives Committee on International Relations, Subcommittee on the Middle East and Central Asia, Washington, DC, October 29, 2003.
25. "Radical Islam in Central Asia: Responding to Hizb ut-Tahrir," International Crisis Group *Asia Report* no. 58, June 30, 2003, 8.
26. Christian Caryl, "Reality Check: The Party's Not Over," *Foreign Policy*, December 22, 2009.
27. Suha Taji-Farouki, *A Fundamental Quest: Hizb ut-Tahrir and the Search for the Islamic Caliphate* (London: Grey Seal, 1996), p.27, 168.
28. See, for instance, *Case of Kasymakhunov and Saybatalov v. Russia*, European Court of Human Rights, "Judgment," March 14, 2013, https://hudoc.echr.coe.int/fre#{"itemid":["001-117127"]}; See also Krishna Mungur, "Islamist Distortions: Hizb ut-Tahrir a Breeding Ground for al-Qaeda Recruitment," *Journal of Strategic Security* 2, no. 4, November/December 2009, https://scholarcommons.usf.edu/cgi/viewcontent.cgi?article=1068&context=jss.
29. Hannah Stuart, "Caliphate Dreaming," *Foreign Policy*, July 5, 2011, http://foreignpolicy.com/2011/07/05/caliphate-dreaming/.
30. "Radical Islam in Central Asia," 7-10.
31. Baran, *Hizb ut-Tahrir: Islam's Political Insurgency*.
32. "Omar Bakri Muhammad," *Counter Extremism Project*, n.d., https://www.counterextremism.com/extremists/omar-bakri-muhammad.
33. Caryl, "The Party's Not Over."
34. Steven Emerson, "Hizb Ut-Tahrir: Islam Has Replaced Communism as Top U.S. Enemy," *The Algemeiner*, July 11, 2011, http://www.algemeiner.com/2011/07/11/islam-has-replaced-communism-as-top-u-s-enemy/.
35. Zeyno Baran, "The Road From Tashkent to The Taliban," *National Review*, April 2, 2004, www.nationalreview.com/article/210139/road-tashkent-taliban-zeyno-baran.
36. Ahmed and Stuart, *Hizb ut-Tahrir: Ideology and Strategy*, 7.-
37. Ibid., 69.

38. Stuart and Ahmed, "Profile: Hizb ut-Tahrir in the UK."
39. "Central Asia: Islamists in Prison," International Crisis Group *Asia Briefing* no. 97, March 15, 2009, 3. See also Emmanuel Karagiannis, *Political Islam in Central Asia: The Challenge of Hizb ut-Tahrir* (New York: Routledge, 2010), 2.
40. Clark McCauley and Emmanuel Karagiannis, "Hizb ut-Tahrir al-Islami: The Challenge of a Non-Violent Radical Islam," *National Consortium for the Study of Terrorism and Responses to Terrorism,* University of Maryland, June 2009, www.start.umd.edu/research-projects/hizb-ut-tahrir-al-islami-challenge-non-violent-radical-islam.
41. Ariel Cohen, Testimony before the U.S. House of Representatives Committee on International Relations, Subcommittee on the Middle East and Central Asia, October 29, 2003, https://www.heritage.org/testimony/radical-islam-and-us-interests-central-asia.
42. "Hizb ut-Tahrir," *Jane's Terrorism and Insurgency Center*, October 26, 2009.
43. Ahmed and Stuart, *Hizb ut-Tahrir: Ideology and Strategy*, 68.
44. Thomas Kunze and Michail Logvinov, "Islamist Threats to Central Asia." *OSCE Yearbook 2015*, 2016, 131, https://doi.org/10.5771/9783845273655-125.
45. Ahmed Rashid, *Jihad: The Rise of Militant Islam in Central Asia* (New York, NY: Penguin Books, 2002), 124; Shiv Malik, "For Allah and the Caliphate," *New Statesman* 17, no. 824 (2004).
46. See "Central Asia: Islamists in Prison."
47. "Andijan Massacre: Uzbek Embassy Picket, 11am 9th May 2015," Hizb ut-Tahrir: The Liberation Party, Britain, May 5, 2015, http://www.hizb.org.uk/current-affairs/andijan-massacre-uzbek-embassy-picket-11am-9th-may-2015.
48. "Radical Islam in Central Asia," 20.
49. Ibid, 13.
50. Ahmed and Stuart, *Hizb ut-Tahrir: Ideology and Strategy*, 55.
51. "Stadium Crowd Pushes for Islamist Dream," *BBC*, August 12, 2009, http://news.bbc.co.uk/2/hi/south_asia/6943070.stm; See also "At massive rally, Hizb ut-Tahrir calls for a global Muslim state," *Christian Science Monitor*, August 14, 2007.
52. Stuart and Ahmed, "Profile: Hizb ut-Tahrir in the UK."
53. Pew Research Center, "Radical Islamist Movements: Jihadi Networks and Hizb ut-Tahrir," September 15, 2010, www.pewforum.org/2010/09/15/muslim-networks-and-movements-in-western-europe-radical-islamist-movements-jihadi-networks-and-hizb-ut-tahrir/.

54. Stuart and Ahmed, "Profile: Hizb ut-Tahrir in the UK."
55. Umm Mustafa, "Why I left Hizb ut-Tahrir," *New Statesman*, February 28, 2008, https://www.newstatesman.com/politics/2008/02/party-hizb-tahrir-members.
56. Ibid.
57. "Hizb ut-Tahrir," *Jane's Terrorism and Insurgency Center*.
58. Ibid.
59. Ibidem.
60. Rauert, "The Next Threat From Central Asia," p.31.
61. Hizb ut-Tahrir Britain, "The Futility of British Elections," April 22, 2015, http://www.hizb.org.uk/election-2015/the-futility-of-british-elections
62. Hizb ut-Tahrir Britain, "Raise your voice, Break the silence, Support you ummah in Aleppo," December 16, 2016, http://www.hizb.org.uk/wp-content/uploads/2016/12/demo-aleppo.jpg
63. Hizb ut-Tahrir Media Office Scandinavia, "Hizb ut Tahrir / Scandinavia Successfully Completed the Friday Prayer and Protest Event in front of the Danish Parliament," March 24, 2019, www.hizb-ut-tahrir.info/en/index.php/press-releases/scandinavia/17147.html.
64. Hizb ut-Tahrir America, "Aleppo, Syrian Crisis and Solution," December 17, 2016, https://hizb-america.org/aleppo-syria-crisis-solution/; Hizb ut-Tahrir America, "Stand up for Aleppo," December 23, 2016, https://hizb-america.org/stand-up-for-aleppo/
65. Taylor Auerbach, "Hizb ut-Tahrir leader Ismail Alwahwah calls for jihad against Jews in inflammatory video*,"* *Daily Telegraph* (London(, March 9, 2015, https://www.dailytelegraph.com.au/news/nsw/hizb-uttahrir-leader-ismail-alwahwah-calls-for-jihad-against-jews-in-inflammatory-video/news-story/ede1315c654f9b2420b507516b-3d1e7f.
66. Rosie Lewis, "Hizb ut-Tahrir: National Anthem is Forced Assimilation," *The Australian*, November 2, 2015, http://www.theaustralian.com.au/in-depth/community-under-siege/hizb-ut-tahrir-national-anthem-is-forced-assimilation/news-story/5aac76c3e-c65454d63f7f323f326e597
67. Rachel Olding, "Muslim men permitted to hit wives in a soft and 'symbolic' way, Hizb ut-Tahrir Australia women say," *Sydney Morning Herald*, April 13, 2017, http://www.smh.com.au/nsw/muslim-men-permitted-to-hit-wives-in-a-soft-and-symbolic-way-hizb-ut-tahrir-australia-women-say-20170413-gvk8rl.html.
68. "Melbourne terror attack: west to blame for Brighton, says Hizb ut-Tahrir," *The Australian*, June 7, 2017, http://www.theaustralian.com.

au/news/nation/melbourne-terror-attack-west-to-blame-for-brighton-says-hizb-uttahrir/news-story/5215a89cfeb225442fbde5bfcdc126fd.

69. Tarek Mahmud, "Hizb-ut Tahrir trying to build support using Rohingya crisis," *Dhaka Tribune*, November 26, 2017, http://www.dhakatribune.com/bangladesh/2017/11/26/hizb-ut-tahrir-trying-build-support-using-rohingya-crisis/.
70. "Hizb ut-Tahrir active again, this time plays Rohingya," *bdnews24.com*, September 17, 2017, https://bdnews24.com/bangladesh/2017/09/17/hizb-ut-tahrir-active-again-this-time-plays-rohingya-card-in-chittagong.
71. "Crimea occupiers detain another eight Crimean Tatars," UNIAN, June 10, 2019, https://www.unian.info/society/10581246-crimea-occupiers-detain-another-eight-crimean-tatars.html.
72. "Five Alleged Members of Banned Hizb ut-Tahrir Arrested in Chelyabinsk," *Radio Free Europe/Radio Liberty*, August 1, 2012, http://www.rferl.org/content/members-hizb-ut-tahrir-arrested/24663122.html
73. "Russia's FSB Detains Six Crimean Tatars Accused Of Being Hizb ut-Tahrir Members," *Radio Free Europe/Radio Liberty*, October 11, 2017, https://www.rferl.org/a/russia-fsb-six-crimean-tatars-detained-hizb-ut-tahrir/28786883.html. It should be noted that, while Russia claimed that the individuals detained were members of HT, Crimean activist groups claimed they were in fact Crimean Tatars who opposed Russia's takeover of Crimea.
74. "Ukraine, United States at OSCE condemn sentences to Crimean Tatars in Hizb ut-Tahrir case,:" UKRINFORM, June 21, 2019, https://www.ukrinform.net/rubric-polytics/2725465-ukraine-united-states-at-osce-condemn-sentences-to-crimean-tatars-in-hizb-uttahrir-case.html.
75. "Eight Crimean Tatars Jailed On Extremism Charges," *Radio Free Europe / Radio Liberty*, June 12, 2019, https://www.rferl.org/a/eight-crimean-tatars-jailed-on-extremism-charges/29995474.html.
76. Bruno De Cordier, "Why Was Hizb ut-Tahrir Protest in Brussels the Biggest?" neweurasia.net, January 28, 2011, http://www.neweurasia.net/photoblog/why-was-hizb-ut-tahrir-protest-in-brussels-the-biggest/
77. Mu Xuequan, "Kyrgyz authorities close websites for publishing extremist materials," Xinhua, January 8, 2018, www.xinhuanet.com/english/2018-01/08/c_136880662.htm.
78. Hu Axia, "Eleven extremists detained in Kyrgyzstan," Xinhua, December 19, 2017, news.xinhuanet.com/en-

glish/2017-12/19/c_136835797.htm.

79. Hizb ut- Tahrir Central Media Office, "Women of Hizb ut-Tahrir Host Historic International Women's Conference," March 8, 2012, http://www.hizb-ut-tahrir.info/en/index.php/press-releases/cmo-women-s-section/1200.html
80. Hizb ut-Tahrir, "Hundreds of Women to Gather at a Critical Press Conference in Jordan Organised by Hizb ut-Tahrir," April 24, 2013, http://www.hizb-ut-tahrir.info/info/english.php/contents_en/entry_24835.
81. Adnan Abu Amer, "Pan-Islamic movement becomes political player in Palestine," *Al-Monitor*, June 19, 2015, https://www.al-monitor.com/pulse/originals/2015/06/palestine-hizb-ut-tahrir-al-aqsa-hamas-islamic-caliphate.html.
82. Hizb ut-Tahrir America, "Al-Quds (Jerusalem) – the First Qiblah," December 6, 2017, https://hizb-america.org/al-quds-jerusalem-the-first-qiblah/.
83. Khaled Abu Toameh, "PA Police Use Force to Prevent Eid al-Fitr Celebration in Hebron," *Jerusalem Post*, June 5, 2019, https://www.jpost.com/Israel-News/Ten-arrested-in-Hebron-following-Ramadan-end-date-debate-591555.
84. "Tunisia radical Islamist party banned for one month," Agence France-Presse, July 6, 2017, https://www.news24.com/Africa/News/tunisia-radical-islamist-party-banned-for-one-month-20170607.
85. "Tunisia radical Islamist party banned for one month," *News 24*, June 7, 2017, https://www.news24.com/Africa/News/tunisia-radical-islamist-party-banned-for-one-month-20170607; "Tunisie – Hizb-Ut-Tahrir prone la Califat et la Chariâa, et organize une manifestation avec la participation d'enfants," *Tunisie Numerique*, March 30, 2019, https://www.tunisienumerique.com/tunisie-hizb-ut-tahrir-prone-la-califat-et-la-chariaa-et-organise-une-manifestation-avec-la-participation-denfants/
86. Massinissa Benlakehal, "Tension, protests mark Tunisia's seventh revolutionary anniversary," *The New Arab*, December 22, 2017, https://www.alaraby.co.uk/english/society/2017/12/22/tension-protests-mark-tunisias-seventh-revolutionary-anniversary.
87. Hizb ut-Tahrir Australia, "Jordan Arrests 15 Senior HT Members Including Respected Scholars," September 30, 2016, http://www.hizb-australia.org/2016/09/jordan-arrests-15-senior-ht-members-including-respected-scholars/
88. Ibrahim Halil Kahraman, "Hizb-ut Tahrir: Zulüm yapılıyor," Şanlıurfa *Olay Gazetesi*, January 9, 2018, http://www.sanliurfaolay.

com/guncel/hizb-ut-tahrir-zulum-yapiliyor/22851; Hizb-ut Tahrir Media Office Wilayah Turkey, "The Banning of our Conference and the Arrest of our Head of the Media Office," March 3, 2017, http://www.hizb-ut-tahrir.info/en/index.php/press-releases/turkey/12586.html; "Yargıda Hizb-ut Tahrir ayrılığı," *Oda TV*, December 25, 2017, https://odatv.com/yargida-hizb-ut-tahrir-ayriligi-2512171200.html.

89. "Hizb ut-Tahrir Indonesia banned 'to protect unity,'" *Al-Jazeera* (Doha), July 19, 2017, http://www.aljazeera.com/news/2017/07/indonesia-hizbut-tahrir-group-banned-protect-unity-170719050345186.html.
90. Matthew Busch, "Jokowi's Panicky Politics," *Foreign Affairs*, August 11, 2017, https://www.foreignaffairs.com/articles/indonesia/2017-08-11/jokowis-panicky-politics.
91. Konradus Epa, "Alarm sounds over outlawed Indonesian militant group," *UCA News*, March 14, 2019, https://www.ucanews.com/news/alarm-sounds-over-outlawed-indonesian-militant-group/84721.
92. Ananth Krishnan, "BRICS declaration names Pakistan terror groups in big diplomatic win for India," *India Today*, September 4, 2017, https://www.indiatoday.in/india/story/brics-summit-declaration-pakistan-india-china-xiamen-terrorism-let-jaish-ttp-1037385-2017-09-04.

68 The Islamic State

Quick Facts

Geographical Areas of Operation: East Asia, Eurasia, Europe, Latin America, Middle East and North Africa, North America, South Asia, Sub-Saharan Africa
Strength: Estimates suggest between 11,000 and 18,000, including several thousand foreign terrorist fightersc (*These estimates only reflect membership in Syria and Iraq*)
Leadership: Amir Mohammed Abdul Rahman al-Mawli al-Salbi, also known as Abu Ibrahim al-Hashimi al-Qurashi
Religious Identification: Sunni Islam

Quick Facts courtesy of the U.S. State Department's Annual Country Reports on Terrorism (2019)

Introduction

The Islamic State (IS) is a Salafi influenced Islamist militant faction that traces its origins to founder Abu Musab al-Zarqawi in 1999. In the two-plus decades since, the movement has grown in size and influence while absorbing dozens of smaller groups.

IS seeks to recreate the caliphate in the Levant region. This caliphate would be run according to the group's Salafi interpretation of Islam, with particular attention to what it calls the "Prophetic method" – ways in which the group claims first generations of Islam were governed. The group has drifted in and out of the al-Qaeda network and is currently its chief rival for supremacy of the global jihadi movement. The establishment of a proto-state, however temporary, inspired other like-minded jihadi groups around the world. IS claims official provinces beyond its core in Iraq and Syria including Khorasan (Afghanistan/Pakistan/Central Asia), Algeria, the Caucasus, Egypt, Libya, Western Africa, Saudi Arabia and Yemen, and works with aspiring affiliates in Bangladesh and East Asia (Indonesia, Malaysia, Singapore, and the Philippines). The temporary success of IS was the result of a combination of many events, personalities, and external factors that attracted other jihadi groups and otherwise passive supporters.

History and Ideology

Ahmed Fadeel al-Khalayleh, better known as Abu Musab al-Zarqawi, was born in 1966 in the small Jordanian town of Al-Zarqa. Zarqawi was imprisoned as a young man for sexual assault and became more religious during his imprisonment.[1] Following his release from jail in 1989, he traveled to Afghanistan to join the *jihad* against the Soviets. However, he arrived too late and the war was already ending. He then worked as a journalist for a few years, writing about the *mujahedeen*, before returning to Jordan, intent on undermining the monarchy. He planned terrorist attacks against Jordan and Israel, but these were quickly exposed, and he was arrested and sentenced to 15 years in jail in 1994. In jail, Zarqawi lifted weights, memorized Quranic verses, and built a network using the strength of his charismatic personality.[2] When Zarqawi was unexpectedly released due to a general amnesty in 1999, he made his way back to Afghanistan where he was hosted and supported by an al-Qaeda network interested in recruiting him.[3] Settling near the western city of Herat, Zarqawi built up a small group of *jihadists* from around the Levant. The 2001 American invasion of Afghanistan disrupted his bucolic commune, and Zarqawi escaped through Iran and settled in the autonomous region of Kurdistan in Iraq.

Zarqawi took refuge with the al-Qaeda affiliated group Ansar al-Islam, a Kurdish-based Salafi militant group. He saw Kurdistan as a base of operations to begin working in other areas of Iraq and possibly in his home country. Zarqawi initially directed his efforts at toppling the Jordanian regime with plans to use his home country as a base to undermine the rest of what he determined were "apostate" Arab regimes.[4] With the U.S invasion of Iraq in 2003, Zarqawi saw in the Iraqi scene a new land of *jihad* and began formulating a new strategy, focusing his growing network's efforts in Iraq. He debuted the group's terror campaign in the late summer of 2003 with massive truck bombs targeting the UN headquarters, the Jordanian embassy, and the Imam Ali shrine in Najaf. This last attack, executed by Zarqawi's father-in-law, killed the most prominent Shi'a cleric in Iraq as well as scores of Shi'a worshippers.[5]

The brutality supported by Zarqawi created an early disagreement between al-Qaeda and Zarqawi's group. While al-Qaeda advocated a focus on the "far enemy," meaning the western countries led by the United States, Zarqawi believed that the "apostates" (Sunni Muslims allied with western powers) and the *rafidah* (Shi'a who reject the legitimacy of Mohammed's immediate successors) would immediately threaten his plans to create an Islamic State in Iraq.[6] Furthermore, the leaders of both groups were divided over *Fiqh* (Islamic jurisprudence). Sayf Adl, the al-Qaeda leader and a mentor to Zarqawi, mentioned that "the controversial issues with [Zarqawi] were neither new nor uncommon. The most important issue with [Zarqawi] was the stance regarding the Saudi regime and how to deal with it in light of the Islamic laws that pertain to excommunication and belief."[7] Nonetheless, the leadership of both groups continued to negotiate a merger of sorts to capitalize on the galvanizing impact of the U.S. presence in Iraq on Muslims around the region and globe.

The continuation of Zarqawi's brutal bombing campaign against Shi'a Iraqis was designed to provoke an uncontrolled Shi'a reaction that would eventually drive Sunnis to his group in search of protection.[8] He also took advantage of environmental factors that fueled Sunni grievances, such as the early De-Baathification programs after the invasion that alienated the overwhelmingly Sunni population of Anbar, where Zarqawi relocated in the summer of 2003.[9] The Anbar region hosted many insurgent groups with different ideologies and characteristics, such as former regime loyalists, nationalists, tribal and Islamists, and proved to be a fertile recruiting ground for the new group.[10]

As the Sunni Triangle – a term used to describe the region north and west of Baghdad including Tikrit, Ramadi, Baqubah, and the capital – developed into a hotbed of insurgency, the religiously conservative city of Fallujah emerged as a nexus for insurgent groups. On March 31, 2004, four Blackwater security contractors were killed in the city; their bodies were mutilated and left hanging on a bridge. The act was broadcasted by different media outlets, influencing an ill-considered U.S. effort to take over the city. However, the operation was deemed a failure as the number of civilian deaths rose to over 800 and resulted in the creation of nearly 60,000 refugees. The operation was called off, and newly created Iraqi security units were installed to maintain order.[11]

However, the new security units mostly melted away or, in some cases, even assisted the insurgents.[12] As the city became a symbol of successful resistance to the new government rule, the Bush administration once again decided to clear the city of insurgents. In early November, the U.S military launched an offensive against the militant coalition in Fallujah resulting in fierce urban fighting and many casualties on both sides. 52 U.S troops, six Iraqi security force members, and nearly 2000 insurgent fighters died in what is considered the bloodiest fight of the Iraq war.[13] These two battles had a large impact on the growth of Zarqawi's group, which at this point was called Tawhid wal-Jihad (Monotheism and Struggle)

The first battle of Fallujah brought Zarqawi's group some notoriety due to its success in frustrating the military offensive, causing it to grow rapidly. By the second battle of Fallujah, Zarqawi's negotiations with al-Qaeda were successful and he pledged allegiance to Osama Bin Laden on October 17th, 2004.[14] Zarqawi leveraged the visibility of his group's participation in the battles for Fallujah to overcome al-Qaeda considerable reticence. In return, the group claimed the brand of al-Qaeda, which set the group apart from Iraqi rivals with no pedigree. The group changed its official name to Tanzim al-Qaeda al-Jihad fi Bilad al-Rafidayn (the Organization of the Base of Jihad in the land of Mesopotamia, better known as al-Qaeda in Iraq [AQI]), and Zarqawi's group began to accrue the benefits of an extensive network of financing, recruiting, and online media dissemination.[15] The honeymoon period between the al-Qaeda leaders and Zarqawi did not last long, however, as Zarqawi's violent attacks against civilians, Shi'a in particular, began to tarnish the global al-Qaeda brand.[16]

In early 2004, before the merger, Zarqawi wrote a letter to his superiors explaining his strategy, naming the Iraqi Shi'a (both the government and the independent religious militias) as "the most evil of mankind," and calling on the *mujahideen* to focus on them over other targets.[17] Zarqawi's soon-to-be superiors in al-Qaeda preferred Zarqawi to focus instead on driving the Americans out, and worry about the Shi'a later. In a 2005 letter addressed to Zarqawi, Bin Laden's then-deputy, Ayman al-Zawahiri, gently reproached Zarqawi and recommended a shift in his strategy.[18] The fact that neither Zarqawi nor his successors ever changed their strategy was an early indicator of an ideological split between the two movements that would continue to worsen over the next decade.[19]

The political backlash resulting from the battles of Fallujah increased Sunni disenchantment of the new government and the occupation.[20] People boycotted the first parliamentary and provincial elections of January 2005.[21] This, coupled with the resultant lack of Sunni participation in the nascent Iraqi government, further exposed the Sunni population to the predation of a wide spread of insurgent groups, especially the newly proclaimed AQI.

The next expansion envisioned by Zarqawi and his lieutenants was a political consolidation of like-minded Salafi groups in Iraq. To facilitate this goal, the Mujahedeen Shura Council (MSC) was established in January 2006 and announced Abdallah Bin Rashid al-Baghdadi, not Zarqawi, as its leader.[22] A top Zarqawi deputy, whose real name was Abdulrahman Mustafa al-Qaduli (and better known as Abu Ali al-Anbari), the first "al-Baghdadi," led a new political front that included AQI and several other groups: Jaysh al-Ta'ifa al-Mansura, Saraya 'Ansar al-Tawhid, Saraya al-Jihad al-Islami, Saraya al-Ghuraba, and Kataib al-Ahwal.[23] This merger was seen as a stepping stone to the formation of a future Islamic State, and had the unintended benefit of preparing for the loss of Zarqawi, who was killed by American forces on June 7th, 2006.[24] Shortly after Zarqawi's death, the MSC announced that Abu Hamza al-Muhajir (also known as Abu Ayub al-Masri) would replace Zarqawi at the head of AQI. The change was temporary; four months later, Abu Hamza announced the dissolution of AQI and the creation of a new, larger merger of resistance groups and tribes called the Islamic State of Iraq (ISI). Abu Hamza pledged allegiance to a completely different and equally unknown "al-Baghdadi," Abu Omar, the newly appointed "emir of the faithful" of the ISI.[25]

Abu Omar al-Baghdadi was born Hamid Dawud Muhammad Khalil al-Zawi in 1964 in Anbar province. He was a police officer in Haditha before being dismissed by the Baathists in the late 1980s/early 90s because of his hardline adherence and promulgation of Salafi ideology.[26] During Saddam's Faith Campaign, a government-sponsored religious program attempting to stifle the rise of Islamist sentiments following the humiliating defeat by a western-led coalition, open Salafi adherence was a sign of disloyalty to the Ba'ath regime.[27] With the invasion of Iraq in 2003, Abu Omar started his own militant group in Haditha before pledging allegiance to Zarqawi's early group. The choice of Abu Omar al-Baghdadi to succeed Zarqawi as the new emir was a strategic move to counter the continuous discontent from the Sunni population. Under Abu Omar, the birth of the ISI transformed the movement into a more structured organization with departments and cabinets, with the hope of increasing legitimacy.[28] Abu Omar inherited an increasingly beleaguered organization that was under fire from the Americans, Iraqi security forces, and the "Awakening Forces," a Sunni tribal force organized to fight the ISI's domination of Sunni Iraq.[29]

Ramadi, the capital of Anbar Province, was a crucial hub of resistance to the occupation.[30] By 2006, the city was the most violent in Iraq and the nascent Islamic State of Iraq designated the "Islamic Emirate of Ramadi" as its "capital."[31] Amid this turmoil, Sunni tribal leaders began a small coalition called the *Sahwa* (Awakening). These figures chafed under the growing domination of Zarqawi's AQI and the soon-to-be Islamic State of Iraq, particularly because of the violence used against the Sunni and the cooption of regular economic trade by the tribes. As a result, the tribal leaders and elements of the large nationalist resistance groups reached a rapprochement with the U.S military to fight together against Zarqawi's successors. The resultant Sunni civil war saw tremendous losses on both sides, but ISI eventually abandoned Ramadi, causing a subsequent drop in violence in the city.[32]

The U.S forces and their Iraqi partners were successful at pushing back against ISI not because they pressed their military advantage, but because they were able to attract an increasingly alienated Sunni population to the side of the government. The Islamic State admitted that the American and Iraqi security forces made potential gains and called for an adjustment of the strategy to keep up with the pace of war.[33]

In addition to the military campaigns that the U.S, Iraqi, and tribal forces led against the ISI, the group suffered from structural and bureaucratic hardships that resulted in a drastic decline in fortunes between 2007 and 2009. The organization lost much of its territory, and its fighters were killed, captured, or deserted in large numbers.[34] Unable to host foreign fighters in tribal areas with hostile *Sahwa* forces, the group's leadership began to limit the flow of foreign fighters to Iraq. The local Iraqi population correctly blamed much of the terrorism, especially suicide bombing, on these foreign fighters.[35]

An ISI after-action review reported several failings, such as a lack of internal communication, poor relations between the emirs and their fighters, and a lack of discipline as contributing to the organization's decline.[36] Brian Fishman argues that "As [ISI] cells proliferated across Iraq, the group's experienced leadership cadre was diluted and communication became more difficult, to the point where the strategic intent of [ISI's] high command was not clear to local cells."[37] The bureaucratic failure pushed the ISI deeper into a crisis that endangered its organizational stability.

In response, the ISI took a series of measures to reestablish political power. The leadership under Abu Omar and his Minister Abu Hamza al-Muhajir prioritized consolidation with other like-minded *jihadi* groups, a reconciliation with tribal leaders, tactical military adjustment, and more lenient behavior toward the Sunni groups. As stated in a 2009 strategy document known as the "Fallujah Memo," "The [Islamic State] should consider unification as one of the most important tactical goals at the current moment and so should the *mujahideen* from other groups."[38] Even Ayman al Zawahiri invited other resistance groups of all types to unify their efforts under the Islamic State banner during this period.

Abu Omar and Abu Hamza also adjusted to the setbacks by offering incentives to tribal leaders to reconsider their new-found allegiance to the Iraqi government.[39] On the one hand, they engaged tribal leaders by establishing "The Awakening Jihadi Council" to incorporate tribal leaders and provide them with financial support.[40] Simultaneously, the ISI leadership ramped up a campaign to kill tribal leaders who continued to sympathize with the government. These assassinations were carefully vetted by the upper echelons of the organization's leadership.[41]

In summary, the ISI spent several years analyzing, and then

mitigating, the causes of its decline after 2007. Under the leadership of Abu Omar and his close partner Abu Hamza, the ISI took a series of pragmatic steps to improve their political standing among Sunnis in Iraq. But their struggles were not over. On April 10th, 2010, a joint Iraqi and U.S operation found and killed Abu Omar al-Baghdadi and Abu Hamza Al-Muhajir, setting the stage for a new leader to emerge: Abu Bakr al-Baghdadi.[42]

Ibrahim Awwad Ibrahim Ali al-Badri al-Samarrai, also known as Abu Bakr al-Husseini al-Hashimi al-Qurashi, is the former *emir* of ISI and its successor —the Islamic State of Iraq and Syria (ISIS or ISIL), and the first caliph of the Islamic State. Abu Bakr was born in 1971 in the city of Samarra (just to the north of Baghdad) to a religious Sunni family with ties to the Salafi movement. He enrolled in Quranic studies at the Saddam University in Baghdad and was taught by several prominent Salafi teachers.[43] The American invasion in 2003 was the catalyst for al-Baghdadi to join the resistance to occupation. Captured in Anbar around the time of the Fallujah battles, he was sent to the notorious Camp Bucca prison in 2004, although his stay in the prison was short due to a lack of evidence. After his release from jail at the end of 2004, Abu Bakr secretly joined AQI and later openly joined the MSC. He rose through the ranks and was appointed to many high positions, including membership in the group's *Shura* (advisory) Council.[44]

The death of Abu Omar and his partner Abu Hamza al-Muhajir paved the way for Abu Bakr to become the new *emir*. By May 2010, he was appointed by the *Shura* as the new *emir* and began working to rebuild a struggling organization that had been hit hard in the wake of security breaches that had led to a decimation of organizational leadership. Abu Bakr continued the expansion of a hierarchical structure that still gave autonomy to members to operate as long as they remained within the ISI framework.[45]

Under Abu Bakr, the Islamic State was able to expand its territorial control to include large parts of Syria after he sent several of his fighters into the country to form al-Nusra Front in 2011, during the rebellion against Bashar al-Assad. Although some parts of al-Nusra Front and its leader Ahmed Hussein Al Shar'a (Abu Mohammad al-Julani) later broke away from ISI/ISIL to become affiliated with al-Qaeda, al-Baghdadi and his lieutenants were able to establish territorial control in Syria as part of their dream of establishing a future caliphate.

The Islamic State saw the Syrian uprising in 2011 as an opportunity to open a new battlefront and expand. By the end of 2011, Abu Bakr sent movement veteran Abu Mohamed al-Julani to establish the group Jabhat al-Nusrah.[46] Within a few months, al-Nusrah was able to absorb a few smaller Syrian resistance groups.[47] It was able to impose its military dominance on the larger resistance, which encouraged even more groups to join. Tensions between ISI and al-Nusrah developed at the end of 2012 as Abu Bakr began to worry about Julani's cooperation with non-*jihadi* groups; he began to assert more influence over his former protégé in Syria. This led to the confrontation and the split – the first and only faction to openly break away from ISI.

Julani's defiance of Abu Bakr's attempt to openly merge the Syrian and Iraqi fronts under one banner led to an intervention by al-Qaeda leader Ayman al-Zawahiri. The proposed compromise – a return to the *status quo* with each theater reporting directly to al-Qaeda – was rejected by Abu Bakr. Battle-tested in Iraq and ruthless when it came to insurgent rivalry, the now newly-renamed ISIL took the major Syrian city of Raqqa, not from the Assad regime but from other rebel groups, including al-Nusra Front.[48] With Raqqa swollen with internally displaced persons from other parts of Syria, for the first time, the Islamic State had uncontested control over a major population area. *Jihadists*, both Arab and foreign, flocked to the group, among them the famed Chechen *jihadist* Abu Omar al-Shishani and his hardened fighters.[49]

Sectarian tensions in Iraq began to rise again in 2010 for the first time in three years during the Parliamentary election of that year. Prime Minister Nouri al-Maliki saw Sunni support for his main rival as a threat to his political career, and began to target Sunni members of the political opposition as a result. Subsequent acts alienated a majority of Anbari political leaders, an opening which benefitted the ISI.[50] In December 2012, the Anbari scene degenerated after Iraqi forces arrested the government finance minister Rafi al-Issawi, a Sunni from al-Fallujah and a member of the influential Albu Issa tribe, and put out warrants for another high-ranking Sunni political leader.[51] In 2013, an ongoing peaceful protest was violently put down by the government, inflaming tensions even further in Anbar.[52] The Islamic State was stepping up its campaign in Iraq at this point, with the ability to surge its forces on alternating sides of the Syrian border. Researchers noted that "in 2013, 7,818 civilians (including police) were killed in acts of terrorism and violence, more than double the 2012 death toll, according to United Nations figures. An additional 17,891 were injured, making 2013 Iraq's bloodiest year since 2008."[53] Al-Baghdadi and his organization took advantage of this opportunity to increase recruiting from the tribes and form new alliances in Sunni dominated areas.[54] By this point, the Islamic State had reemerged as a strong challenger to governments in both Iraq and Syria.

The Islamic State's activity during this period included a wide array of attacks on government forces using guerrilla attacks and terrorism. One of its most important operations in 2013 was the Abu Ghraib prison raid that liberated over 500 senior Islamic State members.[55] Many of these prisoners rejoined the ranks of the movement. Among these prisoners was movement veteran Abu Abdulrahman al-Bilawi, a Zarqawi lieutenant from the early period.

Adnan Ismail Najm al-Bilawi al-Dulaimi was born in 1971 in the Anbar province. A captain in Saddam's Special Forces before joining Zarqawi, Bilawi made it into Zarqawi's inner circle before he was captured in 2005.[56] Despite his long stay in prison, Bilawi's group connections and his skill as a planner led to his appointment to the General Military Council of ISIL after being freed from Abu Ghraib.[57] He was posthumously credited with building the plan to squeeze Mosul in 2014, which fell after a long campaign of unrelenting terror and guerilla attacks.[58] He died early in June 2014 in Mosul, before the fall of the city and the rout of government forces.

As demonstrated with the al-Bilawi example, the Islamic State has been successful at recruiting former military members to play a role in building their guerrilla army. Tarkhan Batirashvili, also known as Umar al-Shishani, was born in 1986 in the Soviet republic of Georgia. Shishani had fought in the 2008 Georgian-Russian war.[59] He was a sergeant in an elite unit before he was diagnosed with tuberculosis and dismissed from the Georgian army in 2010.[60] Shishani was jailed for arms possession, serving 16 months, before adopting the Salafi creed and moving to Syria to fight against Assad's regime early in 2013.[61]

Shishani formed his fighting groups out of foreign fighters and called them Kateebat al-Muhajireen (the Immigrant Battalion). After pledging allegiance to ISIL in 2013, Shishani was appointed as a commander of ISIL forces in northern Syria. He was also invited to be part of the Delegated Committee (the group's new name for the Shura Council), which made him an advisor to Abu Bakr.[62] Before thc capture of Mosul, Shishani was victorious in several battles against Syrian forces in northern and eastern Syria. Abu Bakr later promoted him to de facto war minister.[63] He was eventually killed in July 2016 in a targeted U.S airstrike.

Abu Ali al-Anbari was born in 1959 under the name Abdul Rahman Mustafa al-Qaduli in Tel Afar. He was also known as Abu Ala', Abu Iman, al-Hajji Iman, Abu Hassan, Sayyid Khalil, Abu Zainab, Hajji Taher, Abdullah Rashid al-Baghdadi, Abu Hassan Qardash, Abu Ali al-Anbari, Abu Suhaib al-Iraqi, and Abu Mus'ab al-Shami.[64] The fact that Anbari had so many names confused Iraqi and American forces; often he was described in the same article as two different persons.[65] He completed his graduate studies in *sharia* law in 1982 at the University of Baghdad, and was drafted and fought in Iran-Iraq war.[66] He gave lessons in Tel Afar, where he opposed the Shi'a, the Sufis, and the Ba'athists.[67]

A biography of Anbari written by his son suggests that Anbari was the mastermind of the unification between AQI and other *jihadi* groups to form the MSC, and he became its leader and spokesman for a short period — in fact Anbari was the first "al-Baghdadi" mentioned above.[68] In April 2006, Anbari was captured by the Americans and spent a long time in prison, a fact concealed by the MSC and later ISI. Released as part of a post-occupation amnesty in March 2012, Anbari immediately joined his old organization – and made a pledge of allegiance to its *emir*, Abu Bakr al-Baghdadi. Abu Ali al-Anbari was appointed vice emir and the *sharia* official of the state.

After the announcement of the establishment of the Islamic State in Iraq and the Levant (ISIL) in April 2013, Anbari focused his efforts on the jurisprudence and preaching in the Islamic State and its provinces.[69] Anbari filled several positions for the *emir* before being appointed as the head of Bayt al-Mal (department of treasury), a position he held in his original group in 2003-4. He was killed by a U.S. special operations team while traveling to Mosul from Syria in 2016.

The fall of Mosul, inspired by the planning of al-Bilawi, was a milestone for the Islamic State. Outnumbered sixty to one, determined and ruthless ISIL fighters gained an astonishing victory in the city within a week, and captured U.S. supplied weapons and materials stored within.[70] The northern town of Tal Afar, much of Anbar Province, and several key border crossings all fell to the fighters. Mosul's ancient Christian community was extinguished in one fell swoop as all Christians left *en masse*.[71] ISIL victories displaced as many as 500,000 Iraqi citizens from a variety of religious and ethnic communities. Tikrit and the oil refinery town of Baiji also fell as ISIL forces moved south toward Baghdad, but intervention by Iranian-supported militias prevented the fall of the strategically significant city of Samarra.

Abu Bakr then took the fateful step the Islamic State had repeatedly hinted at since 2006, restoring the Caliphate and declaring himself *Caliph* over all the Muslims. In a unique appearance at Mosul's Nuri Mosque on June 29, 2014, "Caliph Ibrahim" called for Muslims to join the new *caliphate.*

Global Reach

Not long after Abu Bakr's call to unify under one flag, several regional and global *jihadi* organizations were encouraged to join the newly emerging IS. Among these organizations was Ansar Bayt Al Maqdis (ABM), or Supporters of Jerusalem, a *jihadi* terrorist organization that emerged in the northern Sinai Peninsula. Although ABM operates in the Sinai Peninsula bordering Israel, its strategy, similar to that of IS, focuses on attacking the near enemy rather than the far enemy, in this case, the Egypt government and its forces.

In November 2014, ABM became one of the first international organizations to pledge allegiance to the Islamic State and changed their name to *Wilayat* (Province) Sinai.[72] The allegiance brought more than just an ideological, symbolic loyalty; its motivations were also logistical. The devotion to the newly enriched IS, flush with cash from captured Mosul banks and oil resources, provided the new franchise with financial, networking, and recruitment channels.[73] The group was able to maintain a semi-independent territorial authority while its *modus operandi* shifted to align itself with Islamic State strategy to focus its attacks on Egyptian security forces rather than on Israel.[74]

By January 2015, IS was able to extend its power east toward another strategic location of the *jihadi* milieu: Afghanistan. In fact, several Tehrik-e Taliban Pakistan (TTP) factions joined together, pledged allegiance, and became known as the Islamic State in Khorasan (IS-K).[75] Islamic *caliphates* historically referred to territories starting from modern-day Iran to Pakistan and Central Asia as Khorasan.[76] ISIL appointed Hafiz Saeed Khan, a TTP former leader, as the provincial *emir*.[77] Shortly after, the newly formed province absorbed many other members and *jihadi* groups such as Lakshar-e-Taiba, Haqqani network, and Afghan Taliban.[78] However, IS-K was faced by violent opposition from the preexisting groups.[79] According to Amira Jadoon, Nakissa Jahanbani, and Charmaine Willis, the IS-K challenged preexisting tribal group loyalties and threatened their relationship with the Pakistani state. These actions disturbed the relationship between a global sectarian IS-K and local pragmatic groups.[80] Reports indicate that IS-K is currently engaged in several confrontations against local groups (predominantly the Taliban).[81] Nonetheless, they have been able to maintain a steady spate of operations against the Afghan government, including terror attacks in the capital.

Recent Activity

The Islamic State expansion in Iraq and Syria and the corresponding wave of human rights abuses attracted the attention of the international community.[82] As resistance to the IS offensive in central

Iraq stiffened in August 2014, the Islamic State massacred hundreds of Shi'a cadets and Sunni tribal fighters as a warning against any opposition.[83] IS fighters advanced against Kurdish *Peshmerga* (militia) in Ninewa province outside of Mosul, and conducted a genocide against the Yazidi religious minority in the Sinjar region. These acts and others eventually drew the United States into the conflict, along with a coalition of 80 nations to "degrade and ultimately destroy" the Islamic State.[84]

The Iraqi-led campaign to liberate Mosul officially started on October 17th, 2016. By July 2017, Mosul was liberated by Iraqi forces, but its historic "right bank" was destroyed, and the cost in the lives of civilian residents numbered in the thousands. By October 17th of the same year, Raqqa, the self-declared capital of the *caliphate*, was also liberated.[85] While the coalition's airstrike heavy campaign was deemed to be effective in killing large quantities of Islamic State fighters, the Kurdish-led Syrian Democratic Forces were instrumental in ending the physical caliphate in early 2019.[86]

The slow decline of a caliphate that once collected wealth, controlled territory, and had a record number of foreign supporters join it (over 41,000, according to research by Joana Cook and Gina Vale) has incited a series of sharp religious and ideological debates and disputes.[87] The origins of the problem surfaced between two factions: The "Hazemis" and the "Benalis."[88] The Hazemis follow an excommunication concept written by Ahmed Bin Omar al-Hazemi, a Saudi *takfir* scholar. Hazemi is currently arrested in Saudi Arabia.[89] The main ideological difference between the two groups is that Hazemis believe that ignorance is not an excuse to commit a blasphemous act. The leading members of this faction are North African Tunisians and Moroccans, largely due to Hazemi's travels and local influence.[90] Some members of the ultra-orthodox *takfiri* excommunication doctrine even called the Islamic State *caliphate* "the State of the blasphemous," because of a perception that the leaders were soft on those that did not participate in defending the caliphate. On the other hand, the Benalis, who follow the teachings of deceased Bahraini scholar Turki al-Benali, do not believe that ignorance of Islamic duties is a blasphemous act. The "moderate" wing of the Islamic State, including Abu Bakr, were able to crack down on some of the Hazemi leaders and executed several of them.[91] However, many indications show that the Hazemis are still present in the ranks. Right before Benali's death, he tried to push against this ultra-orthodox excommunication ideology by banning these ideas from official discussion, a motion that ultimately failed. Finally, the continued influence of the Hazemis can be seen in the publication of an article in *al-Naba*, Islamic State's official Arabic newspaper, titled "Idols or Symbols," which criticized the glorification of some al-Qaeda affiliated scholars like Abu Musab al-Suri and Abu Yahya al-Libi.[92]

The defeat of the territorial Islamic State is a temporary condition, as we have seen with its predecessor the Islamic State of Iraq. In August 2018, the United Nations estimated that the Islamic State maintains a 41,490 person support network across 80 countries.[93] The same month, the office of the U.S. Department of Defense Lead Inspector General released a report approximating the group to have roughly 30,000 active fighters.[94] Both of these assessments stand in contrast to President Trump's multiple announcements that the Islamic State has been defeated.[95] The continued insurgency in Iraq and Syria, as well as its ties to affiliates around the globe, show that the group has transformed into a lower level of insurgency that does not control much territory (in fact, it controls no territory in Iraq and Syria). Abu Bakr's goal was to bide time until another opportunity arises, much like what happened after 2010.[96] Abu Hassan al-Muhajir, the Islamic State official spokesman, released an audio speech promising to spread the war to different places, stating:

> O lions of the Khilafah and men of the State in Raqqah, Barakah, and Khayr leap like hungry lions, avenge the blood of your brothers and sisters, and declare a raid of revenge that will extirpate the roots of the people of kufr and atheism from Sham. Make these like the days of Zarqawi that will eliminate the ranks of the Crusaders and apostates. Seal the explosive devices, spread the snipers, and launch explosive attacks using boobytraps.[97]

Western intelligence officials are concerned that their citizens who traveled to the caliphate will return and possibly conduct terrorist attacks in home countries.[98] What happens to the thousands of foreigners, and to the tens of thousands of locals in regional prisons, is an important question for the future of regional and European stability.

As of November 2019, the group has announced new leadership following the death of Abu Bakr al-Baghdadi in a U.S. special operation raid near Idlib, Syria, where the *caliph* was hiding. ISIS spokesman Abu Hassan al-Muhajir was also killed in late October in northern Syria. The group confirmed these deaths and announced Abu Ibrahim al-Hashimi al-Quraishi as the emir of the believers and caliph, and Abu Hamza al-Quraishi was named the new spokesman. The identity of neither men is known, but the announcement noted that both men have experience against the Americans as part of AQI/ ISI.[99]

ENDNOTES

1. Jeffrey Gettleman,. 2006. "Abu Musab Al-Zarqawi Lived A Brief, Shadowy Life Replete With Contradictions." *New York Times*, June 9, 2006, https://www.nytimes.com/2006/06/09/world/middleeast/09zarqawi.html.
2. Mary Anne Weaver, "The short, violent life of Abu Musab al-Zarqawi," *The Atlantic*, August 15, 2006, https://www.theatlantic.com/magazine/archive/2006/07/the-short-violent-life-of-abu-musab-al-zarqawi/304983/.
3. Mary Anne Weaver, "The short, violent life of Abu Musab al-Zarqawi," *The Atlantic*, August 15, 2006, https://www.theatlantic.com/magazine/archive/2006/07/the-short-violent-life-of-abu-musab-al-zarqawi/304983/.
4. Aaron Y. Zelin, "The war between ISIS and al-Qaeda for supremacy of the global jihadist movement," Washington Institute for Near East Policy *Research Notes* no. 20, June 2014, 2, https://www.washingtoninstitute.org/policy-analysis/view/the-war-between-isis-and-al-qaeda-for-supremacy-of-the-global-jihadist.
5. Ben Wedeman, "Shiites mourn Najaf bomb victims," *CNN*, August 30, 2003, http://www.cnn.com/2003/WORLD/meast/08/30/sprj.irq.funeral/.
6. Brian Fishman, "After Zarqawi: the dilemmas and future of al Qaeda

in Iraq," *Washington Quarterly* 29, no. 4 (2006), 20.

7. Brian Fishman, "After Zarqawi: the dilemmas and future of al Qaeda in Iraq," *Washington Quarterly* 29, no. 4 (2006), 19-32.
8. Charles R. Lister, *The Islamic State: A Brief Introduction* (Brookings Institution Press, 2015), 8; Weaver, "The short, violent life of Abu Musab al-Zarqawi."
9. James Dobbins, J Seth G. Jones, Siddharth Mohandas, and Benjamin Runkle, *Occupying Iraq: A history of the coalition provisional authority*, vol. 847 (Rand Corporation, 2009), 57; Weaver, "The short, violent life of Abu Musab al-Zarqawi."
10. Ahmed Hashim, *Insurgency and Counter-insurgency in Iraq* (Cornell University Press, 2005).
11. Stephen Graham, "Remember Fallujah: demonizing place, constructing atrocity," *Environment and Planning D: Society and Space* 23, no. 1 (2005), 3.
12. Rajiv Chandrasekaran, "Key general criticizes April attack in Fallujah," *Washington Post*, September 13, 2004, A17.
13. Dan Lamothe, "Remembering the Iraq War's Bloodiest Battle, 10 Years Later," *Washington Post*, November 4, 2014, https://www.washingtonpost.com/news/checkpoint/wp/2014/11/04/remembering-the-iraq-wars-bloodiest-battle-10-years-later/?utm_term=.8f2af90b0125.
14. Jeffrey Pool, "Zarqawi's Pledge of Allegiance to Al-Qaeda: From Mu'asker al-Battar, Issue 21," Jamestown Foundation *Terrorism Monitor* 2, iss. 24, October 16, 2004, https://jamestown.org/program/zarqawis-pledge-of-allegiance-to-al-qaeda-from-muasker-al-battar-issue-21-2/.
15. Zelin, "The war between ISIS and al-Qaeda for supremacy of the global jihadist movement."
16. Fishman, "After Zarqawi: the dilemmas and future of al Qaeda in Iraq."
17. Abu Musab Al-Zarqawi, "February 2004 Coalition Provisional Authority English translation of terrorist Musab Al-Zarqawi letter," U.S Department of State (2004), 2001-2009.
18. Ayman Al-Zawahiri, "Letter from al-Zawahiri to al-Zarqawi," (2005).
19. This term is used by the authors to cover all the evolutions of the group that became the contemporary Islamic State.
20. Patrick B. Johnston et al., *Foundations of the Islamic State: Management, Money, and Terror in Iraq, 2005-2010* (Rand Corporation, 2016), 29-30.

21. Patrick B. Johnston et al., *Foundations of the Islamic State: Management, Money, and Terror in Iraq, 2005-2010* (Rand Corporation, 2016), 29.
22. Fishman, "After Zarqawi: the dilemmas and future of al Qaeda in Iraq."
23. Charles Lister, "Profiling the Islamic state," Brookings Doha Center *Analysis Paper* no. 13, November 2014, 8, https://www.brookings.edu/wp-content/uploads/2014/12/en_web_lister.pdf.
24. Nibras Kazimi, "The Caliphate Attempted: Zarqawi's Ideological Heirs, Their Choice for a Caliph, and the Collapse of their self-styled Islamic State of Iraq," *Current Trends in Islamist Ideology*, July 1, 2008, https://www.hudson.org/research/9854-the-caliphate-attempted-zarqawi-s-ideological-heirs-their-choice-for-a-caliph-and-the-collapse-of-their-self-styled-islamic-state-of-iraq.
25. Lister, "Profiling the Islamic State," 8.
26. Abu Usama al-Iraqi, "Stages in the Jihad of Amir al-Baghdadi," personal blog, May 12, 2012, https://whitesidenwc.wordpress.com/2016/05/25/biography-of-abu-omar-al-baghdadi/.
27. Sam Helfont, *Compulsion in Religion: Saddam Hussein, Islam, and the Roots of Insurgencies in Iraq* (Oxford: Oxford University Press, 2018).
28. Joseph Felter and Brian Fishman, "Al-Qa'ida's foreign fighters in Iraq: A first look at the Sinjar records," Combating Terrorism Center at West Point, January 2, 2007, https://ctc.usma.edu/al-qaidas-foreign-fighters-in-iraq-a-first-look-at-the-sinjar-records/.
29. Craig Whiteside, "Nine Bullets for the Traitors, One for the Enemy: The Slogans and Strategy behind the Islamic State's Campaign to Defeat the Sunni Awakening (2006-2017)," *The International Centre for Counter-Terrorism–The Hague* 9 (2018), 4.
30. Dexter Filkins, "In Ramadi, Fetid Quarters and Unrelenting Battles," *New York Times*, July 5, 2006, https://www.nytimes.com/2006/07/05/world/middleeast/05ramadi.html.
31. Ahmed Hashim, *The Caliphate at War: The Ideological, Organisational and Military Innovations of Islamic State* (Oxford University Press, 2018).
32. Michael Fitzsimmons, *Governance, identity, and counterinsurgency: Evidence from Ramadi and Tal Afar* (U.S. Army War College, 2013), 53; Michael O'Hanlon, Adriana Lins de Albuquerque, and Ian S. Livingston, *Iraq Index: tracking variables of reconstruction & security in post-Saddam Iraq* (Brookings Institution, 2003), 14.
33. Hashim, *The Caliphate at War.*

34. Cameron Glenn, 2016. "Timeline: The Rise, Spread and Fall Of The Islamic State." Wilson Center, October 28, 2019, https://www.wilsoncenter.org/article/timeline-the-rise-spread-and-fall-the-islamic-state.
35. Frederic Wehrey et al., *The Iraq Effect: The Middle East After the Iraq War* (Rand Corporation, 2010), 120-121.
36. Brian Fishman, *Dysfunction and Decline: Lessons Learned from Inside Al-Qa'ida in Iraq* (Combating Terrorism Center at West Point, 2009), 1.
37. Brian Fishman, *Dysfunction and Decline: Lessons Learned from Inside Al-Qa'ida in Iraq* (Combating Terrorism Center at West Point, 2009), 19.
38. Islamic State of Iraq, "Strategy to Improve the Political Position of the Islamic State," (late 2009), provided to the author by researcher Hassan Hassan and translated in its entirety by Anas Elallame from the Middlebury Institute for International Studies, Monterey, CA, 20.
39. Whiteside, "Nine Bullets for the Traitors, One for the Enemy: The Slogans and Strategy behind the Islamic State's Campaign to Defeat the Sunni Awakening (2006-2017)."
40. The Islamic State of Iraq, "Strategy to Improve the Political Position of the Islamic State."
41. Craig Whiteside, "The Islamic State and the Return of Revolutionary Warfare," *Small Wars and Insurgencies* 27, no. 5 (2016).
42. Ahmed S. Hashim, "The Islamic State: From al-Qaeda Affiliate to Caliphate," *Middle East Policy* 21, no. 4 (2014), 69-83.
43. William McCants, *The Believer: How an Introvert with a Passion for Religion and Soccer Became Abu Bakr al-Baghdadi, Leader of the Islamic State* (Brookings Institution Press, 2015).
44. William McCants, *The Believer: How an Introvert with a Passion for Religion and Soccer Became Abu Bakr al-Baghdadi, Leader of the Islamic State* (Brookings Institution Press, 2015).
45. Hashim, "The Islamic State: From al-Qaeda Affiliate to Caliphate."
46. Charles Lister, "Profiling Jabhat al-Nusra," The Brookings Institution, July 2016.
47. Charles Lister, "Profiling Jabhat al-Nusra," The Brookings Institution, July 2016.
48. Sarah Birke, "How al-Qaeda Changed the Syrian War," *New York Review of Books*, December 27, 2013, http://www.nybooks.com/blogs/nyrblog/2013/dec/27/how-al-qaeda-changed-syrian-war/.
49. Counter Extremism Project, "Omar al-Shishani," n.d., http://www.counterextremism.com/extremists/omar-al-shishani.

50. Zachary Laub and Jonathan Masters, "Islamic State in Iraq and Greater Syria," Council on Foreign Relations, June 12, 2014.
51. Kirk H. Sowell, "Iraq's Second Sunni Insurgency," *Current Trends in Islamist Ideology* 17, August 9, 2014, 40, https://www.hudson.org/research/10505-iraq-s-second-sunni-insurgency.
52. Dahr Jamail, "Maliki's Iraq: Rape, Executions and Torture." *Al-Jazeera* (Doha), March 19, 2013, https://www.aljazeera.com/humanrights/2013/03/201331883513244683.html.
53. Laub and Masters, "Islamic State in Iraq and Greater Syria."
54. McCants, *The Believer.*
55. Craig Whiteside, "War, Interrupted, Part II: From Prisoners To Rulers," *War On The Rocks*, November 6, 2014, https://warontherocks.com/2014/11/war-interrupted-part-ii-from-prisoners-to-rulers.
56. Hassan Hassan and Michael Weiss. 2016. "Islamic State: An Invincible Force?" *BBC*, March 8, 2006, https://www.bbc.com/news/world-middle-east-35694297.
57. Arango, Tim, Suadad Al-Salhy, and Rick Gladstone. "Kurdish Fighters Take a Key Oil City as Militants Advance on Baghdad." *New York Times*, June 12, 2014. https://www.nytimes.com/2014/06/13/world/middleeast/iraq.html.
58. Craig Whiteside, "A pedigree of terror: The myth of the Ba'athist influence in the Islamic State movement," *Perspectives on Terrorism* 11, no. 3 (2017).
59. "Iraq: ISIL Says Omar Al-Shishani Killed in Air Strike," *Al-Jazeera* (Doha), July 14, 2016, https://www.aljazeera.com/news/2016/07/iraq-isil-omar-al-shishani-killed-air-strike-160713203202458.html.
60. Murad Batal al-Shishani, "Syria Crisis: Omar Shishani, Chechen Jihadist Leader," *BBC*, December 3, 2013, https://www.bbc.com/news/world-middle-east-25151104.
61. "Iraq: ISIL Says Omar Al-Shishani Killed in Air Strike." *Al-Jazeera*, July 14, 2016. https://www.aljazeera.com/news/2016/07/iraq-isil-omar-al-shishani-killed-air-strike-160713203202458.html.
62. "Treasury Designates Twelve Foreign Terrorist Fighter Facilitators," *Treasury.gov*. United States Department of Treasury, September 24, 2014. https://www.treasury.gov/press-center/press-releases/Pages/jl2651.aspx.
63. Shaun Walker, Shaun, "Isis 'War Minister' Targeted In Syria Had Been In Georgian Army," *Guardian* (London), March 9, 2016, https://www.theguardian.com/world/2016/mar/09/isis-war-minister-targeted-in-syria-had-been-in-georgian-army.
64. Aymen Al-Tamimi, "The Biography Of Abu Ali Al-Anbari: Full

Translation And Analysis." *Aymenn Jawad Al-Tamimi*, December 17, 2018, 11, http://www.aymennjawad.org/21877/the-biography-of-abu-ali-al-anbari-full.

65. Hassan Hassan, "The True Origins Of ISIS," *The Atlantic*, November 30, 2018, https://www.theatlantic.com/ideas/archive/2018/11/isis-origins-anbari-zarqawi/577030/.
66. Al-Tamimi, "The Biography Of Abu Ali Al-Anbari: Full Translation And Analysis."
67. Whiteside, "A pedigree of terror."
68. Al-Tamimi, "The Biography Of Abu Ali Al-Anbari: Full Translation And Analysis."
69. Al-Tamimi, "The Biography Of Abu Ali Al-Anbari: Full Translation And Analysis."
70. Rod Nordland, "Iraqi Forces Attack Mosul, A Beleaguered Stronghold For ISIS," *New York Times*, October 17, 2016, https://www.nytimes.com/2016/10/17/world/middleeast/in-isis-held-mosul-beheadings-and-hints-of-resistance-as-battle-nears.html.
71. Jonathan Krohn, "Has the Last Christian Left Iraqi City of Mosul After 2,000 Years?" *NBC News*, July 27, 2014, http://www.nbcnews.com/storyline/iraq-turmoil/has-last-christian-left-iraqi-city-mosul-after-2-000-n164856.
72. Daniel Milton, "Pledging Baya: A Benefit or Burden to the Islamic State?" *CTC Sentinel* 8, no. 3 (2015), 12.
73. David D. Kirkpatrick, "Militant Group in Egypt Vows Loyalty to ISIS," *New York Times*, November 11, 2014, https://www.nytimes.com/2014/11/11/world/middleeast/egyptian-militant-group-pledges-loyalty-to-isis.html.
74. Milton, "Pledging Baya: A Benefit or Burden to the Islamic State?"
75. "Islamic State Khorasan (IS-K)," Center For Strategic And International Studies, 2018, https://www.csis.org/programs/transnational-threats-project/terrorism-backgrounders/islamic-state-khorasan-k.
76. Adam Taylor, "The Strange Story Behind The 'Khorasan' Group's Name," *Washington Post*, September 25, 2014, https://www.washingtonpost.com/news/worldviews/wp/2014/09/25/the-strange-story-behind-the-khorasan-groups-name/?noredirect=on&utm_term=.0b837eba3cb5.
77. "Islamic State Khorasan (IS-K)."
78. Amira Jadoon, Nakissa Jahanbani, and Charmaine Willis, "Challenging the ISK Brand in Afghanistan-Pakistan: Rivalries and Divided Loyalties," *CTC Sentinel* 11, iss. 4, April 2018, https://ctc.usma.edu/challenging-isk-brand-afghanistan-pakistan-rivalries-divided-loyal-

ties/.

79. Brian J. Phillips, "Terrorist group rivalries and alliances: Testing competing explanations," *Studies in Conflict & Terrorism* (2018), 1-23.
80. Jadoon, Jahanbani, and Willis, "Challenging the ISK Brand in Afghanistan-Pakistan: Rivalries and Divided Loyalties."
81. Amira Jadoon, "Allied & Lethal: Islamic State Khorasan's Network and Organizational Capacity in Afghanistan and Pakistan," *CTC Sentinel*, December 2018, 16.
82. Ben Smith, "ISIS and the Sectarian Conflict in the Middle East," *Economic Indicators* 3 (2015), 48.
83. Martin Chulov, "ISIS kills hundreds of Iraqi Sunnis from Albu Nimr tribe in Anbar province," *Guardian* (London), October 30, 2014, http://www.theguardian.com/world/2014/oct/30/mass-graves-hundreds-iraqi-sunnis-killed-isis-albu-nimr.
84. Mark Landler, "Obama, in Speech on ISIS, Promises Sustained Effort to Rout Militants," *New York Times*, September 10, 2014.
85. "ISIS Fast Facts," *CNN*, August 8, 2014, https://www.cnn.com/2014/08/08/world/isis-fast-facts/index.html.
86. Rukmini Callimachi, "ISIS Caliphate Crumbles as Last Village in Syria Falls," *New York Times*, March 23, 2019, https://www.nytimes.com/2019/03/23/world/middleeast/isis-syria-caliphate.html.
87. Joana Cook and Gina Vale, "From Daesh to 'Diaspora': Tracing the Women and Minors of Islamic State," ICSR, 2018, https://icsr.info/wp-content/uploads/2018/07/Women-in-ISIS-report_20180719_web.pdf.
88. Vera Mironova, Ekaterina Sergatskova and Karam Alhamad, "The Bloody Split Within ISIS," *Foreign Affairs*, December 8, 2017, https://www.foreignaffairs.com/articles/syria/2017-12-08/bloody-split-within-isis.
89. Vera Mironova, Ekaterina Sergatskova and Karam Alhamad, "The Bloody Split Within ISIS," *Foreign Affairs*, December 8, 2017, https://www.foreignaffairs.com/articles/syria/2017-12-08/bloody-split-within-isis.
90. Hani Nsirah, " Hazemis, Post Daesh Extremists," *Aawsat*, September, 25th, 2017.
91. Hani Nsirah, " Hazemis, Post Daesh Extremists," *Aawsat*, September, 25th, 2017.
92. Jones, Christopher W. "Understanding ISIS's Destruction of Antiquities as a Rejection of Nationalism." *Journal of Eastern Mediterranean Archaeology & Heritage Studies* 6, no. 1-2 (2018):

31-58. Accessed May 14, 2020. www.jstor.org/stable/10.5325/jeasmedarcherstu.6.1-2.0031.

93. United Nations, "ISIL Now 'A Covert Global Network' Despite Significant Losses, United Nations Counter-Terrorism Head Tells Security Council," August 23, 2018, https://www.un.org/press/en/2018/sc13463.doc.htm.
94. Department of Defense, Office of the Inspector General, *Overseas Contingency Operation: Operation Inherent Resolve Operation Pacific Eagle-Philippines*, 2018, https://media.defense.gov/2018/Aug/06/2001950941/-1/-1/1/FY2018_LIG_OCO_OIR3_JUN2018_508.PDF.
95. Ellen Mitchell, "16 times Trump said ISIS was defeated, or soon would be," *The Hill,* March 23, 2019, https://thehill.com/policy/defense/435402-16-times-trump-declared-or-predicted-the-demise-of-isis.
96. Haroro Ingram and Craig Whiteside, "Do Great Nations Fight Endless Wars? Against the Islamic State, they Might," *War on the Rocks*, February 25, 2019, https://warontherocks.com/2019/02/do-great-nations-fight-endless-wars-against-the-islamic-state-they-might/.
97. Abu Hassan al-Muhajir, " He Was True to Allah, and Allah Was True to Him," Kyle Orton blog, March 2019, https://kyleorton1991.wordpress.com/tag/islamic-state/.
98. Pieter Van Ostaeyen, "Belgian radical networks and the road to the Brussels attacks," *CTC Sentinel* 9, no. 6 (2016), 7-12.
99. Aymenn al-Tamimi, "Islamic State's Appointment of New Leader: Translation and Notes," blog, October 31, 2019, https://www.aymennjawad.org/2019/10/islamic-state-appointment-of-new-leader.

69 Lashkar-e Taiba

Quick Facts

Geographical Areas of Operation: South Asia
Numerical Strength (Members): Precise numbers are unknown
Leadership: Hafiz Muhammad Saeed
Religious Identification: Sunni Islam (Ahl-e-Hadith)

Quick Facts courtesy of the U.S. State Department's Country Reports on Terrorism (2019)

Introduction

Of the many terrorist groups operating in South Asia, Lashkar-e Taiba (LeT) is among the most potent. Founded in Pakistan in the mid-1980s, LeT was generously supported by Pakistan's Inter-Services Intelligence (ISI) as a proxy in its protracted conflict with India. Since then, LeT has built a substantial infrastructure running schools and social services throughout Pakistan, while simultaneously carrying out deadly, sophisticated attacks throughout India and Afghanistan. From its founding, LeT's ambitions were global in nature, and the group now boasts a presence in some twenty-one countries. After the November 2008 massacre in Mumbai, India—a terrorist attack which claimed the lives of over 180 people and specifically targeted foreigners—the international community has broadly acknowledged that LeT represents a global threat.

History and Ideology

Lashkar-e Taiba (LeT), variously translated from Urdu as "Army of the Pure," "Army of the Righteous," or "Army of the Good," is the armed wing of the radical Pakistani Islamist charitable group Jamaat-ud-Dawa (JuD), or "Society for Preaching." Prior to the 2008 Mumbai attack, LeT was viewed primarily as an actor in the ongoing conflict in Jammu and Kashmir (J&K). Since it was formally founded in

1990, LeT voiced global ambitions and viewed undermining Indian rule in J&K as essential to the ultimate reinstatement of Muslim rule over the Indian sub-continent and beyond.[1]

Hafiz Mohammed Saeed and Zafar Iqbal, a pair of professors at the University of Engineering and Technology in Lahore, founded JuD in 1985 as a small missionary group dedicated to spreading the Ahl-e-Hadith (AeH) interpretation of Islam. LeT's embrace of AeH is unusual for Pakistan-based militant groups, most of which adhere to the Deobandi interpretation of Islam. AeH is closely related to the Wahhabis of the Arabian Peninsula and is a minority sect within Pakistan.[2]

In 1986, JuD merged with an organization that facilitated the *jihad* against the Soviets in Afghanistan. This new organization was called Markaz al-Dawa-wal-Irshad (MDI), or "the Center for Preaching and Guidance."[3] Among MDI's cofounders was Osama bin Laden's religious mentor, Abdullah Azzam.[4] Hafiz Saeed became the *emir* of MDI and subsequently of LeT, when the latter was established as MDI's armed wing.[5]

LeT is unique among the AeH affiliates in Pakistan because it holds *dawa* (preaching) and *jihad* as equal components of Islam. LeT's charitable wings work to convert Pakistanis to their interpretation of Islam. Many LeT recruits undergo military training, and some are sent to fight for LeT in J&K, or more recently, Afghanistan. At the same time, LeT's armed operations help its recruitment and outreach efforts by inspiring disaffected Pakistanis.[6]

LeT's first front was Afghanistan, but by the time LeT was founded, the war against the Soviets was waning. According to one report, only five LeT operatives were killed fighting in Afghanistan before LeT withdrew from the conflict as different factions of the Afghan *mujahideen* turned on each other.[7]

When the people of J&K rebelled against India in the late 1980s and early 1990s, Pakistan's Inter Service Intelligence agency (ISI) sought to take advantage of this turmoil and destabilize its neighbor. One of the lessons Pakistan's generals had drawn from the Afghan war was how to use proxy forces against a more powerful enemy without provoking a full-scale war.[8] Initially, Pakistani strategists supported the Jammu and Kashmir Liberation Front, but found that organization supported an independent Kashmir, rather than Kashmiri absorption into Pakistan. In turn, Pakistan shifted its support to Islamist groups that the ISI believed would be more effective and easier to control.[9] In this regard, LeT was an ideal proxy because it was ideologically committed to *jihad*, had an ethnic composition similar to that of the Pakistani military, swore its loyalty to the state, and represented a minority sect within Pakistan.[10]

For its part, LeT readily shifted its focus to J&K. Despite this local focus, however, LeT's ultimate goal was the establishment of Muslim rule of the Indian subcontinent. To facilitate plausible deniability for Pakistan's role in fomenting violence in Jammu and Kashmir, the ISI urged MDI to split its operations, formally establishing LeT as the organization's militant wing.[11]

The earliest known LeT operation in India took place in 1990, when LeT operatives ambushed a jeep carrying Indian Air Force personnel.[12] In 1993, LeT attacked the army base in Poonch, a major coup in terms of its ability to carry out attacks against hard targets.[13] However, the group's presence was not publicly recognized until early 1996, when a group of LeT terrorists killed 16 Hindus in Kashmir's Doda district.[14] This attack was the first of many massacres that targeted ethnic and religious minority communities such as Sikhs and Hindus within J&K and were intended to provoke ethnic strife.[15] Perhaps the most notable of these massacres occurred on March 20, 2000, on the eve of then-U.S. President Bill Clinton's official visit to India, when LeT terrorists (along with members of Hizbul Mujahideen, another Pakistan-backed terrorist organization) killed 35 Sikhs at Chattisinghpora in Anantnag.[16]

Besides its deadly massacres, LeT has targeted Indian government and military installations and disrupted elections by intimidating voters and targeting political leaders. LeT built IEDs to target Indian army vehicles and adeptly mixed high and low technology to communicate and carry out operations.[17]

The focus on J&K did not mean that LeT lost interest in Afghanistan in the 1990s, however, although Kashmir became its main operational focus. According to LeT expert Stephen Tankel, several possible factors—from LeT's Ahl-e-Hadith background to Pakistani intelligence seeking to separate LeT from other terror groups—could explain why LeT's activities were constrained in Afghanistan during the 1990s.[18]

One of LeT's signature tactics has been *fidayeen* ("those who sacrifice themselves in order to redeem themselves") attacks: small, heavily armed and highly motivated squads strike significant or symbolic targets in an effort to cause mass casualties and humiliate the enemy. LeT has carried out dozens of such *fidayeen* attacks over the years. In November 1999, a team of LeT terrorists infiltrated the headquarters of India's 15 Corps at the Badami Bagh cantonment in Srinagar (the capital of J&K) and killed the detachment's Public Relations Officer and seven of his staffers. The attackers fought off Indian soldiers for almost 10 hours before being killed.[19] A month later, LeT terrorists attacked the Police Special Operations Group Headquarters and killed a dozen Indian security personnel. In January 2001, six LeT operatives attempted to enter Srinagar Airport, and in August 2001, three LeT *fidayeen* killed 11 people inside the Jammu Railway station.[20] And although violence in Kashmir has declined substantially since the mid-2000s, LeT has remained active in the region.[21]

From its beginnings, LeT sought to target India. As early as 1992, Hafez Saeed sent Azam Cheema, a top LeT commander, to India to recruit Indian Muslims. Taking advantage of Hindu-Muslim communal tensions, Cheema had some success, and his network carried out a number of low-level bombings across India.[22] Karim Abdul Tunda, who was arrested on the Indian-Nepal border in August 2013, was one these early LeT recruits. He is suspected of involvement in over 40 terror cases in India, both directly and coordinating operations from Pakistan.[23] Indian police arrested LeT operatives in the 1990s, but LeT was not well known at the time and Indian authorities did not realize the extent of the group's operations.[24]

Just as the ISI supports LeT as a proxy in order to maintain plausible deniability, LeT fosters proxies in India among radical Islamist militias there. LeT's most important ally within India is the Indian Mujahideen (IM). IM's members are primarily drawn from the ranks of the Students Islamic Movement of India (SIMI).[25] LeT, along with several other Pakistani terror groups, provided support to

IM, including training, cash, weapons, explosives, and false travel documents. One of IM's founders, Mohammed Sadiq Israr Sheikh, is believed to have traveled to Pakistan on a legitimate Pakistani passport supplied by ISI through LeT; he met with LeT leaders in Pakistan, attended a LeT training camp, and recruited other Indian Muslims.[26]

Some analysts argue that IM is little more than an outgrowth of LeT and the ISI, established when Pakistan reduced its support for armed operations in J&K.[27] These analysts contend that IM was born of "The Karachi Project" which brought together a number of Pakistani militant groups including LeT to attack India.[28] Other analysts view IM as an independent organization, but allied with LeT.[29]

More of IM's numerous deadly attacks throughout India took place before 2012. While the group's specialty has been IEDs made with pressure cookers packed with ammonium nitrate and fuel oil (a markedly different tactic from LeT's use of *fidayeen*), LeT training and support helped IM build the necessary organizational capabilities to carry out attacks. Indian officials have cracked down hard on IM in recent years, and in March 2014 they claimed to have arrested the group's entire top leadership.[30] Since then, IM has not been particularly active.

LeT runs a vast network of offices, schools, medical centers, and media outlets within Pakistan to proselytize LeT's Ahl-e-Hadith theology as part of the group's belief in *dawa*. LeT's headquarters are located at a 200-acre compound in Muridke designed to be a "pure" Islamic city with a *madrassa*, a hospital, a market, residences, and farmland. To demonstrate the purity of the city, televisions and pictures are banned, with entertainment limited to cassettes of warrior songs.[31]

LeT runs a network of primary and upper-level schools that serve over 18,000 students. They are not, technically, *madrassas*; while LeT pushes its view of Islam, the schools also teach other subjects. However, LeT's worldview is infused into every component of education. The former head of LeT's education department explained that in the basic reader the alphabet is used to emphasize *jihad*, "'*Alif*' for Allah, 'Be' for *Bandooq* (gun), '*Te*' for toop (cannon) and so on." Because of the poor state of Pakistan's public education, LeT schools are an attractive alternative. LeT also subsidizes the fees for those who cannot pay.[32]

LeT is a major healthcare provider, running hospitals, mobile medical centers, and an ambulance service. Over 2,000 doctors volunteer their services part-time and are trained to use their contact with patients as an opportunity to proselytize. LeT believes these activities are necessary to counteract the influence of NGOs and Christian missionaries. As in LeT's education system, the organization is providing a service desperately needed by many impoverished Pakistanis.[33] LeT has also been on the forefront of disaster relief; LeT was one of the first organizations to respond to the 2005 Kashmir earthquake[34] and delivered aid to refugees displaced by the fighting in the Swat Valley in 2008 and the 2010 floods.[35]

The effectiveness of the LeT and JuD as a shadow state cannot be overstated. Consider that, as early as 2005, LeT's assets included a 190-acre campus in Muridke that featured 500 offices, 2200 training camps, 150 schools, 2 science colleges, 3 hospitals, 11 ambulances, a publishing empire, a garment factory, an iron foundry, and woodworks factories. Salaries were in some cases 12 to 15 times greater than those offered for similar jobs in the civilian state sector.[36]

LeT has an extensive media arm, publishing several magazines in Urdu, English, and Arabic that target specific communities such as women and students. The flagship publication, *Majalah al-Dawa,* is an Urdu-language monthly that, as of 2010, had a circulation of about 60,000.[37] *Jihad* is a regular theme in these publications, and they regularly feature testaments to LeT operatives killed in the service of *jihad*.[38] LeT has used the internet to propagate its message, broadcasting an internet radio show and maintaining websites and Facebook pages. However, international scrutiny has led the Pakistani government to shut down these sites. LeT also holds conferences and rallies throughout the country despite the group supposedly being banned.[39] The rallies often feature speeches by Hafez Mohammed Saeed, notwithstanding the $10 million bounty on him under the U.S. Rewards for Justice program.[40]

LeT's large social service and paramilitary operations are expensive to operate. However, the organization has been both creative and systematic in its fundraising. According to one report, donation boxes for the *jihadi* groups are present in "countless" shops across the country.[41] LeT publications include calls for donations. LeT also raises money from wealthy supporters in the Arabian Peninsula and from the global Pakistani expatriate community. Often these donations are channeled through a variety of international Islamist charities, such as the International Islamic Relief Organization and the al-Rashid Foundation.[42]

One notable LeT fundraising operation is collecting the skins of sacrificial animals after holidays and selling them to tanneries. In 2010, JuD reportedly collected 100,000 skins, netting a profit of $1.2 million.[43] LeT uses a range of low and high-tech means to involve people in this campaign. For example, within Pakistan, LeT announces this campaign via loudspeaker; internationally, it allows individuals to contribute to the purchase of a sacrificial animal online and then donate the skin to LeT.[44]

Besides the ISI stipend, the Pakistani civilian government has also contributed to LeT. In June 2010, the Punjab provincial government allocated 80 million rupees (about $1 million) to LeT-affiliated schools and hospitals.[45] In 2019, under pressure from the Financial Action Task Force, a global watchdog that monitors terrorist financing and sanctions countries that it deems not to be combating it, the Pakistani government led by Prime Minister Imran Khan went in a different direction and banned both JuD and its charity wing, the Falah-e-Insaniat Foundation.[46] However, when Pakistani governments have banned LeT- and JuD-affiliated entities in the past, new groups have sprung up with different names.

Another possible source of support for LeT's operations in India is D-company, the organized crime group led by Dawood Ibrahim. Ibrahim's criminal network extends well beyond India and the Subcontinent and into the Middle East. Ibrahim is believed to be a major donor to LeT, with his heroin trade and smuggling networks purportedly used to help LeT move operatives in and out of India.[47]

Global Reach

LeT has allied with other Islamist groups around the world (including al-Qaeda) and has developed its own fundraising and logistical support network. LeT has also become a magnet for Islamists worldwide seeking training. Finally, and most worrisome, LeT is increasingly fighting NATO and Indian military forces in Afghanistan.

LeT statements have long vilified a coalition of Hindus, Jews, and Christians, colorfully termed the "Brahmanic-Talmudic-Crusader" alliance,[48] that seeks to destroy the international Muslim community.[49] LeT rhetoric frequently targets Israel and at one point called for Pakistan to deploy a hydrogen bomb to "make the USA yield before Pakistan."[50]

LeT's affiliation with the global Islamist terror movement is deep and extensive. LeT's links to al-Qaeda, for instance, are rooted in their respective foundations and the legacy of Abdullah Azzam, who was instrumental in the creation of both al-Qaeda and the MDI. LeT has sheltered and trained many notable al-Qaeda figures, including Ramzi Yusuf, the mastermind of the 1993 World Trade Center bombing and nephew of 9/11 organizer Khalid Sheikh Mohammed.[51] After 9/11 and the U.S. invasion of Afghanistan, LeT assisted with the exfiltration of al-Qaeda personnel from Afghanistan, providing safe houses, safe passage, travel documents, and logistical support.[52] Several al-Qaeda operatives trained with LeT. Richard Reid, the notorious "shoe bomber" terrorist, is known to have trained with LeT prior to joining al-Qaeda. Two of the 2005 London subway bombers, Mohammad Siddique Khan and Shehzad Tanweer, may also have received training from LeT.[53]

Many LeT members were embedded in an international network of Islamist organizations, and the group has long offered support to other extremists battling perceived enemies of Islam. For instance, LeT has offered rhetorical – and occasionally financial – support to Islamists in Chechnya, Gaza, the Philippines, and the Balkans.[54] The Islamic Movement of Uzbekistan (IMU), a group working to overthrow the Uzbek regime and to replace it with a *sharia*-based government, has long-standing ties to LeT.[55] LeT is also plugged into the international networks of Islamist fundraisers such as the

Al Akhtar Trust or the Al Rashid Trust, which were founded to fund militant groups.[56]

When al-Qaeda's training infrastructure in Afghanistan was destroyed, LeT's camps were largely untouched due to Pakistan's protection; thus, the camps took up the mantle of training international Islamist movement militants.[57] This training support is provided to militants from numerous organizations in South Asia, such as Hizbul Mujahideen (HuM), Jaish-e-Mohammed (JeM), Harkat-ul-Jihad-ul-Islami (HuJI), and the Taliban, among others.[58] Furthermore, radical Muslims worldwide are known to have travelled to Pakistan to train with the LeT.

LeT has safehouses and supporters in Bangladesh, Nepal,[59] and the Maldives[60] that facilitate the infiltration of operatives into India. It has supporters in the Gulf region who raise funds, but also recruit Indians working there and coordinate travel to Pakistan for training.

LeT's attacks in Afghanistan are consistent with its willingness to serve as a proxy for Pakistani intelligence, which is deeply concerned that increased Indian influence in Afghanistan will leave Pakistan surrounded. At first, LeT's support for the Afghan Taliban in their fight against NATO forces was informal, granting LeT fighters leave to travel to Afghanistan and join the Taliban on their own initiative. In 2004 and 2005, however, LeT began to formally support its members traveling to Afghanistan to fight alongside the Taliban.[61] LeT fighters played a significant role in an attack on a U.S. base in Wanat, Nuristan wherein insurgents nearly overran the base.[62] Additionally, some analysts believe LeT carried out a number of high-profile strikes against Indian targets in Afghanistan, including a July 2008 car-bombing of the Indian Embassy and a February 2010 *fidayeen* attack on Kabul guesthouses hosting Indians.[63]

There is evidence that LeT opened an office in Lodi, California, and counterterrorism officials "cite evidence in recent years of fundraising or recruiting efforts in Canada, Britain, Australia and the United States."[64] LeT has also been active in Germany,[65] a cell that raised money and was armed with explosives was arrested in Spain,[66] and the group maintains an active presence in France.[67]

Recent Activity

Lashkar-e-Taiba currently finds itself in a difficult position. Unlike many other Islamist groups in Pakistan, it has remained loyal to the Pakistani state, and even serves Pakistan's government as an intermediary to other radical groups.[68] At the same time, LeT's primary arena for *jihad*, Jammu and Kashmir, has been increasingly closed off to it. Regional violence has decreased from hundreds of civilians killed annually by terrorists only a decade ago to only a handful today.[69] J&K remain restive, however, and LeT as well as other Pakistani extremists continue to attempt to wage their battle there. Yet LeT has received far less support from the Pakistani government in recent years, as a result of pressure on Islamabad from the international community.[70]

Additionally, LeT has been unable to capitalize on new developments in the global *jihadist* sphere. When the Islamic State announced plans for a franchise in the Afghanistan/Pakistan region in early 2015, some observers noted that LeT could be a logical regional partner, given that both groups adhere to the Salafist sect of Sunni Islam. By contrast, most South Asian terror groups—from the Taliban to the sectarian Lashkar-e-Jhangvi (LeJ)—belong to the Deobandi sect, which ISIS rejects. Observers contended that some renegade LeT members, frustrated with their group's less active role in Kashmir and across India, could jump ship to ISIS.[71]

Instead, ISIS has chosen to partner with other local militant groups, particularly LeJ. ISIS clearly prefers working with groups in South Asia that share its targeting preferences—LeJ, like ISIS, frequently targets Shia Muslims—even if they don't share the Islamic State's Salafist worldview. Another reason for ISIS' lack of interest in LeT is the latter's ties to the Pakistani state, which ISIS wants to destroy. However, one cannot rule out the possibility of a temporary marriage of convenience motivated a common enemy. Still, even these theoretical collaborations would likely only have a limited impact on LeT's capacities.

Several attacks that either involved or were directly executed by LeT in J&K and broader India in 2015 and 2016,[72] but that pace of activity has declined. There were relatively few LeT attacks in 2018 and 2019. Local police in the Kashmiri town of Baramulla blamed the group for an attack that killed three people in April 2018.[73] Otherwise, India and J&K have not suffered any major terror attacks involving LeT since 2016. On the whole, LeT has become notably less relevant; however, it still remains a threat, and Indian officials continue to view it as such[74] and carry out operations against LeT operatives infiltrating Kashmir.[75]

JeM, meanwhile, has significantly elevated its profile in recent years—an emergence that coincided with the return of JeM leader Masood Azhar, who was silent for nearly a decade until 2014. JeM claimed responsibility for several attacks in J&K in early 2019. The reemergence of the "other" India-focused terror threat, marked by a high-profile attack in Kashmir on Valentine's Day 2019 that killed more than 40 Indian security forces, represents a turning point for the region. Indeed, LeT was essentially forgotten during the crisis—and it was JeM, not LeT, that was causing the most concern for India.

Over the course of 2018 and 2019, new pressure prompted Islamabad to crackdown on LeT and JuD. In early 2018, the Financial Action Task Force (FATF)—a global watchdog for terrorist financing—placed Pakistan on a gray list for not sufficiently countering terror finance. Countries placed on FATF's gray list may have trouble conducting business abroad or securing foreign investment. While Pakistan had been put on this gray list in the past, Islamabad is now suffering from a major balance of payments crisis, making the potential designation a significant concern for the country's ailing economy. As a result, the new Pakistani government led by Prime Minister Imran Khan announced a ban on JuD in early 2019 (even though JuD had already technically been banned before).[76] Subsequently, Pakistani police arrested dozens of *jihadists* and shut down their facilities. These steps will pose new challenges for LeT and its affiliates. However, such crackdowns typically do not last long, and shuttered militant charities are reopened under new names.

Despite these setbacks and threats, LeT continues to operate openly in Pakistan. Recent LeT protests have focused on NATO transport vehicles traveling through Pakistan, U.S. drone strikes, Indian water policies, and improved trade relations with India.

LeT has spearheaded a coalition of Islamist groups who opposed these efforts known as the Difa-e-Pakistan Council (Defense of Pakistan).[77]

LeT chief Hafez Muhammed Saeed has continued to travel throughout Pakistan and speak at rallies, despite a $10 million bounty under the U.S. Rewards for Justice program. Saeed also regularly gives academic lectures at colleges in Punjab. Several top LeT leaders are being tried in Pakistan for their role in the Mumbai attacks. But the country's extremely slow judicial process suggests that the Pakistani government is not committed to seeing justice served.[78] Indeed, Zakiur Rehman Lakhvi, a top LeT leader implicated in the Mumbai attacks, has been out on bail since 2015. Saeed, meanwhile, has been rotating in and out of house arrest for years. When Saeed was released in November 2017, he delivered a fiery sermon in which he labeled Nawaz Sharif, Pakistan's prime minister from 2013 until 2017, a traitor for pursuing peace with India. Saeed also vowed to maintain the struggle to "free" Kashmir.[79] And in early 2019, he filed a formal petition with the United Nations requesting that his UN terror designation be removed (his request was refused).[80]

The timing of Saeed's release was notable for two reasons. First, it came several days after the U.S. Congress delinked LeT from aid certification requirements—in other words, Washington decided that it would not need to certify that Pakistan was taking robust action against LeT before releasing aid monies to Pakistan.[81] Why the United States chose to delink LeT is unclear.

Saeed's release was also notable because it came a few days before the 9th anniversary of the 2008 Mumbai terror attacks. For many relatives of the tragedy's victims, the release of Saeed on a date so close to the anniversary was deeply upsetting.[82]

In November 2019, an anti-terrorism court announced that Saeed would be indicted on terrorist financing charges.[83] He was subsequently arrested in a rare indication of the country's willingness to take concrete legal action against the LeT leader. However, this move was likely made in response to FATF pressure, based on past precedent when it comes to Pakistan's handling of terrorists.

For its part, Prime Minister Narendra Modi's administration has shown little interest in improving India's relationship with Pakistan. Modi is a Hindu nationalist whose party has expressed anti-Pakistan views. Due to this point of conflict, LeT's anti-India extremism may continue to resonate with large segments of Pakistani society, particularly in the Punjab province where the group is based. In 2016, Modi threatened to revisit, or even revoke, the Indus Waters Treaty—a water-sharing accord that ensures the Indus, a critical water source for Pakistan, flows downstream unencumbered.[84] Modi's threat provided more ammunition for LeT propaganda, which has long used India's alleged "water theft" as a prominent talking point. India-Pakistan relations were plunged into deep crisis in 2019 – first after a mass casualty attack on Indian security forces in Pulwama, Kashmir, in February, and especially after New Delhi revoked the autonomy of India-administered Kashmir in August. The Indian government insists it will not agree to formal dialogue with Islamabad until Pakistan cracks down conclusively against LeT and its ilk.

Ultimately, LeT considers *jihad* a central tenet of its ideology. The organization may again seek to launch large scale terrorist operations, and possibly do so in more distant places than Kashmir. Alternately, frustrated LeT cadres may begin to plot their own attacks. As a whole, LeT remains ideologically committed to violence and maintains the resources and skills needed to launch major, deadly terror attacks. Revelations that it is embracing technological innovations – including a new mobile application that secures its communications in J&K – highlight the group's willingness to adapt to changing global circumstances.[85]

Endnotes

1. Stephen Tankel, "Lashkar-e-Taiba: Past Operations and Future Prospects," New America Foundation, April 27, 2011, https://www.newamerica.org/international-security/policy-papers/lashkar-e-taiba/.
2. Yoginder Sikand, "Islamist Militancy in Kashmir: The Case of Lashkar-e-Taiba," in Aparna Rao, Michael Bollig and Monika Bock, eds., *The Practice of War: Production, Reproduction and Communication of Armed Violence* (London: Berghahn Books 2007).
3. Ibid.

4. Wilson John, "Lashkar-e-Toiba: New Threats Posed By An Old Organization," Jamestown Foundation *Terrorism Monitor* 3, no. 4, May 5, 2005, http://www.jamestown.org/single/?no_cache=1&tx_ttnews[tt_news]=314.
5. Tankel, "Lashkar-e-Taiba."
6. Muhammad Amir Rana, *A to Z of Jihadi Organizations in Pakistan,* Saba Ansan, trans., (Pakistan: Mashal Books, 2006), 298-300.
7. Ibid., 317-18.
8. Praveen Swami, *India, Pakistan and the Secret Jihad: The Covert War in Kashmir, 1947-2004* (London: Routledge, 2007), 145.
9. Ibid., 170-80.
10. Joshua Adlakha, *The Evolution of Lashkar-e-Tayyiba and the Road to Mumbai*, Unpublished dissertation for Georgetown University, 2010.
11. Ibid.
12. A. Abbas, "In God We Trust," *The Herald*, January 2002.
13. Sikand, "Islamist Militancy in Kashmir: The Case of Lashkar-e-Taiba," 206.
14. South Asian Terrorism Portal, "Incidents and Statements involving Lashkar-e-Toiba: 1996-2007," n.d., http://www.satp.org/satporgtp/countries/india/states/jandk/terrorist_outfits/lashkar_e_toiba_lt2007.htm.
15. Praveen Swami, "Turning the Snow Red," *Frontline* 17, no. 17 (August 19–September 1, 2000), http://www.frontline.in/static/html/fl1717/17170160.htm.
16. Barry Bearak, "A Kashmiri Mystery," *New York Times Magazine*, December 31, 2000, http://www.nytimes.com/2000/12/31/magazine/a-kashmiri-mystery.html?pagewanted=all&src=pm.
17. Peter Chalk & C. Christine Fair, "Lashkar-e-Tayyiba leads the Kashmiri insurgency," *Jane's Intelligence Review* 14, no. 10, October 17, 2002, 1-5.
18. Stephen Tankel, "Lashkar-e Taiba in Perspective: An Evolving Threat," New America Foundation Counterterrorism Strategy Initiative Policy Paper, February 2010, http://carnegieendowment.org/files/Lashkar-e-Taiba_in_Perspective.pdf.
19. Praveen Swami, "A growing toll," *Frontline*, 16, no. 24, November 13-26, 1999, http://www.frontline.in/static/html/fl1624/16240390.htm.
20. For an in-depth chronology of LeT operations, see South Asia Terrorism Portal, "Incidents involving Lashkar-e-Toiba: 1996-2007," http://www.satp.org/satporgtp/countries/india/states/jandk/terrorist_outfits/lashkar_e_toiba_lt2007.htm.

21. "Siege ends at Lal Chowk; 2 militants gunned down," ExpressIndia.com, January 7, 2010, http://expressindia.indianexpress.com/karnatakapoll08/story_page.php?id=564467
22. Praveen Swami, "Pakistan and the Lashkar's Jihad in India," *The Hindu*, December 9, 2008.
23. Dwaipayan Ghosh, "Tunda fed IM sleeper cells via border operations," *Times of India*, September 4, 2013, http://articles.timesofindia.indiatimes.com/2013-09-04/kolkata/41764390_1_indian-mujahideen-terror-attacks-delhi-police.
24. Tankel, "Lashkar-e-Taiba."
25. C. Christine Fair, *Students Islamic Movement of India and the Indian Mujahideen: An Assessment*, (Seattle, WA: The National Bureau of Asian Research, January 2010).
26. "13/7 Accused Haroon Naik met Osama, Lakhvi in Pak: ATS," *The Hindu*, February 7 2012, http://www.thehindu.com/news/national/137-accused-haroon-naik-met-osama-lakhvi-in-pak-ats/article2869467.ece.
27. Vicky Nanjappa, "How the Indian Mujahideen was formed," Rediff.com, July 29, 2008, http://www.rediff.com/news/2008/jul/29ahd9.htm.
28. Unnithan, Sandeep, "The Karachi Project," *India Today*, March 17, 2010, https://www.indiatoday.in/magazine/cover-story/story/20100301-the-karachi-project-742101-2010-02-18.
29. Tankel, *Storming the World Stage,* 144.
30. Rahul Tripathi, "Entire Top Indian Mujahideen Leadership Nabbed in 8 Months," *Indian Express*, March 30, 2014, http://indianexpress.com/article/india/india-others/im-impounded/.
31. Jessica Stern, *Terror in the Name of God: Why Religious Militants Kill* (New York: HarperCollins, 2003), 114.
32. Arif Jamal, "From Madrasa to School," *News*, December 15, 2002.
33. Shushant Sareen, *The Jihad Factory: Pakistan's Islamic Revolution in the Making* (India: Observer Research Foundation, 2005), 243-46.
34. Praveen Swami, "Quake came as a boon for Lashkar leadership," *The Hindu*, November 17, 2005.
35. Saeed Shah, "Pakistan floods: Jamaat-ud-Dawa, Islamists linked to India's Mumbai attack, offer aid," *Christian Science Monitor*, August 4, 2010.
36. Neil Padukone, "The Next Al-Qaeda? Lashkar-e-Taiba and the Future of Terrorism in South Asia," *World Affairs Journal*, November/December 2011, https://www.jstor.org/stable/23210445?seq=1#page_scan_tab_contents

37. Everything You Want to Know About LeT," *Hindustan Times*, February 20, 2010, http://www.hindustantimes.com/Everything-you-want-to-know-about-the-LeT/H1-Article1-511059.aspx.
38. Mariam Abou Zahab, "'I shall be waiting for you at the door of paradise': The Pakistani Martyrs of the Lashkar-e Taiba," in Rao, Bollig and Bock, eds., *The Practice of War: Production, Reproduction and Communication of Armed Violence*, 167.
39. Amir Mir, "The Gates are Open," *Outlook India*, January 19, 2009, http://www.outlookindia.com/article.aspx?239500.
40. Annie Gowen, "Pakistan, India spar in Kashmir in worst border violence in years," *Washington Post,* September 12, 2013, http://articles.washingtonpost.com/2013-09-12/world/41982669_1_indian-controlled-kashmir-india-and-pakistan-muslim-majority-pakistan.
41. Tankel, "Lashkar-e-Taiba: Past Operations and Future Prospects."
42. Sareen, *The Jihad Factory*, 290-93.
43. "Banned Outfits Raise Cash from Sacrifice Day," *Dawn* (Karachi), November 24, 2010, http://www.dawn.com/2010/11/24/banned-outfits-raise-cash-from-sacrifice-day.html.
44. Sareen, *The Jihad Factory,* 298.
45. "Pakistan 'Gave Funds' to Group on UN Terror Blacklist," BBC, June 16, 2010, http://www.bbc.co.uk/news/10334914.
46. "Imran Khan Government Banks Hafiz Saeed's JuD, Its Charity Arm as India Pushes to Put Pak on Terror Blacklist," News 18.com, February 22, 2019, https://www.news18.com/news/world/pakistan-bans-hafiz-saeed-led-jud-and-its-charity-wing-fif-2044527.html.
47. VS Subrahmanian et al., *Computational Analysis of Terrorist Groups: Lashkar-e-Taiba* (New York: Springer Verlag, 2013), 216.
48. C. Christine Fair, testimony before the House Homeland Security Committee, Subcommittee on Transportation Security and Infrastructure Protection, March 11, 2009, http://www.rand.org/pubs/testimonies/CT320/.
49. *Friday Times*, November 21-27, 1998, cited in Sareen, *The Jihad Factory*, 310.
50. Evan Kohlmann, "Expert Witness: Synopsis of Testimony, *Regina v. Mohammed Ajmal Khan, Palvinder Singh, and Frzana Khan*, Exhibit EK/1" (UK: Snaresbrook Crown Court, 2006).
51. Mariam Abou Zahab and Olivier Roy, *Islamist Networks: The Afghan-Pakistan Connection* (New York: Columbia University Press, 2004), 42.
52. Tankel, "Lashkar-e-Taiba."
53. Tankel, 162-66.

54. Peter Bergen, *Holy War Inc.: Inside the secret world of Osama Bin-Laden* (New York: Free Press, 2001).
55. Bill Roggio, "Al Qaeda video highlights fighting in Ghazni," *Long War Journal*, July 13, 2013.
56. South Asian Terrorism Portal, "Al-Rashid Trust," n.d., www.satp.org/satporgtp/countries/pakistan/terroristoutfits/Al-Rashid_Trust.htm.
57. Tankel, "Lashkar-e-Taiba."
58. Neil Padukone, "The Next Al Qaeda? Lashkar-e-Taiba and the Future of Terrorism in South Asia," *World Affairs*, November/December 2011, 67-72.
59. Tankel, *Storming the World Stage*, 144.
60. Animesh Roul, "Jihad and Islamism in the Maldive Islands," Jamestown Foundation *Terrorism Monitor*, February 12, 2010, https://jamestown.org/program/jihad-and-islamism-in-the-maldive-islands/.
61. Tankel, *Storming the World Stage*, 194.
62. "Surge of the Insurgents," *Jane's Terrorism and Security Monitor*, September 5, 2008.
63. Praveen Swami, "Kabul Attack: U.S. Warning was accurate," *The Hindu*, August 3, 2008, http://www.thehindu.com/todays-paper/Kabul-attack-U.S.-warning-was-accurate/article15271791.ece
64. Josh Meyer, "Extremist group works in the open in Pakistan," *Los Angeles Times*, December 18, 2007.
65. Mohit Joshi, "Lashkar-e-Taiba members in Germany, interior minister says." *TopNews*, December 12, 2008.
66. Jesus Duva, Monica Ceberio Balaza, and Jorge A. Rodriguez, "Three Al Qaeda members detained in Spain," *El Pais*, August 2, 2012.
67. Tankel, *Storming the World Stage*, 165.
68. Abou Zahab, "'I shall be waiting for you at the door of paradise:' The Pakistani Martyrs of the Lashkar-e Taiba," 114.
69. South Asia Terrorism Portal, "Fatalities in Terrorist Violence 1988-2013," n.d., http://www.satp.org/satporgtp/countries/india/states/jandk/data_sheets/annual_casualties.htm.
70. Tankel, *Storming the World Stage*, 174-177.
71. Arif Rafiq, "Islamic State Goes Official in South Asia," *The Diplomat*, February 4, 2015, http://thediplomat.com/2015/02/islamic-state-goes-official-in-south-asia/.
72. Praveen Swami, "Pakistan: Lashkar-e-Taiba Claims Uri Attack in Posters in Gujranwala," *Indian Express*, October 26, 2016, http://indianexpress.com/article/india/india-news-india/uri-attack-lashkar-e-taiba-pakistan-terrorism-gujranwala-3103034/; "Lashkar-e-Taiba Behind Gurdaspur Terror Attack, Confirms MHA," *Business*

Standard, July 27, 2015, http://www.business-standard.com/article/news-ani/lashkar-e-taiba-behind-gurdaspur-terror-attack-confirms-mha-115072701297_1.html.

73. "Lashkar-e-Taiba Guns Down 3 Civilians in Kashmir's Baramulla, Probe Ordered," *Business Standard*, April 30, 2018, https://www.business-standard.com/article/current-affairs/kashmir-attack-lashkar-e-taiba-shoots-3-civilians-dead-in-kashmir-s-baramulla-top-updates-118043001119_1.html.
74. Sugam Pokharel and Mukhtar Ahmed, "Indian-Administered Kashmir: Militant Leader's Death Sparks Protests," *CNN*, August 2, 2017, www.cnn.com/2017/08/02/asia/protests-indian-administered-kashmir/index.html.
75. Shuja ul-Haq and Ashraf Wani, "2 Pak Nationals Nabbed near LoC, Planned to Guide LeT Terrorists to Infiltrate J&K," *India Today*, September 4, 2019, https://www.indiatoday.in/india/story/pak-nationals-loc-guide-let-terrorists-kashmir-1595549-2019-09-04.
76. "Imran Khan Govt Bans Hafiz Saeed's JuD, Its Charity Arm as India Pushes to Put Pak on Terror Blacklist," *News18*, February 22, 2019, https://www.news18.com/news/world/pakistan-bans-hafiz-saeed-led-jud-and-its-charity-wing-fif-2044527.html.
77. Arif Rafiq, "The Emergence of the Difa-e-Pakistan Islamist Coalition," *CTC Sentinel*, March 22, 2012.
78. Richard Leiby, "Pakistani militant Hafiz Mohammad Saeed seeks protection from bounty hunters," *Washington Post*, April 22, 2012.
79. Vijaita Singh and Mubashir Zaidi, "Hafiz Saeed Vows to Continue Kashmir Struggle," *The Hindu*, November 24, 2017, http://www.thehindu.com/news/international/hafiz-saeed-calls-nawaz-sharif-a-traitor-for-seeking-peace-with-india/article20787782.ece.
80. Yashwant Raj, "UN Rejects Hafiz Saeed's Appeal to Remove Name from List of Banned Terrorists: Sources," *Hindustan Times*, March 7, 2019, https://www.hindustantimes.com/world-news/un-rejects-hafiz-saeed-s-appeal-to-remove-name-from-list-of-banned-terrorists-report/story-0cdiynrTikKbERlmE5aYKL.html.
81. "Pentagon pressures US congress to delink LeT from Haqqani Network," *The Tribune Express,* November 20, 2017, https://tribune.com.pk/story/1563285/3-pentagon-pressures-us-congress-delink-let-haqqani-network/.
82. Manish Mehta and Rafiq Maqbool, "Families of India Terror Victims Angry at Militant's Release," *Seattle Times*, November 26, 2017, https://www.seattletimes.com/nation-world/families-of-india-terror-victims-angry-at-militants-release/.

83. Rana Bilal, "JuD Chief Hafiz Saeed, Others To Be Indicted in Terror Financing Case on December 7," *Dawn*, November 30, 2019, https://www.dawn.com/news/1519704.
84. Shubajit Roy and Amitabh Sinha, "Blood and Water Can't Flow Together, Says PM Modi at Indus Water Treaty Meeting, Govt Plans Cross-Border River Strategy," *Indian Express*, September 27, 2016, http://indianexpress.com/article/india/india-news-india/indus-water-sharing-treaty-india-pakistan-modi-border-security-underwater-sensor-uri-3051968/.
85. "Terror Goes Hi-Tech: Lashkar-e-Toiba Develops App for its Operations," *Zee News*, October 14, 2015, http://zeenews.india.com/news/india/terror-goes-hi-tech-lashkar-e-toiba-develops-app-for-its-operations_1809936.html.

70 Muslim Brotherhood

Quick Facts

Geographical Areas of Operation: Egypt; Muslim Brotherhood-affiliated groups operate in Algeria, Bahrain, Iraq, Jordan, Kuwait, Libya, Morocco, the Palestinian territories, Qatar, Saudi Arabia, Somalia, Sudan, Syria, Tunisia, Turkey, the United Arab Emirates, and Yemen.
Numerical Strength: Unknown
Founder: Hassan al-Banna
Religious Identification: Sunni

Source: The Counter Extremsim Project, 2020

Introduction

Founded in Egypt in 1928, the Muslim Brotherhood is one of the oldest, largest, and most influential Islamist organizations in the world. The movement was initially intended to spread Islamic morals and create an Islamic state in Egypt by catering to the country's marginalized communities, but quickly became involved in politics. Since 1954, when the Brotherhood was formally outlawed, until Abdel Fattah el-Sisi assumed the presidency of Egypt in 2014, the movement has been sometimes repressed, otherwise tolerated, at one point in charge, but always illegal. While the movement did not immediately join the 2011 Arab Spring uprising in Egypt, its involvement was ultimately pivotal. Since the election of President Sisi, there has been an ongoing crackdown on the group, bringing it to one of its weakest points in history. Moreover, Sisi has taken this effort abroad, attempting to convinced allied countries to declare the Brotherhood a terrorist organization.

History and Ideology

The Jamʿat al- Ikhwan al- Muslimyn (Society of the Muslim Brothers) was founded in 1928 by Hassan al-Banna, a young primary school teacher from the city of Isma'iliyya in southern Egypt.[1] Originally, the Brotherhood began as a community organization, aimed at providing social services. These included education, health, and professional services designed to assist poor and middle class Egyptians[2] that the government was unable to deliver.

The Brotherhood advocated moral reform and a revival of Islam in Egypt and the Middle East as a means to combat what al-Banna viewed as Western-inspired secularization.[3] Al- Banna felt that the weaknesses of the Muslim world could only be cured by implementing Islam as an "all-embracing concept," meaning that Islamic principles as defined by the Brotherhood (or those educated according to the Brotherhood's theories) should govern every aspect of life.[4]

Al-Banna introduced a multi-stage process through which the Brotherhood could achieve its political goals: it would recruit individuals (a process that could last up to one year)[5] and indoctrinate them through *tarbiya* (upbringing, education). Recruitment and indoctrination were designed to weed out dissenters and to ensure that all members were committed to the Brotherhood's vision and willing to follow its leaders' orders. The recruitment process was explicitly designed to prevent government security officials from penetrating the group. Those individuals and their families would lead Islamic lifestyles and promote the Brotherhood's vision in society. Once the society broadly embraced the Brotherhood's vision, it would implement it at the state level until Egypt was an Islamic state. Eventually, as the tactics proliferated to other countries, all would unify under the banner of a new *caliphate*.

Al-Banna outlined his vision through a series of epistles, including one titled "On *Jihad*." In this piece, he argued that too many Muslims were passively watching as their values were overcome by the brand of modernity that Westernization brought. He called supporters to invest themselves in pressing back against the tide of Westernization. However, al-Banna believed that *jihad* was not restricted to the struggle against *kuffar* (apostates) but was in fact a more comprehensive awakening of Muslim hearts and minds.

In the 1930s, al-Banna's opposition to British rule and influence found expression as his organization began to recruit followers who saw the appeal of its ideology on issues ranging from poverty and education to nationalism and the nascent Israeli-Palestinian conflict.

As the movement grew, it faced domestic repression. During this period, a paramilitary wing called the "Special Apparatus" was created, which sought to protect the organization and, more importantly, send operatives to fight against British rule and engage in a campaign of violent activities. Al-Banna's relationship with this apparatus is disputed, but it was blamed for numerous violent incidents during the 1940s, including the 1948 assassination of the country's prime minister.

By the late 1940s, the group was estimated to have around 500,000 members in Egypt.[6] After al-Banna's assassination in 1949, the government accelerated its repression of the group. Nearly 4,000 members were arrested, and most were not released from prison for years. Hassan Al Hudaiby, a judge, succeeded al-Banna as leader, but struggled in the role. The Brotherhood supported the military officers who ousted King Farouk during the 1952 Free Officers Revolution, and thus anticipated having influence in the new government. But, after a brief period of cooperation, the Brotherhood (along with all other political parties) was outlawed by the first president of Egypt, Mohamed Naguib. Following a failed assassination attempt in 1954, then-Prime Minister and future President Gamal Abdel Nasser escalated the crackdown on the organization, imprisoning most of its leadership, sending many Brothers into exile, and effectively eliminating its domestic activities.

During this period, the most radical tendencies within the Brotherhood emerged, propelled by its chief ideologue, Sayyid Qutb.[7] While in prison, Qutb wrote his manifesto, *Milestones*, which has since inspired generations of violent *jihadis*. Published in 1964, *Milestones* argued that the Muslim world had regressed to the pre-Islamic state of ignorance known as *jahiliyya*, and advocated *jihad* as a remedy. Qutb thereby cast contemporary Arab governments, including Egypt's, as non-Islamic, and urged his followers to take up arms against them. The Egyptian government responded by banning *Milestones*, incarcerating Qutb and ultimately executing him in 1966.

In the decades that followed, Qutb and Hudaiby would represent competing trends, both within the organization as well as in the world of Islamism more broadly. "Qutbists" typically favored insularity and ideological purity; more importantly, those Islamists who favored Qutb's call for violent *jihad* gravitated towards it. Meanwhile, those following Hudaiby's teachings favored outreach and working with non-Islamists in pursuit of common short-term objectives.

When Anwar Sadat succeeded Nasser as president in 1970, he gradually gave greater freedom to Islamists, viewing them as a useful counterbalance to Nasserists who threatened his authority. This, combined with the upsurge in Islamist activity that followed the 1967 Arab-Israeli War, catalyzed an explosion of Islamist advocacy on university campuses. Prospective Brotherhood members were recruited from this new generation of Islamists; for the most part, those who joined the Brotherhood during this period rejected violent *jihad* within Egypt.

During President Hosni Mubarak's 30-year reign, which began in 1981, the Brotherhood remained an illegal organization but its members were permitted to participate in parliamentary elections as independents. While the 1984 temporary alliance between the Brotherhood and the liberal *Wafd* party proved effective,[8] the Brotherhood's success at the polls came at a price, as the Mubarak regime viewed its Islamist ideology and its committed following as a significant threat, and thus repressed the movement.[9] Ten years later, after the Brotherhood won an impressive 88 of 444 contested seats in parliament, the Mubarak regime yet again targeted the group: two chief financiers, businessman Hassan Malek and deputy supreme guide Khairat al-Shater, were arrested and each given seven-year sentences, while constitutional amendments issued in 2007 were designed to restrict religious parties from future elections.[10]

Immediately after Mubarak was ousted from power in Egypt on February 11, 2011 as part of what would become the Arab Spring, the Freedom and Justice Party (FJP) was founded by the Brotherhood's internal *Shura* Council in an effort to capitalize on the resulting political vacuum and promote Islamism.[11] By the end of 2011, the FJP, due to its support base, funding network, and estimated 120,000 members,[12] anchored an alliance that won more than 47 percent of the seats. In the FJP-dominated parliament, Brotherhood members held either the chairmanship or deputy chairmanship in 18 of 19 committees. Brotherhood leader Saad al-Katatny was appointed parliamentary speaker.[13] The key issue before this parliament was the selection of the Constituent Assembly, which was tasked with drafting Egypt's next constitution. The Brotherhood had shifted to proposing a balanced system between the president and parliament; a model that was politically popular at the time. In opposition to the Brotherhood's proposal, the Supreme Court of Armed Forces (SCAF), Egypt's highest military body, proposed a system which would ensure the military maintain significant power over the civilian population, something to which the MB strongly objected.[14] The Brotherhood used its dominance in the parliament to chip away at the SCAF's political legitimacy and escalate what had been a dormant power struggle between the junta and the Islamists.

The 2012 presidential elections further ratcheted up tensions between the Brotherhood and the SCAF. The ascension of Muslim Brotherhood leader Abdel Moneim Abouel Fotouh, a moderate who focused his presidential run on social justice,[15] as a leading candidate caused tension within the Brotherhood, in that he disobeyed an intra-group directive that no member should run for President.[16] To quell rising tensions between the FJP and the SCAF,[17] the Brotherhood banished Fotouh.[18] In late March 2012, the Brotherhood nominated FJP chairman Mohammed Morsi from the final list that featured thirteen candidates, after their first choice candidate, Khairat al-Shater, was disqualified.[19] The elections took place on May 23-24, 2012, with Morsi ultimately securing victory.[20]

Due to domestic political instability,[21] when Morsi was sworn in on June 30, 2012, there was no parliament, no new constitution, and his precise powers were undefined. On August 12, Morsi used a major attack in the Sinai the previous week as a pretext for firing leadership in the SCAF, promoting director of military intelligence[22] Abdel Fatah al-Sisi to defense minister, and issuing a new constitutional declaration granting himself legislative power until a new parliament was sworn in.[23] This act (technically) made Morsi Egypt's undisputed power holder.

When court rulings threatened a second constitutional assembly, the makeup of which was favorable to Morsi and the FJP, Morsi issued constitutional declaration that protected it, as well as himself, from court rulings.[24] When mass protests broke out,[25] Morsi used the ensuing political crisis to forcibly ratify a theocratic constitution.[26] Violent protests against Morsi erupted with growing regularity, the economy deteriorated, lines for gas extended around city blocks, and power shortages created outages lasting many hours on end.[27] On June 30, 2013, only one year after the inauguration of Morsi, millions of Egyptians took to the streets demanding Morsi's resignation. When he refused to compromise, the military ousted Morsi from power on July 3, 2013.

After negotiations between the new government and the Brotherhood (whose members filled city streets in protest of the coup)[28] failed, Egyptian security forces stormed two protest camps and violently cleared the protesters on August 14, 2013, killing at least 800 civilians.[29] After the Rabaa massacre, marking the end of the Arab Spring, the government arrested tens of thousands of Brotherhood leaders and supporters and killed at least 1,000.[30] Then, following a massive car bomb in al-Mansoura that killed 15 people in December 2013, the Egyptian government labeled the Muslim Brotherhood a terrorist group.[31] In August 2014, an Egyptian court ruled that the FJP must be dissolved and ordered the government to seize its assets.[32] Following the court ruling, members of the political party were forced underground or exiled to other countries.

Global Reach

Although suppressed and covert for most of its history, the Muslim Brotherhood has nonetheless expanded its activities throughout the Muslim world, most significantly in Egypt's neighboring countries—Lebanon, Syria, Iraq, Sudan, Jordan, and the Palestinian territories—in addition to the Arabian Peninsula: Saudi Arabia, Kuwait, Yemen, Oman, and Bahrain. However, offshoots and affiliates have remained largely autonomous from their Egyptian base, and operate independently from one another, making it inaccurate to characterize the Brotherhood as a coherent, homogenous organization.[33]

Palestinian Territories

In what is today the Palestinian territories, the movement began in 1935 as primarily a social and religious group – one which included the creation of associations, schools, and the establishment of mosques intended to "bring an Islamic generation up."[34] It was only in 1987, in the context of the first *Intifada* (Palestinian uprising), that the Brotherhood became politicized with the Islamic Resistance Movement, more commonly known as Hamas.[35]

Since that time, Hamas has evolved into a powerful geopolitical actor. It ranks as one of the world's most significant extremist organizations, with its military faction – the Izz al-Din al-Qassam Brigades – carrying out a multitude of attacks against Israeli civilian targets and population centers over the past three decades.[36] In late 2006, the organization unexpectedly dominated legislative elections in the Gaza Strip, and thereafter took control of the territory. Hamas' administration of Gaza has been fraught with controversy, and humanitarian conditions there have markedly worsened in recent years as a result of its misrule.[37] Attacks against Israel have also continued, prompting periodic military confrontations and clashes – including 2012's Operation Pillar of Defense and 2014's Operation Protective Edge – designed to erode the movement's military capabilities.

Hamas maintains a contentious relationship with the Palestinian Authority, which governs the Gaza Strip. Repeated attempts for a "unity government" between the two factions (the most recent in September 2020) have so far failed to establish a lasting truce. Notably, Hamas has evolved to function independently from the Brotherhood's original branch in neighboring Egypt, and now maintains a number of positions at odds with those of its Egyptian counterpart – most prominently a significant and ongoing strategic dialogue with the Islamic Republic of Iran, which (despite political differences in recent years) continues to provide the group with funding and materiel.[38]

Syria

Following the 1963 Ba'athist coup in Syria, the Syrian Muslim Brotherhood (SMB) was outlawed and its leader, Isam al-Attar, was exiled. In 1970, the Brotherhood became the main opposition force challenging the ruling Assad clan. This relationship would change several times between then and now, however, oscillating between open armed struggle, devastating repression,[39] and public mutual support. Notably, in 1979, Brotherhood members killed over 80 unarmed Alawi cadets at a military training facility in Aleppo, leading the Assad regime to issue Law Number 49 in 1980. Under Law 49, membership in or association with the SMB became a capital crime.[40] Part of the Brotherhood's acquiescence to the Assad regime in the late 1990s was a product of the revision of Law Number 49, as well as the promise of freedom or repatriation for imprisoned and foreign-exiled Brotherhood members.

The SMB and its then-newly elected leader, Riad al-Shaqfa, supported the Assad regime until the Syrian uprising began in 2011, when the Brotherhood joined the anti-regime movement after the Assad regime killed thousands of protestors.[41] During the course of the Syrian civil war, SMB members chaired relief committees that distributed aid and money to the rebels.[42] In the fall of 2014, al-Shaqfeh stepped down and was replaced as SMB head by Mohammad Hikmat Walid.[43] Over the course of the war, continuing to today, the Syrian Muslim Brotherhood's influence has diminished while much of its leadership remains exiled in Istanbul.[44] However, despite Brotherhood membership remaining punishable by death, some members are reportedly returning to opposition-held regions of the country.[45]

Jordan

In Jordan, the Brotherhood was the country's oldest and largest Islamist organization. The group was initially approved by the government as a charity organization affiliated with the Egyptian Muslim Brotherhood. Known as the Muslim Brotherhood Group (MBG) since 1953, it was authorized as an Islamic religious organization.[46]

Like the SMB, the MBG positioned itself as a leading player in the 2011 anti-government protests that accompanied the onset of the "Arab Spring" by denouncing public corruption and poverty.[47] This drew the attention and ire of King Abdullah II, who has spent the last decade restricting the abilities of the MBG to participate in political and social life while demonizing the group in various media outlets.[48] In July 2020, the Jordanian government formally dissolved the MBG (a decision the group has announced it would appeal).[49] The Brotherhood's political arm in Jordan, the Islamic Action Front (IAF), as well as offshoots born from interparty divisions (including the National Congress Party and the Muslim Brotherhood Society) have attempted to secularize their messages and curry favor from the Jordanian monarchy, likely so they can remain politically relevant and advance their policy goals.[50] Notably, despite the ban on the MBG, the IAF remains a legal entity and has announced that it will participate in the country's November 2020 parliamentary elections.[51]

Iraq

In Iraq, the Brotherhood-affiliated Iraqi Islamic Party (IIP) was established in 1960 and banned almost immediately thereafter by Iraqi nationalists. It remained outlawed under Saddam Hussein's rule (1979-2003), with repressive measures forcing the group underground. The IIP reemerged after the 2003 U.S.-led invasion, and has since grown to become the largest Sunni political party in Iraq, displaying an ambiguous posture, and voicing harsh criticism of the U.S. and Iraq's new political elites, all while still participating in the transitional process.[52] At the outset of the "Arab Spring," the IIP organized demonstrations and strived to gain support for its Islamist messaging among supporters.[53] On May 12, 2018, Iraq held its first parliamentary elections since the fall of the Islamic State. IIP candidates won 14 of 329 seats, the party's worst performance since its return in 2003. The party attributed its weak showing to a global trend of disillusion toward organized politics.[54] There is currently no indicator of how it hopes to regain lost ground in future elections.

Gulf States

While the Brotherhood was being targeted by successive Egyptian regimes,[55] the organization established branches in several countries in the Gulf. Many exiled Brothers found shelter in Saudi Arabia, but their Islamist doctrine came to be seen as a challenge to the country's official *Wahhabbi* creed. In the mid-2000s, the movement thrived in the Kingdom with support from the Saudi ruling family, who granted asylum to exiled leaders, provided it financial support,[56] and helped establish Saudi-based Islamic charities. However, with the ouster of Morsi in the wake of the 2013 Egyptian revolution and the rise of Mohammed bin Salman (known colloquially as MbS) within the Saudi royal family, the Saudi government has increasingly clamped down on Brotherhood activity. While relations between the Morsi government and the Saudi crown were not inherently antagonistic, the latter valued stability, and has welcomed the country's post-religious order.[57] This generated division between the Saudi crown and prominent Muslim Brotherhood clerics, some of whom were previously sympathetic to the government. The culmination came in March 2014, when Saudi Arabia designated the Muslim Brotherhood as a terrorist organization.[58] That estrangement has persisted, and has been exacerbated in recent years by the Saudi-led boycott of Qatar.[59]

Elsewhere, such as in the United Arab Emirates and Qatar, the Brotherhood has relied on a strong intellectual and media presence to influence local populations.[60] Qatar is the GCC's most prominent funder and defender of the MB, a position which has affected its regional relations.[61] As of spring 2020, Qatar's open door policy toward the Muslim Brotherhood (entailing financial and weapons aid,[62] political backing, and provision of safe haven)[63] remains unaltered.

With the exception of Oman, where the Brotherhood has faced severe crackdowns, the movement also managed to gain seats in parliaments across the region: in Kuwait via the Hadas movement,[64] and in Yemen through al-Islah ("Congregation for Reform").[65] Bahrain's Al-Minbar historically had success in the country's 2010 and 2014 Council of Representatives elections, but is now less prominent and only won one seat in the latest election, held in 2018. Al-Menbar, as well as al-Islah, another organization linked to the Muslim Brotherhood, have formally distanced themselves from "any external religious ideology."[66]

Algeria

In Algeria, the Brotherhood emerged in the 1950s as a religious association, members of which joined the uprising against the French during that country's war for independence (1954-1962). Its founders, Abdellatif Soltani and Ahmed Sahnoun, were reportedly inspired by the work of Qutb,[67] and in 1989 formed a political party, the Movement for an Islamic Society (MSI, also known as Hamas, a nickname still in use today). In 1997, Hamas changed its name to the Movement of Society for Peace (MSP) and its slogan from "Islam is the solution" to "Peace is the solution" (amongst other reforms), so that the group could continue operating in the country even as outwardly Islamic parties were banned from politics.[68] Throughout the Algerian civil war (1991-2002), it chose not to go to war with the government alongside other Islamist organizations, and instead worked with it through formal political mechanisms.[69]

From its founding in the 1990s to 2013, the MSP grew increasingly more relevant to Algerian politics. In 1999, MSP leadership backed the nomination and election of Abdelaziz Bouteflika, despite evidence that the election was fraudulent and significant grassroots opposition.[70] MSP party members would later hold positions of influence in Bouteflika's government.[71]

Between May 2013, when the MSP came under new leadership with the rise of Abderrazak Makri, and now, the party has wavered in its support for the central government. It boycotted the 2014 presidential elections, announced a candidate for the same race in 2019, and then later backed out.[72] In parliamentary elections held the same year, MSP won 33 seats after first moving to oppose the Bouteflika administration in 2017, only to later back it.[73]

Tunisia

In Tunisia, the Brotherhood's activities are tied to the political party Ennahda (the Renaissance Party), which was founded in 1989.[74] Formerly outlawed during the Ben Ali regime, Ennahda formally relaunched during the 2011 "Jasmine Revolution"[75] and became a legal party. However, domestic opposition to Islamism has recently forced *Ennahda* to downplay its Islamism; in 2016, Ennahda leader Rachid Ghannouchi formally distanced the movement from political Islam, signaling that it would instead focus on *dawa* (outreach work). In the most recent 2018 municipal elections, Ennahda was able to claim victory alongside its coalition partner, Nidaa Tounes.[76] Despite the party's articulated commitment to move away from Islamism, Ennahda continues to support what would be considered traditional Islamist values.[77]

Ennahda, and more specifically Ghannouchi, has maintained a special relationship with Turkey and its president, Recep Tayyip Erdogan. Ennahda has been compared to Erdogan's Justice and Development Party (AKP), a party with clear Islamic roots which experts have referred to as "effectively the Turkish arm of the Muslim Brotherhood." [78] Since the "Arab Spring," Ghannouchi has pushed for Tunisia to establish a closer relationship with Turkey. Despite some critical scrutiny over Ghannouchi's ties to Turkey, the Muslim Brotherhood, and Qatar,[79] Ennahda remains a powerful political force within Tunisian legislative politics.

Morocco

Until 2013, Morocco's ruling party, the Justice and Development Party (PJD),[80] represented the Moroccan branch of the Brotherhood. This bond, however, was severed after the 2013 military *coup d'état* that removed Morsi from power.[81] Since then, the PJD has repeatedly denied any connection to the Brotherhood.[82] In the country's most recent 2016 election, the PJD won 125 of the 395 total parliamentary seats.[83] The PJD remains influential in Moroccan government, and in 2017 Morocco's monarch, Mohammed VI named former PJD Secretary General Saad Eddine Othmani to the position of Prime Minister.[84]

Libya

The Libyan branch of the Muslim Brotherhood was established in Benghazi in 1949 by Egyptian Muslim Brotherhood members who had been exiled, when King Idris I offered them refuge from persecution. However, after seizing power in a coup in 1969, Muammar al-Qadhafi outlawed the movement. Nevertheless, the Brotherhood managed to maintain a vast network of sympathizers in Libya.[85] The Party of Justice and Construction (JCP), the political arm of the Brotherhood in Libya, formed in 2012, the year after Qadhafi's ouster, and has since gained seats in the country's legislature. It has made clear that it aspires to establish a Libyan *caliphate*.[86]

In the events leading up to the Libyan civil war, the JCP helped form the General National Congress (GNC) and the Government of National Salvation (GNS), both precursors the Libya Dawn

Coalition, one of the conflict's major warring factions.[87] When the Libya Dawn Coalition was dissolved in late 2015 to form the Government of National Accords (GNA), which is now the internationally recognized government of Libya, a number of GNC and GNS leaders joined its rank-and-file and now hold significant influence within it.[88]

Sudan

In Sudan, the Brotherhood branch formed the National Islamic Front (NIF) in 1985, participated in the country's 1986 election and thereafter supported the regime of dictator Omar Hassan al- Bashir.[89] The National Congress Party (NCP) was formally founded in 1998 and led by President Al Bashir following its split from the NIF. In 1999, after being removed from his position as Secretary-General of the NCP by Bashir, Hassan al-Tourabi founded the Popular National Congress Party (PNCP), an Islamist movement that the party claims is not affiliated with the MB movement.[90] Bashir was ousted in a military coup in April 2019.[91]

While a permanent government in Khartoum has not yet formed, the Sudanese transitional government has taken several steps to excise the influence of the Brotherhood. Following the coup, the NCP was disbanded, its militia neutralized, and dozens of its former leaders were arrested.[92] In December 2019, the transitional government announced that it was shuttering the offices of any organization designated as a terrorist group by the U.S. This included Hamas, which had previously used its relationship with al-Bashir to smuggle weapons to the Gaza Strip.[93] In May 2020, it was reported that the Sudanese government would quietly return five members of the violent Muslim Brotherhood offshoot Hasm (who were captured *en route* to Turkey) to Egyptian authorities.[94] However, statements released by Hamas in October 2020 indicate that the group still intends to operate in some underground capacity in Sudan.[95] As of this writing, it is unclear what effect Sudan's announcement of a normalization of ties with Israel will have on the country's Islamist *milieu*, including Hamas and remnants of the Brotherhood.

Europe

The Brotherhood has gained significant ground in Europe through regional forums like the Federation of Islamic Organizations in Europe, the Forum of European Muslim Youth and Student Organizations, and the European Council for Fatwa and Research.[96] Starting as early as the 1960s, group members and supporters moved to Europe and established a vast and sophisticated network of mosques, Islamic charities, and schools. Among them were those in England (the Muslim Association of Britain), France (the Union des Organisations Islamiques de France), Germany (the Islamische Gemeinschaft Deutschland) and Italy (the Unione delle Comunita' ed Organizzazioni Islamiche in Italia).[97] With considerable foreign funding and the tolerance of European governments eager to engage in a dialogue with Muslim minorities,[98] Brotherhood-related organizations have gained positions of prominence on the Continent's sociopolitical scene.

United States

In addition to its presence in Europe, the Brotherhood has also engaged Muslims in the United States, where its members have been located since the 1960s. The movement launched its first long-term strategy in 1975, focusing on proselytizing efforts and the creation of specific structures for youth and newly arrived Muslim immigrants in the U.S. Seeking to exert political influence at the state and federal levels, Muslim Brothers have been represented in multiple religious, civic and communal Muslim organizations in the country, including the Muslim Students' Association (MSA), the Islamic Society of North America (ISNA), the Islamic Circle of North America (ICNA), the Muslim American Society (MAS) and various other activist groups.[99]

In 2015, U.S. Senator Ted Cruz introduced legislation to designate the Muslim Brotherhood a Foreign Terrorist Organization (FTO) and, in 2019, the Trump administration reportedly considered making a similar designation following a visit from Egyptian president Sisi.[100] The previous year, in January 2018, the Trump administration designated two Brotherhood appendages, Harakat Sawa'd Misr (Hasm, or the "Arms of Egypt" Movement) and Liwa al-Thawra (Revolution Brigade, or Banner of the Revolution) as global terrorist organizations. It also designated Ismail Haniyeh, the leader of Hamas, as an international terrorist (Hamas has also been designated by the United States as a global terrorist organization.)[101] However, Senator Cruz's legislation did not pass,[102] and the Trump administration has not yet formally made the decision to move ahead with a blanket designation of the Brotherhood.

Turkey

Much of the Muslim Brotherhood's active leadership has relocated to Istanbul, where the organization and its supporters have found safe haven since the 2013 coup that toppled Morsi.[103] Since then, prominent members of Turkey's ruling AKP party - including now-President Tayyip Erdoğan himself - have provided Muslim Brotherhood members with support, including equipment and grants for asylum from Egypt.[104]

In 2019, when the Trump administration publicly considered designating the Muslim Brotherhood a terrorist organization, a spokesperson for the AKP stated that such a ruling would "damage democracy in the Middle East."[105] Erdoğan has, on several occasions, met with senior Hamas officials. Most recently, the Turkish president held a photo-op with Ismail Haniyeh, the current chief of the terror group, in September 2020.[106]

Recent Activity

Internal fissures and increasingly harsh pressure from the Sisi government has dramatically weakened the Brotherhood in Egypt since 2014.[107] When the Brotherhood's youth wing won internal elections in 2014, the group's "old guard" rejected the results.[108] The younger, "revolutionary" wing of the Brotherhood endorsed and encouraged the use of violence against Egyptian security forces and state infrastructure, and commissioned a Brotherhood *sharia* body to draft an Islamic legal defense of its violence.[109] Meanwhile, the older, more cautious wing argued that such violence would legitimize the state's crackdown and accused the young guard of defying the Brotherhood's internal hierarchy.

Within Egypt, some Brotherhood supporters are believed to

have joined comparatively low-profile militant groups such as Liwaa al-Thawra, Hasm, and the Popular Resistance Movement that have targeted security forces and state infrastructure.[110] While each organization has been involved in its own violent *tête-à-tête* with the Egyptian government and military, none have achieved their goal over overturning the Egyptian government, and their capacity to do appears limited.[111]

Since President Sisi's re-election victory in March 2018, the Muslim Brotherhood has continued to operate outside the political sphere in Egypt.[112] Sisi's subsequent crackdown has targeted a slew of former senior leadership, who have received harsh legal punishments, ranging from life in prison to the death penalty. The Egyptian government has adopted these draconian rulings based on the plaintiffs' membership in the Muslim Brotherhood or their tangential affiliation with it. The Sisi government's crackdown has drawn criticism from human rights organizations; for instance, Amnesty International referred to the mass death sentence given to 75 Muslim Brotherhood members in September 2018 as a "grotesque parody of justice."[113] In 2017, Human Rights Watch released a series of interviews with people detained by the Egyptian interior ministry. According to their accounts, they were tortured by Egyptian authorities while in detention on grounds that some were members of the Muslim Brotherhood.[114]

In the wake of Ezzat's arrest and detention, Ibrahim Mounir, the Muslim Brotherhood's "secretary general," has assumed the position of the organization's acting guide.[115] A member of the its more pragmatic arm, Mounir has, as of this writing, sought to reconcile with the organization's *shura* council and build consensus among its various factions – albeit with what appears to be only mixed success. [116]

Endnotes

1. For an overview of the Muslim Brotherhood's core ideology, see Hassan al-Banna's writings and memoirs, particularly the *Letter To A Muslim Student*, which develops the main principles of the movement. For the English translation, see http://www.jannah.org/articles/letter.html; see also Brynjar Lia, *The Society of the Muslim*

Brothers in Egypt: The Rise of an Islamic Mass Movement, 1928-1942 (New York; Ithaca Press, 1998) and Richard Paul Mitchell, *The Society of the Muslim Brothers* (London & New York: Oxford University Press, 1969).
2. Harvard Divinity School, "Religious Literacy Project: The Egyptian Muslim Brotherhood," n.d., https://rlp.hds.harvard.edu/faq/egyptian-muslim-brotherhood.
3. "Muslim Brotherhood," Counter Extremism Project, n.d., https://www.counterextremism.com/threat/muslim-brotherhood.
4. "Profile: Egypt's Muslim Brotherhood," *BBC News*, December 25, 2013, https://www.bbc.com/news/world-middle-east-12313405.
5. "Muslim Brotherhood," Counter Extremism Project.
6. Ibid.
7. For more on Sayyid Qutb, see Harvard Divinity School, "Sayyid Qutb," n.d., https://rlp.hds.harvard.edu/faq/sayyid-qutb.
8. Samer Shehata, "Egypt: The New Founders," Wilson Center, August 27, 2015, https://www.wilsoncenter.org/article/egypt-the-new-founders.
9. Youssef M. Ibrahim, "Egypt Arrests 15 in 2- Day Sweep Against Muslim Brotherhood," *New York Times*, June 20, 1995, https://www.nytimes.com/1995/07/20/world/egypt-arrests-15-in-2-day-sweep-against-muslim-brotherhood.html.
10. Nathan J. Brown et al., "Egypt's Controversial Constitutional Amendments," Carnegie Endowment for International Peace, March 23, 2007, http://carnegieendowment.org/files/egypt_constitution_webcommentary01.pdf .
11. "Freedom and Justice Party," *Jadaliyya*, July 10, 2017, https://www.jadaliyya.com/Details/24642.
12. "Freedom and Justice Party (Hizb Al-Hurriya Wal-Adala)," Tahrir Institute for Middle East Policy *Parliamentary Elections Monitor*, October 16, 2015, https://timep.org/parliamentary-elections-monitor/freedom-and-justice-party-%E1%B8%A5izb-al-%E1%B8%A5urriya-wal-adala/.
13. Sherif Tarek, "El- Katatni: From prisoner to speaker of the parliament," *Ahram Online* (Cairo), January 24, 2012, http://english.ahram.org.eg/NewsContentP/1/32600/Egypt/ElKatatni-From-prisoner-to-speaker-of-parliament.aspx.
14. Shehata, "Egypt: The New Founders."
15. Yolande Knell, "Egypt Candidate: Moderate Islamist, Abdul Moneim Aboul Fotouh," *BBC News*, April 13, 2012, https://www.bbc.com/news/world-middle-east-17356253.

16. David D. Kirkpatrick, "Egypt Elections Expose Divisions in Muslim Brotherhood," *New York Times*, June 19, 2011, https://www.nytimes.com/2011/06/20/world/middleeast/20egypt.html; Eric Trager, *Arab Fall: How the Muslim Brotherhood Won and Lost Egypt in 891 Days* (Washington: Georgetown University Press, 2016), 127-130.
17. Trager, *Arab Fall,* 126.
18. Ibid., 127- 130.
19. According to a rule banning candidates with prior criminal convictions from running in the elections. See Jeffrey Fleishman, "Egypt disqualifies 3 leading presidential candidates," *Los Angeles Times,* April 14, 2012, https://www.latimes.com/world/la-xpm-2012-apr-14-la-fg-egypt-candidates-20120415-story.html.
20. Although some contest the electoral results. See Borzou Daragahi, "Egypt nervously awaits election results," *Financial Times*, June 22, 2012, https://www.ft.com/content/a17de564-bc5b-11e1-a470-00144feabdc0.
21. Trager, *Arab Fall,* 140-141.
22. Ernesto Londoño, "Egypt's Morsi Replaces Military Chiefs in Bid to Consolidate Power," *Washington Post*, August 12, 2012, https://www.washingtonpost.com/world/middle_east/egypts-morsi-orders-retirement-of-defense-minister-chief-of-staff-names-vp/2012/08/12/a5b26402-e497-11e1-8f62-58260e3940a0_story.html.
23. Trager, *Arab Fall,* 159-161.
24. David Rohde, "Morsi's Power Grab: 'There was a Disease but This Is Not the Remedy,'" *The Atlantic*, November 24, 2012, https://www.theatlantic.com/international/archive/2012/11/morsis-power-grab-there-was-a-disease-but-this-is-not-the-remedy/265555/.
25. Stephanie McCrummen and Abigail Hauslohner, "Egyptians Take Anti-Morsi Protests to Presidential Palace," *Washington Post*, December 4, 2012, https://www.washingtonpost.com/world/middle_east/egyptians-take-anti-morsi-protests-to-presidential-palace/2012/12/04/b16a2cfa-3e40-11e2-bca3-aadc9b7e29c5_story.html.
26. Miriam Rizk and Osman El Sharnoubi, "Egypt's Constitution 2013 vs. 2012: A Comparison," *Ahram Online* (Cairo), December 12, 2013, http://english.ahram.org.eg/NewsContent/1/0/88644/Egypt/0/Egypts-constitution--vs--A-comparison.aspx.
27. David D. Kirkpatrick, "Short of Money, Egypt Sees Crisis on Fuel and Food," *New York Times*, March 30, 2013, https://www.nytimes.com/2013/03/31/world/middleeast/egypt-short-of-money-sees-cri-

sis-on-food-and-gas.html.

28. Carrie Rosefsky Wickham, "The Muslim Brotherhood After Morsi," *Foreign Affairs*, July 11, 2013, https://www.foreignaffairs.com/articles/egypt/2013-07-11/muslim-brotherhood-after-morsi.
29. Ali Omar, "Muslim Brotherhood responds to NCHR Rabaa report," *Daily News Egypt*, March 8, 2014, https://wwww.dailynewssegypt.com/2014/03/08/muslim-brotherhood-responds-nchr-rabaa-report/.
30. "Rabaa: The Massacre That Ended the Arab Spring," *Middle East Eye*, August 14, 2018, https://www.middleeasteye.net/news/rabaa-massacre-ended-arab-spring.
31. Salma Abdelaziz and Steve Almasy, "Egypt's interim Cabinet officially labels Muslim Brotherhood a terrorist group," *CNN*, December 25, 2013, https://www.cnn.com/2013/12/25/world/africa/egypt-muslim-brotherhood-terrorism/.
32. Lin Noueihed, "Egypt Court Dissolves Muslim Brotherhood's Political Wing." Reuters, August 10, 2014. https://www.reuters.com/article/us-egypt-brotherhood/egypt-court-dissolves-muslim-brotherhoods-political-wing-idUSKBN0G90AM20140810.
33. Mohamed-Ali Adroui, "The Unfinished History Between America and the Muslim Brotherhood," *Current Trends in Islamist Ideology*, July 12, 2019, https://www.hudson.org/research/15136-the-unfinished-history-between-america-and-the-muslim-brotherhood
34. Ziad Abu-Amr, "Hamas: A Historical and Political Background," *Journal of Palestine Studies* 22, no. 4, Summer 1993, 5-19.
35. See the Palestinian Territories chapter of the American Foreign Policy Council's *World Almanac of Islamism.*
36. Office of the Director of National Intelligence, "Counterterrorism Guide: Hamas," n.d., https://www.dni.gov/nctc/groups/hamas.html.
37. See, for instance, Hugh Fitzgerald, "In Gaza, Hamas Beats and Tortures Those Who Protest Its Misrule," *New English Review*, March 31, 2019, https://www.newenglishreview.org/blog_direct_link.cfm?blog_id=68238.
38. See, for instance, Michael Bachner and TOI staff, "Iran said increasing Hamas funding to $30m per month, wants intel on Israel," *Times of Israel*, August 5, 2019, https://www.timesofisrael.com/iran-agrees-to-increase-hamas-funding-to-30-million-per-month-report/.
39. See the Syria chapter of the American Foreign Policy Council's *World Almanac of Islamism.*
40. Harvard Divinity School, "The Syrian Muslim Brotherhood," n.d., https://rlp.hds.harvard.edu/faq/syrian-muslim-brotherhood.
41. Khaled Yacoub Oweis, "Syria's Muslim Brotherhood rise from

the ashes," Reuters, May 6, 2012, https://www.reuters.com/article/us-syria-brotherhood-idUSBRE84504R20120506; Youssef Sheikho, "The Syrian Opposition's Muslim Brotherhood Problem," *Al-Akhbar* (Cairo), April 10, 2013, http://english.al-akhbar.com/node/15492.

42. Liz Sly, "Syria's Muslim Brotherhood Is Gaining Influence over Anti- Assad revolt," *Washington Post*, May 12, 2012, https://www.washingtonpost.com/world/syrias-muslim-brotherhood-is-gaining-influence-over-anti-assad-revolt/2012/05/12/gIQAtIoJLU_story.html.
43. Raphaël Lefèvre, "New Leaders for the Syrian Muslim Brotherhood," Carnegie Middle East Center, December 11, 2014, https://carnegie-mec.org/2014/12/11/new-leaders-for-syrian-muslim-brotherhood-pub-57453.
44. Yehuda U. Blanga, "The Role of the Muslim Brotherhood in the Syrian Civil War," *Middle East Policy* XXIV, no. 3, Fall 2017, https://mepc.org/journal/role-muslim-brotherhood-syrian-civil-war.
45. Dasha Afanasieva, "Banned in Syria, Muslim Brotherhood members trickle home," Reuters, May 7, 2015, https://www.reuters.com/article/us-syria-crisis-brotherhood/banned-in-syria-muslim-brotherhood-members-trickle-home-idUSKBN0NR20Y20150507
46. Osama Al Sharif, "Unprecedented rifts splits Jordan's Muslim Brotherhood," Al-Monitor, March 3, 2015, https://www.al-monitor.com/pulse/originals/2015/03/jordan-muslim-brotherhood-revoke-membership-crisis.html.
47. Heather Murdock, "Muslim Brotherhood Sees Opportunity in Jordan," *Washington Times*, March 1, 2011, https://www.washingtontimes.com/news/2011/mar/1/muslim-brotherhood-sees-opportunity-in-jordan/.
48. See, generally, the Jordan chapter in the American Foreign Policy Council's *World Almanac of Islamism*, http://almanac.afpc.org/Jordan
49. "Jordanian court dissolves Muslim Brotherhood branch," *al-Monitor*, July 16, 2020, https://www.al-monitor.com/pulse/originals/2020/07/jordan-muslim-brotherhood-headquarters-dissolve-split-egypt.html
50. See, generally, the Jordan chapter in the American Foreign Policy Council's *World Almanac of Islamism*, http://almanac.afpc.org/Jordan
51. "Jordan's Muslim Brotherhood to take part in parliamentary elections," *Times of Israel*, September 21, 2020, https://www.timesofis-

rael.com/jordans-muslim-brotherhood-to-take-part-in-elections/
52. See the Iraq chapter of the American Foreign Policy Council's *World Almanac of Islamism;* for further details, see "Iraqi Islamic Party," globalsecurity.org, n.d., http://www.globalsecurity.org/military/world/iraq/iip.htm.
53. Mustafa Al- Kadhimi, "Iraq Protests Present Muslim Brotherhood with Opportunity," *Al-Monitor*, January 9, 2013, https://www.al-monitor.com/pulse/originals/2013/01/muslim-brotherhood-iraq.html.
54. Ben Wedeman and Laura Smith-Spark, " Polls close in first Iraqi elections since the defeat of ISIS," *CNN*, May 12, 2018, https://edition.cnn.com/2018/05/12/middleeast/iraq-elections-intl/index.html; Omar Sattar, "Iraq's Sunni lists approach coalition as one bloc," *Al-Monitor*, May 24, 2018, https://www.al-monitor.com/pulse/originals/2018/05/iraq-sunni-coalition-election.html#ixzz5lxBIDZJJ; Muhanad Seloom, "An Unhappy Return: What the Iraqi Islamic Party Gave Up to Gain Power," Carnegie Middle East Center, November 19, 2018, https://carnegie-mec.org/2018/11/19/unhappy-return-what-iraqi-islamic-party-gave-up-to-gain-power-pub-77747
55. Matthew Hedges and Giorgio Cafiero, "The GCC and the Muslim Brotherhood: What Does the Future Hold?" *Middle East Policy* XXIV, no. 1, Spring 2017, https://mepc.org/journal/gcc-and-muslim-brotherhood-what-does-future-hold.
56. John Mintz and Douglas Farah, "In Search of Friends Among the Foes: U.S. Hopes to Work with Diverse Group," *Washington Post*, September 11, 2004, https://www.washingtonpost.com/wp-dyn/articles/A12823-2004Sep10.html.
57. Laurie A. Brand and Joshua Stacher, "Why two islands may be more important to Egyptian regime stability than billions in Gulf aid," *Washington Post*, April 25, 2016, https://www.washingtonpost.com/news/monkey-cage/wp/2016/04/25/why-two-islands-may-be-more-important-to-egyptian-regime-stability-than-billions-in-persian-gulf-aid/
58. Kristin Smith Diwan, "The future of the Muslim Brotherhood in the Gulf," Project on Middle East Political Science, October 2017, https://pomeps.org/wp-content/uploads/2017/10/POMEPS_GCC_Qatar-Crisis.pdf; Mustapha Ajbaaili, "Saudi: Muslim Brotherhood a terrorist group," *Al Arabiya*, March 7, 2014, https://english.alarabiya.net/en/News/middle-east/2014/03/07/Saudi-Arabia-declares-Muslim-Brotherhood-terrorist-group
59. Patrick Wintour, "Gulf Plunged into Diplomatic Crisis as Countries

Cut Ties with Qatar," *Guardian* (London), June 5, 2017, https://www.theguardian.com/world/2017/jun/05/saudi-arabia-and-bahrain-break-diplomatic-ties-with-qatar-over-terrorism

60. See the United Arab Emirates and Qatar chapters of the American Foreign Policy Council's *World Almanac of Islamism.*
61. Hedges and Cafiero, "The GCC and the Muslim Brotherhood: What Does the Future Hold?"
62. "Egypt to repay $2.5 bln Qatari deposit at end-Nov-Cbank source," Reuters, November 6, 2014, https://www.reuters.com/article/egypt-qatar-deposits/egypt-to-repay-2-5-bln-qatari-deposit-at-end-nov-cbank-source-idUSL6N0SW1U420141106.
63. Simone Foxman, "Why the Breach Between Saudis and Qatar-is Goes On and On," *Bloomberg*, March 20, 2018, https://www.bloomberg.com/news/articles/2018-03-20/why-the-breach-between-saudis-qataris-goes-on-and-on-quicktake.
64. See the Kuwait chapter of the American Foreign Policy Council's *World Almanac of Islamism.*
65. See the Yemen chapter of the American Foreign Policy Council's *World Almanac of Islamism*; Amr Hamzawy, "Between Government and Opposition: The Case of the Yemeni Congregation for Reform," Carnegie Endowment for International Peace *Carnegie Papers* no. 18, November 2009, https://carnegieendowment.org/files/yemeni_congragation_reform.pdf.
66. "Muslim Brotherhood in Bahrain," Counter Extremism Project, n.d., https://www.counterextremism.com/content/muslim-brotherhood-bahrain
67. Martin Evans and John Phillips, *Algeria: Anger of the Dispossessed* (New Haven: Yale University Press, 2007), 77.
68. Amel Boubekeur, *Political Islam in Algeria* (Brussels: Centre for European Policy Studies, 2007).
69. Dalia Ghanem, "The Future of Algeria's Main Islamist Party," Carnegie Middle East Center, April 14, 2015, https://carnegie-mec.org/publications/?fa=59769
70. Jacqueline de Gier, "Angry protests but no surprises in Algeria's one-man election," *Guardian* (London), April 17, 1999, https://www.theguardian.com/world/1999/apr/17/6
71. See, for instance, Dalia Ghanem, "The Future of Algeria's Main Islamist Party," Carnegie Middle East Center, April 14, 2015, https://carnegie-mec.org/2015/04/14/future-of-algeria-s-main-islamist-party-pub-59769
72. Lamine Chikhi and Patrick Markey, "Algeria's ruling FLN, allies

win majority after vote marked by apathy," Reuters, May 5, 2017, https://fr.reuters.com/article/us-algeria-election-idUSKBN18116W; "Algeria Islamists name Abderrazak Makri candidate for president," *al-Jazeera* (Doha), January 26, 2019, https://www.aljazeera.com/news/2019/1/26/algeria-islamists-name-abderrazak-makri-candidate-for-president

73. Lamine Chikhi and Patrick Markey, "Algeria's ruling FLN, allies win majority after vote marked by apathy," Reuters, May 5, 2017, https://fr.reuters.com/article/us-algeria-election-idUSKBN18116W; https://www.aljazeera.com/news/2019/1/26/algeria-islamists-name-abderrazak-makri-candidate-for-president
74. Carlotta Gall, "Tunisian Islamic Party Re-elects Moderate Leader," *New York Times*, May 23, 2016, https://www.nytimes.com/2016/05/24/world/africa/tunisia-rachid-ghannouchi-ennahda.html; Aidan Lewis, "Profile: Tunisia's Ennahda Party," *BBC News*, October 25, 2011, https://www.bbc.com/news/world-africa-15442859.
75. "As Tunisians Cheer Egypt, Islamist Leader Returns," NPR, Janury 30, 2011, https://www.wbez.org/stories/as-tunisians-cheer-egypt-islamist-leader-returns/ba73444a-7059-4852-9371-ff915456c6d6.
76. Tarek Amara, "Tunisia's Ennahda claims victory in landmark local elections," Reuters, May 6, 2018, https://www.reuters.com/article/us-tunisia-election/tunisias-ennahda-claims-victory-in-landmark-local-elections-idUSKBN1I708Q.
77. Amel Al-Hilali, "Tunisia's Ennahda struggles to shake political Islam identity," *Al-Monitor*, December 13, 2017, https://www.al-monitor.com/pulse/originals/2017/12/tunisia-ennahda-muslim-brotherhood-terrorist-political-islam.html.
78. Monica Marks, "Erdogan Comes to Tunisia," *Foreign Policy*, June 6, 2013, https://foreignpolicy.com/2013/06/06/erdogan-comes-to-tunisia/; See also "The Muslim Brotherhood's Global Threat," Hearing of the House of Representatives Committee on Oversight and Government Reform Subcommittee on National Security, July 11, 2018, https://docs.house.gov/meetings/GO/GO06/20180711/108532/HHRG-115-GO06-Transcript-20180711.pdf
79. Raul Redondo, "The President of the Tunisian Parliament Faces Plenary Session Focused on Dubious Foreign Diplomacy," *Atalayar*, June 3, 2020, https://atalayar.com/en/content/president-tunisian-parliament-faces-plenary-session-focused-dubious-foreign-diplomacy.
80. Mohammed Hirichi, "Political Islam in Morocco: The Case of the

Party of Justice and Development (PJD)," Association of Concerned Africa Scholars, August 2007, http://concernedafricascholars.org/bulletin/issue77/hirchi/; "Moroccans favor conservative party instead of ushering in Islamic party," Associated Press, September 9, 2007, http://web.archive.org/web/20081014084028/http:/www.iht.com/articles/ap/2007/09/10/africa/AF-GEN-Morocco-Elections.php.

81. Idriss al-Kanboury, "Morocco's Islamists and the Egyptian Muslim Brotherhood," *Al Arabiya* (Riyadh), October 30, 2013, https://english.alarabiya.net/en/perspective/alarabiya-studies/2013/10/30/Morocco-s-Islamists-and-the-Egyptian-Muslim-Brotherhood.html.
82. Betty Chemier and Eduardo Zachary Albrecht, "The PJD in Morocco: Strengths and Weaknesses," *Fair Observer*, September 5, 2014, https://www.fairobserver.com/region/middle_east_north_africa/the-pjd-in-morocco-strengths-and-weaknesses-57321/; "Morocco ruling party says independent of Brotherhood," *Middle East Monitor*, January 11, 2015, https://www.middleeastmonitor.com/20150111-morocco-ruling-party-says-independent-of-brotherhood/.
83. Intissar Fakir, "Morocco's Islamist Party: Redefining Politics Under Pressure," Carnegie Endowment for International Peace, December 28, 2017, https://carnegieendowment.org/2017/12/28/morocco-s-islamist-party-redefining-politics-under-pressure-pub-75121.
84. "Morocco's king names PJD's Othmani as new prime minister," Reuters, March 17, 2017, http://www.reuters.com/article/us-morocco-politics-idUSKBN16O1WU?il=0.
85. Paul Cruickshank and Tim Lister, "Energized Muslim Brotherhood in Libya Eyes a Prize," *CNN*, March 25, 2011, http://articles.cnn.com/2011-03-25/world/libya.islamists_1_moammar-gadhafi-libyan-regime-benghazi?_s=PM:WORLD.
86. Omar Ashour, "Libya's Muslim Brotherhood faces the future," *Foreign Policy*, March 9, 2012, https://foreignpolicy.com/2012/03/09/libyas-muslim-brotherhood-faces-the-future/.
87. "Muslim Brotherhood in Libya," Counter Extremism Project.
88. Ariel Cohen, "Libya Set For Strong Comeback To Global Oil Markets," *Forbes*, October 2, 2020, https://www.forbes.com/sites/arielcohen/2020/10/02/libya-may-stage-a-strong-comeback-to-global-oil-markets/#342581df362d
89. Gabriel R. Warburg, "The Muslim Brotherhood in Sudan: From Reforms to Radicalism," Project for the Research of Islamist Movements (PRISM), August 2006, http://www.e-prism.org/images/Mus-

lim_BROTHERS.PRISM.pdf.

90. "Hassan Abdallah al-Turabi," Global Security, October 7, 2016, http://www.globalsecurity.org/military/world/sudan/turabi.htm.
91. Khalid Abdelaziz, "Sudan's Bashir ousted by military; protesters demand civilian government," Reuters, April 11, 2019, https://www.reuters.com/article/us-sudan-politics/sudans-bashir-ousted-by-military-protesters-demand-civilian-government-idUSKCN1RN0AY.
92. Alex de Waal, "In Sudan, Bashir is Out, Army Takes Over," *New York Times*, April 11, 2019, https://www.nytimes.com/2019/04/11/opinion/sudan-bashir-out.html.
93. Benjamin Weinthal, "Sudan will close office of terrorist groups Hezbollah, Hamas," *Jerusalem Post*, December 16, 2019, https://www.jpost.com/international/sudan-will-close-office-of-terrorist-groups-hezbollah-hamas-611050; Jonathan Schanzer, "Israel's next peace deal will be with Sudan," *New York Post*, September 22, 2020, https://nypost.com/2020/09/22/israels-next-peace-deal-will-be-with-sudan/
94. "Sudan to hand Muslim Brotherhood members to Egypt," *Middle East Monitor*, May 7, 2020, https://www.middleeastmonitor.com/20200507-sudan-to-hand-muslim-brotherhood-members-to-egypt/
95. Ali Hashem, "Hamas leader: 'Sudan has never failed us," *al-Monitor*, October 5, 2020, https://www.al-monitor.com/pulse/originals/2020/10/hamas-leader-uae-israel-sudan-normalization-kadoomi.html
96. Lorenzo Vidino, "The Muslim Brotherhood's Conquest of Europe," *Middle East Quarterly* XII, no. 1 (Winter 2005), 25-34, https://www.meforum.org/687/the-muslim-brotherhoods-conquest-of-europe.
97. Ibid.
98. Ibidem.
99. Adroui, "The Unfinished History Between America and the Muslim Brotherhood."
100. "White House to designate Muslim Brotherhood terrorist organization," *BBC News*, April 30, 2019, https://www.bbc.com/news/world-us-canada-48111594
101. U.S. Embassy in Egypt, "Secretary Tillerson Designates HASM & Liwa Al-Thawra as Specially Designated Global Terrorists," January 31, 2018, https://eg.usembassy.gov/secretary-tillerson-designates-hasm-liwa-al-thawra-specially-designated-global-terrorists/; "U.S. State Department designates Hamas leader as terrorist," Reu-

ters, January 31, 2018, https://www.reuters.com/article/us-usa-palestinians-hamas/u-s-state-department-designates-hamas-leader-as-terrorist-idUSKBN1FK2IA; "Hamas," Counter Extremism Project, n.d., https://www.counterextremism.com/threat/hamas

102. Muslim Brotherhood Terrorist Designation Act of 2015, S. 2230, 114th Congress, November 3, 2015, https://www.govtrack.us/congress/bills/114/s2230
103. Mohammad Abdel Kader, "Turkey's relationship with the Muslim Brotherhood," *Al-Arabiya* (Riyadh), October 14, 2013, https://english.alarabiya.net/en/features/2013/10/14/Turkey-s-relationship-with-the-Muslim-Brotherhood
104. "Muslim Brotherhood in Turkey," Counter Extremism Project, n.d., https://www.counterextremism.com/content/muslim-brotherhood-turkey
105. "Turkey's AK Party: U.S. move against Muslim Brotherhood would damage democracy in Middle East," Reuters, April 30, 2019, https://www.reuters.com/article/us-usa-trump-muslimbrotherhood-turkey/turkeys-ak-party-u-s-move-against-muslim-brotherhood-would-damage-democracy-in-middle-east-idUSKCN1S62JX
106. "Erdogan and Hamas: 'He's presenting himself as leader of Muslim world,'" *Financial Times*, September 8, 2020, https://www.ft.com/content/7447e141-3d3f-4d98-953d-179e15909a7e
107. Eric Trager and Marina Shalabi, "The Brotherhood Breaks Down: Will the Group Survive the Latest Blow?" *Foreign Affairs*, January 17, 2016, https://www.foreignaffairs.com/articles/egypt/2016-01-17/brotherhood-breaks-down.
108. Tadros, Samuel, "The Brotherhood Divided," Hudson Institute. Hudson Institute, August 20, 2015, https://www.hudson.org/research/11530-the-brotherhood-divided.
109. Awad, Mokhtar, "The Rise of the Violent Muslim Brotherhood," Current Trends (27 Jul. 2017): https://www.hudson.org/research/13787-the-rise-of-the-violent-muslim-brotherhood.
110. Awad, Mokhtar, "The Rise of the Violent Muslim Brotherhood," Current Trends (27 Jul. 2017): https://www.hudson.org/research/13787-the-rise-of-the-violent-muslim-brotherhood.
111. U.S. State Department Country Reports on Terrorism 2019, "Egypt," June 24, 2020, https://www.state.gov/reports/country-reports-on-terrorism-2019/egypt/; U.S. State Department Country Reports on Terrorism 2018, "Egypt," https://www.state.gov/reports/country-reports-on-terrorism-2018/#Egypt; U.S. State Department Country Reports on Terrorism 2017, "Egypt," https://www.state.

gov/reports/country-reports-on-terrorism-2017/

112. Davidson, John, and Ahmed Tolba, "Egypt's Sisi wins 97 percent in election with no real opposition," *Reuters*, April 2, 2018, https://www.reuters.com/article/us-egypt-election-result/egypts-sisi-wins-97-percent-in-election-with-no-real-opposition-idUSKCN1H916A.
113. Michaelson, Ruth, and Adham Youssef, "Egypt sentences 75 Muslim Brotherhood leaders to death," *The Guardian*, September 8, 2018, https://www.theguardian.com/world/2018/sep/08/egypt-sentences-75-to-death-in-rabaa-massacre-mass-trial
114. "Torture and National Security in al-Sisi's Egypt," Human Rights Watch, September 5, 2017, https://www.hrw.org/sites/default/files/report_pdf/egypt0917_web.pdf
115. "The Succession Crisis of the Muslim Brotherhood and Their Future Orientation," *European Eye on Radicalization*, October 2, 2020, https://eeradicalization.com/the-succession-crisis-of-the-muslim-brotherhood-and-their-future-orientation/
116. "The Succession Crisis of the Muslim Brotherhood and Their Future Orientation," *European Eye on Radicalization*, October 2, 2020, https://eeradicalization.com/the-succession-crisis-of-the-muslim-brotherhood-and-their-future-orientation/; "Muslim Brotherhood suffers internal rifts, dismiss Secretary General Mahmoud Hussein," *Egypt Today*, September 16, 2020, https://www.egypttoday.com/Article/1/91998/Muslim-Brotherhood-suffers-internal-rifts-dismiss-Secretary-General-Mahmoud-Hussein

71 Tablighi Jama'at

Quick Facts

Geographical Areas of Operation: East Asia, Eurasia, Europe, the Middle East and North Africa, South Asia, and Sub-Saharan Africa
Numerical Strength (Members): Estimated from 12 to 80 million
Leadership: Unknown
Religious Identification: Sunni Islam

Quick Facts Courtesy of 2009 Stratfor Report: Tablighi Jama'at: An Indirect Line to Terrorism

Introduction

Tablighi Jama'at is a vast, transnational, apolitical Sunni Islamic propagation and re-pietization organization, originally founded in India, which has a major support base in South Asia. It is estimated to be active in at least 150 nations throughout the world.[1] *Its annual assembly in Tongi, Bangladesh, is larger than any other in the Islamic world except for the Hajj itself, and estimates of Tablighi Jama'at's membership have ranged from 12 to 80 million.*[2] *Tablighi Jama'at has heretofore flown largely under the analytical radar, unlike other pan-Islamic groups such as Hizb ut-Tahrir and the Muslim Brotherhood, which are more transparently political and occupy a significantly higher profile. Nevertheless, Tablighi Jama'at's global presence and growing influence in both Muslim and non-Muslim majority countries make it arguably the modern world's most dynamic Islamist group.*

History & Ideology

Tablighi Jama'at, or TJ, began in British-ruled India, emerging from the Islamic Deobandi trend.[3] From its inception in 1926, the Deoband movement fused some aspects of Sufism with the study of the *hadith* and a strict adherence to *sharia* law, as well as advocating non-state-sponsored Islamic *dawa* (missionary activity).[4] The

Deoband movement emerged within the context of an increasingly self-aware Muslim minority in British India that felt caught between the resurgent Hindu majority and a small British-supported Christian missionary agenda.

Tablighi Jama'at's founder, Muhammad Ilyas al-Kandhlawi (1885-1944), graduated from the central Deoband *madrassa* in 1910 and, while working among the Muslim masses of Mewat, India (just south of Delhi) questioned whether education alone could renew Islam.[5] He eventually decided that "only through physical movement away from one's place could one leave behind one's esteem for life and its comforts for the cause of God."[6] Some have even described his movement as the missionary arm of the Deobandis.[7] Other Muslim groups in the subcontinent, notably the Barelvis, practiced missionary work—*tabligh*—in order to counter Hindu (and Christian) conversions of Muslims.[8] Ilyas believed that *tabligh* should be the responsibility of each and every individual Muslim.[9] He aimed to recreate the alleged piety and practice of Muhammad and his companions in the 7th century A.D. Ilyas was concerned not only with Hindu or Christian inroads into the Muslim community, but with stemming the rising tide of Westernization and secularization. Unlike other contemporary Islamic reformers, Ilyas did not believe that Islam could be reconciled with Western science, technology and political ideologies.[10]

In the mid-1920s, Ilyas enjoined upon his followers the practice of *gasht* (rounds): summoning Muslims who lived near a mosque to study the Quran and prayer. By the mid-1930s, Ilyas was promulgating a more detailed program of belief expression. This new doctrine included Islamic education, modest dress and appearance, rejection of other religions, propagating Islam, self-financing of *tabligh* trips, lawful means of earning a living, and strict avoidance of divisive and sectarian issues.[11]

Tablighi Jama'at's incursion into new territories follows a regular pattern. An initial "probing mission" is followed by entrenchment into several local mosques which are increasingly controlled by the organization and eventually either taken over by TJ or, barring that, supplanted by TJ-administered mosques.[12] From these mosques, the Tablighi Jama'at teams teach their beliefs and practices to local Muslims, initially approaching local religious leaders, then intellectuals and professionals, followed by businessmen. Lastly, TJ reaches out to the general Muslim community.[13] TJ finds its greatest following among the poor, who are often attracted to the movement's flexibility and openness.

Upon Mawlana Yusuf's death in 1965, Ilyas' grand-nephew Mawlana In 'am al-Hasan assumed leadership of the organization, and subsequently directed the group's activities for the following three decades. Then, beginning in 1995, and for the following decade or so, the organization was supervised by a collective leadership based at Nizamuddin, New Delhi and consisting of Mawlana Said al-Hasan (grandson of Yusuf), Zubair al-Hasan (son of In 'am) and Izhar al-Hasan (another relative of Ilyas').[14]

There is a typology of Islamic renewal/reform movements as 1) emulative (adopters of Western ideas); 2) assimilationist (attempting to reconcile Islamic and Western concepts and practices); or 3) rejectionist (allowing only strictly Islamic answers to the challenges of personal and collective life).[15] Tablighi Jama`at is clearly in the last category, based on its promulgation of strict adherence to the Quran and *sharia*, as well as its emphasis on emulating the lifestyle of Islam's founder, Muhammad. While undeniably conservative, even puritanical, whether TJ serves as an incubator for *jihad* remains a hotly debated topic.

The movement teaches *jihad* primarily as personal purification rather than as holy warfare.[16] This may be because, following Deobandi doctrine, Tablighi Jama'at preaches martial *jihad* as unwise when the *ummah* is weak, rather than disavowing violent *jihad* altogether.[17] However, practical connections between Tablighi Jama'at practitioners and acts of terror (such as the 1998 attacks in Dar es Salaam, Tanzania and Nairobi, Kenya), as well as anecdotal evidence that Ilyas himself believed he was "preparing soldiers" for *jihad*, paint the organization as more complex and possibly dangerous.[18]

Available data indicates that Tablighi Jama'at can be considered, ipso facto, a passive supporter of *jihadist* groups via its reinforcement of strict Islamic norms, intolerance of other religious traditions and unwavering commitment to Islamizing the entire planet in the preponderance of its global locations. TJ is much less political than its transnational Islamic rivals (*Hizb ut-Tahrir*, the Muslim Brotherhood, and the Gülen movement) and is much more focused on personal Muslim piety. As a result, TJ has so far largely escaped government suppression. Whether the organization ever decides to risk state tolerance by transforming into an active supporter of *jihadist* movements remains to be seen.

Global Reach

Tablighi Jama'at expanded out of South Asia and into at least 150 countries,[19] while broadening its mission under Mawlana Yusuf, Ilyas' son. Previously focused on simply re-instilling piety among Muslims, TJ subsequently also attempted to convert non-Muslims to Islam.[20] Most of the Muslim-majority nations of the world saw the infusion of some TJ presence between the end of World War II and the 1960s, with the exception of Soviet Central Asia (that region opened up to TJ influence after the end of the Cold War).[21] Tablighi Jama'at has been perhaps most successful in Africa, where it is known to be active in at least 35 countries on the continent.[22] The Jama'at has its own headquarters in every country it operates in, but its global spiritual center remains the *Markaz* (center) in Delhi.[23]

Africa

Gambia may be the hub of *Tablighi* activity in that part of the continent; the country's population of 1.5 million people is 90% Muslim.[24] TJ's popularity there was limited until the 1990s, when its missionaries' knowledge of English and the global Islamic resurgence made many Gambian Muslims, especially Gambian youth, more receptive to the organization's agenda. Some Gambian Muslim leaders, steeped in West Africa's heavily Sufi tradition, have expressed fears of Tablighi Jama'at coming to dominate the country.[25]

Tablighi Jama'at was introduced to Morocco in 1960 under the name Jama`at al-Tabligh wa-al-Da`wah (JTD), although it was not recognized by the government until 1975.[26] While proselytizing to Moroccan Muslims to re-Islamize their lives, JTD also makes hospital calls upon the sick and indigent. But TJ's focus is on increasing ritualized conduct—persuading Moroccans to eat, drink, prepare for bed and sleep, go to the market, and bathe in the proper ways, emulating the Prophet Muhammad.

Tablighi Jama'at has also committed several teams to Mali, Mauritania and Niger.[27] These three countries have a collective population of some 26 million people, the majority of them Muslim. By the 1990s, TJ had a substantial presence in a region more traditionally aligned with Sufism.[28] Shortly after 9/11, the government of Mali extradited 25 TJ members, though the crackdown did little to slow the group's growth in the region.[29] Tuareg tribal leaders have hastened to point out that the group's activities are totally unconnected to global *jihad*.[30] As the Tuareg's long-running rebellion exploded into a civil war in 2012, the impact of TJ's Salafist inroads became evident. Alongside the traditional Tuareg separatist group, Movement National Pour la Liberation de l'Azawad (MNLA), the Islamist Ansar ud-Dine (Defenders of the Faith) emerged. Ansar ud-Dine established harsh *sharia* law in areas it controlled, including the historic city of Timbuktu, and allied itself with al-Qaeda in the Islamic Maghreb.[31] Mali's Islamists were pushed back when the French intervened, but have continued their violent campaign with high-profile attacks.

South Africa has become a focal point for Tablighi Jama'at's work, despite 85 percent of its population identifying as Christian.[32] South Africa shares a legacy of British rule with India and Pakistan, and some two million of its people are of South Asian origin, of whom perhaps half are Muslim. TJ's "Sufi-lite" orientation and its Deobandi origins give it legitimacy with many South African Muslims, although the more Salafi/*Wahhabbi* groups dislike any hint of Sufism. These groups denigrate TJ for "un-Islamic" practices such as asking for Muhammad's intercession and promoting the reading of other books in tandem with the Quran. Many Muslims in South Africa, encouraged by TJ, became disenchanted with majority Christian rule after rules were relaxed on abortion, prostitution and other "immoral" activities. Tablighi Jama'at appears to have contributed to, and possibly sparked, the polarization of the Muslim community in Africa's southernmost country.[33]

Tablighi Jama'at has a significant presence in Eastern Africa. This is partly because of geographical proximity to the Subcontinent, but also because, like South Africa, there are substantial expatriate Indian and Pakistani communities in Tanzania, Kenya and Uganda. Perhaps one-third of Tanzania's population of 52 million is Muslim (but over 90 percent of the population on the islands of Zanzibar and Pemba is Muslim).[34] Kenya is home to about five million Muslims (out of a population of over 46 million, mostly Christian) and a sizeable 14 percent minority of the Ugandan population identify as Muslim.[35] Jamil Mukulu, the founder of Uganda's Allied Democratic Force (a Muslim separatist group that straddles the border between Uganda and the DRC) converted to Islam under the auspices of TJ. Founded in 1989, in recent years the group's presence in the Eastern DRC has grown and they have claimed responsibility for large-scale massacres. They are also linked to the militant *al-Shabaab* movement in Somalia.[36]

Tablighi Jama'at has been most visible in Tanzania, particularly in Zanzibar. Its message of "return to Islam" has been received as complementary to *Wahhabbi*-Salafi ideology. These two strains of Islamic renewal have come together in the preaching of militant TJ members such as Zahor Issa Omar, who, from his base on Pemba, travels to mainland Tanzania, Kenya and Uganda. Omar advocates *jihad* and is reportedly supported by Saudi *Wahhabbi* money.[37] More traditionalist Tanzanian Muslim leaders consider TJ an intruder bringing a foreign brand of Islam because of the group's opposition to full-blown Sufism.[38] There are anecdotal claims that TJ serves as a conveyor belt, at least indirectly, to Islamic terrorism.[39] Two of the al-Qaeda terrorists indicted in the 1998 bombings of the U.S. embassies in Dar es Salaam and Nairobi—Khalfan Khamis Mohammad and Ahmed Khalfan Ghailani—were Zanzibaris previously involved with Tablighi Jama'at.[40]

There is conflicting data on the relationship between the neo-*Wahhabbi* al-Shabaab militia which controls much of southern and central Somalia and Tablighi Jama'at. In 2009, a story surfaced that al-Shabaab had attacked a TJ mosque, killing at least five of its members.[41] However, in mid-2010 Indian media cited at least one terrorism analyst who claimed that TJ "has been very active in

Somalia, including sending terror fighters to al-Shabaab."[42]

Southeast Asia

Aside from Africa, one of Tablighi Jama'at's primary theaters of operation is Southeast Asia. TJ has been active in Indonesia since 1952, and in its far-eastern province of Irian Jaya (West Papua, the western half of the island of New Guinea) since 1988.[43] Originally a phenomenon of the working classes of large urban areas, it has increasingly penetrated the smaller cities, towns and villages.[44]

Tablighi Jama'at has tried, with limited success, to exploit the Jakarta-supported transmigration of thousands of Muslims from the rest of Indonesia to heavily-Christian West Papua.[45] TJ teams are stymied by indigenous Papuan customs (especially the local affinity for pork) and the large Christian missionary presence there.[46]

Tablighi Jama'at has, counterintuitively, been more successful in majority-Buddhist Thailand.[47] In 2003, some 100,000 Muslims from Southeast and South Asia came to a mass TJ gathering at Tha Sala in Nakhon Si Thammarat province.[48] In two decades, TJ has made inroads not only among the country's roughly 3 million Muslim citizens, but among Buddhists as well. One effective strategy has been to play up the Sufi, mystical side of TJ while also practicing asceticism, which is more familiar to the largely Buddhist population. However, TJ activities have also polarized the Thai Muslim communities; many traditionalist Muslims dislike the long absence of husbands and fathers on TJ mission treks, while more modernist Muslims reject TJ members as "fanatic mullahs" who neglect their families and have given up on the world. However, TJ in Thailand is well on its way to creating an independent mosque network, alternative to the existing national Muslim association created by the Thai government.[49]

The Indian Subcontinent

The heart of Tablighi Jama'at's presence remains in the Indian subcontinent, and the group is significantly prominent in Pakistan. In the 1980s, Pakistan's President, General Zia al-Haq, attended TJ's annual conclave in Raiwind (Pakistan's largest Sunni gathering, attended by hundreds of thousands of people).[50] General Javed Nasir, a former director of Pakistan's Inter-Services Intelligence, was an open member of TJ who expanded ISI engagement with religious extremists, including supporting Tablighi's proselytizing in Chechnya, Dagestan, and Xinjiang.[51]

Pakistan is one of the world's centers of radical Islam and home to numerous terrorist organizations. There is significant cross-fertilization between Tablighi Jama'at and these groups. While TJ's leadership insists that it eschews violence and rejects efforts by terrorist groups to infiltrate their ranks, there is significant evidence that groups like Lashkar-e-Taiba and Lashkar-e-Jhangvi attempt to recruit from TJ's ranks.[52] Harkat-al-Mujahideen, a Pakistani terrorist group active in Kashmir, was reportedly founded by TJ members; thousands of TJ members have since trained in its camps.[53] Anecdotal evidence has also documented that the Pakistani Taliban has in the past used death threats and kidnappings to force singers and actors to renounce their former professions and join TJ —indicating, if true, a troublesome intersection between South Asian Islamic militancy and ostensibly peaceful Islamic missionaries.[54]

Recently, there has been a noticeable uptick in Tablighi Jama'at's presence in Myanmar. The end of socialist autarky in 1988 was a pivotal moment for TJ's national growth. Missionaries from the Arabian Peninsula were able to visit and preach in Myanmar and increasing numbers of Burmese Muslims began travelling to Arabia for work and for the *Hajj*. Arabic and South Asian conservative Muslim styles of dress were on the rise and religious practices became more rigid. This increased conservatism and the rise of Tablighi Jama'at coincided with the Burmese military's push to cement a Burmese identity centered around Buddhist exclusivity. These changing social and political strands resulted in increased Buddhist-Muslim tensions leading to widespread social unrest and sectarian tensions. The movement's popularity in Myanmar has been at least partly built on disaffection with traditional hierarchies and leaders, and the unique opportunities such new affiliation affords.[55]

Russia

Moscow banned TJ activities in 2009 after the Russian Supreme Court recommended the group be added to the country's list of proscribed terrorist organizations. TJ has nonetheless continued to quietly operate within the Russian Federation. In February 2020, the

Russian Federal Secret Service arrested seven members of the group after a counter-terrorism operation in Moscow led to the dismantling of a terror cell closely affiliated with TJ.[56] According to Russian intelligence, the cell was engaging in various activities- recruiting new followers, dissemination of propaganda material and managing training camps- to assist in radicalization. [57]

Europe and the United States

There are an estimated 150,000 Tablighi Jama'at members in Europe, mainly in the UK (primarily among the country's large South Asian diaspora), France, and in Spain (where TJ members from North Africa predominate).[58] TJ's European headquarters is at the Markazi Mosque, which was established in 1978 by Hafiz Patel in the British Midlands.[59] Under Patel's influence, TJ had been a dominant influence in shaping Islam in the UK (Patel himself died in 2016).[60]

In 2007, Tablighi Jama'at's British branch announced plans to build a "mega mosque" with room for over 10,000 worshippers and 190-foot-tall minarets. The site was adjacent to the site of the London 2012 games and engendered substantial community opposition. In 2015, the government made a final decision to block the proposed project.[61]

Some analysts claim that there may be as many as 50,000 Muslims affiliated with Tablighi Jama'at in the United States.[62] They also claim that influential Islamic Circle of North America (ICNA) cooperates with, and hosts, TJ teams and activities.[63]

Tablighi Jama'at's role in the radicalization process is not clear. There have been numerous cases of Western recruits to al-Qaeda who had links to Tablighi Jama'at, but many left the group before committing violence. In the early 2000s, French intelligence asserted that about 80% of French radical Islamists were drawn from TJ's ranks. Richard Reid (the infamous "shoe bomber") had been involved in TJ in the United Kingdom. Several prominent American Muslims have been linked to TJ (including "American Taliban" John Walker Lindh, the "Lackawanna Six," and al-Qaeda operative Jose Padilla).[64] Lindh initially converted to Islam under the auspices of TJ but left them to join the Taliban in Pakistan. The Lackawanna Six, Yemeni-Americans who travelled to Afghanistan and fought with the Taliban, claimed to be members of TJ going to study in Pakistan. However, they were later shown to not have an affiliation with the organization.[65] Padilla was sentenced in 2014 to 21 years in prison charges of terrorism conspiracy and support, 12 years after he was arrested for participation in a plot to set off a radioactive dirty bomb.[66]

Recent Activity

In recent years, Mawlana Said has moved to the fore, once again giving TJ a single spiritual leader.[67] Yet it is also noteworthy that the world's most famous TJ personality is not Said but rather the group's *emir* in Pakistan, Hajji Muhammad Abd al-Wahhab, who was ranked by the Royal Islamic Strategic Studies Centre as the 10th most influential Muslim in the world in 2017.[68]

An internal struggle for leadership of the Tablighi Jama'at has emerged in recent years. A senior Tablighi leader named Professor Mushfiq Ahmed and his followers began a dispute with the current leader of the Bangladeshi branch of TJ, Syed Wasif Islam. This dispute reached new heights when the two factions engaged in a violent clash outside of the Kakrail Mosque in the Bangleshi capital of Dhaka in November 2017.[69]

Even though "the Tablighi's have apparently moved from a fringe phenomenon to the mainstream of Muslim society in South Asia," they still suffer significant backlash.[70] From one side, TJ is attacked by Barelvis, whose mystical Sufi leadership deems the group "a thinly disguised front for the Wahhabis."[71] Some Barelvi propagandists even accuse TJ of being a tool of the British, Americans, and Indians, employed to drain Muslims of *jihadist* zeal.[72] From the other side, the Ahl-i Hadith groups charge TJ with abandoning the concrete concerns of the world for a vacuous mysticism.[73] Jama`at-i Islami, the Islamic political organization established by Sayyid Abu ala `Ali Mawdudi, considers TJ a threat to its own powerful position in Pakistani society. They disparage TJ's alleged lukewarm attitude towards establishing a caliphate.[74]

TJ does not always succeed in its attempts at winning foreign hearts and minds for strict Sunni Islam. In early 2010, almost a hundred members of the organization were arrested in the Central Asian republic of Tajikistan and given lengthy jail sentences for violating local laws against miscreant versions of Islam.[75] In neighboring Kazakhstan, there have been numerous instances of TJ members advocating extremism, although human rights groups accuse that government of repressing religious activity to marginalize potential opposition.[76]

In recent years, TJ has emerged as a possible feeder to the Islamic State, among other extremist groups. A 2017 survey of the more than 50 Indians who had gone to fight for IS in Iraq and Syria found nearly a third were linked to TJ.[77] In one case, a group of French Muslims attended a TJ mosque before traveling to Syria to fight for IS.[78] Syed Rizwan Farook, who, along with his wife Tashfeen Malik committed the San Bernardino massacre in December 2015 and pledged loyalty to IS, had worshipped at a TJ mosque in San Bernardino.[79]

In August 2017, Tablighi Jama'at was banned from the *Darul Uloom* Deoband Islamic seminary. The organization will be reinstated only when the two factions of TJ warring over the title of the organization's *emir* end their dispute[80] – something that has not yet happened.

Most recently, India saw coronavirus breakouts at congregations of TJ members in 2020, involving both Indian nationals and a collection of foreigners from around the world. In response, the government vilified the organization and has virtually persecuted its supporters. For instance, in March, TJ was widely criticized for hosting a congregation in New Delhi, which was blamed for the spread of COVID in the media about two weeks after the event. In the aftermath of the gathering, some 3,500 TJ volunteers from 35 countries were detained at various government and private facilities.[81]

Ultimately, TJ is perhaps the modern world's most effective Islamic group at fostering pan-Islamic identity; one only has to be a Muslim to join and enter a "virtual transnational space" where every Muslim is immediately part of the Dar al-Islam.[82] As such, TJ is both a help and a hindrance to more political Islamic groups.

Endnotes

1. Stanly Johny, "Explained: Who Are the Tablighi Jamaat?" *The Hindu*, April 2, 2020, https://www.thehindu.com/news/national/explained-who-are-the-tablighi-jamaat-the-organisation-at-the-epicentre-of-coronavirus-outbreak-in-india/article31238915.ece.
2. Yoginder Sikand, *The Origins and Development of the Tablighi Jama'at, 1920-2000: A Cross-Country Comparative Survey* (Hyderabad, India: Orient Longman, 2002), 2-12; Pew Forum on Religion and Public Life, "Muslim Networks and Movements in Western Europe: Tablighi Jama'at," September 2010, https://www.pewforum.org/2010/09/15/muslim-networks-and-movements-in-western-europe-tablighi-jamaat/.
3. Sikand, *The Origins and Development of the Tablighi Jama'at, 1920-2000*, 2-77; Muhammad Khalid Masud, ed., *Travelers in Faith: Studies of the Tablighi Jama'at Movement as a Transnational Movement for Faith Renewal* (Leiden, The Netherlands: Brill, 2000), see especially "Introduction" and Chapter One, "The Growth and Development of the Tablighi Jama'at in India."
4. Brannon D. Ingram, "Understanding the Deoband Movement," *Maydan*, November 8, 2018, https://themaydan.com/2018/11/understanding-deoband-movement/.
5. Masud, *Travelers in Faith*, 6.
6. Ibid., 7.
7. Shireen Khan Burki, "The Tablighi Jama'at: Proselytizing Missionaries or Trojan Horse?" *Journal of Applied Security Research* 8, no. 1 (January-March 2013), 98-117.
8. Usha Sanyal, *Ahmad Riza Khan Barelwi: In the Path of the Prophet* (London, United Kingdom: Oneworld Publications, 2005), 129. In Arabic-speaking Islam, the word usually employed for such work is *da`wah*, but in Urdu, India, and, later, Pakistan, *tabligh* ("transmission, communication, propaganda") came to be substituted; founded by Ahmad Riza Khan Bareilly (1856-1921), the *Ahl al-Sunnat* ("Family of the Sunnah") movement—popularly known as Barelvis or Barelwis—advocated Islamic renewal much as did the Deobandis, although Barelvis were (and are) "more inclined toward the emotional or magical," according to Sanyal.
9. Sikand, *The Origins and Development of the Tablighi Jama'at, 1920-2000*, 48.
10. Ibid., 66ff.
11. Masud, *Travelers in Faith*, 10-11.
12. Farish A. Noor, "The Arrival and Spread of the Tablighi Jama'at

in West Papua (Irian Jaya), Indonesia," S. Rajaratnam School of International Studies and Nanyang Technological University *Working Paper* no. 191, 2010, http://library.berry.edu/title/arrival-and-spread-of-the-tablighi-jamaat-in-west-papua-irian-jaya-indonesia/oclc/600808308

13. Masud, *Travelers in Faith*, 134-5.
14. Thomas K. Gugler, "Parrots of Paradise - Symbols of the Super-Muslim: Sunnah, Sunnaization and Self-Fashioning in the Islamic Missionary Movements Tablighi Jama'at, Da'wat-e Islami and Sunni Da'wat-e Islami," Center for Modern Oriental Studies, July 31, 2008, https://www.academia.edu/208898/Parrots_of_Paradise_Symbols_of_the_Super_Muslim_Sunnah_Sunnaization_and_Self_Fashioning_in_the_Islamic_Missionary_Movements_Tablighi_Jamaat_Dawat_e_Islami_and_Sunni_Dawat_e_Islami?auto=download; Dietrich Reetz, "The 'Faith Bureaucracy' of the Tablighi Jama'at: An Insight into Their System of Self-organization (Intizam)," in Gwilym Backerlegge, ed., *Colonialism, Modernity, and Religious Identities: Religious Reform Movements in South Asia* (New Dehli, India: Oxford University Press, 2008), 98-124.
15. Albert Craig et al., *The Heritage of World Civilizations. Volume II: Since 1500. Seventh Edition* (London: Pearson, 2006), 812-16.
16. Barbara Metcalf, "'Traditionalist' Islamic Activism: Deoband, Tablighis, and Talibs," Social Science Research Council, November 1, 2004, http://essays.ssrc.org/sept11/essays/metcalf.htm.
17. Burki, "The Tablighi Jama'at: Proselytizing Missionaries or Trojan Horse?" 102-103.
18. Masud, *Travelers in Faith*, 106.
19. Ibid., 121; Johny, Stanly. "Explained: Who Are the Tablighi Jama'at?"
20. Johny, "Explained: Who Are the Tablighi Jamaat?"
21. Masud, *Travelers in Faith*, 125-130.
22. "Worldwide Tablighi Markaz Address," *All about Tablighi Jamaat*, May 13, 2008, https://tablighijamaat.wordpress.com/2008/05/13/worldwide-tablighi-markaz-address/.
23. "Tablighi Jamaat: The Group Blamed for New Covid-19 Outbreak in India," *BBC News*, April 2, 2020, https://www.bbc.com/news/world-asia-india-52131338.
24. Marloes Janson, "The Prophet's Path: Tablighi Jama`at in The Gambia," *Institute for the Study of Islam in the Modern World Review* 17 (2006), 44-45.
25. Ibid., 45.

26. Masud, *Travelers in Faith*, 161-173.
27. Baz Lecocq and Paul Schrijver, "The War on Terror in a Haze of Dust: Potholes and Pitfalls on the Saharan Front," *Journal of Contemporary African Studies* 25, no. 1 (2007), 141-66.
28. Stephen Harmon, *Terror and Insurgency in the Sahara-Sahel Region: Corruption, Contraband, Jihad and the Mali War of 2012-2013* (New York: Routledge, 2014), 159.
29. Lecocq and Schrijver, "The War on Terror in a Haze of Dust: Potholes and Pitfalls on the Saharan Front," 151.
30. Ibid., 155.
31. David A. Graham, "Mali's Tangled Mix of Jihad and Civil War," *The Atlantic*, November 20, 2015, https://www.theatlantic.com/international/archive/2015/11/mali-hotel-hostage-crisis/417021/.
32. Conor Gaffey, "African Jihadi Groups Unite and Pledge Allegiance to Al-Qaeda," *Newsweek*, March 3, 2017, https://www.newsweek.com/al-qaeda-groups-unite-sahel-563351.
33. William Lloyd-George, "The Man Who Brought the Black Flag to Timbuktu," *Foreign Policy*, October 22, 2012, https://foreignpolicy.com/2012/10/22/the-man-who-brought-the-black-flag-to-timbuktu/.
34. Idrissa Sangare and Adama Diarra, "Al Qaeda-linked Group Claims Deadly Attack at Mali Resort," Reuters, June 18, 2017, https://www.reuters.com/article/us-mali-security/al-qaeda-linked-group-claims-deadly-attack-at-mali-resort-idUSKBN1990TY.
35. Statistics South Africa, *General Household Survey 2013*, 2014.
36. Goolam Vahed, "Contesting Orthodoxy: the Tablighi-Sunni Conflict among South African Muslims in the 1970s and 1980s," *Journal of Muslim Minority Affairs* 23, no. 2 (October 2003), 313-334. https://www.tandfonline.com/doi/abs/10.1080/1360200032000139956; Masud, *Travelers in Faith*, 206-221.
37. Zanzibar was the power base of the Omani Sultans who had taken control of the coastal areas of East Africa and the lucrative Muslim slave trade in the late 17th century and in 1856 was made the capital of the Omani Sultanate there; as such Zanzibar has been, under German, British and then independent Tanzanian rule, a hotbed of Islamic political thought and aspirations.
38. "Kenya." *World Factbook on Intelligence.* March 25, 2019, https://www.cia.gov/library/publications/the-world-factbook/geos/ke.html; "Uganda," *World Factbook on Intelligence*. March 22, 2019, https://www.cia.gov/library/publications/the-world-factbook/geos/ug.html.
39. Sunguta West, "The Rise of ADF-NALU in Central Africa and Its Connections with Al-Shabaab," Jamestown Foundation *Terrorism*

Monitor 13, no. 1, January 9, 2015, https://jamestown.org/program/the-rise-of-adf-nalu-in-central-africa-and-its-connections-with-al-shabaab/#.Vlx70nbhCUl.

40. Gregory Alonso Pirio, *The African Jihad: Bin Laden's Quest for the Horn of Africa* (Trenton, NJ: Red Sea Press, 2007), 167ff.
41. Ibid., 168. For example, Maalim Mohammad Idriss has stated that TJ and Wahhabism both pervert Islam and wrongly undermine Sufi traditions and practices.
42. Fred Burton and Scott Stewart, "Tablighi Jamaat: An Indirect Line to Terrorism," *Stratfor*, January 23, 2008, https://worldview.stratfor.com/article/tablighi-jamaat-indirect-line-terrorism.
43. Gregory Alonso Pirio, *Radical Islam in the Greater Horn of Africa*, IAQ Report, February 2, 2005, http://www.dankalia.com/archive/2005/050202.htm.
44. Mohamed Olad Hassan, "Witnesses: 5 Pakistani preachers killed in Somalia." *Deseret News*, August 12, 2009, https://www.deseretnews.com/article/705322882/Witnesses-5-Pakistani-preachers-killed-in-Somalia.html.
45. Indrani Bagchi, "Indian Jihadis in Qaida's Somalia Arm?" *Times of India*, August 23, 2010, http://timesofindia.indiatimes.com/india/Indian-jihadis-in-Qaidas-Somalia-arm-/articleshow/6399366.cms.
46. Noor, "The Arrival and Spread of the Tablighi Jama'at in West Papua (Irian Jaya), Indonesia," 1-10.
47. Ibid.
48. Ibidem, 18.
49. Ibidem, 14, 16, 22.
50. Alexander Horstmann, "The Inculturation of a Transnational Islamic Missionary Movement: Tablighi Jamaat Al-Dawa and Muslim Society in Southern Thailand," *Sojourn: Journal of Social Issues in Southeast Asia* 22, no. 1 (2007), 107-30, http://www.jstor.org/stable/41308088.
51. Ibid.
52. Noor, "The Arrival and Spread of the Tablighi Jama'at in West Papua (Irian Jaya), Indonesia," 182.
53. Hussain Haqqani, *Pakistan: Between Mosque and Military* (Washington, D.C.: Carnegie Endowment for International Peace, 2005), 151.
54. Bahukutumbi Raman, "Dagestan: Focus on Pakistan's Tablighi Jamaat," South Asia Analysis Group *Paper* 80, September 15, 1999, http://www.southasiaanalysis.org/paper80.
55. Jane Perlez, "Pakistani Group, Suspected by West of Jihadist Ties,

Holds Conclave Despite Ban," *New York Times*, November 19, 2007, http://www.nytimes.com/2007/11/19/world/asia/19jamaat.html.

56. ANI, "Tablighi Jamaat, an 'Antechamber of Terrorism' in Europe?" Big News Network, April 3, 2020, https://www.bignewsnetwork.com/news/264529456/tablighi-jamaat-an-antechamber-of-terrorism-in-europe.
57. Bryan MacDonald, "Russian Cops Bust Banned Radical Islamist Group Tablighi Jamaat's 'Training Camp,' Detain Leaders & Participants." *RT*, February 19, 2020, https://www.rt.com/russia/481226-russian-cops-detained-radical-islamist/.
58. Pew Forum, "Muslim Networks and Movements in Western Europe: Tablighi Jama'at."
59. William Langley et al., "Army of Darkness," *Telegraph* (London), August 20, 2006, https://www.telegraph.co.uk/news/1526793/Army-of-darkness.html.
60. "Hafiz Patel, Influential British Muslim Leader, Dies at 92," *BBC News*, February 19, 2016, https://www.bbc.com/news/uk-35615205.
61. Andrew Gilligan, "Islamic group blocked from building 'Britain's biggest mosque' in London," *Telegraph* (London), October 25, 2015, http://www.telegraph.co.uk/news/uknews/11953462/Islamic-group-blocked-from-building-Britains-biggest-mosque-in-London.html.
62. Burton and Stewart, "Tablighi Jamaat: An Indirect Line to Terrorism." .
63. Alex Alexiev, "Tablighi Jamaat: Jihad's Stealthy Legions." *Middle East Quarterly* 12, no. 1 (Winter 2005), 3-11. https://www.meforum.org/686/tablighi-jamaat-jihads-stealthy-legions.
64. Burki, "The Tablighi Jama'at: Proselytizing Missionaries or Trojan Horse?" 106.
65. Alexiev, "Tablighi Jamaat: Jihad's Stealthy Legions."
66. Greg Allen, "Long, Winding Road Led to Padilla Trial," *National Public Radio*, April 16, 2007, https://www.npr.org/templates/story/story.php?storyId=9598751; Paula McMahon, "Jose Padilla Sentenced to 21 Years in Terrorism Case," *South Florida Sun Sentinel*, September 9, 2014,. https://www.sun-sentinel.com/news/crime/fl-jose-padilla-sentencing-preview-20140908-story.html.
67. Reetz, "The 'Faith Bureaucracy' of the Tablighi Jama'at: An Insight into Their System of Self-organization (Intizam)," 109.
68. Abdallah Schleifer, ed., *The 500 Most Influential Muslims: 2017* (Dabuq, Jordan: Royal Islamic Strategic Studies Centre, 2017), 61-62, https://www.themuslim500.com/wp-content/uploads/2018/05/TheMuslim500-2017-low.pdf.

69. Chowdhury Akbor Hossain, "Tabligh Jamaat Torn Apart by Internal Dispute," *Dhaka Tribune*, November 16, 2017, http://www.dhaka-tribune.com/bangladesh/2017/11/15/tabligh-jamaat-torn-apart-internal-dispute/.
70. Ibid.
71. Yoginder Sikand, "The Tablighi Jamaat's Contested Claims to Islamicity," *New Age Islam*, June 18, 2010, http://www.newageislam.com/islamic-ideology/the-tablighi-jamaat's-contested-claims-to-islamicity/d/3014.
72. Ibid.
73. Ibidem.
74. Ibidem.
75. Mushfig Bayram, "Tajikistan: Jail Terms and Massive Fines—But for What Crimes?" Forum 18 News Service, May 19, 2010, http://www.forum18.org/Archive.php?article_id=1446.
76. Felix Corley, "Kazakhstan: Is Sharing Faith a State Security Issue?" *Occasional Papers on Religion in Eastern Europe* 37, no. 1 (January 2017), 36-45, https://digitalcommons.georgefox.edu/cgi/viewcontent.cgi?referer=&httpsredir=1&article=2006&context=ree.
77. Azaan Javaid, "NIA's study of arrested Indian ISIS fans busts common myths," *Daily News & Analysis*, January 20, 2017, http://www.dnaindia.com/india/report-nia-s-study-of-arrested-indian-isis-fans-busts-common-myths-2294253.
78. Andrew Higgins, "A French Town Linked to Jihad Asks Itself Why," *New York Times*, January 16, 2015, https://www.nytimes.com/2015/01/17/world/europe/french-town-struggles-over-departures-for-jihad.html?_r=0.
79. William Finnegan, "Last Days: Preparing for the Apocalypse in San Bernardino," *New Yorker*, February 22, 2016, http://www.newyorker.com/magazine/2016/02/22/preparing-for-apocalypse-in-san-bernardino.
80. Mohammed Wajihuddin, "Deoband Campus Now off Limits for Tablighi Jama'at," *Times of India*, August 11, 2017, https://timesofindia.indiatimes.com/india/deoband-campus-now-off-limits-for-tablighi-jamaat/articleshow/60012605.cms.
81. Ziya Us Salam, "Tablighi Jamaat: Vindicated, Finally," *The Hindu*, September 15, 2020, https://frontline.thehindu.com/the-nation/vindicated-finally/article32516103.ece.
82. Jerome Taylor and Alex Ward, "Rejected: The Mosque Plan That Grew so Big It Attracted the Wrong Sort of Crowd," *Independent* (London), December 5, 2012, https://www.independent.co.uk/news/

uk/home-news/rejected-the-mosque-plan-that-grew-so-big-it-attract-ed-the-wrong-sort-of-crowd-8386158.html.

72 Taliban

Quick Facts

Geographical Areas of Operation: Europe, South Asia
Numerical Strength (Members): Approximately 60,000 (estimated 2018)
Leadership: Moulavi Haibatullah Akhunzada
Religious Identification: Sunni Islam

Quick Facts Courtesy of the Stanford University's Mapping Militant Organizations

Introduction

The Taliban is a Sunni Islamist fundamentalist militant group that emerged in 1994 during the Afghan Civil War. The Taliban, or "religious students" in Pashto, were primarily madrassa students motivated by restoring peace, eliminating corruption, and enforcing sharia law in Afghanistan. They formed in Kandahar and initiated a military campaign against regional warlords to capture Afghanistan, effectively doing so by 1996. After the September 2001 attacks on the U.S., the Taliban refused to hand over al-Qaeda leader Osama bin Laden, who was, at the time, under their protection in Afghanistan. In response, the U.S. and allied forces invaded Afghanistan and captured Kabul by November 2001, toppling the Taliban regime in the process. In the nearly two decades since, the Taliban has waged a protracted campaign of asymmetric warfare against an assortment of forces, among them the North Atlantic Treaty Organization (NATO) forces, the Northern Alliance, the International Security Assistance Force (ISAF), and the Afghan National Defense and Security Forces (ANDSF). Today, the Taliban continues to attack civilians as well as ANDSF and U.S. military targets even as it negotiates a peace agreement with the latter two parties.

The Taliban's strategic focus remains largely on Afghanistan, as the group seeks to remove the existing government in order to create an Islamic state and to install sharia law within the country. The Taliban's strategic motivations are directly influenced by their ideology. The Taliban's ideological basis is formed by a combination of Pashtunwali, the Pashtun tribal code, and Deobandi Sunni Islam. They combine to form a set of rigid, ultraconservative principles. The group also remains intimately connected to – and supportive of – international Salafi-jihadi groups waging campaigns of terror around the world.

History and Ideology

The Taliban, or "religious students" in Pashto, emerged in 1994 in the midst of an ongoing civil war between *mujahideen* factions prompted by opposition to local warlords and a perceived failure to institute *sharia* law in Afghanistan. Mullah Mohhammad Omar led the fledgling group of primarily Sunni Pashtun *madrassa* students in their early campaign to rid Afghanistan of corrupt and violent warlords. Prior to founding the Taliban, Mullah Omar attended *Darul Uloom Haqqania*, a religious school that promotes Deobandi Sunni Islam and *jihad* against non-Muslims.[1] Mullah Omar took the education to heart, and brought the ideology back to Afghanistan, where it would provide the basis for the Taliban. The Taliban's social, political, and economic ideology rest on a framework that combines Pashtunwali, the tribal code of the Pashtun people who represent the majority of the Taliban, and Deobandi Sunni Islam, the ultra-conservative form of Sunnism often associated with southwest Asian Islamist groups.

The Taliban began their campaign eliminating small time criminals and warlords in southern Afghanistan, ostensibly filling the power vacuum left in the wake of the Afghan Civil War and infighting among the *mujahideen* and atrocities by local authorities.[2] The goals of the organization grew rapidly, as did its membership. Politically, the Taliban sought to install *sharia* law across Afghanistan and to create an Islamic state there and replace the existing government, which they viewed as illegitimate.

The Taliban scored their first major victory in November 1994, when they captured Kandahar. Over the next 22 months, the Taliban grew exponentially in size and in the area they controlled, and by September 1996 had captured Kabul and Jalalabad and seized control of the Afghan government.[3] The Taliban also allowed Osama bin Laden's al-Qaeda to return to Afghanistan in 1996, further worsening the situation in the country. Bin Laden pledged allegiance to Mullah Omar to ensure his organization would be treated as a guest and placed under the Taliban's protection.

Socially, the Taliban's policies are ultraconservative and archaic. While ruling Afghanistan from 1996 to 2001, the Taliban banned many western influences including alcohol, music, television, movies, and sports.[4] They also banned women from being educated and placed extreme restrictions on females.[5] Prayer became compulsory, any person caught breaking any laws was dealt with in extreme and brutal fashion. (Notably, the peace process underway may shift these policies, or at least moderate them somewhat, as the group has agreed to respect women's rights, social progression, and human rights in general as a condition for the negotiations and its ultimate inclusion as a political party in the future government).

Economically, the Taliban banned many illicit forms of revenue generation including opium farming, going so far as attempting to eradicate opium when they ruled Afghanistan. They also heavily taxed all corporations operating in Afghanistan. However, Taliban reneged on these goals after being removed from power, when they shifted to largely rely on the opium trade, as well also conduct weapons, gem, mineral, and timber smuggling, human trafficking, and other illicit forms of financing in order to sustain their campaign against the government.[6]

The Northern Alliance, a group resembling the previous Islamic Unity of Afghanistan Movement, formed in September 1996 from disparate *mujahideen* groups in an effort to combat the surging Taliban.[7] The Northern Alliance consisted of mix of political, religiously, and ethnically aligned militias, including Jamiat-i Islami, Shura-i Nazar Ahmad Shah Massoud, Harakat-i Islami, Bizb-i Wahdat, and Junbish-i Milli.

Prior to 1996, the Northern Alliance groups held territory across Afghanistan. As the war continued, the Taliban pushed the Northern Alliance into the northeastern provinces of Afghanistan with pockets of resistance in major cities including Kunduz and Mazar-i-Sharif remaining outside of Northern Alliance territory. By 2001, the Taliban controlled the majority of the country with the exception of parts of Kunduz, Baghlan, Badakhshan and Takhar provinces in the country's northeast.

On September 9, 2001, al-Qaeda assassinated Northern Alliance Commander Ahmad Shah Massoud in an effort to support the Taliban.[8] Two days later, on September 11, 2001, al-Qaeda launched terror attacks against New York and Washington DC. On September 20, 2001, the U.S. demanded that the Taliban turn Osama bin Laden over and close all al-Qaeda bases in Afghanistan.[9] The Taliban demurred, instead offering to try bin Laden in a Taliban-controlled court in Afghanistan if the U.S. provided evidence of his complicity.[10] The U.S. rejected the Taliban's offer,[11] and launched the invasion of Afghanistan on October 7, 2001. The hostilities were brief; overwhelming U.S. aerial power, as well as collaboration by U.S. Special Forces with the Northern Alliance and Hamid Karzai's militia, led to the fall of the Taliban and the toppling of their government by late November 2001.

Thereafter, a UN-sponsored conference created a provisional Afghan government, bringing together prominent Afghan leaders.[12] The Taliban were deliberately left out of the process. The agreement established a provisional government that would transition power to a permanent government in two years' time, and laid the groundwork for the creation of the International Security Assistance Force (ISAF).

The remnants of the former Taliban government fled Afghanistan to Pakistan over the course of late 2001 and 2002. From Pakistan, the Taliban leadership sought to rebuild the organization and direct operations in Afghanistan. As the Taliban began to spread their influence and regain *de facto* control of some rural areas in southern Afghanistan, the so-called *Quetta Shura* began assigning shadow government positions to various areas and regions where the group maintained a heavy footprint and enjoyed support. The Taliban largely spent 2002 to 2005 recruiting and rebuilding their previous capabilities in an effort to retake Afghanistan. In November 2004, Mullah Omar released a statement that vowed that the Taliban were resurgent and that they would fight the Afghan government and foreign invaders until they once again controlled the country.[13]

But while the Taliban launched attacks and regained some territory between 2003 and 2005, the Taliban did not launch their insurgency in earnest until 2006. The resulting campaign ran from 2006 to 2011, and was defined by bombings and suicide attacks. In response, the U.S. dramatically increased troop levels in the country in September 2008 and February 2009 in efforts to end the fighting. Support for the effort among the U.S. public, however, waned over time and led to troop withdrawals in June 2011. The U.S. and Afghanistan's newly-elected National Unity Government signed a Bilateral Security Agreement in September 2014, which provided the basis for the United States and NATO to leave behind approximately 9,800 U.S. troops and 5,500 coalition troops to support planned operations. The U.S. and NATO halted all combat operations in December of 2014. NATO initiated Operation Resolute Support in January 2015 which remains active and focuses on a train, advise, assist mission set to develop capacities of the ANDSF.

Recent Activity

In April 2013, Mullah Omar died in a Pakistani hospital.[14] News of his death was kept secret for more than two years, and during that period the Taliban released official statements under their former leader's name to ensure the movement remained cohesive. Furthermore, the group published Omar's biography in April 2015 to mark his 19th year as the Taliban supreme leader. In July 2015, Afghan intelligence officials revealed the Taliban leader had died years earlier – something which the Taliban subsequently confirmed.[15] Mullah Akhtar Mansour succeeded Mullah Omar after a hasty selection process that was disputed by high-ranking leaders of the movement.[16] Soon after, fractures began to appear in the movement. Some Taliban leaders protested that the late Mullah Omar's son, Mullah Mohammad Yaqoub, should become leader instead and argued that Pakistan had orchestrated Mansour's selection.[17] They accused Mansour of "hijacking the movement because of personal greed," which led to the creation of a splinter group, the High Council of the Afghanistan Islamic Emirate, led by Mullah Mohammad Rasool.[18] The split soon erupted into infighting between the two sides, with Mansour's side gaining the upper hand.[19] Intense clashes under the leadership of Mullah Mohammad Rasool continued well into the Spring of 2016.

The Taliban continued to splinter as the Islamic State's Afghan faction grew in power in eastern Afghanistan. In January 2015, news emerged that Mullah Abdul Rauf Alizai swore allegiance to the or Islamic State Khorasan Province (ISK), and had been appointed its deputy commander, after falling out with the Taliban. The following month, however, Alizai was killed by a U.S. drone strike in Helmand province.[20]

In May 2016, Mullah Mansour was killed by a U.S. drone strike in Balochistan, Pakistan.[21] Mansour was reportedly returning from a scheduled trip to Iran. The Taliban confirmed Mullah Mansour's death and announced that Mawlawi Haibatullah Akhunzada, a Taliban religious scholar with no military experience, would lead the organization.[22] They also announced that Sirajuddin Haqqani and Mullah Mohammad Yaqoub, son of Mullah Mohammad Omar, would serve as deputies. Akhunzada effectively left the operational command of the movement in the hands of his deputies.[23] The two deputies divided Afghanistan in two with each wanting to control his own front. The Afghan government urged the new Taliban leadership to consider joining a peace process to end the fighting, but Taliban leadership announced the Taliban would not participate in peace talks and would remain committed to fighting.[24] The decision was driven by the conviction of many of the movement's commanders that a political settlement to the conflict is not a desired option, given that military victory over the Afghan government is attainable. This view was strengthened by the movement's 2015 and 2016 offensives across the country's 34 provinces. The capture of major cities including Kunduz in September 2015 and again in August 2016 provide symbolic and strategic significance to the Taliban.[25] The ANDSF retook Kunduz both times with significant help from U.S. special operations and air support. The Taliban primarily focused on capturing smaller district centers, but would launch attacks on major cities to initiate the summer fighting season each year.

Since assuming power in September 2014, Afghan President

Ashraf Ghani prioritized reconciling with the Taliban by reaching out to Pakistan to facilitate negotiations. He has also helped establish a Quadrilateral Coordination Group (QCG), which includes Afghanistan, Pakistan, China, and the United States, in pursuit of a peace settlement with the Taliban. However, the Taliban continued their offensives and refused to come to the negotiating table to engage in peace talks. As a result, in the first quarter of 2016, Ghani effectively eschewed amnesty and passivity as a policy option toward the insurgency but continued to welcome those Taliban members who wished to reconcile.[26]

On August 21, 2017, the Trump administration announced a new Afghanistan and South Asia strategy that shifted to a conditions-based approach for a peace process and withdrawal of US troops.[27] The strategy loosened rules of engagement for U.S. commanders in Afghanistan, took a harsher stance on Pakistan attempting to address duplicitous behavior in fighting terrorism, and called on India to assume a large role in Afghanistan's development. The White House reaffirmed the importance of the peace process and that the door was open for negotiations with the Taliban while increasing both the number of US troops in Afghanistan and combat operations. On February 14, 2018, the Taliban released a letter addressed to the United States and the American people; in it, the group attempted to remind the American people of the costs of the war in Afghanistan, the Taliban's continued willingness to negotiate peace with the US government, and corruption in the Afghan government.[28] The letter spurred the Afghan government to move towards peace. On February 28, 2018, President Ashraf Ghani made an overture to the Taliban by outlining a bold peace proposal during the Kabul Process Conference in front of high-level international representatives from 25 countries.[29] Ghani's peace proposal invited the conciliatory Taliban members to enter peace talks without any preconditions. The peace proposal states that the Afghan government will recognize the Taliban as a legitimate political group, issue Taliban members and their families passports, release Taliban prisoners, remove sanctions on Taliban leaders, and provide amnesty, security, and financial guarantees to Taliban members who resettle in Afghanistan. The Taliban would in turn be required to respect the rule of law, women's rights, and the sovereignty of the Afghan government. In December of 2018, Taliban leadership announced that they were ready to restart negotiations.[30] The Taliban excluded the Afghan government from their list of parties with which they wished to negotiate, as the group believes the government is illegitimate and does not represent the population effectively.

In January 2019, Taliban and U.S. delegations met in Doha, Qatar for six days of peace negotiations, after which both sides stated that progress was made, but several issues remain unresolved.[31] On February 6, 2019, Taliban and GIROA delegations met in Moscow, Russia for a subsequent two days of peace negotiations, during which the two sides charted out a peace process that relied on the removal of foreign forces from Afghanistan and the Taliban committing to protecting human rights.[32] On February 25, 2019, Taliban co-founder and chief of the Taliban political office Mullah Abdul Ghani Baradar met with U.S. Special Representative for Afghanistan Zalmay Khalilzad to discuss the peace process.[33] The meeting suggested increasing seriousness on part of the Taliban to reach a peaceful resolution.

But, Taliban officials made clear, that peaceful resolution would only come if the group's demands were met. On June 1, 2019, Taliban Leader Mullah Hibatullah Akhunzada pledged to continue fighting until the organization's goals were achieved.[34] The message proclaimed that the Taliban wanted a government that is representative of all Afghans and an end to the conflict in Afghanistan. As the same time, continued Taliban military action – such as the September 2019 killing of foreign soldiers and Afghan civilians with a vehicle borne improvised explosive device (VBIED)[35] – infuriated the White House and caused at least temporary derailments and delays in peace talks with Washington.[36]

The conflict between U.S. and Taliban forces remained violent throughout the year, despite sporadic diplomatic contacts between the group and Washington, with 180 U.S. troops wounded and 17 killed in action.[37] However, Taliban-U.S. peace negotiations picked up speed at the beginning of 2020 and, on February 21, 2020, the two sides initiated a seven day reduction in violence.[38] The reduction in violence held between the two sides over the course of the week and, on February 29, 2020, the U.S. and the Taliban signed a formal peace agreement.[39]

The agreement is broken down into four parts, including prevention of the use of Afghanistan as a base by groups that threaten the security of the United States and allies, removal of all foreign forces from Afghanistan, initiation of negotiations between the Afghan government and the Taliban, and a permanent ceasefire between the Afghan government and the Taliban. The U.S. and Afghan governments also signed a joint declaration on February 29 demonstrating continued commitment to find a peaceful solution to the conflict.[40]

On March 1, 2020, however, President Ghani stated that the government would not abide by the terms set for prisoner release in the U.S.-Taliban peace agreement signed days earlier.[41] The agreement envisioned 5,000 Taliban prisoners and 1,000 Afghan government prisoners being released prior to the upcoming March 10th peace talks between the Afghan government and the Taliban. President Ghani's statement led to the Taliban refusing to attend then-upcoming peace talks in Oslo, Norway. Ghani relented somewhat, and after some delays, a smaller number of prisoners (100 total) were released by the Afghan government in support of the peace agreement.[42] The Taliban, however, were dissatisfied by this, and stepped up their violent activity in the late Spring and early Summer of 2020, resulting in the deaths of scores of civilians and members of the Afghan military.[43] On May 20, 2020, the U.S., the Afghan government, and Taliban leaders met to revive the faltering U.S.-Taliban and Afghan-Taliban peace deals.[44] Those talks were ultimately successful, leading to a reconciliation – still in process as of this writing – between the Taliban and the government of Afghanistan.[45]

The United States is also forging ahead with its plans made under its 2020 truce with the Taliban. As of late May 2020, the Trump administration appears to be well ahead of its troop withdrawal schedules as enumerated under the February deal.[46] This does not, however, mean that U.S.-Taliban hostilities have ceased; throughout the summer of 2020, Taliban attacks against Afghan military and civilian targets precipitated U.S. airstrikes.[47]

Global Reach

Taliban operations are largely restricted to within the borders of Afghanistan, although violent clashes in the frontier areas with Iran, Pakistan, and Tajikistan have occasionally been reported. The Taliban have occasionally threatened attacks against NATO countries whose soldiers are operating in Afghanistan including the US, UK, Spain, and Germany although none of the terrorist attacks in any of these countries have ever been attributed to the Taliban. Despite those threats, the Taliban have never truly sought a global agenda. In the fall of 2009, the Taliban tried to promote a new "foreign policy" by releasing several statements on their website declaring the movement poses no regional or international security threat. Mullah Omar repeated this rhetoric in one of his two annual *Eid* statements to the Afghan people, which appeared in mid-November 2010.[48] The Taliban do maintain connections to and are supportive of foreign Salafi-*jihadists* with international missions and motivations including al-Qaeda, al-Qaeda in the Indian Subcontinent, Jaish-e Mohammad, Lashkar-e Taiyba, and Tehrik-e Taliban Pakistan.[49]

Within Afghanistan, the Taliban have demonstrated the capability to reach all corners of the country. Over the course of the war in Afghanistan, the Taliban have controlled territory and district centers in all 34 of Afghanistan's provinces. They also maintain the ability to execute suicide attacks, indirect fire attacks, insider attacks, and raids across the country on ANDSF, U.S. and NATO military, and Afghan civilian targets. The Taliban focus on military and Afghan targets, but occasionally attack non-government civilian targets.

Endnotes

1. Frud Bezhan, "'University of Jihad' Gets Public Funds Even as Pakistan Fights Extremism" *Radio Free Europe/Radio Liberty*, March 11, 2018, https://www.rferl.org/a/pakistan-jihad-university-haqqania-government-funding-haq-taliban-omar/29092748.html
2. Carlotta Gall, "Mullah Muhammad Omar, Enigmatic Leader of Af-

ghan Taliban, is Dead" *New York Times*, July 31, 2015, https://www.nytimes.com/2015/07/31/world/asia/mullah-muhammad-omar-taliban-leader-afghanistan-dies.html

3. Kathy Evans and Phil Goodwin, "From the Archive: Kabul Falls to Islamist Taliban Militia" *Guardian* (London), September 28, 2009, https://www.theguardian.com/theguardian/2009/sep/28/taliban-afghanistan-kabul.
4. Nicholas Wroe, "A Culture Muted" *Guardian* (London), October 13, 2001, https://www.theguardian.com/world/2001/oct/13/afghanistan.books
5. Heather Barr, "A Crucial Moment for Woman's Rights in Afghanistan" Human Rights Watch, March 5, 2020, https://www.hrw.org/news/2020/03/05/crucial-moment-womens-rights-afghanistan
6. Justin Rowlatt, "How the US Military's Opium War in Afghanistan was Lost" *BBC*, April 29, 2019, https://www.bbc.com/news/world-us-canada-47861444
7. Fiona Symon, "Afghanistan's Northern Alliance" *BBC*, September 19, 2001, http://news.bbc.co.uk/2/hi/south_asia/1552994.stm
8. Joseph Fitchett, "Assassination of Massoud Removed Potential Key Ally for US" *New York Times*, September 17, 2001, https://www.nytimes.com/2001/09/17/news/assassination-of-massoud-removed-a-potential-key-ally-for-us-did-bin.html.
9. "White House warns Taliban: 'We will defeat you'" *CNN*, September 21, 2001, https://www.cnn.com/2001/WORLD/asiapcf/central/09/21/ret.afghan.taliban/
10. "Taliban say bin Laden under their control" *CNN*, September 30, 2001, https://www.cnn.com/2001/WORLD/asiapcf/central/09/30/ret.taliban.binladen/index.html
11. "U.S. rejects Taliban offer to try bin Laden" *CNN*, October 7, 2001, https://edition.cnn.com/2001/US/10/07/ret.us.taliban/
12. "Agreement on Provisional Arrangements in Afghanistan" *Washington Post*, December 5, 2001, https://www.washingtonpost.com/wp-srv/world/texts/bonnagreement.html
13. Carlotta Gall, "Afghanistan: Taliban Leader Vows Return" *New York Times*, November 13, 2004, https://www.nytimes.com/2004/11/13/washington/world/world-briefing-asia-afghanistan-taliban-leader-vows-return.html.
14. Jane Onyanga-Omara and Katharine Lackey, "Afghan Intel Agency: Taliban Leader Died Two Years Ago" *USA Today*, July 29, 2015, https://www.usatoday.com/story/news/world/2015/07/29/taliban-leader-mullah-omar/30819359/.

15. "Taliban Admit Covering up Death of Mullah Omar," *BBC*, August 31, 2015, http://www.bbc.com/news/world-asia-34105565.
16. Kenneth Katzman, "Afghanistan: Post-Taliban Governance, Security, and U.S. Policy," Congressional Research Service, June 2016, http://www.fas.org/sgp/crs/row/RL30588.pdf.
17. Ibid.
18. Dawood Azami, "Why are the Taliban Resurgent in Afghanistan?" *BBC*, January 5, 2016, http://www.bbc.com/news/world-asia-35169478.
19. Ibid.
20. "Afghanistan Drone Strike 'Kills IS Commander Abdul Rauf,'" *BBC*, February 9, 2015, http://www.bbc.com/news/world-asia-31290147; U.S. Department of State, Bureau of Counterterrorism, "Foreign Terrorist Organizations," n.d., http://www.state.gov/j/ct/rls/other/des/123085.htm.
21. Kenneth Katzman, "Taliban Leadership Succession," Congressional Research Service, May 26, 2016, https://www.fas.org/sgp/crs/row/IN10495.pdf.
22. Camila Domonoske, "Taliban Name New Leader, Confirm Death of Mullah Mansour" *NPR*, May 25, 2016, https://www.npr.org/sections/thetwo-way/2016/05/25/479428701/taliban-name-new-leader-confirm-death-of-mullah-mansour.
23. Katzman, "Taliban Leadership Succession."
24. Mirwais Harooni,"Afghan Taliban Appoint a New Leader, Kabul Urges Peace," Reuters, May 25, 2016, https://www.reuters.com/article/us-afghanistan-taliban/afghan-taliban-appoint-a-new-leader-kabul-urges-peace-idUSKCN0YG0DW.
25. Katzman, "Taliban Leadership Succession."
26. Samimullah Arif, "Ashraf Ghani's New Plan to Win Afghanistan's Long War Against the Taliban," *The Diplomat*, April 28, 2016, http://thediplomat.com/2016/04/ashraf-ghanis-new-plan-to-win-afghanistans-long-war-against-the-taliban/.
27. Jim Garamone, "President Unveils New Afghanistan, South Asia Strategy" *DOD News*, August 21, 2017, https://www.defense.gov/Explore/News/Article/Article/1284964/president-unveils-new-afghanistan-south-asia-strategy/.
28. "Taliban Letter Addresses 'American People' Urges Talks," Associated Press, February 14, 2018, https://apnews.com/bb443b16da2a4e3285f19fb6dd627777/Taliban-letter-addresses-'American-people,'-urges-talks
29. Hamid Shalizi and James Mackenzie, "Afghanistan's Ghani Offers

Talks with Taliban 'Without Preconditions,'" Reuters, February 28, 2018, https://www.reuters.com/article/us-afghanistan-taliban/afghanistans-ghani-offers-talks-with-taliban-without-preconditions-idUSKCN1GC0J0.

30. "Taliban Appear Ready to Discuss Peace Talks," *New York Times*, December 17, 2018, https://www.nytimes.com/2018/12/17/world/asia/taliban-afghanistan-peace-talks.html.
31. Eshan Popalzai and Kara Fox, "US-Taliban Peace Talks in Doha a 'Significant Step,'" *CNN*, January 27, 2019, https://www.cnn.com/2019/01/27/asia/us-taliban-afghan-peace-talks-doha-intl/index.html.
32. Andrew Higgins and Mujab Mashal, "Taliban Peace Talks in Moscow End with Hopes the U.S. exits, if not too Quickly" *New York Times*, February 6, 2019, https://www.nytimes.com/2019/02/06/world/asia/taliban-afghanistan-peace-talks-moscow.html?module=inline.
33. "Afghan Peace Talks: Taliban Co-Founder Meets with Top White House Envoy," *BBC*, February 25, 2019, https://www.bbc.com/news/world-asia-47351369.
34. "Afghan Taliban Leader Pledges to Keep Fighting Until Goals Met" Reuters, June 1, 2019, https://www.reuters.com/article/us-afghanistan-taliban/afghan-taliban-leader-pledges-to-keep-fighting-until-goals-met-idUSKCN1T22ZJ
35. Tameem Akhgar and Cara Anna, "Taliban Blast Kills US Soldier, Several Civilians in Kabul," Associated Press, September 5, 2019, https://apnews.com/874989f36e364304b757186340dc9e6d.
36. Phil Stewart and Jason Lange, "Trump Says He Canceled Peace Talks with Taliban over Attack," Reuters, September 7, 2019, https://www.reuters.com/article/us-usa-afghanistan-mckenzie-idUSKCN1VS0MX
37. "New in 2020: Army Combat Casualties Trend Upwards into 2020," *Army Times*, December 30, 2019, https://www.armytimes.com/news/your-army/2019/12/30/new-in-2020-army-combat-casualties-trend-upwards-into-2020/.
38. Eshan Popalzai, "Seven-Day Reduction in Violence in Afghanistan to Begins" CNN, February 21, 2020, https://www.cnn.com/2020/02/21/politics/us-taliban-reduction-in-violence-afghanistan/index.html.
39. "Agreement for Bringing Peace to Afghanistan between the Islamic Emirate of Afghanistan which is not recognized by the United States as a state and is known as the Taliban and the United States of America," February 29, 2020, https://www.state.gov/wp-con-

tent/uploads/2020/02/Agreement-For-Bringing-Peace-to-Afghanistan-02.29.20.pdf.

40. "Joint Declaration between the Islamic Republic of Afghanistan and the United States of America for Bringing Peace to Afghanistan," February 29, 2020, https://www.state.gov/wp-content/uploads/2020/02/02.29.20-US-Afghanistan-Joint-Declaration.pdf.
41. Kathy Gannon, "Afghan Peace Deal Hits First Snag over Prisoner Releases" Associated Press, March 1, 2020, https://apnews.com/8cfce4344ad386697c78b033a3cb3dc6
42. "Afghan government frees 100 Taliban Prisoners as Part of Peace Process" Reuters, April 8, 2020, https://www.reuters.com/article/us-usa-afghanistan-taliban/afghan-government-frees-100-taliban-prisoners-as-part-of-peace-process-idUSKCN21Q2EA
43. Fahim Abed, "Afghan War Casualty Report: May 2020," *New York Times*, May 7, 2020, https://www.nytimes.com/2020/05/07/magazine/afghan-war-casualty-report-may-2020.html
44. Kathy Gannon and Tameem Akghar, "US Envoy Working to Resuscitate Flagging Afghan Peace Deal" Associated Press, May 21, 2020, https://apnews.com/6b39a152a914e9de830de87bb9a85cb9.
45. Kathy Gannon, "Taliban, Ghani Declare Three-Day Cease Fire for Eid Holiday," Associated Press, May 23, 2020, https://apnews.com/8325cb19bfa0ad5b3d610de92a3be8e1
46. Idrees Ali and Rupam Jain, "US Troop Strength in Afghanistan Down to close to 8,600 Ahead of Schedule," Reuters, May 27, 2020, https://www.reuters.com/article/us-usa-afghanistan-taliban-exclusive/exclusive-u-s-troop-strength-in-afghanistan-down-to-close-to-8600-ahead-of-schedule-sources-idUSKBN233147.
47. "U.S. forces conduct airstrikes on Taliban in Afghanistan," Reuters, June 5, 2020, https://www.reuters.com/article/us-usa-afghanistan-taliban/u-s-forces-conduct-airstrikes-on-taliban-in-afghanistan-idUSKBN23C27W
48. "Taliban Leader Mullah Omar Issues Statement on Eid Al-Adha, Rejects Media Reports of Peace Talks as 'Baseless Propaganda' Aimed at 'Wrongfully Raising Hollow Hopes in the Hearts of... People,'" Middle East Media Research Institute *Special Dispatch* no. 3380, November 15, 2010, http://www.memri.org/report/en/0/0/0/0/0/0/4769.htm.
49. "UN Security Council Analytical Support and Sanctions Monitoring Team Report," United Nations, May 2020, https://www.undocs.org/S/2020/415.

73 Contributors

Afghanistan

Cody Retherford

Cody Retherford joined the American Foreign Policy Council as a Junior Fellow in May 2020. He has conducted research on counterterrorism, counterinsurgency, and state proxy, cyber, and information operations and strategy. He also has a background in market research and geopolitical risk analysis. Cody holds a BA in International Affairs and Middle East Studies. He is currently a graduate student at Johns Hopkins University School of Advanced International Studies (SAIS) pursuing an MA in International Economics and International Affairs. Prior to attending SAIS, Cody served as a US Army Officer on active duty for 5 years in light infantry and special operations organizations. He deployed to Afghanistan in support of Operation Freedom's Sentinel and Operation Resolute Support. He has also supported combat operations against terror groups across the Middle East.

Al-Qaeda

Kyle Orton

Kyle Orton is an independent researcher focused on the Syrian war and related terrorist groups. His work has been published in various outlets, including Foreign Policy, The Wall Street Journal, and The New York Times. He obtained his masters in social science from Liverpool University, completing his thesis on the conditions of the Syrian refugees in Lebanon, and previously worked at a London think tank.

Albania

Christopher Deliso

Christopher Deliso is an American journalist and author concentrating on the Balkans. Over the past decade, Chris has established a dedicated presence in teh Balkans, and published analytical articles on related topics in numerous relevant media outlets, such as UPI, the Economist Intelligence Unit, and *Jane's Intelligence Digest*. Chris is also the founder and director of the Balkan-interest news and current affairs website, www.balkanalysis.com, and the author of *The Coming Balkan Caliphate: The Threat of Radical Islam to Europe and the West*.

Algeria

Yahia Zoubir

Yahia H. Zoubir is Professor of International Studies and Director of Research in Geopolitics at KEDGE Business School, France. Prior to joining KEDGE in September 2005, he taught in the United States. He has been Visiting Faculty in various universities in the China, Europe, the United States, and India, His numerous publications include books, such as North African Politics: Change and Continuity (Routledge, 2016); Global Security Watch—The Maghreb: Algeria, Libya, Morocco, and Tunisia (ABC/CLIO, 2013); North Africa: Politics, Region, and the Limits of Transformation (Routledge, 2008) and articles in scholarly journals, such as Third World Quarterly, Mediterranean Politics, International Affairs, Journal of North African Studies, Middle East Journal, Journal of Contemporary China, etc.. He has also contributed many book chapters and various entries in encyclopedias. He is currently collaborating on the Project on Rivalries in the Middle East & North Africa and another on Sahel Security and the Mediterranean.

Argentina

David Grantham

David A. Grantham currently serves as a Senior Fellow with the Center for a Secure Free Society and is the Director of Intelligence for the Tarrant County Sheriff's Office. Prior to that, David served as Senior Fellow of National Security at the National Center for Policy Analysis (NCPA) and as an officer in the United States Air Force with the Air Force Office of Special Investigations (AFOSI).

David holds a PhD in History from Texas Christian University and a Master of Science in International Relations from Troy University. He earned his Bachelor of Art in History from University of South Florida in 2004. David is author of Consequences: An Intelligence Officer's War.

Australia

Michael Sobolik and Tilly Moross
Michael Sobolik joined AFPC as a Fellow in Indo-Pacific Studies in September 2019. His work covers American and Chinese grand strategy, regional economic and security trends, America's alliance architecture in Asia, and human rights. Michael also serves as editor of AFPC's Indo-Pacific Monitor e-bulletin, AFPC's review of developments in the region. His analysis has appeared in The Diplomat, The Hill, The National Interest, National Review, Newsweek, and Providence.

Prior to joining AFPC, Michael served as a Legislative Assistant to Sen. Ted Cruz from 2014 to 2019 and managed his Indo-Pacific policy portfolio. While in the Senate, Michael drafted legislation on China, Russia, India, Taiwan, North Korea, and Cambodia, as well as strategic systems and missile defense.

Michael is a graduate of Texas A&M University, where he studied political philosophy as an undergraduate. He also earned his Master of International Affairs degree in American grand strategy and U.S.-China relations at the Bush School of Government and Public Service.

Tilly Moross is a former researcher with the American Foreign Policy Council.

Azerbaijan

Svante E. Cornell
Svante E. Cornell joined the American Foreign Policy Council as Senior Fellow for Eurasia in January 2017. He also servs as the Director of the Central Asia-Caucasus Institute & Silk Road Studies Program, and a co-founder of the Institue for Security and

Development Policy, Stockholm. His main areas of expertise are security issues, state-building, and transnational crime in Southwest and Central Asia, with a specific focus on the Caucasus and Turkey. He is the Editor of the Central Asia-Caucasus Analyst, the Joint Center's bi-weekly publication, and of the Joint Center's Silk Road Papers series of occasional papers.

Cornell is the author of four books, including Small Nations and Great Powers, the first comprehensive study of the post-Soviet conflicts in the Caucasus, and Azerbaijan since Independence. Cornell is an Associate Research Professor at Johns Hopkins University's Paul H. Nitze School of Advanced International Studies. He was educated at the Middle East Technical University, received his Ph.D. in Peace and Conflict Studies from Uppsala University, and holds an honorary degree from the National Academy of Sciences of Azerbaijan. He is a member of the Swedish Royal Academy of Military Science, and a Research Associate with the W. Martens Center for European Studies in Brussels. Formerly, Cornell served as Associate Professor of Government at Uppsala University.

Bahrain

Dr. Courtney Freer
Courtney Freer is an assistant professorial research fellow at the Middle East Centre at the London School of Economics and Political Science (LSE). She is the author of Rentier Islamism: The Role of the Muslim Brotherhood in the Gulf Monarchies (Oxford University Press, 2018), the first English language book focused on the Muslim Brotherhood in the Gulf states and specializes in domestic politics and foreign policies of the states of the Gulf Cooperation Council.

Bangladesh

Michael Kugelman
Michael Kugelman is the Asia Program Deputy Director and Senior Associate for South Asia at the Woodrow Wilson Center, where he is responsible for research, programming, and publications on the region. His main specialty is Pakistan, India, and Afghanistan

and U.S. relations with each of them. Mr. Kugelman writes monthly columns for Foreign Policy's South Asia Channel and monthly commentaries for War on the Rocks. He also contributes regular pieces to the Wall Street Journal's Think Tank blog. He has published op-eds and commentaries in the New York Times, Los Angeles Times, Politico, CNN.com, Bloomberg View, The Diplomat, Al Jazeera, and The National Interest, among others. He has been interviewed by numerous major media outlets including the New York Times, Washington Post, Financial Times, Guardian, Christian Science Monitor, National Geographic, BBC, CNN, NPR, and Voice of America. He has also produced a number of longer publications on South Asia, including the edited volumes Pakistan's Interminable Energy Crisis: Is There Any Way Out? (Wilson Center, 2015), Pakistan's Runaway Urbanization: What Can Be Done? (Wilson Center, 2014), and India's Contemporary Security Challenges (Wilson Center, 2013). He has published policy briefs, journal articles, and book chapters on issues ranging from Pakistani youth and social media to India's energy security strategy and transboundary water management in South Asia.

Mr. Kugelman received his M.A. in law and diplomacy from the Fletcher School at Tufts University. He received his B.A. from American University's School of International Service.

Boko Haram/Islamic State West Africa Province

Jacob Zenn

Jacob Zenn is an analyst of African and Eurasian Affairs for The Jamestown Foundation and author of the Occasional Report entitled "Northern Nigeria's Boko Haram: The Prize in al-Qaeda's Africa Strategy," published by The Jamestown Foundation in November 2012. In 2012, he conducted field research in Nigeria, Niger, Chad and Cameroon on the socio-economic factors behind the Boko Haram insurgency. Mr. Zenn earned a J.D. from Georgetown Law, where he was a Global Law Scholar, and a graduate degree in International Affairs from the Johns Hopkins SAIS Center for Chinese-American Studies in Nanjing, China. He has spoken at international conferences on Boko Haram and is frequently interviewed and cited in international media.

Bolivia

Joseph M. Humire

Joseph M. Humire is a global security expert, focusing on the nexus between security, defense and economic freedom. Humire's research and investigations on the crime-terror nexus, radical Islam and Iran's influence in Latin America has been sought after by various entities within the U.S. government as well as think tanks and private sector clients throughout the hemisphere. Currently the Executive Director of the Center for a Secure Free Society (SFS), Humire is developing a global network of security and defense specialists that are focused on the intersection of security, intelligence, defense and economic development. Prior to his, Humire spent seven years with the United States Marine Corps, deployed to many hot spots around the world, including Iraq and Liberia, and partook in the first multinational military exercise in Latin America—Unitas 45-04. He is also a graduate from George Mason University with a degree in Economics and Global Affairs.

Brazil

Nathalia Watkins

Nathalia Watkins works at Dataminr, where she monitors, track and analyzes political, economic and security developments for a number of clients at one of the world's leading businesses in AI and Machine Learning innovation. Nathalia Watkins holds a Master of Arts in International Public Policy with a concentration in Global Risk Analysis and Latin America. Nathalia worked as a foreign affairs journalist at Veja magazine, the largest weekly in Brazil, covering major international political events. Nathalia has also worked for outlets like Exame, Estado de S. Paulo, TV Bandeirantes, and RFI. Internationally, Nathalia worked at Reuters in Jerusalem and at Yedioth Aharonot, Israel's largest newspaper. She has received numerous awards for her work.

Nathalia was a research fellow at Eurasia Group, the world's leading political risk consultancy, where she assisted the Latin America team in assessing the impact of policy decisions on the business environment.

Nathalia graduated from the Pontificia Universidade Catolica (PUC-RJ) in 2005 with a BA in Journalism and from the Hebrew University of Jerusalem in 2009 with an MA in International Relations with focus on conflict resolution.

Canada

Candice Malcolm

Candice Malcolm is a best-selling author, a nationally syndicated columnist with the Toronto Sun and Postmedia papers, and an international fellow with the Centre for a Secure Free Society in Washington, D.C. She is the founder of the True North Initiative – an independent, non-profit research and educational organization in Canada that seeks to champion sound immigration and security policies for the 21st century. Candice is the author of two best-selling books, Generation Screwed and Losing True North. She is a former advisor to the Minister of Citizenship and Immigration Canada, the former director of research at Sun News Network, and the former Director of the Canadian Taxpayer's Federation in Ontario.

Born and raised in Vancouver, British Columbia, Candice is a ninth generation Canadian and loves to travel; she has visited over 80 countries. Candice has master's degrees in international relations and international law, and splits her time between Toronto and San Francisco, with her husband Kasra.

China

Michael Sobolik

Michael Sobolik joined AFPC as a Fellow in Indo-Pacific Studies in September 2019. His work covers American and Chinese grand strategy, regional economic and security trends, America's alliance architecture in Asia, and human rights. Michael also serves as editor of AFPC's Indo-Pacific Monitor e-bulletin, AFPC's review of developments in the region. His analysis has appeared in The Diplomat, The Hill, The National Interest, National Review, Newsweek, and Providence.

Prior to joining AFPC, Michael served as a Legislative Assistant to Sen. Ted Cruz from 2014 to 2019 and managed his Indo-Pacific policy portfolio. While in the Senate, Michael drafted legislation on China, Russia, India, Taiwan, North Korea, and Cambodia, as well as strategic systems and missile defense.

Michael is a graduate of Texas A&M University, where he studied political philosophy as an undergraduate. He also earned his Master of International Affairs degree in American grand strategy and U.S.-China relations at the Bush School of Government and Public Service.

Denmark

Kirstine Sinclair

Kirstine Sinclair is Associate Professor (PhD) at the Centre for Contemporary Middle East Studies, Department of History, University of Southern Denmark. Her theoretical interests involve modernity theory, social movement theory, place, space and the sensory turn. Empirically, her work focuses on Muslim minorities in the West, as well as on transnational Muslim organisations and Islamism.

Egypt

Dr. Ofir Winter

Dr. Ofir Winter, a research fellow at INSS, holds a PhD from the Department of Middle Eastern and African History at Tel Aviv University. His doctoral research focused on Egypt and Jordan's quest to legitimize their peace treaties with Israel between the years 1973-2001. He is the author of the book Zionism in Arab Discourses (Manchester University Press, 2016, with Uriya Shavit), and the author of several articles on the politics of Egypt, the Arab-Israeli conflict, church and state in the Arab world, and contemporary Muslim law.

ETHIOPIA

Dr. J. Peter Pham
J. Peter Pham is Vice President for Research and Regional Initiatives at the Atlantic Council as well as Director of the Council's Africa Center. From 2008 to 2017, he also served as Vice President of the Association for the Study of the Middle East and Africa (ASMEA) and was founding Editor-in-Chief of its refereed Journal of the Middle East and Africa. He is currently on a leave of absence from the Atlantic Council to serve in the U.S. Department of State. Dr. Pham's contributions were made before his entry into government service.

FETULLAH GÜLEN MOVEMENT

Gareth Jenkins
Gareth Jenkins is a British national who has been living and working in Istanbul since 1989. He is currently a Non-resident Senior Fellow at the Central Asia-Caucasus Institute & Silk Road Studies Program Joint Center, a transatlantic research and policy initiative between the American Foreign Policy Council in Washington and the Institute for Security and Development Policy in Stockholm. He is also a Country of Origin Information (COI) expert for the International Refugee Rights Initiative in Oxford, United Kingdom, and a Consulting Fellow with the International Institute for Strategic Studies (IISS), which has its headquarters in London, United Kingdom.

During his first ten years in Turkey, Gareth Jenkins worked primarily as a journalist for international wire services, newspapers and periodicals, covering a range of political, economic and social issues related to Turkey and the surrounding region. Amongst others, he has written for Reuters, Time magazine, Newsweek, the Economist Intelligence Unit, the International Herald Tribune, Bridge News, the Sunday Times, the Daily Telegraph, the European, the Financial Times, Global Agribusiness, Farm Journal magazine, Doing Business in Turkey, Jane's Intelligence Review, International Affairs, Al Ahram Weekly, Turkey Analyst, Eurasia Daily Monitor,

Survival, Strategic Comment, Strategic Survey, Turkey Analyst, Foreign Report and National Geographic.

Although he has continued to write and provide commentaries for the international media on various aspects of Turkish politics and economics, over the last 15 years Gareth Jenkins has increasingly concentrated on consulting, analysis and research related to Turkey and its region. During this time, he has provided services to a wide range of companies, professional bodies, governmental institutions and international organizations in numerous fields, including political analysis, risk analysis, security issues and the business environment.

France

Doug Dubrowski

Doug Dubrowski is a former researcher with the American Foreign Policy Council.

Germany

Benjamin Weinthal

Benjamin Weinthal is a research fellow at the Foundation for Defense of Democracies. A widely published journalist based in Berlin, he serves as FDD's eyes and ears in Europe. Benjamin's investigative reporting has uncovered valuable information on Iran's energy links to European firms, as well as Hamas and Hezbollah's terror-finance operations in Europe. He has also examined the growth of the Islamic State in Europe, growing anti-Semitism on the Continent, and neo-Nazism.

Benjamin's work has appeared in The Wall Street Journal Europe, Slate, The Guardian, The New Republic, The Weekly Standard, National Review Online, the Israeli dailies Haaretz and The Jerusalem Post, and broadcast outlets including the BBC and Fox News. A fluent German speaker, Benjamin has also written columns and articles in the German newspapers Frankfurter Rundschau, Berliner Morgenpost and Der Tagesspiegel.

Hezbollah

Hanin Ghaddar

Hanin Ghaddar is the inaugural Friedmann Visiting Fellow at The Washington Institute's Geduld Program on Arab Politics, where she focuses on Shia politics throughout the Levant.

The longtime managing editor of Lebanon's NOW news website, Ghaddar shed light on a broad range of cutting-edge issues, from the evolution of Hezbollah inside Lebanon's fractured political system to Iran's growing influence throughout the Middle East. In addition, she has contributed to a number of U.S.-based magazines and newspapers, including the New York Times and Foreign Policy.

Prior to joining NOW in 2007, Ghaddar wrote for the Lebanese newspapers As-Safir, An-Nahar, and Al-Hayat, and also worked as a researcher for the United Nations Development Program regional office. A native of Al-Ghazieh, Lebanon, Ghaddar holds a bachelor's degree in English literature and a master's degree in Middle East studies, both from the American University of Beirut.

Hizb ut-Tahrir

Kevin Truitte

Kevin Truitte is an independent researcher and graduate student pursuing an MA in Security Studies at Georgetown University. He previously worked as a Research Assistant at Hudson Institute, where he focused on state instability and security challenges in the Middle East and North Africa. He holds a BA in Political Science and Islamic Civilization and Societies from Boston College.

India

Dr. Ajai Sahni

Dr. Ajai Sahni is Founding Member & Executive Director of the Institute for Conflict Management; Editor, South Asia Intelligence Review; Executive Director, South Asia Terrorism Portal; Executive Editor, Faultlines: Writings on Conflict & Resolution. He has researched and written extensively on issues relating to conflict, politics and development in South Asia, and has participated in advisory projects undertaken for various National or State Governments. He jointly edited (with K.P.S. Gill) Terror & Containment: Perspectives on India's Internal Security; and The Global Threat of Terror: Ideological, Material and Political Linkages. He has lectured at numerous professional institutions.

Indonesia

Dr. Namrata Goswami

Dr. Namrata Goswami is an independent strategic analyst, author and consultant on counter-insurgency, counter-terrorism, alternate futures, and great power politics. After earning her Ph.D. in international relations, she served for nearly a decade at India's Ministry of Defense (MOD) sponsored think tank, the Institute for Defence Studies and Analyses (IDSA), New Delhi, working on ethnic conflicts in India's Northeast, counter-terrorism and China-India border conflict. Her research and expertise generated opportunities for collaborations abroad, and she accepted visiting fellowships at the Peace Research Institute, Oslo, Norway; the La Trobe University, Melbourne, Australia; and the University of Heidelberg, Germany. In 2012, she was selected to serve as a Jennings-Randolph Senior Fellow at the United States Institute of Peace (USIP), Washington D.C. where she studied India-China border issues, and was awarded a Fulbright-Nehru Senior Fellowship that same year. Shortly after establishing her own strategy and policy consultancy in 2016 after relocating to the U.S., she won the prestigious MINERVA grant awarded by the Office of the U.S. Secretary of Defense (OSD) to study great power competition in the grey zone of outer space. In 2017, she was awarded a contract with Joint Special Forces University (JSOU) to write a monograph on ISIS in Asia, in which one of her field of study was Indonesia.

Iraq

Dr. Renad Mansour

Since 2008, Renad has held research and teaching positions focusing on issues of comparative politics and international relations in the Middle East. His research at Chatham House explores the situation of Iraq in transition and the dilemmas posed by state-building.

Prior to joining Chatham House, Renad was an El-Erian fellow at the Carnegie Middle East Centre, where he examined Iraq, Iran and Kurdish affairs. Renad is also a research fellow at the Cambridge Security Initiative based at Cambridge University and from 2013, he held positions as lecturer of International Studies and supervisor at the faculty of politics, also at Cambridge University. Renad has been a senior research fellow at the Iraq Institute for Strategic Studies in Beirut since 2011 and was adviser to the Kurdistan Regional Government Civil Society Ministry between 2008 and 2010. He received his PhD from Pembroke College, Cambridge.

Islamic Republic of Iran

Ilan Berman
Ilan Berman is the Senior Vice President of the American Foreign Policy Council in Washington, DC. An expert on regional security in the Middle East, Central Asia, and the Russian Federation, he has consulted for both the U.S. Central Intelligence Agency and the U.S. Department of Defense, and provided assistance on foreign policy and national security issues to a range of governmental agencies and congressional offices. Berman is the author or editor of five books:Tehran Rising: Iran's Challenge to the United States (Rowman & Littlefield, 2005),Dismantling Tyranny: Transitioning Beyond Totalitarian Regimes (Rowman & Littlefield, 2005), Taking on Tehran: Strategies for Confronting the Islamic Republic (Rowman & Littlefield, 2007), Winning the Long War: Retaking the Offensive Against Radical Islam (Rowman & Littlefield, 2009), and, most recently, Implosion: The End of Russia and What it Means for America (Regnery Publishing, 2013).

The Islamic State

Anas Elallame and Craig Whiteside
Anas Elallame is an Intelligence Analyst at Pinkerton at Facebook.

He is also a Native level linguist in Arabic and French. He co-authored "The Logistics of Terror: The Islamic State's Immigration and Logistics Committee," and has translated primary material sources tied to several jihadi organizations.

Craig Whiteside is an associate professor of national security affairs for the U.S. Naval War College at the U.S. Naval Postgraduate School in Monterey, California. He researches the Islamic State and is a fellow at the ICT - The Hague, George Washington University's Program on Extremism, and USIP's Resolve Network.

Israel

Yaakov Lappin

Yaakov Lappin is a military and strategic affairs correspondent and researcher. He is an Associate Researcher at the Begin-Sadat Center for Strategic Studies at Bar-Ilan University, and the Israel correspondent for Jane's Defense Weekly and the military correspondent for Jewish News Service. Yaakov is a regular guest commentator on international TV and radio outlets, including Sky News, BBC World Service, and I24, to provide commentary on defense issues. In 2010, he published Virtual Caliphate – Exposing the Islamist state on the internet, a book that explored the jihadist online presence.

Italy

Dr. Francesco Marone

Dr. Francesco Marone is Research Fellow for the Program on Radicalization and International Terrorism at ISPI - Italian Institute for International Political Studies, in Milan, and Adjunct Lecturer in International Politics at the University of Pavia. He is also an Associate Fellow at the International Centre for Counter-Terrorism – The Hague (ICCT). He is the author of several publications in the field of security studies. In particular, his research interests focus on radicalization and terrorism.

Jordan

Ehud Rosen
Ehud Rosen is an expert on modern political Islam, focusing on the ideology and history of the Muslim Brotherhood in the Middle East and Europe. He is a senior researcher at the Jerusalem Center for Public Affairs and teaches at Bar-Ilan University. Among his relevant publications are "The Muslim Brotherhood's concept of education", Current Trends of Islamist Ideology (vol. 7, November 2008), and "Reading the runes? The United States and the Muslim Brotherhood as seen through the Wikileaks cables" (co-authored with Dr. Martyn Frampton), The Historical Journal, Cambridge (forthcoming 2013).

Kazakhstan

Julian Tucker
Mr. Julian Tucker is a Research Fellow and Research Coordinator at the Stockholm China Center of ISDP. He recently completed his Master of Arts in Central Asian Studies at the Humboldt University in Berlin, Germany. He also pursued Uzbek language and history courses at the Samarkand State Institute of Foreign Languages in Uzbekistan. He holds a BA in Anthropology and Middle Eastern Languages from McGill University in Montreal, Canada. Mr. Tucker's research interests include the implications of regional authority and security structures in Central Asia for international development efforts. At the China Center his work will focus primarily on the One Belt One Road Initiative and Maritime Security in the South China Sea.

Kosovo

Christopher Deliso
Christopher Deliso is an American journalist and author concentrating on the Balkans. Over the past decade, Chris has established a dedicated presence in teh Balkans, and published analytical articles on related topics in numerous relevant media outlets, such as UPI, the Economist Intelligence Unit, and *Jane's Intelligence Digest*. Chris is also the founder and director of the Balkan-interest news

and current affairs website, www.balkanalysis.com, and the author of *The Coming Balkan Caliphate: The Threat of Radical Islam to Europe and the West*.

Kuwait

Dr. Courtney Freer

Dr. Courtney Freer is an assistant professorial research fellow at the Middle East Centre at the London School of Economics and Political Science (LSE). She is the author of Rentier Islamism: The Role of the Muslim Brotherhood in the Gulf Monarchies (Oxford University Press, 2018), the first English language book focused on the Muslim Brotherhood in the Gulf states and specializes in domestic politics and foreign policies of the states of the Gulf Cooperation Council.

Kyrgyzstan

Dr. Meena Singh Roy

Dr. Meena Singh Roy is a Research Fellow and heads the West Asia Centre at the Institute for Defence Studies and Analyses (IDSA). Her area of specialisation is Central Asia and West Asia. Prior to joining IDSA, she was a senior research scholar in the Department of African Studies, Delhi University. She was associated with Institute of Commonwealth Studies, School of Oriental and African Studies and London School of Economics for her research work. She was a visiting Research Fellow with German Institute of Global and Area Studies Institute of Asian Studies (GIGA) in 2014.

Dr. Singh Roy has several peer-reviewed articles and papers focused on West Asia and Central Asia. She has also been involved in net assessment reports and strategic gaming on West Asia and Central Asia. She has published a monograph titled The Shanghai Cooperation Organization: India Seeking New Role in the Eurasian Regional Mechanism (2014), books titled, International and Regional Security Dynamics: Indian and Iranian Perspectives (ed.) (July 2009); Emerging Trends in West Asia: Regional and Global Implications (ed.), (2014), Persian Gulf 2016-17 India's Relations with the Region (co-edited with Prof. P. R. Kumaraswamy), 2017; Ideology, Politics and New Security Challenges in West Asia (ed.) , 2018 and completed the joint Delhi Policy Group and the IDSA Task Force report on West Asia in Transition in 2015.

Lashkar-e Taiba

Michael Kugelman

Michael Kugelman is the Asia Program Deputy Director and Senior Associate for South Asia at the Woodrow Wilson Center, where he is responsible for research, programming, and publications on the region. His main specialty is Pakistan, India, and Afghanistan and U.S. relations with each of them. Mr. Kugelman writes monthly columns for Foreign Policy's South Asia Channel and monthly commentaries for War on the Rocks. He also contributes regular pieces to the Wall Street Journal's Think Tank blog. He has published op-eds and commentaries in the New York Times, Los Angeles Times, Politico, CNN.com, Bloomberg View, The Diplomat, Al Jazeera, and The National Interest, among others. He has been interviewed by numerous major media outlets including the New York Times, Washington Post, Financial Times, Guardian, Christian Science Monitor, National Geographic, BBC, CNN, NPR, and Voice of America. He has also produced a number of longer publications on South Asia, including the edited volumes Pakistan's Interminable Energy Crisis: Is There Any Way Out? (Wilson Center, 2015), Pakistan's Runaway Urbanization: What Can Be Done? (Wilson Center, 2014), and India's Contemporary Security Challenges (Wilson Center, 2013). He has published policy briefs, journal articles, and book chapters on issues ranging from Pakistani youth and social media to India's energy security strategy and transboundary water management in South Asia. Mr. Kugelman received his M.A. in law and diplomacy from the Fletcher School at Tufts University. He received his B.A. from American University's School of International Service.

Lebanon

Hanin Ghaddar
Hanin Ghaddar is the inaugural Friedmann Visiting Fellow at The Washington Institute's Geduld Program on Arab Politics, where she focuses on Shia politics throughout the Levant.

The longtime managing editor of Lebanon's NOW news website, Ghaddar shed light on a broad range of cutting-edge issues, from the evolution of Hezbollah inside Lebanon's fractured political system to Iran's growing influence throughout the Middle East. In addition, she has contributed to a number of U.S.-based magazines and newspapers, including the New York Times and Foreign Policy.

Prior to joining NOW in 2007, Ghaddar wrote for the Lebanese newspapers As-Safir, An-Nahar, and Al-Hayat, and also worked as a researcher for the United Nations Development Program regional office. A native of Al-Ghazieh, Lebanon, Ghaddar holds a bachelor's degree in English literature and a master's degree in Middle East studies, both from the American University of Beirut.

Libya

Emily Estelle
Emily Estelle is the research manager for the Critical Threats Project at the American Enterprise Institute. She is also a senior al Qaeda analyst and the Africa team lead. She studies the Salafi-jihadi movement in Africa, including al Qaeda, ISIS, and associated groups. She specializes in the Libya conflict and the Sahel. Ms. Estelle led a yearlong planning exercise to produce a recommended US strategy for Libya in 2017. She has testified before Congress on US interests in Ethiopia. Ms. Estelle has appeared on MSNBC and published for numerous news outlets, including the Wall Street Journal, the LA Times, National Interest, The Hill, and FoxNews.com. She also coordinates CTP's training and tradecraft and manages the integration of technology into the research process. She graduated Summa Cum Laude from Dartmouth College with a BA in Anthropology modified with Arabic Language.

Malaysia

Dr. Prashanth Parameswaran

Dr. Prashanth Parameswaran is a fellow with the Wilson Center's Asia Program, where he produces analysis on Southeast Asian political and security issues, Asian defense affairs, and U.S. foreign policy in the Asia-Pacific. He is also a director at the consultancy Bower Group Asia and a senior columnist at The Diplomat, one of Asia's leading current affairs publications.

A political scientist by training, Dr. Parameswaran is a recognized expert on Asian affairs and U.S. foreign policy in the region, with a focus on Southeast Asia and politics and security issues. He has conducted grant-based field research across the region, consulted for companies and governments, and taught courses affiliated with the U.S. Department of Defense and the U.S. Department of State. His policy insights, research and commentary have been published widely in the United States and across the region in leading publications and journals including CNN, The Washington Post, The South China Morning Post, The Straits Times, Asia Policy and Contemporary Southeast Asia.

Dr. Parameswaran has held roles across think tanks, government, media and business in the United States and in the region, including most recently the Foreign Service Institute and The Diplomat, where he served as senior editor. In those capacities, he advanced research and analysis on key Asian political and security trends using rigorous research methodologies and extensive in-country networks, with an emphasis on Southeast Asia.

Dr. Parameswaran holds a Ph.D. and a Master of Arts from the Fletcher School of Law and Diplomacy at Tufts University focused on international security, international business and U.S. foreign policy, and received a bachelor's degree from the University of Virginia where he studied foreign affairs and peace and conflict studies and graduated Phi Beta Kappa.

Maldives

Animesh Roul

Animesh Roul is the Executive Director at Society for the Study of Peace and Conflict, a Delhi-based policy research think-tank. In his earlier stint he worked as a Research Associate at New Delhi-based Institute for Conflict Management, which hosts a leading terrorism database on South Asia. He holds a Master of Philosophy degree from the School of International Studies, Jawaharlal Nehru University, New Delhi and has a master's degree in Modern Indian History. Mr. Roul specializes in counterterrorism, radical Islam, terror financing, armed conflict and issues relating to arms control and proliferation in South Asia. He has written for Terrorism Monitor, the CTC Sentinel, Jane's Intelligence Review, Militant Leadership Monitor, and CBW Magazine, among others. He is also serving as executive editor of South Asia Coflict Monitor (SACM), a monthly E-bulletin on armed conflicts and terrorist violence in South Asia.

Mali

James Wholley
James Wholley is a program management professional monitoring security threats in sub-Saharan Africa, with a focus on the Sahel and northern Mozambique. He was formerly a Program Assistant in the Atlantic Council's Africa Center. In 2016, he supported the Mandela Washington Fellowship as part of the International Research and Exchanges Board. James has a Bachelor of Arts from McGill University.

Mauritania

Martin Ewi
Martin A. Ewi joined the Institute for Security Studies in July 2010, as a Senior Researcher, International Crime in Africa Programme (ICAP), Pretoria Office. He previously served as a Political Affairs Officer at the headquarters of the Organisation for the Prohibition of Chemical Weapons (OPCW) based in The Hague, the Netherlands from 2005 to 2010. Before joining the OPCW, Mr Ewi was in charge of the African Union Commission's counter-terrorism programme in Addis Ababa, Ethiopia, where he was concurrently in charge of security strategic issues from 2002 to 2005.

Mr. Ewi holds a MA degree in International Peace Studies from the University of Notre Dame, at Southbend, Indiana, United States of America. He also holds a BA (with Distinction) in Peace Studies and International Politics from Juniata College in Huntingdon, Pennsylvania, United States of America. His research focus is in the area of counterterrorism and the competences of regional organisations in Africa on strategic security issues.

MOROCCO

Dr. J. Peter Pham
J. Peter Pham is Vice President for Research and Regional Initiatives at the Atlantic Council as well as Director of the Council's Africa Center. From 2008 to 2017, he also served as Vice President of the Association for the Study of the Middle East and Africa (ASMEA) and was founding Editor-in-Chief of its refereed Journal of the Middle East and Africa. He is currently on a leave of absence from the Atlantic Council to serve in the U.S. Department of State. Dr. Pham's contributions were made before his entry into government service.

THE MUSLIM BROTHERHOOD

Ilan Berman and Jacob McCarty
Ilan Berman is the Senior Vice President of the American Foreign Policy Council in Washington, DC. An expert on regional security in the Middle East, Central Asia, and the Russian Federation, he has consulted for both the U.S. Central Intelligence Agency and the U.S. Department of Defense, and provided assistance on foreign policy and national security issues to a range of governmental agencies and congressional offices. Berman is the author or editor of five books:Tehran Rising: Iran's Challenge to the United States (Rowman & Littlefield, 2005),Dismantling Tyranny: Transitioning Beyond Totalitarian Regimes (Rowman & Littlefield, 2005), Taking on Tehran: Strategies for Confronting the Islamic Republic (Rowman & Littlefield, 2007), Winning the Long War: Retaking the Offensive Against Radical Islam (Rowman & Littlefield, 2009), and, most recently, Implosion: The End of Russia and What it Means for

America (Regnery Publishing, 2013).

Jacob McCarty joined the American Foreign Policy Council in January 2019 as a Research Fellow and Program Officer. He currently serves as the Managing Editor of the Council's World Almanac of Islamism project. His commentary can be found in The Hill, Jane's Defence Weekly, The National Interest, and The Washington Times. Prior to joining AFPC, Jacob conducted research into defense acquisition reform, force modernization, international trade, global cities, and African politics for a number of policy institutions, and oversaw several development projects on two continents.

A graduate of Ohio University, he has lived in North Africa and the South Pacific. He completed a Masters of Science in Defense & Strategic Studies in August 2019, focusing on the role of global cities and African politics and their impact on U.S. foreign policy and international institutions. He is proficient in the French language.

The Netherlands

Margot van Loon

Margot van Loon is a former Junior Fellow at the American Foreign Policy Council. She conducts research, editing, and analysis in support of multiple AFPC publications. She currently serves as the Project Coordinator for AFPC's World Almanac of Islamism. A graduate of American University, her research focuses on U.S. foreign policy and public diplomacy. Her commentary has appeared in U.S. News and World Report.

Nicaragua

Christine Balling

In 2009, Ms. Balling founded Fundación ECCO, a Colombian-registered nonprofit organization that promoted democracy and youth leadership in areas of conflict. She executed projects in areas where the FARC (Revolutionary Armed Forces of Colombia) insurgency operated, working with the Colombian Army, Air Force and the National Police. She received grants from USAID, U.S. Special Operations Command South, the International Organization for Migration and Spirit of America.

From 2013 to 2014, Ms. Balling served as a Subject Matter Expert to the U.S. Special Operations South commander and partnered with U.S. Army Civil Affairs teams downrange in Colombia. In this role, she interviewed numerous female demobilized FARC and ELN (National Liberation Army) fighters and worked with the Colombian military's demobilization group to create the first tactical guide on individual demobilization. In 2015, Ms. Balling was pinned by the Colombian Minister of Defense with the Colombian Armed Forces' "Medal of Distinguished Service."

In 2016 and 2017, Ms. Balling organized and led two solo expeditions to Iraqi Kurdistan to deliver humanitarian aid and embed with a company of female Yazidi peshmerga soldiers who survived the 2014 genocide by ISIS.

From 2015 to 2020, Ms. Balling was the Senior Fellow for Latin American Affairs at the American Foreign Policy Council. She has published articles in Foreign Affairs, The National Interest, the Small Wars Journal and The Hill. She has lectured at the Escuela Superior de Guerra in Bogotá, the National Defense University's William J. Perry Center, the Institute of World Politics and Harvard Summer School. In 2019, Ms. Balling testified as an expert witness at a Senate Foreign Relations sub-committee hearing on U.S./Colombia relations.

Ms. Balling received her B.A.in English Literature at Barnard College, Columbia University and earned an Executive M.A. in National Security Affairs at the Institute of World Politics. She serves as a member of the Board of Trustees of the Universidad El Bosque in Bogotá, Colombia and is a 2020 recipient of the Phillips Academy Andover Alumni Award of Distinction.

Nigeria

Jacob Zenn

Jacob Zenn is an analyst of African and Eurasian Affairs for The Jamestown Foundation and author of the Occasional Report entitled "Northern Nigeria's Boko Haram: The Prize in al-Qaeda's Africa Strategy," published by The Jamestown Foundation in November

2012. In 2012, he conducted field research in Nigeria, Niger, Chad and Cameroon on the socio-economic factors behind the Boko Haram insurgency. Mr. Zenn earned a J.D. from Georgetown Law, where he was a Global Law Scholar, and a graduate degree in International Affairs from the Johns Hopkins SAIS Center for Chinese-American Studies in Nanjing, China. He has spoken at international conferences on Boko Haram and is frequently interviewed and cited in international media.

North Macedonia

Christopher Deliso
Christopher Deliso is an American journalist and author concentrating on the Balkans. Over the past decade, Chris has established a dedicated presence in teh Balkans, and published analytical articles on related topics in numerous relevant media outlets, such as UPI, the Economist Intelligence Unit, and *Jane's Intelligence Digest.* Chris is also the founder and director of the Balkan-interest news and current affairs website, www.balkanalysis.com, and the author of *The Coming Balkan Caliphate: The Threat of Radical Islam to Europe and the West.*

Pakistan

Michael Kugelman
Michael Kugelman is the Asia Program Deputy Director and Senior Associate for South Asia at the Woodrow Wilson Center, where he is responsible for research, programming, and publications on the region. His main specialty is Pakistan, India, and Afghanistan and U.S. relations with each of them. Mr. Kugelman writes monthly columns for Foreign Policy's South Asia Channel and monthly commentaries for War on the Rocks. He also contributes regular pieces to the Wall Street Journal's Think Tank blog. He has published op-eds and commentaries in the New York Times, Los Angeles Times, Politico, CNN.com, Bloomberg View, The Diplomat, Al Jazeera, and The National Interest, among others. He has been interviewed by numerous major media outlets including

the New York Times, Washington Post, Financial Times, Guardian, Christian Science Monitor, National Geographic, BBC, CNN, NPR, and Voice of America. He has also produced a number of longer publications on South Asia, including the edited volumes Pakistan's Interminable Energy Crisis: Is There Any Way Out? (Wilson Center, 2015), Pakistan's Runaway Urbanization: What Can Be Done? (Wilson Center, 2014), and India's Contemporary Security Challenges (Wilson Center, 2013). He has published policy briefs, journal articles, and book chapters on issues ranging from Pakistani youth and social media to India's energy security strategy and transboundary water management in South Asia. Mr. Kugelman received his M.A. in law and diplomacy from the Fletcher School at Tufts University. He received his B.A. from American University's School of International Service.

The Palestinian National Authority

Neri Zilber

Neri Zilber is a journalist and analyst on Middle East politics and culture, an adjunct fellow of The Washington Institute for Near East Policy, and a senior fellow at BICOM, a U.K think tank. He is a regular contributor to The Daily Beast, Foreign Policy, and Politico Magazine, and his work has appeared in the New York Times, Washington Post, Guardian, The Atlantic, New Republic, and Foreign Affairs, among other outlets. He is the co-author of State with No Army, Army with No State: Evolution of the Palestinian Authority Security Forces 1994-2018, and the contributing author on Israel's social protest demonstrations for The Occupy Handbook (Little, Brown), a chronicle of the global «Occupy» movement. He has held fellowships at the Heinrich Boell Stiftung (Transatlantic Media Fellow 2019), the Washington Institute for Near East Policy (Visiting Scholar 2014-2015), the Institute of Current World Affairs (2011-2013), and the U.S. Library of Congress (2005-2006). In addition to reportage and analysis, Neri has consulted for the private sector on political and economic risk. Neri holds a bachelor's degree from the School of Foreign Service, Georgetown University and a master's degree from the Department of War Studies, King's College

London.

The Philippines

Richard Javad Heydarian

Richard Javad Heydarian is a Manila-based academic, having taught political science at Ateneo De Manila University and De La Salle University, Philippines. He is a regular contributor to Centre for Strategic and International Studies (CSIS) and Council on Foreign Relations (CFR), and is the author of, among others, "Asia's New Battlefield: US, China & the Struggle for Western Pacific" & "Rise of Duterte: A Populist Revolt Against Élite Democracy". He has written for/or interviewed by Aljazeera English, BBC, Bloomberg, The New York Times, Foreign Affairs, The Guardian, The Washington Post, The Financial Times, Wall Street Journal, The Economist, The Atlantic, South China Morning Post, Nikkei Asia Review, Straits Times, among other leading publications.

Qatar

Varsha Koduvayur

Varsha Koduvayur is a senior research analyst at FDD focusing on the Gulf States, where she covers internal dynamics, regional geopolitics, illicit financing, and political and economic reform trends. Varsha was previously a researcher for the Middle East practice at Eurasia Group, and a junior fellow at the Carnegie Endowment for International Peace. She studied Arabic language in Morocco through the Language Flagship program, completing her capstone year in Meknes. Varsha has a BA in International Relations from Michigan State University.

Russia

Ilan Berman

Ilan Berman is the Senior Vice President of the American Foreign Policy Council in Washington, DC. An expert on regional security in the Middle East, Central Asia, and the Russian Federation, he has consulted for both the U.S. Central Intelligence Agency and the U.S. Department of Defense, and provided assistance on foreign policy and national security issues to a range of governmental agencies and congressional offices. Berman is the author or editor of five books:Tehran Rising: Iran's Challenge to the United States (Rowman & Littlefield, 2005),Dismantling Tyranny: Transitioning Beyond Totalitarian Regimes (Rowman & Littlefield, 2005), Taking on Tehran: Strategies for Confronting the Islamic Republic (Rowman & Littlefield, 2007), Winning the Long War: Retaking the Offensive Against Radical Islam (Rowman & Littlefield, 2009), and, most recently, Implosion: The End of Russia and What it Means for America (Regnery Publishing, 2013).

Saudi Arabia

Varsha Koduvayur
Varsha Koduvayur is a senior research analyst at FDD focusing on the Gulf States, where she covers internal dynamics, regional geopolitics, illicit financing, and political and economic reform trends. Varsha was previously a researcher for the Middle East practice at Eurasia Group, and a junior fellow at the Carnegie Endowment for International Peace. She studied Arabic language in Morocco through the Language Flagship program, completing her capstone year in Meknes. Varsha has a BA in International Relations from Michigan State University.

Senegal

Jonathan Gass
Jonathan obtained his BA in history, politics, and French from the University of Toronto, where his studies focused on sub-Saharan Africa. Prior to joining McLarty Associates, he served as the Associate Director of the Atlantic Council's Africa Center, where he concentrated on geopolitical, commercial, and security issues in Central and West Africa and managed the Center's publications and events portfolio. He has also worked at Oxfam France, helping to plan the organization's annual Trailwalker fundraiser. Jonathan was

born and raised in England. He is fluent in French.

Somalia

Dr. J. Peter Pham

J. Peter Pham is Vice President for Research and Regional Initiatives at the Atlantic Council as well as Director of the Council's Africa Center. From 2008 to 2017, he also served as Vice President of the Association for the Study of the Middle East and Africa (ASMEA) and was founding Editor-in-Chief of its refereed Journal of the Middle East and Africa. He is currently on a leave of absence from the Atlantic Council to serve in the U.S. Department of State. Dr. Pham's contributions were made before his entry into government service.

Spain

Margot van Loon

Margot van Loon is a former Junior Fellow at the American Foreign Policy Council. She conducts research, editing, and analysis in support of multiple AFPC publications. She currently serves as the Project Coordinator for AFPC's World Almanac of Islamism. A graduate of American University, her research focuses on U.S. foreign policy and public diplomacy. Her commentary has appeared in U.S. News and World Report.

Sri Lanka

Jeff M. Smith

Jeff M. Smith is a research fellow in the Heritage Foundation's Asian Studies Center, focusing on South Asia. He is the author/editor of "Asia's Quest for Balance: China's Rise and Balancing in the Indo-Pacific" (2018), and of "Cold Peace: China-India Rivalry in the 21st Century" (2014). He has contributed to multiple books on Asian Security issues, testified as an expert witness before multiple congressional committees, served in an advisory role for several presidential campaigns, and regularly briefs officials in the executive and legislative branches on matters of Asian security.

His writing on Asian security issues has appeared in Foreign Affairs, The Wall Street Journal, Foreign Policy, the Harvard International Review, Jane's Intelligence Review, The National Interest, and The Diplomat, among others. In recent years his expert commentary has been featured by The Economist, The New York Times, FOX News, The Washington Times, Reuters, and the BBC, among others. Smith formerly served as the Director of Asian Security Programs at the American Foreign Policy Council.

Syria

Kyle Orton
Kyle Orton is an independent researcher focused on the Syrian war and related terrorist groups. His work has been published in various outlets, including Foreign Policy, The Wall Street Journal, and The New York Times. He obtained his masters in social science from Liverpool University, completing his thesis on the conditions of the Syrian refugees in Lebanon, and previously worked at a London think tank.

Tablighi Jama'at

Sagar Wadgaonkar
Sagar was born and raised in New Orleans, Louisiana; his family is from Pune, India, and he has retained a keen interest in Indian and South Asian affairs, history, and politics since his childhood. Sagar graduated with a double BA from Boston College in 2013 in Political Science and Islamic Civilization and Societies, during which time he attended numerous study abroad programs in Kuwait, Israel/Palestine, and India. He also received a prestigious advanced study grant to conduct field research in Haiti, detailing sustainable relief efforts in the post-earthquake environment. Sagar spent over a year living in Tel Aviv and Jerusalem, working with a risk consulting firm, the Levantine Group, and studying Arabic.

Tajikistan

Kamoludin Abdullaev

Kamoludin Abdullaev, an independent historian from Tajikistan, has more than forty years of experience in study and teaching the modern history of Central Asia with a focus on Tajikistan, Afghanistan, Uzbekistan. Since 1992, Dr. Abdullaev is a policy analyst and independent consultant in international non-governmental research organizations involved in conflict resolution, conflict prevention, peace-building, civil society building, and education in Central Asia. From 1994-2014 he actively participated of the international research exchange programs in the field of history and social sciences. Awards include: Fulbright Scholar (1994, the George Washington University and 2005, Allegheny College, PA); Regional Exchange Scholar (1995, Kennan Institute for Advanced Russian Studies, Woodrow Wilson International Center for Scholars); the British Academy visiting fellow (SOAS, 1996); Visiting scholar at the University of Toronto (2009); Jennings Randolph Senior Fellow at the United States Institute of Peace (USIP) in 2010-2011; Visiting Research Fellow at the Humboldt University of Berlin, Crossroads Asia (2014) and others. Dr. Abdullaev taught Central Asian subjects from multidisciplinary perspectives at Yale, the Ohio State University from 2001-2013. He authored and edited 10 books in English and Russian including Historical Dictionary of Tajikistan. Third Edition. Lanham-Toronto-Plymouth, UK: The Scarecrow Press Inc., 2018 and Ot Sintsiana do Khorasana. Iz Istorii Sredneaziatskoi Emigratsii 20 veka. (From Xinjiang to Khurasan. From the History of the 20th Century Central Asian Emigration). Dushanbe: Irfon, 2009, as well as over 70 articles in English, Russian, Tajik, and translated into French, Farsi and Japan.

Taliban

Cody Retherford

Cody Retherford joined the American Foreign Policy Council as a Junior Fellow in May 2020. He has conducted research on counter-terrorism, counterinsurgency, and state proxy, cyber, and information operations and strategy. He also has a background in market research and geopolitical risk analysis. Cody holds a BA in International Affairs and Middle East Studies. He is currently a graduate student at Johns Hopkins University School of Advanced International Studies (SAIS) pursuing an MA in International Economics and International Affairs. Prior to attending SAIS, Cody served as a US Army Officer on active duty for 5 years in light infantry and special operations organizations. He deployed to Afghanistan in support of Operation Freedom's Sentinel and Operation Resolute Support. He has also supported combat operations against terror groups across the Middle East.

Tanzania

Kelsey Lilley
Kelsey Lilley is a former Policy Analyst with Yorktown Solutions, a foreign policy and national security strategic advisory firm in Washington, DC, and Associate Director of the Atlantic Council's Africa Center, where she coordinated the Council's Sudan Task Force and led two delegations to Sudan to undertake consultations with government, civil society, and private sector stakeholders. Her expertise is in U.S. foreign and security policy in Africa, with a focus on the political and security dynamics of East Africa. Prior to the Atlantic Council, Kelsey lived and worked in Addis Ababa, Ethiopia and at the Africa Center for Strategic Studies at the National Defense University. She holds an MA in Security Studies from Georgetown University's School of Foreign Service, which supported her 2018 research on security issues in Dar es Salaam and Zanzibar, Tanzania, and a BA in Political Science from Davidson College.

Thailand

Richard Javad Heydarian
Richard Javad Heydarian is a Manila-based academic, having taught political science at Ateneo De Manila University and De La Salle University, Philippines. He is a regular contributor to Centre for Strategic and International Studies (CSIS) and Council on Foreign Relations (CFR), and is the author of, among others, "Asia's New Battlefield: US, China & the Struggle for Western Pacific" & "Rise of

Duterte: A Populist Revolt Against Élite Democracy". He has written for/or interviewed by Aljazeera English, BBC, Bloomberg, The New York Times, Foreign Affairs, The Guardian, The Washington Post, The Financial Times, Wall Street Journal, The Economist, The Atlantic, South China Morning Post, Nikkei Asia Review, Straits Times, among other leading publications.

Tunisia

Emmanuel Cohen-Hadria

Emmanuel Cohen-Hadria is the Head of the Euro-Mediterranean Policies Department at the European Institute of the Mediterranean (IEMed). With his team, he coordinates the activities of EuroMeS-Co, a network of Euro-Mediterranean think tanks, as well as the annual publication of the Mediterranean Yearbook. His main fields of expertise are EU-Mediterranean relations, EU foreign policy and Tunisia. He published a number of articles on the transition in Tunisia as well as on EU-Tunisia relationships. Before joining the IEMed in 2015, Emmanuel Cohen-Hadria worked eight years for the European Commission and the European External Action Service (EEAS). Between 2012 and 2015, he worked in the office of the then Deputy Secretary General for Political Affairs of the EEAS, where he was in charge of Mediterranean issues. He graduated from Sciences Po Paris and holds a master's from the College of Europe/ Bruges. He lectures in various universities in Barcelona.

Turkey

Svante E. Cornell

Svante E. Cornell joined the American Foreign Policy Council as Senior Fellow for Eurasia in January 2017. He also servs as the Director of the Central Asia-Caucasus Institute & Silk Road Studies Program, and a co-founder of the Institue for Security and Development Policy, Stockholm. His main areas of expertise are security issues, state-building, and transnational crime in Southwest and Central Asia, with a specific focus on the Caucasus and Turkey. He is the Editor of the Central Asia-Caucasus Analyst, the Joint Cen-

ter's bi-weekly publication, and of the Joint Center's Silk Road Papers series of occasional papers.
Cornell is the author of four books, including Small Nations and Great Powers, the first comprehensive study of the post-Soviet conflicts in the Caucasus, and Azerbaijan since Independence. Cornell is an Associate Research Professor at Johns Hopkins University's Paul H. Nitze School of Advanced International Studies. He was educated at the Middle East Technical University, received his Ph.D. in Peace and Conflict Studies from Uppsala University, and holds an honorary degree from the National Academy of Sciences of Azerbaijan. He is a member of the Swedish Royal Academy of Military Science, and a Research Associate with the W. Martens Center for European Studies in Brussels. Formerly, Cornell served as Associate Professor of Government at Uppsala University.

Turkmenistan

Slavomir Horak
Slavomir Horak holds a Ph.D. in International Area Studies at the Institute of International Studies, Charles University in Prague. He currently holds a tenure track position as an Assistant Professor in the Department of Russian and East European Studies at the Institute of International Studies, Charlies University in Prague. His research covers political, social, and economic issues in the former USSR, with a focus on Central Asia, particularly Turkmenistan's domestic issues, as well as its informal politics and state and nation-building.

He is the author of several books on Central Asian and Afghanistan internal developments as well as numerous articles published in Czech, Russian, and English scholarly journals. He has also provided expert consultation for the Czech Republic's Ministry of Foreign Affairs, Bertelsmann Transformation Index, and other companies.

United Arab Emirates

Dr. Malcolm Peck
Now retired, Peck was a senior program officer at Meridian

International Center in Washington, DC, where he designed and implemented professional study programs for participants in the State Department's International Visitor Leadership Program, from 1984 to 2015. Most of those programs were conducted for visitors from the Arab world, exploring such subjects as the role of religion, the rule of law, education at the secondary and post-secondary levels, and local and state government. Previously, he served as the Arabian Peninsula analyst in the State Department's Bureau of Intelligence and Research, 1981-83, and was director of programs at the Middle East Institute, 1970-81. He is the author of The United Arab Emirates: A Venture in Unity (1986) and of The Historical Dictionary of the Gulf Arab States (1997 and 2007), with a co-authored third edition of the Dictionary scheduled for publication in 2018. Additionally, he has contributed chapters on Arab world issues to ten books and published over 150 articles and encyclopedia entries on Middle East subjects. He served as the president of the National Committee to Honor the Fourteenth Centennial of Islam, which exhibited art expressive of Islamic culture in Houston, Pittsburgh, and Washington, DC in 1982. Peck was born in Boston in 1939. Although he has lived and worked in the Washington, DC area for nearly 50 years, he remains a proud Bostonian. He received an AB in European History (honors) and an AM in Middle East Studies from Harvard University, and holds MA and PhD degrees from the Fletcher School of Law and Diplomacy, Tufts University.

He was married to Aida Ravelo Peck, a nurse originally from the Visayan region of the Philippines, who specialized in assisting open heart surgery. Son John is an architect working in Portland, Oregon.

The United States

Sam Westrop

Sam Westrop is director of Islamist Watch, a project of the Middle East Forum. He is a fellow of the Gatestone Institute, Freedom Association, Scholars for Peace in the Middle East and the American Islamic Forum for Democracy. He writes on the subject of extremism, radicalization and terror finance, and has published in dozens of newspapers and online publications based in the United

States, Canada, United Kingdom, India, Bangladesh, Israel and the United Arab Emirates. Along with his frequent appearances on radio and television, on stations that include the BBC and Al Jazeera, he is the author of Hidden in Plain Sight: Deobandis, Islamism and British Multiculturalism Policy, which was published as part of an edited book by Palgrave Macmillan in 2016. His work has been cited in the British Parliament and Congress and by prominent thinktanks around the world.

Uzbekistan

Svante E. Cornell

Svante E. Cornell joined the American Foreign Policy Council as Senior Fellow for Eurasia in January 2017. He also servs as the Director of the Central Asia-Caucasus Institute & Silk Road Studies Program, and a co-founder of the Institue for Security and Development Policy, Stockholm. His main areas of expertise are security issues, state-building, and transnational crime in Southwest and Central Asia, with a specific focus on the Caucasus and Turkey. He is the Editor of the Central Asia-Caucasus Analyst, the Joint Center's bi-weekly publication, and of the Joint Center's Silk Road Papers series of occasional papers. Cornell is the author of four books, including Small Nations and Great Powers, the first comprehensive study of the post-Soviet conflicts in the Caucasus, and Azerbaijan since Independence. Cornell is an Associate Research Professor at Johns Hopkins University's Paul H. Nitze School of Advanced International Studies. He was educated at the Middle East Technical University, received his Ph.D. in Peace and Conflict Studies from Uppsala University, and holds an honorary degree from the National Academy of Sciences of Azerbaijan. He is a member of the Swedish Royal Academy of Military Science, and a Research Associate with the W. Martens Center for European Studies in Brussels. Formerly, Cornell served as Associate Professor of Government at Uppsala University.

Venezuela

Joseph M. Humire

Joseph M. Humire is a global security expert, focusing on the nexus between security, defense and economic freedom. Humire's research and investigations on the crime-terror nexus, radical Islam and Iran's influence in Latin America has been sought after by various entities within the U.S. government as well as think tanks and private sector clients throughout the hemisphere. Currently the Executive Director of the Center for a Secure Free Society (SFS), Humire is developing a global network of security and defense specialists that are focused on the intersection of security, intelligence, defense and economic development. Prior to his, Humire spent seven years with the United States Marine Corps, deployed to many hot spots around the world, including Iraq and Liberia, and partook in the first multinational military exercise in Latin America—Unitas 45-04. He is also a graduate from George Mason University with a degree in Economics and Global Affairs. Humire co-edited the first English book on "Iran's strategic penetration of Latin America," scheduled to be released in the fall of 2013 by Lexington Books.

Yemen

James Barnett

James Barnett is an independent researcher focusing on African and Middle Eastern security issues. He was previously an al-Qaeda analyst at the Critical Threats Project at the American Enterprise Institute. He received a BA with Highest Honors from the University of Texas at Austin and was a 2016-17 Boren Scholar in Tanzania.